HANDBOOK OF ARCHITECTURAL TECHNOLOGY

HANDBOOK OF ARCHITECTURAL TECHNOLOGY

edited by
Henry J. Cowan

VAN NOSTRAND REINHOLD
New York

Copyright © 1991 by Van Nostrand Reinhold

Library of Congress Catalog Card Number 90-45339
ISBN 0-442-20525-2

All rights reserved. No part of this work covered by the
copyright hereon may be reproduced or used in any form or
by any means—graphic, electronic, or mechanical, including
photocopying, recording, taping, or information storage and
retrieval systems—without written permission of the
publisher.

Manufactured in the United States of America

Published by Van Nostrand Reinhold
115 Fifth Avenue
New York, New York 10003

Chapman and Hall
2-6 Boundary Row
London, SE1 8HN

Thomas Nelson Australia
102 Dodds Street
South Melbourne 3205
Victoria, Australia

Nelson Canada
1120 Birchmount Road
Scarborough, Ontario M1K 5G4, Canada

16 15 14 13 12 11 10 9 8 7 6 5 4 3 2 1

Library of Congress Cataloging-in-Publication Data

Handbook of architectural technology / edited by Henry J. Cowan.
    p. cm.
  Includes bibliographical references and index.
  ISBN 0-442-20525-2
  1. Building. I. Cowan, Henry J.
TH19.H36 1991
690—dc20   90-45339
                                      CIP

To
Judith Cowan and David Hartstein

Contributors

Richard M. Aynsley, BArch, MS (Arch Eng), PhD, FRAIA, RIBA MAIB, Head of the School of Architecture, University of Auckland, Auckland 1030, New Zealand. *Chapter 10.*

Kevin Bach, Hydraulic Services Consultant, Julius Poole and Gibson, Consulting Engineers, 9 Atchison Street, Leonards NSW 2065, Australia. *Part of Chapter 24.*

John Ballinger, BArch, Head of the School of Architecture and Director of the Solar Architecture Research Unit, University of New South Wales, Kensington NSW 2033, Australia. *Chapter 21.*

Alan D. Bendtsen, Project Leader, Engineering Properties of Wood, Forest Products Laboratory, 1 Gifford Pinchot Drive, Madison, WI 53705, USA. *Part of Chapter 4.*

Ronald E. Bucknam, PhD, President, Converse Consultants NW, 3131 Elliott Avenue, Seattle, WA 98121, USA. *Part of Chapter 15.*

Louis Challis, MSc (Arch), BSc, Acoustic Consultant, 248 Dowling Street, Kings Cross NSW 2011, Australia. *Chapter 17.*

William W. S. Charters, ME, MSE, BSc, FIMechE, FIEAust, FAIEnergy, Dean of the Faculty of Engineering, University of Melbourne, Parkville VIC 3052, Australia. *Part of Chapter 22.*

Henry J. Cowan, DEng, Hon DArch, PhD, MSc, MArch, Hon FRAIA, FIEAust, FIStructE, FASCE, Professor Emeritus of Architectural Science, University of Sydney, Sydney NSW 2006, Australia. *Parts of Chapters 1, 2, 3, 5, and 11.*

Alan D. Freas, Retired Assistant Director, Forest Products Laboratory, 1 Gifford Pinchot Drive, Madison, WI 53705, USA. *Parts of Chapters 4 and 14.*

Thomas M. Gavin, MS, Senior Geotechnical Engineer, Converse Consultants NW, 3131 Elliott Avenue, Seattle, WA 98121, USA. *Part of Chapter 15.*

Baruch Givoni, PhD, BArch, Professor of Architecture, University of California, Los Angeles, CA 90024, USA. *Chapter 18.*

K. I. Guthrie, BE, MEngSc, MIEAust, Section Head, Energy Systems, Scientific Services Department, Gas and Fuel Corporation of Victoria, 1136 Nepean Highway Highett, Vic. 3190 Australia.

Tibor Z. Harmathy, MechEng, DrEng, PEng, Retired Head of the Fire Research Section, National Research Council of Canada, Ottawa K1H 5S1, Canada. *Chapter 26.*

Warren Julian, PhD, MSc (Arch), BE, BSc, DipBdgSc, FIESAust, Dean of the Faculty of Architecture, University of Sydney NSW 2006, Australia. *Chapter 19.*

Anita Lawrence, MArch, FRAIA, MAAS, Associate Professor, Graduate School of the Built Environment, University of New South Wales, Kensington NSW 2033, Australia. *Chapter 16.*

Bruce Martin, MA, AADip (Hon), FRIBA, FRSA, Chartered Architect, The New Studio, Little Hadham, Ware, Herts. SG11 2ET, England. *Chapters 6 and 7.*

Madan Mehta, PhD, MBdgSc, BArch, FIIA, Professor of Architecture, University of Texas, Arlington, TX 76019, USA. *Chapter 13.*

Russell C. Moody, Project Leader, Engineered Wood Products and Structures, Forest Products Laboratory, 1 Gifford Pinchot Drive, Madison, WI 53705, USA. *Part of Chapter 14.*

Spiro N. Pollalis, PhD, MBA, DiplEng, Associate Professor of Architectural Technology, Graduate School of Design, Harvard University, Cambridge, MA 02138, USA. *Part of Chapter 9.*

Daniel L. Schodek, PhD, MS, MA (Hon), Professor of Architectural Technology, Graduate School of Design, Harvard University, Cambridge, MA 02138, USA. *Part of Chapter 9.*

J. Max Sherrard, BE, FIEAust, Director, Julius Poole and Gibson, Consulting Engineers, 9 Atchison Street, St. Leonards NSW 2065, Australia. *Part of Chapter 24.*

Peter R. Smith, PhD, MArch, FRAIA, Head of the Department of Architectural Science, University of Sydney, Sydney NSW 2006, Australia. *Chapter 25, and Parts of Chapters 1, 2, 3, 5, and 11.*

Anthony D. Stokes, PhD, BE, FIEAust, Associate Professor of Electrical Engineering, University of Sydney, Sydney NSW 2006, Australia. *Chapter 23.*

S. V. Szokolay, PhD, MArch, DipArch, FRAIA, RIBA, MInstEnvSc, MAIRAH, Head of the Department of Architecture, University of Queensland, St. Lucia QLD 4067, Australia. *Chapter 20.*

Lambert Tall, PhD, Professor of Civil Engineering, Florida International University, Tamiami Campus, Miami, FL 33199, USA. *Chapter 12.*

Forrest Wilson, PhD, Senior Editor, *Architecture*, Emeritus Professor of Architecture, The Catholic University of America, Washington, DC 20064, USA. *Chapter 8.*

Contents

Preface / xvii

1. MATHEMATICS / 1
Henry J. Cowan and Peter R. Smith

1.1. Trigonometric and Hyperbolic Functions and the Number *e* / 1
1.2. Logarithms, Quadratic Equations, and Infinite Series / 2
1.3. Differentiation and Integration / 3
1.4. Measurement of Circumferences, Areas, and Volumes / 4
1.5. A List of Statistical Terms / 4
1.6. Decimal Equivalents of Fractions / 8
1.7. Arabic Equivalents of Roman Numerals / 8
Suggestions for Further Reading / 9
Notation / 9

2. METALS / 10
Henry J. Cowan and Peter R. Smith

2.1. Metals, Ceramics, and Plastics / 10
2.2. The Deformation and Fracture of Metals / 11
2.3. Wrought Iron, Cast Iron, and Carbon Steel / 14
2.4. The Properties and Treatment of Steel / 15
2.5. Corrosion Protection / 16
2.6. Alloy Steels / 17
2.7. Aluminum and Its Alloys / 18
2.8. The Classification and Treatment of Aluminum Alloys / 20
2.9. Other Nonferrous Metals / 22
2.10. Methods of Joining Metals / 23
References / 24
Suggestions for Further Reading / 25
Notation / 25

3. CERAMIC MATERIALS / 26
Henry J. Cowan and Peter R. Smith

3.1. Traditional and Modern Uses of Natural Stone / 26
3.2. Classification of Stone / 26
    Sedimentary Rocks / 27
    Igneous Rocks / 27
    Metamorphic Rocks / 27
    The Industrial Classification of Stone / 28
3.3. The Deterioration of Natural Stone / 28
3.4. The Preservation and Repair of Natural Stone / 30
3.5. Stone Veneer / 31
3.6. Lime, Lime Mortar, and Lime Wash / 31
3.7. Gypsum and Gypsum Plaster / 32
3.8. Portland Cement / 33
    The Testing of Cement / 33
    Modifications of Ordinary Portland Cement / 33
    White and Colored Portland Cement / 34
    Cement Mortar and Plaster / 34
3.9. Other Cements / 34
3.10. Concrete and Concrete Aggregate / 34
    Particle Size of Concrete Aggregates / 35
    Classification of Concrete Aggregate / 35
    Alkali-Aggregate Reaction / 35
    Unsound Particles and Deleterious Substances / 35
    Moisture Content of Aggregate / 35
    Bulk Density and Specific Gravity / 36
    Abrasion Resistance and Strength / 36
3.11. Mixing, Placing, and Curing of Concrete / 36
    Testing Concrete for Workability / 37
    Testing Concrete for Strength / 38
    Transportation and Placing of Concrete / 38
    Curing of Concrete / 40
3.12. Concrete Admixtures / 40
    Air Entrainment / 40
    Water-Reducing Admixtures and Superplasticizers / 40
    Shrinkage Compensation / 41

Integral Waterproofers / 41
Accelerators / 41
Retarders / 41
3.13. Concrete Surface Finishes / 41
3.14. Cement-Based Insulating Materials / 43
3.15. Precast Concrete and Concrete Products / 43
3.16. Clay Brick and Other Bricks / 44
Cavity Walls and Brick Veneer Walls / 45
Reinforced Brickwork / 45
Face Brick and Plastered Brick / 45
Mortar and Plaster for Bricks / 46
Other Types of Brick / 47
3.17. Other Clay Building Products / 47
3.18. The Manufacture of Glass / 48
3.19. Special Glass / 49
3.20. The Thermal and Acoustic Properties of Glass / 50
References / 51
Suggestions for Further Reading / 52
Notation / 52

4. TIMBER AND TIMBER PRODUCTS: PROPTERIES, DETERIORATION, PROTECTION / 53
B. Alan Bendtsen and Alan D. Freas

4.1. Introduction / 53
4.2. Structure / 53
Cell Types / 53
Macrostructure / 54
Chemical Composition / 55
4.3. Physical Properties / 55
Anisotropy / 55
Moisture in Wood / 56
Dimensional Stability / 56
Density / 57
Resistance to Weathering / 57
Durability / 57
Electrical Properties / 58
Thermal Properties / 58
4.4. Mechanical Properties / 58
Clear Wood Mechanical Properties / 59
Factors that Influence Clear Wood Properties / 62
4.5. Protection of Wood / 68
Weathering / 68
Decay / 69
Fire / 69
4.6. Wood and Wood-Based Products / 69
Lumber / 69
Glued-Laminated (Glulam) Timber / 71
Laminated Veneer Lumber / 72
Round Timbers / 73
Appearance Products / 74
Structural-Use Panels: Reconstituted Wood / 75
Particle- and Fiber-Based Panel Products / 76
References / 78
Suggestions for Further Reading / 78
Notation and Abbreviations / 78

5. PLASTICS, FLOOR COVERING MATERIALS, SEALANTS, ADHESIVES, AND PAINT / 79
Henry J. Cowan and Peter R. Smith

5.1. The Categorization of Plastics / 79
5.2. Thermoplastic Materials / 79
5.3. Thermosetting Materials / 82
5.4. Fabrication and Durability of Plastics / 83
5.5. Woodchip Board and Polymer Concrete / 84
5.6. Floor Covering Materials / 85
5.7. Waterproofing Materials / 86
5.8. Sealants / 86
5.9. Adhesives / 87
5.10. Paint and Paint Vehicles / 88
5.11. Pigments / 88
5.12. Paint as a Protective Coating / 89
5.13. Paints for Special Purposes / 89
5.14. Varnishes, Stains, Lacquers, and Clear Coatings / 90
References / 90
Suggestions for Further Reading / 91
Notation / 91

6. DEFORMATION AND JOINTING / 92
Bruce Martin

6.1. Joints / 92
6.2. Movement Joints / 92
6.3. Contraction Joints / 93
6.4. Expansion Joints / 93
6.5. Movement at a Joint / 95
6.6. Sealants / 96
6.7. Sealing Strips / 97
6.8. Gaskets / 97
6.9. Joint Fillers / 98
References / 99
Suggestions for Further Reading / 99
Notation / 99

7. EXCLUSION OF WATER BY ROOFS, WALLS, AND FLOORS / 100
Bruce Martin

7.1. Water / 100
7.2. Exclusion of Rainwater from Roofs / 101
7.3. Exclusion of Condensate from Roofs / 102
Pitched Roofs / 102
Flat Roofs / 103
Flat Roofs with Warm Deck / 103
7.4. Exclusion of Rainwater from External Walls / 103
Solid Walls / 103
Fully Sealed Walls / 104
Protected Walls / 104
Drained Joints / 104
7.5. Exclusion of Condensate from External Walls / 105
Mass Walls / 105
Fully Sealed Walls / 105
Protected Walls / 105

7.6. Exclusion of Water from Ground Floors / 105
  Slabs on Grade and Groundwater / 106
  Suspended Floors and Groundwater / 106
7.7. Exclusion of Condensate from Ground Floors / 106
  Standards / 107
  Suggestions for Further Reading / 107
  Notation / 107

8. DURABILITY AND MAINTENANCE / 108
Forrest Wilson

8.1. A Question of Value / 108
  Services and Scenery / 109
8.2. State of the Art / 110
8.3. Life-Cycle Costing / 111
8.4. Testing / 111
8.5. Reminders / 112
  Environment / 112
  Roofing / 113
  Flooring / 113
  Excessive Moisture / 113
  References / 114
  Suggestions for Further Reading / 114

9. LOADS / 115
S. N. Pollalis and D. L. Schodek

9.1. Loads on Buildings / 115
9.2. The Applicable Building Code / 116
9.3. Dead Loads / 116
9.4. Live Loads / 116
  Occupancy Loads / 118
  Snow Loads / 118
  Moving and Impact Loads / 119
9.5. Wind Loads / 120
9.6. Earthquake Loads / 120
  Nature of Earthquake Loads / 120
  Effects of the Structural System and its Foundation on Earthquake Loads / 121
  Earthquake Design According to the Applicable Code / 122
  Dynamic Analysis and Appropriateness / 122
  Experimental Alternatives / 122
  Design Hints / 122
9.7. Other Loads / 122
9.8. Calculation of Loads / 123
9.9. Loads On Floors / 124
9.10. Loads On Roofs / 124
9.11. Loads on Beams, Columns, and Walls / 126
  Exerior Walls / 127
9.12. Foundation Loads / 127
  Retaining Walls / 127
9.13. Loads On Railings, Sidewalks, and Driveways / 128
9.14. Horizontal Forces on the Building / 128
  Wind Forces / 128
  Earthquake Forces / 129
9.15. Load Combinations and Partial Live Loads / 131
  References / 132
  Suggestions for Further Reading / 132

10. WIND EFFECTS / 133
Richard M. Aynsley

10.1. Wind Climate / 133
  Hurricanes / 133
  Frontal Storms / 134
  Tornadoes / 134
  Slope and Valley Winds / 134
  Description of Strong Winds / 134
10.2. Structure of Wind / 134
  Mean Wind Speed Profile / 135
  Integral Scale of Longitudinal Turbulence / 136
  Turbulence Intensity and Spectra / 136
10.3. Wind Records / 136
  Estimation of Wind Conditions at Sites Remote from an Airport Recording Station / 137
  Wind Frequency Analysis / 137
  Probabilistic Descriptions of Wind / 137
10.4. Bluff Body Aerodynamics / 138
  Reynolds Number / 138
  Flow Regions around Bluff Bodies, and Static and Dynamic Pressure / 139
  Vortex Shedding and Turbulent Wake Flow / 140
  Influence of Architectural Features on Airflow / 140
  Computational Fluid Mechanics / 140
10.5. Wind Loads / 141
  Dynamic Response of Structure to Wind Gusts / 141
  Localized Dynamic Loads on Claddings / 142
  Knowledge-Based Expert Systems and Wind Tunnel Assessments of Wind Loads / 142
10.6. Environmental Wind Effects / 142
  Wind Effects on Pedestrians / 142
  Wind Chill Index / 143
  Air Movement for Thermal Comfort / 144
  Infiltration / 144
  Wind Transport of Particulates / 145
  Wind Effects on Building Mechanical Systems / 145
  Wind Dispersion of Gaseous Wastes / 146
  References / 146
  Suggestions for Further Reading / 147
  Notation / 147

11. STRUCTURAL SYSTEMS / 148
Henry J. Cowan and Peter R. Smith

11.1. Structural Members and Structural Assemblies / 148
11.2. Ties and Struts / 149
11.3. Statically Determinate Beams / 151
11.4. Fixed-Ended and Continuous Beams / 153
11.5. Trusses / 155

xii CONTENTS

- 11.6. Portal Frames and Arches / 161
- 11.7. Multistory Frames / 164
- 11.8. Cable-Stayed Beams / 167
- 11.9. Space Frames / 169
- 11.10. Domes / 169
- 11.11. Suspension Structures / 171
- 11.12. Cylindrical Structures / 173
- 11.13. Saddle Surfaces / 174
- 11.14. Fabric and Pneumatic Structures / 176
  - References / 177
  - Suggestions for Further Reading / 177
  - Notation / 177

12. STEEL STRUCTURES / 178
Lambert Tall

- 12.1. Design Principles / 178
- 12.2. Width-Thickness Ratio / 179
- 12.3. Tension Members / 180
- 12.4. Beams / 181
- 12.5. Compression Members / 183
- 12.6. Beam-Columns / 185
- 12.7. Bolted Connections / 186
- 12.8. Welded Connections / 187
- 12.9. Rigid Frames / 188
- 12.10. Plate Girders / 189
- 12.11. Plastic Design / 190
- 12.12. Load and Resistance Factor Design (LRFD) / 190
- 12.13. Computer-Aided Design / 191
- 12.14. Fabrication / 191
  - References / 191
  - Suggestions for Further Reading / 192
  - Notation / 192

13. CONCRETE AND MASONRY STRUCTURES / 193
Madan Mehta

- 13.1. Reinforced Concrete Codes of Practice / 193
- 13.2. Reinforced Concrete Materials / 193
  - Concrete / 193
  - Steel Reinforcement / 194
- 13.3. Methods of Design in Reinforced Concrete / 194
  - Safety Provisions / 194
- 13.4. Flexure in Reinforced Concrete Members / 195
  - Failure Modes / 195
  - Design Assumptions / 196
  - Singly Reinforced Beams / 196
  - Doubly Reinforced Beams / 198
  - T-Beams / 199
- 13.5. Shear and Torsion in Reinforced Concrete Members / 200
  - Shear / 200
  - Torsion / 202
- 13.6. Deflection in Reinforced Concrete Members / 202
- 13.7. Reinforcement Detailing / 203
  - Concrete Cover / 203
  - Reinforcement Spacing / 203
  - Crack Control / 203
  - Anchorage and Bar Development / 204
- 13.8. Analysis of Reinforced Concrete Structures / 204
  - ACI Coefficients for Beams and One-Way Slabs / 205
- 13.9. Reinforced Concrete Floor Systems / 205
  - One-Way Systems / 205
  - Two-Way Systems / 207
  - Design of One-Way Solid Slabs / 208
- 13.10. Reinforced Concrete Columns / 211
  - Reinforcement in Columns / 211
  - Short and Slender Columns / 212
  - Design of a Short Column / 212
- 13.11. Reinforced Concrete Walls / 212
- 13.12. Reinforced Concrete Footings / 213
  - Design of an Isolated Column Footing / 215
- 13.13. Prestressed Concrete / 215
  - Stresses in Prestressed Concrete Members / 216
- 13.14. Composite Construction / 218
  - Composite Beam with Slab on Removable Forms / 218
  - Composite Beam with Slab on Metal Deck Forms / 220
  - Composite Trusses and Open-Web Joists / 221
  - Composite Columns / 221
- 13.15. Load-Bearing Masonry / 221
  - Design of Masonry Walls / 223
  - Progressive Collapse / 226
  - References / 226
  - Suggestions for Further Reading / 226
  - Notation / 227

14. TIMBER STRUCTURES / 228
Russell C. Moody and Alan D. Freas

- 14.1. History / 228
- 14.2. Structural Wood Elements / 229
  - Joists, Rafters, and Studs / 229
  - Beams and Girders / 230
  - Posts and Columns / 231
  - Trusses / 233
  - Curved Members / 234
  - Stressed-Skin and Sandwich Panels / 234
  - Design of Wood Structural Elements / 236
- 14.3. Light-Frame Buildings / 236
  - Foundations / 237
  - Floors / 238
  - Exterior Walls / 238
  - Ceiling and Roof / 240
  - Sources of Additional Information / 241
- 14.4. Heavy Timber Buildings / 242
  - Log and Timber Frame Houses / 242
  - Pole and Post Frame Buildings / 243
  - Mill-Type Construction / 243
  - Glulam Beam Systems / 244
  - Arch Structures / 244

Domes / 244
Sources of Additional Information / 244
14.5. Special Considerations / 245
Connections / 246
Grades of Lumber and Panel Products / 247
Moisture Content and Shrinkage / 249
Directional Properties / 249
Erection and Bracing / 249
References / 250
Suggestions for Further Reading / 251

15. FOUNDATIONS / 252
Ronald E. Bucknam and Thomas M. Gavin

15.1. Structure and Classification of Soils / 252
Gradation / 252
Soil Classification Symbols / 253
Soil Constituents / 253
General Characteristics of Major Soil Types / 253
15.2. Engineering Properties of Soil / 253
Soil Shear Strength / 254
Compressibility / 254
Permeability / 254
15.3. Soil Exploration and Testing / 255
15.4. Foundation Systems / 256
Shallow Foundations / 256
Deep Foundations / 257
15.5. Design Considerations / 259
Building Loads / 259
Frost Protection / 259
Presence of Unsuitable Soils / 259
Shallow Foundations / 260
Stepped Footings / 260
Preloading and Surcharging / 260
Pile Foundations / 261
Preaugering or Spudding / 261
Downdrag or Negative Skin Friction / 261
Pile Hammer Selection / 261
Test Piles / 261
Pile Spacing / 262
Pile Length Prediction / 262
15.6. Retaining Walls / 262
Cantilevered Retaining Walls / 262
Braced Retaining Walls / 262
15.7. Construction Considerations / 262
Site Preparation / 263
Excavations / 263
Fill Placement and Compaction / 264
Foundation Installations / 265
15.8. Problem Soils / 266
Fill / 266
Organic Soils and Peat / 267
Collapsing Soils / 267
Swelling Soils / 267
Liquefaction / 267
Permafrost / 268

References / 268
Suggestions for Further Reading / 268

16. NOISE CONTROL / 269
Anita Lawrence

16.1. Sound and Sound Propagation / 269
16.2. Sound Perception / 270
Decibels / 271
Loudness / 271
16.3. Sound Analysis / 271
16.4. Vibration Perception / 272
16.5. Criteria for Acceptable Sound Levels in Buildings / 272
Speech Intelligibility / 272
Annoyance Criteria / 272
16.6. Airborne Sound Transmission / 272
Rating Systems for Airborne Sound Transmission Loss / 275
16.7. Structure-Borne and Impact Sound Transmission / 275
Rating Systems for Impact Sound Transmission / 275
Whole Building Vibration / 276
16.8. Building Services Noise Control / 276
16.9. Noise and the Building Envelope / 277
16.10. Detailing, Supervision, and Acceptance Testing / 278
References / 279
Suggestions for Further Reading / 280
Notation / 280

17. ROOM ACOUSTICS / 281
Louis A. Challis

17.1. Planning for Acoustical Requirements / 281
17.2. Behavior of Sound in an Enclosed Space / 282
17.3. Reflection and Diffraction of Sound in Rooms / 283
The Reflection of Sound / 283
The Diffraction of Sound / 284
Diffraction of Sound from Reflective and Absorptive Surfaces / 284
17.4. Sound Absorptive Materials / 284
Determination of Sound Absorption Coefficients / 285
Frequency Selective and Additive Systems / 285
17.5. Rating of Acoustical Absorptivity of Materials / 286
Noise Reduction Coefficient of Sound Absorptive Systems and Typical Sound Absorption Coefficients / 286
17.6. Growth and Decay of Sound in Rooms / 286
The Eyring Reverberation Time Formula / 288
The Fitzroy Reverberation Time Formula / 289

xiv CONTENTS

- 17.7. Classification of Auditoriums / 289
  - Acoustics for Speech / 289
  - Amplification of Music / 290
  - Concert Halls and Music Auditoriums / 291
  - Shapes of Auditoriums / 291
  - References / 291
  - Suggestions for Further Reading / 292
  - Notation / 292

18. WINDOWS IN BUILDINGS / 293
Baruch Givoni

- 18.1. Functions of Windows in Buildings / 293
  - Architectural Role of Glazed Areas and Shading Devices / 294
- 18.2. Spectral-Optical Properties of Windows / 294
  - Spectral Properties of Different Glasses / 294
  - Types and Treatment of Glass / 294
  - Control of the Reflected Radiation / 295
  - Control of the Absorbed Radiation / 295
  - Electrochromic Glazing / 296
- 18.3. Thermal Properties (U Values) and Effect of Windows / 296
  - Effect of Air Spaces between Window Panes / 296
  - Effect of Unshaded Windows on Cooling Loads of Air-Conditioned Buildings (Heat Gain through Unshaded Windows) / 296
  - The Shading Coefficient of Unshaded Windows with Different Glazing / 297
- 18.4. Characteristics and Efficiency of Various Shading Devices / 297
  - Fixed Shading / 297
  - Operable External Shading / 298
  - Operable Internal Shading / 299
- 18.5. Effect of Windows on Indoor Temperatures / 300
  - Effect of Unshaded Windows in Different Orientations / 300
  - Effect of Windows Shaded by Various Devices in Different Orientations / 300
- 18.6. Windows as Daylighting Elements / 302
  - Windows as Daylighting Elements in Nonresidential Buildings / 302
- 18.7. Windows as Natural Ventilation Elements / 303
  - Ventilation Functions and Requirements / 303
  - Physical Mechanisms of Natural Ventilation / 303
  - Window Design for Effective Natural Ventilation / 304
- 18.8. Windows as Solar Heating Elements / 305
  - Direct Gain through Solar Windows / 305
  - Location of Solar Windows / 306
  - Size of the Solar Windows / 306
  - Choice of the Glazing Type / 306
  - Thermal Mass in Direct Gain Solar Buildings / 306
  - References / 306
  - Suggestions for Further Reading / 307
  - Notation / 307

19. LIGHTING / 308
W. G. Julian

- 19.1. The Objectives of Lighting Design / 308
- 19.2. The Visual Basis of Lighting Design / 309
- 19.3. Units and Concepts / 310
- 19.4. Lighting Standards and Their Bases / 311
- 19.5. Lighting Design Methods / 311
  - Direct Illuminance / 313
  - The Lumen Method / 313
  - Daylight Illuminances / 314
  - Sports Lighting / 314
  - Roadlighting / 314
  - Obtrusive Light / 314
  - Emergency Lighting / 314
  - Computer-Aided Design / 315
- 19.6. Light Sources / 316
  - Daylight / 316
  - Electric Lamps / 316
- 19.7. Windows and Luminaires / 319
  - Windows and Rooflights / 319
  - Luminaires / 319
  - Lighting Control Systems / 320
- 19.8. Energy Considerations / 320
- 19.9. Lighting Maintenance / 321
  - References / 322
  - Suggestions for Further Reading / 322
  - Notation and Abbreviations / 322

20. HEATING AND COOLING OF BUILDINGS / 323
S. V. Szokolay

- 20.1. Thermal Quantities / 323
- 20.2. Heat Transfer / 324
- 20.3. Psychrometry / 327
- 20.4. Thermal Comfort / 330
- 20.5. Climate / 334
- 20.6. Climatic Data / 335
- 20.7. Thermal Insulation / 337
- 20.8. Condensation / 344
- 20.9. Heat Loss Calculation / 344
- 20.10. Thermal Behavior of Buildings / 349
- 20.11. Thermal Response Simulation / 350
- 20.12. Climatic Design / 351
- 20.13. Mechanical Ventilation / 354
- 20.14. Heating / 356
- 20.15. Air Conditioning / 358
- 20.16. Energy Conservation / 361
  - References / 364
  - Design Handbooks / 364
  - Suggestions for Further Reading / 364
  - Notation / 364

21. PASSIVE SOLAR ENERGY-EFFICIENT BUILDING DESIGN / 366
John A. Ballinger

- 21.1. Introduction / 366
- 21.2. Historical Perspective / 367
- 21.3. Site Planning and Orientation / 368
  - Passive Solar Design / 368
  - Solar Access / 370
  - Landscaping / 373
- 21.4. Thermal Insulation Materials and Their Application / 373
- 21.5. Thermal Mass and Its Effects / 374
  - Thermal Storage Capacity / 375
  - Interior Finishes and Furniture / 377
- 21.6. Passive Solar Heating Systems / 377
  - Direct Gain / 377
  - Thermal Storage Wall (Trombe Wall) / 378
  - Attached Sunspace / 379
  - References / 379
  - Suggestions for Further Reading / 380

22. ACTIVE SOLAR ENERGY SYSTEMS / 381
W. W. S. Charters and K. I. Guthrie

- 22.1. Solar Thermal and Power Systems / 381
  - Solar Thermal Systems / 381
  - Solar Power Systems / 381
- 22.2. Hot Water Services and Swimming Pool Heating / 382
  - Swimming Pool Heating / 382
  - Energy and Temperature / 382
- 22.3. Solar Water Heaters / 382
  - Systems / 382
  - Collector Types / 383
  - Solar Heat Pumps / 385
  - Hot Water Storage Cylinders / 385
  - System Design Aspects / 385
  - Installation / 387
- 22.4. Swimming Pool Heating / 387
  - Siting Features / 388
- 22.5. Solar Space Heating and Cooling / 389
  - Solar Space Heating / 389
  - Solar Space Cooling / 390
- 22.6. Stand-Alone Power Supplies / 391
  - Sizing of Solar Systems / 391
  - References / 392
  - Suggestions for Further Reading / 392

23. ELECTRICITY IN BUILDINGS / 393
Anthony D. Stokes

- 23.1. Introduction / 393
- 23.2. Fundamentals / 394
- 23.3. Electric Power Distribution / 396
- 23.4. Three-Phase, Single-Phase, and Load Balancing / 398
- 23.5. Circuits, Switchboards, and Substations / 398
- 23.6. Power Distribution Paths / 399
- 23.7. Lightning Protection / 400
- 23.8. Communications / 401
- 23.9. Quality of Supply / 401
  - Ordinary Supply Quality / 401
  - Uninterruptible Supplies / 402
- 23.10. Flicker as an Example of a Calculation in an AC Series Circuit / 403
- 23.11. Power-Factor Correction in an AC Parallel Circuit / 404
  - References / 404
  - Suggestions for Further Reading / 405
  - Notation / 405

24. WATER SUPPLY, DRAINAGE, AND REFUSE DISPOSAL / 406
Max Sherrard and Kevin Bach

- 24.1. Water Supply / 406
- 24.2. Water Reticulation (Distribution) / 406
- 24.3. Cold Water / 408
  - Valves and Faucets (Taps) / 409
  - Metering / 409
  - Maintenance / 409
  - Sizing / 409
- 24.4. Hot Water / 410
  - Hot Water Storage / 411
  - Gas Heaters / 411
  - Planning / 411
- 24.5. Fire Services / 411
  - Fire Hose Reels / 413
  - Fire Hydrants / 414
  - Detector Systems / 414
  - Sprinkler Systems / 415
  - Fire Extinguishers / 415
- 24.6. Roof, Surface, and Subsoil Drainage / 415
  - Roof Drainage / 415
  - Stormwater Drainage / 416
  - Surface Drainage / 417
  - Subsoil Drainage / 417
- 24.7. Sewerage and Waste Disposal / 417
  - Soil and Waste Pipes / 419
  - Vent Pipes / 420
- 24.8. Refuse Disposal / 420
  - Reference / 422
  - Suggestions for Further Reading / 422

25. THE MOVEMENT OF PEOPLE AND GOODS / 423
Peter R. Smith

- 25.1. The Need for Access and Egress / 423
  - Size and Shape of Building / 423
  - Normal Access—Able-Bodied People / 424
  - Normal Access—Handicapped People / 424

Emergency Access and Egress / 424
Access for Goods and Equipment / 425
25.2. Rates of Arrival and Departure, and Queueing / 425
25.3. Size and Capacity of Corridors / 425
Minimum Widths / 425
Widths Based on Traffic Flow / 426
25.4. Stairways / 426
25.5. Escalators and Moving Walkways / 428
Urban People-Moving / 428
Mechanical Details / 429
Physical Sizes / 429
Speeds and Capacities / 429
25.6. Elevators (Lifts) / 430
Criteria for Design of an Elevator Installation / 430
Layout of Elevator Groups / 431
Mechanical Details that Affect Performance / 432
Layout of Elevator Equipment / 433
25.7. Estimating Elevator Performance / 435
Speeds and Capacities / 435
Performance and Performance Criteria / 435
Zoning / 437
Skylobbies / 437
Multilevel Elevator Cars / 439
References / 439
Suggestions for Further Reading / 440

26. SAFETY IN BUILDINGS / 441
T. Z. Harmathy

26.1. Building Codes / 441
26.2. Protection from Fire—Safety Aspects / 442
Safety: As the Insurer Sees It / 442
Safety: As the Building Designer Sees It / 442
The Building before the Outbreak of Fire / 442
26.3. Spread of Fire / 443
Ignition / 443
Preflashover Fire Growth / 444
Fully Developed Fires / 446
26.4. Defense Against the Spread of Fire / 446
Defense Against Fire Spread by Destruction / 446
Defense Against Fire Spread by Convection / 449
26.5. Smoke, and Fire Safety Decisions / 450
The Smoke Problem / 450
Logic Trees and Tradeoffs / 452
Psychological and Sociological Factors / 453
26.6. Protection from Crime / 453
Paucity of Regulatory Measures / 453
Security Systems for Small Buildings / 453
Security Systems for Large Buildings / 454
"Smart" Buildings / 455
26.7. Protection from Floods and Lightning / 455
References / 455
Suggestions for Further Reading / 458
Notation / 458

APPENDIX: UNITS OF MEASUREMENT / 459

A.1. Abbreviations Used for Units of Measurement / 459
A.2. Definitions of Units, and Conversion Factors Between British/American and Metric Units / 460

INDEX TO CONTRIBUTORS / 465

INDEX TO AUTHORS CITED / 467

SUBJECT INDEX / 473

Preface

Many years have passed since the publication of the last handbook of architectural technology. In the meantime the design of the interior environment and of the building services, which were relatively minor problems prior to World War II, have become more sophisticated and much more expensive. Hence they occupy far more space in the present Handbook than had been considered appropriate in the past.

The first chapter on mathematics is very elementary; it is to provide a ready reference for people who no longer own a school or college mathematics book. The four following chapters deal with the physics and chemistry of building materials. Next there are three chapters on jointing, exclusion of water, and durability.

The chapter on loads includes a discussion of wind forces and earthquake forces: the numerical data are those applicable in the USA; similar rules apply in most other countries. There is also a separate chapter on wind which discusses environmental wind effects. The long chapter on structural systems is essentially descriptive, and it covers conventional framed structures, as well as the more complex shell, fabric, and cable-stayed structures.

We debated whether chapters on steel and concrete structures should be included. They have been a prominent feature of previous handbooks of architectural technology, and the subjects are still taught in most architecture schools, even though the actual design is now generally done by engineers. We have therefore included only an elementary treatment, and confined it to American practice, since it would have taken too much space to include the different provisions of British, Canadian, and Australian codes. The chapter on concrete structures includes a brief treatment of prestressed concrete, composite construction, and load-bearing masonry. The chapter on timber structures also has an American bias; however, North American timber is widely used in Britain, the European continent, and Australia. The structural section concludes with a discussion of foundations.

There are two chapters on acoustics, one on the reduction of (unwanted) noise, and the other on the design of auditoriums. A special chapter on windows deals with the positive contribution they make and the problems they create. The chapter on lighting includes a discussion of daylight, and the energy savings that can be achieved by making more use of it.

The long chapter on the heating and cooling of buildings is mainly concerned with the contribution made by the fabric of the building, a part of the design which often rests with the architect. The mechanical equipment used for heating and air conditioning, whose design is the task of a consulting engineer, is considered in less detail at the end of that chapter. There are separate chapters on passive and active solar energy.

The next three chapters deal with the other building services: electricity, water, drainage, sewerage, fire-fighting equipment, elevators (lifts), and escalators. The final chapter is concerned with safety in buildings, notably protection from fire. The appendix describes both the British/American and SI metric systems of measurement, and gives conversion factors between the two.

Each chapter has a bibliography, and a list of the symbols and abbreviations used in it. The abbreviations of the units of measurement are in the Appendix.

A variety of smaller topics are covered in the various chapters, and the best way to locate a particular piece of information in this Handbook is to consult the index.

Thirteen of the contributors are American, ten are Australian, and there is one each from England, Canada, and

New Zealand. We have tried to make the information useful to as many English-speaking people as possible (with the exceptions noted above, where this proved impossible), and both British/American and metric units are used throughout the Handbook.

In conclusion I would like to thank all the contributors, particularly those from overseas who have so successfully overcome the "tyranny of distance." I am indebted to Dr. Forrest Wilson, himself a contributor, who offered much helpful advice on several of the chapters, and to Ms. Wendy Lochner and Mr. Everett Smethurst, who administered this project for Van Nostrand Reinhold.

Henry J. Cowan
Sydney, Australia

HANDBOOK
OF
ARCHITECTURAL TECHNOLOGY

1
Mathematics

Henry J. Cowan and Peter R. Smith

Trigonometric, hyperbolic, and exponential functions, logarithms, and infinite series are defined. Formulas are given for simple problems involving these, and also for quadratic equations, differential coefficients and integrals. Two tables give the circumferences and areas of some plane figures, and the surface areas and volumes of some solids. The principal technical terms used in statistics are defined.

This chapter does not include tables of powers of numbers; of trigonometric, exponential and hyperbolic functions; of decimal or natural logarithms; nor of compound interest, as these are now readily obtainable from moderately priced digital calculators. However, a table of the decimal equivalents of fractions (in sixty-fourths) is given, and also the Arabic equivalents of Roman numerals.

1.1. TRIGONOMETRIC AND HYPERBOLIC FUNCTIONS, AND THE NUMBER e

Figure 1.1.1 shows a circle, center C, with a radius CA at an angle θ to the horizontal. The vertical line through A intersects the horizontal radius at B.

$$ACB = \theta \quad \text{and} \quad CBA = 90°.$$

The *trigonometric functions* (also called circular functions) are sine (abbreviated sin), cosine (cos), tangent (tan), cotangent (cot), secant (sec), and cosecant (csc or cosec). They are defined as follows:

$$\sin \theta = AB/AC, \quad \cos \theta = BC/AC,$$
$$\tan \theta = AB/BC, \quad \cot \theta = BC/AB, \quad (1.1)$$
$$\sec \theta = AC/BC, \quad \csc \theta = AC/AB.$$

The angle θ can be expressed in *degrees* (which is an arbitrary measure derived from the ancient Babylonians), or in *radian measure*, which is an absolute measure: 1 radian is the angle subtended at the center of a circle of unit radius by an arc of unit length (Figure 1.1.2). Since the entire circumference of a circle of unit radius is 2π, which corresponds to an angle of $360°$, 1 radian = $360/2\pi$ = $57°17'45''$.

The sign convention used for normal (Cartesian) coordinates also applies to trigonometric functions: Positive is up and to the right, and negative down and to the left of the origin (or center of the circle). The quadrants are customarily numbered counterclockwise, as shown in Fig. 1.1.1, and the trigonometric functions are therefore:

θ is in quadrant	$\sin \theta$	$\cos \theta$	$\tan \theta$	$\cot \theta$	$\sec \theta$	$\csc \theta$
I	+	+	+	+	+	+
II	+	−	−	−	−	+
III	−	−	+	+	−	−
IV	−	+	−	−	+	−

Inverse trigonometric functions are generally written $\sin^{-1} x$, etc., (or on calculators arc sin x or inverse sin x), where $\sin^{-1} x$ is the angle whose sine is x.

The following equations are useful in trigonometric calculations:

$$\tan \theta = \frac{\sin \theta}{\cos \theta}, \qquad \cot \theta = \frac{1}{\tan \theta},$$
$$\sec \theta = \frac{1}{\cos \theta}, \qquad \csc \theta = \frac{1}{\sin \theta},$$
$$\sin^2 \theta + \cos^2 \theta = 1, \qquad \sin 2\theta = 2 \sin \theta \cos \theta,$$
$$\cos 2\theta = \cos^2 \theta - \sin^2 \theta. \qquad (1.2)$$

2 HANDBOOK OF ARCHITECTURAL TECHNOLOGY

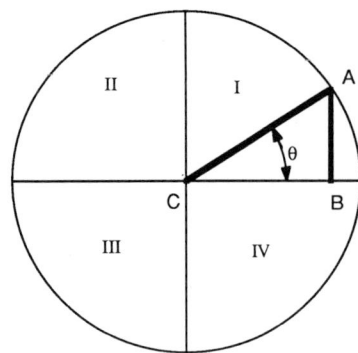

Fig. 1.1.1. Definition of trigonmetric functions.

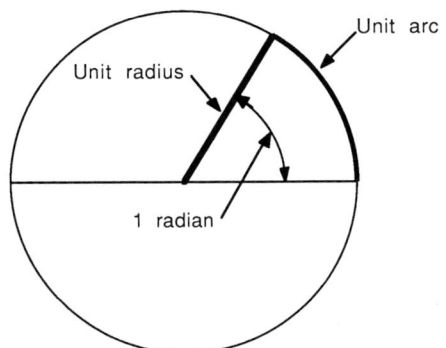

Fig. 1.1.2. Definition of radian measure.

The *number e* is defined by the series*

$$e^x = 1 + \frac{x}{1!} + \frac{x^2}{2!} + \frac{x^3}{3!} + \cdots \quad (1.3)$$

which gives $e = 2.7183\ldots$ when $x = 1$.
  The first derivative of e^x is e^x, and its integral is also e^x. e^x is also written $\exp x$.

Hyperbolic functions are related to the properties of the hyperbola, but they are more conveniently derived from e^θ:

$$\sinh \theta = \tfrac{1}{2}(e^\theta - e^{-\theta}), \quad \cosh \theta = \tfrac{1}{2}(e^\theta + e^{-\theta}),$$

$$\tanh \theta = \frac{\sinh \theta}{\cosh \theta}, \quad \coth \theta = \frac{1}{\tan \theta}, \quad (1.4)$$

$$\operatorname{sech} \theta = \frac{1}{\cosh \theta}, \quad \operatorname{csch} \theta = \frac{1}{\sinh \theta}.$$

The following equations are useful for calculations:

$$\cosh^2 \theta - \sinh^2 \theta = 1, \quad \sinh 2\theta = 2 \sinh \theta \cosh \theta,$$

$$\cosh 2\theta = \cosh^2 \theta + \sinh^2 \theta. \quad (1.5)$$

Tables of trigonometric and hyperbolic functions and of e^x were at one time customarily included in handbooks of

*The exclamation point means "factorial," that is, $3! = 1 \times 2 \times 3$.

this type. They have been omitted because they have now been readily available for more than ten years on moderately priced digital calculators.

1.2. LOGARITHMS, QUADRATIC EQUATIONS, AND INFINITE SERIES

$$\text{If } y = a^x, \text{ then } x = \log_a y. \quad (1.6)$$

This means that x is the *logarithm* of y to the base a. Any number can serve as a base, but in practice only two are used: decimal logarithms (to the base 10), and natural logarithms (to the base $e = 2.7183\ldots$). One is converted to the other by

$$\log_{10} y = \log_e y / \log_e 10, \quad \text{where} \quad \log_e 10 = 2.3026$$

$$\log_e y = \log_{10} y / \log_{10} e, \quad \text{where} \quad \log_{10} e = 0.4343$$

$$(1.7)$$

Logarithms were at one time widely used as an easy way of performing multiplications, divisions, and other calculations. They are less important today, because most of the calculations for which logarithms were once used are now done with digital calculators or computers. Logarithmic tables are not included in this handbook, partly for this reason, and partly because both decimal and natural logarithms can be obtained from many digital calculators.

The *quadratic equation*

$$x^2 + ax + b = 0$$

can either be solved by "completing the square" or directly from the equation

$$\begin{aligned} x_1 &= -\tfrac{1}{2}a + \sqrt{\tfrac{1}{4}a^2 - b} \\ x_2 &= -\tfrac{1}{2}a - \sqrt{\tfrac{1}{4}a^2 - b} \end{aligned} \quad (1.8)$$

The *sum of the series*

$$\sum x = 1 + 2 + 3 + \cdots + n = \tfrac{1}{2}n(n + 1)$$

$$\sum x^2 = 1^2 + 2^2 + 3^2 + \cdots + n^2$$

$$= \tfrac{1}{3}n(n + 1)(n + \tfrac{1}{2}) \quad (1.9)$$

$$\sum x^3 = 1^3 + 2^3 + 3^3 + \cdots + n^3 = \tfrac{1}{4}n^2(n + 1)^2$$

The *binomial series*

$$(x + y)^n = x^n + nx^{n-1}y + \frac{1}{2!}n(n - 1)x^{n-2}y^2$$

$$+ \frac{1}{3!}n(n - 2)x^{n-3}y^3 + \cdots \quad (1.10)$$

has $n + 1$ terms, if n is a positive integer:

$$(x + y)^2 = x^2 + 2xy + y^2 \quad (1.11)$$

$$(x + y)^3 = x^3 + 3x^2y + 3xy^2 + y^3$$

etc. (1.12)

When n is a negative integer, the series is infinite:

$$(1 + x)^{-1} = \frac{1}{1 + x} = 1 - x + x^2 - x^3 + \cdots$$

$$(1 - x)^{-1} = \frac{1}{1 - x} = 1 + x^2 + x^3 + \cdots \quad (1.13)$$

The series is also infinite if n is a fraction:

$$(1 + x)^{1/2} = \sqrt{1 + x} = 1 + \frac{x}{2} - \frac{x^2}{8} + \frac{x^3}{16} + \cdots \quad (1.14)$$

$$(1 + x)^{-1/2} = \frac{1}{\sqrt{1 + x}} = 1 - \frac{x}{2} + \frac{3x^2}{8} - \frac{5x^3}{16} + \cdots \quad (1.15)$$

The series in Eqs. (1.13)–(1.15) converge if x^2 is smaller than 1, that is, $-1 < x < 1$.

The series for e^x has already been given in the previous section, Eq. (1.3). Trigonometric and hyperbolic functions can also be expressed as infinite series:

$$\sin x = x - \frac{x^3}{3!} + \frac{x^5}{5!} - \frac{x^7}{7!} + \cdots \quad (1.16)$$

$$\cos x = 1 - \frac{x^2}{2!} + \frac{x^4}{4!} - \frac{x^6}{6!} + \cdots \quad (1.17)$$

$$\sinh x = x + \frac{x^3}{3!} + \frac{x^5}{5!} + \frac{x^7}{7!} + \cdots \quad (1.18)$$

$$\cosh x = 1 + \frac{x^2}{2!} + \frac{x^4}{4!} + \frac{x^6}{6!} + \cdots \quad (1.19)$$

The series in Eqs. (1.16)–(1.19) are convergent for all values of x.

1.3. DIFFERENTIATION AND INTEGRATION

The following equations are commonly used for differentiation (u, v, and w are functions of x, and c is a constant):

$$\frac{d}{dx} c = 0 \quad (1.20)$$

$$\frac{d}{dx}(cu) = c\frac{du}{dx} \quad (1.21)$$

$$\frac{d}{dx}(u + v - w) = \frac{du}{dx} + \frac{dv}{dx} - \frac{dw}{dx} \quad (1.22)$$

$$\frac{d}{dx}(uv) = u\frac{dv}{dx} + v\frac{du}{dx} \quad (1.23)$$

$$\frac{d}{dx}\left(\frac{u}{v}\right) = \frac{u\frac{du}{dx} - v\frac{dv}{dx}}{v^2} \quad (1.24)$$

$$\frac{d}{dx} u^n = nu^{n-1}\frac{du}{dx} \quad (1.25)$$

$$\frac{d}{dx} \sqrt{u} = \frac{1}{2\sqrt{u}}\frac{du}{dx} \quad (1.26)$$

$$\frac{d}{dx} \log_e u = \frac{1}{u}\frac{du}{dx} \quad (1.27)$$

$$\frac{d}{dx} \sin u = \cos u \frac{du}{dx} \quad (1.28)$$

$$\frac{d}{dx} \cos u = -\sin u \frac{du}{dx} \quad (1.29)$$

$$\frac{d}{dx} \tan u = \sec^2 u \frac{du}{dx} \quad (1.30)$$

$$\frac{d}{dx} e^u = e^u \frac{du}{dx} \quad (1.31)$$

$$\frac{d}{dx} \sinh u = \cosh u \frac{du}{dx} \quad (1.32)$$

$$\frac{d}{dx} \cosh u = \sinh u \frac{du}{dx} \quad (1.33)$$

The table of standard integrals, which is reproduced in many textbooks and handbooks is very lengthy. The following are those most frequently used:

$$\int c\, dx = cx \quad (1.34)$$

$$\int cu\, dx = c\int u\, dx \quad (1.35)$$

$$\int (u + v - w)\, dx = \int u\, dx + \int v\, dx - \int w\, dx \quad (1.36)$$

$$\int x^n\, dx = \frac{x^{n+1}}{n + 1} \quad \text{(provided } n \neq -1\text{)} \quad (1.37)$$

Eq. (1.37) applies to $x^{1/2} = \sqrt{x}$; $x^{-1/2} = 1/\sqrt{x}$; and $x^{-2} = 1/x^2$; however, for $n = -1$, Eq. (1.38) applies:

$$\int \frac{dx}{x} = \log_e x \quad (1.38)$$

4 HANDBOOK OF ARCHITECTURAL TECHNOLOGY

$$\int e^x \, dx = e^x \tag{1.39}$$

$$\int a^x \, dx = a^x / \log_e a \tag{1.40}$$

$$\int x e^x \, dx = e^x(x - 1) \tag{1.41}$$

$$\int \sin x \, dx = -\cos x \tag{1.42}$$

$$\int \sin^2 x \, dx = \tfrac{1}{2}(x - \sin x \cos x) \tag{1.43}$$

$$\int \cos x \, dx = \sin x \tag{1.44}$$

$$\int \tan x \, dx = -\log_e \cos x \tag{1.45}$$

$$\int \sin^{-1} x \, dx = x \sin^{-1} x + \sqrt{1 - x^2} \tag{1.46}$$

$$\int \cos^{-1} x \, dx = x \cos^{-1} x - \sqrt{1 - x^2} \tag{1.47}$$

$$\int \tan^{-1} x \, dx = x \tan^{-1} x - \log_e \sqrt{1 + x^2} \tag{1.48}$$

$$\int \sinh x \, dx = \cosh x \tag{1.49}$$

$$\int \cosh x \, dx = \sinh x \tag{1.50}$$

$$\int \tanh x \, dx = \log_e \cosh x \tag{1.51}$$

1.4. MEASUREMENT OF CIRCUMFERENCES, AREAS, AND VOLUMES

The information is presented in tabular form in Tables 1.1 and 1.2.

1.5. A LIST OF STATISTICAL TERMS

Statistic. A quantity computed from observation on a sample.
Observation. The value of a quality characteristic observed or measured on a unit.
Statistical Unit. One of a number of similar pieces of material of a similar type. A unit may possess several different quality characteristics.
Sample. A group of units from a larger number.
Random Sample. A sample selected so that every unit has an equal chance of inclusion.
Representative Sample. A sample taken so that units are selected from each of the different sub-portions of the whole.
Population. A large collection of units from one source; for example, all the concrete test pieces produced from one structure.

Arithmetic Mean, also called **Average,** or **Mean.** The sum of all the observations, divided by the number of observations.
Geometric Mean. If there are n observations, the geometric mean is the nth root of their product.
Median. The middle item in a group, arranged in order of magnitude. For example, if there are 21 observations, the median is the 11th; if there are 20, the median is the mean of the 10th and the 11th.
Mode. The most common item in a group. If the observations are plotted as a bar chart, or histogram, the mode is the observation corresponding to the longest bar.
Histogram or Bar Chart. A diagram in which observations are represented by rectangles or bars with one side equal to the interval over which the observations occurred, and the other equal to the frequency of occurrence of the observations within that range.
Range. The difference between the largest and the smallest observations.
Deviation. The departure of an observation from the arithmetic mean of all observations.
Variance. The average of the squares of the deviations of a number of observations from their mean value.
Standard Deviation. The square root of the variance. This is the most commonly used measure of the spread of a number of observations. A small standard deviation thus indicates good quality control. The exact value of the standard deviation is

$$\sigma = \sqrt{\frac{1}{n - 1} \sum (x_i - x_m)^2} \tag{1.52}$$

where σ = standard deviation,
n = number of observations,
x_i = an observation in the group $x_1, x_2, x_3, \ldots, x_n$,
x_m = the arithmetic mean of the values in the group.

Coefficient of Variation. The ratio of the standard deviation and arithmetic mean, expressed as a percentage.
Distribution Curve. The idealized form of a histogram. When the interval over which the observations occur becomes infinitely small, the bar chart becomes a continuous distribution curve.
Normal (Gaussian) Distribution Curve. The distribution curve found from experience to result when the number of observations is very large and there are no unusual circumstances to distort the distribution (Fig. 1.5.1). The equation of this curve is

$$y = K e^{-(1/2)t^2} \tag{1.53}$$

where K is a constant,
e is the base of the natural logarithms, 2.7183 . . . ,

Table 1.1. Circumferences and Areas of Some Plane Figures.

Name and Dimensions	Circumference	Area
1. Circle	πd	$\frac{1}{4}\pi d^2$
2. Segment of a Circle	$d\left[\theta + \sin\frac{1}{2}\theta\right]$	$\frac{1}{8}d^2(\theta - \sin\theta)$
3. Sector of a Circle	$d(\theta + 1)$	$\frac{1}{8}\theta d^2$
4. Annulus	πd_1 (External) πd_2 (Internal)	$\frac{1}{4}\pi(d_1^2 - d_2^2)$
5. Triangle	$a + b + c$	$\frac{1}{2}bh$
6. Square	$4a$	a^2
7. Rectangle	$2(a + b)$	ab

6 HANDBOOK OF ARCHITECTURAL TECHNOLOGY

Table 1.1. (*Continued*)

Name and Dimensions	Circumference	Area
8. Parallelogram 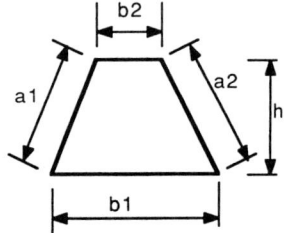	$2(a + b)$	bh
9. Trapezoid 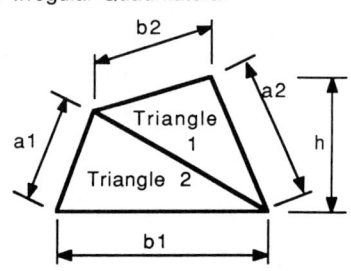	$a_1 + a_2 + b_1 + b_2$	$\frac{1}{2}(b_1 + b_2)h$
10. Irregular Quadrilateral	$a_1 + a_2 + b_1 + b_2$	The sum of the areas of two triangles into which the quadrilateral can be divided.

Table 1.2. Surface Areas and Volumes of Some Solids.

Name and Dimensions	Surface Area	Volume
1. Sphere 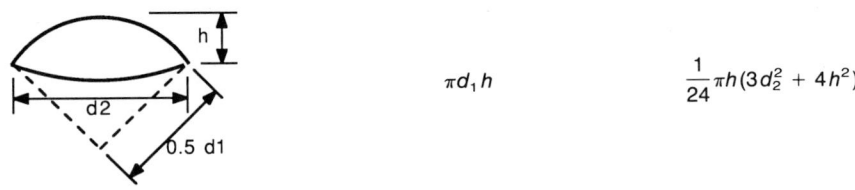	πd^2	$\frac{1}{6}\pi d^3$
2. Segment of a Sphere	$\pi d_1 h$	$\frac{1}{24}\pi h(3d_2^2 + 4h^2)$
3. Sector of a Sphere 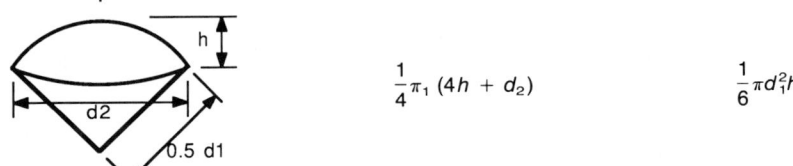	$\frac{1}{4}\pi_1 (4h + d_2)$	$\frac{1}{6}\pi d_1^2 h$

MATHEMATICS 7

Table 1.2. (*Continued*)

Name and Dimensions	Surface Area	Volume
4. Hollow Sphere Outer diameter = d_1 Inner diameter = d_2	Outer surface area: πd_1^2	$\frac{1}{6}\pi(d_1^3 - d_2^3)$
5. Cylinder	$\pi dh + \frac{1}{4}\pi d^2$	$\frac{1}{4}\pi d^2 h$
6. Hollow Cylinder or Pipe Outer diameter = d_1 Inner diameter = d_2	$\pi d_1 h + \frac{1}{2}\pi(d_1^2 - d_2^2)$	$\frac{1}{4}\pi h(d_1^2 - d_2^2)$
7. Torus or Ring of Circular Cross Section	$\frac{1}{4}\pi(d_1 + d_2)\cdot(d_1 - d_2)$	$\frac{\pi^2}{32}(d_1 + d_2)\cdot(d_1 - d_2)^2$
8. Cube	$6a^2$	a^3
9. Rectangular Column	$2ab + 2ah + 2bh$	abh
10. Cone	$\frac{1}{4}\pi d\sqrt{d^2 + 4h^2} + \frac{1}{4}\pi d^2$	$\frac{1}{12}\pi d^2 h$

8 HANDBOOK OF ARCHITECTURAL TECHNOLOGY

Table 1.2. *(Continued)*

Name and Dimensions	Surface Area	Volume
11. Pyramid 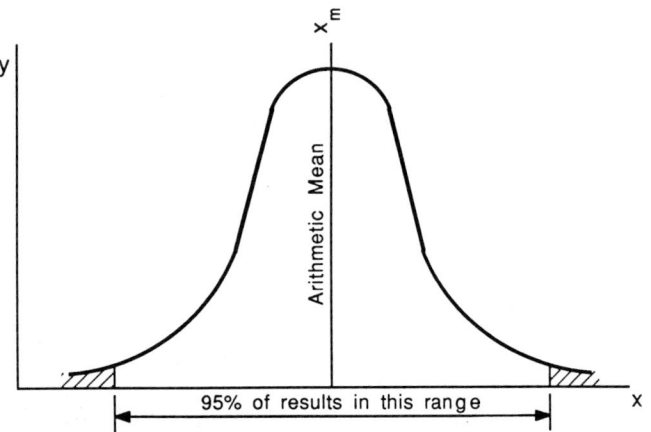 Area of base = A	Area of base + areas of sides	$\frac{1}{3}Ah$

Fig. 1.5.1. The normal, or Gaussian, distribution curve, and the range for which quality control tests are normally devised.

$$t = (x_i - x_m)/\sigma$$

x_i is the observation plotted on the curve,
x_m is the arithmetic mean, and
σ is the standard deviation.

The Gaussian curve contains a few very high and a few very low observations. Quality control tests are generally devised for 90 or 95 per cent of the results (Fig. 1.5.1).

Level of Significance. The figure selected as the criterion for accepting a hypothesis about a population. Common tests include the *Chi-Square Test* for goodness of fit, the *t-Test* for comparing population means, and the *F-Test* for comparing population variances.

1.6. DECIMAL EQUIVALENTS OF FRACTIONS

In the American (British) system of measurements, fractions are frequently made dividing by 2, instead of dividing by 10. For the purpose of calculation these fractions must be converted to decimals. The following table gives the decimal equivalents of fractions advancing in sixty-fourths.

$\frac{1}{64}$ = .015625	$\frac{25}{64}$ = .390625	$\frac{49}{64}$ = .765625
$\frac{1}{32}$ = .03125	$\frac{13}{32}$ = .40625	$\frac{25}{32}$ = .78125
$\frac{3}{64}$ = .046875	$\frac{27}{64}$ = .421875	$\frac{51}{64}$ = .796875
$\frac{1}{16}$ = .0625	$\frac{7}{16}$ = .4375	$\frac{13}{16}$ = .8125
$\frac{5}{64}$ = .078125	$\frac{29}{64}$ = .453125	$\frac{53}{64}$ = .828125
$\frac{3}{32}$ = .09375	$\frac{15}{32}$ = .46875	$\frac{27}{32}$ = .84375
$\frac{7}{64}$ = .109375	$\frac{31}{64}$ = .484375	$\frac{55}{64}$ = .859375
$\frac{1}{8}$ = .125	$\frac{1}{2}$ = .50	$\frac{7}{8}$ = .875
$\frac{9}{64}$ = .140625	$\frac{33}{64}$ = .515625	$\frac{57}{64}$ = .890625
$\frac{5}{32}$ = .15625	$\frac{17}{32}$ = .53125	$\frac{29}{32}$ = .90625
$\frac{11}{64}$ = .171875	$\frac{35}{64}$ = .546875	$\frac{59}{64}$ = .921875
$\frac{3}{16}$ = .1875	$\frac{9}{16}$ = .5625	$\frac{15}{16}$ = .9375
$\frac{13}{64}$ = .203125	$\frac{37}{64}$ = .578125	$\frac{61}{64}$ = .953125
$\frac{7}{32}$ = .21875	$\frac{19}{32}$ = .59375	$\frac{31}{32}$ = .96875
$\frac{15}{64}$ = .234375	$\frac{39}{64}$ = .609375	$\frac{63}{64}$ = .984375
$\frac{1}{4}$ = .25	$\frac{5}{8}$ = .625	
$\frac{17}{64}$ = .265625	$\frac{41}{64}$ = .640625	
$\frac{9}{32}$ = .28125	$\frac{21}{32}$ = .65625	
$\frac{19}{64}$ = .296875	$\frac{43}{64}$ = .671875	
$\frac{5}{16}$ = .3125	$\frac{11}{16}$ = .6875	
$\frac{21}{64}$ = .328125	$\frac{45}{64}$ = .703125	
$\frac{11}{32}$ = .34375	$\frac{23}{32}$ = .71875	
$\frac{23}{64}$ = .359375	$\frac{47}{64}$ = .734375	
$\frac{3}{8}$ = .375	$\frac{3}{4}$ = .75	

1.7. ARABIC EQUIVALENTS OF ROMAN NUMERALS

Roman numerals are based on the digits of both hands:

Roman numerals: I V X L C D M
Arabic equivalents: 1 5 10 50 100 500 1000

The digits are read from left to right. Four and nine are written by subtracting 1 from 5 and 10. A smaller number preceding a larger one is subtracted from it; otherwise they are added together. There is no symbol for zero.

I = 1; II = 2, III = 3; IV = 4, V = 5; VI = 6, VII = 7; VIII = 8; IX = 9; X = 10; XI = 11; XIX = 19; XL or XXXX = 40; XC or LXXXX = 90; CD or CCCC = 400 etc. For example MCMLXXXIV = 1984.

Roman numerals are rarely used for numbers above

3000. Higher numerals, if needed, are produced by placing a bar above the numeral, which multiplies it by 1000.

SUGGESTIONS FOR FURTHER READING

Milton Abramowitz and Irene A. Stegun (Eds.). *Handbook of Mathematical Functions with Formulas, Graphs, and Mathematical Tables.* National Bureau of Standards Applied Mathematics Series 55. 9th Printing. U.S. Government Printing Office, Washington, DC, 1970.

C. B. Allendoerfer and C. O. Oakley. *Principles of Mathematics.* McGraw-Hill, New York. 1986.

A. Beck et al. *Excursions into Mathematics.* Worth, New York, 1972.

M. Boas. *Mathematical Methods in the Physical Sciences.* Wiley, New York, 1983.

H. J. Cowan (Ed.). *Encyclopedia of Building Technology.* Prentice-Hall, Englewood Cliffs, NJ, 1988.

H. J. Cowan and P. R. Smith. *Dictionary of Architectural and Building Technology.* Elsevier Applied Science, London and New York, 1986.

L. Garding. *Encounter into Mathematics.* Springer Verlag, New York, 1977.

J. Heading. *Mathematical Methods in Science and Engineering.* Edward Arnold, London, 1963.

L. Hogben. *Mathematics for the Million.* Pan, London, 1973.

W. G. Johnson and L. N. Zaccaro. *Modern Introductory Mathematics.* McGraw-Hill, New York, 1966.

M. Kline. *Mathematics in the Physical World.* John Murray, London, 1960.

J. R. Newman. *The World of Mathematics.* Novello, London, 1961.

Mathematics and the Modern World: Readings from the Scientific American. W. H. Freeman, San Francisco, 1968.

I. H. Rose. *A Modern Introduction to College Mathematics.* Wiley, New York, 1959.

I. S. Sokolnikoff and R. M. Redheffer. *Mathematics of Physics and Modern Engineering.* McGraw-Hill, New York, 1966.

George N. Thomas and Ross L. Finney. *Calculus and Analytical Geometry,* 6th Ed. Addison-Wesley, Reading, MA, 1983.

J. P. Trembley and R. Mancher. *Discrete Mathematics with Applications to Computer Science.* McGraw-Hill, New York, 1975.

NOTATION

x	independent variable
y	dependent variable
θ	angle (independent variable)
u, v, w	functions of x
a, b, c, K	constants
n	number
$n!$	n factorial $= 1 \times 2 \times 3 \times \ldots \times n$
e	$2.7183\ldots$
$\exp x$	a method of writing e^x on one line, without the use of a superscript
π	$3.14159\ldots$
Σ	sum of
$\dfrac{d}{dx}$	differential coefficient of, first derivative of
$\int$	integral of
σ	standard deviation

2
Metals

Henry J. Cowan and Peter R. Smith

This chapter deals with the physical and chemical properties of the metals used in building construction. The manufacture of iron and steel, their properties, and their treatment are described. Special consideration is given to corrosion protection and to alloy steels, including stainless steel. In the discussion of the nonferrous metals, particular attention is given to aluminum and its alloys. The final section deals with methods for joining metals. The structural properties of steel are considered in Chapters 12 and 13.

2.1. METALS, CERAMICS, AND PLASTICS

The fundamental particles of matter combine to form over 100 elements, each consisting of a nucleus and a number of electrons that revolve around the nucleus (Fig. 2.1.1). The innermost orbit, or shell, can hold a maximum of 2 electrons, the next a maximum of 8 electrons, the next after that a maximum of 16 electrons, and so on.

The elements are arranged in accordance with their increasing number of electrons in a periodic table (Fig. 2.1.2). The great majority of the elements are metals, and these are on the left of Figure 2.1.2.

Metals have a characteristic "metallic" appearance; they are good conductors of heat and electricity (which may or may not be a desirable property for any particular application); and unless formed into very, very thin sheets, they are opaque to light. These properties are due to the structure of the atom (Fig. 2.1.1).

As the atomic weight increases, more electrons are added to an atom; as vacant positions in the outer shell of electrons are filled, a new shell further from the nucleus is formed. This outer shell may contain far fewer than the maximum possible number of electrons, and these "free" electrons are comparatively mobile in an electric field, a characteristic that gives metals their high electrical conductivity. The high thermal conductivity of metals is also associated with the mobility of the outer electrons, which can thus transfer thermal energy more easily from a high to a low temperature level. The opaqueness of metals is due to the readiness with which free electrons in the outer shell absorb light energy.

The chemical elements with the larger number of electrons in the outer shell are the nonmetals. In materials science, the branch of engineering that deals with the physical properties of materials, any compound of a metal and a nonmetal is called a *ceramic*.

In everyday parlance the word *ceramic* refers to pottery, porcelain, bricks, and tiles, all made from clay, which is a hydrated aluminum silicate. In materials science, however, the term *ceramic* has the wider meaning just given, and thus it includes natural stone, concrete, plaster, and all metallic ores.

Because of their "free" electrons, metals readily form chemical compounds. Some, like aluminum or sodium, oxidize immediately on being exposed to air, that is, they form a "ceramic" oxide skin. With the exception of gold, no metal has been found in its metallic state on the earth's surface in significant quantities. Iron, which has become the most widely used metal in buildings, is produced from ores, most of which are various forms of iron oxide. The reduction of the oxide to the metal requires thermal energy; but the oxidation of the metal produces energy.

In ceramics, the free metallic electrons are combined with the electrons of the nonmetal; ceramics are therefore usually poor conductors of heat and electricity.

Many ceramics are chemically stable compounds, and they are therefore common on the earth's surface. Natural ceramics and the materials made from them include natural

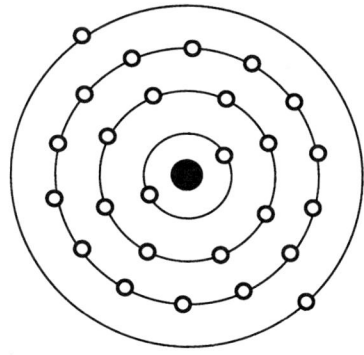

Fig. 2.1.1. An atom consists of a nucleus and a number of electrons which revolve around it. This illustration shows the atom of iron, which has 26 electrons, the atomic number 26, and an atomic weight of 55.85. (Hydrogen has an atomic weight of 1.008.) The outermost orbit, or shell, contains only two electrons, and this accounts for the metallic character of the atom.

stone, brick, and concrete. These are important to the building industry because they are durable, plentiful, and cheap; but they are brittle and have poor tensile strength (see Section 3.1, Chapter 3).

In common parlance *plastics* have chain or ring molecules, based mostly on carbon atoms (see Section 5.1, Chapter 5). However, in materials science this term also has a wider meaning, including all compounds of nonmetals. Thus all organic compounds are plastics in this terminology, and that includes timber.

2.2. THE DEFORMATION AND FRACTURE OF METALS

All metals form crystals, and some non-metals and ceramics also form crystals. A crystal can be visualized by taking a number of billiard or ping-pong balls and close-stacking them in the various ways possible. The three principal types are the face-centered cubic, the body-centered cubic, and the hexagonal close-packed structure (Ref. 2.1).

The deformation of a crystal (Fig. 2.2.1) therefore increases the distance between some of the atoms, and the attractions between the atoms resist this deformation (Fig. 2.2.1b). When the force causing the deformation is removed, the crystal resumes its original form (Fig. 2.2.1a); this is called *elastic deformation*. A sufficiently great force,

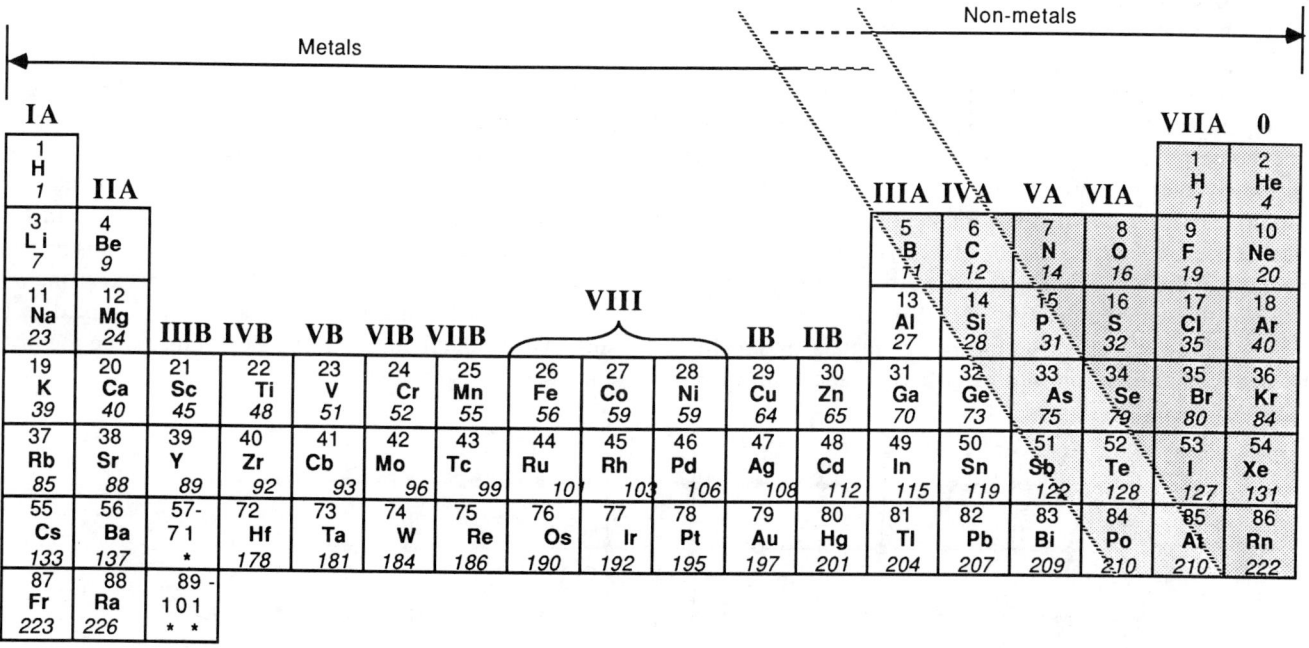

Fig. 2.1.2. The periodic table of the elements. The elements are arranged in the order of increasing *atomic weights* (which are here given only to the nearest whole number). Each is given a serial number, which is called the *atomic number*. The elements are arranged in vertical columns, according to their chemical behavior, which depends mainly on the number of electrons in the outer shell of the atom. Since elements with few electrons in the outer shell behave like metals, this arrangement shows metals on the left of the table and nonmetals on the right; a few intermediate elements behave sometimes like metals and sometimes like nonmetals.

The names of the elements of particular interest to the study of building materials, along with their abbreviations, are as follows: H = hydrogen; He = helium; C = carbon; N = nitrogen; O = oxygen; F = fluorine; Ne = neon; Na = sodium; Mg = magnesium; Al = aluminum; Si = silicon; P = phosphorus; S = sulfur; Cl = chlorine; Ar = argon; K = potassium; Ca = calcium; Cr = chromium; Mn = manganese; Fe = iron; Ni = nickel; Cu = copper; Zn = zinc; Br = bromine; Sn = tin; W = tungsten; Hg = mercury; Pb = lead.

*Elements 57–71: The rare-earth elements of atomic weight 139–175.

**Elements 89–101: Actinium, thorium, uranium, and a number of radioactive elements which have been produced in the laboratory, but do not exist in nature; their atomic weights are 227–256.

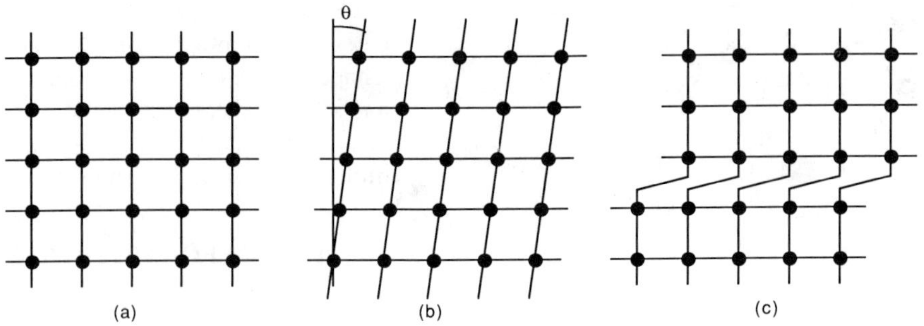

12 HANDBOOK OF ARCHITECTURAL TECHNOLOGY

Fig. 2.2.1. Deformation of a crystal of pure, unalloyed iron at room temperature. At room temperature iron occurs in the form of *ferrite* or *alpha iron* (Section 2.4), which forms body-centered cubic crystals (a). A small force causes elastic deformation (b), which is fully recovered when the force is removed (a). A larger force causes plastic deformation (c), which is not recovered.

however, causes some atoms to move further from their original neighbors than from adjacent atoms, and the interatomic forces then cause a jump of one atomic space (Fig. 2.2.1c). This is called *plastic deformation*; unlike elastic deformation, it is permanent, and not recovered when the force is removed.

The elastic and the plastic deformation of perfect crystals can be calculated from atomic theory. Observed elastic deformations agree quite well with the theory, but the force needed in practice to produce plastic deformation in pure metals (which are not, in fact, very strong) is only a small fraction of that theoretically required. The reason for this discrepancy is that most metal crystals have imperfections. One common imperfection is the *dislocation*, a defect caused by the intrusion of an extra line of atoms (Fig. 2.2.2a). These imperfections make plastic deformation much easier, because a smaller force is then required for the atom at the end of the dislocation to make a new interaction with another atom (Fig. 2.2.2b).

It is relatively easy to deform *pure* metals plastically, and metals are therefore normally used in the form of alloys. Even the gold and silver used for jewelry are alloys; for example, sterling silver contains $7\frac{1}{2}$ percent of copper.

The addition of an atom of another material increases strength, because it deforms the crystal lattice, and thus makes the movement of a dislocation more difficult (Fig. 2.2.3). Thus about 0.1 percent of carbon greatly increases the strength of pure iron; this impure iron is called *steel*. Impure metals, or *alloys*, are much stronger than the pure metal, provided suitable alloying elements are used (see Sections 2.4, 2.6, and 2.7).

Most metals used in buildings are *ductile*, that is, they have the capacity for large plastic deformation. The opposite property is *brittleness*. Brittle materials rupture with little or no warning, but their strength may be higher than that of some ductile materials with a similar composition.

Because of their large plastic deformation, ductile materials give warning of impending failure, and this provides a factor of safety against collapse. For this reason, reinforced concrete (Chapter 13) is normally designed to ensure that the ductile reinforcing steel fails before the brittle concrete.

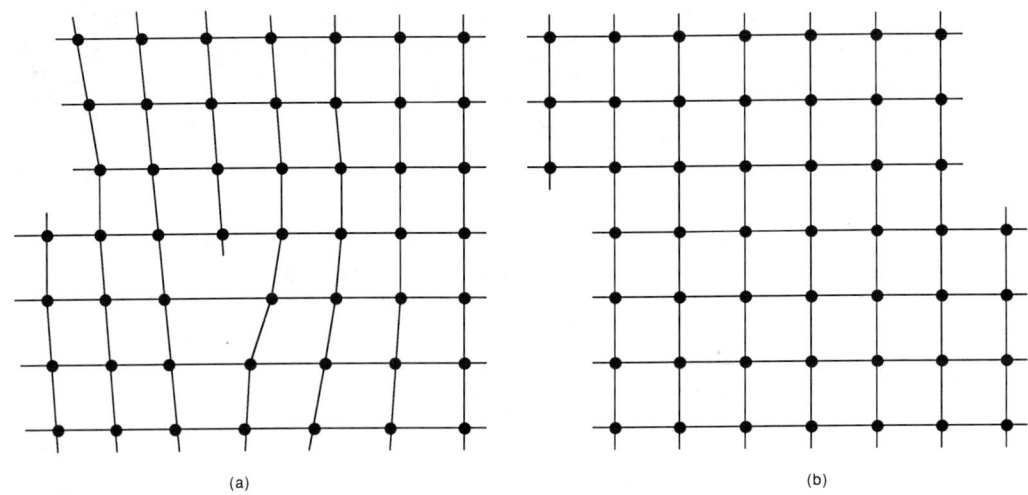

Fig. 2.2.2. Plastic deformation at a dislocation, which is a defect caused by the intrusion of an extra line of atoms (a). This reduces the force required to cause plastic deformation (b).

METALS 13

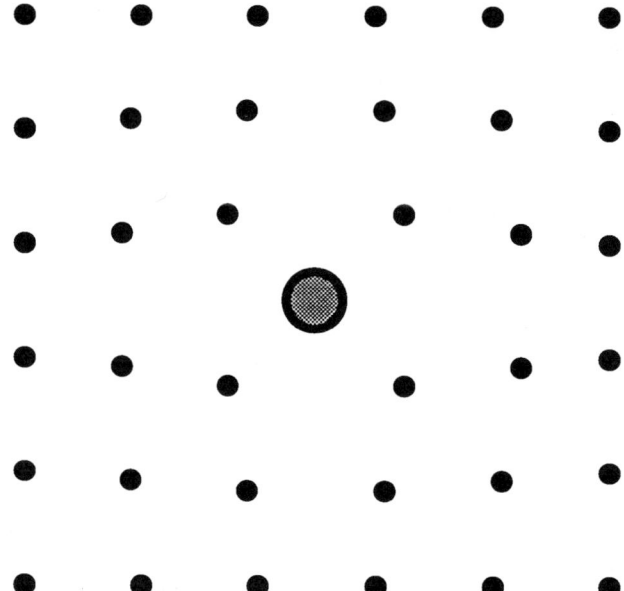

Fig. 2.2.3. The addition of a carbon atom into an interstitial space in the iron crystal lattice increases strength, because it makes the movement of a dislocation more difficult.

Ductile materials can absorb stress concentrations without failure. Thus, when a sheet of glass is scratched with a glass cutter, it will easily break along the line drawn because of the stress concentrations produced by the scratch, but a sheet of steel cannot be broken along a scratch line because the stress concentrations merely cause local plastic deformations.

In spite of their limitations, we make extensive use of brittle materials. They usually have good compressive strength, they are often hard and abrasion resistant, and they are frequently the cheapest materials that fulfill the functional requirements.

Ductility and brittleness are not inherent properties of a material; they depend on temperature and pressure. Thus rocks are brittle; but they were once deformed plastically at high temperatures and pressures, as the geological record shows. Ductile structural steel turns brittle at extremely low temperatures, and the danger of a brittle failure is increased in very cold weather.

Boiling a material and fracturing it both involve rupture of the atomic bonds, and one would theoretically expect that the energy needed to fracture a material would be the same as the latent heat required for its vaporization. In practice, however, the energy needed for fracture is very much less, and the discrepancy is due to the presence of minute flaws, or microcracks. These cracks are distributed in a random manner, but the probability of encountering a large flaw is greater in a large piece of material than in a small piece. Thus the average strength of large pieces of brittle material is lower than that of small pieces of the same material. Thus it is important to specify the size of the test piece for testing strength, particularly if a brittle failure is expected.

The addition of carbon to steel increases its strength, because it blocks more of the dislocations, but it reduces the ductility of high-carbon steels, frequently used in the past because of their high strength; it is now customary to use other low-alloy steels (see Section 2.6) in order to maintain the ductility of the steel.

The ductility or brittleness of a metal are immediately apparent from an inspection of its *stress-strain diagram*. *Stress* is defined as the force per unit area, and *strain* as the elongation or contraction per unit length. Both are therefore independent of the actual dimensions of a test piece. The elastic strain of a metal is small compared to its later plastic strain, and it is generally directly proportional to the stress. The ratio of elastic stress to elastic strain is a constant called the *modulus of elasticity*.

Figure 2.2.4 shows three carbon steels. With increasing carbon content from Fig. 2.2.4 (a) to (c), the material becomes less ductile and more brittle, and its strength increases. The *toughness* of steel is defined as the energy required to break the material, and it is thus represented by the area under the stress-strain diagram, shown shaded in Figure 2.2.4.

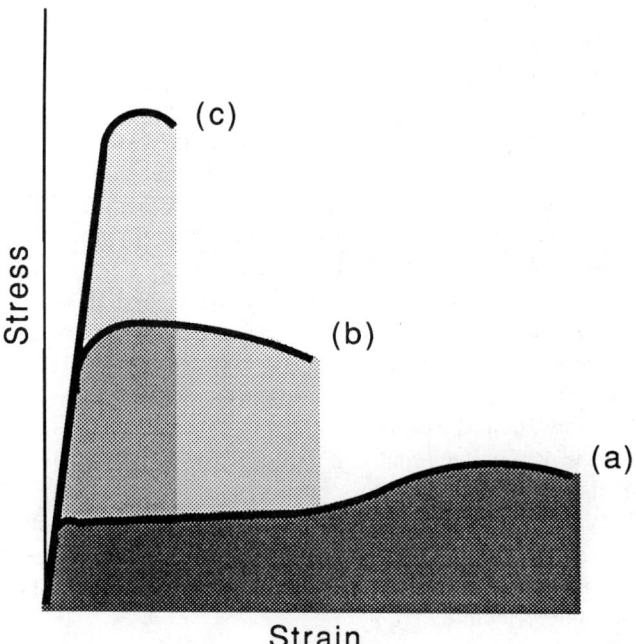

Fig. 2.2.4. Definition of strength, ductility, brittleness, and toughness. *Strength* is the ability to sustain a high stress without yielding or breaking. *Ductility* is the ability to sustain a high strain without breaking; *brittleness* is the opposite of ductility. *Toughness* is the ability to absorb energy without breaking, and it is proportional to the shaded area under the stress-strain curve. Thus the steel of curve (a) has the highest ductility, the steel of curve (b) has the highest toughness, and the steel of curve (c) has the highest strength.

2.3. WROUGHT IRON, CAST IRON, AND CARBON STEEL

Copper (whose melting point is 1981°F or 1083°C) has been used for tools since about 4000 B.C. Iron (whose melting point is much higher, 2797°F or 1536°C) was not produced in significant quantities until 1400 B.C. The fuel technology to produce temperatures high enough to melt pure iron did not exist until modern times; instead, iron was made by the more complex process of heating iron ore on a charcoal fire and reducing it to a soft sponge without actually melting it. This spongy iron could be worked (or wrought) into the desired shape at white heat. It then became possible to make *steel* from this traditional form of *wrought iron* by heating and hammering it for a prolonged period in a charcoal fire, from which it absorbed some carbon. It was very difficult to ensure that the material uniformly absorbed sufficient carbon for the strength required, without absorbing so much that it became brittle; hence steel was a very expensive material until modern times.

The other traditional form of iron is *cast iron*. Whereas wrought iron is almost pure iron, cast iron contains 1.8–4.5 percent of carbon, and it is an alloy of iron and iron carbide. Its melting point is 630°F (350°C) lower than that of wrought iron, and this temperature can be produced with a charcoal fire and bellows. The Chinese discovered this process in the 6th Century B.C., but it was not discovered in Europe until the 12th Century A.D., and the metal did not become a serious competitor to wrought iron until the 18th century.

A small quantity of wrought iron is still made by the traditional *puddling process*, in which the iron is not melted, but remains in a pasty condition. In this process it absorbs some slag which gives it a fibrous structure, and also gives it a better rust resistance than steel. This iron is easily worked, and it is used mainly for decorative gates, etc. Cast iron still has substantial uses because it provides hard wearing surfaces and rusts less easily than steel. However, most iron is used in building in the form of steel.

Before Henry Bessemer invented the process named after him, in 1856, steel could be produced only laboriously in small quantities. The Bessemer convertor blows hot air through liquid pig iron (that is, unrefined cast iron) until most of the carbon is burned, and the resulting steel is then cast into molds. Other modern steel-making processes use the same principle.

Most iron ores are oxides, although some are iron carbonates or silicates. They contain impurities, notably sulfur, phosphorus, silicon, and manganese. Most substances other than iron are burned during the process of steel making, or converted into materials that float to the surface as a *slag*. A *flux*, usually limestone, is added to promote the formation of this slag.

Steel furnaces are made from steel, but since this would itself melt or soften in contact with the molten steel, it is lined with *refractory bricks* which melt at a higher temperature (but do not have the strength to be used for a furnace without the support of the steel). The choice between *acid* refractories (usually bricks of silicon oxide) and *basic* refractories (usually bricks of magnesium oxide or of magnesium and calcium oxide derived from dolomite rock) depends on the ores used, and the desired composition of the steel. Basic refractories are more common, because they remove most of the sulfur and phosphorus which some ores and fuels contain in excessive quantities.

After the ingots have cooled, they are removed from the molds, reheated to a white heat, and passed through a *blooming mill*, which turns them into longer and thinner shapes called *blooms*. Another mill then further reduces the section and increases the length to produce *billets*. Billets are then further hot-rolled into structural sections (Fig. 2.3.1), into plates, or into bars for reinforced concrete.

Hot-rolled steel has a rough, brown surface formed by the oxide skin that results when the steel cools. This improves the bond between steel and concrete or light struc-

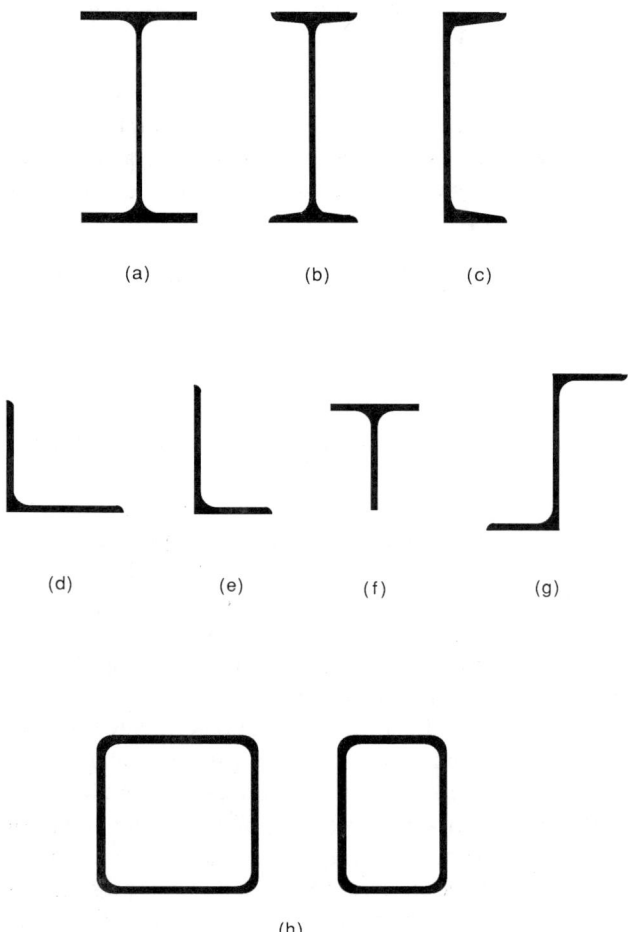

Fig. 2.3.1. American standard steel sections produced by hot rolling. (a) Wide-flange beams and stanchions; (b) standard beams; (c) standard channels; (d) equal angles; (e) unequal angles; (f) tees; (g) zees; (h) hot-rolled square and rectangular tubing.

tural fire protection. For many purposes, however, a smoother surface is required, and this can be produced by *cold-rolling* the steel so that it does not oxidize when the rolling process is complete. Cold steel offers more resistance to rolling, so that only thin sections can be rolled cold.

2.4. THE PROPERTIES AND TREATMENT OF STEEL

The properties of iron and steel, and their improvement by heat treatment, are best explained with the help of the phase diagram in Fig. 2.4.1. Iron occurs in different crystalline forms, but only *alpha iron*, also called *ferrite*, and *gamma iron*, also called *austenite*, are of practical importance. Ferrite is a ductile and comparatively soft metal, and it crystallizes with a body-centered cubic space lattice (see Section 2.2). Austenite has a face-centered cubic lattice. In carbon steels it exists only above a temperature of 730°C, but in some alloy steels (Section 2.6) it can exist at room temperature.

The two materials alloyed in carbon steel and cast iron are iron and iron carbide (Fe_3C); the latter is a hard and brittle white compound, also called *cementite*, and it occurs at room temperature. The eutectoid *pearlite* also occurs at room temperature. It consists of ferrite and cementite which alternate in a fine and regular pattern; as a result, when viewed under a metallurgical microscope it looks somewhat like mother-of-pearl.

The traditional wrought iron, which is mostly ferrite, is the material on the extreme left of the phase diagram (Fig. 2.4.1). Low-carbon steel made in the normal manner consists mainly of ferrite and pearlite. But steels with a carbon content higher than 0.8 percent contain the brittle cementite, and as the carbon content increases they become more brittle. Although they have high strength and hardness, they have now been mostly replaced in structures by low-alloy steels (see Section 2.6).

The performance of most metals can be improved by heat treatment and/or by cold working. The three principal properties desired in metals are high strength, and/or high ductility, and/or toughness. It is usually necessary to compromise if all three are required (Fig. 2.2.4).

Hardness is also needed for some applications, and steels that are strong are usually also hard.

Heat treatment has been used at least since medieval times to improve the properties of steel. Low-carbon steel can be hardened by *quenching*, that is, heating to a bright red heat, and then rapidly cooling it in water or, less drastically, in oil. At a bright red heat the steel temperature is above 850°C, above the A1 line, so that the iron is in the form of austenite. If this were to be cooled slowly, it would be transformed into ferrite and pearlite, both soft, ductile materials. On rapid cooling, however, another material is formed, called *martensite*. Because of the rapid cooling, the carbon atoms that are in solid solution in the austenite

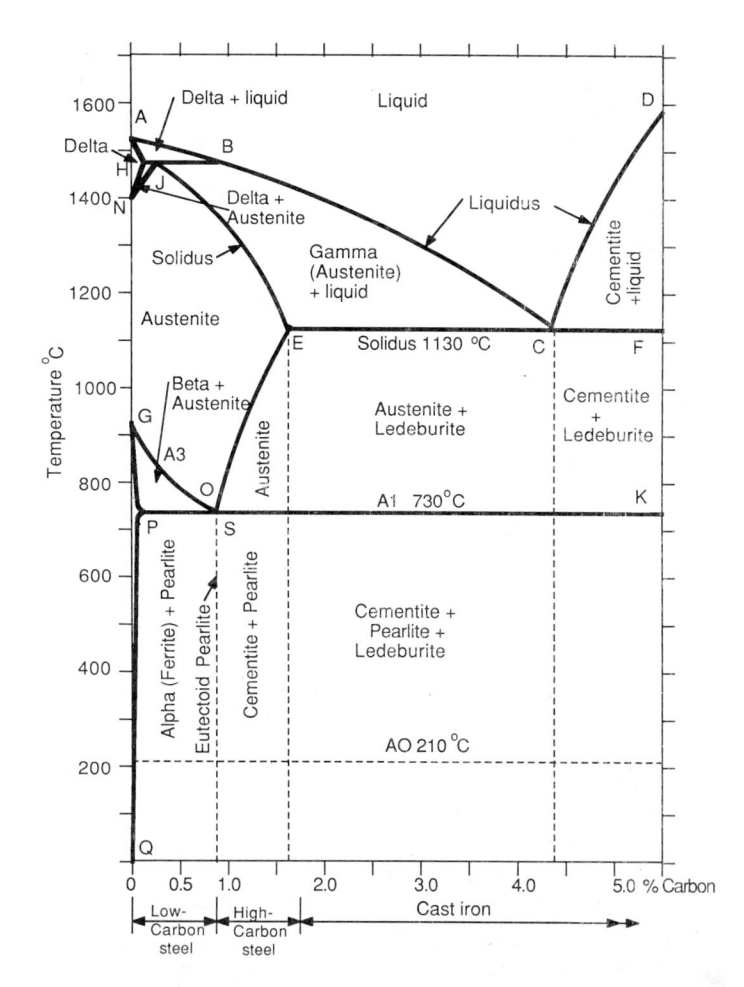

Fig. 2.4.1. The phase diagram of iron and iron carbide for the range covering cast iron, steel, and wrought iron. The phase diagram shows the temperature on the vertical axis, and the percentage of carbon in the iron on the horizontal axis. It thus shows the various forms in which alloys of iron and iron carbide can exist at various temperatures.

Above the *liquidus* lines all material is liquid. Below the *solidus* lines all material is solid. Between the liquidus and the solidus the alloys are partly liquid and partly solid.

A *critical point* is a point where the liquidus or solidus lines have a minimum. The alloy formed at a critical point on cooling from a liquid is called a *eutectic*. This phase diagram shows the formation at 1130°C of a eutectic alloy called *ledeburite*, with a carbon content of 4.3 percent.

The alloy formed on cooling from a solid solution at a critical point, that is from a dip in the solidus line, is called a *eutectoid*. This phase diagram shows the formation of a eutectoid, called *pearlite*, at a temperature of 730°C, with a carbon content of 0.8 percent.

do not have enough time to form cementite, which is a constituent of pearlite; instead they distort the body-centered cubic lattice of the ferrite. Under the microscope, martensite looks like a large number of fine needles scattered at random. It is very hard and strong, but also very brittle. Thus quenching hardens the steel, but also turns it brittle.

The other traditional heat treatment is *annealing*, which consists of heating the steel to a bright red heat, holding at that temperature for at least half a minute, and then cooling it slowly in air. This produces the structure shown for room temperature in Fig. 2.4.1, that is, ferrite and pearlite, which are both ductile.

Evidently annealing merely reverses the heat treatment given by quenching. However, we can obtain a compromise by heating the hardened low-carbon steel to a lower temperature, and then cooling it slowly in air. This is called *tempering*. The steel is heated above the A0 line in Fig. 2.4.1, which occurs at 210°C, but kept well below the A1 line (730°C). In this range the steel does not turn red hot, but it acquires a color due to the formation of an oxide coating; the characteristic colors acquired by carbon steel during tempering are shown in Table 2.1.

Let us assume we wanted to give some ductility and toughness (see Fig. 2.2.4) to a carbon steel after quenching. We heat it, say, to a dark blue temper color, and then cool it slowly. The result is a compromise. The steel is not now as ductile as it was before quenching, but it has recovered sufficient ductility and increased its toughness. *Normalizing* and *aging* (or *age-hardening*) are similar processes (see also Section 2.7).

Work-hardening is the name given to a number of processes that deform the crystal structure of the steel by mechanical working and in the process increase its strength, although with some loss of ductility. The original crystal structure can be restored by annealing. Thus if two pieces of steel whose strength has been increased by work hardening are welded together, the increased strength is lost at the welded joint if it is allowed to cool slowly in air.

The most drastic method of work hardening is *wire drawing*, that is, drawing a bar through a succession of dies to form a wire. Each drawing operation reduces the diameter slightly and increases the strength greatly. The material becomes brittle in the process, and the coils of wire are usually *stress relieved*, which is a form of tempering.

Bars too large in diameter for wire drawing can be work-hardened by stretching or twisting.

Case hardening is a surface treatment applied to steel to increase the hardness of the skin without reducing the ductility of steel below the surface layer. It is achieved by packing the steel in a box tightly surrounded by charcoal or sodium cyanide (which is more effective) and heating it to about 925°C, so that the surface layer of the steel absorbs additional carbon. Case hardening has now been largely superseded by *nitriding*, which forms hard particles of nitride in the surface layer of the steel. This is done by heating the steel in ammonia at about 500°C.

2.5. CORROSION PROTECTION

We distinguish today between *ferrous metals* (which consist predominantly of iron) and *nonferrous metals* (which contain little or no iron). This in itself is a clear indication of the important place which iron occupies in our technology. It was not always so. In the early days of the Iron Age (that is, the era of Ancient Greece and the late period of Ancient Egypt) copper and its alloys were used far more than iron and steel. Iron gradually became more and more important, partly because with improved technology it became cheaper than copper and lead, and partly because it is a very strong material. Iron and steel have one great disadvantage, however. They rust easily unless protected against corrosion; stainless steel is an exception, and it is often considered as a separate material (see Section 2.6). The nonferrous metals used in buildings, however, generally have good resistance to corrosion.

Heat is needed to produce a metal from its ores, which are usually its oxides after impurities are removed. When a metal oxidizes, on the other hand, heat is generated. Iron combines with oxygen in dry air to produce a mixture of *ferrous oxide*, FeO, and *ferric oxide*, Fe_2O_3. These oxides form a skin which slows further oxidation. In the presence of moisture, however, the ferrous oxide is oxidized to ferric oxide, and *hydrated ferric oxide*, $2Fe_2O_3 \cdot 3H_2O$, is formed. This is rust, a red-brown porous substance. No energy is required for the formation of rust; it actually generates some energy. Rusting continues indefinitely in the presence of oxygen and moisture until there is no metallic iron left.

One method of corrosion protection is therefore to protect the steel physically by a coating that cuts off the supply of oxygen. Another approach is to rely on sacrificial protection by coating the steel with a metal that is nearer to the anodic end of the electrochemical series than iron (Table 2.2).

Zinc meets both criteria, and zinc coating is therefore the most common form of corrosion protection for steel sheet. The zinc coating cuts off the supply of oxygen to the steel, and any corrosion that occurs does so in the zinc coating, because zinc is nearer to the anodic end of the electrochemical series (Table 2.2) than steel. The most common method of zinc coating is *galvanizing*, which may be accomplished by hot-dipping the steel in molten zinc, or by electrodeposition in a chemical bath. Another method is called *sherardizing*, and this utilizes hot zinc dust.

In *zincalume* sheeting the coating consists of 45 percent zinc and 55 percent aluminum.

Table 2.1. Colors Acquired by Carbon Steels Heated for a Normal Period during Tempering.

Color	Temperature, °C
Straw	225
Yellow-brown	255
Red-brown	265
Purple	275
Violet	285
Dark blue	295
Light blue	310

Table 2.2. The Electrochemical Series of Metals and Alloys.

An electrolyte is any liquid that conducts electricity, for example impure water. If a metal is in contact with an electrolyte, it tends to dissolve slightly and send positive ions into solution, leaving the metal negatively charged. This reaction produces an electric potential between the metal and the solution. Different metals have different electric potentials, and they can be arranged in a series of increasing potentials; this is the electrochemical series shown below.

There are two exactly opposite definitions of anode and cathode. It was originally assumed that a direct current passed from the anode to the cathode. Later it was discovered that the "cathode," as originally defined, supplied the electrons, and that the electrons traveled in the electrolyte from the cathode to the anode. The exactly opposite terminology is now used in physical chemistry and in materials science, and also in this table: "the anode is the pole that supplies the electrons, and the cathode is the pole that receives them."

Cathodic end	gold
	silver
	stainless steel
	bronze
	copper
	brass
Reference	hydrogen
	nickel
	tin
	lead
	iron and steel
	cadmium
	aluminum
	zinc
Anodic end	magnesium

In *terne plate* the coating consists of 80 percent lead and 20 percent tin. Unlike zinc, this coating does not give sacrificial protection, because both metals are above iron in the electrochemical series. However, the flexibility of the lead insures that terne plate can be bent or otherwise deformed without causing a break in the physical barrier provided by the coating.

Steel can also be protected by coating it with a substance that is corrosion resistant, and which firmly adheres to the steel.

Porcelain enamel has been used for this purpose since the early 1930s. The coating is produced by melting frit, a glass-forming substance (see Section 3.18, Chapter 3), and fusing it to the steel sheet at a temperature of 1400–1600°F (760–870°C). The first coat is applied to both sides, so that the steel is enclosed in an envelope of glass. Further coats are applied only to the visible side.

During the 1980s steel coated with durable and tough plastics has been used increasingly. In addition to coated steel sheet (corrugated or plain), coated tubes and bars are available.

The most common protective coating for steel is paint (see Section 5.10) which may be applied before or after fabrication of the steel.

The nonferrous metals used in buildings are mostly protected by the oxide skin which forms very quickly after the metal is exposed to air (for example, by cutting ing).

In *aluminum*, which is a silvery metal when it is cut, an oxide skin forms within a few seconds. This can be strengthened by *anodizing*, a process described in Section 2.8. Pure aluminum has better corrosion resistance than most of its alloys. Hence aluminum alloys that require weathering resistance are often given a thin surface coating of pure aluminum, and this material is called *alclad*.

Gold is the only metal that does not tarnish or corrode on exposure to air, and that is the reason why it is found in nature in its metallic state. *Copper* is the best of the common metals in this regard, and it can retain its characteristic metallic appearance for many days, even years in a dry climate. The metallic appearance can be restored by polishing, which removes the oxide skin by abrasion. The metallic appearance can also be preserved with a transparent varnish which seals the copper from the oxygen. Over a period of time copper changes to a dull brown because of the formation of an oxide skin. Prolonged exposure on a roof transforms the oxide to copper sulfate and basic copper carbonate. This is the green *patina* of copper roofs, caused by the color of the sulfate. However, the process is slow, and copper is very resistant to a polluted atmosphere.

Lead is also a silvery metal when cut, but it oxidizes rapidly, and the oxide film absorbs carbon dioxide from the atmosphere to form lead carbonate. This dull patina adheres to the metal strongly, is insoluble in all inorganic acids, and provides the lead with chemically excellent and mechanically flexible corrosion resistance.

The effectiveness of zinc coating on steel, as already mentioned, is due to the fact that is on its anodic side in the electrochemical series (Table 2.2), so that it protects the iron by sacrificial corrosion; the steel does not corrode, the zinc does. However, zinc does not corrode readily. The silvery metal immediately forms a zinc oxide coating, about one hundredth of a millimeter (a thousandth of an inch) thick; this is gradually changed in air to zinc carbonate, which is highly resistant to further corrosion.

2.6. ALLOY STEELS

Another method of protecting steel against corrosion is to alloy the iron with certain nonferrous metals. *Stainless steel* was discovered in 1913 during experiments for producing stronger gun barrels. The essential element which makes it stainless is chromium. Stainless steel contains between 12 and 20 percent of chromium, and a small amount of carbon. It may contain up to 20 percent of nickel, and small quantities of copper, aluminum, molybdenum, and titanium.*

The phase diagram for carbon steels (Fig. 2.4.1) shows that austenite can exist only above a temperature of 1350°F

---

*Molybdenum and titanium are, respectively, Nos. 42 and 22 in the Periodic Table, Fig. 2.1.2.

(730°C). In some stainless steels, however, notably those with a high nickel content, austenite, which is much tougher than ferrite, occurs at room temperature. These *austenitic stainless steels* have high strength and good ductility. A common alloy in this class contains 18 percent chromium and 8 percent nickel. It is an alloy frequently used for sanitary fittings, kitchen sinks, and curtain walls; but it is expensive, and cheaper alloys are used if less wear and/or weathering is required.

The corrosion resistance of stainless steel is due to the formation of a chromium-rich oxide film on the surface of the steel. This very thin film is not visible to the naked eye, and it immediately reforms if it is damaged, for example by scratching, to maintain the corrosion protection.

In spite of the high alloy content, the modulus of elasticity of stainless steel is almost as high as that of ordinary steel, and as a result stainless steel sheet has a low deflection. When backed with an insulating or other material, 22 U.S. standard-gauge (see Appendix for conversion to in. and mm) can be used. Very thin plain panels pose, however, a visual problem, because it is impossible in practice to produce and maintain a perfectly flat surface. The eye instantly detects departures from flatness, particularly because of the reflective nature of stainless steel. Thin sheets should therefore be corrugated for extra stiffness, or impressed with a decorative pattern that detracts the eye from imperfections in flatness. This problem does not arise with aluminum, which is used in greater thicknesses (Section 2.7). The insulation of curtain walls is considered in Section 2.7, since aluminum is used more for that purpose than the more expensive stainless steel.

Because of its high strength and durability, stainless steel is useful for protecting columns; 14-gauge sheet is sufficient if the column is unlikely to be bumped by cars, baggage, etc.; otherwise 10-gauge sheet is required.

Stainless steel has better corrosion resistance than copper, and it is increasingly being used for gutters and downspouts (downpipes), where a long life is required. However, much cheaper gutters and downspouts that last a number of years can be made from galvanized steel or plastics.

While the durability and strength of stainless steels are excellent, their use is limited by their relatively high cost.

A limited amount of corrosion protection for structural steel can, however, be obtained by the use of a low-alloy *weathering steels*. These steels are made by several manufacturers; the best known is the USX's Cor-Ten. These steels contain up to ten alloying elements, but the total alloying material is generally less than 2 percent. The carbon content is low, less than 0.1 percent. Phosphorus is generally regarded as an undesirable impurity, but in this type of steel it contributes to corrosion resistance. Other beneficial elements are silicon, chromium, and nickel. All weathering steels are high-tensile steels, in spite of their low carbon content.

The weathering steels rust, but the thin layer of brownish black rust that forms over a period of two or three years firmly adheres to the steel, and protects it from further corrosion. Continuous wetting may, however, restart surface corrosion, hence buildings should be designed so that all weathering steel parts can shed the water that falls on them. Furthermore, the rust is not entirely insoluble, and parts of the building below weathering steel are liable to be stained brown by water running off the steel, at least during the first few years. The buildings must therefore be designed so that water draining off weathering steel does not run over concrete, brick, or stone, but is drained into a sink, or into a gravel bed or flower bed which can periodically be renewed, or on asphalt paving that does not show the stains. These requirements evidently impose limitations on design.

We noted in Section 2.4 that high-carbon steels have higher strength than low-carbon steels (Fig. 2.4.1), but have lower ductility and toughness. These steels were at one time used as high-tensile structural steels, but they have now been replaced by low-alloy steels, which have high strength as well as good ductility and toughness.

These *high-strength low-alloy structural steels* usually contain less than 0.25 percent of carbon, and vanadium or columbium (called niobium in Europe). Some also contain silicon, boron, molybdenum, nickel, chrome, titanium, and zirconium.* The total amount of alloying elements is generally less than 2 percent.

Carbon, however, remains the essential alloying element, because it is the iron carbide that makes hardening and tempering possible. The small quantities of the other elements merely modify these heat treatments. Most low-alloy high-tensile steels can be welded.

The structural design of steel is discussed in Chapter 12.

2.7. ALUMINUM AND ITS ALLOYS

Aluminum is the only metal used today in buildings which was not known to the ancient world. A globule of aluminum the size of a pinhead was first produced in 1845, from which some of the metal's properties, including its light weight, were determined. It remained a precious metal until 1886, when Paul Héroult in France and Charles Martin Hall in the United States independently invented the electrolytic Martin-Héroult process still used today. Aluminum is produced by electrolysis from *alumina* (aluminum oxide, Al_2O_3). This in turn is produced from *Bauxite*, a mineral which contains 40–60 percent of alumina, 5–30 percent of ferric oxide, 10–30 percent of water, and some other materials. The process for extracting the alumina from bauxite was invented by Karl Joseph Bayer in 1892. Both processes require a great deal of electricity. It is therefore expedient to take the bauxite, or at least the alumina produced from it, to a place where electricity can be generated cheaply. Even then the cost of the electricity needed to

---

*Vanadium, columbium, boron, molybdenum, titanium, and zirconium are, respectively, Nos. 23, 41, 5, 42, 22, and 40 in the Periodic Table, Fig. 2.1.2.

reduce the bauxite to aluminum makes the metal more expensive than steel.

Most aluminum is turned into aluminum alloy, and its fabrication depends to some extent on the nature of the alloy, as some are suited to hot-rolling, some to cold-rolling, some to casting, and some to two or all three. The aluminum ingots produced by the Martin-Héroult process can be hot-rolled in a blooming mill, like steel (Section 2.3), or they can be cut with a saw to reduce their size. Aluminum alloy can be hot-rolled into standard sections somewhat similar to the steel standard sections (Fig. 2.3.1), but these are rarely used in building.

The melting point of aluminum alloys is between 1000 and 1200°F (540 and 650°C), so that it can be worked at much lower temperatures than steel. This makes it possible to form aluminum by *extrusion*, that is, squeezing the hot metal through a die, within the temperature range of 750 and 930°F (400 and 500°C), depending on the alloy. The hot aluminum emerges from the die of the extrusion press with a smooth surface and a protective oxide coating, and it can be used thus without any further surface treatment, or the oxide coating can be made thicker (and/or colored) by anodizing (Section 2.8). Very complex sections can be made by extrusion (Fig. 2.7.1), and their shape can be varied by cutting a new die, which is much cheaper than making new rollers for a rolling mill.

Aluminum, like structural steel and stainless steel, can be cold-rolled.

The principal properties of the metals discussed in this chapter are given in Table 2.3, except for their strengths, which vary according to the alloys used and the manner in which they have been treated. Some aluminum alloys are as strong as structural steel, and a few are as strong as high-tensile steel. Aluminum is much lighter than steel or copper, and many building components, which would require power hoists if made from steel, stainless steel or copper, can be manhandled if made from aluminum alloy. However, aluminum also has a much lower modulus of elasticity than steel or stainless steel, and it therefore deflects more and buckles more easily (Sections 2.6 and 11.2). It also has a greater thermal expansion than steel.

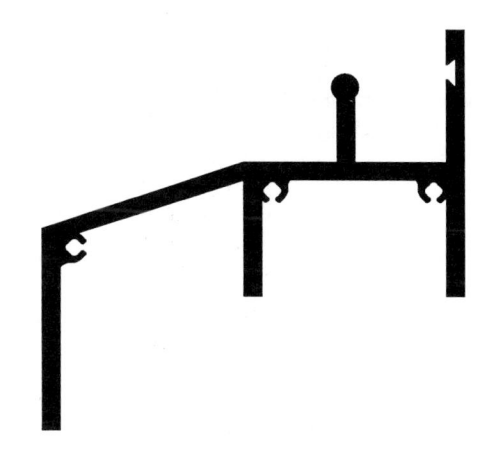

Fig. 2.7.1. Window frame made from extruded aluminum sections. These very complex sections can easily be produced by extrusion of the hot metal through a die; they would be impossible to produce by a (hot or cold) rolling mill. Door and window frames at present use more aluminum than any other single use in the building industry.

Most aluminum alloys have a more favorable strength per unit weight than structural steel, but it is no better than that for most kinds of laminated timber.

The main advantages of aluminum alloys over structural and low-alloy steels are good appearance and better corrosion resistance. The lower weight is also frequently an advantage. Their main disadvantages are their higher cost and lower fire resistance. In a severe fire aluminum is not merely going to soften, like steel, but it may melt. Fire-protective coatings are not normally used on aluminum, because its main advantages would then be lost.

Aluminum alloy is generally cheaper than stainless steel, but its corrosion resistance is not as good; one would not, for example, use it for urinals. Because of its lower mod-

Table 2.3. Comparison of the Physical Properties of Steel, Aluminum, Copper, and Lead.

Property	Steel	Stainless Steel	Aluminum	Copper	Lead
Specific gravity	7.9	7.9	2.7	9.0	11.34
Density,					
lb/ft²	493	493	169	559	708
kg/m³	7900	7900	2700	8960	11,340
Melting point,					
°F	2780	2640	1220	1980	621
°C	1530	1450	660	1080	327
Coefficient of thermal expansion,					
per °F × 10⁶	7	7	13	10	16
per °C × 10⁶	13	13	24	19	29
Modulus of elasticity,					
ksi	29,000	28,000	10,000	17,000	*
MPa	200,000	190,000	69,000	117,000	*

*Although lead is elastic at very low temperatures, it is not elastic at room temperature.

20 HANDBOOK OF ARCHITECTURAL TECHNOLOGY

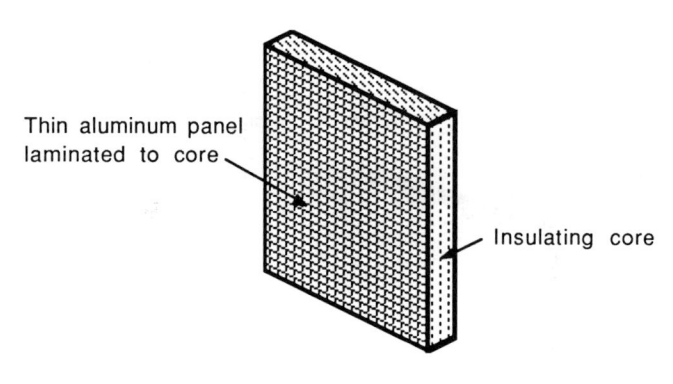

Fig. 2.7.2. Aluminum sheet by itself has neglegible thermal insulation, and it also has inadequate resistance to deflection and buckling. The insulation is therefore an integral part of a curtain wall panel.

ulus of elasticity and its consequent higher deflection and greater tendency to buckle, aluminum alloys are generally used in thicker sheets than stainless steel.

Aluminum is thus useful as a structural material where weight is a dominant design factor, that is, for very long spans, or when a substantial part of a structure is to be hoisted into position in one piece.

It is an economical material for curtain walls (Fig. 2.7.2), and it can be colored by anodizing to look like bronze (see Section 2.8).

It is a lighter material for roof sheets than galvanized steel. It has replaced steel as the principal material for metal windows and doors. It is widely used for framing partitions (Fig. 2.7.3).

Aluminum is increasingly replacing lead for damp-proof courses; however, unlike lead, it needs a protective coating of asphalt. It is also used in competition with lead and copper for flashings.

Aluminum foil with a thickness of the order of 0.0004 in. (0.01 mm) is used as reflective insulation in conjunction with thermal insulating materials (see Section 20.7). It reflects thermal radiation (see Section 20.1) and also acts as a vapor barrier (see Sections 7.3 and 20.9).

Aluminum castings, sometimes anodized to look like brass or bronze, can be used for door furniture, and they have been used to replace cast iron in the restoration of 19th Century houses.

2.8. THE CLASSIFICATION AND TREATMENT OF ALUMINUM ALLOYS

There are many more alloys of aluminum than there are of steel, and each is available in more than one form of hardness and temper. There are thus several hundred materials to choose from. The first distinction is between casting alloys and wrought alloys, that is, materials which can be worked by hot or cold rolling, extrusion, or stamping. Since casting aluminum alloys are used in building only for small

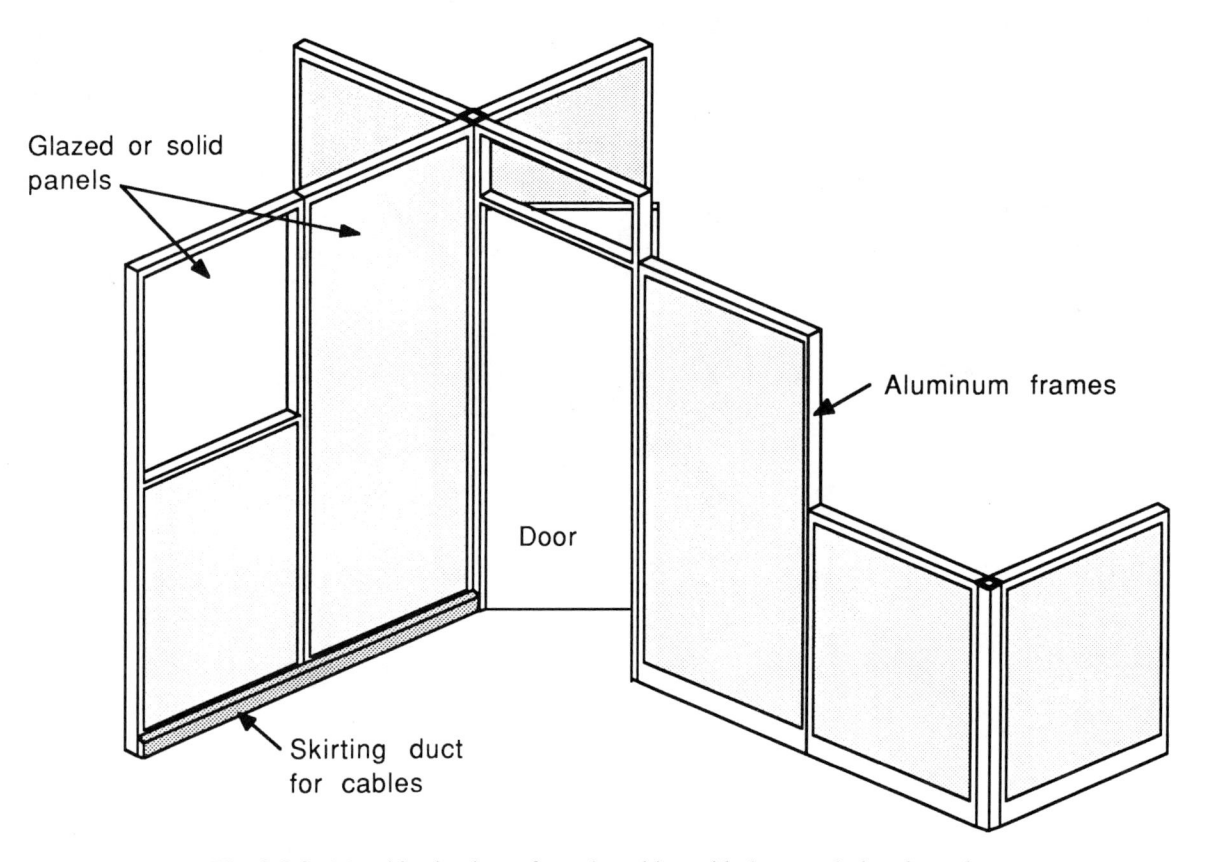

Fig. 2.7.3. Movable aluminum-framed partition with doors and glazed panels.

manufactured components, this discussion is confined to the *wrought alloys*.

The international classification consists of four numbers. The first of these describes the principal alloying material:

1. Pure aluminum
2. Copper alloys
3. Manganese alloys
4. Silicon alloys
5. Magnesium alloys
6. Magnesium-silicon alloys
7. Zinc alloys

Series 1, 3, 4, and 5 are *non-heat-treatable* alloys; series 2, 6, 7 are *heat-treatable* alloys. There is a secondary coding system for each type.

The strength of the *non-heat-treatable alloys* can be increased by work-hardening; most of this occurs while the alloys are cold-rolled. However, this increase is accompanied by a reduction of ductility which may be excessive, and the material is then annealed (see Section 2.4), either at the conclusion of the cold-rolling process or during it—that is, the reduction in thickness is interrupted, the material is annealed, and the cold rolling is then resumed. Each non-heat-treatable alloy is therefore given one of the following *temper designations:*

0	Annealed and recrystallized
H1	Strain-hardened only
H2	Strain-hardened and then partially annealed
H3	Strain-hardened and then stabilized, that is, stress-relieved

One or two further digits are added to follow these designations; for example a second digit 8 means full-hard; 4 means half-hard; and 2 means quarter-hard.

The *heat-treatable alloys* are instead given one of the following *thermal heat treatment designations:*

T1	Cooled from an elevated-temperature shaping process and naturally aged to a substantially stable condition. (Natural aging means precipitation from a solid solution that occurs slowly at room temperature, and results in an improvement in an alloy's properties)
T2	Annealed
T3	Solution-heat-treated and then cold-worked. (Solution heat treatment involves heating an alloy at a suitable temperature for a sufficient time to allow soluble constituents to enter into a solid solution, and then quenching it so that these constituents are retained in a supersaturated state. Quenching means rapid cooling of the alloy from a high temperature by immersion in a liquid or a gas)
T4	Solution-heat-treated and naturally aged to a substantially stable condition, that is, without cold working
T5	Cooled from an elevated-temperature shaping process and then artificially aged. (Artificial aging means that the precipitation from the solid solution occurs more rapidly at a high temperature)
T6	Solution-heat-treated and then artificially aged
T7	Solution-heat-treated and then stabilized, that is, stress-relieved
T8	Solution-heat-treated, cold-worked, and then artificially aged
T9	Solution-heat-treated, artificially aged, and then cold-worked
T10	Cooled from an elevated-temperature shaping process, artificially aged, and then cold-worked

Additional digits can be added to give further information, for example, whether stress relieving is by stretching, compressing, or thermal treatment.

Each of the alloys has its own phase diagram (see Fig. 2.4.1), and its own specific properties.

The 1000 series consists of aluminum of 99 percent or higher purity. These materials have excellent corrosion resistance and low strength. Their main use in building is for cladding: a thin sheet is placed above and below a thicker sheet of another alloy before cold rolling, and the alloy sheet emerges from the cold-rolling mill with a protective sheet or pure aluminum on each side; it is thus called *alclad*.

The alloys in the 2000 and 7000 series have the highest strength, but these are used mainly in the aircraft industry. The alloys with the main architectural applications are to be found in the 3000, 4000, 5000, and 6000 series.

As mentioned in Section 2.5, aluminum forms an oxide skin as soon as it is cut or scratched, and this protects it from further corrosion, as the skin reforms if it is damaged. This is one of the major advantages that aluminum alloys have over structural and low-alloy high-tensile steels. This oxide skin can be strengthened by an electrolytic process known as *anodizing*, which is particularly useful if the aluminum is designed to be exposed to the weather. This process is quite different from galvanizing and other methods of coating. The aluminum oxide coat is not *added* to the existing aluminum surface, but the top layer of aluminum metal is *transformed* into oxide. There are several processes (Ref. 2.2). The most common is the sulfuric acid process, in which the aluminum to be anodized is immersed in a 10 percent solution of sulfuric acid, connected to the positive end of a direct-current electric supply.

The oxide coating formed by anodizing has tiny pores, and color can be deposited in these during the anodizing process. Organic dyes fade in sunlight, but they have been used successfully for interior surfaces, and entire pictures can be printed on aluminum by offset litho or silk-screen printing during the anodizing process.

Inorganic pigments which do not fade on exterior surfaces have been used successfully since the 1960s. The most popular colors are various shades of bronze. Bronze-anodized aluminum looks almost exactly like oxidized copper or bronze, but is cheaper and weighs less. The color is produced by introducing salts (usually the sulfates) of copper, nickel, tin, or cobalt, or a combination of these, into the electrolyte. Various other light-fast colors are possible, notably blue-gray and gold.

Anodized coatings must be sealed before they are exposed to the weather. For the sulfuric acid process this can be done by immersion in water close to its boiling point for a period ranging from 10 minutes to 2 hours, depending on the thickness of the oxide film. Transparent lacquers can also be used for sealing.

Aluminum alloys vary in their suitability for anodizing (Ref. 2.2, p. 7).

2.9. OTHER NONFERROUS METALS

The visible use of *copper* in buildings is declining, as it has been replaced for many purposes by aluminum and by plastics. However, more copper is used for building than ever before, because it is the principal material for electric wiring, as it has the second-highest electrical conductivity of any material (silver is slightly better). The discovery that copper is made harder and stronger by a small addition of tin is very ancient. About 500 B.C. the Greeks made *bronze* from 9 parts of copper and 1 part of tin. Today the term *bronze* is used not merely for copper-tin alloys, but also for copper-zinc and copper-silicon alloys that have a bronze color.

Brass was first used in the 18th Century as an alloy of 60 percent copper and 40 percent zinc. Both bronze and brass have in the past had military uses, reflected in the names of some alloys: cartridge brass—30 percent zinc; naval brass—38 percent zinc; gunmetal—2 percent zinc and 8 percent tin. The remainder in each case is copper.

The international coding system for copper alloys is similar to that for aluminum alloys discussed in Section 2.8. The principal alloys used in building are:

110 Copper: 99.9 percent copper.

122 Copper: 99.9 percent copper, 0.02 percent phosphorus (the principal alloy used for copper pipes)

220 Commercial Bronze: 90 percent copper, 10 percent zinc (a bronze-colored metal)

230 Red Brass: 85 percent copper, 15 percent zinc (the principal alloy used for brass pipes)

260 Cartridge Brass: 70 percent copper, 30 percent zinc (a yellow brass)

280 Muntz Metal: 60 percent copper, 40 percent zinc (a reddish-yellow brass)

385 Architectural Bronze: 57 percent copper, 40 percent zinc, 3 percent lead

655 Silicon Bronze: 97 percent copper, 3 percent silicon (a reddish old gold alloy)

745 Nickel Silver: 65 percent copper, 25 percent zinc, 10 percent nickel (a silver-colored alloy)

796 Leaded Nickel Silver: 45 percent copper, 42 percent zinc, 10 percent nickel, 2 percent manganese, 1 percent lead (a silver-colored alloy)

Most of these alloys are very durable (see Section 2.5). Copper alloys can be fabricated by hot rolling, cold rolling, extrusion, stamping, or casting, but only certain alloys are suitable for each process.

As already mentioned, copper is the principal material for electrical wiring.

Copper and brass pipes and fittings are used for conveying hot and cold water. Galvanized steel pipes are also used for cold water, but they need periodic renewal. Plastic pipes are now used for both hot and cold water supply (see Section 24.3). Copper is an excellent material for hot-water tanks, and solar collectors used in conjunction with hot-water systems. All these uses are largely hidden from view.

Copper is still used as a roofing material where a high-quality, completely waterproof finish is required; but this use, once common and prominently visible, is now rare. Since copper is heavy and expensive, sheets ranging in thickness from 0.01 to 0.04 in. (0.25 to 1 mm) are used, and these are specified in terms of weight per unit area of sheet. This thin sheet is fully supported on a timber or concrete surface. Pure 110 copper is commonly used, and this is sometimes given a surface coating of lead, in which case the roof looks like a lead roof.

Copper is used for gutters and downspouts, to avoid the periodic renewal required when galvanized steel or plastics are used; stainless steel or aluminum are the alternative materials for this purpose. Copper is used for flashings in place of lead or aluminum, particularly where appearance is important.

Copper is now rarely used for curtain walls, because a very similar appearance can be obtained with the cheaper and lighter anodized aluminum. Brass and nickel silver are still widely used for door furniture, but they are now in competition with aluminum alloys and with plastics. Nickel silver is a useful alternative to stainless steel for kickplates for doors.

Lead was an important building material at least from the time of Ancient Rome until the 19th Century. It was widely used for water pipes; indeed, the word *plumber* comes from the Latin word for lead, *plumbum*. Today it is still used occasionally for waste pipes, but no longer for water supply pipes (Chapter 24). It was used extensively for fully supported roof covering, and some of the world's most famous domes, such as St. Peter's in Rome and the Aya Sofya in Istanbul, are still covered with lead. However, lead, which was a cheap material in Roman times, has now become comparatively expensive, and its present use as a roof covering is mostly for restorations. Because of its flexibility, it must always be used fully supported. Lead sheet is now often made from an alloy containing 6 percent of antimony (Sb, No. 51, in the Periodic Table, Fig. 2.1.2). This increases the strength and stiffness, so that thinner sheets can be used.

Lead is one of the most weather-resistant materials, and in this respect it surpasses even stainless steel and zinc. It is still used for weather protection in the form of terne coating (see Section 2.5) and a coating for copper.

Lead is still extensively used for flashing because of the ease with which it can be shaped in position on a building at a complex junction of surfaces. It is being replaced as a material for damp-proof courses by the cheaper aluminum and plastics (see Sections 2.7 and 5.2).

Because of its high density, lead is an excellent material for protection against X-rays and gamma rays in research laboratories and medical centers.

The use of lead for sound insulation and vibration absorption depends both on its density and on its softness. A panel of sheet lead placed loosely between two walls, not touching either, acts as an effective sound insulator, partly because of its mass, and partly because it cannot vibrate since it is not an elastic material. Lead can also be used to absorb ground vibrations, say, from underground railroads, by placing a sheet of lead between steel columns and their footings. However, a pad of rubber or of certain plastics serves the same purpose.

2.10. METHODS OF JOINING METALS

The oldest method for joining two pieces of wrought iron or steel is by riveting. The rivets must be used at a *red heat*, and since the handling of red-hot rivets is unpleasant, riveting is now rarely used for steel structures.

Riveting is still a common method for joining pieces of aluminum, and occasionally of copper, since satisfactory joints can be produced with *cold rivets*. The rivets have a head at one end, and the other head is formed with a power tool after the rivet has been inserted in its previously drilled hole. Aluminum rivets up to $\frac{3}{8}$ in. (10 mm) can be driven cold, and larger aluminum rivets are unlikely to be needed in buildings.

It is possible to make riveted joints where only one side of the material is accessible, for example in assembling a tube, by using *explosive rivets*. The shaft of these rivets is hollow, and filled with a small quantity of explosive which is set off with a blow from a hammer. The far end of the rivet is blown out and forms a secure joint.

Prior to the invention of high-tensile bolts, there were two kinds of bolts. *Black bolts* fitted loosely into the holes of the two members to be joined. A stronger joint was made with "*bright*" bolts which fitted perfectly into the holes and thus made a stronger joint. Black-bolted joints are still used for connections of minor importance, but structural steel joints are now made with *high-tensile bolts* (see Section 12.7). These are tightened with a *calibrated torsion wrench*, which must be calibrated at frequent intervals. As the bolt is tightened with a standard torque, it applies a standard pressure to the two pieces of steel to be joined. The calibrated wrench ensures that there is sufficient pressure, but also that the tension in the bolt is not so high that it is liable to break.

Bolted joints are rarely used in aluminum structures. If they are needed, steel bolts are often used in preference to aluminum bolts. Since steel and aluminum in contact produce galvanic corrosion (see Section 2.5), the steel bolts must be galvanized or *cadmium-plated*. Cadmium plating is more effective because cadmium is very close to aluminum in the electrochemical series (Table 2.2).

Welding can be done on the building site, but it is better suited to the factory. It generates heat and glare, and the job is well suited to performance by robots if sufficiently repeated.

Care must be taken if work-hardened high-tensile steel is welded, since it may lose its high strength if heated and then cooled slowly during welding. Most high-strength low-alloy steels and most stainless steels can be welded.

Some aluminum alloys can be welded, but others cannot. Specifications normally state whether welding can be used.

Welding is a fusion process: some of the metal in each of the pieces to be joined is melted and the two pieces are then fused together by pressure (as in spot welding and tube welding) or by additional metal of the same composition.

The necessary heat can be generated by a gas flame or by electricity. In *electric welding* the steel rod that supplies the weld metal forms one electrode. It is essential that the fused metal not oxidize during welding, since the inclusion of an oxide particle would seriously weaken the weld. The *flux* used for this purpose forms the coating on the electrode and automatically melts as welding proceeds.

Aluminum alloys, which oxidize more rapidly than steel, need extra protection. The operation is carried out in an atmosphere of the chemically inert gas *helium*, which is directed into the weld area through a sheath surrounding the electrode, thus preventing oxidation of both the electrode and the weld pool. *Heliarc welding* is also used for stainless steel. Helium is an expensive gas outside America, and the inert gas *argon* is used instead in Europe and Australia.

The pieces to be joined by welding must be prepared by cleaning them of all dirt and oxide, and by cutting them back if necessary to form a *throat*, to make it easier to fuse them with weld metal (Fig. 2.10.1).

In *brazing* and *soldering* the metal pieces to be joined are not fused, and the strength of the joint depends on the adhesion of the solder, and the strength of the solder. The two methods differ only in the nature of the solder used.

The solder must have a lower melting point than that of the pieces to be joined. The surfaces must be kept free from

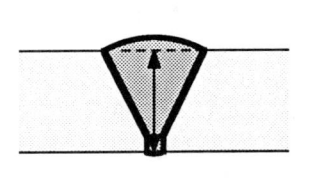

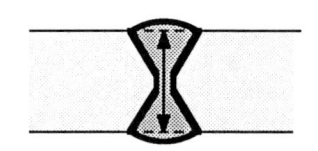

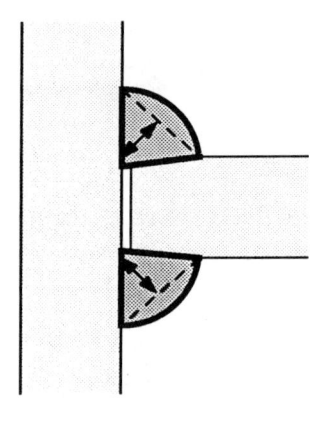

Fig. 2.10.1. The throat of welded joints. In most welded joints, the parent metal is cut back to make it easier for the weld metal to penetrate into the joint and produce perfect fusion between the two metals. The strength of the joint is calculated by multiplying the maximum stress of the metal by the cross-sectional area of the *throat*, indicated by the arrows.

oxide films. Oxidation during soldering is prevented by a *flux* that melts at a lower temperature than the solder. The flux is often supplied as a core within the solder.

Galvanized iron, copper, brass, and lead can all be soldered. Some aluminum alloys can be soldered.

A variety of low-melting-point alloys can be used as solders. *Soft solders* consist of lead and tin. Low-melting-point aluminum alloys are sometimes used for soldering aluminum. Silver solders are stronger, and have a higher melting point; they are mostly alloys of silver, copper, and zinc. Brazing solders are stronger still, and they have a slightly higher melting point. The high-copper brazing alloys are used for brazing copper, brass, and steel. High-aluminum alloys are used for brazing aluminum; they can be used for some aluminum alloys that are nonweldable.

Metals can also be joined with *adhesives* (see Section 5.9), although special care must be taken if the metal is to be used externally. Glued joints are particularly suitable for light-gauge metals. Adhesives are always used if metals are used as a facing for plywood.

REFERENCES

2.1. T. J. Lewis and P. E. Secker. *Science of Materials*. George Harrap, London 1965. pp. 96–104; or most other textbooks on materials science.

2.2. A. W. Brace and P. G. Sheasby. *The Technology of Anodizing Aluminium*. Technicopy, Stonehouse (England), 1979. 321 pp.

Standards of the American Society for Testing and Materials

ASTM Standards in Building Codes. 25th Edn. American Society for Testing and Materials, Philadelphia 1988. 4100 pp.

A 6-87d	General requirements for rolled steel plates, shapes, sheet-piling, and bars for structural use
A 36-87	Structural steel
A 529-85	Structural steel with 42 ksi (290 MPa) minimum yield point ($\frac{1}{2}$ in. (12.7 mm) maximum thickness)
A 570-85	Hot-rolled carbon steel sheets and strip, structural quality
A 321-81	Quenched and tempered carbon steel bars
A 615-87	Deformed and plain billet-steel bars for concrete reinforcement
A 616-86	Rail-steel deformed and plain bars for concrete reinforcement
A 617-87	Axle-steel deformed and plain bars for concrete reinforcement
A 663-85	Mechanical properties of merchant quality carbon steel bars
A 82-85	Plain steel wire for concrete reinforcement
A 496-85	Deformed steel wire for concrete reinforcement
A 497-86	Welded deformed steel wire fabric for concrete reinforcement
A 185-85	Plain steel wire fabric for concrete reinforcement
A 29-876	General requirements for hot-rolled and cold-finished carbon and alloy steel bars
A 242-87	High-strength low-alloy structural steel with 50,000 psi minimum yield point to 4 in. thick
A 441-85	High-strength low-alloy structural manganese vanadium steel
A 706-86	Low-alloy steel deformed bars for concrete reinforcement
A 331-87	Cold-finished alloy steel bars
A 666-87	Austenitic stainless steel, sheet, strip, plate, and flat bar for structural applications
A 416-87a	Uncoated seven-wire stress-relieved strand for prestressed concrete
A 421-80 (1985)	Uncoated stress-relieved wire for prestressed concrete
A 361-85	Steel sheet, zinc-coated (galvanized) by the hot-dip process for roofing and siding
A 755-83	Steel sheet, zinc-coated (galvanized) by the hot-dip process and coil-coated for roofing and siding, general requirements
A 527-85	Steel sheet, zinc-coated (galvanized) by the hot-dip process, lock-forming quality
A 586-86	Zinc-coated parallel and helical steel wire structural strand
A 308-86	Aluminum-alloy standard structural shapes, rolled or extruded
B 221-85a	Aluminum-alloy extruded bars, rods, wire, shapes, and tubes
B 429-82	Aluminum-alloy extruded structural pipe and tube
B 241-87	Aluminum-alloy seamless pipe and seamless extruded tube
B 313-82a	Aluminum and aluminum-alloy round welded tubes
B 370-84a	Copper sheet and strip for building construction

B 36-87	Brass plate, sheet, strip, and rolled bar
B 101-83	Lead-coated copper sheets
B 121-86	Leaded brass plate, sheet, strip, and rolled bar
B 88-86	Seamless copper water tube
B 280-86	Seamless copper tube for air conditioning and refrigeration field service
B 447-86	Welded copper tube

SUGGESTIONS FOR FURTHER READING

Lawrence H. Van Vlack. *Elements of Materials Science and Engineering*, 5th Ed. Addison-Wesley, Reading, MA 1985. 550 pp.

Michael F. Ashby and David R. H. Jones. *Engineering Materials*. Pergamon Press, Oxford, 1980. 278 pp.

Herman W. Pollack. *Materials Science and Metallurgy*, 4th Ed. Prentice-Hall, Englewood Cliffs, NJ, 1988. 554 pp.

W. Alexander and A. Street. *Metals in the Service of Man*, 8th Ed. Penguin Books, Harmondsworth (England), 1983. 312 pp.

Mars G. Fontana and Norbert D. Greene. *Corrosion Engineering*, 2nd Ed. McGraw-Hill, New York, 1978. 465 pp.

Lionel Luis Shreir (Ed.). *Corrosion*, 2nd Ed. Newnes-Butterworth, London 1976. Two volumes.

A. K. Osborne. *An Encyclopaedia of the Iron and Steel Industry*. Technical Press, London, 1967. 558 pp.

Aluminum: Properties and Physical Metallurgy. The Aluminum Association, Washington 1984. 417 pp.

P. C. Varley. *The Technology of Aluminium and its Alloys*. Newnes-Butterworth, London, 1970. 161 pp.

NOTATION

Al	aluminum
Fe	iron
H	hydrogen
O	oxygen

A list of abbreviations of the units of measurement, definitions of these units, and conversion factors between British/American and metric units and thickness gauges are given in the Appendix.

3
Ceramic Materials

Henry J. Cowan and Peter R. Smith

This chapter deals with natural stone, and with the materials manufactured from soils and from stone: lime, gypsum, concrete, bricks and other clay products, and glass. These ceramic materials are chemically stable compounds, and as a result they are mostly durable. As the raw materials are readily available, they are relatively cheap. However, they are brittle materials which are liable to form cracks. They are also not as strong in tension as they are in compression. These disabilities must be allowed for when they are used as building materials.

3.1. TRADITIONAL AND MODERN USES OF NATURAL STONE

The term *ceramic materials* is used in this chapter in the sense defined in Section 2.1: chemical compounds of metals and nonmetals. The ceramic building materials are soils and natural stone, and materials manufactured from them: lime, gypsum, plaster, cement, concrete and concrete products, bricks, clay tiles, and glass.

Because ceramic materials are chemically stable compounds, they are mostly durable. Soil and most varieties of stone are widely distributed over the earth's surface, and they are readily obtainable and relatively cheap. Ceramic materials are therefore, together with timber (which is discussed in Chapter 4), the traditional building materials, as opposed to the "modern" metals and plastics (discussed in Chapters 2 and 5).

Ceramic materials are brittle, and therefore much stronger in compression than in tension. The compressive strength of some is very high, and the lack of tensile strength can be overcome in the traditional manner by the use of arches, domes, or vaults (Section 11.6) or in the modern manner by the use of reinforcement (Section 13.4).

Soils as foundation materials are discussed in Chapter 15, and soils used in adobe and pisé construction in Section 3.17. In addition clay is a raw material for bricks, terracotta, tiles, and cement; sand is a raw material for concrete and glass.

Natural stone is the principal raw material for concrete, and lime, gypsum, and cement are made from various types of rock.

Thus stone is still a very important building material. However, prior to the 19th Century it was an even more widely used material, since the most important buildings (except in China, Japan, and some other parts of East Asia) were built from it. Many of these buildings survive as part of our heritage.

Thus natural stone has today three distinct uses:
1. As a raw material for other ceramic materials (Sections 3.6 to 3.17);
2. In the repair of old stone buildings, which are mostly of a type no longer built today (Section 3.4);
3. As a facing material in relatively thin slabs (Section 3.5).

3.2. CLASSIFICATION OF STONE

Sedimentary rocks were deposited in layers by water or by air from fragments of preexisting rock, or from materials produced by small animals or by plants. The *igneous rocks* used in building are not part of the original crust of the earth, but molten rock material that solidified subsequently. *Metamorphic rocks* are sedimentary or igneous rocks whose structure has been drastically altered by great heat and pressure.

Sand and clay were produced in the first instance by the

disintegration of igneous rocks. Sand is mostly silica, and clay is produced by weathering from the feldspars, which are the chief minerals in granite rock.

Sedimentary rocks were then produced from these soils. Sands became sandstones, and clays became shales and slates. Limestones and marbles resulted from the deposition of the shells of small marine animals, or from chemical deposition. Coal was produced from plants.

Sedimentary Rocks

The geological classification of sedimentary rocks by composition and by age is discussed in detail in textbooks on geology (for example, Ref. 3.1). The older rocks are generally denser, stronger, and more durable than those deposited more recently, but this is not necessarily so. Deposits laid down in the last few million years are usually soils that have not yet been formed into rocks.

Coal is an important source of energy, but not used as a building material. Shale is used as a raw material for the manufacture of portland cement and of clay bricks, but it is not used directly as a building material.

Most *sandstones* are formed from small particles of silica (SiO_2), but they contain other fragments of rock. These sand particles are cemented into sandstone by the deposition of silica (*siliceous sandstones*), or of iron oxide (*ferruginous sandstones*), or of lime (*calcareous sandstones*), or of clay (*argillaceous sandstones*).

Limestones consist mainly of calcium carbonate, usually with some addition of magnesium carbonate. *Dolomite* (which should not be confused with the igneous rocks dolerite or diorite, listed in Table 3.1) contains the double carbonate of calcium and magnesium ($CaCO_3 \cdot MgCO_3$).

Many limestones contain fossil shells that are easily visible to the naked eye. *Oolitic limestone* is made up of round grains formed by the deposition of several coats of calcium carbonate on fragments of shell or grains of sand. It weathers evenly, and is easily cut and carved. Hence the stronger varieties have been very popular as building stones. *Chalk* is a soft white limestone from recent geological formations.

Limestones can be cemented by substances other than lime. Thus there are siliceous, ferruginous, and argillaceous limestones; the terms imply the same type of binders as for sandstones, discussed above.

Limestone can also be produced by chemical deposition from saturated solutions. *Tufa* is formed around calcareous springs. *Travertine* is a variety of tufa into which vegetable matter was embedded which subsequently rotted, leaving cavities in the rock. Travertine was already highly esteemed in Ancient Rome. Its popularity for floors is partly due to its good and even abrasion resistance, and partly to its variable texture, which is not only attractive in itself, but hides dirt marks that would be very obvious on white marble. The travertine quarries near Rome are still worked today.

Flint is a form of silica, probably derived from sponges. It is found in irregularly shaped nodules in chalk deposits in some countries. It is very brittle and breaks with a sharp fracture, hence it has been used extensively for tools and weapons in the Stone Age. The flint nodule is unattractive in appearance, but the split or *knapped* flint has a smooth surface, and in this form it was used as a building stone.

Igneous Rocks

Igneous rocks are classified by their texture and by their chemical composition (Table 3.1). The chemical composition is into *acid rocks*, which contain more silica (SiO_2), and *basic rocks*, which contain a higher proportion of metallic oxides. Free silica occurs only in acid rocks; the dark-green olivine occurs only in basic rocks. Basic rocks are generally darker in color than acid rocks. *Feldspars* (alumino-silicates of potassium, sodium or calcium) and *micas* (hydrous alumino-silicates of iron, magnesium, potassium, etc. which can be split into thin sheets) occur in most types of igneous rock. There are more than thirty minerals that can occur in igneous rock, and these are discussed in detail in textbooks on geology (for example, Ref. 3.1).

The texture division is into very fine-grained or glassy *extrusive rocks*, fine-grained *minor intrusive rocks*, and coarse-grained *major intrusive rocks*. Extrusive rocks are produced by volcanic action, and thus cool rapidly. Intrusive rocks are produced by molten magma from the earth's interior that solidifies before reaching the surface (Figs. 3.2.1 and 3.2.2).

Metamorphic Rocks

Metamorphic rocks are sedimentary or igneous rocks whose structure has been modified by the action of heat and/or pressure.

Marble is metamorphic limestone. If the stone was white and the recrystallization is complete, the result is a white marble free of any texture. Most marbles contain some materials other than calcium carbonate, and these may produce color and texture.

Table 3.1. Classification of Igneous Rocks.

Texture	Chemical Composition		
	Acid	Intermediate	Basic
Extrusive (Volcanic) Glassy or very fine-grained	Rhyolite	Andesite	Basalt
Minor intrusive (Dykes and sills) Fine-grained	Quartz-porphyry*	Porphyrite	Dolerite
Major intrusive (Plutonic) Coarse-grained	Granite	Diorite	Gabbro

*The term *porphyry* in common parlance means a fine-grained igneous rock containing large isolated crystals; it could have any chemical composition. The most decorative porphyries, however, are microgranites with some large white or red crystals of plagioclase feldspar (a mixture of $NaAlSi_3O_8$ and $CaAl_2Si_2O_8$).

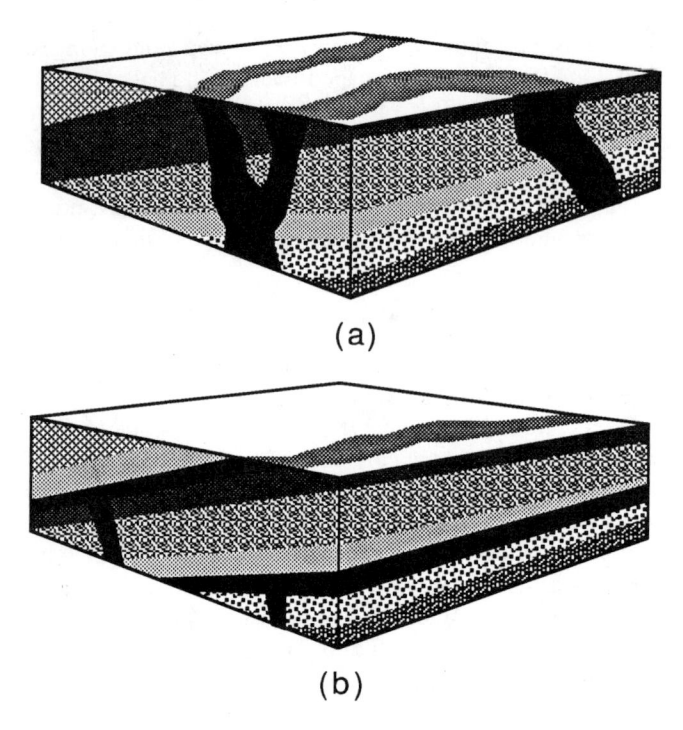

Fig. 3.2.1. Minor intrusive rocks may be *dykes* or *sills*. Dykes are cross-cutting fissures filled with igneous rocks which have not reached the surface. Sills are intrusions between beds of sedimentary rock. (a) Dykes. (b) Sills formed on top of dykes.

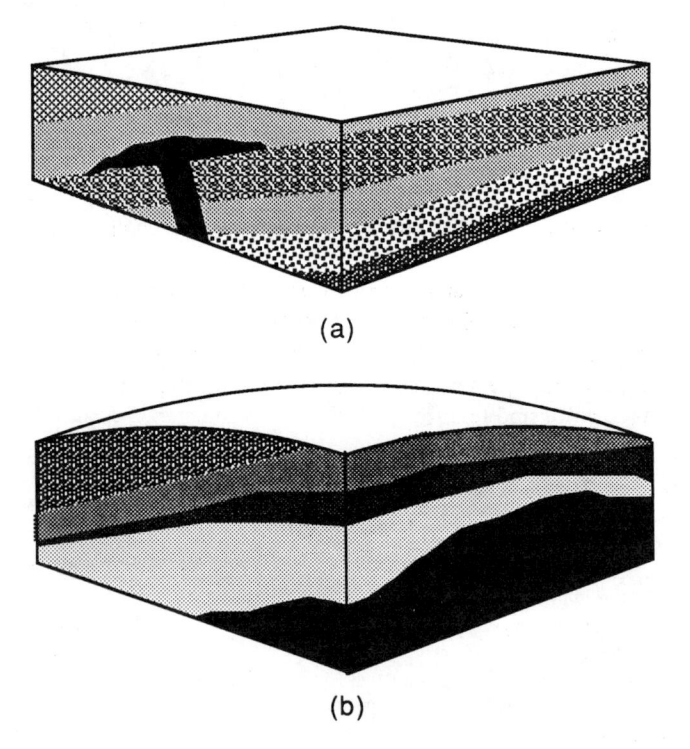

Fig. 3.2.2. Major intrusions of magma, forming *plutonic* rocks. (a) Major intrusion between beds of sedimentary rock, called *laccolith*. (b) Major intrusion pushing the entire sedimentary rock upwards, called *batholith*. The sedimentary rock may subsequently be eroded so that it exposes the harder plutonic rock on the surface.

Slate is metamorphized shale. The metamorphic action produces cleavage planes, so that it can be split into thin slabs.

Quartzite is a sandstone in which the sand grains and siliceous cement are recrystallized, sometimes with partial fusion.

Gneiss, produced by metamorphism of an igneous or sedimentary rock, has alternate light and dark bands.

The Industrial Classification of Stone

The building stone industry uses a simpler classification than the geological classification discussed above.

The term *limestone** has a more restricted meaning, since the more decorative stones capable of taking a polish are classified as marble (see below).

Sandstone* has the same meaning as in the geological classification. It is divided according to grain size into coarse-grained, medium-grained, and fine-grained sandstone. Most sandstones used for buildings are medium-grained.

Slate also has the same meaning, but slates are today used less for roofs, where the thinnest slates are the best, and more for covering walls and floors, where thinness is not necessarily an advantage.

The term *granite* includes all igneous rocks and the metamorphic gneiss. Commercial granites thus range from pink or red (for acid rocks) to dark gray or black (for basic rocks), and in grain size from coarse to fine. *Porphyry*, which includes large crystals in a fine-grained matrix, and *gneiss*, which is banded, are sometimes identified as such, instead of being called granite.

The term *marble* includes both the true metamorphic marbles and limestones that can take a polish. These "sedimentary marbles" may have fossils showing on their polished surface. *Serpentine*, a green ultrabasic igneous rock consisting mainly of hydrous magnesium silicate, $Mg_6Si_4O_{10}(OH)_8$, is also classified as a marble. Marbles are thus available in a wide range of colors. *Travertine* is sometimes described as marble, because it takes a high polish, and sometimes as limestone.

3.3. THE DETERIORATION OF NATURAL STONE

Granite, slate, and the harder sandstones are barely affected by wind and rain, but the softer sandstones and limestones gradually show signs of erosion (Fig. 3.3.1a). In fact, many sandstones and limestones weather to a greater extent than a strong mortar; after a time mortar joints would then project beyond the wall's surface, which is unsightly. To ensure that this does not happen, a mortar should always be used that is weaker than the stone. Any cracks that form

---

*The term *freestone* is used both for limestone and sandstone that can be cut and carved easily.

Fig. 3.3.1. Replacement of a weathered stone carving by a new carving. (a) Original stone carving in the stone-mason's yard after removal; note that the upper part of the pinnacle had been repaired previously. (b) New carving after installation. The original quarry was no longer in existence, and the new stone came from a quarry which worked stone from the same geological formation. The new carving is similar to, but not identical with the original. (*Courtesy of Mr. Robert Marsh, Clerk of Works, University of Sydney.*)

will then run through the joints (Fig. 3.3.2), which can be repaired by repointing. Limestones should be laid in mortar that contains more lime than portland cement.

Stone weathers more readily along its bedding planes, and it should therefore preferably be used so that its bedding planes are horizontal; indeed, if a bedding plane is placed vertically parallel to the wall surface, a piece of stone might fall off because of preferential weathering of a bedding plane. As a result of the movement of the earth's crust, the bedding planes could be at any angle, and they are not always visible, although they may become so during the quarrying operation, or be known from past experience.

Cracks in stone can give rise to serious deterioration, particularly in climates with frequent cycles of freezing and thawing, because the cracks enlarge if water within them turns into ice. This provides points of entry for chemical deterioration. Apart from weathering of bedding planes, cracks may result from the excessive use of pneumatic tools and explosives in quarries in place of the traditional hammer and chisel, or from careless handling or cutting of the stone. They may also result from temperature and moisture movement, unless adequate expansion joints are provided. Consequently if stone is used as a veneer, the method of connection must make due allowance for differential movement between the stone veneer and the structure of the building (see Section 3.5).

Some stones contain soluble salts that may rise gradually to the surface and form unsightly deposits, called *efflorescence*. These can often be completely removed by washing.

Sulfur dioxide (SO_2) resulting from industrial processes, which can be carried in the atmosphere a considerable distance from its source, combines with water to form sulfurous acid, and with water and the oxygen in the air to form sulfuric acid. These, in turn, combine with the calcium carbonate of limestones or calcareous sandstones to form insoluble calcium sulfite and calcium sulfate.

Calcium carbonate is water-soluble, and limestone is therefore normally washed clean by rainwater; but if lime-

30 HANDBOOK OF ARCHITECTURAL TECHNOLOGY

Fig. 3.3.2. Cracks in stonework laid with mortar that is weaker than the stone. The cracks run through the joints, and the stone is undamaged. Repair can be effected by repointing the joints.

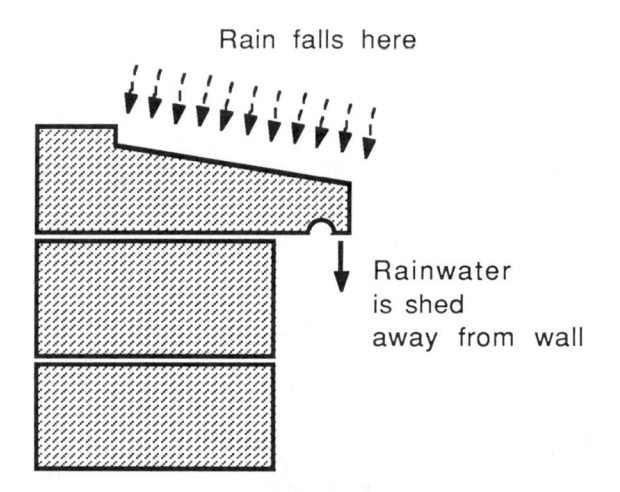

Fig. 3.3.3. Throat cut on the underside of a stone window sill, near the edge, to collect water running off the top of the sill, and throw it clear off the wall. Dirt deposited during a dry period on the top face of a projecting stone is washed off by rain, and this dirty water would produce stains if it fell on the stone surface. Throats are usually cut hemispherical or square.

stone is sheltered from the rain, an insoluble skin may form, and this may blister and fall off in scales, ruining the stone surface. Such deterioration can be avoided by designing buildings to be washed evenly by rain, or where this is not possible, by washing the sheltered parts from time to time.

Sandstones are not water-soluble; indeed they absorb water, and they are not washed clean by rain. Horizontal projections on which water can collect, such as copings, cornices and window ledges, should be fitted with a throat that collects dirty water (Fig. 3.3.3), and throws it clear off the stone wall, so that it does not stain the wall (Fig. 3.3.4).

3.4. THE PRESERVATION AND REPAIR OF NATURAL STONE

In the past, the normal response to deterioration has been to cut back the damaged stone and replace it with new stone from the same quarry, or with compatible stone of similar chemical composition if the original quarry is no longer in operation (Fig. 3.3.1). For some old buildings the cost of repeated repairs already exceeds the original cost, even when allowance is made for increases in the price of labor and materials. Preservative treatments are therefore of great interest, even though their result is less certain than replacement of the damaged stone.

Waterglass (sodium or potassium silicate) has been employed as a preservative for the more porous stones since the 16th Century. Better results are obtained using *silica* (SiO_2) dissolved in alcohol. The alcohol evaporates and

Fig. 3.3.4. Staining and deterioration of a sandstone surface by water dripping from a window air conditioner.

leaves bars of silica as reinforcement between the grains of stone.

More controversial are treatments with modern synthetics. *Silicones* (see Section 5.3) have been used as stone preservatives since the 1940s. The British Directorate of Ancient Monuments has reported that the arrest of decay was only short-lived (Ref. 3.2), but satisfactory results have been reported of the use of silicones, acrylic resins, and epoxies as preservatives and as fillers to repair damage from restoration work in Venice (Ref. 3.3).

For less important buildings reconstituted stone can be used to replace damaged natural stone. This consists of particles of the stone to be replaced, or a very similar stone, and a cement. The cheaper reconstituted stones use white or colored portland cement. A better result is obtained with synthetic adhesives, such as epoxy resin (Fig. 3.4.1).

3.5. STONE VENEER

Except for small monuments and restorations of old buildings, natural stone is today used mainly as a veneer. These veneers have in recent years become much thinner, partly because of the increasing cost of natural stone, and partly because of improved stone-cutting technology. For interior use veneers of strong stone need only be a fraction of an inch (a few millimeters) thick. These are fixed with adhesives, such as epoxies (Section 5.9). These thin pieces are usually not much larger than tiles.

Floor surfaces require stones with a hard surface, such as slates, quartzites, granites, the harder marbles, and travertine. Wall surfaces in exposed locations should also be abrasion resistant. Corners that are liable to be damaged can be protected by bronze or stainless steel.

Adhesives can be used externally for fixing stones, but their durability should be carefully examined to ensure that they do not stain the stone, and that the adhesion is lasting, lest stone slabs fall from a wall on pedestrians.

A better method of fixing, particularly for large pieces of stone, is the use of metal cramps. There should be an air space of a fraction of an inch (or a few millimeters) between the stone slabs and the supporting structure to allow for differential and temperature movement (Fig. 3.5.1). For the same reason at least some of the joints between the stone slabs should be open, or filled with a flexible mastic.

The cramps are usually made from stainless steel, but gun metal or phosphor bronze can be used. Ordinary steel is unsatisfactory, even when heavily galvanized or terneplated. The stone slabs must have sufficient thickness to resist local bending. This depends partly on the size of the slabs and the spacing of the cramps, and partly on the strength of the stone.

3.6. LIME, LIME MORTAR, AND LIME WASH

Quicklime (which is calcium oxide, CaO) is produced by burning limestone, chalk, or seashells (all consisting of

Fig. 3.4.1. Replacement of deteriorated sandstone carvings with reconstituted stone castings made with epoxy resin in the Queen Victoria Building, Sydney. (*By courtesy of the architects, Rice Daubney, Sydney.*)

32 HANDBOOK OF ARCHITECTURAL TECHNOLOGY

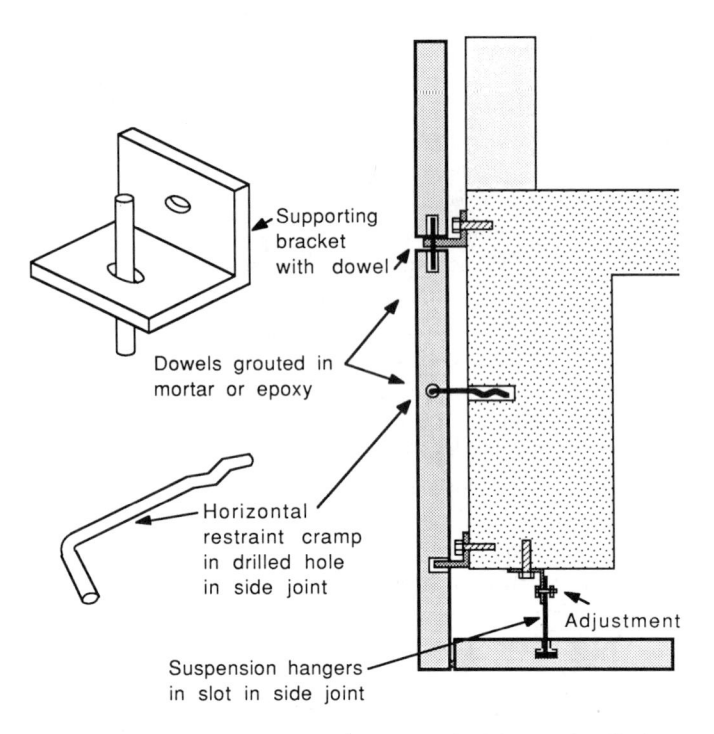

Fig. 3.5.1. Fixing of stone veneer to vertical face and soffit (underside) of reinforced-concrete structure with cramps, angle brackets, and suspension hangers.

calcium carbonate, $CaCO_3$) in a kiln; carbon dioxide (CO_2) is released as a gas. The resulting lumps of quicklime are pulverized, and water is added in a hydrator to produce *hydrated lime powder* (which is calcium hydroxide, $Ca(OH)_2$). This is packaged in large paper bags. *Lime putty* is produced by adding water to hydrated lime powder.

Until the end of the 19th Century, lime was universally used in masonry of brick and natural stone for *mortar*, made by mixing it with 2 to 5 parts of sand; the inert sand is needed to reduce the shrinkage of the lime. The gluing action of the mortar is physical rather than chemical; it is mainly caused by the stiffening of the paste as water is lost by evaporation or absorbed by the brick or stone.

Pure lime mortar is used today only for the restoration of old buildings, because portland cement mortar is much stronger (see Section 3.8). Lime mortar is, however, still used widely as an additive to cement mortar to improve its workability and water retention; an alternative to the addition of lime is the use of masonry cement (see Section 3.8), which contains an inert filler.

Pure lime mortar has been used in the past for *plastering* walls, often mixed with animal hair or vegetable fiber to give it some reinforcement; it is, however, very soft, and if used today it is mixed with portland cement or gypsum in various proportions, depending on the hardness required.

Whitewash or *limewash* is a cheap form of white paint for external use, and for use internally in agricultural buildings. Limewash can be made from quicklime and tallow, from hydrated lime and common salt, and from hydrated lime, alum, and animal glue. A small quantity of blue pigment makes the lime wash appear "whiter".

3.7. GYPSUM AND GYPSUM PLASTER

Gypsum (calcium sulfate dihydrate, $CaSO_4 \cdot 2H_2O$) occurs in nature as an off-white crystalline material. *Alabaster* is a decorative, generally translucent variety.

When heated in the range 262–325°F (128–163°C), gypsum gives up three quarters of its water, and the resulting *hemihydrate* is called *plaster of Paris*. If gypsum is heated above 400°F (200°C), all the water is driven off (*anhydrous gypsum plaster* if manufactured, *anhydrite* if found in nature).

All gypsum plasters expand when they set, in sharp contrast to cement plaster, which shrinks on setting. Gypsum cast into a mold therefore copies its shape precisely, and gypsum plaster has no shrinkage cracks.

When water is added to plaster of Paris, it changes back to the dihydrate, and forms an interlocking mass of fine, needle-shaped crystals. It sets in 5 to 20 minutes. This is useful for casting the material into a mold, or for repairs of minor damage. When it is used for plastering, that is, applied with a trowel to timber or metal laths, more time is needed, and a retarder, such as *keratin*, is added; it is then called *retarded hemihydrate gypsum plaster*.

Anhydrite or *hard-burnt plasters* have a much longer setting time than plaster of Paris. *Keene's cement* is a variation made by heating gypsum first in the 262–325°F range to form the anhydrite; the material is then given a bath in alum, and heated further to 400°F. This produces a much harder plaster with a faster setting time than anhydrite.

Gypsum plasters have been used for several centuries both in precast units, and applied wet to brick or concrete block walls, or to lathing; wooden lathing has now been replaced by metal laths. Wet plaster is applied in two or three coats, which may be plaster and sand (sometimes with the addition of lime putty) or neat plaster. In three-coat work the final coat is usually neat gypsum plaster to give a smooth finish. Gypsum is not suitable for external plastering. *Fibrous plaster* is reinforced with animal hair or vegetable fibers to make it self-supporting.

By far the largest present use of gypsum, however, is in the form of *gypsum drywall construction*, which utilizes precast gypsum sheet sandwiched between sheets of treated paper (*plasterboard*). The sheets are usually joined by adhesive tape, embedded in a jointing compound, and then sanded. They can be used for ceilings, partitions, and the interior lining of walls.

Gypsum plaster with an aggregate of perlite (an expanded volcanic rock) or exfoliated vermiculite (a platelike mineral which expands on heating) can be used for the *fire-protection* of structural steel.

Gypsum plaster with the same type of aggregate can be used as an *acoustic plaster* for sound absorption. Alternatively, aluminum powder can be mixed with the plaster to produce bubbles of hydrogen in the set plaster.

On the other hand, gypsum without aggregate can be used to produce a hard, smooth surface that acts as a sound reflector.

Graffito (or *sgraffito*) has been used in Italy and some other countries for many centuries for decorative plaster work. Two or three coats of differently colored plaster are used. While the plaster is still wet, a pattern is scored on it which exposes the lower, differently colored layer(s). The technique can also be used with portland cement plaster.

3.8. PORTLAND CEMENT

Hydrated portland cement is not water-soluble, and is therefore weather-resistant. Hence it is now generally used in mortar and plaster where lime was used until the early years of this century. It has also replaced gypsum for internal plastering.

Portland cement is manufactured from clay (or shale) and limestone (or chalk). Clay and shale consist mainly of kaolinite ($Al_2O_3 \cdot 2SiO_2 \cdot 2H_2O$); on heating, this dissociates into alumina (Al_2O_3) and silica (SiO_2), and the water evaporates. Limestones and chalk consist mainly of calcium carbonate ($CaCO_3$), which dissociates into calcium oxide (CaO) and carbon dioxide which is given off as a gas. In addition there are some impurities present in the clay and the limestone, of which iron oxide is the most common.

These materials are first ground and then heated to a temperature of 2650°F (1450°C) while they travel slowly along a rotary kiln. In the process calcium silicates, calcium aluminates, and some other compounds are formed. The cement clinker which emerges from the rotary kiln is mixed with gypsum to retard the initial setting of the cement, and is then ground to a very fine powder, with a particle size of the order of 5 to 50 μm.

Tricalcium silicate ($3CaO \cdot SiO_2$) constitutes about half the volume of the cement. It is responsible for the early gain in the strength of the cement, which is called *hardening*. About one-quarter of the cement is dicalcium silicate ($2CaO \cdot SiO_2$). This takes more time to hydrate (that is, combine with water), and it is responsible for the long-term gain in strength, called *aging*:

$$2(3CaO \cdot SiO_2) + 6H_2O$$
$$= 3CaO \cdot 2SiO_2 \cdot 3H_2O + 3Ca(OH)_2$$

and

$$2(2CaO \cdot SiO_2) + 4H_2O$$
$$= 3CaO \cdot 2SiO_2 \cdot 3H_2O + Ca(OH)_2$$

Thus the hydration of both tricalcium silicate and of dicalcium silicate produces $3CaO \cdot 2SiO_2 \cdot 3H_2O$, a compound that occurs naturally in California, Ireland, and South Africa. It is called *afwillite*, and current research indicates that it is the material primarily responsible for the strength of portland cement.

About one-tenth of the volume of cement consists of the amorphous tricalcium aluminate ($3CaO \cdot Al_2O_3$), whose hydration is very rapid. It causes the cement to *set*, that is change from a liquid to a stiff paste. The setting must allow sufficient time for the concrete, in which the cement is used, to be placed in the formwork, and to be worked into every corner of it.

To provide this time, the setting of portland cement is retarded by the addition of gypsum, whose hydration produces calcium sulfoaluminate ($3CaO \cdot Al_2O_3 \cdot 3CaSO_4 \cdot 32H_2O$), which also occurs as a natural mineral, called *ettringite*. The formation of ettringite is an expansive reaction. Prior to hardening, the cement is in a plastic condition, and it can thus absorb the expansion. After it has hardened, the expansion is liable to produce cracks. The amount of gypsum added to the cement clinker must therefore be carefully controlled.

The principal hydration products of portland cement are basic, and they protect reinforcing steel from corrosion, provided there is adequate cover, no large cracks, and no concrete additives that produce corrosive anions, such as chlorides.

The Testing of Cement

In America the *fineness of cement* is measured with a Wagner turbidimeter (ASTM C 115-86). The British standard test uses the Lea and Nurse permeability apparatus (Ref. 3.3).

The setting time is determined with the Vicat apparatus (ASTM C 191-82).

Several tests are in use for checking the *soundness* of cement. Unsoundness is a tendency for hardened cement to expand which could lead to disruption. The three main causes are an excess of free lime, an excess of crystalline magnesia, and an excessive proportion of sulfates. Soundness is tested by autoclaving (ASTM C 151-84) or boiling (Ref. 3.4) a standard specimen of hardened cement paste.

The strength of cement is measured by standard tension and/or compression tests on cement mortar (ASTM C 190-85 and C 109-84).

Modifications of Ordinary Portland Cement

In *low-heat portland cement* the tricalcium silicate is reduced and the dicalcium silicate increased, because the slower chemical reaction of the latter generates less heat.

The reverse steps are taken for *high-early-strength cement* (called *rapid-hardening cement* in Britain) to increase the rate at which strength develops. In addition the cement is ground finer so as to offer a larger surface to the water.

Masonry cement is portland cement with a finely ground inert filler, usually limestone, and an air-entraining agent (see Section 3.12). It is an alternative, particularly in the U.S.A., to a cement-lime mortar (see Section 3.6) for laying bricks, concrete blocks, or natural stone.

In *sulfate-resistant portland cement* the tricalcium aluminate is kept low enough for only a small amount of gypsum (which is a sulfate) to have to be added; thus the risk of the formation of an excessive amount of ettringite is reduced.

Portland-pozzolan cement contains an additive that turns the calcium hydroxide ($Ca(OH)_2$) produced during hydration (which does not contribute significantly to strength) into calcium silicate hydrates, which do. The name comes from the natural cement used in Ancient Rome, which in turn took its name from the Italian town of Pozzuoli, whence it came. Modern pozzolans are, however, chemically different. They are waste products which contain reactive silica and cost very little, such as fly ash and blast-furnace slag.

White and Colored Portland Cement

The color of portland cement is gray because of small quantities of iron oxide and manganese oxide introduced by the raw materials and the grinding process. A perfectly white cement can be made by using china clay, white limestone, and pebbles or nickel-molybdenum alloy balls for grinding. Its properties are the same, but the cost is much higher.

Off-white cement, which costs only a little more than gray cement, is made with light-colored clay, white limestone, and ordinary grinding procedures.

Colored cement is made by the addition of mineral pigments. The lighter colors need white or off-white cement as a base. Colored concrete fades over a period of time due to the formation of a surface film of white calcium carbonate. This can be removed by washing with 1:10 solution of hydrochloric acid, followed by washing with water.

Cement Mortar and Plaster

Mortar made only from portland cement and sand is rarely used because it lacks adequate workability. This can be remedied by using instead masonry cement which, as mentioned above, contains an inert filler and an air-entraining agent, *or*, as mentioned in Section 3.6, by adding some lime to the portland cement.

Portland cement is used for external plaster work, because lime plaster is gradually dissolved by rain water, and gypsum is not suitable for exterior work. It is now also commonly used for interior plastering. One coat is sufficient, but a second coat containing more cement and less sand is frequently used. However, as neat cement cannot be used for plastering, it is not possible to obtain the same smooth finish as with gypsum plaster.

Graffito work is briefly described in Section 3.7.

3.9. OTHER CEMENTS

A cement known as *aluminous cement, high-alumina cement*, or *calcium-aluminate cement* is made by burning together limestone and bauxite. The cement is darker than portland cement, it is stronger and develops its strength more quickly, and it has better resistance to attack by sulfates and sea water. When water is added, hydrated monocalcium aluminate ($CaO \cdot Al_2O_3 \cdot 10H_2O$) is formed, and that is the main cementing compound. It has always been known that this may convert to another hydrate at high temperatures:

$$3(CaO \cdot Al_2O_3 \cdot 10H_2O)$$
$$= 3CaO \cdot Al_2O_3 \cdot 6H_2O + 2(Al_2O_3 \cdot 3H_2O)$$
$$+ 18H_2O.$$

This *conversion* results in disintegration of the concrete. During the 1960s a number of structures built with aluminous cement failed because of conversion of the cement at ordinary temperatures. Aluminous cement is therefore now rarely used merely because high strength or high early strength is required, but it is still considered useful where resistance to sulfates or sea water is needed.

Magnesium oxychloride is manufactured from magnesite ($MgCO_3$) which is heated until it turns into lightly burnt reactive magnesia (MgO). This is ground and mixed with a 20 percent solution of magnesium chloride to produce magnesium oxychloride ($3MgO \cdot MgCl_2 \cdot 11H_2O$). This is a strong and hard material; however, it is not water-resistant and it corrodes steel. Its most common use is for interior surfaces (*magnesite flooring*) with an inert aggregate, usually colored with a mineral pigment. After casting, the surface is ground and polished with wax dissolved in turpentine to give it protection against water.

3.10. CONCRETE AND CONCRETE AGGREGATE

Concrete has become the most widely used material for large buildings, as it was in Imperial Rome, and for the same reasons: it is relatively cheap, it is durable, it is fire-resistant, and an entire structure can be cast monolithically (that is, as if it was carved from one piece of stone).

Unlike natural stone, which must be cut to its desired shape, concrete can be cast in a mold, and it can be reinforced. The chemical reactions which formed stone occurred long ago, whereas concrete remains chemically active for many years. On the one hand it continues to gain strength due to aging, on the other it *shrinks* when it is cast and it continues to deform under load (*creep*). Both shrinkage and creep must be accommodated in the design of reinforced concrete (see Chapter 13).

Particle Size of Concrete Aggregates

Normal concrete used in buildings has *fine aggregate* of which 95 percent passes through a $\frac{3}{16}$ in. (5 mm) sieve, and 95 percent is retained on a No. 100 sieve (British BS and American ASTM sieve sizes differ slightly, but the No. 100 sieve is the same, 0.0060 in. or 0.15 mm).

Ninety-five percent of the *coarse aggregate* passes through a $\frac{3}{4}$ in. (20 mm) sieve, and 95 percent is retained on the $\frac{3}{16}$ in. (5 mm) sieve.

Classification of Concrete Aggregate

Fine particles of rock can be used for *fine aggregate*, but sand, which produces a more workable concrete, is usually preferred. The sand may come from a river or the sea, or more commonly from a pit. It may be necessary to wash it to remove salt, organic material, or clay particles. Most sand consists predominantly of particles of silica, but white coral sand or black sand of volcanic origin can be used.

Limestone, sandstone, or granite (which includes all hard igneous rocks, Section 3.2) may be used for *coarse aggregate* as crushed rock, crushed gravel, or gravel of the right size. Crushed artificial materials, such as blast-furnace slag, can be used if they are strong enough and free from deleterious substances.

The strength of concrete can be no higher than the strength of the coarse aggregate, although it may be less. The softer limestones, sandstones, and bricks are therefore not suitable.

Silica changes from its alpha to its beta phase at about 1100°F (600°C), and this may disintegrate the concrete. The aggregate of a concrete that requires fire resistance should therefore be limestone or a basic rock, such as dolerite, since sandstones and acid rocks contain silica.

Lightweight aggregates may be light volcanic rocks, such as pumice or scoria, or processed materials, such as expanded clay or shale. They generally weigh about 20 percent less than normal aggregates, but the concrete made with them has a strength comparable to that of normal concrete. Hence there is a substantial saving in the dead load of the structure (ASTM C 330-87). However, the cost of these aggregates is often higher. The term *lightweight aggregate* is also used for much lighter materials, such as expanded perlite and exfoliated vermiculite (see Section 3.14).

No-fines concrete is a lightweight concrete made only from coarse aggregate and cement. Because it has large pores, its strength is low, but it provides insulation and there is no capillary moisture movement. It has been used mainly for the walls of low-cost houses; external walls must be rendered with cement mortar.

Alkali-Aggregate Reaction

Opaline silica and other reactive forms of silica react expansively with any potassium or sodium oxide (K_2O or Na_2O), and this often causes disintegration of the concrete. Such rocks occur in the U.S.A., Australia, New Zealand, India, and the Scandinavian countries. The reaction takes place only when reactive aggregates are used together with high-alkali cement. One or the other on their own cause no damage (Ref. 3.6). Liability of alkali-aggregate reaction can be checked by chemical tests (Ref. 3.7), or by measuring the expansion of test pieces.

Unsound Particles and Deleterious Substances

Organic materials are usually derived from decayed vegetable matter. They may interfere with the hydration of the cement. Their presence can be determined by placing the aggregate in a 3 percent solution of sodium hydroxide (NaOH); if the color is deeper than that in a standard solution, the aggregate must be washed (ASTM C 40-84).

Clay, silt, or crusher dust coating the aggregate surface interferes with the adhesion of the cement to the aggregate (ASTM C 117-87).

Sand or gravel from sea or estuarine shores may contain salt, and this may cause efflorescence on the surface of the concrete; however, some specifications permit the use of unwashed sea sand.

Sugar is a very deleterious substance. Even a 1 percent solution almost completely inhibits the setting and hardening of concrete (Ref. 3.8).

Some coarse aggregates contain unsound particles such as lumps of clay, particles of coal, or particles with veins where igneous rock has decayed into clay. The maximum permissible content of unsound particles is usually of the order of 1 percent (ASTM C 142-78 (1984)).

Moisture Content of Aggregate

Concrete aggregate, even if protected from rain, is likely to contain an appreciable amount of moisture (Fig. 3.10.1). This must be allowed for when determining the amount of water to be used for the concrete mix. The moisture content of surface-dry aggregate need only be determined once for any given type of aggregate; this is done by drying surface-dry aggregate in an oven. It ranges from 0.25–4 percent. The *free moisture* (Fig. 3.10.1d), for which adjustment must be made, is then the excess of the actual moisture content over the surface-dry moisture content (Fig. 3.10.1c). The actual moisture content of any given batch of aggregate can also be determined by drying in an oven, but this is rather time-consuming. A faster, if less accurate method, is to use an electric moisture meter, which measures the change of electrical resistance in various parts of the aggregate pile.

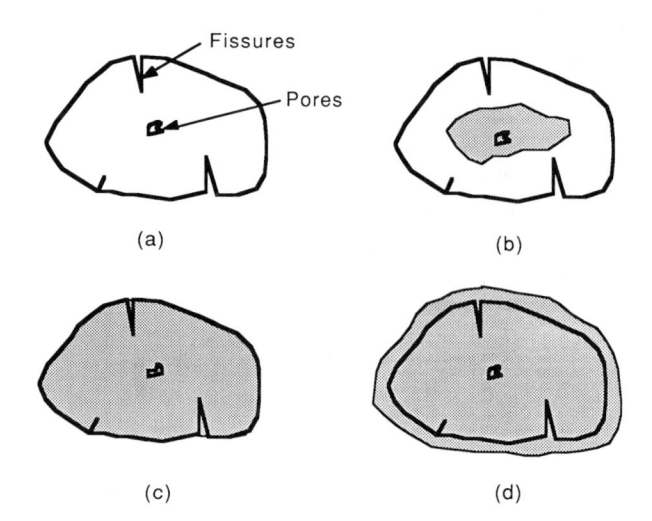

Fig. 3.10.1. The moisture content of aggregate. (a) The moisture content is zero (*oven-dry*). When it is used for making concrete, absorption by the aggregate reduces the water/cement ratio (W/C). (b) The aggregate contains interior moisture (*air-dry*). Absorption by the aggregate reduces the W/C slightly. (c) The aggregate is saturated, so that all pores are full of moisture (*surface-dry*). The W/C is not affected by aggregate. (d) Moisture adheres to aggregate surface (*moist*). When the aggregate is used for making concrete, the W/C increases due to this *free moisture* on the surface of the concrete.

The volume of sand increases as its moisture content increases by up to 25 percent (at about 8 percent moisture content), and with higher content the volume decreases again. This is a problem that need be considered only if concrete aggregates are measured by volume instead of weight, and this is now rare.

Bulk Density and Specific Gravity

The bulk density of aggregate is measured by weighing the contents of a standard cylinder, and dividing the weight by its volume. There are two bulk densities. For measuring *loose bulk density* the cylinder is filled loosely with the aggregate. To measure *compacted bulk density* the aggregate is compacted with a tamping rod.

Bulk density depends on the moisture content, the shape of the aggregate particles, and their specific gravity. For most concrete aggregates the specific gravity is between 2.5 and 2.8, which corresponds to a density of 156–175 lb/ft^3 (2500–2800 kg/m^3).

Abrasion Resistance and Strength

Abrasion resistance of aggregate is important only for concrete to be used for floor surfaces. There are several machines for testing it. The most common utilizes a tumbling barrel into which the aggregate is placed together with a number of standard steel balls. The dust formed is removed, and the loss of weight of the aggregate is measured.

The strength of aggregate is determined by a compression test. The aggregate is placed into a standard cylinder, consolidated by tamping, and loaded through a piston that fits into the cylinder.

3.11. MIXING, PLACING, AND CURING OF CONCRETE

The 1:2:4 rule for proportioning the concrete mix goes back to the early years of the 19th Century, and it is still a good rule where concrete is mixed by hand or with a small mixer. It means that concrete consists of one part of cement, two parts of sand, and four parts of coarse aggregate. The unit of cement is usually one bag of cement (94 lb in the U.S.A., and 40 or 50 kg in metric countries); the aggregate is measured by volume in a gauge box. As the technology of weighing heavy materials improved, concrete has been increasingly proportioned by weight, which is more accurate (see discussion of bulk density in Section 3.10).

Since the middle of the present century, concrete for building sites has been increasingly supplied from *ready-mix plants* which produce very large quantities of concrete mix, so that it is economical and practical to spend a considerable amount of time on determining the best mix possible for the available aggregates, using a mix of two or more types of coarse aggregates, and occasionally more than one type of fine aggregate.

Strength does not depend on the absolute content of cement or water, but on the water/cement ratio (Fig. 3.11.1). However, the relationship holds good only as long as the

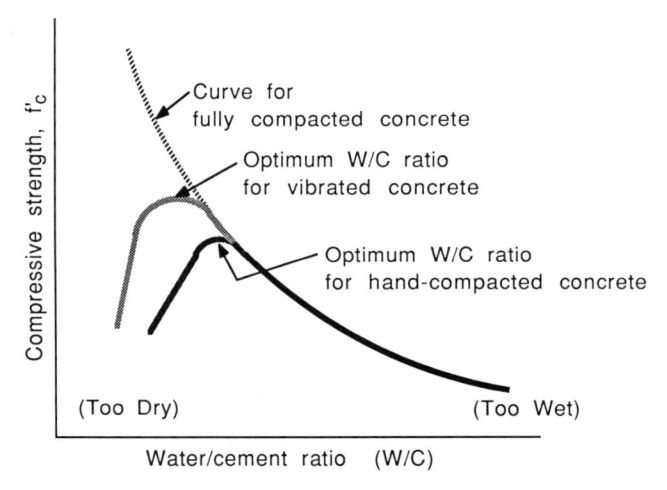

Fig. 3.11.1. Relation between the water/cement ratio W/C and the specified compressive strength of the concrete, f'_c. The strength f'_c is inversely proportional to W/C, provided that the concrete is fully compacted. Hence the curve for fully compacted concrete is a hyperbola. This was established in 1919 by Duff Abrams from experiments carried out at the Lewis Institute, a precursor of the Illinois Institute of Technology [Ref. 3.9]. The range of full compaction can be extended by vibration. When the concrete is too dry for full compaction, its strength falls rapidly below the ideal curve.

concrete is fully compacted. Hence workability has an important influence on strength.

In theory the fine aggregate is required to fill the spaces between the coarse aggregate particles, and the cement the spaces between the fine aggregate particles. In practice these proportions have to be altered appreciably by the need for a workable (that is, sufficiently fluid) mix. All the corners of the formwork and all the spaces between the reinforcing bars or prestressing tendons must be filled with concrete, and there must be no air pockets anywhere. In heavily reinforced concrete it may therefore be necessary to use more water than is necessary for maximum strength in order to achieve the necessary fluidity.

Thus workability depends partly on the aggregate proportions, and partly on the water content. Since strength depends on the water/cement ratio, an increase in strength for a given water content calls for an increase in the cement content. This increases the cost of the concrete, and it also increases its shrinkage and creep, which are entirely due to the cement content. High-strength concrete is therefore usually made with chemical additives (see Section 3.12), rather than a very high cement content.

American and British practice for the design of concrete mixes employs the same principles, but the procedure differs. The American method is based on calculations of the absolute volume for the estimated unit weights of the materials (Ref. 3.10), whereas the British method uses a series of charts and tables (Ref. 3.11).

The concrete mix having been chosen, the weights of the materials to be used for a trial mix are calculated; only a small batch of concrete is needed, sufficient to test the workability and specified compressive strength. If the desired results are not achieved, the trial mix is modified empirically on the basis of the results obtained.

Once the correct mix proportions have been determined, they can be used until it becomes necessary to vary the workability and/or the compressive strength, or until it becomes necessary to switch to different concrete aggregates.

When concrete is transported from a ready-mix plant to a building site in a mixer truck, the water is usually added to the dry concrete mix just before it reaches the building site.

Testing Concrete for Workability

Workability is the property of freshly mixed concrete or mortar that determines the ease with which it can be placed and compacted to fill every part of the formwork, and given a satisfactory surface finish.

The *slump test* (ASTM C 143-78) is the oldest and most widely used workability test. A hollow truncated cone of sheet metal (Fig. 3.11.2) is filled with concrete; the mold is lifted, and the concrete allowed to slump (Fig. 3.11.3). The test gives a satisfactory answer when a true slump occurs. However, shear slumps give less accurate results, and collapses may be produced either by very dry or very wet concrete, so that a collapse as such does not indicate whether the concrete mix is very harsh or very fluid.

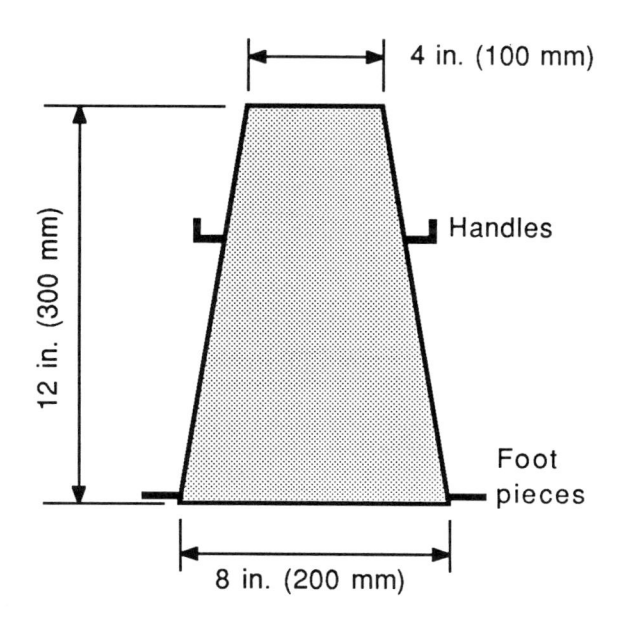

Fig. 3.11.2. Mold for the slump test. The mold is filled through the 4-in. (100-mm) circular hole at the top of the mold in three layers, compacted with 25 strokes of a steel rod, and the mold is then lifted to allow the concrete to slump.

Several other tests have been devised, and some give better results in a laboratory or a ready-mix plant. They measure either the flow of wet concrete, its capacity for remolding, or penetration into wet concrete.

For the *flow test* the concrete is placed in a mold, similar to a slump-test mold, on a flow table. The mold is then lifted, and the table raised and dropped several times. The resulting outward flow of the concrete is measured (ASTM 230-83).

The *remolding test* is a variation on the flow test. A slump test mold is placed on a flow table and filled, the mold is lifted and the concrete is allowed to slump, as in the slump test. A cylinder mold of larger diameter is then placed over the slumped concrete, and the flow table is raised and dropped until the concrete fills the cylinder mold. (U.S. Army Corps of Engineers Standard CRD-C 6-63; there is no ASTM Standard).

The *Vebe test* is another remolding test devised by V. Bährner in Sweden, and widely used throughout the world. It uses a glass plate on top of the cylinder mold, which makes it easier to determine when full compaction is achieved, and it uses a vibrating table instead of a mechanically jolted flow table (Ref. 3.12).

The *compacting factor test* is standardized by the British specification BS 1881. The concrete is allowed to drop into a cylinder under standardized conditions, and its weight is determined. The compacting factor is the ratio of the experimentally determined weight to that of an equal volume of fully compacted concrete (Ref. 3.13).

The *Kelly ball test* (ASTM C 360-82) is the most widely used penetration test (Fig. 3.11.4). The slump test and the

Normal slump · Shear · Collapse

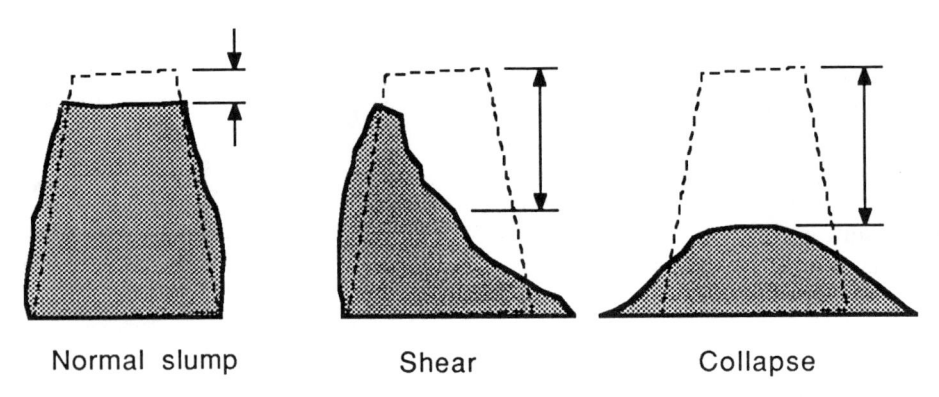

Fig. 3.11.3. The slump test for the workability of concrete. (a) The slump can be measured with some accuracy for a *true slump*, which is obtained from mixes that contain a high proportion of cement and/or fine sand. Mass concrete and lightly reinforced concrete should have a slump of the order of 1 to 2 in. (25 to 50 mm); normal reinforced concrete requires a slump of 2 to 4 in. (50 to 100 mm).

(b) Harsher mixes produce a *shear slump*, which is measured to the middle of the slump on each side of the cone. The result is much less accurate than for a true slump.

(c) A *collapse* may be due to the concrete being so wet that it flows outwards into a shallow heap. It may also occur with a very dry mix which, had it been a little more cohesive and not collapsed, would have produced zero slump. No satisfactory measurement can be made when the cone collapses.

Kelly ball test are simple field tests. The Kelly test, unlike the slump test, can be used on harsh mixes which would produce a collapsed slump. However, slump remains the most popular measure of workability. The other tests are laboratory tests.

Testing Concrete for Strength

The strength of concrete is determined by compression tests on concrete cylinders (in America and Australia) or on concrete cubes (in Europe). The cylinders are normally 6 in. (150 mm) in diameter and 12 in. (300 mm) high, and the cubes are normally 6 in. (150 mm) in each direction. They are tested in a hydraulic press, and the maximum load they can support before breaking is measured (ASTM C 39-86). The strength in direct tension and in diagonal tension due to shear is normally derived from the compressive strength.

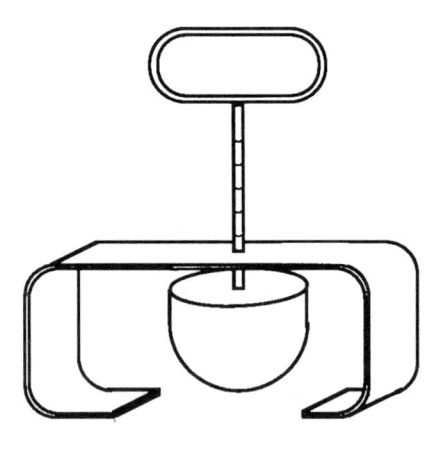

Fig. 3.11.4. The Kelly ball test. A hemispherical plunger, weighing 30 lb (13.6 kg) and fixed to a supporting frame, is placed on the concrete surface, and allowed to penetrate into the concrete under its own weight. The depth of the penetration is measured by the graduations on the handle.

The *specified compressive strength* f'_c, on which design calculations for reinforced and prestressed concrete are based (see Chapter 13), is the guaranteed minimum strength, except for a few very low results. From statistics the required average strength of the concrete is determined to be $1.34s$ higher for a probability of 1 in 10,000 that the concrete structure will not suffer any significant damage, and 1 in 1,000,000 that it will not collapse (Fig. 3.11.5); s is the standard deviation, and this depends on the degree of quality control (Fig. 3.11.5d). Evidently for large concreting operations using high-strength concrete the best quality control will result in a considerable saving of material. The same degree of control is not warranted for work of less importance.

Transportation and Placing of Concrete

Segregation is defined as a separation of the constituents of concrete so that their distribution ceases to be sufficiently uniform. It is due to differential settlement of the larger and/or heavier aggregate particles, which travel faster down a pipe or slope, or settle faster in the liquid concrete when they reach their final destination. It is thus more likely to occur when concrete is pumped and then allowed to descend a long gravity chute, than when it is delivered directly by bucket or barrow. Another type of segregation, which occurs particularly in wet mixes, results in the separation of the cement and the water from the aggregate by forming a layer on top of the concrete.

Segregation is unlikely to occur when a concrete mix is *cohesive*, but a *workable* mix is not necessarily cohesive. The slump test, the Kelly ball test, and the compacting-factor test all measure workability, but not cohesiveness. Good results for workability in the various flow tests, however, indicate cohesiveness. Air-entraining agents (Section 3.13) reduce segregation.

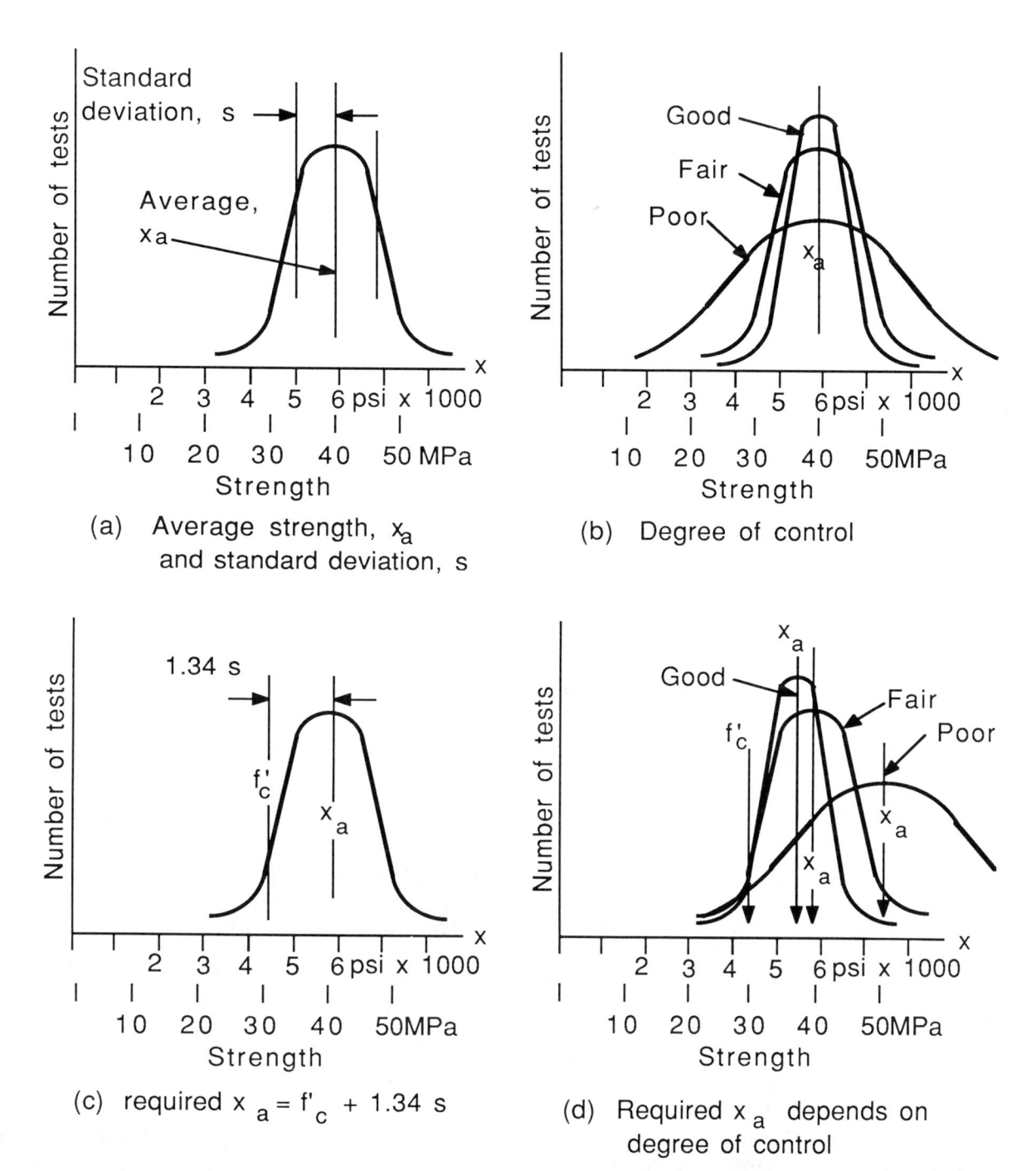

Fig. 3.11.5. Determination of the characteristic strength of concrete. The strength of concrete varies over an appreciable range, partly because it is a brittle material and thus of variable strength and partly because it is a cheap material mass-produced from aggregates and cement that are themselves of variable strength. The strength of concrete that matters is the guaranteed *minimum strength* f'_c, not the *average strength* which is much higher.

(a) The *average strength* x_a and the *standard deviation* s (these terms are defined in Section 1.5).

(b) The spread of test data, and hence the standard deviation, depends on the degree of control. Good control is essential for concrete of the highest quality; but fair control, which costs less, may be appropriate for small concreting operations requiring only concrete of ordinary strength.

(c) The *specified compressive strength* f'_c is the minimum strength, except for a few very low results. Its location on the curve is based on a probability of 1 in 10,000 that the concrete structure will not suffer any significant damage, and 1 in 1,000,000 that it will not collapse. This strikes a reasonable balance between the increased cost of stronger concrete and the social acceptability of failure; complete certainty that no collapse will *ever* occur is not attainable. The equation

$$x_a = f'_c + 1.34s$$

is derived by statistics, based on these probabilities.

(d) Given a specified compressive strength f'_c, the average strength of the concrete x_a to be aimed for is lower when good quality control is exercised, than when the control is poor.

Bleeding is related to segregation; it is the collection of mixing water, which may carry some of the cement with it, on the surface of freshly placed concrete. Bleeding is a form of subsidence, which can be expressed quantitively as the total settlement per unit depth of concrete. Tests set out in ASTM Standard C 232-71 can be used to determine experimentally the capacity of concrete mix for bleeding, and its likely rate of bleeding.

Bleeding water may become trapped under large aggregate particles or under reinforcing bars, where it forms voids on evaporation. These may have an adverse effect on durability, particularly on resistance to frost. Bleeding is not necessarily harmful if the water collects on the surface and evaporates or is removed before the concrete's surface is given its final finish. If, however, the water brings cement to the surface, a layer of set cement, called *laitance*, is formed on the surface; this produces a dusty surface and a plane of weakness. The laitance must be removed before any further concrete is placed on top of the old concrete. It is advisable to use a wooden rather than a steel float to finish the concrete, as this avoids working an excess of cement to the surface.

The tendency toward bleeding can be reduced by the use of finer cement, a greater proportion of fine aggregate, and a lower water/cement ratio; but the most effective method is to use an air-entraining agent (see Section 3.12).

Curing of Concrete

Curing is the term given to protecting the concrete against evaporation of its mixing water during the early stages of the chemical hardening process, when it requires additional moisture to sustain the hydration of the cement. The concrete also requires protection from extremes of temperature during cold nights and hot days.

The concrete surface can be covered with sand or with *burlap* (a coarse fabric of jute or hemp, called *hessian* in Britain and Australia), which is kept moist by spraying or periodic watering. Precast concrete units and site-cast concrete slabs may be covered with water.

A more effective method is to cover the concrete with a *curing membrane*. This may be a sheet of waterproof building paper, or of a plastic, such as polyvinyl chloride or polyethylene, about 0.001 in. (0.2 mm) thick. Alternatively a liquid can be sprayed on the concrete, which dries within a few hours to a continuous adhesive film; a dye may be added to the liquid to aid the operator to provide complete coverage. Various plastics and various wax and oil emulsions can be used as liquid curing compounds.

Both high and low temperatures adversely affect the hydration of cement. If the temperature during the casting of the concrete is likely to be below 40°F (4°C), special precautions need to be taken. Concrete should be kept above a temperature of 59°F (15°C). To achieve this, the concrete aggregates and the water may be heated, but not above 150°F (65°C) to avoid a flash set of the cement. The use of a *high-early-strength cement* (*rapid-hardening cement*, see Section 3.9) generates additional heat. *Calcium chloride* (see Section 3.13) is an accelerator which increases the rate of hydration and thus generates additional heat; it also turns the mixing water into a salt solution, and thus lowers its freezing point. However, it has a tendency to corrode reinforcement, and many specifications forbid its use.

If frost is likely to occur, the concrete must be given additional cover during curing.

Freshly cast concrete should not be allowed to get too hot. The temperature of new concrete should be kept below 90°F (32°C), and if possible below 85°F (30°C). This may be accomplished by keeping all materials in the shade, and by using crushed ice instead of mixing water. The heat of hydration of the cement can be reduced by using a *low-heat cement* (Section 3.8). In addition, the concrete must be given additional protection during curing.

Reinforced and prestressed concrete are considered in Chapter 13.

3.12. CONCRETE ADMIXTURES

Substances which are added to the cement, such as pozzolans, inert fillers (in masonry cement), and colors (for colored cement) have been discussed in Section 3.8.

The following substances are added later, usually when the cement and the aggregates are mixed in the concrete mixer.

Air Entrainment

About 5 percent of freshly mixed concrete consists of air in cavities. This is called *entrapped air*; it is in contact with the outside air through capillary channels, and this may lead to deterioration of the concrete, particularly during freezing and thawing. *Air-entraining agents*, on the other hand, produce minute air bubbles, ranging in size from 0.04 to 0.004 in. (1 to 0.1 mm), that are uniformly distributed through the concrete and closed off from it. These bubbles act as additional "fine aggregate," and increase the workability of the concrete mix. Air-entraining agents "capture" the entrapped air, which then becomes part of the enclosed bubbles of entrained air. By thus reducing the capillarity of the hardened concrete, air-entraining agents increase durability, particularly during freezing and thawing. On the other hand, the air bubbles reduce the strength of the concrete by about 10 percent.

Air-entraining agents, which are usually sold as proprietary compounds, are made from wetting agents or synthetic detergents, or alternatively from wood resins, or from vegetable or animal fats or oils, or from the fatty acids or soaps of the latter.

Water-Reducing Admixtures and Superplasticizers

It was noted in the previous section that the strength of concrete depends mainly on the water/cement ratio (Fig.

3.11.1), and that its workability depends mainly on the water content. Any substance which increases the workability therefore serves as an agent permitting a reduction in the water content; if the cement content is unaltered, the water/cement ratio is reduced, and the strength increased. The water-reducing admixtures, which have recently been renamed *superplasticizers*, can greatly increase the strength of the concrete. They are therefore used extensively in structures where strength is important. This has been an important factor in making reinforced concrete more economical for tall buildings. The principal water-reducing admixtures are modified lignosulfates and sulfonated naphthalene or melamine formaldehyde condensates.

Air-entraining agents and superplasticizers are the most commonly used concrete admixtures; but there are others that are used less frequently.

Shrinkage Compensation

The chemistry of *expansive cements* is not yet fully understood, but it is known that their expansion is due to the formation of *ettringite* ($3CaO \cdot Al_2O_3 \cdot 3CaSO_4 \cdot 32H_2O$), discussed in Section 3.8. This can be accommodated while concrete is still in a plastic condition. Once the concrete has hardened, however, the expansion causes internal stresses which may lead to disintegration of the concrete. Hence expansive cement must be used with great care.

Shrinkage-compensating cements are portland cements with a small admixture of expansive cement, which is just sufficient to cause an expansion equal to the shrinkage of the concrete. This relatively small expansion can usually be safely achieved (Ref. 3.14).

Much larger expansions are possible (Ref. 3.15), and these can be used to prestress concrete chemically without the use of prestressing jacks. However, these highly expansive cements have so far only been used experimentally.

Integral Waterproofers

Water-repellent materials, such as resins and waxes, have been used successfully to make *cement render* and *cement plaster* more waterproof.

The same materials have been used as *integral waterproofers* for concrete. Another group of materials that have been used for this purpose are pore-filling substances, such as sodium silicate or talc (Ref. 3.16). Neither has been entirely satisfactory, and many engineers consider that better waterproof concrete can be produced by increasing the cement content without any admixture.

Accelerators

Accelerators increase the rate of hydration of cement, and thus generate additional heat. They are useful in cold weather, and when high early strength is needed.

High-early-strength cement (rapid-hardening cement) achieves this result without chemical additives, by increasing the proportion of tricalcium silicate in the cement, and by grinding the cement clinker to finer particles (see Section 3.8).

More drastic acceleration can be achieved by chemical additives, of which *calcium chloride* is the most common. However, calcium chloride is liable to corrode reinforcing bars and prestressing tendons, and many specifications therefore forbid its use.

Retarders

All portland cement contains some gypsum in order to retard the setting of the cement, and allow sufficient time for placing concrete in its formwork (see Section 3.8).

If surface retarders are required, they are usually employed as coatings on the formwork to retard the setting of the cement in the surface layer of the concrete. The most common objective is to allow the cement to be removed and expose the aggregate (see Section 3.13). A number of materials can be used as surface retarders; the most commonly available are sugar or molasses.

3.13. CONCRETE SURFACE FINISHES

Concrete has many admirable qualities as a building material (see Section 3.10 and Chapter 13), but it is difficult to give it a surface finish which is aesthetically comparable to that normally achieved on natural stone, brick, timber, glass, or metal. The Ancient Romans normally covered their concrete with stone or brick, and so did most designers in the 19th and early 20th Century. As the theory of Modern Architecture (the International Style) began to dominate the design of concrete, it was increasingly exposed with a minimum of surface treatment (*béton brut*), on the principle that materials should be used truthfully. As a result, many concrete surfaces were built which became shabby and ugly within a few years (Fig. 3.13.1).

Untreated concrete surfaces are unattractive (1) because their color is a dirty gray when ordinary portland cement is used, and (2) because concrete easily collects dirt, particularly when it is on the exterior, since has a rough surface, and since it remains chemically active for many years so that tiny cracks form, which are barely visible when they occur, but become so when they fill with dirt particles.

Concrete surfaces can therefore be improved by one or more of the following measures:

1. By masking the blemishes or dirt on a concrete surface with a stronger pattern;
2. By removing the cement from the concrete surface;
3. By changing the color of the cement; or
4. By covering the concrete with another material.

1. Most concrete is still constructed with the cement showing on the surface. If the concrete is troweled smooth on the surface, or if the concrete is cast against hard, flat

42 HANDBOOK OF ARCHITECTURAL TECHNOLOGY

Fig. 3.13.1. The dark irregular streaks on this concrete surface were formed within two years of construction by rainwater which dissolved wind-blown soot and dirt. The remedy is (i) to prevent the water from running down the wall by placing a coping with a throat or drip groove (see Fig. 3.3.3) on top of the wall; and (ii) to use a surface finish which *either* does not collect dirt to the same extent (for example, an exposed aggregate finish using smooth gravel) *or* has a rougher texture that hides the dirt.

Fig. 3.13.2. A rough concrete surface finish, intended to be viewed from a distance. Ropes are cast into the concrete near the surface, and pulled out after the concrete has hardened, leaving a rough surface between the textures imprint made by the ropes. This looks somewhat brutal at close quarters, but it is a remarkably effective finish when seen from a distance where the lack of readability of exposed aggregate (Table 3.3) makes it an unsuitable concrete surface finish.

surfaces, the resulting finish is smooth and looks attractive when new. It soon deteriorates as fine shrinkage cracks form on this smooth surface.

A *surface pattern* helps to mask these cracks and other surface imperfections. The texture of timber boards used as formwork provides a shallow pattern, which can be made stronger if the timber is naturally or artificially weathered to emphasize the texture of the timber growth rings.

A stronger pattern is formed by the deliberate breakage of concrete surfaces. This can be accomplished by casting wire ropes into the concrete, and pulling them out after the concrete has hardened (Fig. 3.13.2), by casting reinforcing bars or timber laths into the concrete and pulling them out, or by marking the concrete with blows from a sledge hammer. This is a cheap finish which is moderately satisfactory when viewed from a distance of 200 ft (60 m) or more; but it is not suitable for surfaces seen at close quarters.

2. The cement skin can be removed from the concrete surface either mechanically or chemically. The mechanical removal is by *sandblasting* or by the use of a serrated pneumatic tool called a *bush hammer*.

The chemical removal is by coating the formwork with a *retarder* (see Section 3.12), and then scrubbing the surface of the concrete with water, or with dilute hydrochloric acid followed by scrubbing with water, to remove the cement skin.

Either method removes a large part of the gray cement, and instead exposes a concrete aggregate with a more interesting color (which depends on the aggregate used).

Better *exposed aggregate finishes* can be produced by using an attractively colored and textured aggregate which is used purely for its visual effect, and which need not have a high strength. This can be used on site-cast concrete by using the *aggregate transfer process*. The concrete mold is coated with a suitable adhesive, such as paraffin wax, and the aggregate is sprinkled on it before it sets. After the concrete has hardened, any adhesive still adhering to the aggregate is removed.

If concrete wall units are precast, as they very often are, to be used as permanent formwork, or as facing panels to be fixed to the structure at a later stage, the concrete can be cast with ordinary aggregate, and the decorative aggregate is then sprinkled on while the concrete is still wet, and rolled lightly into the surface.

Exposed aggregate surfaces look attractive at close quarters, if good aggregates are chosen, and this presents no practical problems. However, it is difficult to distinguish the aggregate particles at a distance (Table 3.2). Since the upper parts of tall buildings are of necessity viewed from a distance, rough finishes, such as that shown in Fig. 3.13.1, may be more suitable. Alternatively an exposed aggregate of a single color can be used. The most suitable color is white. There are two suitable types of white aggregate: marble chips, which are a dull white, or quartz chips, which are a shiny white; both are used with white or off-white cement.

3. White cement is expensive (Section 3.8), but the much cheaper off-white cement is suitable for most white

Table 3.2. Readability of Exposed Aggregate, i.e., Maximum Distance at Which Its Texture Is Visible.

British Units		Metric Units	
Size of Aggregate Particles in.	Distance ft	Size of Aggregate Particles mm	Distance m
$1\frac{1}{2}$	350	40	110
1	300	25	90
$\frac{3}{4}$	200	20	60
$\frac{1}{2}$	115	15	40
$\frac{3}{8}$	75	10	25
$\frac{1}{4}$	60	6	18

exposed aggregate finishes. The replacement of the dirty gray of portland cement by off-white greatly improves the appearance of concrete, not merely in exposed aggregate finishes, but also in board-marked off-the-form concrete, and in sculptured surfaces produced by placing a patterned plastic panel inside the formwork; the pattern may be repeated or varied.

Colored cement is usually used in conjunction with colored exposed aggregate. Colored glass can be used as an aggregate provided it is in a location where nobody is likely to be cut by sharp edges on the glass.

Exposed aggregate finishes can also be used on floor surfaces, particularly on garden paths and swimming pool surrounds. Small, well rounded gravel should be used for comfortable walking.

4. Although a *terrazzo floor* is a concrete floor, it may be considered as the first category of "covering the concrete." A typical terrazzo mix consists of colored cement, a fine aggregate of crushed marble, and a coarse aggregate of crushed colored marble. Divider strips of brass, copper, or a suitable plastic are cast into the concrete to provide control joints to prevent cracking. After the concrete has been cured, it is ground wet and any surface blemishes are repaired with mortar. This process is repeated several times with progressively finer grades of carborundum. Finally the surface is given several coats of wax, and treated with a sealer.

In Southern Europe, concrete floors are frequently paved with natural stone or with tiles. In Northern Europe, America, and Australia, concrete floors are more often covered with carpet, except in kitchens and bathrooms, where tiles are commonly used. Quarry tiles (see Section 3.17) provide a good surface in heavily trafficked areas. All these facing materials cover the concrete surface, and thus solve the problem of its finish.

There have been few arguments about the ethics of covering concrete used on floor surfaces with other materials, because concrete floors are dusty unless they are especially treated.

However, for several decades there was a trend to use exposed concrete on vertical surfaces, partly because it was considered appropriate that the concrete used in the building should also be shown on the facade, and partly because concrete surfaces were generally cheaper than other finishes.

In recent years stone has increasingly returned as a facing material. It is not, however, used today as it was in Ancient Rome and in the early years of this century as permanent formwork for concrete structures, but as a veneer which is fixed subsequently (Fig. 3.5.1).

3.14. CEMENT-BASED INSULATING MATERIALS

Most modern insulating materials are based on plastics, and these are generally lighter and provide greater insulation than cement-based materials. However, some burn easily, and none are fire-resistant. The cement-based materials can be used for fire protection, as well as thermal insulation and sound absorption.

Concrete for fire protection, particularly that of structural steelwork (see Chapter 12), is made with a very light aggregate, such as expanded perlite or exfoliated vermiculite. Perlite is a glassy, acid, igneous rock which contains combined water. Vermiculite is the collective name of a number of minerals in the mica group (Section 3.2) which, like all micas, have cleavage planes. They also contain combined water. The expansion of the perlite and the exfoliation of the vermiculite result from the conversion of water into steam within confined spaces.

These materials have specific gravities ranging from 0.06 to 0.3, and the lightweight concrete made from them has a specific gravity in the range from 0.3 to 1.0, corresponding to densities of 20 to 65 lb/ft^3 (300 to 1000 kg/m^3). However, its strength is only 100 to 800 psi (0.7 to 6 MPa), so that it can only be used for fire protection, thermal insulation, or sound absorption.

Even lighter materials can be made by using only sand, cement, water, and air or gas bubbles. They become lighter still if the sand is left out. These materials are known as *cellular concretes* or *aerated concretes* (not to be confused with air-entrained concretes, see Section 3.12). The same materials that are used for producing the air bubbles for air-entrained concrete can also be used for making aerated concrete. However, a much greater proportion of additive is needed. An alternative method is to add aluminum powder to the cement. This combines with the mixing water to produce hydrogen bubbles. A *wetting agent* is normally used to control the distribution and uniformity of size of the air or gas bubbles. Aerated concrete can be poured liquid into the spaces where it is required as a thermal insulating material.

3.15. PRECAST CONCRETE AND CONCRETE PRODUCTS

Concrete bricks, blocks, floor tiles, and roof tiles were originally made as substitutes for clay bricks and tiles in places where this was cheaper. They have, however, acquired a character of their own (Fig. 3.15.1), and they offer a wider range of colors.

44 HANDBOOK OF ARCHITECTURAL TECHNOLOGY

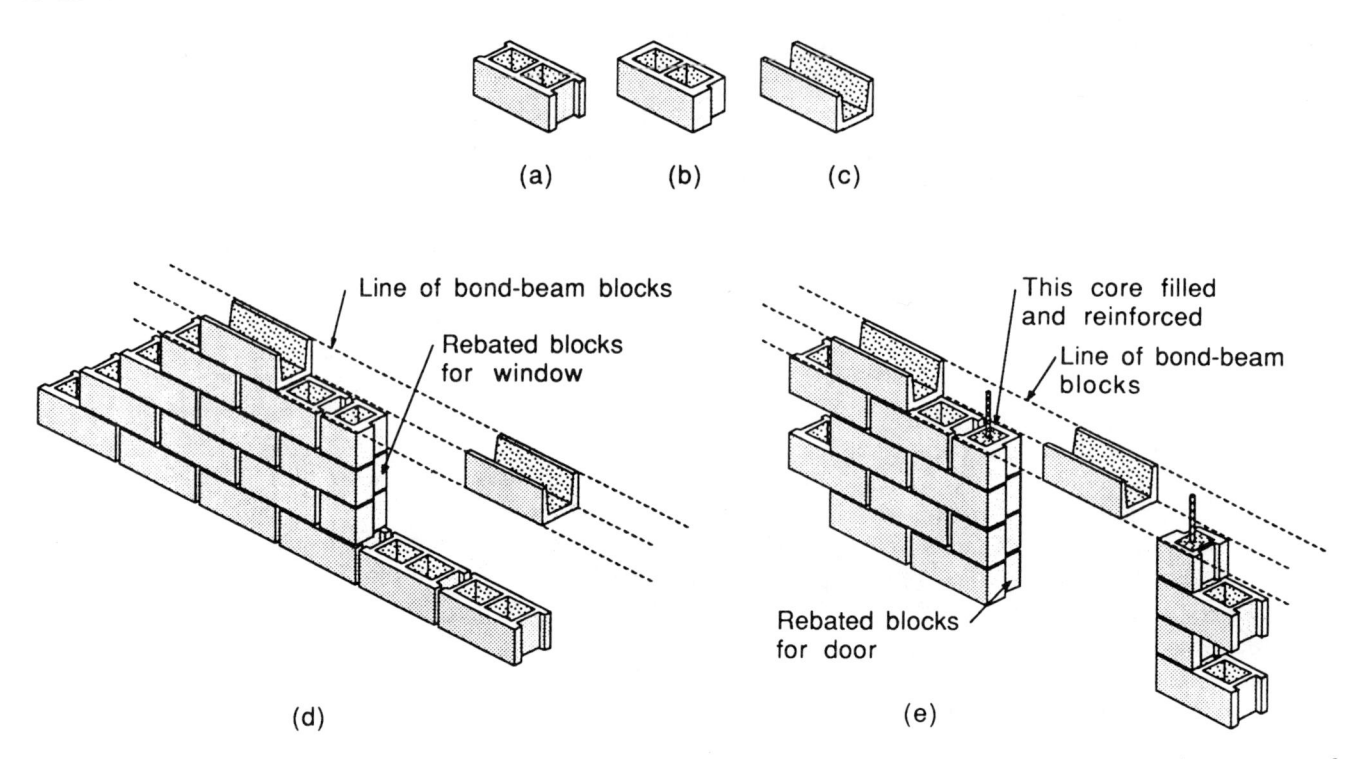

Fig. 3.15.1. Concrete blocks. (a) Normal cored block. (b) Blocks are available with square or rabbeted ends, for turning corners, or for door and window openings. (c) Bond-beam blocks, for reinforcing and filling with concrete. (d) Use of rabbeted blocks for window opening. (e) Use of reinforced vertical cores to strengthen a door opening.

The term *precast concrete* is normally reserved for concrete units that are reinforced or prestressed (see Chapter 13). Precasting has several advantages over site casting, and also several disadvantages. If a sufficient number of castings are to be made from the same mold, then it is economical to make it of steel with quick-release and reassembly mechanisms. The mold can be filled, vibrated, and the concrete finished on a mechanized assembly line. Concrete surfaces can be given a better surface finish than is possible on the building site. In particular, *vertical surfaces* can be cast and finished horizontally, which gives much better results (see Section 3.13). Precast units can thus be used as permanent formwork for site-cast concrete, as load-bearing walls, or with dry construction as curtain walls.

The main disadvantages are the cost of transportation, and the problems of jointing. Floor and roof units can be transported and lifted into position horizontally. Wall panels, however, must either be transported and handled vertically, or else they must be given sufficient additional reinforcement to support their own weight in a horizontal position, which adds to their cost. The transportation of large units, particularly through narrow city streets, is another problem.

3.16. CLAY BRICKS AND OTHER BRICKS

A brick is a masonry unit which is used in "wet" construction with mortar joints, and it is small enough to be lifted with one hand, so that the bricklayer can use his other hand to lay the mortar with a trowel. Consequently the size of a brick does not vary greatly from one region to another; it generally weighs 7 to 9 lb (3 to 4 kg). Modern bricks are twice as long as they are wide, so that they can be bonded (Fig. 3.16.1). Sizes generally range from 8 to 9 in. (200 to 230 mm) long, and 2 to 3 in. (50 to 75 mm) high. Blocks are usually larger, and some are laid dry without mortar.

Pure clay is hydrous aluminum silicate ($Al_2O_3 \cdot 2SiO_2$

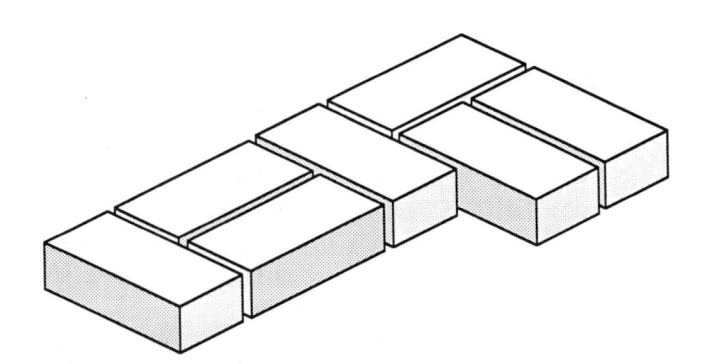

Fig. 3.16.1. Headers and stretchers. Bricks are made twice as long as they are wide (including an allowance for one mortar joint) so that they can be bonded to interrupt the continuity of the mortar joints, and thus increase the strength of the brick wall. The two heads of the *headers* are visible on both sides of the walls, while the *stretchers* are the bricks which visibly stretch their long side parallel to the wall. Headers and stretchers can be used together in the same *course* (or horizontal layer) of brickwork, or they can be used in alternate courses (Fig. 3.16.3).

$\cdot 2H_2O$). On heating, the alumina and the silica dissociate and the water evaporates. Pure clay melts only at very high temperatures, and for that reason it is used as a refractory material in furnaces. However, most natural clay contains impurities such as soda (Na_2O), potash (K_2O), and lime (CaO), which act as fluxes when the clay is heated.

Bricks are made by pressing or extruding moist clay, or a mixture of clay and shale, into the desired shape. *Dry-pressed bricks* are made from raw material ground with only a little moisture to a crumbly consistency, which is pressed into molds with appreciable force. A *frog* (a depression) is usually formed on one of the longer surfaces of the brick to aid the bonding of the bricks. *Semi-dry-pressed* or *stiff-plastic bricks* are made with a slightly moister mix.

Extruded or *wire-cut bricks* are made from clay mixed to a plastic consistency, which is extruded through a die. The extrusion frequently includes holes made through the thickness of the bricks, which aids bonding, reduces the weight of the brick, improves thermal insulation, and speeds up the drying and firing processes. After extrusion the bricks are cut to the required thickness with a taut wire.

The bricks produced by any of these processes must be strong enough to be handled and stacked. To avoid distortion during firing, they are first dried gradually in warm air. They are then fired in a kiln and allowed to cool slowly.

During firing the clay is partially *vitrified*, that is a glassy substance is formed by the clay and fluxes which binds the material. Vitrification is visible on the surface of some bricks, particularly hard bricks fired at a relatively high temperature. Depending on the type of brick, this visual vitrification may be considered a defect, or it may be a desirable feature which gives a texture to *face bricks*. The temperature and the time of firing must be carefully adjusted for each particular type of clay, and for the type of brick to be produced. Too little firing produces a brick that lacks durability and strength. Too much firing causes the brick to melt partially, so that it loses its shape and adheres to other bricks. These overburnt bricks are called *clinker bricks*. They are sometimes produced deliberately; some architects consider that they blend better with natural stone walls, where a modern brick-walled addition is to be built.

All but the most hard-burnt bricks can absorb an appreciable amount of water, and they expand slightly as they do so, and contract again as they dry out. All bricks expand slightly in warm weather, and contract again as the temperature drops. A more important phenomenon is *brickwork growth*, which is an expansion that occurs after the bricks are removed from the kiln. For most bricks all the growth that is likely to occur will have taken place after six months, but for some the expansion continues at a reducing rate for many years. Before bricks from an unfamiliar source are used, one should ascertain whether they are subject to significant and/or prolonged brickwork growth. This must be allowed for when deciding on the spacing of *control joints*. Concrete (including concrete bricks) shrinks during hydration; when concrete and bricks are used together, this differential movement must be allowed for, and it may require additional control joints.

Some types of brick suffer from *efflorescence*. This is caused by salts contained in the bricks being washed to the brick surface by rain water, where they form an unsightly, usually white, deposit. Most types of efflorescence can be removed completely by washing or brushing.

Cavity Walls and Brick Veneer Walls

Although bricks absorb water, brick walls can be made resistant to water penetration by making them sufficiently thick; the thickness required depends on the porosity of the bricks. An alternative is to use a cavity wall (Fig. 3.16.2), which drains away any water that penetrates the outer skin. Cavity walls cannot be used in regions with prolonged periods of frost, as the cavity is liable to fill with ice.

Brick veneer walls are single-leaf brick walls used for the outer walls of a timber-framed house; the inner wall is generally plasterboard (see Section 3.7). Brick veneer houses have better fire resistance than houses with timber siding (weatherboards), and they require less maintenance.

Reinforced Brickwork

In the 19th Century openings in brick walls over windows and doors were generally bridged by arches or by natural-stone lintels. Both methods are now considered too expensive. Reinforced concrete lintels are sometimes used, but because concrete shrinks and bricks expand during the early life of the building, their combination is liable to result in the formation of cracks. Steel reinforcement lintels or reinforcing bars are neater in appearance (Fig. 3.16.3).

Reinforcement is also sometimes used to strengthen brick walls generally. Because of the difficulty of arranging the reinforcement between the bricks (Fig. 3.16.4) it is better to use reinforced concrete if a great deal of reinforcement is required.

Face Brick and Plastered Brick

There is a variety of brick bonds, some of only regional significance; their names also vary from region to region. However, all are variations on two basic types (Fig. 3.16.5). Bond is particularly important when face brick is used, because it is a significant factor in its appearance.

Brick is a durable material, and external plastering does not improve its durability, although it may increase its water resistance slightly. Face brick is virtually maintenance-free, while plastered brick requires periodic repainting.

The reason for plastering is partly historical. During the European Middle Ages bricks were relatively expensive, and they were used almost exclusively in regions where natural stone was not available. During the 17th and 18th Century bricks became cheaper, and they were increasingly substituted for natural stone. The brickwork was plastered and painted, including lines for the mortar joints,

46 HANDBOOK OF ARCHITECTURAL TECHNOLOGY

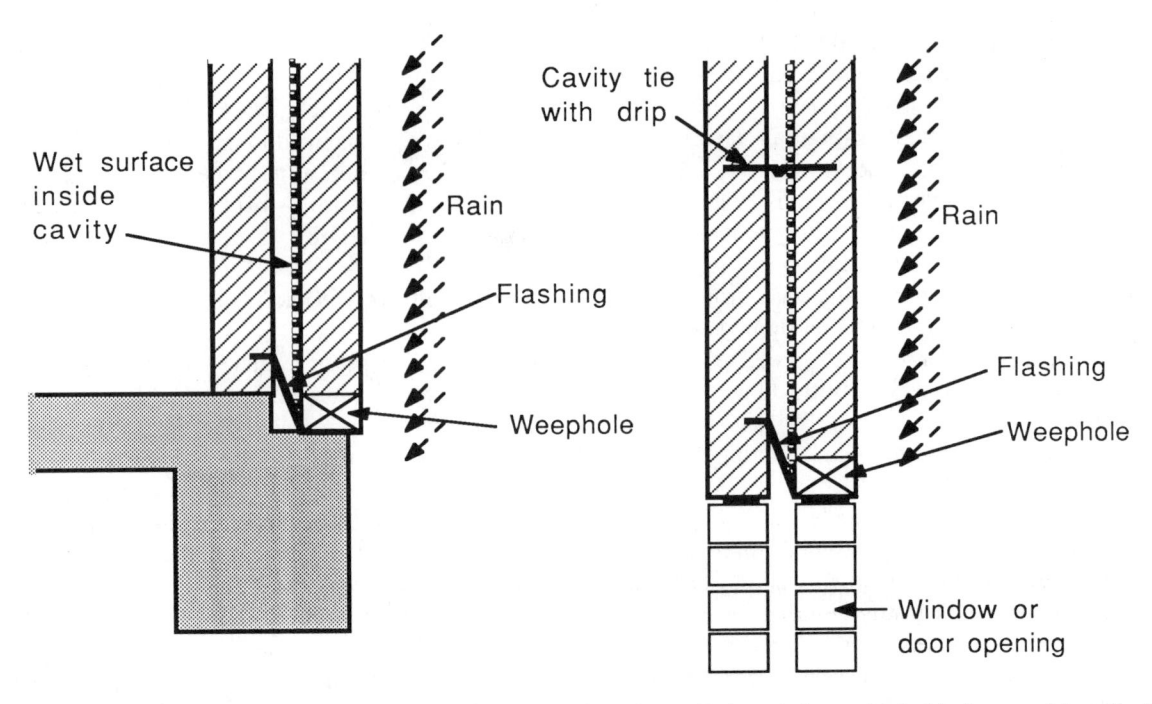

Fig. 3.16.2. Cavity walls. If rainwater penetrates the outer skin of a cavity wall, it runs down the inside face, and is collected by the flashing, where it is allowed to escape through weepholes. Cavity walls need to be tied together with metal ties, and these are formed with a drip to prevent water from traveling across to the inner brick skin. The metal ties must be of galvanized or stainless steel.

so that it looked like natural stone from a distance. The practice of painting joint lines on the plaster disappeared completely only in the early 19th Century. Plastered brickwork is still more common in the traditional stone regions of Europe than in the traditional brick regions, where face brick predominates.

Generally a better quality brick with an attractive color and texture is chosen for face bricks, which need to be laid with greater care. However, face brick is generally cheaper than plastered brick, particularly if allowance is made for the capitalized maintenance cost of periodic repainting.

Brick walls are usually plastered inside, except where a "feature wall" of face brick is used, because the rough texture of the bricks and the joints have the potential for holding dust. The internal plaster, in turn, needs to be painted or papered.

Mortar and Plaster for Bricks

The traditional lime mortar had little strength, and its main function was to take up irregularities; the strength of brick walls depended mainly on their bond. Portland cement

(a)   (b)

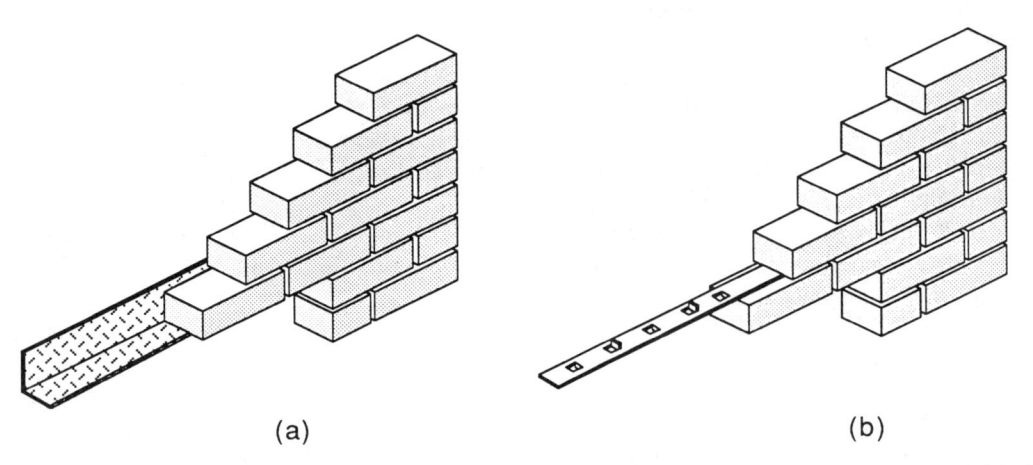

Fig. 3.16.3. Steel lintels over window or door openings in brickwork. The steel lintel is required to carry the bricks in a triangular area over the opening; the other bricks are supported by arching action within the brickwork. (a) The simplest method is to carry the bricks on a steel angle, which has much better bending resistance than a flat bar. However, this is visible unless it is covered. (b) A neater method is to use a lugged steel bar which forms a reinforced brick beam over the opening. The bricks must be temporarily supported while the mortar sets, since the lower layer of bricks is part of the beam.

CERAMIC MATERIALS 47

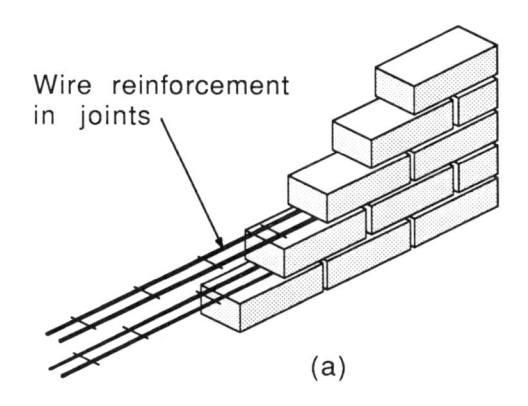

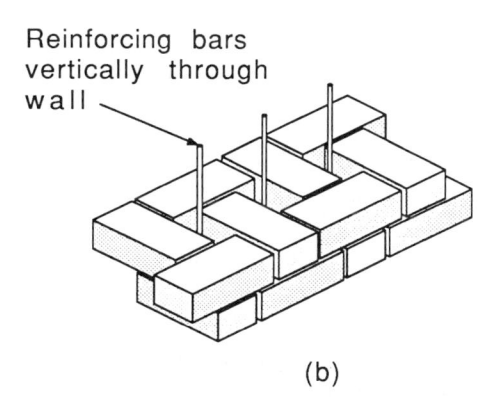

Fig. 3.16.4. Reinforcement for brickwork. Reinforcement may be needed to resist horizontal forces. Unreinforced brickwork should not be used in seismic areas (see Section 9.3). (a) Horizontal reinforcement can be laid within the thickness of the joint, using either a wire mesh or small-diameter reinforcing bars. Any thickness of brickwall can be reinforced in this manner. (b) Vertical reinforcement can be placed in mortar cores in the middle of the brickwork. A wall at least $1\frac{1}{2}$ bricks thick is required.

mortar, however, has a strength comparable to that of the bricks. As mentioned in Sections 3.6 and 3.8, portland cement used for brick mortar or for plastering brick is usually given additives to make it more workable and less harsh. In the U.S.A. a finely ground inert filler, usually limestone, and an air entraining agent are added to portland cement for this purpose, and the material is prepackaged and sold under the name of masonry cement. An alternative method, used less frequently in the U.S.A., but common practice in Europe and Australia, is to add some lime to the portland cement.

The amount of water used must be controlled to allow for the initial rate of water absorption of the bricks, which varies appreciably with the type of brick used.

Other Types of Brick

Mention has already been made of *concrete bricks* (Section 3.15), which are concrete blocks made to the same size as clay bricks. They are laid and generally used like clay bricks; they shrink when they are new, while clay bricks expand.

Calcium-silicate bricks, also called *sand-lime bricks*, are used in some regions. They are made from sand (SiO_2) and lime ($Ca(OH)_2$), which are mixed together, pressed into molds, and subjected to high-pressure steam in an autoclave; this causes the lime and part of the sand to form calcium silicate. Their natural color ranges from white through off-white to yellow. They are usually made to the same sizes as clay bricks, and are used the same way. Calcium-silicate bricks shrink when they are new.

3.17. OTHER CLAY BUILDING PRODUCTS

The term *earthenware* is used to describe products made from clay, and fired at a temperature below vitrification. They are porous and may have a low strength. The term *stoneware* is used for products made from clay, and fired

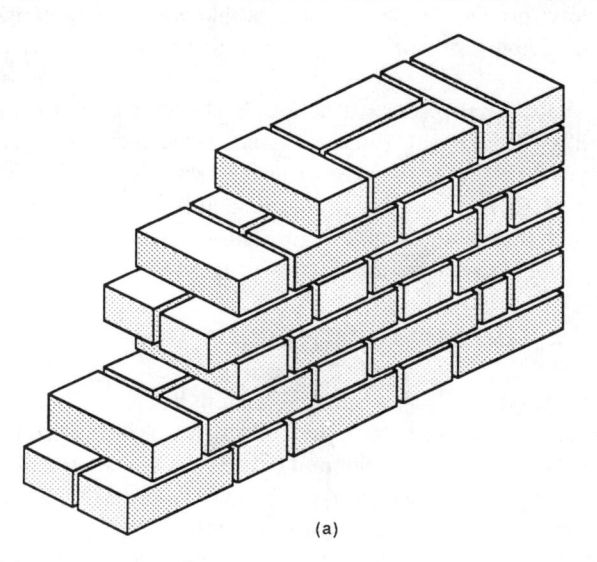

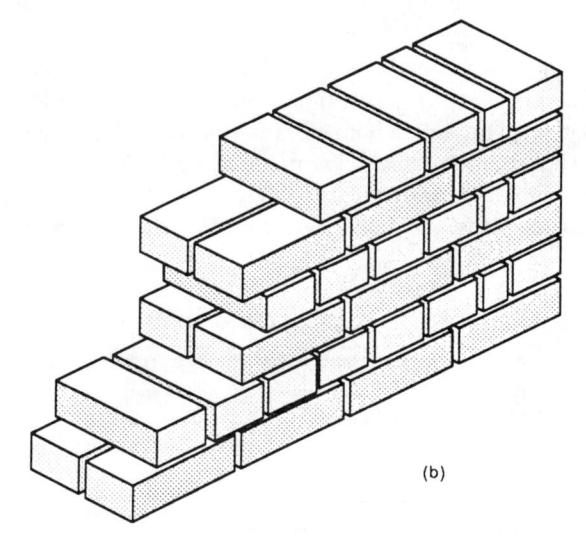

Fig. 3.16.5. The two basic brick bonds. There are numerous other types of bond, which are all variations on these. (a) Flemish bond has alternate headers and stretches in each course. (b) English bond has courses entirely of headers alternating with courses entirely of stretchers.

at a temperature of about 2300°F (1260°C), which is above vitrification. They are hard and waterproof without further treatment.

Earthenware products can be made waterproof by *glazing*. The cheapest glaze is made by throwing common salt (NaCl) into the kiln near the end of the firing operation. The sodium combines with the clay to form a thin layer of soda glaze on all the products which are in the kiln at the time. This is a satisfactory method for waterproofing earthenware pipes.

Quarry tiles are made of stoneware, usually about 1 in. (25 mm) in thickness, in natural earth colors. They have a naturally rough surface which makes them nonslippery, and they are extremely durable. However, they are more difficult to clean than the smoother glazed tiles. Quarry tiles are fired in pairs back-to-back to reduce distortion in the kiln, and are split apart before use.

The term *terracotta* is used for earthenware or stoneware made from a mixture of natural clay and finely ground prefired clay, known as *grog*. Since the grog does not distort during firing, products can be made more accurately to shape and size than would be possible if only natural clay was used. Terracotta is used extensively for roof tiles, floor tiles, and wall tiles. Roof tiles are generally more durable if they are not glazed. Floor tiles and wall tiles are glazed for easy cleaning; they are usually about $\frac{1}{4}$ in. (6 mm) thick, and made to close tolerances. They generally need two layers of glaze, or more if several colors are used. Floor tiles must have a non-slip surface, and for this reason the top layer of glazing is usually spattered on to give a rougher surface.

Hollow, unglazed terracotta blocks are widely used in Europe, Asia, and Latin America in the construction of reinforced concrete floors (Fig. 3.17.1) and in partitions (Fig. 3.17.2). The hollow terracotta blocks are extruded with walls about $\frac{1}{2}$ in. (12 mm) thick, and burned at high temperatures to produce hard and strong lightweight blocks. They have a good fire rating and good thermal insulation, and they are exceptionally light; however, their sound insulation is poor. A partition of hollow terracotta blocks must be plastered on both sides for the sake of appearance.

The extent to which clay products other than bricks are used is declining, because plastics are now increasingly used for pipes, and concrete for roofing tiles. Fixed parti-

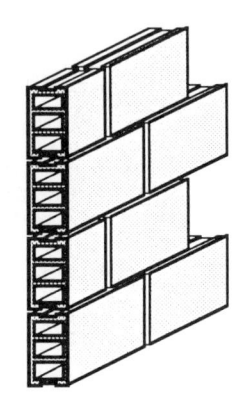

Fig. 3.17.2. Terracotta block partition.

tions are increasingly being replaced by movable, factory-made partitions.

Unburned earthen construction was at one time very widely used, even for prestige buildings such as the royal palaces of Ancient Egypt. It is still an important material in developing countries, but in America and Western Europe the high labor content makes it an uneconomical form of construction, unless an owner-builder does a large part of the work.

Adobe is construction with *mud bricks*, which are dried in the sun only. The bricks can be formed by hand or in a hand-operated press. Adobe bricks are generally large, about 16 by 12 in. and 6 in. thick (400 × 300 × 150 mm), so that they must be lifted with both hands. They must contain some clay to act as binder for the earth, but if they consist of pure clay, cracks will develop during drying. Some fiber, such as grass or straw, may be added. Unsuitable earth can be improved by stabilizing it with a little portland cement or lime.

Pisé is construction with earth rammed into formwork. Each layer is about 6 in. (150 mm) deep, as in a course of adobe bricks. The earth must be allowed to dry partially before the formwork is raised and another layer placed on top.

Adobe and pisé construction can only be used for thick walls. This is not a disadvantage, since the raw material costs very little; the cost is in the labor. The thick walls have excellent thermal insulation and high thermal inertia, which makes them suitable for arid (hot and cold) climates, but not for hot-humid climates.

3.18. THE MANUFACTURE OF GLASS

The glass used as a building material is soda-lime-silica glass, made from a mixture of silicon oxide (SiO_2) and smaller quantities of calcium oxide (CaO) and sodium oxide (Na_2O). It is a supercooled liquid, a solid in which the atoms are arranged amorphously as in a liquid. There are several types of silica glass. Window glass is made by melting together sand (which is mostly silica), soda ash, limestone, dolomite, and feldspar at a temperature of about 2700°F (1500°C).

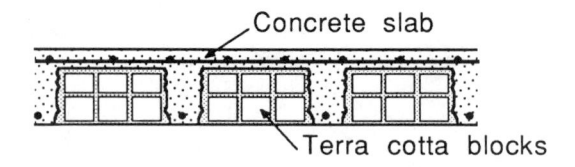

Fig. 3.17.1. Reinforced concrete floor built with terracotta blocks between the reinforced concrete joists, which act as permanent formwork. The entire ceiling is then plastered to give a uniform flat surface. This form of construction is frequently used in Europe. In America the space between the joists is commonly left open (see Fig. 13.9.2).

Normally when a liquid cools and reaches the temperature at which it changes to solid crystals, there is a contraction of its volume because solid crystals occupy less space. This contraction does not occur in the normal glass-making process; instead the material passes through its normal freezing point and gradually turns into a solid supercooled liquid. However, partial or complete crystallization may occur if the liquid glass is kept at its freezing point for a sufficiently long time, particularly if a glass crystal is placed in the melt to act as a nucleus.

As glass is cooled past its freezing point, its viscosity increases rapidly, which impedes atomic migration and thus the formation of crystals. The attainment of the glassy state thus depends on fairly rapid cooling through this critical temperature range.

The *transparency* of glass, which is the main reason for its use as a building material, is due to its amorphous state. Like a single crystal or a liquid, glass consists of one large molecule. It contains no internal boundaries with dimensions of the same order of magnitude as the wavelength range of visible light, and it therefore does not offer any obstruction to the passage of light or of the infrared thermal radiation emitted by the sun, whose wavelengths overlap with those of visible light. Soda-lime-silica glass is not, however, transparent to the long-wave thermal radiation emitted by the surfaces of a building. This gives rise to the *greenhouse effect*: solar radiation can enter through the glass and heat up the walls and floors of the building, but the radiation which this heating produces cannot be returned to the outside air because soda-lime-silica glass is opaque to it.

Glass is the most *corrosion-resistant* of all the common building materials, because it consists entirely of fully oxidized substances. Glass is also the most *brittle* of the common building materials, because a fracture, once started at a weak point, can travel through the supercooled liquid without being stopped by a grain boundary or a polymer chain. The brittleness of glass poses a serious fire hazard (see Chapter 26). It is also vulnerable to accidental or deliberate damage, but this can be overcome by toughening or lamination (see Section 3.19).

The oldest glass found, dating from about 2500 B.C., was made by casting. The first blown glass was made about 300 B.C. Glass is the only building material that can be formed by blowing. Because it is a supercooled liquid it softens gradually and extends uniformly. Unlike a metal it does not form a "neck" when it is extended. This ability of glass to be drawn uniformly is the basis of most processes for making window glass.

By the late Middle Ages glass was made in Europe and the Middle East increasingly by blowing rather than casting because this produced a better surface. However, the glass cylinder had to be flattened on some kind of surface after blowing, and that contact impaired the blown glass surface. This problem was solved by the crown glass process, in which the blown glass was flattened by rotating the bubble in air until it became a flat disk; since the glass did not touch any solid surface before it solidified, it was perfectly clear. The crown glass process was introduced into England in the 17th Century, and the brilliantly clear, slightly curved crown glass windows became a characteristic feature of Georgian architecture. It could, however, be made only in comparatively small window panes.

The first plate glass was made in France in the 18th Century by polishing cast glass; however, larger and thicker sheets of glass have since the 19th Century been made increasingly by the cheaper method of blowing the glass or drawing it directly from the furnace. The American Libbey-Owens Company developed in 1905 a process for drawing glass directly from the furnace as a continuous ribbon, and cooling it as quickly as possible with water coolers. It is then reheated and straightened in an annealing furnace. The British Pilkington Brothers Company invented *float glass* in 1955. After being drawn from the furnace, the glass is floated on a bed of molten tin, and heat is applied from above and below to give it the brilliance achieved in the traditional crown glass.

3.19. SPECIAL GLASS

Glass is easily colored by adding a small amount of the appropriate metallic oxide. As little as 1 part in 1000 may be sufficient to produce a deep color. Virtually any color can be produced in glass.

A pattern can be rolled on the surface of glass by engraving the rollers through which the soft glass passes. *Cathedral glass* has a wavy texture, sufficient to prevent visibility through the glass and thus ensure privacy. *Figured glass* has a definite, usually repeated pattern, and it is sometimes colored.

A *matte* or *frosted* glass surface is made by sand blasting or acid etching; either process can be used for writing or a pattern on the glass.

Opal glass is produced by including minute crystals in clear glass. It can be made in a range of opacities, from fully opaque to faintly milky.

Glass can be given an *opaque ceramic coating* which is fused to its surface. A wide range of colors is available.

Mirrors are made by coating glass with a thin film of metal. This is usually applied to the back of the glass, which then protects the film. The normal metal is silver, but others are occasionally used. Pink or blue mirrors are produced by combining a suitable metal with tinted glass.

A striped mirror, consisting of bands of silver coating about $\frac{3}{4}$ in. (20 mm) wide separated by strips of clear glass about $\frac{1}{16}$ in. ($1\frac{1}{2}$ mm) wide, acts as a *one-way mirror*. From a distance it has the appearance of a fully silvered mirror; at close quarters it is possible to see through the stripes of clear glass.

Wired glass is ordinary glass which contains a steel-wire mesh. This can be fed in between two separate glass ribbons which converge to embed it, or it can be forced into a single glass ribbon with a roller. Wired glass is often patterned. It is not a reinforced glass, and its breaking strength is no higher than that of glass without the wire mesh. However, when the glass is broken, the pieces do not fall apart, so that it is a safer glass.

Tempered or *toughened glass* is produced by heating the glass, and then rapidly cooling both sides with air jets or by immersion. This cooling is stopped before it can reach the interior of the glass, which is allowed to cool slowly. The external layers of the glass are therefore put into compression, and brittle fracture can occur only after this compression has been reversed. As the compressed layers must have reasonable depth, the minimum thickness of toughened glass is $\frac{3}{16}$ in. (4 mm).

Toughened glass is much stronger than ordinary glass, and its fracture pattern is different. Because of its highly stressed condition the formation of cracks is delayed, but when eventually one forms, it is quickly propagated so that the entire sheet of glass disintegrates into small fragments that normally lack the sharp edges ordinarily formed when glass breaks. Since any cutting may result in fracture, toughened glass cannot be drilled or cut, and all holes or cuts must be made before the toughening treatment.

Laminated glass is made by placing a layer of a suitable transparent plastic, such as vinyl butyral, between two layers of glass in an atmosphere free from moisture and dust, and pressing them together with heated rollers. Laminated glass may crack, but the laminations hold the pieces together. A single layer of plastic is sufficient to withstand flying debris generated by a hurricane (cyclone), or an attack with a brick or a hammer. Several layers of laminate are needed to stop bullets.

3.20. THE THERMAL AND ACOUSTIC PROPERTIES OF GLASS (See also Chapters 16, 18, and 20)

Large windows greatly increase the *heating load in winter*, unless suitable precautions are taken. The poor insulating value of window glass is not due to thermal conductivity, which is about the same as that of concrete, but to the small thickness of window glass. A great improvement can be achieved by using two sheets of glass with an insulating air space between them. *Double windows* are traditional in the northern countries of the European Continent, and in some parts of North America.

In buildings with curtain walls, double glazing produces a great improvement in thermal performance, and *triple glazing* is warranted in severe climates. A double window should be sealed and all moisture removed to avoid condensation. The thermal path through metal window frames should be broken by plastic inserts. The heat loss caused by the leakage of warm air from the inside of the building, which is a major source of loss in traditional windows, is thus greatly reduced. Heat loss by thermal radiation is not affected by double or triple glazing, because it depends only on the overall thickness of the glass.

Another approach to the problem is utilize the greenhouse effect (see Section 3.18) in climates where winter days are predominantly sunny. Since soda-lime-silica glass is transparent to the thermal radiation emitted by the sun, but opaque to the long-wave thermal radiation produced by the surfaces of a building after absorbing solar radiation, the heat cannot escape, and it can be stored by the thermal inertia of the building (see Chapter 21).

The *hot-weather problem* is created by the solar radiation transmitted by the glass. The windows can be shaded in summer to prevent the entry of solar radiation, while admitting it in winter when the building needs heat (see Chapter 21). Alternatively, the windows can be shaded throughout the year. The simpler shading devices may compensate for the extra cost of winter heating.

Neither solution is possible if the building is to be designed with an unencumbered curtain wall, and particularly if that wall is to be entirely of glass. In that case the entry of heat must be reduced by the use of *solar-control glass*.

Body-tinted glass is manufactured by adding color to the glass melt to give a uniform color throughout the glass thickness. The first such glass was produced with a green tint resulting from the addition of ferrous oxide (FeO). This absorbs a substantial part of the solar heat radiation, but also some visible light. For example, a $\frac{1}{4}$ in. (6 mm) thick sheet transmits 49 percent of the solar heat and 78 percent of the visible light; a $\frac{3}{8}$ in. (10 mm) thick sheet transmits 36 percent of the solar heat and 69 percent of the visible light. The more recently developed gray and bronze glasses have similar properties, but give daylight of more agreeable color.

Since the solar heat absorbed by the body-tinted glass is reradiated partly to the outside and partly to the inside, thermal efficiency is greatly improved if it is used as the outer leaf of a sealed, double-glazed window. The inner leaf is made of clear glass, and an air space of about $\frac{1}{2}$ in. (12 mm) is left between them. The clear glass is transparent to solar radiation, but opaque to the heat reradiated by the body-tinted glass, which has a longer wavelength than that of the solar heat.

Heat-reflecting glass reflects solar heat by means of a metallic coating. However, it also reflects some of the visible light. A sheet of glass $\frac{1}{4}$ in. (6 mm) thick transmits 43 percent of the solar heat and 33 percent of the visible light. The glass appears like a mirror when seen from the outside during the day, and it transmits a bronze-colored light to the interior.

Heat-absorbing and heat-reflecting glasses significantly alter the interior appearance of buildings by changing the color of daylight. They also have a marked effect on the exterior thermal environment, because the heat, whether absorbed or reflected, does not disappear; it is merely redirected.

The *sound insulation* of windows presents problems that can be almost as difficult as those of thermal insulation. Insulation against airborne sound is governed by the mass law (see Section 16.9), and the mass of window glass is low because the sheets are thin. The most common complaints about noise occur, nevertheless, in summer in non-air-conditioned buildings whose windows are left open for ventilation. Even a single sheet of glass greatly reduces the noise that enters through an open window.

The sound attenuation of two sheets of glass is in principle the same as that of a single sheet of double thickness. In practice, however, it is possible to obtain much higher sound insulation by the use of double glazing (i) by surrounding the air space between the two sheets of glass with a sound-absorbing material such as fiberglass, and (ii) by sealing all air gaps and thus preventing the entry of sound through spaces around the window. The sound attenuation of windows in traditionally built houses is much lower because sound can enter through the narrow unobstructed spaces around them.

REFERENCES

3.1. F. G. H. Blyth and M. H. Freitas. *A Geology for Engineers*, 7th ed. Edward Arnold, London 1984. 325 pp.
3.2. B. L. Clarke and A. J. Ashurst. *Stone Preservation Experiments*. Department of the Environment, London, 1972. 78 pp.
3.3. G. G. Amoroso and V. Fassina (Eds.). *Stone Decay and Preservation Experiments*. Elsevier, Amsterdam, 1983. 453 pp.
3.4. *Methods of Testing Cement*. BS 4550, Section 3.3—Fineness Test. British Standards Institution, London, 1978.
3.5. Ibid. Section 3.7—Soundness Test.
3.6. F. M. Lea. *The Chemistry of Cement*. Edward Arnold, London, 1970, pp. 569–576.
3.7. Ibid., pp. 575–579.
3.8. Ibid., p. 302.
3.9. Duff A. Abrams. "Design of Concrete Mixes." Bulletin 1, Structural Materials and Research Laboratory, Lewis Institute, Chicago, 1919. 20pp.
3.10. "Recommended Practice for Selecting Proportions for Normal, Heavyweight and Mass Concrete (ACI Committee 211)," in *ACI Manual of Concrete Practice*, Part 1, Section 211.1-81. American Concrete Institute, Detroit, 1988. 34 pp.
3.11. *Design of Normal Concrete Mixes*, 2nd Ed. BRE Report 106. H. M. Stationery Office, London, 1987. pp. 42.
3.12. *Methods of Testing Concrete*. BS 1881, Part 104—Method for Determining Vebe Time. British Standards Institution, London, 1983.
3.13. Ibid., Part 103—Method for Determination of Compacting Factor.
3.14. "Standard Practice for the Use of Shrinkage-Compensating Concrete," in *ACI Manual of Concrete Practice, Part 1*. American Concrete Institute, Detroit, 1988, Section 223-83. 36 pp.
3.15. V. V. Mikhailov. "Self-Stressed Concrete." *Proceedings of the Sixth Congress. Fédération Internationale de la Précontrainte (FIP)*, Prague, 1970, pp. 3–15.

Standards of the American Society for Testing and Materials

ASTM Standards in Building Codes, 25th Ed. American Society for Testing and Materials, Philadelphia, 1988. 4100 pp.

C 616-85.	Sandstone building stone.
C 615-85.	Granite building stone.
C 503-85.	Marble building stone.
C 629-80 (1985).	Slate building stone.
C 406-84.	Roofing slate.
C 241-85.	Test method for abrasion resistance of stone subjected to foot traffic.
C 170-87.	Test method for compressive strength of natural building stone.
C 97-83.	Test method for absorption and bulk specific gravity of natural building stone.
C 51-71 (1986).	Definitions of terms relating to lime and limestone.
C 5-79 (1984).	Quicklime for structural purposes.
C 206-84.	Finishing hydrated lime.
C 207-79 (1984).	Hydrated lime for masonry purposes.
C 110-87.	Physical testing of quicklime, hydrated lime, and limestone.
C 22-83.	Gypsum.
C 28-86.	Gypsum plasters.
C 61-76 (1981).	Gypsum Keene's cement.
C 59-83.	Gypsum casting and molding plaster.
C 842-85.	Application of interior gypsum plaster.
C 36-85.	Gypsum wallboard.
C 557-73 (1985).	Adhesives for fastening gypsum wallboard to wood framing.
C 475-81.	Joint treatment materials for gypsum wallboard construction.
C 514-84.	Method for physical testing of gypsum plasters and gypsum concrete.
C 473-87a.	Method for physical testing of gypsum board products, gypsum lath, gypsum partition tile or block.
C 150-86.	Portland cement.
C 91-87a.	Masonry cement.
C 618-85.	Fly ash and raw or calcined natural pozzolans for use as a mineral admixture in portland cement concrete.
C 311-87.	Methods of sampling and testing fly ash or natural pozzolans for use as a mineral admixture in portland cement concrete.
C 115-86.	Test method for fineness of portland cement by the turbidimeter.
C 151-84.	Test method for autoclave expansion of portland cement.
C 191-82.	Test method for time of setting of hydraulic cement by the Vicat needle.
C 807-83.	Test method for time of setting of hydraulic cement mortar by the Vicat needle.
C 109-84.	Test method for compressive strength of hydraulic cement mortars (using 2 in. or 50 mm cube specimens).
C 190-85.	Test method for tensile strength of hydraulic cement mortars.
C 33-86.	Concrete aggregates.
C 330-87.	Lightweight aggregates for structural concrete.
C 331-87.	Lightweight aggregates for concrete masonry units.
C 117-87.	Test method for material finer than No. 200 (75 μm) sieve in mineral aggregates by washing.
C 40-84.	Test methods for organic impurities in fine aggregate for concrete.
C 142-78 (1984).	Test method for clay lumps and friable particles in aggregates.
C 94-86b.	Ready-mix concrete.
C 171-69 (1986).	Sheet materials for curing concrete.
C 309-81.	Liquid membrane-forming compounds for curing concrete.
C 143-78.	Test method for slump of portland cement concrete.
C 230-83.	Flow test for use in tests of hydraulic cement mortars.
C 360-82.	Test method for ball penetration in fresh portland cement concrete.
C 31-87a.	Practices for making and curing concrete test specimens in the field.

C 192-87.	Method of making and curing concrete test specimens in the laboratory.
C 39-86.	Test method for compressive strength cylindrical concrete specimens.
C 260-86.	Air entraining admixtures for concrete.
C 494-86.	Chemical admixtures for concrete.
C 98-87.	Calcium chloride.
C 332-87.	Lightweight aggregates for insulating concrete.
C 55-85.	Concrete building brick.
C 145-85.	Solid load-bearing concrete masonry units.
C 90-85.	Hollow load-bearing concrete masonry units.
C 129-85.	Hollow non-load-bearing concrete masonry units.
C 73-85.	Calcium silicate face brick (sand-lime brick).
C 270-87a.	Mortar for unit masonry.
C 476-83.	Mortar and grout for reinforced and non-reinforced masonry.
E 518-80.	Test method for flexural bond strength of masonry.
C 62-87.	Building brick (solid masonry units made from clay or shale).
C 216-87a.	Facing brick (solid masonry units made from clay or shale).
C 652-87a.	Hollow brick (hollow masonry units made from clay or shale).
C 67-87.	Method for sampling and testing brick and structural clay tile.
C 126-86.	Ceramic glazed structural clay facing tile, facing brick, and solid masonry units.
C 212-60 (1986).	Structural clay facing tile.
C 34-84.	Structural clay load-bearing wall tile.
C 56-71 (1986).	Structural clay non-load-bearing tile.
C 530-70 (1986).	Structural clay non-load-bearing screen tile.
C 57-57 (1983).	Structural clay floor tile.

SUGGESTIONS FOR FURTHER READING

John Pitts. *A Manual of Geology for Civil Engineers.* Halsted Press, New York, 1985. 228 pp.

R. J. Shaffer. *The Weathering of Building Stones.* Building Research Special Report No. 18. H. M. Stationery Office, London, 1983. 149 pp.

E. M. Winkler. *Stone: Properties and Durability in Man's Environment.* Spinger Verlag, New York 1973. 230 pp.

R. H. Bogue. *Chemistry of Portland Cement.* Reinhold, New York, 1955. 793 pp.

Martin Grayson (Ed.). *Encyclopedia of Glass, Ceramics, and Cement.* Wiley, New York, 1984. 925 pp.

A. M. Neville. *Properties of Concrete.* Pitman, London, 1963. 532 pp.

W. H. Taylor. *Concrete Technology and Practice.* McGraw-Hill. New York, 1977. 846 pp.

D. Popovics. *Fundamentals of Portland Cement Concrete: A Quantitative Approach.* Volume 1: *Fresh Concrete.* Wiley, New York, 1982. 477 pp.

A. B. Searle. *Modern Brickmaking.* Ernest Benn, London, 1956. 734 pp.

C. Beall. *Masonry Design for Architects, Engineers, and Builders.* Prentice-Hall, Englewood Cliffs, NJ, 1971. 290 pp.

S. Sahlin. *Structural Masonry.* Prentice-Hall, Englewood Cliffs, NJ, 1971. 290 pp.

Raymond McGrath and A. C. Frost. *Glass in Architecture and Decoration.* Architectural Press, London, 1961. 712 pp.

John Peter. *Design with Glass.* Reinhold, New York, 1965. 159 pp.

R. Persson. *Flat Glass Technology.* Butterworths, London, 1969. 167 pp.

Technical data on the sizes and physical properties of glass for use in buildings are readily obtainable from the glass manufacturers.

NOTATION

Al	aluminum
C	carbon
Ca	calcium
Cl	chlorine
f'_c	characteristic strength of concrete
H	hydrogen
K	potassium
Mg	magnesium
Na	sodium
O	oxygen
s	standard deviation
S	sulfur
Si	silicon
W/C	water/cement ratio
x_a	average strength

A list of abbreviations of the units of measurement, definitions of these units, and conversion factors between British/American and metric units are given in the Appendix.

4

Timber and Timber Products: Properties, Deterioration, Protection

B. Alan Bendtsen and Alan D. Freas

Wood is a biological material. It shrinks and swells in response to changing environmental conditions, and it is subject to degrading agencies such as decay, insects, and fire. These factors must be accounted for in design with timber and timber products.

The mechanical and physical properties of wood and factors that influence these properties are discussed. In place of solid sawn timber, timber products are often used, such as plywood, glued-laminated (glulam) timber, laminated veneer lumber (LVL), insulation board, hardboard, and particleboard.

4.1. INTRODUCTION

Beginning with prehistory, man has used wood for shelter, stream crossings, furniture, and fuel. Because of the many desirable characteristics of wood, it continues to be in demand for these and other uses. Because wood is a renewable resource, it has a unique quality of availability in contrast to materials of a finite nature. With care and prudent use of forests, generations to come will be able to avail themselves of this material.

For the architect, the wide ranges in color, figure, strength, and other characteristics available from a variety of species permit the creation of a wide range of architectural effects. An array of new materials based on wood has evolved from research to vastly broaden the potential for architectural designs of span, form, and appearance.

4.2. STRUCTURE

Wood comes from two broad classes of trees—softwoods and hardwoods. These classifications really are not related to the hardness of the wood, since some hardwoods are softer than some of the denser softwoods. Rather, the groupings are biological in nature. Hardwoods, for the most part, have broad leaves that in temperate climates are lost in the fall or winter. Softwoods, on the other hand, have needlelike or scalelike leaves that, with a few exceptions, remain on the tree all through the year; hence the name *evergreen* is frequently applied to the softwoods.

Cell Types

Wood is the hard, fibrous material found beneath the bark in the stems and branches of trees. Wood contains a variety of cell forms, but the primary building blocks are the fibers (also called *tracheids*). Fibers are elongated and pointed at the ends and are oriented generally parallel to the axis of the tree trunk. While fiber length varies greatly in a single tree and among species, softwood fibers average from $\frac{1}{8}$ to $\frac{1}{3}$ in. (3 to 8 mm) in length and hardwood fibers are about $\frac{1}{25}$ in. (1 mm) long.

Besides fibers, hardwoods have large-diameter cells, known as *vessels* or *pores*, that serve as arteries for longitudinal sap movement. Softwoods do not have such vessels or pores, since the fibers serve the sap-conducting function.

Both hardwoods and softwoods have some cells with their longitudinal axes oriented horizontally between the pith and the bark. They conduct sap radially across the grain and are known as *ray cells*; as groups they are known as *rays*.

Macrostructure

The cross section of a tree, seen when viewing the end of a log or the top of a stump, may be divided into three principal parts: the bark, the cambium, and the wood (Fig. 4.2.1.). The *bark* is the outer layer, most of which is corky material with a thin inner layer of living cells. Bark functions mainly to protect the tree against loss of water, abrasion, and fire. The *cambium* is a thin ring of living, reproductive tissue located directly beneath the bark. It is in this layer that wood and bark cells are formed. The material between the cambium and the pith is *wood*, which provides support for the tree and stores and conducts nutrients. The woody area has two parts: sapwood and heartwood. *Sapwood* occupies the outer portion of the wood area, has both active and inactive cells, and functions primarily for food storage and transport of sap. *Heartwood*, which was sapwood at the time it was formed, is composed mostly of inactive cells. In most species, the heartwood contains extraneous materials, many of which can be extracted from the wood by solvents. These *extractives* are deposited in the cells during conversion from sapwood to heartwood and, in most cases, give the heartwood a darker color than the sapwood; in a few species, the sapwood and heartwood are virtually the same color. The extractives also make the heartwood of some species more resistant to attack by decay fungi and insects. Other extraneous materials are described in the discussion on chemical composition.

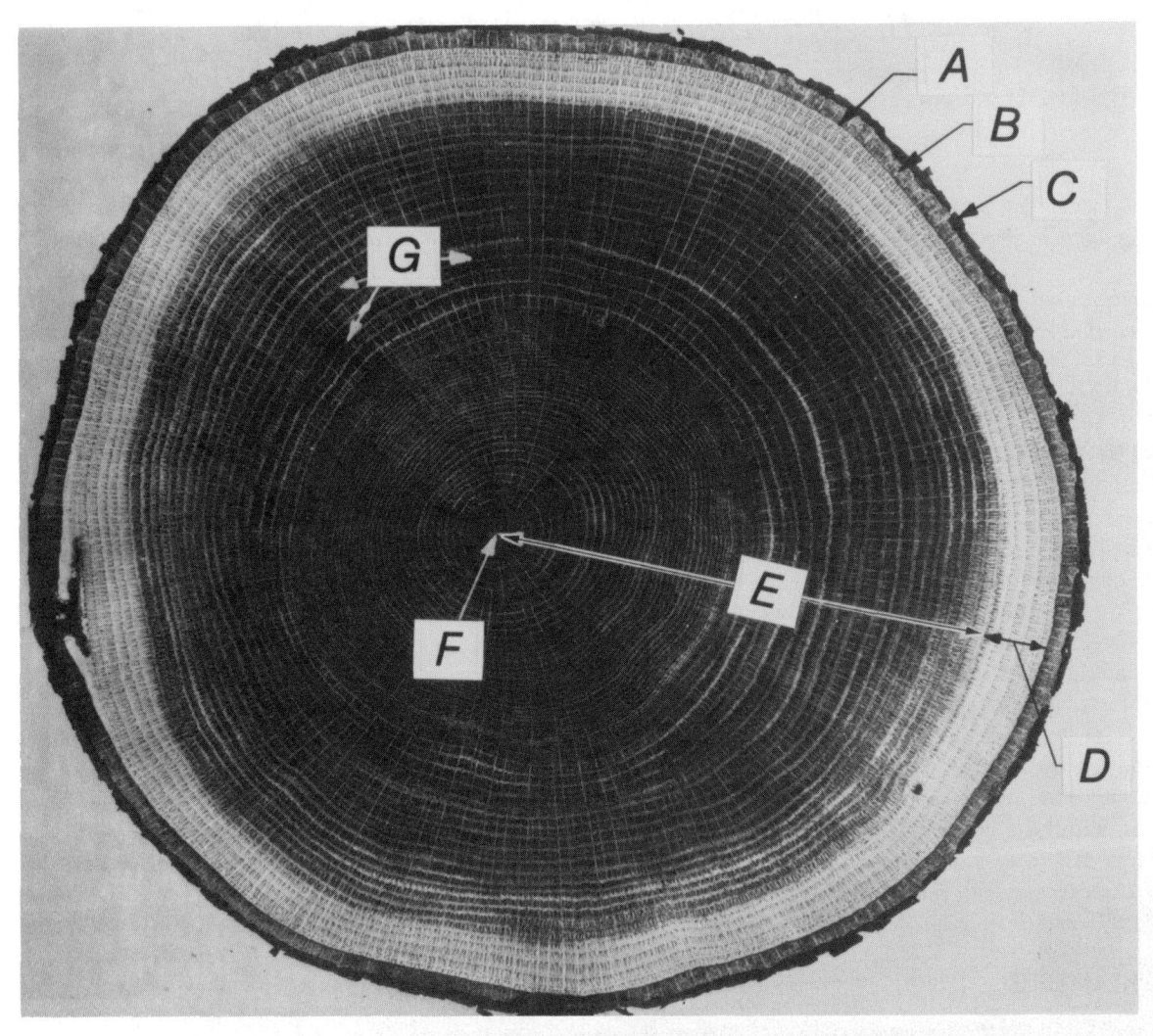

Fig. 4.2.1. Cross section of a white oak tree trunk. *A*: Cambium layer (microscopic) is inside inner bark and forms wood and bark cells. *B*: Inner bark is moist, soft, and contains living tissue. It carries prepared food from leaves to all growing parts of tree. *C*: Outer bark containing corky layers is composed of dry dead tissue. It gives general protection against external injuries. *D*: Sapwood, which contains both living and dead tissues, is the light-colored wood beneath the bark. It carries sap from roots to leaves. *E*: Heartwood (inactive) is formed by a gradual change in the sapwood. *F*: Pith is the soft tissue about which the first wood growth takes place in the newly formed twigs. *G*: Wood rays connect the various layers from pith to bark for storage and transfer of food.

In temperate climates, growth occurs only in the warmer part of the year. Wood formed early in the growing season is termed *earlywood* (sometimes called springwood), and wood formed later in the growing season is termed *latewood* (sometimes called summerwood). Together, each layer of earlywood and latewood form an *annual ring*. Earlywood fibers are characterized by thin walls and large cavities (called *lumens*), while latewood fibers have thicker walls and smaller lumens. In many species, such as the oaks and the ashes in the hardwoods and the southern pines and Douglas-fir in the softwoods, the contrast between earlywood and latewood is apparent as the prominent annual ring structure when viewed on a cross section. In others, such as aspen and sweetgum, there is little differentiation between earlywood and latewood in the growth rings, making the rings difficult to recognize. In many tropical regions, growth is practically continuous, and well-defined rings are not formed. Annual growth rings may be affected by climatic conditions occurring when the rings are formed. A drought, for example, may slow the growth of the tree and the rings may be quite narrow, while those grown during a favorable period may be much wider. Such variations in ring patterns, corresponding to changes in climatic conditions, can sometimes be used for dating the age of a piece of wood.

Earlywood is lighter, softer, and weaker than latewood because the proportion of wood substance per unit of volume is less in earlywood. Because it is the wood substance that provides strength, the latewood portion is stronger. The proportion of latewood is therefore indicative of clear wood strength. In some species, such as Douglas-fir and the southern pines, a higher proportion of latewood (combined with a normal rate of growth) permits assignment of higher design stresses for stress-rated lumber.

Chemical Composition

Dry wood is made up mainly of cellulose, lignin, and hemicelluloses, with a small proportion (about 5 to 10 percent) of extraneous materials. *Cellulose* is the major constituent, comprising about half of the wood substance by weight. During growth of the tree, the cellulose molecules form themselves into small elements called fibrils, which are organized into larger elements forming the cell wall of the fibers. It is the cellulose that imparts strength to wood. *Lignin* constitutes a much smaller percentage of the fibers, on the order of 23 to 33 percent for softwoods and 16 to 25 percent for hardwoods. Lignin is a complicated polymer, not well understood. It is found throughout the cell wall but at a higher concentration toward the outside of the wall. It serves, in part, to bind together adjoining cells. It is difficult to remove lignin to obtain individual fibers for papermaking or chemical conversion for manufacture of such things as textiles and films.

Hemicelluloses are associated with the cellulose and are polymers based on several kinds of sugar monomers. Relative amounts of the different sugars vary widely with species. The sugars are of interest for conversion into chemical products.

Extraneous materials (including extractives) mentioned earlier are not structural components of wood and are both organic and inorganic in nature. The organic extractives contribute to such properties of wood as color, odor, taste, decay resistance, density, hygroscopicity, and flammability. Extractives are so named because they can be removed by extraction with solvents such as water, alcohol, benzene, and ether. The extractives include tannins and other polyphenolics, coloring matter, essential oils, and other compounds. They range from about 5 to 30 percent, depending upon such factors as species, age of the wood, conditions under which the tree grew, and the time of year the tree was cut.

The inorganic component generally amounts to 0.2 to 1.0 percent of the wood substance although higher volumes are occasionally reported. Most abundant are calcium, potassium, and magnesium, while others, such as phosphorus, sodium, and iron, occur in trace amounts.

4.3. PHYSICAL PROPERTIES

Anisotropy

Many structural materials are *isotropic*, that is, they have the same properties in all directions. The arrangement of fibers in wood, with the long axes of the fibers parallel (or essentially so) to the axis of the trunk of the tree, suggests that wood may have characteristics that vary with direction in the wood: (1) longitudinal or parallel to the axis of the trunk or (2) perpendicular to the longitudinal axis and either radial in the trunk or tangent to the annual growth rings. Research has shown this to be true and thus wood is *anisotropic*, not isotropic. Actually, wood is considered to be *orthotropic*, with different characteristics parallel to three mutually perpendicular axes: longitudinal, radial, and tangential (Fig. 4.3.1). Many wood properties, including mechanical properties and dimensional change with changes in moisture content, differ in the three directions.

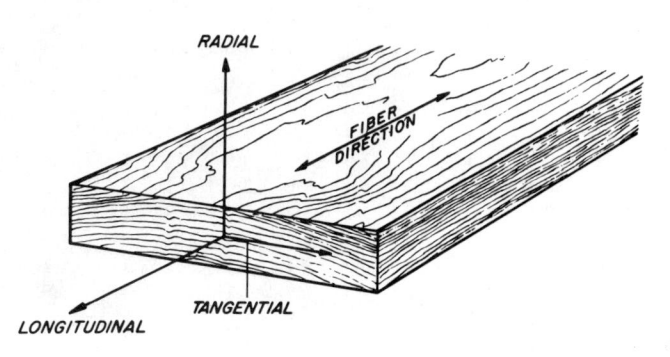

Fig. 4.3.1. The three principal axes of wood with respect to grain direction and growth rings.

Moisture in Wood

The moisture content within and between living trees varies widely, from about 30 percent of the ovendry weight of wood to 200 percent or perhaps more. This moisture in the green wood is, in part, adsorbed in the cell walls and, in part, is present in the cell cavities or lumens. The moisture in the cell walls is termed bound water and that in the cavities is termed free water. A piece of wood fresh from a live tree will begin to dry as soon as it is exposed to the air. The free water comes off first, followed by the bound water. The point in drying at which the cell walls are still fully saturated and the cell cavities are empty is known as the *fiber saturation point*. This point, which varies with species, is generally in the neighborhood of 30 percent moisture content, and when the true value is not known, the fiber saturation point is generally taken to be 30 percent. The significance of the fiber saturation point will be explained in later sections.

Wood gives off moisture to a relatively dry atmosphere and takes on moisture from a very humid atmosphere until it comes into balance with atmospheric conditions and thus is said to be *hygroscopic*. In other words, it comes to an *equilibrium moisture content* (EMC). The EMC is related to the relative humidity and the temperature of the atmosphere, although temperature has a relatively minor effect (Table 4.1). The value of the EMC for a specific combination of relative humidity and temperature varies slightly with species, but the values in the table are generally representative. For most uses of wood, it is desirable that the end product be put into service at a moisture content as close as possible to that which it may be expected to reach in service. The EMC values in the table thus provide a guide to the conditions that should be used in drying wood for a specific end use. It is apparent that service conditions in the arid southwest require a lower initial moisture content than would be required for the damp Gulf Coast.

Dimensional Stability

Wood shrinks as it dries and swells as it picks up moisture, as evidenced by dresser drawers that stick in summer but move freely in winter. Wood shrinks and swells at different amounts per unit of distance along the three principal axes: longitudinal, radial, and tangential. Longitudinal shrinkage is generally minor, with radial shrinkage being greater and tangential shrinkage about twice the radial. These differential shrinkages cause lumber to warp as it dries. Radial and tangential shrinkage values for a few selected species are given in Table 4.2. Thus if a piece of wood is machined to final size while it is green, it will be less than that size when it comes to equilibrium under most service conditions. Because not every piece of wood shrinks and swells exactly the same, it is obviously desirable to machine wood products to final size at a moisture content as close as possible to that expected in service so that pieces for a particular use will not change too much in size as they equilibrate in service.

Table 4.1. Moisture Content of Wood in Equilibrium with Stated Dry-Bulb Temperature and Relative Humidity.[1]

Temperature (dry-bulb)		\multicolumn{20}{c}{Moisture Content (%) at Various Relative Humidity Levels (%)}
(°C)	(°F)	5	10	15	20	25	30	35	40	45	50	55	60	65	70	75	80	85	90	95	98
−1.3	30	1.4	2.6	3.7	4.6	5.5	6.3	7.1	7.9	8.7	9.5	10.4	11.3	12.4	13.5	14.9	16.5	18.5	21.0	24.3	26.9
4.2	40	1.4	2.6	3.7	4.6	5.5	6.3	7.1	7.9	8.7	9.5	10.4	11.3	12.3	13.5	14.9	16.5	18.5	21.0	24.3	26.9
9.8	50	1.4	2.6	3.6	4.6	5.5	6.3	7.1	7.9	8.7	9.5	10.3	11.2	12.3	13.4	14.8	16.4	18.4	20.9	24.3	26.9
15	60	1.3	2.5	3.6	4.6	5.4	6.2	7.0	7.8	8.6	9.4	10.2	11.1	12.1	13.3	14.6	16.2	18.2	20.7	24.1	26.8
21	70	1.3	2.5	3.5	4.5	5.4	6.2	6.9	7.7	8.5	9.2	10.1	11.0	12.0	13.1	14.4	16.0	17.9	20.5	23.9	26.6
26	80	1.3	2.4	3.5	4.4	5.3	6.1	6.8	7.6	8.3	9.1	9.9	10.8	11.7	12.9	14.2	15.7	17.7	20.2	23.6	26.3
32	90	1.2	2.3	3.4	4.3	5.1	5.9	6.7	7.4	8.1	8.9	9.7	10.5	11.5	12.6	13.9	15.4	17.3	19.8	23.3	26.0
38	100	1.2	2.3	3.3	4.2	5.0	5.8	6.5	7.2	7.9	8.7	9.5	10.3	11.2	12.3	13.6	15.1	17.0	19.5	22.9	25.6
43	110	1.1	2.2	3.2	4.0	4.9	5.6	6.3	7.0	7.7	8.4	9.2	10.0	11.0	12.0	13.2	14.7	16.6	19.1	22.4	25.2
49	120	1.1	2.1	3.0	3.9	4.7	5.4	6.1	6.8	7.5	8.2	8.9	9.7	10.6	11.7	12.9	14.4	16.2	18.6	22.0	24.7
54	130	1.0	2.0	2.9	3.7	4.5	5.2	5.9	6.6	7.2	7.9	8.7	9.4	10.3	11.3	12.5	14.0	15.8	18.2	21.5	24.2
60	140	0.9	1.9	2.8	3.6	4.3	5.0	5.7	6.3	7.0	7.7	8.4	9.1	10.0	11.0	12.1	13.6	15.3	17.7	21.0	23.7
65	150	0.9	1.8	2.6	3.4	4.1	4.8	5.5	6.1	6.7	7.4	8.1	8.8	9.7	10.6	11.8	13.1	14.9	17.2	20.4	23.1
71	160	0.8	1.6	2.4	3.2	3.9	4.6	5.2	5.8	6.4	7.1	7.8	8.5	9.3	10.3	11.4	12.7	14.4	16.7	19.9	22.5
76	170	0.7	1.5	2.3	3.0	3.7	4.3	4.9	5.6	6.2	6.8	7.4	8.2	9.0	9.9	11.0	12.3	14.0	16.2	19.3	21.9
82	180	0.7	1.4	2.1	2.8	3.5	4.1	4.7	5.3	5.9	6.5	7.1	7.8	8.6	9.5	10.5	11.8	13.5	15.7	18.7	21.3
88	190	0.6	1.3	1.9	2.6	3.2	3.8	4.4	5.0	5.5	6.1	6.8	7.5	8.2	9.1	10.1	11.4	13.0	15.1	18.1	20.7
93	200	0.5	1.1	1.7	2.4	3.0	3.5	4.1	4.6	5.2	5.8	6.4	7.1	7.8	8.7	9.7	10.9	12.5	14.6	17.5	20.0
99	210	0.5	1.0	1.6	2.1	2.7	3.2	3.8	4.3	4.9	5.4	6.0	6.7	7.4	8.3	9.2	10.4	12.0	14.0	16.9	19.3
104	220	0.4	0.9	1.4	1.9	2.4	2.9	3.4	3.9	4.5	5.0	5.6	6.3	7.0	7.8	8.8	9.9	*	*	*	*
110	230	0.3	0.8	1.2	1.6	2.1	2.6	3.1	3.6	4.2	4.7	5.3	6.0	6.7	*	*	*	*	*	*	*
115	240	0.3	0.6	0.9	1.3	1.7	2.1	2.6	3.1	3.5	4.1	4.6	*	*	*	*	*	*	*	*	*
121	250	0.2	0.4	0.7	1.0	1.3	1.7	2.1	2.5	2.9	*	*	*	*	*	*	*	*	*	*	*
126	260	0.2	0.3	0.5	0.7	0.9	1.1	1.4	*	*	*	*	*	*	*	*	*	*	*	*	*
132	270	0.1	0.1	0.2	0.3	0.4	0.4	*	*	*	*	*	*	*	*	*	*	*	*	*	*

[1] Asterisks indicate conditions not possible at atmospheric pressure.

Table 4.2. Shrinkage Values of Some U.S. Woods.

Species	Radial	Tangential	Volumetric
	Shrinkage from Green to Ovendry Moisture Content[1]		
White ash	4.9	7.8	13.3
Quaking aspen	3.5	6.7	11.5
Yellow birch	7.3	9.5	16.8
Shagbark hickory	7.0	10.5	16.7
Northern red oak	4.0	8.6	13.7
Sugar maple	4.8	9.9	14.7
White oak, white	5.6	10.5	16.3
Western redcedar cedar	2.4	5.0	6.8
Coast Douglas-fir[2]	4.8	7.6	12.4
White fir	3.3	7.0	9.8
Walnut, black	5.5	7.8	12.8
Yellow-poplar	4.6	8.2	12.7
Western hemlock	4.2	7.8	12.4
Eastern white pine	2.1	6.1	8.2
Loblolly pine	4.8	7.4	12.3
Longleaf pine	5.1	7.5	12.2
Young-growth redwood	2.2	4.9	7.0
Black spruce	4.1	6.8	11.3

[1] Expressed as a percentage of the green dimension.
[2] Coast Douglas-fir is defined as Douglas-fir in the States of Oregon and Washington west of the summit of the Cascade Mountains. Interior West includes the State of California and all counties in Oregon and Washington east of but adjacent to the Cascade summit. Interior North includes the remainder of Oregon and Washington and the States of Idaho, Montana, and Wyoming.

Average longitudinal shrinkage values from green to ovendry are between 0.1 and 0.2 percent for most species. However, abnormal types of wood, such as compression wood (in the softwoods), tension wood (in the hardwoods), and juvenile wood (wood formed early in the life of the tree), commonly have unusually high longitudinal shrinkage. Thus a piece of wood composed of normal wood on one edge and abnormal wood on the other may be expected to warp. The difference in longitudinal shrinkage between abnormal and normal wood is so high (as much as 10 times that of normal wood) that a strip of abnormal wood in the center of a piece of lumber can actually fail from the tensile stress parallel to grain set up by restraint of the shrinkage in the abnormal wood caused by lack of shrinkage in the surrounding normal wood.

Density

The density of wood is determined mainly by two factors: the amount of wood substance per unit volume and the moisture content. The amount of extractives and minerals has only a minor effect. Density, exclusive of moisture (i.e., at an ovendry condition), differs greatly between species and even within a species depending upon such things as climatic conditions during growth and the geographic area of growth. Because wood is used under a wide range of conditions and thus a wide range of moisture contents, and because wood in use does contain moisture, values of density are usually reported on a moisture-condition-in-use basis. The density of most species falls between about 20 and 45 lb/ft^3 (320 and 720 kg/m^3), but the full range extends from less than 10 lb/ft^3 (160 kg/m^3) for balsa to more than 65 lb/ft^3 (1,040 kg/m^3) for some tropical species. Many characteristics of wood are affected by density. Because it is the wood substance present that imparts strength, wood of high density is stronger and stiffer than wood of low density, other things (including moisture content) being the same. Woods of high density tend to shrink and swell more with changes in moisture content than do those of low density.

Resistance to Weathering

Unless wood has some protective treatment, such as a paint coating, exposure to weather will cause all woods to become gray. The color changes are accompanied by photodegradation and a gradual loss of wood cells at the surface that are slowly eroded. Since the weathering process is a surface phenomenon and the process is so slow, weather-exposed wood may be expected to lose only about $\frac{1}{4}$ in. (6 mm) in thickness in a century.

In addition to color change and erosion, surface checking, warping, and roughening may be expected. While all woods turn gray under weather exposure, usually there is a surface growth of fungi; the spores and mycelia of the fungi may give a dark gray, blotchy, and unsightly appearance to the wood.

Exposure to sunlight results in chemical degradation, with the ultraviolet portion of the spectrum causing the most severe effects. As the wood is wetted and dried repeatedly over a period of time, the wood checks, with the higher-density woods tending to develop more checks than do lower-density woods. Vertical-grained (quarter sawed) boards check less than do flat-grained (plain sawed) boards because of the lower shrinkage in the radial direction.

Some boards tend to warp, particularly to cup, as they weather and may pull out their fastenings. The tendency to cup is greater for high-density boards, for those wide in proportion to thickness, and for flat-grained as opposed to edge-grained boards.

Color changes may also result from biological attack. Dark-colored fungal spores and mycelia on the surface give wood an unsightly dark gray, blotchy appearance. The desired, light gray, silvery sheen on weathered wood is most common in areas where attack by organisms is inhibited by a hot and dry climate or a salt atmosphere near a coast.

Durability

Age. Wood is commonly thought to be a short-lived material because it is organic. However, its useful life may be measured in centuries if it is protected from adverse conditions in service. Wood structures several centuries old exist in Japan. In the United States, one can see wood houses that date back to the early days of the country and covered bridges that are nearly as old. A well-known wood structure, the Tabernacle of the Church of Jesus Christ of Latter-Day Saints, is used regularly even though it is more than 100 years old, and there are wooden structures in Europe and Asia that were built more than 6 centuries ago.

Decay. Decay is one of the principal hazards facing wood. Decay is the result of action by wood-destroying fungi that use the wood substance as a food source. Wood-destroying fungi, as do all fungi, require favorable conditions of moisture, temperature, and air as well as a food source (the wood); lack of any one of the four inhibits fungal growth. The simplest of these to control in most uses is moisture content, and keeping wood at moisture contents of about 20 percent or less is an effective way of preventing decay. Wood fully saturated with water lacks air; hence, piles constantly submerged in fresh water will not support fungal growth. Wood species vary greatly in the natural resistance of their heartwood to decay. Sapwood of any species has, at best, minimal resistance. Thus wood having decay-resistant heartwood or wood treated with preservative chemicals is needed for use under severe service conditions or where the moisture content cannot be controlled.

Action of Other Organisms. Fungi that cause stain and mold on wood get sustenance from materials in cell cavities and thus do not attack the wood substance; their principal effect will be in changing the appearance of the wood. Soft-rot fungi, found in wood at high moisture content, for example, in cooling tower slats, do cause deterioration. Bacteria in water may attack the cell walls, slowly reducing strength and increasing porosity over very long periods. Bacteria-attacked wood may also adsorb abnormal amounts of water or preservative chemicals during treatment.

Insects and borers attack wood, with termites probably being the most destructive. Termites are most prevalent in the tropics and subtropics, such as the Southern United States, although there are some spots of termite infestation in cooler areas. Carpenter ants can destroy wood, although they use the wood only for shelter, whereas termites feed on wood. Carpenter ants prefer moist or decayed wood; therefore, keeping the wood dry is an effective way of limiting the damage they may cause. Preservative treatments that control decay will generally control insects, but soil poisoning is the most common method of controlling termites. Marine borers may be active in salt and brackish water and can cause extensive damage to piles and other wood members. Treatment with creosote generally controls marine borers except for *Limnoria*. To control *Limnoria* an initial treatment with waterborne salts followed by creosote is needed.

Electrical Properties

Electrical properties of most importance are conductivity, dielectric constant, and dielectric power factor. At low moisture content, wood may be classified as an insulator rather than as a conductor. The distinction is important in wood power line poles and in tool handles and ladders used around electrical lines. The DC electrical resistance varies greatly with moisture content, especially below the fiber saturation point, increasing tenfold as the moisture content decreases from about 25 to 7 percent. Many electric moisture meters operate on this principle. Effects of factors such as temperature and species must be accounted for in converting the meter reading to moisture content.

Thermal Properties

Four thermal properties of wood are important. Thermal conductivity of wood is a small fraction of that for metals. For example, structural softwood lumber has a conductivity of about 0.75 Btu/in./h/ft^2/°F (0.11 W/(m · K)) compared with 1,500 (215 W/(m · K)) for aluminum, 310 (45 W/(m · K)) for steel, and 6 (0.9 W/(m · K)) for concrete. Thermal conductivity is on the order of two to four times that of mineral wool, a common insulating material.

Specific heat of wood depends on the temperature of the wood but is practically independent of species and density. Specific heat is approximately related to temperature t in degrees Fahrenheit by the relation

$$\text{Specific heat (cal/gm} \cdot \text{°F)} = 0.25 + 0.0006t$$

or

$$\text{Specific heat (kJ/kg} \cdot \text{K)} = 1.88 + 0.0045t$$

for ovendry wood. Moisture in wood causes the specific heat to increase because the specific heat of water is greater than that of ovendry wood.

The thermal diffusivity of wood is much smaller than that of other structural materials. A typical value for wood is 0.00025 in.^{2}/s (0.16 mm^2/s) compared with 0.021 in.^{2}/s (13.5 mm^2/s) for steel and 0.001 in.^{2}/s (0.645 mm^2/s) for mineral wool.

Coefficients of thermal expansion for completely dry wood are positive in all directions; that is, wood expands on heating and contracts on cooling. Tests of a variety of species, both hardwoods and softwoods, have given values parallel to grain in the range of 1.7 to 2.5 × 10^{-6}/°F (3 to 4.5 × 10^{-6}/°C). Values perpendicular to grain (radial and tangential) range from about 5 to over 10 times those parallel to grain.

4.4. MECHANICAL PROPERTIES

Mechanical properties of wood, such as strength, stiffness, hardness, and resistance to impact, affect the utility of wood for some uses even if that use is not as a primary structural element such as a beam. For example, resistance to shock (or impact) is important in use of wood as baseball and cricket bats, hockey sticks, and tennis rackets. Hardness is important for flooring, particularly that used in industrial plants, where heavy loads may be moved to and from processing machinery. Strength and stiffness are, of course, vital to such uses as girders and columns in buildings or bridges. Thus, knowledge of mechanical properties for various species has always been important to structural designers, architects, and builders, as well as to the producers of wood products for those uses.

In the early history of stress-grading timbers in the United States, mechanical properties as a basis for structural design were derived from tests of full-sized lumber and timber elements of specific grades. The utility of such data was limited because lumber and timber grades were not well standardized and were subject to frequent change. Later, the idea was conceived that structural design properties could be derived from the basic properties of a species, evaluated by means of tests on small, clear, straight-grained specimens. The "small, clear" properties are modified by factors that account for the effects of factors such as knots, cross grain, and other strength-reducing characteristics permitted in lumber and timber grades, together with adjustments for variability, seasoning, duration of load, safety, and member depth. Design values are currently being derived from small clear properties.

Because lumber and timber grades are more standardized, it is now considered feasible to evaluate the mechanical properties of specific grades and sizes as a basis for deriving design values. A program of "in-grade" testing of commercial lumber has provided data on a large number of grades and sizes [Ref. 4.1]. Design values will be derived from these test results as quickly as appropriate consensus standards are completed and approved. Such data are expected to be particularly useful in load and resistance factor design (LRFD), now in use for structural design with steel and concrete, when this design procedure is fully developed for wood structures.

Clear Wood Mechanical Properties

Clear wood mechanical properties are commonly evaluated using methods outlined in American Society for Testing and Materials (ASTM) Standard D143 [Ref. 4.2]. Average properties obtained by these methods for a few species are given in Tables 4.3a and 4.3b.

Wood is anisotropic, not isotropic, and thus has unique and independent mechanical properties in the directions of three mutually perpendicular axes: longitudinal, radial, and tangential. The longitudinal axis (L) is parallel to the fiber (grain) direction (Fig. 4.3.1); the radial axis (R) is normal to the growth rings (perpendicular to grain in the radial direction); and the tangential axis (T) is perpendicular to grain but tangent to the growth rings. Because of these directional characteristics, mechanical properties are generally evaluated in each of the three directions L, R, and T.

Elastic Properties. Twelve values, nine of which are independent, describe the elastic behavior of wood: three moduli of elasticity (E); three moduli of rigidity (G); and six Poisson's ratios (μ). Moduli of elasticity and Poisson's ratios are related by expressions having the form

$$\frac{\mu_{ij}}{E_i} = \frac{\mu_{ij}}{E_j} \; (i \neq j; i, j = L, R, T)$$

Values of E_L, E_R, and E_T may be derived from a compressive test, but such data are very limited. Thus, most commonly, the value of E_L determined from a bending rather than an axial test is the only E value available (Table 4.3). The E_L as determined from a bending test includes an effect of shear deflection. Comparison of E_L from bending tests with those derived from compression tests shows a difference of about 10 percent. Thus the E_L in compression, if not available from test data, may be estimated by increasing the E_L from bending by 10 percent.

Data on modulus of rigidity, too, are limited. Values of the various moduli of rigidity (G_{LR}, G_{LT}, G_{RT}) from limited tests of a few species are given in Table 4.4 as ratios to E_L. Poisson's ratios are shown in the same table and are designated as μ_{LR}, μ_{RL}, μ_{LT}, μ_{TL}, μ_{RT}, and μ_{TR}. The first subscript refers to the direction of the applied stress, and the second refers to the direction of lateral deformation. For example, μ_{LR} is the Poisson's ratio for deformation along the radial axis caused by stress along the longitudinal axis.

Strength Properties. Strength properties most commonly measured are modulus of rupture in bending, maximum stress in compression parallel to grain, compression strength perpendicular to grain, and shear strength parallel to grain. Additional measurements may be made of work to maximum load in bending, impact bending strength, tensile strength perpendicular to grain, and hardness. Table 4.3 presents average values of these properties and E_L from bending tests for a few selected species. Such data for a wide range of species may be found in Ref. 4.3.

Modulus of rupture in bending reflects the maximum load-carrying capacity of the member and is proportional to the maximum bending moment borne by the specimen. Work to maximum load is a measure of the energy absorbed by the specimen as it is slowly loaded to failure in bending, while height of drop in an impact test is related to the energy absorption due to a rapid or falling load. Hardness is the load required to embed a ball having a diameter of 0.444 in. (projected area of 1 cm^2) to half its diameter in a direction perpendicular to grain.

Strength properties less commonly measured by clear wood tests include tensile strength parallel to grain, torsional shear strength, creep under constant load, rolling shear strength, and resistance to fatigue. Relatively few data exist on tensile strength parallel to grain; modulus of rupture is considered to be a conservative estimate of tensile strength for clear wood. Torsional shear strength is commonly taken as equal to shear strength parallel to grain, and two-thirds of this value is often taken as torsional shear

60 HANDBOOK OF ARCHITECTURAL TECHNOLOGY

Table 4.3a. Mechanical Properties[1] of Some Commercially Important Woods Grown in the United States.

Common Names of Species	Moisture Condition	Specific Gravity[2]	Static Bending — Modulus of rupture, lb/in.²	Static Bending — Modulus of elasticity,[3] ×10⁶ lb/in.²	Static Bending — Work to maximum load, in.-lb/in.³	Impact Bending — Height of Drop Causing Complete Failure,[4] in.	Compression Parallel to Grain — Maximum Crushing Strength, lb/in.²	Compression Perpendicular to Grain — Fiber Stress at Proportional Limit, lb/in.²	Shear Parallel to Grain — Maximum Shearing Strength, lb/in.²	Tension Perpendicular to Grain — Maximum Tensile Strength, lb/in.²	Side Hardness — Load Perpendicular to Grain, lb
Hardwoods											
White ash	Green	0.55	9,500	1.44	15.7	38	3,900	670	1,350	590	960
	Dry	0.60	15,000	1.74	16.6	43	7,410	1,160	1,910	940	1,320
Quaking aspen	Green	0.35	5,100	0.86	6.4	22	2,140	180	660	230	300
	Dry	0.38	8,400	1.18	7.6	21	4,250	370	850	260	350
Yellow birch	Green	0.55	8,300	1.50	16.1	48	3,380	430	1,110	430	780
	Dry	0.62	16,600	2.01	20.8	55	8,170	970	1,880	920	1,260
Shagbark hickory	Green	0.64	11,000	1.57	23.7	74	4,580	840	1,520	—	—
	Dry	0.72	20,200	2.16	25.8	67	9,210	1,760	2,430	—	—
Sugar maple	Green	0.56	9,400	1.55	13.3	40	4,020	640	1,460	—	970
	Dry	0.63	15,800	1.83	16.5	39	7,830	1,470	2,330	—	1,450
Northern red oak	Green	0.56	8,300	1.35	13.2	44	3,440	610	1,210	750	1,000
	Dry	0.63	14,300	1.82	14.5	43	6,760	1,010	1,780	800	1,290
White oak	Green	0.60	8,300	1.25	11.6	42	3,560	670	1,250	770	1,060
	Dry	0.68	15,200	1.78	14.8	37	7,440	1,070	2,000	800	1,360
Walnut, black	Green	0.51	9,500	1.42	14.6	37	4,300	490	1,220	570	900
	Dry	0.55	14,600	1.68	10.7	34	7,580	1,010	1,370	690	1,010
Yellow-poplar	Green	0.40	6,000	1.22	7.5	26	2,660	270	790	510	440
	Dry	0.42	10,100	1.58	8.8	24	5,540	500	1,190	540	540
Softwoods											
Western redcedar	Green	0.31	5,200	0.94	5.0	17	2,770	240	770	230	260
	Dry	0.32	7,500	1.11	5.8	17	4,560	460	990	220	350
Coast Douglas-fir[5]	Green	0.45	7,700	1.56	7.6	26	3,780	380	900	300	500
	Dry	0.48	12,400	1.95	9.9	31	7,230	800	1,130	340	710
White fir	Green	0.37	5,900	1.16	5.6	22	2,900	280	760	300	340
	Dry	0.39	9,800	1.50	7.2	20	5,800	530	1,100	300	480
Western hemlock	Green	0.42	6,600	1.31	6.9	22	3,360	280	860	290	410
	Dry	0.45	11,300	1.63	8.3	23	7,200	550	1,290	340	540
Eastern white pine	Green	0.34	4,900	0.99	5.2	17	2,440	220	680	250	290
	Dry	0.35	8,600	1.24	6.8	18	4,800	440	900	310	380
Loblolly pine	Green	0.47	7,300	1.40	8.2	30	3,510	390	860	260	450
	Dry	0.51	12,800	1.79	10.4	30	7,130	790	1,390	470	690
Longleaf pine	Green	0.54	8,500	1.59	8.9	35	4,320	480	1,040	330	590
	Dry	0.59	14,500	1.98	11.8	34	8,470	960	1,510	470	870
Young-growth redwood	Green	0.34	5,900	0.96	5.7	16	3,110	270	890	300	350
	Dry	0.35	7,900	1.10	5.2	15	5,220	520	1,110	250	420
Black spruce	Green	0.38	6,100	1.38	7.4	24	2,840	240	739	100	370
	Dry	0.42	10,800	1.61	10.5	23	5,960	550	1,230	—	520

[1] Results of tests on small, clear, straight-grained specimens. Values in the first line for each species are from tests of green material; those in the second line are from tests of seasoned material adjusted to a moisture content of 12 percent.
[2] Specific gravity based on weight ovendry and volume at moisture content indicated.
[3] Modulus of elasticity measured from a simply supported, center-loaded beam, on a span-depth ratio of 14/1. The modulus can be corrected for the effect of shear deflection by increasing it 10 percent.
[4] 50-lb hammer.
[5] Coast Douglas-fir is defined as Douglas-fir growing in the States of Oregon and Washington west of the summit of the Cascade Mountains. Interior West includes the State of California and all counties in Oregon and Washington east of but adjacent to the Cascade summit. Interior North includes the remainder of Oregon and Washington and the States of Idaho, Montana, and Wyoming. Interior South is made up of Utah, Colorado, Arizona, and New Mexico.

Table 4.3b. Mechanical Properties[1,2] of Some Commercially Important Woods Grown in the United States.

Common Names of Species	Moisture Condition	Specific Gravity[4]	Static Bending — Modulus of rupture, kPa	Static Bending — Modulus of elasticity,[5] MPa	Static Bending — Work to maximum load, kJ/m³	Impact Bending — Height of Drop Causing Complete Failure,[3] mm	Compression Parallel to Grain — Maximum Crushing Strength, kPa	Compression Perpendicular to Grain — Fiber Stress at Proportional Limit, kPa	Shear Parallel to Grain — Maximum Shearing Strength, kPa	Tension Perpendicular to Grain — Maximum Tensile Strength, kPa	Side Hardness — Load Perpendicular to Grain, N
Hardwoods											
White ash	Green	0.55	66,000	9,900	108	970	27,500	4,600	9,300	4,100	4,300
	Dry	0.60	106,000	12,000	114	1,090	51,100	8,000	13,200	6,500	5,900
Quaking aspen	Green	0.35	35,000	5,900	44	560	14,800	1,200	4,600	1,600	1,300
	Dry	0.38	58,000	8,100	52	530	29,300	2,600	5,900	1,800	1,600
Yellow birch	Green	0.55	57,000	10,300	111	1,220	23,300	3,000	7,700	3,000	3,500
	Dry	0.62	114,000	13,900	143	1,400	56,300	6,700	13,000	6,300	5,600
Shagbark hickory	Green	0.64	76,000	10,800	163	1,880	31,600	5,800	10,500	—	—
	Dry	0.72	139,000	14,900	178	1,700	63,500	12,100	16,800	—	—
Sugar maple	Green	0.56	65,000	10,700	92	1,020	27,700	4,400	10,100	—	—
	Dry	0.63	109,000	12,600	114	990	54,000	10,100	16,100	—	6,400
Northern red oak	Green	0.56	57,000	9,300	91	1,120	23,700	4,200	8,300	5,200	3,300
	Dry	0.63	99,000	12,500	100	1,090	46,600	7,000	12,300	5,500	5,700
White oak	Green	0.60	57,000	8,600	80	1,070	24,500	4,600	8,600	5,300	4,700
	Dry	0.68	105,000	12,300	102	940	51,300	7,400	13,800	5,500	6,000
Black walnut	Green	0.51	66,000	9,800	101	940	29,600	3,400	8,400	3,900	4,000
	Dry	0.55	101,000	11,600	74	860	52,300	7,000	9,400	4,800	4,500
Yellow-poplar	Green	0.40	41,000	8,400	52	660	18,300	1,900	5,400	3,500	2,000
	Dry	0.42	70,000	10,900	61	610	38,200	3,400	8,200	3,700	2,400
Softwoods											
Coast Douglas-fir[6]	Green	0.45	53,000	10,800	52	660	26,100	2,600	6,200	2,100	2,200
	Dry	0.48	85,000	13,400	68	790	49,900	5,500	7,800	2,300	3,200
White fir	Green	0.37	41,000	8,000	39	560	20,000	1,900	5,200	2,100	1,500
	Dry	0.39	68,000	10,400	50	510	40,000	3,700	7,600	2,100	2,100
Western hemlock	Green	0.42	46,000	9,000	48	560	23,200	1,900	5,900	2,000	1,800
	Dry	0.45	78,000	11,200	57	580	49,700	3,800	8,900	2,300	2,400
Eastern white pine	Green	0.34	34,000	6,800	36	430	16,800	1,500	4,700	1,700	1,300
	Dry	0.35	59,000	8,500	47	460	33,100	3,000	6,200	2,100	1,700
Loblolly pine	Green	0.47	50,000	9,700	57	760	24,200	2,700	5,900	1,800	2,000
	Dry	0.51	88,000	12,300	72	760	49,200	5,400	9,600	3,200	3,100
Longleaf pine	Green	0.54	59,000	11,000	61	890	29,800	3,300	7,200	2,300	2,600
	Dry	0.59	100,000	13,700	81	860	58,400	6,600	10,400	3,200	3,900
Young-growth redwood	Green	0.34	41,000	6,600	39	410	21,400	1,900	6,100	2,100	1,600
	Dry	0.35	54,000	7,600	36	380	36,000	3,600	7,600	1,700	1,900
Black spruce	Green	0.38	42,000	9,500	51	610	19,600	1,600	5,100	700	1,600
	Dry	0.40	75,000	11,100	72	580	41,100	3,800	8,500	—	2,300

[1] Results of tests on small clear specimens in the green and air-dry condition, converted to metric units directly from Table 4-3a.
[2] Values in the first line for each species are from tests of green material; those in the second line are adjusted to 12 percent moisture content.
[3] 22.6-kg hammer.
[4] Specific gravity is based on weight when ovendry and volume when green or at 12 percent moisture content.
[5] Modulus of elasticity measured from a simply supported, center-loaded beam, on a span-depth ratio of 14/1. The modulus can be corrected for the effect of shear deflection by increasing it 10 percent.
[6] Coast Douglas-fir is defined as Douglas-fir growing in the States of Oregon and Washington west of the summit of the Cascade Mountains. Interior West includes the State of California and all counties in Oregon and Washington east of but adjacent to the Cascade summit. Interior North includes the remainder of Oregon and Washington and the States of Idaho, Montana, and Wyoming. Interior South is made up of Utah, Colorado, Arizona, and New Mexico.

Table 4.4. Elastic Ratios for Several Species.

Species	Approximate Specific Gravity[1]	Approximate Moisture Content, %	E_T/E_L	E_R/E_L	G_{LR}/E_L	G_{LT}/E_L	G_{RT}/E_L	μ_{LR}	μ_{LT}	μ_{RT}	μ_{TR}	μ_{RL}	μ_{TL}
Balsa	0.13	9	0.015	0.046	0.054	0.037	0.005	0.23	0.49	0.67	0.23	0.02	0.01
Birch, yellow	0.64	13	0.050	0.078	0.074	0.068	0.017	0.43	0.45	0.70	0.43	0.04	0.02
Douglas-fir	0.50	12	0.050	0.068	0.064	0.078	0.007	0.29	0.45	0.39	0.37	0.04	0.03
Spruce, Sitka	0.38	12	0.043	0.078	0.064	0.061	0.003	0.37	0.47	0.44	0.24	0.04	0.02
Sweetgum	0.53	11	0.050	0.115	0.089	0.061	0.021	0.32	0.40	0.68	0.31	0.04	0.02
Walnut, black	0.59	11	0.056	0.106	0.085	0.062	0.021	0.50	0.63	0.72	0.38	0.05	0.04
Yellow-poplar	0.38	11	0.043	0.092	0.075	0.069	0.011	0.32	0.39	0.70	0.33	0.03	0.02

[1]Based on ovendry weight and volume at the moisture content shown.

strength at proportional limit. Toughness represents the energy required to rapidly cause complete failure in a centrally loaded bending specimen. In some applications, resistance of wood to fatigue is important in design. The fatigue strength of wood is generally a higher proportion of static strength than that for metals. The term *rolling shear* describes the shear strength of wood where the shearing force is in a longitudinal-transverse plane and perpendicular to grain so that the force may be said to "roll" the fibers about their long axes. Tests for this property are a relatively recent development; consequently, data are sparse. From limited tests, rolling shear strengths are in the order of 10 to 20 percent of shear strength parallel to grain.

Factors that Influence Clear Wood Properties

Specific Gravity. Wood substance is actually heavier than water, with a specific gravity of about 1.5 regardless of the species of wood. Wood floats because of the presence of cell cavities and pores. Variations in the sizes of these cavities and the thickness of cell walls cause some species to have more wood substance per unit volume than do others and thus to have higher specific gravity. Specific gravity is a good index of the amount of wood substance present in a piece of dry wood. Because it is obvious that it is the wood substance rather than the cavities that imparts strength and other mechanical properties, specific gravity is also a good index of the level of mechanical properties so long as the wood is clear, straight-grained, and free of defects. Relationships between specific gravity and various mechanical properties are given in Tables 4.5a and 4.5b for clear, straight-grained wood based on tests of more than 160 species. These relationships are admittedly approximate, and for any species, more accurate results may be obtained from data on that species.

Moisture Content. Many mechanical properties are affected by changes in moisture content of the wood, most properties increasing with decreasing moisture content as indicated by the following relationship:

$$P = P_{12}\left(\frac{P_{12}}{P_g}\right)^{(12-M)/(M_p-12)}$$

where P is the value of the property at moisture content M, P_{12} is the value at 12 percent moisture content, P_g (green condition) is the value of the property for all moisture contents greater than M_p, which is the moisture content at the intersection of a horizontal line representing the strength of green wood and an inclined line representing the logarithm of the strength-moisture content relationship for dry wood. Values of M_p are given in Table 4.6 for a few species; for other species a value of 25 percent may be taken. Values of P_{12} and P_g are commonly given in tables of clear wood values. The formula is not valid for estimating the effect of moisture content change on work to maximum load, impact bending, and tension perpendicular to grain, all of which respond erratically to moisture change. The formula also assumes that no deterioration of the product has occurred in the drying process. The drying process or other exposure to high temperature may cause degrade such as checking and honeycombing that may affect strength.

Temperature. At constant moisture content and temperatures below about 400°F (200°C), mechanical properties are approximately linearly related to temperature. The changes that occur when wood is quickly heated or cooled and then tested at that condition are called *immediate* effects. At temperatures below about 200°F (93°C), the immediate effect is essentially reversible, or in other words, properties will return to the value at the original temperature if the temperature change is rapid. This immediate effect is indicated by Figures 4.4.1 to 4.4.3 based on a composite of test results. Permanent effects of heating are illustrated by Figures 4.4.4 to 4.4.7. Repeated exposure to heat has a cumulative effect.

Table 4.5a. Functions Relating Mechanical Properties to Specific Gravity of Clear, Straight-Grained Wood.

	Specific Gravity-Strength Relation[1]					
	Green wood			Wood at 12 percent moisture content		
Property	Softwoods	Hardwoods	All species[2]	Softwoods	Hardwoods	All species[2]
Static bending						
Fiber stress at proportional limit, lb/in.^{2}	$8,420\,G^{0.92}$	$8,480\,G^{1.04}$		$14,200\,G^{0.91}$	$12,200\,G^{0.80}$	
Modulus of elasticity, $\times 10^6$ lb/in.^{2}	$2.44\,G^{0.81}$	$1.91\,G^{0.64}$		$3.13\,G^{0.90}$	$2.33\,G^{0.65}$	
Modulus of rupture, lb/in.^{2}	$16,230\,G^{1.04}$	$16,700\,G^{1.12}$		$25,600\,G^{1.05}$	$24,400\,G^{1.10}$	
Work to maximum load, in.-lb/in.^{3}	$20.7\,G^{1.16}$	$31.4\,G^{1.48}$		$24.2\,G^{1.24}$	$29.7\,G^{1.47}$	
Total work, in.-lb/in.^{3}			$103\,G^{2.00}$			$72.7\,G^{1.75}$
Impact bending, height of drop causing complete failure, in.			$114\,G^{1.75}$			$94.6\,G^{1.75}$
Compression parallel to grain:						
Fiber stress at proportional limit, lb/in.^{2}	$5,400\,G^{0.90}$	$4,930\,G^{0.96}$		$10,100\,G^{1.02}$	$6,210\,G^{0.57}$	
Modulus of elasticity, $\times 10^6$ lb/in.^{2}	$3.24\,G^{0.92}$	$2.03\,G^{0.55}$		$3.72\,G^{0.91}$	$2.70\,G^{0.63}$	
Maximum crushing strength, lb/in.^{2}	$7,740\,G^{1.02}$	$6,630\,G^{1.02}$		$14,600\,G^{1.04}$	$10,600\,G^{0.83}$	
Shear parallel to grain, lb/in.^{2}	$1,560\,G^{0.72}$	$2,510\,G^{1.20}$		$2,430\,G^{0.86}$	$3,200\,G^{1.15}$	
Compression perpendicular to grain:						
Fiber stress at proportional limit, lb/in.^{2}	$1,360\,G^{1.60}$	$2,380\,G^{2.32}$		$2,540\,G^{1.65}$	$2,920\,G^{2.03}$	
Hardness						
End lb			$3,740\,G^{2.25}$			$4,800\,G^{2.25}$
Side, lb			$3,420\,G^{2.25}$			$3,770\,G^{2.25}$

[1]The properties and values should be read as equations; for example, modulus of rupture for green wood of softwoods = $16,230\,G^{1.04}$, where G represents the specific gravity based upon weight ovendry and volume green. For the air-dry properties, the specific gravity is based upon the weight ovendry and the volume at 12 percent moisture content.
[2]As reported in USDA Bulletin No. 676, "The Relation of the Shrinkage and Strength Properties of Wood to its Specific Gravity," by J.A. Newlin and T.R.C. Wilson, 1919.

Table 4.5b. Functions Relating Mechanical Properties to Specific Gravity of Clear, Straight-Grained Wood.

	Specific Gravity-Strength Relation[1]					
	Green wood			Wood at 12 percent moisture content		
Property	Softwoods	Hardwoods	All species[2]	Softwoods	Hardwoods	All species[2]
Static bending						
Modulus of elasticity, MPa	$16,800\,G^{0.81}$	$13,200\,G^{0.64}$		$21,600\,G^{0.90}$	$16,100\,G^{0.65}$	
Modulus of rupture, kPa	$111,900\,G^{1.04}$	$115,100\,G^{1.12}$		$176,500\,G^{1.05}$	$168,200\,G^{1.10}$	
Impact bending, height of drop causing complete failure, mm			$2,900\,G^{1.75}$			$2,400\,G^{1.75}$
Compression parallel to grain:						
Modulus of elasticity, MPa	$22,300\,G^{0.92}$	$14,000\,G^{0.55}$		$25,000\,G^{0.91}$	$18,000\,G^{0.63}$	
Maximum crushing strength, kPa	$53,400\,G^{1.02}$	$45,700\,G^{1.02}$		$100,700\,G^{1.04}$	$73,100\,G^{0.83}$	
Shear parallel to grain, kPa	$10,800\,G^{0.72}$	$17,300\,G^{1.20}$		$16,800\,G^{0.86}$	$22,100\,G^{1.15}$	
Compression perpendicular to grain:						
Fiber stress at proportional limit, kPa	$9,400\,G^{1.60}$	$16,400\,G^{2.32}$		$17,500\,G^{1.65}$	$20,130\,G^{2.03}$	
Hardness						
End N			$16,600\,G^{2.25}$			$21,400\,G^{2.25}$
Side, N			$5,200\,G^{2.25}$			$3,770\,G^{2.25}$

[1]The properties and values should be read as equations; for example, modulus of rupture for green wood of softwoods = $16,230\,G^{1.04}$, where G represents the specific gravity based upon weight ovendry and volume green. For the air-dry properties, the specific gravity is based upon the weight ovendry and the volume at 12 percent moisture content.
[2]As reported in USDA Bulletin No. 676, "The Relation of the Shrinkage and Strength Properties of Wood to its Specific Gravity," by J.A. Newlin and T.R.C. Wilson, 1919.

Shape and size of wood pieces are important when considering the effects of temperature. For short-time exposure, the inner parts of a piece of large cross section will not reach the temperature of its surroundings and the immediate effect will be less than for outer parts of the piece. For members stressed in bending, the outer fibers are subjected to the greatest stress and will generally govern the load-carrying capacity; the fact that the inner part is at a lower temperature may not be significant. For extended noncyclic exposures such as girders close to steam pipes, it must be assumed that all parts of the member are subject to permanent strength loss. It is, however, unlikely that wood will reach the daily extremes of temperature of the air around it.

Time Under Load. Handbook data for mechanical properties of wood usually are derived from the results of tests in which the maximum load is reached in about 5 min and are generally referred to as *static* strength values. Higher values are obtained for clear wood loaded at more

Table 4.6. Intersection Moisture Content Values for Selected Species.[1]

Species	M_p, %
Ash, white	24
Birch, yellow	27
Chestnut, American	24
Douglas-fir	24
Hemlock, western	28
Larch, western	28
Pine, loblolly	21
Pine, longleaf	21
Pine, red	24
Redwood	21
Spruce, red	27
Spruce, Sitka	27
Tamarack	24

[1] Intersection moisture content is the point at which mechanical properties begin to change when drying from the green condition.

rapid rates and lower values are obtained for wood loaded at slower rates. For example, the load required to produce failure of a wood member in one second is about 10 percent higher than that obtained in a standard test. Over a wide range of loading rates, the trend is approximately an exponential function of rate as illustrated in Figure 4.4.8.

When first loaded, a wood member initially deforms elastically. If the load is maintained, however, additional time-dependent deformation called *creep* takes place and can continue over a period of years. If loads are sufficiently

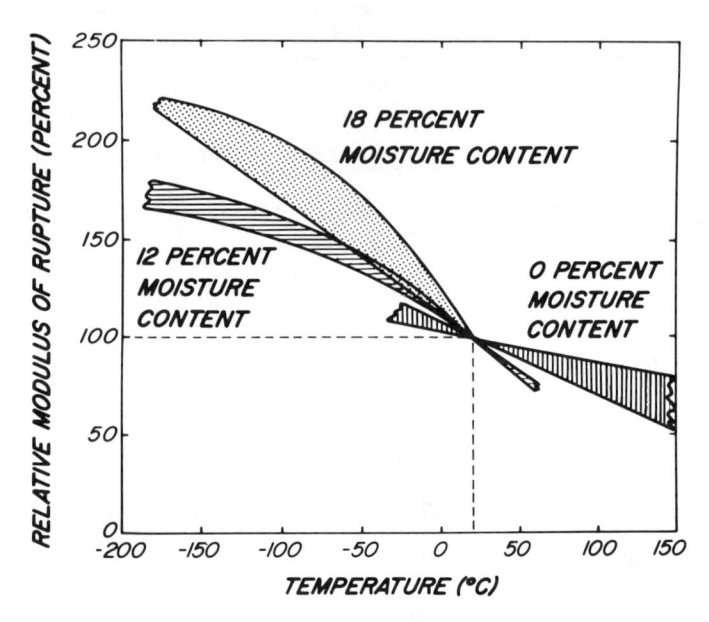

Fig. 4.4.2. The immediate effect of temperature on modulus of rupture in bending at three moisture contents relative to value at 20°C. The plot is a composite of results from several studies. Variability in reported trends is illustrated by the width.

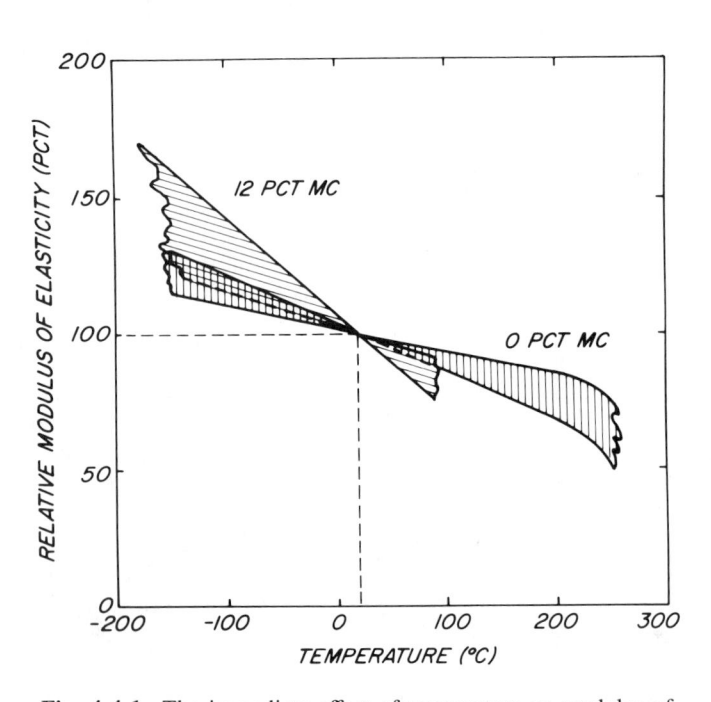

Fig. 4.4.1. The immediate effect of temperature on modulus of elasticity parallel to the grain at two moisture contents relative to value at 20°C. The plot is a composite of results from several studies. Variability in reported trends is illustrated by the width of bands.

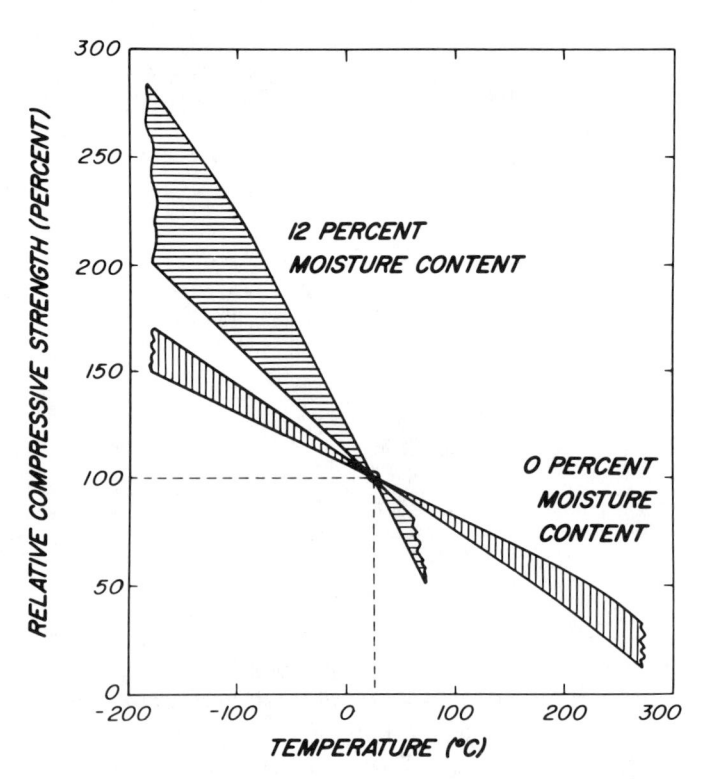

Fig. 4.4.3. The immediate effect of temperature on compressive strength parallel to the grain at two moisture contents relative to value at 20°C. The plot is a composite of results from several studies. Variability of reported trends is illustrated by the width of bands.

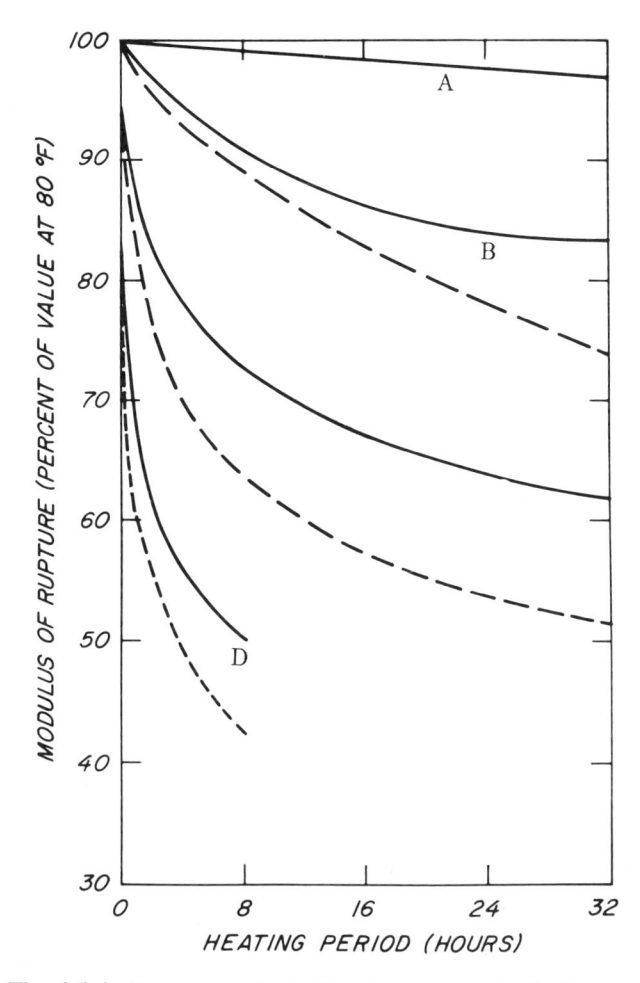

Fig. 4.4.4. Permanent effect of heating in water (solid line) and in steam (dashed line) on the modulus of rupture. A, 200°F (93°C); B, 250°F (121°C); C, 300°F (149°C); D, 350°F (176°C). All data based on tests of Douglas-fir and Sitka spruce tested at room temperature.

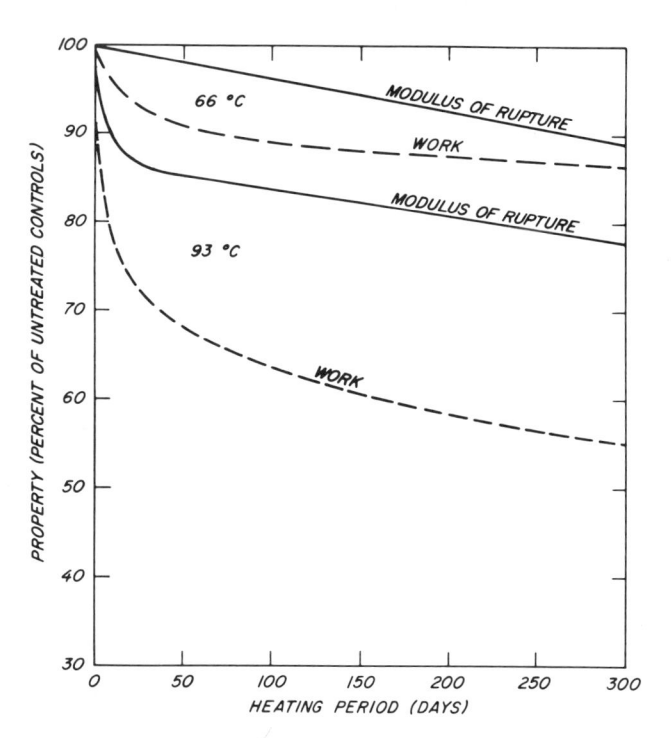

Fig. 4.4.5. Permanent effect of heating in water on work to maximum load and on modulus of rupture. All data based on tests of Douglas-fir and Sitka spruce tested at room temperature.

high, failure will eventually occur. This phenomenon is called *duration of load effect*. For typical design levels and use environments, the deformation due to creep will equal the initial instantaneous elastic deformation over a period of a few years. This is illustrated in Figure 4.4.9. Usual variations in temperature or humidity will cause creep to increase; an increase of 50°F (28°C) in temperature can cause creep to increase two to three times, and green wood may creep five to six times the initial elastic deformation as it dries under load. If this load is removed, an immediate recovery equal to the original elastic deformation will occur, and with time, the recovery will be about half of the creep deformation.

If, instead of controlling load (or stress), a constant deformation is imposed, the initial stress relaxes at a decreasing rate to about 60 to 70 percent of its original value within a few months. The duration of stress (or the time during which a load acts on a member) is important in determining the load that the member can safely carry.

The constant stress that a wood member can carry is approximately an exponential function of time to failure as shown in Figure 4.4.10 where the relationship is a composite of results from studies on small, clear wood specimens conducted at constant temperature and relative humidity. From this figure, it is clear that the load required to cause failure is much smaller than that determined from standard tests. For example, a wood member under bending stress for 10 years may carry only about 60 percent of the load that would cause failure in a few minutes. Conversely, if the duration is very short, the load-carrying capacity may be higher than that determined in the usual test.

Fatigue. The term *fatigue* in engineering is defined as the progressive damage that occurs when a material is subjected to cyclic loading. This loading may be *repeated* when the stresses are always of the same sign (for example, always compression), or *reversed* when the stresses are of alternating sign. If the stresses are high enough and there are enough repetitions, cyclic loadings can cause fatigue failure.

Fatigue life is a term used to define the number of cycles that are sustained before failure. *Fatigue strength*, the maximum stress reached in the stress cycle used to determine fatigue life, is approximately exponentially related to fatigue life. Fatigue strength and fatigue life depend upon other factors as well: frequency of cycling; whether loading is repeated or reversed; range factor (ratio of minimum to maximum stress per cycle); and other factors such as

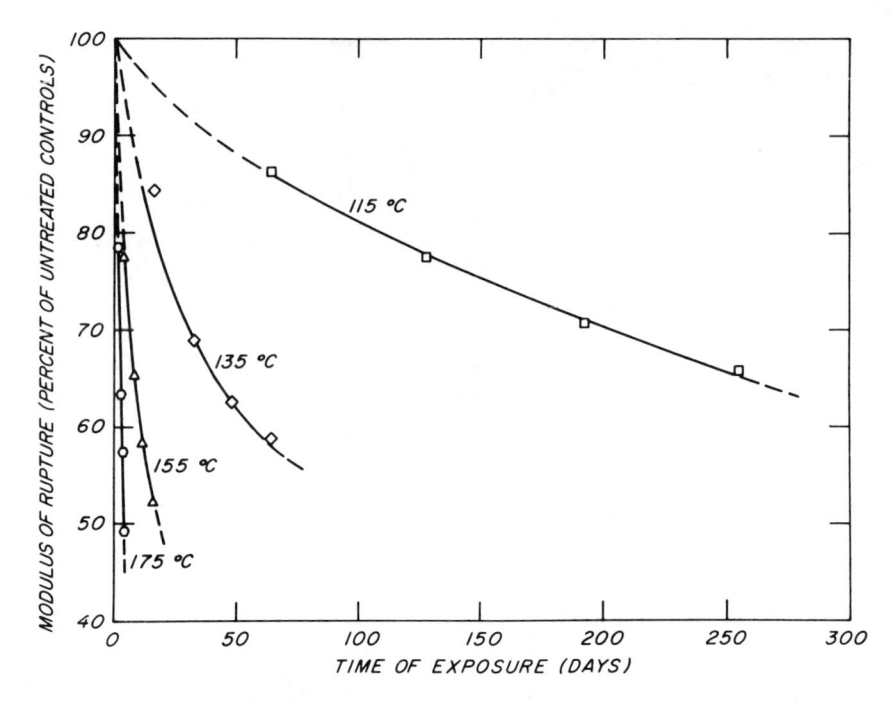

Fig. 4.4.6. Permanent effect of oven heating at four temperatures on the modulus of rupture, based on four softwood and two hardwood species. All tests conducted at room temperature.

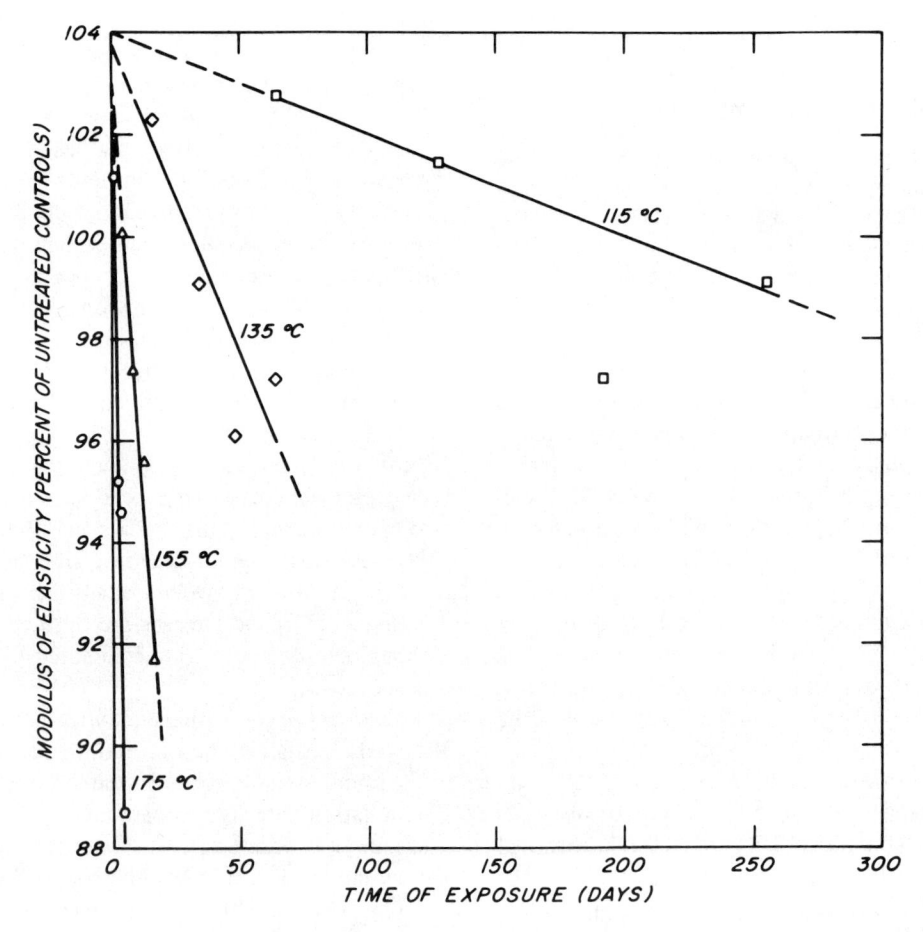

Fig. 4.4.7. Permanent effect of oven heating at four temperatures on modulus of elasticity, based on four softwood and two hardwood species. All tests conducted at room temperature.

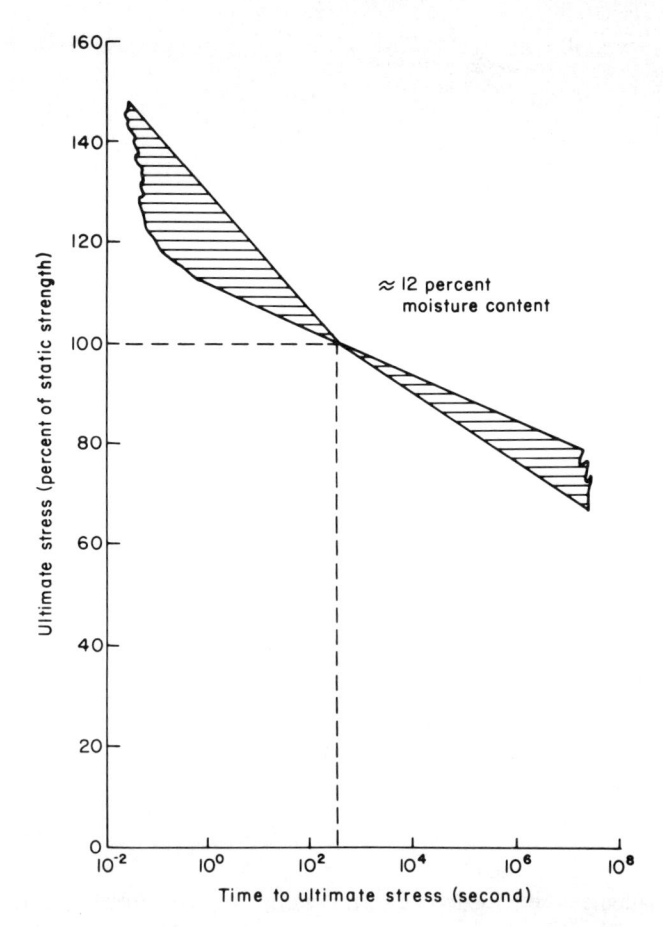

Fig. 4.4.8. Relationship of ultimate stress at short-time loading to that at 5-min loading, based on a composite of results from rate of loading studies on bending, compression, and shear parallel to the grain. Variability in reported trends is indicated by width of band.

temperature, moisture content, and specimen size. Results from several studies of fatigue in wood are summarized in Table 4.7. Positive range ratios imply repeated loading, while negative ratios imply reversed loading.

Chemicals. Effects of chemical solutions on clear wood mechanical properties depend on the specific type of

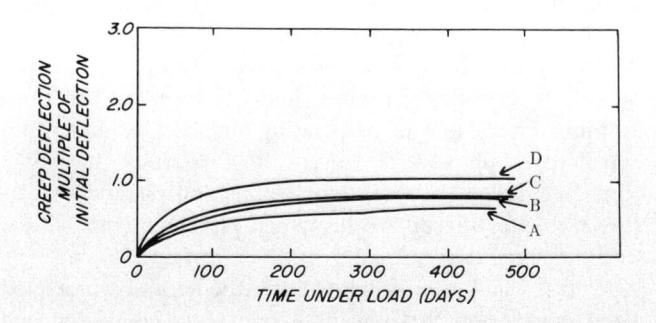

Fig. 4.4.9. An illustration of creep as influenced by four levels of stress: A, 500 lb/in.² (3.5 MPa); B, 1,000 lb/in.² (7 MPa); C, 2,000 lb/in.² (14 MPa); D, 4,000 lb/in.² (28 MPa). (*Adapted from Kingston.*)

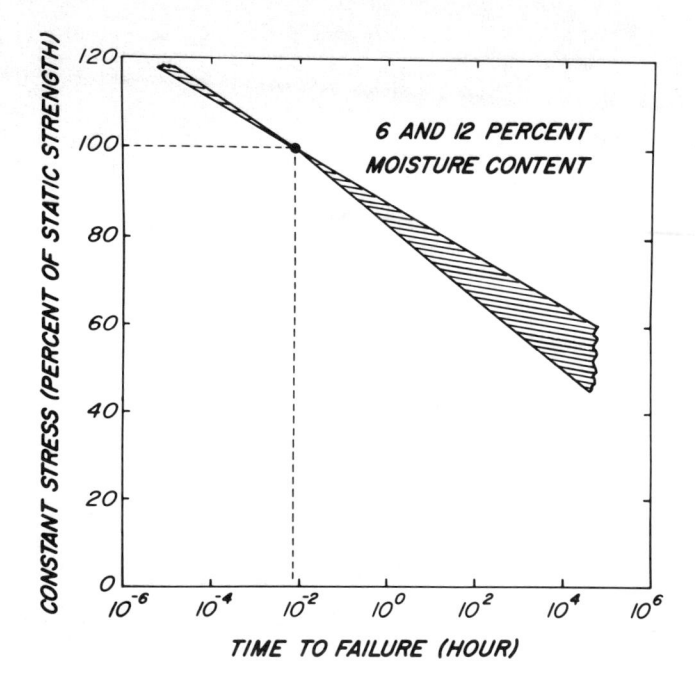

Fig. 4.4.10. Relationship between stress due to constant load and time to failure for small clear wood specimens, based on 28 s duration at 100 percent stress level. The figure is a composite of trends from several studies, mostly dealing with bending but with some on compression parallel to the grain and bending perpendicular to the grain. Variability in reported trends is indicated by the width of band.

chemical. Nonswelling liquids such as petroleum oils or creosote are inert to wood and have no appreciable effect. Properties of wood are lowered by water, alcohol, or other wood-swelling organic liquids because they in essence decrease the specific gravity, even though they do not cause chemical degradation of the wood. Loss of properties in such instances depends largely on the amount of swelling, and this loss is regained when the swelling liquid is removed and the wood returns to its original dimensions. Liquid ammonia markedly reduces strength, but most of the reduction is regained as the ammonia is removed.

Chemical solutions that degrade wood substance have a permanent effect on strength. Following are some generalizations on this point: (1) some species are quite resistant to attack by dilute mineral and organic acids; (2) oxidizing acids such as nitric acid degrade wood more than do nonoxidizing acids; (3) alkaline solutions are more destructive than acidic solutions; and (4) hardwoods are more susceptible to attack by both acids and alkalies than are softwoods.

Wood products are sometimes treated with fire-retardant or preservative salts, usually in water solution, to impart resistance to fire or decay and the wood products are usually kiln-dried after treatment. Preservative chemicals applied in the amounts required for underground or ground contact service generally do not reduce properties except for those related to resistance to shock loads (work to maximum load, height of drop in impact bending, and toughness). Heavy salt treatments for protection in marine environments may

Table 4.7. A Summary of Reported Results on Cyclic Fatigue.[1]

Property	Range Ratio	Cyclic Frequency Hz	Maximum Stress per Cycle, Percentage of Estimated Static Strength	Approximate Fatigue Life, $\times 10^6$ cycles
Bending, clear, straight grain				
Cantilever	0.45	30	45	30
Cantilever	0	30	40	30
Cantilever	−1.0	30	30	30
Center-point	−1.0	40	30	4
Rotational	−1.0	–	28	30
Third-point	0.1	$8\frac{1}{3}$	60	2
Bending, third-point				
Small knots	0.1	$8\frac{1}{3}$	50	2
Clear, 1 : 12 slope of grain	0.1	$8\frac{1}{3}$	50	2
Small knots, 1 : 12 slope of grain	0.1	$8\frac{1}{3}$	40	2
Tension parallel to grain:				
Clear, straight grain	0.1	15	50	30
Clear, straight grain	0	40	60	3.5
Scarf joint	0.1	15	50	30
Finger joint	0.1	15	40	30
Compression parallel to grain, clear, straight grain	0.1	40	75	3.5
Shear parallel to grain, glue laminated	0.1	15	45	30

[1] Starting moisture contents about 12 to 15 percent.

reduce bending strength by 10 percent or more, and shock-resistance properties may be reduced by as much as 50 percent. If drying and treatment processes (temperature and pressure) are not kept within acceptable limits, further loss in mechanical properties may result.

Fire-retardant treatments also affect mechanical properties, with the effects resulting from both the chemicals and the treating and drying processes. Studies have shown that modulus of rupture may be reduced by as much as 20 percent, and work to maximum load and toughness may be reduced by as much as 45 percent.

4.5. PROTECTION OF WOOD

Weathering

Wood exposed to the elements without protection is degraded in several ways: photodegradation by ultraviolet light; leaching, hydrolysis, and swelling by water; and discoloration and degradation by microorganisms. These factors cause changes in color, roughness, checking, and erosion. In general, these factors affect only a very thin layer at the surface of the wood. Their effects on strength are minimal for solid wood but may be more important for bonded products, such as plywood and particleboard, because they may affect the adhesive bonds. Wood siding (weatherboard) or fences may be left to weather naturally, and in fact, some homeowners prefer the appearance of weathered wood siding.

Protection from weathering is usually to maintain or enhance the appearance of the wood surface. Protection is provided basically in two ways: by film-forming finishes or by penetrating finishes. Film-forming finishes include paints and varnishes. Paints are by far the most often used because they are available in a variety of colors and thus offer a range of choice to the homeowner and because they are longer lasting. Varnishes offer an attractive initial appearance because the natural color and grain or figure of the wood shows through (see Sections 5.10 to 5.14).

Film-forming finishes themselves are subject to degradation from effects of shrinkage and swelling of the wood beneath them, ultraviolet (UV) light, water from outside and inside the structure, and certain organisms. All contribute to failure of the finish by cracking, peeling, and blistering, with the natural finishes such as varnish having a much shorter life than good-quality paints properly applied over a well-prepared surface.

Penetrating finishes do not leave a film and are not subject to cracking, peeling, and blistering as are film-forming finishes. The penetrating finishes include water repellents, pigmented penetrating stains (inorganic pigments added to water repellents), and chemical treatments such as preservatives, which protect against weathering to some degree.

Wood, whether finished or unfinished, can be protected from weathering to some degree by care in design and construction and by proper maintenance. Wide roof overhangs, for example, protect exterior walls against summer sunlight and thus reduce the effects of UV light. Roof leaks, poor drainage from roof valleys, and ice dams increase the amount of water passing over the surface of the wood and, as well, admit water into the walls, from which it can work its way out and damage exterior finishes.

Decay

As was discussed in the section on durability, wood is subject to deterioration from the activity of decay fungi. Practically all sapwood has little or no resistance to decay, and resistance of heartwood to decay varies greatly depending upon the species. When the hazard of decay is high, as in foundations, bridges, and other exposed structures, particularly those whose repair or replacement is difficult or costly, protection from decay by treatment with preservative chemicals is necessary.

For the more severe exposures, treatment is commonly carried out by injecting protective chemicals under pressure into the wood. In other instances, more superficial protection may be satisfactory. Window parts, for example, are commonly dipped in a preservative solution for a short period.

The types of preservative chemicals vary greatly. Creosote, for example, is generally used for severe exposures such as piles or utility poles. Creosote is dirty and unpaintable and has a disagreeable odor; thus, it is unsuitable for uses such as residential construction. Combinations of water-soluble chemicals are frequently used, some of which are suitable for uses where a high degree of protection is required. They are, however, clean and paintable. Pentachlorophenol in light solvents or in liquid petroleum gas may be used. Pentachlorophenol in heavier oils would be unsuitable for many architectural uses. As noted above, preservative chemicals in combination with water repellents may be used to protect millwork. Whatever the chemical used, it cannot give optimum protection unless proper amounts of the chemical are carried deeply enough into the wood. Careful control of the treating process is therefore necessary; this is usually provided by competent inspection of the treating process and of the finished product. All preservative chemicals have some degree of toxicity; thus, only chemicals registered by the U.S. Environmental Protection Agency should be used and then only in applications prescribed in the registration and in the manner and at the concentration prescribed. The list of registered chemicals varies from time to time and prospective users should be sure to obtain current information. In some instances, the use of preservative chemicals is limited to people trained in their use.

Fire

In some instances, building codes require that wood products be treated with fire retardants to improve their resistance to the spread of flame. Two methods are generally used to accomplish this. One involves pressure impregnation of the wood with waterborne or organic solvent-base chemicals. The second involves applying fire-retardant coatings to the wood surface. The first is usually more effective and longer lasting. In existing structures, the second offers a practical method to reduce flame spread.

Inorganic salts, including monoammonium and diammonium phosphate, ammonium sulfate, zinc chloride, sodium tetraborate, and boric acid are the chemicals most commonly used for pressure impregnation to impart fire retardancy. They are commonly combined in formulations that develop good fire performance, while retaining acceptable levels in the treated product of such characteristics as hygroscopicity, strength, corrosivity, and machinability. The salts make the treated wood somewhat corrosive, with the possibility of damage to metal fastenings in humid environments. In general, truss plates are not used in salt-treated wood because of the corrosion hazard and the small gauge of the plates. The salts are leachable and thus not suitable for exterior use as in wood shingles or shakes. The salts also are known to cause some loss in wood strength and must be accounted for in engineering design. Water-soluble fire retardants (that become fixed in the wood upon curing) have been developed to meet the need for nonleachable systems. One type involves resins polymerized in the wood after treatment. The second involves graft polymer fire retardants attached to the cellulose. Wood members treated with waterborne chemicals must be redried after treatment before most uses.

4.6. WOOD AND WOOD-BASED PRODUCTS

The number of wood and wood-based products available for use in architectural applications has increased greatly in the past 50 years or so. Lumber is probably the most familiar wood product because of the long time it has been available. Glued-laminated timber and plywood are examples of 20th Century wood products.

Lumber

Lumber is sawed directly from the log, generally to rectangular cross section, and cut to length. It is produced from both softwood and hardwood species. Species with similar properties are commonly produced and marketed as a group under a "commercial species" name. Most lumber is manufactured and graded for quality by standardized rules that make lumber purchasing more or less uniform across the country. Producers of lumber from the same species or group of species commonly form associations and issue rules by which their products are manufactured and graded. These rules limit or prohibit the number, character, and location of features that affect the strength, durability, appearance, or utility of the lumber. Features affecting utility of lumber include knots, checks, pitch pockets, shakes, stain, decay, and sloping grain.

Lumber that is to be used where appearance is important may be free or practically free of knots or other features affecting appearance. Lumber that is intended for structural use may contain knots, cross grain, and other features, but with strict limitations. Stress-graded lumber intended for engineered structures has such features limited in order to permit the assignment of design stresses to the grades.

Lumber for construction purposes is mostly from softwood species. Hardwoods are more commonly found in such applications as millwork, flooring, or furniture.

Softwood Lumber. If softwood lumber is to be marketed as American Standard lumber, the grading rules under which it is produced must conform to the requirements of the National Bureau of Standards (NBS) Voluntary Product Standard PS20-70, American Softwood Lumber Standard [Ref. 4.4]. The rules published by the various rules-writing organizations are reviewed by the Board of Review of the American Lumber Standards Committee for conformance to the overall requirements of PS20-70. Similarly, the allowable design values for structural lumber are reviewed for conformance.

Softwood lumber is classified in several ways:

By intended use—

1. Yard lumber—for ordinary construction and general building purposes
2. Structural lumber—lumber 2 in. or more (more than 50 mm) in nominal thickness and width for uses where design stresses are required
3. Factory and shop lumber—primarily for remanufacturing purposes

By manufacturing classifications—

1. Rough lumber—has not been dressed (surfaced) but has been sawed, edged, and trimmed at least to the extent of showing saw marks in the wood on the four longitudinal surfaces of each piece over the full length
2. Dressed (surfaced)—has been dressed by a planing machine (to attain smoothness of surface and uniformity of size) on one side (S1S), two sides (S2S), one edge (S1E), two edges (S2E), or a combination of sides and edges (S1S1E, S1S2E, S2S1E, S4S)
3. Worked lumber—in addition to being dressed, has been matched, shiplapped, or patterned
   (a) Matched—worked with a tongue on one edge and a groove on the opposite edge to provide a close tongue-and-groove joint by fitting the pieces together; may be end-matched, with tongue and groove on the ends also
   (b) Shiplapped—has been rabbeted on both edges to provide a close lapped joint by fitting two pieces together
   (c) Patterned—shaped to a pattern or to molded form in addition to being dressed, matched, or shiplapped or any combination of these workings

By size—

1. Nominal size[1]
   (a) Boards—less than 2 in. (50 mm) in nominal thickness and 2 or more in. in nominal width; if less than 6 in. (150 mm) in nominal width, may be classified as "strips"
   (b) Dimension—from 2 in. to 4 in. (50 to 100 mm) in nominal thickness and 2 or more in. in nominal width; may be classified using terms such as framing, joists, planks, rafters, studs, or small timbers
   (c) Timbers—5 in. (125 mm) or more nominally in least dimension; may be classified by using terms such as beams, stringers, posts, caps, sills, girders, or purlins
2. Roughdry size—minimum roughdry thickness of finish, common boards, and dimension of sizes 1 in. (25 mm) or more in nominal thickness not less than $\frac{1}{8}$ in. (3 mm) thicker than the corresponding minimum finished dry thickness, except that 20 percent of a shipment may be not less than $\frac{3}{32}$ in. (2 mm) thicker than the corresponding minimum finished dry thickness; minimum roughdry widths of finish, common boards, and dimension not less than $\frac{1}{8}$ in. (3 mm) wider than the corresponding minimum finished dry width
3. Dressed sizes—not less than the minimum sizes specified in Table 4.8

As already mentioned, the grades established for construction lumber by rules-writing agencies will prohibit some characteristics (decay, for example); will limit some material characteristics (such as knots, cross grain, and shakes); and will limit manufacturing imperfection (such as planer skip and torn grain). Degree of seasoning (moisture content) may be specified. Sometimes the provisions of the rules and the grade names differ among rules-writing agencies. For detailed information on grades, specific rules should be consulted.

Grades of dimension lumber, however, are covered in the National Grading Rule for Dimension Lumber, with each grade having the same name and the same requirements regardless of species. Design allowables, however, vary with the species or group of species from which the dimension lumber is produced according to the clear wood mechanical properties of that species or group.

Members in timber sizes are graded as "beam and stringer" or "post and timber." Beam and stringer grades are generally used as bending members, while post and timber grades are more often used as columns and as bearing timbers.

A large proportion of lumber grading is done visually;

---

[1]Relations between nominal and actual sizes are shown in Table 4.8.

Table 4.8. American Standard Lumber Sizes for Stress-Graded and Non-stress-Graded Lumber for Construction.[1,2]

Item	Thickness, in. Nominal	Minimum dressed Dry	Minimum dressed Green	Face Width, in. Nominal	Minimum dressed Dry	Minimum dressed Green
Boards	1	$\frac{3}{4}$	25/32	2	$1\frac{1}{2}$	$1\frac{9}{16}$
	$1\frac{1}{4}$	1	$1\frac{1}{32}$	3	$2\frac{1}{2}$	$2\frac{9}{16}$
	$1\frac{1}{2}$	$1\frac{1}{4}$	$1\frac{9}{32}$	4	$3\frac{1}{2}$	$3\frac{9}{16}$
				5	$4\frac{1}{2}$	$4\frac{5}{8}$
				6	$5\frac{1}{2}$	$5\frac{5}{8}$
				7	$6\frac{1}{2}$	$6\frac{5}{8}$
				8	$7\frac{1}{4}$	$7\frac{1}{2}$
				9	$8\frac{1}{4}$	$8\frac{1}{2}$
				10	$9\frac{1}{4}$	$9\frac{1}{2}$
				11	$10\frac{1}{4}$	$10\frac{1}{2}$
				12	$11\frac{1}{4}$	$11\frac{1}{2}$
				14	$13\frac{1}{4}$	$13\frac{1}{2}$
				16	$15\frac{1}{4}$	$15\frac{1}{2}$
Dimension	2	$1\frac{1}{2}$	$1\frac{9}{16}$	2	$1\frac{1}{2}$	$1\frac{9}{16}$
	$2\frac{1}{2}$	2	$2\frac{1}{16}$	3	$2\frac{1}{2}$	$2\frac{9}{16}$
	3	$2\frac{1}{2}$	$2\frac{9}{16}$	4	$3\frac{1}{2}$	$3\frac{9}{16}$
	$3\frac{1}{2}$	3	$3\frac{1}{16}$	5	$4\frac{1}{2}$	$4\frac{5}{8}$
	4	$3\frac{1}{2}$	$3\frac{9}{16}$	6	$5\frac{1}{2}$	$5\frac{5}{8}$
	$4\frac{1}{2}$	4	$4\frac{1}{16}$	8	$7\frac{1}{4}$	$7\frac{1}{2}$
				10	$9\frac{1}{4}$	$9\frac{1}{2}$
				12	$11\frac{1}{4}$	$11\frac{1}{2}$
				14	$13\frac{1}{4}$	$13\frac{1}{2}$
				16	$15\frac{1}{4}$	$15\frac{1}{2}$
Timbers	5 and greater		$\frac{1}{2}$ less than nominal	5 and greater		$\frac{1}{2}$ less than nominal

[1] Nominal sizes in the table are used for convenience. No inference should be drawn that they represent actual sizes.
[2] There are no metric equivalent sizes for lumber in the United States. In Canada a straight soft conversion is used. For example, the metric equivalent for nominal 2- by 8-in. dimension lumber is 38.10 by 184.15 mm.

that is, the size, position, and effects of various factors are judged by eye, generally as pieces of lumber move rapidly past an inspector. Mechanical grading, or machine stress rating (MSR), introduced early in 1960, is based on a relation between a strength property and the modulus of elasticity of a member. Usually, the modulus of elasticity is evaluated by measuring the load corresponding to a fixed deflection imposed by a set of rollers through which the piece is passed. Some visual requirements are included in the rules; most important are limitations on the size of edge knots.

Allowable design stresses for visually graded and MSR dimension lumber, beams and stringers, and posts and timbers are given in the National Design Specification [Ref. 4.5].

Factory and shop lumber is of no direct interest to the architect. Because factory and shop lumber is intended for remanufacture into other wood products, the principal grading criterion is an estimate of the number of cuttings of given sizes and qualities that can be obtained from the lumber. The architect has a direct interest in the products made from these cuttings (such as windows and doors), not in the lumber itself.

Hardwood Lumber. Little hardwood lumber is used for structural purposes in North America and Europe. Hardwood lumber is classified in several ways but is graded mostly for cuttings, as are factory and shop softwood lumber. Some material goes directly into products such as flooring. Hardwoods are graded under the rules of the National Hardwood Lumber Association, the National Dimension Manufacturers Association, the Maple Flooring Manufacturers Association, and the National Oak Flooring Manufacturers Association. The term *dimension* as used here should not be confused with the same term used for softwoods and described in the section on softwoods. For hardwoods, the term *dimension parts* signifies stock that is produced in specific thicknesses, widths, and lengths, or multiples thereof.

Glued-Laminated (Glulam) Timber

Glulam is an assembly of two or more layers (laminations) of lumber bonded together with an adhesive and with the grain direction of all layers approximately parallel. It may be either straight or curved, for use as an arch, as a column, as a beam, as a truss chord, or as a member of a dome framework. Laminations are not generally over 2 in. (50 mm) in nominal thickness ($1\frac{1}{2}$ in. (38 mm) actual), and are usually thinner in curved members. Available lengths of lumber do not limit the lengths of laminations because long laminations may be produced by finger jointing available lengths of lumber end to end. For exterior uses such as bridges and waterfront structures, the adhesives used in glulam manufacture must be waterproof and commonly are of the phenol-resorcinol type, which when properly applied and cured, are not affected by moisture or high temperature. For interior applications, casein adhesives may be used, but it is rather common practice to use waterproof adhesives for all members.

Glulam members generally are fabricated in a shop in order to control quality. Size limitations thus are generally set by limitations in the manufacturing process, by transportation problems such as bridge clearances, and if preservative treatment is required, by the size of the treating facilities. However, arches spanning 300 ft (90 m) and simple beams with spans of 150 ft (45 m) and depths of 7 ft (2 m) are in service. Laminated members have been used in dome frameworks with clear spans exceeding 500 ft (150 m).

If glulam members are to be used under conditions that could result in a moisture content higher than about 20 percent, the wood should be treated with approved preservative chemicals and only wet-use adhesives should be used. It is known that some oil-borne preservatives, besides providing protection from fungi and insects, also retard moisture changes at the surface of the wood and thus inhibit checking. If the size and shape of the members permit, glulam timbers can be treated with some preservatives after gluing but penetration perpendicular to the glue joints will be distinctly retarded at the first glueline. Treatment of large glulam timbers with waterborne preservatives after gluing is not recommended because of difficulties in subsequent drying and associated checking. It is general practice, therefore, to treat the individual laminations.

American National Standard for Wood Products, Structural Glued Laminated Timber, ANSI/AITC A190.1 [Ref. 4.6], is the national standard for this product. The American Institute of Timber Construction (AITC) sponsored and contributed in a significant way to the development of the standard. Its members manufacture, fabricate, assemble, erect, and design wood structural systems and related wood products for construction. The Institute develops and maintains standards and technical literature related to the design, manufacture, and construction of glulam structures.

The ANSI standard requires strict quality control for glulam manufactured in the United States. Assurance that the products conform to the requirements of the standard requires continuing inspection and evaluation of plant procedures, qualification of bonded joints, and maintenance of records. Plant quality control that meets specific qualification requirements outlined in the standard is monitored by a third-party inspection and testing agency. AITC operates such an oversight agency as its Inspection Bureau. It is evident that substantial effort is expended to insure the production of high-quality products.

There are no glulam "grades" in the sense outlined earlier for lumber. Because glulam is made by bonding together a number of laminations of lumber, higher grades of lumber are often placed in more highly stressed portions of the cross section and laminations of lower quality in portions less highly stressed. Load-carrying ability is a function not only of the characteristics of the constituent laminations but of how they are combined in the final member. Thus, glulam members are identified by a symbol that represents the combination of lumber grades used in manufacturing the member.

Some of these combinations are designed specifically for members intended for use as beams or girders, while others are intended for use under axial rather than bending stress. Both types may be used under either type of loading but may require lower allowable stresses than when used in the primary function. It is advisable and more efficient to use the member in the manner originally intended.

Glulam members are essentially not limited in cross section or length. Standard finished widths are established having a range from $2\frac{1}{8}$ to $14\frac{1}{4}$ in. (54 to 360 mm) for members made from western species and from 3 to $10\frac{1}{2}$ in. (75 to 270 mm) for members made from the southern pines. There are minor width differences between the two species within the ranges. Member depths are multiples of lamination thickness; that is, a 12-lamination member made of $1\frac{1}{2}$-in.- (38-mm-) thick lumber would have a depth of 18 in. (450 mm). Normally, sizes given for glulam members are actual, not nominal.

Where members for some reason cannot be made in the full length required, partial lengths may be fabricated and end joined by a mechanical connection. For example, an arch may be of such form and size that it cannot be transported from manufacturer to construction site as a single unit. In such a case a hinge may be used at a central point, or a moment-resisting connection may be used. In the case of a member spanning several supports, if the spanning member cannot be made as a single, continuous beam, it may be possible to use beams that cantilever past supports with another (simple) beam supported on the ends of the cantilevers.

Laminated Veneer Lumber

Laminated veneer lumber (LVL) is a material made by the parallel lamination of veneers into thicknesses common to solid sawn lumber ($\frac{3}{4}$ to $2\frac{1}{2}$ in.; 19 to 64 mm). Generally, veneers $\frac{1}{10}$ to $\frac{1}{8}$ in. (2.5 to 3.2 mm) thick are hot pressed, with phenol-formaldehyde adhesive, into lengths from 8 to 60 ft. (2.4 to 18 m) or more. End joints between adjacent sheets of veneer in a layer are staggered to avoid large strength-reducing defects. Commonly, these end joints are simply butted or overlapped to provide load transfer, or scarf joints may be used. Eight-foot panels would have no end joints, and a number of such panels can be scarf jointed together to produce longer elements. The veneers can be visually graded as for PS1 [Ref. 4.7] veneers, except that lack of a cross grain requirement limits the effectiveness of this method for assessing strength characteristics. Some producers segregate veneer into various stiffness classes by ultrasonic methods, which reduces variability in mechanical properties of the finished product.

No national standard exists for LVL manufacture. Manufacturers have individually obtained approvals for their products from the model building codes for use in structural applications. One continuous-length product (up to 80 ft (24 m) long) has three grades—1.8E, 2.0E, and 2.2E corresponding to the modulus of elasticity ($\times 10^6$ lb/in.^{2} (6,890 MPa)) associated with each grade. Code approval for this product covers thicknesses of $\frac{3}{4}$ to $2\frac{1}{2}$ in. (19 to 64 mm) and member depths from $2\frac{1}{2}$ to 24 in. (64 to 600 mm). Laminated veneer lumber manufactured in panel lengths may be end-jointed to provide longer stock and is approved in two grades: (1) with end joints between panel lengths, a flexural stress of 2,600 lb/in.^{2} (17,900 kPa) is allowed and (2) for unjointed material, an allowable of 3,000 lb/in.^{2} (20,700 kPa) is allowed.

Dispersion of cross grain and compression wood among the veneers in a cross section reduces the amount of warp as compared with sawn lumber, and splitting is minimized. Treatment with preservatives and fire retardants after layup is enhanced by the lathe checks in the veneers and by end joints between veneers.

Laminated veneer lumber is used in a variety of applications. Cut to proper width, it may, for example, be used in parallel-chord trusses, in I-beams using LVL as flanges to which plywood or structural flakeboard webs are bonded into a machined slot in the flanges, for wide floor joists, for large window and door headers, and for long-span beams. Laminated veneer lumber is being used in scaffold planks because of the uniformity of its properties and its resistance to splitting. Other limited uses include ladder rails and special tension lamination grades for glulam.

Round Timbers

Round timbers (poles, piles, and logs) represent efficient use of the forest resource. Round timbers require a minimum amount of processing from harvesting the tree to marketing a structural product. Poles and piles are debarked or peeled, seasoned, and often treated with preservatives prior to use. Construction logs are usually cut to specific shapes to facilitate construction.

The architectural applications of round timbers (construction poles, piles, and construction logs) require straightness. For construction poles and piles, strength is an important factor; thus, such things as number and size of knots and slope of cross grain are limited. Strength, however, is generally not an important factor for construction logs. Standards and specifications for requirements of round timbers applicable in the United States are shown in Table 4.9.

Resistance to decay is important in most applications of round timbers because of their exposure to hazardous conditions. Thus poles and piles generally require preservative treatment, even those made from species with natural resistance to decay. Temporary piles, piles in fresh water permanently below the permanent water level, and construction logs, however, may not need treatment if their natural decay resistance is high. Any construction logs in ground contact should be pressure treated, and logs within two or three levels above a concrete foundation should be brush treated with a waterborne salt solution.

Poles function as both foundation and wall systems for agricultural and storage buildings (Fig. 14.4.3) and sometimes are used in residences to perform the same functions. In some constructions, posts (short poles) may serve as foundation support for a platform on which the rest of the structure has conventional framing.

Log homes are no longer limited to primitive summer cottages, but may be of substantial size (Fig. 14.4.1). A number of volume builders construct log homes. The logs forming the walls may be machined to any of a variety of cross-sectional forms. The forms of the vertical faces of the logs reflect aesthetic considerations, while the

Table 4.9. Standards and Specifications for Round Timbers.

	Material Requirements	Preservative Treatment	Engineering Design Stresses Procedures	Design values
Construction poles	ANSI O 5.1[1]	TT-W-571 AWPA C 23[2]	ASTM D 3200[3]	ASAE EP 388[4]
Piles	ASTM D 25	TT-W-571 AWPA C1, C3	ASTM D 2899	NDS[5]
Construction logs	(See material supplier)	—	ASTM D 3957	(See material supplier)

[1] American National Standards Institute.
[2] American Wood-Preserver's Association.
[3] American Society for Testing and Materials.
[4] American Society of Agricultural Engineers.
[5] National Design Specifications.

horizontal surfaces reflect thermal considerations. The exterior surfaces of the logs are generally rounded, whereas the interior surfaces may be either flat or rounded. The interface between logs is machined to form an interlocking joint.

Species that can be used in round form are many, but are generally softwoods. The southern pines (principally loblolly, longleaf, shortleaf, and slash) account for a high percentage of the poles treated with preservatives in the United States. They generally have a thick and easily treated sapwood, favorable strength properties and form, and are readily available in lengths that would be required for use in pole buildings. Douglas-fir is used throughout the United States for transmission poles in utility systems and in the Pacific Coast region for building poles. When properly treated, Douglas-fir poles are expected to have the same serviceability as treated southern pines. Western redcedar poles are primarily used for utility lines but could be used for pole buildings. Lodgepole pine and western larch have limited use in building construction.

Appearance Products

Completion of a construction project usually depends on the variety of lumber items available in finished or semifinished form. The following items often may be stocked in only a few species and finishes, or may be stocked in limited sizes depending on the yards.

Finish. Finish boards usually are available in a local yard in one or two species principally in grade C&BTR. Redwood and cedar have different grade designations. Grades such as Clear Heart, A, or B are used in cedar; Clear All Heart, Clear, and Select are typical redwood grades. Finish boards are usually a nominal 1 in. (25 mm) thick, dressed two sides to $\frac{3}{4}$ in. (19 mm). The widths usually stocked are nominal 2 to 12 in. (51 to 300 mm) in even-numbered inches.

Siding. Siding, as the name implies, is intended specifically to cover exterior walls. Beveled siding is ordinarily stocked only in white pine, ponderosa pine, western redcedar, cypress, or redwood. Drop siding, also known as rustic siding or barn siding, is usually stocked in the same species as beveled siding. Siding may be stocked as B&BTR or C&BTR, except in western redcedar where Clear, A, and B may be available and redwood where Clear All Heart and Clear will be found. Vertical grain (VG) is sometimes a part of the grade designation. Drop siding sometimes is stocked also in sound knotted C and D grades of the southern pines, Douglas-fir, and hemlock. Drop siding may be dressed and matched, or shiplapped.

Flooring. Flooring is made chiefly from hardwoods, such as oak and maple, and from the harder softwood species, such as Douglas-fir, western larch, and southern pines. At least one softwood and one hardwood often are stocked. Flooring is usually nominal 1 in. (25 mm) thick. Thicker flooring is available for heavy-duty floors. Thinner flooring is available especially for recovering old floors. Vertical- and flat-grained (also called quartersawed and plainsawed) flooring is manufactured from both softwoods and hardwoods. Vertical-grained flooring shrinks and swells less than does flat-grained flooring, is more uniform in texture, wears more uniformly, and its joints do not open as much.

Softwood flooring is usually available in B&BTR grade, C Select, or D Select. The chief grades in maple are Clear No. 1 and No. 2. The grades in quartersawed oak are Clear and Select, and in plainsawed Clear, Select, and No. 1 Common. Quartersawed hardwood flooring has the same advantages as vertical-grained softwood flooring. In addition, the silver or flaked grain of quartersawed flooring is frequently preferred to the figure of plainsawed flooring.

Casing and Base. Casing and base are standard items in the more important softwoods and are stocked by most yards in at least one species. The chief grade, B&BTR, is designed to meet the requirements of interior trim for dwellings. Many casing and base patterns are dressed to $\frac{11}{16}$ by $2\frac{1}{4}$ in. (17 by 57 mm); other sizes used include $\frac{9}{16}$ by 3, $3\frac{1}{4}$, and $3\frac{1}{2}$ in. (14 by 76, 83, and 89 mm). Hardwoods, such as oak and birch, to be used for the same purposes may be carried in stock in the retail yard or may be obtained on special order.

Shingles and Shakes. Shingles that are usually available are sawn from western redcedar, northern white-cedar, and redwood. The shingle grades for western redcedar are No. 1, No. 2, and No. 3; for northern white-cedar, Extra, Clear, 2nd Clear, Clearwall, and Utility; for redwood, No. 1, No. 2 VG, and No. 2 MG.

Shingles that are all heartwood give greater resistance to decay than do shingles that contain sapwood. Edge-grained shingles are less likely to warp and split than are flat-grained shingles; thick-butted shingles less likely than thin-butted shingles; and narrow shingles less likely than wide shingles. The standard thicknesses of thin-butted shingles are described as $4/2$, $5/2\frac{1}{4}$, and $5/2$ (four shingles to 2 in. (50 mm) of butt thickness, five shingles to $2\frac{1}{4}$ in. (57 mm) of butt thickness, and five shingles to 2 in. (50 mm) of butt thickness). Lengths may be 16, 18, or 24 in. (400, 450, or 600 mm). Random widths and specified widths ("dimension" shingles) are available in western redcedar, redwood, and baldcypress.

Shingles are usually packed four bundles to the square. A square of shingles will cover 100 ft^2 (9.3 m^2) of roof area when the shingles are applied at standard weather exposures.

Shakes are handsplit or handsplit and resawn from western redcedar. Shakes are of a single grade and must be 100 percent clear. Handsplit and resawn shakes are graded from the split face. Handsplit shakes are graded from the best face. Shakes must be 100 percent heartwood. The standard thickness of shakes ranges from $\frac{3}{8}$ to $1\frac{1}{4}$ in. (10 to 30 mm). Lengths are 18 and 24 in. (450 to 600 mm), and a 15-in. (380 mm) "Starter-Finish Course" length.

Structural-Use Panels: Reconstituted Wood

Structural-use panels is a term used to identify a class of wood-based panel products used for construction and industrial applications. The structural wood panel products industry's primary market is the light-frame construction industry. Panel products are shipped to suppliers and contractors for onsite assembly of residential and commercial structures or to manufacturers of factory built homes. These wood panel products are commodities manufactured and distributed in standard sizes and grades [Ref. 4.8]. The structural panel products include plywood, waferboard, oriented strandboard, and veneer/particle composite panels.

Plywood. Plywood is a glued wood panel product made up of relatively thin layers of veneer with the grain direction of adjacent layers at right angles. Or plywood may be made up of veneers in combination with a core of lumber or reconstituted wood. Most plywood constructions have an odd number of layers to maintain balance and thus dimensional stability. In some instances, one or more layers may be made with two plies of veneer having their grain directions parallel.

Two broad classes of plywood are made. One, covered by Product Standard PS 1, covers construction and industrial plywood [Ref. 4.7] and the second, American National Standard ANSI/HPMA HP, covers hardwood and decorative plywood [Ref. 4.9]. Most structural uses are served by plywood made in accordance with PS 1, while paneling and other decorative applications are served by plywood made in accordance with ANSI/HPMA HP.

Construction and industrial plywood includes both appearance grades and engineered grades, together with several types. The term *type* refers to resistance to moisture, which is a function of the adhesive used and the veneer grade. *Exterior type*, for example, will retain its glue bond when repeatedly wetted and dried or otherwise subjected to permanent outdoor exposure. It has a minimum veneer grade of C in any ply and is bonded with a waterproof adhesive. Three levels of adhesive bond durability are included in the *interior type* for PS 1 panels: (1) *interior*—bonded with interior adhesives and intended only for interior applications; (2) *exposure 2*—bonded with an intermediate adhesive and intended for protected construction and industrial uses where moderate delay in providing protection may be expected or conditions of high humidity or water leaks may exist; (3) *exposure 1*—bonded with waterproof adhesives and intended for protected construction and industrial uses where protection against moisture during long construction delays or conditions of similar severity, such as pressure preservative treatment, are involved. Most sheathing, such as C-D, is rated exposure 1.

All construction and industrial grades of plywood have limitations: on knots and other factors in the veneers; on constructions, including veneer thicknesses, number of layers, veneer grades; and on species groups permitted in various plies through the thickness. These limitations permit assignment of allowable design stresses. Engineered grades include Structural I, Plyform, 2-4-1, C-C EXT, and C-D. Grademarks on plywood panels suitable for subfloors, roof sheathing, and the like may include span ratings, which indicate the distance between supports (floor joists or roof rafters or trusses) on which the panel may be safely used. For example, a rating of 32/16 indicates that the panel may be safely used as roof sheathing with rafters or trusses spaced at 32 in. (810 mm) and as subfloor over joists or trusses spaced at 16 in. (405 mm). A rating of 24/0 indicates that the panel may be safely used as roof sheathing over supports spaced at 24 in. (610 mm) but that it may not be used as subfloor. Decorative grades of construction and industrial plywood have similar requirements but have less structural capacity if sanded thinner.

Hardwood and decorative plywood finds only limited structural use, and that mainly in marine applications. Like construction plywood, it is produced in several types; Technical (exterior), Type I (exterior), Type II (interior), and Type III (interior). Technical and Type I are fully waterproof, Type II is water resistant, and Type III is moisture resistant. Veneer characteristics and panel constructions are specified for each type. Both hardwood and softwood veneers may be used in ANSI/HPMA HP plywood. The same is true of construction and industrial plywood, although hardwoods are not commonly used for those products.

Waferboard and Oriented Strandboard. Waferboard and oriented strandboard (OSB) are made from flakes or strands of wood that are produced directly from the log. This differentiates them from industrial particleboards, which are produced from mill residue. Flakes and strands are much larger than particles from typical mill residue. The boards are commonly made from low-density species such as aspen or pine, and are bonded with an exterior-type adhesive, basically phenolic resins or the newer class of isocyanate resins.

Waferboard and oriented strandboard differ in the shape of the flake and the orientation of the flake in the board. The flakes in waferboard are referred to as wafers, are more or less square, and range from 20 to 50 mm on a side. The flakes are uniformly distributed across the board in a random orientation.

In oriented strandboard, the flakes are called strands, which are rectangular in cross section with the length along the grain three to five times the width. Strands are typically 30 to 60 mm long and 10 to 25 mm in width. The oriented strandboard is formed in a mat of three to five layers with the strands in each layer aligned in a direction at right angles to those in adjacent layers, much as the veneers of plywood. The bending properties of the oriented strandboard in the alignment direction are generally superior to those of the randomly oriented waferboard. The properties are highly dependent on the manufacturing process used to make the board.

Waferboards and oriented strandboards are finding increasing use in light-frame construction for applications usually dominated by plywood. Among these applications are wall and roof sheathing, single-layer flooring, and underlayment. Waferboards and oriented strandboards have been approved by some codes for siding applied either over sheathing or nailed directly to the studs. Exterior ceilings, soffits, and interior walls or ceilings in light-frame construction are other areas of use. In nonresidential construction, waferboards and oriented strandboards may be used for sheathing/siding of farm structures, for industrial packaging, for crates, and for pallet decks.

Veneer/Particle Composite Panels. Veneer/particle composite panels are made with veneer faces bonded to a core layer made from oriented strands or randomly oriented particles. Sometimes referred to as COM-PLY, veneer/particle composite panels are marketed as a plywood product and are considered to be interchangeable with construction grades of plywood. Thicknesses of $\frac{3}{8}$ to $\frac{1}{2}$ in. (9.5 to 13 mm) are used for sheathing, and thicknesses up to $1\frac{1}{8}$ in. (29 mm) have been produced for single-layer floors. The performance standard for structural-use panels sponsored by the American Plywood Association covers this material as well as plywood, waferboard, and oriented strandboard [Ref. 4.8].

Particle- and Fiber-Based Panel Products

This group of panel products is based on wood that has been broken down into particles, fibers, or fiber bundles and then put back together by special forms of manufacture into panels of relatively large size and moderate thickness. Many if not all may play a role in construction. These products may be separated into different groups and subgroups based in part on product density and in part on intended use.

Fiberboard. Fiberboard is a broad term for a homogeneous panel made from lignocellulose fibers (usually wood or bagasse) that has been interfelted and consolidated into homogeneous panels with a density between 10 and 31 lb/ft^3 (160 to 500 kg/m^3). Sometimes ingredients other than wood or bagasse may be incorporated to impart specific physical properties. Fiberboard is dried in an oven, but it is not consolidated under heat and pressure during manufacture.

Insulation board usually has a density of less than 15 lb/ft^3 (240 kg/m^3). Sizes from 2 by 4 ft (0.61 by 1.2 m) up to 4 by 8 ft (1.2 by 2.4 m) are available. This material is normally used for roof insulation where R-values are determined by thickness and density. One-half-inch- (13-mm-) thick panels are laminated to gain thicknesses as great as 4 in. (100 mm).

Sheathing is an important use for fiberboard and is produced in three forms: regular density, intermediate density, and nail-base. The first has a density of about 18 lb/ft^3 (290 kg/m^3). It is made in 2- by 8-ft (0.61- by 2.4-m) or 4- by 8-ft (1.2- by 2.4-m) panels and in thicknesses of $\frac{1}{2}$ or $\frac{25}{32}$ in. (13 or 20 mm). The narrower panels, when used as sheathing, are generally applied with the long dimension horizontal, while the wider panels are usually applied with the long dimension vertical. When the regular density material is applied vertically, racking resistance requirements for residential walls are usually met, but $\frac{1}{2}$-in. (13-mm) panels usually require additional bracing when panels of either thickness are applied horizontally. Intermediate density sheathing usually has a density of about 22 lb/ft^3 (352 kg/m^3). It is produced only in the $\frac{1}{2}$-in. (13-mm) thickness but will meet residential racking resistance requirements. Nail-base is about 25 lb/ft^3 (400 kg/m^3). Nail-base sheathing has sufficient nail-holding capability to allow siding to be nailed directly to it with special annular-grooved nails. With other sheathing grades, the siding must be nailed into framing members or other backup.

Ceiling tiles and lay-in panels are also important uses for fiberboard. These tiles and panels generally have a factory-applied paint finish for decoration and to improve resistance to flame spread. When perforated or formed with special fissures or other sound traps, they reduce sound reflectance. *Ceiling tiles* are generally 12 by 12 in. (0.30 by 0.30 m) or 12 by 24 in. (0.30 by 0.61 m) in size and $\frac{1}{2}$ in. (13 mm) in thickness. Edges may be square or tongued-and-grooved. They may by applied to nailing strips with nails, staples, or special fastenings, or may be applied directly to the ceiling surface with an adhesive. *Lay-in ceiling panels* are typically 24 by 48 in. (0.61 by 1.2 m), at least $\frac{1}{2}$ in. (13 mm) thick, and are installed in metal tees and angles in a suspended ceiling system.

Other forms of fiberboard are manufactured for specific purposes. Sound deadening board is used in walls to control sound transmission. Building board serves as a base for interior finishes. Insulating formboard is used as a permanent form for poured-in-place gypsum or light weight concrete roofs. Shingle backer serves as an undercourse for wood or asbestos cement shingles. Insulating roof deck serves as a roof decking for open-beamed ceiling construction. Insulating wallboard is a general-purpose product used for decorative wall and ceiling coverings.

Hardboard. Hardboard is a generic term for a panel manufactured from interfelted lignocellulose fibers that are consolidated under heat and pressure to a density of 31 lb/ft^3 (500 kg/m^3) or more. Other materials may be added to the fibers to improve specific properties. About 65 percent of the hardboard manufactured is used as the base for prefinished paneling and siding. An additional 25 percent is for industrial uses, including cut-to-size and molded products.

Medium- and high-density hardboard 31 to 50 lb/ft^3

(500 to 800 kg/m^3) and 50 lb/ft^3 (500 kg/m^3) or more may be produced as S-1-S (screen-backed) or S-2-S (smooth two sides). This is basically a matter of how wet this mat is when pressed. In the wet process the mat is formed from a water slurry. If the mat is not predried before pressing, a screen must be used to permit the steam to escape. The screen pattern is left on the back. If the mat is predried and then hot-pressed, no screen is required, and the panel is smooth on both faces. When dry process hardboard is air felted, no screen is required, and again an S-2-S panel is produced.

Most medium-density hardboard is made for use as house siding. It is mostly $\frac{7}{16}$ in. (11 mm) thick, although $\frac{1}{2}$ in. (13 mm) is becoming more common, and may be applied as either panel siding or lap siding. Panel siding is 4 ft (1.2 m) wide and 8, 9, or 10 ft. (2.4, 2.7, or 3.0 m) long. It may be grooved to simulate reversed board and batten or may be pressed with ridges to simulate a raised batten. Various grain and stucco surfaces are also available. Lap siding is generally 6, 8, 10, 12, or 16 in. (150 to 400 mm) wide and up to 16 ft (4.9 m) long. Self-aligning lap sidings are gaining popularity. Most siding is preprimed, with finish coat or coats applied onsite [Ref. 4.10].

High-density hardboard is made in three qualities. Standard hardboard has a density of about 60 to 65 lb/ft^3 (960 to 1,040 kg/m^3) and is unmodified except for humidification and trimming after hot pressing. Tempered hardboard is a standard board that has been treated with a blend of resins after hot pressing. Tempering improves water resistance, hardness, and strength but makes the board less shock resistant. A third quality, service hardboard, is of lower density (about 50 to 55 lb/ft^3 (800 to 880 kg/m^3)) for uses where the higher strength of the standard quality is not needed. Most of the high-density board is made for industrial use, but service quality board, surfaced to a thickness of about 0.200 in. (5 mm), is used as underlayment for resilient flooring.

Special densified hardboard is used for industrial purposes rather than for construction, being used mainly as diestock and in electrical panels. It has a density in the range of 84 to 90 lb/ft^3 (1,350 to 1,440 kg/m^3).

Medium-density fiberboard (MDF) is manufactured from wood fibers combined with a synthetic resin or other suitable binder, and bonded under heat and pressure to a density of between 31 and 55 lb/ft^3 (500 and 880 kg/m^3). Because of its homogenous construction, MDF has an extremely smooth face and a tight machinable core. Occasionally MDF is used as molding stock, but its primary uses are for industrial applications such as furniture and cabinets. The accepted industry standard for MDF is Ref. 4.11.

Particleboard. Particleboard is a wood panel manufactured from wood particles or combinations of wood particles and fibers, bonded together with synthetic resins under heat and pressure. Particleboard can range from 27 to 55 lb/ft^3 (430 to 880 kg/m^3) in density and from $\frac{1}{4}$ to $1\frac{3}{4}$ in. (6 to 44 mm) in thickness. Panel sizes range from 3 to 9 ft (0.91 to 2.7 m) and often up to any length transportable. Most particleboard is made with urea-formaldehyde adhesive, which limits its applications to interior uses. Several manufacturers make board from phenol-formaldehyde and other exterior adhesives.

The primary use of particleboard is for industrial applications such as office and residential furniture, fixtures, and cabinets. The most common construction applications of particleboard are for underlayment, manufactured home decking, stair treads, and shelving. Particleboard floor underlayment, $\frac{1}{4}$ to $\frac{3}{4}$ in. thick (6.4 to 19 mm), provides a smooth, stiff, and hard surface for floor coverings. Exterior grades of particleboard also serve as siding, combined siding-sheathing, soffit linings, ceilings for carports, porches, and other protected exterior applications.

For manufactured homes, particleboard may be made in almost any size the home manufacturer can transport and handle, often up to 6 by 14 ft (1.8 by 4.3 m). Particleboard is used for manufactured home decking (MHD) to provide a combined subfloor and underlayment. It is typically made with urea-formaldehyde resins and so requires protection from moisture.

Some other wood-based particle panel products are Mende-process particleboard, molded particle products, and cement-bonded particle products. Mende-process particleboard is produced by continuous pressing of the mat (particles may range from fibers to flakes) by applying heat and pressure through a large rotating cylinder. The board thickness ranges up to $\frac{1}{4}$ in. (6.4 mm), which permits it to be formed on this cylindrical platen and subsequently flattened. The product may be used as wall paneling (with printed overlay or other surface finish), furniture backing, drawer bottoms, and case goods.

Molded particle products include parts that are formed from furnish blended with less than 25 percent binder resin and cured in dies under heat and pressure. Limited flow of the furnish during pressing restricts the kinds of items that may profitably be molded. Among the products that have been produced are exterior siding, door jambs, and window sills.

Cement-bonded particle products are made by bonding wood particles with Portland cement. The particles are typically excelsior (or wood wool), which are long (up to 10 in. (250 mm)) and stringy. Among products produced in this fashion are roof decking (good sound absorption and fire resistance properties), building blocks, and panels that can be used in doors, floors, walls, partitions, concrete forms, and exterior siding.

The National Particleboard Association publishes several standards covering performance of particleboard and medium density fiberboard, including Ref. 4.12.

Laminated Paperboard. This board is made in both interior and weather-resistant qualities, the main differences being in the type of adhesive used to bond the layers together and in the amount of sizing used in the pulp stock for making the layers. Its principal construction applications are in prefabricated housing and mobile home construction as interior wall and ceiling finish.

REFERENCES

4.1. D. W. Green. "In-Grade Testing: Impetus for Change in the Utilization of Structural Lumber." In: T. J. Corcoran and R. Douglas, eds., *Recent Advances in Spruce-Fir Utilization Technology*, Society of American Foresters, Pub. No. 83-13, Bethesda, MD, 1983.
4.2. "Standard Methods for Testing Small Clear Specimens of Timber." ASTM D143-83 (1987). American Society for Testing and Materials, Philadelphia, 1987.
4.3. *Wood Handbook: Wood as an Engineering Material.* U.S. Department of Agriculture. Agriculture Handbook 72, Revised 1987. U.S. Department of Agriculture, Washington, DC, 1987. 466 pp.
4.4. "American Softwood Lumber Standard." Product Standard 20-70. Rev. Jan. 1986. National Bureau of Standards, Washington, DC, 1986. 26 pp.
4.5. *National Design Specification for Wood Construction.* National Forest Products Association, Washington, DC, 1986.
4.6. "American National Standard for Wood Products—Structural Glued Laminated Timber. ANSI/AITC A190.1.-1983." American Institute of Timber Construction, Englewood, CO, 1983.
4.7. "Construction and Industrial Plywood." U.S. Product Standard PS 1-83. U.S. Department of Commerce, Washington, DC, 1983.
4.8. "Peformance Standards and Policies for Structural-Use Panels." APA PRP 108.-1986. American Plywood Association, Tacoma, WA, 1986.
4.9. "American National Standard for Hardwood and Decorative Plywood." ANSI/HPMA HP.-1983. American National Standards Institute, New York, 1983.
4.10. "American National Standard for Hardboard Siding." ANSI/AHA A135.6. American Hardboard Association, Palatine, IL, 1984.
4.11. "American National Standard for Medium Density Fiberboard for Interior Use." ANSI A208.2. American Hardboard Association/National Particleboard Association, Palatine, IL, 1980.
4.12. "American National Standard for Wood Particleboard." ANSI A208.1. National Particleboard Association, Gaithersburg, MD, 1989.

SUGGESTIONS FOR FURTHER READING

Forest Products Research Laboratory. *A Handbook of Softwoods*, 2nd Ed. H. M. Stationery Office, London, 1977.
Forest Products Research Laboratory. *A Handbook of Hardwoods*, 2nd Ed. H. M. Stationery Office, London, 1972.
H. E. Desch. *Timber: its Structure, Properties and Utilization*, 6th Ed. Macmillan, London, 1981.
K. R. Bootle. *Wood in Australia*. McGraw-Hill, Sydney, 1983. 443 pp.
M. Chudnoff. *Tropical Timbers of the World*. Agriculture Handbook 607. U.S. Department of Agriculture, Washington, DC, 1984. 464 pp.
G. M. Lavers. *The Strength Properties of Timbers*. Ministry of Technology, Forest Products Research, Bulletin No. 50. H. M. Stationery Office, London, 1967.
Canadian Woods: Their Properties and Uses. 3rd Ed., University of Toronto Press, Toronto, ON, 1981.
The International Book of Wood. Simon & Schuster, New York, 1976.
H. Burgess. *Wood as a Structural Material*. Timber Research and Development Association, U.K., 1968.
"Voluntary Standard for Formaldehyde Emission from Medium Density Fiberboard (MDF)." NPA 9-87. National Particleboard Association, Gaithersburg, MD, 1987.

NOTATION AND ABBREVIATIONS

AITC	American Institute of Timber Construction
ANSI	American National Standards Institute
DC	direct current
E	modulus of elasticity
G	modulus of rigidity
M	moisture content
NBS	National Bureau of Standards
t	temperature
UV	ultraviolet
μ	Poisson's ratio

A list of abbreviations of the units of measurement, definitions of these units, and conversion factors between British/American and metric units are given in the Appendix.

5
Plastics, Floor Covering Materials, Sealants, Adhesives, and Paints

Henry J. Cowan and Peter R. Smith

The division of plastics into thermoplastic and thermosetting materials, and the difference in their physical behavior and their fabrication are discussed. The principal types of plastics are considered individually, including their durability and fire resistance.

Although plastics still form only about 1 percent of the materials used by the building industry, they play an important role, and they have transformed the technologies of a number of other building materials, notably sealants, adhesives, paint, varnishes, and lacquers. The use of plastic materials has also greatly extended the utilization of timber, and improved the quality of concrete for special purposes. Many floor covering materials are now made from plastics; however, the section in this chapter considers also materials made from natural organic substances.

5.1. THE CATEGORIZATION OF PLASTICS

Plastics are materials that can be formed into complex shapes during the manufacturing process. It is rarely necessary to cut or machine them like natural stone, timber, or metal, and they are therefore *plastic* in the sculptural sense. This is one reason why their use is economical, and why they have replaced traditional materials for many building applications.

Some are "plastic" in the sense in which that word is used in describing the deformation of metals at high stresses (see Section 2.2), that is, they deform permanently at normal temperatures. On the other hand, some plastics do the exact opposite: they fail by brittle fracture. The term *plastics* does not imply that the material is necessarily capable of plastic deformation (see Fig. 2.2.4).

With the exception of the silicones (see Section 5.3), all plastics contain carbon. The carbon atom has four vacancies in its outer shell (see Section 2.2, and Figs. 2.1.1 and 2.1.2), and it therefore has a valency of four. Unlike other elements, however, carbon atoms can combine with other carbon atoms, and thus form either long chains (Figs. 5.1.1 and 5.1.2), or rings (Fig. 5.1.3). These chains and rings can be modified in a variety of ways as shown, for example, in Figs. 5.1.4 and 5.1.5.

Most plastics consist of much larger molecules formed by *polymerization* (from the Greek *polys*, many and *meros*, part). The short molecules that are being polymerized are called *monomers*, and the resultant chains are called *polymers* (Figs. 5.1.6 and 5.1.7).

Solid plastics are divided broadly into *thermoplastic* and *thermosetting* materials. Thermoplastic materials are formed by heat or pressure, or both. They retain that shape at normal temperature and pressure, but they soften again if heated or subjected to pressure. Thermosetting materials undergo chemical changes at high temperatures by forming cross linkages, so that the material becomes rigid and is not thereafter softened by heat and/or pressure (Fig. 5.1.8).

5.2. THERMOPLASTIC MATERIALS

As shown in Fig. 5.1.6, *polyvinyl chloride* (PVC) is the polymer of vinyl chloride. It can be produced in rigid or flexible form. Rigid PVC is self-extinguishing when set on

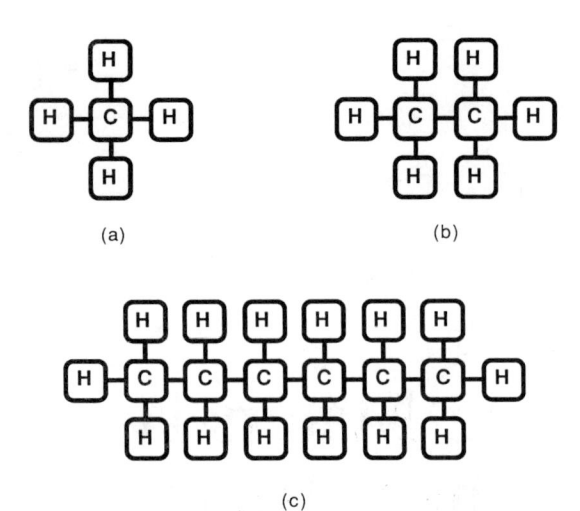

Fig. 5.1.1. Formation of carbon-chain molecules. (a) Methane, CH_4; (b) ethane, C_2H_6, formed by a link between two carbon molecules; (c) hexane, C_6H_{14}, formed by further links between carbon molecules. Methane and ethane are gases, and hexane is a liquid at a normal temperature. The longer carbon chains are solid at a normal temperature.

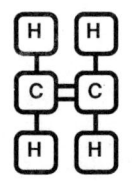

Fig. 5.1.2. Multiple links between carbon atoms. If the two carbon atoms (Fig. 5.1.1b) are joined by a double bond, two bonds fewer are available for joining them to hydrogen atoms; this is the gas ethylene, C_2H_4.

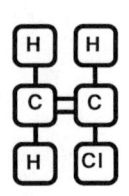

Fig. 5.1.4. Structure of vinyl chloride. One monovalent hydrogen atom of ethylene (Fig. 5.1.1b) is replaced by one monovalent chlorine atom, to form $C_2H_3 \cdot Cl$. This can be more clearly expressed by the formula $CH_2:CH \cdot Cl$, where the : indicates a double bond. The resulting material is chlorethylene, more commonly called vinyl chloride.

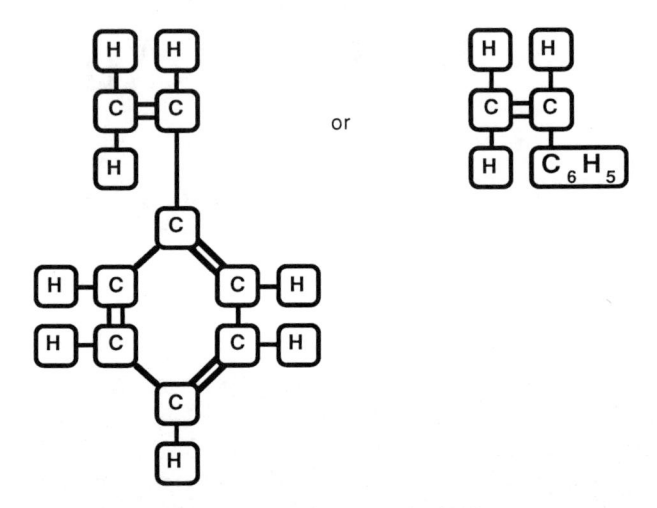

Fig. 5.1.5. Structure of styrene. One monovalent hydrogen atom of ethylene (Fig. 5.1.1b) is replaced by a benzene ring, minus one of its hydrogen atoms, which thus also is monovalent $[C_2H_3 \cdot C_6H_5]$. This can also be written as $CH_2:CH \cdot C_6H_5$, where : denotes a double bond, and · a single bond. The material is called styrene.

fire, but some of the flexible types of PVC burn because the plasticizers used to make them flexible burn. Flexible PVC remains flexible at temperatures well below the freezing point, but neither flexible nor rigid PVC can be used at elevated temperatures. Most types of PVC have good resistance to ultraviolet radiation, but some trans-

parent types are degraded by it. The specific gravity of PVC ranges from 1.2 to 1.7. It has good resistance to water and to many chemicals, excellent resistance to tearing, and its cost is relatively low.

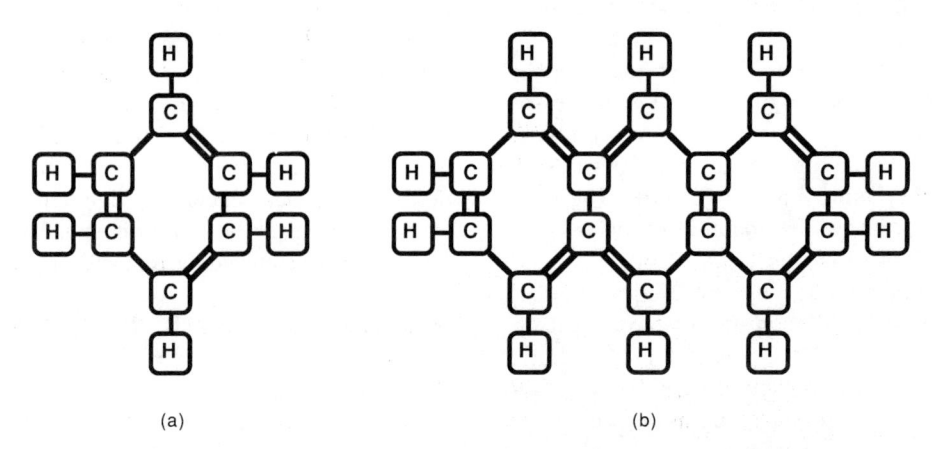

Fig. 5.1.3. Formation of carbon-ring molecules. (a) Benzene, C_6H_6; (b) anthracene, $C_{14}H_{10}$.

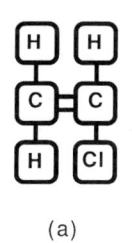

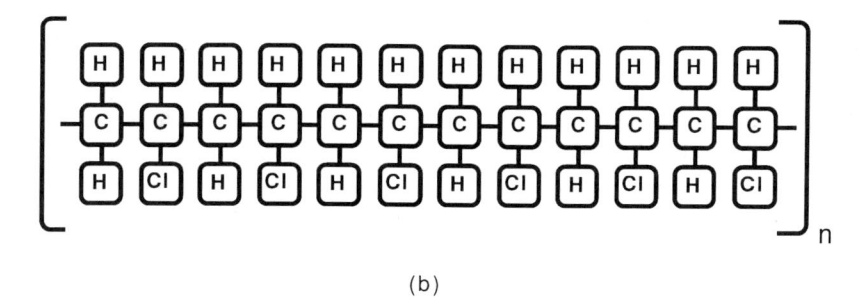

PLASTICS, FLOOR COVERING MATERIALS, SEALANTS, ADHESIVES, AND PAINTS 81

Fig. 5.1.6. Polyvinyl chloride. (a) The monomer vinyl chloride, $CH_2:CH \cdot Cl$. (b) The polymer polyvinyl chloride, $(CH_2:CH \cdot Cl)_n$.

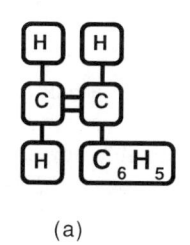

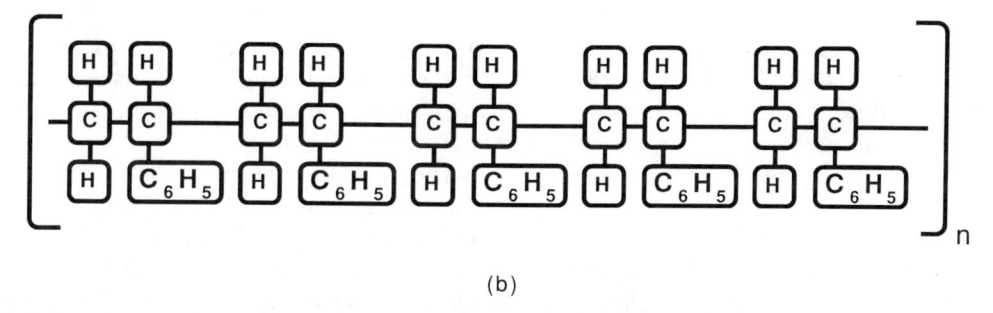

Fig. 5.1.7. Polystyrene. (a) The monomer styrene, $CH_2:CH \cdot C_6H_5$. (b) The polymer polystyrene $(CH_2:CH \cdot C_6H_5)_n$.

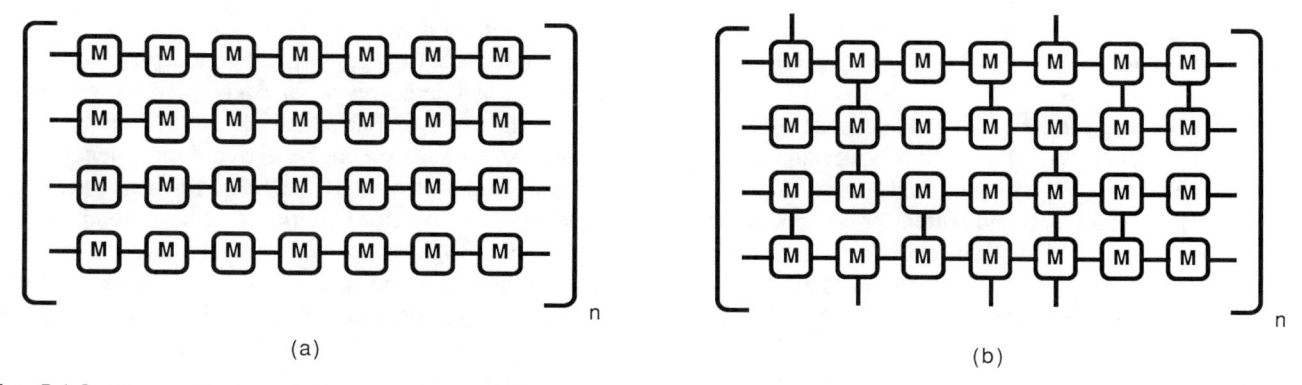

Fig. 5.1.8. Thermoplastic and thermosetting materials. (a) The monomer chains in thermoplastic materials have no crosslinkages. (b) There are some crosslinkages between the monomer chains in thermosetting materials.

Polyvinyl acetate (PVA) is the polymer of vinyl acetate (CH$_2$:CH · OOC · CH$_3$). It has a high rate of flow, and good adhesion to most materials. It is therefore used as a vehicle in emulsion paints (Section 5.10); it cannot be used for moldings or extrusions.

As shown in Fig. 5.1.7, *polystyrene* is the polymer of styrene. Its specific gravity ranges from 1.04 to 1.08, and its Vicat softening point (defined as the temperature at which a standard needle penetrates into the material by a standard distance under a standard load) ranges from 172 to 200°F (78 to 93°C). It can be made transparent and colorless. Polystyrene burns only slowly if ignited. It is easy to mold, turn, drill, glue, and polish. Its surface can be decorated by printing, metallizing, or lacquering.

However, its most important use for building is as *expanded lightweight polystyrene* for insulation, with a specific gravity of about 0.018. A hydrocarbon with a low boiling point, such as pentane, is introduced into the polystyrene beads during the polymerization process. When the beads are heated and the polystyrene softens, the pentane vaporizes and expands the beads. They are left in warm air until the air diffuses into the beads, and are then reheated and either extruded or molded to fuse into an apparently solid mass which consists, however, mainly of air.

High-impact polystyrene (HIPS) is produced by dissolving butadiene rubber (CH$_2$:CH · CH:CH$_2$) in styrene before polymerization. HIPS has better shock resistance than polystyrene, but is otherwise similar.

Styrene-acrylonitrile copolymer (SAN) is made by polymerizing a mixture of styrene (CH$_2$:CH · C$_6$H$_5$) and acrylonitrile (CH$_2$:CH · CN). *Acrylonitrile butadiene styrene* (ABS) is an alloy of SAN copolymer with polymerized butadiene rubber (CH$_2$:CH · CH:CH$_2$). Both materials are stronger, tougher, and more shock-resistant than polystyrene but otherwise similar to it.

Polyethylene is the polymer of ethylene (C$_2$H$_4$, see Fig. 5.1.2). Its specific gravity ranges from 0.91 to 0.97 and its Vicat softening point from 185 to 265°F (85 to 130°C). It is easily processed, and has good flexibility, good resistance to water and many chemicals, and good electrical insulation; however, it is degraded by ultraviolet radiation.

Polypropylene is the polymer of propylene (C$_3$H$_6$). Its specific gravity ranges from 0.89 to 0.92, and its properties are similar to those of polyethylene; however, it has a higher tensile strength, greater stiffness, and greater resistance to heat.

Polymethyl methacrylate or *acrylic plastic* is the polymer of methyl methacrylate (Fig. 5.2.1). It is better known by the trade names *Plexiglas*, *Perspex*, and *Lucite*. It has a specific gravity of about 1.2, and softens at a temperature between 265 and 300°F (130 and 150°C), when it can easily be formed into complex shapes. Acrylics have excellent weather resistance, and they can be exposed to ultraviolet light. Acrylic can be made clear and transparent, with a light transmission of about 92 percent, and it is therefore an important alternative to glass in locations where the brittleness of glass is a disadvantage (see Section 3.18); the

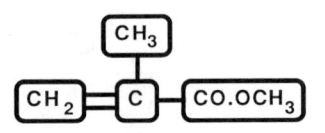

Fig. 5.2.1. Methyl methacrylate, the monomer from which the acrylic resins are made.

polymer chains delay the propagation of cracks. Acrylic scratches more easily than glass, but its scratch resistance is quite high for a plastic material, and it is about the same as that of aluminum. The scratches are more in evidence because the material is transparent.

Acrylic can be made clear or colored transparent or opaque. Like other plastics, it can be produced as a granular material for subsequent injection molding, or it can be cast into sheets or rods. Its cost is in the medium range.

Polycarbonate has a complex chemical structure, and reference should be made to a specialized textbook (for example Ref. 5.1, pp. 499–521). It is the strongest and toughest of the transparent plastics, and it retains its strength at temperatures well below the freezing point and above the boiling point of water. It is an expensive material.

Polyacetal, a polymer of formaldehyde (H · CHO), has high strength, toughness, and stiffness and good wear resistance. This makes it suitable for applications for which metals have previously been used. It is one of the more expensive materials.

The *polyamides* also have a complex structure, and reference should be made to a specialized textbook (for example, Ref. 5.1, pp. 435–466). The best known member of the group is generally known by its trade name *Nylon*. It is a tough and abrasion resistant material with a very low coefficient of friction, which makes it suitable for slides and guide rails.

The *cellulose plastics* were the first thermoplastic materials to be made; *celluloid* was first produced in 1870. The principal material in this group is now *cellulose acetate*, which is used in solid form, and also as a lacquer for wood and for metals (see Section 5.14).

5.3. THERMOSETTING MATERIALS

The thermosetting materials are often called *resins*, because most naturally occurring resins are thermosetting polymers. The oldest synthetic resin is *bakelite*, first produced commercially by Leo Baekeland in 1910. It is a *phenol formaldehyde (PF)* resin, polymerized from phenol (Fig. 5.3.1) and formaldehyde (H · CHO). PF resins are used in solid form as low-cost materials that have good dimensional stability, high heat resistance, and resistance to many chemicals; however, they are available only in dark colors. PF resins are also used as adhesives for plywood and as the binder for hardboard and for thermal insulation.

Urea formaldehyde UF resin, polymerized from urea (Fig. 5.3.2) and formaldehyde, is a low-cost material with uses similar to PF, but with a light color.

Fig. 5.3.1. Phenol. Phenol is a benzene ring (Fig. 5.1.3a) in which one hydrogen atom (—H) has been replaced by a hydroxyl (—OH).

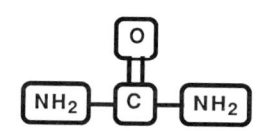

Fig. 5.3.2. Urea.

Melamine formaldehyde (MF) resin is polymerized from melamine (Fig. 5.3.3) and formaldehyde. It is a much more expensive material that has excellent scratch and heat resistance, and produces surfaces that are transparent and very hard. It is the principal material for decorative laminates and other hard-wearing surface finishes.

Polyurethane is polymerized from materials that contain a urethane link (Fig. 5.3.4). Most polyurethane is used as a foam, made by introducing a volatile liquid that is vaporized during the production process. Polyurethane foam may be flexible or rigid (although the latter is more common in buildings), and the rigidity of the foam depends on the number of crosslinks between the polymer chains (Fig. 5.1.8b). Polyurethane is also used for sealants, adhesives, and coatings.

Alkyd resins (a name derived from the words alcohol and acid) are a diverse group of materials that have in common an ester (—COO—) link that enhances the flexibility of the polymer chains. They are also known as *polyester resins*. They are used in solid form on their own, but they are more commonly reinforced with glass fibers, which may be random short fibers or fibers woven into a mat. This

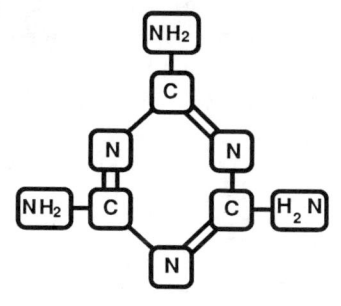

Fig. 5.3.3. Melamine.

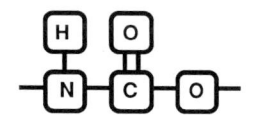

Fig. 5.3.4. The urethane link.

material is frequently called *glass reinforced plastic (GRP)*, or simply *fiberglass*, although it is in fact polyester sheet reinforced with glass fibers. Polyester is also used for textiles: *Dacron*, *Terylene*, and *Mylar* are extruded from it.

Epoxy resins contain an epoxy group (Fig. 5.3.5) at the end of each polymer chain. They are mainly used as adhesives (Section 5.9), but also as coatings, and for the repair of damaged concrete.

Silicones differ from all the other plastics discussed so far. Instead of the long chains of carbon atoms, they are built around long chains of silicon and oxygen atoms. The main use of silicones in buildings is as water repellants and as adhesives (Sections 5.5, 5.6, 5.8, and 5.9).

5.4. FABRICATION AND DURABILITY OF PLASTICS

Most plastics are manufactured from the byproducts of the destructive distillation of coal, which turns it into coke; and from the cracking of crude oil, which produces gasoline and fuel oil. The substances obtained from these processes are mostly monomers which are then polymerized or copolymerized (see Figs. 5.1.6–5.1.8), usually by heat and/or pressure. Fabrication of thermoplastic materials is often facilitated by a *plasticizer*; this is a small quantity of material that is added to facilitate the separation of the polymer chains by heat and pressure, and thus reduce the force and the temperature needed to achieve the necessary deformation.

Most plastic raw materials can only be made in large chemical plants. These raw materials can, however, be fabricated into plastic building components and other articles in relatively small factories.

Most plastics are delivered to the fabricators in the form of small particles. These may be tiny spheres, cubes, or cylinders, or irregular particles, or flakes, or powder. The acrylics are an exception as most are produced immediately in the form of transparent sheets and rods. Plastics are generally *fabricated* by extrusion or by molding.

Extrusion is used mainly for thermoplastics. The material enters the extruder through a screw conveyor, and the heat

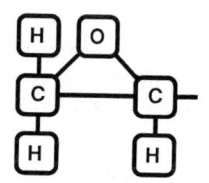

Fig. 5.3.5. The epoxy group.

generated may be sufficient to soften the material; if it is not, additional heat can be applied in the extruder before it is squeezed through a die which gives it the desired shape.

It is less common to use extrusion for forming thermosetting resins. In that case the extrusion press has a plunger, instead of a screw conveyor.

Blow molding is a process whereby thermoplastics are blown through an extrusion die against a mold, which is not restricted in size as in injection molding. Large components can be produced by this method. When thermoplastics are formed by *injection molding*, the material is rendered fluid in a chamber outside the mold, and then injected into the mold and cooled therein.

Thermosetting resins achieve their strength through chemical action and do not need to cool before they are removed from the mold. In *compression molding* a weighed quantity of thermosetting resin grains is fed into the mold, and liquefied by heat and pressure. The molding emerges from the press completely finished, except for a thin flange where the parts of the mold join, and this is removed by grinding.

Most plastics can be *cut*, *drilled*, *turned*, or *shaped* with metalworking machines used at an appropriate speed. Most plastics can be welded and glued. *Welding* can be done with a welding rod, as it is for metal; this is melted by a jet of hot air or, preferably, by an inert gas such as nitrogen or carbon dioxide. Alternatively the two pieces to be joined can be softened and butted together under pressure or ultrasonically. *Gluing* is best accomplished with a glue made from the material to be joined dissolved in a suitable solvent.

Many plastic components, such as light fittings, pipes, basins, taps, toilet seats, rain gutters, downspouts, ducts, vapor barriers, and floor tiles can be made from a number of different plastics. Their appearance, strength, and durability, and their cost, will vary with the material used.

PVC has proved particularly suitable as a floor covering; acrylics as transparent materials for normal use; polycarbonate as a transparent material where extra strength is needed. Melamine formaldehyde resin is used as the finishing material for laminates to impregnate the decorative sheet of paper and serve as a protective transparent outer cover; however, the cheaper phenolic resins are used for impregnating the lower layers.

The specific gravity of plastics varies roughly over the same range as that of the various species of timber. However, plastic components can usually be made thinner, so that for the same purpose plastic components usually weigh less than those of timber. When plastics are substituted for metal and clay products, there is a great saving in weight.

Since the strength of plastics varies from 1.5 to 150 ksi (10 to 1000 MPa), it should be possible to find a suitable plastic for any given strength requirement. Many plastics have excellent resistance to tearing, and for the same tensile strength this is usually superior to that of wood and metals.

However, most plastics have a low modulus of elasticity, and excessive elastic deflection is often a problem, particularly if the component is thin. In addition, most thermoplastics have a high rate of creep, and the resulting creep deflection can continue for several years. This limits the use of plastics for load-bearing members where deflection is critical.

Plastics have a wide range of hardness and abrasion resistance, and there should be little difficulty in finding a suitable material. Few plastics deteriorate as a result of contact with water, and some are resistant to various acids and alkalies.

Some plastics soften in contact with very hot water, and these cannot be used for hot-water or waste-water pipes.

Many plastics are degraded by the *ultaviolet radiation*, which is a part of the solar radiation during daylight hours. The only reliable test is exposure of a component on a test site over a period of several years. However, a prediction can be made with a *weatherometer*, in which the material is subjected to speeded-up cycles of ultraviolet radiation, and any other components of the weather that may be critical, such as wetting and drying, freezing and thawing, and so on. Weatherometers can reproduce in a few weeks weather cycles that would occur naturally only over a period of years. They are useful for comparing two plastics, one of known performance and one to be tested. They are much less reliable if there is no similar component of known performance with which a comparison can be made.

Many plastics pose a *fire hazard*. Some produce combustible vapors in quantities greater than are necessary to sustain combustion, so that a fire of this sort, once started, continues to burn until the available fuel is exhausted. Some burning thermoplastics melt and throw off drops that may spread the fire.

Some plastics produce a great deal of smoke. Others are virtually incombustible. Some of the latter, referred to as *intumescent*, are converted into a swollen carbonaceous mass as they burn; this acts as an insulator, and inhibits further combustion to the point of making these materials self-extinguishing (see Section 26.5).

Silicones, rigid polyvinyl chloride (PVC), and the melamine laminates have substantial fire resistance. Cellulose plastics, polyethylenes, polypropylenes, polystyrenes, and acrylics, on the other hand, pose a fire risk unless treated with fire retardants.

Fire retardants have been used at least since the time of Ancient Rome. Modern treatments are based on the halogens (mainly chlorine), phosphorus, nitrogen, and antimony. The chemistry of these compounds and their action in fire is complex, and reference should be made to specialist textbooks (for example, Refs. 5.2 and 5.3).

5.5. WOODCHIP BOARD AND POLYMER CONCRETE

Woodchip board is reconstituted wood. Wood offcuts that would otherwise be wasted can be used, but specially prepared wood chips made from relatively small trees are also used. To produce a high quality product, the wood chips must be of the right shape, size, and moisture content (see Chapter 4). The most common adhesive is urea formaldehyde, using about 5 to 10 percent of the weight of the timber. The sheet is compressed to the required thickness and density at a temperature of about 300°F (150°C).

Polymer concrete is concrete (see Section 3.10) in which portland cement is replaced by a polymer. It has a lower water absorption, and consequently better resistance to cycles of freezing and thawing, than portland cement concrete. The most commonly used resins are acrylics and polyesters, but the more expensive epoxy concrete has better adhesion to other building materials. The plastic material is mixed with the aggregate either as a monomer or as a partial polymer, together with a hardener, that is, a cross-linking agent, and a catalyst to produce full polymerization.

Polymer concrete is concrete in which all the cement is replaced by plastics; it is sometimes reinforced with metal fibers, glass fibers, or glass fiber mats. *Polymer-cement concrete* is a similar material in which the plastic material replaced only part of the portland cement.

Polymer-impregnated concrete is hardened portland cement concrete that has been impregnated with monomers in the form of a low-viscosity liquid or a gas, using a vacuum or pressure. The monomers are polymerized by a catalyst, by heat, or by ultraviolet radiation. While only a surface layer of the concrete is impregnated, it forms a layer free of any voids. Acrylics are at present the most commonly employed monomers.

5.6. FLOOR COVERING MATERIALS

The use of natural stone (including marble, travertine, and slate), concrete (including terrazzo), magnesium oxychloride, and quarry tiles has been discussed in Chapter 3, and the use of timber in Chapter 4. Plastic flooring materials will be considered in this section, and also flooring materials made with natural organic substances.

The most common plastics for floor surfaces are *polyvinyl chloride* (PVC) and *synthetic rubber*. They can be used as sheets cut to the shape of the floor surface, but more conveniently in the form of tiles, which are easier to lay and cut.

Organic sheet materials used for floor surfaces are *cork* and *linoleum*. Cork comes from the bark of the cork oak. As a flooring material it is turned into shavings and then compressed into sheets, which are cut into tiles.

Linoleum can also be used in the form of tiles, but as it is a flexible material that is easily cut, it is more commonly used in sheets. It is made from linseed oil, which is heated (but not boiled) to oxidize it, and a natural resin. Chalk, sometimes with wood flour or cork dust, is added as a filler, together with pigments to give the material its color. The "marble" effect often seen in linoleum is achieved by using a blend of two or more colors.

The use of *carpets* as flooring materials was until the early Twentieth Century restricted by the limited size of carpet that could be made. Wall-to-wall carpet became popular when the broadloom process was introduced whereby carpets could be made to a width of 12 ft (3.65 m); this was later extended to 18 ft (5.48 m).

Carpets can be made from natural or synthetic fibers. The most important natural fiber is wool, shorn from unimproved breeds of sheep which yield a wool that is more resistant to wear. Cotton can be used, but its durability is inferior. Silk is used, mostly in China, for high-quality carpets.

Synthetic fibers used in carpets are made from Nylon, polypropylene, or acrylic yarn, and to a lesser extent polyester yarn. Viscose Rayon, a cellulose fiber made from purified wood pulp, is used for cheaper carpets of inferior durability. Wool and the synthetic fibers may be used singly or as a mixture.

Since wool and the other animal hairs occasionally used for carpets scorch and burn slowly, they are more resistant to fire than the synthetic fibers which melt as they burn. Scorch marks on wool are easier to remove than melted material on synthetic carpets. The spread of fire can be inhibited by the use of flame retardants. Wool carpets are usually mothproofed.

Staining and dirt absorption can be reduced by treating carpets with a water-repellent, such as silicone. Nylon carpets are liable to accumulate static electricity when the humidity falls below 65 percent; the same happens in wool carpets when the humidity falls below 20 percent (which is rare). This poses problems particularly in rooms where computers or electrical instruments are used. The static electricity can be controlled by the use of stainless steel threads in the carpet.

The durability of nylon and propylene under normal wear is superior to that of wool and acrylics, and much superior to that of Rayon and cotton; however, wool carpets are less liable to accidental damage that cannot be removed by cleaning.

Durability and the comfort generated by a carpet otherwise depend on the weight of the pile. This is partly determined by its density (the number of tufts per unit area), and partly by its thickness (the height of the pile above its backing). The cost in turn depends largely on the weight of material used.

Machine-made carpets, as distinct from the traditional hand-woven carpets, are woven in one process. They are usually classified as *Axminster*, *Brussels*, and *Wilton* carpets. These names do not nowadays signify a place of origin or a company, but a process of manufacture. In an Axminster carpet the pile is made by weaving separate short tufts of pile yarn with the backing threads; the other two types are made by looping the pile yarn over rods, which are then withdrawn. In a Brussels carpet the loops of the pile are left uncut, while in the other two types they are cut to form a "velvet" pile.

Carpets are excellent absorbers of impact noise. They provide the best means of sound insulation against footsteps and dropping objects. They are also good thermal insulators, and thus give a "warm" feeling to persons walking on them in cold weather; in this respect they are greatly superior to the ceramic flooring materials discussed in Chapter 3. On the other hand, carpets cannot be used if it is desired to utilize the floor as a thermal store of passive solar energy (Chapter 21), because they insulate the concrete on which they are laid.

5.7. WATERPROOFING MATERIALS

The solid or semisolid hydrocarbons obtained from the distillation of coal or petroleum are excellent for waterproofing basements, on-grade floors, and flat roofs (see Chapter 7). They are called *asphalt* in America, and *bitumen* in England (where the term *asphalt* is used for a natural or artificial mixture of bitumen and limestone). They can be liquified by heating, and then laid to form a continuous layer that produces a waterproof membrane when cooled.

The traditional waterproofing membranes are of three kinds: asphalt (bitumen) laid and rolled to about $\frac{3}{4}$ in. (20 mm) thick; built-up roofing of felt impregnated with asphalt (bitumen), usually in three layers stuck together with asphalt (bitumen); and single-layer asphaltic (bituminous) sheets, welded at the edges with a blowtorch. More recently these have been improved by using glass or plastic fibers instead of asbestos or paper felt.

In recent years *elastomeric membranes* have been used to an increasing extent for flat roofs in place of asphalt (bitumen). They may be applied as fluids or as sheets of materials such as butyl rubber, neoprene, chlorinated polyethylene, or silicone rubber. These materials can also be used on curved concrete roofs, such as shell structures, for which asphalts (bitumens) are unsuitable. They are less expensive, but also less durable than copper sheet (see Section 2.9).

A heavy *polyethylene film*, sealed at all overlaps between adjoining sheets, can be used for waterproofing below on-grade concrete slabs and in basements, provided it can be protected against puncture. It cannot, however, be used on roofs, because it is degraded by ultraviolet radiation.

Asphalt shingles are used in North America to cover sloping roofs. They are made of heavy felt impregnated and coated with asphalt (bitumen). Because they have no bending strength and are very flexible, they must be fully supported by the roof structure.

Bituminous paint consists of asphalt (bitumen) dissolved in a volatile solvent or suspended in water as an emulsion. It is used for waterproofing, and for repairing bituminous flat roofs.

5.8. SEALANTS

Most of the joints in brick and concrete construction are made "wet" with mortar or concrete (see Chapter 3). The term *sealant* is usually reserved for flexible materials in joints to control temperature and moisture movement. In the interior of the building, soft sealing compounds are needed in the joints between floor slabs and the walls below because of the movement that occurs between them.

The job of sealants in exterior walls and roofs is much more demanding, particularly in curtain walls where they are used to make all the joints. Sealants must prevent the entry of rainwater driven by wind (see Chapter 10) which may hit a wall at a variety of angles, even in an upward direction. Since curtain-wall buildings are invariably heated or air-conditioned, the joints should also prevent leakage of air, which would greatly increase the expenditure of energy for heating and cooling. The design of these joints is discussed in Chapter 6.

Sealants can be divided into caulking compounds, elastomeric compounds, and preformed sealants.

Caulking compounds (also called *mastics*) are soft, doughlike materials that adhere to the surfaces with which they are in contact. Prior to 1950 all caulking compounds were made with a base of linseed oil. Window putty, for example, consists of about 12 percent of linseed oil and 88 percent of whiting (powdered chalk, $CaCO_3$). In traditional construction it is placed with a putty knife, allowed to harden in air, and then given a coat of paint as surface protection.

Caulking compounds of greater plasticity can be produced by the addition of castor oil or soybean oil. These can be applied with a knife or with a caulking gun under pressure, which requires less labor.

Oil-based caulking materials have been largely replaced by synthetic materials. Most latex caulking compounds have a polyvinyl acetate (PVA) base (see Section 5.2). This is water-soluble, so that tools and hands can be cleaned with water, and spills can be removed with a damp cloth. Latex caulks, which are supplied in cartridges for application with a caulking gun, are used mostly for smaller buildings, particularly for window glazing, for door and window perimeters, for sealing around air conditioners, and for sealing cracks in concrete. The material adheres well to concrete, brick, wood and aluminum.

The curtain walls of large buildings are sealed with *elastomeric sealants*, but these materials are also used for other purposes, such as control joints in concrete, brick and steel, and repair of cracks in concrete. Their adhesion characteristics vary. Some require that adjacent materials be cleaned with a solvent and/or painted with a primer; others can be applied directly.

Some sealants are used with a *filler*. This reduces the cost of the sealant, and it usually increases its strength, because it acts as reinforcement. It may also color the sealant. Suitable filters are powdered chalk, mineral fibers, and pigments such as carbon black.

All polymers used as curtain-wall sealants must be resistant to ultraviolet radiation.

Acrylic and butyl sealants cure by evaporation of their

solvent; that is, they change from a doughlike material to a rubbery one. They are normally applied by extrusion from a cartridge with a caulking gun.

Acrylic polymer is thermoplastic (see Section 5.2), and its cartridge must be heated to about 120°F (50°C) before use. Butyl sealant has a base of synthetic rubber. Both materials remain tacky for a day or two after application, and complete curing of the sealant bead takes a few weeks.

Polysulfide, silicone, and polyurethane sealants cure by chemical action, that is, they are converted from a doughlike material to a rubbery one. Polysulfide polymer is a two-component sealant. It is a thick liquid which is converted gradually into a rubbery solid by the addition of lead dioxide. The two materials are supplied separately, and mixed together immediately before use. Silicone is a one-component sealant. Polyurethane sealant (usually called urethane sealant) is also a one-component material. It can be used by itself, or combined with acrylic or epoxy resin.

Preformed gaskets can be made from neoprene, butyl, styrene-butadiene, vinyl, silicone, or other rubber (see Sections 5.2 and 5.3). The gasket is usually fixed without an adhesive, and the seal is produced by compression of the gasket (see Section 6.9).

There are two types of *sealing tapes*. One consists of ribbons of sealing compound, supplied in rolls with a paper backing that is peeled off during installation. These tapes eliminate the need for a caulking gun and the subsequent cleanup, but the joint must be designed so that the ribbon can be inserted (see Section 6.8). The ribbons are made from various polymers, and most incorporate a filler. Depending on the polymer used and its method of curing, the tapes are either resilient (like rubber) or nonresilient (soft like a caulking compound).

The resilient tapes are used mainly for window glazing, and they are sometimes coated with a tacky rubber solution to provide adhesion for easier installation. The nonresilient tapes are used mainly for sealing joints between walls and floor or ceilings, for sealing joints between external doors and windows and the surrounding walls, and for sealing around air conditioner units. They can also be used for glazing, but their softness requires a protective cover; this can be supplied by a bead of compatible sealant from a caulking gun.

The second type are the *pressure-sensitive adhesive tapes*. These consist of a backing material and rubber-based or resin-based adhesive that adheres to most materials when a light pressure is applied. The backing material may be a transparent or pigmented polymer, such as cellophane, cellulose acetate, polyester, or vinyl; cloth, paper with or without fiber reinforcement; or aluminum foil.

These tapes are used for sealing joints between dry components, such as gypsum drywall construction (see Section 3.7), using an automatic taper with a long arm, which eliminates the need for scaffolding. They are also used for joining bats of insulation and sections of air conditioning ducts. They are wrapped around sprayed insulation on hot-water pipes and heating ducts as protection for the friable insulating material.

Pressure-sensitive adhesive tapes have temporary uses during construction as masking tapes during painting, and for fixing temporary protective sheets of polyethylene.

5.9. ADHESIVES

Until the 1930s adhesives were produced almost exclusively from natural materials: animal glues, casein, vegetable glues, and cements made from natural rubber. Since then a variety of synthetic adhesives have been developed from the thermosetting resins (see Section 5.3).

The most important and versatile high-strength adhesives are the *epoxy resins*. Epoxy resins cure by chemical action at room temperature; the resin and its catalyst are supplied in separate parts and mixed just before use. It is not necessary to apply a high contact pressure during curing.

Epoxy resin adheres well to portland cement concrete and to natural stone, and it can therefore be used for the repair of small damaged sections of concrete, or the restoration of natural stone (see Section 3.4). It is, however, an expensive material, and cheaper adhesives are used where a substantial quantity is required.

Wood products are today among the biggest users of synthetic adhesives in the building industry. The reconstitution of woodchips into woodchip board (see Section 5.5) would not have been possible without cheap synthetic resin, such as urea formaldehyde, since it constitutes 5 to 10 percent of the finished board (see Chapter 4).

Plywood contains less than 4 percent by weight of adhesive, but the strength of the glue is more critical, and the more durable (and more expensive) *phenol formaldehyde* or *resorcinol formaldehyde* is usually preferred. For exterior use the even more expensive *melamine formaldehyde* may be required. The same materials are suitable for laminated timber and for finger joints in timber.

For all adhesives, the glue line should be as thin as possible, since the strength of a properly bonded joint, both in shear and in tension, is invariably much higher than the strength of the adhesive itself. In this respect adhesives differ from portland cement mortar, where a substantial joint thickness is acceptable, and indeed desirable.

To perform satisfactorily, all adhesives must wet both surfaces to be glued together. To insure proper wetting, both surfaces, particularly of metals, must be cleaned and degreased before the adhesive is applied.

Although manufacturers often prescribe and supply a specific adhesive, most building materials can be glued with any one of several different materials. Furthermore, consideration should be given to the alternative methods of fixing that are available for some materials. For example, ceramic tiles and thin stone slabs can be laid on a relatively thick bed of portland cement mortar, or fixed with a thin layer of adhesive. Nonferrous metal sheets can be joined by soldering (see Section 2.10) or with adhesives. Several thermoplastic materials can be joined with an adhesive at room temperature or welded through the application of heat and pressure, but without adhesive.

5.10. PAINT AND PAINT VEHICLES

Paintings covering large areas have been found in Egyptian tombs made more than five thousand years ago. By that time, craftsmen had discovered vehicles for binding their pigments so that they would not rub off. These consisted of animal products, such as raw egg and milk, and plant resins, such as water-soluble gum. Paintings made with water-soluble vehicles are now called *tempera* or *distemper* paintings. *Fresco* painting is a more durable technique. It was discovered more than once, for the first time by the Minoan civilization in Crete about 1700 B.C. The pigments dissolved in a vehicle of lime water are painted on wet lime plaster. The carbon dioxide in the air reacts with the lime to form calcium carbonate, and the colors are thus rendered insoluble in water. Although this technique was used by many of the greatest painters of the Renaissance, it is very restrictive, because of the need to complete the painting while the lime plaster is wet.

Oil painting, using *linseed oil* as a vehicle, has been used since the Fourteenth Century as a method to produce durable paintings which did not have to be completed to a strict time schedule, and during the last three centuries fresco painting has rarely been used.

At the beginning of the Twentieth Century there were thus two main types of vehicle: water and water-soluble glues, used in limewashes and distempers; and linseed oil, fish oil, tung oil, and dehydrated castor oil, used in oil paints.

The introduction of new synthetic vehicles has completely transformed paint technology since the 1930s. Synthetic polymers, such as alkyd resins (which belong to the polyester group) and phenolic resins (see Section 5.3) have been used as an alternative to oil, and in conjunction with oil. A *resin paint* has a vehicle of synthetic resin only, an *oil paint* has as its vehicle a traditional drying oil, and an *oleoresinous paint* has as its vehicle a mixture of both.

All three types of paint are classified as *enamel* (very high gloss), *high-gloss*, *semi-gloss*, and *flat-paints*. The degree of gloss depends on the ratio of vehicle to pigment; the higher the ratio, the glossier is the finish of the paint.

The vehicle in which the pigment is dispersed must adhere to the *substrate*, that is, the surface of wood, metal, concrete, etc. Wetting agents may have to be added to ensure that the liquid paint wets the substrate. The lower the wetting ability of the paint, the more thoroughly must the substrate be cleaned and smoothed to insure adhesion of the paint film.

Paint that has been stored for some time may no longer contain sufficient volatile constituents, and in that case a *thinner* must be added. This is usually mineral turpentine or white spirit (a petroleum distillate). The same material can be used to clean the rollers or brushes used for painting.

On *drying* the liquid oil, oleoresinous or resin paint is converted into a paint film containing the pigment particles. This is a chemical process initiated by the oxygen in the atmosphere. It results in cross-linkages between the polymer chains, and thus in film formation. Plasticizers are added to some paint vehicles to impart the necessary degree of flexibility to the dried paint film.

An even more significant innovation was the introduction in 1949 of *water-based paints using synthetic polymers* under the name of *emulsion paints*. The most common vehicles for these paints are polyvinyl acetate (PVA) and the acrylics (see Section 5.2). The formation of the paint film results from physical rather than chemical action. As the water evaporates, capillary forces deform the long-chain polymers to fill the voids left by the water, so that fusion takes place, and a continuous film is formed.

Water-based emulsion paints can be thinned with water, and the rollers and brushes can be cleaned with water. Because of the ease with which they can be used, they have largely displaced the traditional water-based paints, and also flat oil paints. Most emulsion paints give a flat or matte finish, but gloss and semi-gloss finishes can be obtained.

5.11. PIGMENTS

The range of pigments, which was already quite substantial during the Roman Empire, has been greatly augmented since the beginning of the Nineteenth Century, and some expensive natural pigments have been replaced by much cheaper synthetics. For example ultramarine, worth more than its weight in gold during the Middle Ages, was successfully analyzed in the 1820s, and found to be a complex aluminosilicate ($3Na_2O_3 \cdot 3Al_2O_3 \cdot 6SiO_2 \cdot 2NaS$). It is now manufactured quite cheaply by heating a mixture of china clay, soda, sulfur, and coal. Many pigments that occur naturally at a reasonable cost are now also produced synthetically because a better control over the color can be obtained that way.

Paint generally has a white base into which the pigment is blended. It can be mixed shortly before use, or earlier in a factory. If it is stored for some time, it needs to be remixed, to insure that the pigment, the vehicle, and its solvent are uniformly distributed throughout the container. Most of the colors produced by paint manufacturers are blends of standard pigments.

The *opacity* or *hiding power* of white paint is therefore of particular importance. It is defined as the weight of paint needed to obliterate a standard board of alternating black and white squares. A thin layer of an opaque paint may have the same hiding power as a thicker layer of a more transparent paint.

A modern stable, opaque, and nontoxic white pigment is titanium dioxide (TiO_2), made from the mineral ilmenite. Other opaque whites are zinc oxide (ZnO) and antimony oxide (Sb_2O_3); the latter has fire-retardant properties. The traditional white opaque pigment, white lead, is poisonous, and therefore rarely used today.

Other traditional white pigments lack the necessary opacity, and are therefore today considered extenders rather than pigments. These are china clay, or kaolin ($Al_2O_3 \cdot 2SiO_2 \cdot 2H_2O$); whiting, or chalk ($CaCO_3$); French chalk, or talc ($H_2Mg_3Si_4O_{12}$); and *blanc fixe*, or barytes ($BaSO_4$).

Bentonite, a very fine clay, is used as a thickener in emulsion paints. Powdered mica (see Section 3.2) improves the moisture resistance and helps seal porous surfaces in primer coats; it does that through the alignment of the tiny flat plates from which it is formed parallel to the surface.

The pigments which color white paint are a mixture of the traditional and the modern. Red iron oxide (Fe_2O_3) is a traditional *red* pigment. Cadmium red is a modern pigment produced by blending cadmium selenide (CdSe) and cadmium sulfide (CdS); several shades of red can be produced by varying the proportions.

Hydrated yellow iron oxide ($Fe_2O_3 \cdot nH_2O$) is a traditional pigment which can vary from bright *yellow* to dark yellow-brown. It is now generally made synthetically for better control of color. The modern yellow pigments are cadmium yellow (CdS), zinc chromate ($ZnCrO_4$), and lead chromate ($PbCrO_4$).

The traditional *blue* pigment ultramarine has already been mentioned earlier in this section; it is now made synthetically. Prussian blue, which is ferric ferrocyanide ($Fe_4(Fe(CN)_6)_3$), is a different shade of blue. Another widely used blue pigment is copper phthalocyanine blue, a complex organic pigment containing a large number of benzene rings (see Fig. 5.1.3).

In traditional paint technology *green* was generally made by mixing blue and yellow, and this is still sometimes done today: Brunswick green is a mixture of Prussian blue and lead chromate. Two other widely used green pigments are chromium oxide (Cr_2O_3) and copper phthalocyanine green, which is similar to the blue pigment of the same name, except that most of the hydrogen atoms in the benzene rings have been replaced by chlorine atoms.

These are just some of the more common pigments that are now used for buildings.

5.12. PAINT AS A PROTECTIVE COATING

Three coats are required when paint serves as a protective coating. The *primer* is chosen for its chemical compatibility with the substrate. The *undercoat* and the *topcoat* are mainly decorative, but the topcoat must also have adequate resistance to weathering or abrasion, depending on its location.

Two coats are adequate where the paint is purely decorative. A single top coat without an undercoat may be sufficient if the material to be painted is of a very similar color.

Some materials are entirely durable without a protective coat of paint, but they are often painted to improve their appearance. These are concrete, fiber-reinforced cement panels, cement plaster and render, gypsum plaster, and gypsum panels used in drywall construction. Some of these materials, however, require special paints (see Section 5.13).

Some species of timber, such as the American softwoods *Redwood* and *Western Red Cedar*, and several Australian hardwoods can be used without a protective coating, and these are always chosen for wooden shingles and sometimes for wooden siding (weatherboards). Timber window and door frames, however, are usually made of cheaper softwood, and these must be protected by paint when used externally. Internally a decorative treatment with lacquer, varnish or stain (see Section 5.14) can be used.

Timber is usually given three coats of paint (see Chapter 4). The *primer* serves mainly to protect the paint from the timber's exudations, such as resin that continues to form at knots in the timber. It also acts as a filler for any irregularities in the wooden surface. The primer and second coat, or *undercoat*, have a matte finish, but the *topcoat* is usually given a high gloss as weather protection. Titanium dioxide (see Section 5.11) is particularly suitable for white and light-colored topcoats for timber, because it is a nontoxic, stable pigment with a high opacity, and protects it against ultraviolet radiation.

Nonferrous metals and stainless steel are painted only rarely. They do not require protection against corrosion. However, copper and brass are sometimes given a coat of lacquer (see Section 5.14) when used indoors to retain their bright metallic appearance; lacquer cannot be used externally because it lacks the necessary durability.

Ordinary steel requires corrosion protection. This may be accomplished by galvanizing (Section 2.5), or by means of an anticorrosive coat of paint. Before this *primer* is applied, all traces of rust must be removed by pickling in hot dilute acid, or by blast cleaning with an air jet containing grit, or by descaling with a very hot flame that loosens the rust (followed by scraping or wire brushing).

Red lead ($PbO_2 \cdot 2PbO$) is a traditional primer with excellent rust-inhibiting properties, but as it is poisonous it is now used only where the exposure is severe. Zinc tetroxychromate ($ZnCrO_4 \cdot 4Zn(OH)_2$) or zinc chromate are used in an oleoresinous or resinous vehicle. Zinc dust gives sacrificial protection (see Section 2.5); a suitable primer contains 90 percent of zinc dust in a vehicle of chlorinated rubber.

Galvanized steel is frequently painted, partly for additional protection against corrosion, and partly to improve its appearance.

5.13. PAINTS FOR SPECIAL PURPOSES

Building materials containing portland cement cannot be used with certain pigments and paint vehicles, because the cement contains free alkaline oxides when it is new. This is a particular problem with site-cast concrete. The alkali attack diminishes as the chemical action becomes neutralized by aging, but this takes several years.

The principal pigments whose color changes through alkali attack are ultramarine, Prussian blue, lead chromate, and Brunswick green. The paint vehicles affected are alkyds and oils, except tung oil. Alkalies turn oil into a soapy material; in fact, toilet soap is made from various vegetable oils and caustic soda.

The most suitable vehicles for alkaline surfaces are those that are highly polymerized, such as copolymer emulsions of polyvinyl acetate (PVA) and acrylics. Alternatively cement paints can be used on cement surfaces. These consist (see Section 3.8) of pigmented white portland cement.

Concrete swimming pools are painted partly for the sake of appearance, but the paint very significantly contributes to the waterproofing of the concrete. Chlorinated rubbers, epoxies, and styrene-butadiene copolymers are suitable vehicles.

Gypsum wallboard used in drywall construction (see Section 3.7) does not interact with paint. An emulsion paint is suitable as a first coat, and the same type of paint or an alkyd-based or oil-based paint can be used as a topcoat.

The time required for the ignition of wood can be increased by as much as 200 percent by the use of fire-retardant paints. They are usually applied in several coats, and the first coat is often *intumescent*, that it, it swells on heating to form a thick viscous foam that acts as an insulator. Since this does not weather well, the top coat must be both weather-resistant and fire-retardant. Antimony oxide (Sb_2O_3) is a stable and opaque white pigment with fire-retardant properties which can serve as a base for colored pigment.

5.14. VARNISHES, STAINS, LACQUERS, AND CLEAR COATINGS

Varnishes have been used since Antiquity. They were made from the resins of certain trees and shrubs, and from shellac, which was prepared from the excretions of certain tropical insects. Today varnishes are mostly made from synthetics, such as phenolic and alkyd resins.

An *oil varnish* is made by cooking the resin in a drying oil until partial polymerization occurs, and then adding a drier and a solvent to the ingredients after they have cooled. The varnish dries slowly if the proportion of resin to oil is low, and the coating has good elasticity. If more resin is used, the varnish dries faster and becomes harder, but it is more brittle and has poorer exterior durability. The formation of the oil varnish film is mainly due to the oxidation of the oil. The normal finish of an oil varnish is glossy, but eggshell or flat finishes can be produced by adding a suitable wax.

A *spirit varnish* is made by dissolving the resin in spirit. The film of a spirit varnish is formed mainly by the evaporation of the spirit.

Stains are water-soluble dyes used to decorate and protect wood used in the interior of a building. Since the dye is absorbed more readily by the softer part of the wood, it emphasizes the grain. Stains can be made in a variety of colors, but most are yellow or brown. Traditional stains were made from vegetable dyes, but today most are made synthetically. They are applied with wax, varnish, oil, spirit or water as a medium.

The term *lacquer* was used in the Nineteenth Century mainly for Chinese and Japanese varnish of superior quality. It is now used for synthetic materials that form a solid film by the rapid evaporation of a volatile solvent. Lacquers are easily applied by spraying, and since the dried film is soluble in the original solvent, it can be repaired. The most widely used synthetic lacquers are solutions of nitrocellulose, but lacquers can also be made from vinyl, polyurethane, and acrylics.

Clear coatings are skins with a very high abrasion resistance made with polyurethane or epoxy resins (see Section 5.3), used as sealers for wooden floors.

The term *clear coating* is also used for clear alkyd and polyurethane varnishes employed to retain a bright metallic surface on copper and its alloys, brass and bronze, by preventing oxidation.

The same result can be achieved with an abrasive, such as brass polish, but this is laborious, and it is impracticable for many metal fittings in buildings. These varnishes are not sufficiently durable for use on the exterior of buildings, but used internally they last many years before they need to be renewed.

REFERENCES

5.1. J. A. Brydson. *Plastics Materials*, 4th Ed. Butterworths, London, 1982. 800 pp.
5.2. P. Thiery. *Fireproofing*. Elsevier, Amsterdam, 1970. 156 pp.
5.3. M. Lewin, S. M. Atlas, and E. Pearce (Eds.). *Flame-Retardant Polymeric Materials*. Plenum Press, New York, 1978. 333 pp.

STANDARDS

Uniform Building Code. International Conference of Building Officials (ICBO), Whittier CA 1988. Chapter 52. *Light-Transmitting Plastics*. pp. 781-785.
Annual Book of ASTM Standards. American Society for Testing and Materials. Philadelphia 1989.
Volume 04.04. Roofing, Waterproofing and Bituminous Materials. 110 standards.
Volume 04.07. Building Seals and Sealants; Fire Standards; Building Construction. 155 standards.
Volumes 06.01, 06.02, and 06.03 Paint. 728 standards.
Volumes 08.01, 08.02, 08.03, and 08.04 Plastics. 547 standards, including:
  D 2843-70. Chamber Method of Test for Measuring the Density of Smoke from the Burning or Decomposition of Plastic Materials.
  D 1929-68 (1975). Ignition Properties of Plastics.
  D 635-74. Method of Test for Determining Classification [in relation to fire] of Approved Light-Transmitting Plastics.
Voluntary Specifications and Test Methods for Sealants. American Architectural Manufacturers Association, Des Plaines, IL, 1986. 24 pp.

SUGGESTIONS FOR FURTHER READING

R. Montella. *Plastics in Architecture*. Marcel Dekker, New York, 1985. 219 pp.

J. Frados (Ed.). *Plastics Engineering Handbook*, 4th Ed. Van Nostrand Reinhold, New York, 1976. 832 pp.

H. Olin, L. Schmidt, and W. H. Lewis. *Construction: Principles, Materials and Methods*, 5th Ed. Institute of Financial Education, Chicago, 1983. Chapter 209, "Plastics," pp. 209-1-18.

J. Heger, R. E. Chambers, and A. H. Dietz. *Structural Plastics Design Manual*. ASCE Manual on Engineering Design Practice No. 63. American Society of Civil Engineers, New York, 1984.

A. Blaga and J. J. Beaudoin. *Polymer Concrete*. Canadian Building Digest No. 242. National Research Council, Ottawa, 1985. 4 pp.

L. Moillett (Ed.). *Waterproofing and Water-Repellency*. Elsevier, Amsterdam, 1963. 502 pp.

Sealants: The Professionals Guide. Sealants and Waterproofers Institute, Chicago, 1987. 75 pp.

R. Panek and J. P. Cook. *Construction Sealants and Adhesives*. Wiley, New York, 1984. 348 pp.

R. Lambourne. *Paint and Surface Coatings: Theory and Practice*. Ellis Harwood-Wiley, Chichester (England), 1987. 860 pp.

NOTATION

Al	aluminum
Ba	barium
C	carbon
Ca	calcium
Cd	cadmium
Cl	chlorine
Cr	chromium
Fe	iron
H	hydrogen
Mg	magnesium
N	nitrogen
O	oxygen
Pb	lead
S	sulfur
Sb	antimony
Si	silicon
Zn	zinc

A list of abbreviations of the units of measurement, definitions of these units, and conversion factors between British/American and metric units are given in the Appendix.

6
Deformation and Jointing

Bruce Martin

Joints that permit movement are needed in buildings to permit expansion and contraction due to elastic deformations resulting from the addition and removal of loads; from changes in the temperature; from changes in the moisture content of building materials such as concrete and timber; and the initial shrinkage or expansion of cementituous materials, gypsum plaster, and clay products.

These joints are normally sealed with sealants, sealing strips, or gaskets.

6.1. JOINTS

A building is commonly considered to be a very solid form of structure that is constructed on firm foundations and is not liable to move even when subjected to high winds. A ship, in contrast, is subject to the buffeting of waves and wind and has to be designed to take account of these forces. In the design of ships the action of these forces is taken into account in such a way that the complete ship structure is intended to move and deflect in response to them. Otherwise, the ship would be liable to break up, as was the case with certain ships that had all-welded hulls.

New forms of building that make use of new and stronger materials and light structural frameworks are not as solid as some traditional structures so that, when subjected to wind, weather, and ground forces, movements take place. To prevent cracks and structural failure the design must be such as to take account of and allow for such movements. The main causes of movement that affect buildings and their effects are shown in Table 6.1. An important way of allowing for movement in a building structure is to design special joints. Such joints are referred to as *movement joints*.

Joints occur throughout a building. Wherever two or more products or components meet, the construction that is used to put together, fix or unite them forms a joint. Joints are an essential part of building construction, for without a joint that performs properly the building element that contains it may fail and so lead in due course to the failure of other parts of the building. During the building process joints can also facilitate the positioning and fixing of the components. The performance of a joint in a building: the way it behaves in use, often under conditions of stress, may be affected by all kinds of energy and by living organisms. The functions of joints are listed in Table 6.2.

6.2. MOVEMENT JOINTS

Certain joints are designed especially to accommodate the movement that may occur between adjoining parts. Where and when changes in temperature or moisture content induce corresponding changes in the dimensions of certain materials movement may occur. Joints that occur between such materials must allow for expansion or contraction or both movements. The joint is designed so as to accept variations of joint clearance sufficient to accommodate the calculated movements likely during the life of the joint.

There are a number of alternative ways of forming movement joints in blockwork walls. In the first method (Fig. 6.2.1), the blocks are bonded and laid to give a continuous vertical joint which is filled with mortar as the work proceeds. The mortar is then raked out on both sides of the joint to a depth of not more than $\frac{3}{4}$ in. (20 mm) and the gap is then filled with a sealant. In the second method the blockwork is built with a continuous open joint $\frac{3}{8}$ in.

DEFORMATION AND JOINTING

Table 6.1. Types of Movement and their Principal Causes.

Cause	Effect	Duration	Examples of Materials Affected
1. Temperature changes	Expansion and contraction	Intermittent diurnal, seasonal	All: see Table 2
2. Moisture content changes			
(a) Drying	Shrinkage	Principally short-term, due to loss of initial moisture	Mortar, concrete, and lime bricks, unseasoned timber
(b) Wetting	Expansion	Short-term, due to initial take-up of moisture	Ceramic products
(c) Drying alternating with wetting	Expansion and contraction	Seasonal	Poorly protected joinery, shrinkable clay soils
3. Other physical changes:			
(a) Loss of volatiles	Contraction	Short-term or long-term	Mastics
(b) Ice or crystalline salt formation	Expansion (in building materials; frost heave	Intermittent, dependent on weather conditions	Porous natural stones and other building materials; soils
4. Loading			
(a) On structure			
(i) Dead and imposed loading within design limits	Normally insignificant		
(ii) Structural overloading	Excessive deflection and distortion		
(b) On ground	Settlement	Extent of settlement varies with seasons	Silts and peaty ground particularly susceptible
5. Soil movements, e.g., mining subsidence, holes made by birds and rodents, landslips, soil creep, earthquakes	Settlement		
6. Vibration from traffic, machinery, sonic booms			Authenticated cases of damage are rare
7. Chemical changes:			
(a) Corrosion	Expansion	Continuous	(a) Metals
(b) Sulfate attack	Expansion	Continuous	(b) Portland cement and hydraulic lime products, e.g., concrete and mortar
(c) Carbonation	Shrinkage	Continuous	(c) Porous Portland cement products, e.g., lightweight concrete, asbestos cement

Tables 6.1, 6.2, and 6.3 are adapted from Ref. 6.1 by courtesy of the Controller of H. M. Stationery Office, Crown Copyright reserved.

(10 mm) wide. The center of the joint is then filled with a compressible filler, such as cellular polyethylene or cellular polyurethane, which serves as a backup material and also acts as a bond breaker. A sealant is then used to fill the gap on both sides of the joint (Fig. 6.2.2). A third method that may be used in the case of internal facing blockwork walls and partitions that are not required to be weather-resistant, the joint is raked out to give a groove $\frac{3}{4}$ in. (20 mm) deep and $\frac{3}{8}$ in. (10 mm) wide that is then filled with a weak mortar (Fig. 6.2.3).

6.3. CONTRACTION JOINTS

A contraction joint is a movement joint designed to accommodate shrinkage movement, especially the contraction of concrete, due to loss of moisture or loss of heat from the heat of hydration. Shrinkage movement can normally be considered irreversible, but cyclic movement may continue to occur due to variations in moisture content and temperature. Shrinkage or reduction in size of plastic concrete may occur during the hours following placing in position due to the loss of water from the concrete by evaporation or, sometimes, by absorption into adjacent materials. Hot weather and drying winds promote shrinkage and may produce cracking of the concrete. Shrinkage is a long-term process and may continue over many months. It will vary with the size of the section, the mix of concrete, the amount of reinforcement and the surrounding environmental conditions. The amount of movement in materials due to thermal and moisture changes is given in Table 6.3.

6.4. EXPANSION JOINTS

An expansion joint is a movement joint designed to accommodate both expansion and contraction movements of materials caused by cyclic variations in moisture content and temperature. The joint clearance must be large enough to accommodate the calculated maximum movement in the

Table 6.2 The Function of Joints.

Joints may be affected by living organisms and by energy of all kinds. As essential parts of a building process they must facilitate the fixing and the positioning of the components. As part of the architectural design, they must be visually acceptable.

An analysis of the many functions of a joint in building construction has been made in recent years and is contained in the International Standard, ISO 3447.

The list is reproduced here:

A1	To control passage of insects and vermin
A2	To control passage of plants, leaves, roots, seeds and pollen
A3	To control passage of dust and inorganic particles
A4	To control passage of heat
A5	To control passage of sound
A6	To control passage of light
A7	To control passage of radiation
A8	To control passage of air and other gases
A9	To control passage of odors
A10	To control passage of water, snow and ice
A11	To control passage of water vapor
A12	To control condensation
A13	To control generation of sound
A14	To control generation of odors

To resist stress in one or more directions due to:

B1	compression
B2	tension
B3	bending
B4	shear
B5	torsion
B6	vibrations (or any other type of stress which may induce fatigue)
B7	impact
B8	abrasion (indicate, for each particular case, the type of wear)
B9	shrinkage or expansion
B10	creep
B11	dilation or contraction due to temperature variations
C1	To control passage of fire, smoke, gases, radiation and radioactive materials
C2	To control sudden positive or negative pressures due to explosion or atmospheric factors
C3	To avoid generation of toxic gases and fumes in case of fire
C4	To avoid harboring or proliferation of dangerous micro-organisms
D1	To accommodate variations in the sizes of the joint at assembly due to deviations in the sizes and positions of the joined components (induced deviations)
D2	To accommodate continuing changes in the sizes of the joint due to thermal, moisture and structural movement, vibration and creep (inherent deviations)
E1	To support joined components in one or more directions
E2	To resist differential deformation of joined components
E3	To permit operation of movable components
F1	To have acceptable appearance
F2	To avoid promotion of plant growth
F3	To avoid discoloration due to biological, physical or chemical action
F4	To avoid all or part of the internal structure showing
F5	To avoid dust collection
G1	To have known first cost
G2	To have known depreciation
G3	To have known maintenance and/or replacement costs

Table 6.2 (Continued)

H1	To have specified minimum life, taking into account cyclic factors
H2	To resist damage or unauthorized dismantling by man
H3	To resist action of animals and insects
H4	To resist action of plants and micro-organisms
H5	To resist action of water, water vapor or aqueous solutions or suspensions
H6	To resist action of polluted air
H7	To resist action of light
H8	To resist action of radiation (other than radiation of light)
H9	To resist action of freezing of water
H10	To resist action of extremes of temperatures
H11	To resist action of airborne or structure-borne vibrations, shock waves or high-intensity sound
H12	To resist action of acids, alkalis, oils, fats and solvents
H13	To resist abrasive action
J1	To permit partial or complete dismantling and reassembly
J2	To permit replacement of decayed jointing products
K1	To perform required functions over a specified range of temperatures
K2	To perform required functions over a specified range of atmospheric humidity
K3	To perform required functions over a specified range of air or liquid pressure differentials
K4	To perform required functions over a specified range of joint clearance variations
K5	To exclude from the joint if performance would be impaired: a) insects b) plants c) micro-organisms d) water e) ice f) snow g) polluted air h) solid matter
K6	To perform required functions over a specified range of driving rain volume

adjoining building elements, such as, for example, a length of wall. A particular kind of expansion is permanent moisture expansion in fired clay units, which decreases with time and is dependent on the type of clay and its method

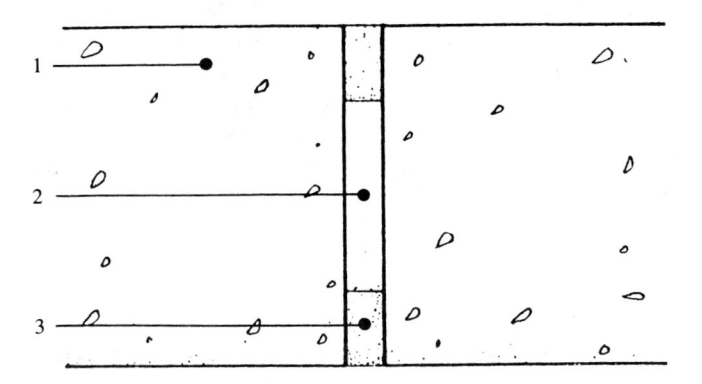

Fig. 6.2.1. Movement joint in blockwork. 1 = Concrete block; 2 = portland cement : lime : sand mortar, 1 : 1 : 6; 3 = sealant. Masonry cement may be substituted for the cement-lime mix.

DEFORMATION AND JOINTING

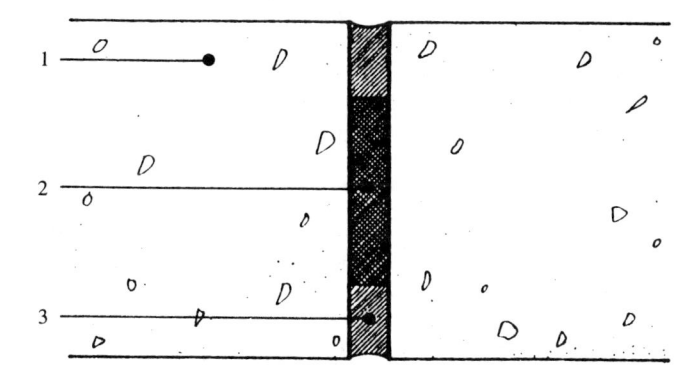

Fig. 6.2.2. Movement joint in blockwork. 1 = Concrete block; 2 = cellular polyethylene backup material and bond-breaker; 3 = sealant.

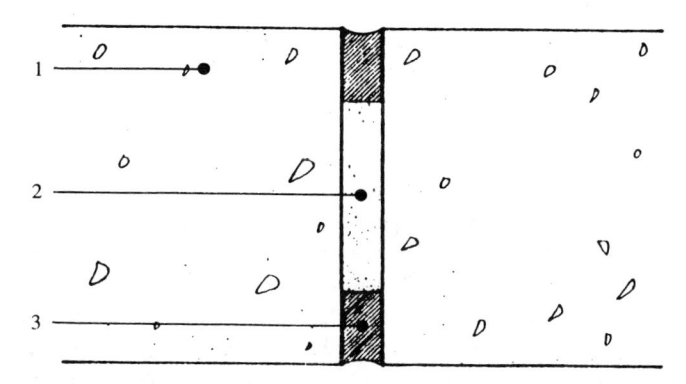

Fig. 6.2.3. Movement joint in blockwork. 1 = Concrete block; 2 = portland cement : lime : sand mortar, 1 : 1 : 6; 3 = cement : lime : sand mortar, 1 : 2 : 9. Masonry cement may be substituted for the cement-lime mix.

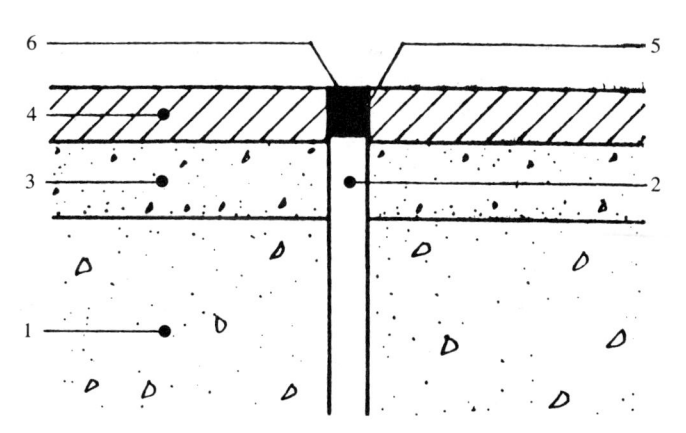

Fig. 6.4.1. Expansion joint in a concrete slab finished with clay floor tiles. An expansion joint across a floor of clay tiles is recommended when any floor dimension exceeds 50 ft (15 m). Gaps with a clearance of up to $\frac{3}{8}$ in. (10 mm) are filled with a compressible filler board, a seperating strip, and a sealant. The filler must be tightly packed so that no voids remain at the base of the gap. 1 = Concrete base; 2 = compressible filler board; 3 = cement : sand bed (mixture 1 : 4); 4 = clay floor tile; 5 = separating strip; 6 = sealant.

of burning. Changes in moisture content that cause reversible movement will affect timber, especially when it is not protected by a suitable paint. For a typical expansion joint in a concrete floor slab with a clay tile floor finish see Fig. 6.4.1.

6.5. MOVEMENT AT A JOINT

Movement that takes place at a joint is characterized by its mode, frequency, rate and magnitude.

Table 6.3 Approximate Unrestrained Movement.

Material	Thermal Movement in. per ft per °F	Thermal Movement mm per 3 m per 30°C	Moisture Movement (Dry to Saturated) 0.001 in. per ft	Moisture Movement (Dry to Saturated) mm per 3 m length
Steel	4.2–4.9	0.9–1.05	–	–
Aluminum	9.7	2.1	–	–
Copper	6.7	1.45	–	–
Glass	4.4	0.95	–	–
Clay bricks	2.0–2.3	0.4–0.6	0.3–1.2	0.08–0.3
Sand-lime bricks	5.6	1.2	1.2–7.2	0.3–1.5
Dense concrete, mortar, cement plaster	3.8–5.6	0.8–1.2	2.4–7.2	0.6–1.8
Neat gypsum plaster	6.9–8.1	1.5–1.8	Negligible	
Sanded gypsum plaster	4.6–5.8	1.0–1.3	Negligible	
Asbestos cement	3.2	0.7	2.4–9.6	0.6–2.4
Marble, dense limestone	2.2	0.5	Negligible	
Plastic (other than polyethylene)	5.8–40	1.3–9	Usually negligible	
Wood along the grain			0.1	0.03
Wood across grain, tangential			600–1800	150–450
Wood across grain, radial			360–600	90–150
Initial drying shrinkage of portland-cement products			2.4–6	0.6–1.5

The initial expansion of fired-clay products varies greatly.

Note: A temperature range of 54°F (30°C) may be greatly exceeded in practice. Color, orientation, and thermal conductivity all play a part. Thus a black panel, insulated at its back, can reach 158°F (70°C).

Mode. Forces may be applied perpendicular to the joint reference plane to produce tension, as in a simple butt joint. (Fig. 6.5.1) Alternatively, forces may be applied parallel to the joint reference plane to produce shear, as in a simple lap joint. (FIg. 6.5.2)

Frequency. Movement may be a steady one in one direction during a period of time or a cyclical movement that may correspond to climatic temperature changes. Cyclic movement may be inhibited by frictional forces that develop between adjoining components as, for example, between two roofing sheets, one of which overlaps another.

Rate. Movement may be rapid as a result of changes in weather conditions and temperature combined with particular kinds of materials and construction. A component such as aluminum alloy siding (walling sheet), especially if it is painted a dark color, has a relatively high coefficient of thermal expansion and low thermal capacity. Where subjected to changes of temperature, movement is rapid due to rapid heat gain and loss. The positioning of insulation immediately behind the sheet will further increase the temperature changes of the sheet due to the lower rate of dissipation of heat from the sheet by radiation or convection.

Magnitude. The total amount of movement of adjoining components at a joint can be estimated by using methods such as that described in Refs. 6.2, 6.3, 6.4, and 6.5. When the calculation has been made, the minimum and maximum joint clearance can then be determined. Jointing products are then selected to accommodate the estimated total movement. In the case of a sealant, its use for a particular joint will be governed by its Movement Accommodation Factor (MAF). The movement accommodation factor of a sealant is the maximum movement which the sealant is capable of tolerating throughout its working life, expressed as a percentage of the minimum joint width.

6.6. SEALANTS

The simplest way of accommodating movement at a joint is to leave the joint gap unfilled. For example, floor tiles can be laid with a gap around the perimeter of the flooring that allows for movement of the tiles and a variation in the gap width. (Fig. 6.6.1) However, it is often necessary to fill the gap with a jointing product for other purposes, such as to provide a seal against wind or weather. In such cases the material used to fill the joint space and be capable of movement is referred to as a sealant, sealing strip, or gasket (see also Section 5.8). A sealant is an unformed flexible material that is applied to a joint to prevent the passage of dust, moisture, wind, etc. Sealants are described as elastic, plastic, elastoplastic, and plastoelastic according to their reaction to an applied force.

An elastic sealant is one where stresses induced in the sealant are almost proportional to the strain. A plastic sealant is one where the stresses induced in the sealant are rapidly relieved. An elastoplastic sealant has predominantly elastic properties but shows some plastic properties when stressed for other than short periods. A plastoelastic sealant, on the other hand, has mainly plastic properties with some elastic recovery when stressed for short periods. A sealant is applied with a gun or with a knife, or is poured into position. The main types of material are polysulfide: one-part; polysulfide: 2-part; silicone: one-part; polyurethane: one-part; polyurethane: two-part; acrylic: one-part; butyl; oil-based; bituminous; bitumen rubber; and asphalt (pitch) polymer.

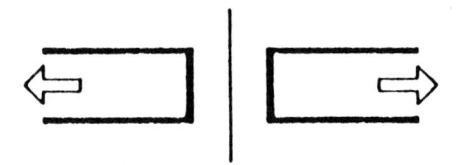

Fig. 6.5.1. Tension in a simple shear joint.

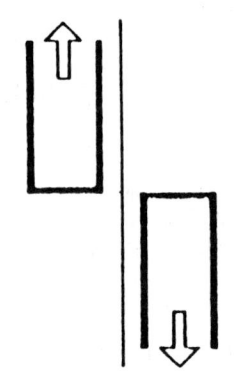

Fig. 6.5.2. Shear in a simple lap joint.

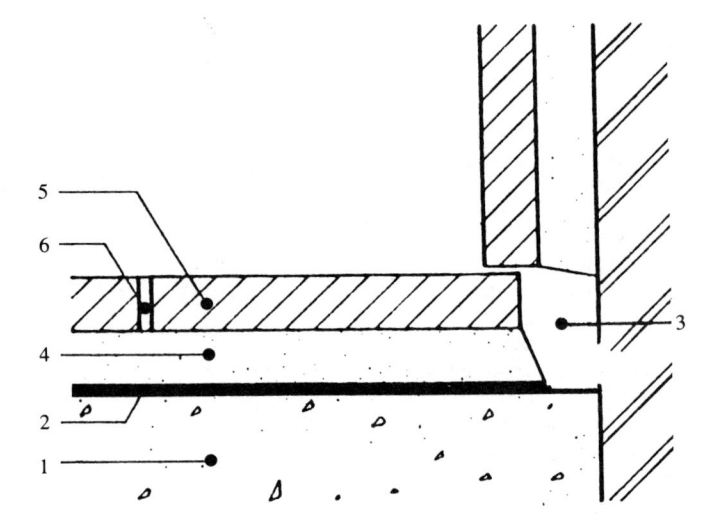

Fig. 6.6.1. Joints between tiles, and movement joints around flooring. 1 = Concrete base; 2 = separating layer; 3 = movement joint (unfilled gap); 4 = cement : sand bedding (1 : 4); 5 = clay floor tile; 6 = joint $\frac{1}{8}$ in. (3 mm) thick, filled with cement-sand grout.

DEFORMATION AND JOINTING 97

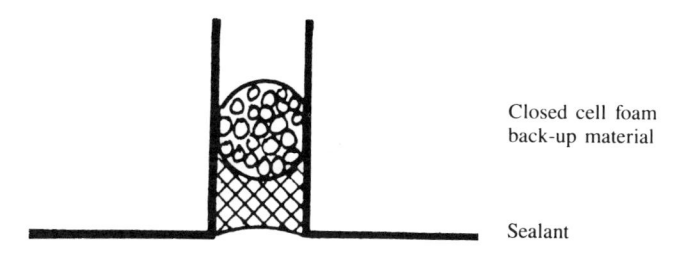

Fig. 6.6.2. Joint with sealant and backup material.

A sealant must be applied against a firm backing so that it adheres well to the joint faces when forced into position. The backing, called *backup material*, is inserted into a joint so as to limit the depth of sealant that is required and maintain the correct depth of sealant (Fig. 6.6.2). For joint gap widths of between $\frac{1}{2}$ and 2 in. (12 and 50 mm) the depth of sealant should be one-half of the joint width. The minimum depth of sealant is $\frac{1}{4}$ in. (6 mm). In concrete and masonry joints where structural movement is expected the depth of sealant should be between $\frac{1}{2}$ and $\frac{3}{4}$ in. (12 and 20 mm), depending on the gap width. If the gap width is less than $\frac{1}{2}$ inch (12 mm), the depth should be between $\frac{1}{4}$ and $\frac{1}{2}$ in. (6 and 12 mm). If the joint width is $\frac{1}{4}$ inch (6 mm), the depth should be $\frac{1}{4}$ inch (6 mm) (Fig. 6.6.3).

Backup material is cellular, fibrous, or granular and is in the form of sheet or strip, or is unformed. Materials used for backup material are wood fiber/bitumen, bitumen/cork, cork/resin, cellular plastic, cellular rubbers, mineral fiber, synthetic fiber, and mortar. The sealant must not adhere to the backup material, as it would then be held on three sides and not be free to expand and contract at right angles to the joint gap. To prevent adhesion to the backup material a *bond breaker* is used. A bond breaker is usually in the form of a film or tape. Closed-cell foam backup material, because it has release properties, itself acts as a bond breaker. In practice, it is important that the film or tape only extend over the joint clearance and not up the joint faces where it would reduce the area of adhesion of the sealant (Fig. 6.6.4).

6.7. SEALING STRIPS

A sealing strip is a jointing product preformed to a definite cross section and of unspecified length. It may be cellular or noncellular and is formed by extrusion from sealant material that has properties of elasticity, plasticity or a combination of the two. A sealing strip is usually used to act as a backup for a sealant. When the sealing strip is made of cellular foam polyethylene it also acts as a bond breaker. Some sealing strips are manufactured with an adhesive layer on the outer faces that serve to help locate the strip during installation.

6.8. GASKETS

A gasket is a jointing product used in a joint to act as a barrier to the passage of wind and rain. It may be inserted

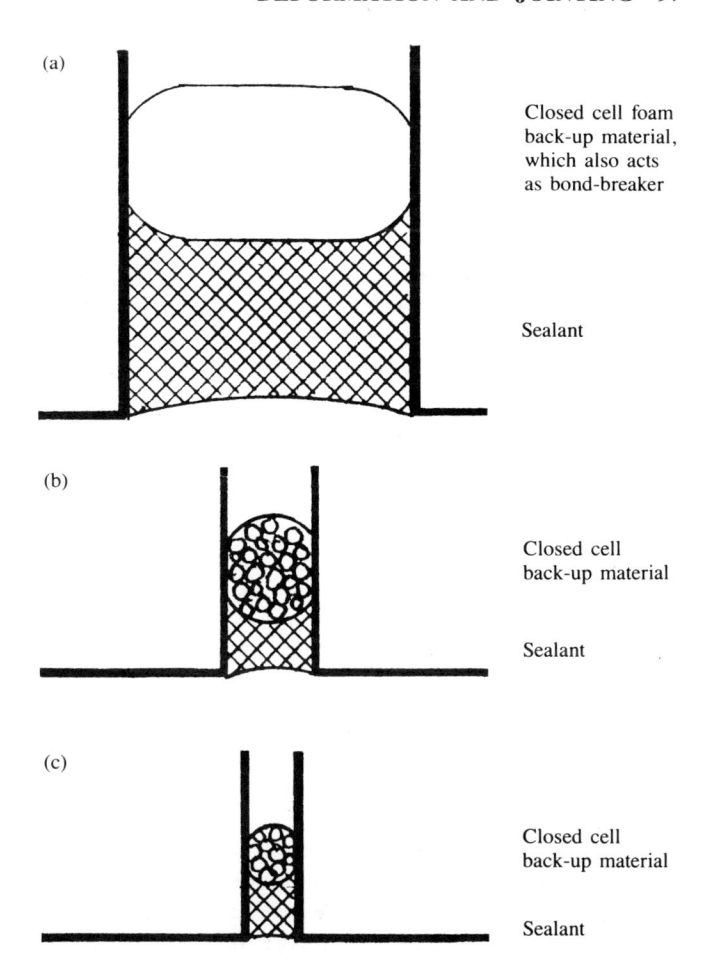

Fig. 6.6.3. Width and depth of sealant. (a) In concrete and masonry movement joints, the depth of the sealant should be between $\frac{1}{2}$ and $\frac{3}{4}$ in. (12 and 20 mm). (b) If the gap width is less than $\frac{1}{2}$ in. (12 mm), the depth of the sealant should be at least $\frac{1}{4}$ in. (6 mm). (c) If the gap width is $\frac{1}{4}$ in., the depth of the sealant should be $\frac{1}{4}$ in. (6 mm).

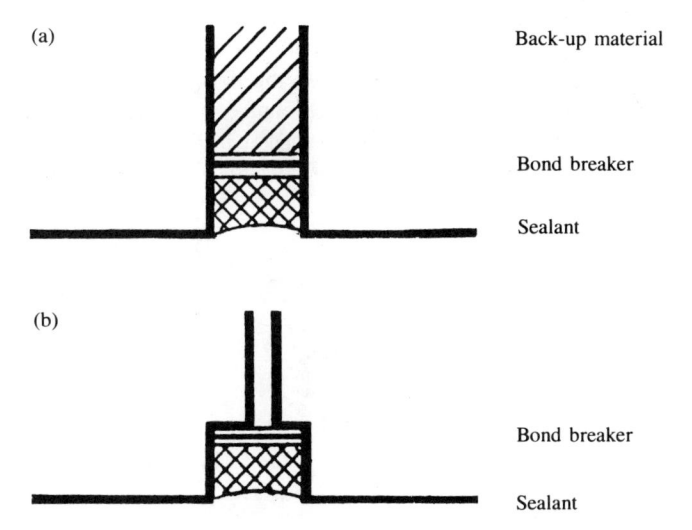

Fig. 6.6.4. Joint with bond breaker. (a) Bond breaker between sealant and backup material. (b) Bond breaker at base of slot for sealant without backup material.

prior to assembly in one of the adjoining components or during erection of the components or after the components have been placed in position.

A gasket should be compressible and resilient and have a long life. Sometimes a gasket may be needed to be resistant to the effects of oils and a suitable material should be selected in this case.

Materials for gaskets include non cellular and cellular chloroprene, butyl, chlorobutyl, ethylene propylene, rubbers, styrene butadiene and isoprene rubbers, neoprene, polyurethene, polyethylene, ethylene vinyl acetate, silicone, cork, and mineral fiber.

Gaskets are formed with solid, hollow, or finned cross-sections or combinations of these, and may be cellular or noncellular. Gaskets may be manufactured with or without an adhesive outer covering. The shape of the gasket depends upon its position when assembled and should provide for contact with the component in at least two positions so as to provide an air space between the points of contact and give a second barrier to the passage of wind and rain (see Figs. 6.8.1, 6.8.2, and 6.8.3).

The profile of the cross section of the gasket should be related to the joint profile of the component and the sizes must be designed to take account of the calculated minimum and maximum joint clearance.

The junctions between gaskets positioned in vertical joints and those positioned in horizontal joints must be designed to be water and wind resistant by means of effective overlaps, the use of sealants, or the use of specially fabricated corner pieces. Butt joints between gaskets, without the use of adhesives, should be avoided. The type of gasket must be related to the type of joint profile of the components and especially to the sequence of assembly. Examples of typical gaskets that are related to each stage of assembly are shown in Figs. 6.8.1, 6.8.2, and 6.8.3.

Gaskets when in position in a joint must remain under compression for all calculated and actual gap widths and during the whole life of the gasket material. Otherwise, the gaskets may have to be replaced during the life of the building. If this is the case, then the design should allow for the removal and the replacement of the aged gasket. The method of insertion of the gasket in the joint and the sequence of assembly must be such as to ensure proper

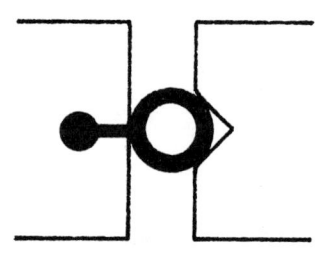

Fig. 6.8.1. Joint with gasket fixed to one component during manufacture.

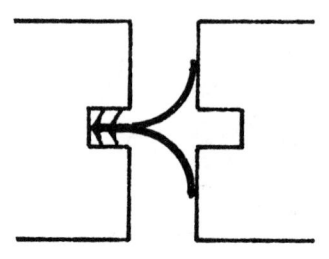

Fig. 6.8.2. Joint with gasket fitted during assembly on site.

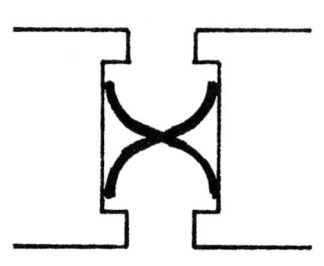

Fig. 6.8.3. Joint with gasket fitted after erection of both components.

compression of the gasket and the maintenance of that compression throughout its life, especially where and when there is a variation of gap width as, for example, in a movement joint. However, the gasket must not be compressed beyond the limit of recovery of the material from stress. During assembly, the joint faces of the component designed to accept a gasket must be clean and smooth. The joint gap before insertion of the gasket must be open and clear of dust and debris.

6.9. JOINT FILLERS

A joint filler is a jointing product that is used to fill a joint during construction to permit movement between its adjoining components. It provides a temporary barrier during construction to maintain the joint gap and prevent it being filled with dirt and debris which could subsequently prevent movement of the components. Sometimes the joint filler may also act as a support for a sealant and be located to maintain the correct depth of the sealant in the joint.

A joint filler should be compressible to permit variation in the gap width, resilient so as not to be squeezed out of the joint, nonstaining, and resistant to damage when handled. In certain positions, the joint filler may need to be fire resistant and a suitable material selected accordingly. The material of a joint filler should be compatible with the sealants and primers, resistant to solvents, and be stable over a range of temperature.

Materials for joint fillers, together with their properties, are shown in Table 6.4.

Table 6.4. Fillers for Movement Joints.

Joint Filler Type	Typical Uses	Form	Density Range lb/ft³	Density Range kg/m³	Pressure for 50% Compression psi	Pressure for 50% Compression N/mm² or MPa	Resilience (recovery after compression), %	Tolerance to Water Immersion
Wood fiber/bitumen	General purpose expansion joints	Sheet, strip	12–24	200–400	100–750	0.7–5.2	70–85	Suitable if infrequent
Bitumen/cork	General purpose expansion joints	Sheet	30–37	500–600	100–750	0.7–5.2	70–80	Suitable
Cork/resin	Expansion joints in water-retaining structures where bitumen is not acceptable	Sheet, strip	12–18	200–300	70–500	0.5–3.4	85–95	Suitable
Cellular plastics and rubbers	Low load transfer joints	Sheet, strip	2.4–3.7	40–60	10–50	0.07–0.34	85–95	Suitable if infrequent
Mineral or synthetic fibers	Fire-resistant joints: low movement	Loose fiber or braided	Dependent upon degree of compaction		Dependent upon degree of compaction		Slight	Not suitable

REFERENCES

6.1. *Cracking in Buildings.* Digest No. 75. Building Research Establishment, Garston, England, 1966. 4 pp.

6.2. *Estimation of Thermal and Moisture Movements and Stresses. Parts 1, 2, and 3.* Digests No. 227, 228, and 229. Building Research Establishment, Garston, England, 1979. 4 pp. each.

6.3. *Differential Movement—Cause and Effect.* Technical Note 18, 1984.
Differential Movement—Expansion Joints. Technical Note 18A, 1980.
Differential Movement—Flexible Anchorage. Technical Note 18B, 1980.
Brick Institute of America, Reston, VA.

6.4. *Joint Movement and Sealant Selection.* Canadian Building Digest No. 155, 1973. 4 pp.
Joints in Conventional Bituminous Roofing Systems. Canadian Building Digest No. 202, 1979. 4 pp.
Division of Building Research, National Research Council, Ottawa.

6.5. *Movement Control Joints in Masonry Walls.* NSB 57, 4 pp.
Differential Movement in Buildings Clad with Clay Bricks. NSB 134, 1974, 4 pp., and NSB 135, 1975, 4 pp.
Notes on the Science of Building. Experimental Building Station, Sydney.

STANDARDS

Joints in Building—General Check List of Joint Functions. ISO 3447. International Standards Organization, Geneva, 1975.

Code of Practice for Design of Joints and Jointing in Building Construction. BS 6093. British Standards Institution, London, 1981.

Modular Coordination in Buildings. BS 6750. Part A.4. *Joints and Fit.* British Standards Institution, London, 1986.

SUGGESTIONS FOR FURTHER READING

Building Research Establishment. *Clay Tile Flooring.* Digest No. 79. 1967. 4 pp.
Floor Screeds. Digest No. 104, 1969. 4 pp.
Principles of Joint Design. Digest No. 137, 1977. 4 pp.
Calcium Silicate Brickwork. Digest No. 157, 1973. 4 pp.
Getting Good Fit. Digest No. 199, 1977. 4 pp.
Wall Cladding: Designing to Minimize Defects Due to Inaccuracies and Movement. Digest No. 223, 1979. 4 pp.
Building Research Establishment, Garston, England.

Institute for Research in Construction. *Use of Sealants.* Canadian Building Digest (CBD) No. 96. 1967. 4 pp.
Look at Joint Performance. CBD No. 97. 1967 4 pp.
Requirements for Exterior Walls. CBD No. 48. 1963. 4 pp.
Thermal and Moisture Deformations in Building Materials. CBD No. 56. 1964. 4 pp.
Some Implications of the Properties of Wood. CBD No. 86. 1967. 4 pp.
Volume Change and Creep of Concrete. CBD No. 119. 1969. 4 pp.
Institute for Research in Construction, National Research Council, Ottawa.

W. Brewer. "Use of Flexible Closures in High-Performance Joints." *Construction Specifier*, 41 (N 5), 27–30 (May 1988).

C. T. Grimm. "Design for Differential Movement in Brickwork." *J. Structural Div., Amer. Soc. Civil Engineers.* **101**(11), 2385–2403 (1975).

Bruce Martin. *Joints in Buildings.* Godwin, London, 1977; Wiley, New York, 1977.

NOTATION

A list of abbreviations of the units of measurement, definitions of these units, and conversion factors between British/American and metric units are given in the Appendix.

7

Exclusion of Water by Roofs, Walls, and Floors

Bruce Martin

Moisture may enter buildings as rain water, as condensate forming as the temperature falls below the dew point, or as water rising from the ground. Since this moisture can cause decay of building materials, and create a damp, unhealthy atmosphere within the building, it must be controlled, while permitting the passage of air. The various control measures are discussed in turn.

7.1. WATER

Water is a clear, colorless, tasteless, odorless liquid that is an effective solvent. It can exist in a gaseous state as water vapor and in a solid state as ice or snow. Water is present in the atmosphere as clouds or rain or condensate. It is moved by gravity, changes of temperature and pressure. In the atmosphere it can lose its purity by absorption of chemicals or similar substances that may be produced as a waste product by an industrial process.

Rain or snow consists of drops of water that are formed by the condensation of water vapor in the atmosphere. Under the action of gravity they become rainfall or snowfall. The amount of rainfall in a particular place over a specified period of time is measured by a rain gauge (also called a pluviometer).

A given building in a particular position anywhere in the world will be subjected to an annual rainfall that varies to a limited extent from year to year. But at certain times in a given place a building will be subjected to a large amount of rainfall over a short period. Such rainstorms may occur at different times of the year but when they do occur the building must be designed to remove such a sudden quantity of stormwater in such a way that it does not penetrate the building or affect its foundations.

A building in its simplest form consists of a roof, walls, and a floor. One of its main functions is to *provide shelter*, especially from the weather: that is to say, the conditions in its locality of temperature, cloudiness, rain and wind. However, while providing shelter, the building, if it is to be used by people, must also *provide for the circulation of fresh air*. To meet both these functions, the envelope and fabric of the building must keep out rain and permit the passage of air.

Rainfall, as it falls vertically, will not affect the walls of buildings. When, however, it is combined with wind, it is called *driving rain*. The amount of rain driven onto a wall is directly proportional to the product of the rainfall on the ground and the speed of the wind during rainfall. The effect of driving rain on the wall of a building will, of course, depend upon the direction of the wind, but during heavy storms the wind may blow from any direction. The presence of the building itself and of adjoining buildings will affect the direction of driving rain and its intensity.

Water or water vapor can also be produced inside a building as a result of human activities: by human breathing, cooking of food, washing and drying of clothes, and combustion of gas that is used for heating or cooking. A household can generate from 1.8 to 3 gallons (7 to 11 liters) or 19 to 30 lb (7 to 11 kg) per day. As the quantity of water vapor inside the building increases, the pressure will rise above that of the outside atmosphere and the water vapor will tend to flow outwards. It can do so through flues, roof window vents, open windows and porous walls. But where these do not exist, water vapor indoors will become excessive and form mist or water by the *process of condensation* (see Section 20.3).

Condensation takes place when a given volume of air is saturated with water vapor and the temperature drops. The quantity of water vapor carried in air is proportional to its temperature: the higher the temperature the more water vapor it can carry. When condensation takes place in air, water vapor forms mist and when it takes place on a cold surface it forms water. The proportion of water vapor that can be carried in air is known as the *Relative Humidity* and is expressed as a percentage (see Section 20.3). Saturated air has a relative humidity of 100 percent. When air changes in a building are maintained at a specified rate, as, for example, by means of an air-conditioning system, the relative humidity is kept down to about 50 percent and the possibility of condensation is greatly reduced.

7.2. EXCLUSION OF RAINWATER FROM ROOFS (See also Section 24.6)

One of the principal requirements of roofs is that they shall be waterproof, especially in areas of heavy rainfall and places subject to snowfalls. The ability of the roofing to shed water is related to its slope, which is in turn related to the type of roofing material (see Table 7.1). In countries with very low rainfall, roofs can be and often are flat. In countries subject to heavy rainfall or extremes of snow, ice, and cold, roofs are usually steep. Furthermore, roofs protect the walls, especially on single-story buildings and to some extent on two-story buildings, and especially if the eaves are wide or there is a veranda.

On *pitched roofs* the roofing (the upper layer or layers of a roof that provide a waterproof surface) is usually formed of components that overlap one another. The amount of overlap is related to the pitch of the roof and the nature of the roofing material. The overlap is intended to check driving rain and also to increase the capillary path formed by two overlapping components such as slates, tiles, shingles, or metal sheets. Apart from the overlaps on the main pitch of a roof, there are important junctions of roofing such as at the ridge, eaves, verges, hips, valleys, rooflights, and roof windows, where the design of joints that exclude water is essential. It follows that the simpler the design of a roof, and the fewer are the interruptions and junctions in the surface of the roofing, the more likely is it to exclude water. Furthermore, too low a pitch for the roofing material used will increase the likelihood of rain penetration and may cause gradual disintegration of the slates or tiles due to their retention of water for a longer period and its freezing in cold weather.

Flat roofs are not exactly flat and generally have a slope of 1 : 50 to 1 : 100 that is intended to remove rainwater as it accumulates. The roofing of flat roofs necessarily cannot

Table 7.1. Inclination of Roofs.

Roofing Material for Ordinary Exposed Roof	in. per ft	Slope	Angle, degrees
Corrugated steel or aluminum sheet in one single length:			
on steel battens	$\frac{1}{4}$	1 : 50	1
on timber battens	$\frac{1}{2}$	1 : 28	2
in corrosive atmosphere	1	1 : 12	5
Roll roofing	1–3	1 : 12–1 : 4	5–14
Asphalt shingles; Corrugated steel with overlaps; Glass with overlaps	3–4	1 : 4–1 : 3	14–18
Wood shakes (handsplit) with underlayment	4	1 : 3	18
Wood shingles (sawn) without underlayment	3–5	1 : 4–1 : 2.4	14–24
Large slates	5	1 : 2.4	24
Ordinary slates	6–7	1 : 2–1 : 1.7	27–30
Roman tiles, Spanish tiles, or pan tiles of clay or concrete	4–8	1 : 3–1 : 1.5	18–34
Interlocking clay or concrete tiles	4–8	1 : 3–1 : 1.5	18–34
Plain tiles of clay or concrete	8–12	1 : 1.5–1 : 1	34–45
Thatch	15	1 : 0.8	50

1. Pitch is defined as the ratio of rise to span, and it is therefore normally one half of the slope.
2. Roof slopes can generally be reduced if an underlayment or sarking is used.
3. A steeper slope may be used for aesthetic reasons, or because it is traditional in the region.

be made of small overlapping components and a continuous weatherproof surface has to be provided. With large areas of flat roofs thermal movement of the roof and its roofing can become important and joints must be designed to take movement into account as well as to resist the passage of rainwater.

The principal sheeting roofing materials for flat roofs are bitumen roofing, sheet roofing, built-up felt roofing, and single-ply roofing.

Bitumen roofing may consist of asphalt roofing laid in two or more layers applied in a molten state to a substrate of insulation, normally cork or polyisocyanurate. Alternatively, it may be formed of two or more layers of bituminous materials completely bonded together.

Sheet roofing is formed of roofing sheets that are made of metal, plastics, or similar material, flat or profiled in cross section and sufficiently rigid to be self-supporting between supports. Roofing sheets are used on both flat and pitched roofs and are fixed with exposed or concealed fixings. When the span of the roof exceeds the length of the manufactured sheet, end laps are required; they can be difficult to make weatherproof, especially on low slopes. There are many kinds of longitudinal lap and few that are entirely satisfactory at the present time. Long sheets are subject to considerable thermal movement that must be allowed for in the method of fixing: holes, for example, should be slotted. The cut edges of coated steel sheets may deteriorate. Openings in the sheeting for roof windows, rooflights, ventilation, or pipes are difficult to weatherproof, especially when the sheeting has a troughed profile. Repairs to damaged sheets are not easily carried out and may necessitate total replacement of the damaged sheet. Nevertheless, such sheeting is quick to erect and relatively economical, especially on large areas of building with a simple plan shape and spans carefully related to the lengths of roofing sheet.

Built-up felt roofing consists of two or more layers of bitumen felt bonded together. Bitumen felt is fiber-based material saturated with asphalt (bitumen). The material should provide a base that does not rot, strength to permit flexibility to accommodate continuous thermal movement and resistance to aging and hardening of the asphalt (bitumen) due to the combined action of ultraviolet light, ozone, and oxygen. It should not be easily damaged or torn and be able to accept knocks and wear over many years of service. The development of roofing membranes to meet some of these requirements has consisted in the addition to the bitumen of a polymer such as rubber, SBS (styrene butadiene styrene) or APP plastic (atactic polypropylene). Felt with SBS additive has increased elasticity and is normally bonded in hot asphalt (bitumen). Felt with APP additive has improved resistance to high temperature and better resistance to weather, and is normally bonded by torching (a method of applying heat to fuse and weld the felts together).

High performance polyester-based roofing felt is manufactured in different weights with either oxidized asphalt (bitumen) coating or SBS modified bitumen coating.

Two-layer fully bonded high performance roofing consists of a first layer of a lightweight polyester and a top layer of a heavier weight. Partially bonded roofing usually consists of a first layer of perforated felt laid on the concrete or insulation, a second layer of felt and an APP modified torch-on polyester based top layer.

Single-ply roofing consists of a single layer of roofing sheet of thermoplastic or elastomeric material. Thermoplastic sheets such as polyvinyl chloride (PVC), or chlorinated polyethylene (CPE), are generally welded by solvent or heat at the laps (see Section 5.4). Elastomeric sheets, such as butyl, polyisobutene (PIB), or ethylene-propylene-diene monomer (EPDM) are normally bonded adhesively at the laps (see Section 5.9). Single-layer membranes may be loose-laid and covered with ballast, mechanically fixed, or fully adhered to the substrate.

7.3. EXCLUSION OF CONDENSATE FROM ROOFS

Condensate is the water formed by the process of condensation. Condensation from saturated air (air that contains water vapor about to be deposited as water) will take place in a roof when any surface of the roofing is colder than the saturated air below the surface. The temperature at which the saturated air becomes saturated is described as the *dewpoint* (see Section 20.3).

Pitched Roofs

To prevent condensation on the underside of the roofing or roofing support structure, ventilation should be provided to remove the saturated or partially saturated air in the rooms below before it reaches the roof space. Nevertheless, to lessen the amount of saturated air that may enter the roof space, a *vapor barrier* should be provided at ceiling level and all access doors and holes through the ceiling should be properly sealed. Reinforced felt used under the roofing tiles or roofing slates should be of a kind to permit the passage of water vapor and also be absorbent, since impermeable material allows condensate to form in its undersurface, and nonabsorbent material will not take up condensate that if absorbed would evaporate subsequently (Fig. 7.3.1).

When there is no roof space below the roofing and when the roofing is resistant to the passage of water vapor, as is the case with metal roofing sheet, condensation may occur below the ceiling or below the reinforced felt or below the roofing sheet. To prevent condensation under the ceiling, insulation should be provided immediately above the ceiling and a vapor barrier should be positioned below the insulation (Fig. 7.3.2).

To prevent condensation under the roofing felt or roofing sheet water vapor entering the felt must be minimized and there must be adequate ventilation of the space below the felt or sheet.

To limit the amount of water vapor, the vapor barrier should be a minimum of 500 gauge (0.05 mm) polyethylene sheet with properly sealed joints between the sheets. To provide for ventilation under the roofing felt or roofing sheet an air space of 2 in. (50 mm) should be provided between the insulation and the felt or sheet.

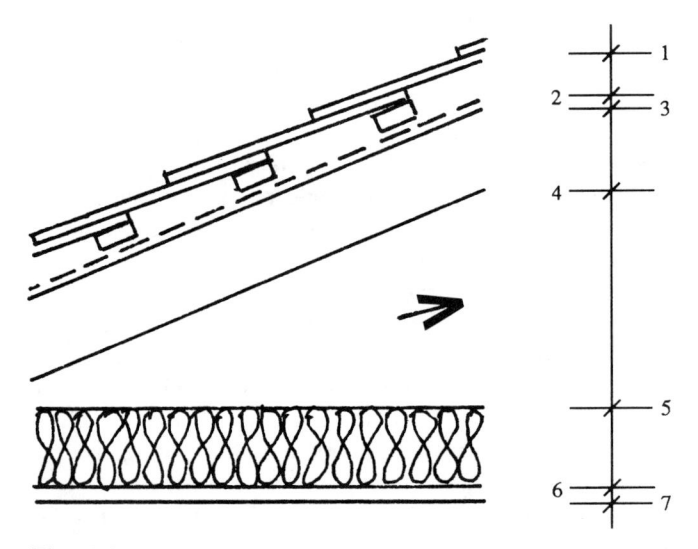

Fig. 7.3.1. Pitched roof with roof space: (1–2) tiles, slates, shingles, corrugated metal, etc. on battens; (2–3) underlayment, sarking felt, or reflective insulation, if used; (3–4) rafters; (4–5) ventilated air space; (5–6) thermal insulation, if used; (6–7) ceiling.

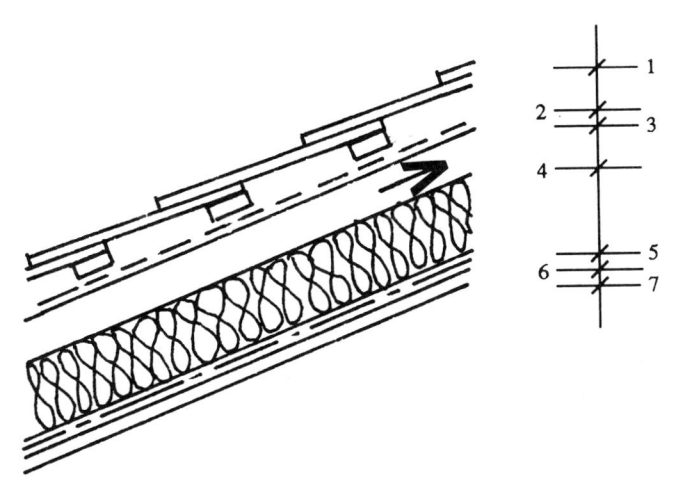

EXCLUSION OF WATER BY ROOFS, WALLS, AND FLOORS 103

Fig. 7.3.2. Pitched roof with ceiling: (1–2) tiles, slates, shingles, corrugated metal, etc. on battens; (2–3) underlayment, sarking felt, or reflective insulation, if used; (3–4) rafter and ventilated air space (minimum 2 in. or 50 mm); (4–5) thermal insulation, if used; (5–6) vapor control layer; (6–7) ceiling.

Flat Roofs

Condensation in flat roofs may occur on the underside of the ceiling or on the underside of the roof decking or roof finish (Fig. 7.3.3).

To prevent condensation on the surface of the ceiling adequate insulation should be provided immediately above the ceiling over the whole area so as to avoid a cold ceiling.

To prevent condensation under the roof decking or roof finish a vapor barrier should be provided under the insulation to exclude the passage of water vapor from the room into the air space below the roof deck. In addition, the air space should be at least 2 in. (50 mm) wide and should be properly ventilated.

Flat Roofs with Warm Deck

Condensation in flat roofs with a warm deck may occur on the underside of the waterproof finish (Fig. 7.3.4). To prevent condensation on the underside of the roof finish,

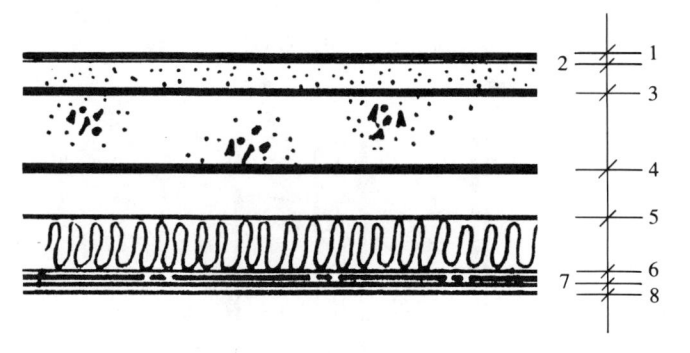

Fig. 7.3.3. Flat roof: (1–2) weatherproof roof finish; (2–3) roof screed; (3–4) structural concrete deck; (4–5) airspace; (5–6) thermal insulation; (6–7) vapor control layer; (7–8) ceiling.

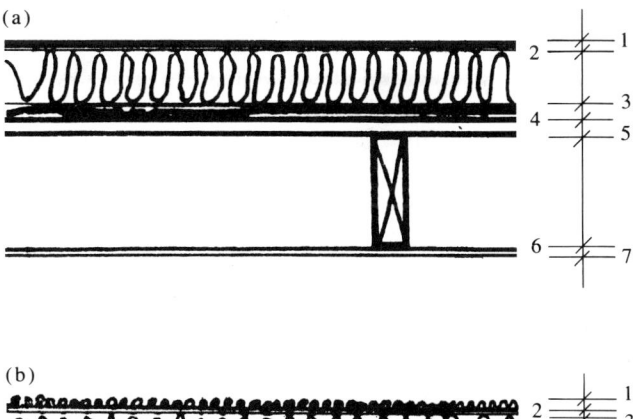

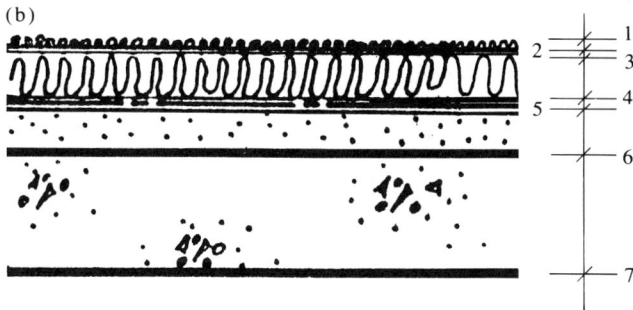

Fig. 7.3.4. Flat roof with warm deck: *(a) using a timber structure*: (1–2) weatherproof roof finish; (2–3) thermal insulation; (3–4) vapor control layer; (5–6) unventilated air space; (6–7) ceiling.

(b) Using a concrete structure: (1–2) solar reflective chippings; (2–3) weatherproof roof finish; (3–4) thermal insulation; (4–5) vapor control layer; (5–6) roof screed; (6–7) structural concrete deck.

an effective control barrier should be provided under the layer of insulation over the whole area of the roof so as to stop water vapor penetrating the insulation and reaching the roof finish. For example, the use of a high performance roofing felt laid in hot asphalt (bitumen) with laps properly sealed.

7.4. EXCLUSION OF RAINWATER FROM EXTERNAL WALLS

As with roofs, a principal requirement of external walls is that they shall be waterproof. They must be protected from groundwater and also from the effects of driving rain and snow. In considering the movement of water across the face of external walls, they can be classified into three main types: solid external walls, fully sealed walls and protected walls.

Solid Walls

To provide protection against driving rain and snow a solid wall must be of sufficient thickness to release water in a dry period before it penetrated to the inner face or causes damage to the construction. The solid wall, usually constructed of brick, stone, or concrete, absorbs water, stores it and allows it to evaporate before it affects the inner surface of the wall or the building. To do so, it should be constructed of rendered brickwork at least 14 in. (350 mm) thick, or rendered aerated autoclaved concrete blockwork at least 9 in. (225 mm) thick. The rendering on the outer face should have a total thickness of at least $\frac{3}{4}$ in. (18 mm). The type and mix of the rendering depends on the material of the bricks or blocks and the degree of exposure to wind, rain, and snow. The provision of a wide eaves to the roof will reduce the quantity of rainwater reaching the wall, especially on building of one story (Fig. 7.4.1). Additional protection of the external wall against water is required above and below openings and at the base of the wall. Such protection should be provided by means of damp-proof courses or components such as water-resistant sills.

Fully Sealed Walls

The fully sealed wall is constructed of a nonabsorbent material such as glass or metal sheet that provide an impervious outer face. It acts as a waterproof cladding and, with its system of joints, must exclude water completely. Sealed cladding should resist completely the penetration of rain and snow and should not deteriorate or be damaged by the action of the weather (Fig. 7.4.2).

Protected Walls

A protected wall is formed of an outer leaf or screen (sometimes called a rainscreen) that is intended to break the force of the weather, allow a certain amount of rainwater to pass through it and drain downwards either on its inside face or to be redirected outward. The material of the outer leaf may be porous and its joints may admit water as, for example, with the outer leaf of a masonry cavity wall.

To provide adequate protection against penetration of rain and snow, the external cavity wall should have an outer leaf of masonry (brickwork, blockwork, or stonework or concrete slabs), an open cavity with a thickness of at least 2 in. (50 mm) that is bridged by wall ties and an inner leaf of masonry or timber frame. An insulation material may be provided; it is positioned on either side of the inner leaf, the open cavity being maintained (Fig. 7.4.3). If the material of the external wall is impervious, then water flows across the outer face in large quantities and in all directions and enters the joints that are designed to form drainage channels as, for example, with certain types of wall cladding where rain or snow that enters a joint is directed outwards. These joints should also be designed to accommodate structural and thermal movement and can be designed as open joints that do not necessarily depend upon the use of sealants or gaskets (Fig. 7.4.4).

Drained Joints

In a drained joint a rain screen is provided at the face outdoors, and an air seal only is provided at the face indoors. A drainage system must be provided that allows the water to drain, and that equalizes the pressure in the drainage cavity so that the water can drain by gravity. The sealants or gaskets in drained joints need therefore only serve as air seals (see Section 5.8).

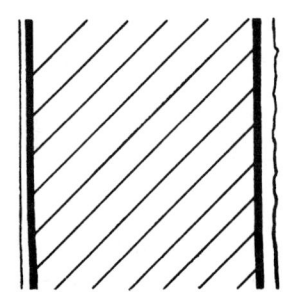

Fig. 7.4.1. Solid wall.

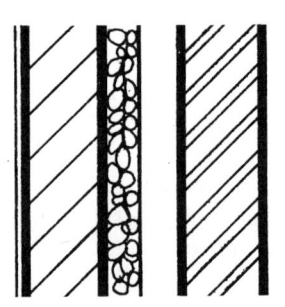

Fig. 7.4.3. Protected wall.

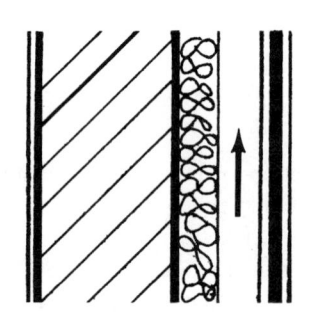

Fig. 7.4.2. Fully sealed wall.

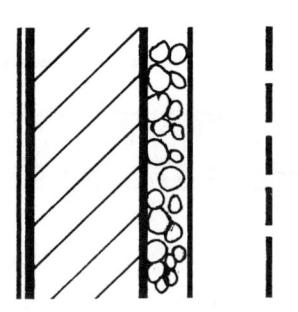

Fig. 7.4.4. Wall with open joints.

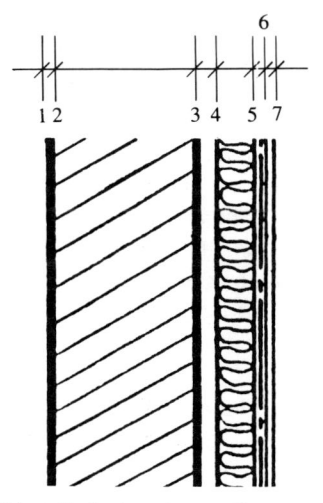

EXCLUSION OF WATER BY ROOFS, WALLS, AND FLOORS 105

Fig. 7.5.1. Solid wall designed to collect condensation: (1-2) weather protection, if required; (2-3) masonry; (3-4) vented air space; (4-5) thermal insulation; (5-6) vapor control layer, if required; (6-7) internal lining.

7.5. EXCLUSION OF CONDENSATE FROM EXTERNAL WALLS

Mass Walls

Condensation on the inner surface of a mass wall is likely to occur if its surface temperature is below the dewpoint: the temperature at which air becomes saturated with water vapor. To prevent such condensation, adequate insulation should be provided on the face of the inner side facing the room together with a vented air space behind the insulation (Fig. 7.5.1).

Fully Sealed Walls

Condensation may occur on the inside face of the outer screen or wall cladding. To prevent such condensation the cavity between the cladding and the inner wall should be ventilated and drained. In addition, a vapor barrier should be provided on the inside face of the insulation on the inner leaf of the wall (Fig. 7.5.2).

Protected Walls

Condensation on the inner surface of the inner leaf of the wall is likely to occur if its surface temperature is below the dew point. To prevent such condensation, adequate insulation should be provided on the face of the inner leaf facing the room (Fig. 7.5.3).

7.6. EXCLUSION OF WATER FROM GROUND FLOORS

There are five possible causes of dampness in ground floors:

1. Ground water;
2. Condensation in the floor construction;

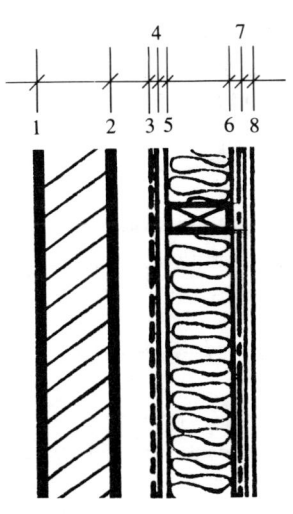

Fig. 7.5.2. Fully sealed wall designed to collect condensation. (1-2) masonry; (2-3) vented and drained air space; (3-4) breather membrane; (4-5) sheathing; (5-6) timber frame, and thermal insulation if required; (6-7) vapor control layer; (7-8) internal lining.

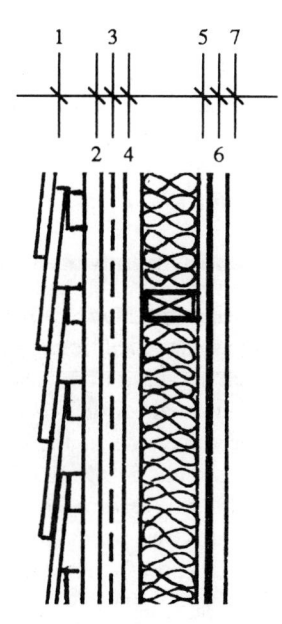

Fig. 7.5.3. Protected wall designed to collect condensation: (1-2) vertical tiles or shingles on battens; (2-3) counter battens; (3-4) breather membrane; (4-5) timber frame, and thermal insulation if required; (5-6) vapor control layer; (6-7) internal lining.

3. Condensation on the surface of the flooring;
4. Water remaining in the floor construction following completion of the construction;
5. Accidental spillage or leakage of water inside the building.

Ground floors are of two main types:

1. *Ground-supported floors* (*slabs on grade*), where the floor construction rests directly on prepared ground. The damp-proof membrane is required under, through, or on top of a slab on grade.

2. *Suspended floors* where the floor construction spans between supports and has an air space between the construction and the ground.

Damp-proof courses are required below the wall plate and below the bearers.

A ground floor should be designed to prevent water and water vapor from groundwater reaching the flooring (the upper layer of a floor that provides a finished surface).

Slabs on Grade and Groundwater

To prevent groundwater penetrating a *slab on grade* (*ground-supported floor*) the ground should be covered with a layer of dense concrete laid on a rough stone (hardcore) bed and provided with a damp-proof membrane positioned above or below the concrete. The damp-proof membrane should be continuous with the damp-proof courses in the walls or piers of the building. If necessary, a vertical damp-proof course should be provided to join the horizontal membrane to the damp-proof courses in the walls. When the ground-supported floor is subject to water pressure, a continuous waterproofing lining should be provided to the walls, floors and foundations below ground. The damp-proof membranes should be applied to the structurally sound concrete bases and walls, or walls of structurally sound brickwork or blockwork.

Suspended Floors and Groundwater

Suspended Timber Ground Floor. To prevent groundwater from reaching a suspended timber ground floor, there should be a ventilated air space of at least 6 in. (150 mm), measured from the ground surface (or the surface of a concrete slab) to the underside of the timber floor joists. Damp-proof courses should be provided under the timber wall plates or other kind of external walls.

In the British Isles it is also necessary that the ground be covered with a damp-proof membrane overlaid with concrete at least 2 in. (50 mm) thick.

It is important that the ground, or the top of this concrete ground-covering slab be graded to fall to a drainage outlet above the lowest level of adjoining ground.

Suspended Concrete Ground Floor. To prevent groundwater from reaching a suspended concrete floor, a damp-proof membrane should be provided where the depth of the air space between the concrete floor and the ground is less than 3 in. (75 mm), or where the air space is unventilated, or where the ground below the floor is below the level of the ground adjoining the building.

7.7. EXCLUSION OF CONDENSATE FROM GROUND FLOORS

Ground-Supported Floors (Slabs on Grade). To prevent condensation on the surface of flooring on a ground-supported floor, a vapor barrier should be provided on the warm side of insulation that should be positioned either below or above the floor slab (Fig. 7.7.1).

Suspended Timber Floors. To prevent condensation on the surface of the flooring of a timber floor with insulation below the floor joists, the air space below the floor should be at least 6 in. (150 mm) deep and should be adequately ventilated. The insulation and its supporting material should be of a low vapor resistance to minimize high timber moisture content in the floor construction (Fig. 7.7.2).

Suspended Concrete Floors. To prevent condensation on the surface of the flooring adequate continuous insulation

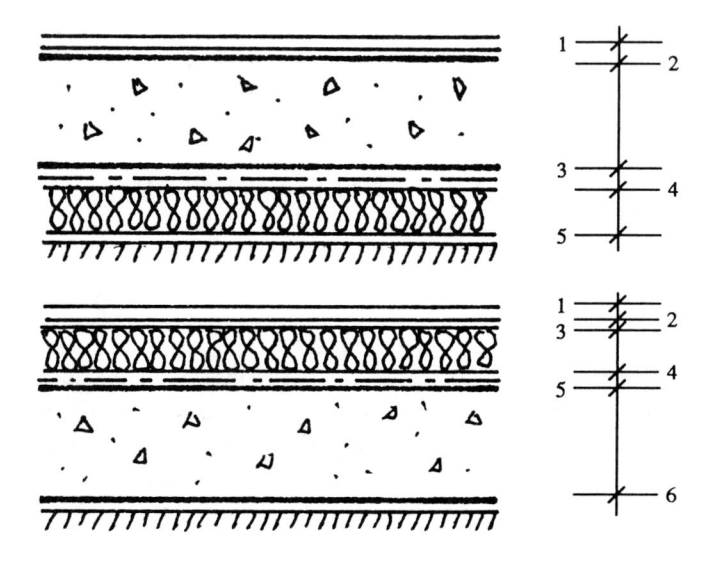

Fig. 7.7.1. Exclusion of condensate from ground-supported floors (slabs on grade): (a) if the thermal insulation is below the concrete slab: (1–2) floor finish; (2–3) concrete slab; (3–4) damp-proof membrane, also acting as vapor barrier; (4–5) rigid thermal insulation.

(b) If the thermal insulation is above the concrete slab: (1–2) floor finish; (2–3) vapor control layer, if required; (3–4) rigid thermal insulation; (4–5) damp-proof course (which may alternatively be placed below the concrete slab); (5–6) concrete slab.

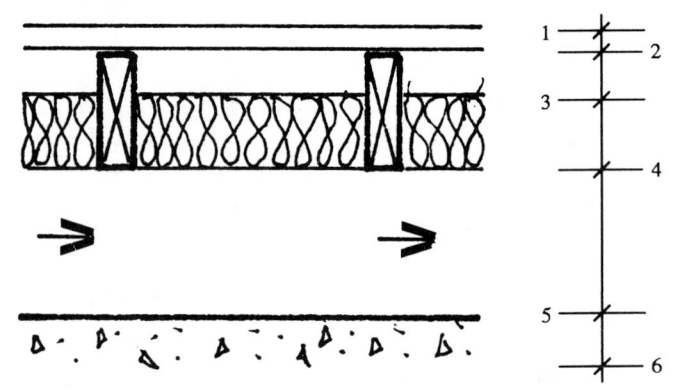

Fig. 7.7.2. Exclusion of condensate from suspended timber floor: (1–2) timber floor deck; (2–3) air space; (3–4) thermal insulation; (4–5) ventilated air space; (5–6) oversite concrete, if required.

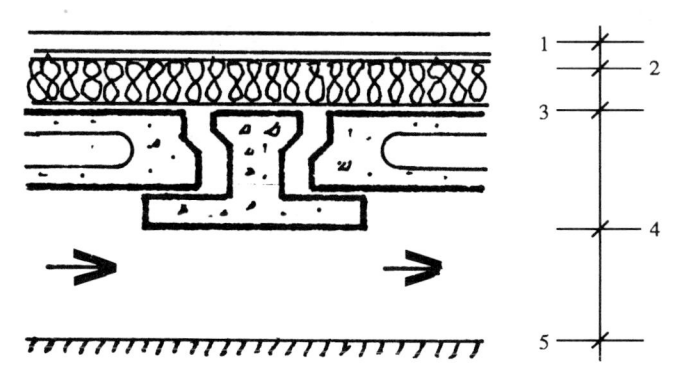

Fig. 7.7.3. Exclusion of condensate from suspended concrete floor: (1-2) floor finish; (2-3) rigid thermal insulation; (3-4) precast concrete beams and filler blocks, or site-cast concrete structure; (4-5) ventilated air space.

should be provided above the concrete floor construction and a vapor barrier should be provided above the insulation and below the flooring. The air space below the floor construction should be adequately ventilated to minimize underfloor dampness (Fig. 7.7.3).

STANDARDS

The Control of Condensation in Buildings. BS 5250. British Standards Institution, London, 1988.
ASHRAE Handbook—Fundamentals. American Society of Heating, Refrigerating, and Air Conditioning Engineers, Atlanta, 1985. Chapter 21. *Moisture in Building Construction*, pp. 21.1-21.20.
Voluntary Test Method for Condensation Resistance of Windows, Doors, and Glazed Wall Sections. AAMA 1502.7. Architectural Aluminum Manufacturers Association, Chicago, IL, 1981. 19 pp.
Building Code of Australia. Australian Uniform Building Regulations Coordinating Council, Canberra, 1988. Section F.1. *Damp and Weatherproofing*, pp. F1.3-F1.6.

SUGGESTIONS FOR FURTHER READING

Building Research Establishment. *Condensation.* Digest No. 110, 1972. 4 pp.
  Condensation in Roofs. Digest No. 180, 1986. 4 pp.
  Condensation in Insulated Domestic Roofs. Digest No. 270, 1983. 4 pp.
  Principles of Natural Ventilation. Digest No. 210, 1982. 4 pp.
  Ventilation Requirements. Digest No. 206, 1977. 4 pp.
  Control of Lichens, Moulds and Similar Growths. Digest No. 139, 1988. 4 pp.
  Rising Damp in Walls: Diagnosis and Treatment. Digest No. 245, 1986. 4 pp.
  Flat Roof Design: the Technical Options. Digest No. 312, 1986. 4 pp.
  Building Research Establishment, Garston, England.
Institute for Research in Construction. *Water and Building Materials.* Canadian Building Digest (CBD) No. 30, 1962. 4 pp.
  Rain Penetration and its Control. CBD No. 40, 1963. 4 pp.
  Rain Penetration of Walls of Unit Masonry. CBD No. 6, 1960. 4 pp.
  Silicone Water-Repellents for Masonry. CBD No. 162, 1974. 4 pp.
  Fundamentals of Roof Design. CBD No. 67, 1965. 4 pp.
  Drainage from Roofs. CBD No. 151, 1973. 4 pp.
  Moisture Considerations in Roof Design. CBD No. 73, 1966. 4 pp.
  Sliding Snow on Sloping Roofs. CBD No. 228, 1983. 4 pp.
  Ice on Roofs. CBD No. 89, 1967. 4 pp.
  Venting of Flat Roofs. CBD No. 176, 1976. 4 pp.
  Protected-Membrane Roofs. CBD No. 150, 4 pp.
  Shrinkage of Bituminous Roofing Membranes. CBD No. 181, 1976. 4 pp.
  Precast Concrete Walls: Problems with Conventional Design. CBD No. 93, 1967. 4 pp.
  Moisture and Thermal Considerations in Basement Walls. CBD No. 161, 4 pp.
  Groundwater. CBD No. 82, 4 pp.
  Flood-Proofing of Buildings. CBD No. 198, 1978. 4 pp.
  Institute for Research in Construction, National Research Council, Ottawa.
Forest Products Laboratory. *Condensation Potential in High Thermal Performance Walls: Cold Winter Climate.* FPL 433, 1983 19 pp.
  Condensation Potential in High Thermal Performance Walls: Hot, Humid Summer Climate. FPL 455, 1985. 28 pp. Forest Products Laboratory, Madison WI.
Brick Institute of America. *Dampproofing and Waterproofing Masonry Walls.* Technical Note 7, 1980.
  Flashing Clay Masonry. Technical Note 7A, 1983.
  Moisture Control in Brick and Walls—Rain Penetration. Technical Note 7B, 1980.
  Moisture Control in Brick and Tile Walls—Condensation. Technical Note 7C, 1981.
  Moisture Control in Brick and Tile Walls—Condensation Analysis. Technical Note 7D, 1981.
  Colorless Coatings for Brick Masonry. Technical Note 7E, 1976.
  Moisture Resistance of Brick Masonry—Maintenance. Technical Note 7F, 1986.
  Brick Institute of America, Reston, VA.
National Bureau of Standards. *Effect of Edge Insulation upon Temperature and Condensation on Concrete-Slab Floors.* Building Materials and Structures Report (BMS) No. 138, 1953. 21 pp.
  Effect of Outdoor Exposure on the Water Permeability of Masonry Walls. BMS No. 76, 1941. 21 pp.
  Water Permeability of Walls Built of Masonry Units. BMS No. 82, 1942. 37 pp.
  Moisture Condensation in Building Walls. BMS No. 63, 1940. 14 pp.
  Laboratory Observations of Condensation in Wall Specimens. BMS No. 106, 1946. 9 pp.
  National Bureau of Standards, Washington.

J. L. Heiman, E. H. Waters, and R. C. McTaggart. "Treatment of rising damp." *Architectural Science Review,* **16,** 170-177 (1973).

NOTATION

A list of abbreviations of the units of measurement, definitions of these units, and conversion factors between British/American and metric units are given in the Appendix.

8
Durability and Maintenance

Forrest Wilson

The life expectancy of a contemporary building is measured by its continued usefulness. The definition of its durability and maintenance may thus be completely different from that of traditional buildings of the past, since it is determined by design and finance. Life-cycle costing is therefore required by many building owners. Design for maintenance which permits repair, adjustment and cleaning of a reasonable cost means major savings for building owners and tenants. The prediction of wear and durability of building materials, while not an exact science, can be greatly aided by testing.

8.1. A QUESTION OF VALUE

The life expectancy of contemporary buildings is measured by continued usefulness. Durability and maintenance are design decisions. For example a building constructed to last 50 years may have a foundation durable for 500 years and wall coverings that will last 5 years, mechanical equipment that will have to be replaced in 15 years, and communications equipment to be updated every 3 years. Some parts will be repaired, others replaced and others discarded.

Design decisions preserve or force destruction of durable, well maintained building elements. Replacement of a poorly chosen toilet fixture requires destruction of ceramic tile walls in excellent condition. The energy crisis and the rapid improvement of telecommunication equipment found many buildings unable to adapt to new technical demands. The buildings, otherwise in workable condition with many more years of useful life in other respects, were torn down.

Design requires value judgments. In the past designers set standards of value on the proven worth of traditional building materials. Historically stone is more durable than wood or metal and did not burn. The more expensive stones were the most valuable, they were the most beautiful and often the most impervious to wear. But the use of expensive stone today may force a building's obsolescence.

Durability and maintenance in a contemporary office building may have a completely different meaning than in traditional buildings. Office buildings are used here as examples because there is a great deal of information about them and because most work in western cultures takes place in office settings. It is here that change is most pronounced and cost decisions are most crucial in estimating the projected life and upkeep of building elements.

There has been a significant change in office building design costs in the last quarter century, according to Dr. Francis Duffy, a British architect. Duffy divided the building into shell, services, scenery, and set:

Shell. This consists of the structure, roof and perimeter walls, which are expected to endure for many decades and to accommodate many generations of user organizations;

Services. This term describes major elements such as elevators, air-conditioning plants (chillers and main ducts), and the main ducting for power, electronic data, and telecommunications. Services are generally expected to have a life no longer than two decades, and to be replaced two or three times in the existence of a major office building.

Scenery. This term describes the shorter life of the interior fittings: partitions, furniture, lighting, the more adaptable parts of air conditioning, as well as finishes and decorations, which are often designed to last no longer than a lease of five or seven years.

Set. This is the arrangement of the parts.

Taking a typical 1965 high quality British office building

as standard, the equivalent price today is 50% higher, says Duffy. This is a significant increase. But of far more interest, he pointed out, is how these costs are apportioned. In 1965, 70 percent of the cost was spent on Shell, 20 percent on Services, and very little, say 10 percent on Scenery. Today the proportions are quite different: 40 percent on Shell, 40 percent on Services, and 20 percent on Scenery. In other words, "good old-fashioned architecture," as Duffy puts it, is diminishing in importance. Services and scenery are absorbing more and more of an already large but increasing budget.

Expenditures examined in the context of the life of the office building show the shell is relatively insignificant. More money is spent on services, replaced every fifteen to twenty years, which may be three or more times during the life of the building. More is spent on scenery which is torn out and replaced six or seven times during the same period. Obviously this influences decisions concerning durability and maintenance.

The exact conditions may vary in North America or Australia with different tax laws, incentives, and zoning ordinances, but the principle holds.

Services and Scenery

Traditionally, offices were powered through direct access from the building distribution system; desks and equipment radiated out from columns and walls that housed fixed power outlets. The power system adapted itself to structural and architectural systems and its maintenance was tied to them. Today the reverse is true.

The crucial consideration in offices today is access to power. As commercial transactions are increasingly electrified they need more and more flexible wiring and cabling (see Chapter 23). Blocking easy access to power locks a firm out of business. The computer is the nerve center of corporate telecommunications, mail and message delivery, and data and information transmission between people and computers and between computers.

Core design determines power distribution, structural design and architectural features. Vertical core space limits the amount of power that can be transmitted through the electrical system from the utility's main feeder line to the floors. Structural components can not limit power access by blocking conduits that distribute wires and cables through floors and ceilings. If they do the building itself cannot accommodate its occupants.

PLEC (power, lighting, electronic, and communication) distribution systems radiate from the building core through either ceiling or floor. Ceiling distribution systems use conduit, metal raceways, or flexible conduit cable to run wires and cables through the plenum (the space between the ceiling and the floor above it). Wires and cables are routed from the plenum to work stations through vertical hollow "power poles" or through flexible "infeed" cables. Ceiling distribution can also incorporate a standard "poke-through" system of delivery in which access to the floor above is gained from the plenum below. As much as possible of the building is activated or capable of activation.

Furniture panels and components act as the means of distributing wires and cables through the space to each equipment location. Hollow channels in panels, work surfaces, and attachable components allow vertical and horizontal distribution throughout an area at various heights. Some furniture surfaces and panels come already electrically wired at the factory. Furniture panels and components store excess wiring and cabling safely and out of sight. Expanded distribution channels in the furniture can be used for storage, or trays and hooks can be mounted under work surfaces. The furniture becomes an electric appliance and is treated like a household toaster or mixer. It is replaced rather than maintained.

Twenty-five years ago, a typical office plant consisted of closed rooms furnished with free-standing file cabinets, desks, chairs, and credenzas. An open "secretarial pool" was the center of information processing. There was optimum security and little flexibility, but flexibility was not needed, for this system had worked well for well over 50 years.

The majority of today's offices are open, with only fixed exterior walls. Partitions of various heights provide spatial separation and privacy and support work surfaces, storage bins, shelves, files, and other office furnishings. What formerly were walls is now furniture. Walls were painted and repaired, furniture is refinished or replaced. Given today's "churn rate," replacement is the most common practice.

Today's business organizations are increasingly dynamic; on the average, an organization will relocate 40 to 50 percent of its microcomputers per year. Some report up to 110 percent annual move rate. An office in a state of constant flux, heavily reliant on equipment, cannot easily function in a setting where power outlets and cable access are fixed and limited. The cost of change is an initial design decision.

The rapid advances in communication and information technology changes traditional concepts of durability and maintenance which now must be adjusted to consider the following design decisions:

1. Building changes must take place with minimal disruption in the work place. The design is not successful if simple tasks such as moving wires, partitions or light fixtures involves the interruption of daily tasks.

2. Change is essential if the building is to retain its economic value. Unless changes are easily facilitated they will not be made. Neglected minor changes become major costly obstructions. The building is a container for operations much more expensive than itself.

The more expensive and durable traditional building materials such as bronze and marble are difficult and costly to alter. The wrecker's ball generally smashes more expensive and finer materials and workmanship than will be used in the new buildings built on the site cleared.

3. On-site manufacture is more costly and less efficient than factory production. The controlled environment, heavy machinery, and assembly line techniques reduce costs of factory products compared to on site work. The tendency is to replace rather than to maintain.

4. Mechanical systems of the building are kinetic parts constantly responding to climatic changes, the number of people in the building, and the heat emitted and varying amounts of energy consumed by machines. Mechanical equipment is subject to the highest level of maintenance, breakdown, and improvement. If the building is designed for easy removal and replacement of equipment, then it is economically beneficial to replace rather than repair and maintain.

5. In addition, mechanical equipment must be constantly upgraded. The owner pays a penalty if it is not. If the cost of change is too high the entire building is too expensive to operate. The major distribution system of ducts and pipes does not change as frequently as the mechanical plant. Upgraded mechanical units are attached to them.

6. Minor mechanical distribution systems servicing individual rooms are in a constant state of flux. The purpose and size of rooms is constantly altered. Those parts of the system that require constant maintenance and tuning in a well designed facility are located in public movement spaces so that maintenance men or women do not enter building function zones.

7. Each system, component, or element designed to plug in and out, bolt on and off, lessens the danger of obsolescence.

8. An ability to change is the governing factor. Timelessness is not determined by how long a building stands but by how long it remains useful. Its usefulness is now dependent on entirely different concepts than those held of traditional durability and maintenance (Refs. 8.1 and 8.2).

This description is not true of all buildings, but indicates a direction. Only about 2 percent of the building stock is built new each year. The remainder is either retrofitted or continues to struggle with traditional problems.

8.2. STATE OF THE ART

The conditions that will determine a building's durability and maintenance is determined by design and finance. Those that contribute to poor maintenance and durability are listed below:

- Building products are sold with little or no data on continued performance.
- Construction emphasizes speed and economy of erection and use of materials.
- There is little mention in product literature and less understanding of the mechanisms of deterioration or the influence on them of the environmental factors responsible for deterioration.

The increasing frequency of building decay can be measured in the increasing cases of litigation against designers, builders, and product manufacturers. There is no coordinated approach to the problem of building deterioration. There are fundamental weaknesses in sources of fundamental knowledge:

- Manufacturers' data are not relevant to a particular application.
- Manufacturers change the formulation of their products before long life experience is gained, or they cannot afford the luxury of long-term monitoring.
- Research results are difficult to relate to practice.
- Government laboratories are reluctant to recommend particular manufacturer products.
- Searching for the results of relevant research overseas takes too long and is avoided.
- Most tests are of too short duration for life assessment, and are therefore dangerous to use with confidence.
- Standard tests bear little relation to reality and therefore provide little support to performance evaluation.
- There is little, if any feedback on performance in service.
- Few technologists and professionals are trained to cope with the diverse range of disciplines involved in deterioration processes.

There is a pressing need to establish a sound basis for evaluating the durability and maintenance of building materials and products to meet a specific, or a range of, operating conditions over a projected building lifetime.

A comprehensive plan would encompass the many aspects of deterioration and their effects on building materials and components. It would consider material science, strength of materials over time, aging, environmental influence, experimental laboratory, and field testing and monitoring techniques, life cycle costing, stress analysis, construction practice, and the analysis of in service performance.

To illustrate the wide range of analysis that must take place we can take the simple debonding of a tile on a building facade. An examination may find that the cause to have been:

- Differential thermal movement between the tile, the adhesive and the backing under solar and air temperature variations;
- Lack of bond at the tile/adhesive or the adhesive/backing interface due to aging, moisture, or thermal causes;
- Lack of understanding of the temperature and moisture conditions;

- Incorrect application of the adhesive and lack of surface preparation;
- Failure to allow for structural movement of the reinforced concrete frame over time caused, for example, by creep and shrinkage;
- Lack of appreciation of the cost of materials in relation to performance therefore avoiding the use of more expensive and more stable adhesive;
- Little or no in service monitoring.

Early testing of the system under simulated or exaggerated field conditions could have identified a problem before use on building, avoiding costly remedial action and possible litigation.

Some design firms, as part of their contract, compose and turn over to the owner a maintenance manual which delineates in detail the procedures the owner should follow to maintain the architectural components of the building. This resembles the practice demanded of mechanical systems contractors, who must turn over all manuals concerning the operation of mechanical systems. It has been proposed that maintenance be made a permanent division of specifications.

This division would spell out in detail the appropriate materials to use in the care and maintenance of every part of the building. The design professional is ultimately responsible for the performance of the materials and systems, and is therefore in the best position to instruct the owner in the techniques best suited to assure continued satisfactory performance (Ref. 8.3).

8.3. LIFE CYCLE COSTING

Owning and operating costs of buildings have increased at a steady rate. The cost of ownership is a growing concern. As a result a number of private owners, the U.S. government and state governments specify mandatory Life Cycle Cost (LCC) procedures be followed before commissioning a building. An essential feature of LCC is the durability and maintenance of the building, its systems and materials.

Life cycle costing involves multidisciplinary analysis. Traditionally design was dictated by the architect, and other disciplines responded to his or her direction. In multidisciplinary design evaluations for laboratories, high-tech facilities, and automated offices the maintenance and durability of mechanical and electrical systems may take precedence over architectural decisions.

Total building costs include initial and all other costs over the buildings life time. Maintenance may be as high 22.5 percent of this total, while the initial design cost will be as low as 2 percent.

If the cost of changing, altering, and replacement is factored in with maintenance and durability, the percentage may be higher. The denial of the use of working space is taken into consideration in life cycle costs. As an illustration, an expensive partition system which may be rearranged over a weekend by a bank's maintenance staff is compared with an initially less expensive system that means shutting down operations while outside contracting crews reconfigure the space; the cost of shut down would also be a factor in the life cycle costs, not just the initial cost.

Life cycle costs analyze an item, area, system, or facility considering all significant costs of ownership over an economic life expressed in terms of equivalent costs. Life cycle cost = purchase and installation costs − salvage value + maintenance and repair costs + replacement costs.

The baseline for all costs must be the same if comparisons are to be made. All cash amounts are generally converted to either present value or annual value dollars. *Present value* is defined as the equivalent value of past and future dollars corresponding to today's value. *Annual value* means that all past, present, and future costs are converted to an equivalent constant amount recurring annually over the evaluation period. The conversion process for present value and annual value dollars is called *discounting*.

The value of money is time dependent, and constant inflation means that a given dollar amount today will be worth more than that same dollar amount in a year's time. To evaluate the economic efficiency of life cycle analysis it is necessary to estimate the values of the various expenditures and savings that accrue over time and convert them to values in a common base year. Usually, all past and future values are converted to equivalent present values, or all past, present, and future values are converted to equivalent annual values.

The cost of building elements is measured in *first cost*, which is the cost installed, and in *life cycle cost*. Life cycle cost includes first cost and the expected lifetime of the finish system including maintenance costs.

Trends in interior finish systems have been toward lighter dry materials away from heavy clay tiles, wooden and terrazzo floors. Lighter systems reduce the dead load of the building, shipping costs and installation costs. First costs are lowered but life cycle costs may be increased, since the older materials are more durable with better wear characteristics. In addition, new materials do not have a history of use. The specifier either relies on manufacturers claims or some form of testing.

8.4. TESTING

The prediction of wear and durability of building materials is not an exact science. Observation of older materials over time results in fairly accurate predictions of their performance. New materials are usually subjected to some form of testing. This may be done in a laboratory following testing methods described by standards organizations such as ASTM (American Society for Testing and Materials) or the manufacturers' data may be used.

Manufacturers, laboratories, and building research establishments place materials on racks in the open air monitored by weather recording instruments for a number of years and the results are published. There are also instruments and devices used to accelerate wear and weathering. "Weatherometers" simulate and accelerate weather heating cooling cycles, humidity extremes and the simulation of air pollution.

Many do not consider these instruments sufficiently accurate or reliable to predict weathering properties directly. They are, however, useful for measuring comparative performance between known and new materials. The value of the tests depends upon the sophistication of the instrument and integrity of the laboratory doing the testing.

Wear is measured by abrasion machines simulating the wearing conditions of actual exposure. However, those responsible for setting durability and maintenance standards prefer actual conditions. Decisions are usually made based on personal experience or the opinions of those with field experience. For example, carpet testing may be conducted by putting carpet squares in a busy corridor, recording the number of walkers, and inspecting the results.

Museums are an exception. They do a great deal of instrument measuring and testing variations of humidity control and interior climatic conditions including sunlight effects. As a result museum designers and curators have accumulated considerable information concerning the sensitive environments required to preserve their precious exhibits.

Preservationists also tend to accumulate information concerning durability and maintenance. The Ehrenkrantz Group, responsible for major restoration projects in the U.S., including that of the Woolworth Building in New York City, issue maintenance manuals to their clients. The manuals generally schedule five-year cycles of continued care and include exact instructions for constant evaluation of the building's exterior and interior condition.

Restorers, in contrast to those working with new material, can consult a history of wear under specific conditions. In contrast, a maintenance manual given to the owner of a new building is based on manufacturers' recommendations.

A great deal of valuable information concerning durability and maintenance is in the heads of preservationists and is not yet part of preservation science. The New York City Department of Parks and Recreation conducts roundtable discussions as a means of capturing this information for life cycle cost analysis. Ten or twelve people from different disciplines, including experienced tradesmen, analyze the project.

The National Park Service (Ref.8.4), National Trust for Historic Preservation (Ref.8.5), and the Association for Preservation Technology realize that maintenance is essential to historic preservation. They have actively involved the building trades and maintenance personnel since 1974. The programs they have inaugurated in partnership with maintenance workers are based on periodic inspection and frequent examination. Deterioration is most easily arrested in its early stages and the physical closeness of the building's maintenance staff to the building and its materials encourages swift response based on a day-to-day familiarity with the building's systems.

8.5. REMINDERS

Design for maintenance which permits repair, adjustment, and cleaning at a reasonable cost means major savings for the owner and tenants of buildings. A minor reduction in maintenance costs over the life span of the building add to major economic benefits.

Problems can occur with new materials that do not have a maintenance record. Specification of a limited number of finish materials simplifies maintenance by the use of standardized items.

Much of maintenance and durability is thinking ahead and finding the requirements of the equipment and the expected wear life of materials. Where it is not found in manufacturers' literature, personal observation will have to take its place:

- Permanent drawings must be kept of plumbing systems.
- Plugged T's should be used for cleanouts rather than elbows.
- Locate mechanical equipment in open or extended positions to assure accessibility. Be sure that mechanical equipment is well lit. Use drains where spillage may occur.
- Soft, blown-on mineral materials cannot be cleaned. Be sure that the surfaces adjacent to diffusers are smooth and easily cleaned.
- Use daylight, but avoid skylights wherever possible.
- Put wall-mounted cigarette urn/waste-receptacle unit on landings.
- Provide electric receptacle for each stair landing.

Many of these are simple design decisions that have to be weighed in terms of the first or life cycle costs of the building.

Environment

Among the factors in the environment that affect the rate and extent of deterioration of materials, the dominant ones are moisture, high temperature, aggressive chemical components, radiation, and load.

Polymeric materials such as plastics can be seriously affected by a range of natural phenomena, such as ultraviolet light degradation, oxygen diffusion causing oxidation, water ingress causing hydrolysis, thermal aging, and biological attack.

For reinforced concrete the initiation of corrosion is predominantly dependent on:

- Chloride deposition on concrete surfaces in marine and de-icing salt environments;

- CO_2 and O_2 present in the atmosphere;
- The relative humidity of the air and its effect on the moisture content of the concrete.

Roofing

The durability of a roofing material is determined by its quality, suitability, climatic conditions, quality of workmanship in laying, effectiveness of maintenance, and other factors, but these are primary. Therefore it is difficult to compare roofing materials. However, given the best quality, proper installation, and good maintenance, roofing materials can be arranged in an ascending scale of durability.

1. Sheet copper, lead, stainless steel, aluminum, clay tile, slate, concrete tile;
2. Terne plate, galvanized steel, asbestos-cement tile, built-up roofing;
3. Wood shingles;
4. Asphalt shingles;
5. Roll roofing.

Copper, aluminum, lead, and stainless steel roof coverings are noncorrosive and do not require painting. Built-up roofs require very little maintenance. Terne plate and galvanized sheet steel require periodic painting because of the tendency of the base metal to corrode when defects develop in the coatings.

The tiles and slate may be broken by large hailstones or other projectiles, natural or man made, and require repair. The life of wood shingles may be prolonged by coatings and the life of smooth-surfaced asphalt roll roofings can be prolonged by recoating with asphalt roof coatings.

All of the above should be considered in life cycle costing.

Flooring

The durability of floors is their resistance to wear, temperature changes, humidity, decay, and disintegration from various sources including cleaning agents, and adhesion of the material to its base.

The most durable surfaces for foot traffic are slate, terrazzo, ceramic tile, and concrete. Terrazzo floors have a tendency to crack if not separated by dividing strips or laid as tile. Marble is used in floors subject to severe wear, but is not as durable as the other materials and softer marbles may wear very poorly. If concrete surfaces are to be durable the aggregates must be durable.

Hardwood, vinyl plastic, and rubber tile wear comparatively well; cork and asphalt tile are not quite as durable. None of these materials, except concrete, is suitable for heavy traffic such as trucking; brick, end-grain wood block, and heavy maple are best for this purpose.

Maintenance must include the ease of cleaning and the application of surface treatment such as waxing and painting. The necessity of repairs and their cost has to be factored in.

Ceramic tile, marble, terrazzo, slate, vinyl plastic, and rubber tile are easily cleaned and require little care. Asphalt and carpet tile are easily cleaned, but require surface treatment occasionally. Cork is not cleaned easily and requires surface treatment. Hardwood floors are fairly easy to clean if in good condition but require frequent surface treatment. Concrete is not easy to clean, unless it is painted or waxed.

Monolithic floors of terrazzo and concrete are difficult to repair, while floors composed of tiles or separate units are easily repaired.

Maintenance costs of wood block, heavy asphalt mastic, brick, and concrete are relatively low except under extremely severe traffic. With the exception of concrete, these materials are easily repaired and need no surface treatment.

Excessive Moisture

Building materials differ markedly in their ability to resist damage from moisture. A moisture level that might cause slight staining or other tolerable minor damage in one material may produce severe staining, decay or spalling in another.

Wood. When the moisture content of wood exceeds 20 percent, mold growth and decay set in. Timbers anchored in a damp wall could be seriously weakened, and decorative skirting boards, chair rails, and cornices could become so damaged that replacement would be necessary.

Brick. Moisture does not necessarily damage brick. In fact, most brick could remain submerged for decades and not be affected. Damage does occur, however, when the expansive forces of subflorescence and freezing exceed the strength of the brick, resulting in spalling or cracking. Efflorescence, or surface salt crystallization, does not adversely affect brick. But wherever there is efflorescence there will also be subflorescence, so its presence indicates potential damage. Damage from subflorescence, however, takes many years and often decades to result. Freeze damage, on the other hand can occur overnight if the conditions exist.

Sandstone, Limestone, Mortar, Stucco, and Plaster. Like brick, these materials can be adversely affected by the expansive forces of subflorescence and freezing. Like brick also, these materials are not damaged by efflorescence beyond the resultant visual blemish. Since these materials (with the exception of some varieties of sandstone) contain calcium, they are susceptible to damage from continued contact with water. Both calcium carbonate and calcium sulfate will precipitate out of the material, leaving a weakened physical structure and often an intractable encrustation. Weaker materials, such as plaster and lime mortars, can be seriously damaged from this action because they dissolve and begin to crumble. Durable stones, on the other hand, require hundreds of years of continued moisture saturation before their strength is seriously weakened.

Iron, Steel, Tin and Zinc. These materials are quite susceptible to deterioration from any contact with moisture and they must be properly painted or protected to preclude moisture contact. Rusting or corrosion are the undesirable results of prolonged moisture contact.

Wall Coverings. Paint, whitewash, wallpaper and other surface coverings can become stained from dampness or efflorescence. This can be a nuisance and can require unplanned repainting or repairs. But the resultant damage is primarily visual, not physical. Subflorescence, however, is more troublesome. Permeable paints and other coatings are normally not affected by subflorescence to any greater extent than the base material. Impervious coatings, however will often become separated from their base because of subflorescence. The expansive forces of freezing could affect either permeable or impermeable surface coatings if the baste materials were saturated and a hard freeze occurred (Ref. 8.4.).

REFERENCES

8.1. F. Wilson. "Industrialized Buildings." *Architectural Technology (Washington)*, 6–19 (Fall 1984).
8.2. F. Wilson. "Industrialized Buildings." *Architecture (Washington)*, 50–59 (March 1987).
8.3. R. Brown. "Building Deteriorology—The Study and Prediction of Building Performance." *Chemistry and Industry*, 837–842 (15 December 1986).
8.4. B. A. Smith. *Moisture Problems in Historic Masonry Walls, Diagnosis and Treatment*. Preservation Assistance Division of the National Park Service. U. S. Government Printing Office, Washington, DC, 1986, p. 31.
8.5. *Conservation of Historic Stone Buildings and Monuments—Report of the Committee on Conservation of Historic Stone Buildings and Monuments*. Building Materials Advisory Board of the National Research Council. National Academy Press, Washington, DC, 1982.

SUGGESTIONS FOR FURTHER READING

R. E. Billow. *Facilities Management: A Manual for Physical Plant Administration*. Association of Physical Plant Administrators of Universities and Colleges, Alexandria, VA, 1986.

H. S. Conover. *Grounds Maintenance Handbook*, 3rd Ed. McGraw-Hill, New York, 1976.

E. B. Feldman. *Building Design for Maintainability*. Service Engineering Associates, Atlanta, GA, 1983

E. B. Feldman. "Building Maintenance," in *Encyclopedia of Architecture, Design, Engineering, and Construction*, McGraw-Hill, New York, 1989, Vol. 3, pp. 345–350.

L. R. Higgins and L. C. Morrow. *Maintenance Engineering Handbook*, 3rd Ed. McGraw-Hill, New York, 1977.

H. Olin, L. Schmidt, and W. H. Lewis. *Construction: Principles and Methods*, 5th Ed. Institute of Financial Education, Chicago, 1983.

9
Loads

S. N. Pollalis and D. L. Schodek

Vertical loads result from the weight of the construction materials, from the weight of occupants and objects in the building, and from the weight of snow or water accumulation. Loads from other sources such as winds, earthquakes or blasts, earth pressure, or temperature changes can have several orientations. It is the horizontal component of these loads that require special consideration.

This chapter explains how these loads are calculated for the various parts of the building, in accordance to the applicable U.S.A. Building Codes.

9.1. LOADS ON BUILDINGS*

Buildings must support their loads without exceeding the allowable state of stresses in the structural members, as described by the applicable building code. The magnitude of the loads is determined from the weight of the construction materials, the use of the building, its location and exposure to the elements of nature. In all cases, the loads should not be less than the magnitudes specified by the applicable building code.

Vertical (gravity) loads result from the weight of the construction materials, from the weight of occupants and objects in the building, and from the weight of snow or water accumulation (ponding). Vertical loads are supported by the bearing elements of the building. Loads from other sources such as winds, earthquakes or blasts, earth pressure or temperature changes can have several orientations. The horizontal components of these loads are the *horizontal (lateral) loads* which are resisted by the lateral stiffness of the building.

A load is *static* if it is applied slowly and reaches a peak magnitude. Under a static load, the building responds slowly to the load and reaches a maximum deflection and maximum stresses corresponding to the maximum magnitude of the load. The weight of construction materials, equipment and snow loads are static loads. Occupancy loads can also be considered static loads.

A load is *dynamic* if it changes rapidly in magnitude as it is applied to the building and its frequency is near the natural frequency of the building. Under a dynamic load, the building, or a part of it, responds rapidly to the load and develops inertia forces that relate to its mass. The maximum deflection and maximum stresses do not coincide with the maximum magnitude of the load and depend on the frequency of the applied load, its peak magnitude and the released energy. Typical dynamic loads are transient loads such as wind loads, earthquake loads and loads resulting from traffic or blasts, and steady-state dynamic loads such as those resulting from working machinery. The dynamic characteristics of a building determine the spectrum of loads that have dynamic effects on it. Thus, wind loads may have dynamic effects on certain buildings but only static effects on others. The building codes suggest the employment of dynamic analysis when dynamic loads are involved but treat these loads as static loads for ordinary buildings after they properly amplify their magnitude.

---
*Building: An enclosed structure including all service equipment. The term will be used here as if followed by the phrase "structure or part thereof."

9.2. THE APPLICABLE BUILDING CODE

There is uncertainty associated with the loads acting on a building. The magnitude of the future loads, the location of the movable loads, and the various loading combinations cannot be accurately predicted in advance. Similarly, there is uncertainty with the strength of the building. The introduction of safety margins lowers the probability of failure resulting from the uncertainty of both the loads and the strength of the building to accepted levels.* Thus, the loads acting on a building and the acceptable state of stresses in the structural members should be based both on the same building code, which should specify the minimum design loads, and on the maximum allowable state of stresses.

The design loads specified by the codes are the *working loads*, the maximum expected loads to occur during the life of the building typically with a probability of occurrence once every 50 or 100 years. In elastic design, the codes require that, under the working loads, the stresses do not exceed a percentage of the yielding stress for each structural member. In an alternative design method, called ultimate strength design, the working loads are amplified to obtain the *ultimate loads*. The amplification factors depend on the type of loads and may be different for dead and live loads and for combinations of different loads. The structural members and joints should reach their *ultimate strength* if subject to the ultimate loads.

In the U.S.A., the designer should use the relevant city building code in conjunction with the state code. For the specification of loads† on buildings, city and state codes are based on the BOCA National Building Code (Building Officials and Code Administrators International, Inc., Ref. 9.1), the Uniform Building Code (International Conference of Building Officials, Ref. 9.2) and the ANSI Standard Reference A58.1-82 (American National Standards Institute, Inc., Ref. 9.3). For loads on bridges, city and state codes usually reference the Standard Specifications for Highway Bridges (American Association of State Highway and Transportation Officials (AASHTO), 12th Ed., Washington, DC, 1977) and the Specifications for Steel Railway Bridges (American Railway Engineering Association (AREA)). In Australia (Ref. 9.4), Britain (Ref. 9.5), Canada (Ref. 9.6), New Zealand (Ref. 9.7), and in other parts of the world, the corresponding national building codes should be used.

If the applicable code does not specify the applicable design load, then the designer should determine the load based on reasonable assumptions. In such cases, most building codes require that the officials approve these loads.

The requirements presented in this chapter for the loads acting on buildings are based on the BOCA National Building Code (Ref. 9.1), the Uniform Building Code (Ref. 9.2), ANSI Standard Reference A58.1-82 (Ref. 9.3), the Building Code of the City of New York (Ref. 9.8), the Building Code of Chicago (Ref. 9.9), the Massachusetts Building Code (Ref 9.10), and the California State Building Code (Ref. 9.11). Normally the code with the most simplified version on a particular loading condition is presented. Earthquake loads follow the BOCA National Building Code (Ref. 9.1) and the Uniform Building Code (Ref. 9.2), which is adopted by the California State Building Code (Ref. 9.11).‡

9.3. DEAD LOADS

Dead loads are vertical static loads that result from the weight of the construction materials and from the weight of the permanent service equipment supported in, on or by the building (including its own weight) that are intended to remain permanently in place.

The actual weight of the construction materials, including the bearing§ and the nonbearing elements, should be computed from the unit weights of the materials. As a preliminary design aid, Table 9.1 provides an estimate of the weight of various structural slab systems. These values are intended to be used as a starting point and they should be verified after the structural slab is designed.

Structural assemblies should be analyzed and the weight of their individual components should be calculated. The unit weights of the materials should be based on the applicable building code (see Table 9.2). Codes usually provide the weight of the most common assemblies as a uniform distributed load‖ applicable to the floor area (see Table 9.3).

The weight of the service equipment, permanently installed in the building, should be computed from the specifications of the manufacturer. Service equipment includes plumbing stacks, piping, electrical, heating, ventilation and air conditioning equipment, escalators, elevators and other fixed equipment.

The weight of partitions should be included in the dead loads and can be determined from the unit weights of the components of such partitions. Codes usually provide an average uniformly distributed load to be used for the partitions (see Table 9.4). This average uniformly distributed partition load should be added to the other loads acting on the same area.

9.4. LIVE LOADS

Live loads are static loads resulting from the weight of all occupants, vehicles, snow and water supported in, on or

---

*Accepted levels of the probability of failure vary with the risk that the owner is willing to take. Probabilities of failure between 0.001 and 0.0001 are implied for the specification of minimum loads and maximum state of stresses.

†The term *loads* will be used instead of *working loads*, unless otherwise specified.

‡For a complete list of the applicable codes in the U.S.A., please see Ref. 9.12.

§*Bearing member*: the member supports the applicable vertical loads, in addition to its own weight.

‖*Uniformly distributed load*: A conventionalized representation of an element of dead or live load as a load of uniform intensity, distributed over an area.

Table 9.1. Initial Estimate of Slab Self-Weight

Concrete Slab with Beams
Approximate dead weight of a concrete slab (slab + beams)
Average loads are assumed (60–125 psf[a] for live load, ceiling and floor)

Beam span:		10	20	30	40	50 ft
Slab span:	10 ft:	60	65	75	90	110 psf
	20 ft:		110	115	125	135 psf
	30 ft:			155	165	175 psf

Average loads are assumed (3–6 kPa for live load, ceiling and floor[b])

Beam span:		3	6	9	12	15 m
Slab span:	3 m:	2.8	3.1	3.6	4.2	5.1 kPa
	6 m:		5.1	5.5	5.9	6.5 kPa
	9 m:			7.4	7.8	8.3 kPa

Concrete Mushroom Slab
Approximate dead weight of a concrete mushroom slab

Average loads are assumed (60–125 psf for live load, ceiling and floor)

Span:	10	20	30	40 ft
Self-weight:	60	100	155	220 psf

Average loads are assumed (3–6 kPa for live load, ceiling and floor)

Span:	3	6	9	12 m
Self-weight:	2.8	5	7.5	10.5 kPa

Concrete Flat Plate
Approximate dead weight of a concrete flat plate

Average loads are assumed (60–125 psf for live load, ceiling and floor)

Span:	10	20	30	40 ft
Self-weight:	60	115	190	270 psf

Average loads are assumed (3–6 kPa for live load, ceiling and floor)

Span:	3	6	9	12 m
Self-weight:	3.0	5.5	9.0	13.0 kPa

Ribbed slab on Prestressed Concrete Beams
Approximate dead weight of a ribbed slab (slab and beams)

Average loads are assumed (60–125 psf for live load, ceiling and floor)

Beam span:		10	20	30	40	50 ft
Slab span:	10 ft:	60	65	75	90	105 psf
	20 ft:		105	115	125	135 psf
	30 ft:			155	165	175 psf

Average loads are assumed (3–6 kPa for live load, ceiling and floor)

Beam span:		3	6	9	12	15 m
Slab span:	3 m:	2.8	3.1	3.6	4.2	5.1 kPa
	6 m:		5.1	5.5	5.9	6.5 kPa
	9 m:			7.4	7.8	8.3 kPa

Steel Decking with Steel Beams
Approximate dead weight of a steel decking (slab and beams)

Average loads are assumed (60–125 psf for live load, ceiling and floor)

Beam span:		20	30	40	50 ft
Slab span:	8 ft:	45	50	55	60 psf
	12 ft:	65	70	75	80 psf
	16 ft:	95	100	105	110 psf

Table 9.1. (Continued)

Steel Decking with Steel Beams
Approximate dead weight of a steel decking (slab and beams)
Average loads are assumed (3–6 kPa for live load, ceiling and floor)

Beam span:		6	9	12	15 m
Slab span:	2.4 m:	2.1	2.3	2.5	2.7 kPa
	3.6 m:	3.2	3.4	3.6	3.8 kPa
	4.8 m:	4.7	4.9	5.1	5.3 kPa

Timber Decking with Timber Beams
Approximate dead weight of a timber decking (deck and beams)

Average loads are assumed (60–85 psf for live load, ceiling and floor)

L_x span:		12	24	36 ft
L_y span	10 ft:	20	23	25 psf
	20 ft:	30	35	38 psf
	30 ft:	40	45	52 psf

Average loads are assumed (3–4 kPa for live load, ceiling and floor)

Beam span:		4	8	12 m
Slab span:	3 m:	1.0	1.1	1.3 kPa
	6 m:	1.5	1.7	1.9 kPa
	9 m:	2.0	2.2	2.6 kPa

Timber Decks

Type	Weight, psf (kPa)	Depth, in. (mm)
Simple deck, made of planks	4 (0.2)	1.50 (40)
Heavier deck with exposed beams, without insulation	4 (0.2)	2.00 (50)
Heavier deck with exposed beams, with a floating slab cover, without insulation	8 (0.4)	4.75 (120)
Deck with covered ceiling, hollow	16 (0.8)	4.00 (100)
Deck with covered ceiling, filled with sound insulation	40 (2.0)	4.00 (100)
Deck with covered ceiling, filled with sound insulation and with a floating slab cover	45 (2.2)	6.75 (170)

Source: Prof. Hans H. Hauri, ETH, Zürich, Switzerland.
[a] Pounds per square foot.
[b] 1 kPa (kN/m^2) is equal to 20.885 psf. Unit conversions are rounded. The conventional American unit is derived from the application code and governs.

Table 9.2. Unit Weight of Various Materials.

Material	pcf[a]	kN/m^{3}[b]
Aluminum	175	26.5
Cinder fill	57	8.5
Earth (dry)	96	14.5
Earth (wet)	120	18
Lightweight concrete	100	15
Masonry	140–170	21–26
Reinforced concrete	150	23
Steel	500	76
Timber	30–45	4.5–7
Water	64	9.8

[a] Pounds per cubic foot.
[b] 1 kN/m^3 is equal to 6.3637 pcf. Unit conversions are rounded. The conventional American unit is derived from the applicable code and governs.

Table 9.3. Unit Dead Loads for Design Purposes.[a]

Floor Finish

Type	Weight, psf	(kPa)	Depth, in.	(mm)
3/4–2 in. (20–50 mm) mortar or underlayment, light covering	25	(1.25)	2.00	(50)
3/4–2 in. (20–50 mm) mortar or underlayment, heavy covering (plates)	50	(2.50)	4.00	(100)
Floating floor, light covering	30	(1.50)	4.00	(100)
Floating floor, heavy covering (plates)	60	(2.75)	6.00	(150)
Flat roof covering without thermal insulation	50	(2.50)	6.50	(160)
Flat roof covering with thermal insulation	60	(2.75)	8.50	(220)
Waterproofing	5	(0.25)	2.00	(50)

Ceiling

Type	Weight, psf	(kPa)	Depth, in.	(mm)
Plaster or gypsum board	12.5	(0.6)	1.25	(30)
Suspended ceiling	12.5	(0.6)	8.00	(200)
Suspended ceiling with services	25.0	(1.2)	variable	

Source: Prof. Hans H. Hauri, ETH, Zürich, Switzerland.
[a] For a detailed set of dead loads please see BOCA National Building Code (Ref. 9.1) Appendix B, which has been adopted by most state and city codes in the U.S.A.

Table 9.4. Unit Dead Loads of Partitions for Design Purposes.[a]

	psf	kPa
Unplastered walls and partitions:		
Clay brick (4–22 in.), per in.	8.5	0.40
Concrete brick (4–22 in.), per in.	10	0.50
Concrete block (8–12 in.), per in.	7	0.35
4-in. glass block	18	0.85
Lath and plaster partitions	10–25	0.50–1.2
Plaster work (gypsum, or cement on wood or metal lath)	5–10	0.25–0.5

[a] For a detailed set of dead loads please see BOCA National Building Code (Ref. 9.1) Appendix B, which has been adopted by most state and city codes in the U.S.A.

by the building, as well as materials and equipment, that will be or are likely to be moved or relocated during the expected life of the building. Live loads are vertical, except for moving loads which, amplified to reflect their dynamic effect, are either vertical or horizontal. Live loads are either uniformly distributed over an area or concentrated* loads.

Occupancy Loads

The occupancy loads depend on the intended use of the space. The designer should calculate them as uniformly distributed or concentrated loads based on reasonable assumptions. Their minimum magnitude for design purposes, however, is specified by the applicable code. The

---

Concentrated load: The load is assumed to act at a point or within a limited area.

---

codes also specify if the concentrated loads should be used in conjunction with the uniformly distributed loads, or if they should be considered independently from the uniformly distributed load. Table 9.5 shows typical values for the minimum live loads for design purposes, according to the type of the building.[†]

If the applicable code does not include a provision for the intended use of the space, then the designer should derive the distributed live load according to the expected assembly of people or equipment in the space. While the density of the equipment can be determined from design considerations, Table 9.6 can assist the designer in predicting the number of people located in a specific space.[‡] Most building codes require officials to approve the live load to be used for structural design if it is not explicitly specified by the code.

The codes allow a reduction of the uniformly distributed occupancy loads for large areas. The load reduction depends on the use and the size of the space and the particular structural elements.[§]

In statically indeterminate structural systems (frame action), partial occupancy loads can increase the stresses at certain parts of the structure. Partial loading for determining the most critical state of stresses will be discussed in Section 9.14, as specified by the codes.

Snow Loads

The snow load on the roof depends on the geographic location of the building, the shape of the roof and its proximity to other taller buildings. The load from snow is always presented as a uniformly distributed load per projected area on the horizontal plane. The applicable city and state codes provide the ground snow load for each geographical location.

The ground snow load is the design snow load on flat roofs and on pitched roofs with a slope less than 20°. Pitched roofs with a slope more than 20° have a reduced snow load and as the pitch increases, the snow load becomes smaller. Roofs with valleys or roofs next to a taller building accumulate more snow and therefore the applicable snow load is more than a flat roof with the same projected area. Wind may also affect the snow accumulation on a roof. Under wind conditions, the snow accumulation on each part of a pitched roof will be different and most codes require that a series of unbalanced load combinations be considered.

The Uniform Building Code (Ref. 9.2) references city and state codes for determining the applicable snow load. The BOCA National Building Code (Ref. 9.1) provides the ground snow load on a map of the U.S.A. In some areas of the U.S.A., however, the variation of snow loads is so

---

[†] For an alternative presentation, please see Ref. 9.13.
[‡] For design purposes, the average weight of a person is estimated to be 200 lb (900 N).
[§] Reduction of live loads will be discussed in section 9.9.

Table 9.5. Minimum Live Loads for Design.

Use of Space	Uniform psf	Uniform kPa	Concentrated[a] lb	Concentrated[a] kN
One & two family houses:				
1st floor[b]	35	1.5	200	0.80
upper floors	25	1.3	200	0.80
unoccupied attics	15	0.8	250	1
inaccessible roof			250	1
Apartment buildings:				
private space	40	2	200	0.80
lobbies, exits and stairways	100	4.5		
1st floor corridors[b]	100	4.5		
corridors above 1st floor[b]	60	3		
balconies	100	4.5		
roof gardens	100	4.5		
Assembly areas:				
dance floors	100	4.5		
gymnasiums, skating rings	100	4.5		
museums	100	4.5		
restaurants	100	4.5		
Churches/courthouses:				
auditorium—fixed seats	60	3		
auditorium-movable seats	100	4.5		
Garages:				
passenger cars only	50	2.5	2,500	10
unloaded buses and light trucks	125	6	6,000	25
general purpose	250	11	20,000	80
Hospitals:				
patient rooms	40	2	1,000	4
operating rooms, labs	60	3	2,000	8
other areas	100	4.5		
Hotels:				
guest rooms	40	2		
conference rooms	50	2.5		
lobbies, exits and stairways	100	4.5		
balconies	100	4.5		
roof gardens	100	4.5		
Libraries:				
reading rooms	60	3	1,000	4
stack areas	150	7	1,500	6
lobbies, exits and stairways	100	4.5		
Manufacturing & storage:				
light	125	6	2,000	8
heavy	250	11	3,000	12
Office buildings:				
office space, conference rooms	50	2.5	2,000	8
toilets	50	2.5		
lobbies, exits and stairways	100	4.5		
1st floor[b] corridors	100	4.5		
corridors above 1st floor[b]	80	3.5		
Plaza areas, including landscape portions	100	4.5		
Recreation areas:				
bowling alleys	40	2		
poolrooms	75	3.5		
Schools:				
classrooms	50	2.5	1,000	4
other areas	100	4.5		
Sideways & driveways, subject to trucking	250	11		
Stadiums, grandstands and seating areas	100	4.5		
Stores:				
retail—basement & 1st floor[b]	100	4.5	2,000	8

Table 9.5. (Continued)

Use of Space	Uniform psf	Uniform kPa	Concentrated[a] lb	Concentrated[a] kN
retail—upper floors	75	3.5	2,000	8
wholesale	125	6	3,000	12
Theaters:				
dressing rooms	40	2		
auditorium—fixed seats	60	3		
auditorium—movable seats	100	4.5		
projection room	100	4.5		
stage floor	150	7	2,000	8

[a] Nonconcurrent with the uniformly distributed load, acting on an area of 2.5 ft^2 (0.25 m^2).
[b] In some countries (including Britain) this is called the ground floor, and the 1st floor is the one above that.

extreme that specific values cannot be included in the scale of this map.

Moving and Impact* Loads

If applicable, moving loads from the weight and impact of passenger cars and trucks, crane runways and supports, monorail beams and supports, elevators, dumbwaiters, escalators, machinery supports, assembly structures, and

Impact load: A kinetic load of short duration.

Table 9.6. Occupant Load Requirements.

Occupancy	Net Floor Area per Occupant ft^2	Net Floor Area per Occupant m^2
Classrooms	20	2
Dance floors	10	1
Dining spaces (nonresidential)	12	1.2
Exhibition spaces	10	1
Garages and open parking structures	250	25
Gymnasiums	15	1.5
Habitable rooms	140	14
Industrial shops	200	20
in schools	30	3
Institutional sleeping rooms:		
adults	75	7.5
children	50	5
infants	25	2.5
Kindergartens	35	3.5
Kitchens (nonresidential)	200	20
Laboratories	50	5
preparation rooms	100	10
Libraries	25	2.5
Locker rooms	12	1.2
Offices	100	10
Retail sales area:		
basement and 1st floor	25	2.5
upper floors	50	5
Seating areas—movable seats	10	1
Skating rings	15	1.5
Standing room (audience)	4	0.4
Storage rooms	200	20

Source: Building Code of the City of New York (Ref. 9.8), Table 6.2.

heliports and helistops should be considered in the design of the building.

The building codes treat these loads as static loads for ordinary buildings. As a compensation for their dynamic nature, the loads are amplified (impact load increase) and than a *quasi-static* analysis* is executed. The impact increase of the load depends on the frequency of the applied load, the natural frequency of the building, and the dumping (energy dissipation) of the building.

In most cases, the required impact increase of the vertical loads ranges between 10 and 25 percent. For working machinery, the vertical impact increase should be between 25 and 50 percent, and for elevators, the vertical impact increase should be 100 percent. The horizontal impact increase required is up to 25 percent of the actual vertical load.

9.5. WIND LOADS

As discussed in Chapter 10, wind loads develop from wind blowing on the exterior of the building, resulting in pressure on some parts of the building and suction on other parts. Both the pressure and the suction are proportional to the square of the wind velocity and act perpendicular to the corresponding building surface, such as the roof or the walls. A reference wind pressure related to the wind velocity, the height above grade, the nature of the terrain around the building, and the importance of the building (I) are all used by most building codes to determine the wind forces on buildings. The wind velocity is measured at 30 ft (10 m) above grade and depends on the geographical location of the building. The codes usually distinguish three different exposures for each geographical area: A, B, and C. Exposure A refers to urban areas with high-rise buildings, B refers to urban and suburban areas, and C to flat rural areas. The codes also provide the wind pressure profile along the height of the building, assuming that the maximum wind velocity occurs at 1,800 ft (550 m) for exposure A, at 1,100 ft (335 m) for exposure B, and at 900 ft (275 m) for exposure C.

The reference wind pressures for exposures B and C and the importance factor I for various types of buildings are given in Tables 9.7, 9.8, and 9.9.

The direction of the wind determines whether the wind force on each exposed building surface is a pressure or a suction. Assuming a certain direction of the wind, the pressure or suction on each part of the building is calculated from the reference wind pressure, the importance of the building, and the pressure coefficients. The pressure coefficients, defined by the applicable code for each part of the building, are based on the wind direction and the shape of the building (see Section 9.9). A positive coefficient suggests wind pressure, while a negative coefficient implies suction. For a particular part of the building, both a positive and a negative coefficient may be provided, implying that either pressure or suction can act on that part of the building. In such cases, the designer should determine which results in a more critical loading condition for each load bearing member of the building.

Wind gusts can cause a dynamic excitation of a building, if its natural frequency is near the frequency of the wind; this is most likely to occur in tall buildings. Wind tunnel tests and computer-based dynamic analysis should be employed to predict the behavior of a building, if it is determined that its dynamic characteristics are near those of the wind or if the shape of the buildings is irregular. In such cases, records of the 100-year wind force† should be used as the load input. The obtained forces on the building as a whole and on its various members, however, should not be less than 80 percent of the forces obtained following the quasi-static analysis based on the wind forces specified by the applicable code (see Section 9.9).

9.6. EARTHQUAKE LOADS

Nature of Earthquake Loads

Earthquakes result from the sudden movement of plates on the earth's surface along geological faults. Earthquake waves propagate along the earth's surface and shake the foundations of buildings, thus causing inertia forces.

The displacement, velocity, and acceleration of the foundation of a building depend on the magnitude of the earthquake, the location of its source, and the soil strata between the source of the earthquake and the building. The magnitude of the earthquake is commonly measured on the Richter scale, a logarithmic scale from 0 to 12 that measures the released energy at a distance of 60 miles (100 km) from the source. The energy released by the earthquake attenuates logarithmically with distance, thus the energy

---

*A quasi-static analysis is a static analysis with an amplified static load.

†Mean expected occurrence every 100 years.

Table 9.7. Minimum Design Wind Pressures, psf (kPa); Exposure B (Ref. 9.1).

Height above Grade, ft (m)		Basic Wind Speed, mph (km/h)				
		70 (110)	80 (130)	90 (145)	100 (160)	110 (175)
0–40	(0–12)	10 (0.5)	13 (0.6)	16 (0.75)	20 (0.95)	24 (1.15)
40–100	(12–30)	14 (0.7)	17 (0.8)	23 (1.1)	28 (1.35)	33 (1.55)
100–200	(30–60)	18 (0.85)	23 (1.1)	29 (1.4)	35 (1.65)	42 (2.0)
200–300	(60–90)	20 (0.95)	26 (1.25)	33 (1.6)	41 (2.0)	50 (2.4)
300–400	(90–120)	23 (1.1)	30 (1.45)	37 (1.75)	46 (2.2)	56 (2.7)
above 400	(120) per ANSI A58.1 (Ref. 9.3)					

Table 9.8. Minimum Design Wind Pressures, psf (kPa); Exposure C (Ref. 9.1).

Height above Grade, ft (m)		\multicolumn{5}{c}{Basic Wind Speed, mph (km/h)}				
		70 (110)	80 (130)	90 (145)	100 (160)	110 (175)
0–40	(0–12)	16 (0.75)	21 (1.0)	26 (1.25)	32 (1.55)	39 (1.85)
40–100	(12–30)	20 (0.95)	26 (1.25)	33 (1.6)	41 (1.95)	50 (2.4)
100–200	(30–60)	24 (1.15)	31 (1.5)	39 (1.85)	49 (2.35)	59 (2.8)
200–300	(60–90)	25 (1.2)	33 (1.6)	42 (2.0)	51 (2.45)	62 (2.95)
300–400	(90–120)	28 (1.35)	36 (1.7)	46 (2.2)	56 (2.7)	68 (3.25)
above 400	(120) per ANSI A58.1 (Ref. 9.3)					

Table 9.9. Building Importance Factor I for Wind Loads (Ref. 9.1).

Nature of Occupancy	100 Miles (160 km) from Hurricane Oceanline	At Hurricane Oceanline
All buildings except those listed below	1.00	1.10
Buildings for assembly use (more than 300 persons in one room)	1.15	1.23
Essential facilities:	1.15	1.23
Hospitals for emergency treatment		
Fire, rescue, police stations		
Communications and power stations		
National defense structures		
Buildings that represent low hazard in the event of failure	0.90	1.00

reaching the building depends on both the magnitude of the earthquake and the building's distance from the source. The soil strata between the earthquake's source and the building also affect the earthquake waves. The attenuation of the earthquake energy depends on the soil properties; soft deposits under the building tend to increase its natural period, usually bringing it closer to the earthquake's.

The Modified Mercalli Intensity (MMI) of an earthquake relates the intensity of the earthquake to the physical damage caused by the earthquake. It ranges from I to XII and is described in Table 9.10.

Effects of the Structural System and its Foundation on Earthquake Loads

Earthquake waves cause motion in the base of a building, resulting in its swaying and rocking in all directions. As the earthquake shakes the building, inertia forces develop both horizontally and vertically. The short duration of the motion is usually close to the natural frequency of the building, so the mass and stiffness of the building determine how the building will respond to the earthquake waves. A stiff building, such as a shear wall building, will most likely move together with its foundation during the earthquake (small relative displacement), but it will move significantly with respect to its initial position. Thus, it will develop high inertia forces but small deformations. Stiff buildings absorb a small amount of strain energy and absorb the earthquake energy as kinetic energy. Upper floors of flexible buildings, such as high-rise frame buildings or timber low-rise buildings, hardly move from their initial position, while their foundation and lower floors follow the earthquake motion. This results in large relative displacements of the upper floors with respect to the ground but in small absolute displacements. Thus, flexible buildings

Table 9.10. Abridged Modified Mercalli Intensity (MMI) Scale[a]

I	Detected only by sensitive instruments
II	Felt by a few persons at rest, especially on upper floors; delicate suspended objects may swing
III	Felt noticeably indoors, but not always recognized as a quake; standing autos rock slightly, vibration like passing truck.
IV	Felt indoors by many, outdoors by a few; at night some awaken; dishes, windows, doors disturbed; cars rock noticeably
V	Felt by most people; some breakage of dishes, windows, and plaster; disturbance of tall objects
VI	Felt by all; many are frightened and run outdoors; falling plaster and chimneys; small damage
VII	Everybody runs outdoors; damage to buildings varies, depending on quality of construction; noticed by car drivers
VIII	Panel walls thrown out of frames; fall of walls, monuments, chimneys; sand and mud ejected; car drivers disturbed
XI	Buildings shifted off foundations, cracked, thrown out of plumb; ground cracked, underground pipes broken.
X	Most masonry and framed structures destroyed; ground cracked; rails bent; landslides.
XI	Few structures remain standing; bridges destroyed; fissures in ground; pipes broken; landslides; rails bent
XII	Total damage; waves seen on ground surface; lines of sight and level distorted; objects thrown up into air

Source: R. L. Wiegel (Ref. 9.14), Table 4.9.
[a]This scale is a subjective measure of the effect of the ground shaking and is not an engineering measure of the ground acceleration.

develop small inertia forces but large deformations, absorbing a large amount of strain energy. Actual buildings usually have an in-between behavior, with varying amounts of relative and absolute movements.

Earthquake Design According to the Applicable Code

Most of the U.S.A. state codes are based on the BOCA National Building Code (Ref. 9.1) and the Uniform Building Code (Ref. 9.2). These codes suggest that an earthquake generates horizontal forces only and require a quasi-static analysis. Vertical loads, which can reach up to a third of the horizontal loads are not taken into consideration, since an increase of stresses of 33 percent is allowed for superimposing the earthquake loads* and, most likely, the maximum allowable live loads would not coincide with a maximum intensity earthquake.

Static horizontal forces are specified for each floor and for the top of the building. These forces create an overturning moment that should be resisted by axial loads on each floor and the foundation from columns, shear walls, and elevator and stair wells. Earthquake forces depend on the geographical location of the building. If the building is in a low seismic area, then the earthquake load is small. For buildings in high seismic areas, earthquake loads can be high and usually dominate the design of buildings higher than several floors. The U.S.A. is divided into 5 seismic zones, with zone 0 being seismically the least active and zone 4 being the most active.

The calculated forces acting on each level of the building are distributed among all the elements that provide the lateral stiffness of the floor, including columns, cross-bracing, shear walls, and elevator and stair wells. In addition, the applicable horizontal force should reflect any eccentrically distributed mass and it should always be applied with a 5 percent eccentricity. The torsional resistance will be provided by all elements providing torsional resistance on each floor.

The deflections of the building caused by earthquake loads should also be considered. Independent structures should have minimum distances between them, so that they do not collide during an earthquake.

Dynamic Analysis and Appropriateness

Due to the nature of earthquake loads and the development of inertia forces and dumping in the building, a dynamic analysis is usually appropriate (especially for high-rise buildings) and it is recommended by the building codes. A rigorous dynamic analysis takes into consideration the distribution of the mass and the stiffness of the building, and the frequency spectrum and the magnitudes of the loads. A detailed dynamic analysis can be executed on computers only. Even a dynamic analysis is not absolutely precise, however, because of uncertainties in the properties of the building and the dynamic characteristics of the earthquake that will be used as the input load. Recorded earthquakes are few and their characteristics vary significantly. Thus, buildings can be studied subject to one of the few recorded earthquakes or subject to an artificial earthquake derived from a frequency spectrum, a peak acceleration and a random generator. Nevertheless, computer-based dynamic analysis is highly recommended for high-rise buildings, or buildings with irregular shapes or irregular distribution of mass.

If a dynamic analysis is performed, the building codes require that the smooth earthquake spectrum, or the earthquake record provided as input to the dynamic analysis, be consistent with the geographic location of the building. The applicable codes also limit the computer-based dynamic analysis so that the computed base shear is not less than 90 percent of the base shear determined by the quasi-static method specified by the codes.

Experimental Alternatives

The use of scale models on shaking tables and the electronic capturing of the model's behavior is the experimental alternative to the dynamic analysis under earthquake loading. Scale models can be large in size, depending on the experimental facility, and experiments on shaking tables are costly and long when compared to a computer-based analysis. Such experiments are dependable and extensively used, however, for determining the behavior of high-rise buildings in seismic areas, together with predictions from computer-based models.

Design Hints

Buildings should be designed for horizontal loads resulting from earthquakes by having the necessary ductility to absorb energy so they do not experience a progressive collapse. Thus, the strength and ductility of the individual structural members and particularly the connections between the members are of fundamental importance for seismic design.

The applicable codes specify the required properties of reinforced concrete, steel, timber and masonry for seismic design and give specific design details.

9.7. OTHER LOADS

In addition to dead, live, snow, wind and earthquake loads, other loads may apply to a particular building.

Earth Pressure on Retaining Walls. Retaining walls should be designed to resist the lateral pressure of retained materials. Walls retaining drained earth should be designed to withstand a lateral hydrostatic pressure from a fluid weighing at least 30 pcf (4.7 kN/m^3) and depth equal to

---

*For elastic design.

the retained earth. All surcharged loads should be additional to the hydrostatic pressure.

Water Pressure on Foundation. The foundation should be designed to resist water pressure from the water table. The uplift pressure is determined from the distance between the water table and the level of the foundation.

Fluid Pressures. The design of the building should consider pressures from confined fluids or gases.

Construction and Erection Loads. The building should be designed so that it can withstand temporary loads during construction, including wind loads. Temporary structures to assist the building's erection can also be employed if necessary.

Thermal Forces. Expansion joints in the building should allow for an unrestrained expansion or contraction due to temperature changes. Enclosed buildings more than 250 ft (80 m) in plan dimension between expansion joints should be designed for the forces and the movements resulting from a temperature difference of 40°F (20°C). For exterior exposed frames, arches, trusses or shells, the building should be designed for the forces and the movements resulting from a temperature difference of 40°F (20°C) for concrete buildings or 60°F (30°C) for steel buildings.

9.8. CALCULATION OF LOADS

Loads act on specific elements of the building that should be designed to carry them within the allowable state of stresses. The structural hierarchy of the building determines the forces acting on the various load-bearing elements.

On the structure shown in Fig. 9.8.1, a uniformly distributed floor load is applied on the deck. The deck is supported on joists, so the deck load is transferred to the joists as a uniformly distributed load per unit length of the joist. The joists are supported on beams which carry the

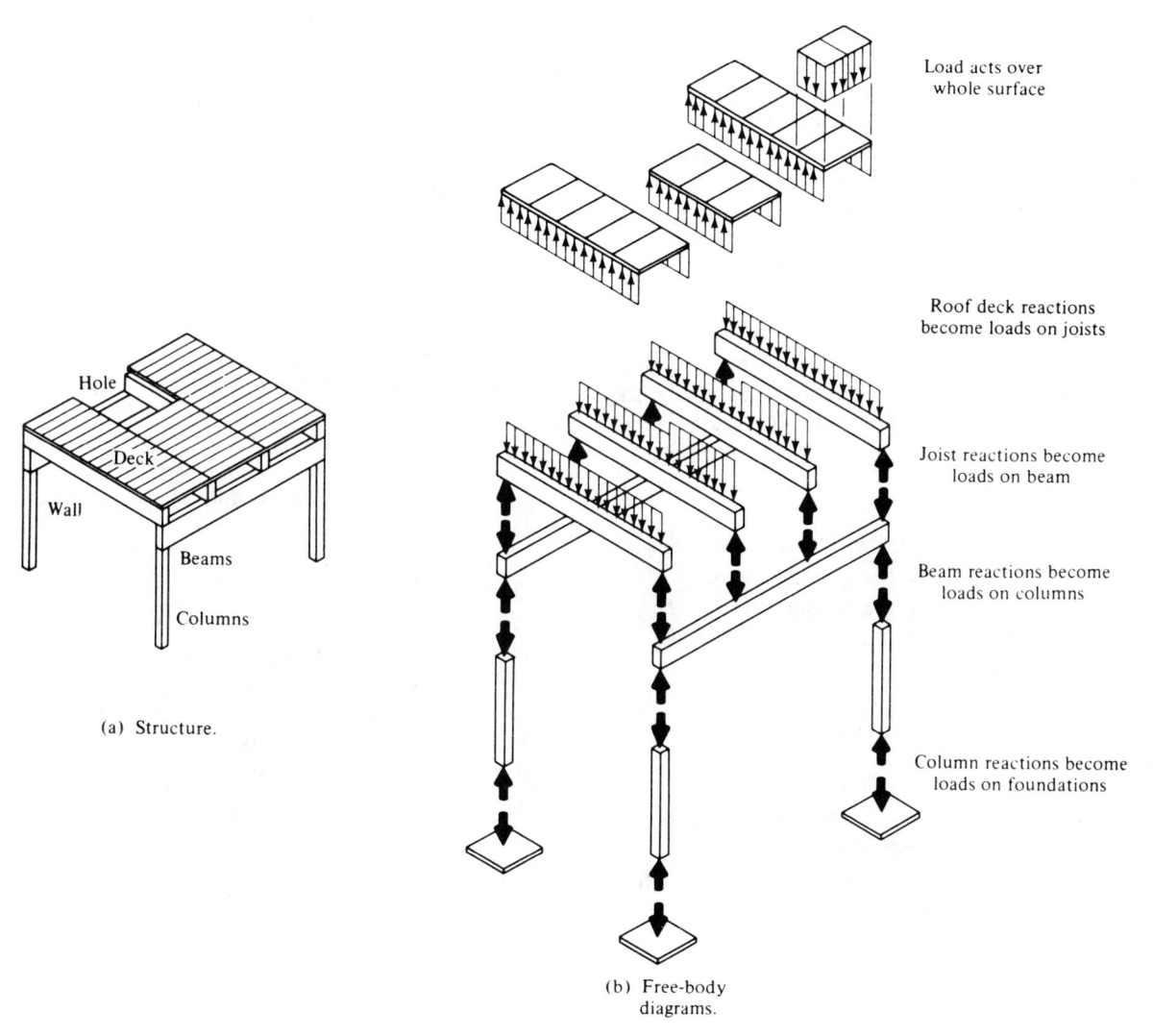

Figure 9.8.1. Load modeling. Reproduced from *Daniel L. Schodek, Structures,* © *1980, p. 114,* by permission of Prentice Hall, Inc., Englewood Cliffs, New Jersey.

forces to the columns and, finally, to the foundation. The magnitude of the forces on each structural element can be easily determined for statically determined systems by using the contributory areas for surface areas and then the established structural hierarchy. The distribution of forces in statically indeterminate systems involves the material stiffness and the geometry of each member. Thus, the calculation of the forces on each member for a large structure requires either a computer-based analysis or a simplified approach based on distribution coefficients.

The wind loads are applied directly to the exposed elements of the building, such as the roof and the walls. Thus, each element and its connections, including glass panels, should be designed to support the applicable wind forces. In addition to the individual elements, the building as a unit should be designed to withstand the horizontal wind force and the resulting overturning moment.* Similarly, each element and its connections must resist the element's inertia forces during an earthquake and the building as a unit must withstand the horizontal force and the overturning moment from earthquakes. The building supports the horizontal loads and the overturning moment from both wind and earthquakes either by a structural frame,† a bracing core, such as an elevator well or a stairwell, or a series of shear walls or braced frames. Thus, structural elements such as beams and columns carry a combination of loads, both vertical and horizontal, concurrent or not. In the following paragraphs, the loads for some typical structural members will be presented and in Section 9.14. the required load combinations will be presented.

9.9. LOADS ON FLOORS

The types of loads described in Section 9.2. apply to various parts of a building. In this section, the loads on the structural elements of the building will be presented, together with the applicable information for structural design.

Floors should be designed for dead loads, occupancy loads, both uniformly distributed and concentrated loads, and moving loads, if applicable (see Sections 9.3. and 9.4.)

For large floor areas the uniform live load can be reduced to reflect a smaller probability of the load to be applied on a large area. The building codes allow a reduction of the live loads, based on the size of the loaded area. The applicable live load, as a percentage of the reference live load, is shown in Table 9.11. A reduction of the load is not allowed for floors used for assemblies, manufacturing, parking, storage or sales. No reduction will be allowed for the calculation of shearing forces at the column capitals for flat plate or flat slab construction. The live loads on columns, piers or walls supporting a floor should be reduced to 80 percent of their reference live loads.

---

*A horizontal force, applied at a distance from grade, produces an overturning moment.
†Columns and beams rigidly connected.

Table 9.11. Percentage of Live Loads.

Contributory Area ft² (m²)	Ratio of Live Load to Dead Load[a]		
	0.625 or less	1	2 or more
150 or less (15 or less)	100%	100%	100%
150–300 (15–30)	80%	85%	85%
300–450 (30–45)	60%	70%	75%
450–500 (45–60)	50%	60%	70%
600 or more (60 or more)	40%	55%	65%

Source: Building Code of the City of New York (Ref. 9.8), Table 9.1.
[a]For intermediate values of live load/dead load, the applicable percentages of live load may be interpolated.

Beams and trusses in the ceilings of spaces used for garages or manufacturing areas should be designed for a concentrated 2,000 lb (8 kN) load applied at their lower cord. This load is concurrent with all other loads acting on the floor.

Calculation of Dead and Live Loads Applied on a Floor. The floor of a residential apartment building, for private space occupancy, will be constructed of a reinforced concrete flat plate. The column grid is 15 ft × 15 ft (4.5 m × 4.5 m). The ceiling will be suspended and the floor cover will be 2 inches (50 mm) of mortar and light covering. The wall partitions will be 4-inch (100 mm) clay brick. The applicable loads on such a floor are:

	psf	kPa
Estimate of the weight of the slab (Table 9.1)	90	4.3
Floor cover (Table 9.3)	25	1.25
Suspended ceiling (Table 9.3)	12.5	0.6
4-in. clay brick partitions (Table 9.4)	4 × 8.5	4 × 0.4
TOTAL DEAD LOAD	161.5	17.75
Reference occupancy live load (Table 9.5)	40	2
Live load after reduction; factor 80% (Table 9.11)	32	1.6

Concentrated live load (Table 9.5): 200 lb (0.8 kN) nonconcurrent with the uniformly distributed load, acting on an area of 2.5 ft² (0.25 m²).

9.10. LOADS ON ROOFS

Roofs should be designed for dead load, snow load, occupancy load, wind load, water accumulation, and special loads, in combinations specified in Section 9.14. The shape of the roof determines the magnitude of the applicable loads. A reduction of live loads is not allowed in the design of roofs.

Occupancy Load. If the roof is accessible to the public, it should be designed according to its intended use and the applicable live load for floor loads should be employed. If the roof is landscaped, the weight of the saturated soil and landscape materials must be considered. All areas adjacent to the landscaped areas and not specifically restricted to the public are considered as assembly areas and should be designed according to the applicable provision for floor loads. For roofs that are not accessible to the public, the provision for a single person visiting the roof requires 250 lb (1 kN*) applied on an area of 2 ft × 2 ft (0.60 m × 0.60 m), nonconcurrent† with snow load.

Ceiling Load. Beams and trusses in the roofs of buildings used for garages or manufacturing areas should be designed for a concentrated 2,000 lb (8 kN) load applied at their lower cord. This load is concurrent with all other loads acting on the roof.

Snow Load. The snow load on the roof is always vertical, applied on the projection of the roof on a horizontal plane. The snow load is calculated based on the ground snow load, the shape of the roof, and the structure's proximity to other taller buildings.

For flat roofs or for pitched roofs with a slope less than 20° and standing away from other buildings, the snow load on the roof is the same as the ground snow load. For pitched roofs with a slope more than 20°, the snow load is considered to act on a projected area‡ and should be reduced by 1/30 of the ground snow load for every degree more than 20°. Pitched roofs with a slope more than 50° are considered free of snow load. Wind reduces the snow accumulation on the windward side of pitched roofs and increases the snow accumulation of the leeward side. Thus, unbalanced snow loads should be considered on pitched roofs. If the roof slope is less than 20°, the snow load on the windward side will be reduced by 50 percent, while the load on the leeward side will be unchanged. Pitched roofs with a slope between 20° and 50° will have no snow load on the windward side, but a 25 percent snow load increase on the leeward side (Fig. 9.10.1).

For multiple folded-plate sawtooth roofs, the snow load will be the same as the ground snow load, regardless of the slope of the folded plates. The unbalanced snow load will be reduced 50 percent at the crown, but will be three times larger at the ridge of the folded plates. In any case, the snow surface at the ridge should not exceed the elevation of the crown.

For curved roofs, the snow load on the roof will be determined using the ground snow load and the coefficients shown in Table 9.12 for the shape of the roof. If the roof rise-to-span ratio of curved roofs is more than 0.2, an unbalanced snow load should be considered. In such cases the windward side will be free of snow, while the snow load on the leeward side will be triangular, with a maximum magnitude twice the ground snow load at eaves and zero at the crown of the roof.

Wind also causes more snow to accumulate on roofs less than 20 ft (6 m) away from a taller building. The snow accumulation on the lower roof depends on the relative height of the two buildings and the area of the roof of the taller building. For more information, please see the BOCA National Building Code (Ref. 9.1) Section 1111.7.

Water Accumulation (Ponding). Roofs should be designed for the weight of water that may be accumulated on the roof due to its geometry, assuming that the drainage system is clogged.

Wind Load. The direction of the wind and the shape of the roof determine the magnitude of the wind load and whether the wind force on each part of the roof is a pressure or a suction. The pressure or suction on each part of the roof is calculated from the reference wind pressure P_e (see Tables 9.7 and 9.8), the importance of the building (factor I, see Table 9.9), and the pressure coefficients C_p (see Table

Table 9.12. Design Snow Load for Curved Roofs.

Rise-to-Span Ratio	Percentage of Ground Snow Load
0–0.2	100%
0.2–0.3	80%
0.3–0.6	60%
more than 0.6	40%

Source: Massachusetts State Code (Ref. 9.10), Fig. 711.4.

---

*1 kPa (kN/m²) equals 20.885 psf. Unit conversions are rounded. The conventional American unit is derived from the applicable code and governs.
†*Concurrent loads*: loads acting simultaneously on the building.
‡The projection of the roof area on the horizontal plane.

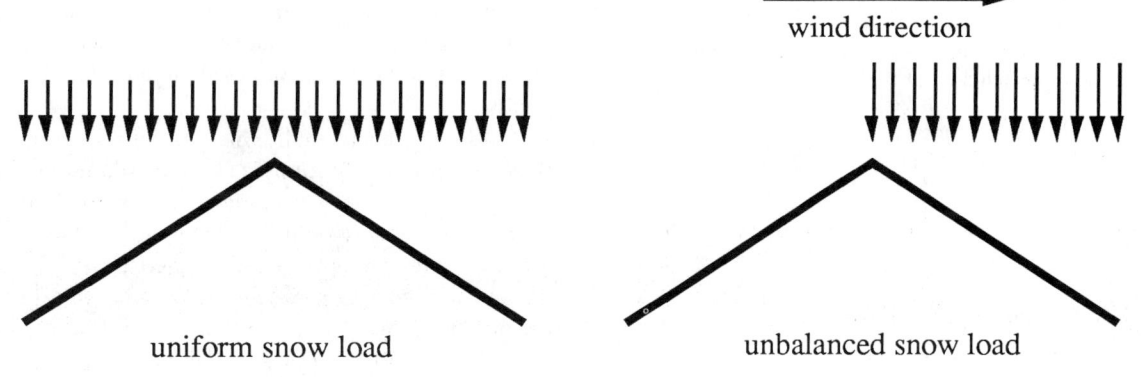

Figure 9.10.1. Snow load on a pitched roof (slope 20° to 50°).

Table 9.13. Roof Pressure Coefficients C_p.

Roof Pitch	Pressure coefficients	
	Windward slope	Leeward slope
0°–20°	−0.6	−0.6
20°–30°	0.2 or −0.5	−0.6
30°–40°	0.3 or −0.4	−0.6
40°–50°	0.4 or −0.3	−0.6
50°–90°	0.6	−0.6

Wind direction normal to ridge. For wind direction parallel to ridge, windward and leeward, $C_p = -0.70$.

Table 9.14 External Pressure Coefficients C_p for Arched Roofs.

Rise-to-Span Ratio	Windward Quarter	Center Half	Leeward Quarter
Less than 0.2	0.2 or −0.9	−0.7	−0.4
0.2 to 0.3	0.3	−0.8	−0.4
0.3 to 0.6	0.6	−1.0	−0.4

9.13 for pitched roofs and Table 9.14 for arched roofs) according to the equation:

$$P = I \times C_p \times P_e$$

The wind load on a pitched roof with a slope less than 50° and wind direction normal to the ridge is shown schematically in Fig. 9.10.2.

The codes specify that wind pressure acts perpendicular to the roof surface and that the design should be based on winds from any direction, despite the prevailing winds in each area. As a result, the designer should study the stresses on the various structural members of the roof from wind

As a result, the following combinations of snow loads should be considered:

	Windward snow load, psf (kPa)	Leeward snow load, psf (kPa)
Case I	15 (0.75)	15 (0.75)
Case II	0	18.75 (0.95)

The above snow loads should be applied to the horizontal projection of the roof.

According to Table 9.8, the reference wind pressure for exposure C (rural area) up to 40 ft (12 m) high is 26 psf (1.25 kPa). According to Table 9.9, the importance factor of the building $I = 1$. For a wind direction normal to the ridge, the windward slope has a pressure coefficient $C_p = 0.3$ or $C_p = -0.4$. The pressure coefficient for the leeward slope is $C_p = -0.6$. For a wind direction parallel to the ridge, both windward and leeward coefficients are $C_p = -0.7$. As a result, the following combinations of wind pressures (suctions) should be considered:

	Windward pressure, psf (kPa)	Leeward pressure, psf (kPa)
Case I	0.3 × 26 = 7.8 (0.375)	(−0.6) × 26 = −15.6 (−0.750)
Case II	(−0.4) × 26 = −10.4 (−0.500)	(−0.6) × 26 = −15.6 (−0.750)
Case III	(−0.7) × 26 = −18.2 (−0.875)	(−0.7) × 26 = −18.2 (−0.875)

The calculated wind pressures (suctions) should be applied perpendicular to each roof surface, resulting to both horizontal and vertical forces.

loads resulting from all possible wind directions. For the design of purlins and other roof elements supporting small contributory areas, the wind pressure should be amplified by 50% to accommodate wind gusts and increased local pressure.

Calculation of the Snow and Wind Loads on a Pitched Roof. A building with an inaccessible pitched roof with slopes to the horizontal 35° is located in a rural area with reference ground snow load 30 psf (1.5 kPa) and wind velocity 90 mph (145 km/h). The roof's ridge is 40 ft (12 m) above grade. The snow load on the projected area of the roof is

$$30 - 30 \times \frac{35° - 20°}{30} = 15 \text{ psf } (0.75 \text{ kPa})$$

The unbalanced snow load, due to snow movement by the wind, is

windward side: 0 (the slope is more than 20°)

leeward side: 1.25 × 15 = 18.75 psf (0.95 kPa)

9.11. LOADS ON BEAMS, COLUMNS, AND WALLS

Beams and columns transfer the vertical loads from the roof and the floors to the foundation. In the absence of a bracing system, such as an elevator well, a shear wall or any other stiff bearing element extending from the basement to the top of the building, beams and columns provide the lateral stiffness of the building, resisting the applicable horizontal forces from wind or earthquakes. In such cases, beams and columns and their structural connections should be designed to withstand the horizontal loads in addition to the vertical loads.

Cars may accidentally hit columns in parking areas. Unless specifically protected, such columns should be designed to absorb an impact horizontal force. This horizontal force should be considered as acting simultaneously with all other loads carried by the column. For areas accessible to passenger cars only, this force should be at least 2,500 lb (10 kN) acting at a height of at least 21 inches (0.50 m). For areas accessible to trucks or heavy pressure on windward slope   suction on windward slope

Figure 9.10.2. Wind load on a pitched roof.

vehicles, the impact force should be determined accordingly.

Exterior Walls

Walls should support the wind pressure obtained by multiplying the wall pressure coefficients C_p, shown in Table 9.15, with the reference wind pressure P_e, shown in Tables 9.7 and 9.8, and the importance of the building for wind loads, factor I, shown in Table 9.9. The equation would read:

$$P = I \times C_p \times P_e$$

The wind forces on the vertical walls are shown schematically in Fig. 9.11.1.

Table 9.15. Wall Pressure Coefficients C_p.

Surface	L/B	C_p	To Be Evaluated at
Windward wall	all values	0.80	each floor
Leeward wall	0 to 1	−0.50	the mean roof height
	2	−0.30	
	more than 4	−0.20	
Side walls	all values	−0.70	the mean roof height

L is the horizontal dimension of the building, parallel to wind direction.
B is the horizontal dimension of the building, normal to wind direction.

As with the design of roofs, the codes specify that the design should be based on winds coming from all directions. For the design of wall elements supporting contributory areas less than 1,000 ft² (95 m²), the wind pressure should be amplified by 50 percent to accommodate wind gusts and increased local pressures.

9.12. FOUNDATION LOADS

The foundation loads result from the total load of the column, pier or wall, after the appropriate live load reduction, plus the dead weight of the foundation plus the weight of any overlaying soil. Impact forces can be omitted, unless the soil is of a loose granular consistency, or if the foundation supports heavy machinery, cranes or moving loads, or if the live load causing impact is more than one third of the total live (excluding impact) and dead loads. The foundation loads are used in computing the soil bearing pressure and for the design of the foundation.

Retaining Walls

Retaining walls provide resistance from earth pressure, as described in Section 9.7., and should be designed accordingly.

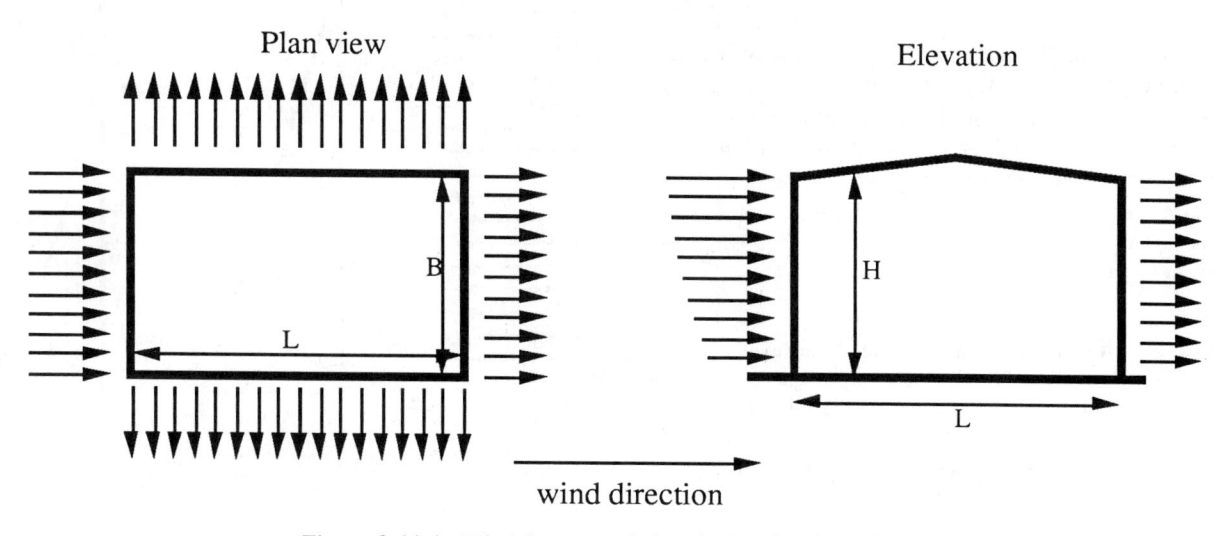

Figure 9.11.1. Wind forces on the vertical walls of a building.

9.13. LOADS ON RAILINGS, SIDEWALKS, AND DRIVEWAYS

Top, intermediate and bottom handrailings should carry a horizontal load of 200 lb (0.8 kN) and a vertical load of 200 lb (800 N). In addition, handrailings should carry a horizontal load of 40 plf* (0.5 kN/m) and a vertical load of 50 plf (0.6 kN/m) acting simultaneously. In theaters, the horizontal load should be 50 plf and the vertical load 100 plf (1.2 kN/m). In single family and two-family dwellings, the required loads are 20 plf (250 N/m) for each. Solid panel railings should be designed for a uniform lateral load of 20 psf (1 kPa).

Railings used in parking areas should resist 300 plf (4.4 kN/m) applied at least 21 inches (0.50 m) above the roadway and a minimum of 2500 lb (10 kN) per vehicle. The live load on sidewalks and driveways should be at least 100 psf (5 kPa). If subject to wheel loads, the live load should be at least 600 psf (39 kPa) or the maximum vehicular wheel load. Live loads on sidewalks and driveways should conform to the specifications of the relevant State's Department of Highways.

9.14. HORIZONTAL FORCES ON THE BUILDING

The building as a unit should be designed to withstand the horizontal forces and the resulting overturning moments from wind and earthquakes. The horizontal forces are distributed along the height of the building and are supported by a structural frame, a bracing core, such as an elevator well or a stairwell, or a series of shear walls or braced frames.

Wind Forces (see also Chapter 10)

In lieu of a dynamic analysis, wind forces along the height of a building are considered to be static and are determined according to the applicable codes. Wind pressures are assumed to act simultaneously, perpendicular to all exterior surfaces of the building. The forces on the roof and the exterior walls, as specified by the codes and presented in Sections 9.10. and 9.11., should produce the horizontal forces acting as each floor level. The building should be designed to withstand these forces and the resultant overturning moment.

Calculation of Wind Forces on a Building. As an example, the horizontal wind forces on a 30-story building will be determined based on the code requirements. The building is 360 ft (110 m) high with a square base 150 ft × 150 ft (45 m × 45 m), and it is located in an area with wind exposure B and wind velocity 80 mph (130 km/h) at 30 ft (9 m) above ground. The horizontal force on the windward wall, calculated at each pressure level, is equal to

$$F = P \times H \times B = I \times C_p \times P_e \times H \times B$$
$$F = 1 \times 0.80 \times 150 \times (40 \times 13 + 60 \times 17 + 100 \times 23 + 100 \times 26 + 60 \times 30)$$
$$= 989 \text{ kips } (4,400 \text{ kN})$$

and the total force on the leeward wall, calculated at the mean height of the roof, is equal to

$$F = 1 \times 0.50 \times 150 \times 360 \times 30 = 810 \text{ kips } (3,603 \text{ kN})$$

The base shear force is

$$F = 989 + 810 = 1,799 \text{ kips } (8,003 \text{ kN})$$

The bending moment (overturning moment) at grade is

$$M = 1 \times 0.80 \times 150 \times \left[\frac{40^2}{2} \times 13 + 60 \times \left(40 + \frac{60}{2}\right) \right.$$
$$\times 17 + 100 \times \left(100 + \frac{100}{2}\right) \times 23 + 100$$
$$\times \left(200 + \frac{100}{2}\right) \times 26 + 60$$
$$\left. \times \left(300 + \frac{60}{2}\right) \times 30 \right] + 1 \times 0.50 \times 150 \times \frac{360^2}{2} \times 30$$
$$= 346,300 \text{ kips-ft } (470 \text{ MNm})$$

The distribution of horizontal forces and the shearing forces and bending moments diagrams along the height of the building are shown in Fig. 9.14.1.

wind forces   shearing forces   bending moments

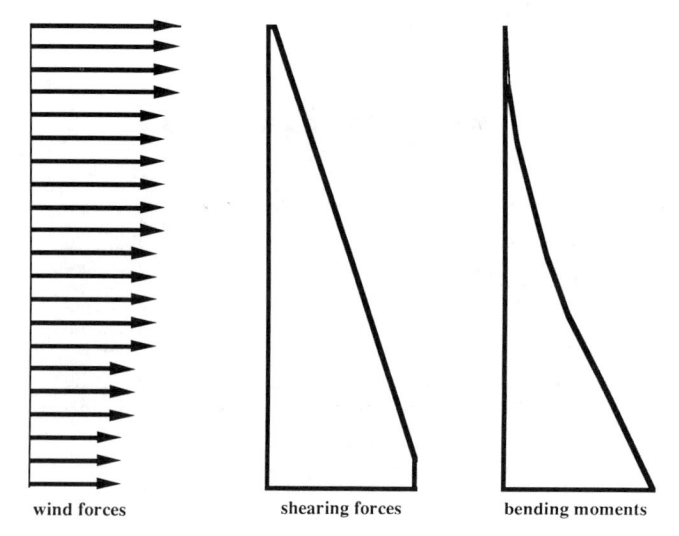

Figure 9.14.1. Wind forces, shearing and bending moment diagrams along the building height.

---

*Plf: pounds per linear foot.

Earthquake Forces

In lieu of a dynamic analysis, the earthquake forces along the height of the building are considered to be static and are determined according to the BOCA National Building Code (Ref. 9.1) and the Uniform Building Code (Ref. 9.2) as it is presented in the following paragraphs.

The Total Shear Force at Base. The total horizontal force at the base of a building (V) depends on the seismic zone (coefficient Z), the importance of the building occupancy (factor I), the stiffness of the structural system of the building (factor K), the natural period of the building (factor C), the soil profile on which the building resides (factor S), and the weight of the building (W). Thus the total horizontal force at the base of the building (V) is represented by the equation:

$$V = Z \times I \times K \times C \times S \times W$$

The coefficient Z depends on the seismic zone and is shown in Table 9.16. Factor I depends on the building occupancy and is shown in Table 9.17. Factor K depends on the lateral stiffness of the building and is shown in Table 9.18.

Factor C depends on the natural frequency of the building occupancy and is represented by the equation

$$C = \frac{1}{15\sqrt{T}}, \quad \text{but not more than } 0.12.$$

Table 9.16. Coefficient Z for Earthquake Loads

Seismic Zone	Z
4	1 (1.000)
3	$\frac{3}{4}$ (0.750)
2	$\frac{3}{8}$ (0.375)
1	$\frac{3}{16}$ (0.1875)
0	$\frac{1}{8}$ (0.125)

Table 9.17. Factor I for Earthquake Loads.

Nature of occupancy	I
All buildings except those listed below	1.0
Buildings for assembly use (more than 300 persons in one room)	1.25
Essential facilities:	1.5
Hospitals for emergency treatment	
Fire, rescue, police stations	
Communications and power stations	
National defense structures	

Table 9.18. Factor K for Earthquake Loads.

Arrangement of lateral force-resisting elements	K
All buildings except those listed below	1.00
Reinforced concrete or reinforced masonry bearing wall system	1.33
Buildings with a dual bracing system	0.80

The natural frequency of the building can be derived either by a computer-based dynamic analysis, or it can be approximated by the following equations. For frame buildings, where the lateral stiffness is provided by the frame only, the natural period is approximated as:

$$T = 0.1 \times N$$

where N is the number of floors of the building.

For braced frames, or for shear walls not interconnected with the frames, the natural period is represented by the equation:

$$T = \frac{0.05\, H}{\sqrt{L_s}} \quad (H, L_s \text{ in feet})$$

$$T = \frac{0.09\, H}{\sqrt{L_s}} \quad (H, L_s \text{ in meters})$$

where H is the height of the building and L_s is the longest dimension of a shear wall or a braced frame in the direction of the applied forces.

For shear walls or exterior reinforced concrete frames with deep beams or piers, the natural period is approximated as:

$$T = \frac{0.05\, H}{\sqrt{L}} \quad (H, L \text{ in feet})$$

$$T = \frac{0.09\, H}{\sqrt{L}} \quad (H, L \text{ in meters})$$

where L is the dimension of the building in the direction of the applied forces.

Factor S depends on the soil profile and is shown in Table 9.19. If the soil profile is not known, a soil profile of type S_3 should be used.*

Distribution of the Horizontal Forces. The base shear force is distributed along the height of the building to a single force F_t at the top of the building and a series of forces at each floor level.

For structures with regular shapes or framing systems, the force F_t at the top of the building depends on the natural frequency of the building (T) and is represented by the equation

$$F_t = 0.07 \times T \times V, \quad \text{but no more than } 0.25 \times V$$

*Or S_2, whichever gives the larger value of $C \times S$, if the natural period of the building is calculated using the soil properties.

Table 9.19. Factor S for Earthquake Loads.

Soil Profile Type	S
S_1: Rock, stiff soil less than 200 ft (60 m) deep	1.0
S_2: Stiff soil more than 200 ft (60 m) deep	1.2
S_3: Soft to medium-stiff soil	1.5

For very stiff buildings ($T < 0.7$ second), the force at the top is equal to zero. Similarly, for structures with regular shapes or framing systems, the force F_x at floor x, is given as a fraction of the remaining horizontal force and it is proportional to the weight of the floor (w_x) and its distance from the base (h_x), according to the equation:

$$F_x = (V - F_t) \frac{w_x h_x}{\sum_{i=1}^{n} w_i h_i}$$

The above magnitudes for the top horizontal force and the horizontal force at each floor apply even if a regularly shaped building has setbacks along each dimension up to 75 percent between a tower and the lower plan.

For structures with irregular shapes or framing systems, the distribution of horizontal forces along the height of the building depends on its stiffness between adjacent storeys and the dynamic characteristics of the structure. A detailed structural analysis should determine the distribution of the horizontal forces along the height of an irregularly shaped building.

The calculated forces acting on each level of the building are distributed among all the elements that provide the lateral stiffness of the floor, including columns, cross-bracing, shear walls, and elevator and stair wells. In addition, the applicable horizontal force should reflect any eccentrically distributed mass that will cause torsion of the floor. Even for symmetrical buildings, a 5 percent eccentricity of the horizontal force on each floor should be employed to produce the minimum torsion specified by the codes. The torsional resistance of the floor should be provided by all elements that provide lateral stiffness to the floor.

The building should also be designed for the overturning moment at each floor, as derived by the distribution of the horizontal forces. The overturning moments are resisted as axial forces by columns, shear walls and elevator and stair wells.

The deflection of the building due to earthquake loads should also be considered. Regardless of the structural soundness of the building, the maximum permissible displacement between two adjacent floors should not exceed 0.005 of the height between the two floors. For buildings with unreinforced masonry, the maximum displacement should be less than 0.0025. Under design constraints, the designer can accept a higher tolerance of horizontal forces, as long as it can be proved that such a displacement can be tolerated by the structural and nonstructural elements of the building. The restriction of allowable displacements ensures the intactness of nonstructural elements such as gypsum boards, plasters, fixtures, and so forth, and is also based on the psychological distress that an extensive displacement would produce. Independent structures should have a minimum distance between them, so that they do not collide during an earthquake. This distance can be obtained from the calculated displacements along each building, assuming that each building moves toward the other during an earthquake.

Calculation of Earthquake Forces on a Building. As an example, the earthquake forces on a 30-story building will be determined based on the code requirements. The building is 360 ft (110 m) high with a square base 150 ft × 150 ft (45 m × 45 m).* Assuming an average unit weight equal to 12 pcf (1.9 kN/m^3), soil profile of type S_1, and a seismic zone 3, the shear force at the base of the building is:

$$V = Z \times I \times K \times C \times S \times W$$

$$T = 0.1 \times N = 3 \text{ seconds}, \quad C = \frac{1}{15 \times \sqrt{3}} = 0.0385$$

$$W = 12 \times 360 \times 150 \times 150 = 97,200 \text{ kips } (432,427 \text{ kN})$$

$$V = \tfrac{3}{8} \times 1 \times 1 \times 0.0385 \times 1 \times 97,200$$

$$= 1403 \text{ kips } (6,242 \text{ kN})$$

The horizontal force acting on the top of the building is:

$$F_t = 0.07 \times T \times V, \quad \text{but no more than } 0.25 \times V$$

$$F_t = 0.07 \times 3 \times 1403 = 295 \text{ kips } (1,312 \text{ kN}),$$

which is less than $0.25 \times 1403 = 350$ kips (1,557 kN)

Assuming that each floor has the same height and the same weight, each floor's height is 12 ft and weighs on average 97,200 ÷ 30 = 3,240 kips (14,414 kN) each.

The horizontal force distribution along the height of the building is:

$$F_x = (V - F_t) \frac{w_x h_x}{\sum_{i=1}^{n} w_i h_i}$$

$$V - F_t = 1108 \quad \text{and} \quad \sum_{i=1}^{30} 3240 \, h_i = 3240 \times 12 \times 465$$

$$F_x = 1108 \, \frac{3240 \times 12 \times n}{3240 \times 12 \times 465} = 1108 \, \frac{n}{465}$$

where n is the nth floor. According to the equations, the force at the 1st and the 30th floors are:

$$F_1 = 1108 \, \frac{1}{465} = 2.4 \text{ kips } (10.7 \text{ kN})$$

$$F_{30} = 1108 \, \frac{30}{465} = 71.5 \text{ kips } (318 \text{ kN})$$

The bending moment (overturning moment) at grade is

$$M = \sum_{i=1}^{n} F_i h_i = 380,000 \text{ kips-ft } (515 \text{ MNm})$$

*Same geometry with the building subject to wind forces in a previous example.

The distribution of horizontal forces and the shearing forces and bending moments diagrams along the height of the building are shown in Fig. 9.14.2.

Comparison between Wind and Earthquake Forces on Buildings. Both wind and earthquake loads produce horizontal forces on buildings, according to the applicable codes. Wind and earthquake loads, however, should not be combined for design purposes. The wind pressures on the building, the seismic zone, and the shape and type of the building determine the relative magnitude of both wind and earthquake loads. In the previous examples, the comparison between the wind and the earthquake forces on the 30-story building showed that the base shear from the wind load is 1,799 kips (8,003 kN) versus 1,403 kips (6,242 kN) of the base shear due to the earthquake. If the seismic zone were zone 4, however, the base shear due to the earthquake for the same building would be 3,741 kips (16,643 kN). The earthquake forces, according to the code, are significantly larger at the upper floors, in contrast to the wind forces, which are more uniformly distributed along the height of the building. As a result, the overturning moment from the wind (346,300 kips-ft or 470 MNm) is lower than the overturning moment from the earthquake forces (380,000 kips-ft or 515 MNm) for the specific building that was subject to both wind and earthquake forces.

A more general comparison between wind and earthquake forces, based on the code requirements,* follows. If the average pressure along the building is p, the base shear from the wind load is:

$$V_W = p \times B \times H$$

Assuming $S = 1$ and $I = 1$, the base shear from the earthquake is:

$$V_E = Z \times K \times C \times W$$

*As a result, the obtained results cannot be generalized beyond the applicability of the quasi-static methods provided by the codes.

earthquake forces   shearing forces   bending moments

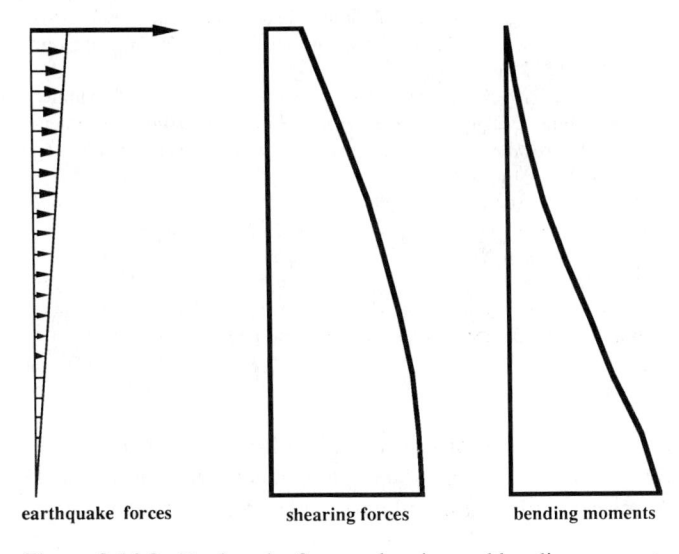

Figure 9.14.2. Earthquake forces, shearing and bending moment diagrams along the building height.

For simplification, assume that $T = 0.01 H$ (i.e., the height of each floor is 10 ft). Then the ratio of the wind to the earthquake force becomes:

$$\frac{V_W}{V_E} = \frac{1.5 \times \sqrt{H} \times p}{Z \times K \times L \times w}$$

where H is the height of the building, L is the length of the building parallel to wind direction, and w is the average unit weight of the building.

Substituting the values for a frame building in Boston, Massachusetts: $Z = 3/8$, $K = 1$, $w = 12$ pcf (1.9 kN/m^3) and $L = 100$ ft (30 m), the wind load becomes greater for a building height higher than 225 ft (70 m), based on an average wind pressure $p = 20$ psf (1 kPa). A similar building in seismic zone 4 ($Z = 1$) and under the same wind velocity needs to be more than 1600 ft (485 m) tall for the wind forces to exceed the earthquake forces, based on an average wind pressure $p = 30$ psf (1.5 kPa).

As shown in this example, the taller the building the more flexible it is and the earthquake forces become smaller compared to the wind forces. Furthermore, the relative importance of the wind load is greater when the wind direction is along the short dimension of the building, because the projected area of the building is larger. The earthquake load, according to the applicable codes, is indifferent to the orientation of the building.

9.15. LOAD COMBINATIONS AND PARTIAL LIVE LOADS

Due to the nature of different loads, it is quite unlikely to have a load combination that includes the maximum loads of each type.

Dead loads are always present in the building and provide the basis for all required load combinations. According to most codes, the following combinations of loads should be examined:

1. dead   + live + snow
2. dead   + live + snow + (wind or earthquake or thermal)

The allowable stresses for elastic design and the soil bearing stresses will be increased by 33 percent, when considering either wind or earthquake forces.

Different load cases may predict reverse stresses in structural elements, especially in columns, piers, walls and footings. The structural element must be designed so that it can withstand a reversal in the state of stress. If the effect of any load counteracts the dead load, then the dead load should be decreased by 33 percent. This is done to study the stability of a particular structural element or the structure.

The combination of vertical and horizontal loads should be properly examined. Under horizontal loads, the building will experience horizontal displacements, which will cause eccentricity of the vertical loads. Such an eccentricity can result in significantly higher stresses on the structural elements of the building (P-Δ effect).

By definition, the live loads may or may not be applied at all parts of the building at any given time. For structural design purposes, therefore, the live loads should be positioned in a way that produces the maximum stresses in the structural members. Live loads applied on all spans should always be considered, followed by alternative loading patterns that live load is present in certain parts of the building only.

For continuous beams, in addition to acting along the entire length of the beam, the live load should be positioned in alternating spans, so they produce maximum stresses in the midspans of the loaded segments. Subsequently, live loads should be positioned at both sides of each support with the rest of the beam unloaded.* This loading will produce the maximum stresses at the support loaded at both sides. A series of all possible loading conditions should be considered for a continuous beam to determine the higher stresses at all critical sections of the beam.

For frames, the live load should be positioned in alternating spans, along the floor and along the height of the building, so the loads produce maximum stresses in the midspans of the loaded members. Subsequently, live loads should be positioned at both sides of a joint and then alternate. This loading will produce the maximum stresses at the supports loaded at both sides. Similarly to the case of a continuous beam, a series of loading conditions should be considered for a frame to determine the higher stresses at all critical locations. Some codes allow for a simplified approach to obtain the most critical loading on each section of the frame. They suggest that designers consider each floor independently from the other floors of the building. In such cases, the far ends of the columns above and below that floor can be considered fixed. Then, the same loading conditions apply as in a continuous beam.

The live load on arches and gabled frames should also be positioned in such a way to produce maximum stresses on each section of the structure. The live load should be applied on the entire length of the arch, and then at half the arch adjacent to one support, at the center quarter length of the arch, and finally on the 3/8 of the span adjacent to each support.

Moving concentrated loads should also be positioned in such a way that they produce maximum stresses in the structural elements. Only moving loads that physically can occur simultaneously with other live loads should be considered as acting concurrently. If the moving loads and the other live loads cannot be applied simultaneously, then they should be examined independently for maximum stresses on the building.

---

*The rest of the segments should be loaded in an alternate manner. This may be omitted, however, since it makes a small difference in the obtained stresses.

REFERENCES

9.1. *BOCA National Building Code*. Building Officials & Code Administrators International, Inc., Country Club Hills, IL, 1987.

9.2. *Uniform Building Code*. International Conference of Building Officials, Whittier, CA, 1982.

9.3. *Reference Standard A58.1-82: Loads Minimum Design in Buildings and other Structures*. American National Standards Institute, Inc., New York, 1982.

9.4. (a) *Minimum Design Loads on Structures, Part 1: Dead and Live Loads*. Standards Association of Australia, Sydney, 1981.
(b) *Minimum Design Loads on Structures, Part 2: Wind Loads*. Standards Association of Australia, Sydney, 1989.

9.5. (a) *Loading for Buildings, Part 1, Dead and Imposed Loads, BS 6399*. British Standards Institution, London, 1989.
(b) *Wind Loading, CP3, Chapter 5, Part 2*. British Standards Institution, London 1972.

9.6. *National Building Code of Canada 1976*. Associate Committee on the National Building Code, National Research Council, Ottawa, Canada, 1978.

9.7. Standards Association of New Zealand. *NZS 4203: 1984 Code of Practice for General Structural Design and Design Loadings for Buildings*. Private Bag, Wellington, New Zealand.

9.8. *Building Code of the City of New York* (Titles 26 and 27 of the Administrative Code). Gould Publications, Binghamton, NY, 1988.

9.9. *Building Code of Chicago*. Index Publishing Corp., Chicago, IL, 1988.

9.10. *Commonwealth of Massachusetts State Building Code*. State Building Code Commission, Boston, MA, 1988.

9.11. *California State Building Code*. (Title 24, Part II of the Administrative Code). Division of Codes and Standards, Sacramento, CA, 1988.

9.12. *Directory of State Building Codes and Regulations*. National Conference of States on Building Codes and Standards, Inc., Herndon, VA, 1985.

9.13. John H. Callender (Ed.). *Time-Saver Standards for Architectural Design Data*. McGraw-Hill, New York, 1974.

9.14. Robert L. Wiegel (Ed.). *Earthquake Engineering*. Prentice Hall, Englewood Cliffs, NJ, 1970.

SUGGESTIONS FOR FURTHER READING

B. Ellingwood et al. "Development of a Probability Based Load Criterion for American National Standard A58—Building Code Requirements for Minimum Design Loads for Buildings and Other Structures." NSB Special Publication 577. National Bureau of Standards, Washington, DC, 1980, 222 pp.

Joint Committee on Structural Safety. "General Principles on Reliability for Structural Design." *Reports of the Working Commissions. International Association for Bridge and Structural Engineering*, **35**, 41–58 (1981).

H. S. Lew, E. Stein, and B. Ellingwood. "Loads," in *Building and Structural Design Handbook*, edited by R. N. White and C. G. Salmon. John Wiley, New York, 1987, pp. 9–43.

T. Y. Lin and S. D. Stotesbury. *Structural Concepts and Systems for Architects and Engineers*, 2nd Ed. Van Nostrand Reinhold, New York, 1988, Chapter 5, "Structural Loads and Responses," pp. 129–156.

NOTE

A list of abbreviations of the units of measurement, definitions of these units, and conversion factors between British/American and metric units are given in the Appendix.

10
Wind Effects

Richard M. Aynsley

Wind results from atmospheric pressure differences, and wind climate is determined by the pattern and magnitude of pressure gradients. Air flow around buildings produces wind pressure and suction, which create structural loads on entire buildings, and also localized dynamic loads on cladding. Also important are the environmental wind effects on pedestrians near a building, and on the inhabitants of the building.

10.1. WIND CLIMATE

All winds result from pressure differences within the atmosphere. These pressure differences are caused by uneven heating of the earth's surface between the equator and the polar regions. In turn, heat is transferred to surface layers of the air by conduction and convection, providing energy for large-scale convective circulation in the atmosphere.

This circulation is evidenced by wind flow between the pressure systems which may be seen as part of daily television weather reports. These large pressure systems consist of cyclones (low pressure) and anticyclones (high pressure). Because of the rotation of the earth about its axis, air moves from high- to low-pressure systems in a rotational manner, flowing into low-pressure regions in a clockwise direction in the southern hemisphere and a counterclockwise direction in the northern hemisphere.

Hurricanes

Large pressure systems are typically hundreds of kilometers across. When low-pressure systems develop over warm tropical oceans, the high moisture content of the air provides additional convective energy from the condensation of moisture in the cooler upper atmosphere. Under conditions where the central pressure of cyclones fall to a low level, tropical storms are generated which can intensify into hurricanes. Hurricanes are known by different names in various parts of the world. In Southeast Asia they are called *typhoons*, while in Oceania they are referred to as *tropical cyclones*.

These storms pose the greatest economic threat to buildings and service infrastructure due to their large scale, up to 600 miles (970 km) in diameter with the most intense wind speeds, 90–200 mph (40–90 m/s), occurring over a 40–60 mile (64–97 km) diameter region. The strong upward flow in the center of hurricanes creates an eye at the center of the storm, typically 10 miles in diameter, where wind speeds are very low. Duration of hurricanes depends on the forward path of the storm continuing over a warm body of water and given this condition, hurricanes can have lifespans of a number of weeks.

Most of the damage from hurricanes occurs in coastal areas. These storms lose most of their energy and degenerate into tropical rain depressions if they move more than about 50 miles (80 km) inland from the sea. Most of the damage to buildings by hurricanes occurs due to impact of windborne debris, wave action, or uplift forces on roofs in nonengineered buildings such as housing (Ref. 10.1).

Most structural failures in buildings during hurricanes are due to inadequate framing connections. Wind speeds are highest in the quadrant of the storm in which the forward velocity of the storm system augments the storm's rotational wind speed. The Cyclone Structural Testing Station at James Cook University in Townsville, Australia, is the leading research center for studies of hurricane resistance of housing. A number of full size buildings have been tested to destruction under hydraulically simulated wind forces determined from data derived from meteorological records and wind tunnel studies of model buildings.

Frontal Storms

More localized damage can be caused by winds associated with thunderstorms that form along the squall lines and boundaries of air masses with large differences in temperature. The general air circulation in large pressure systems is a spiral movement out of the high-pressure centers moving horizontally near the ground. In the case of local frontal thunderstorms, air movement can have a much greater vertical component, or "wind shear," with large masses of air descending rapidly from high altitudes. Detailed information on these winds is beginning to appear in the literature as a result of doppler radar studies (Ref. 10.2). Individual storms of this type are short-lived, usually lasting less than an hour, but many storms may develop over a period of two or three hours, typically during the late afternoon. Wind from these storms is of great interest to aviation authorities as wind shear has been identified as the cause of a number of recent crashes of large passenger airliners during landing.

Tornadoes

The most violent forms of wind are the very intense, small-scale, rotating winds known as *tornadoes*, or in their less intense form willy-willys, dust devils, and waterspouts. Tornadoes are associated with the vertical atmospheric instability in thunderstorms created by temperature inversions. Such instability can reach up to 50,000 feet (15,000 m) above ground.

A tornado is a violently rotating column of air extending in a funnel-shaped cloud from a thunderstorm cloud to the ground. The destructive path of tornadoes along the ground is typically 4 miles (6.4 km) long, but some have exceeded 100 miles (160 km), with typical widths of 900 to 1200 feet (300–400 m) but sometimes reaching 1 mile (1.6 km). Windborne debris is a major problem during the passage of a tornado, with typical missiles being fragments of damaged buildings. Maximum tornado wind speeds are difficult to determine but recent estimates by researchers suggest 275 mph (123 m/s) as the maximum possible tornado wind speed (Ref. 10.3).

A six point scale from F0 to F6, developed by Prof. T. Fujita in 1971 (Ref. 10.4), is often used to classify tornadoes by characteristics of the damage generated. The wind speeds suggested in the upper classifications of this scale are now considered to be overestimated and F6 is often omitted.

Slope and Valley Winds

Other forms of local winds are slope and valley winds. These winds are caused by local differential solar heating of ground surfaces which results in changes in density of adjacent air. These winds can become quite severe where they are channeled through narrow valleys as cold air masses drain toward lower elevations. However, they are short-lived, occurring during daily heating and cooling cycles. Less is known about these winds than other types of wind as they rarely occur near airport recording anemometers (Ref. 10.5).

Description of Strong Winds

Care must be taken when using wind data for wind load purposes in foreign countries as the methods of describing strong winds can vary significantly. The reason for this variation stems from the primitive nature of early instrumentation. The U.S. National Weather Service began recording strong winds using a simple counting procedure. This procedure measures strong winds by the time taken for the number of revolutions of a cup anemometer when a mile of wind passes the instrument and is still used today, although more sophisticated instruments are now available. The standard "Fastest Mile Wind Speed" of 60 mph wind means that it takes 60 seconds for a mile of wind to pass the anemometer.

In the U.S. wind loading code, ANSI A58.1-82 (Ref. 10.6), a map provides isopleths of fastest mile wind speeds at 33 ft above ground in flat, open (airport) terrain with a return period of 50 years. The Canadian wind loading code NBCC 1985 (Ref. 10.7) uses a "mean hourly"—a mean wind speed over an hour—but moves are underway to reduce this to a 10 minute interval. A 10 minute mean wind speed is approximately 1.06 times its equivalent mean hourly wind speed. British CP3 1972 (Ref. 10.8) and Australian AS 1170 Pt.2 1983 (Ref. 10.9) wind loading codes use the "peak gust" wind speed based on the response characteristics of standard recording anemometers, which is from 1 to 3 seconds. A 2 second gust wind speed is approximately 1.59 times its equivalent mean hourly wind speed.

10.2. STRUCTURE OF WIND

Discussion so far has indicated some of the difficulties in describing wind due to its variability in wind speed and direction. These descriptions have only attempted to describe a standard reference wind at 10 meters above ground level. In reality the wind is much more complex. One complexity which must be dealt with in order to understand the impact of wind on buildings is the *boundary layer*.

A boundary layer is a layer of airflow adjacent to a stationary surface. This layer of airflow is disturbed by friction and roughness such as buildings and trees on the surface over which it is passing. The complex structure of a boundary layer is reduced to a number of mean characteristics in order to simplify its use in the design of structures. These characteristics are clearly described in Ref. 10.10.

Mean Wind Speed Profile

One important characteristic of boundary layers is the mean hourly vertical profile of wind speed. This indicates the increase in mean horizontal component of wind speed with height above the ground. Alternatively, this change in mean wind speed with height can be considered as the retardation of wind close to the ground by obstacles such as trees and buildings, as shown in Fig. 10.2.1.

In the case of very rough terrain, such as the central business districts of large city areas, this retardation can effect airflow up to heights of 1600 feet (500 m), known as the *gradient height*. In less rough terrain, such as suburban areas, the retardation extends to 1300 feet (400 m). In open, flat terrain, such as around airports, the retardation effect extends to 1000 feet (300 m). The flattest terrain, over open sea, retards wind speeds up to a height of 800 feet (250 m).

This increase in speed with height above the ground level is not a linear relationship. In the lower levels of a boundary the velocity profile tends to follow a logarithmic relationship, while at higher levels a simple power law, developed by Davenport in 1960 (Ref. 10.11), adequately describes the velocity distribution.

The Power Law Mean Wind Speed Profile Equation is:

$$V_z = V_g \left(\frac{z}{z_g}\right)^a$$

where V_z = mean wind speed at height z
V_g = mean wind speed at gradient height z_g
a = an exponent related to terrain roughness (see Table 10.1).

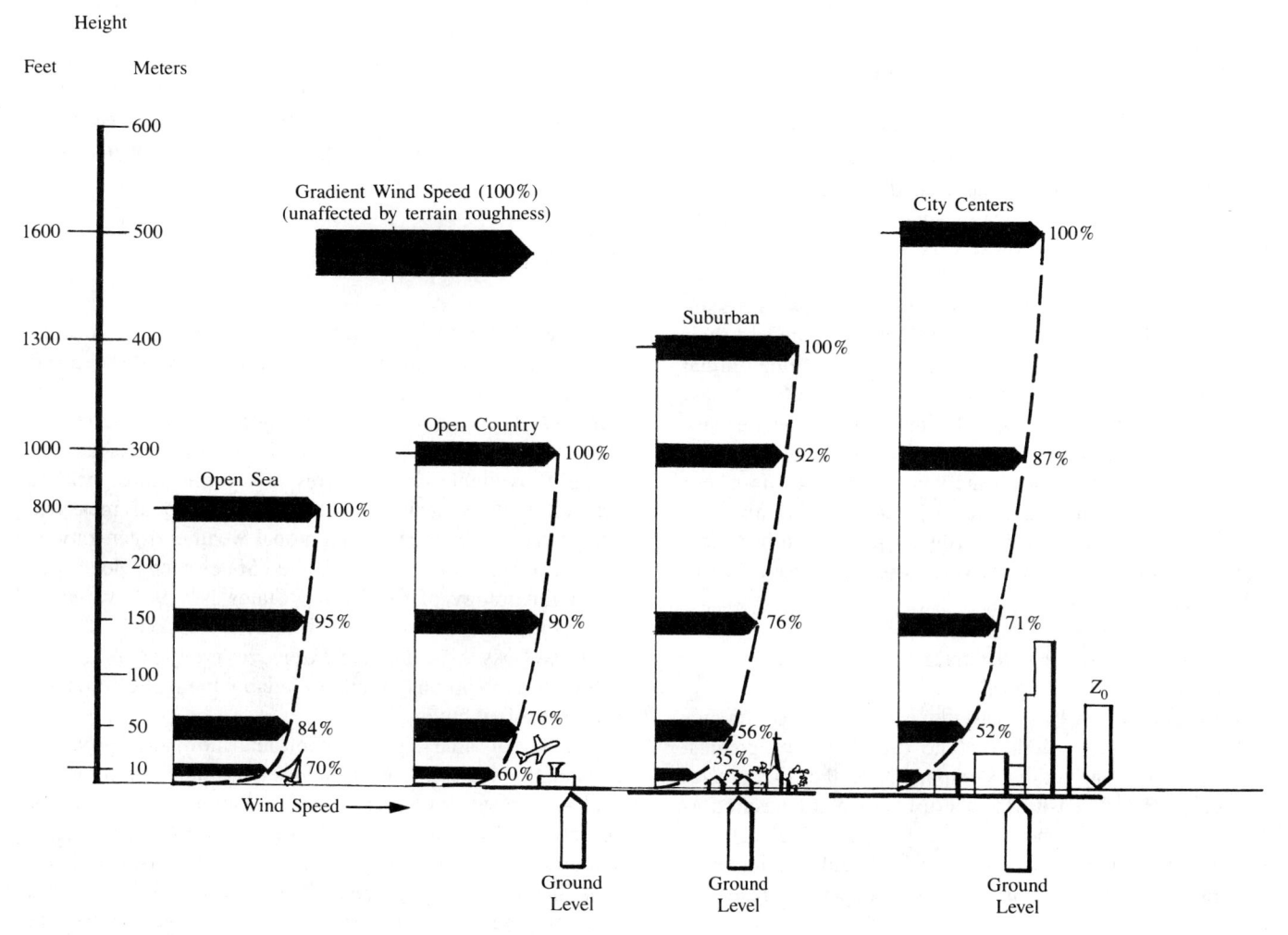

Fig. 10.2.1. Vertical profiles of mean wind speed over various terrains.

Table 10.1. Terrain Constants for the Earth's Boundary Layers.

Terrain Description	z_g, Gradient Height, ft (m)	z_0, Roughness Length, ft (m)	a, Mean Wind Speed Exponent	b, Gust Speed Exponent
Open sea, ice, tundra, desert	800(250)	0.003(0.001)	0.11	0.07
Open country with low bushes or scattered trees	1000(300)	0.1(0.03)	0.15	0.09
Suburban areas, small towns, well wooded areas	1300(400)	1.0(0.3)	0.25	0.14
Numerous tall buildings, city centers, dense industrial development	1600(500)	10(3)	0.36	0.20

The Log Law Mean Wind Speed Profile Equation is:

$$V_z = V_1 \log_e \left(\frac{z}{z_0}\right) \Big/ \log_e \left(\frac{z_1}{z_0}\right)$$

where V_z = mean wind speed at height z
 V_1 = mean wind speed at some reference height z_1
 z_0 = roughness length, about 5–10 percent of the height of terrain roughness elements, e.g., trees, houses, etc. (see Table 10.1).

Integral Scale of Longitudinal Turbulence

Many slender buildings with height-to-breadth ratios greater than approximately 4 or 5 to 1 can be sensitive to the impact of wind gusts. The mass distribution, stiffness, and damping characteristics of such structures determine the frequencies at which these structures are most sensitive to wind gusts.

In order to estimate the impact of wind gusts on such structures, the distribution of wind gusts in time and their size must be determined. Integral scales of longitudinal turbulence are measures of the average size of turbulent eddies in an airflow. The size of eddies is important because only those eddies large enough to envelop a whole building have a significant effect on the whole building's response to wind gusts. In strong winds, over flat terrain, the horizontal dimensions of wind eddies approximately 36 feet (11 m) above ground level typically range from 360 to 1900 feet (120 to 630 m).

Turbulence Intensity and Spectra

Disturbance of airflow near the earth's surface creates turbulence in all directions. The turbulence of greatest interest is the longitudinal component (in the direction of the wind). The intensity of this turbulence is measured as the ratio of the root mean square of longitudinal velocity fluctuations to the mean wind speed. Turbulence intensity is greatest close to the surface roughness which creates it, and decreases with height above ground.

As the dynamic response of buildings to the impact of wind gusts is described in frequency of vibration and deflection for a range of deflection modes, a description of turbulent wind energy related to frequency or period of gusts is desirable. For this reason turbulence spectra as illustrated in Fig. 10.2.2 are used to describe the contribution of gusts with various frequencies or periods to the mean square value fluctuations at a specified point in the flow, usually 10 meters above ground level (Ref. 10.12). These curves can show the effects of solar flares, which reoccur roughly every seven years, down to small scale wind gusts with frequencies of a fraction of a second.

Wind energy in the lower frequencies of this spectrum is relevant to establishing a design wind speed for static loading on buildings. Only a small, higher frequency portion of the spectrum is directly relevant to the dynamic structural response of buildings and structures, as indicated in Fig. 10.2.2.

10.3. WIND RECORDS

Any detailed assessment of wind conditions in a locality must make use of wind records. Records of wind speed and direction are kept in great detail by most national weather services. These data are often summarized for a variety of particular applications. Summarized wind records are usually available in a series of publications printed annually. Very detailed records of individual measurements can be obtained from national weather organizations in printed summaries. In the United States such a document is "Climatology of the United States No. 90" which is available from the National Climatic Data Center, Greenville, NC. As these data are extensive, many people prefer to purchase them on computer readable magnetic computer tape for a few hundred dollars.

An initial analysis of such data normally produces seasonal or average effects such as maximums, minimums, and wind roses, which indicate distribution with respect to direction. These wind records are derived from measurements with cup anemometers mounted on a mast at a specified height above ground. The international standard mounting height is 10 meters (33 feet) above ground, but many nonstandard installations exist and the height of the anemometer should be determined when wind records are

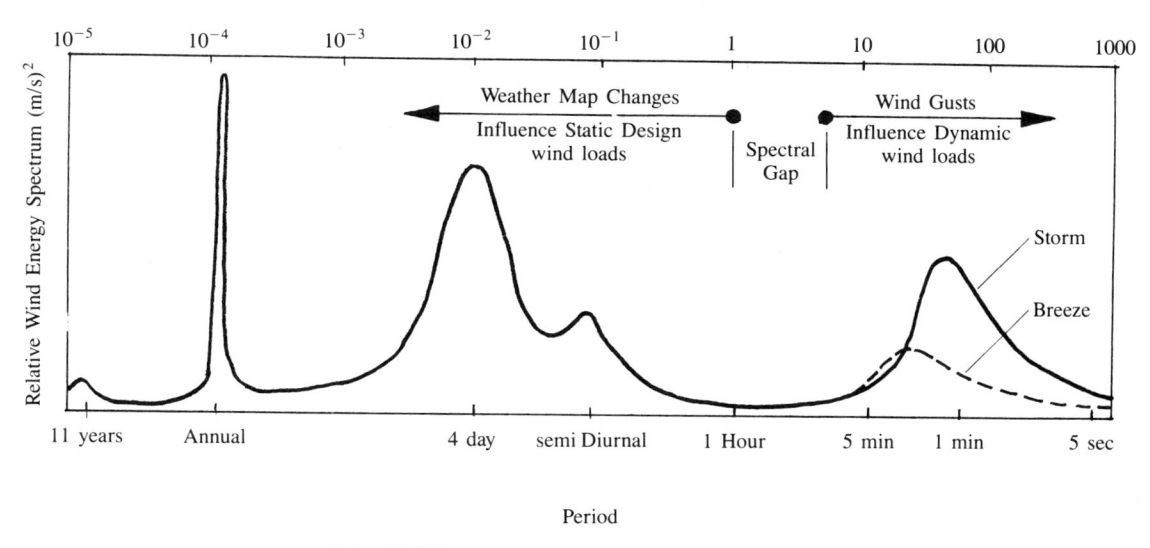

Fig. 10.2.2. Spectrum of horizontal wind energy.

sought. Many US anemometers are mounted about 20 feet above ground level.

Care must be taken in using recorded wind data, as in many cases difficulty in achieving standard mounting conditions results in the anemometer being mounted at nonstandard heights and possibly in positions shielded by buildings or other nearby obstructions. Adjustments can be made to records made at nonstandard heights. Records from anemometers mounted on buildings or shielded from some wind directions should be discarded in favor of anemometers with a more standard exposure.

The majority of anemometers are sited at airports, as their data are required daily for aircraft operations. This means that the measurements are usually made in an open, flat terrain with scattered buildings. Wind conditions will vary from these conditions when the terrain roughness is greater or surrounding topographic features such as hills, valleys, and escarpments cause significant changes in wind speed, direction, and turbulence.

Estimation of Wind Conditions at Sites Remote from an Airport Recording Station

Corrections can be made to wind data from such standard anemometer installations to account for the approximate wind conditions at a site distant from the recording station using an equation described by Swami and Chandra (Ref. 10.13). The factors taken into account are the distance from the recording station, the intervening terrain characteristics and the height of measurement above ground.

Wind Frequency Analysis

While seasonal mean wind speeds and directions are often sufficient for general assessment or comparison of wind conditions, for more detailed analyses or comparison, wind frequencies and probabilities are required. Wind frequency relates to the number of occurrences of wind in various wind speed ranges from each of the principal wind directions, normally 16 points of the compass, N, NNE, NE, etc. These data are often assembled into wind frequency analyses, where the number of occasions when wind has blown from a particular direction within a particular wind speed range is counted.

An inexpensive source of wind frequency data for North American cities has been published on floppy computer disks as part of the Bin and Degree Hour Weather Data for Simplified Energy Calculations by the American Society of Heating, Refrigerating and Air-Conditioning Engineers, Inc. (Ref. 10.14). An example of this type of wind frequency data is provided in Table 10.2.

Probabilistic Descriptions of Wind

By comparing these frequencies of occurrence with the total number of observations in the wind record, it is possible to calculate the percentage of time that wind blows within a wind speed range from each particular direction. These wind frequency analyses often have curves fitted to them to allow the frequency of occurrence at other particular wind speeds to be estimated. At the extreme high and low wind speed ends of the wind record, *Weibull distributions* have been found to provide a good fit to most wind records and provide a continuous function for estimating the probabilities of extreme high wind events as well as low wind speed events.

Weibull distributions take the form:

$$P(>V, \theta) = A(\theta) \exp\left[-\left(\frac{V}{C(\theta)}\right)^{k(\theta)}\right]$$

138 HANDBOOK OF ARCHITECTURAL TECHNOLOGY

Table 10.2. Wind Frequencies (for a Chosen City and Month of Year).

Time Groups	1–4 am	5–8 am	9–12 am	13–16 pm	17–20 pm	21–24 pm	Total
Wind Speed Interval	\multicolumn{6}{c}{HOURS OF OCCURRENCE (PREVAILING DIRECTION)}	
<2.5 m/s	90(N)	75(N)	19(ESE)	11(E)	24(E)	75(ESE)	294(N)
2.5–6.4 m/s	30(ESE)	50(ESE)	98(ESE)	105(ESE)	98(ESE)	48(E)	429(ESE)
6.5–10 m/s	0(—)	1(ESE)	8(ESE)	8(ESE)	3(ESE)	1(ENE)	21(ESE)
>10 m/s	0(—)	0(—)	0(—)	0(—)	0(—)	0(—)	0(—)

where $P(>V, \theta)$ is the probability of exceeding a wind speed V from a chosen direction θ, A and C are characteristics of wind speed for the site for the chosen direction, and k is the exponent parameter used to fit data to the curve.

After wind data have been fitted to a continuous Weibull function (Fig. 10.3.1) it is possible to estimate the probability of occurrence of any wind speed from a particular direction. When the exponent of a Weibull distribution is 2 the distribution is known as a *Rayleigh distribution*. The advantages of using probability data fitted to a continuous function is that it allows simple statements to be made in terms of the number of hours per year when any chosen wind speed is likely to prevail. This type of wind description is often more readily understood by nontechnical people.

10.4. BLUFF BODY AERODYNAMICS

When describing airflow around a body, it is common practice to classify bodies into two groups, *streamlined* and *bluff*. In the case of streamlined bodies, where body surfaces follow the curvature of flow streamlines, the airflow tends to remain attached to the surfaces of the body. In the case of a bluff body, such as a rectangular building, the airflow is attached to the windward faces, but separates at the sharp corners of the downwind edges of the windward faces.

Reynolds Number

The attachment of the flow around bodies depends on the ratio of the inertia force to the viscous force on each air molecule in the flow. This dimensionless ratio of inertia force to viscous force on molecules in a fluid is known as Reynolds number.

$$R_e = \frac{\rho V L}{\mu}$$

where R_e is the Reynolds number, ρ is the mass density of the fluid, V is the velocity of the flow approaching the body, L is the cross-flow dimension of the body, and μ is the dynamic viscosity of the fluid.

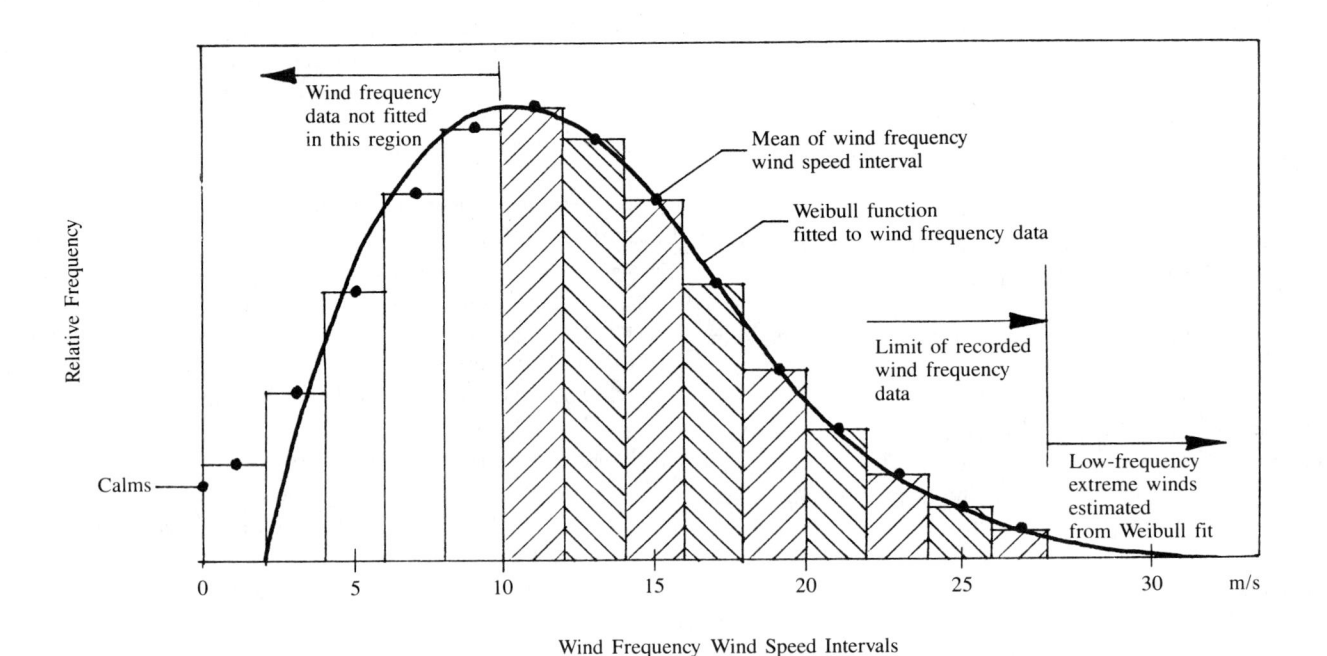

Fig. 10.3.1. Weibull function fits to wind frequency data.

When inertia forces in an airflow are small compared to viscous forces (low Reynolds Number), which is the case at very low velocities or in highly viscous fluids, the viscous forces hold adjacent molecules together. When some molecules are accelerated much more than adjacent molecules the inertia forces can overcome the viscous bond between molecules (high Reynolds numbers) and separation will occur in the flow. Low Reynolds numbers are those less than the transition range of approximately 2,000 to, say, 10,000. Reynolds numbers above the transition range are referred to as high Reynolds numbers.

When separation occurs in a flow the whole flow pattern changes from streamline flow, where adjacent layers of air slip smoothly past one another, to a flow pattern where flow separates from body surfaces and turbulent shear layers are formed which enclose a turbulent wake on the leeward side of rectangular (bluff body) buildings in the flow.

Flow separation occurs at sharp corners at virtually all wind speeds. Flow separation will not occur in airflow around streamlined bodies until the approach velocity is increased to a point where the inertia forces overcome viscous forces in the flow near the body's surface. This flow separation will initially occur near the leeward edge of a curved, streamlined body and will move toward the windward end of the body with further increases in flow velocity. This means that there can be an infinite number of Reynolds-number-dependent flow patterns and associated surface pressure distributions around a streamlined body for a given flow direction, depending on the approach flow velocity.

Because the flow always separates at the sharp corners of a bluff building shape, the airflow pattern and associated relative surface pressure distribution remain constant over a wide range of Reynolds numbers for a given wind direction regardless of the approach wind speed.

Flow Regions Around Bluff Bodies, and Static and Dynamic Pressure

Airflow around buildings with sharp corners (bluff bodies) can be divided into three regions. The major regions are those associated with the relatively undisturbed flow, the wake region on the leeward side of the building, and the turbulent shear layers that separate these two major flow regions, as illustrated in Fig. 10.4.1.

Static pressure can be considered as local atmospheric pressure created by the force of gravity acting on the earth's atmosphere of air extending some 500 miles up from the surface of the earth. Static pressure acts equally in all directions. It is a maximum, around 14.7 psi (101.3 kPa),

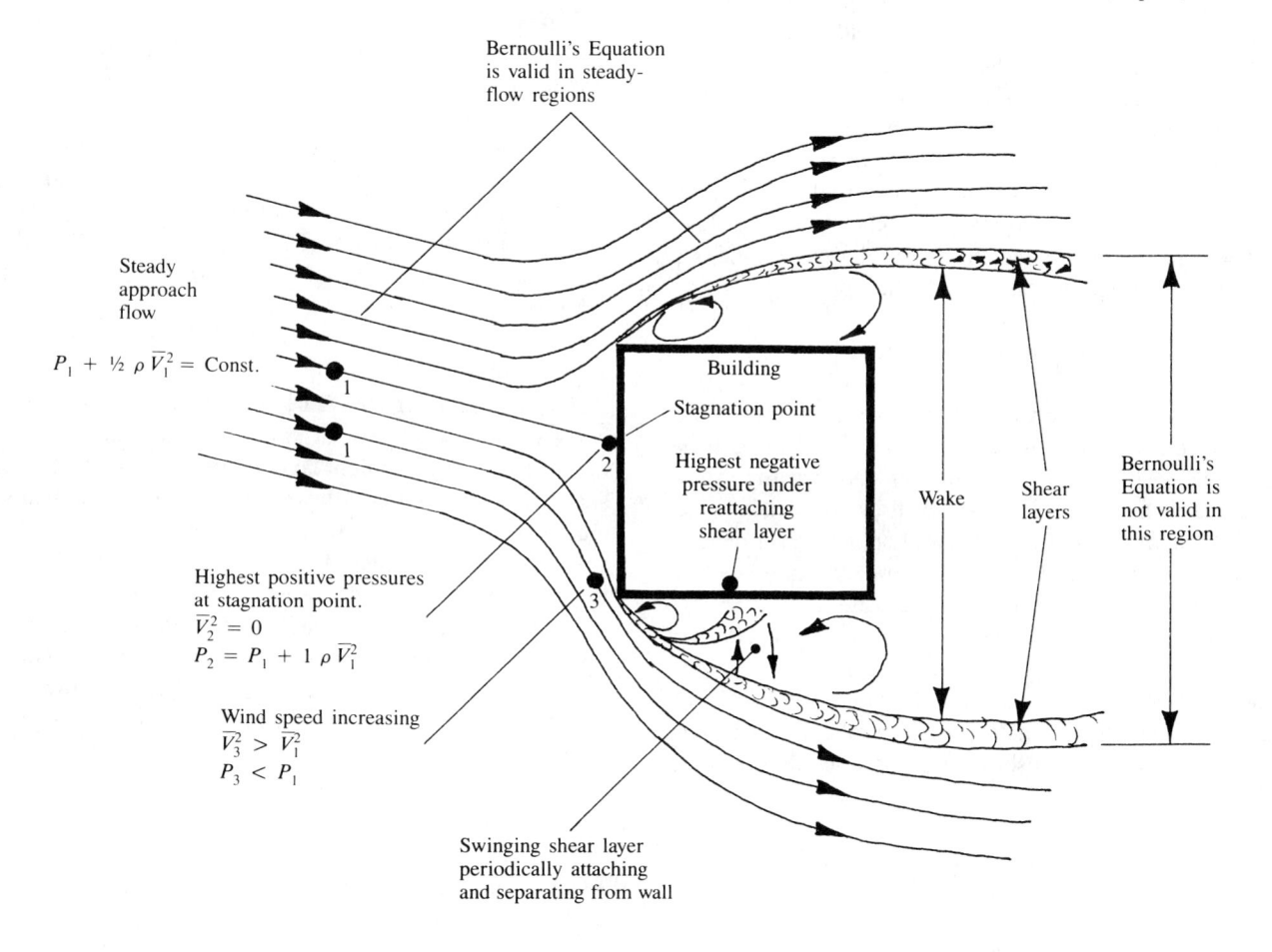

Fig. 10.4.1. Flow regions around a bluff-body, rectangular building.

when winds are calm in regions of high pressure. Suction or negative pressures are local air pressures in high-speed flow where static pressures fall below local atmospheric pressure.

Dynamic or velocity pressure is derived from the kinetic energy of a moving mass of air. Air typically has a mass of 1.2 kg/m^3 (0.0024 slugs/ft^3) at a temperature of 60°F (16°C) and standard atmospheric pressure. Dynamic pressure can be exerted only in the direction of movement of the air mass.

Bernoulli's equation states that the sum of static and dynamic pressures is constant along a streamline.

$$p + \tfrac{1}{2}\rho \overline{V}^2 = \text{constant}$$

where p is the static pressure in psi (kPa), and $\tfrac{1}{2}\rho \overline{V}^2$ is the dynamic pressure in psi (kPa), sometimes referred to as velocity pressure. The mass density of air ρ, is typically 0.0024 slugs/ft^3 (1.2 kg/m^3). Mean velocity $\overline{V}$ is in ft/s (m/s). This means that where wind speeds are high, static pressures are low; and conversely where the wind speed is zero, static pressure is at its maximum.

A stagnation point occurs on the windward face where the flow parts to flow around both sides of a body. At stagnation points the velocity is zero, and all the energy in the flow is in the form of static pressure. Stagnation points experience the maximum positive wind pressure (acting toward a surface) on a building.

Maximum negative wind pressures (suctions, acting away from a surface) are experienced where wind speeds parallel to a surface are maximum. The highest suctions occur downstream from flow separations. A typical flow separation occurs downwind from the windward edges of roofs, where strong vortices form in the flow.

Vortex Shedding and Turbulent Wake Flow

Large slowly rotating vortices known as eddies form in the wake-region behind buildings, and grow in size until they are no longer shielded by the building. At that time they are carried away in the downstream flow. In steady wind this shedding of vortices is surprisingly periodic for rectangular shapes. The vortex shedding frequency is related to the mean velocity of the approaching wind and the cross-wind dimension and shape of the building by a number referred to as the *Strouhal number*. Strouhal numbers are Reynolds-number-dependent at low Reynolds numbers, but generally constant at high Reynolds numbers for rectangular shapes. This relationship is expressed in the following equation:

$$n = \frac{S\overline{V}}{D} \text{ Hz}$$

where n is the frequency of vortex shedding in Hz, D is the cross-wind dimension (ft or m) of the building, $\overline{V}$ is the mean velocity (ft/s or m/s) of the approaching wind, and S is the Strouhal number, which varies from about 0.1 for rectangular sections to 0.25 for circular sections. Strouhal numbers for circular shapes are highly Reynolds number dependent at high Reynolds numbers.

Flow in the region of the wake is extremely irregular and complex as eddies are shed downstream. Wind speeds in this region tend to be less than 10 percent of the approach wind speed and vary constantly in speed and direction. Building surfaces exposed to this region of the flow experience low to moderate suction pressures. A chief concern in these regions is not wind loading, but entrapment and recirculation of polluted air. This issue will be addressed with other environmental matters later in this chapter.

Influence of Architectural Features on Airflow

The shape of buildings is a prime determinant of airflow patterns around buildings. This extends from the overall building geometry to projections from its surfaces, such as eaves, columns, beams, and floor slabs, to attached elements such as sun-screens. The variety and scale of such projections prevents a detailed description, but detailed wind tunnel studies have been conducted to measure local wind pressure distributions near such architectural details.

Parapet walls tend to give some protection to flat roofs from high suctions generated by vortex flows at roof edges. Projecting eaves, walls and floor slabs, used together, prevent cross-flow across the surface of windward walls, and provide a more even distribution of positive wind pressure for more efficient natural ventilation of buildings. Projecting floor slabs on tall buildings encourage lateral flow around buildings which minimizes flow of strong winds down windward faces. This strong downward flow referred to as "downwash," can create undesirable, and sometimes even dangerous, conditions for pedestrians at street level.

Projecting columns have been used on tall buildings with curved surfaces to prevent streamline flow and to ensure the presence of a turbulent layer of airflow near the building surface. This practice allows more accurate estimates of local surface pressures to be made than can be made on smooth curved surfaces, which are strongly influenced by Reynolds number effects. Projecting columns on tall buildings can also create the undesirable effect of channeling strong winds down a windward face to street level. To overcome this effect podiums are often formed at the lowest few floors to deflect this downwash laterally above ground level.

Computational Fluid Mechanics

Many of the common points of interest in airflow around buildings are near corners where flow separates from the surface. This flow separation results in intense vortex flows. Bernoulli's equation is only valid where flow is steady, inviscid (viscous forces are negligible), and irrotational (there is no rotation in the flow as streamlines change direction).

If a numerical study of flows near separation points in shear layers or in turbulent wakes is proposed, other more sophisticated computational fluid mechanics techniques have to be used. These methods include the discrete-vortex method and other techniques using Navier-Stokes equations which contain terms to describe the shear stresses (viscous forces) and vorticity (rotational characteristics) in a fluid flow. Computational fluid mechanics is a rapidly growing area of building aerodynamics.

10.5. WIND LOADS

Chapter 9 of this book deals with typical code provisions for design loads for buildings including wind loads. While these provisions are used to design most simple, small buildings, tall or wind sensitive structures are usually designed using pressures, forces, and moments determined from model studies in boundary-layer wind tunnels.

Most failures in smaller buildings due to wind loads occur because of the combination of internal pressurization and external suction loads on buildings and the fact that inadequate connections are made between individual components of the building which may hold together quite well under normal wind conditions. It is essential to identify continuously adequate load paths from the roof through the building to the foundations.

When the normal gravity load direction is reversed by wind forces, joint connections between framing elements become the major source of load resistance. In traditional timber-frame residential-scale construction a few nails are all that hold joints together under wind-induced uplift forces. This deficiency can be overcome by utilizing a wide range of readily available, inexpensive framing anchors, hurricane clips, or galvanized metal straps, as recommended in recent editions of building codes for hurricane-prone areas. Alternatively, plywood sheathing can be used in the section of a load path between the top plates and bottom plates of external walls.

Large windows in external walls reduce the opportunity for vertical structural connections and restrict the location for load paths. Large windows, if they are broken during a hurricane, can cause internal pressurization and a large increase in wind loading on the structure.

Dynamic Response of Structures to Wind Gusts

The response of a structure to the impact of wind gusts is dependent on the size of the gust and the effectiveness of energy transfer at each gust frequency.

Basically the transfer of wind energy into the building is determined by the building's shape and size. The proportion of wind energy transferred to the building across the spectrum is referred to as the building's aerodynamic admittance. The resulting spectrum of wind force on the building is the product of incident wind energy and the building's aerodynamic admittance. The dynamic response of the building in terms of deflections at various gust frequencies, is the product of the spectrum of wind force and the spectrum of the building's mechanical vibration and damping characteristics. These relationships can be traced through the series of graphs in Fig. 10.5.1.

The impact of normal wind gusts on buildings is lessened because of their random size and frequency. More critical conditions arise when gusts impact with a definite frequency equal or close to the natural frequency of a building. Impact of these gusts leads to forced vibration and significant building motion. Such motion is only opposed by structural and aerodynamic damping (Ref. 10.15).

Structural damping occurs through dissipation of elastic strain energy (created by deflections) in heat from friction at frame joints. To increase structural damping special purpose viscous material (acting in shear) is built into joints in lateral diagonal bracing.

Aerodynamic damping occurs when periodic separation in the flow around a building generates cross-wind lift forces (normal to the direction of flow) that oppose the periodic cross-wind deflections. Aerodynamic damping can be negative and lead to increased deflections. This occurs when periodic fluctuations in cross-wind forces reinforce periodic cross-wind building deflections.

Dynamic wind loads on buildings due to the natural gusting of the approaching wind are referred to as buffeting. Generally of more concern are cross-wind fluctuations in wind loads (normal to the wind). These occur even in relatively smooth airflow due to the turbulence generated by the periodic shedding of vortices from alternate sides of

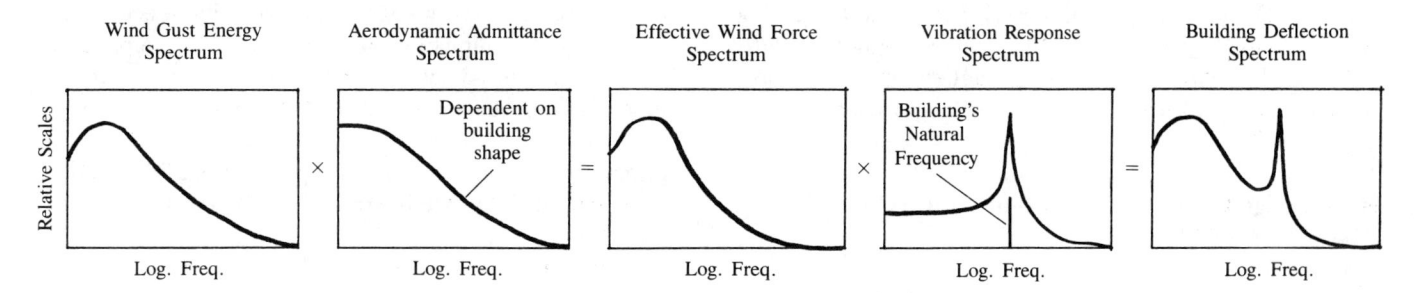

Fig. 10.5.1. Spectral impact and response sequence for dynamic loads on buildings.

bluff body buildings themselves, or vortices shed by upstream buildings.

When wind speeds are low the shedding frequency tends to be much higher than the natural frequencies of tall buildings, typically 0–0.67 Hz (0–30 Hz for low buildings). Under these conditions, the lateral dynamic wind forces are minimal and their only impact is to contribute slightly to the quasi-static wind load.

At higher wind speeds, wind energy increases and shedding frequencies close to the natural frequencies of tall building deflection modes will excite lateral dynamic responses. These dynamic responses have caused structural collapse in highly elastic, lightly damped circular structures such as tall steel chimneys. Normal buildings tend to have broader ranging shedding frequencies and are usually more highly damped. These characteristics provide some protection from their own shed vortices. Some common problems that are caused by shed vortices include deflections that damage building claddings and building motions that lead to motion sickness in building occupants, as described by Simiu and Scanlan (Ref. 10.16). Specialist wind engineering consultants are normally commissioned to assess these dynamic effects on tall buildings. An outline of these effects can be found in Ref. 10.12.

Localized Dynamic Loads on Claddings

Another service provided by specialist consultants is the detailed load analyses for cladding on the surface of buildings. These local cladding loads are determined from detailed studies of surface pressures in a boundary layer wind tunnel.

Vortex flows resulting from flow separations generate very high suction pressures on surfaces with which they come in contact. These high suctions, at least twice the maximum local positive pressures, occur over small areas of a few square feet at any time and have short duration times in the order of 1/50th of a second. While these local load conditions do not pose serious problems for the overall structure, they do create real problems in terms of local fatigue failures of cladding materials such as glass and other external surface panels.

Failure of cladding on tall buildings poses particular problems in relation of the safety of pedestrians on sidewalks around the base of the buildings where falling claddings such as glass and sheet metal can be a serious hazard. Classic examples of these failures was the glazing on the John Hancock building in Boston during the 1970s (Ref. 10.17) and the loss of sheet metal roofing from almost all the houses in Darwin, Australia, during tropical cyclone Tracy in December 1974.

Knowledge-Based Expert Systems, and Wind Tunnel Assessments of Wind Loads

Rapid advances and increasing complexity in wind engineering design practices have led to the development of knowledge-based expert systems to aid the less expert designer. These systems are particularly useful for the design of small timber and concrete masonry residential buildings in high-wind areas where the cost of wind tunnel studies is difficult to justify in comparison to the building cost. As wind loading codes become more complex, expert systems in the form of user-friendly software are beginning to appear.

Wind tunnel studies are essential in the detailed design of tall, slender, wind-sensitive buildings, flexible roofs (suspended or air supported), snow loads on complex roof shapes, buildings of unusual shape not covered by the appropriate loading code, or buildings sited near steep hills or in narrow valleys which increase local wind speeds.

Current practice in wind-tunnel studies of tall buildings as described in the ASCE's Manual on Engineering Practice No. 67 (Ref. 10.18) include detailed measurement of surface pressures for design of cladding including glazing and overall forces and moments at the building's base.

10.6. ENVIRONMENTAL WIND EFFECTS

In recent years a number of environmental wind effects have gained importance as a result of wind induced injuries to pedestrians in strong winds near tall buildings and resulting law suits. These environmental wind effects fall into categories such as pedestrian safety, thermal effects, particle erosion, impact on mechanical systems, and pollution control, particularly in street canyons of urban centers.

Wind Effects on Pedestrians

High-speed upper-level winds deflected down the windward face of tall buildings into pedestrian areas, referred to as *downwash*, are a common problem in many cities, as illustrated in Fig. 10.6.1. Another type of pedestrian-level wind problem occurs when high-speed winds pass through openings between high-pressure air near a windward wall and a low-pressure region on the leeward side of a large building. A range of wind speeds and their environmental impacts are shown in Table 10.3.

These effects can be measured using wind-tunnel studies. A number of internationally accepted criteria are available for a variety of dining and pedestrian activities. These criteria include some measure of probability of occurrence, typically in the number of hours per year when a particular wind speed will be equaled or exceeded. It is important to note whether the wind speed is a gust wind speed measured over a few seconds or a mean wind speed measured over a minute or so. One of the more popular sets of criteria is that suggested by Melbourne (Ref. 10.19) and listed in Table 10.4.

Interest in pedestrian-level wind effects was spurred by the death of a number of elderly people who while walking past tall buildings were knocked to the ground by strong

WIND EFFECTS

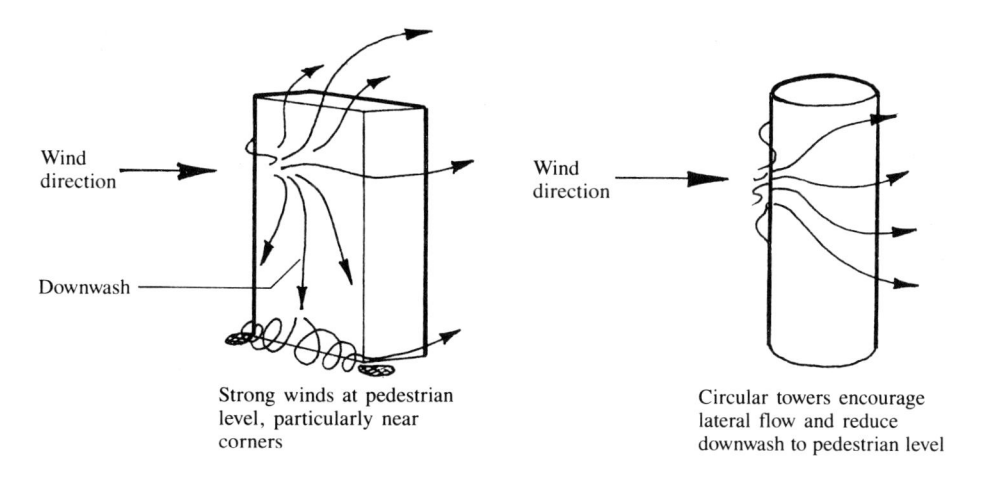

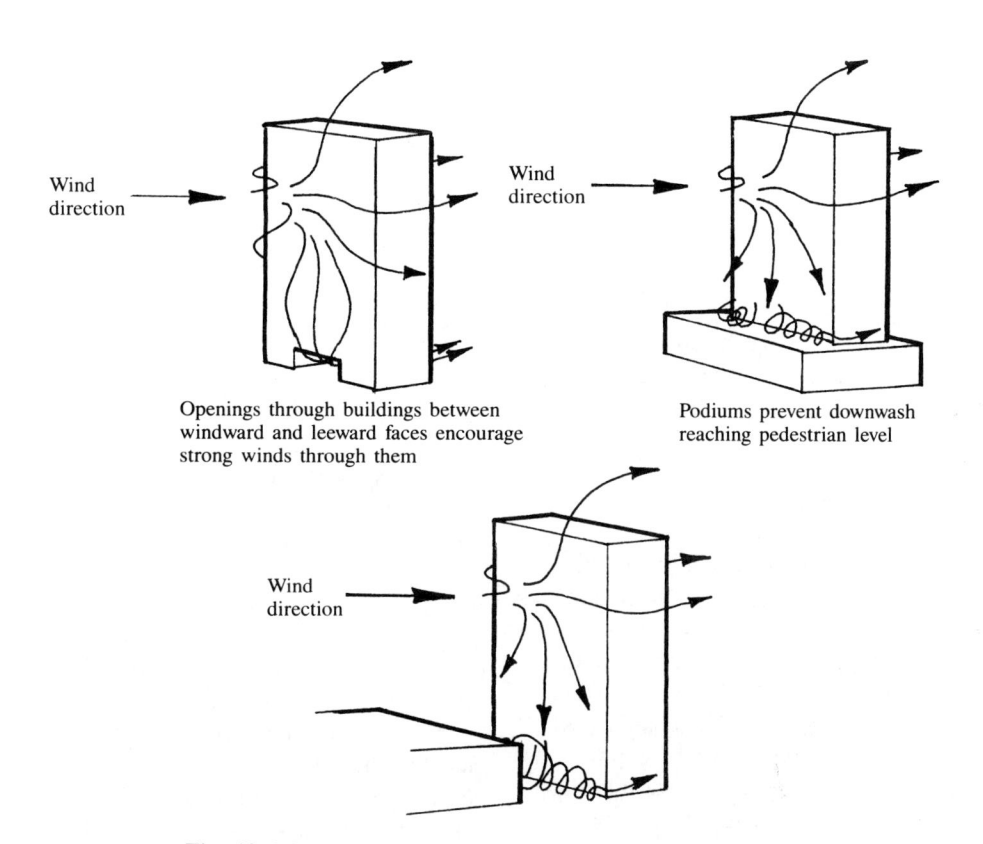

Fig. 10.6.1. Some typical wind flow patterns around tall buildings.

wind gusts and fatally injured. Wind-tunnel studies of potential pedestrian-level wind problems, which are mandatory in some cities, are a routine part of all major tall building design these days.

Wind Chill Index

The human body's heat exchanges are affected by airflow past the skin. In cold conditions this is referred to as the chill effect. This information is often given on local weather forecasts to indicate the chilling effects of the wind. Wind chill index can be calculated using the following equations:

$$WCI = 91.4 - [(10.45 + 6.69(RV) - 0.447(V))(91.4 - F)]/22$$

or in SI units:

$$WCI = 33 - [(10.45 + 10(RV) - V)(33 - C)]/22$$

where WCI, the wind chill index, is a still air temperature (°F or °C) that would give the same rate of body heat loss

Table 10.3. Impact of Ground-Level Winds on People and Their Environment.

Description	Beaufort No.	Wind Speed, mph (m/s)	Effects
Calm	0	0	smoke rises vertically
Light air	1	0–3(0–1.3)	wind not noticed
Light breeze	2	4–7(1.8–3.1)	wind felt on face
Gentle breeze	3	8–12(3.6–5.4)	wind extends light flag, people's hair is disturbed, loose clothing flaps
Moderate breeze	4	13–18(5.8–8.1)	raises dust, dry soil and loose paper, people's hair is disarranged
Fresh breeze	5	19–24(8.5–10.7)	force of wind felt on body, drifting snow becomes airborne
Strong breeze	6	25–31(11.2–13.9)	difficulty using umbrellas, hair blown straight, difficult to walk steadily, unpleasant wind noise in ears, snow windborne above head height (blizzard conditions)
Near gale	7	32–38(14.3–17.0)	loss of balance while walking
Gale	8	39–46(17.4–20.1)	wind generally impedes progress, frequent loss of balance due to gusts
Strong gale	9	47–54(19.8–24.1)	people frequently blown to the ground by gusts

as the combined effects of air temperature and airflow; V is the wind speed in mph or m/s; RV is the square root of V; and F is the dry bulb air temperature in °F, and C is the dry bulb air temperature in °C.

Air Movement for Thermal Comfort

While the chill effect is seen as detrimental in cold climates, in warmer, humid climates airflow past the skin can be quite beneficial in restoring thermal comfort. This cooling effect is limited, however, to conditions where the air temperature is less than skin temperature—98°F (37°C)—and relative humidities are low enough (less than about 95 percent) to allow evaporative cooling from exposed, sweating skin. The wind speed needed to restore thermal comfort in warm, humid environments can be estimated using the following equations:

$$WS_c = 30[DBT - 81 + 1.5(RH - 60)/10] \text{ fpm}$$

Table 10.4. Suggested Criteria for Pedestrian-Level Winds.

Exposure	Limit of Acceptable Wind Speed with an Occurrence of Once per Year During Daylight Hours
Sitting long	peak wind speed < 10 m/s
Sitting short	peak wind speed < 13 m/s
Walking	peak wind speed < 16 m/s
Dangerous	peak wind speed > 16 m/s (if 23 m/s is exceeded, people are blown over)

or in SI units

$$WS_c = 0.15[DBT - 27.2 + 0.56(RH - 60)/10] \text{ m/s}$$

where WS_c is the wind speed (fpm or m/s) needed to restore thermal comfort; DBT is the dry bulb temperature (°F or °C); and RH is the relative humidity in percent.

This beneficial cooling effect is often incorporated in the design of buildings for tropical areas where insulated roofs are provided to eliminate radiant heat gains of occupants and wall openings are large to allow generous airflow through the building.

This natural ventilation for comfort cooling can be designed using local wind data in combination with thermal comfort criteria. Airflow patterns and velocities can be studied in models in a wind tunnel. The velocities at various locations within the model are expressed as wind speed coefficients relating local wind speeds to an external reference local wind speed, say, 33 feet (10 m) above ground. These wind speed coefficients can then be related to the wind speed frequencies from records for that particular location. This allows estimates to be made of the probability of occurrence of various comfort or wind speed conditions within the building.

Infiltration

Where buildings rely on air conditioning or heating and cooling systems to maintain indoor thermal comfort, ventilation (fresh air changes) and infiltration of outdoor air represent significant loads on the system.

Air-conditioned buildings are usually expected to be well sealed, but achieving a well sealed building is more difficult than many people imagine. Airflow through cracks and holes in the building's external envelope is referred to as *infiltration*. Most of the cracks are around doors and windows, or small openings in the construction for utility conduits.

Infiltration can be estimated using pressure differences due to wind and relative buoyancy of warm indoor air to cold outside air. An equation for this thermosyphonic ventilation effect is given in Chapter 18, Section 18.7. Generally, pressure differences from air buoyancy are relatively small compared to pressure differences due to wind, with the possible exception of very tall buildings. Wind pressures dominate on most buildings when wind speeds exceed approximately 5 mph (2.2 m/s) (Ref. 10.20).

Wind Transport of Particulates

Another aspect of wind effects around buildings is that of erosion, where surface material particulate can be lifted by strong wind gusts and moved. This process is often referred to as *saltation*. Serious problems have arisen as a result of wind erosion of ballast pebbles used on flat roofs. When airborne these pebbles can impact on adjacent buildings causing extensive glass failures. Much of the recent research on wind effects on roofing systems has been carried out in Aachen, Germany.

Wind erosion can also be a problem around beach front properties where beach sand becomes airborne in wind and results in scouring around the windward footings of buildings. The airborne sand is deposited in drifts in the wakes of the buildings where velocities have fallen and wind can no longer carry the sand particles.

A similar type of problem is encountered in pedestrian plazas with ponds and fountains, where water is blown out of the fountain. This problem can be reduced in the case of fountains by installing an anemometer-operated switch nearby which turns off the fountain pumps during strong wind conditions. Water spray from wind-generated waves in ornamental ponds in plazas can also be a problem.

Wind-driven snow has been studied in wind tunnels both for determining snow loads on roofs and for checking accessibility of building entrances and exits and roadways under heavy snow drift conditions.

Wind Effects On Building Mechanical Systems

Rather than locating mid-level plant room exhaust fan outlets near the centers of walls facing strong prevailing winds where positive pressures are high, locations near

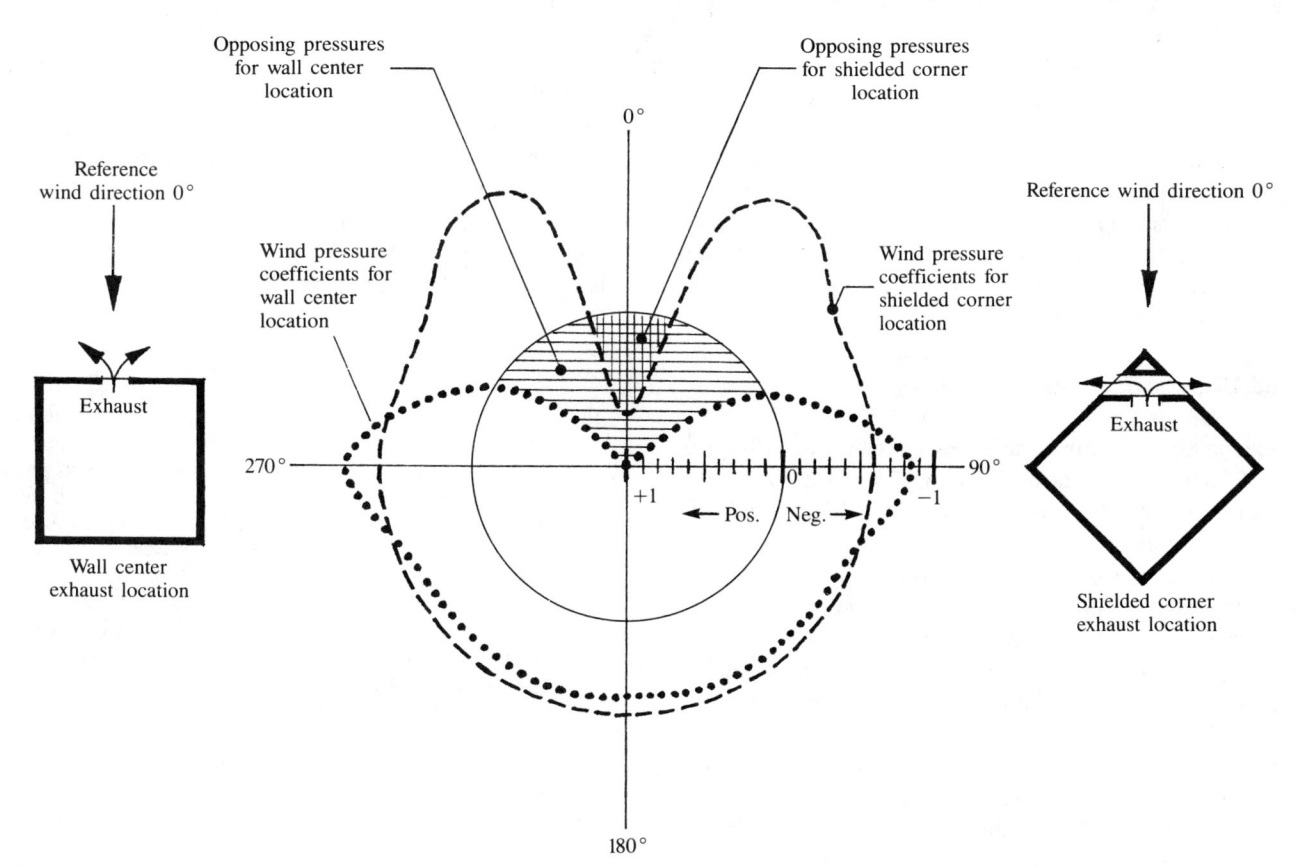

Fig. 10.6.2. Wind pressure distributions on the mid-level plant room exhaust fan outlets of a tall building at the wall-center and shielded-corner locations.

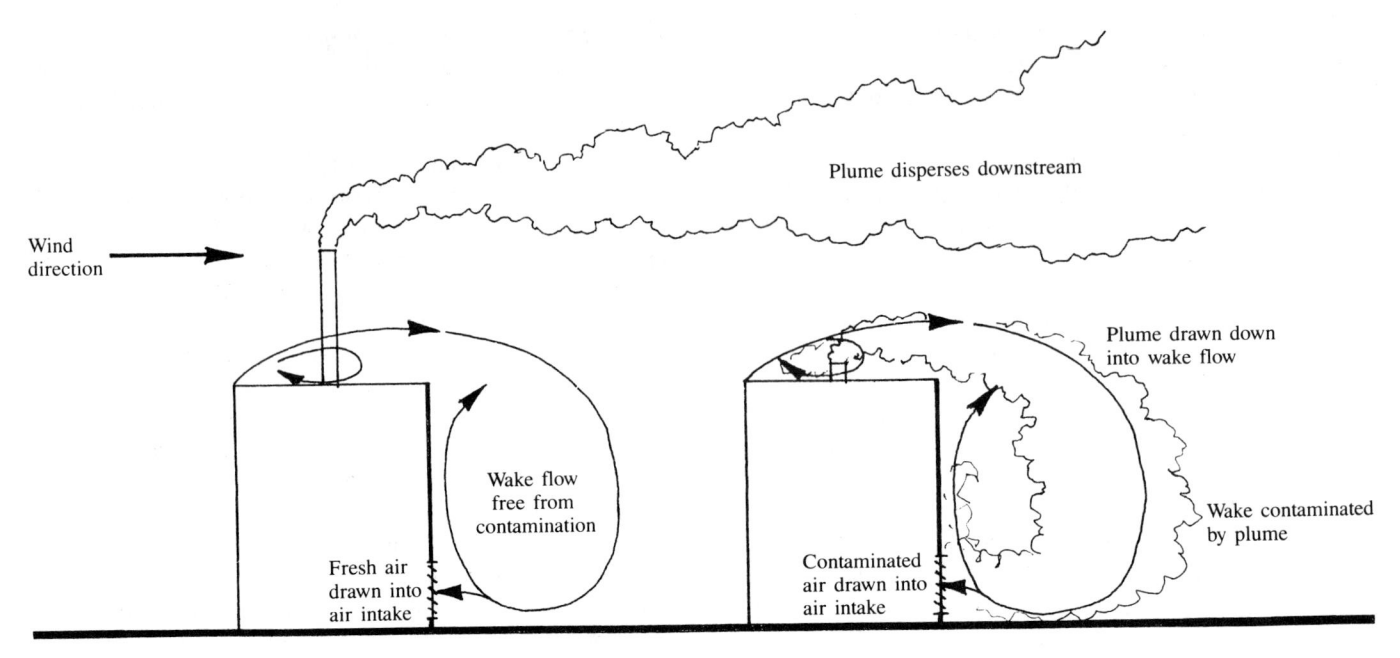

Fig. 10.6.3. Wind effects on the plumes from tall and short rooftop slacks.

corners should be selected. Slots through the corners of rectangular buildings as in Fig. 10.6.2 usually have good flow through them because of the wind pressure difference across the corner for many wind directions. By discharging exhaust fans into such a slot exhaust fans are assisted by low wind pressures for a wide range of wind directions, as illustrated in Fig. 10.6.2.

If elevator (lift) cars are exposed to the elements, as they sometimes are on communication towers with high-level observation decks or restaurants, elevator cables can become tangled by wind-induced motions. One solution to this problem is to have retractable arms at suitable spacing down the cable to restrict cable sway due to wind. When the elevator car approaches a set of arms they are swung clear to allow the car to pass.

Wind Dispersion of Gaseous Wastes

Extensive high rise urban development can lead to stagnation of air movement at the bottom of street canyons and result in unacceptable concentrations of vehicular exhaust gases. Orientation of the streets to align with prevailing winds can minimize these conditions. The shapes of individual large buildings can influence the ventilation of street canyons by wind. City planners in New York City have used data from boundary layer wind tunnel dispersion studies to evaluate the likely impact of proposals for new large buildings.

Tall stacks can be avoided to some degree by increasing the exit velocity of contaminated gases so that the momentum of the jet from the stack is sufficient to place materials clear of the recirculating eddies, as illustrated in Fig. 10.6.3 (Ref. 10.21). Another approach for buildings with many gaseous waste outlets and fresh air intakes is a rooftop manifold leading to a single tall stack. This approach allows the stack to be taller than is feasible with smaller-diameter stacks and for it to be placed in the best position on the site with respect to prevailing wind directions.

Another problem with mechanical ventilation systems in buildings is where both the exhaust opening and the fresh air intakes occur on the leeward face of large buildings. In this case the stale, contaminated air exhausted from the building recirculates in the wake flow of the building and is reingested and circulated within the building. Similar problems can occur when there are fires in buildings. It is important to endeavor to locate air intakes in such a location that smoke issuing from a building will not reenter the fresh air intakes.

REFERENCES

10.1. *Coastal Construction Manual*, FEMA-55. Federal Emergency Management Agency, Washington, DC, 1986.
10.2. E. Gossard, A. Frisch, R. Kropfli, L. Miller, and R. Strauch. "Middle Scale Wind Patterns Revealed by Dual-Doppler Radars." *Proceedings Second U.S. National Conference on Wind Engineering Research*. Colorado State University, Fort Collins, 1975, pp. I-4-1 to I-4-4.
10.3. J. Minor, J. McDonald, and K. Mehta. *The Tornado: An Engineering-Oriented Perspective*. NOAA Technical Memorandum ERL NSSL-82. National Severe Storms Laboratory, Norman, OK, December 1977.
10.4. T. Fujita. *Proposed Characterization of Tornadoes and Hurricanes by Area and Intensity*. SMRP Research Paper 91. Departmental of Geophysical Sciences. The University of Chicago. Chicago 1971.
10.5. R. Geiger. *The Climate Near the Ground*, 4th Ed. Harvard University Press, Cambridge, MA, 1966.
10.6. *Minimum Design Loads for Buildings and Other Structures*. ANSI A58.1-1982. American National Standards Institute. New York, 1982.

10.7. *National Building Code of Canada 1985, Section 4.1.8 Live Loads Due to Wind*. National Research Council of Canada, Associate Committee on the National Building Code, Ottawa, 1985.
10.8. *Code of Basic Data for the Design of Buildings, CP3: Chapter V Part 2*. British Standards Institution, London, 1972.
10.9. *AS1170 Pt. 2, Minimum Design Loads on Structures, SAA Loading Code Part 2—Wind Forces*. Standards Association of Australia. Sydney, 1983.
10.10. Council on Tall Buildings and Urban Habitat. *Monograph on the Planning and Design of Tall Buildings*, Vol. CL. American Society of Civil Engineers, New York, 1980, Chapter CL-3, pp. 145-248.
10.11. A. Davenport. "Rationale for determining design wind velocities." *J. Struct. Div. Am. Soc. Civ. Engrs.*, **86** (1960).
10.12. Council on Tall Buildings and Urban Habitat. *Monograph on the Planning and Design of Tall Buildings*, Vol. PC. American Society of Civil Engineers, New York, 1981, Section 13.2. pp. 805-862.
10.13. M. Swami and S. Chandra. "Correlations for Pressure Distribution on Buildings and Calculation of Natural-Ventilation Airflow." *ASHRAE Transactions*, **94**(Pt. 1) (1988).
10.14. L. O. Degelman. *Bin and Degree Hour Weather Data for Simplified Energy Calculations*. American Society of Heating, Refrigeration and Air-Conditioning Engineers, Atlanta, 1986, RP-385.
10.15. N. Isyumov and T. Tschanz. *Building Motion in Wind*. American Society of Civil Engineers, New York, 1986.
10.16. E. Simiu and R. Scanlan. *Wind Effects on Structures*, 2nd Ed. John Wiley, New York, 1986.
10.17. N. Cobb. "The Panes of Big John." *Boston Globe* (Newspaper), Boston, MA, April 22, 1973, pp. 5-26.
10.18. *Wind Tunnel Model Studies of Buildings and Structures*. Manual on Engineering Practice No. 67. American Society of Civil Engineers, New York, 1987.
10.19. W. Melbourne. "Criteria for Environmental Wind Conditions." *Journal of Wind Engineering and Industrial Aerodynamics*. **3**, 241-249 (1978).
10.20. M. Liddament. "The Calculation of Wind Effect on Ventilation." *Transactions, American Society of Heating, Refrigerating and Air-Conditioning Engineers*, **94**(Pt. 2), 1645-1660 (1988).
10.21. *ASHRAE 1989 Handbook of Fundamentals*. American Society of Heating, Refrigerating and Air-Conditioning Engineers, Atlanta, GA, 1989, Chapter 14.

SUGGESTIONS FOR FURTHER READING

Wind Loading and Wind-Induced Structural Response. American Society of Civil Engineers, New York, 1987.

R. Aynsley, W. Melbourne, and B.J. Vickery. *Architectural Aerodynamics*. Applied Science, London, 1977.

R. Aynsley. "Reducing the Effects of Wind on Mid-Level Exhaust Fans in Tall Buildings." *Architectural Science Review*, **21**, 109-110 (1978).

J. Cermak (Ed.). *Wind Engineering*, Vols. 1 and 2. Pergamon Press, Oxford, 1980.

H. J. Critchfield. *General Climatology*. Prentice Hall, Englewood Cliffs, NJ, 1983.

R. Edwards and C. Irwin. "Four-Cell Ventilation and Air Movement Measurements Using a New Multiple Tracer Gas Technique." *Air Infiltration Review*. **9**(4), 5-6 (Aug. 1988).

J. Francis. *Fluid Mechanics for Engineering Students*, 4th Ed. Edward Arnold, London, 1975.

E. L. Houghten and N. B. Carruthers. *Wind Forces on Buildings and Structures: An Introduction*. Edward Arnold, London, 1976.

A. Kareem (Ed). *Proceedings, Sixth U.S. National Conference on Wind Engineering*, Vols. I and II. University of Houston, Houston, TX, 1989.

H. Leutheusser. "Influence of Architectural Features on Static Wind Loading of Buildings," in R. Marshall and H. Thom (Eds.), *Proceedings of Technical Meeting Concerning Wind Loads on Buildings and Structures*, National Bureau of Standards, Gaithersburg, MD, 1970, pp. 73-86.

K. Mehta and R. Dillingham. *Proceedings of the Fifth U.S. National Conference on Wind Engineering*. Texas Technical University, Lubbock, TX, 1985.

J. Morgan and V. Beck. *Sheet Metal Roof Failures by Repeated Loading*. Australian Department of Housing and Construction, Housing Research Branch, Technical Report No. 2, Canberra, ACT, 1975.

A. Penwarden. "Acceptable Wind Speeds in Towns." *Building Science*, **8**(3), 259-267 (Sept. 1973).

J. Peterka. "Structure and Circumstance." *Progressive Architecture*. **4**(12), 50-57 (1980).

R. Peyret and T. Taylor. *Computational Methods for Fluid Flow*. Springer-Verlag, New York, 1983.

J. Reardon and C. Shaw. "Balanced Fan Depressurization Method for Measuring Component and Overall Air Leakage in Single- and Multi-family Dwelling." *Air Infiltration Review*, **9**(4), 7-8 (Aug. 1988).

T. Reinhold (Ed.). *Wind Tunnel Modeling for Civil Engineering Applications*. Cambridge University Press, Cambridge, UK, 1982. pp. 8-26.

V. L. Streeter. *Fluid Mechanics*, 4th Ed. McGraw-Hill, New York, 1958.

B. Vickery and A. Clark. "Lift or Across-Wind Response of Tapered Stacks." *J. Structural Division ASCE*, **98**(St1), 1-20 (Jan. 1972).

NOTATION

DBT	dry bulb temperature
Hz	hertz (= cycles per second)
p	static pressure
R_e	Reynolds number
RH	Relative humidity
S	Strouhal number
V	wind velocity
WCI	wind chill index
z	height
μ	dynamic viscosity
ρ	mass density

A list of abbreviations of the units of measurement, definitions of these units, and conversion factors between British/American and metric units are given in the Appendix.

11
Structural Systems

Henry J. Cowan and Peter R. Smith

This Chapter considers the basic principles of the performance of structural members and of structural systems, which are assemblies of structural members.

The properties of the structural materials were discussed in Chapters 2–5, and the loads to which structures are subjected in Chapters 9 and 10. The detailed design of steel, concrete, masonry, and timber structures will be covered in Chapters 12–14, and the design of foundations in Chapter 15.

The design of individual beams, columns, and tension members is considered first. The most common structural systems are trusses and single-story and multistory frames; these are discussed in some detail.

The various other methods used for long-span and/or lightweight roof structures are then surveyed.

11.1. STRUCTURAL MEMBERS AND STRUCTURAL ASSEMBLIES

Structures are assemblies of structural members capable of resisting the loads considered in Chapters 9 and 10. The structural members must be big enough to resist these loads without failing, but no bigger than is necessary, otherwise material is wasted. In this chapter only the structural systems are discussed. The design of actual steel, concrete, masonry, and timber structures will be considered in Chapters 12, 13, and 14.

Structures exist in a three-dimensional world, and they are therefore themselves three-dimensional. However, most practical structures can be reduced to two-dimensional systems. They are easier to visualize and to draw in two dimensions, and the design calculations are much simpler. There are, however, some *space frames* (see Section 11.9), which can only be considered in three dimensions, and their solution is accordingly more laborious.

A two-dimensional system of forces is in equilibrium if the horizontal components of all the forces balance, the vertical components of all the forces balance, and if the moment of all the forces about any convenient point (which may or may not lie within the structural system) balance:

$$\left. \begin{array}{l} \Sigma H = 0 \\ \Sigma V = 0 \\ \Sigma M = 0 \end{array} \right\} \qquad (11.1)$$

This is proved in many elementary textbooks on the theory of structures (for example, Ref. 11.1, p. 65). The state of statical equilibrium thus yields three equations which can be used to find up to three unknown forces. For some structures these *equations of statical equilibrium* are sufficient to determine all the forces in the structure. These are called *statically determinate structures*. If there are more unknown forces, the structure is *statically indeterminate*. The structure cannot then be solved by the equations of statical equilibrium alone, and some other equations must be found.

There are two distinctively different methods for designing statically indeterminate structures. We can consider the behavior of the structure under the action of the actual *working* or *service loads*. The structure remains *elastic* under the action of these loads, and its elastic deformation at certain critical points can be calculated. This provides the additional equations needed to solve the statically indeterminate structure.

The second method considers the state of the structure *at failure* under loads which are much higher than the working or service loads. Before a statically indeterminate structure can fail, a number of hinges must form which provide the necessary mechanism for collapse. The additional equations needed to solve a statically indeterminate structure can be derived from these considerations.

Most structural design of statically indeterminate structures is at present based on the elastic method, and this is the only one which will be considered in this chapter.

A distinction must also be made between *structural analysis* and *structural design*. In structural analysis the dimensions of the structure and of the structural members are given, and also the maximum stresses which are permitted in the structural material. From these we can determine the load-bearing capacity of the structure. This analysis can be performed for both statically determinate and for statically indeterminate structures, because we have all the data required for the solution of the necessary equations.

Structural design is the more useful procedure. We are given the overall dimensions of the structure, the maximum stresses permitted in the structural material, and the loads which the structure is required to carry. From these we determine the sizes required for the structural members. This can be done only for statically determinate structures, for whose design only the equations of statical equilibrium are needed. We cannot set up any elastic equations until we know the sizes of the structural members, and hence we cannot design statically indeterminate structures directly.

To design a statically indeterminate structure we must therefore assume the dimensions of the structural members, using information obtained from previous structural analysis, and then modify them as the result of our analysis. Since all structural analyses are today done with the aid of a computer, this presents no practical problems, but it is a more complex procedure.

Since this is a Handbook of Architectural Construction, we shall concern ourselves in this chapter mainly with the structural design of statically determinate structures, and we will consider approximate solutions for more complex structures by converting them into statically determinate structures (see Section 11.6). These are the methods used in *preliminary design*, which is the part of structural design primarily of interest to architects.

For a more detailed discussion of structural systems for statically indeterminate structures, readers may be referred to a handbook or a textbook on structural design (for example Ref. 11.2).

11.2. TIES AND STRUTS

Before we consider structural assemblies, we will consider the individual structural members. There are two basic types:

1. Structural members in line with the direction of the loads. These are *ties* or *struts* (*columns* or *load-bearing walls*) (Fig. 11.2.1).
2. Structural members at right angles to the direction of the loads. These are *beams* or *slabs* (Fig. 11.2.1.), and they are considered in Section 11.3.

If a *tie* or *tension member* with a cross-sectional area A carries a load P (Fig. 11.2.2), then the stress in the material is

$$f = P/A \qquad (11.2)$$

If we want to design a tie made of a structural material whose maximum permissible stress is f to carry a load P, then the cross-sectional area must be at least

$$A = P/f \qquad (11.3)$$

The design of *struts, compression members*, or *columns* is more complex, because there are two types of failure:

1. *Short-column* failure is caused by overstressing of the material. This is analogous to the failure of the tie. If the column has a cross-sectional area A, and the maximum permissible stress of the material is f, then its permissible short-column load is

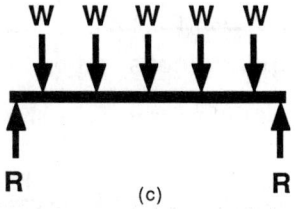

$$P_s = fA \qquad (11.4)$$

Fig. 11.2.1. Structural members: (a) tie; (b) strut or column; (c) beam.

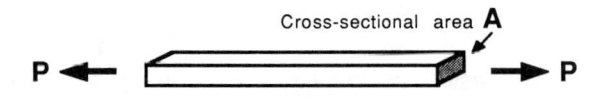

Fig. 11.2.2. Tensile stress. The stress in a tie is $f = P/A$. Its load-carrying capacity is $P = fA$, where f is the maximum permissible stress.

2. *Long-column* failure is caused by buckling of the column sideways (Fig. 11.2.3). This is, initially at least, an elastic phenomenon; if the load is removed, the column recovers its original shape. However, a column that has buckled sideways has ceased to be a useful column, so that buckling constitutes failure. The theory of buckling is too complex for this chapter, and reference should be made to a textbook on the theory of structures (for example, Ref. 11.1, p. 185). The result is that the long-column load is

$$P_l = \pi^2 EI/L^2 \qquad (11.5)$$

where
- π is the circular constant = 3.1416...,
- E is the modulus of elasticity (which is a constant for the structural material),
- L is the effective length of the column,
- $I = Ar^2$ is the second moment of area, also called moment of inertia (see Section 11.3),
- A is the cross-sectional area, and
- r is the radius of gyration, which is simply a convenient term for $\sqrt{I/A}$.

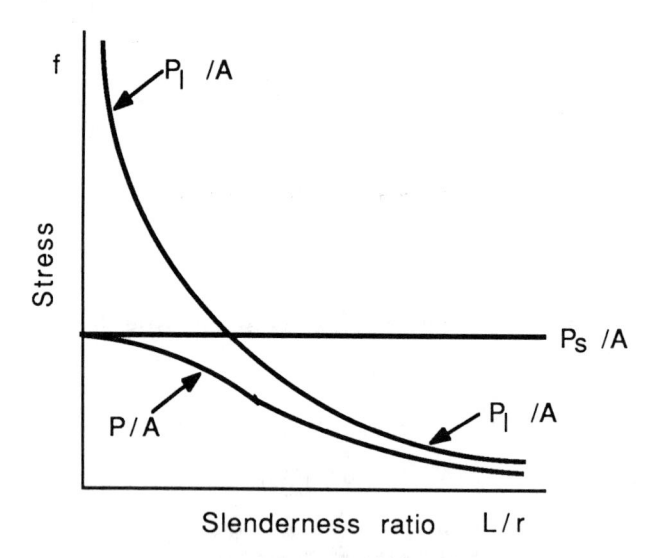

Fig. 11.2.3. Variation of column load with slenderness ratio. When the slenderness ratio is 0, the stress in the column is the maximum permissible stress for a short column, P_s/A. When it is infinity, the maximum stress permissible is P_l/A. The maximum stress permissible in a column of intermediate slenderness ratio is shown by the lowest of the three curves, P/A. It can be determined theoretically or empirically.

Equation (11.5) can thus be written

$$P_l = \pi^2 EA(r/L)^2 = (\text{constant})A(r/L)^2 \qquad (11.6)$$

The constant in this equation depends on the modulus of elasticity of the structural material, whereas in Eq. (11.4) it is the maximum permissible stress (which depends on the strength of the material).

Let us consider three materials: (a) ordinary structural steel; (b) a high-strength aluminum alloy which has the same strength as structural steel; and (c) a high-strength steel which is stronger than structural steel, but has the same modulus of elasticity. Materials (a) and (b) have the same short-column load capacity P_s, and materials (a) and (c) have the same long-column load capacity P_l. The short-column load capacity of material (c) is much higher than that of (a), and the long-column load capacity of material (b) is much lower than that of (a).

The effective length of a column, L, depends on its end supports. For many columns it is the actual length. It may be as high as twice the actual length for a cantilevered column (an unlikely contingency in a building), or as low as half the actual length for a column firmly fixed at both ends. The effective length is specified in the building codes for the structural material (see Fig. 12.5.2).

The radius of gyration r is a geometric property of the section. It is proportional to the depth d of the section in the direction in which it will buckle. This is the smallest depth or thickness, unless the column or strut is restrained from buckling in some direction, for example, by being firmly fixed to the material forming a wall or floor. The value of r is $0.25d$ for a solid circular section, $0.29d$ for a rectangular section, and $0.42d$ for an I-section with relatively thin flanges (refer to a textbook on the theory of structures, for example, Ref. 11.1, p. 188).

The ratio L/r is called the *slenderness ratio*. The variation of the stresses due to long-column load P_l and the short-column load P_s are shown in Fig. 11.2.3. Most practical columns lie in the intermediate range, which is represented by the lowest of the three curves in Fig. 11.2.3. The compressive stress permitted in columns and struts is thus less than the stress permitted in a short compression member. The variation of this stress with the slenderness ratio is given in the appropriate building code either as a formula (see Equations 12.10 and 12.11) or as a table.

The stress reduction due to buckling is only small in concrete and masonry columns and load-bearing walls, because these are relatively thick, and thus have low slenderness ratios. The slenderness ratios tend to be greater in timber, and they are still greater in steel structures, because steel sections can be made relatively thin, which is economical in material, but increases the tendency to buckling.

Buckling may become a dominant consideration in the design of aluminum structures, because the modulus of elasticity of aluminum is only one third of that of steel, and thus its tendency to buckle is much greater.

Please refer to Chapters 12 and 13 for examples of the design of ties, struts, and columns.

11.3. STATICALLY DETERMINATE BEAMS

Structural members at right angles to the direction of the loads are called *beams*, or *lintels* if they are in walls (Fig. 11.2.1).

The loads at right angles to a beam set up both bending moments and shear forces. The bending moments are needed to satisfy the moment equilibrium equation $\Sigma M = 0$ of Eq. (11.1), and the shear forces the vertical equilibrium equation $\Sigma V = 0$. The third equation, $\Sigma H = 0$, gives in this instance merely $0 = 0$ (Fig. 11.3.1).

In practice the bending moments usually determine the size of beams in buildings. The beams must be big enough to resist both the bending moments and the shear forces, but the larger and therefore critical beam size is usually obtained from the bending moment equations. The shear forces must be considered in the detail design of the beams (see, for example, Section 13.5). However, as this Chapter is concerned with *preliminary design* we will not consider shear forces further in this Chapter.

Nor will we consider the limitations imposed by excessive deflection. These depend to a large extent on the choice of the nonstructural materials; cracks can be produced in brittle materials (see Chapter 3) by relatively small elastic deformations of the load-bearing structure.

Figure 11.3.1 shows that the loads acting on a beam or slab and the reactions which support it set up a bending moment at any section chosen. Similar bending moments are set up at other sections. We design the beam for the maximum bending moment, which we shall determine presently for different types of beam.

It is customary to define a *positive bending moment* as one which causes compression at the top and tension at the bottom (Fig. 11.3.2). Thus in most structures the bending moments in beams and slabs over the supports (which may be other beams, or columns, or load-bearing walls) are negative, and those near mid-span are positive.

The *theory of bending* is derived in most textbooks on the theory of structures (for example, Ref. 11.1, p. 160). The solution is:

$$\frac{M}{I} = \frac{f}{y} \qquad (11.7)$$

where M is the bending moment to be resisted,
f is the maximum stress set up by that bending moment,
I is the second moment of area (also called the moment of inertia), which is a geometric property of the cross section, and
y is the greatest distance from the neutral axis (Fig. 11.3.2); if the section is unsymmetrical, y_c and y_t have different values.

The *section modulus* is defined as

$$S = I/y$$

(If y has different values for tension and compression, there are two section moduli, one for tension and one for compression.)

Equation (11.7) then becomes

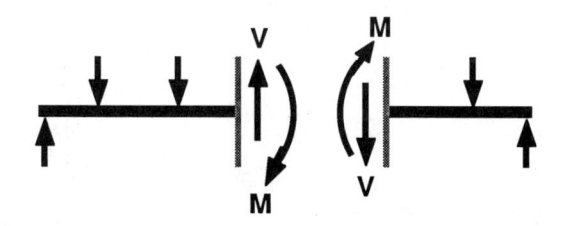

$$M = fS \qquad (11.8)$$

Fig. 11.3.1. Bending moments and shear forces set up in a beam by a system of loads. We cut the beam at some section along its length, and consider the equilibrium of the left-hand portion. For vertical equilibrium, a shear force V is needed to balance the two vertical loads and the vertical reaction acting on that part of the beam. If we take moments about that section, we find that a bending moment M is needed to balance the two loads and the reaction for moment equilibrium. We obtain exactly the same result if we consider the equilibrium of the right-hand portion instead.

At the section we are considering, the beam is therefore being subjected to a bending moment M which is bending the beam and a shear force V which is tending to shear (or cut through) the beam. The beam must have sufficient structural material to resist both the bending moment and the shear force.

Fig. 11.3.2. The theory of bending. Positive bending moments are defined as those which bend a beam downwards. They thus set up compression on the top of the beam, and tension on its bottom. Between there is a *neutral axis* where there is neither compression or tension. The greatest compression occurs at a distance y_c, which is the greatest distance from the neutral axis. Similar considerations apply to the tensile part of the beam. If the section is symmetrical, which is usual, $y_c = y_t$. If the section is not symmetrical, the theory of bending becomes slightly more complicated.

The section moduli for various sections of steel, aluminum and wood are listed in section tables produced by companies that manufacture, fabricate or sell the various structural sections available.

Reinforced concrete consists of two materials, and it is convenient to use a different type of equation (see Section 13.4).

It remains to determine the bending moments for which beams must be designed. There are three types of statically determinate beam:

1. Cantilevers
2. Simply supported beams
3. Simply supported beams with cantilever overhangs

The simply supported beams are by far the most common type in buildings.

Let us first consider a cantilever carrying a single concentrated load at its end (Fig. 11.3.3). The maximum bending moment evidently occurs at the support, where the cantilever is built in.

To obtain the maximum bending moment for a simply supported beam at midspan (Fig. 11.3.4) we make an imaginary cut in the beam, just to one side of the concentrated load, and take moments about that point.

In practice most loads are considered to be uniformly distributed (Section 9.3). To obtain the maximum bending moment for a simply supported beam carrying a uniformly distributed load (Fig. 11.3.5) we make an imaginary cut at midspan, and replace the uniformly distributed load with a single concentrated load which has the same effect.

Instead of being built into a wall, a cantilever can also project over the supports of a beam. The cantilever's support bending moment is then transmitted to the beam supporting it (Fig. 11.3.6).

Thus the maximum bending moment of a simply supported beam with cantilever overhangs is less than that of a beam without them (Fig. 11.3.7).

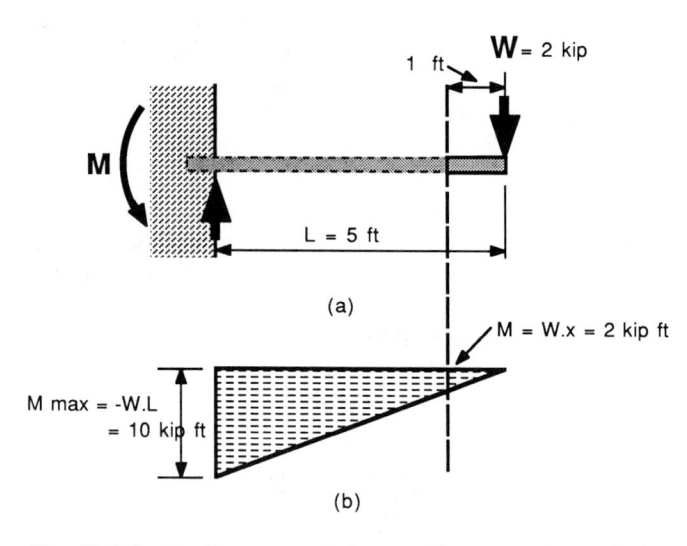

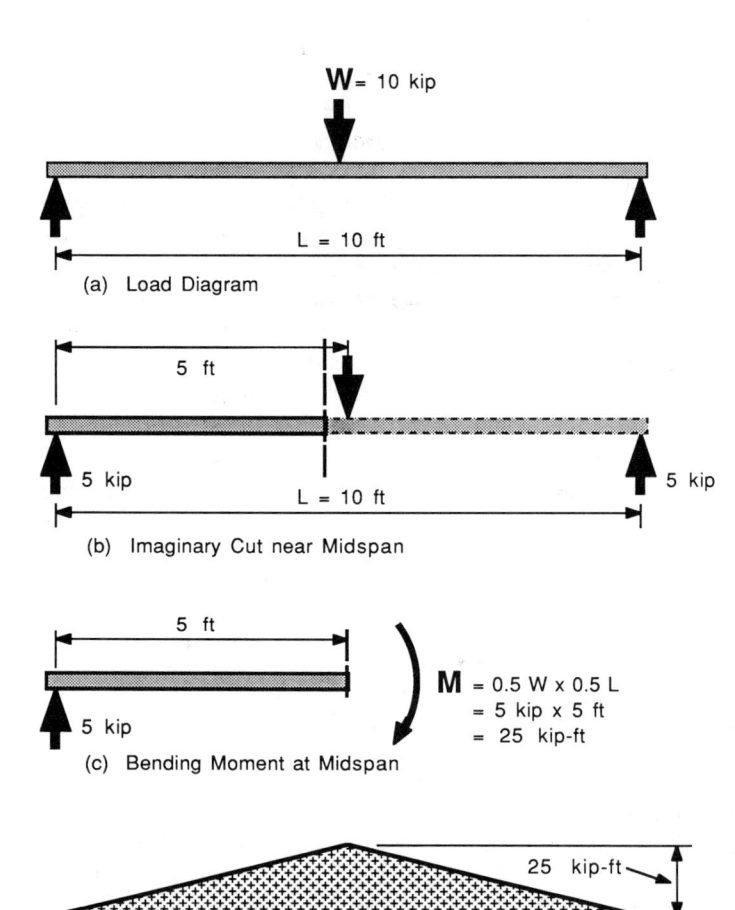

Fig. 11.3.3. Bending moments in a cantilever carrying a single concentrated load at its end: (a) load diagram (variation of load along the span); (b) bending moment diagram (variation of bending moment along the span).

At the free end of the cantilever the bending moment is zero: if we consider the equilibrium of the forces to the right of the end of the cantilever about the end, the result is zero, because there are no forces.

We will next consider the moments about a section 1 ft to the left of the end of the cantilever:

$$M = -Wx = -2 \text{ kip} \times 1 \text{ ft} = -2 \text{ kip ft}$$

Evidently the bending moment increases uniformly until we get to the support, where it reaches its maximum:

$$M = -WL = -10 \text{ kip ft}$$

Fig. 11.3.4. Bending moments in a simply supported beam carrying a central concentrated load: (a) The reactions must by symmetry be equal, and therefore equal to 5 kip. (b) We make an imaginary cut a fraction of an inch to the left of the concentrated load. (c) The only force acting on the left-hand portion of the beam is the reaction of 5 kip, which is 5 ft to the left of the cut. (d) Thus the maximum bending moment, which occurs at midspan, is 25 kip ft.

STRUCTURAL SYSTEMS 153

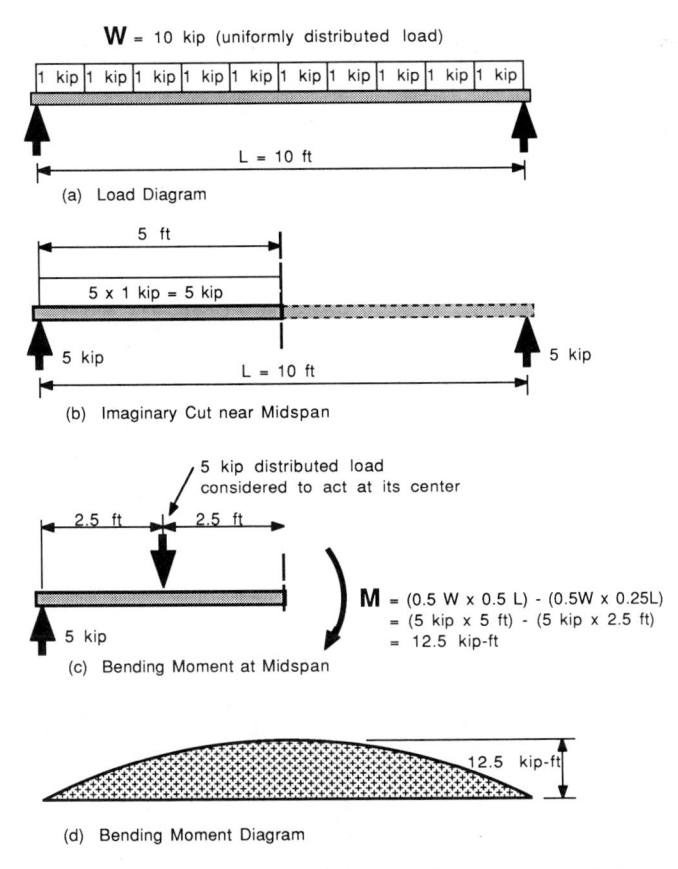

Fig. 11.3.5. Bending moments in a simply supported beam carrying a uniformly distributed load. (a) By symmetry, the reactions are 5 kip each. (b) We make an imaginary cut at midspan. (c) We replace the uniformly distributed load on the left-hand portion of the beam with a single concentrated load acting at its center of gravity, that is, 2.5 ft from the cut. We now have two forces acting on the left-hand part of the beam, each 5 kip; one acts 5 ft from the cut, and the other 2.5 ft. (d) The resulting bending moment at mid-span, which is obviously the maximum, is

$$5 \times (5 - 2.5) = 12.5 \text{ kip ft}$$

11.4. FIXED-ENDED AND CONTINUOUS BEAMS

Beams are statically determinate if their supports impose only two reactions. Simply supported beams, including those with cantilever overhangs, have two supports, which may be other beams, load-bearing walls, or columns. We can determine these vertical reactions from the equations of equilibrium. Cantilevers also have two reactions, a vertical reaction and a moment reaction where they are fixed into the wall or column. Eq. (11.1) has three parts, but since there are no horizontal forces, $\Sigma H = 0$ yields only $0 = 0$, so that only two support reactions can be determined.

Any beams that have more reactions are therefore statically indeterminate. *Fixed-ended beams* have vertical and moment reactions at *each* end, so that we need an extra two equations to obtain the bending moments in them.

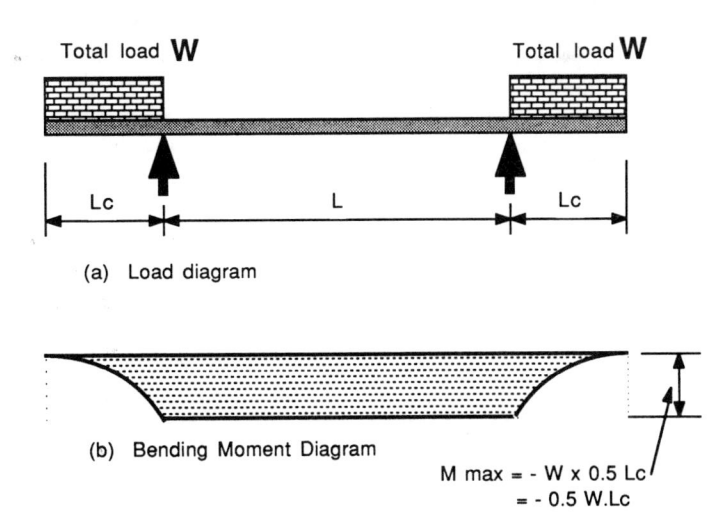

Fig. 11.3.6. Bending moments in cantilevers projecting over the ends of a simply supported beam. The distribution of bending moment in the two cantilevers projecting over the ends of a simply supported beam is exactly the same as for a cantilever built into a wall. If the beam carries no loads between its supports, there is nothing to change the maximum cantilever bending moment, which remains constant between the supports of the beam.

(Fixed-ended beams are called *built-in beams* or *encastré* beams in British books.) *Continuous beams* have one additional vertical reaction for each additional span. In both cases the solution is obtained from the geometry of the deformed beams, which supplies the additional equations needed (Figs. 11.4.1 and 11.4.2).

Both problems were already solved in the first half of the 19th Century, and tables of bending moments for standard loading conditions are readily available. The most important results are given in Tables 11.1 and 11.2.

The loads covered include uniformly distributed loading (by far the most common case in practice), single concentrated loads, which are needed where load concentrations occur (see Section 9.3). The two equally spaced concentrated loads (third-point loading) are needed for systems which employ secondary beams (Fig. 11.4.3).

Table 11.1 gives in addition bending moments for triangularly distributed loading; these are used for two-way slabs (Fig. 11.4.4) and for lintels supporting brick or blocks over an opening (Fig. 11.4.5).

Table 11.2 gives bending moments for continuous beams up to 4 spans. The maximum bending moments do not vary greatly as the number of continuous spans increases.

While the tables make a sharp distinction between simply supported and fixed-ended beams, and between beams that are continuous and those that are not, this is sometimes blurred in practice. However, it is generally possible to choose one or the other as appropriate. Most connections in steel and timber can be classified either as rigid or flexible. Site-cast concrete may be assumed to have rigid connections, while precast concrete is generally simply

154 HANDBOOK OF ARCHITECTURAL TECHNOLOGY

(a) Load Diagrams

(b) Bending Moment Diagrams

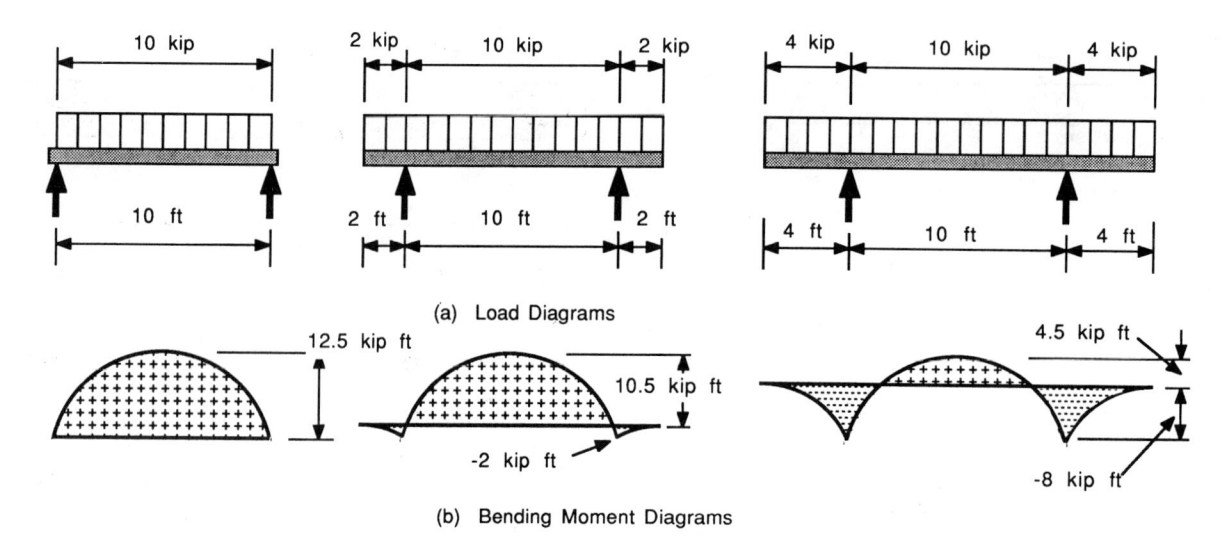

Fig. 11.3.7. Bending moments in simply supported beams with cantilever overhangs. Between the supports, the positive bending moment due to the load acting between the supports is reduced by the maximum negative bending moment due to the load acting on the cantilevers (see Fig. 11.3.6). As the cantilevers get longer, the maximum negative bending moment becomes larger than the maximum positive bending moment, and it then determines the size of the beam. The positive equals the negative bending moment when the ratio of the cantilever span to the span between the supports is 0.354 (which is $1/\sqrt{8}$).

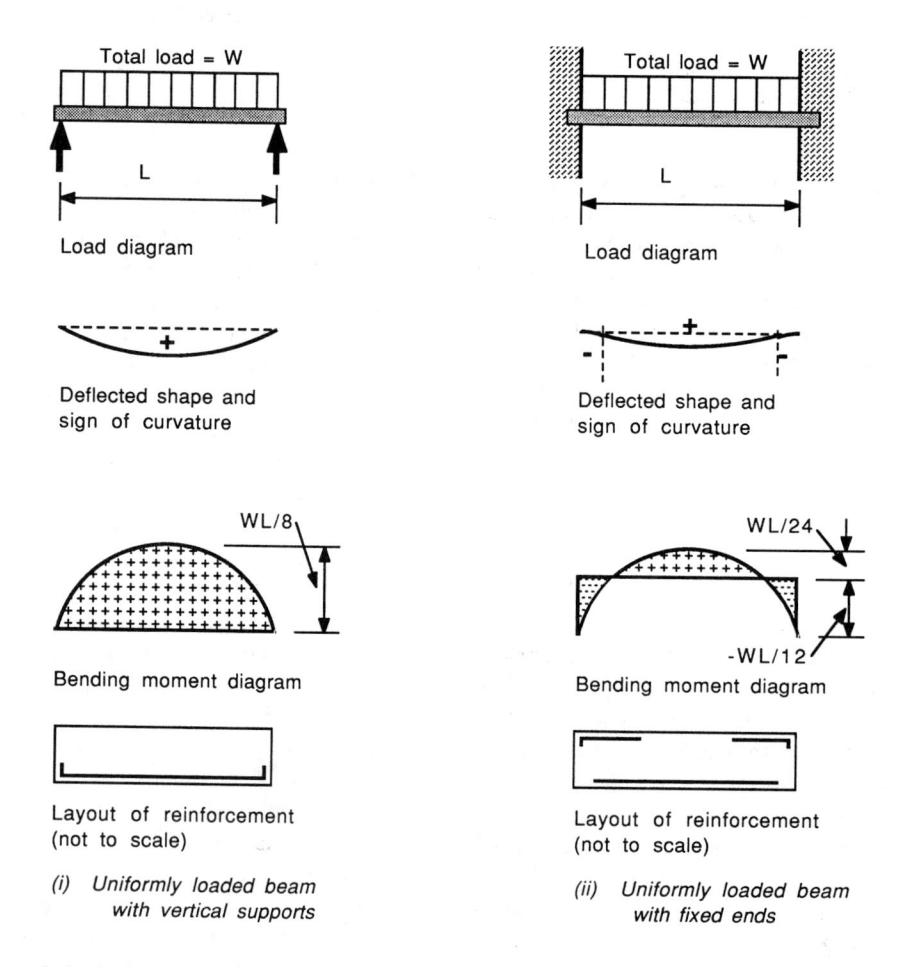

(i) Uniformly loaded beam with vertical supports

(ii) Uniformly loaded beam with fixed ends

Fig. 11.4.1. Bending moments in fixed-ended beams. Fixed-ended beams are rigidly restrained at the ends, in the same way as cantilevers (Fig. 11.3.3). At each end of the beam there is a vertical reaction and a moment reaction, and thus the beam has two more reactions than can be determined with the equations of statical equilibrium, Eq. (11.1).

The solution is obtained from the geometry of the beam. If the ends are rigidly restrained (ii), then the slope at both ends of the beam must be zero. The bending moment diagram is therefore the same as for a beam with two cantilever overhangs (Fig. 11.3.7), with overhangs just sufficient to produce zero slope over the supports. *Caption continued at bottom of p. 155.*

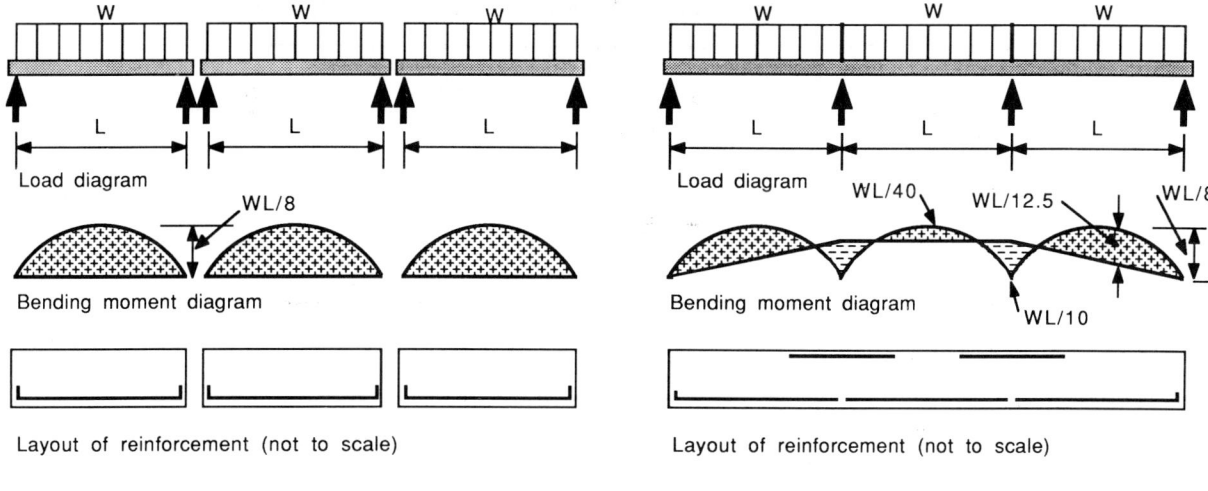

Fig. 11.4.2. Bending moments in continuous beams. If a number of beams are firmly joined together to form a continuous beam, or if the same beam extends in one piece over several spans, we have a statically indeterminate problem, because each intermediate support of the beam is a statically indeterminate reaction; we can only determine two vertical supports for a beam with the equations of statical equilibrium. However, we can make use of the fact that the curvature of the beam is also continuous over the supports. Thus the right-hand end of the left-hand span is also the left-hand end of the middle span, and the slope is the same (except that one points up and the other down). This gives us the additional equations needed to solve the problem.

As for the fixed-ended beam, the maximum bending moment is reduced, but the continuous beam is subject to both positive and negative bending moments. In a reinforced concrete beam or slab, reinforcement must be provided both near the top and near the bottom.

supported. Departures from these rules are usually clearly stated.

A site-cast concrete slab that is supported by much larger beams is best assumed as fixed-ended, because the relative rigidity of its supports; a site-cast concrete beam supported on relatively flexible columns should be treated as continuous. However, most final designs now treat the entire structure as a frame (see Section 11.7) instead of calculating the beams as separate structural members.

11.5. TRUSSES

The simplest *structural system* which can be assembled from *structural members* is a triangular frame with flexible joints (Fig. 11.5.1a).

A perfectly flexible joint is commonly called a *pin joint*, because pins were frequently used to make flexible joints in the early iron structures of the 19th Century; they were pushed through holes left in iron castings or through loops forged at the ends of wrought iron bars.

If we want to make the structure of Fig. 11.5.1a bigger, we must add two structural members for each additional structural joint (Fig. 11.5.1b). If the joints are pin joints, there can be no bending in any of the structural members, which are either in tension or in compression. The structure is statically determinate, and there are several simple methods for designing it, which are given in textbooks on the theory of structures (for example, Ref. 11.1, p. 81).

For a preliminary design, however, we can obtain a quicker approximate solution by treating the truss as if it was a very deep beam into which large holes had been cut; they are mainly in the part of the beam where the bending stresses are low, so that we make good use of the structural material that way. Thus we have two ways of looking at trusses: (1) as assemblies of tension and compression members (see Section 11.2) with pin joints, or (2) as deep beams, in which the horizontal members on top are in

---

From this consideration the bending moments at the supports can be determined as $-WL/12$ (please refer to a textbook on the theory of structures, for example Ref. 11.1, p. 234).

The sum of the maximum positive and negative bending moments remains $WL/8$, as for a simply supported beam. Thus the maximum positive bending moment in a fixed-ended beam carrying a uniformly distributed load is $WL/24$. The maximum bending moment that determines the size of the beam is $-WL/12$.

The fixed-ended beam has a maximum bending moment that is 33 percent less than that for a simply supported beam. However, it has both positive and negative bending moments. In a reinforced concrete beam or slab, reinforcement must be provided both near the top and near the bottom.

Table 11.1. Maximum Bending Moments for Single-Span Beams.

	Loading Diagram Cantilevers	Maximum Bending Moment Is*	Occurs at
1	Point load W at free end, length L	$-WL$	Support
2	Point load W at distance L from support	$-WL$	Support
3	Total Load W uniformly distributed over length L	$-\tfrac{1}{2}WL$	Support
4	Total Load W** uniformly distributed over length L	$-\tfrac{1}{3}WL$	Support
5	Total Load W uniformly distributed over partial length L	$-\tfrac{1}{2}WL$	Support

	Loading Diagram Simply Supported Beams	Maximum Bending Moment Is*	Occurs at
6	Point load W at mid-span, $\tfrac{1}{2}L$ each side, total span L	$+\tfrac{1}{4}WL$	Mid-span
7	Point load W at distances a and b from supports, span L	$+\dfrac{ab}{L}W$	Under the Load
8	Two point loads W at third points, $\tfrac{1}{3}L$ spacing, span L	$+\tfrac{1}{3}WL$	Mid-span and Under the Load

Table 11.1 (*Continued*)

	Loading Diagram Simply Supported Beams	Maximum Bending Moment Is*	Occurs at
9	Total Load W, span L (uniform)	$+\frac{1}{8}WL$	Mid-span
10	Total Load W**, span L (triangular)	$+\frac{1}{6}WL$	Mid-span

	Loading Diagram Built-in Beams	Maximum Bending Moment Is*	Occurs at
11	W at mid-span, $\frac{1}{2}L$ each side, span L	$-\frac{1}{8}WL$ $+\frac{1}{8}WL$	Supports Mid-span
12	$\frac{1}{2}W$ and $\frac{1}{2}W$ at third points, $\frac{1}{3}L$ spacing, span L	$-\frac{1}{9}WL$	Supports
13	Total Load W, span L (uniform)	$-\frac{1}{12}WL$	Supports
14	Total Load W**, span L (triangular)	$-\frac{1}{10}WL$	Supports

*A *positive bending moment* produces tensile stresses near the bottom of a beam or slab. A *negative bending moment* produces tensile stresses near the top of a beam or slab.
**The total load W varies uniformly as shown.

158 HANDBOOK OF ARCHITECTURAL TECHNOLOGY

Table 11.2. Maximum Bending Moments for Continuous Beams.

	Loading Diagram	Maximum Bending Moment Is*	Occurs at
1	Load W at Center Point of each Span of Length L	− 0.188 W L	Interior Support
2		− 0.150 W L	Interior Supports
3		− 0.161 W L	First Interior Supports
4	Loads W at Third Points of Each Span. Total Load W per Span of Length L	− 0.167 W L	Interior Support
5		− 0.134 W L	Interior Supports
6		− 0.143 W L	First Interior Supports
7	Total Load W Uniformly Distributed Over Each Span of Length L	− 0.125 W L	Interior Support

Table 11.2 (*Continued*)

	Loading Diagram	Maximum Bending Moment Is*	Occurs at
8	Total Load W Uniformly Distributed Over Each Span of Length L	−0.100 W L	Interior Supports
9		−0.107 W L	First Interior Supports

*A *positive bending moment* produces tensile stresses near the bottom of a beam or slab. A *negative bending moment* produces tensile stresses near the top of a beam or slab.

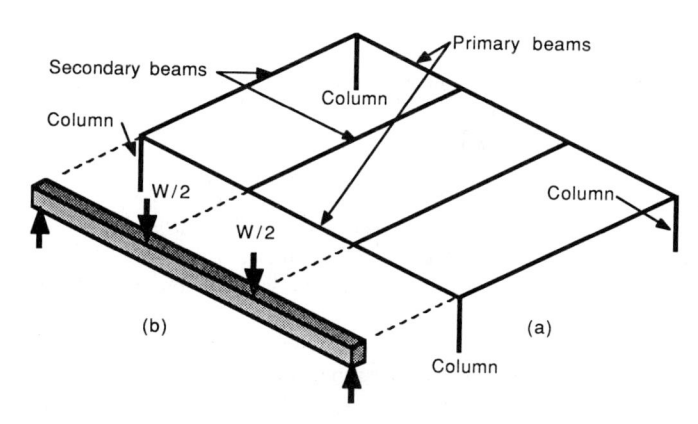

Fig. 11.4.3. Third-point loading. The slab is supported by secondary beams (joists). These are in turn supported by primary beams (girders), which transfer their load to the columns (a). It is generally convenient to divide the panel into three equal divisions. Two of the secondary beams transmit their load directly to the columns. The other two transmit it to the columns via the primary beam, which thus carries two loads $\tfrac{1}{2}W$ at third points (b).

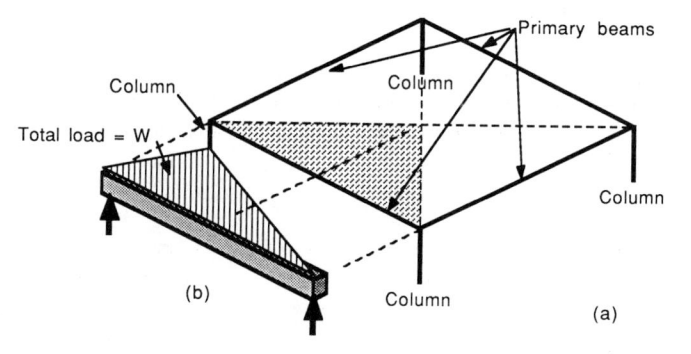

Fig. 11.4.4. Triangular load distribution produced by the reactions of a two-way slab. The load transmitted by the concrete slab is shared by the four primary beams which support it. It is generally assumed that the load is distributed in accordance with the diagonals shown dotted in (a). Each beam then carries a triangularly distributed load as shown at (b).

compression, and the horizontal members on the bottom are in tension; together these form a resistance moment which resists the bending moment due to the loads (Fig. 11.5.1c). The internal structural members resist the shear force at that section.

There are three principal types of trusses with parallel chords. They differ in the arrangement of the internal structural members; these provide the lever arm that holds the compression and tension members apart, and they also resist the shear force (Fig. 11.5.2).

Most sloping roofs are supported by trusses. The principal types are illustrated in Fig. 11.5.3a–d, and a simple method for preliminary design is shown in 11.5.3e.

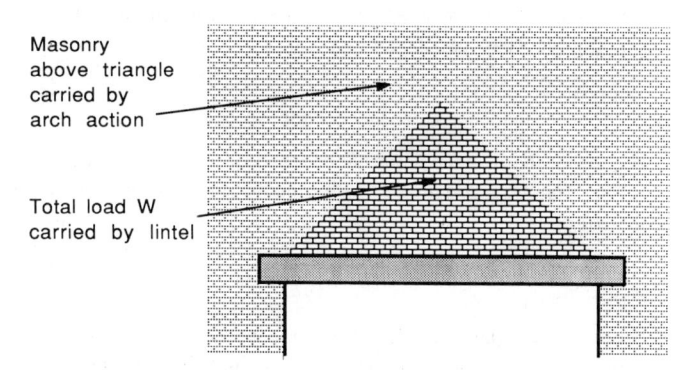

Fig. 11.4.5. Triangular load distribution produced by masonry. If an opening is cut into a wall of stone, brick, or concrete blocks, it is necessary to support some of the masonry units with a lintel (a short beam) or an arch. This needs to carry only the triangular portion above the opening; the remainder is carried by the arch action of the masonry.

160 HANDBOOK OF ARCHITECTURAL TECHNOLOGY

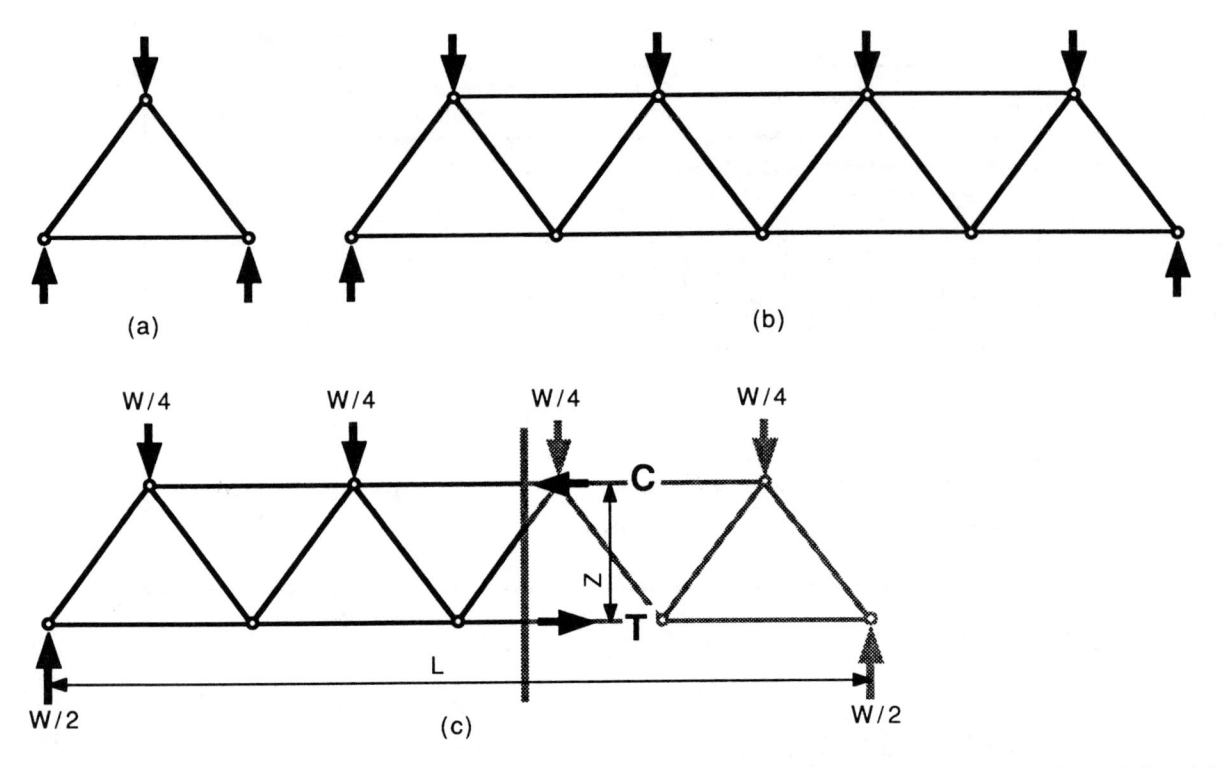

Fig. 11.5.1. The concept of triangulated trusses. (a) The simplest assembly of structural members consists of three members joined by *pin joints* (joints that in theory are perfectly flexible, and approach that ideal in practice).

(b) Two additional members are needed for each additional joint to produce a structure, so that

$$n = 2j - 3$$

where *n* is the number of members in the truss and *j* is the number of joints. The result is a triangulated truss, which is a *statically determinate structure*. If fewer members are used, we obtain a *mechanism*, which can be deformed by quite small loads. If more members are used, we obtain a *statically indeterminate truss*.

Trusses with parallel tension and compression members (or *chords*) can be used for flat roofs or for supporting long-spanning floor structures (Fig. 11.5.2). Trusses with sloping compression members (or *rafters*) are used for sloping roofs (Fig. 11.5.3). These are the most common types; but other configurations can be used.

(c) For a *preliminary design* the sizes of the most important structural members can be obtained quickly by treating the truss as a simply supported beam into which holes have been cut. The bending moment due to a uniformly distributed load *W* over a span *L* is

$$M = WL/8$$

at midspan. This is resisted by the forces in the compression and tension members at midspan; the contribution of the inclined members is negligible. This resistance moment is

$$M = Cz = Tz$$

where *z* is the distance from the centroid of the compression chord to the centroid of the tension chord.

This may be made clearer with a numerical example. We want to carry a load of 50 kips over a span of 50 ft = 600 in. The bending moment is

$$M = \tfrac{1}{8} \times 50 \times 600 = 3750 \text{ kip in.}$$

Let us try a pair of 3 in. × 3 in. $\tfrac{5}{16}$ in. steel angles for the compression flange (which will be larger than the tension flange). Each angle has a cross-sectional area of 1.78 in.^{2}. We must make a guess at the slenderness ratio, and look up the maximum permissible compressive stress: we find this is 16 ksi. Therefore we require

$$z = 3750/16 \times 2 \times 1.78 = 65.84 \text{ in.}$$

The overall depth of the girder must be slightly greater, say 5 ft 8 in.

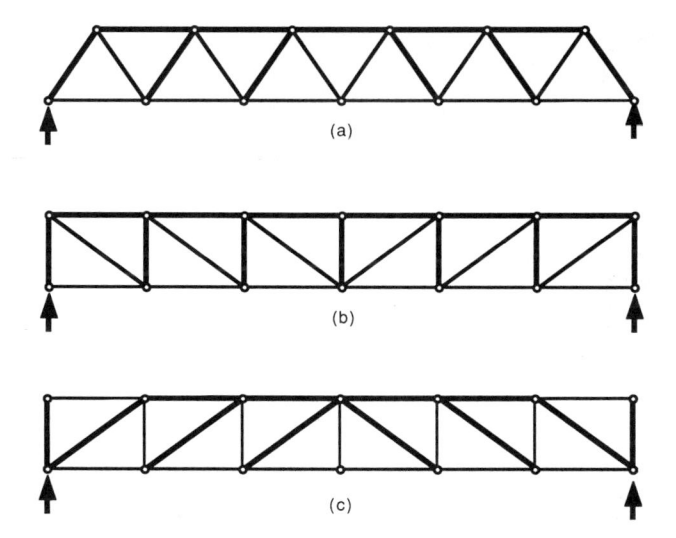

Fig. 11.5.2. Parallel-chord trusses. (a) Warren truss, in which all internal members are inclined; half are in tension and half are in compression.

(b) and (c) Pratt trusses, in which half the internal members are vertical, and half are inclined. Truss (b) is the more efficient; the vertical members are in compression, and since they are shorter, they have a lower slenderness ratio and a higher permissible compressive stress. In truss (c) the vertical members are in tension, and the inclined members in compression.

Warren was a British and Pratt an American engineer; both invented their trusses in mid-19th Century.

11.6. PORTAL FRAMES AND ARCHES

Triangulated structures are easy to design, and they are economical in material. However, story-high inclined members interfere with the movement of people and goods, and they are therefore used mainly as roof structures, or as structures built into walls or partitions.

We can avoid the use of triangulation by using *rigid joints* instead of the pin joints employed in Section 11.5. Structural systems in which the vertical members (or columns) are connected to the horizontal members (or beams) with rigid joints (Fig. 11.6.1a) are called *portal frames*.

Portal frames can be used singly (Fig. 11.6.1) or as a series of bays joined together, and sharing vertical members (Fig. 11.6.2). Portal frames can also be stacked vertically. These are considered in Section 11.7.

A portal frame must have rigid connections between the beam on top and the vertical members, otherwise we need an inclined member (which we wish to avoid). If it also has rigid joints at the base (Fig. 11.6.3a) we have a structure with three *redundant reactions*, that is, it is statically indeterminate. We can, however, make it statically determinate by inserting three pin joints. Thus if we have an actual portal frame with rigid joints, and we wish to know its approximate dimensions for a preliminary design, we can find them easily by placing three *imaginary* pin joints

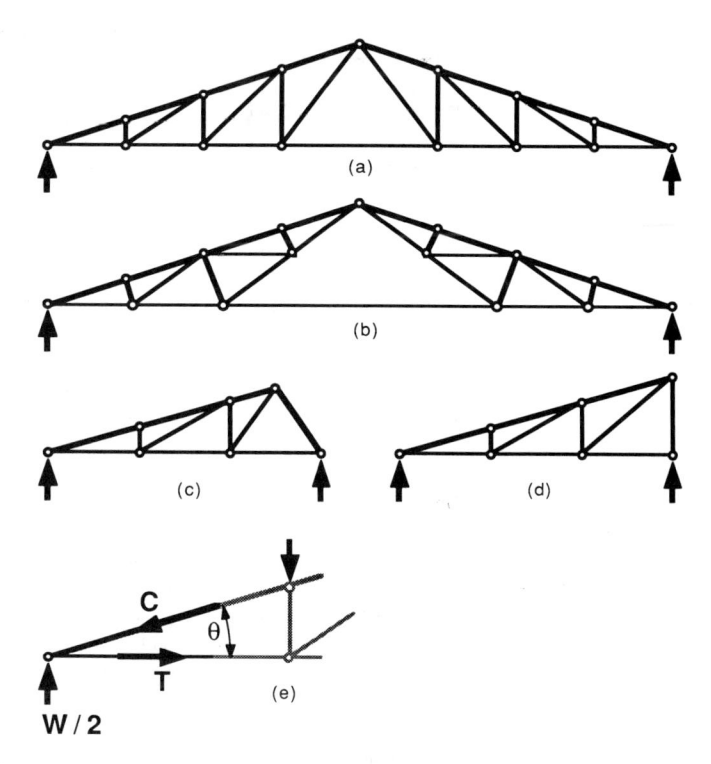

Fig. 11.5.3. Roof trusses. The two principal types of roof truss are: (a) the Pratt roof truss, which is triangulated like a parallel-chord Pratt truss, with shorter vertical members in compression and the longer inclined members in tension; and (b) the trussed-rafter type of roof truss, which for longer spans can be made as two trussed rafters, which are then joined on the site with the long tie in the center panel.

North-light roof trusses are used to admit daylight through high-light windows facing north, without admitting direct sunlight, which might cause overheating of the building. Type (c) is used in the temperate zone, and type (d) in subtropics. In the southern hemisphere these trusses must face south.

The method described in Fig. 11.5.1c cannot be used for trusses with sloping rafters, because the highest tensile and compressive forces occur at the support, unless the slope of the rafters is very shallow. However, the sizes of the rafter and the bottom tie can be obtained by resolving forces at the support, as shown at (e).

If the roof truss is symmetrical, as shown at (a) or (b), half the load, $\frac{1}{2}W$, is carried by each support. This must be balanced by the compressive force in the rafter, C, and the tensile force in the bottom tie, T. Resolving vertically:

$$\tfrac{1}{2}W = C \sin \theta$$

so that

$$C = \tfrac{1}{2}W / \sin \theta$$

Resolving horizontally:

$$T = C \cos \theta$$

so that

$$T = \tfrac{1}{2}W \cot \theta$$

We thus obtain the forces C and T, and from them the sizes needed for the rafter and the bottom ties can be calculated.

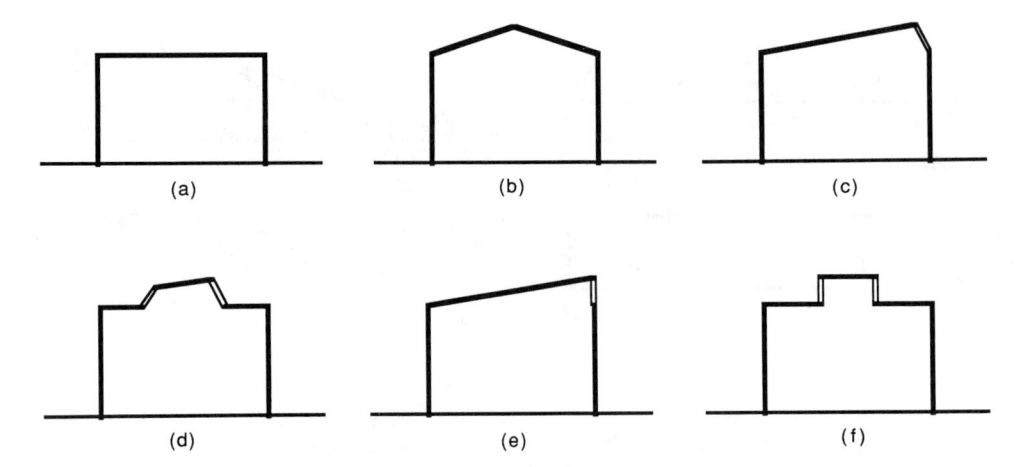

Fig. 11.6.1. Single-bay portal frames. (a) Standard portal frame in which the beam supporting the story above (or a flat roof) is connected to the columns with *rigid joints*.

(b) Portal frame forming sloping roof. Note that this roof structure avoids the clutter of inclined members of the triangulated roof trusses in Fig. 11.5.3, and also gives a greater clear height for the movement of manufactures or stores within the building.

(c) and (e) Portal frame with north-light roof (see also Fig. 11.5.3c).

(d) and (f) Portal frame with monitor. It contains high-light windows, which admit daylight near the center of the building.

(c) and (d) are suitable for the temperate zone, (e) and (f) for the subtropics. In the southern hemisphere the windows must face south.

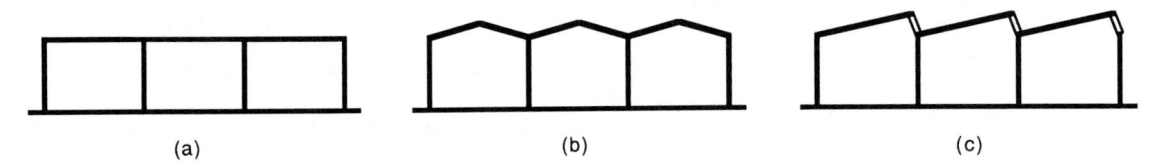

Fig. 11.6.2. Multi-bay portal frames. Long spans should be used only where they are needed, since bending moments go up as the square of the span, and the cost rises accordingly. Multi-bay portal frames, which subdivide the floor area to be covered, can utilize the columns of adjacent spans.

(a) Standard portal frames.
(b) Portal frames for sloping roofs.
(c) Portal frames for north-light roofs.

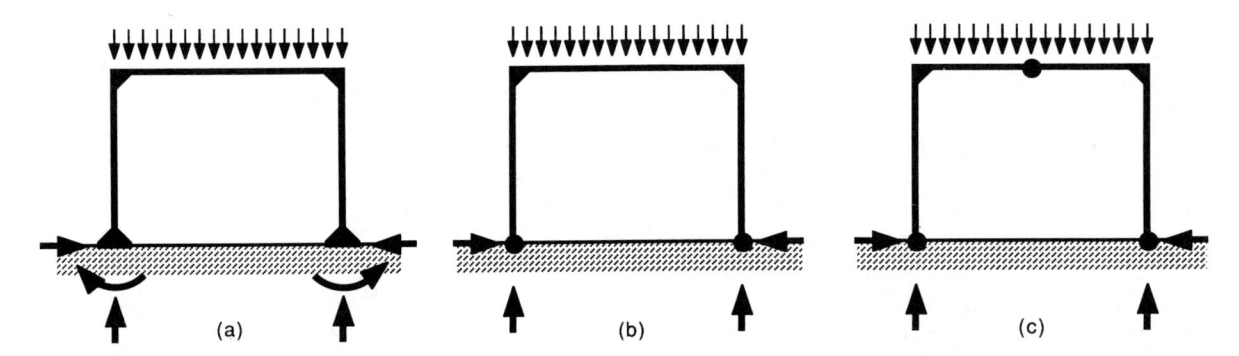

Fig. 11.6.3. The three-pin portal frame. (a) A portal frame with four rigid joints (which is the simplest type to use in practice), has at its base two vertical reactions, two horizontal reactions, and two moment reactions. Eq. (11.1) enables us to determine two of these from $\Sigma M = 0$ and $\Sigma V = 0$. $\Sigma H = 0$ merely tells us that the two horizontal reactions are equal, which is obvious. We therefore have three *redundant reactions*, that is, three more reactions than we can determine by statics.

(b) If we insert pin-joints at the base, we still have one redundant reaction, and the portal is still statically indeterminate.

(c) If, however, we insert a third pin-joint in the beam, say, at its center, the frame becomes statically determinate, because now have an additional point where the bending moment is by definition zero; this gives us the extra equation that we need.

This *three-pin portal* is important not so much for its practical use, although it is useful particularly for precast concrete and laminated-timber portals, but because the size of its structural members can be calculated very easily for a *preliminary design*. A rigid portal with the same dimensions, carrying the same load, will need slightly less structural material.

into it (Fig. 11.6.4). The actual portal frame without pin joints will require slightly less material.

This method can be applied to other types of portal frame (Fig. 11.6.5), both single-bay and multi-bay (see Figs. 11.6.1 and 2).

The maximum bending moment for the portal frame with the sloping roof is less than that for the flat-topped portal. This is due to the fact that the former resembles more closely the shape of the parabolic bending moment diagram for the uniformly distributed load.

For the same reason, arches require less structural material than beams or portals, and they have therefore been used since antiquity for long spans, particularly when the structural material is stone, brick, or concrete, which has poor tensile strength, and therefore poor bending resistance (see Chapter 3). They are still used today for long spans.

The bending moment diagram for a three-pinned semicircular arch is derived in Fig. 11.6.6. The more commonly used rigid arch has an even lower maximum bending moment.

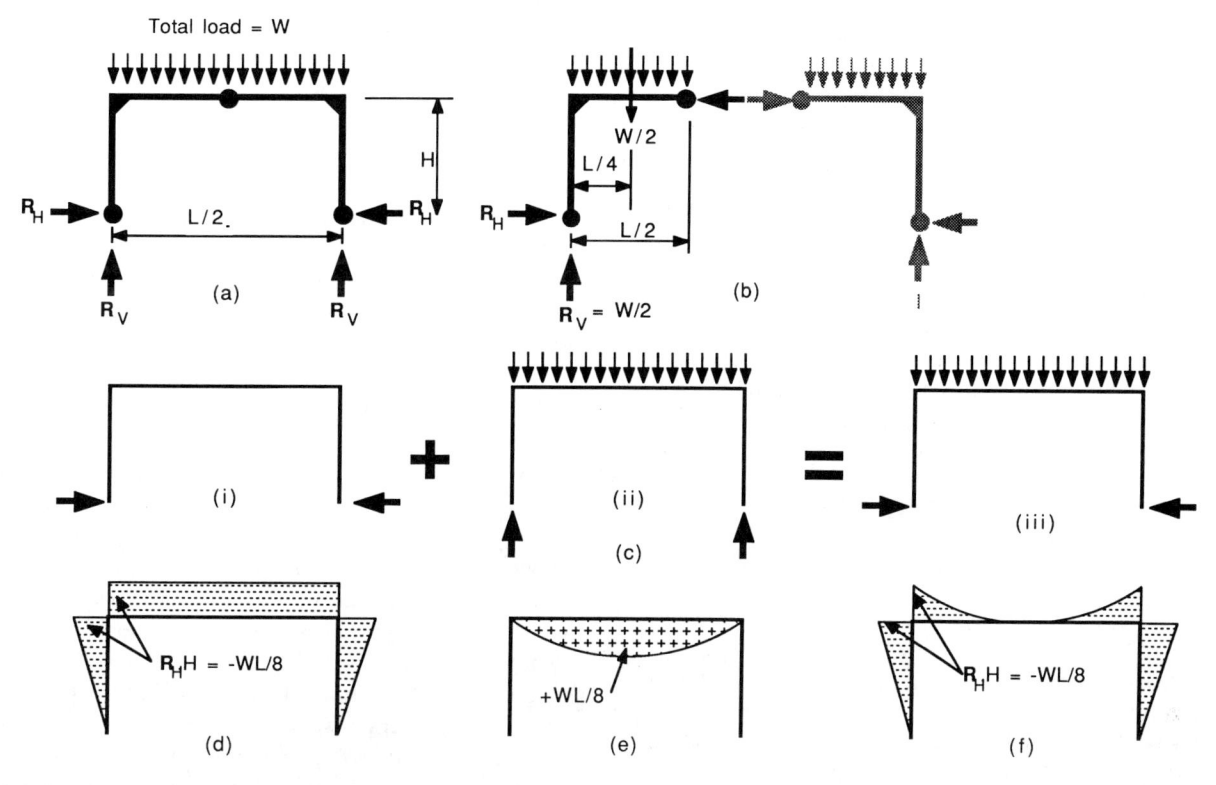

Fig. 11.6.4. Maximum bending moment in a rectangular portal frame. (a) The portal frame carries a uniformly distributed load W on its beam. It has three pin-joints.

(b) The vertical reactions are by symmetry $\frac{1}{2}W$ each. To determine the horizontal reactions, we separate the two halves of the portal frame at the top pin, and take moments about that pin:

$$R_H H = \tfrac{1}{2}W(\tfrac{1}{2}L - \tfrac{1}{4}L)$$

so that

$$R_H = WL/8H$$

(c) The bending moment distribution becomes clearer if we separate the forces acting on the portal frame into two parts: (i) the horizontal reactions, and (ii) the vertical loads and the vertical reactions, which are exactly the same as for a simply supported beam (Fig. 11.3.5).

(d) The bending moment due to the horizontal reaction increases uniformly until it reaches its maximum at the rigid joint. Nothing happens thereafter to change that bending moment until we reach the other rigid joint, when it decreases uniformly to zero. The maximum bending moment is $-H \times WL/8H = -WL/8$.

(e) The bending moment diagram for the vertical loads is exactly the same as for a simply supported beam carrying a uniformly distributed load.

(f) If these two bending moment diagrams are added, we obtain the bending moment diagram for the portal frame. The maximum bending moment, which occurs at the rigid joint, is $M = -WL/8$. This reduces to zero at the pin-joints, as it must, because no bending moments can exist at a pin-joint.

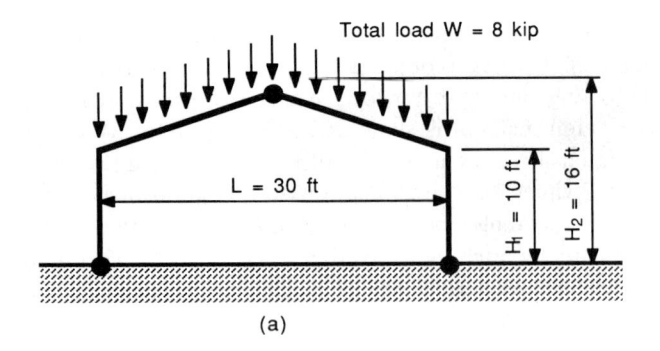

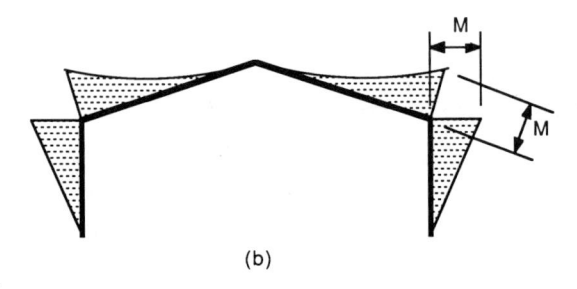

Fig. 11.6.5. Maximum bending moment in a portal frame with a sloping roof. (a) The moment distribution for a portal frame with a sloping roof is slightly more favorable, because the maximum bending moment occurs nearer to the ground.

(b) As in Fig. 11.6.4b, the horizontal reaction is obtained by taking moment about the top pin:

$$R_H = WL/8H_2$$

The maximum bending moment occurs at the rigid joint:

$$M = -R_H \times H_1 = -WLH_1/H_2$$

This may be made clearer with the aid of an example. Let us assume that the portal frame carries a total uniformly distributed vertical load of 8 kip, and that the dimensions of the frame are as shown in (a). The horizontal reaction is

$$R_H = 8 \times 30/8 \times 16 = 1.875 \text{ kip}$$

The bending moment due to that horizontal reaction is

$$M = -1.875 \times 10 = -18.75 \text{ kip ft} = -225 \text{ kip in.}$$

If the maximum permissible stress for steel in bending is 24 ksi, we need a steel section with a section modulus of

$$S = 225/24 = 9.38 \text{ in.}^3$$

This allows only for the bending stresses induced by the loads in the columns of the portal frame. Superimposed on that are compressive stresses due to the column load. These make, however, little difference to the result, and they can be neglected in a preliminary design.

Evidently the bending moment can be entirely eliminated if the shape of the arch is the same as that of the bending moment diagram due to the load it carries. For a load uniformly distributed in plan this requires a parabolic arch. If the load is uniformly distributed along the line of the arch, we need a catenary-shaped arch. The mathematical equation of the catenary is

$$y = a \cosh(x/a) \qquad (11.9)$$

where a is a constant (see note on hyperbolic functions in Section 1.1). However, its shape is quite close to that of a parabola.

Arches with shapes similar to catenaries have been used since antiquity, presumably based on observations of failures. The Gothic arch is an approximation to the shape of the catenary, made with circular arcs. In the early 18th Century it was proved (Ref. 11.3 p. 182) that an arch shaped as a catenary is indeed entirely in compression under its own weight, and thus the most economical shape of the masonry arch. However, the cost of fabricating or forming a catenary shape over that of a circular arch or dome may be more than the cost of the material saved.

The introduction of steel and reinforced concrete has made the design of long-span structures much easier, and thus reduced the significance of curved structures in architecture.

11.7. MULTISTORY FRAMES

If we stack several portal frames of the type shown in Fig. 11.6.1a or 11.6.2a on top of one another, we have a multistory frame. This is inherently statically indeterminate, because is has a large number of rigid or semi-rigid joints. As a result a large number of simultaneous equations have to be solved. This was very laborious until suitable computer programs were developed.

A number of solutions were devised in the late 19th and early 20th Centuries, which rendered the frame statically determinate by inserting imaginary pin-joints at locations in the frame where the bending moment is approximately zero, so that the insertion of a pin-joint makes little difference to its *theoretical* behavior. These are still useful today for visualizing the behavior of the frame as a structural system.

Small steel frames (Fig. 11.7.1) and small reinforced concrete frames (Fig. 11.7.2) carrying only vertical loads can be rendered statically determinate by inserting imaginary pin joints between the beams and the columns.

A different set of imaginary pin-joints is needed to visualize the behavior of multistory frames under the action of horizontal loads due to wind and earthquakes (see Chapters 9 and 10), because the frames shown in Figs. 11.7.1 and 2 have no resistance whatever to horizontal forces. Fig. 11.7.3 shows that we can insert imaginary pin-joints at the middle of each column and each beam to render the structure statically determinate; we can then draw its bending moment diagram due to the wind loads (Fig. 11.7.4). The bending moments due to the wind loads must now be combined with those due to the vertical loads (Fig. 11.7.5) to obtain the total bending moments.

STRUCTURAL SYSTEMS 165

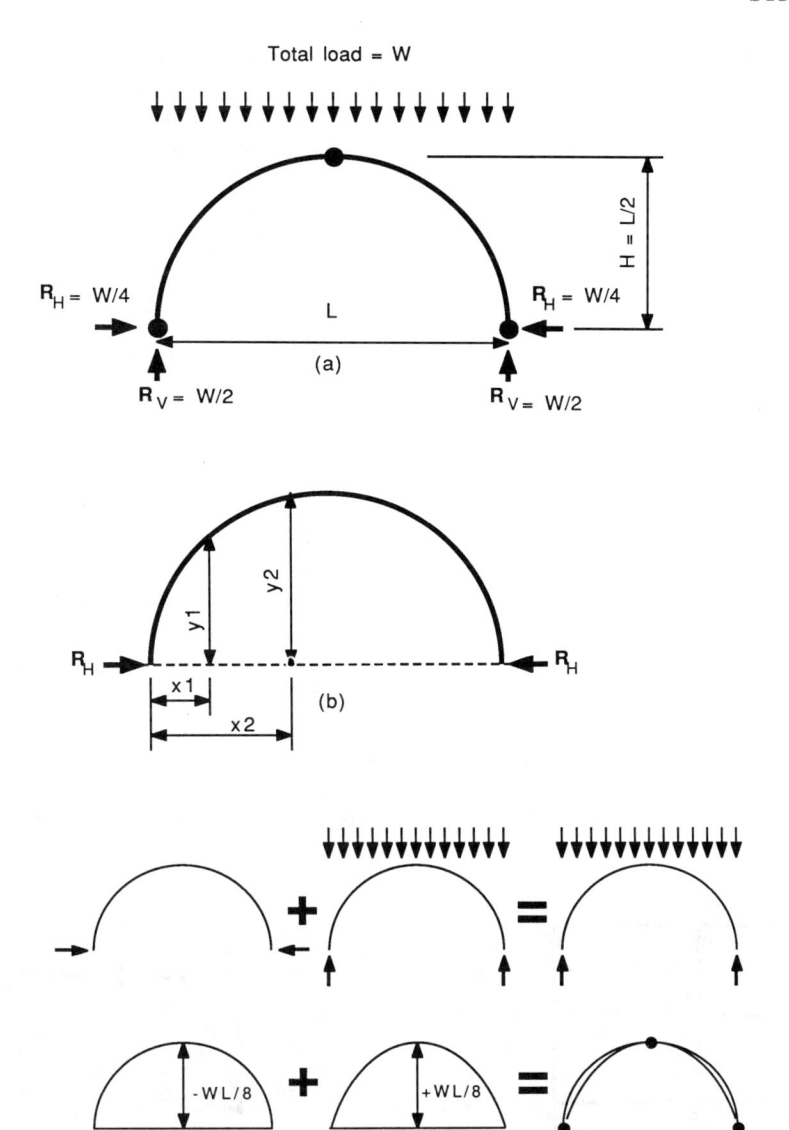

Fig. 11.6.6. The semicircular arch. (a) A semicircular arch comes vertically on its supports, also called its *springings*. We will assume that the arch has three pin-joints, and is thus statically determinate. We can then take moments about the top pin, and obtain, as for the portal frames considered in Figs. 11.6.4 and 11.6.5:

$$R_H \times H = \tfrac{1}{2}W(\tfrac{1}{2}L - \tfrac{1}{4}L)$$

For a semicircular arch the height to the top pin or *crown* is $H = \tfrac{1}{2}L$, so that

$$R_H = WL/8 \times \tfrac{1}{2}L = \tfrac{1}{4}W$$

(b) The bending moment due the horizontal reaction at a distance x_1 along the span is $R_H y_1$, and so on. Consequently the bending moment diagram is a semicircle, like the arch.

(c) The bending moment diagram due to the entire load system is therefore the sum of the negative bending moment due to the horizontal reactions *and* the usual positive bending moment for a uniformly distributed load, which is a parabola. The net bending moment for the three-pinned circular arch is therefore the difference between the semicircle and the parabola. It can be shown (see, for example, Ref. 11.1, p. 144) that the maximum is $-WL/32$.

This is only a quarter of the bending moment for a simply supported beam. In addition the arch is subject to a compressive force, or *thrust*, which has a maximum at the supports, or *springings*, where it equals the vertical reaction, which is $\tfrac{1}{2}W$. However, the size of the arch cross section is mainly determined by the bending moment, even though it is small. When the effect of the thrust is included, the section size is only slightly modified.

The thrust determines the arch size, however, if the bending moment is entirely eliminated by using an arch whose shape is the same as that of the bending moment diagram for the load it carries. In this instance, the arch would have to be parabolic.

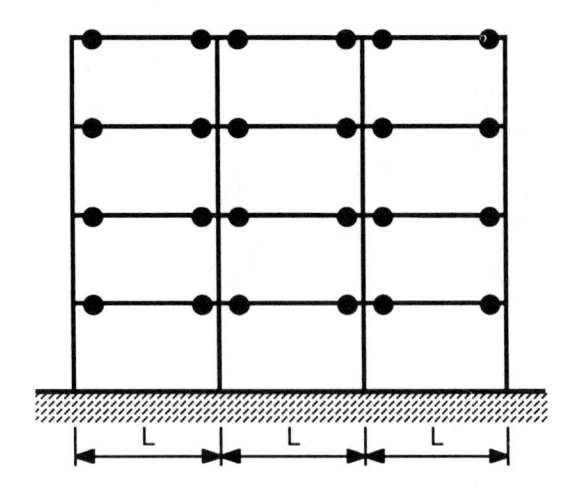

Fig. 11.7.1. Simple steel skeleton frame carrying vertical loads only. If the steel beams are supported on the columns by relatively flexible connections, which is commonly the case in small steel frames, we may treat them as simply supported on the columns. If that assumption is made, the structure becomes statically determinate.

High-rise buildings cost more per unit floor area than low-rise buildings. If the floor loads remain identical, the cost of the floor structure to carry the vertical loads is the same for the 6th floor and the 60th floor. The part of the cost of the columns due to their capacity to carry the vertical loads increases proportionally with the number of stories, as each column has to carry the vertical loads on *all* the floors above. The bending moments due to the wind load, however, increase parabolically with the height of the building, and so does the additional cost of the columns (Fig. 11.7.6) unless we take measures to reduce it.

This can be achieved by taking advantage of the substantial load-bearing capacity of the service core, which is generally surrounded by a reinforced concrete wall for fire protection (Fig. 11.7.7). For very tall buildings it becomes economical to eliminate all interior columns, so that the load-bearing structure consists of a *tube within a tube* formed by the columns and beams on the facade of the building, and the service core (Fig. 11.7.8).

It is frequently desirable to have an open space unencumbered by columns at ground level, either within the building, or as an open space under the building. This can be achieved by using a transfer girder with a depth equal to the height of a full story, or even two stories. The most economical way of doing this is to use a triangulated truss (see Section 11.5). However, if this interferes with the fenestration, it is possible to use a *Vierendeel girder* (Fig. 11.7.9).

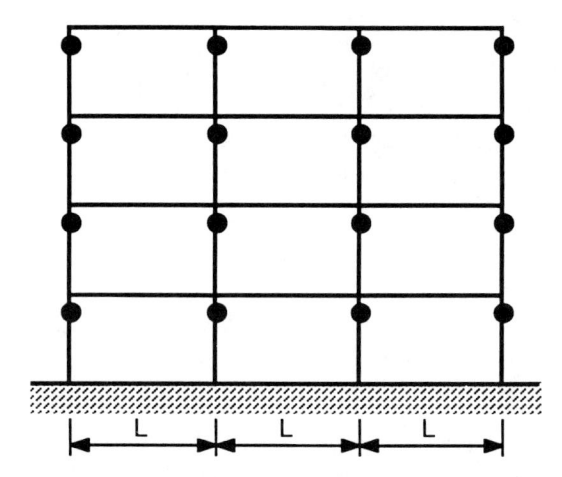

Fig. 11.7.2. Simple reinforced concrete skeleton frame carrying vertical loads only. The floor structure of a site-cast reinforced concrete frame is much stiffer than the columns which support it. This is not merely true of a concrete slab together with its supporting beams, but also of a concrete flat plate or flat slab (without supporting beams). The floor structure is therefore continuous over the supporting columns, which by comparison are sufficiently flexible to permit the necessary rotation at the supports of a continuous beam or slab. Bending moments in continuous beams are easily determined (see Table 11.2).

Although the columns are sufficiently flexible to allow the rotation to occur, bending moments are nevertheless induced in the columns in addition to the vertical loads they carry, and these must be allowed for in the design (Fig. 11.7.5b).

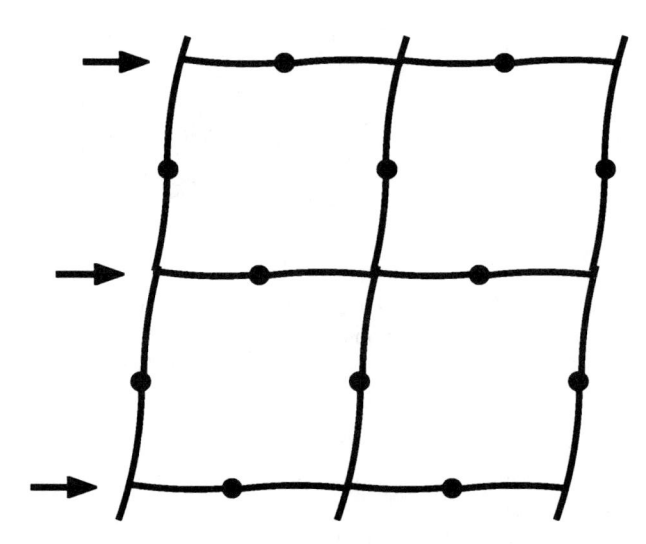

Fig. 11.7.3. Deformation of a rectangular frame under the action of horizontal forces. If a rectangular frame is subjected to horizontal forces only, it deforms as shown in the figure. At the middle of each beam and of each column the curvature changes from convex to concave. This is known as a *point of inflexion* (called a *point of contraflexure* in British textbooks).

It can be shown that at a point of inflexion the bending moment is always zero (this is proved in many textbooks on the theory of structures, for example. Ref. 11.1 p. 242). At a point of zero bending moment we can insert a pin-joint without altering the stresses in the frame.

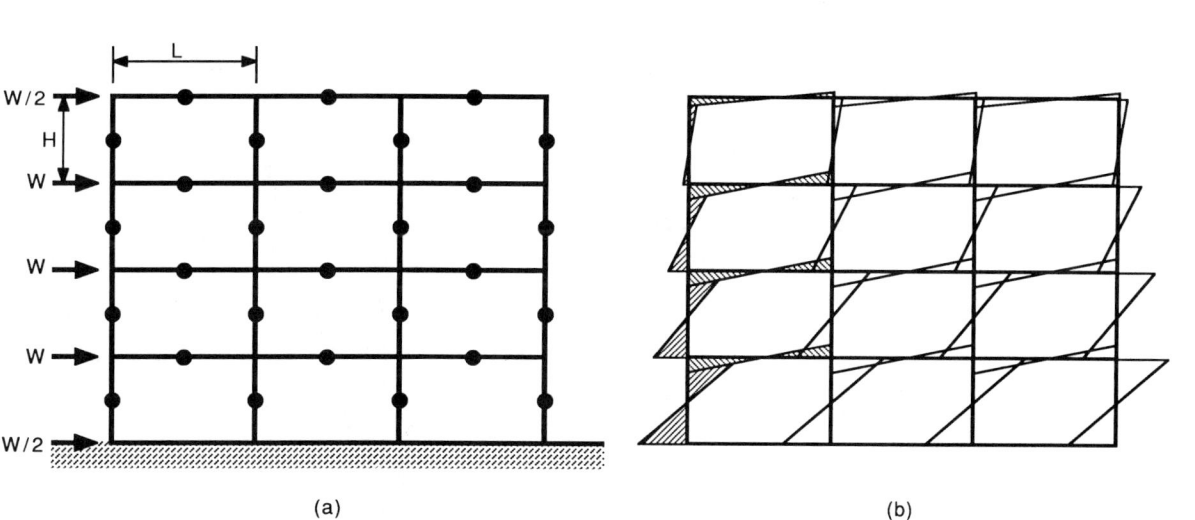

Fig. 11.7.4. Bending moments due to wind loads. As shown in Fig. 11.7.3, the bending moment is approximately zero at the middle of each beam and column for a multistory frame subject to a uniform wind load. We can therefore place imaginary pin-joints at those points, as shown at (a).

The problem is similar to that of the three-pinned portal frame in Fig. 11.6.4. The bending moments due to the horizontal forces increase uniformly from zero at the pin-joints to a maximum at the rigid joint; they are then transmitted around the corner, and decrease uniformly to zero at the pin-joint, as shown at (b).

11.8. CABLE-STAYED BEAMS

In the previous sections we considered the structures that are used in everyday architectural construction. The following sections deal with structural systems for roofs that enable us to use longer spans unobstructed by interior columns. Some of these systems are more interesting or attractive in appearance. Most save structural material, but some do so at a greatly increased cost of construction.

In cable-stayed roof structures cables are used to provide

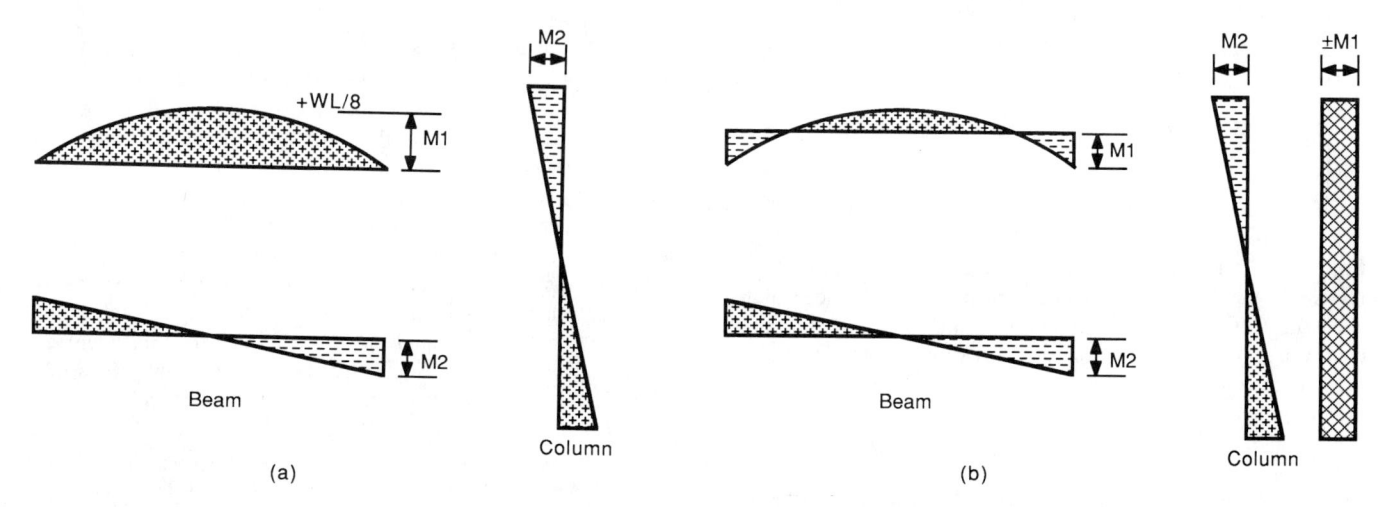

Fig. 11.7.5. Combined bending moments due to vertical and horizontal loads in multistory frames. (a) Assuming that the beams of a steel frame may be regarded as simply supported on the columns (Fig. 11.7.1) for the purpose of considering the vertical loads, the bending moment due to the vertical loads, M_1, is entirely positive. The bending moments due to the horizontal loads, M_2 (Fig. 11.7.4), must be added to that.

(b) Assuming that the beams or slabs of a reinforced concrete frame are continuous over the columns, the bending moment M_1 in the beams due to the vertical loads is negative near the columns, and positive near midspan. The bending moment M_2 due to the horizontal loads must be added to that.

The bending moment in the columns also has two components. The component M_1 due to the vertical loads, transmitted to the columns by the rotation of the floor structure at its supports, may be positive or negative.

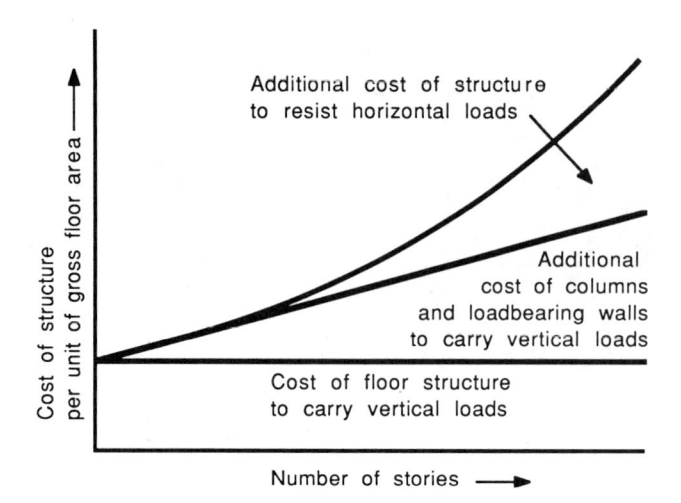

Fig. 11.7.6. The contribution to the cost of the structure of a multistory building made by the vertical loads and the horizontal loads.

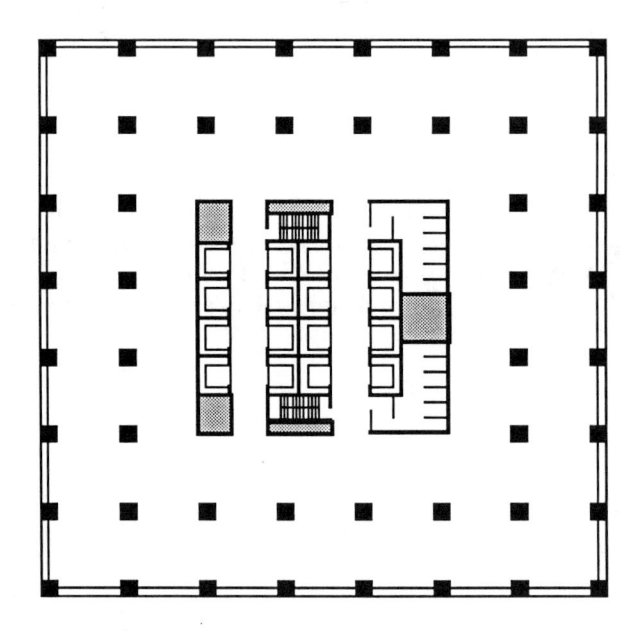

Fig. 11.7.7. The service core. As the height of a building increases, the size of the service core increases, because more elevators (lifts), fire stairs, and ventilating or air conditioning ducts are required. The service core has substantial load-bearing capacity, particularly for resisting horizontal forces, because of the fire protection required.

supports while avoiding the obstruction caused by columns. The upper end of the cable is raised above the level of the roof so that the cable meets the roof structure at an angle. If this angle is too small, the cable is largely ineffective as a support for the roof structure, and it induces too much compression in it. On the other hand, if the supporting struts are too high above the roof, they are unsightly.

Cable stays were originally introduced to increase the

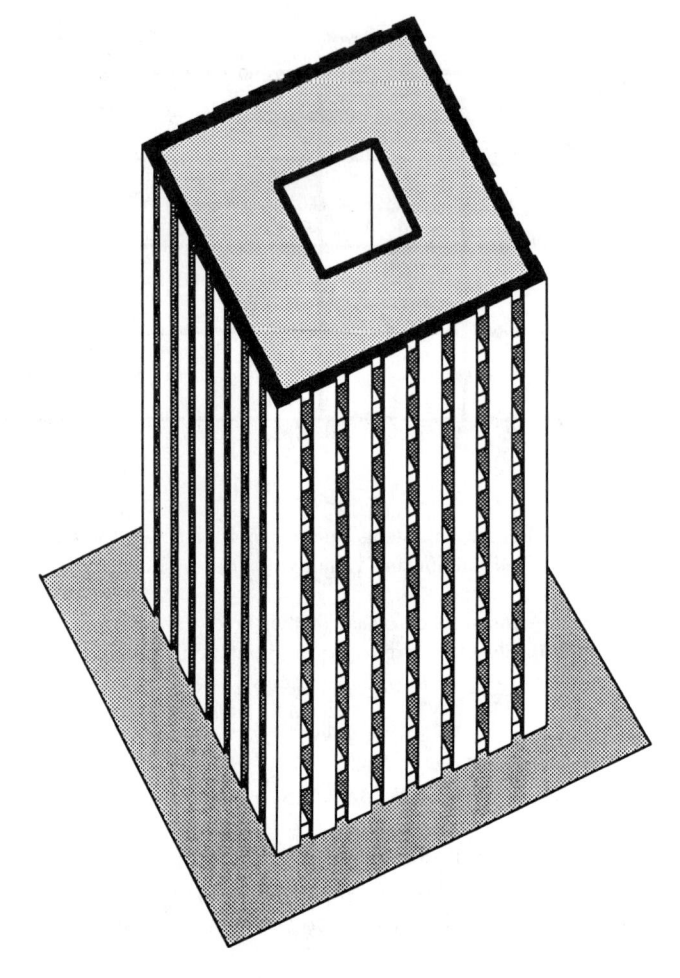

Fig. 11.7.8. The tube concept. External columns can, if need be, project beyond the facade; however, the interior columns occupy useful floor space, particularly on the lower stories where they have to resist large loads. As the height of the building increases, it becomes more and more economical to eliminate the interior columns, and to allow the floor structure to span directly from the service core to the facade. This can be facilitated by using high-strength materials and prestressing (see Section 13.13).

The structure then becomes a tube (the service core) within a tube (the facade). It has been customary to think of vertical members as columns and of horizontal members as beams. However, in a very tall building there are large horizontal as well as large vertical loads, and the vertical and horizontal members of the facade are therefore both columns and beams. It is then appropriate to think of the facade as a tube (with holes in it) which resists both the vertical and the horizontal forces. The service core is also a tube (with only a few holes in it for doors). These two tubes are interconnected at each level by the floor structure, and by the roof structure.

potential span of cantilever roofs (Fig. 11.8.1), but they are now also used to increase the column spacing in single-story flat-roofed or curved structures (Fig. 11.8.2) without resorting to deep trusses or space frames under the roof, or using complex shell structures.

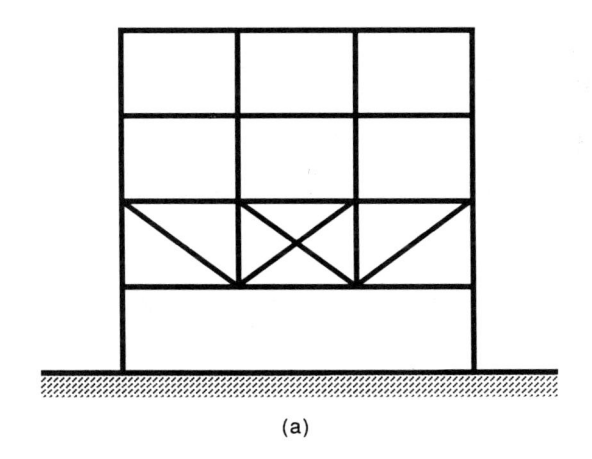

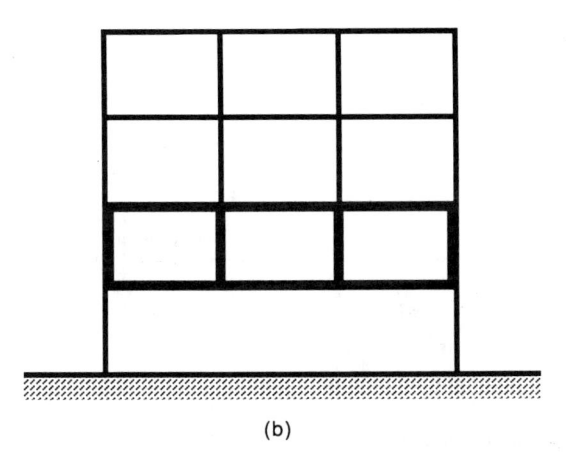

Fig. 11.7.9. Elimination of the columns of a multistory building at ground level. The elimination of the columns at the level where they carry their highest load is evidently not economical from the structural viewpoint; but it is frequently desirable to have an open space at this level. If the building is tall, a very deep transfer girder is needed; the deeper the truss, the less material is required for it (see Fig. 11.5.1). It is generally convenient to make the depth of this girder equal to the height of one story or of two stories.

(a) The most economical solution is a triangulated truss (see Section 11.5). However, if windows are required, it becomes necessary to use a rigid frame (see Section 11.6), called a *Vierendeel girder* (b). In addition to requiring more structural material, this has a greater elastic deflection than a triangulated truss.

Cable stays provide tensile forces as supports at selected points in the roof structure; but they do not counteract the weight of the roof directly as does a suspension structure (see Section 11.11).

11.9. SPACE FRAMES

Parallel-chord trusses (Fig. 11.5.2) are economical for supporting flat roofs with wide column spacing. However, if the trusses become too deep, they need lateral support to prevent buckling sideways, and the roof structure becomes effectively a space frame. It is then more appropriate to use a fully triangulated space frame (Fig. 11.9.1), especially if the column spacing is approximately the same in both directions (Fig. 11.9.1a).

The simplest triangulated space frame is a triangular pyramid; when all its sides are equal, this is called a *tetrahedron*. It has 4 joints and 6 structural members. Whenever we add a joint, we need another 3 structural members. Consequently the number of members needed for a triangulated space frame is

$$n = 3j - 6 \qquad (11.10)$$

where j is the number of joints.

Although space frames are mainly used as structures for flat roofs, they can easily be adapted to any shape. They are an economical solution to free-shaped roof structures or large sculptures, particularly if it is difficult to define their geometry. They have also proved more economical than concrete shells for long-spanning domes and for cylindrical roofs.

11.10. DOMES

We noted in Section 11.6 that bending moments in semicircular arches were small, because the shape of the arch resembled that of the bending diagram due to the imposed loads. This was due to the opposing bending moments set up by the horizontal reactions (see Fig. 11.6.6). The absorption of these horizontal reactions is greatly simplified if the arches are arranged about a vertical axis to form a dome (Fig. 11.10.1).

In a *hemispherical dome* the meridional forces, which constitute the arch action, come vertically on the springings, and they thus have no horizontal component acting outward. The hoop forces in the lower part of the dome are tensile, and these tie the dome together to form a self-contained structure with only vertical reactions. Thus the hemispherical dome is very efficient for long spans.

In practice this theory is correct only if the dome is thin, and if it can expand freely on its supports (the *springings*) under the action of the hoop tension; as neither condition can be met completely, there are bending moments in the lower part of the dome, which in a reinforced concrete dome require thickening of the shell and additional reinforcement.

Hemispherical and other tall domes with large spans are rarely built today, partly because they no longer have a strong symbolic significance in religious architecture, but more particularly because they enclose too much air, which has to be heated or cooled. The hoop forces in *shallow domes* are entirely compressive, so that the entire dome is

170 HANDBOOK OF ARCHITECTURAL TECHNOLOGY

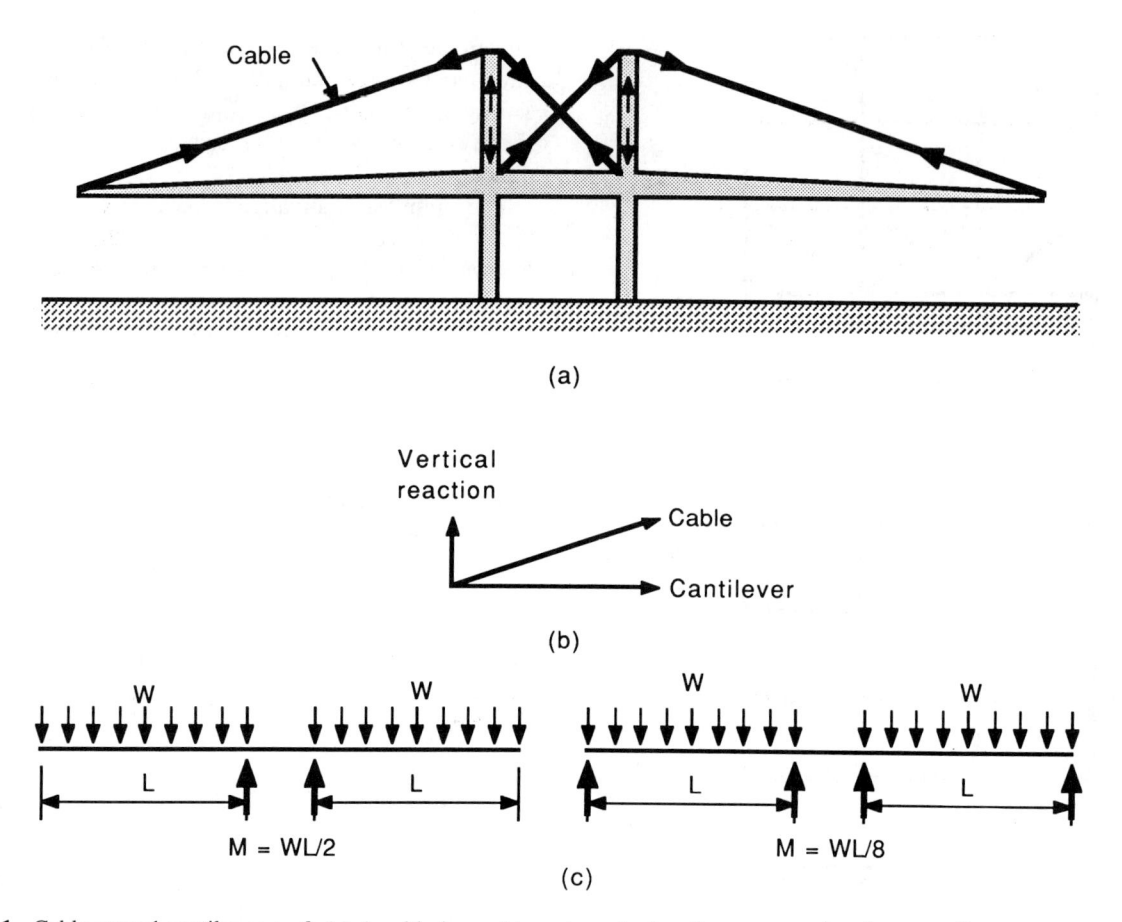

Fig. 11.8.1. Cable-stayed cantilever roof. (a) A cable is used to reduce the bending moment in a long cantilever.

(b) The vertical component of the cable tension provides a vertical support at the free end of the cantilever, but its horizontal component produces compression in the cantilever.

(c) The bending moment is reduced by 75 percent from $WL/2$ to $WL/8$, while leaving the space under the cantilever free from additional columns. The size of the cantilever is therefore greatly reduced, although a small amount of this material is needed to absorb the horizontal (compressive) component of the cable.

On the debit side we have to pay for the cost of the cables, the cost of their installation, and the cost of the supporting struts.

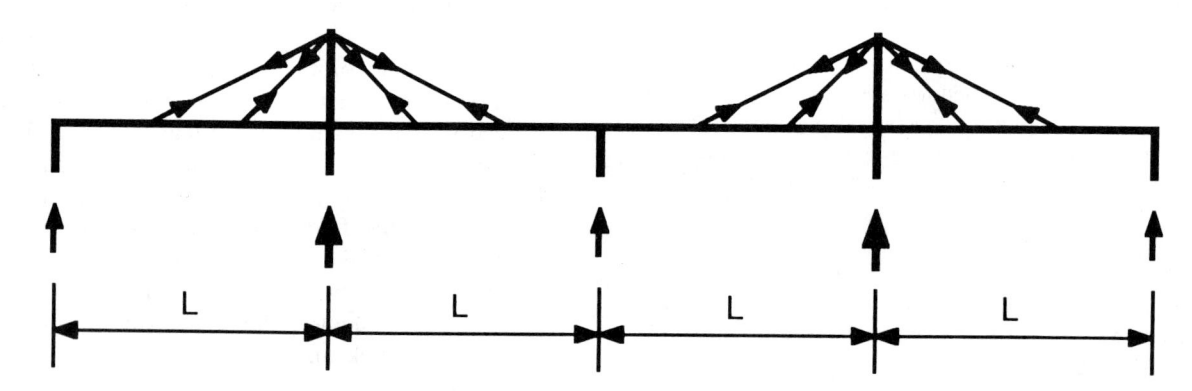

Fig. 11.8.2. Cable-stayed continuous roof structure. The cables provide the equivalent of supporting columns at third points. For a four-span continuous beam carrying a uniformly distributed load, the maximum bending moment is (see Table 11.2)

$$-0.107WL$$

The cable supports reduce the spans to one-third, and the loads on each span to one-third, so that the bending moment for the twelve-span continuous beam is reduced to

$$-0.012WL$$

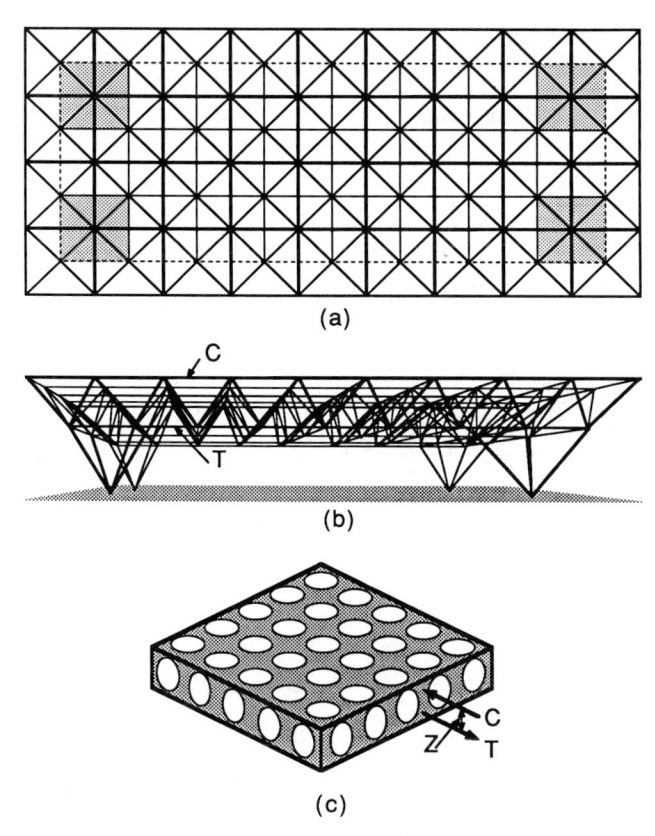

Fig. 11.9.1. Space frame. (a) A fully triangulated space frame is an assembly of tetrahedra. It can form a flat structure, or a structure with complex surfaces.

(b) Triangulated space frames can be used to provide flat roofs with wide column spacing. They may be considered as flat plates (see Section 13.9) into which very many large holes have been cut.

(c) They provide a resistance moment in both directions, formed by the compressive force C and the tensile force T, and the lever arm z. If the space frame is simply supported, the compressive force is always in the top chord; if it is continuous, it will vary between the two chords.

in compression. Only nominal reinforcement is therefore required in a concrete shell dome. However, as the dome does not come vertically on its springings, horizontal reactions are set up, and these must be absorbed by a tie (or else by buttresses, which is rare today). This creates bending stresses in the adjacent part of the concrete shell (Fig. 11.10.2), for which adequate reinforcement must be provided. In addition the thickness of the shell must be increased in the region near the tie.

Domes can be built from steel sections or tubes. The overall structural behavior of steel domes is essentially the same (Fig. 11.10.3).

11.11. SUSPENSION STRUCTURES

We noted in Section 11.6 that bending moments in an arch are small because its shape resembles that of the bending

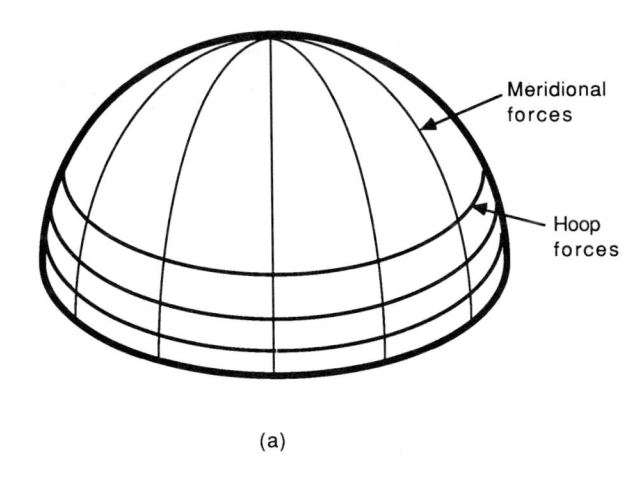

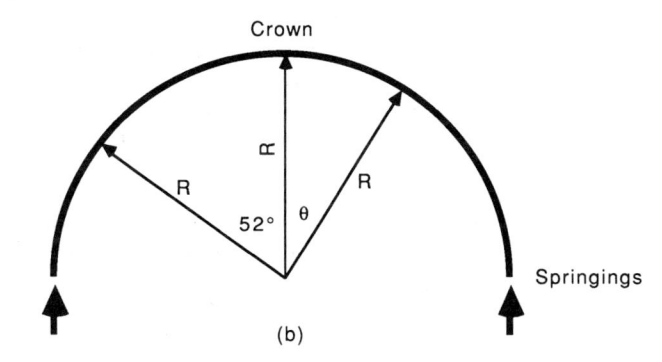

Fig. 11.10.1. The hemispherical dome. In analyzing domes it is convenient to use coordinates similar to those of the earth's surface, the meridians of longitude and the circles of latitude, for defining the internal forces. If a reinforced concrete dome is sufficiently thin to be considered a shell structure, the meridional forces are entirely compressive. They act like arches intersecting at the *crown* (a), and they come vertically on the *springings*.

The hoop forces are compressive near the crown, and tensile near the springings. The change from tension to compression occurs at a hoop which subtends an angle of 104° at the center of the sphere, that is, it makes an angle of 52° with the crown (b).

Thin hemispherical domes are statically determinate; however, the solution of the basically simple equations is complicated by the need to use spherical geometry. The answer is given in a number books (for example Ref. 11.4, p. 6). The meridional forces are

$$N_\theta = -wR \frac{1}{1 + \cos \theta}$$

and the hoop forces are

$$N_\phi = wR \left(\frac{1}{1 + \cos \theta} - \cos \theta \right)$$

where w is the vertical load per unit area of shell,
 R is its radius of curvature (which is half the diameter or span of the hemispherical dome), and
 θ is the angle subtended by the point under consideration with the crown.

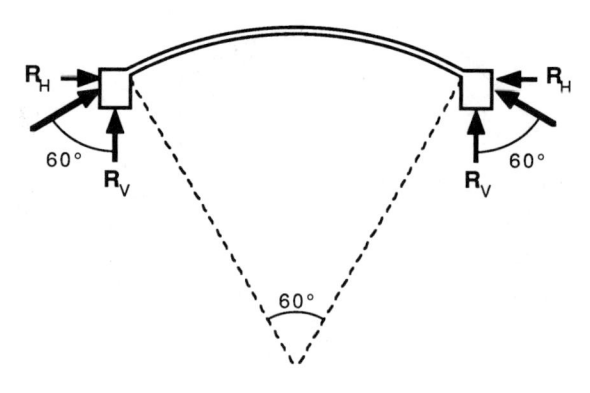

Fig. 11.10.2. The shallow dome. In a shallow dome the hoop forces are entirely compressive; however, the meridional forces do not come vertically on the springings. The vertical components of these forces are easily absorbed by the vertical reactions R_V, but in addition horizontal reactions R_H are required. In Byzantine architecture these were absorbed with buttresses, and this is still occasionally done in modern architecture.

It is much more convenient to absorb them in a reinforced concrete dome with a tie. This tie, being in tension, expands. However, in the adjacent portion of the shell dome the hoop forces are in compression, so that the shell contracts. This differential elastic deformation sets up bending stresses, which must be resisted by thickening the shell and providing it with suitable reinforcement near the tie.

moment due to the load it carries. A cable is even more efficient structurally. It is flexible, and thus unable to resist bending. It adapts itself to the shape needed so that it is in pure tension under the action of the loads it carries. Its shape is a catenary if its load is distributed uniformly along its length, a parabola if it is distributed uniformly in plan, or a triangle if it is a concentrated load (see Sections 11.3 and 11.6).

While arches, being compression members, can buckle if they become too thin, suspension cables are in tension and thus cannot buckle. Furthermore, suspension cables are made from hard-drawn high tensile steel, the strongest material available for use in architectural structures (see Section 2.6). The material is so hard that it cannot be used for anything other than cables or prestressing tendons (see Section 13.13).

Thus cables are particularly efficient for long-span structures. The world's fourteen longest-spanning *bridges* are suspension bridges, followed by two arch bridges. Suspension structures are not as efficient in *architecture* because of the very flexibility of the cables which make them so useful structurally; a roof that is too flexible cannot be made weathertight, and it is liable to vibrate due to wind (Fig. 11.11.1); to avoid that, stiff beams, or a separate set of prestressed cables, or a saddle surface (Section 11.13) must be used.

Today the longest-spanning *architectural* structures are domes, as they have been since the days of Ancient Rome.

While suspension structures have limited potential when

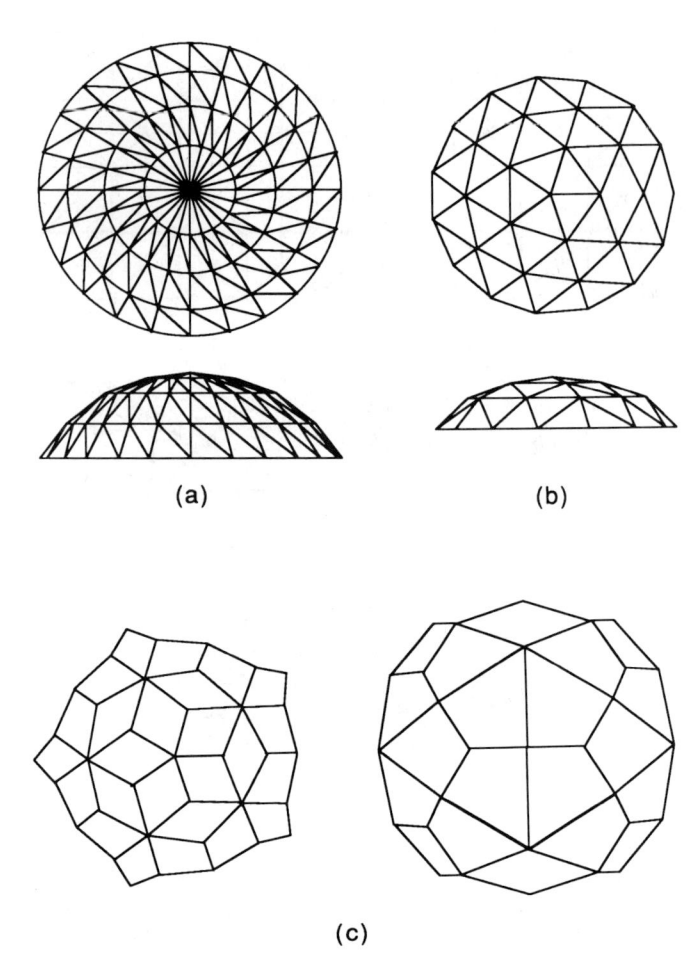

Fig. 11.10.3. Steel domes. The overall structural behavior of a steel dome is the same as that of a reinforced concrete dome. The vertical components of the structural steel members resist the meridional forces (Fig. 11.10.1), and the horizontal components resist the hoop forces.

For design of the structural details, however, it is necessary to treat the structure as a triangulated frame. The single-layer steel dome is a two-dimensional frame on a curved surface, not a true space frame. Thus the number of members needed is $n = 2j - 3$, not $n = 3j - 6$ (see Sections 11.5 and 11.9). For domes with longer spans, however, a double-layer dome, which has resistance to bending, is used. It must be triangulated within its depth, so that a space frame results.

There are three principal types of steel dome: (a) the *Schwedler dome* (named after a German 19th Century engineer who first used it), in which the steel members follow the lines of latitude and longitude, the third set being diagonals to complete the triangulation; (b) the *triangulated geodesic dome*, in which all three sets of lines forming the triangulation are great circles intersecting at 60°; and (c) The *geodesic dome with rigid joints*, in which a number of triangles are combined into polygons, such as quadrilaterals, pentagons, or hexagons.

used with conventional roofing materials, they have proved themselves particularly useful for producing lightweight structures in conjunction with structural membranes (see Section 11.14).

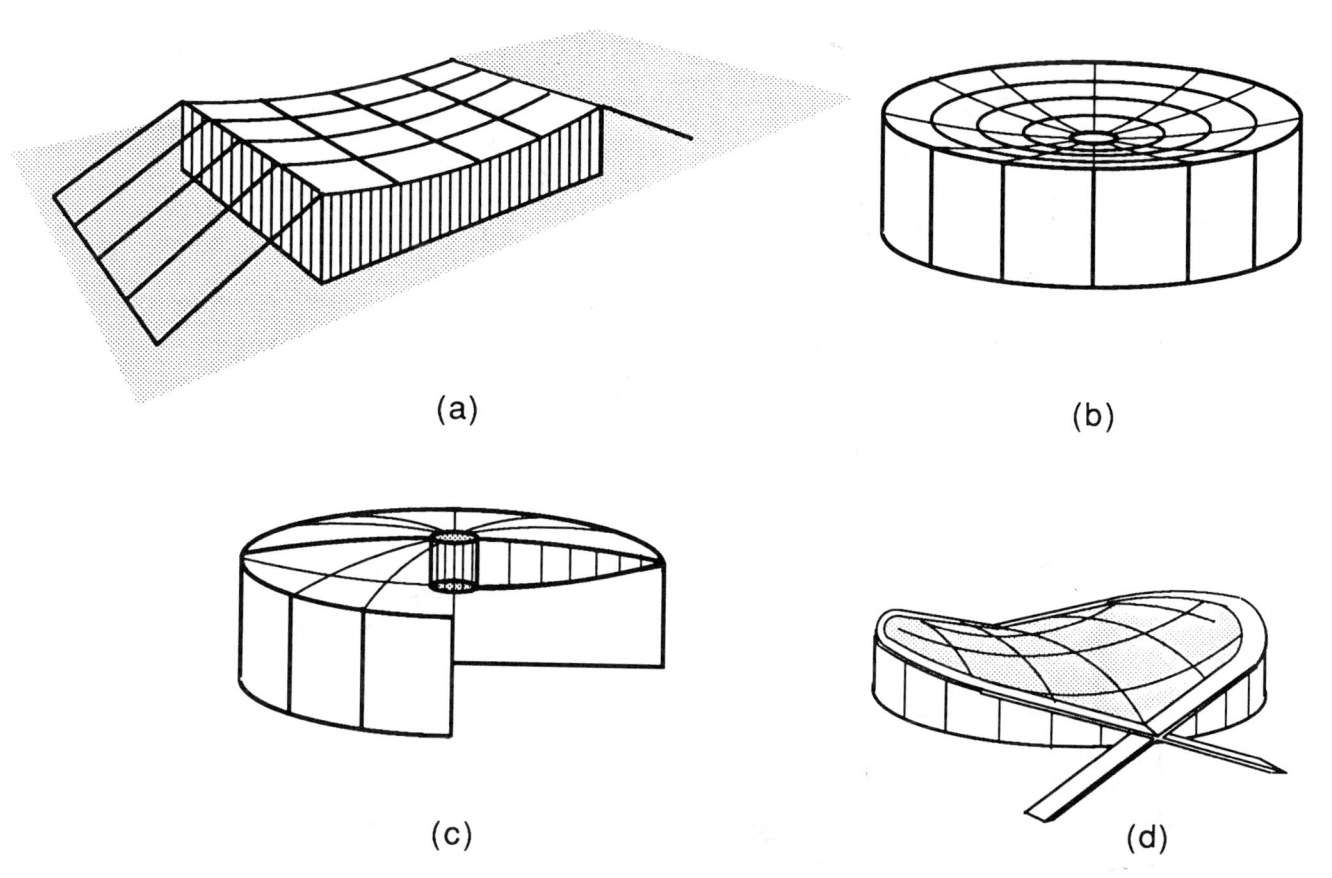

Fig. 11.11.1. Suspension structures. (a) Simple linear suspension roof. The catenary cables that carry the roof are vertically supported at two faces of the building. A structure of this type is particularly suitable for a sporting arena flanked by banked seats. The supporting structure for these seats can incorporate the vertical supports, and the cables can then be joined through the floor structure to provide the horizontal reactions, so that the inclined cables required in a suspension bridge can be avoided. In a suspension bridge this efficient method of absorbing the horizontal reactions is not possible because there is generally open water between the vertical supports. The parallel cables are, however, likely to move differentially because of the uplift caused by wind (see Chapter 10), and it is thus necessary to incorporate in the roof stiff beams or prestressing cables at right angles to the suspension cables.

(b) Simple circular suspension roof. Dished domes can be, and have been, built, but the roof must be heavier than any uplift forces due to wind that are likely to occur in that location. Rainwater must either be collected by a downspout (downpipe) in the center of the roof, or else it must be removed by a pump.

(c) Double circular suspension roof. The use of two sets of cables, separated by short struts, solves the problem of vibration due to wind which is inherent in the simple roofs (a) and (b). If movement of the roof reduces the tension in one set of cables, the struts cause an increase in cable tension in the other set of cables. The roof drainage problem is also solved by the convex shape of the upper set of cables.

(d) Cables suspended from crossed arches. The catenary cables running between the arches carry the weight of the roof. Prestressed cables are needed at right angles to ensure that the roof remains weathertight, and to resist uplift and vibrations due to wind. The resulting roof has a saddle shape, which increases its stability (see Section 11.13).

11.12. CYLINDRICAL STRUCTURES

Cylindrical vaults were used widely prior to the 20th Century for fireproof structures of medium span, and cylindrical reinforced concrete shells were popular in the 1950s for the same purpose. However, cylindrical shells do not have the same potential for long spans as domes, and for medium spans the cost of the formwork now limits their use.

Cylindrical structures must be built either with ties (Fig. 11.12.1a) to prevent the vault from spreading, or else with rigid frames that are stiff enough to perform the same function (Fig. 11.12.1b).

The load-carrying capacity of the cylindrical structure is largely due to its curved shape. In one direction it acts as an arch whose supports are prevented from spreading; in the other direction it acts like a deep beam of cylindrical cross section. If the span L is greater than the width B, the beam action predominates (Fig. 11.12.1a and d); if L is smaller than B, the arch action predominates (Fig. 11.12.1c).

While few cylindrical concrete shells have been built in

174 HANDBOOK OF ARCHITECTURAL TECHNOLOGY

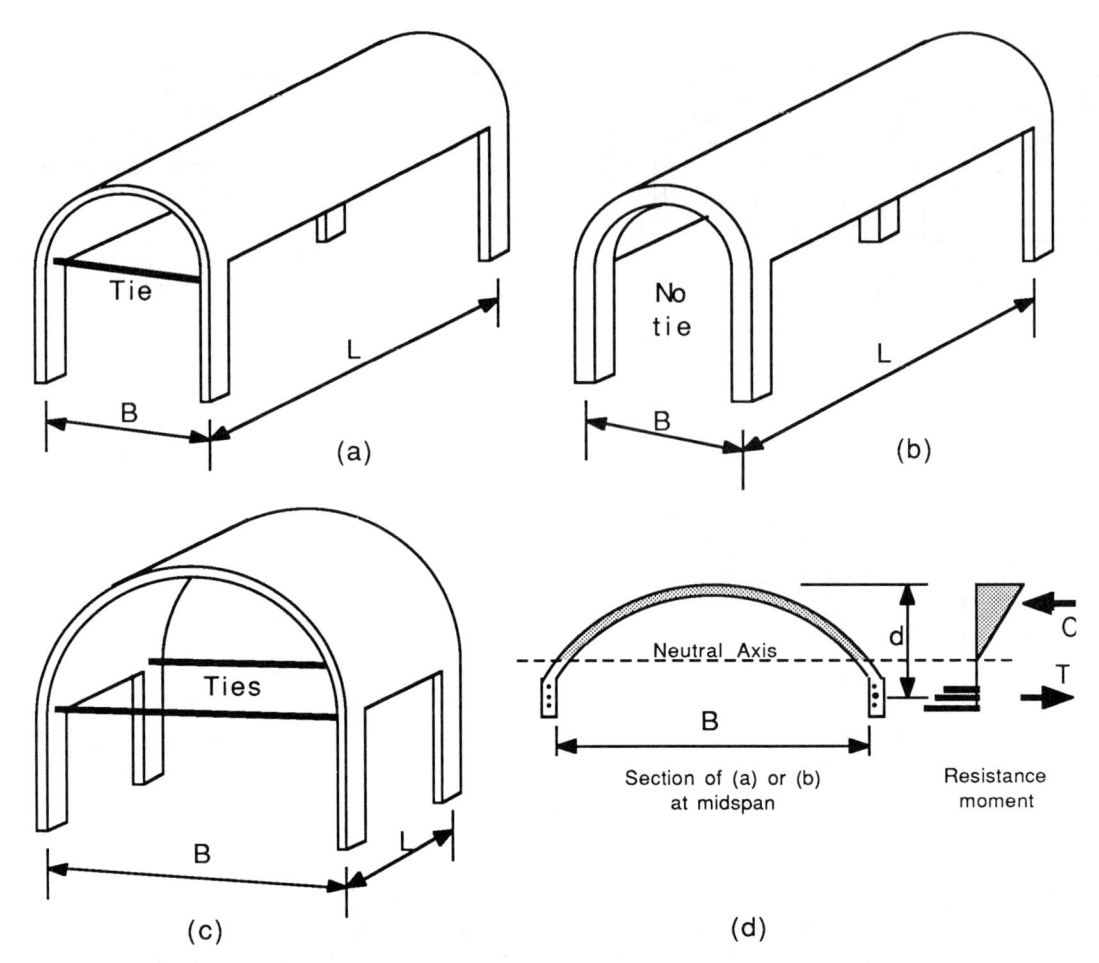

Fig. 11.12.1. Cylindrical reinforced concrete shell. (a) A cylindrical shell whose span *L* is greater than its width *B*, so that *beam action* predominates.

(b) The same shell, but without a tie. It has rigid frames at both ends which are sufficiently stiff to perform the same function as the ties between columns across the width *B*.

(c) A cylindrical shell whose width *B* is greater than its span *L*, so that *arch action* predominates.

(d) The shell shown at (a) may be considered as an arch-shaped beam which resists the bending due to the loads it carries over the span *L*. The neutral axis must be determined from the theory of reinforced concrete design. Above the neutral axis the concrete, shown shaded, is in compression, and it provides the force *C*; below the neutral axis the reinforcement provides the tensile force *T*; *z* is the lever arm between the two forces which produces the resistance moment of the shell. Since the overall depth of the shell is considerable, the shell has appreciable load-bearing capacity.

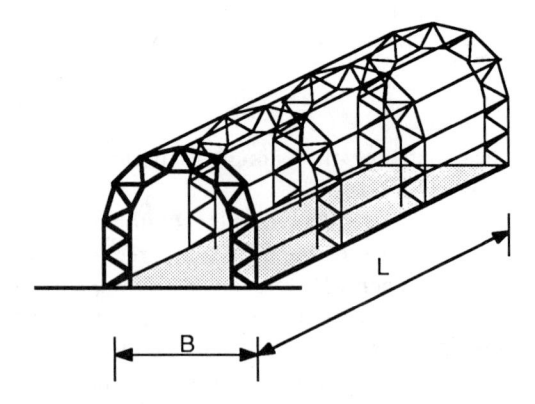

Fig. 11.12.2. Cylindrical steel structure. If the structure has a double-layer triangular grid, it behaves like a space frame, and it does not need a tie at the base of the arch (see Fig. 11.12.1a and b).

recent years, cylindrical steel structures (Fig. 11.12.2) have become more common since the development of coated and pre-painted steel tubes.

11.13. SADDLE SURFACES

The curved surfaces used in buildings can be classified according to the type of their curvature. *Cylindrical surfaces* have straight lines in one direction; a cut made at right angles to the straight lines is curved (Figs. 11.12.1 and 2). If two cuts are made in a *dome* at right angles to one another, both are curved in the same direction (Figs. 11.10.1 and 3). These are the two traditional curved surfaces used in architecture.

The third type of surface, not used in architecture prior to the 20th Century, is the *saddle*. If two cuts are made at right angles to one another, one is curved upward and the other downward. Using a topographic analogy, a dome is a mountain top, a cylindrical structure a mountain ridge, and a saddle a pass in a range of mountains.

We can flatten a cylindrical surface in a model. We can buckle a thin dome. However, it is much harder to flatten or buckle a saddle surface.

Another useful classification of curved surfaces is into those that cannot and those that can be *ruled* (that is, have straight lines drawn on them). Domes cannot be ruled; it is impossible to draw a straight line on them in any direction. Cylindrical surfaces can be ruled in one direction. Not all saddle surfaces can be ruled, but some can be ruled in two directions, not necessarily at right angles to one another (Figs. 11.13.1 and 11.13.2). It is easier to build timber formwork for a concrete structure or to fabricate a steel structure if a surface is singly ruled, and even more so if it is doubly ruled.

It is also easier to prestress a ruled surface, because this can be done with straight wires or cables. Prestressing increases the stiffness of cable networks and membranes, and eliminates wrinkling.

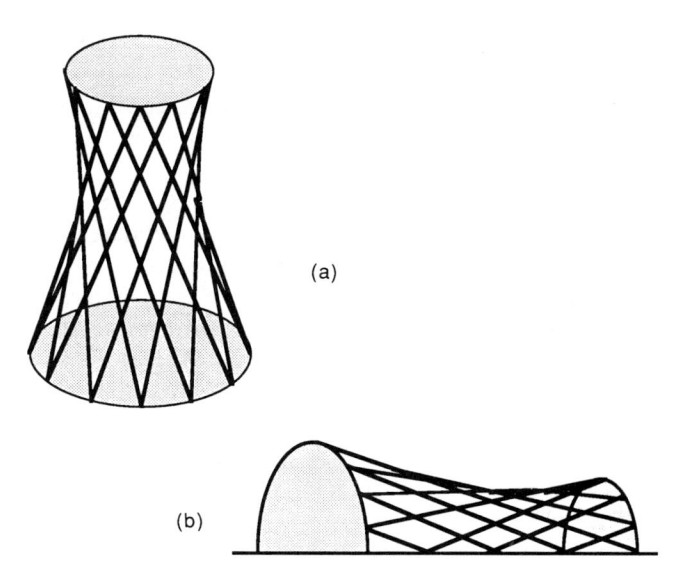

Fig. 11.13.2. The hyperboloid. The hyperboloid is generated by two straight lines rotating about a central axis. (a) The hyperboloid used vertically. This the shape familiar from cooling towers, which were originally built with straight pieces of timber. (b) The hyperboloid used horizontally.

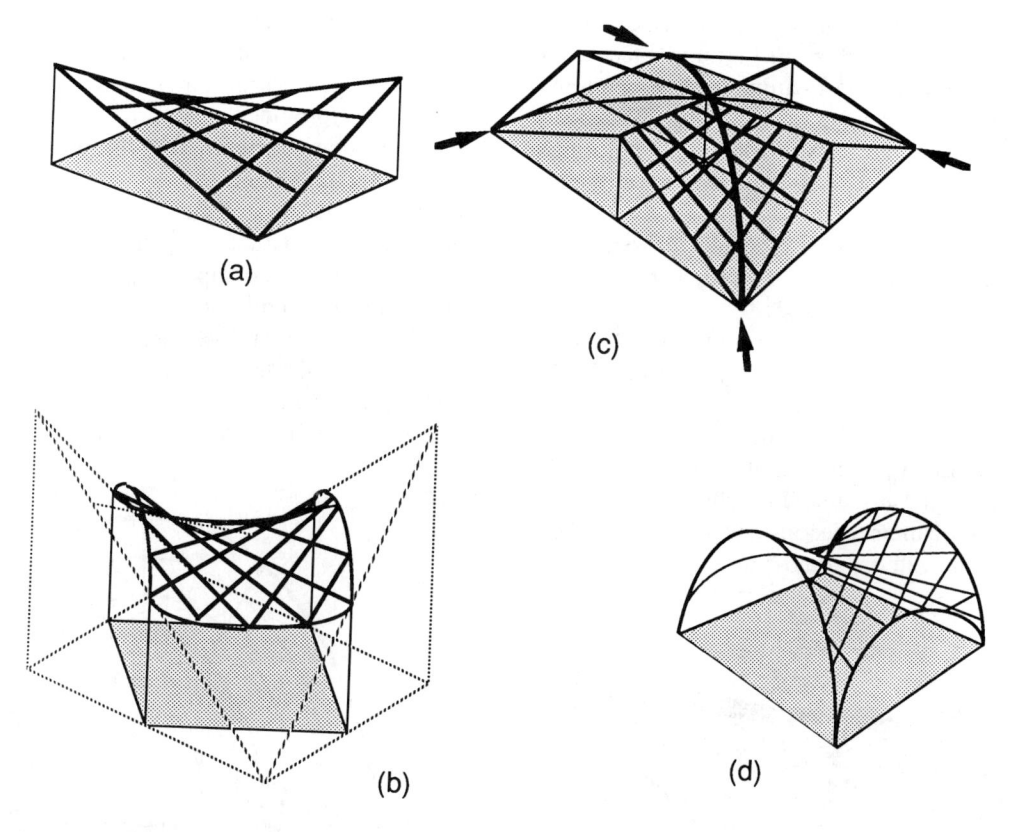

Fig. 11.13.1. The hyperbolic paraboloid (also called hypar) used as a shell structure. (a) The hyperbolic paraboloid is generated by two straight lines at right angles to one another. It is a saddle surface which consists of interacting "suspension cables" (the internal tensile forces), and "arches" (the internal compressive forces in the shell). (b) If the surface generated at (a) is cut at 45°, a different-looking surface results, which resembles a vault rather than a linear roof. (c) A roof shape resulting from a combination of several surfaces of type (a). (d) A roof shape resulting from a combination of several surfaces of type (b). Surfaces (a) and (c) can also be used in fabric structures (Section 11.14).

11.14. FABRIC AND PNEUMATIC STRUCTURES

Saddle surfaces are also useful for fabric structures. They are more resistant to deformation and vibration due to wind than flat surfaces (Fig. 11.14.1).

Tents have been used for many centuries, but they have until recently been considered temporary structures, to be dismantled from time to time, packed, and moved elsewhere. The development of stronger and more durable fabrics has led to the construction of permanent fabric structures.

The fabrics may be woven materials coated with thermoplastics, thermosetting resins, or rubbers; they may be plastic materials reinforced with short fibers; or they may for short spans be plastic foils without reinforcement. Suitable fibers are:

- Natural fibers: linen, cotton
- Metal fibers: steel, stainless steel (a chrome alloy steel, see Chapter 2)
- Mineral fiber: glass fiber
- Plastic fibers: polyester yarn, Nylon (a polyamide), kevlar [poly-(p-phenyleneterephthalimide)] (see Chapter 5)

Suitable coatings are: PVC (polyvinyl chloride), PTFE (polytetrafluoroethylene), Teflon FEP (fluorinated ethylene-propylene), acrylic lacquer, natural rubber, neoprene, silicone rubber (see Chapter 5).

Suitable plastic foils are: PVC (polyvinyl chloride), mylar (a polyester), teflon FEP (fluorinated ethylene-propylene) (see Chapter 5).

The fabric panels are tensioned by cables or ropes, and in addition struts (tentpoles) may be used, particularly if extra height is needed (Fig. 11.14.2).

The mechanics of *pneumatic structures* are entirely different from all the structures previously discussed in this chapter. They are supported by an air pressure slightly in excess of atmospheric pressure, which is more than that necessary to counteract the weight of the roof. Because the weight of the fabrics and any stiffening cables used is small, the additional air pressure needed inside the building is less than 1 percent of the external atmospheric pressure. It can

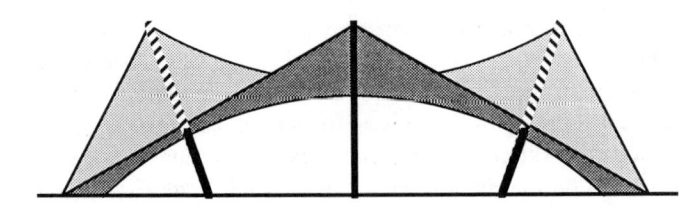

Fig. 11.14.2. Tent structure in which the fabric is tensioned by struts ("tentpoles").

be supplied by a small air compressor for a moderately sized span.

The building is usually entered through revolving doors that are reasonably airtight. The resulting loss of pressure is restored by the air compressor.

Pneumatic roofs are particularly useful for demountable structures, such as temporary store rooms, or roofs placed over swimming pools in winter to turn them into indoor pools (Fig. 11.14.3).

In theory there is no limit to the span of a pneumatic structure. The weight of the roof structure is resisted everywhere by the excess air pressure, and the span of the structure does not enter into this equation.

In practice, however, large pneumatic roofs present special problems. The wind will vary in direction and in velocity. In most cases it will exert an unevenly distributed uplift on the roof. This can be corrected by varying the internal air pressure, but unless automatic sensors and controls are provided, the correction will be too slow in a variable wind. Furthermore, the wind may excite vibrations in the membrane.

The chance of an accidental puncture of the pneumatic membrane is small, but if the puncture is larger than the air compressor can compensate, an unreinforced pneumatic membrane will collapse. All but the smallest pneumatic membranes are therefore used in conjunction with suspension cables which give them sufficient stiffness under wind loading, and a safety net in the event of a puncture, unless the membrane has sufficient strength by itself.

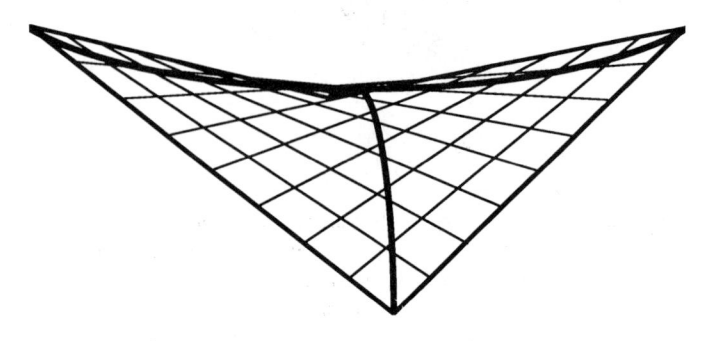

Fig. 11.14.1. Saddle surface formed by fabric panel.

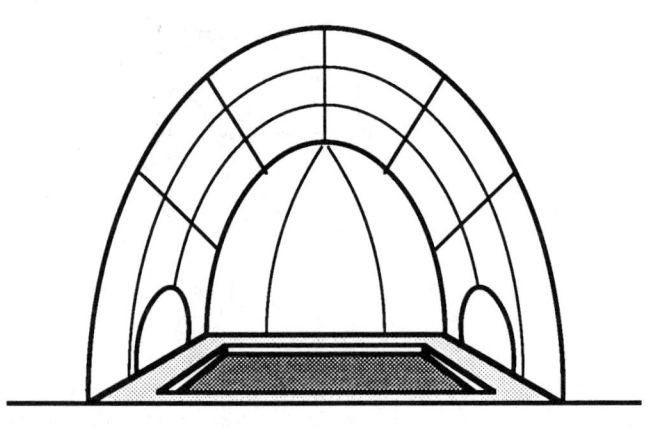

Fig. 11.14.3. Pneumatic roof structure. The membrane is supported by small excess internal air pressure. This type of structure is used for small spans.

The materials used for fabric and pneumatic structures may be opaque, translucent or, for small spans, transparent. A building whose roof contains large areas of translucent panels is generally well lit by daylight, even if it has no windows, but it may require provision for opening the roof to prevent overheating on sunny days.

REFERENCES

11.1. H. J. Cowan. *Architectural Structures*, 2nd Ed. American Elsevier, New York, 1976. 448 pp.

11.2. R. N. White and C. G. Salmon. *Building Structural Design Handbook*. Wiley, New York, 1987. 1197 pp.

11.3. H. J. Cowan. *The Masterbuilders*. Wiley, New York, 1977; Krieger, Malabar, FL, 1985. 299 pp.

11.4. A. Pflüger. *Elementary Statics of Shells*, 2nd Ed. McGraw-Hill, New York, 1961. 122 pp.

SUGGESTIONS FOR FURTHER READING

H. J. Cowan. *Science and Building*. Wiley, New York, 1978. 374 pp.

H. J. Cowan. *An Historical Outline of Architectural Science*, 2nd Ed. Elsevier, New York, 1977. 202 pp.

M. Salvadori and M. Levy. *Structural Design in Architecture*, 2nd Ed. Prentice-Hall, Englewood Cliffs, NJ, 1981. 458 pp.

D. L. Schodek. *Structures*. Prentice-Hall, Englewood Cliffs, NJ, 1980. 572 pp.

R. Coleman. *Structural Systems Design*. Prentice Hall, Englewood Cliffs, NJ, 1983. 320 pp.

T. Y. Lin and S. D. Stotesbury. *Structural Concepts and Systems for Architects and Engineers*, 2nd Ed. Van Nostrand Reinhold, New York, 1988. 507 pp.

D. Guise. *Design and Technology in Architecture*. Wiley, New York, 1985. 275 pp.

W. P. Moore, H. D. Eberhart, and H. J. Cowan (Eds.). *Monograph on Planning and Design of Tall Buildings*, Volume SC: *Tall Buildings Systems and Concepts*. American Society of Civil Engineers, New York, 1980. 651 pp.

G. S. Ramaswamy. *Design and Construction of Concrete Shell Roofs*. McGraw-Hill, New York, 1968. 641 pp.

C. Faber. *Candela: Shell Builder*. Reinhold, New York, 1963. 240 pp.

Z. Makowski. *Steel Space Structures*. Michael Joseph, London, 1963. 213 pp.

P. L. Nervi (transl. M. and G. Salvadori). *Structures*. Dodge, New York, 1956. 118 pp.

E. Torroja. *Philosophy of Structures*. University of California Press, Los Angeles, 1958. 366 pp.

Proceedings of the First International Conference on Lightweight Structures in Architecture, University of New South Wales, Sydney, 1986. Two volumes. 1037 pp.

P. Drew. *Frei Otto: Form and Structure*. Crosby Lockwood Staples, London 1976. 160 pp.

Ove Arup and Partners 1946–1986. St. Martin's Press, New York, 1986. 216 pp.

P. Drew. *Tensile Architecture*. Granada, London, 1979. 237 pp.

T. Herzog. *Pneumatic Structures*. Crosby Lockwood Staples, London, 1977. 192 pp.

International Symposium on Pneumatic Structures. Delft University of Technology, Delft, The Netherlands, 1972. 3 volumes.

NOTATION

A	cross-sectional area
C	compressive force
E	modulus of elasticity
f	stress
H	horizontal force
I	second moment of area (moment of inertia)
j	number of joints in truss or frame
L	span
M	moment
n	number of members in truss or frame
P	load acting on tension or compression member
R	reaction; radius
r	radius of gyration $= \sqrt{I/A}$
S	section modulus
T	tensile force
V	vertical force; shear force
W	total load acting on beam
w	load per unit area
x	horizontal distance
y	vertical distance
z	lever arm between the forces C and T
θ	angle
π	circular constant $= 3.1416\ldots$

A list of abbreviations of the units of measurement, definitions of these units, and conversion factors between British/American and metric units are given in the Appendix.

12
Steel Structures

Lambert Tall

This chapter deals mainly with allowable stress design, based on elastic considerations. Beams, columns, and beam-columns are considered in turn, together with bolted and welded connections. Rigid frames and plate girders are briefly discussed. Finally there are sections on plastic design, based on ultimate strength; computer-aided design; and the problems of fabrication. Composite construction of structural steel and reinforced concrete is considered in Section 13.14.

12.1 DESIGN PRINCIPLES

The basic objectives of a structural design are to meet *fundamental requirements*, to *carry the loads*, and to be *economical*. The American Society of Civil Engineers has stated this as: "An engineering structure is satisfactorily designed if it can be built with needed economy and if, throughout its useful life, it carries its intended loads and otherwise performs its intended function (Ref. 12.1)."

The various aspects and their interactions involved in the design are collectively called "systems engineering" (Ref. 12.2). The design objectives require a knowledge of the properties of the material (see Chapter 2), the methods of structural analysis (see Chapter 11), and the specifications and codes. The design process goes through a number of steps: the establishment of the purpose of the structure, the type of structure to be used and its loading, a preliminary design where the structural member sizes are estimated, a structural analysis, which then leads to the final member sizes. Thus, structural design is iterative.

The function of the structure and its intended use will reflect the type of structure chosen: a frame, truss, plate girder, or other (see below). These structures may be designed on the basis of their component elements or as a complete structural system designed as a unit.

Steel is the material considered in this chapter. In many ways, this is a remarkable and extraordinary material offering high strength at a relatively low cost (see Chapter 2). The two basic properties of structural steel are its strength and ductility, as shown in Fig. 12.1.1a. While the importance of its strength is obvious, the ductility is equally important, as this property of "giving" but not breaking under load is a major safety feature. It is of interest also that most structures behave in a way that resembles the stress-strain curve of a simple tension test (see Fig. 12.1.1b) for a rigid frame which exhibits first elastic behavior and then plastic behavior under a maximum and constant load. It is the ductility of steel which allows a redistribution of load in an overloading situation such that no negative effects occur.

An important but simple thing to check in the design procedure, and one easily overlooked, is the availability of the steel shape or plate. Because of the limitations of the manufacturing process, the heavier and thicker shapes and plates do not receive as much hot-rolling as lighter shapes, and so higher yield strengths can not be developed for them; there is also a limitation on the amount of carbon and other chemicals that can be added to raise the strength (Ref. 12.3). Thus, not all shapes and plates are available in all grades of steel; see Tables 1 and 2, Part 1 of the AISC Specifications (Refs. 12.4 and 12.5.).

There are different philosophies of structural design. Most design has been *allowable stress design*, or elastic design, which simply requires the actual stress in the structure not to exceed an allowable stress as given by the code. *Limit states design* was introduced into the U.S.A. in 1986 (Ref. 12.5) after having been in use in Canada since 1974 (Ref. 12.6) and in many European countries since the

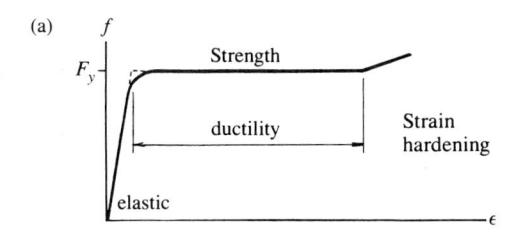

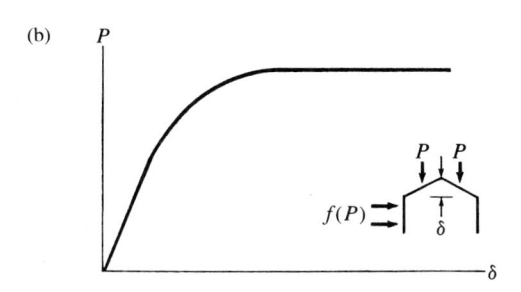

Fig. 12.1.1. Behavior of material and structure under load.

1960s. Limit states design is "a method of proportioning structures so that no applicable limit state is exceeded when the structure is subjected to all appropriate factored load conditions (Ref. 12.5)." This design is based on probability studies of the strength (or "reliability") of structural elements under loads which are factored depending on the knowledge of them. *Plastic design*, or maximum strength design, or collapse design, is based on the ultimate strength of the structure or structural member, and considers the development of complete plastification at certain points in the structure.

For structural design purposes buildings may be classified as either industrial-type, multi-story, or special buildings (see Chapter 11). Industrial-type buildings are typified by rigid frames or mill-type (Fig. 12.1.2a and b), which include columns, beams, and trusses, as well as corner connections. Multi-story buildings, Fig. 12.1.2c, contain a system of columns, beams, and corner connections. Special buildings have unique shapes and framing schemes, and may be used for churches, houses, auditoriums, observation towers, and the like.

In this chapter, the basic specification referred to and used in the examples is that of the American Institute of Steel Construction (AISC) (Ref. 12.4). This specification is part of the AISC Manual, 9th Edition, which contains much additional material needed in the design process; the Specification is a part of the Manual, but the two terms are often used synonymously.

12.2. WIDTH-THICKNESS RATIO

Width-thickness (b/t) limitations are used to prevent local buckling and the premature failure of a member which is wholly or partly in compression. The local buckling limita-

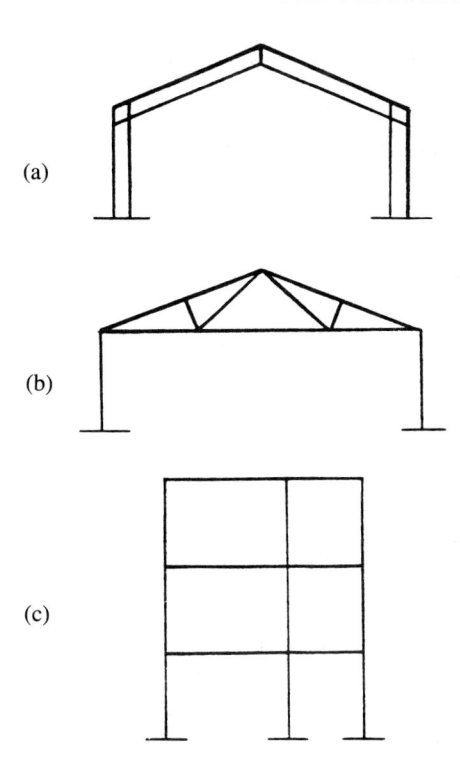

Fig. 12.1.2. Industrial-type buildings. (a) Rigid frame; (b) mill type; (c) multistory frame.

tions for structural shapes are listed in specifications for the various elements of the shape. Those of major interest, which are discussed here, are the flange and web of wide-flange and I-shapes.

Local buckling is a localized buckling under compression of a plate element (e.g., flange, web) that makes up the shape. Local buckling distorts the shape of the structural member and leads to failure at loads much lower than if local buckling was not present. The simplest way to prevent local buckling is to make the plate element thick enough with respect to its width; that is, the width-thickness, or b/t, limitation. Although b/t is the general term used, the specific dimensions are $b/2t$ for the flange, and d/w for the web (see Fig. 12.2.1). These values are tabulated in the AISC Manual for each shape.

The AISC limitations for flange and web are:

$$\frac{b}{2t_f} \leq \frac{95}{\sqrt{F_y}} = 15.8 \text{ for } F_y = 36 \text{ ksi} \qquad (12.1)$$

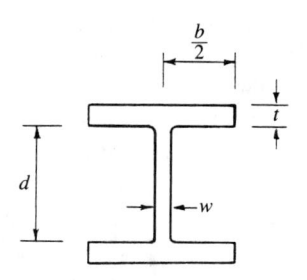

Fig. 12.2.1. Critical dimensions for local buckling.

180 HANDBOOK OF ARCHITECTURAL TECHNOLOGY

$$\frac{d}{t_w} \le \frac{253}{\sqrt{F_y}} = 42.2 \text{ for } F_y = 36 \text{ ksi} \quad (12.2)$$

These limitations are for the flange and web in compression, as would occur for a column, or, in the case of a beam, for the compression flange. The limitation is not valid for the web of a beam, since such a member is in compression over one half, and in tension over the other. For a web in a beam or girder, the AISC limitation is:

$$\frac{14000}{\sqrt{F_y(F_y + 16.5)}} = 322 \text{ for } F_y = 36 \text{ ksi} \quad (12.3)$$

where F_y is the yield strength of the material in the element under consideration.

12.3. TENSION MEMBERS

Tension members are used in a wide spectrum of situations, from members in trusses to eyebars and cables supporting hangers and special tower structures. Almost any cross section may be used as a tension member, a rolled shape, a bar, or a cable.

The length of a tension member is restricted by AISC to $L/r = 300$. This is to decrease the flexibility and to prevent whipping in the wind, which could create problems with fatigue and with the fastening arrangement.

The basic design of tension members is simple. Determine the actual tensile stress

$$f_t = \frac{P}{A} \quad (12.4)$$

where f_t = actual stress in tension
P = load on tension member
A = net area of tension member.

It is required that

$$f_t \le F_t \quad (12.5)$$

where F_t is the allowable stress in tension. In the AISC Specification, F_t shall not exceed $0.6F_y$ on the gross area nor $0.50F_u$ on the net area (Ref. 12.4), where F_u is the specified minimum tensile strength of the steel, tabulated in the Specification.

The net section must be determined. This is simple for one hole in the cross section, but may become complicated when stagger of the failure path is involved (see Fig. 12.3.1). Consider the plate on the right, which shows the gage and stagger. Two possible failure paths exist, No. 1 and No. 2. Failure path No. 2 involves a stagger and the net area needs to be computed from the empirical relationship

$$A_{\text{net}} = t w_n$$

$$= t \left(w_g - \Sigma d + \Sigma \frac{s^2}{4g_n} \right) \quad (12.6)$$

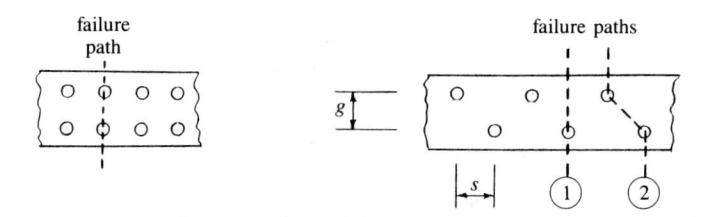

Fig. 12.3.1. Effective width of plates in tension.

where t = thickness of plate
w_n = net width of plate
w_g = gross width
d = diameter of hole (= diameter of bolt + $\frac{1}{8}''$)
s = stagger (see Fig. 12.3.1b)
g = gage (see Fig. 12.3.1b).

Example 12-1 shows the computation of the maximum load that may be carried by a joint, using the AISC Specification.

Example 12-1. What is the allowable load for the joint shown in Fig. 12.3.2? The steel is A36 and the bolts are $\frac{3}{4}''$ diameter.

Solution

There are three possible failure paths:

1. A-B
2. A-C-D
3. A-C-D-F

Path	Net width (AISC Section B2)	
1 (2 holes)	$9 - (2 \times \frac{7}{8}) + 0$	$= 7.25''$
2 (3 holes)	$9 - (3 \times \frac{7}{8}) + \frac{3^2}{4(1.5)}$	$= 7.87''$
3 (4 holes)	$9 - (4 \times \frac{7}{8}) + 2\left(\frac{3^2}{4(1.5)}\right)$	$= 8.50''$

Path 1 is smallest width and controls.

$$\therefore A_n = 7.25 \times \tfrac{1}{2} = 3.62 \text{ in.}^2$$

Check AISC Section B3 (85 percent rule):

$$0.85 A_g = 0.85 \times 9 \times \tfrac{1}{2} = 3.83 \text{ in.}^2$$

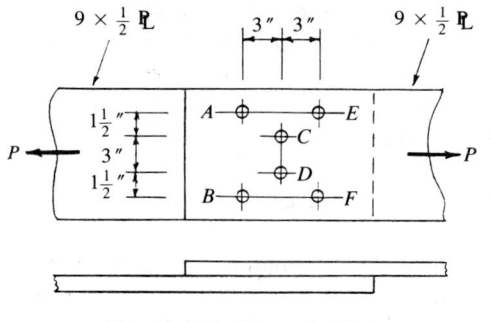

Fig. 12.3.2. Example 12.1.

Use smaller of A_n or $0.85 A_g$.

$$\therefore \text{Use } A_n = 3.62 \text{ in.}^2$$

Allowable stresses (from AISC Section D1):

$$F_t = 0.60 F_y = 22.0 \text{ ksi on gross area}$$

or

$$F_t = 0.50 F_u = 29.0 \text{ ksi on net area}$$

(from Tables 1, 2, pages 5-117, 118). Thus,

$$P = 22.0 \times (9 \times \tfrac{1}{2}) = 99.0 \text{ K}$$

or

$$P = 29.0 \times 3.62 = 105.0 \text{ K}$$

Take smaller value:

$$P = 99.0 \text{ K} \qquad \text{Answer.}$$

12.4. BEAMS

Beams are structural members which carry loads transverse to their length, and so resist bending and shear, and sometimes, depending of the placement of the load, torsion. Typical beams are purlins and floor beams. The design of beams includes a check that the allowable stresses are not exceeded for bending and shear, and also, that the deflection is within the specified limit. This chapter does not consider torsion which is a complicated analytical problem.

For simple bending (Fig. 12.4.1), the bending stress f_b is given by

$$f_b = \frac{Mc}{I} = \frac{M}{S} \qquad (12.7)$$

where M = moment at section considered
c = distance from axis of bending (neutral axis) to extreme fiber
I = moment of inertia of cross section about axis of bending
S = section modulus about axis of bending.

The design requires that $f_b \leq F_b$, where F_b has been based on the assumption that the beam does not buckle laterally under load. The allowable stress F_b is not a single number, but depends on the yield strength of the steel, and, most importantly, on the lateral support that the beam has. The basic value of F_b is $0.6 F_y$. However, compact

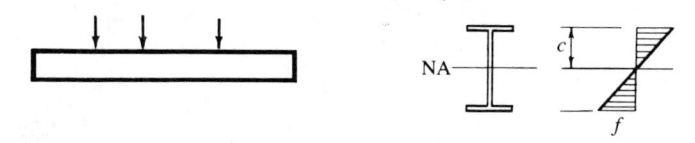

Fig. 12.4.1. Simple bending.

sections are allowed $F_b = 0.66 F_y$, while noncompact sections with insufficient lateral support have F_b no greater than $0.6 F_y$, and equal to the larger of the values from AISC equations F1-6 or F1-7 and F1-8, given as Eqs. (12.8a,b) and (12.9), below. For

$$\sqrt{\frac{102 \times 10^3 C_b}{F_y}} \leq \frac{L}{r_T} \leq \sqrt{\frac{510 \times 10^3 C_b}{F_y}} \qquad (12.8a)$$

$$F_b = \left[\frac{2}{3} - \frac{F_y \left(\frac{L}{r_T}\right)^2}{1530 \times 10^3 C_b} \right] F_y$$

For

$$\frac{L}{r_T} \geq \sqrt{\frac{510 \times 10^3 C_b}{F_y}} \qquad (12.8b)$$

$$F_b = \frac{170 \times 10^3 C_b}{\left(\frac{L}{r_T}\right)^2}$$

and

$$F_b = \frac{12 \times 10^3 C_b}{\frac{Ld}{A_f}} \qquad (12.9)$$

where L = distance between lateral supports
r_T = radius of gyration of top sixth of beam, taken about axis in plane of web (this is tabulated for each shape in the AISC Manual)
A_f = area of compression flange (d/A_f is tabulated for each shape in the AISC Manual)
C_b = a factor to account for nonuniform moment; see details in AISC Section F1.3
F_y = yield strength in ksi.

Sections are defined as compact if they meet a number of criteria listed in the AISC Specification, mainly width-thickness and lateral support distance requirements (Ref. 12.4).

After the bending stress f_b has been checked, the beam design should be checked for shear although this normally is not expected to be critical. Basically, the shear stress $f_v \leq F_v$, where F_v is the allowable shear stress and $F_v = 0.4 F_y$ in the AISC Specification.

Example 12-2 shows the check for whether a beam is suitable to carry its load with the lateral bracing specified.

Example 12-2. Check the design for the W14 × 30 section used (Fig. 12.4.2). Is the section acceptable?

$F_y = 45$ ksi; X = lateral bracing

182 HANDBOOK OF ARCHITECTURAL TECHNOLOGY

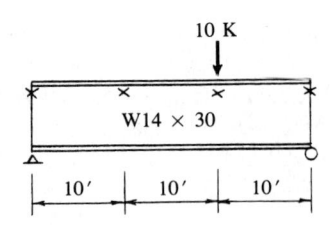

Fig. 12.4.2. Example 12.2.

Solution

W14 × 30. From Manual:

$$S_x = 42.0 \qquad b = 6.73$$
$$w = 0.27 \qquad d = 13.84 \qquad T = 12.0$$
$$r_T = 1.74 \qquad \frac{d}{A_f} = 5.34$$
$$\frac{L}{r_T} = \frac{10 \times 12}{1.74} = 68.97 \qquad \left(\frac{L}{r_T}\right)^2 = 4757$$

The moment diagram is given in Fig. 12.4.3. Check Section F1.1 if we can use $F_b = 0.66F_y$: from Eq. F1-2, L must not be greater than

$$\frac{76b}{\sqrt{F_y}} \quad \text{and} \quad \frac{20{,}000}{\frac{d}{A_f} F_y}$$

which gives

$$76.2'' \quad \text{and} \quad 83.2''$$

Does not satisfy, since $L_1 = L_2 = L_3 = 10$ ft,

i.e., $F_b \ne 0.66F_y$

Use F_b as given in Section F1.3.

C_b values:

$L_1 \qquad C_b = 1.75$

$L_2 \qquad C_b = 1.75 + 1.05(-\tfrac{1}{2}) + 0.3(-\tfrac{1}{2})^2$
$\qquad\qquad = 1.30$

$L_3 \qquad C_b = 1.75$

$\dfrac{L}{r_T}$ limit in AISC Eq. F1-6:

Fig. 12.4.3. Example 12.2.

$$\frac{L}{r_T} = \sqrt{\frac{510 \times 10^3 C_b}{45}}$$
$$= \sqrt{11333\, C_b}$$

Span $L_1 \quad \left.\dfrac{L}{r_T}\right|_{\text{limit}} = 141$

$L_2 \qquad\qquad\qquad 121$ — all greater than 68.97

$L_3 \qquad\qquad\qquad 141$

So, use AISC formulas Eqs. F1-6 and F1-8 for all spans.
AISC Eq. F1-6:

$$\max F_b = 0.60 F_y = 27.0 \text{ ksi}$$

Span L_1: $\quad F_b = \left[\dfrac{2}{3} - \dfrac{(45)4757}{1530(10^3)1.75}\right]45 = 26.4$

L_2: $\qquad\quad \left[\dfrac{2}{3} - \dfrac{(45)4757}{1530(10^3)1.3}\right]45 = 25.2$

L_3: $\qquad\qquad = 26.4$

AISC Eq. F1-8

$$F_b = \frac{12 \times 10^3 C_b}{\frac{Ld}{A_f}} = \frac{12 \times 10^3 C_b}{10(12)5.34} = 18.73\, C_b$$

Span L_1: $\quad F_b = 18.73(1.75) = \cancel{32.8} \quad 27.0$

L_2: $\qquad\qquad 18.73(1.3) = 24.3$

L_3: $\qquad\qquad\qquad\quad = \cancel{32.8} \quad 27.0$

Summary for F_b:

Span L_1: $\quad F_b = 27.0$

L_2: $\qquad\qquad 25.2$

L_3: $\qquad\qquad 27.0$

Use $F_b = 25.2$ for all spans.

Check stresses:

Max. bending stress:

$$f_b = \frac{M}{S} = \frac{66.7(12)}{42} = 19.1 < 25.2 \qquad \text{OK}$$

Max. shear stress:

$$f_v = \frac{V}{A_w} = \frac{6.67}{(0.27)13.84} = 1.8 \qquad \text{OK}$$

b/t check:

$$\frac{b}{2t_f} = 8.7 \qquad \frac{T}{w} = \frac{12}{0.27} = 44.4$$

limits:

$$\frac{b}{2t_f} = \frac{95}{\sqrt{F_y}} = 14.2 \qquad \text{OK}$$

$$\frac{d}{w} = \frac{14{,}000}{\sqrt{F_y(F_y + 16.5)}} = 261 \qquad \text{OK}$$

Existence check: shape exists for 46 ksi.   OK
Conclusion: Shape OK, but overdesigned. Try smaller shape.

Lateral support is one of the most important design details for a beam. It is critical that the compression flange of the beam be supported laterally. If the beam is embedded in concrete, then the lateral support is continuous and local buckling is not possible, such that $F_b = 0.66F_y$. Normally, lateral supports are placed wherever there is a concentrated load or a beam reaction support—the lateral supports are smaller structural members which must be fixed to the *compression* flange or very close to it. A large distance between lateral supports in a beam will require a small F_b, and vice-versa, although the maximum value of F_b is $0.6F_y$, or $0.66F_y$ for a compact shape.

The design is not complete until the width-thickness and the maximum deflection are checked and shown to be within limits. The AISC Specification does not specify a deflection limitation except for plastered ceilings where it is span/360. The local building code may specify a deflection limitation. The Commentary to the AISC Specification (Ref. 12.4) suggests a guide:

$$\frac{d}{L} \leq \frac{F_y}{800} \quad \text{for fully stressed floor beams}$$

and

$$\frac{d}{L} \leq \frac{F_y}{1000} \quad \text{for fully stressed roof purlins}$$

12.5. COMPRESSION MEMBERS

A compression member carries compression, and if the member is vertical, is referred to as a column. A column has its length considerably greater than its cross-sectional dimensions. A column loaded along its center of gravity is referred to as an axially loaded column or a centrally loaded column or a simple column. Such columns do not normally exist in practice, yet their strength and behavior form the basis for specifying the strength of practical columns, the beam-column.

The strength of a column is defined by its ultimate strength which, in the case of a simple column, is the load at which the column buckles. This buckling load is a function of the slenderness ratio (see Section 11.2) of the column, L/r, which defines the geometric shape, and of the magnitude and distribution of the residual stresses present within the column. For design purposes, all that is

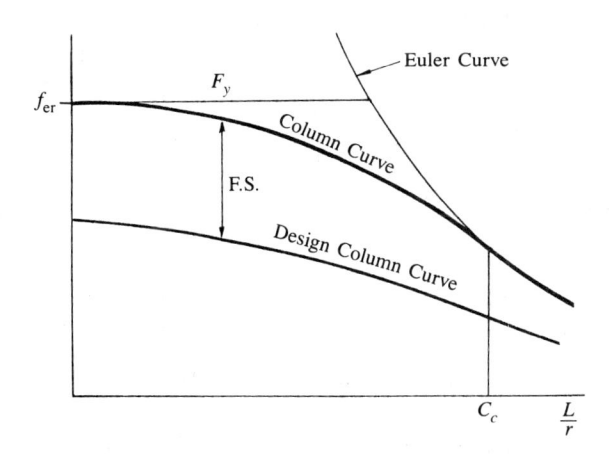

Fig. 12.5.1. Column curves.

needed is the column curve, Fig. 12.5.1, which plots maximum strength versus slenderness ratio. The column curve is a line of best fit to a wide scatterband of test results and theoretical analyses and may take any convenient form, such as a straight line or a parabola. When a factor of safety is applied, the resulting curve is the column design curve which plots F_a, the allowable compressive stress, versus the slenderness ratio. The AISC uses a parabola which takes into account the presence of residual stresses but which is a compromise insofar as it is an average for both axes of bending (Ref. 12.4). The AISC column design curve is limited by the yield strength of the material and by the Euler buckling curve, and is defined by Eqs. (12.10) and (12.11):

For $KL/r \leq C_c$:

$$F_a = \frac{\left[1 - \frac{\left(\frac{KL}{r}\right)^2}{2C_c^2}\right] F_y}{\frac{5}{3} + \frac{3}{8}\frac{\frac{KL}{r}}{C_c} - \frac{\left(\frac{KL}{r}\right)^3}{8C_c^3}} \qquad (12.10)$$

where $C_c = \sqrt{\dfrac{2\pi^2 E}{F_y}}$

For $KL/r > C_c$:

$$F_a = \frac{12\pi^2 E}{23\left(\dfrac{KL}{r}\right)^2} \qquad (12.11)$$

The denominator of Eq. (12.10) is the factor of safety, and C_c is the value of L/r at the point in the column curve where the parabola meets the Euler curve. Equation (12.11) is the Euler curve; it is valid for elastic buckling only, which occurs for very long columns.

184 HANDBOOK OF ARCHITECTURAL TECHNOLOGY

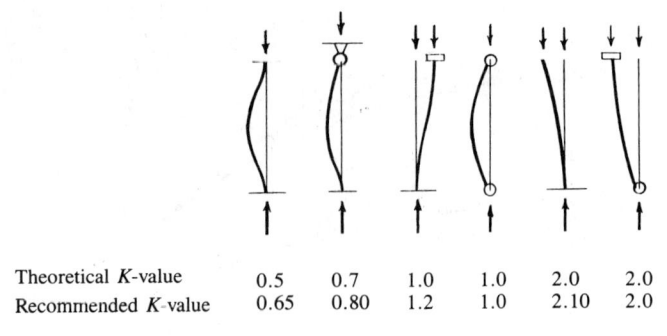

Theoretical K-value	0.5	0.7	1.0	1.0	2.0	2.0
Recommended K-value	0.65	0.80	1.2	1.0	2.10	2.0

Fig. 12.5.2. Effective-length factors.

The expression KL/r used in Eqs. (12.10) and (12.11) is the effective slenderness ratio, where K is the effective length factor which takes into account the end conditions of the column. The effective length factors of centrally loaded columns with various idealized end conditions are shown in Fig. 12.5.2 (Ref. 12.7). Alignment charts are available (Refs. 12.4 and 12.7) for a more general determination of effective length factors in continuous frames. KL/r is preferably limited to 200 by AISC.

Multiple column curves are in use in Canada and in a number of European countries, but not in the U.S.A. despite having been under discussion for over two decades. The term "multiple column curves" describes the use of more than one column curve for design, and the specific column curve to be used in the design is chosen from a table according to the size of the structural shape used as well as its method of fabrication.

Example 12-3 gives the design of a compression member, and Example 12-4 shows the determination of the K-factors in a frame using the alignment chart.

Example 12-3. Design the column shown in Fig. 12.5.3 using the AISC Specification. Use A36 steel.

Solution

From AISC Table C-C2.1 (p. 5-135), $K = 0.8$.
Try W14 × 132; from p. 1-26:

$$A = 38.8$$

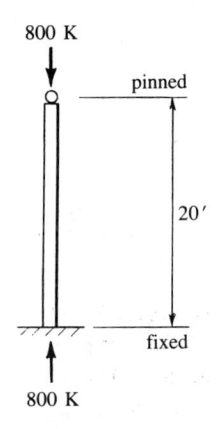

Fig. 12.5.3. Example 12.3.

$$r_x = 6.28$$
$$r_y = 3.76$$

buckling about y-axis gives smaller F_a:

$$\frac{KL}{r_y} = \frac{0.8 \times 20 \times 12}{3.76} = 51.06$$

from Table C-36, $F_a = 18.25$ ksi.

$$\therefore \text{Carrying capacity} = A \times F_a = 38.8 \times 18.25$$
$$= 708 \text{ K} < 800 \quad \text{NO GOOD}$$

Try W14 × 145 (one size up):

$$A = 42.7; \quad r_y = 3.98$$
$$\frac{KL}{r} = \frac{0.8 \times 20 \times 12}{3.98}$$
$$= 48.25, \quad \text{i.e.,} \quad F_a = 18.5$$
$$A \times F_a = 42.7 \times 18.5 = 790 \text{ K} \quad \text{NO GOOD}$$

Try W14 × 159:

$$A = 46.7; \quad r_y = 4.0$$
$$\frac{KL}{r} = \frac{0.8 \times 20 \times 12}{4.0}$$
$$= 48, \quad \text{i.e.,} \quad F_a = 18.53$$
$$P_{\text{all}} = A \times F_a = 18.53 \times 46.7 = 865 \text{ K} \quad \text{OK}$$

Check b/t:

$$\text{flange } \frac{b}{2t_f} = 6.5 < 15.8$$
$$\text{web } \frac{d}{t_w} = 20.1 < 42.2 \quad \text{OK}$$

Check

$$\frac{KL}{r} = 48 < 200 \quad \text{OK}$$

Check existence, AISC Tables 1, 2 (pages 1-7, 1-8). OK
Use W14 × 159

Example 12-4. Find K-values for columns C1 and C2 for the frame shown in Fig. 12.5.4. Sidesway is allowed. All columns W8 × 40; all beams W16 × 40. The frame is braced laterally. Joints 1 and 4 are pinned, Joint 7 fixed.

Solution

Use alignment charts of AISC p. 3-5.

W8 × 40: $I_x = 146$
W16 × 40: $I_x = 518$

Fig. 12.5.4. Example 12.4.

Column I/L

C1 $\dfrac{146}{12 \times 14} = 0.87$

C2 $\dfrac{146}{12 \times 12} = 1.01$

Beam I/L

$\left.\begin{array}{l} B1 \\ B2 \end{array}\right\} \dfrac{518}{15 \times 12} = 2.88$

G values:

Column C2 $\left\{\begin{array}{l} G_3 = \dfrac{1.01}{2.88} = 0.35 \\ G_2 = \dfrac{1.01 + 0.87}{2.88} = 0.65 \end{array}\right\}$ K = 1.16

Column C2 $\left\{\begin{array}{l} G_2 = 0.65 \\ G_1 = 10.0 \\ \text{(pinned end)} \end{array}\right\}$ K = 1.80

12.6. BEAM-COLUMNS

Most columns in practice are actually beam-columns, that is, they carry significant amounts of compression and bending. The design strength of a beam-column is defined by an interaction curve, the simplest form of which is the straight line (see Fig. 12.6.1). The design of the beam-column using the straight-line interaction curve merely requires that the following formula is satisfied, as also indicated in Fig. 12.6.1:

$$\dfrac{f_a}{F_a} + \dfrac{f_b}{F_b} \leq 1.0 \qquad (12.12)$$

The straight-line interaction curve is empirical, and not entirely satisfactory, since it overestimates the strength of many members and underestimates that of others. Beam-column strength has now been defined very accurately by research, and the current AISC interaction equation, although set in the form of Eq. (12.12), is actually a curve:

$$\dfrac{f_a}{F_a} + \dfrac{f_b}{F_b} \dfrac{C_m}{\left(1 - \dfrac{f_a}{F'_e}\right)} \leq 1.0 \qquad (12.13)$$

where C_m is a coefficient that takes into account the variation in the moment applied. $C_m = 0.85$ for a frame which sways (that is, it has no bracing), and for no sway, $C_m = 0.6 - 0.4 M_1/M_2$, or more for transverse loading. Equation (12.13) is empirical in that it uses the form of Eq. (12.12), but modified so that it represents beam-column behavior very accurately. Because of some of the approximations in its development, a second interaction equation must be checked:

$$\dfrac{f_a}{0.6F_y} + \dfrac{f_b}{F_b} \leq 1.0 \qquad (12.14)$$

Thus, beam-column design requires that both AISC formulas, Eqs. (12.13) and (12.14), must be satisfied simultaneously, as shown in Example 12-5.

Example 12-5. Design the beam-column:
  top end moment = 3700 k-in.
  bottom end moment = 5700 k-in.
  (where moment application causes single curvature)
    axial load = 510 k
    length = 24 ft
    K = 1.0

Use a rolled W-shape, A36 steel, strong-axis bending, and the AISC Specification. Assume $F_b = 22$ ksi. (A simplifying assumption for this example only.)

Solution

To obtain trial shape, assume $M = 0$; from AISC p. 3-26, this gives W12 × 136. Add 4 or 5 sizes to account for moment, which gives W12 × 279. (If needed, a more exact method to obtain the trial shape is given in AISC, p. 3-9).

Try W12 × 279:

$A = 81.9;$ $r_x = 6.16$

$S_x = 393;$ $r_y = 3.38$

$\dfrac{KL}{r_y} = \dfrac{1 \times 24 \times 12}{3.38} = 85.2$

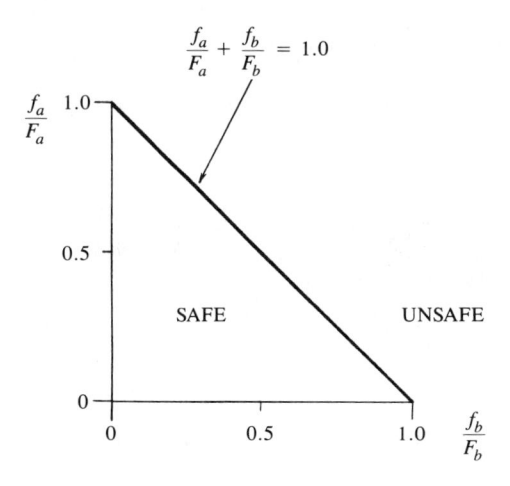

Fig. 12.6.1. Simple interaction design curve for beam-columns.

$$F_{ay} = 14.75, \text{ i.e., } F_a = 14.75$$

$$f_a = \frac{510}{81.9} = 6.23$$

Check:

$$\frac{f_a}{F_a} > 0.15$$

so, use AISC Eqs. H1-1, 1-2.

$$f_b = \frac{M}{S} = \frac{5700}{393} = 14.5$$

$$F_b = 22, \text{ as specified}$$

Reduction factor:

$$C_m = 0.6 - 0.4\left(-\frac{3700}{5700}\right) = 0.86$$

Amplification factor:

$$\frac{KL}{r_x} = \frac{1 \times 24 \times 12}{6.16} = 46.75, \text{ i.e., } F'_e = 68.3$$

(from Table 8 AISC p. 5-122). Therefore,

$$1 - \frac{f_a}{F'_e} = 1 - \frac{6.23}{68.3} = 0.909$$

Check interaction equations:

AISC Eq. H1-1 $\dfrac{6.23}{14.75} + \dfrac{0.86\,(14.5)}{22\,(0.909)} = 1.04$ NO GOOD

AISC Eq. H1-2 $\dfrac{6.23}{22} + \dfrac{14.5}{22} = 0.94$

Try W12 × 305:

$$A = 89.6; \quad r_x = 6.29$$

$$S_x = 435; \quad r_y = 3.42$$

$$\frac{KL}{r_y} = 85.2 \rightarrow \quad F_a = 14.75$$

$$f_a = \frac{510}{89.6} = 5.69; \quad f_b = \frac{5700}{435} = 13.10$$

$$F_b = 22.0$$

$$C_m = 0.86$$

$$\frac{KL}{r_x} = \frac{1 \times 24 \times 12}{6.29} = 45.79 \quad 1 - \frac{f_a}{F'_e} = 1 - \frac{5.69}{68.4} = 0.92$$

$$F'_e = 68.4$$

AISC Eq. H1-1: $\dfrac{5.69}{14.75} + \dfrac{0.86\,(13.10)}{22\,(0.92)} = 0.94$ OK

AISC Eq. H1-2: $\dfrac{5.69}{22} + \dfrac{13.10}{22} = 0.85$

Check b/t, d/w: OK.
Check shape existence: OK.
Use W12 × 305. (Note: W14 × 257 also OK.)

12.7. BOLTED CONNECTIONS

Before the 1950s, rivets were used almost exclusively as the mechanical fasteners in connections. The introduction of the high strength bolt resulted in accurately defined and greater strengths, simplicity of erection, and simplicity in the connection details—thus, after a period of transition, rivets are no longer used today. Connections which use mechanical fasteners are splices in a structural member, beam-to-beam and beam-to-column connections, and connections to brackets or gusset plates.

Bolted connections may be designed as bearing joints or as friction joints. As shown in Fig. 12.7.1, the bearing joint transfers load directly through the bolt which bears on each plate, while the friction joint transfers the load through the faying (or mating) surfaces of the plates, which are gripped tightly together by the bolt. Despite the differences between the two types of joint, both are designed on the basis of the shear stress in the bolt. This is a matter of convenience for the friction joint, since its bolt is not in shear but is actually in tension. Thus, the allowable shear stresses for design of the bolt in the friction joint are less than those in the bearing joint.

The bolt transmits load either in single shear or in double shear (Fig. 12.7.2). In double shear, the bolt has two shear fracture surfaces, and thus has twice the strength as in single shear.

In addition to the shear stress, the joint also needs to be checked for bearing stress, that is, to check that the stress between the bolt and the bearing surface of the hole of the plate is within the allowable limits: If the plate is not thick enough, it will crumple and fail under load. There are also requirements for the minimum edge distance for the hole in the plate.

It is assumed that all bolts in a connection carry the same load, despite the fact that the bolts at the ends carry

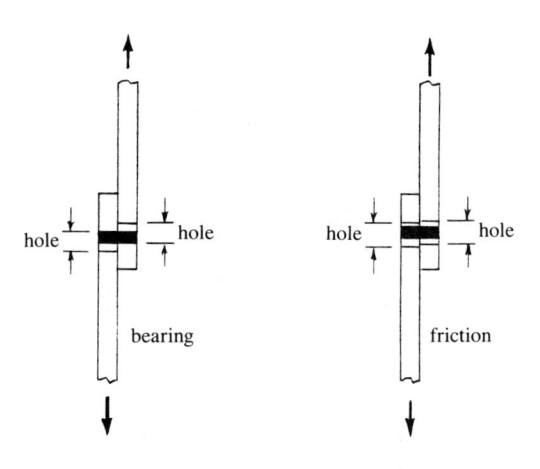

Fig. 12.7.1. Bearing and friction joints.

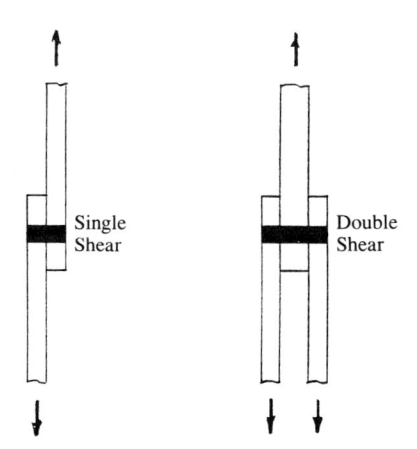

Fig. 12.7.2. Bolts in single shear and in double shear.

substantially more than those in the middle. This assumption depends on the ductility of the steel which allows the end bolts to deform, redistributing the load in the joint. This redistribution is not possible in a very long joint with a single row of bolts where the end bolts will shear off under load, leading to failure of the whole joint by "unbuttoning." Thus, bolted joints need to be compact with many rows and not long with a single row of bolts.

High strength bolts are available in two grades, ASTM A325 and A490, and with threads either over the whole length of the bolt or over a specified length such that the allowable stress for the bearing-type connection depends on whether the threads are excluded or not from the shear planes.

Example 12-6. Design a maximum strength, single-lap joint, bearing-type connection, between two $6 \times \frac{1}{2}$-in. plates. $F_y = 36$ ksi. Use $\frac{5}{8}$-in.-diameter A325 bolts.

Solution

For one bolt, area = 0.307 in.² (see AISC p. 4-3). Assume threading *not* excluded; then, from AISC Table J3.2 allowable stress, single shear = 21.0 ksi, i.e.,

$$\text{allowable load} = 21.0 \times 0.307$$
$$= 6.5 \text{ K per bolt}$$

From AISC Section J3.7,

allowable stress, bearing = $1.2 F_u$
$$= 1.2(58) = 69.6 \text{ ksi},$$

i.e.,

$$\text{allowable load} = 69.6 \times \left(\frac{5}{8} \times \frac{1}{2}\right) = 21.8 \text{ K}.$$

So, design for shear, since $6.5 < 21.8$.
Assume 1 row of fasteners, i.e., $A_g = 6 \times \frac{1}{2} = 3$ in.²:

$$A_n = \left[6 - \left(\frac{5}{8} + \frac{1}{8}\right)\right]\frac{1}{2} = 2.62 \text{ in.}^2.$$

Check the 85 percent rule:

$$0.85 A_g = 2.55 \text{ in.}^2$$

$$\therefore \text{Use } A_n = 2.55$$

From AISC Section D1, for $P_{\max}$, use

$$F_t = 0.60 F_y \text{ on gross area} = 22 \text{ ksi}$$

or

$$F_t = 0.50 F_u \text{ on effective net area} = 29 \text{ ksi}$$

i.e.,

$$\left.\begin{array}{l}P_{\max} = 22(3) = 66 \text{ K}\\ \text{or } = 29(2.55) = 74 \text{ K}\end{array}\right\} \rightarrow P_{\max} = 66.0 \text{ K}$$

$$\text{Number of bolts} = \frac{66}{6.5} = 10.2$$

Use 11 bolts.

12.8. WELDED CONNECTIONS

There are approximately 40 welding processes classified by the American Welding Society (Ref. 12.8). Arc-welding normally is used for structural steel, and may be manual but is more often the automatic process, typically using the shielded metal-arc or the submerged-arc process (Refs. 12.3 and 12.8). A welded connection is both simpler to fabricate and more esthetically pleasing than a bolted connection, and further, gives a continuity between the connected parts. On the other hand, the welding process needs great care to ensure a sound connection; the choice of a weldable steel, the use of qualified welders, the design of the joint, the choice of the welding sequence to ensure no distortion, and the use of pre-heat or post-heat, all play a role.

Welding gives the best results when carried out in the down-hand position, and a "positioner" may be used to place the joint in the desired position for welding. The specification of the electrode is critical; electrodes use a numbering system to describe the basic properties, for example, E*abcd*: E indicates an electrode for metal arc-welding; *ab* is the minimum tensile strength in ksi; *c* is the welding position where 1 = all positions, 2 = flat and horizontal, and 3 = only flat; and *d* indicates such items as the current supply and welding technique variables. Thus, E7012 is a common electrode for structural steel: it is all position, either DC straight polarity or AC welding machine, and a minimum tensile strength of 70 ksi. The structural design specifies this electrode as an E70 electrode, which defines its strength, while the other criteria would be of interest to the fabricating shop in achieving a sound weld.

There are two basic welds, the groove weld and the fillet weld, and a number of joints, including butt joints and lap joints (see Fig. 12.8.1). The joints need edge preparation,

groove weld
(butt joint)

fillet weld
(lap joint)

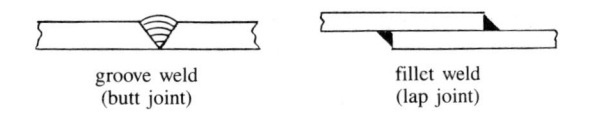

Fig. 12.8.1. Basic welds.

even if this is only a square cut at the end of the plate, using flame-cutting. Butt joints usually have a V-preparation, as shown in Fig. 12.8.1, but also may use J-grooves or other shapes. Preparation of the joint for welding is important—it adds to the cost but results in a better and stronger joint. Many joints are "prequalified" (Refs. 12.8 and 12.9); such joints may be specified for use without testing. Other joints must first be fabricated and tested to check for soundness and strength.

Groove welds do not need to be checked for stress, as the weld will normally be stronger than the parent material. Fillet welds do need to be checked for the stress they carry. There are two basic assumptions for the strength of a fillet weld: the load is distributed uniformly over the weld, and the strength of the weld is the same irrespective of the direction of the load. Neither of these assumptions reflects actual behavior but their use is a major simplification in the design process (Ref. 12.3).

The shear strength of the weld is the basis for fillet weld design. The design is based on the allowable shear stress on the minimum throat dimension (see Fig. 12.8.2 for definitions). Thus, the length of the weld, L, required to resist a load P, may be determined from the throat area of the weld length times the allowable stress in shear,

$$L = \frac{P}{(0.707\,S)F_v} \qquad (12.15)$$

The AISC (in Table J2.5 of Ref. 12.4) specifies the allowable stress in shear as

shear on throat,

$$F_v = 0.30 \times \text{nominal tensile strength of weld metal}$$

The AISC (in Art. J2.2a) allows the throat dimension of Fig. 12.8.2 to be increased by 0.11 in. for fillet welds with a size over $\frac{3}{8}$ in. which are made by the submerged-arc process. This recognizes the deeper weld penetration in comparison with that of the shielded-arc process.

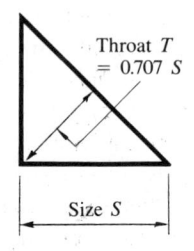

Fig. 12.8.2. Fillet-weld cross section.

Example 12-7 repeats the connection of Example 12-6 for a welded connection.

Example 12-7. Design a maximum strength, single-lap, fillet-welded joint, for the two $6 \times \frac{1}{2}$-in. plates of Example 12.6. $F_y = 36$ ksi.

Solution

$$A_g = A_n = 6 \times \frac{1}{2} = 3 \text{ in.}^2$$

$$P_{max} = (22)3 = 66 \text{ K}$$

Use weld size $\frac{3}{8}''$, use E70 electrodes.

From AISC Table J2.5:

$$F_v = (0.3)70 = 21.0 \text{ ksi on effective area}$$

Length of weld:

$$L = \frac{P}{(0.707\,S)F_v} = \frac{66}{(0.707)\frac{3}{8}(21)} = 11.9 \text{ in.}$$

∴ Need 12 in. of $\frac{3}{8}''$ weld, E70 electrodes.
Placement of weld: Fig. 12.8.3, weld = $2 \times 6'' = 12''$

If the answer had been more than 12 in., the additional length of weld would be obtained by using a slot, or by cutting plates at an angle (Fig. 12.8.4).

12.9. RIGID FRAMES

Rigid frames, also called continuous frames, derive their name from the fact that moment is transferred from one member to another without any loss. These frames are esthetically very pleasing, and achieve their continuity and their appearance through the use of welded connections. Regular frames do not have rigid connections and their design is relatively simple and involves the design of the

Fig. 12.8.3. Example 12.7: insufficient length of weld.

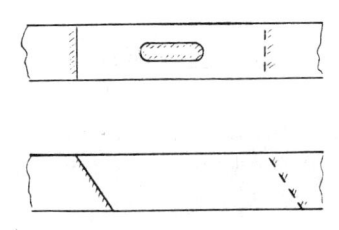

Fig. 12.8.4. Example 12.7: adequate length of weld.

separate elements. Rigid frames, on the other hand, may be designed as a unit, which also reflects their actual behavior: the design may be based on elastic or inelastic behavior, that is, on allowable stress design, plastic design, or limit states design (Refs. 12.3, 12.4, and 12.5). The design is relatively simple for a single-story frame and becomes lengthy and complex for multistory frames.

The strength of rigid frames depends on the continuity of the joints, that is, on the corner connections, haunched connections, and beam-to-column connections (see Fig. 12.9.1). Although approximate elastic methods exist for design, corner connections, haunched connections, and beam-to-column connections may be designed most simply using plastic analysis. Haunched connections need lateral bracing at the ends and at the inside of the knee, and this is a particularly important design check as the lack of lateral bracing will lead to lateral buckling of the inside flanges when they are in compression. The placement of the lateral brace may be a nuisance, as it does not contribute to the esthetics, yet it *must* be used for structural reasons.

The cost of fabricating and welding rigid connections is high, but this needs to be balanced against the overall gains in strength and esthetics.

12.10. PLATE GIRDERS

Plate girders are very deep beams which are deeper than rolled shapes and thus must be fabricated by connecting flange and web plates. Today, plate girders are fabricated by welding. The deep shape of the plate girder with its thick flanges and thin web supplies a relatively large section modulus, Fig. 12.10.1, and thus these members are used to span large distances, as would be needed, for example, in the ground floor foyer level of a multistory building (Fig. 12.10.2).

The design of plate girders (Refs. 12.4 and 12.5) follows a simple although time-consuming procedure (Ref. 12.3) which is based on their actual ultimate strength. Thus, the

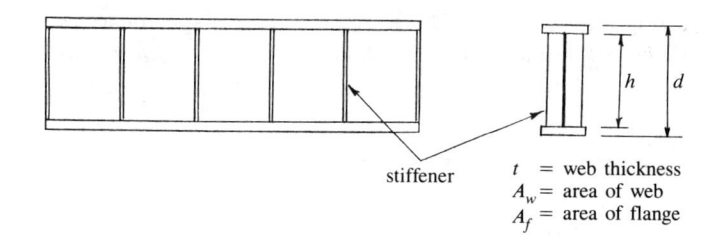

t = web thickness
A_w = area of web
A_f = area of flange

Fig. 12.10.1. Plate girder.

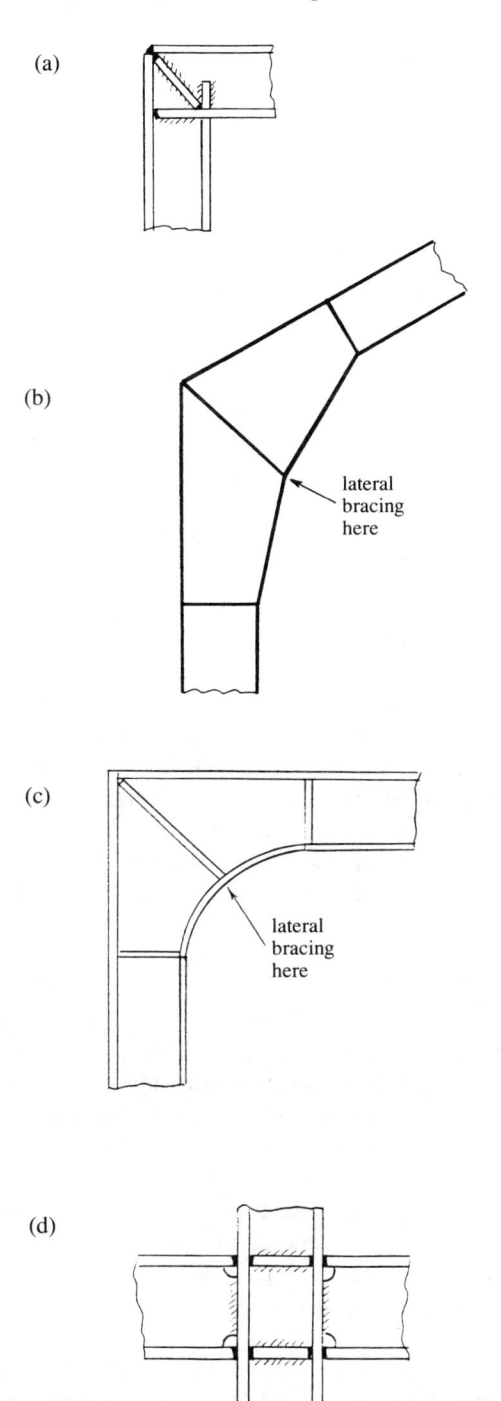

Fig. 12.9.1. Welded connections. (a) Corner connection; (b) haunched connection; (c) curved knee; (d) beam-to-column connection.

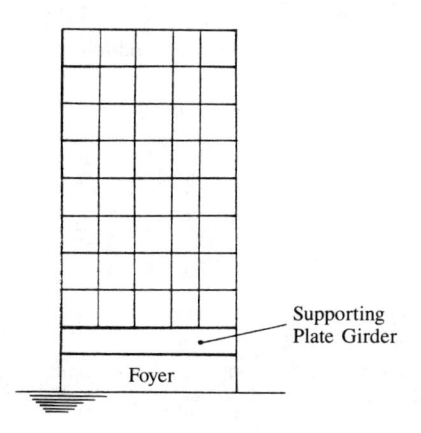

Fig. 12.10.2. Multistory building with plate girder.

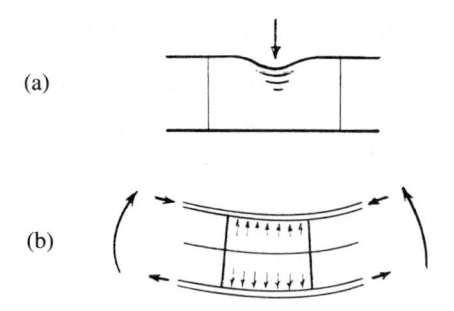

Fig. 12.10.3. Forces to be considered in the design of a plate girder. (a) Failure due to web being too thin; (b) forces acting on a panel of the girder.

web must be thick enough to resist vertical buckling of the flange (Fig. 12.10.3). Equilibrium of all the forces involved leads to an expression for the h/t ratio, and thus the web thickness. The flange is designed so that it resists bending moment, as in a beam; however, in a plate girder the compression web buckles and relieves itself of load, thus increasing the stress in the compression flange (Fig. 12.10.4). This results in a complicated expression for the maximum stress in the compression flange, which is a function of h/t and A_w/A_f. There are further modifications to the expression to prevent lateral buckling, and the local buckling criteria also must be met.

The spacing of the transverse stiffeners results from a consideration of tension field action (Ref. 12.3). As a plate girder is loaded, parts of the web start acting as tension members, so that the plate girder becomes, in effect, a Pratt truss (Fig. 12.10.5). The spacing of the stiffeners is obtained from a consideration of the equilibrium forces acting on the panels. There are tables in the specifications (Refs. 12.4 and 12.5) which facilitate this. The size of the

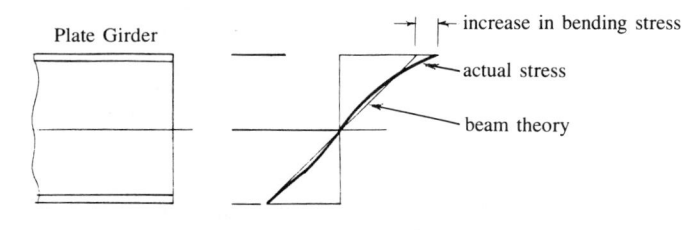

Fig. 12.10.4. Bending stress distribution in plate girder.

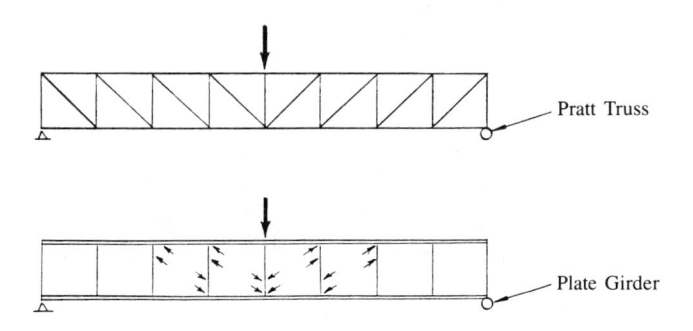

Fig. 12.10.5. Tension-field action in plate girder.

intermediate and end stiffeners also may be obtained at this time. It should be noted that intermediate stiffeners are not mandatory, but that their use allows considerably greater loads to be carried than otherwise.

12.11. PLASTIC DESIGN

Plastic analysis and design is a method based on the ultimate or collapse strength of a structure, unlike allowable stress design, which considers only elastic behavior (Refs. 12.1 and 12.10). In plastic analysis, the structure is allowed to reach the yield at its points of maximum stress, and then is allowed to carry additional load until the entire cross section at those points has yielded so that no further load may be carried. Plastic analysis and design uses the ductility of steel, which allows considerable yielding and readjustment of stress to occur. The method is not only simple but also results in more economical designs than those using elastic methods, and it also gives a better estimate of strength. It is particularly advantageous to use for continuous beams and simple rigid frames.

Plastic analysis and design is covered by the 1989 AISC Specifications in Chapter N (Ref. 12.4) and is an integral part of, and a limiting condition of, load and resistance factor design of the 1986 AISC Specifications (Ref. 12.5).

12.12. LOAD AND RESISTANCE FACTOR DESIGN (LRFD)

Limit states design is based on probability studies of the strength (or "reliability") of structural elements under loads which are factored depending on the accuracy of the knowledge of their magnitude. Limit states design is called load and resistance factor design (LRFD) in the U.S.A., and is covered by the 1986 AISC Specification (Ref. 12.5).

The basic equation governing LRFD is (Ref. 12.5)

$$\sum \gamma_i Q_i \leq \phi R_n \qquad (12.16)$$

where
i = type of load (DL, LL, wind load, etc.)
Q_i = nominal load effect
γ_i = load factor corresponding to Q_i (this takes account of uncertainties of load)
$\sum \gamma_i Q_i$ = required resistance
R_n = nominal resistance
ϕ = resistance factor corresponding to R_n (this accounts for the uncertainties inherent in the determination of resistance)
ϕR_n = design strength

Note that $\gamma > 1$ and $\phi < 1$. It should also be noted that the left-hand side of Eq. (12.16) is the required resistance, which is computed by structural analysis based on assumed loads, and that the right-hand side of the equation is the limiting structural capacity provided by the members considered.

LRFD has many basic requirements which are similar to, if not identical with, those of allowable stress design, so that in those cases the main difference from allowable stress design comes from the use of load factors and resistance factors in place of the factors of safety used in allowable stress design.

As an example of LRFD, consider the design of a tension member. Chapter D of the 1986 AISC Specification (Ref. 12.5) states, in part:

The design strength, $\phi_t P_n$, shall be the lower value obtained according to the limit states of yielding in the gross section, and fracture in the net section:

(a) for yielding in the gross section,

$$\phi_t = 0.90$$

$$P_n = F_y A_g \quad (12.17)$$

(b) for fracture in the net section,

$$\phi_t = 0.75$$

$$P_n = F_u A_e \quad (12.18)$$

where A_e is the effective net area, P_n is the nominal axial strength, ϕ_t is the resistance factor for tension members, and the other symbols are identical to those used in allowable stress design.

For ASTM A36 steel, $F_y = 36$ ksi and $F_u = 58$ ksi, so that Eqs. (12.17) and (12.18) become

(a) $\quad \phi_t P_n = 0.9(36) A_g = 32.4 A_g \quad (12.19)$

(b) $\quad \phi_t P_n = 0.75(58) A_e = 43.5 A_e \quad (12.20)$

Example 12-8. Determine the design strength of a W10 × 30 shape of A36 steel used as a tension member. What dead load can it carry when the only load is the dead load? Assume that there are no holes in the member. Use LRFD.

Solution

Since there are no holes, $A_e = A_g$, and Eq. (12.19) governs, since 32.4 < 43.5, (in comparing Eqs. (12.19) and (12.20). Thus,

$$\phi_t P_n = 32.4 A_g = 32.4(8.84) = 286 \text{ kip}$$

Since DL is the only load, the load to be considered is $1.4D$. (This is Eq. A4-1 of AISC-86 (Ref. 12.5), one of six equations in Chapter A4, Loads and Combinations, which defines the load factors to use with various combinations of DL, LL, wind, snow, and earthquake loads.) That is,

$$1.4 P_{DL} \leq \phi_t P_n = 286 \text{ kip}$$

and

$$P_{DL} \leq \frac{286}{1.4} = 204 \text{ kip}$$

Thus, 204 kip is the maximum dead load that can be supported by the member.

12.13. COMPUTER-AIDED DESIGN

The use of computers has developed to such an extent that the design and drawing of many structures can be carried out completely with them. (Computer-aided design and drawing, or CADD.) It has been suggested that failure to use computerized databases and their presentation of the latest information may constitute a legal liability in the case of a failure (Ref. 12.11). There are computer programs for structural analysis, for structural design, and for the preparation of engineering drawings and construction specifications, and all design offices are equipped to handle them to a lesser or greater degree. Thus, the AISC has available a computerized database for the properties and dimensions of the structural shapes listed in its Manual.

The legal aspects of using prepared computer programs for structural design has not kept pace with the technical developments. There is a tendency for computer programs to be purchased and used, with little attention paid to the validity of the results, even though a cursory examination of suspicious results would alert the user. The user normally will have neither the time nor the expertise to correct an error in the computer program. Thus, the possibility for structural failure resulting from a program error, and then the lack of attention or recognition of a suspicious result, is not unreal.

12.14. FABRICATION

The fabrication of the structure is of critical importance and should be part of the design engineer's responsibility. The structure must be fabricated according to the intention of the designer; otherwise, there is the very real possibility of different load and stress situations which could lead to potential failure.

Fabrication using welding needs particular care, although this is not as critical with buildings as it is with bridges and other structures where dynamic loading situations can cause fatigue problems.

REFERENCES

12.1. WRC-ASCE Joint Committee. *Commentary on Plastic Design in Steel*, ASCE Manual No. 41, 2nd Ed., American Society of Civil Engineers, New York 1969.

12.2. T. C. Kavanagh and S. M. Johnson. "Maintenance—The Systems Approach," *Civil Engineering* (New York), July 1966.

12.3. L. Tall (Ed.). *Structural Steel Design*, 2nd Ed. Ronald/Wiley, New York 1974.

12.4. *Specification for Structural Steel Buildings, Allowable Stress Design and Plastic Design*. American Institute of Steel Construction, Chicago, 1989. (Part of *AISC Manual*, 9th Ed., Ref. 12.9.)

12.5. *Load and Resistance Factor Design Specification for Structural Steel Buildings*. American Institute of Steel Construction, Chicago, 1986. (Part of *AISC LRFD Manual*, 1st Ed.)

12.6. *Steel Structures for Buildings—Limit States Design*, CSA Standard

S16.1-1974. Canadian Standards Association, Rexdale, Ontario, 1974.
12.7. T. V. Galambos (Ed.). *Guide to Stability Design Criteria for Metal Structures*, 4th Ed. Wiley/Interscience, New York, 1988.
12.8. *Welding Handbook*, 8th Ed., Sect. 1—*Fundamentals*. American Welding Society, Miami, 1988.
12.9. *Manual of Steel Construction, Allowable Stress Design*. 9th Ed. American Institute of Steel Construction, Chicago, 1989.
12.10. L. S. Beedle. *Plastic Design of Steel Frames*. Wiley, New York, 1958.
12.11. P. M. Lurie and B. D. Weiss. "Computer Assisted Mistakes." *Civil Engineering* (New York), December 1988.

SUGGESTIONS FOR FURTHER READING

American Institute of Steel Construction. *Manual of Steel Construction*, 8th Ed. AISC, Chicago, 1980.
L. Tall (Ed.). *Structural Steel Design*, 2nd Ed. Ronald/Wiley, New York, 1974.
CONSTRADO. *British Steel Designers' Manual*, 4th Ed. Granada, London, 1983.
B. Gorenc and R. Tinyou. *Steel Designers' Handbook*, 5th Ed. New South Wales University Press, Sydney, 1984.
The Structural Use of Steel in Buildings—BS 5950. British Standards Institution, London. Part 1, 1985. Part 2, 1985. Part 4, 1985, Part 5, 1987.
Australian Steel Structures Code—AS 1250. Standards Association of Australia, Sydney 1981.

NOTATION

A	area of member
A_e	net effective area
A_f	area of flange
A_g	gross area
A_n, A_{net}	net area
A_w	area of web
b	width of flange
C	a factor
c	distance from neutral axis to extreme fiber
D, DL	dead load
d	depth of cross section; depth of web; diameter of hole
f_a	actual stress in compression
f_b	actual stress in bending
f_{cr}	critical stress
f_t	actual stress in tension
f_v	actual stress in shear
F_a	allowable stress in compression
F_b	allowable stress in bending
F_t	allowable stress in tension
F_v	allowable stress in shear
FS	factor of safety
F_y	yield strength
F_u	ultimate strength
g	gage
h	depth of web of plate girder
I	moment of inertia (second moment of area)
K	effective length factor of column; kilo pounds (=1000 pounds)
L	length of member; distance between lateral supports of beam; length of weld; live load
LL	live load
L/r	slenderness ratio
M	moment
NA	neutral axis
P, Q	load on member
r	radius of gyration
S	section modulus; size of weld
t, t_f	thickness of flange
t_w	thickness of web
w	thickness of web; width of plate
γ	load factor
δ	deflection
ϵ	strain
ϕ	resistance factor

A list of abbreviations of the units of measurement, definitions of these units, and conversion factors between British/American and metric units are given in the Appendix.

13
Concrete and Masonry Structures

Madan Mehta

This chapter deals with some of the fundamental aspects of the design of reinforced concrete, prestressed concrete and masonry structures. It begins with an introduction to the ultimate strength design method in reinforced concrete and its underlying assumptions. The next few sections deal with flexure, shear, torsion, crack control, and deflection in reinforced concrete members.

The design of one-way slabs is covered in greater detail since they occur frequently in small buildings which an architect might like to design without the services of a structural consultant. Prestressed concrete and composite construction are covered in Sections 13.13 and 13.14 respectively. The final section deals with contemporary load-bearing masonry structures.

13.1. REINFORCED CONCRETE CODES OF PRACTICE

Although the basic theory of structural design in reinforced concrete is itself universal, there are several differences in its application from country to country. In the United States and Australia, for example, 6 × 12 in. (150 × 300 mm) concrete cylinders are tested for compressive strength; in Britain, the test specimens are 6 in. (150 mm) concrete cubes. Most countries, similarly, have their own individual national concrete codes of practice. In the United States, the *Building Code Requirements for Reinforced Concrete* published by the American Concrete Institute (ACI) is followed. This code is updated every few years to include the latest developments in concrete design and construction. The current edition of the code (ACI 318-83) was comprehensively updated in 1983 with a few modifications incorporated in 1986.

A code of practice has no legal authority by itself until adopted by the building code of a central, state or local government. The ACI code has been adopted by almost all cities in the United States. Many other countries which at present do not have their own codes, have also adopted it. The material presented in this chapter (Sections 13.2 to 13.13) is based on the current ACI code (ACI 318-83, revised 1986) to which a general reference will be made using the word "code" and a specific reference by indicating in parentheses its relevant section number.

13.2. REINFORCED CONCRETE MATERIALS

Concrete

This has been covered in Chapter 3. Note that the fundamental property of concrete is its specified compressive strength, f'_c. All other properties such as shear strength, flexural tensile strength, modulus of elasticity, etc. are derived from the value of f'_c.

The most commonly specified compressive strength of concrete for buildings varies between 3 and 4 ksi (approximately 20 to 30 MPa), although concrete up to 22 ksi (150 MPa) compressive strength has been produced in laboratories and up to 19 ksi (130 MPa) used in buildings (Ref. 13.1). For foundations, the lower strength is usually specified; up to 8 ksi concrete (sometimes stronger) may be required in ground floor columns of a tall building. For prestressed concrete components, 5 to 6 ksi concrete is generally used.

Steel Reinforcement

The properties of steel have been covered in Chapter 2. In buildings, reinforcing steel bars of grades 40 and 60 which correspond to yield strength $f_y = 40$ ksi (300 MPa), and 60 ksi (400 MPa) respectively, are normally used. The Concrete Reinforcing Steel Institute (CRSI) of the United States recommends the use of grade 60 bars in buildings for economy (Ref. 13.2) and it is this grade that is commonly used. Grade 40 steel is recommended where deflection and flexural cracks must be limited, such as in water-retaining structures and thin concrete roofs (shells and folded plates) exposed to weather. It is also preferred for use in field-bent dowels because of its higher ductility.

The bars are rolled with surface ribs for better bonding to concrete. Smooth bars are not allowed except as spirals for columns. Eleven standard sizes of bars, referred to (in the customary American units) as #3, #4, #5, etc. are available in the United States. Their diameters and cross-sectional areas are given in Table 13.1; Table 13.1a gives the diameters and cross-sectional areas of metric bars.

Reinforcing steel is also produced as *welded wire fabric*, which consists of a rectangular grid of bars or wires welded at intersections. It is available in rolls or sheets, depending on the size of wires, and is widely used as reinforcement in slabs and walls. Its main advantage is the economy of labor in placing the reinforcement, but it also provides better distribution of reinforcement because of its small closely spaced bars.

13.3. METHODS OF DESIGN IN REINFORCED CONCRETE

There are two methods of structural design in reinforced concrete: the *working stress method* and the *ultimate strength method*.

In the working stress method, the material is assumed to behave elastically under *service loads* with a linear stress-strain relationship. The size of a structural member is determined by the fact that the stresses in the member under service loads must be less than the *allowable stresses*. Service load is defined as the actual maximum load to which a member will be subjected. The allowable stress is a fraction of the stress at which the member will fail and is obtained by dividing the failure stress (or the ultimate stress) by a factor of safety.

The working stress method makes no prediction as to the ultimate load carrying capacity of a member, the maximum load it can sustain before failure. In the ultimate strength or simply the strength design method, the size of the member is determined by its ultimate load carrying capacity. The design is not concerned with service loads but with the behavior of the member under loads that will cause complete collapse of the structure.

The working stress method is attractive for its simplicity but has two major disadvantages: (i) it does not represent the true behavior of the member, since concrete behaves inelastically under service loads, and (ii) various types of loads acting on the member namely, dead loads, live loads, wind loads, etc. are assigned the same factor of safety, although the uncertainty in determining their magnitudes varies. For example, the dead loads on a member can be predicted with greater certainty than live loads or wind loads.

For a long time, the working stress method was the only design method in use. The strength design method was introduced in the code for the first time in 1956 and is almost exclusively the method accepted by the current code. The working stress method is permitted only for the design of non-prestressed members as an alternative design approach.

The strength design method has the advantage in that the strength of a member is computed based on the actual (nonlinear) stress-strain behavior of concrete and the safety provisions are based on more realistic considerations than those assumed in the working stress method. It consequently gives a more economical design and it is this method that is further discussed.

Safety Provisions

In the strength design method, the safety of the structure is provided through two factors: the load factor and the strength reduction factor.

Table 13.1. Diameters and Areas of U.S. Standard Bars.

Bar size	Nominal diameter (in.)	Area (in.²)
#3	$\frac{3}{8}$	0.11
#4	$\frac{1}{2}$	0.20
#5	$\frac{5}{8}$	0.31
#6	$\frac{3}{4}$	0.44
#7	$\frac{7}{8}$	0.60
#8	1	0.79
#9	$1\frac{1}{8}$	1.0
#10	$1\frac{1}{4}$	1.27
#11	$1\frac{3}{8}$	1.56
#14	$1\frac{3}{4}$	2.25
#18	$2\frac{1}{4}$	4.0

Table 13.1a. Diameters and Areas of U.S. Standard Metric Bars.

Bar size	Nominal diameter (mm)	Area (mm²)
#10	11.3	100
#15	16.0	200
#20	19.5	300
#25	25.2	500
#30	29.9	700
#35	35.7	1000
#45	43.7	1500
#55	56.4	2500

Load Factors. These are factors (numbers greater than 1) by which the service loads are multiplied to give the design loads. Their values vary with the uncertainty inherent in the determination of a particular type of load. A load whose magnitude and distribution can be ascertained with greater accuracy is assigned a smaller value of load factor than one about which predictions cannot be made with the same degree of accuracy.

The load factors prescribed by the code are given in Table 13.2. The design load or the factored load U is obtained by multiplying the service loads by appropriate load factors and adding the resulting products. Thus, if a member is subjected to dead loads and live loads only, the factored load, U, is:

$$U = 1.4D + 1.7L$$

Recognizing the improbability of the maximum values of various types of loads to occur simultaneously, the code allows suitable reduction for various load combinations. Thus, if a member is subjected to dead loads, live loads, and wind loads, then:

$$U = 0.75(1.4D + 1.7L + 1.7W)$$

Similar provisions exist in the code for other load combinations. Obviously, the structure must be adequate under all possible load combinations. For example, the live loads may not always be present on the structure. Since the gravity loads counteract the effect of the lateral loads, the structure must be checked for stability and strength by assuming the live loads as zero. Thus, the following load combination must also be considered in addition to other combinations:

$$U = 0.9D + 1.3W$$

The axial forces, shear forces, bending moments, etc. produced by factored loads are called factored axial forces, factored shear forces, factored bending moments, represented by P_u, V_u, M_u, respectively.

Strength Reduction Factors. A structural member of given dimensions has a limited capacity to withstand applied forces and moments. The maximum values of these quantities that a member can sustain are called its *nominal strengths*. Thus, the maximum bending moment that a member can resist is called its nominal moment strength, M_n. Similarly, the maximum shear force that a member can resist is called its nominal shear strength, V_n.

To account for adverse variations in material strength due to inadequate quality control of materials, workmanship, supervision etc. the code requires that the nominal strength of a member be multiplied by a factor less than 1, called the strength reduction factor, ϕ (Table 13.3). Thus, the flexural strength of a member, as assumed by the code, is not M_n but ϕM_n; similarly, its shear strength is assumed as ϕV_n. For a member to be structurally adequate, the factored moments and forces must be less than or equal to the corresponding strengths of the member, i.e.,

$$P_u \leq \phi P_n; \quad M_u \leq \phi M_n; \quad V_u \leq \phi V_n$$

Strength reduction factors constitute the second part of the safety provision in the strength design method. Their values, Table 13.3, vary with the type of stress, depending on the severity of failure caused by such a stress. For example, the value of ϕ for compressive stresses is lower than that for flexural stresses since the failure of a column (which is primarily under compression) can be more catastrophic than the failure of a beam (which is primarily under flexural stresses).

13.4. FLEXURE IN REINFORCED CONCRETE MEMBERS

Failure Modes

A reinforced concrete section may fail in flexure (bending) in three modes depending on the relative areas of steel and concrete:

(i) The concrete in the compression zone may reach its crushing strength before the steel in the tension zone reaches yield stress. Such a section, called an *overreinforced section*, gives a brittle failure because the crushing of the concrete is sudden. Since steel deforms extremely little below its yield stress, there is very little overall deformation in the beam, giving virtually no warning of impending failure.

(ii) The steel may yield before the concrete in the compression zone attains the maximum (crushing) stress. Such a section has relatively small amount of reinforcement and is called an *underreinforced section*. Since the

Table 13.2. Load Factors.

Type of Load	Load Factor
Dead load, D	1.4
Live load, L	1.7
Wind load, W	1.7
Earth pressure, H	1.7
Fluid pressure, F	1.4
Earthquake load, E	1.87

Table 13.3. Strength Reduction Factors, ϕ.

Type of Stress	ϕ
Bending with or without axial tension, and axial tension	0.9
Shear and torsion	0.85
Bending in plain concrete	0.65
Bearing on concrete	0.70
Axial compression with or without bending:	
members with spiral reinforcement	0.75
members with ties	0.70

yielding of steel is accompanied by large deformations, ample warning of failure is available, resulting in a ductile mode of failure. The final collapse of the beam, however, is due to the crushing of the concrete, because the stresses in concrete in the compression zone increase after the tension steel yields and undergoes strain hardening.

(iii) The concrete in the compression zone may reach the maximum compressive stress at the same time as the yielding of the steel in the tension zone. Such a section is called a *balanced section*.

To avoid a brittle failure of reinforced concrete members, the code (10.3.3) prescribes an upper limit on the area of steel in members subjected to flexure. It requires that a section under flexure be designed as an underreinforced section with the steel area A_s not to exceed 75 percent of the steel area required for a balanced section, A_{sb}; that is,

$$A_{s\max} = 0.75 A_{sb}$$

However, if the area of steel is extremely small, the member may fail by the sudden snapping of steel (tensile failure). The code, therefore, prescribes a lower limit on the steel area in the section. The maximum and minimum prescribed steel areas are given later in this section.

Design Assumptions

The following assumptions are made in designing reinforced concrete members in bending.

(i) There is a perfect bond between steel and concrete so that the strains in both materials are the same.

(ii) Except for prestressed concrete or plain concrete, the tensile strength of concrete is negligible. Therefore, the entire tensile force in concrete sections at failure is provided by the steel.

(iii) The value of E_s for all grades of steel is 29,000 ksi (2×10^5 MPa).

(iv) The actual shape of compressive stress distribution in concrete sections at failure is approximately parabolic, similar to the stress-strain curve obtained from test cylinders. However, to make computations simple, the code (10.2.7) permits the use of rectangular stress distribution in which the stress in concrete at failure is $0.85 f'_c$ and the depth of stress block, a, is such that: $a = \beta_1 c$ (Fig. 13.4.1). β_1 is a constant whose value is 0.85 for $f'_c \leq 4$ ksi (30 MPa). For $f'_c > 4$ ksi, the value of β_1 is reduced by 0.05 for every additional 1 ksi. Thus, if $f'_c = 5$ ksi, β_1 is 0.80 and if $f'_c = 6$ ksi, β_1 is 0.75. (In the SI system, the corresponding reduction in the value of β_1 is 0.008 for each 1 MPa in excess of 30 MPa). β_1 is not allowed to be less than 0.65, regardless of the strength of concrete.

(v) The strain in concrete is linearly proportional to the distance from neutral axis. The maximum strain in extreme compression fibers of concrete at failure is 0.003.

Singly Reinforced Beams

Consider a rectangular beam with tension steel only (singly reinforced beam), Fig. 13.4.2. Since the code requires the steel to yield at failure, the stress in steel is f_y. Thus the tensile force T and compressive force C on the section are:

$$T = A_s f_y \quad \text{and} \quad C = 0.85 f'_c a b$$

For equilibrium, T must be equal to C. Thus,

$$a = \frac{A_s f_y}{0.85 f'_c b} \tag{13.1}$$

The nominal moment strength of the section, M_n, is:

$$M_n = C\left(d - \frac{a}{2}\right) = T\left(d - \frac{a}{2}\right)$$

Substituting the value of a, as obtained above, and $\rho = A_s/bd$, the following is obtained for the moment strength of the section, ϕM_n:

$$\phi M_n = K b d^2 \tag{13.2}$$

where

$$K = 0.9 \rho f_y \left[1 - \frac{\rho f_y}{1.7 f'_c}\right] \tag{13.3}$$

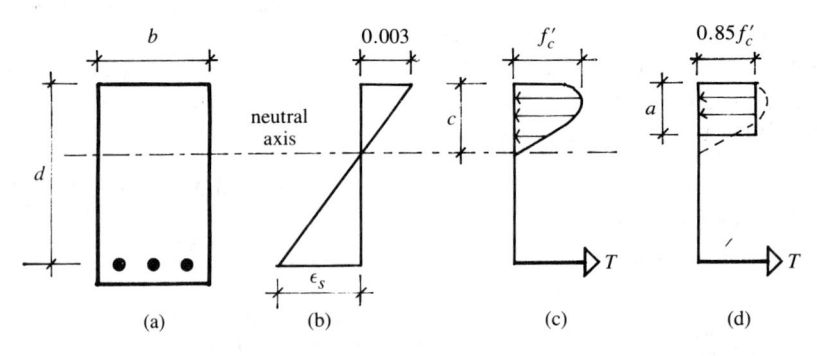

Fig. 13.4.1. Distribution of stress and strain in a reinforced concrete section. (a) Beam cross-section; (b) strain distribution in the section at failure; (c) stress distribution in the section at failure; (d) equivalent rectangular compressive stress distribution at failure: the depth of rectangle $a = \beta_1 c$, where c is the depth of the neutral axis.

CONCRETE AND MASONRY STRUCTURES 197

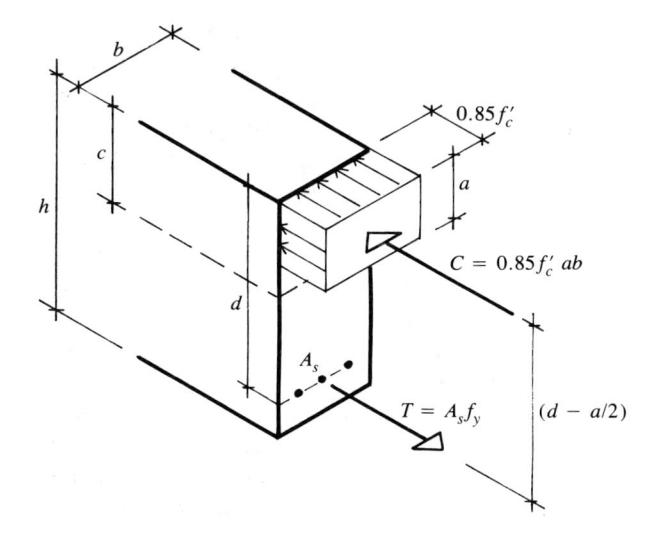

Fig. 13.4.2. Equivalent stress block for a singly reinforced beam.

In the above expression for K, the value of $\phi = 0.9$ in flexure has been substituted. The term ρ is called the *steel ratio*, since it is the ratio of the steel area and the gross area of concrete in the section, i.e. $\rho = A_s/bd$. Note that the units of K are the same as those of the stress; psi in customary American units and MPa (or N/mm^2) in the SI system (Tables 13.4 and 13.4a).

Maximum Steel Ratio. In a balanced section, the yielding of the steel and the crushing of the concrete occur simultaneously. The maximum strain in concrete is 0.003, Fig. 13.4.3. Thus,

$$c_b = \left[\frac{0.003}{\frac{f_y}{E_s} + 0.003}\right] d$$

Since $E_s = 29,000$ ksi, this gives:

$$c_b = \frac{87}{87 + f_y} d$$

Table 13.4. Values of K for $f'_c = 4$ ksi and $f_y = 60$ ksi, Obtained from Eq. (13.3).

ρ, %	K, ksi	ρ, %	K, ksi
0.1	0.054	1.2	0.580
0.2	0.106	1.3	0.620
0.3	0.158	1.4	0.662
0.4	0.208	1.5	0.700
0.5	0.258	1.6	0.742
0.6	0.307	1.7	0.780
0.7	0.355	1.8	0.818
0.8	0.400	1.9	0.853
0.9	0.447	2.0	0.890
1.0	0.492	2.1	0.924
1.1	0.536	2.14	0.936

$\rho_{max} = 2.14\%$, from Eq. (13.4), and $\rho_{min} = 0.33\%$, for beams only.

Table 13.4a. Values of K for $f'_c = 30$ MPa and $f_y = 400$ MPa, Obtained from Eq. (13.3).

ρ, %	K, MPa	ρ, %	K, MPa
0.1	0.357	1.3	4.203
0.2	0.709	1.4	4.487
0.3	1.054	1.5	4.765
0.4	1.395	1.6	5.037
0.5	1.729	1.7	5.304
0.6	2.058	1.8	5.565
0.7	2.382	1.9	5.821
0.8	2.699	2.0	6.071
0.9	3.011	2.1	6.315
1.0	3.318	2.2	6.553
1.1	3.618	2.3	6.786
1.2	3.913	2.4	7.014
		2.45	7.125

$\rho_{max} = 2.45\%$, from Eq. (13.4), and $\rho_{min} = 0.35\%$, for beams only.
Note: 1 MPa = 1 N/mm^2.

Using Eq. (13.1) and the fact that $a_b = \beta_1 c_b$, the following is obtained;

$$A_{sb} = 0.85\beta_1 \left[\frac{f'_c}{f_y}\right] \frac{87}{87 + f_y} bd$$

Since, $A_{s\,max} = 0.75 A_{sb}$, i.e., $\rho_{max} = 0.75\rho_b$,

$$\rho_{max} = 0.64\beta_1 \left[\frac{f'_c}{f_y}\right] \frac{87}{87 + f_y} \quad (13.4)$$

where f'_c and f_y are in ksi. In the SI system, Eq. (13.4) is:

$$\rho_{max} = 0.64\beta_1 \left[\frac{f'_c}{f_y}\right] \frac{600}{600 + f_y}$$

where f'_c and f_y are in MPa.

Minimum Steel Ratio. The code (10.5.1) requires that the minimum steel ratio for positive moment, $\rho_{min} = 0.2/f_y$, where f_y is in ksi ($\rho_{min} = 1.4/f_y$, where f_y is in MPa). This limitation does not apply to one-way slabs, see Section 13.9.

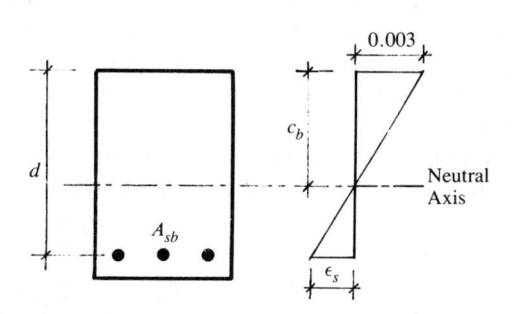

Fig. 13.4.3. Strain distribution in a balanced section. Note that $\epsilon_s = f_y/E_s$.

In the design of singly reinforced beams for bending, two quantities must first be chosen: f'_c and f_y. The next step is to determine the values of b, d and ρ, so that $M_u \le \phi M_n$. If the calculations are done by hand, tables, such as Table 13.4, are used to simplify the process. Obviously, there are a large number of combinations of b, d and ρ that satisfy the requirement. Their values are chosen based on other code requirements as well as on architectural and economic considerations.

Example 13.1. Select the steel for a singly reinforced beam section to resist a factored moment of 2800 k in. Architectural considerations require the beam to be 10 in. wide. $f'_c = 4$ ksi and $f_y = 60$ ksi.

Solution. From Table 13.4, $\rho_{max} = 2.14$ percent and $\rho_{min} = 0.33$ percent. Arbitrarily choose $\rho = 1.4$ percent, although this should depend on the relative costs of concrete (including the cost of formwork) and steel. $\rho = 1.5$ percent has been suggested as an optimum value for singly reinforced beams (Ref. 13.3). Thus, $K = 0.662$ ksi. From Eq. (13.2),

$$2800 = 0.662(10 \times d^2). \quad \text{Hence,} \quad d = 20.6 \text{ in.}$$

$$A_s = \rho b d = 0.014(10 \times 20.6) = 2.88 \text{ in.}^2$$

Provide 3 #9 bars ($A_s = 3.0$ in.^{2}), see Table 13.1.

Example 13.1a. Select the steel for a singly reinforced beam section to resist a factored moment of 300 kN m ($= 300 \times 10^6$ N mm). Architectural considerations require the beam to be 250 mm wide. $f'_c = 30$ MPa and $f_y = 400$ MPa.

Solution. From Table 13.4a, $\rho_{max} = 2.45$ percent and $\rho_{min} = 0.35$ percent. Choose $\rho = 1.4$ percent (see Example 13.1). Thus, $K = 4.487$ N/mm^2. From Eq. (13.2).

$$300 \times 10^6 = 4.487(250 \times d^2). \quad \text{Hence,} \quad d = 517 \text{ mm}$$

$$A_s = \rho b d = 0.014(250 \times 517) = 1810 \text{ mm}^2$$

Provide 3 #30 bars ($A_s = 2100$ mm^2), see Table 13.1a.

Doubly Reinforced Beams

These are beams which are reinforced in the tension as well as the compression zone. Since steel is just as strong in compression as in tension (if restrained against buckling), compression steel increases the moment strength of the beam. Thus, a doubly reinforced beam requires a smaller cross-section than a singly reinforced beam carrying the same loads.

To fully utilize the benefit of compression steel, the steel area in the tension zone in a doubly reinforced beam must be more than the maximum allowed for a singly reinforced beam of the same cross-sectional dimensions. In a beam with less than the maximum allowable tension steel, the tensile force provided by the steel can be fully equilibrated by the compressive force generated by the concrete. Consequently, the provision of compression steel in such a beam does not greatly add to its strength, since it adds strength where it is not really required. Compression steel should, therefore, be provided to increase the moment capacity of a section beyond that given by a singly reinforced section with maximum allowable steel area. Otherwise, the compression steel will not significantly reduce beam cross-section.

The provision of compression steel has advantages other than reducing beam cross-section. (In fact, it is for these other reasons that the compression steel is commonly used). It increases the ductility of the beam and provides safety against the reversal of stresses in members. Since seismic ground motions may cause stress reversal, several building codes require that in buildings located in seismic zones, flexural members have a certain minimum area of compression steel. In addition, since steel has a higher modulus of elasticity than concrete, the compression steel reduces creep deflection and increases the stiffness of the beam.

Since the steel under compression has the tendency to buckle outward, and if not restrained may burst through the concrete cover, the code (7.11.1) requires that compression steel when provided to give additional moment strength must be enclosed laterally by ties in the same way as columns, see Section 13.10. Alternatively, stirrups which meet the size and spacing requirements of ties may be used.

The theory of the design of doubly reinforced beams is as follows.

Since a ductile failure of the beam is required, the tension steel must yield at failure. As for the compression steel at failure, there are two possibilities: (i) it yields or (ii) it does not yield.

(i) Consider the first possibility (i.e., the compression steel yields). From Fig. 13.4.4, the total compressive force $C = C_1 + C_2$, where

$$C_1 = 0.85 f'_c ab, \quad \text{and} \quad C_2 = A'_s f_y$$

where A'_s is the area of compression steel.

The tensile force T may be split in two components, one to balance C_1 and the other to balance C_2. If A_s is the area of tension steel in the beam, then:

$$T = A_s f_y = A_{s1} f_y + A_{s2} f_y$$

so that

$$A_{s1} f_y = 0.85 f'_c ab, \quad \text{and} \quad A_{s2} = A'_s f_y$$

From the above equations,

$$A_{s2} = A'_s \quad \text{and} \quad A_{s1} = A_s - A'_s$$

Thus, the moment strength of the section, ϕM_n, can be calculated in two parts so that $\phi M_n = \phi M_{n1} + \phi M_{n2}$, Fig. 13.4.5. ϕM_{n1} is given by the singly reinforced section with tension steel $= A_{s1}$, and

$$\phi M_{n2} = \phi A'_s f_y (d - d')$$

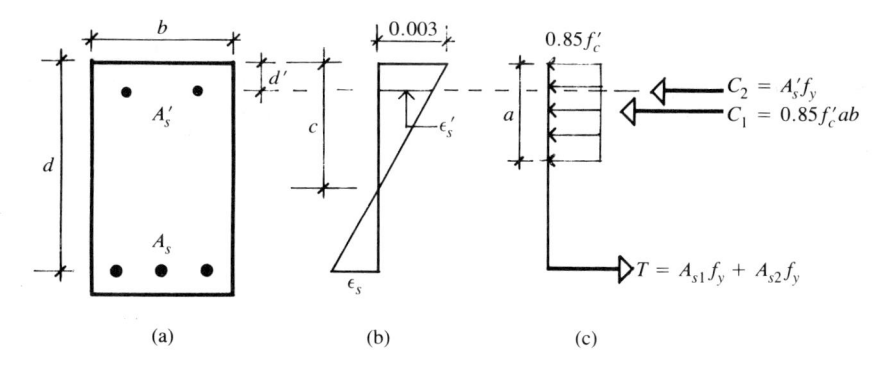

Fig. 13.4.4. (a) A doubly reinforced section. The areas of tension and compression steel are A_s and A'_s, respectively. (b) Strain distribution at failure. (c) Stress distribution at failure.

The restriction for maximum steel is the same as for a singly reinforced section, i.e., $A_{s1} \leq A_{s\,max}$, or $\rho_1 \leq \rho_{max}$, where ρ_{max} is given by Eq. (13.4). This restriction means that the difference between the tension steel and compression steel must not exceed the maximum steel area allowed for a singly reinforced section.

The above analysis assumes that the compression steel yields. With reference to Fig. 13.4.4b, it may be seen that for this to occur, the compression steel should be placed as close as possible to the compression edge of the beam. Mathematically, the condition becomes (Ref. 13.4):

$$d' \leq \left[\frac{87 - f_y}{87}\right] \frac{A_{s1} f_y}{0.85 \beta_1 f'_c b} \quad (13.5)$$

where f'_c and f_y are in ksi, d' and b in in., and A_{s1} in in.².

(ii) If the compression steel does not yield, the force provided by it is small. In this case, a simpler (but conservative) approach is to neglect the compression steel altogether and consider the section as singly reinforced. Alternatively, a detailed analysis of the section may be performed, which is quite lengthy.

Example 13.2. Select the steel for a beam to resist factored moment of 4800 k in. The values of b and d are limited to 10 in. and 20 in. respectively. $f'_c = 4$ ksi and $f_y = 60$ ksi.

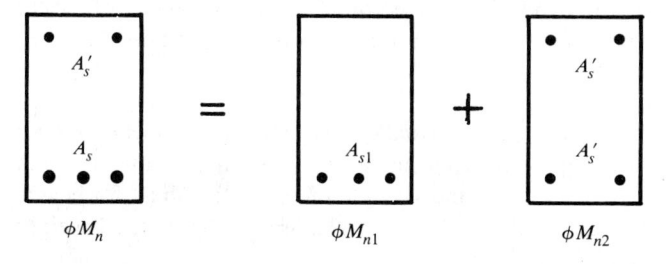

Fig. 13.4.5. The moment strength of a doubly reinforced section, ϕM_n, may be considered as the sum of two components: (i) ϕM_{n1}, due to singly reinforced section with tension steel area A_{s1} and (ii) ϕM_{n2}, due to compression steel area A'_s and with an equal area of tension steel. Note that $A_{s1} + A'_s = A_s$.

Solution. Let $d' = 2.5$ in. The value of K for $\rho_{max} = 2.14$ percent, is 0.936 ksi, Table 13.4. From Eq. (13.2), the moment strength of a singly reinforced section with maximum permissible tensile steel,

$$\phi M_{n1} = 0.936 \times 10 \times 20^2 = 3744 \text{ k in.}$$

Thus,

$$A_{s1} = 2.14\% (10 \times 20) = 4.28 \text{ in.}^2$$

The remaining strength, $\phi M_{n2} = 4800 - 3744 = 1056$ k in., must be provided by compression steel, A'_s, and an equal amount of tension steel. If the compression steel yields, then

$$\phi M_{n2} = 1056 = \phi A'_s f_y (d - d') = 0.9 A'_s (60)(20 - 2.5)$$

Thus, $A'_s = 1.12$ in.². Hence $A_s = 4.28 + 1.12 = 5.40$ in.².

Provide 6 #9 bars (in two layers, giving $A_s = 6.0$ in.²) in the tension zone and 2 #7 bars ($A'_s = 1.2$ in.²) in the compression zone.

That the compression steel yields can be verified from Eq. (13.5).

T-Beams

T-beams occur naturally in a poured-in-place concrete floor slab-and-beam assembly. While the slab must bend under the action of loads in a direction perpendicular to the beams supporting it, the monolithic nature of a poured-in-place concrete structure forces the slab to bend in the direction of the beams also. The floor slab therefore has a two-way bending, one perpendicular to the supporting beams and the other along the beams as their integral part. The latter bending action means that the beam does not act as a rectangular beam but as a T-beam (or an L-beam if it is a spandrel beam) in which the slab forms the flange and the portion of the beam below the slab forms the web of the T-beam.

The code limits the width of the slab that can be considered to act integrally with the beam. This width, called the effective flange width b_e, is the least of the dimensions given in Fig. 13.4.6.

T-beam behavior in a slab-beam assembly increases the

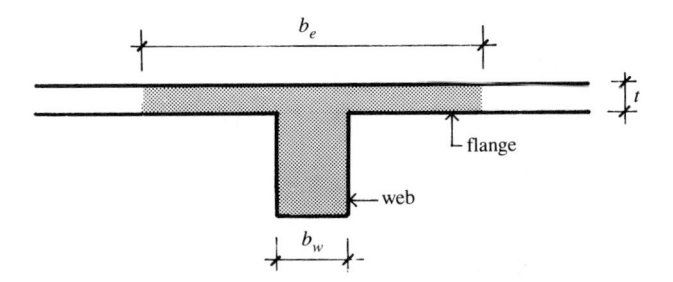

Fig. 13.4.6. In a monolithically poured slab-and-beam assembly, the width of the slab considered effective as the flange of a T-shape, b_e, is the smallest of the following dimensions: (i) $16t + b_w$; (ii) $0.25 L$, where L is beam span; (iii) the distance between centerlines of adjacent beams. The code specifies similar restrictions for a spandrel (L-shape) beam in which the slab is only on one side of the beam.

moment strength of the beam because the flange provides extra compression area to resist moments. But this benefit is available only where the flange is in compression—the parts of the beam where the bending moment is positive. In a continuous beam or a beam with fixed supports, parts of the beam are subjected to negative moments. In these parts, the beam behaves as a rectangular beam (with a width equal to that of the web) since the flange, being in tension, cannot contribute to the moment strength of the beam. To compensate for the smaller moment strength of a T-beam in regions of negative moment, it is usually provided with compression steel there to give a doubly reinforced section.

However, the code (10.6.6) requires that in these regions (where the flanges of a T-beam are in tension), a part of the flexural tension reinforcement should be provided over the entire effective flange width or over a width equal to $\frac{1}{10}$ the clear span of the beam, whichever is smaller. If the effective flange width exceeds $\frac{1}{10}$ the span, an additional longitudinal reinforcement should be provided in the outer portions of the flange.

The theory of the design of T-beams is similar to that of the doubly reinforced beams and may be looked up in one of the books suggested at the end of the chapter (Ref. 13.4, 13.6, or 13.7).

13.5. SHEAR AND TORSION IN REINFORCED CONCRETE MEMBERS

Shear

If a small three-dimensional cubic element is isolated from a beam made of an isotropic material, it will be seen to be acted upon by axial and shear stresses shown in Fig. 13.5.1. The horizontal and vertical shear stresses give rise to tensile stresses on one diagonal plane of the element and compressive stresses on the other, called the *diagonal tension* and *diagonal compression*, respectively. Concrete is strong in compression; therefore we are less concerned about the diagonal compression.

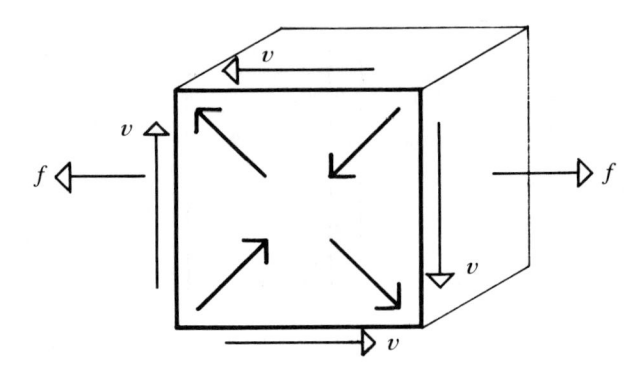

Fig. 13.5.1. Shear and axial stresses (v and f, respectively) on a small rectangular element isolated from a beam. The shear stresses, which must be all equal for rotational equilibrium of the element, produce diagonal compression and diagonal tension in the element. Note that the axial stress on the element may be tensile or compressive, depending on whether the element has been isolated from the tension or the compression zone of the beam.

Concrete will resist some shear (diagonal tension) but if the latter exceeds the tensile strength of concrete, shear reinforcement is required. This is usually provided in the form of vertical stirrups. The variation of shear along the length of a beam is accommodated by changing the spacing of stirrups. In regions of high shear (near the supports of beams), the stirrups are placed closer together than in regions where the shear is low (center of the beam). The bar diameter of stirrups should not be varied in a beam. The most commonly used bar size is #3 although #4 or #5 bars are used if the shear in the beam is large. Stirrup spacings in a beam should be as few as possible, preferably not exceeding three.

An alternative to stirrups is the use of bars bent at an angle of 30° or more to the longitudinal axis of the beam, but this is not common.

The total shear strength of a beam section, ϕV_n, is the sum of shear strengths provided by concrete and shear reinforcement, that is,

$$\phi V_n = \phi(V_c + V_s)$$

where V_c is the nominal shear strength of concrete in the section and V_s the nominal shear strength of shear reinforcement. For a member to be adequate in shear, $V_u \leq \phi V_n$.

Shear Strength Provided by Concrete. The shear strength provided by concrete increases with an increase in beam cross section and the strength of concrete. Thus, for beams subjected only to shear and flexure, V_c for normal weight concrete is given by:

$$V_c = 2\sqrt{f'_c}\,bd \qquad (13.6)$$

where V_c is in pounds, f'_c in psi; b and d in inches. In the SI system, the corresponding equation is: $V_c = (\sqrt{f'_c}/6)bd$, where f'_c is in MPa, b and d in mm, b is the width of the beam (or the width of the web, for a flanged beam).

Shear Strength of Stirrups. It can be shown (Ref. 13.5) that the shear strength of vertical stirrups spaced at a distance s from each other is

$$V_s = A_v f_y (d/s)$$

where A_v is the cross-sectional area of the stirrup legs. For a two-leg #3 stirrup, $A_v = 0.22$ in.^{2}, being twice the area of one #3 bar, Table 13.1.

The code does not allow the use of steel with $f_y > 60$ ksi (400 MPa) for stirrups. In addition, several other restrictions, as given below, are prescribed.

(i) V_s should not exceed $8\sqrt{f'_c}\,bd$, which is four times the shear strength of the concrete section. This restriction is a safeguard against excessive shear on the section causing shear failure (which is a brittle failure) of the member prior to flexural failure (ductile failure). If $V_s > 8\sqrt{f'_c}\,bd$, the section must be enlarged. This, however, occurs rarely, since shear does not usually govern the design of reinforced concrete beams in buildings.

(ii) Stirrup spacing should exceed neither $d/2$ nor 24 inches. But if $V_s > 4\sqrt{f'_c}\,bd$, spacing should not exceed $d/4$. The $d/2$ requirement for stirrup spacing is to ensure that each diagonal tension crack will be crossed by at least one stirrup.

(iii) Theoretically, no shear reinforcement is required if $V_u \leq \phi(2\sqrt{f'_c}\,bd)$, but since a member without shear reinforcement may have a sudden failure on first cracking, a minimum shear reinforcement area A_v, as given below, should be provided in beams unless $V_u \leq \phi\sqrt{f'_c}\,bd$):

$$A_v \text{ (minimum)} = (50bs)/f_y$$

where f_y is in psi, b and s in in., and A_v in in.^{2}.

Floor slabs, floor joists, footings, and shallow beams (the definition of a shallow beam is given in the code (11.5.5)) may be designed without any minimum requirement for shear reinforcement.

Critical Section for Shear. Although the maximum shear force occurs at the face of the support, the code (11.1.2) stipulates that sections located at a distance less than d from the face of support may be designed for the same shear force as the one which occurs at distance d, called the *critical section*. This provision recognizes the additional shear strength available in sections near a support due to compression caused by support reaction. Such condition exists in a flexural member bearing on another member, e.g., a slab or a beam resting on a masonry wall, a slab framing into a beam, or a beam framing into a column.

A typical support condition where the above provision is not applicable is a member hung from another member. Here, the critical section is located at the face of the support. The code requires that in such a situation, a detailed investigation of the state of stress within the connection must be made.

Stirrup Shapes. Three basic stirrup shapes are in common use: U-shape, closed shape, and galloping type, Fig. 13.5.2. The most frequently used is the U-shape, of which type (a), in which the hooks are turned in, is more popular. However, type (b) is preferred if the beam has flanges on both sides to accommodate hooks turned out, since it gives less obstruction to the placement of concrete.

Closed-shape stirrups give greater torsional resistance. They are mandatory if compression steel is used in the beam to increase its flexural strength. They can either be in one piece, type (c), or in two pieces, type (d). The two-piece stirrups help in bar placing but require a certain minimum depth of member in order to provide adequate development length (Ref. 13.6). If one-piece stirrups are used, prefabrication of the entire beam's reinforcement cage is required, which makes the junction between column and beam very difficult.

While the U-shape and closed stirrups are two-leg stirrups, the galloping stirrup, type (e), is a single-leg stirrup. It is used in narrow beams and floor joists. Three- or four-leg stirrups may be used if the shear is high, but their use is relatively uncommon.

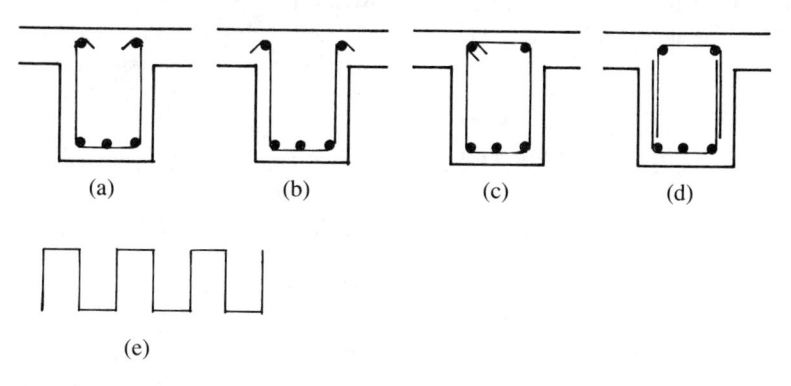

Fig. 13.5.2. Commonly used stirrup shapes. (a) and (b) are U-shape stirrups, (c) and (d) are closed stirrups, and (e) is the galloping stirrup. The hooks at the ends of stirrups may be 90° or 135° hooks.

Torsion

Torsion is the twisting of a member around its axis and is fairly common in reinforced concrete structures. Its magnitude is usually small in the case of an interior beam of a monolithic floor system, but in spandrel beams, curved beams, and girders supporting secondary beams on one side only, torsional moments are substantial and must be considered in their design.

Torsion produces diagonal tension and compression similar to that of a shear force, but (unlike a shear force) torsion also produces axial tension. Thus, both the vertical reinforcement (stirrups) and longitudinal reinforcement are required to resist torsion. These reinforcement areas are additive; that is, the reinforcement area required for torsion is in addition to that required to resist shear forces, bending moments, and axial forces.

Since the twisting of a member creates torsional shear stresses on all faces of the member, all four sides of stirrups are stressed. Closed stirrups, anchored by hooks, are therefore mandated for torsional resistance. In addition, longitudinal reinforcement (not less than #3 bar) must be distributed uniformly around the perimeter of the stirrups spaced not more than 12 in. on center. Out of this, at least one bar is required in each corner of the stirrup.

For a detailed discussion of torsional effects in reinforced concrete members, the reader is referred to books on reinforced concrete (Ref. 13.4, 13.6, or 13.7).

13.6. DEFLECTION IN REINFORCED CONCRETE MEMBERS

The structural continuity of poured-in-place concrete members makes deflection a less critical design parameter in reinforced concrete structures than those of wood or steel. The negative moments at supports and the positive moments at midspan tend to balance the opposite curvatures, giving smaller overall deflections. However, in heavily loaded and long-span members, deflection may be excessive and must be held to specified limits. Excessive deflection in beams and slabs, although safe, may cause the following problems: (i) damage to elements such as walls and partitions supported on them, (ii) cracking of surface applied finishes, e.g., plaster and stucco, (iii) jamming of windows and doors, (iv) ponding of roof with rainwater, which has caused several structural failures in large span roofs, and (v) aesthetic and psychological unacceptability.

Two approaches are given in the code to satisfy deflection criteria: (i) provide minimum thickness of flexural members, and (ii) compute deflections and insure that these are less than those specified by the code (9.5.2).

Minimum Thickness. The code stipulates that, for beams and one-way slabs, if minimum thickness as given in Table 13.5 is used, there is no need to compute deflections. The only restriction in the use of the method is that the member should not support or be attached to a partition which is likely to be damaged by large deflections. Since this is usually not the case in most building structures, the minimum thickness approach is commonly used to satisfy the deflection criterion.

Computation of Deflection. A reinforced concrete member has two types of deflections: instantaneous deflection and long-term deflection. Long-term deflection is caused by the effect of creep in concrete. Since concrete creeps over a period of time under the effect of sustained loads, long-term deflection is a time-dependent quantity. It increases with time, reaching its maximum value in five years. For a singly reinforced beam, the maximum value of long-term deflection is twice the instantaneous deflection due to sustained loads. In fact, the long-term deflection is not calculated separately but is obtained by multiplying the instantaneous deflection with a time-dependent factor. Since steel has a higher modulus of elasticity than concrete and because steel does not creep, a doubly reinforced beam has a smaller long-term deflection than a singly reinforced beam.

The computation of instantaneous deflection for a reinforced concrete member is based on the elastic theory under service loads (not factored loads). It is the same theory that is used in calculating the deflection of steel and wood beams. According to this theory, the maximum deflection of a member is a function of the load and its distribution, the span of the member, modulus of elasticity of the material, E, and the moment of inertia, I, of the section.

In applying this theory to reinforced concrete members, only two modifications are made. E is replaced by E_c, the

Table 13.5. Minimum Thickness of Beams and One-Way Slabs.

Member	f_y, ksi	Simply Supported	One End Continuous	Both Ends Continuous	Cantilever
Solid one-way slab	40	span/25	span/30	span/35	span/12.5
	60	span/20	span/24	span/28	span/10
Beams or joist	40	span/20	span/23	span/26	span/10
floors	60	span/16	span/18.5	span/21	span/8

Source: ACI Code Table 9.5a.

Note: For continuous beams and slabs, the span is the center-to-center distance between supports. For members not built integrally with supports, the span is either the center-to-center distance between supports, or the clear span plus the thickness of the member, whichever is smaller.

modulus of elasticity of (plain) concrete, and I by I_e, called the *effective moment of inertia* of the reinforced concrete section. The effective moment of inertia differs from the elastic moment of inertia I (which is equal to $bh^3/12$ for a rectangular section made of a homogeneous material) because, first, reinforced concrete is a heterogeneous material consisting of steel and concrete (concrete itself is not homogeneous), and second, the concrete section is a cracked section under service loads.

The method of calculating I_e is lengthy. Briefly, I_e depends on how much cracking of the section takes place under service loads. Apparently, if the cracking is small, the section is stiffer than if the cracking is large. At best, I_e is equal to I, which is the case when no cracking of the section takes place. Thus, I_e is always less than (or equal to) I. The actual value of I_e depends on the ratio of two moments: M_{cr}/M_a. M_a is the applied moment and M_{cr}, called the cracking moment, is the (smaller) moment that will just cause flexural failure of a plain concrete section of the same dimensions as the reinforced concrete section under consideration. The larger the applied moment in comparison to the cracking moment, the greater the cracking of the section and hence smaller the value of I_e.

13.7. REINFORCEMENT DETAILING

Concrete Cover

Concrete protects reinforcing steel from corrosion by the environment. The minimum concrete covers for various situations as required by the code (7.7.1) are given in Table 13.6. These requirements are for normal environments and must be suitably increased for more corrosive or other abnormal conditions. Apart from providing adequate cover, severe environments may also require such other measures as the minimization of cracks, greater attention to curing and compaction of concrete to provide a less permeable concrete. Greater concrete cover may also be required for the protection of steel against fire, since steel loses its strength substantially at elevated temperatures.

Reinforcement Spacing

The code (7.6) gives requirements for minimum and maximum spacing for longitudinal bars. The minimum spacing requirement ensures that the concrete flows easily between bars to prevent honeycombing and to give proper bar anchorage. For example, the minimum clear spacing between parallel bars in one layer in a beam should neither be less than one bar diameter nor 1 in. (25 mm) and the minimum clear vertical distance between bars, when placed in more than one horizontal layer, is 1 in. (25 mm). In addition, the largest size of coarse aggregate should not be greater than three-quarters of the clear distance between bars.

The maximum spacing ensures an even distribution of cracks and in the case of slabs and walls, it also ensures that a concentrated load will be distributed over an area larger than that on which the load acts.

Crack Control

The tensile strength of concrete being extremely low, concrete begins to crack at very low stresses. Cracks are therefore an inevitable part of a concrete structure, but their size must be kept under control. Cracks reduce the effectiveness of concrete cover and decrease the stiffness and shear resistance of the member. Because the cracked portion of the section cannot resist any shear, the area of the section available for shear resistance is reduced.

Longitudinal reinforcement cannot eliminate cracks but reduces their width while increasing their numbers, giving small but closely spaced cracks.

Three types of cracks occur in a reinforced concrete member: (i) shrinkage cracks, (ii) cracks resulting from temperature-induced stresses, and (iii) flexural cracks.

Shrinkage and Temperature Cracks. In one-way slabs, although the reinforcement is required in one direction only, called the *principal reinforcement*, the code requires that steel bars must also be provided perpendicular to the direction of the principal reinforcement to reduce shrinkage and temperature-induced cracking; see Section 13.9.

Flexural Cracks. Since steel and concrete are perfectly bonded in a reinforced concrete structure, the deformations in steel and concrete are the same. Crack widths due to flexure are therefore a function of the stress in the steel and the spacing of steel bars. To minimize the width of flexural cracks, the stresses in steel bars and their spacing must be as small as possible. The code (10.6.4) requires that, in tension zones of beams and one-way slabs, if $f_y > 40$ ksi (300 MPa), the quantity z, as defined below, must not be greater than 175 k/in. (30 MN/m) for interior exposures and 145 k/in. (20 MN/m) for exterior exposures. When z equals the values given above, the average crack width in concrete members is approximately 0.016 in. (0.4 mm) and 0.013 in. (0.3 mm), respectively (Ref. 13.4, p. 187):

$$z = 0.6 f_y \sqrt[3]{d_c A} \qquad (13.7)$$

Table 13.6. Minimum Concrete Cover.

(a) Concrete cast against and permanently exposed to earth	3 in.
(b) Concrete exposed to earth or weather:	
#5 bars or smaller	$1\frac{1}{2}$ in.
#6 bars and above	2 in.
(c) Concrete not exposed to weather or in contact with earth:	
Beams and columns	$1\frac{1}{2}$ in.
Slabs, walls, and joists:	
#11 bars and smaller	$\frac{3}{4}$ in.
#14 bars and above	$1\frac{1}{2}$ in.

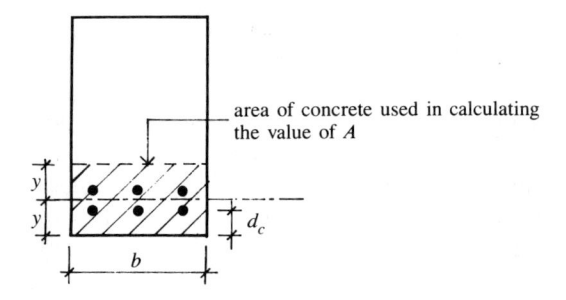

Fig. 13.7.1. Quantities for checking crack control in flexural members. (i) d_c is the thickness of concrete cover measured to the center of the outermost bar in in. (or mm); (ii) A is the area of concrete, in in.^{2} (or mm^2), surrounding the tensile reinforcement and having the same centroid as the reinforcement, divided by the number of bars; thus, $A = b(2y)/$(number of bars); (iii) f_y is in ksi (or MPa).

A and d_c are defined in Fig. 13.7.1. $0.6f_y$ is approximately the magnitude of tensile stress in steel under service loads. If the area of steel provided is more than that calculated from flexural considerations resulting in a smaller stress in steel bars, then that value of stress may be used in place of $0.6f_y$. In fact, a greater tension steel area than that required, and/or lower grade steel, is often used in the design of structures in which crack control is critical.

Anchorage and Bar Development

It is a fundamental assumption made in all reinforced concrete design that the steel bars are bonded sufficiently by the concrete so that no slippage occurs between the two. The assumption means that because of the interaction between steel and concrete, a shear type of stress, called *bond stress*, is developed on the surface of contact between concrete and steel bars whenever a load is applied on the member.

To appreciate the implication of the bond between steel and concrete, consider the equilibrium of a bar of cross-sectional area A_b, embedded a length equal to l in. concrete, and subjected to a pull-out force T, Fig. 13.7.2. If the stress generated in the bar equals f_s, then $T = A_b f_s$. If the bond stress is denoted by u, the internal force due to bond resisting the applied tensile force $= Olu$, where O is the circumference of the bar. For equilibrium, $T = Olu$. Apparently, there is a limit on the maximum value of bond stress, u_{max}, that can be developed between the steel and the concrete. Thus, the maximum internal force that can be generated by the bar is equal to Olu_{max}. Since bond failure is a sudden failure, it is necessary that the steel must yield prior to bond failure, i.e., $Olu_{max} \geq A_b f_y$. If the bar diameter is d_b, the above inequality simplifies as

$$l \geq (d_b f_y)/(4u_{max})$$

The value of l gives the minimum embedment length of the bar to prevent bond failure. It means that a bar must extend on either side of the point of maximum stress by a prescribed minimum length, called the *development length* of the bar.

Several factors affect the development length of a bar. They are: the strength of concrete, bar size, amount of concrete below the bar, actual stress in steel, and the amount of concrete around bars. The code, therefore, uses the concept of *basic development length*, and gives its values for bars under tension and compression. The basic development length when multiplied by the applicable modification factors, gives the value of the development length.

As stated previously, development length must be provided at sections of maximum stress. Such sections occur at midspan of a simply supported uniformly loaded beam, fixed end of a cantilever, and at supports as well as at midspan of a continuous beam. The other critical sections for development length are sections within the span at which a part of the reinforcement is terminated because it is no longer required for moment strength. Wherever such termination occurs, peak stress is caused in the remaining reinforcement, which necessitates development length beyond the point of termination.

Enough length may not be available in the member to use a straight development length, particularly at the ends. In such a case, 90° or 180° hooks are used which require smaller development length. Note that a hook is effective only in tension. The dimensions and bend diameters of hooks have been standardized by the code and may be looked up in a book on reinforced concrete (Ref. 13.4, 13.6, or 13.7).

The detailing of reinforcement for development length and termination of bars can be quite tedious. Standard bar cutoff diagrams are therefore prepared for commonly occurring situations. Such diagrams for a single span simply supported slab and a continuous slab are given in Fig. 13.7.3. For other conditions, refer to Ref. 13.8.

13.8. ANALYSIS OF REINFORCED CONCRETE STRUCTURES

Before any structural design of concrete members can be taken up, the values of factored moments and forces that

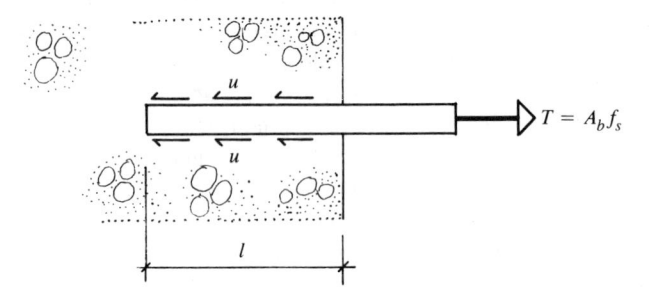

Fig. 13.7.2. Bond stress u developed at the interface of a bar and the concrete, when the bar is subjected to a pull-out force.

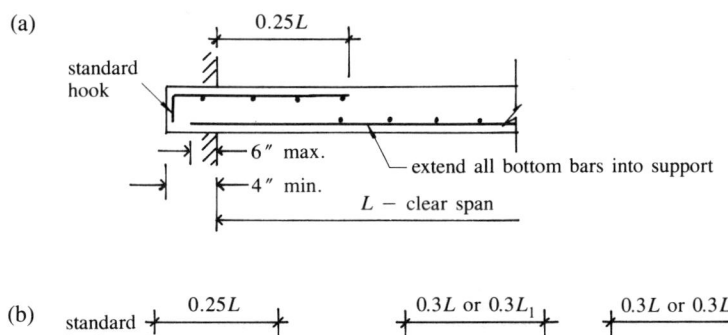

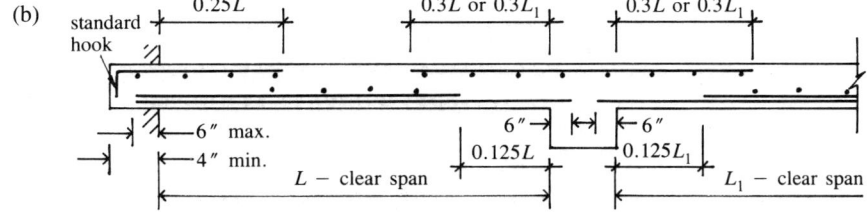

Fig. 13.7.3. Recommended bar details for one-way slabs. (a) Single-span simply supported slab; (b) continuous slab.

act on members must be determined. The code permits the use of elastic analysis for this purpose (see Chapter 11) although the strength design method, based on the inelastic behavior of concrete, is used for the design of sections.

Reinforced concrete beams and slabs are usually continuous over several spans. Due to their monolithic construction, the joints between slabs and beams and between beams and columns are rigid joints. Indeterminate structural analysis is therefore required for all but single-span beams or slabs on simple supports such as the masonry walls. The analysis is usually done with a digital computer for both the gravity as well as the lateral loads.

If structural walls are incorporated into the framing system (in fact, they are often required for architectural reasons) to provide lateral load resistance and lateral bracing for the columns, the beam-column frames can then be designed for gravity loads only and the walls mainly for lateral loads. This separation of structural systems for gravity and lateral loads simplifies the analysis considerably and works quite well for buildings of moderate height. The moment distribution method or other more sophisticated methods can be used for gravity load analysis of continuous beams and slabs.

ACI Coefficients for Beams and One-Way Slabs

An alternative to structural analysis for gravity loads is the use of ACI coefficients for bending moments, Fig. 13.8.1. They are applicable to beams and one-way slabs and are convenient for a small structure since no structural analysis is required. However, the following conditions must be satisfied for the use of the coefficients: (i) There are two or more spans which are all approximately equal; the longer span ≤ 1.2 times the shorter span; (ii) the loads are uniformly distributed; (iii) the ratio of live load to dead load ≤ 3; (iv) the members are prismatic with the same cross section in all spans of the continuous slab or beam.

The use of the coefficients is explained in Example 13.4.

13.9. REINFORCED CONCRETE FLOOR SYSTEMS

If a reinforced concrete slab is supported along two opposite edges, it will bend only in one direction, perpendicular to the supporting edges and carry the entire load of the slab in that direction. Such a slab is called a *one-way slab*.

If the slab is supported on all four edges, it will bend in both directions, in double curvature, and is called a *two-way slab*. If such a slab is a square slab, the load on the slab is transferred equally along both spans; that is, all the four supporting edges carry equal load. In a rectangular slab, greater load is carried by the short span; it can be shown (Ref. 13.5 p. 177) that the ratio of the loads carried by the short and the long spans is approximated by $(L_1/L_2)^4$ where L_1 and L_2 are long and short spans, respectively. Thus, a rectangular slab, with $L_1/L_2 \geq 1.5$, behaves as a one-way slab, bending primarily along the short span, since nearly 83 percent of the load is carried in that direction (Note that $(1.5)^4$ is approximately equal to 5.0, so that if $L_1/L_2 = 1.5$, five times as much load is carried along the short span as along the long one.)

One-Way Systems

Two types of one-way slabs are used in practice: (i) one-way solid slabs, and (ii) joist floors.

One-way Solid Slabs. A one-way solid slab is a slab of uniform thickness spanning across parallel lines of support provided by walls or beams. Since bending takes place in

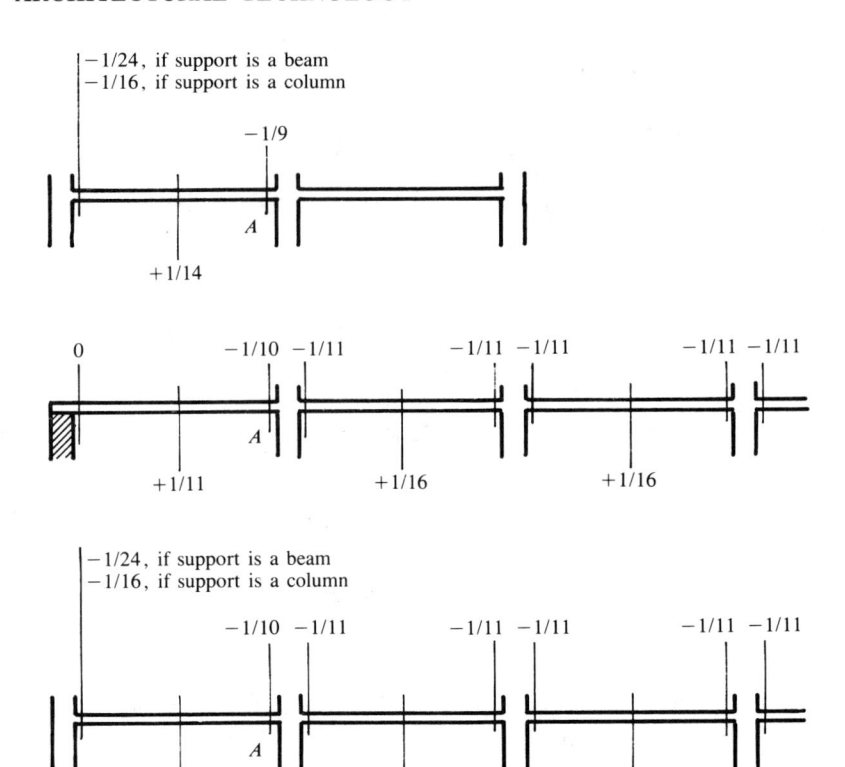

Fig. 13.8.1. ACI coefficients for beams and one-way slabs.

1. M_u = coefficient in Fig. 13.8.1 $\times$ $(w_u L^2)$, where L is the clear span for positive moment and average of the adjacent spans for negative moment and w_u is the factored dead load plus live load.
2. V_u at all supports is $(0.5 w_u L)$ except at the interior support of the end span (section A) where $V_u = 1.15\,(0.5 w_u L)$.
3. For slabs with span ≤ 10 ft, negative moment at the face of all supports is $\frac{1}{12}(w_u L^2)$.

one direction only, the structural behavior of the slab is identical to that of a series of individual beams placed side by side. Since the concrete below the neutral axis in a beam is ineffective, a one-way solid slab contains a large amount of concrete that is structurally redundant. This creates an unnecessary burden on the slab itself and also on supporting beams and columns. It is, therefore, uneconomical to use a one-way solid slab for spans exceeding 15 to 20 ft (4.5 to 6 m). Larger column spacings may, however, be provided by using a system in which one-way solid slabs are supported on secondary beams which in turn rest on primary beams (also called girders), Fig. 13.9.1. The structural design of one-way solid slabs is described later in this section.

Joist Floors. A more economical solution to the above system (secondary beams and girders) is the joist floor, also called the *ribbed slab*. This consists of closely spaced beams, called ribs or joists, resting on a set of parallel beams. The spacing between joists is normally about 3 ft (900 mm), so that the slab spanning over the joists need only be about 2 in. (50 mm) thick unless greater thickness is required for increased fire resistance and/or sound insulation.

The joists are generally formed with inverted U-shape reusable metal, or glass-reinforced plastic pans. They have tapered sides for easy removal. The joist width can be varied simply by placing the pans closer together or farther apart. Instead of the removable forms, hollow concrete or clay blocks may be used as permanent forms giving a flat soffit and increased sound insulation.

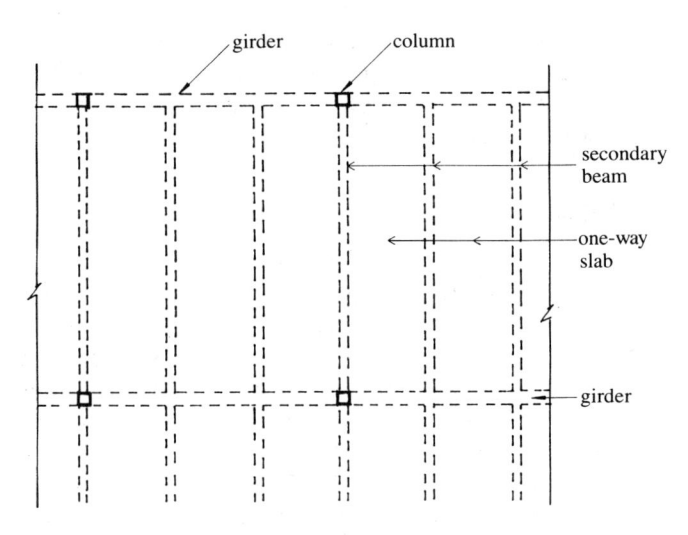

Fig. 13.9.1. Secondary beam and girder system (in plan).

The ends of joists near the supports are broadened for greater shear resistance, Fig. 13.9.2a. This generally obviates the need for shear reinforcement but if required, galloping stirrups are used, see Fig. 13.5.2.

Distribution ribs are provided perpendicular to the main joists to distribute loads. Usually one rib is provided at midspan for joist spans of up to 30 ft (9 m) and two, if the span exceeds 30 ft. These ribs are usually 5 in. wide, reinforced at the top and bottom with one #5 bar. Concrete cover for joists is $\frac{3}{4}$ in. (20 mm), Table 13.6, and their minimum depth requirement is the same as for beams, Table 13.5.

A typical joist is designed as a singly reinforced beam. The slab is designed assuming that the joists provide a fixed support to it. Thus, the flexural reinforcement for the slab, perpendicular to the joists, is calculated assuming $M_u = (w_u L^2)/12$, but it should not be less than that required for shrinkage reinforcement, provided parallel to the direction of the joists. The reinforcement is located at the centerline of the slab to resist both the positive and negative moments.

The beams supporting the joists are usually designed with the same depth as the joists, giving wide but shallow beams, Fig. 13.9.2b. This gives economy of formwork since the entire floor (joist floor and the supporting beams) can be formed with pans laid side by side on one horizontal deck. Deeper supporting beams may, however, be required if the distance between the columns is large.

The joist floor system is economical for joist spans of 25 to 40 ft (7.5 to 12 m).

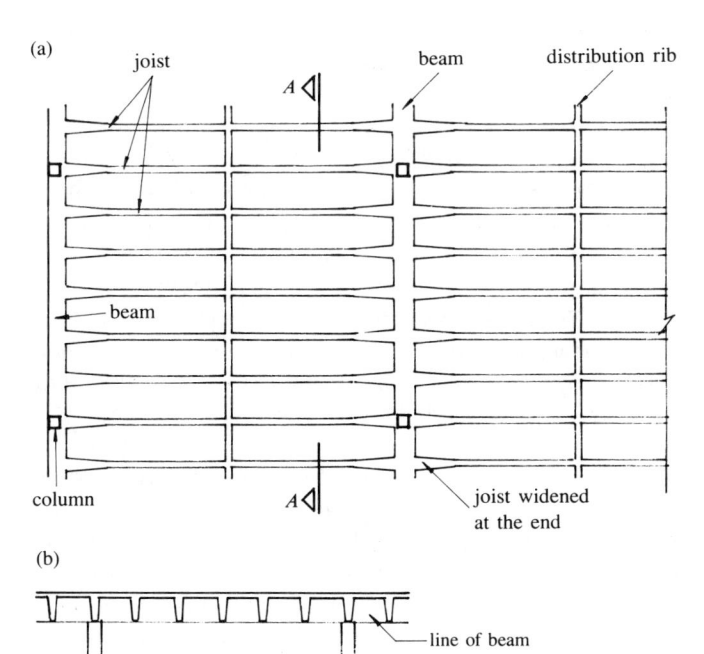

Fig. 13.9.2. One-way joist floor formed by using removable pans. (a) Plan, looking up; (b) section *AA*; note the equal depths of joists and supporting beams which simplifies the formwork considerably.

Two-Way Systems

Two-way slabs are of three types, Fig. 13.9.3: (i) slabs with edge beams on all sides (the beams may be replaced by walls in a masonry structure), and (ii) slabs resting directly on columns (without any beams) called *flat slabs* or *flat plates* depending on whether or not the slab is thickened around columns, and (iii) waffle slab.

A flat plate/flat slab behaves virtually as a shallow (but wide) beam in both directions. Thus, the slab is designed to carry 100 percent of the load in each direction. In a two-way slab with edge beams, the load on the slab is shared between the two principal directions. A two-way slab with edge beams is, therefore, structurally more efficient than a flat slab or flat plate and requires less material for the same column spacing. This presumes that the edge beams are much stiffer than the slab. If this is not so, the behavior of a two-way slab with edge beams lies somewhere between that of a two-way slab with very stiff beams and a flat plate/flat slab. Only square or nearly square panels are permitted for flat plates and flat slabs, a restriction that is relaxed somewhat for two-way slabs with edge beams.

Two-way Slabs with Edge Beams. They are quite popular, particularly in countries where formwork costs are low (due to cheap labor). If the cost of concrete and steel is relatively high, the use of flat plate/flat slab floors becomes uneconomical. Two-way slabs with edge beams are structurally efficient up to a maximum span of nearly 25 ft (7.5 m).

Flat Plates and Flat Slabs. The completely flat soffit of a flat plate results in lower formwork costs and allows partitions to be placed anywhere without changing their heights. It requires greater thickness than a flat slab of the same size, due to its lower shear resistance, as the columns tend to punch through a flat plate. Consequently, shear governs the thickness of a flat plate. Thus, a flat plate system is suitable only for lightly loaded floors with small column spacing such as in apartments and hotels. Column spacing of 15 to 24 ft (4.5 to 7.2 m) is suggested for reinforced concrete flat plates and 24 to 33 ft (7.2 to 10 m) for posttensioned flat plates (Ref. 13.3 page 171). Posttensioning reduces the deflection of flat plate floors and the posttensioning cables tend to carry some of the shear directly to the columns.

Flat slabs are suitable for heavily loaded buildings such as storage and industrial-type buildings. Their structural behavior is similar to that of flat plates. The thickening of the slab around the columns increases the shear strength of the slab and its moment capacity at supports. It also reduces the maximum moment in the slab by reducing its clear span. Traditionally, this thickening was accomplished by a drop panel and a mushroom capital but today, only drop panels are used to achieve a simpler formwork.

Waffle Slabs. A waffle slab is a two-way version of the one-way joist floor and is therefore much stiffer than the

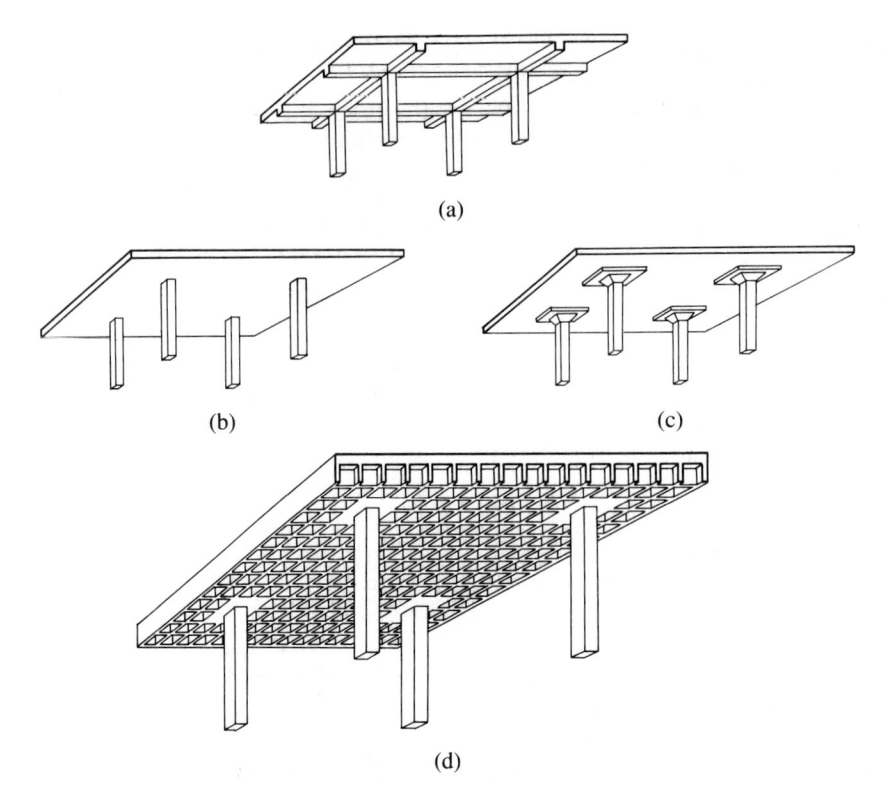

Fig. 13.9.3. Two-way floor slabs. (a) Two-way slab with edge beams; (b) flat plate; (c) flat slab; (d) waffle slab.

latter. Reinforced concrete waffle slabs are recommended for spans of 35 to 50 ft (10 to 15 m), and posttensioned slabs for 50 to 70 ft (15 to 20 m).

The slab is formed with reusable metal or plastic forms, called domes. Square domes are most popular and are usually about 3 ft (1 m) wide. Solid heads are formed over the columns by leaving a few domes out of the formwork to improve the shear resistance of the slab. The slab panel over the waffles need only be about 2 in. (50 mm) thick. However, a greater thickness is normally used to meet building code requirements for fire resistance.

Design of One-Way Solid Slabs

A one-way solid slab is designed as a singly reinforced beam of unit width (12 in. in U.S. customary units and 1 m in the SI system) whose overall depth is equal to the slab thickness and whose span is equal to the distance between the two supporting edges.

Principal Reinforcement. The steel area A_s calculated from flexural considerations gives the area required for 12 in. (or 1 m) width. This is converted into bar size and spacing so that the steel area available in any 12 in. (or 1 m) wide strip of the slab is greater than or equal to the calculated area. The requirements for principal reinforcement are:

(i) The maximum spacing of bars is $s = 3h$ but not greater than 18 in. (450 mm), where h is slab thickness, and (ii) the area of principal reinforcement must be greater than or equal to the area of shrinkage and temperature reinforcement, A_{ss}; that is, $A_s \geq A_{ss}$.

Shrinkage and Temperature Reinforcement. Shrinkage and temperature reinforcement (also called secondary reinforcement) is required in a direction perpendicular to that of the principal reinforcement. Apart from minimizing cracks, it helps in distributing the loads on the slab in the transverse direction and, during construction, in holding the principal reinforcement in place by forming a mesh. The secondary reinforcement should be placed above the principal reinforcement to maximize the effective depth of the slab. The requirements for secondary reinforcement are:

(i) The maximum spacing of bars is $s = 5h$ but not greater than 18 in. (450 mm), and (ii) $A_{ss} \geq 0.2\%(bh)$ for grade 40 steel and $0.18\%(bh)$ for grade 60 steel.

Other Considerations. Shear does not normally govern the design of a one-way slab but a check must be made. Since stirrups are not provided, shear is resisted by the concrete only. The slab must also satisfy the minimum thickness requirements, unless the computed deflection meets code requirements. Crack control needs to be checked. The minimum cover required is $\frac{3}{4}$ in. (20 mm), Table 13.6. The following examples illustrate the design of one-way slabs.

Example 13.3. Design the slab for a room 12 ft × 24 ft (clear). The slab is supported on four masonry walls which provide simple supports to the slab. $f'_c = 4$ ksi and $f_y = 60$ ksi. Live load on slab

= 60 psf. Assume dead load on the slab due to floor finish, ceiling, etc. as 50 psf, and the density of reinforced concrete as 150 pcf.

Solution. The slab is a (simply supported) one-way slab (since $L_1/L_2 = 24/12 = 2 > 1.5$). For the purpose of calculating its minimum thickness, the span of the slab = 12 ft + slab thickness = 12.6 ft, see Table 13.5. From the same table, the minimum thickness of slab, h = span/20 = $(12.6 \times 12)/20$ = 7.56 in., or say 7.5 in. We shall assume this as the required thickness of the slab unless flexure or shear considerations require greater thickness. Therefore:

$$d = h - \text{cover} - \text{half bar diameter}$$
$$= 7.5 - 0.75 - 0.25 = 6.5 \text{ in.}$$

Considering 12 in. wide strip of slab,

$$\text{self load of slab} = (7.5/12)150 = 94 \text{ lb/ft}$$

$$\text{Total dead load} = 94 + 50 = 144 \text{ lb/ft}$$

Therefore,

$$w_u = 144 \times 1.4 + 60 \times 1.7 = 304 \text{ lb/ft} = 0.304 \text{ k/ft}$$

$$M_u = w_u L^2/8 = 0.304(12^2/8) = 5.47 \text{ k ft} = 65.7 \text{ k in.}$$

(Note that the clear span has been used in calculating the moment, see Fig. 13.8.1)

From Eq. (13.2), $65.7 = Kbd^2 = K(12 \times 6.5^2)$. Thus, $K = 0.13$ ksi. From Table 13.4, $\rho = 0.25$ percent.

$$A_s = \rho bd = 0.25\%(12)6.5 = 0.20 \text{ in}^2.$$

Use #3 bar 6 in. on center as principal reinforcement (from Table 13.1, the area of #3 bar is 0.11 in.^{2}, which gives $A_s = 0.22$ in.^{2} per foot of slab length). Check if A_s is at least equal to A_{ss}:

$$A_{ss} = 0.18\% bh = 0.18\%(12 \times 7.5) = 0.16 \text{ in.}^2$$

Since $A_s(0.22 \text{ in.}^2) > A_{ss}(0.16 \text{ in.}^2)$, this is OK.
Check spacing of principal reinforcement:

$$6 \text{ in.} < 3h\ (= 22.5 \text{ in.}) \quad \text{OK}$$

Provide shrinkage reinforcement as #3 bar 8 in. on center (which gives $A_{ss} = 0.17$ in.^{2} per foot of slab length). Note that the spacing requirement for shrinkage reinforcement is satisfied.
Check for crack control. With reference to Fig. 13.9.4a and Eq. (13.7),

$$z = 0.6 f_y \sqrt[3]{d_c A} = 0.6(60)\sqrt[3]{12}$$
$$= 82.4 \text{ k/in.} < 175 \text{ k/in.} \quad \text{OK}$$

Check for shear:

$$V_u = 0.5 w_u L = 0.5(304 \times 12) = 1824\#$$

From Eq. (13.6), $\phi V_c = \phi 2\sqrt{f'_c} bd$, see Section 13.5. Thus,

$$\phi V_c = 0.85 \times 2\sqrt{(4000)}(12 \times 6.5) = 8386\# > 1824\# \quad \text{OK}$$

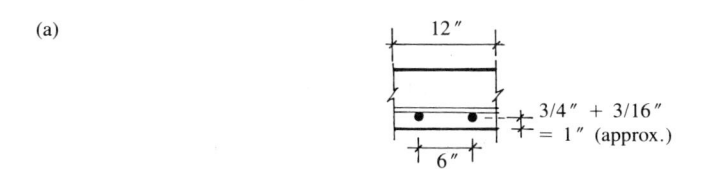

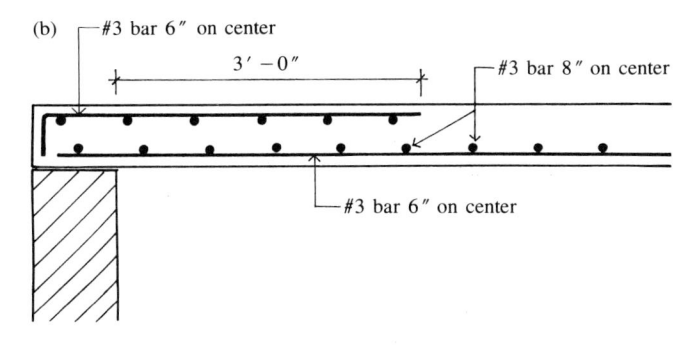

Fig. 13.9.4. Example 13.3. (a) 12-in.-wide strip of slab; note that $d_c = (0.75 + 0.375/2) = $ approximately 1 in.; $A = 2(1)(12)/2 = 12$ in.^{2}; (b) part layout of reinforcement in the slab.

Note that it is not necessary to use the lower value of V_u (at the critical section) since $\phi V_c > V_u$. The (part) layout of reinforcement is shown in Fig. 13.9.4b.

Example 13.3a. Design the slab for a room 3.6 m × 7.2 m (clear). The slab is supported on four masonry walls which provide simple supports to the slab. $f'_c = 30$ MPa and $f_y = 400$ MPa. Live load on slab = 3.0 kN/m^2. Assume dead load on the slab due to floor finish, ceiling, etc. as 2.5 kN/m^2, and the density of reinforced concrete as 2400 kg/m^3.

Solution. The slab is a (simply supported) one-way slab (since $L_1/L_2 = 3.6/7.2 = 2 > 1.5$). For the purpose of calculating its minimum thickness, the span of the slab = 3.6 m + slab thickness = 3.79 m, see Table 13.5. From the same table, the minimum thickness of slab, h = span/20 = $(3.79 \times 1000)/20$ = 190 mm. We shall assume this as the required thickness of the slab unless flexure or shear considerations require greater thickness. Therefore,

$$d = h - \text{cover} - \text{half bar diameter} = 190 - 20 - 5 = 165 \text{ mm}$$

Considering 1 m wide strip of slab:

$$\text{self load of slab} = (190/1000)23.5 = 4.5 \text{ kN/m}$$

Note that a concrete density of 2400 kg/m^3 translates into a slab self load of 23.5 kN/m^3 (= 2400 × 9.8 N/m^3)

$$\text{Total dead load} = 4.5 + 2.5 = 7.0 \text{ kN/m}$$

Therefore,

$$w_u = 7.0 \times 1.4 + 3.0 \times 1.7 = 14.9 \text{ kN/m}$$

$$M_u = w_u L^2/8 = 14.9((3.6^2/8) = 24.1 \text{ kN m}$$
$$= 24.1 \times 10^6 \text{ N mm}$$

(Note that the clear span has been used in calculating the moment, see Fig. 13.8.1.)

From Eq. (13.2),

$$24.1 \times 10^6 = Kbd^2 = K(1000 \times 165^2)$$

Thus, $K = 0.885$. From Table 13.4a, $\rho = 0.25$ percent.

$$A_s = \rho bd = 0.25\% (1000)165 = 413 \text{ mm}^2$$

Use #10 bar 200 mm on center as principal reinforcement. Note that from Table 13.1a, the area of #10 bar is 100 mm² which gives $A_s = (1000/200)(100) = 500$ mm² per meter of slab length, which is greater than the required area of 413 mm².
Check if A_s is at least equal to A_{ss}:

$$A_{ss} = 0.18\% bh = 0.18\%(1000 \times 190) = 342 \text{ mm}^2$$

Since $A_s(500 \text{ mm}^2) \geq A_{ss}(342 \text{ mm}^2)$, this is OK.
Check spacing of principal reinforcement:

$$200 \text{ mm} < 3h(= 570 \text{ mm}) \qquad \text{OK}$$

Provide shrinkage reinforcement as #10 bar 250 mm on center which gives $A_{ss} = 400$ mm² per meter of slab length. Note that the spacing requirement for shrinkage reinforcement is satisfied.
Check for crack control: With reference to Eq. (13.7),

$$z = 0.6f_y \sqrt[3]{d_c A} = 0.6(400)\sqrt[3]{25 \times 1000} \qquad \text{OK}$$
$$= 15113 \text{ N/mm} = 15.1 \text{ MN/m} < 30 \text{ MN/m}$$

Check for shear:

$$V_u = 0.5 w_u L = 0.5(14.9 \times 3.6) = 26.8 \text{ kN}$$
$$\phi V_c = \phi(\sqrt{f_c'}/6)bd$$

(see Section 13.5). Thus,

$$\phi V_c = 0.85(\sqrt{30}/6)(1000 \times 165) = 128,030 \text{ N} \qquad \text{OK}$$
$$= 128.0 \text{ kN} > 26.8 \text{ kN}$$

Note that it is not necessary to use the lower value of V_u (at the critical section) since $\phi V_c > V_u$. The layout of reinforcement is similar to that shown in Fig. 13.9.4b.

Example 13.4. Design the slab, shown in Fig. 13.9.5, continuous over three equal spans, 12 ft clear. The beams (each 12 in. wide) are simply supported with a clear span of 24 ft. The other data are the same as in Example 13.3.

Solution. For minimum thickness calculation, the span of each slab is 13 ft. The two end slabs have each one end continuous and the middle slab has both ends continuous. From Table 13.5, the minimum thicknesses of slabs are:
For the end spans,
$$h = \text{span}/24 = (13 \times 12)/24 = 6.5 \text{ in.}$$
For the middle span,
$$h = \text{span}/28 = (13 \times 12)/28 = 5.6 \text{ in.}$$
Adopt a uniform thickness, $h = 6.5$ in. for all spans. Hence, $d = 5.5$ in.
$$\text{Self load of slab} = (6.5/12)150 = 81 \text{ psf}$$
Hence,
$$w_u = (81 + 50)1.4 + (60)1.7 = 285 \text{ \#/ft}$$
$$= 0.285 \text{ k/ft}$$
$$w_u L^2 = 0.285(12^2) = 41.0 \text{ k ft} = 492 \text{ k in.}$$
$$0.5 w_u L = 1710 \text{ \#}$$

As shown in Fig. 13.9.5, there are five sections (A, B, C, D, and E) where the values of M_u must be determined. The calculations of moments are given in Table 13.7; the values of moment coefficients have been obtained from Fig. 13.8.1. Note that all the restrictions stipulated by the code for using moment coefficients are satisfied, see Section 13.8.
First work out A_{ss}. This will give the minimum area required for principal reinforcement.

$$A_{ss} = 0.18\% bh = 0.18\%(12 \times 6.5) = 0.14 \text{ in.}^2$$

Use #3 bar 9 in. on center, which gives $A_{ss} = 0.146$ in.².
In Table 13.7 the asterisk shows that the calculated value of A_s is less than A_{ss}; hence the latter value has been adopted for A_s. For the sake of simplicity, only two different spacings of #3 bars have been used, 8 in. and 9 in. The values of K have been obtained by dividing M_u by bd^2, where $bd^2 = 12(5.5)^2 = 363$ in.³.
Check for shear: From Fig. 13.8.1, the maximum value of shear on the beam is:

$$V_u = 1.15(0.5 w_u L) = 1.15(1710) = 1967 \text{ lb}$$
$$\phi V_c = 0.85 \times 2\sqrt{(4000)}(12 \times 5.5) = 7096 \text{ lb} > 1911 \text{ lb}$$

(OK)

The reader may verify that the above design is also satisfactory for (i) spacing of principal and secondary reinforcements and (ii) crack control. The layout of reinforcement may be prepared using details of Fig. 13.7.3.

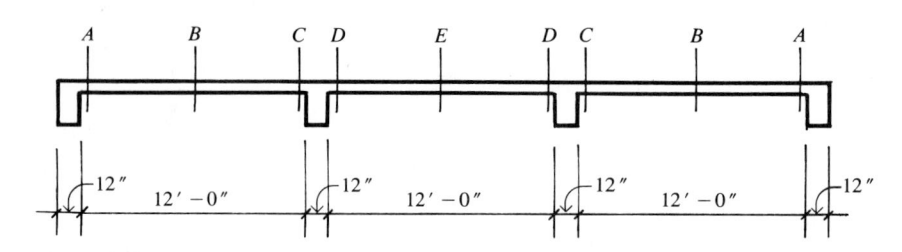

Fig. 13.9.5. Example 13.4.

Table 13.7. (Example 13.4).

Section	Coeff.	M_u (k in.)	K (ksi)	ρ	A_s (in.²)	Bar Size & Spacing
A	−1/24	−20.5	0.056	0.11%	0.14*	#3, 9 in. o.c.
B	+1/14	+35.1	0.097	0.18%	0.14*	#3, 9 in. o.c.
C	−1/10	−49.2	0.135	0.25%	0.17	#3, 8 in. o.c.
D	−1/11	−44.7	0.123	0.23%	0.15	#3, 8 in. o.c.
E	+1/16	+30.8	0.085	0.16%	0.14*	#3, 9 in. o.c.

13.10. REINFORCED CONCRETE COLUMNS

The code (2.1) defines a column as that element of the building which is used primarily to support compressive loads. In actual fact, most reinforced concrete columns in a building are subjected to shear and bending moments in addition to axial compressive forces. The compressive force on a column is caused mainly by gravity loads.

The bending moments in a column may be caused by both the gravity as well as the lateral loads. If the beams frame into an interior column from both sides, the moment in such a column due to gravity loads is present only if the respective moments in the beams at the beam-column junction are unequal. The moment in the column is simply the difference between the two beam moments, since the beams tend to bend the column in opposite directions. If the two beams have equal spans with equal loads, their moments at the junction will be equal but opposite and hence the net moment on the column will be zero. However, the unbalanced moment on an interior column resulting from the presence of live load on one side and its absence on the other, must be considered. This unbalanced moment is distributed to the column above and below the junction.

An exterior column has large unbalanced gravity load moment due to the unsymmetrical loading along one direction and a corner column is subjected to biaxial moments due to unsymmetrical loading along both directions.

Moments in a column due to lateral loads can be substantial, particularly on the lower floor of a multistory building, unless separate structural elements, such as shear walls and shear cores are provided to absorb them. In such a case, the columns are designed for gravity loads only.

Reinforcement in Columns

Since the longitudinal reinforcement of a column may buckle under axial loads and burst through concrete cover, lateral reinforcement is provided in the form of either individual ties placed at intervals or a continuous spiral wound around the longitudinal reinforcement, Fig. 13.10.1. The lateral and longitudinal reinforcements form a cage which keeps both reinforcements securely in place while the concrete is poured in the forms.

Tied columns are generally square, rectangular, or L-shaped. The ties must be out of a minimum of #3 bar, if the longitudinal reinforcement is #10 bar or less and out of #4 bar if the longitudinal reinforcement is #11 bar and

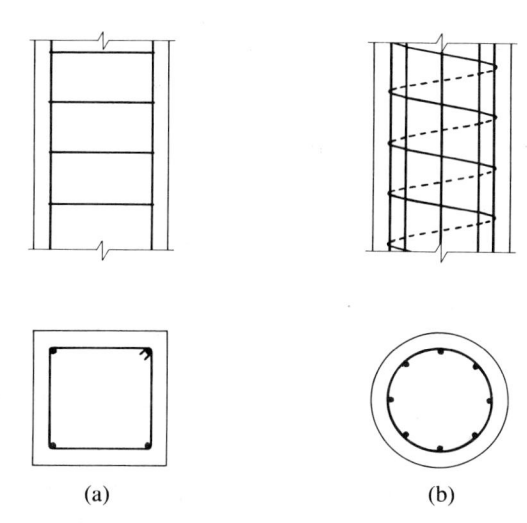

Fig. 13.10.1. (a) Tied and (b) spiral columns.

above. The required maximum spacing of ties is the smallest of the following dimensions: (i) 48 times the tie diameter, (ii) 16 times the longitudinal bar diameter, and (iii) the least dimension of the column.

Spiral columns are more expensive than the tied columns but have much greater ductility. They deform several times more than the tied columns before failure, Fig. 13.10.2, and are, therefore, preferred for buildings in seismic zones. A spiral column is either circular or square, but even a square column must have a circular reinforcement cage. The minimum diameter for the spiral is $\frac{3}{8}$ in. (10 mm) and the maximum clear spacing of spiral (pitch) is 3 in. (75 mm).

The longitudinal reinforcement in a column must be at least 1 percent. Even columns which carry only concentric loads must have this minimum reinforcement. This is to

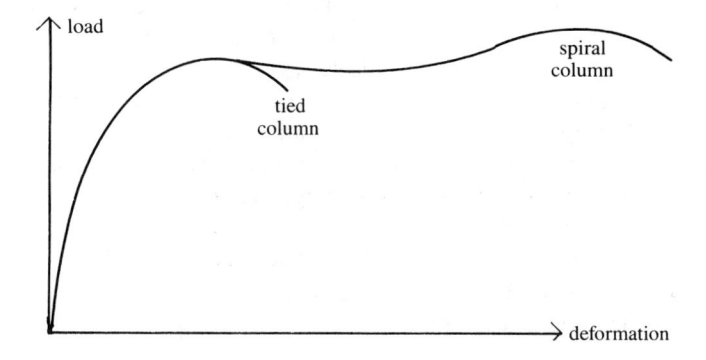

Fig. 13.10.2. Behavior of tied and spiral columns under load.

resist any bending stresses caused by unintentional eccentricity of the load and also to reduce the effects of creep and shrinkage in the column. The maximum reinforcement is 8 percent, although it is generally difficult to accommodate more than 5 to 6 percent longitudinal reinforcement in a column.

A minimum of four bars are required for a tied circular or rectangular column and six bars for a spiral column. The code does not place any limitation on the cross-sectional dimension of a reinforced concrete column, although in practice the smallest dimension is about 8 in. (200 mm).

Short and Slender Columns

Unlike steel or wood columns, reinforced concrete columns are seldom so long that they will fail by buckling alone. However, reinforced concrete columns are separated into two categories: short and slender columns. A precise definition of a slender column is provided in the code (10.11); suffice it to note here that the slenderness of a column is a function of the ratio of the column's height to its cross-sectional dimensions and whether or not the column is braced against side-sway. A slender column has lower strength than a short column of the same cross-sectional dimensions and steel area, and its analysis is more complicated. Fortunately, however, most reinforced concrete columns in buildings are short. A study of over 20,000 reinforced concrete columns indicated that nearly 90 percent of all braced columns and 40 percent of all unbraced columns were short columns (Ref. 13.7). Only short columns will be briefly discussed here.

Design of a Short Column

Axial Loads. Theoretically, the nominal strength of a column under a concentric load (zero eccentricity) P_0 is simply the sum of the strengths provided by concrete area and the steel area; that is,

$$P_0 = f'_c(A_g - A_{st}) + f_y A_{st}$$

where A_g is the gross area of concrete section and A_{st} is the area of steel in the column.

Tests on actual columns have, however, shown that the strength of a column is better predicted if f'_c is replaced by $0.85 f'_c$ in the above equation. The reason is that the concrete in a test cylinder is stronger than the concrete in a column mainly because of better compaction and curing of concrete in a cylinder than in a column at the job site.

To account for any unintentional eccentricity in the load, the code requires that the strength of a tied column be reduced by a factor of 0.80. This is in addition to the reduction due to the ϕ-factor, whose value for a tied column is 0.70, Table 13.3. Thus, the strength of a tied column under concentric loads is given by

$$\phi P_n = \phi(0.80)\left[0.85 f'_c(A_g - A_{st}) + f_y A_{st}\right]$$

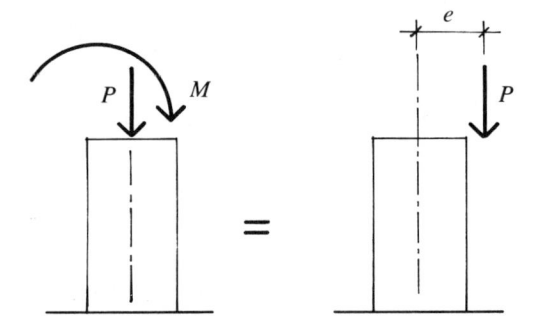

Fig. 13.10.3. The behavior of a column under the combined action of a concentric load P and a bending moment M is equivalent to the column's behavior under load P located at an eccentricity e. Note that $M = Pe$.

Axial Loads and Bending Moment. The combined action of a concentric load P and a bending moment M on a column is equivalent to the action of the load P acting on the column at an eccentricity e, where $e = (M/P)$, Fig. 13.10.3. Thus, a column, subjected to a concentric load and a bending moment, can be designed assuming that it is subjected to an eccentric load of the same magnitude as the concentric load.

If the strength of a column under a concentric load has been calculated as ϕP_n, it is obvious that its strength under an eccentric load will be less than ϕP_n; the decrease in strength will be in direct proportion to the magnitude of eccentricity. The larger the eccentricity of the load, the smaller the load itself which the column will be able to carry. Thus, a given column will support a large number of load-eccentricity combinations (load-moment combinations). This means that a curve giving a relationship between the load and moment strength of the column, called the *load-moment interaction curve*, can be prepared. A point on this curve will give the values of load and moment which a given column will be able to support.

The design of columns subjected to the combined action of concentric load and bending moment is accomplished through the use of load-moment interaction curves (if a computer is not used) prepared for various column sizes and reinforcement percentages. For additional details on load-moment interaction curves, refer to Ref. 13.4, 13.6 or 13.7.

13.11. REINFORCED CONCRETE WALLS

Reinforced concrete walls are used in buildings as: (i) walls supporting axial loads, (ii) retaining walls, (iii) basement walls, and (iv) shear walls. Often, a wall is required to serve more than one of the above functions.

Regardless of the type of wall, the code (14.3) specifies a few general requirements for a reinforced concrete wall with respect to the minimum thickness, minimum area of reinforcement, its spacing, anchorage to supporting elements, etc. As in slabs, reinforcement in walls must be provided in both directions and if the thickness of the wall exceeds 10 in. (250 mm), two layers of reinforcement are required, one near each face of the wall. Vertical reinforcement need not be enclosed by lateral ties if its area is less than 1 percent of the gross concrete area or if the vertical reinforcement is not required as compression reinforcement. At least two #5 bars are required at each corner of an opening to resist diagonal cracking there. These bars must extend at least 24 in. (600 mm) beyond corners to develop the tensile strength of the bars.

Walls Supporting Axial Loads. These may carry uniformly distributed loads, such as those resulting from the reactions of roofs or floors, or concentrated loads from columns or beams. In the latter case, the horizontal length of the wall to be considered effective in carrying each concentrated load, must not exceed center-to-center distance between loads nor the width of bearing plus 4 times the thickness of the wall.

They may be designed as wide but narrow columns, in which case the design must satisfy all the requirements of column design. Alternatively, if the resultant of all the factored loads on the wall lies within the middle third of the wall thickness, they may be designed using the empirical method given in the code (14.5), which is much simpler. The minimum thickness of such walls is $\frac{1}{25}$ times the supported height or length but not less than 4 in.

Retaining Walls. These are constructed below ground to retain the earth and resist its pressure. The pressure of the earth is assumed to be hydrostatic, i.e., it acts normal to the wall and its value at any point is obtained by multiplying the depth of the point below ground by an equivalent fluid density, which usually lies between 30 and 62.5 pcf (62.5 pcf is the density of water). Granular soils (sand and gravel) have a smaller equivalent fluid density than cohesive soils (silt and clay). In some situations, where a cohesive soil is fully saturated with water, equivalent fluid density may exceed 62.5 pcf (1000 kg/m^3).

Retaining walls are usually free standing and occur as isolated walls. Although reinforced concrete is commonly used, they may also be constructed of masonry or plain concrete particularly if the height of the wall is small. They may be of several shapes depending on the height of the wall and its location with respect to the property line. The most widely used shape is an inverted tee, Fig. 13.11.1, whose flange functions as the footing of the wall and also provides stability against overturning and sliding of the wall.

Under the action of horizontal loads, the wall has tendency to overturn about the lower end of the "toe." This overturning moment must be balanced by an opposite moment caused by vertical forces due to the wall's own weight and that due to the weight of the soil above the "heel." Both the toe and the heel help to increase this balancing moment. A larger toe gives a greater moment arm and a larger heel provides a greater vertical force. Both

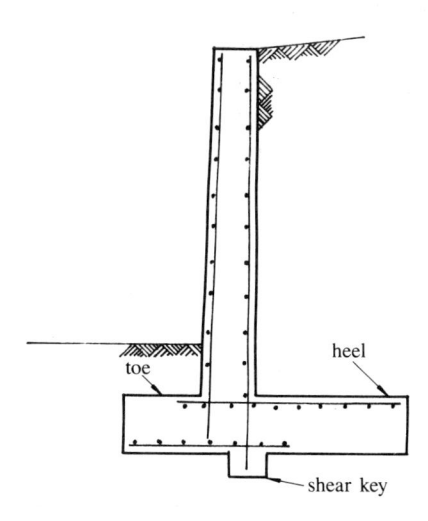

Fig. 13.11.1. Section through a cantilever retaining wall.

the toe and the heel behave as cantilevers, bending in opposite curvatures. A shear key is provided in the footing to increase the resistance of the wall against sliding.

Basement Walls. These are supported laterally at the top and the bottom by floor slabs, and also at intermediate points if the basement is more than one story deep. Apart from supporting horizontal load due earth pressure, they also support vertical loads due to their own weight and the superstructure loads. The vertical load cancels some of the tension in the wall due to the earth pressure.

Shear Walls. These are provided to resist lateral loads due to wind and earthquake. They behave as cantilevers against in-plane forces and are designed to resist bending, shear and torsion (if any).

13.12. REINFORCED CONCRETE FOOTINGS
(see also Chapter 15)

Following are some of the commonly used foundation (or footing) types in buildings, Fig. 13.12.1.

An *isolated column footing* is usually square in plan but a rectangular shape may be used if dimensional limitations require its use. It may be with or without a pedestal or have a sloping profile. It is used when the columns are spaced far apart and the bearing capacity of the soil is high, Fig. 13.12.1a.

If two or more columns are spaced close together, it is more economical to use a *combined footing* which may be rectangular or trapezoidal in shape depending on the magnitudes of loads on columns and the physical limitations of space, Fig. 13.12.1b.

A combined footing may also be used if one of the columns is very close to the property line for which it is impossible to design an isolated footing. However, if the distance between the columns is large, a *strap* or *cantilever footing* may be more economical. This consists of two

214 HANDBOOK OF ARCHITECTURAL TECHNOLOGY

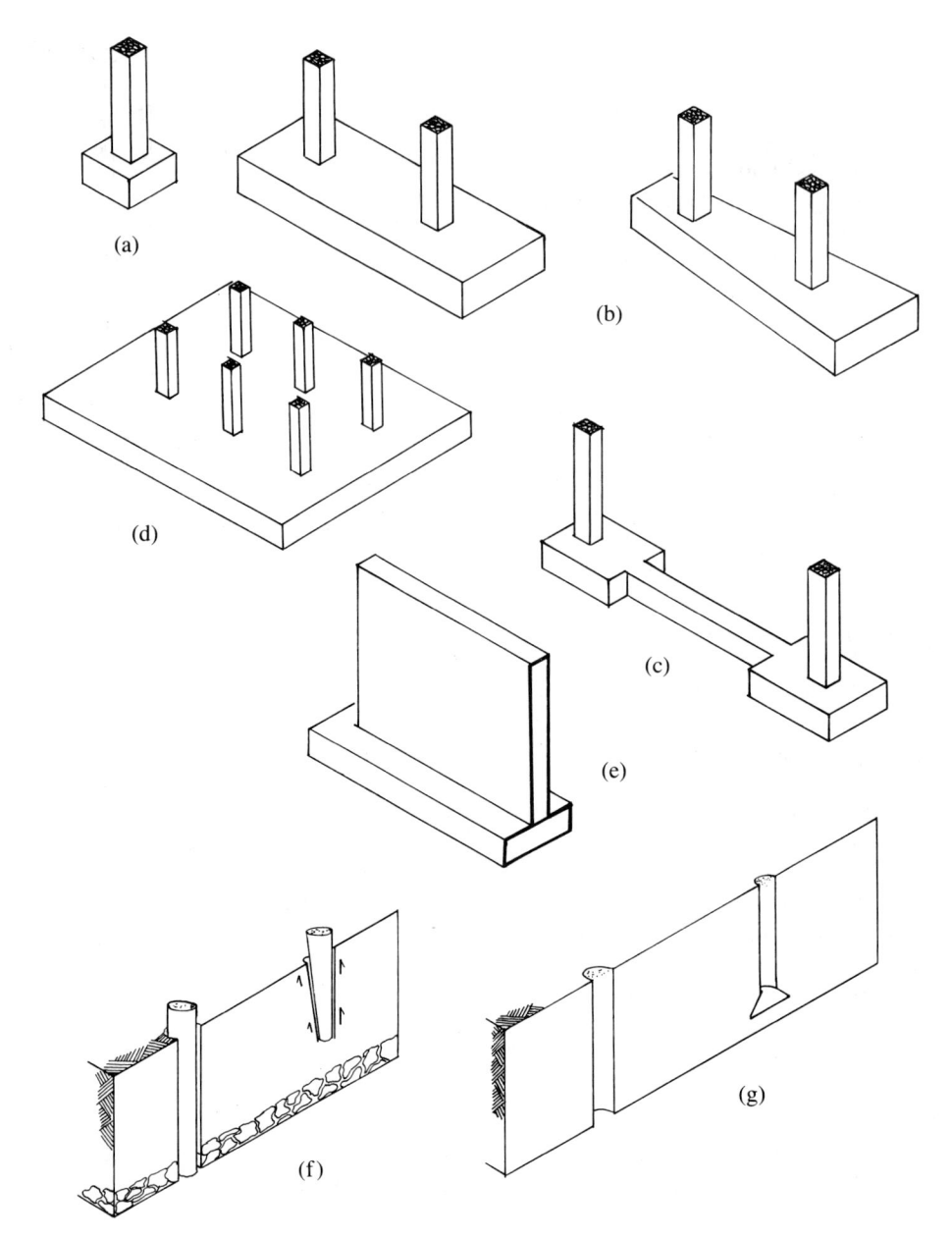

Fig. 13.12.1. Various types of reinforced concrete foundations. (a) Isolated column footing; (b) combined footing; (c) strap footing; (d) mat footing; (e) wall footing; (f) bearing and friction piles; (g) drilled piers.

isolated footings connected by a (strap) beam, Fig. 13.12.1c. The beam transfers the bending moment in the exterior footing to the interior footing.

If the bearing capacity of soil in comparison to the loads on columns is low, the areas of isolated footings become unduly large. In such a case, it is more economical to merge them into one large footing placed under the entire building, called a *raft* or *mat footing*, Fig. 13.12.1d. A raft also reduces the differential settlement in the building.

A *wall footing*, Fig. 13.12.1e is a linear footing provided under a load-bearing or a non-load-bearing wall. Since the intensity of load on a wall is small, it is usually more economical to use a plain concrete footing under walls.

If satisfactory soil conditions do not exist fairly close to the surface below the lowest floor level of the building, *piles* or *drilled piers* may be used. They carry the load from the building to an underlying firmer stratum, either by bearing at the bottom of the pile (or pier) or by friction along their sides, Fig. 13.12.1f. Piles are driven into the ground and may be of timber, steel, concrete or a combination of these materials.

A pier (also called a caisson) is made by drilling a shaft with a rotating auger and subsequently filling the shaft with concrete, Fig. 13.12.1g. Pier footings are commonly used in locations where the top soil is expansive, so that footings rest on a more stable soil below. In such situations, the piers are usually widened at the base, in the shape of bells, to resist uplift on them due to soil expansion.

Design of an Isolated Column Footing

The design of an isolated column footing involves determining (i) the area of footing, (ii) amount of steel, (iii) thickness of footing, and (iv) its depth into the ground. The last factor depends on how far below the ground, satisfactory soil conditions are available (see Chapter 15). In cold climates, the footings must be located below the frost line to prevent instability resulting from freeze thaw cycles.

The area of footing, A_f, is obtained by dividing the service loads on the column by the net bearing capacity of soil, q_n. The net bearing capacity is obtained by subtracting the pressure caused by soil surcharge and the weight of the footing itself from the allowable bearing capacity q_a.

The structural behavior of an isolated footing is like that of a slab cantilevered from the column in all directions and loaded by the soil pressure. Since the design of footing cross-section must be based on the strength design, the factored soil pressure q_u is obtained by dividing the factored load on the column, P_u, by the area of footing; that is, $q_u = P_u/A_f$.

Since shear reinforcement is not generally used in footings, the entire shear resistance must be provided by the concrete. The thickness of an isolated column footing is, therefore, usually governed by shear (not flexural) considerations.

Shear considerations in a footing require lengthy calculations. The reader is referred to books on reinforced concrete for a detailed discussion of this topic (Ref. 13.4, 13.6, or 13.7). Suffice to note here that two types of shear must be considered in a column footing: (i) punching shear since the column tends to punch through the footing, and (ii) one-way shear, which is same as the shear in beams.

A simpler procedure for the design of an isolated column footing is to disregard shear considerations altogether and determine the thickness of the footing based only on flexural considerations. The limitations of this procedure are: (i) it works only for square footings supporting square or circular columns, and (ii) the thickness of the footing is calculated using the minimum permissible flexural reinforcement. Because the reinforcement area is small, a large concrete thickness is required for flexural resistance, which eliminates the need for shear calculations (Ref. 13.2, p. 7-6).

The minimum permissible flexural reinforcement for footings is the same as the shrinkage reinforcement in one-way slabs; that is 0.18% bh for grade 60 steel and 0.2% bh for grade 40 steel.

The critical section for flexure is at the face of the column. The footing is designed as a one-way slab in both directions. Thus, for a square footing of width b supporting a square column of width c the overhang of the footing beyond the face of the column is $0.5(b - c)$. Considering one foot width of footing (as is done in the design of one-way slabs), the design moment for the footing is (see Fig. 13.12.2):

$$M_u = \tfrac{1}{8} q_u (b - c)^2$$

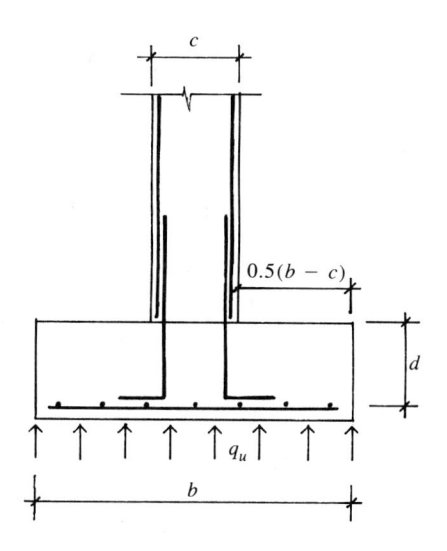

Fig. 13.12.2. An isolated square column footing. The footing is designed as a one-way slab cantilevered from the column and loaded by soil pressure q_u.

The effective thickness of the footing, d, can be worked out from Eq. (13.2). A check must be made for the development length of flexural reinforcement and also that of the dowels between the column and the footing.

13.13. PRESTRESSED CONCRETE

To prestress a component is to induce stresses in it which fully or partially counteract the undesirable stresses in the component resulting from the external loads. Since concrete is weak in tension, the prestressing of concrete is done to produce compression in regions where tension would occur under the action of loads. This reduces tensile stresses and hence the cracking of concrete. Prestressed concrete is therefore more durable than reinforced concrete, which is of particular importance for structures in corrosive atmospheres.

The absence of cracks in a prestressed concrete member allows the full utilization of the material, unlike that of a reinforced concrete member in which the concrete in the tension zone is structurally ineffective. The sections are therefore stiffer and have greater shear resistance. In addition, as explained later, a higher strength concrete must be used for prestressed concrete members. Thus, in comparison to conventional reinforced concrete, prestressed concrete flexural members have smaller sections and weigh less which yields economy of material not only for the member itself but also for the supporting columns and foundations.

Prestressing of concrete is done with high-strength steel wires, cables, or bars, called *tendons* (a generic term for all types of prestressing steel), that are elastically tensioned by hydraulic jacks. When the tensile forces are removed, the tendons tend to return to their original lengths but are prevented from doing so by the surrounding concrete, which as a result comes under compression.

Two methods are used to prestress concrete. The difference between them is based on whether the tendons are tensioned before or after the concrete has been cast. The former is called *pretensioning* and the latter *posttensioning*.

Pretensioning is done in precasting plants on long horizontal slabs called *casting beds*, which are typically several hundred feet long. Their great length allows a number of identical components to be cast in a line and prestressed simultaneously. Rigid abutments at both ends of a casting bed allows tendons to be stretched between them and anchored at their ends. After the tendons have been tensioned, ordinary reinforcing steel, which is required in most prestressed components to resist diagonal tension and handling stresses, is placed in position. The forms are then assembled around the steel and the concrete cast. After the concrete hardens, the tendons are cut. As the tendons tend to return to their original lengths, the prestressing force gets transferred to concrete. The components are now removed from casting beds, stored at a convenient location for subsequent transportation to the construction site, and the casting beds reprepared for a new batch of components. The use of high early strength portland cement and steam curing allows a 24 hour production cycle.

Pretensioning is particularly popular for precast floor slabs. Four types of such units are commonly produced as standard components, Fig. 13.13.1. The solid slabs are used for small spans (8 to 20 ft), hollow core slabs for intermediate spans (15 to 40 ft), and for long spans double tees (up to 100 ft) and single tees (up to 120 ft) are used. They are generally made with a rough top surface to produce a stronger bond with the structural lightweight concrete which is poured on them after they have been assembled in place. This integrates the units and also improves their structural action against concentrated loads.

In posttensioning, a void is left between the tendons and the concrete to prevent the two from bonding to each other. This is done with the use of ducts or waterproof paper that surrounds the tendons. The concrete is cast around the tendons and allowed to harden sufficiently before the steel is stretched and anchored with the help of mechanical devices against the anchorage seats fixed to the ends of the component. The void between prestressing steel and the concrete is later grouted to prevent the corrosion of tendons.

Although precast components may be posttensioned in prestressing plants, posttensioning is usually performed at construction sites. Posttensioning of long-span cast-in-place reinforced concrete beams and slabs is fairly common in countries where such technology is available.

The success of prestressing depends on the fact that the prestressing steel, once stressed, will maintain its stress without any relaxation over time. This is possible only if the concrete can resist the return of steel to its original length. The shrinkage, creep and the elastic shortening of concrete gradually reduces the initial elongation in tendons and hence the initial prestress in concrete. This *loss of prestress* is also contributed by two other factors: friction between the tendons and the concrete, and the slipping of anchorage seats.

It is estimated that the loss of prestress due to shrinkage, creep and elastic shortening is between 35 and 45 ksi (240 to 310 MPa) (Ref. 13.7, p. 444). This does not include losses due to other factors. Ordinary reinforcing steel (f_y = 40 or 60 ksi; 300 or 400 MPa), therefore, cannot be used for prestressing, since it will lose all or most of its prestress in due course. High-strength steel, which will stretch substantially before failure, is mandatory for prestressing so that the loss of prestress represents only a small fraction of its total strength.

The most common type of prestressing steel is a seven-wire strand with an ultimate strength of 250 to 270 ksi (1700 to 1900 MPa).

The concrete used in prestressed work must be sufficiently strong to absorb the high initial prestress. A high-strength concrete is therefore required. Other reasons for using a high-strength concrete are: (i) lower creep or shrinkage strain (ii) lower transportation costs due to smaller member sizes, and (iii) a higher early strength, which gives a shorter production cycle. A 5 to 6 ksi (35 to 40 MPa) concrete is normally used; a higher strength is not desirable, since the mix is more difficult to produce and requires a smaller water-cement ratio, making concrete less workable. There is also the cost factor, which makes a higher-strength concrete increasingly uneconomical.

Stresses in Prestressed Concrete Members

The simplest way to prestress a member is through the use of a straight tendon placed at the centroid of the section. This will apply a uniform compressive prestress over the entire section. Thus, if the cross-sectional area of the member is A, and the prestressing force P, the prestress on the section will be P/A. Now, if the bending moment on the beam due to external loads is M, and the beam's section modulus S, then the extreme fiber stresses on the section will be $(P/A + M/S)$, and $(P/A - M/S)$, Fig. 13.13.2a, where the positive sign in the above expressions indicates

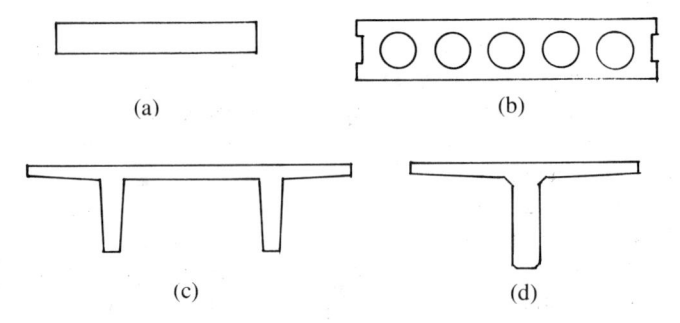

Fig. 13.13.1. The four most commonly used pretensioned slab elements. (a) Solid slab; (b) hollow core slab; (c) double tee; and (c) single tee.

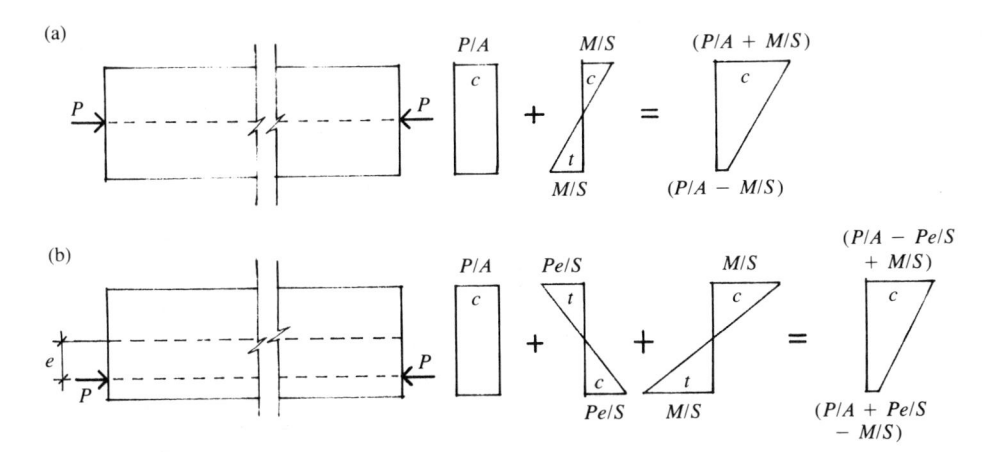

Fig. 13.13.2. Stresses in a prestressed component. P is the prestressing force and M the bending moment due to the applied loads; c and t denote compression and tension, respectively. (a) Prestressing force applied by a straight tendon placed at the centroid of the section; (b) prestressing force applied by an eccentrically placed straight tendon.

compression and the negative sign, tension. If no tension is permitted on the section, then in the extreme case when the tension is zero, $P/A = M/S$. In other words, the maximum permissible bending moment due to the loads (self load + external loads) is

$$M_{max} = P(S/A)$$

Although a concentric prestressing force reduces tensile stresses caused by the loads, it also increases compressive stresses in the section. The effectiveness of prestressing force is improved by using a straight tendon with an eccentricity e. Since, the net effect of an eccentric force is a concentric force plus a bending moment (Fig. 13.10.3), the prestressing force produces a compressive stress equal to P/A and a bending moment equal to Pe. Now, if the bending moment on a section of the member due to the loads is once again M, then the net extreme fiber stresses on that section will be $(P/A - Pe/S + M/S)$, and $(P/A + Pe/S - M/S)$, Fig. 13.13.2b. In the extreme case when the tension in the section, after the application of the load, is zero, we have

$$M_{max} = [P(S/A) + Pe]$$

Thus, compared to a concentric prestressing force, an eccentric prestressing force allows a larger bending moment to be applied to the member.

The moment due to the loads generally varies throughout the length of the member. If this moment is balanced at every section by an equal but opposite moment produced by the prestressing force (i.e., $M = Pe$), then the component can be completely free of bending. All sections will be under uniform compression—an ideal state of stress for concrete.

This concept, called *load balancing*, requires a variable eccentricity in order to respond to the variation of the applied bending moment along the length of the member. In posttensioned members, a continuously varying eccentricity can be obtained by the use of curved tendons. In pretensioned members, however, because of the nature of the prestressing process itself, only approximate curves, produced by a few straight segments, are possible, Fig. 13.13.3.

In practice, load balancing can be done for only one set of loading condition since the live load on the member varies in time. It is generally economical to balance the whole of the dead load and one half of the live load. The member is therefore subject to some bending moment but a much smaller one. Since load balancing reduces bending moments, both the instantaneous and the creep deflections are reduced.

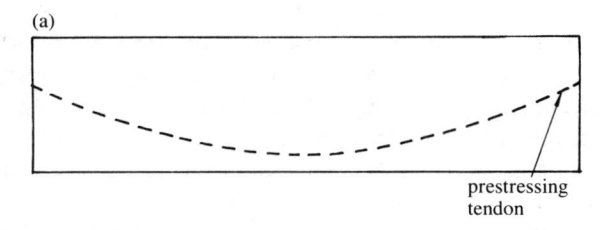

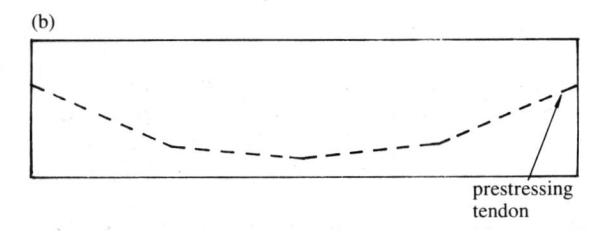

Fig. 13.13.3. (a) In posttensioned members, the tendons can be placed in smooth curves. (b) In pretensioned members, only approximate curves formed by straight segments, can be achieved.

13.14. COMPOSITE CONSTRUCTION

A reinforced concrete frame building may not require any structural steel component. But the same is not true of a building using a steel frame (steel beams and columns), which almost always requires the use of reinforced concrete for floor slabs and foundations, and in some buildings, for shear walls. In fact, steel beams or trusses topped with a cast-in-place reinforced concrete slab (usually on a metal deck) is a standard floor system for contemporary multistory steel buildings. Compared with a reinforced concrete frame, the steel frame offers the benefits of prefabrication, faster construction, lighter weight, and smaller beam depths, which substantially reduces the overall height of a tall building. The concrete slab gives diaphragm rigidity and sound insulation to the floor.

If the horizontal shear at the interface of a steel beam or truss and the concrete slab is effectively resisted, the two components act as a unit, in a composite manner, yielding a more economical design of steel members (beams or trusses). For a long time, the advantage of this interaction could not be realized in buildings because of the unavailability of suitable shear connectors. This was so even when a concrete slab and steel beam floor system was in use. The development of welded shear connectors in the early 1960s provided the necessary thrust for the development of this construction (Ref. 13.9).

The above construction is called *composite construction*. In the United States, its use is regulated by Section 1.11 of the Specifications for the Design, Fabrication and Erection of Structural Steel for Buildings prepared by the American Institute of Steel Construction (AISC). This section is based on the above specifications (Ref. 13.10).

Composite Beam with Slab on Removable Forms

The flexural action of a concrete slab and steel beam assembly in composite construction is similar to that of a cast-in-place reinforced concrete T-beam (Section 13.4) in which the slab works as the flange and the steel beam as the web of the T-beam. The neutral axis of this assembly usually lies in the beam portion; consequently, the entire concrete slab is under compression and (most of) the steel beam under tension. In a provision similar to that of reinforced concrete T-beams, AISC limits the width of the concrete slab that participates with the steel beam in composite action. This provision is shown in Fig. 13.14.1.

Example 13.5. Determine the effective flange width b_e for the interior beam of a composite floor assembly given that the beam span is $L = 40$ ft, slab thickness is $t = 5.5$ in., and the spacing of beams is 9 ft. Each beam is W 16 × 57 and is simply supported.

Solution. From Ref. 13.10, the flange width b_f of a W 16 × 57 beam is 7.12 in. From Fig. 13.14.1, b_e is the least of the following:

(i) $0.25L = 0.25(40 \times 12) = 120$ in.

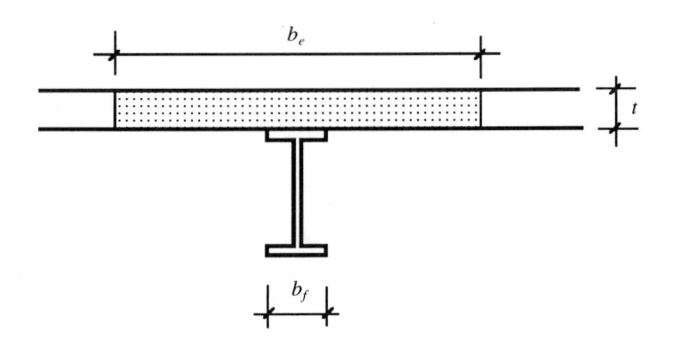

Fig. 13.14.1. For a slab extending on both sides of a beam, the effective flange width of slab, b_e, which works compositely with the beam is the least of the following values:
  (i) $0.25 L$, where L is beam span
  (ii) center-to-center distance between beams
  (iii) $16t + b_f$, where t is slab thickness and b_f the width of beam flange

For the effective flange width of a slab extending only on one side of the beam, see Ref. 13.10 p. 5-36.

(ii) the distance between the centerlines of beams = 9×12 = 108 in.
(iii) $16t + b_f = 16 \times 5.5 + 7.12 = 95$ in.

Hence, $b_e = 95$ in.

Shear Connectors. The shear resistance between the slab and the beam is provided by welding shear connectors to the top flange of the beam. There is undoubtedly some shear resistance developed due to the natural concrete-steel bond and the friction between beam flange and the slab but it is not relied upon. The most commonly used shear connector is a headed round stud, although hooked studs and short sections of steel channels are sometimes used, Fig. 13.14.2. The studs are field welded to the flanges of the beams after the beams have been erected and the formwork for concrete slab placed in position; welding the studs in the shop carries the risk of their being damaged during shipment and the construction crew tripping over them during the steel erection process.

AISC requires that in composite construction, the total horizontal shear V_h to be resisted by shear connectors be the smaller of the two values obtained from the following equations:

$$V_h = 0.85 f'_c A_c / 2 \qquad (13.8)$$

$$V_h = A_s f_y / 2 \qquad (13.9)$$

where A_c = cross-sectional area of the effective concrete flange (in.^{2})
 = $b_e t$
A_s = cross-sectional area of steel beam (in.^{2})
f_y = yield strength of steel beam; usually steel with a yield strength of 36 ksi is used in buildings.

Note that in the above equations, V_h represents the total horizontal shear between the points of maximum positive

Table 13.8. Allowable Horizontal Shear Load for One Connector (q), kips.[a]

Connector[b]	Specified Compressive Strength of Concrete, f'_c, ksi		
	3.0	3.5	≥ 4.0
$\frac{1}{2}$ in. diam. × 2 in. hooked or headed stud	5.1	5.5	5.9
$\frac{5}{8}$ in. diam. × $2\frac{1}{2}$ in. hooked or headed stud	8.0	8.6	9.2
$\frac{3}{4}$ in. diam. × 3 in. hooked or headed stud	11.5	12.5	13.3
$\frac{7}{8}$ in. diam. × $3\frac{1}{2}$ in. hooked or headed stud	15.6	16.8	18.0
Channel C 3 × 4.1	$4.3w^c$	$4.7w^c$	$5.0w^c$
Channel C 4 × 5.4	$4.6w^c$	$5.0w^c$	$5.3w^c$
Channel C 5 × 6.7	$4.9w^c$	$5.3w^c$	$5.6w^c$

Source: AISC (Ref. 13.10) Table 1.11.4, reprinted with permission.
[a] Applicable only to concrete made with ASTM C33 aggregates.
[b] The allowable horizontal loads tabulated may also be used for studs longer than shown.
[c] w = length of channel in inches.

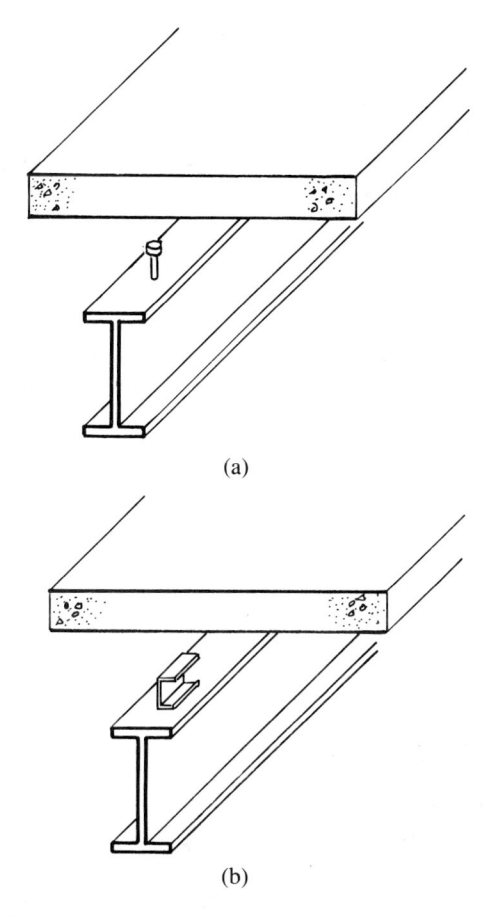

Fig. 13.14.2. Types of shear connectors. (a) Headed shear studs; (b) channel section.

moment and zero moment in a beam. Thus for a simply supported beam, the total shear for the entire length of a beam = $2V_h$. To obtain the total number of connectors, the total shear is divided by the shear capacity of an individual shear connector, q, which depends on the type of shear connector used, and the type of concrete, and its strength. The values of q for normal weight concrete are given in Table 13.8. For lightweight concrete, Ref. 13.10 should be consulted.

The benefit of composite action is not available in regions of negative moment (e.g., near the supports of a continuous beam) because here the concrete slab is in tension. AISC, however, recognizes some composite action in negative moment regions by permitting the use of slab reinforcement which runs parallel to the beam in resisting the tension in the beam. This provision gives an enhanced negative moment capacity of the beam, and if used shear connectors are required in negative moment regions as specified by AISC.

The shear connectors are welded at uniform spacing throughout the length of the beam. Although the uniform spacing provision may appear to contradict the laws of mechanics, which predict higher shear intensity near the supports requiring closer spacing of shear connectors there, experimental testing has shown that beams with uniformly spaced connectors have virtually the same ultimate moment strengths and the same deflection at working loads as those in which the connector spacing is varied according to the intensity of static shear (Ref. 13.10, p. 5-135).

AISC requires that if shear studs are used, the center-to-center distance between them along the longitudinal axis of the beam must not be more than 8 times the slab thickness but not less than 6 times the stud diameter. Usually a single row of studs is provided in the center of beam flange but if two or more rows are required, the center-to-center distance between studs in the transverse direction should not exceed 4 stud diameters. Minimum concrete cover above the top of studs is 1 in.

Example 13.6. Determine the number of $\frac{7}{8}$ in.-diameter headed studs required for the composite construction of Example 13.5 given that $f'_c = 4$ ksi and $f_y = 36$ ksi.

Solution. From Ref. 13.10, A_s (for W 16 × 57 beam) = 16.8 in.². From Eqs. (13.8) and (13.9), V_h is the lower of the following values:

$$V_h = 0.85(4)(95 \times 5.5)/2 = 888 \text{ k}$$

$$V_h = (16.8 \times 36)/2 = 302 \text{ k}$$

From Table 13.8, $q = 18$ k. Hence, the number of studs required for the entire length of beam = $2V_h/q = (2 \times 302)/18 = 34$. Since the span of the beam is 40 ft, provide studs at intervals of $40 \times 12/34 = 14$ in. Note that this spacing satisfies the maximum and minimum spacing requirements given above.

Calculation of Stresses. All AISC provisions for composite construction are based on the ultimate strength of the assembly but adjusted for use in the working stress design method under service loads. The stresses in the assembly are calculated using the elastic analysis and the *transformed area procedure*, a standard procedure, used in the working stress design of members consisting of two different materials that act in full structural cooperation. According to this method, the cross section of the structural member is transformed to an equivalent cross section of only one material. In composite beam-slab assembly, it is usual to transform the entire cross section into steel by multiplying the effective flange width of a concrete slab by a factor equal to $1/n$; n is called the modular ratio and is equal to (E_s/E_c), the ratio of the modulus of elasticity of steel and concrete. The transformed area procedure is based on the fact that if the two materials act compositely, the deformations at any point in the two materials must be equal.

Once the transformed section has been obtained, its neutral axis is located and section modulus S calculated. Usually the neutral axis will not lie at mid-height of the section and hence there will be two values of S: S_{top} and S_{bottom} (see Section 11.3). The extreme fiber stresses in the section are simply M/S, where M is the maximum applied moment on the beam. The allowable stresses in flexure in steel and concrete are taken as $0.66 f_y$ and $0.45 f'_c$, respectively.

The increase in the strength of steel beam due to its composite action with the concrete slab is available only after the concrete has hardened. The steel beams may therefore be shored (with temporary vertical supports) to prevent the sagging of the beam before the concrete has hardened. However, since the shoring of beams adds to construction costs, it is often omitted. Unshored beams, therefore, must also be designed to carry their own loads, the load of wet concrete, and the supporting formwork without considering any composite action.

The slabs in composite construction are normally one-way slabs and are designed as described in Section 13.9.

Composite Beam With Slab on Metal Deck Forms

In place of the removable form (which is normally a plywood deck) for the concrete slab, a ribbed steel deck made from cold-formed steel sheets may be used as permanent form. It is this version of composite construction that is popular in North America, since the removable form is labor intensive except for irregular slab areas. The most widely used deck type is a composite deck, defined as a deck which serves both as a permanent form and as tensile reinforcing for the slab. The noncomposite deck functions only as a permanent form. Both decks, however, act compositely with steel beams with the help of shear studs which are welded to steel beams directly or by melting through the deck.

Composite decks are available in various profiles, thickness of steel sheets, and rib depths. The required sheet thickness and rib depth is a function of the center-to-center distance between supporting beams. Deck manufacturers usually provide the load carrying capacities of their decks. A depth of 3 in. is the maximum permitted by AISC.

Since a composite deck functions as longitudinal reinforcing for the slab, there must be adequate bond between the concrete and the deck. The composite decks are therefore fabricated with embossed patterns in their inclined webs, Fig. 13.14.3a, a device that is similar to surface deformations provided in steel reinforcing bars. Minimum reinforcement is however required in the slab for shrinkage and temperature changes, which is usually given in the form of welded wire fabric. In addition, some reinforcement may be needed at the top of the slab over the beams to resist negative moments produced because of slab continuity.

Figure 13.14.3b shows a composite deck in which transverse wires welded to the top surface of the deck replace the embossments. In another version of the deck, a flat steel sheet is attached to the underside of the deck, which greatly enhances the strength of the deck in addition to providing ducts for services such as the electrical and telephone cables, Fig. 13.14.3c.

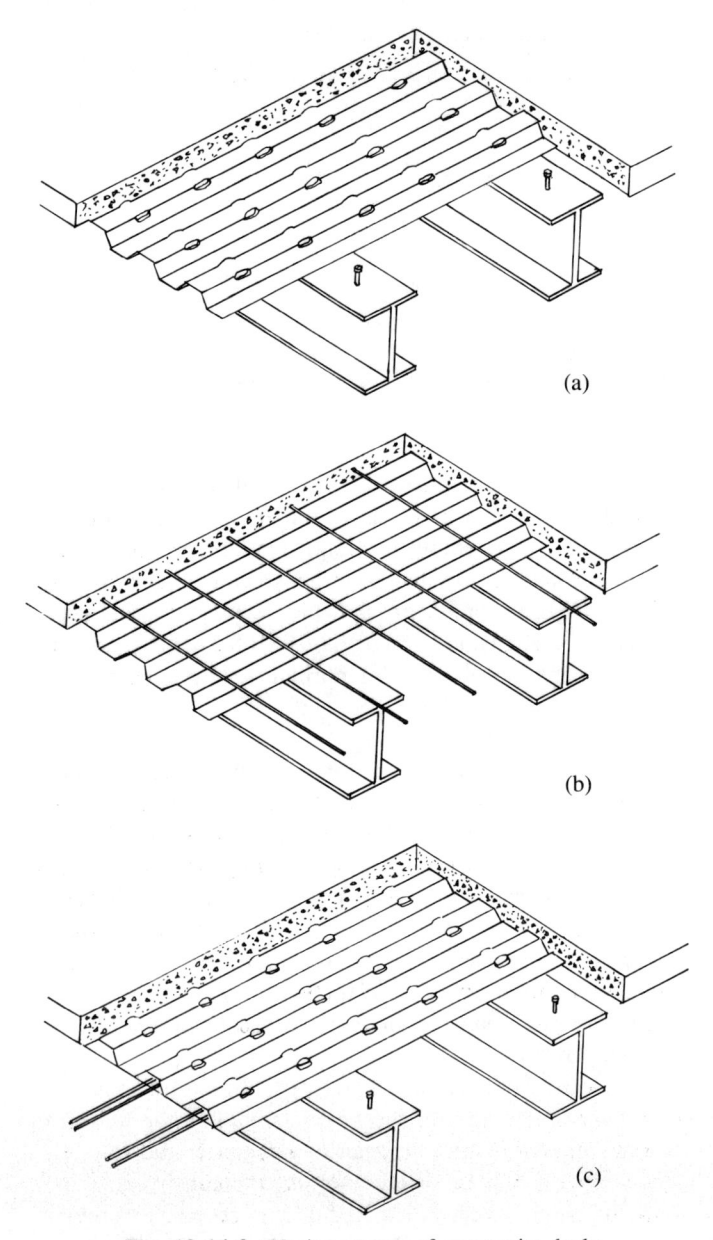

Fig. 13.14.3. Various types of composite decks.

The deck must be anchored to the steel beams by spot welding at intervals not exceeding 16 in. (400 mm) including the connections through the studs. The beam design procedure is similar to that of beams with slab on removable forms. Only the concrete that is above the top of the deck is considered in calculating the transformed section and the value of A_c. The allowable shear capacity of studs is obtained by multiplying the values of Table 13.8 by a reduction factor specified by AISC. The studs must extend at least 1.5 in. above the top of the deck and the stud diameter must not exceed 0.75 in. (20 mm).

Composite Trusses and Open-Web Joists

In the case of composite trusses or open-web joists, the bottom chord and web members are designed noncompositely, while the design of the top chord is based on composite action. The trusses/joists must also be designed to carry the load of wet concrete without considering any composite action, a requirement that is similar to the design of an unshored beam described earlier.

Composite Columns

A composite column is a combination of a structural steel section and concrete. The steel section is usually an H-shape which is encased with concrete, or a pipe section which is filled with concrete, Fig. 13.14.4a. The encasing or filling of a steel section increases the load carrying capacity of the steel column by increasing the column's buckling strength. The main advantage of this construction lies in the fire protection provided by concrete; even the concrete fill inside a pipe column provides some increase in its fire resistance. However, the success of spray-on fireproofing materials has greatly reduced the use of composite columns.

Longitudinal and lateral reinforcement is required in encased composite columns. Transfer of axial loads from steel to concrete is accomplished by welding to steel columns elements that come under direct bearing such as small angle clips, plates, or lugs, Fig. 13.14.4b. The design of composite columns is covered by the ACI code, Section 10.14.

13.15. LOAD-BEARING MASONRY

Until the beginning of this century, most buildings were constructed with load-bearing masonry walls, particularly those that were more than two to three stories high. The invention of the skeleton frame and concurrent developments in structural theories of reinforced concrete and steel led to a rapid decline in the use of load-bearing masonry. By comparison with a frame structure, the structure of a masonry building was extremely heavy giving a much smaller usable floor area. Additionally, because of the greater strength of the materials, reinforced concrete and

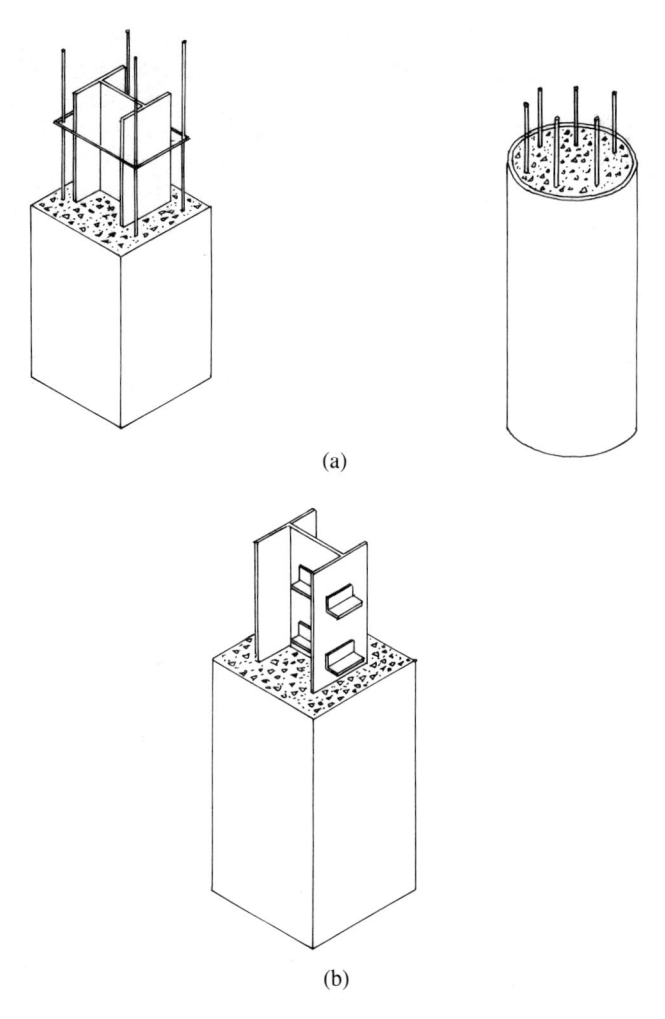

Fig. 13.14.4. (a) Composite columns; (b) connectors for composite columns.

steel frame allowed the construction of much taller buildings than were possible in masonry. Consequently, a concrete or steel frame became the preferred structural system for most buildings except the low-rise (two to three story high) buildings for which masonry walls could also be used.

But concrete and steel were (and still are) more expensive compared with masonry materials, and also in short supply after World War II, when several European countries began to rebuild their demolished cities; most could not afford the cost of concrete or steel frame construction (Ref.13.11). Architects and engineers were therefore forced to make innovations in the use of masonry materials as economical alternatives to concrete and steel. This led to the production of bricks and mortars with high compressive strengths and the use of reinforced masonry, but more importantly, it led to a better understanding of the structural behavior of masonry buildings. At the same time, extensive structural testing of masonry components led to the introduction of masonry codes allowing for the first time a rational structural design of masonry, similar to that of concrete and steel.

Before the introduction of the rational design of masonry, the design of load-bearing masonry buildings was governed by the building codes which required that the walls be made progressively thicker toward the lower floors. Thus, the walls of 16 story Monadnock Building in Chicago, constructed in 1893 (and still standing), varied from nearly 1 ft (0.3 m) thick at the top floor to 6 ft (1.8 m) thick at the ground. The code requirements were empirical and were based on the assumption that, in resisting the lateral loads, each wall functioned in isolation, without any interaction with other components. The contemporary masonry wall design concept, on the other hand, takes into account the contribution made to the strength and stability of the building by floor and roof diaphragms, and the intersecting walls. Thus, a bearing wall does not act in isolation but as part of a three-dimensional box in which all its elements participate in resisting the lateral loads. As a result, buildings of approximately the same height as the Monadnock Building have been built with only 7.5 in. (190 mm) thick (reinforced) masonry walls (Ref. 13.12).

Consider the simple structure of Fig. 13.15.1a with four walls and a flat roof, and assume that a uniform wind load acts on wall C in the direction of the arrows. Under the load, the wall behaves as a one-way slab, transferring the loads to the roof diaphragm and the foundations. The roof diaphragm acts as a (deep) beam and develops end reactions on the cross-walls (walls A and B) through shear resistance between the roof and the walls. Thus, the loads which acted perpendicular to wall C have been changed to in-plane loads on the cross-walls. This results in a more efficient use of structural elements, since both cross-walls act as shear walls, in which case it is not the thickness of the walls that is of primary importance but their lengths. If no tension is allowed to develop in the walls, the resultant of the in-plane and gravity loads on each cross-wall must lie within the middle-third of its length. If wall C were to act in isolation, it would require a much greater thickness, since in this case it is the thickness of the wall (not its length) that is important in resisting the lateral loads.

The shear wall action produced in cross-walls is also produced in walls C and D, when the lateral act in the other direction. Thus, all the walls of the building in Fig. 13.15.1a must resist in-plane loads. In addition, each wall must also carry vertical (gravity) loads and lateral loads perpendicular to the plane of the wall. All the three different types of loads to which wall C is subjected are shown in Fig. 13.15.1b.

The interaction of various building components as described above also applies to a multistory building in which both the exterior and interior cross-walls may function as shear walls. Thus, the walls of a load-bearing masonry building serve a dual function: as structural elements and also as nonstructural elements (cladding material and space dividing partitions), giving a more efficient system compared to the one in which the skeleton frame is used structurally and the walls as space dividing elements.

The walls in masonry building should be oriented along both principal axes of the building so that shear wall action is developed almost equally in these directions. The arrangement is not particularly critical from the structural viewpoint as long as a reasonable balance is maintained between the walls along each axis. An unlimited number of different wall arrangements satisfy this requirement (Ref. 13.13). However, a masonry structure is most appropriate for occupancies in which the space is subdivided on a permanent basis into small to medium size rooms and the plan is repeated at every floor. Typical examples are single-family residences, apartments, student dormitories, hotels, and motels.

The intersecting wall patterns resulting from the two-way orientation of walls add to the rigidity of crosswalls (shear walls) since, instead of behaving as rectilinear walls, they behave as flanged walls (C-shape, T-shape, Z-shape, I-shape, etc.), Fig. 13.15.2. The length of the perpendicular portion (the return) which can be assumed to act as a flange is, however, limited. This limitation is similar to the limitation of flange width in reinforced concrete T- or L-beams (see Fig. 13.4.6). For instance, the Uniform Building Code (Ref. 13.14) limits the dimension of the flange to a maximum of six times the thickness of the flange. For the walls to function as flanged walls, it is

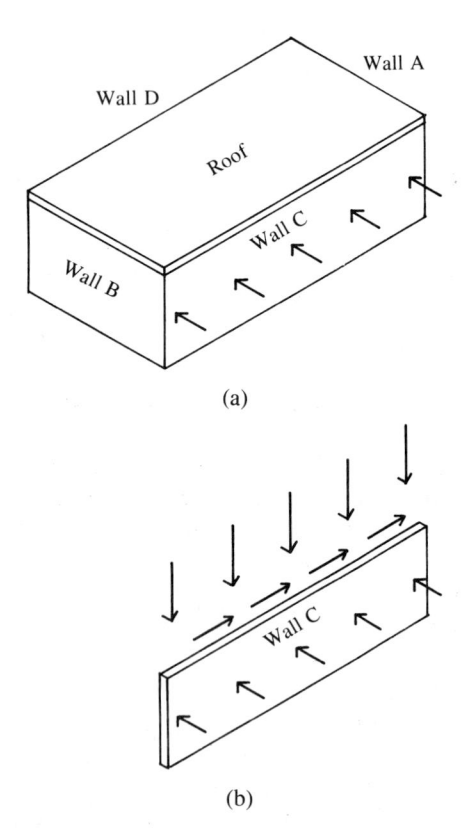

Fig. 13.15.1. (a) A simple box-type structure under the action of lateral loads. (b) A wall in a box-type structure is designed to resist vertical loads, in-plane loads and loads acting perpendicular to the plane of the wall. The in-plane loads, as shown, are caused by the reaction of the roof when the wind loads act on wall *B*.

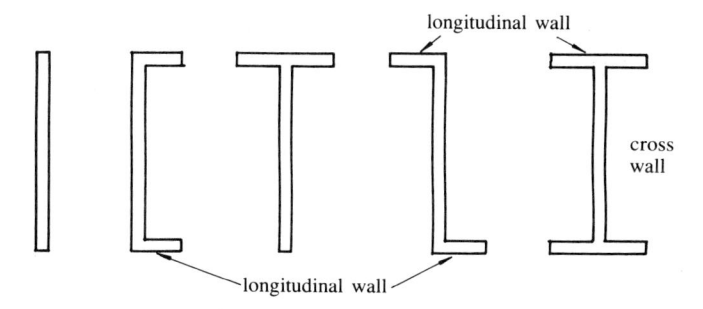

Fig. 13.15.2. When longitudinal walls are bonded with crosswalls, creating an intersecting wall pattern, they change the shape of a crosswall from a simple rectilinear shape to a C, T, Z, or I section. This gives the crosswall increased stiffness and greater stability than the rectilinear wall.

important that the expansion or control joints in them should be located away from their intersections.

The floors of a masonry building should preferably be of heavy construction, such as cast-in-place or precast concrete slabs. The added dead load increases the stability of shear walls against overturning and the additional compression produced in walls tends to balance the tension produced by in-plane and out-of-plane bending, which is similar to the principle of prestressing and is particularly helpful in the case of unreinforced masonry walls. The dead loads also increase the shear resistance of walls; the codes provide for an increase in the allowable shear stresses in unreinforced masonry in direct proportion to the compression stresses caused by the dead loads (Ref. 13.14, p. 193). As described later, cast-in-place concrete floors also increase the robustness of masonry buildings.

Due to its rigidity, a concrete floor is better able to resist torsional stresses produced in the building due to unsymmetrical arrangement of shear walls. Flexible floor diaphragms (plywood or metal deck without concrete topping) cannot develop much torsional resistance. Additionally, a rigid diaphragm distributes lateral loads on shear walls in proportion to their individual rigidities; thus a more rigid wall has to resist a larger load. A flexible diaphragm, on the other hand, distributes lateral loads on a tributary area basis. In this case, a less rigid wall may have to carry a larger load than a more rigid wall—an inefficient structural action. Very unsymmetrical wall arrangements should, however, be avoided in all masonry buildings since torsional effects produce undesirable stress conditions and are difficult to calculate (Ref. 13.13, p. 86-2).

Design of Masonry Walls

In the United States, the design of individual masonry elements is based on the working stress method, i.e., the stresses in the element are calculated based on elastic analysis under service load conditions. The element is so proportioned that the actual stresses do not exceed the allowable stresses, which are a fraction of the ultimate stresses, see also Section 13.3.

The most referenced masonry code at present in the United States is chapter 24 of the Uniform Building Code and it is this code that will be referred to in the remainder of this section. A national consensus code for masonry, similar to the ACI-318 code for reinforced and prestressed concrete, is currently (1989) in its final stages of development by the American Concrete Institute and the American Society of Civil Engineers which, when ready, is expected to be adopted by all the model building codes in the United States.

The fundamental strength property of masonry is its specified compressive strength f'_m. This is similar to the specified compressive strength of concrete, f'_c. The value of f'_m is a function of both the masonry unit strength and the strength of mortar. Three types of masonry mortars, M, S, and N are allowed by the code for use in load-bearing masonry. They differ from each other in respect of the proportion of hydrated lime to portland cement in the mortar mix. Type M contains the least amount of hydrated lime and has the highest compressive strength, approximately 2500 psi. Type N contains the highest amount of hydrated lime but has the least compressive strength (750 psi), and type S lies in between types M and N with a strength of 1800 psi.

The value of f'_m is established by testing masonry prisms, similar to the testing of concrete cylinders (a masonry prism is a rectangular assemblage of masonry units and mortar). Due to a large variation in the size of masonry units that are used, the size of masonry test prisms cannot be rigidly specified (unlike that of the concrete test cylinders). The code requires that the test prisms should not be less than 12 in. (300 mm) high with a height-to-thickness ratio of not less than 1.5 and not more than 5.0 (Ref. 13.15).

As an alternative to prism testing, the value of f'_m may be selected from the code table, Table 13.9. The values obtained from this table are conservative estimates of f'_m and should be used only when the size of the project does not justify the expenditure involved in the testing of prisms.

The allowable stresses in masonry (in compression, flexure, shear, bearing, etc.) are all a function of f'_m. The code requires that the allowable stresses in masonry be reduced by 50 percent if (i) f'_m has not been established from prism tests prior to and during construction and (ii) if the construction is not subject to on-site quality control as defined in the codes. The modulus of elasticity of masonry is taken as $750 f'_m$ and is not subject to 50 percent reduction. Similarly, the allowable stresses in steel are also not subject to 50 percent reduction since they are not masonry stresses. All allowable stresses are permitted one-third increase if the element is acted upon by wind or seismic loads either acting alone or in combination with gravity loads. No increase is allowed for gravity loads acting alone.

Unreinforced Masonry. The values of allowable stresses in unreinforced (plain) masonry are given below.

1. Allowable axial compressive stress F_a:

$$F_a = 0.20 f'_m R$$

Table 13.9. Specified Compressive Strength of Masonry[2], f'_m, in psi, Based on the Compressive Strength of Masonry Units.

Compressive Strength of Clay Masonry Units[1] (psi)	Specified Compressive Strength of Masonry, f'_m	
	Type M or S Mortar[3] (psi)	Type N Mortar[3] (psi)
14,000 or more	5,300	4,400
12,000	4,700	3,800
10,000	4,000	3,300
8,000	3,350	2,700
6,000	2,700	2,200
4,000	2,000	1,600

Compressive Strength of Concrete Masonry Units[4] (psi)	Specified Compressive Strength of Masonry, f'_m	
	Type M or S Mortar[3] (psi)	Type N Mortar[3] (psi)
4,800 or more	3,000	2,800
3,750	2,500	2,350
2,800	2,000	1,850
1,900	1,500	1,350
1,250	1,000	950

[1] Compressive strength of solid clay masonry units is based on gross area. Compressive strength of hollow clay masonry units is based on minimum net area. Values may be interpolated.
[2] Assumed assemblage: the specified compressive strength of masonry f'_m is based on gross area strength when using solid units or solid grouted masonry and net area strength when using ungrouted hollow units.
[3] Mortar for unit masonry, proportion specification, as specified in UBC Table No. 24-A. These values apply to portland cement-lime mortars without added air-entraining materials.
[4] Net area compressive strength of concrete masonry units is determined in accordance with U.B.C. Standard No. 24-7. Values may be interpolated. In grouted concrete masonry the compressive strength of grout shall be equal to or greater than the compressive strength of the concrete masonry units.
Source: Unified Building Code (Ref. 13.14) Table 24-C, reprinted with permission.

The reduction factor R in the above equation accounts for the slenderness of the wall (P-Δ effect) and is equal to $[1 - (h'/42t)^3]$, where h' is the effective height of the wall and is a function of the wall's actual height (distance between floors) and the type of support provided to the wall by the floors. In most masonry buildings, the floors provide simple supports to walls and hence h' is equal to the actual height floors. In the case of a cantilevered wall (garden wall), h' is twice the actual height. t is the effective thickness of the wall. For a single wythe wall, t is its actual thickness. For a cavity wall, t is a function of the thicknesses of both wythes (Ref. 13.14, p. 197).

2. Allowable flexural compressive stress F_b:

$$F_b = 0.33 f'_m \leq 2000 \text{ psi } (14 \text{ MPa})$$

3. Allowable flexural tensile stress F_t varies with the type of masonry unit (clay or concrete), the type of mortar, and whether the bending of the wall causes tension normal to head joints or normal to the bed joints.

(a) F_t normal to bed joints (type M or S mortar):

	clay units	concrete units
solid units	36 psi (250 kPa)	40 psi (280 kPa)
hollow units	22 psi (150 kPa)	25 psi (170 kPa)

(b) F_t normal to head joints (type M or S mortar):

	clay units	concrete units
solid units	72 psi (500 kPa)	80 psi (550 kPa)
hollow units	44 psi (310 kPa)	50 psi (340 kPa)

Note that the values of F_t given above are for M or S mortar. If N-type mortar is used, these values are to be reduced by 50 percent for clay units and 25 percent for concrete units.

4. Allowable shear stress, F_v:

(a) Flexural

$$F_v = (f'_m)^{0.5} \leq 50 \text{ psi } (340 \text{ kPa})$$

(b) Shear walls:
clay units:

$$F_v = 0.3 (f'_m)^{0.5} \leq 80 \text{ psi } (550 \text{ kPa})$$

concrete units:

$$F_v = 34 \text{ psi } (230 \text{ kPa}) \quad \text{for M/S-type mortar}$$

$$F_v = 23 \text{ psi } (160 \text{ kPa}) \quad \text{for N-type mortar}$$

As stated earlier, the design of plain masonry is based on linear elastic behavior of masonry. If the element is subjected to combined axial and flexural compression, the following equation (unity formula) must be satisfied.

$$(f_a/F_a) + (f_b/F_b) \leq 1 \qquad (13.10)$$

Example 13.7. A $7\frac{5}{8}$ in. (8 in. nominal) thick clay masonry wall carries a reinforced concrete roof which delivers a (concentric) load of 1200 lb/ft on the wall. The wind load on the wall is 15 psf. Investigate the structural adequacy of the wall in axial compression and flexure, given that:

clay masonry unit strength = 6000 psi, mortar type S
dead load of wall = 75 psf (of wall elevation)
height of wall between roof and foundations = 10 ft
no special inspection is provided

Solution. Assume that the wall is simply supported between the foundation and roof. The bending of the wall will, therefore, cause flexural tension normal to the bed joints.
From Table, 13.9, $f'_m = 2700$ psi.

$$R = 1 - [120/(42 \times 7.625)]^3 = 0.95$$

All allowable stresses are to be reduced by 50 percent for noninspection and increased by one-third for lateral loading. Hence, the multiplication factor = $0.5 \times 1.333 = 0.67$. The allowable stresses are:

$$F_a = 0.67 \times 0.2(2700)0.95 = 344 \text{ psi}$$
$$F_b = 0.67 \times 0.33(2700) = 600 \text{ psi}$$
$$F_t \text{ (normal to bed joints)} = 0.67(36) = 24 \text{ psi}$$

Consider a 1 ft width of wall. The loads on the wall are shown in Fig. 13.15.3. The critical section of wall is its mid-height. Here the total gravity load on wall = load of slab + load of half the wall = $1200 + 75(5) = 1575$ lb. Thus, axial stress, f_a, in the wall is:

$$f_a = P/A = 1575/(7.625 \times 12) = 17.2 \text{ psi}$$

The bending moment at mid-height, M, is:

$$M = wL^2/8 = 15(10)^2/8 = 187.5 \text{ lb. ft} = 2250 \text{ lb in.}$$

The section modulus of the wall is

$$S = bh^2/6 = 12(7.625)^2/6 = 116.3 \text{ in.}^3$$

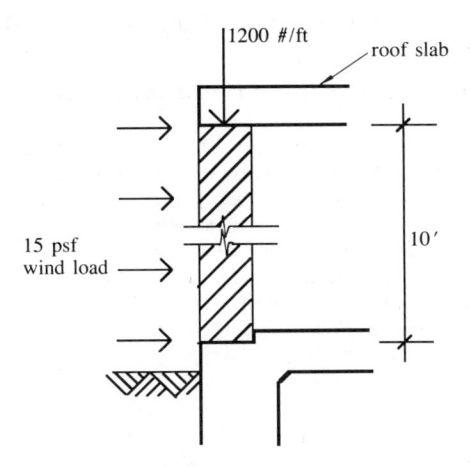

Fig. 13.15.3. Example 13.7.

Hence, the flexural stress in the wall is

$$f_b = M/S = 2250/116.3 = 19.3 \text{ psi}$$

The extreme fiber tension on section is

$$f_t = 19.3 - 17.2 = 2.1 \text{ psi} < 24 \text{ psi} \qquad \text{OK}$$

The extreme fiber compression on section

$$= 19.3 + 17.2 = 36.5 \text{ psi}$$

Check Eq. (13.10):
$$(17.2/344) + (19.3/600) = 0.08 < 1.0 \qquad \text{OK}$$

Reinforced Masonry. Since the flexural tensile strength of masonry is low, it normally governs the design of plain masonry. A large wall thickness is, therefore, required for buildings subjected to small gravity loads and/or high lateral loading. In such buildings, reinforcement can substantially reduce wall thickness and is commonly used. In addition, reinforced masonry is mandated in areas of moderate to high seismic activity, or high wind velocities. Both horizontal and vertical reinforcements are required. For example, the code (Ref. 13.14, p. 200) requires that walls in seismic zone 2 be provided with a minimum reinforcement area equal to 0.2 in.^{2} spaced not more than 4 ft on center for vertical reinforcement and not more than 10 ft on center for horizontal reinforcement. Boundary reinforcement is required in each wall in the form of continuous vertical reinforcement from support to support at each corner of the wall, and continuous horizontal reinforcement at each floor and roof level. Reinforcement requirements are more stringent for seismic zones 3 and 4, while no special requirements are called for zones 0 and 1. (The continental United States is divided into six seismic risk zones, 0, 1, 2A, 2B, 3, and 4 in order of increasing seismic risk, see Chapter 9).

The two additional ingredients of reinforced masonry (in addition to masonry units and mortar) are the grout and the steel reinforcement. The more commonly used reinforcement is grade 40, since there is little reason for using a high-grade steel (grade 60) with low-strength masonry. The code recognizes this fact by restricting the allowable tensile stress in steel to $0.5 f_y$ but not to exceed 24 ksi. Thus in the case of grade 40 steel, the allowable tension is 20 ksi and in grade 60 steel 24 ksi.

The grout is an extremely fluid concrete (8 to 10 in. slump) with a minimum strength of 2000 psi. A large slump is required for two reasons: (i) to compensate for the absorption of water in grout by masonry units and (ii) to allow the grout to easily flow into and fill the (usually) small spaces and cells in masonry.

For the design of reinforced masonry elements (walls and beams), the reader is referred to books suggested at the end of this chapter.

Progressive Collapse

Masonry structures must be able to withstand their *progressive collapse*, a term used to describe the behavior of a structure when one structural element (column, wall, beam, etc.) fails due to an accidental damage, causing adjoining elements to fail and leading to a chain reaction in which the entire structure or a major part of it collapses. The phenomenon assumed importance after the collapse of 22 story Ronan Point Tower in London in 1968 (Ref. 13.16). In this building, a gas explosion destroyed the precast concrete panels on the 18th floor. The loss of support for the upper floors caused them to collapse. As the upper floor panels fell on the lower floors, a complete collapse of one corner of the building resulted.

It is unlikely that a masonry building, if properly designed and constructed, would suffer the same kind of damage as the Ronan Point Tower, which was constructed of rectangular precast concrete panels. (It is believed that if the panels in this building had returns giving C-shape panels, the damage to the building would have been much smaller). Several masonry structures in Europe were seriously damaged during World War II, but did not collapse. Masonry buildings have much greater structural continuity between various elements than that in a precast concrete building. In addition, masonry walls have the innate ability to arch which helps them to span and cantilever over openings caused by the removal of structural supports below. The intersecting wall patterns and the interaction of walls and floors gives a masonry structure the capacity to withstand local damages. However, the codes require that the *robustness* of a masonry structure must be checked. This requirement is to ensure the availability of alternative routes of load transfer in the structure in the event of an unexpected collapse of a wall or a part of it.

The robustness of a masonry structure can be improved by using cast-in-place reinforced concrete slabs continuous over external and internal walls. The relative robustness of various types of floors is shown in Fig. 13.15.4. Continuous boundary reinforcement in walls from end to end and floor to floor (as if the wall is tied all around by a strap) also adds to the robustness of the structure. In this case, the wall functions as a tied arch so that if the wall underneath collapses, the loads will be transferred to the side walls.

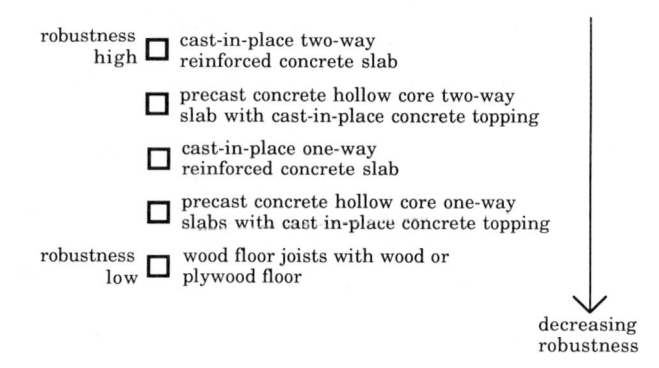

Fig. 13.15.4. Relative robustness of floor diaphragms.

REFERENCES

13.1. K. A. Godfrey. "Concrete Strength Record Jumps 36%." *Civil Engineering* (Publication of the American Society of Civil Engineers, New York), (Oct. 1987).

13.2. G. B. Neville. *Simplified Design: Reinforced Concrete Buildings of Moderate Size and Height.* Portland Cement Association, Skokie, IL, 1984, p. 8-2.

13.3. T. Y. Lin and S. D. Stotesbury. *Structural Concepts and Systems for Architects and Engineers.* Van Nostrand Reinhold, New York, 1988, p. 183.

13.4. N. Hassoun. *Design of Reinforced Concrete Structures.* PWS Publishers, Boston, 1985, p. 78.

13.5. H. J. Cowan. *Design of Reinforced Concrete Structures.* Prentice Hall, Englewood Cliffs, NJ, 1989, p. 163.

13.6. R. S. Fling. *Practical Design of Reinforced Concrete.* John Wiley, New York, 1987, p. 144.

13.7. K. Leet. *Reinforced Concrete Design.* McGraw Hill, New York, 1982, p. 261.

13.8. *ACI Detailing Manual.* American Concrete Institute, Detroit, 1988.

13.9. C. Salmon and J. Johnson. *Steel Structures—Design and Analysis.* Harper and Row, New York, 1980, p. 911.

13.10. *Manual of Steel Construction*, 8th Ed. American Institute of Steel Construction, Chicago, 1987.

13.11. C. Beall. *Masonry Design and Detailing for Architects, Engineers and Builders.* McGraw Hill, New York, 1987, p. 6.

13.12. J. Mock. "Modern Loadbearing Masonry Construction in the Western United States." *Proceedings of the First North American Masonry Conference*, University of Colorado, Boulder, Colorado, 1978, p. 110-1.

13.13. A. Hendry. "Some Fundamental Factors in the Structural Design of Masonry Buildings." *Proceedings of the First North American Masonry Conference*, University of Colorado, Boulder, Colorado, 1978, p. 86-1.

13.14. *Uniform Building Code 1988 Edition*, International Conference of Building Officials, Whittier, CA, Section 2407, p. 197.

13.15. *Uniform Building Code Standards 1988 Edition*, International Conference of Building Officials, Whittier, CA, p. 92.

13.16. J. Amrhein. *Reinforced Masonry Engineering Handbook.* Masonry Institute of America, Los Angeles, 1983, p. 67.

SUGGESTIONS FOR FURTHER READING

Reinforced Concrete and Prestressed Concrete

Building Code Requirements for Reinforced Concrete. ACI318-83, Revised 1986. American Concrete Institute, Detroit, 1986.

Commentary on Building Code Requirements for Reinforced Concrete (ACI318-83): American Concrete Institute, Detroit, 1986.

Building Code Requirements for Reinforced Concrete (Metric). ACI318-M-83. American Concrete Institute, Detroit, 1986.

The Structural Use of Concrete. BS 8110, 3 parts. British Standards Institution, London, 1985.

Australian Concrete Structures Code. AS 3600. Standards Association of Australia, Sydney, 1988.

Design of Concrete Structures for Buildings. CAN3-A23.3-M84. Canadian Standards Association, Rexdale, Ontario, Canada, 1984.

G. B. Neville. *Notes on ACI 318-83 Building Code Requirements for Reinforced Concrete.* Portland Cement Association, Skokie, IL, 1984.

C. E. Reynolds and J. E. Deedham. *Reinforced Concrete Designer's Handbook*, 9th Ed. View Point Publications (Cement and Concrete Association), London, 1988.

R. R. Warner, B. V. Rangan, and A. S. Hall. *Reinforced Concrete*, 3rd Ed. Pitman, Sydney, 1989.

S. U. Pillai and D. W. Kirk. *Reinforced Concrete Design*. McGraw Hill-Ryerson, Toronto, Canada, 1988.

M. P. Collins and D. Mitchell. *Prestressed Concrete Basics*. Canadian Prestressed Concrete Association, Ottawa, Canada, 1987.

Composite Construction

R. Amon et al. *Steel Design for Engineers and Architects*. Van Nostrand Reinhold, New York, 1982.

Load-Bearing Masonry

Code of Practice for Use of Masonry. BS 5628, 3 parts. British Standards Institution, London, 1985.

J. J. Roberts et al. *Concrete Masonry Designer's Handbook*. View Point Publications, London, 1983.

R. Schneider and W. Dickey. *Reinforced Masonry Design*. Prentice Hall, Englewood Cliffs, NJ, 1987.

W. G. Curtin, G. Shaw, J. K. Beck, and W. A. Bray. *Structural Masonry Designers' Manual*. BSP Professional Books, London, 1987.

A Manual of Facts on Concrete Masonry. National Concrete Masonry Association, Herndon, VA, 1988.

NOTATION

a	depth of equivalent rectangular stress block, see Fig. 13.4.1
A_s	area of tension reinforcement in beam or one-way slab
A_{sb}	area of tension reinforcement in a balanced section
A_s'	area of compression reinforcement
A_{ss}	area of secondary reinforcement in one-way slab
A_{st}	area of longitudinal reinforcement in column section
b	width of beam; width of square footing, see Section 13.12
b_w	width of the web of a flanged beam
c	distance from extreme compression fiber to neutral axis of beam
c_b	distance from extreme compression fiber to neutral axis of beam for a balanced section
d	distance from extreme compression fiber to the centroid of tension reinforcement
d'	distance of extreme compression fiber to the centroid of compression reinforcement
e	eccentricity of axial load on member
E_c	modulus of elasticity of concrete
E_s	modulus of elasticity of steel
f_c'	specified compressive strength of concrete
f_y	specified yield strength of steel
h	overall thickness of beam or slab
k	kilopounds (=1000 pounds)
K	a factor defined by Eq. (13.3)
M_n, M_u	nominal and ultimate (factored) moment strengths, respectively, of member
P_n, P_u	nominal and ultimate (factored) strengths, respectively, of member under axial loads
V_c	nominal shear strength of concrete
V_n, V_u	nominal and ultimate (factored) shear strengths, respectively, of member
V_s	nominal shear strength of shear reinforcement
w_u	factored loads on member. Thus, if the member is subjected to dead load D and live load L, then $w_u = 1.4D + 1.7L$
β_1	a factor defined in Section 13.4
ϵ	strain
ρ	steel ratio $= A_s/bd$
ρ_b	steel ratio in a balanced section
ϕ	strength reduction factor, see Section 13.3

A list of abbreviations of the units of measurement, definitions of these units, and conversion factors between British/American and metric units are given in the Appendix.

14

Timber Structures

Russell C. Moody and Alan D. Freas

Chapter 14 first describes structural wood elements, particularly linear elements; trusses, curved members, and stressed-skin panels are also discussed. The chapter then considers light-frame buildings, which constitute the majority of timber-framed buildings. The discussion of heavy-timber buildings includes glulam systems, arch structures, and domes. The final section on special considerations covers connections, lumber grades, and shrinkage.

14.1. HISTORY

From the earliest days of human history, people found shelter from the elements in natural caves. As our ancestors developed and began to provide their own shelter—where they wanted and needed it, and not only where nature had provided it—wood was usually the most available material. Nomadic cultures used sapling-size supports for coverings of hide or cloth because of easy assembly, disassembly, and transport. As civilizations developed, their needs grew to include shelter not only for people and animals, but also for storage of materials and foodstuffs, for various manufacturing or converting processes, for retail stores, and the like. Thus, larger and larger structures were needed, for both family use and commerce and industry.

In North America, two types of construction prevailed for dwellings in the days of the early settlers (Ref. 14.1). One type, prominent on the East Coast, was the New England timber frame house, which was based on the English timber frame house. The second type, more suited to the frontier, used logs that were placed horizontally. The log house has often been thought of as an American development, although it was introduced by Scandinavians in the early 17th Century. The size of log houses was limited by the length of the logs, and the structures were generally built as separate modules as needed, with the modules sometimes connected by a roofed area without walls.

With the appearance of sawmills in the early 19th Century, sawn lumber became available in quantities sufficient to meet the demands of the growing population. From this evolved the light-frame construction that currently forms the basis for the greatest proportion of American homes and for a significant proportion of low-rise retail, agricultural, commercial, and light-industrial buildings. In the nonresidential sector, mill-type or heavy timber construction was commonly found in industrial or warehouse facilities. As originally built, heavy timber construction used members of large cross section, which provided good resistance to fire, and structures were designed with attention to details such as avoiding concealed spaces and limiting the number of openings in walls to ensure adequate fire resistance. This type of construction is still recognized in many building codes.

Both light-frame and heavy timber constructions have adapted to the use of modern materials and techniques. For example, where floor, wall, and roof sheathing for light-frame construction was once commonly made from wood boards, sheathing now is commonly made from panel products such as plywood, structural flakeboards, particleboards of various types, or fiberboards. All of these are faster to install than boards and provide improved structural resistance to wind and earthquake loadings. Furthermore, prefabricated floor and wall panels along with prefabricated roof and floor trusses are replacing piece-by-piece on-site construction. Factory-made and hauled to the site, a structure can be enclosed within a short time using panelized systems.

In the case of larger structures, the development of glued-laminated timbers (glulam) has greatly widened the horizons. No longer are the spans in a post-and-beam structure limited by the lengths of available timbers. Rather, spans may be of almost any length, and beams 100 feet (30 m) or longer and several feet (meters) in depth are relatively commonplace.

Building systems use many types of structural wood elements. The following section describes joists, rafters, and studs; beams and girders; posts and columns; trusses; curved members; and stressed-skin and sandwich panels. The section also describes the design of such elements.

14.2. STRUCTURAL WOOD ELEMENTS

Wood structural elements are required to resist loads in a wide variety of structures. Dimension lumber (usually nominal 2 in. (50 mm) in thickness) commonly provides the structural framework for light-frame buildings, particularly individual homes, but also small apartment and office buildings, and small retail or warehouse structures. In larger structures, structural timbers may provide the structural framework, including posts and girders, with wood decking for the floor. The roof over a large area (a particularly long span) may be supported by deep glued-laminated girders.

Over the years, many technological developments have led to improvements in structural wood elements. These developments and their applicability to the architecture are briefly described in the following sections. The materials have been discussed in Chapter 4.

Joists, Rafters, and Studs

Joists and rafters of dimension lumber have traditionally been the primary elements for resisting bending loads in floors and roofs of light-frame structures.

Typically, building codes specify different design loads for various areas of light-frame buildings, so grades and sizes for floor and ceiling joists vary with the requirements and cannot be generalized. Most lumber joists are nominal 2 by 8 in. (50 by 200 mm), nominal 2 by 10 in. (50 by 250 mm), or nominal 2 by 12 in. (50 by 300 mm). Grade, species, and size are related to allowable spans in tables prepared by lumber-producing organizations, with oversight from regulatory bodies (Ref. 14.2).

Wood-plywood or other composite members in either I or box sections can be made in sizes suitable for use as joists. The I-joist arrangement (Fig. 14.2.1) is the most common and is best adapted to a high-speed, automated manufacturing process. The flanges in such members may be sawn lumber or laminated veneer lumber (LVL). The webs are generally either plywood or structural flakeboard, and they are commonly glued into slots machined in the flanges.

Another option for floor joists is the flat truss (Fig. 14.2.2J), which is most frequently made with metal plate connections between wood truss members. This type of

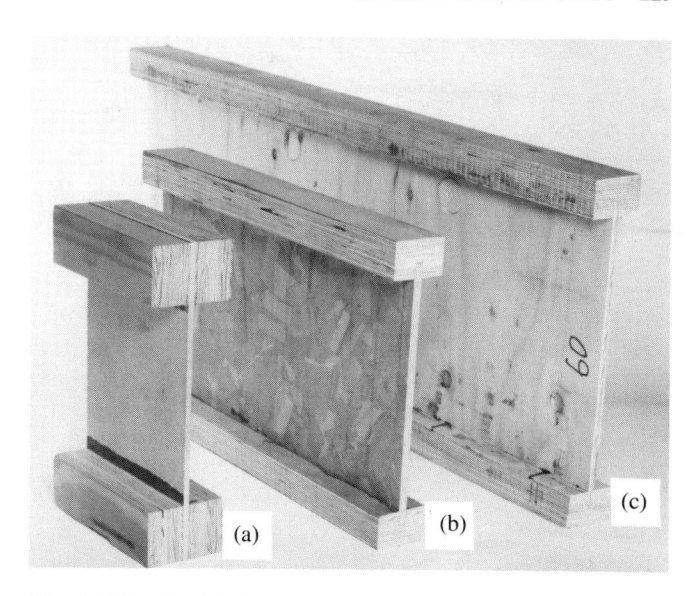

Fig. 14.2.1. Prefabricated I-joists are made with lumber flanges and panel webs. Products shown all have laminated veneer lumber (LVL) flanges; small sections of dimension lumber may also be used. (a) experimental product with hardboard web; (b) commercial product with structural flakeboard web; (c) commercial product with plywood web.

truss is more fully discussed in a later section. A variation of this type of truss employs wood chords and two types of metal webs: a light-duty type with wood flanges and stamped steel webs with integral truss plates, and a heavy-duty type with wood flanges and tubular steel webs flattened at the ends and pinned into the flanges.

Roof systems are commonly made with triangular trusses of any of the wide variety of forms shown in Fig. 14.2.2. These are most commonly made with metal truss plates, although nail-glued plywood gusset plates are also used to a limited extent.

Where rafter systems are used, suitable spans vary with lumber grade and size, with roof slope, and of course, with anticipated loadings. Span tables for rafters are available (Ref. 14.2). The present trend is to replace the wide dimension lumber used for joists and rafters with I-joists and trusses. One advantage of prefabricated I-joists and trusses (both floor and roof) is that they can be designed for spans longer than those feasible with lumber alone, eliminating the need for central beams and load-bearing partitions.

Studs are the main framing members in exterior walls of light-frame structures. They are most commonly nominal 2 by 4 in. (50 by 100 mm), although nominal 2- by 5-in. (50- by 125-mm) and nominal 2- by 6-in. (50- by 150-mm) studs may be used to provide space for greater amounts of insulation, and in larger structures, to accommodate greater loads than are normal in typical houses. Stud spacing may range from 12 to 24 in. (300 to 600 mm) depending upon loading; common spacing is 16 in. (400 mm). Although a variety of species may be used, stud grades are generally used. No. 2 or better lumber, sized to match the studs, is commonly used for the top and bottom

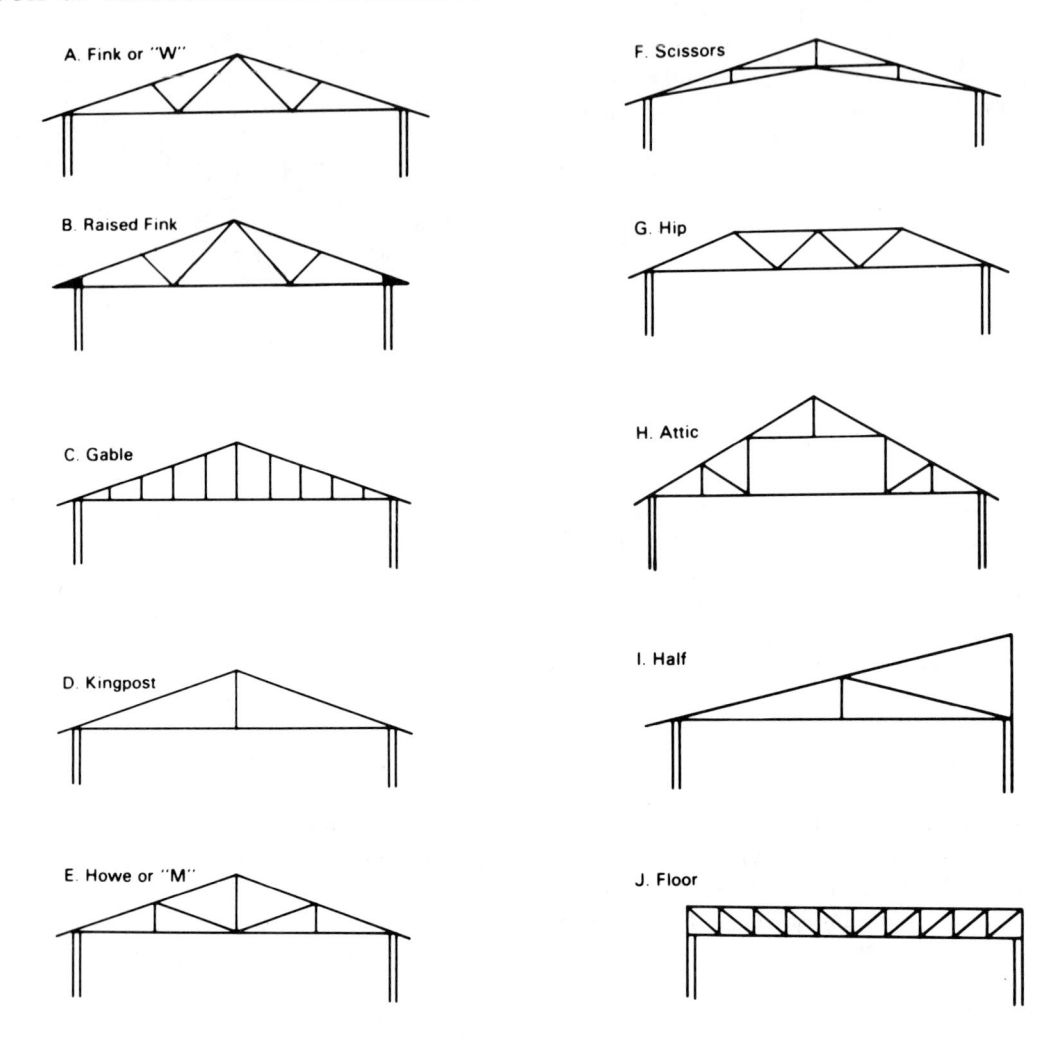

Fig. 14.2.2. Types of trusses commonly used for roof and floor systems.

plates to which the studs are attached. A double top plate is often used for additional stiffness.

Interior load-bearing partitions are framed in the same way and with the same lumber grades as exterior walls. Depending upon the building code, studs for non-load-bearing partitions may be 2 by 3 in. (50 by 75 mm) in size and spaced up to 24 in. (600 mm) apart using single top and bottom plates.

Beams and Girders

In light-frame construction, perhaps the most common central beam in the foundation system is a built-up beam consisting of several 2-in. (50-mm) planks (commonly three) set on edge and nailed together. The limited lengths of the sawn lumber used in the beam necessitate posts at frequent intervals to support such a beam. The butt joints between abutting pieces must be staggered between adjacent layers so that they are separated by 16 in. (400 mm). The beam is supported by posts positioned within 12 in. (300 mm) of the butt joints. Alternatively, a steel or glulam beam is used.

Mill-type or heavy timber construction has been widely used for warehouse and manufacturing structures, particularly in the Eastern United States. As previously noted, this type of construction is recognized as fire resistant because of the use of heavy (large cross section) timbers for beams, girders, and other structural elements.

To qualify as heavy timber construction, beams and girders of solid-sawn timber must be not less than 6 by 10 in. (150 by 250 mm) in cross section, and columns must be not less than 8 by 8 in. (200 by 200 mm) in cross section.

Stress-graded timbers classified as beams and stringers, as discussed in Chapter 4, are desirable for beams and girders in mill-type construction. These grades are described and allowable design stresses are provided in grading rule books of the associations that produce timbers in this classification.

For spans too long for ordinarily available lengths of sawn timbers, glulam members, whose lengths are relatively unlimited, may be manufactured for specific situations (that is, made to order). Such beams are straight or curved to meet job requirements. Stock glulam members, commonly straight beams, are available through distributors nationwide (Ref. 14.3). For situations where stock beams are not suitable, beams may be made in a number of forms to fit special situations. To meet architectural and other requirements, the beams may be made in the forms shown in Fig. 14.2.3, including single- or double-tapered straight beams, double-tapered curved beams, and double-tapered pitched and curved beams.

In some situations, headroom or other limitations may dictate the use of continuous beams to take advantage of the reduced bending moments in such beams. If the greater length of a continuous beam creates problems, a cantilevered-suspended system may be indicated, as shown in Fig. 14.2.4.

Composite beams of various types with mechanical fasteners may be used (Fig. 14.2.5). Some slip between layers must take place before mechanical fasteners come into play, so that the efficiency of such beams in both strength and stiffness suffers somewhat. Despite reduced efficiency, such beams may serve well in such applications as door and window headers and garage door headers. Headers at floor openings in light-frame construction where joists are interrupted are commonly made of lengths of joist-size lumber face nailed together and set with the wide dimension of the components vertical.

Posts and Columns

Posts supporting central beams in residences or other light-frame structures are commonly made of solid-sawn lumber or pipe columns. In heavier construction (like mill-type construction), they are commonly solid sawn or glulam. In some instances, such columns may be built up from a number of pieces of dimension lumber (Fig. 14.2.6). As with built-up beams, built-up columns lose some efficiency because the components are connected with mechanical fasteners. In the case of types (a) and (b) of Fig. 14.2.6, the strength may be estimated by applying certain multipliers to the strength of a comparable solid column. These multipliers range from about 0.65 to about 0.82; details are given on p. 328 of Ref. 14.4.

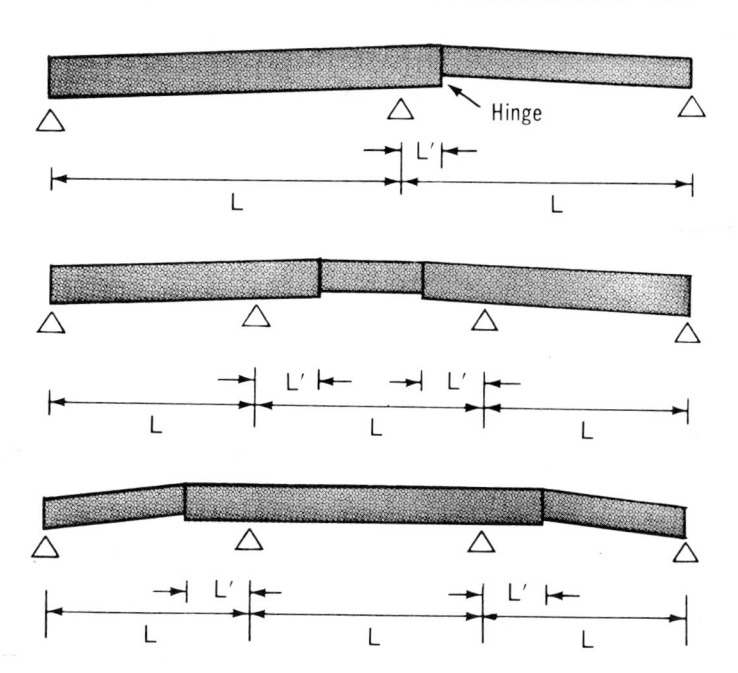

Fig. 14.2.4. A structural system of cantilevered and supported beams is efficient in multi-span structures (Ref. 14.40). (By permission of the American Institute of Timber Construction.)

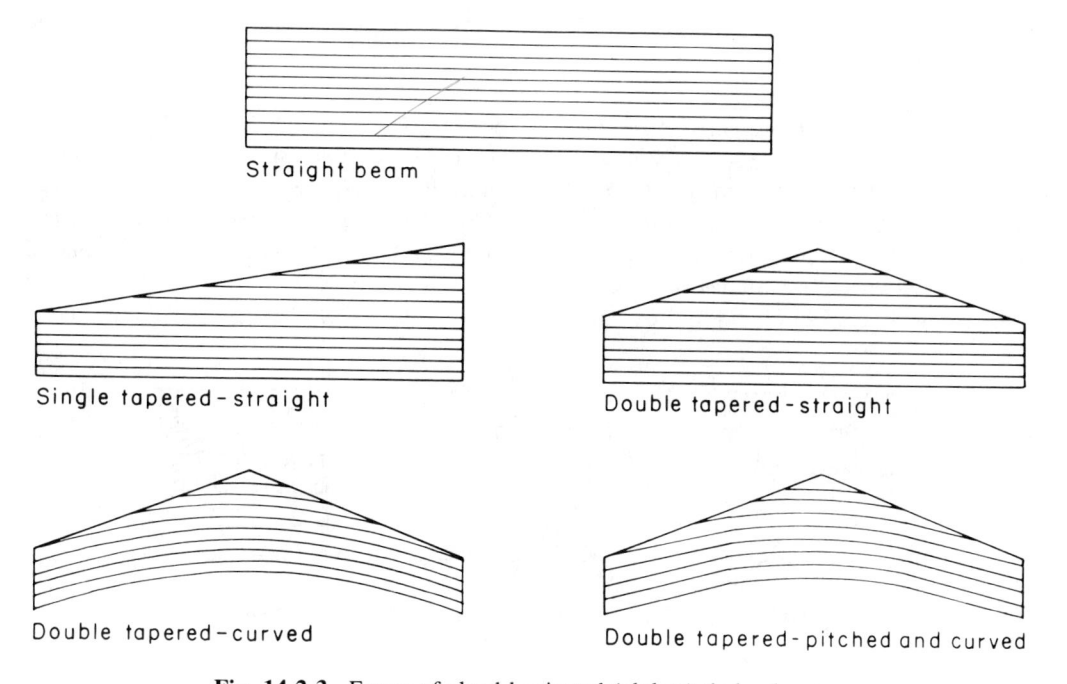

Fig. 14.2.3. Forms of glued-laminated (glulam) timber beams.

232 HANDBOOK OF ARCHITECTURAL TECHNOLOGY

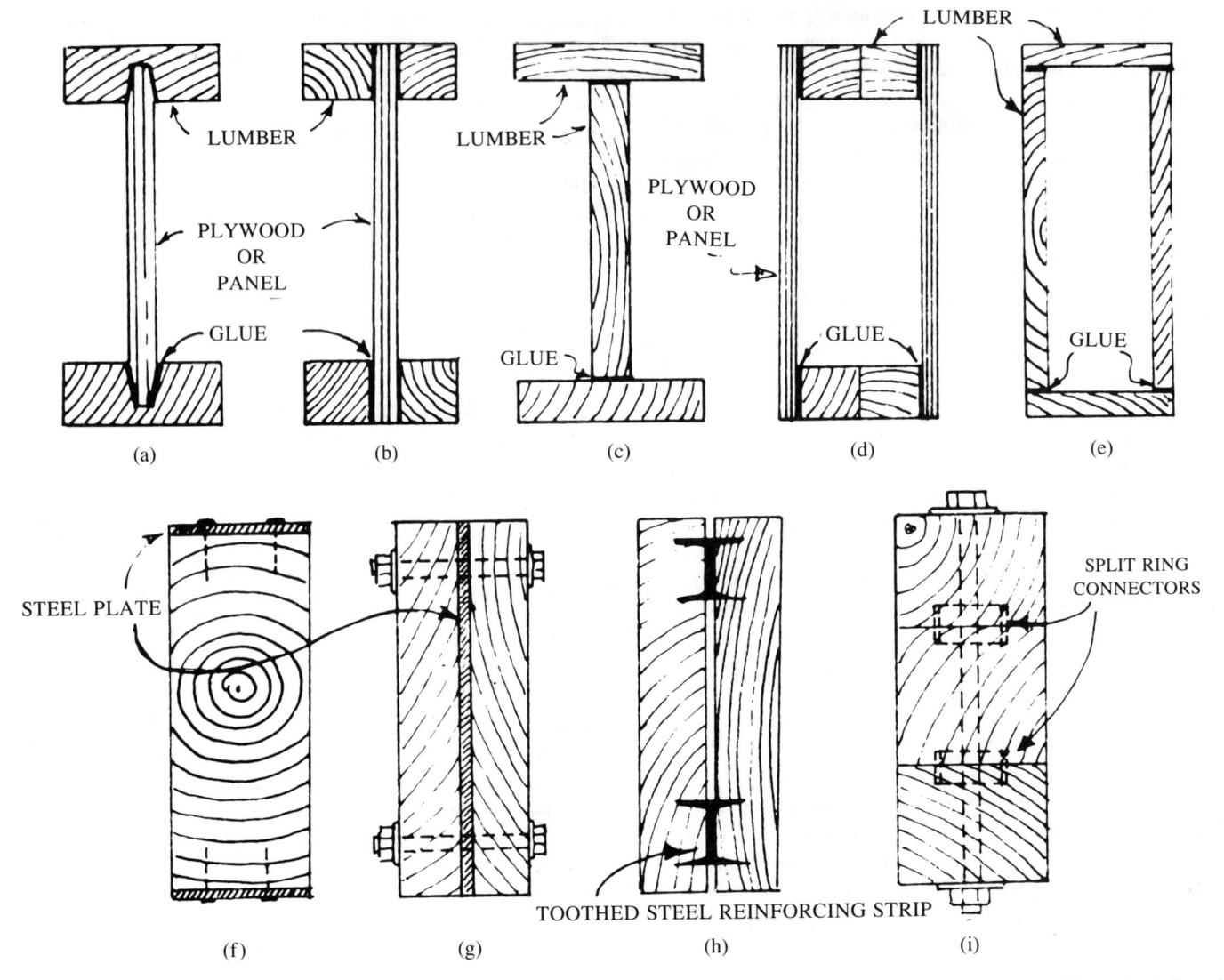

Fig. 14.2.5. Composite and mechanical fasteners. Composite I-beams (a–c) and box beams (d, e); solid wood beam with steel reinforced edges (f); beams connected with mechanical fasteners (g–i).

The poles in a pole-supported building carry compressive loads, as do foundation and marine piles. The lower portions of such members may be subjected to sizable axial forces. All of these represent tapered-column forms; the poles and piles are naturally tapered. In structures supported by Tudor arches, the vertical legs of the arches are tapered by design requirements with respect to both shear and bending forces. Architectural considerations may lead to single- or double-tapered columns. Special methods of analysis are required for tapered columns (Ref. 14.4).

Spaced columns are sometimes used when solid members of adequately sized lumber are not available or to facilitate the column-to-beam connection; that is, the beam forms one end-block of the spaced column. The spaced column

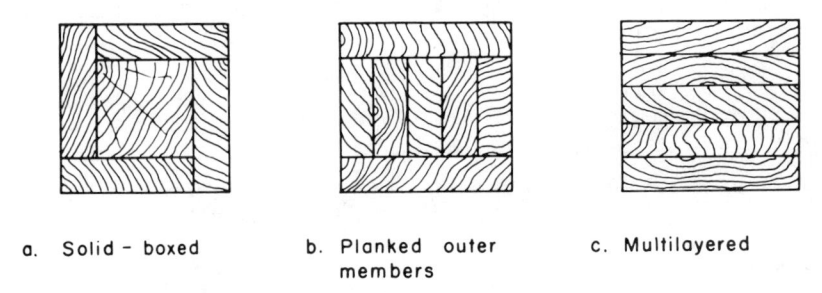

a. Solid-boxed   b. Planked outer members   c. Multilayered

Fig. 14.2.6. Configurations of columns built up from lumber components.

consists of two (rarely more) individual column members separated by spacer blocks. The individual members are connected to the end blocks by timber connectors or, somewhat rarely, by bolts or nails. A center spacer block is usually held in place by a bolt. Slippage between the end blocks and the individual members is restrained by the connectors more effectively than would be the case for bolts or nails. Thus, the elements of the column act together rather than individually. Regardless of the type of mechanical connector, spaced columns generally require more board feet of lumber than does a solid column of the same capacity. Compression members in timber trusses often act as spaced columns.

Design procedures for glulam columns are the same as for solid columns except that the lower variability in stiffness for glulam offers some design advantages. Glulam members intended to support axial loads should be specified differently from beams; often, the glulam combinations intended for axial loading can be used efficiently (see Ref. 14.5).

Trusses

Developments of the 20th Century have widened the application of wood trusses. Split-ring and shear-plate connectors have improved trusses in long-span, wide-spaced, heavy-load applications such as industrial buildings and military facilities.

The nail-glued plywood gusset plate connector has facilitated the greater use of light wood trusses or trussed rafters for residential, agricultural, and other light-frame structures. Another type of connector, the toothed metal-plate connector, has teeth stamped at right angles to the plane of the metal sheet; when the teeth are pressed into the wood of the truss members, they serve to transmit shear, axial, and moment forces from one member to another. This type of connector dominates the light truss market today.

Wood trusses are available in a wide variety of forms (Fig. 14.2.2) commonly used in residential construction as well as commercial-industrial and agricultural structures. They are manufactured by fabricators nationwide and are available through lumber yards and building material suppliers. The designs are generally provided by plate manufacturers or structural designers who specialize in trusses. Building codes generally require that trusses be made to designs approved by licensed structural engineers.

Trusses are designed for light or heavy applications. One light-duty truss consists of dimension lumber chords and stamped steel webs; integral toothed metal plates hold the webs and chords together. A heavy-duty metal web truss is made from high grade lumber, LVL, or glulam chords with tubular metal web members flattened at the ends and pinned to the chords. Heavy-duty trusses are also manufactured with 4-in. (100-mm)-thick lumber or glulam chords and heavy metal truss plates (Fig. 14.2.7).

Competition from metal-plate trusses, laminated beams,

Fig. 14.2.7. Long-span trusses made with toothed metal-plate connectors and double nominal 4- by 6-in. (100- by 150-mm) lumber chords and webs.

bar joists, and metal-web trusses has radically reduced the use of heavy wood trusses. Heavy trusses are still used to give a rustic appearance to a building. These trusses are primarily parallel-chord and full triangular types. Bowstring trusses are found in many buildings erected in the first half of the century.

Curved Members

Glue-laminating techniques remove the limitations on member size and form caused by the cross-section size and length of structural timbers.

Pitched and tapered beams were described under the heading Beams and Girders. Two-hinged arches are seldom used except for short spans; transporting such arches over long distances is troublesome because of limited clearances at railway or highway crossings. Three-hinged arches (hinges at supports and at a point within the arch, usually at the peak) are likely to be easier to transport than the two-hinged arch. Most commonly, three-hinged arches are some variation of the forms shown in Fig. 14.2.8. Arches of especially long span or of a form that is difficult to ship may be made in several segments and then connected in the field with moment-resisting joints.

Stressed-Skin and Sandwich Panels

Units consisting of plywood or structural flakeboard "skins" glued to wood stringers are often called stressed-skin panels (Fig. 14.2.9). These panels provide efficient structural units for floor, roof, and wall components of buildings. They can be designed to provide the necessary stiffness, bending strength, and shear strength for use in building construction. The panel skins provide resistance to bending and the wood stringers provide resistance to shear.

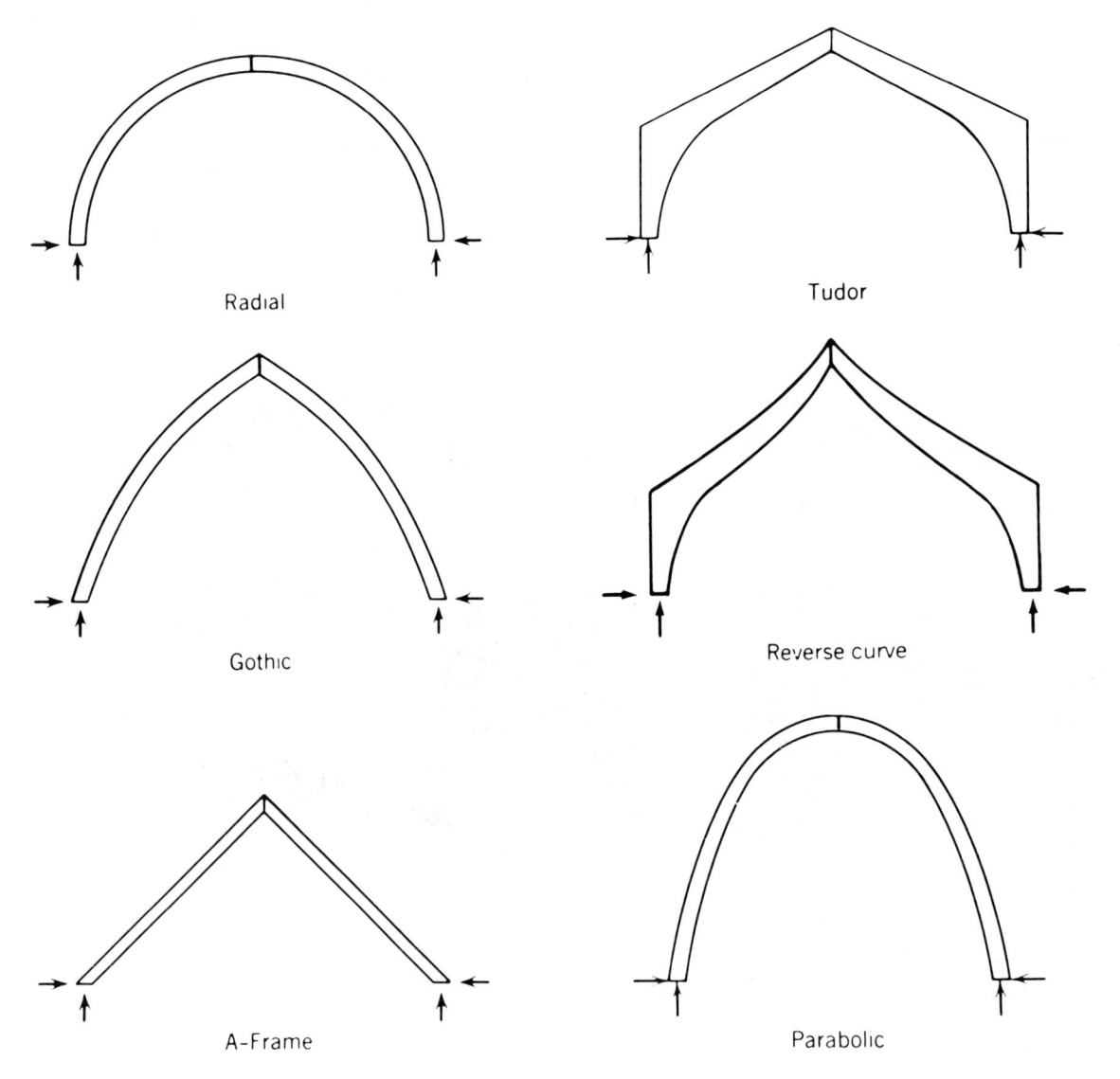

Fig. 14.2.8. Two-hinged and three-hinged glulam arches. Other more complex shapes may also be fabricated (Ref. 14.3). (By permission of the American Institute of Timber Construction.)

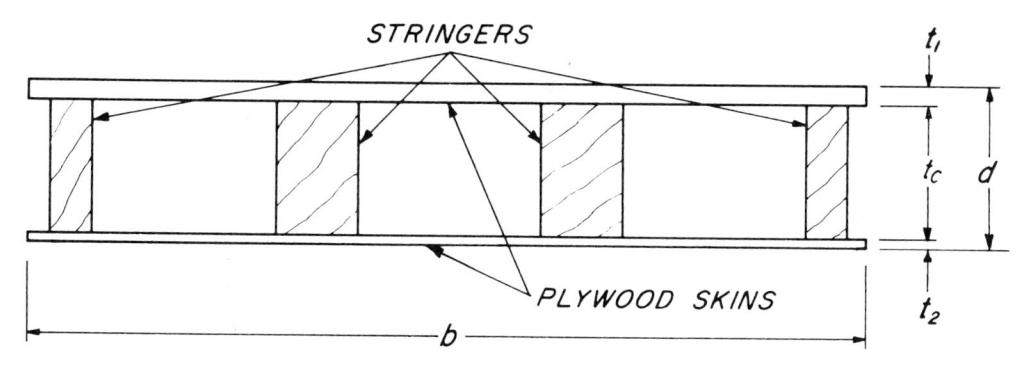

Fig. 14.2.9. Cross section of a stressed skin panel.

Sandwich panels are also of layered construction; the faces provide bending resistance and the core, shear resistance. Fig. 14.2.10 shows the application of one of many possible sandwich constructions. Because the core provides nearly continuous support for the faces, as contrasted with stressed-skin panels, the faces may be thinner than those of stressed-skin panels and a greater variety of materials may be used. Facings include plywood, veneer, plywood overlaid with a resin-treated paper, fiberboard, structural flakeboard, particleboard, glass-fiber-reinforced plastic, veneer bonded to metal, or metal (aluminum, enameled steel, stainless steel, magnesium, or titanium).

Sandwich cores have been made from many light-weight materials: balsa wood, rubber foam, resin-impregnated paper, reinforced plastic, perforated chipboard, expanded plastic, foamed glass, light-weight concrete, clay products, and formed sheets of cloth, metal, or paper. Cores made of formed sheet materials are often called honeycomb cores. Cores are made in a wide range in densities by varying the sheet material, sheet thickness, and cell size and shape.

(a)

(b)

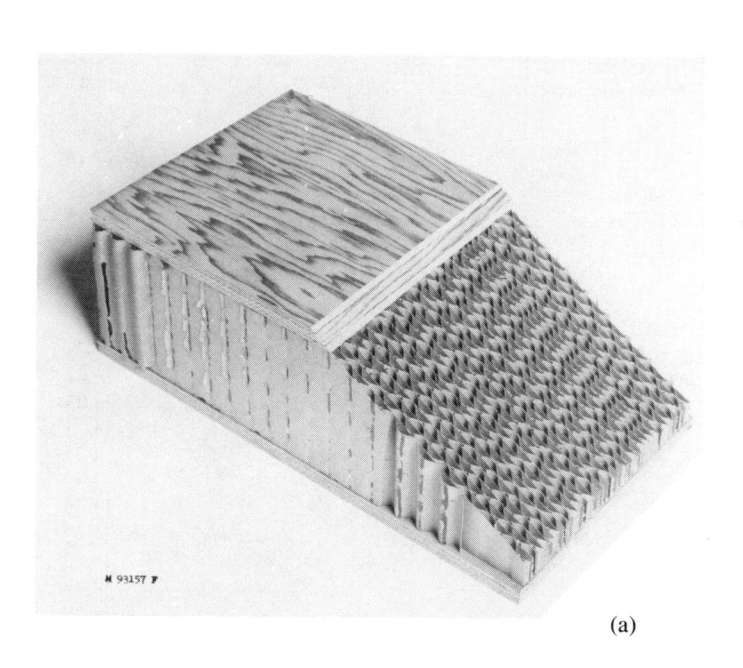

Fig. 14.2.10. Sandwich panels with plywood facings and paper honeycomb core. (a) Closeup view of construction; (b) panel used in an experimental structure.

Special properties can be imparted to the panels by careful selection of facing and core. An impermeable facing can act as a moisture barrier, and an abrasion-resistant facing can serve as the top facing of a floor panel. Plywood or plastic facings can produce a decorative effect. Both sandwich and stressed-skin panels may serve as structural elements in construction. Because such panels are relatively light weight, they can be economical in some nonstructural applications such as curtain walls.

Design of Wood Structural Elements

Wood has some special characteristics that differentiate it from other structural materials. For example, wood is hygroscopic, taking on moisture from the atmosphere or giving it off. Because important properties vary with moisture content, wood elements must be protected from excessive exposure to moisture change. Wood is also isotropic in nature and thus has different properties in the three major directions. Since strength properties perpendicular to grain are characteristically only a fraction of those parallel to grain, elements must be designed to avoid or to minimize stresses perpendicular to grain.

Years of experience with many types of timber structures, large and small, together with continuing research have resulted in design procedures that take into account the unique characteristics of wood. A number of publications devoted to the design of wood structures are available to the structural designer who is not already experienced in wood design. These include design handbooks, specifications, and textbooks (Table 14.1).

14.3. LIGHT-FRAME BUILDINGS

In the 1980s, light-frame construction has dominated the housing market and is widely used in agricultural, commercial, and light industrial applications. In many respects, contemporary light-frame construction differs from this type of building 50 years ago in the use of new and innovative materials, panel products for floor and roof sheathing, and prefabricated components and modules as opposed to stick-built or on-site construction. Additional

Table 14.1 Publications on Wood Design.

Type of Publication	Information	Reference
Design handbook	National Design Specification for Wood Construction	14.7
	Timber Construction Manual	14.8
	Australian Timber Construction Manual	14.9
	Timber Design Manual (Canada)	14.10
Specifications[a]	American Plywood Association (APA) design specifications	14.11
	TPI-85, metal plate connected trusses	14.12
	AITC 117, glulam	14.5
	PCT-80, parallel-chord trusses	14.13
	TPIC-88, metal plate connected trusses (Canada)	14.14
	CAN 3-086, engineering design of wood in Canada	14.15, 16
	National Building Code of Canada 1985	14.17
	AS 1720, Timber Structures Code	14.18
	AS 1684, Timber Framing Code	14.19
	CIB Structural Timber Design Code	14.20
Textbook	Design of Wood Structures	14.21
	Wood Technology in the Design of Structures	14.22
	Wood Engineering	14.23
	Wood Engineering and Construction Handbook	14.24
	Structural Design in Wood	14.25
	Wood: Engineering Design Concepts, Heritage Memorial Series on Wood, Vol. IV	14.4
	Timber Design and Construction Handbook	14.26
	Limit States Design of Wood Structures	14.27
	Timber Designers Manual	14.28
	Structural Timber Design and Technology	14.48
Miscellaneous	Wood Handbook	14.29
	Wood Structures: A Design Guide and Commentary	14.30
	Evaluation, Maintenance, and Upgrading of Wood Structures	14.31
	Designs for Glued Trusses	14.32
	Wood Frame Design	14.33
	Southern Pine Use Guide	14.34
	Wood Frame House Construction	14.35
	Canadian Woods	14.37
	APA Design/Construction Guide: Residential and Commercial	14.38
	Wood: Its Structure and Properties, Heritage Memorial Series on Wood, Vol. I	14.39
	Wood as a Structural Material, Heritage Memorial Series on Wood, Vol. II	14.40

[a]Some associations that publish specifications for wood structural elements also have publications on wood design.

information on construction of residential buildings using platform-type construction is given in Refs. 14.35 and 14.36.

Foundations

The light-frame building is typically supported on cast-in-place concrete walls or by concrete block walls supported by footings. This type of construction with a basement is common in northern climates. Some buildings, commonly in southern climates, have no foundation as such; the frame is supported by a concrete slab, so there is no basement or crawl space. The central supporting structure for a house with a basement may consist of wood posts on suitable footings that carry a built-up beam, which is frequently composed of planks the same width as the joists (2 by 8 in. to 2 by 12 in. (50 by 200 mm to 50 by 300 mm)), face-nailed together and set on edge. Because planks are seldom sufficiently long to span the full length of the beam, butt joints are required in the layers. The joints are staggered in the individual layers near the column supports (see Section 14.2, Beams and Girders). The girder may also be a steel H-section, perhaps supported on steel pipe columns. Similar details may be used in a house over a crawl space. In some instances, a glulam girder may be used rather than a built-up beam.

A fairly recent innovation is the use of treated wood for basement foundation walls. Basically, such foundations consist of prefabricated wood-frame wall sections of treated studs and treated plywood sheathing supported on treated wood plates (Fig. 14.3.1). The plates are laid on a layer of crushed stone or gravel to distribute the loads on the plates. The exterior surface of the foundation wall below grade is draped with a continuous sheet of 6-mil (0.15-mm) polyethylene to prevent direct water contact with the surface of the prefabricated panels. Because a foundation wall needs to be permanent, the preservative treatment of the plywood and framing is highly important. Therefore, a special foundation (FDN) treatment has been established with strict requirements for the treatment results, both as to depth of chemical penetration and amount of chemical

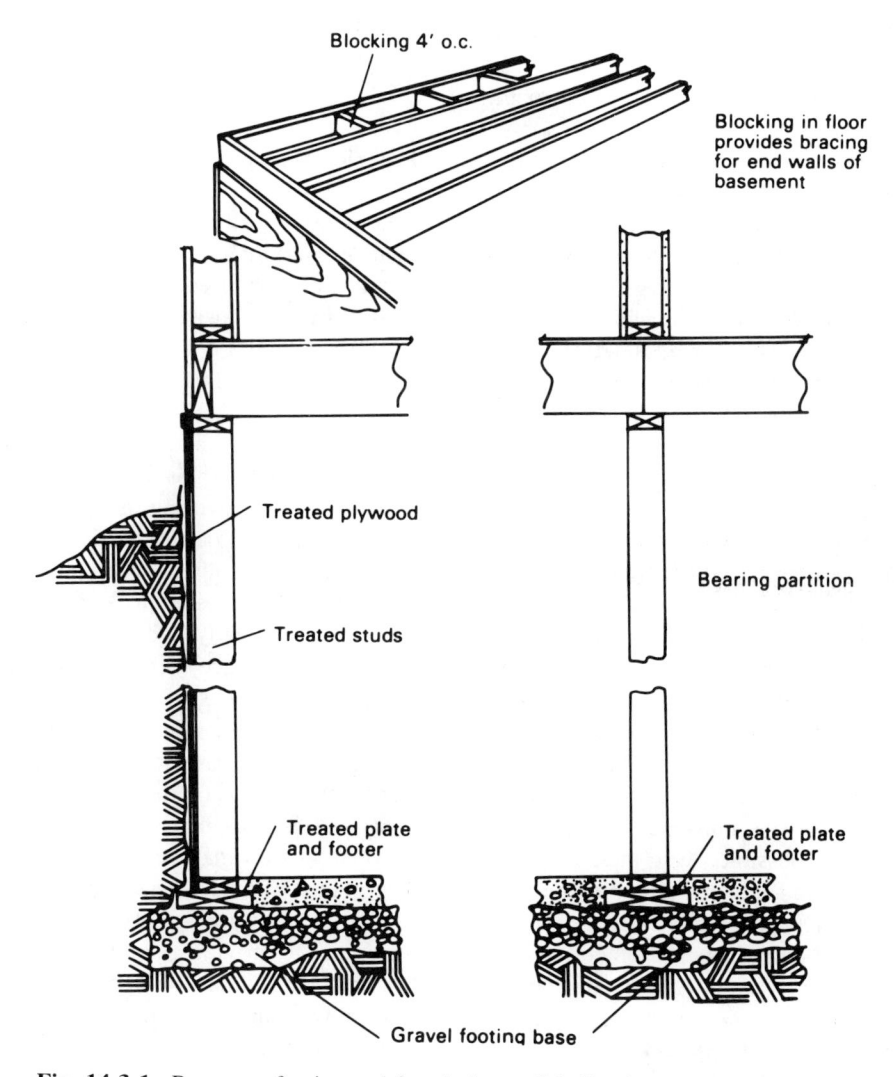

Fig. 14.3.1. Basement footing and foundation wall built with pressure-treated wood.

retention. The foundation wall requires noncorrosive nails (stainless steel or aluminum).

Floors

The floor framing in residential structures typically consists of wood joists on 16- or 24-in. (400- or 600-mm) centers supported by the foundation walls and the center girder (Fig. 14.3.2). The joists may bear directly on top of the girder and on top of the foundation walls or, more commonly, on a sill plate that is anchored to the walls. This arrangement carries the potential for problems if the lumber in the beam and the joists has not been adequately dried before installation in the building; if the joists and girder dry in service, the greater depth of wood (joist plus girder) can result in greater shrinkage at the center of the building than at the perimeter, where shrinkage occurs in the joists alone or the joists and sill plate, resulting in a sloping floor. To reduce this possibility, the joists may be framed into the sides of the center beam so that the tops of the joists are just below the top of the girder to allow for possible beam shrinkage. The joists may be supported on ledger strips or on joist hangers attached to the sides of the beam. Joists may be butted into the side of a steel beam with support provided by a wood ledger attached to the beam.

Joist size depends on the anticipated loading, spacing between joists, distance between supports (span), and species and grade of lumber. Joists are usually spaced 16 or 24 in. (400 or 600 mm) apart. Span tables are available for allowable spans for loadings and spacings (Ref. 14.2), and other tables list allowable stresses and moduli of elasticity assigned to various stress grades (Ref. 14.7). Conversely, when spans are set by other considerations, the span tables provide a basis for choosing grade, species, and size.

Floor openings, as at stairwells, fireplaces, and chimneys, may interrupt one or more joists. Preferably, such openings should be parallel to the length of the joists to reduce the number of joists that will be interrupted. At the interruption, a support (header) is placed between the uninterrupted joists and attached to them. A single header is usually adequate for openings up to about 4 ft (1.2 m) in width, but double headers are required for wider openings. Special care must be taken to provide adequate support at headers (by joist hangers, for example).

Cutting of framing members for installation of plumbing lines, heating ducts, and the like must be carefully done and should be avoided if possible. Cut members may require a reinforcing scab or a supplementary member may be needed. Areas of highly concentrated loads, such as under bathtubs, require doubling of joists or other measures to provide adequate support. One advantage of framing floors with parallel-chord trusses or prefabricated I-joists is the elimination of interior supports. An additional advantage is that plumbing, electrical, and heating ducts and piping may pass through the web area of these types of components.

Floor sheathing, or subfloor, is used over the floor framing to provide a working platform and a base for the finish flooring. Old homes have board sheathing but new homes generally use panel products. Common sheathing materials include plywood and structural flakeboard, which may be obtained in a number of types to meet sheathing requirements. Exterior-type panels with water-resistant adhesive are desirable for locations where moisture may be a problem, as in floors near plumbing fixtures or in situations where the subfloor may be exposed to the weather for some time during construction.

Plywood should be installed with the grain direction of the face plies at right angles to the joists. Structural flakeboard also often has a preferred direction of installation. Nailing patterns are either prescribed by code or recommended by the manufacturers. About $\frac{1}{8}$ in. (3 mm) of space should be left between edges and ends of abutting panels to provide for dimensional changes associated with moisture content changes.

The literature of the American Plywood Association (APA) should be consulted for selection and installation of the types of structural panels suitable for subfloors (Ref. 14.38).

Exterior Walls

The exterior walls of light-frame structures are generally load bearing: they support upper floors and roof. An exception are the gable ends of one-story buildings. Basically, wall framing consists of vertical studs and horizontal members, including top and bottom plates and headers (or lintels) over window and door openings. The studs are generally nominal 2- by 4-in. (50- by 100-mm) members spaced between 12 and 24 in. (300 and 600 mm) on center depending on the loads the wall is to carry and the need for support of wall-covering materials. Sometimes, 2- by 5-in. (50- by 125-mm) or 2- by 6-in. (50- by 150-mm) studs are used when required by the loading or if the walls will be filled with more than $3\frac{1}{2}$ in. (90 mm) of insulation. Headers are usually 2 by 6 in. (50 by 150 mm), nailed together face to face with spacers, which brings the headers flush with the faces of the studs. Wall framing is erected over the platform formed by the first-floor joists and subfloor. In most cases, a whole wall is framed in a horizontal position on the subfloor and then tilted into place. If a wall is too long to make this procedure practical, sections of wall may be formed horizontally and tilted up, then joined to adjacent sections.

Corner studs are usually prefabricated in such a configuration as to provide a nailing edge for interior finish (Fig. 14.3.3). Studs are sometimes doubled at the points of intersection with an interior partition to provide backup support for the interior wall finish. Alternatively, a horizontal block is placed midheight between exterior studs to support the

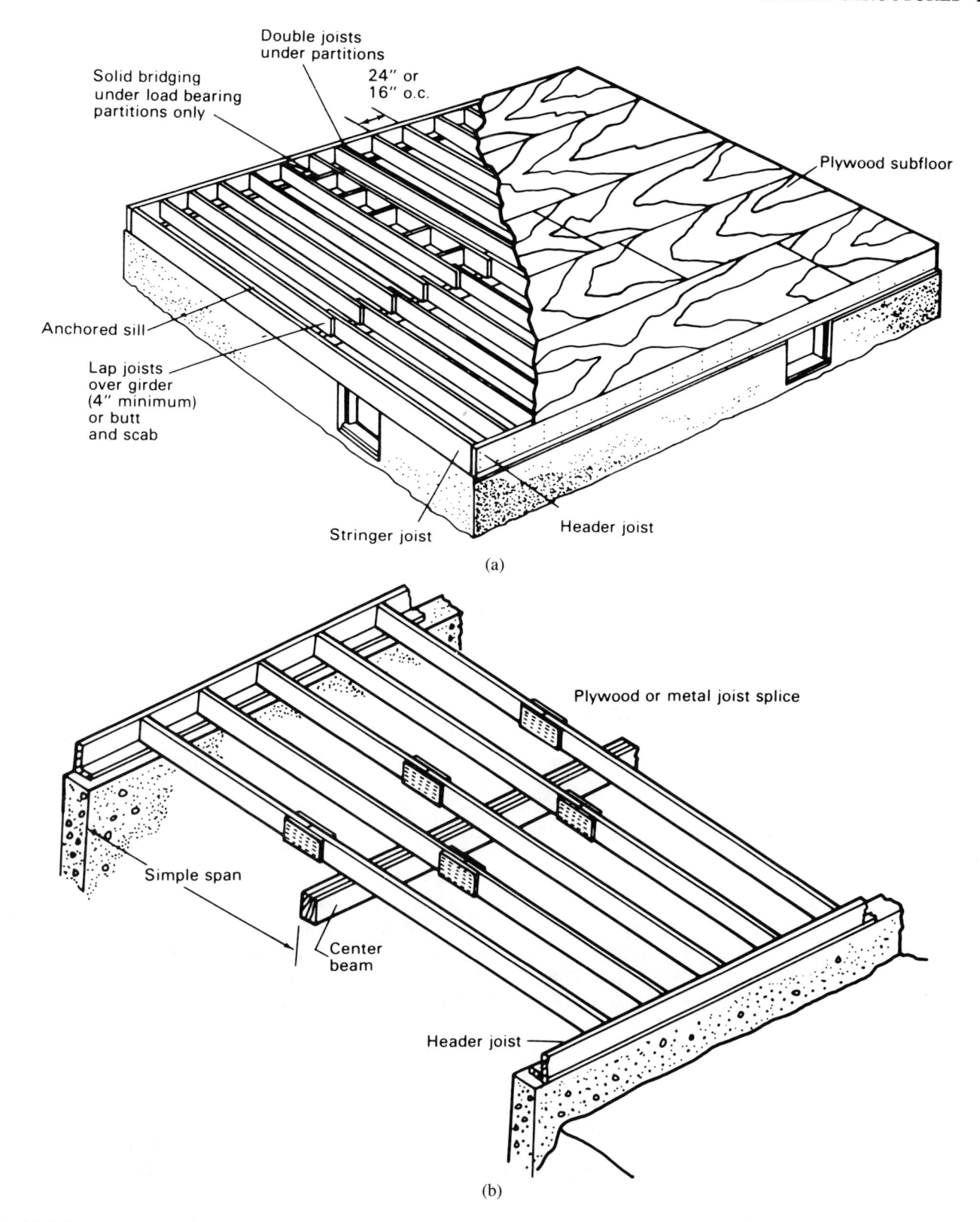

Fig. 14.3.2. Typical floor details for platform type of construction. (a) Joists spliced on center beam; (b) off-center splices allowing use of shorter pieces of lumber.

partition wall. In such a case, backup clips on the partition stud are needed to accommodate the interior finish.

Upper plates are usually doubled, especially when rafters will bear on the top plate between studs. The second top plate is added in such a way that it overlaps the first plate at corners and at interior wall intersections. This provides a tie and additional rigidity to the walls. In areas subject to high winds or earthquakes, ties should be provided between

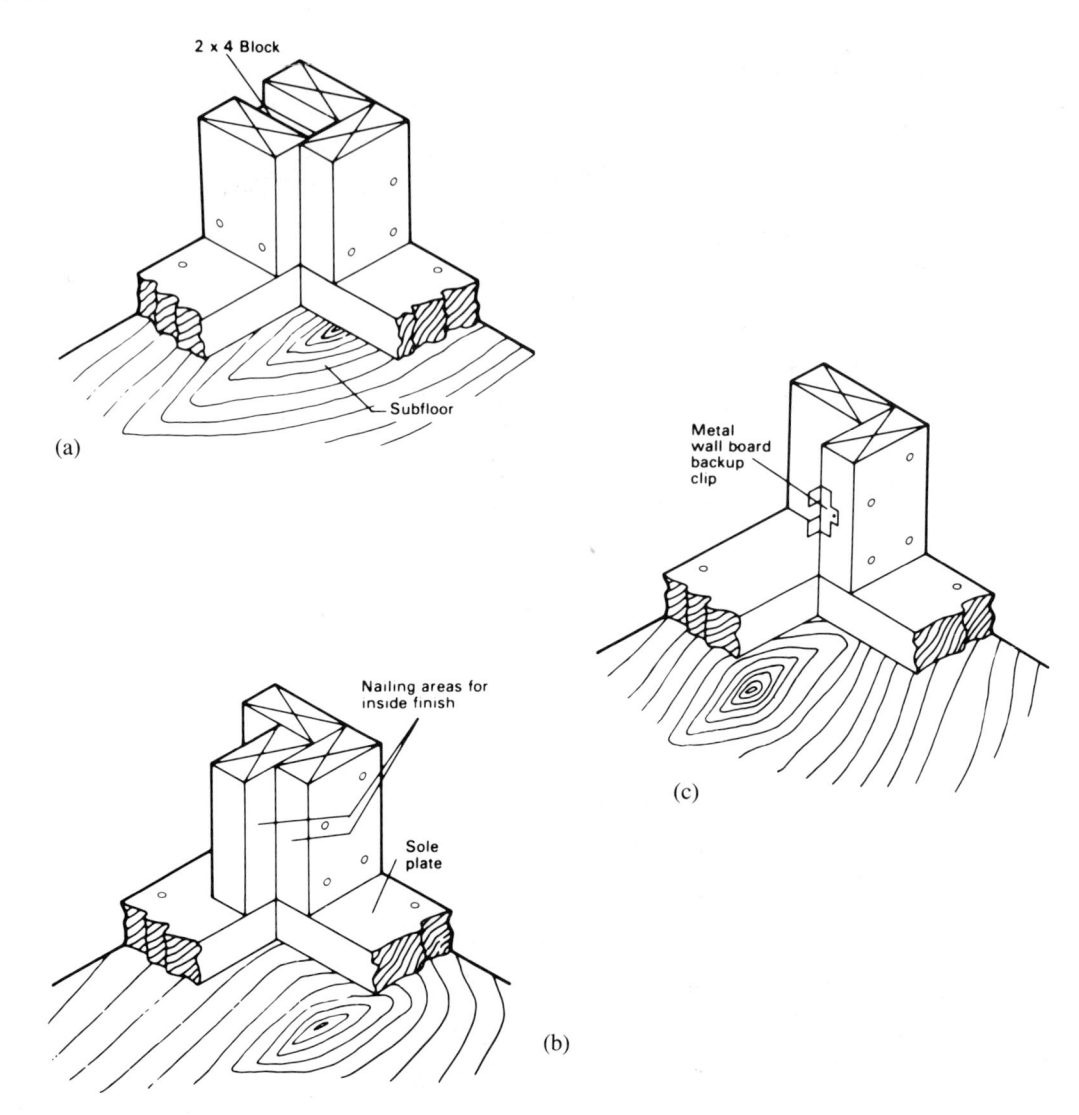

Fig. 14.3.3. Corner details for wood stud walls that provide support for interior sheathing. (a) Traditional 3-stud corner with blocking; (b) 3-stud corner without blocking; (c) 2-stud corner with wallboard backup clips.

the wall, floor framing, and sill plate, which is anchored to the foundation. If a second story is to be added to the structure, the edge floor joist is nailed to the top wall plate, and subfloor and wall framing are added in the same way as for the first floor.

Sheathing for exterior walls is commonly some type of panel product. Here again, as for subfloors, plywood or structural flakeboard may be used. Fiberboard that has been treated to impart some degree of water resistance is another option. Several types of fiberboard are available. Regular-density board sometimes requires additional bracing to provide necessary racking resistance. Intermediate-density board is used where structural support is needed. Numerous foam-type panels are also used to impart greater thermal resistance to the walls. However, because many foam sheathings cannot provide racking resistance, diagonal braces must be placed at the corners, or structural panels must be applied over the first 4 ft (1.2 m) of the wall from the corner. In cases where the sheathing cannot provide the required racking resistance, diagonal bracing must be used. When light-weight insulating foam sheathings are used, bracing is commonly provided by let-in 1- by 4-in. (25- by 100-mm) lumber or by steel strapping.

Ceiling and Roof

Prefabricated roof trusses are used to form the ceiling and sloped roof of over 80 percent of current light-frame buildings. The remainder are framed with ceiling joists and rafter systems. Trusses reduce on-site labor and can span greater distances without intermediate support, thus eliminating the need for interior load-carrying partitions. This provides greater flexibility in the layout of interior walls.

In the past, sloping rafters were common. Such rafters are supported on the top plate of the wall and attached to a ridge board at the roof peak. However, because the rafters slope, they tend to push out the tops of the walls. This is prevented by nailing the rafters to the ceiling joists and nailing the ceiling joists to the top wall plates (Fig. 14.3.4a).

A valley or hip is formed where two roof sections meet perpendicular to each other. A valley rafter is used to support short-length jack rafters that are nailed to the valley rafter and to the ridge board (Fig. 14.3.4b). In some cases, the roof does not extend to a gable end but is sloped from some point down to the end wall to form a "hip" roof. A hip rafter supports the jack rafters, and the other ends of the jack rafters are attached to the top plates (Fig. 14.3.4c). In general, the same materials used for wall sheathing and subfloors are used for roof sheathing.

Sources of Additional Information

Additional information on the use of wood in housing and other light-frame construction is available from several organizations:

American Plywood Association
7011 South 19th Street
Tacoma, WA 98466

Canadian Wood Council
55 Metcalfe Street
15th Floor, Suite 1550
Ottawa, Ontario
Canada K1P 6L5

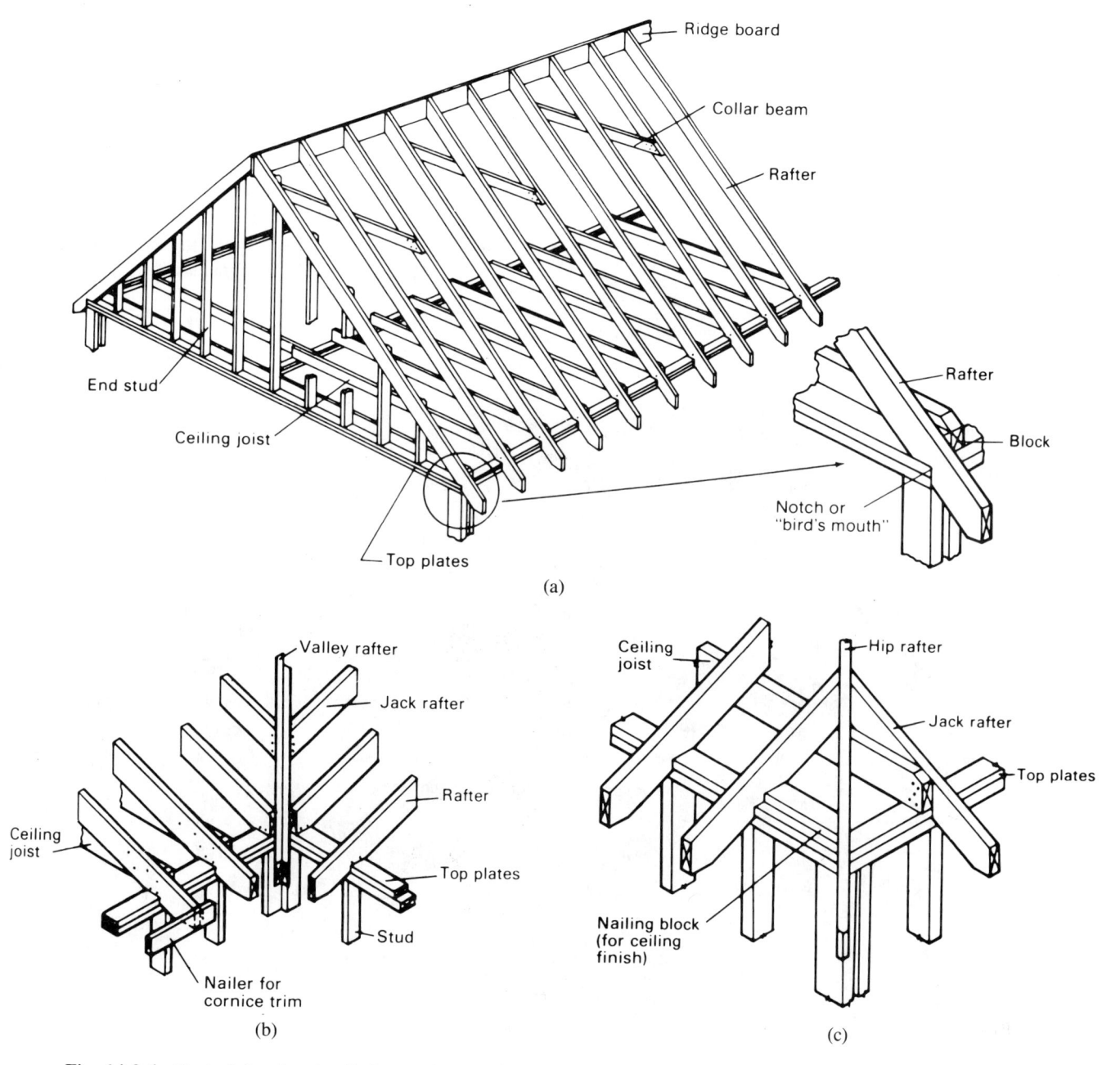

Fig. 14.3.4. Typical framing details for a rafter-type roof (a) showing framing details at a valley (b) and a hip corner (c).

National Association of Home Builders
15th and M Streets, NW
Washington, DC 20005

National Forest Products Association
1250 Connecticut Avenue
Washington, DC 20036

Small Homes Council
Building Research Council
University of Illinois
One East St. Mary's Road
Champaign, IL 61820

Timber Development Association
55 Elizabeth Street
Sydney, NSW 2000
Australia

Timber Research and Development Association
Stocking Lane
Hughenden Valley
High Wycombe, Bucks
England HP14 4ND

Truss Plate Institute
583 D'Onofrio Drive
Madison, WI 53719

14.4. HEAVY TIMBER BUILDINGS

Log and Timber Frame Houses

Interest is growing in log houses—from small, simple houses for vacation use to large, permanent residences. Fig. 14.4.1 illustrates a modern residential log structure. Several firms in the United States furnish designs and materials for log houses. In general, walls, roofs, and floor systems are built from logs rather than framed with dimension lumber. The companies tend to categorize log types into two systems. In the round log system, the logs are machined to a smooth, fully rounded surface, and they are generally all the same diameter. In the other system, the logs are machined to specific shapes, generally not fully round. The exterior surfaces of the logs are generally rounded, whereas the interior surfaces may be either flat or rounded. The interface between logs is machined to form an interlocking joint.

Consensus standards have been developed to conform log houses to building code requirements (Ref. 14.41). Builders and designers need to realize that logs may reach the building site at moisture content levels higher than ideal; the effects of moisture change and the consequences of associated shrinkage should be considered.

Fig. 14.4.1. Modern log homes are available in a variety of designs.

The popularity of "timber frame" structures is also increasing. This type of construction was used in early American houses, barns, and factory buildings (Fig. 14.4.2). The frame is made of large solid-sawn timbers connected to one another by hand-fabricated joints such as mortise and tenon. Construction of such a frame involves rather sophisticated joinery, as illustrated in Fig. 14.4.2.

Because the timber frame is characteristically quite rigid, wall bracing or structural sheathing are not needed to resist racking. Frequently, a prefabricated, composite, 4- by 8-ft (1.2- by 2.4-m) sheathing panel is applied directly to the frame. This panel may consist of an inside layer of $\frac{1}{2}$-in. (12-mm) gypsum, a core layer of rigid foam insulation, and an outside layer of exterior plywood. Finish siding is applied over the composite panel. In some cases, a layer of 1-in. (25-mm), tongue-and-groove, solid-wood boards is applied to the frame, and a rigid, foam-exterior, plywood composite panel is then applied over the boards to form the building exterior. Local fire regulations should be consulted about the suitability of foam insulation for such a use, since some types of foams emit hazardous fumes in a fire.

Because the framing members are cut in large cross sections, seasoning them before installation is difficult, if not impossible. Thus, the builder (and the owner) should recognize the dimensional changes that may occur as the members dry in place. The structure must be designed to accommodate these dimensional changes as well as seasoning checks, which are almost inevitable.

Pole and Post Frame Buildings

Round poles, or square or rectangular posts, may serve as the foundation of a building and simultaneously as the principal framing element. This type of construction is known as the wood pole (or wood post) foundation-framing system. For relatively low structures, such as shown in Fig. 14.4.3, light wall and roof framing is nailed to poles or posts set at fairly frequent centers, commonly 8 to 12 ft (2.4 to 3.6 m). For larger buildings, the center-to-center separation of poles or posts may be greater. This type of construction was originally used for agricultural buildings, but the structural principle has been extended to both commercial buildings and residences.

Attachment of framing may be difficult if round poles are used. This problem may be eased by slabbing the outer face of the pole, and for corner poles, two faces may be slabbed at right angles. This permits better attachment of both light and heavy framing by nails or timber connectors. In some cases, the pole is left round, but it is inserted in the foundation hole so that the outer face of the pole is vertical. Poles may be notched to provide seats for beams.

Posts may be solid sawn, glulam, or built up by nail laminating. Built-up posts are advantageous because only the bases of the posts must be treated. The treated portion in the ground may have laminations of varying lengths that are matched with the lengths of untreated laminations in the upper part of the post. The design of these types of posts must consider the integrity of the splice between the treated and untreated lumber.

Mill-Type Construction

Mill-type construction has been widely used for warehouse and manufacturing structures, particularly in the Eastern United States. This type of construction uses timbers of large cross sections; columns are spaced in a grid according to the available lengths of beam and girder timbers. As previously noted, the size of the timbers makes this type of construction resistant to fire. The good insulating qualities of wood (and char) result in slow penetration of fire into the large members, and the members thus retain a large proportion of their original load-carrying capacity and stiffness for a relatively long period after the onset of fire exposure. Consequently, fire fighting is safe for longer periods in mill-type construction than in light-frame construction. Mill-type construction is recognized by some building codes as 1-h fire-resistant construction, with some limitations.

To be recognized as mill-type construction, the structural elements must not be less than specific sizes—columns cannot be less than a nominal 8 in. (200 mm) in dimension, and beams and girders cannot be less than 6 by 10 in. (150 by 250 mm) in cross section. Other limitations must be observed as well. For example, walls must be made of masonry, and concealed spaces must be avoided. Construction details are illustrated in Ref. 14.26. The structural frame has typically been constructed of solid-sawn timbers, which should be stress graded. These timbers can now be supplanted with glulam timbers, and longer spans are permitted.

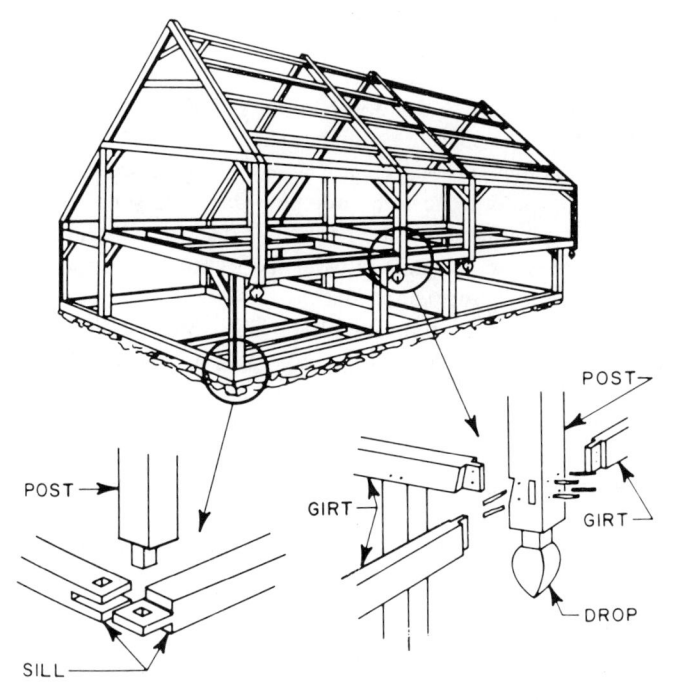

Fig. 14.4.2. Timber frame structure with typical joint details.

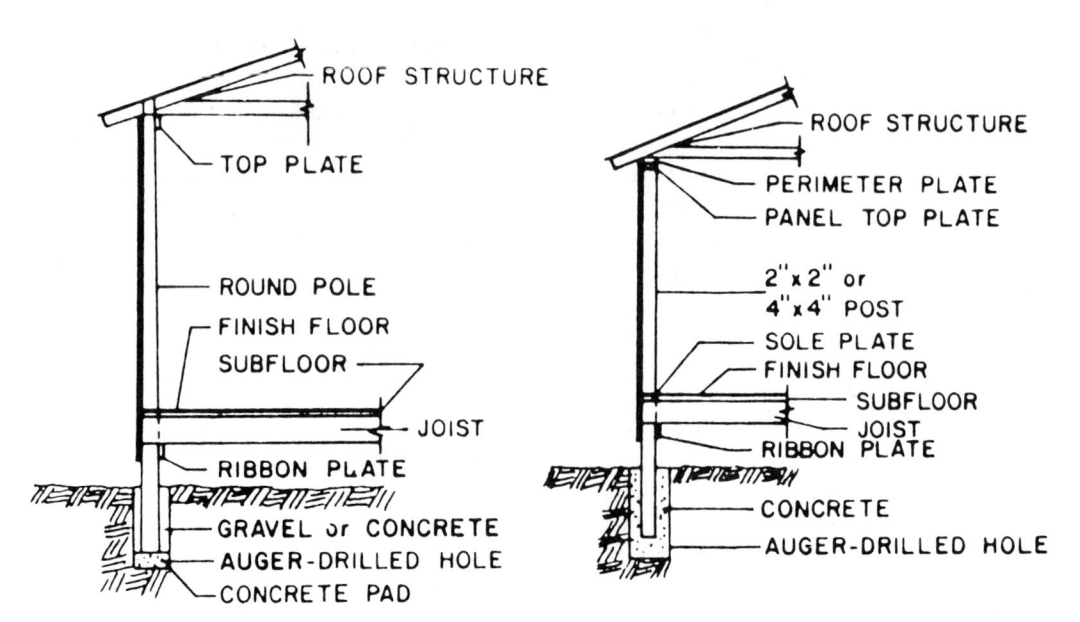

Fig. 14.4.3. Function of pole in pole and post-frame buildings. (*Left*) pole forms both foundation and wall; (*right*) pole forms only the foundation (conventional platform-framed structure).

Glulam Beam Systems

Various forms of glulam beams were described earlier in this chapter. A panelized roof system using glulam roof framing is widely used in the Southwestern United States. This system is based on supporting columns located at the corners of preestablished grids. The main glulam beams support glulam or sawn purlins, which in turn support preframed structural panels. The basic unit of the preframed system is a 4- by 8-ft (1.2- by 2.4-m) structural panel nailed to 2- by 4-in. (50- by 100-mm) or 2- by 6-in. (50- by 150-mm) stiffeners (subpurlins). The stiffeners run parallel to the 8-ft (2.4-m) dimension of the structural panel. One stiffener is located at the centerline of the panel; the other is located at an edge, with the plywood edge at the stiffener centerline. The stiffeners are precut to a length equal to the long dimension of the plywood less the thickness of the purlin, with a small allowance for the hanger.

In some cases, the purlins are erected with the hangers in place, the prefabricated panels are lifted and set into place in the hangers, and the adjoining basic panels are then attached to each other. In other cases, the basic panels are attached to one purlin on the ground. A whole panel is lifted into place to support the loose ends of the stiffeners. This system is fully described in Ref. 14.42.

Arch Structures

Arch structures are particularly suited to applications in which large, unobstructed areas are needed, such as churches, recreational buildings, and aircraft hangars. Although a number of basic arch forms are shown in Fig. 14.2.8, the variety of possible forms seems to be limited only by the imagination of the architect. Churches have used arches from the beginning of the manufacture of glulam in the United States (Ref. 14.6).

Domes

Radial-rib domes consist of curved members extending from the base ring (tension ring) to a compression ring at the top of the dome and ring members at various elevations between the tension ring and compression ring (Fig. 14.4.4). The ring members may be curved or straight. If they are curved to the same radius as the rib and have their centers at the center of the sphere, the dome will have a spherical surface. If the ring members are straight, the dome will have an umbrella look. Design of the radial-rib dome is fairly straightforward because it is statically determinate. Connections between the ribs and the ring members are critical because of the high compressive loads in the ring members. Erection is not overly complicated, but care must be taken to stabilize the dome, since it has a tendency to rotate about the central vertical axis.

Other dome patterns called Varax and Triax are also used. Their geometries are quite complex, and specialized computer programs are used for their design. The key to these domes are the steel hubs at the joints and supports. Most hubs are proprietary and are designed by either the manufacturer or its representative. The 530-ft- (190-m-) diameter Tacoma Dome, a Triax type, is shown under construction in Figure 14.4.5; its structural design is described in Ref. 14.43.

Sources of Additional Information

The following organizations have information on heavy timber structures:

American Institute of Timber Construction
11818 SE Mill Plain Blvd.
Suite 415
Vancouver, WA 98684

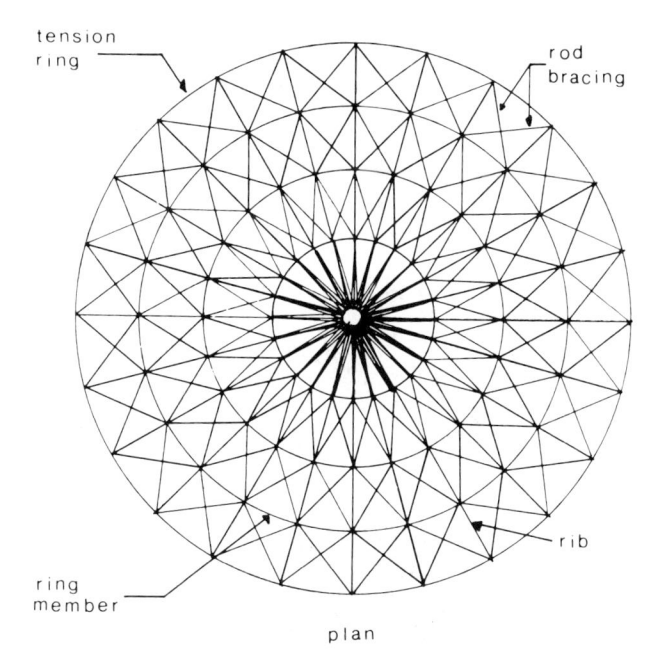

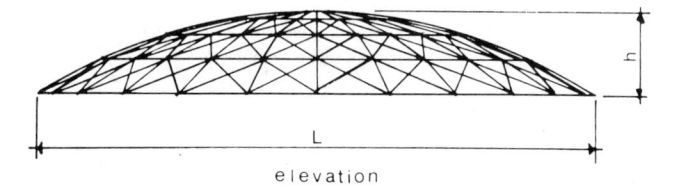

Fig. 14.4.4. Member layout and geometry of a radial rib dome.

Canadian Wood Council
55 Metcalfe Street
15th Floor, Suite 1550
Ottawa, Ontario
Canada K1P 6L5

Log Home Council
15th and M Streets, NW
Washington, DC 20005

National Forest Products Association
1250 Connecticut Avenue, NW
Washington, DC 20036

Timber Development Association
55 Elizabeth Street
Sydney, NSW 2000
Australia

Timber Research and Development Association
Stocking Lane
Hughenden Valley
High Wycombe, Bucks
England HP14 4ND

14.5. SPECIAL CONSIDERATIONS

As discussed in Chapter 4, wood has a number of special characteristics that distinguish it from other materials. In many cases, these characteristics affect the behavior of products made from wood. Thus, the success or failure of a project may rest to a greater or lesser degree on the care

Fig. 14.4.5. The 530-ft- (190-m-) diameter Tacoma Dome built in 1982–83 in the state of Washington is both the largest wood dome structure and one of the longest clear roof spans in the world.

with which that product is chosen or the way in which it is used in the overall project. This suggests the desirability of careful specification writing and design, together with attention to detail in the construction process. The following sections outline some precautions.

Connections

Connections between the load-carrying members of a building or other structure are essential to the proper functioning of that structure. Obviously, individual parts of a truss must be interconnected or the truss would not function as a single unit. What may not be quite so obvious is that structural units must be interconnected. This is especially true in areas subject to high winds, earthquakes, high water, or waves, where experience has shown that failure to provide adequate connections between roof systems and walls and between walls and foundation can result in disastrous damage to the structure. Such damage frequently can be prevented by careful attention to the details of connections between elements and units. Many fastener types, such as nails, screws, lag screws, dowels, drift pins, and bolts, have been available for many years. More recent fasteners include special nails, staples, split rings, shear plates, spike grids, toothed metal plates, clamping plates, framing anchors, joist and purlin hangers, and special fasteners. Some of these fasteners are illustrated in Figs. 14.5.1 and 14.5.2.

Nails are commonly used when loads are low, and they are the fastener of choice in most light-frame construction as well as for diaphragms and shear walls. Screws are not generally used to join structural members.

Lag screws, bolts, and timber connectors are used for loads of relatively large magnitude. They are used in heavy timber construction and may be used in light-frame construction when exceptional loads are anticipated.

Bolts are less efficient than split rings and shear plates, but they are adequate for many situations. Lag screws are used in place of bolts under special conditions, such as in a connection for a very thick member or when one face of a member is not accessible for installation of washers and nuts. Both bolts and lag screws may be used with split rings and shear plates.

Split rings and shear plates (Fig. 14.5.1) are used for joints in heavy timber construction. They may be used in light wood trusses designed for long spans or wide spacings.

Thin-gauge steel plate connectors (Fig. 14.5.2) are used to join structural elements in fastening subassemblies and to anchor a structure to its foundation. Joist and purlin hangers, beam seats, column caps, strap ties, framing anchors, and like fasteners are commonly available for these purposes.

Toothed metal plates are used extensively in light wood trusses for both roof and floor systems. Such systems are used in a very high percentage of residential structures as

Fig. 14.5.1. Joints with shear-plate connectors. (a) Wood side plates; (b) steel side plates.

well as in some commercial and institutional buildings. The plates are commonly galvanized, but when used with either preservative-treated or fire-retardant-treated wood, stainless steel is recommended because of the corrosive nature of the treating salts. Design handbooks, such as those listed in Table 14.1, describe connection design in detail. In addition, AITC 104 (Ref. 14.44) gives details on connections particularly applicable to glulam.

Some special characteristics of wood can affect not only member design, but also connection design. This problem is covered in considerable detail in *Wood: Engineering Design Concepts* (Ref. 14.4, chapter on design of connections). Among the subjects treated are the effects of connection details that impose tensile stress perpendicular to grain; for instance, when a load is suspended near the bottom of a beam or shrinkage resulting from moisture change is restrained by widely separated fasteners. This book also describes details that result in accumulation of moisture in a wood member, such as encasing the end of a column in a concrete floor or supporting the end of an arch or a column in a concrete floor or a steel box. The problems that result from undesirable stresses accompanying the use of eccentric joints in trusses are also covered. Because more extensive coverage of this subject is not feasible here, references in this area are "must" reading for both architects and structural designers.

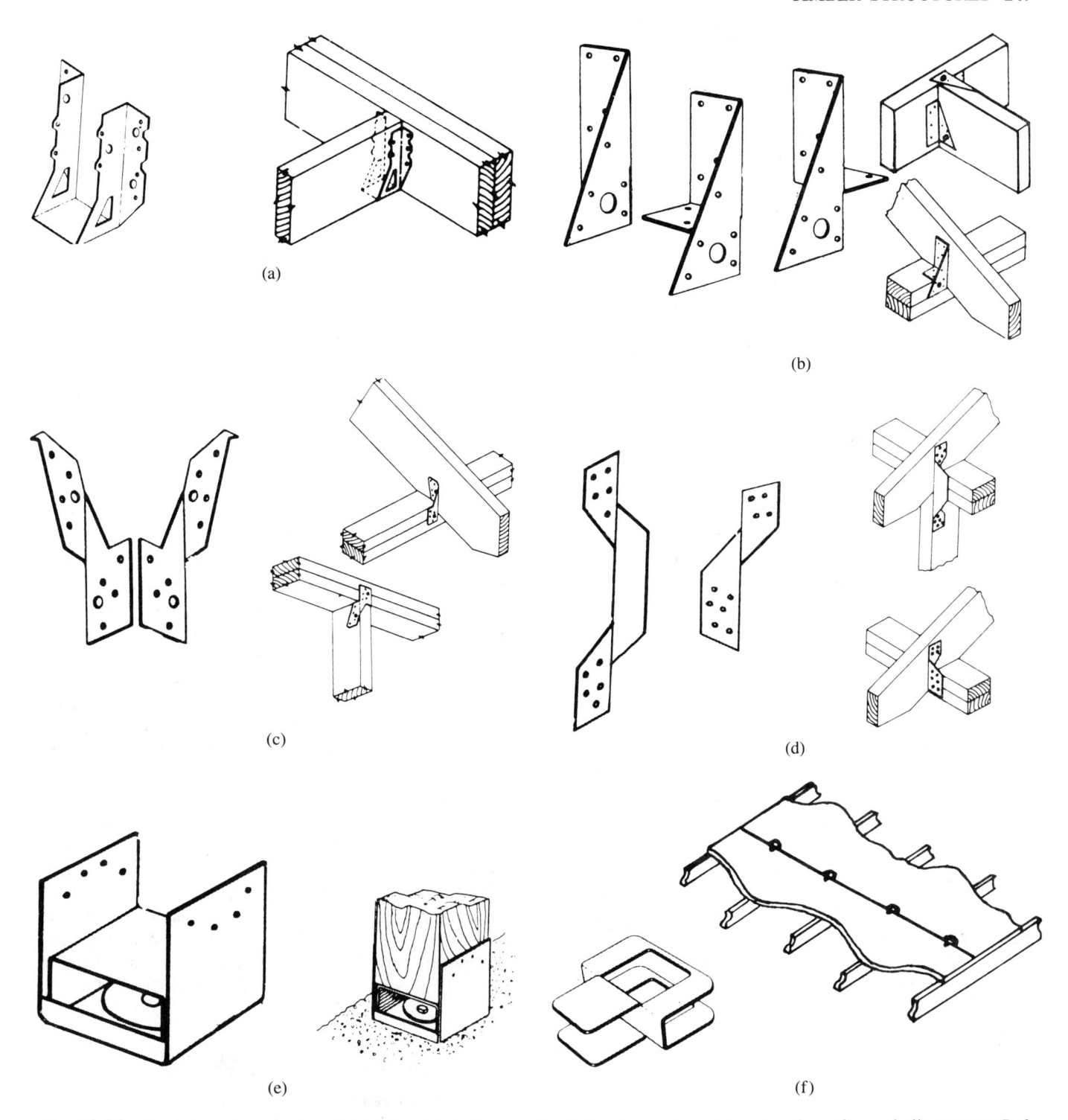

Fig. 14.5.2. Special wood connectors. (a) Joist and beam hanger; (b–d) framing anchors; (e) post anchor; (f) panel clip support (Ref. 14.30). (By permission of the American Society of Civil Engineers.)

Grades of Lumber and Panel Products

In effect, the grading rules for lumber are descriptions of products for specific purposes. One set of grades is designed for structural uses of lumber, such as joists, truss members, or scaffold planks. Accordingly, the factors that affect strength and stiffness are properly limited or perhaps prohibited. Another set of grades describes lumber intended to be cut into smaller pieces for parts of doors, windows, and the like, setting limits on the size and quality of the pieces that can be produced by cutting between defects, such as large knots. Such grades in softwoods are called "shop" grades. However, even though a piece of shop grade lumber might be of the same species, general appearance, and size as a piece graded for a joist and plank grade, this does not make it suitable for use as a joist. The size and location of large knots are not specified in the "shop" rules and consequently not limited in the piece. Use of such a piece for structural purposes, such as a joist, could result in disaster. Therefore, the selection of lumber grade should be guided by the end use of the wood.

Certain specifications refer to a grade name that is not an accepted grade—"commercial" grade, for example—and this "grade" is not described anywhere. This practice can only result in confusion. Thus, the architect should specify only a fully described and accepted grade of lumber that bears a grade mark, such as that shown in Fig. 14.5.3.

Some light-frame structures are built after an engineering analysis. In such instances, the lumber chosen for structural elements should be stress graded to provide assurance that the structural elements meet the strength and stiffness requirements established by the engineering analysis. In other instances, such as in some dwellings, the framing systems may copy those that had been used earlier and had worked well even though they were not based on engineering analysis. If no stress grades are available and new grades have to be chosen, guides to the selection of such grades are available. Span tables can be used for choosing grades and sizes of joists for specific spans or conversely, for choosing suitable spans for available materials. Span tables are based on allowable values of strength and assigned values of modulus of elasticity, coupled with anticipated loadings. Stress grades should be used to ensure that the requirements implicit in the span tables will be met by the structure (Ref. 14.7).

Plywood and other panel products made in accordance with the APA performance standard (Ref. 14.45) and PS 1-83 (Ref. 14.46) include some engineered grades and some appearance grades; both kinds of grades are made for exterior or interior use—that is, with or without waterproof adhesives. In addition, allowable design stresses are available for the engineered grades of plywood (Ref. 14.11). Engineered grades suitable for use as subfloor or roof sheathing, when marked under APA supervision, carry an identification index that indicates the safe distance between supports (Fig. 14.5.4). For example, an identification index of 42/20 indicates that the plywood panel is suitable for use as roof sheathing when roof rafters or trusses are spaced as much as 42 in. (1.1 m) between centers; when used as subfloor, the support spacing may not be more than 20 in. (500 mm). An index of 24/0 indicates that supports for roof sheathing may be spaced as much as 24 in. (600 mm) on center, but that the panel may not be used as subfloor. Such indices provide a good guide to proper usage of plywood and other panel products.

Interior-type panels may have adhesive bonds with three levels of moisture resistance: interior, intermediate, and exterior. When bonded with an interior adhesive, the panel is intended for interior use only. When bonded with an intermediate adhesive, the panel is intended for use in protected construction and industrial applications where protection from weather may be delayed for short periods or conditions of high humidity or water leakage may prevail. When bonded with an exterior adhesive, the panel is intended for construction and industrial uses where construction delays or other conditions may expose the wood to moisture for long periods. Obviously, exterior adhesive is also necessary when the panels will be treated with preservatives.

Exterior-type plywood will retain its glue bond when repeatedly wetted and dried or otherwise subjected to weather or other conditions of comparable severity such as pressure preservative treatment.

Thus, the load and moisture resistance of plywood and panel products covers a wide range, and it should be considered when selecting a type of panel for specific uses.

Plywood produced under the American National Standards Institute (ANSI) HP 1983 (Ref. 14.47) is

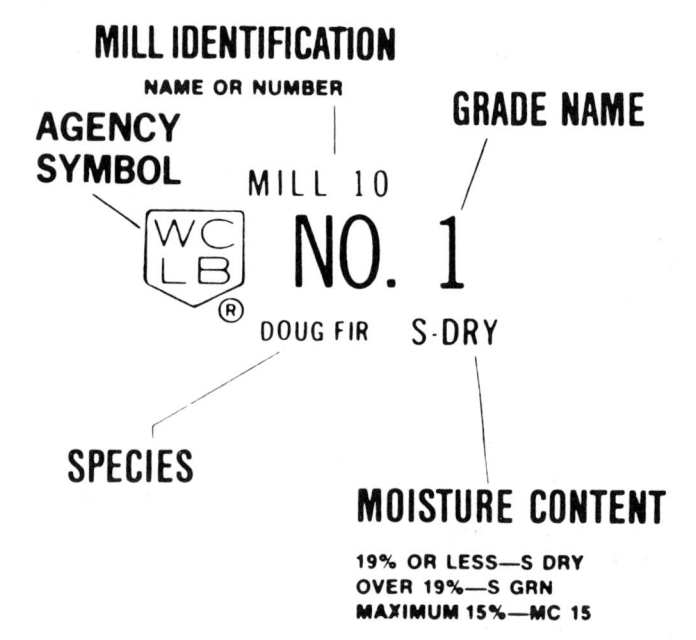

Fig. 14.5.3. Example of a lumber grade mark. All structural lumber should bear a grade mark.

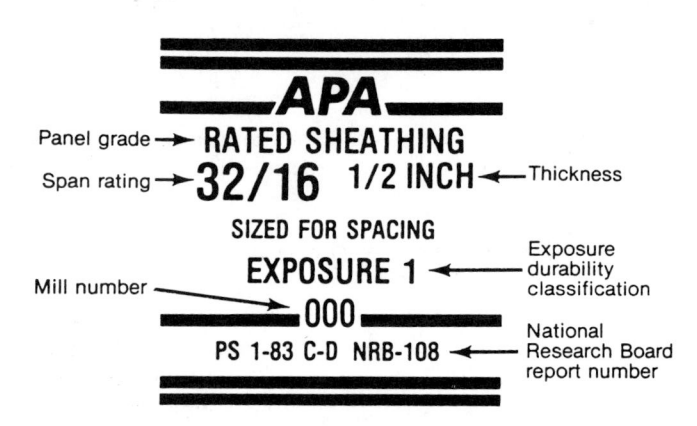

Fig. 14.5.4. Example of identification index for sheathing panels.

basically intended for use as decorative wall panels; cut-to-size and stock panels for furniture, cabinets, containers, and specialty products; and marine applications.

Moisture Content and Shrinkage

The growing tree has large amounts of moisture. When wood is cut from the tree, it immediately begins to lose moisture to the surrounding atmosphere. Conversely, when wood that has been dried encounters a humid atmosphere or is wetted by water, it gains moisture. Thus, outside the tree, wood has the property of changing its moisture content in an attempt to achieve equilibrium with the surroundings (i.e., wood is hygroscopic). When wood is below the fiber saturation point (see Chapter 4), certain properties change with changing moisture content. Below this point, for example, strength and modulus of elasticity increase as moisture content decreases and decrease as moisture content increases. Thus, allowable design stresses are different for wood at low moisture content than at high. The structural designer must anticipate conditions in service and choose appropriate design specifications from which to calculate member sizes.

Reduction in moisture content after a wood member is placed in service may have undesirable effects. For example, green wood placed in service in a structure, even a relatively unprotected structure, will lose moisture with time, with the potential of warping, reduction of cross-sectional dimensions, splitting, and other defects.

As wood loses moisture below the fiber saturation point, it shrinks; conversely, wood swells with increases in moisture content. These effects are demonstrated in dresser drawers (or doors) that operate freely in winter but may be all but impossible to operate after a siege of high summer humidity. Shrinkage is least in the fiber direction (parallel to grain), more in the perpendicular-to-grain direction radial to the annual growth rings, and still more in the perpendicular-to-grain direction parallel to a tangent to the growth rings. Specific shrinkage coefficients for different species are given in the *Wood Handbook* (Ref. 14.29). A general rule of thumb is that wood will change about 1 percent in dimension perpendicular to the grain for each 4 percent change in moisture content below about 30 percent moisture content.

In lumber, the width of edge-grained lumber is parallel to the radial direction, whereas that of a flat-sawn board or plank is more or less parallel to the tangential direction. An edge-grained board will consequently have less shrinkage in width than will a flat-sawn board. In such applications as siding, the tendency for cupping is greatly reduced by using edge-grained wood; cupping is not only unsightly but may also result in splitting and pulling of the nails that attach the siding to the framing. Although edge-grained siding costs more than other types of siding, it can be expected to give better performance over time.

Directional Properties

Unlike many other materials, wood does not have the same properties, mechanical and otherwise, in all directions. The ratio of mechanical properties at right angles to the grain to those parallel to grain may range from perhaps 0.03 to 0.12 or, roughly, from $\frac{1}{30}$ to $\frac{1}{8}$. This strongly suggests that design details that permit large forces to be developed perpendicular to grain, especially in tension, are highly undesirable. For example, a hanger carrying a concentrated load and supported by a bolt a short distance above the bottom of a girder would not be good practice because of the likelihood of failure in tension perpendicular to grain. In many instances, compressive loads perpendicular to grain cannot be avoided, as where girders bear on the supports or where posts bear against caps, as in the bents of a trestle. Although catastrophic failure is not likely in such locations, excessive crushing perpendicular to grain may occur and result in such things as sloping floors in buildings. Consideration should be given to potential problems that might result from anisotropy. Properties other than strength and stiffness may also be anisotropic in nature. Shrinkage with changes in moisture content varies with respect to both fiber direction and annual ring orientation; the potential effects of shrinkage were discussed previously.

Erection and Bracing

Proper erection and bracing are essential for the satisfactory performance of timber structures. Many engineered wood products have low lateral stiffness and must be handled carefully to prevent damage. Without proper lateral bracing, many long-span engineered wood products such as trusses, I-beams, and glulam timbers are unstable during erection or under a fraction of their design load. For example, the top chord of many trusses will buckle unless properly restrained.

Wood members of any kind should not be lifted with steel cables in direct contact with their edges. Special blocking or fabric slings should be used to protect the edges from indentations, which can disproportionately weaken the members. Trusses must be carefully handled during erection, and often a spreader bar or strongback must be used to prevent damage.

Once in place, temporary bracing is often required for many engineered wood products until the permanent sheathing is attached. This temporary bracing should be a part of the building design, but may be the responsibility of the construction contractor. The first member erected must be securely braced because the common practice is to brace the other members to the first member. Bracing of the top chord of trusses is more important because the top chord is particularly susceptible to lateral buckling. This bracing is often placed at the ridge line and at intervals of

8 to 10 ft (2 to 3 m) along the span. To permit the addition of sheathing or permanent bracing with the temporary bracing intact, the temporary bracing is often installed on the underside of the top chord.

Handling and erection of trusses are discussed in detail in Ref. 14.49.

The design of many engineered wood products requires that the compression side of bending members be laterally supported either continuously or at specific intervals. The designer must ensure that the bracing system provides stability for the building under service loads. In many instances, panel-type sheathing is attached to the compression side of bending members and provides the needed lateral support. If sheathing is attached to purlins, these purlins can be designed to assure stability. Suggested bracing for wood truss systems is given in Ref. 14.50. Sometimes, compression web members of trusses also require additional diagonal bracing. All permanent bracing should be installed as soon as practical after the structure is erected because some parts of a structure are subjected to heavy loads during construction.

REFERENCES

14.1. G. Hans. "The American Home in Another Perspective." *Forest Prod. J.*, **26**(7), 14–20 (1976).

14.2. National Forest Products Association. *Span Tables for Joists and Rafters*. Washington, DC, 1977.

14.3. American Institute of Timber Construction. *Glulam Beams*. Vancouver, WA, 1985.

14.4. A. D. Freas, R. C. Moody, and L. A. Soltis (eds.). *Wood: Engineering Design Concepts*. Vol. IV, Clark C. Heritage Memorial Series on Wood. Pennsylvania State University, University Park, PA 1986.

14.5. American Institute of Timber Construction. *Design—Standard Specifications for Structural Glued Laminated Timber of Softwood Species*. AITC 117. Vancouver, WA, 1987.

14.6. American Institute of Timber Construction. *A Portfolio of Religious Structures*. Vancouver, WA, undated.

14.7. National Forest Products Association. *National Design Specification for Wood Construction*. Washington, DC, 1986.

14.8. American Institute of Timber Construction. *Timber Construction Manual*. John Wiley and Sons, New York, 1985.

14.9. Australian Timber Research Institute. *Australian Timber Construction Manual*. Sydney, Australia, 1989.

14.10. Laminated Timber Institute of Canada. *Timber Design Manual*. Ottawa, Ontario, Canada, 1980.

14.11. American Plywood Association. *Plywood Design Specification*. Tacoma, WA, 1983.

14.12. Truss Plate Institute. *Design Specifications for Metal Plate Connected Wood Trusses*. TPI-85. Madison, WI, 1985.

14.13. Truss Plate Institute. *Design Specifications for Metal Plate Connected Parallel Chord Wood Trusses*. PCT-80. Madison, WI, 1980.

14.14. Truss Plate Institute of Canada. *Truss Design Procedures and Specifications for Light Metal Plate Connected Wood Trusses*. TPIC-88 (1-88), 1988.

14.15. Canadian Standards Association. *Engineering Design in Wood (Working Stress Design)*. CAN 3-086-M84. Ottawa, Ontario, Canada, 1984.

14.16. Canadian Standards Association. *Engineering Design in Wood (Limit States Design)*. CAN 3-086-M84. Ottawa, Ontario, Canada, 1986.

14.17. National Research Council of Canada. *National Building Code of Canada 1985*. Publication No. 2374. Ottawa, Ontario, Canada, 1985.

14.18. Standards Association of Australia. *Timber Structures Code*. AS 1720. Sydney, Australia, 1988.

14.19. Standards Association of Australia. *Timber Framing Code*. AS 1684. Sydney, Australia, 1979.

14.20. International Council for Building Research Studies and Documentation. *CIB Structural Timber Design Code*. Publication 86. Rotterdam, Netherlands, 1983.

14.21. D. E. Breyer. *Design of Wood Structures*, 2nd Ed. McGraw-Hill, New York, 1988.

14.22. R. Hoyle and F. Woeste. *Wood Technology in the Design of Structures*, 5th Ed. Iowa State Univ. Press, Ames, IA, 1989.

14.23. G. Gurfinkel. *Wood Engineering*. Southern Forest Products Association, New Orleans, LA, 1973.

14.24. K. F. Faherty and T. G. Williamson. *Wood Engineering and Construction Handbook*. McGraw-Hill, New York, 1989.

14.25. J. J. Stalhaker and E. G. Harris. *Structural Design in Wood*. Van Nostrand Reinhold, New York, 1989.

14.26. Timber Engineering Company. *Timber Design and Construction Handbook*. F. W. Dodge, New York, 1956.

14.27. F. J. Keenan. *Limit States Design of Wood Structures*. Morrison Hershfield Ltd., Toronto, Ontario, Canada, 1986.

14.28. E. C. Ozelton and J. A. Baird. *Timber Designers Manual*. Granada Publishing, London, England, 1976.

14.29. Forest Products Laboratory. *Wood Handbook*. USDA Forest Service Agricultural Handbook 72. U.S. Government Printing Office, Washington, DC, 1987.

14.30. American Society of Civil Engineers. *Wood Structures: A Design Guide and Commentary*. New York, 1975, 416 pp.

14.31. American Society of Civil Engineers. *Evaluation, Maintenance, and Upgrading of Wood Structures: A Guide and Commentary*. New York, 1982.

14.32. Midwest Plan Service. *Designs for Glued Trusses*. Midwest Plan Service, Iowa State University, Ames, IA, 1981.

14.33. Western Wood Products Association. *Wood Frame Design*. Publication No. 1305/556. Portland, OR, 1987.

14.34. Southern Pine Marketing Council. *Southern Pine Use Guide*. Southern Forest Products Association, New Orleans, LA [see latest edition].

14.35. G. E. Sherwood and R. Stroh. *Wood Frame House Construction*. USDA Forest Service Agricultural Handbook 73. U.S. Government Printing Office, Washington, DC, 1989. (Also available from Armonk Press, Armonk, NY).

14.36. Timber Research and Development Association. *Structural Recommendations for Timber Frame Housing*. The Construction Press, Lancaster, England, 1980.

14.37. Canadian Wood Council. *Canadian Woods*. Ottawa, Ontario, Canada [see latest edition].

14.38. American Plywood Association. *APA Design/Construction Guide: Residential and Commercial*. Tacoma, WA [see latest edition].

14.39. F. F. Wangaard (Ed.). *Wood: Its Structure and Properties*. Vol. I, Clark C. Heritage Memorial Series on Wood. Pennsylvania State University, University Park, PA, 1981.

14.40. A. G. H. Dietz, E. L. Schaffer, and D. S. Gromala (Eds.). *Wood as a Structural Material*. Vol. II, Clark C. Heritage Memorial Series on Wood. Pennsylvania State University, University Park, PA, 1982.

14.41. American Society for Testing and Materials. *Standard Methods for Establishing Stress Grades for Structural Members Used in Log Buildings*. ASTM D 3957-80. Philadelphia, PA, 1988.

14.42. American Institute of Timber Construction. *Glued Laminated Timbers for Industrial, Commercial, and Institutional Buildings—1989*. Vancouver, WA, 1989.

14.43. R. W. Eshelby and R. J. Evans. "Design Procedures for Reticulated Timber Domes." *Proceedings of the 1988 International Conference on Timber Engineering*. R. Y. Itani (Ed.), Vol. 1, pp. 283–287. Forest Products Research Society, Madison, WI.

14.44. American Institute of Timber Construction. *Typical Construction Details*. AITC 104. Vancouver, WA [see latest edition].

14.45. American Plywood Association. *Performance Standards and Policies for Structural-Use Panels*. Tacoma, WA, 1982.

14.46. National Bureau of Standards Institute. *U.S. Product Standard PS 1-83 for Construction and Industrial Plywood*. Office of Product Standards Policy, Washington, DC, 1983.

14.47. American National Standards Institute. *American National Standard for Hardwood and Decorative Plywood*. HP 1983. Hardwood Plywood Manufacturers Assoc., Reston, VA, 1983.

14.48. C. J. Mettem. *Structural Timber Design and Technology*. Longman, London, England, 1986.

14.49. Truss Plate Institute. *Commentary and Recommendations for Handling and Erecting Wood Trusses*. Truss Plate Institute HET-80. Madison, WI, 1980.

14.50. Truss Plate Institute. *Commentary and Recommendations for Bracing Wood Trusses*. Truss Plate Institute BWT-76, Madison, WI, 1976.

SUGGESTIONS FOR FURTHER READING

American Institute of Timber Construction. *Timber Construction Manual*. John Wiley, New York, 1985.

D. E. Breyer. *Design of Wood Structures*, 2nd Ed. McGraw-Hill, New York, 1988.

Timber Research and Development Association. *Structural Recommendations for Timber House Framing*. The Construction Press, Lancaster, England, 1980.

Laminated Timber Institute of Canada. *Timber Design Manual*. LTIC, Ottawa, Canada, 1980.

Australian Timber Research Institute. *Australian Timber Construction Manual*. ATRI, Sydney, 1980.

15

Foundations

Ronald E. Bucknam and Thomas M. Gavin

The practice of foundation engineering, which constitutes a major portion of geotechnical engineering, should not be regarded as a science. Rather, it is an art based on specific scientific principles developed from soil mechanics and tempered to a large degree by experience, common sense and sound engineering judgment.

Whereas manufactured materials, such as steel and concrete, have physical properties which are controlled within relatively narrow, definable ranges, soils are products of natural weathering or depositional processes and therefore can exhibit engineering properties which vary substantially, even within relatively small distances on a given site.

As a result, it is imperative for the successful completion and performance of a project that a geotechnical engineering consultant be carefully selected based on previous experience and familiarity with the same type of project and knowledge of the subsurface soil, bedrock and groundwater conditions in the vicinity of the project site. The selection should not be made solely on the basis of the estimated cost of the geotechnical services to be provided. In addition, due to the present emphasis on potential liability issues, it is recommended that the limits of the geotechnical consultant's general and professional liability insurance coverage be defined prior to finalizing a contract for these services.

15.1. STRUCTURE AND CLASSIFICATION OF SOILS

Gradation

Soils are normally classified by the equivalent diameter or maximum dimension of the constituent particles. The ASTM Test Designation D 2487 soil classification system (Ref. 15.1) is considered the standard of practice and is an outgrowth and refinement of what previously was referred to as the Unified Soil Classification System. The grain size distribution of soils is determined by passing a composite soil sample through a series ("nest") of sieves having increasingly smaller square openings and recording the percentage of the total sample retained on each sieve. The results are presented as a gradation or grain size distribution curve which plots the percent retained (by dry weight) versus the sieve opening size in mm, to a log scale. Sometimes this procedure is termed *mechanical analysis*.

Coarse-grained soils are defined by ASTM D 2487 as those materials having more than 50 percent, by dry weight, with maximum dimensions greater than 0.074 mm, which is the equivalent opening size of a US Standard No. 200 sieve. This sieve designation indicates that there are 200 square openings per linear inch along the sieve surface. Coarse-grained soils include the overall terms of *gravel* and *sand*. Gravels are defined as soils having a particle size greater than the No. 4 sieve (4.75 mm opening). Gravels having a particle size greater than 3 in. (75 mm), but less than 12 in. (300 mm), are termed *cobbles*, while particles larger than 12 in. (300 mm) are designated as *boulders*. Sands are subdivided into fine, medium, and coarse, and range in size from the No. 200 sieve (0.074 mm) to the No. 4 sieve (4.75 mm).

For coarse-grained soils, the term *well-graded* applies to those soils which have a mixture of soil types ranging from fine sand to gravel sizes. In well-graded soils, the finer particles tend to fill in the voids between the larger particle sizes. The results of a grain size distribution test for a well-graded soil exhibits a typical S-shaped gradation curve. *Uniform* or poorly graded soils are those coarse-grained materials which contain particles of essentially a single size, or a very narrow range of particle sizes, and plot as a very steep or nearly vertical line on a gradation curve.

Fine-grained soils are defined as those having more than 50 percent of the particles, by dry weight, smaller than the No. 200 sieve. These soils are classified as either *silt* or *clay*, where silts generally exhibit little or no strength or cohesion when air dried, while clays exhibit high strengths or large cohesion when air dried. Individual clay particles are extremely small and can only be discerned by use of an electron microscope.

Fine-grained soils are also separated on the basis of *plasticity*, which is a measure of the ability of the soil to maintain a plastic consistency over a large range of moisture contents. As a result, both silts and clays may be classified as having either low or high plasticity. The engineering significance of these terms is discussed in Section 15.2.

Organic soils are those which contain sufficient organic matter to significantly influence the engineering behavior of the material. Typically, the term *organic* is applied to silts and clays, but not to coarse-grained soils.

Peats are fine-grained soils containing large amounts of vegetable matter in various stages of decomposition. The texture of peats may vary from amorphous (mucks) to highly fibrous. Such highly fibrous soils encountered in subarctic or arctic environments are often termed *muskeg*.

In general, organic silts and clays, as well as peats, are not suitable for support of building foundations and should be removed from the site or used for nonstructural landscaping features.

Soil Classification Symbols

Abbreviated symbols are used to characterize soils in accordance with the ASTM D 2487 classification system, and are included on logs of subsurface explorations, in addition to expanded word descriptions of each soil stratum encountered. Table 15.1 presents these symbols.

When the soil symbols shown in Table 15.1 are combined, the resultant designation is termed the Soil Group Symbol. For example:

```
GW = well graded gravel
SP = poorly graded sand
CH = highly plastic clay
OL = organic soil with low plasticity
```

Table 15.1. Soil Classification Symbols.

Major Constituents		Modifiers	
G	gravel	Coarse-grained soils	
S	sand	W	well graded
M	silt	P	poorly graded
C	clay	Fine-grained soils	
Pt	peat	L	low plasticity
		H	high plasticity
		O	organic

Soil Constituents

For purposes of understanding the basic terms applied to soil masses, it is possible to separate a soil mass conceptually into three basic constituents or phases: water, air or gas, and condensed solids, realizing that real soils are a combination of these phases. By determining the relative weights and volumes of each of these phases for a given soil sample in the field or laboratory, it is possible to define the following terms:

- *Void ratio*, expressed as a decimal, equals the volume of the voids (space occupied by air and water) divided by the volume of the solids
- *Moisture content*, expressed as a percentage, equals the weight of the water divided by the weight of the solids
- *Degree of saturation*, expressed as a percentage, equals the volume of water divided by the total available void space
- *Unit weight*, expressed in lb per ft^3 (kN per m^3), equals the total weight divided by the total volume
- *Dry unit weight*, expressed in lb per ft^3 (kN per m^3), equals the weight of the soil solids divided by the total volume of the soil sample for a condition where the moisture content is 0 percent

While geotechnical engineers use a variety of other terms from time to time, those described above have been shown to be the most pertinent when dealing with foundations and site-related earthwork.

General Characteristics of Major Soil Types

The general engineering characteristics of coarse and fine-grained soils are shown in Table 15.2.

15.2. ENGINEERING PROPERTIES OF SOILS

As with steel and concrete as structural materials, the two major engineering criteria when working with soils as foundation materials are the strength and deformation

Table 15.2. General Characteristics of Soil Types.

	Coarse Grained	Fine Grained
Drainage	moderate to excellent	poor
Strength	high	low
Sensitivity to moisture content changes	low	high
Compressibility	low	moderate to high
Compaction potential	good to excellent	fair to poor
Workability in wet weather	moderate to good	poor to virtually impossible (without expensive treatment)

(compressibility) characteristics under applied building loads. In addition, the permeability of the soils plays an important role since the rate at which water drains out of soil strata can have a substantial influence on the selection and design of suitable foundation systems for a project. Soil permeability is also a key factor in determining the necessity for installation of perimeter and underslab drains, as well as drains behind basements and site retaining walls.

Soil Shear Strength

Soil shear strength may be defined as the ability of a soil stratum to withstand shear stresses induced from loads applied through building foundations, the placement of fills or the construction of braced excavations for basements or retaining structures. Accurate determination of soil shear strength is also required for assessing the stability of natural or man-made slopes.

The three basic parameters required to determine the shear strength of a soil are, (1) the hydrostatic pressure in the water in the soil voids (termed porewater pressure), (2) the angle of internal friction of the soil mass, and (3) the cohesion of the soil. In coarse-grained soils the shear strength is derived from the grain-to-grain friction between particles. These soil types are termed *cohesionless*. The amount of friction developed is a function of the *effective stress* between the particles (similar to the stress developed between a block and an inclined frictional plane). This effective stress is equal to the total stress in the soil mass at the point in question, minus the hydrostatic porewater pressure at that point.

In fine-grained soils the shear strength results partially from internal friction and partially from cohesion. Cohesion occurs from the fact that large concentrations of unbalanced electromagnetic charges are present on the surfaces of the very small, platy clay particles. These unbalanced charges act as small magnets, causing the adsorption of water molecules (which are dipoles) and cations in the porewater to the clay surfaces, thereby binding the soil mass together cohesively.

The presence of porewater in coarse-grained soils has a relatively minor influence on shear strength, since the shear strength is derived primarily from grain-to-grain friction. As a result, the more compact or dense the granular mass, the greater the resultant shear strength. However, in fine-grained soils, especially clays, the greater the volume of porewater, the larger the separation between clay particles, resulting in a decrease in shear strength. Causing drainage of porewater from clays increases the shear strength of the soil substantially, while drainage of porewater from coarse-grained soils generally has a small effect on shear strength, since the orientation of the granular particles does not usually change significantly.

Methods of testing for shear strength in the laboratory commonly include direct shear devices, triaxial shear tests in which the soil sample is encapsulated in a confining chamber and subjected to vertical and horizontal stresses simulating field conditions, and vane shear tests run on cohesive soils by inserting and rotating an X-shaped vane in the sample to determine the resultant cohesion on the cylindrical soil failure surface.

When the shear strength of a soil is exceeded, the result is usually manifested as a rapid punching and/or rotation of foundations into the supporting strata, or as a downhill movement of substantial portions of natural or man-made slopes. If the extent of the movement and volume of material involved is sufficiently large, it is called a landslide.

Compressibility

The vertical deflection or settlement occurring in soils under foundations or other superimposed loads results from the compressibility of the supporting soil strata. In coarse-grained soils the amount of settlement which occurs is a function of the relative density of the bearing soils, or how closely oriented the particles are with respect to each other.

For saturated, fine-grained soils, as soon as the additional stress from foundations or superimposed loads is applied to the soil, it is instantaneously transmitted to the porewater, creating an excess hydrostatic head which in turn induces flow of the porewater out of the soil voids or interstitial spaces. As this drainage occurs, the fine-grained soil particles come into progressively closer proximity, thereby transferring an increasing percentage of the new stresses to the grain-to-grain soil structure. This process of drainage and transfer of stress to the soil grain structure in fine-grained soils is called *primary consolidation*, and continues until all of the additional stress has been transferred to the soil structure, at which time drainage ceases.

An additional phenomenon, known as *secondary consolidation*, is often observed in clays and most organic soils and peats, in which very gradual, progressively decreasing settlements continue to occur over a protracted time period. These secondary consolidation settlements, when they occur, usually are on the order of 20 percent or less of the primary consolidation settlement, however in some instances they can be considerably greater. This potential for secondary consolidation should be evaluated on the basis of the results of appropriate long-term laboratory consolidation tests.

Permeability

Permeability is the ability of a soil mass to accommodate fluid flow (usually water) as a function of time, and is expressed in cm per sec. Coarse-grained soils have relatively high permeabilities, ranging from approximately 10^{-4} cm per sec for clean sand and gravel mixtures to 10^2 cm per sec for clean gravels (Ref. 15.2). On the other hand, fine-grained soils, such as clays, may be nearly impervious, exhibiting permeabilities as low as 10^{-8} cm per sec to 10^{-9} cm per sec.

The rate at which settlements occur under stresses

induced from foundations or other superimposed loads is dependent on the permeability or rate at which porewater can drain from the bearing soils. As a result, settlements of foundations on coarse-grained bearing soils occur within a short time of the application of the additional loads, whereas consolidation and the resultant settlements of fine-grained soils may require from several weeks to several months or more for completion, depending on the permeability of the fine-grained soil.

15.3. SOIL EXPLORATION AND TESTING

Most of the technical specialists associated with building construction (e.g., architectural, structural, mechanical, and electrical engineers) may generally commence the design process almost immediately upon inception of a new project. The manufactured materials they are using in design (e.g., wood, metals, concrete, etc.) possess physical properties that are controlled in the manufacturing process and are described as given, i.e., known factors available from handbooks or other sources.

For the foundation engineer, the inception of a new project usually means a unique geographic site underlain by site-specific natural soil deposits with not only the nature and physical characteristics, but also the vertical and lateral extent, both unknown and likely to vary significantly across the site. Consequently, the foundation engineer cannot begin the design process until he has developed a reasonably accurate conception of the arrangement of the subsurface soil deposits, as well as the physical properties of the soils that will affect the final design. The field and laboratory methods utilized to obtain this essential information are commonly referred to as *soil exploration and testing*.

Development of sufficient information regarding site-specific soil conditions to permit an adequate yet economical design typically involves a significant expenditure of design funds. Therefore, careful planning and execution of exploration work should be supervised by an experienced foundation engineer. Without such guidance, inordinate or inappropriate expenses might be incurred, perhaps without generating the necessary information to permit a suitable design.

To plan an efficient exploration and testing program, a competent foundation engineer will first perform an office literature review of any available information that might provide some clues regarding site soil conditions. The appropriate literature might include such published information as topographic and geologic maps and reports, soil surveys for agricultural purposes, air photos, and prior explorations in the vicinity (e.g., borings or water well logs). The architect can provide valuable assistance at this stage by providing the foundation engineer with as much preliminary information as is available regarding the specifics of the project, such as configuration and on-site location (vertical and horizontal) of buildings and other facilities and estimated structural loads. Once this information has been assimilated, a site visit and reconnaissance should be made by the engineer to observe general site conditions, plan exploration accessibility, and modify as appropriate any preliminary plans for exploration and testing.

Site exploration most commonly consists of drilling a borehole into the ground and extracting samples of subsurface materials for identification, classification, and possible testing. Many variations exist in the equipment and procedures utilized for both drilling and sampling operations. The choice of methods should be based on the anticipated nature of subsurface materials and conditions and the type of design information needed for the specific project. Equipment and methods that proved very useful and economical for one site and project might be inappropriate, or perhaps even useless, in developing adequate information for another site or project. Because this process is an exploration of unknown conditions, methods chosen initially for the anticipated conditions might prove inefficient or ineffective if somewhat different or unanticipated conditions are encountered. Consequently, the exploration and testing program should remain flexible and be modified as appropriate based on subsurface information developed during the early stages. Where project size and importance permit, an exploration program consisting of two or more phases (e.g., preliminary, design, and construction phases) is often utilized for more efficient and productive use of exploration expenditures.

Drilling of exploratory borings is most often accomplished by truck-mounted rotary or auger (especially hollow-stem auger) drill rigs. For sites with equipment mobility problems (such as steep terrain or poor traction on soft, wet soils), track-mounted vehicles might be used to transport or assist drill equipment. Some smaller drills and light-weight equipment can even be transported by helicopter to highly inaccessible sites. Other drilling methods less commonly used include wash-borings, percussion drilling, large-diameter or bucket augers, air-rotary, and others. Each of these drilling methods has their own advantages and disadvantages which could render them relatively suitable or unsuitable for specific site subsurface conditions.

For smaller projects with relatively light structural loads on sites known to have good foundation soils near the ground surface, an economical yet adequate exploration program can often be accomplished with test pits excavated to maximum depths of about 10 feet (3 meters) by relatively inexpensive backhoe equipment. Because such excavations disturb the soils within the relatively large volume excavated, it is generally advised to locate such test pits outside the area of planned buildings and foundations.

Soil samples extracted from explorations vary in quality and usefulness depending on the procedures used and the degree of disturbance to the soils associated with excavation, drilling, and sampling methods. A *representative* sample contains all soil constituents in their proper proportions and is therefore suitable for proper identification and classification of soil type, including classification tests such as grain size analysis or Atterberg limits. However, a representative sample may have experienced a change in the arrangement of soil constituents relative to one another. This possible disturbance to the in-situ (in-place) soil structure, void ratio, or unit weight could alter the physical properties of the soil from the natural condition existing prior to sample extraction. Consequently, such samples are not suitable for tests to determine characteristics directly relevant to engineering behavior such as shear strength, compressibility, and in-place permeability to water flow.

If a sample is extracted in such a manner that it experiences negligible deformation during sampling, the soil structure, void ratio, and unit weight should not have been altered appreciably. As a result, a relatively *undisturbed* sample is obtained. Such a sample would not only be *representative* but would also be suitable for all tests to determine physical (engineering) properties.

Materials removed from the ground through the drilling or excavation procedures are usually sufficiently mixed and altered that the soil constituents are not in their proper proportions. These *nonrepresentative* samples might consist of materials removed from the ground by an auger drill, cuttings or choppings washed up in the drilling fluid of rotary or other wash boring methods, or materials excavated by a backhoe test pit. These samples are not suitable for proper identification and classification of soils and much less for physical property tests; however, they may have limited value in indicating changes in soil type encountered in drilling.

The most common and generally most economical method to obtain a high-quality, relatively undisturbed sample is to push a thin-wall steel tube (Shelby tube) into the soil and extract the tube with the contained sample by a steady pulling action. This may be accomplished at the bottom of a test boring using two- to three-inch-diameter tubes attached to the end of a string of drill rods. Unfortunately, this method is generally successful only for soils having sufficient cohesion to remain intact within the sample tube during extraction from the ground.

Cohesionless soils, such as sand and gravel, will fall out of a sample tube unless a core "catcher" device is added to the bottom of the tube. This device, however, results in disturbance of the soil. In addition, a sample tube can generally not be pushed into these soils but must be driven using a heavy drop hammer. The resulting vibrations also tend to alter or disturb the sample obtained. This procedure generally results in significant disturbance of the arrangement of soil particles but usually maintains soil constituents in their proper proportions. Thus, the *representative* sample usually obtained is suitable for proper identification and classification of soil type.

With the difficulties of obtaining undisturbed samples (especially in cohesionless soils), soil exploration programs often utilize methods that attempt to measure (directly or indirectly) pertinent soil properties in place on the site. A commonly utilized method is to measure the resistance to penetration of a sampler or other probe into the soil. One method is to count the number of blows to drive a split barrel sampler a given distance into the soil. To be consistent and useful in correlating with relevant engineering properties, the method of measurement must be standardized, as in the commonly utilized Standard Penetration Test (SPT) (ASTM Test Method D-1586). Using a standard two-inch-outside-diameter split barrel sampler driven by a standard 140-pound drop hammer free-falling 30 inches, the SPT resistance is stated as the number of blows (N-value) to advance the sampler one foot.

Another commonly used penetration test utilizes hydraulic rams to advance the standardized Dutch cone penetrometer (CPT) with measurement of the force necessary for advancement. Although this method obtains no soil sample, comparison of the measured point and friction sleeve resistance can be correlated with general soil type (cohesive versus cohesionless) and soil consistency or relative density. Although the CPT penetrometer is limited in use to soils of low to moderate hardness, it is considerably less expensive to use on a footage basis than typical drilling and sampling techniques.

15.4. FOUNDATION SYSTEMS

The purpose of a foundation system for a building is to transfer dead and live loads from the roof, floors, walls and columns into the underlying supporting soil strata. Various types of foundation systems are used depending on the intensity of the loads transmitted to the foundation level and the ability of the bearing soils to accommodate these loads.

Shallow Foundations

Shallow foundations are defined as those where the ratio of the depth to the bottom of the foundation element from the lowest adjacent finished grade compared to the width of the foundation unit is less than 4. The most common shallow foundation is the *footing*, where footings under single columns are termed *isolated* or *spread* footings. Footings supporting more than one column are called *combined* footings. Footings beneath walls are called *strip* or *continuous* footings (see Fig. 15.4.1). The purpose of footings is to distribute the loads carried by walls and columns over a

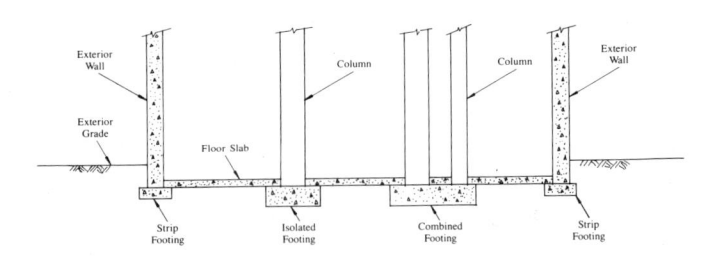

Fig. 15.4.1. Foundations for footings.

sufficiently large basal area so that the stresses induced in the underlying soils will not cause a shear strength failure or excessive settlements of the supported building elements.

Where the subsurface soils are competent at and below the foundation level, footings are the most economical means of building support since they require a minimal amount of labor to form, and the soil bearing surface is usually readily accessible for inspection prior to casting the concrete.

As indicated in Ref. 15.3, *mats* are foundations which cover a substantial area of the building footprint, if not the entire building area, and are used in relatively specialized cases where the underlying soils are so weak that the cumulative spread footing areas calculated on the basis of the allowable soil bearing pressure equal 50 percent or more of the building area. These mats are typically constructed as thick, reinforced concrete slabs (see Fig. 15.4.2). Mats are also used where the subsurface soils are highly compressible and the anticipated total settlements, or the differential settlements between adjacent columns carrying substantially different loads, cannot be tolerated. In such cases, the mat is often constructed after excavating several feet of soil in order to reduce the additional stresses transmitted to the underlying bearing soils. If the total weight of the soil excavated is sufficient to equal the weight of the proposed building, the resulting mat is called a *raft*, and is a *fully compensated* or *floating foundation*.

Deep Foundations

Deep foundations are installed to transmit superstructure loads through weak or compressible upper soils down to competent underlying strata; in instances where design of the building superstructure results in very high, concentrated column loads; for structures sensitive to unequal or differential settlements; for projects where it is necessary to transfer loads to depths equal to or greater than the foundations for existing adjacent structures; and to provide uplift resistance and/or lateral load capacity.

Driven Piles. Driven piles consist of long, relatively slender units made of timber, concrete, or steel which are installed into subsurface soil strata by use of a pile-driving hammer which imparts energy through the pile material to the pile tip. An adequate amount of energy must reach the tip in order to advance the pile through the soil. Support of these piles is derived through bearing of the tip on or in a dense soil stratum (*end-bearing piles*), through friction mobilized between the soil and the sides of the pile (*friction piles*), or through a combination of end-bearing and friction, depending on the properties of the subsurface soils (see Fig. 15.4.3).

Usually at least three piles are used to support a column, while single piles are often used for support of points along wall sections. For heavily loaded structures, it is not unusual to install clusters of up to 12 or more piles at a column location. The group or cluster of piles is normally imbedded in a pile cap, which in turn supports the building column positioned at the centroid of the pile cluster. If the pile cluster is expected to resist uplift loads which may occur from forces such as wind loads or seismic events, it is necessary to structurally tie the tops (butts) of the piles into the pile cap.

Timber piles typically carry maximum allowable loads of 25 tons (222 kN) or less for each pile, while concrete and steel piles may be installed to support individual loads of up to 120 tons (1,070 kN) or more, depending on the pile diameter and the properties of the bearing soils. *Concrete piles* are precast in horizontal casting beds and usually are prestressed with high-strength steel strands to resist the bending moments induced during removal of the piles from the casting bed, transportation to the project site, and pickup and vertical positioning under the hammer in the pile driving leads. *Steel piles* may consist of rolled H-sections, or a steel pipe section driven into the ground and subsequently filled with concrete (*concrete-filled steel pipe piles*). Usually these piles are driven with a circular closure plate welded to the tip of the pile to preclude intrusion of soil or water into the pipe. Upon occasion the pipe pile may be driven open-ended (without a closure plate on the tip), and later cleaned out before placement of the concrete fill in the pipe.

Cast-in-place concrete piles are installed by driving a heavy fabricated steel unit (mandrel) into the subsurface soils with a light-weight, corrugated metal sheath encompassing the mandrel. Once the mandrel/sheath combination has been driven to the required depth or final penetration

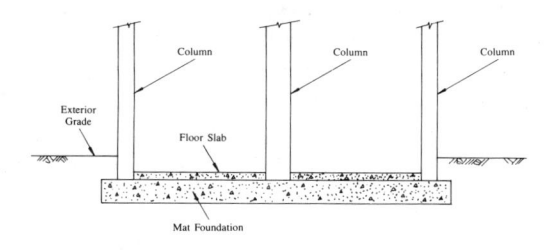

Fig. 15.4.2. Mat foundation.

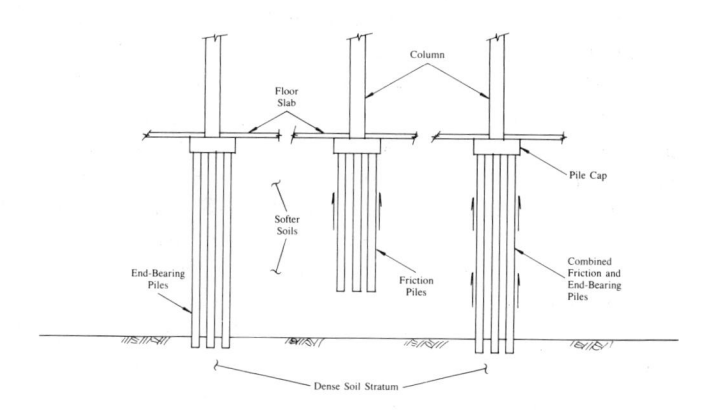

Fig. 15.4.3. Pile foundations.

resistance, the mandrel is withdrawn and the remaining corrugated metal form filled with concrete.

Conventional pile-driving hammers include single-acting and double or differential-acting hammers, as well as diesel-powered hammers. The *single-acting hammer* is powered by either steam or compressed air pressure lifting a heavy internal ram, which then falls by gravity, imparting energy to the top of the pile through an anvil attached to the bottom of the hammer configuration. *Double/differential-acting hammers* utilize steam or air pressure to lift a lighter internal ram, as well as to force the ram down in addition to gravity effects. These hammers are therefore lighter, operate approximately twice as fast, and tend to experience less mechanical wear than single-acting hammers. *Vibratory hammers* are used upon occasion, especially for the installation of sheetpile walls or bulkheads in granular soils, and for extracting piles or sheetpile sections from the ground where necessary.

Augered Piles. The most common type of augered pile is installed by advancing a single-flight auger having a hollow shaft into the ground, and then pumping cement grout through the hollow stem as the auger is slowly withdrawn. This type of pile is particularly effective in subsurface conditions where a significant portion of the support capacity can be derived from the skin friction developed between the grouted shaft and the surrounding soil. However, it should be noted that this pile is effective only where the installation can be completed without the risk of the surrounding soil caving or squeezing into the augered hole, causing a reduction in the grouted shaft diameter, or complete disruption of the grouted shaft. Because of this concern, it is important that the contractor be carefully screened on the basis of previous experience with successful installations in similar subsurface soil and groundwater conditions.

Pressure-Injected Footings. A specialized foundation unit called the pressure-injected footing, or compacted concrete pile, was originated by Franki International for use primarily in deep deposits of loose to medium dense, clean sands where installation of conventional, high-capacity, driven piles is not economical due to the excessive lengths required to penetrate to a dense or hard bearing stratum. This installation process involves driving a large diameter, thick-walled steel tube into the ground by dropping a cylindrical ram on a plug of zero-slump concrete placed in the bottom of the drive tube prior to driving. The energy generated by the falling ram is approximately 140,000 ft-lb (190 kN-m), which is several times greater than most conventional pile-driving hammers. Once the drive tube has reached the required depth, it is held stationary while the original and successive plugs of zero-slump concrete are driven out of the bottom of the tube. This process results in the formation of a relatively dry concrete bulb in the sand stratum, and the creation of a large, highly densified sphere of compacted sand surrounding the concrete plug. The drive tube is then withdrawn slowly as concrete is extruded through the tube to form the pile shaft. If weak soils are present in the subsurface profile above the compacted concrete base, a corrugated metal pipe is used as a form for the shaft concrete. These units have been shown to be capable of successfully supporting loads in excess of 140 tons (1,245 kN).

Piers. Foundation piers (not to be confused with waterfront docks or with bridge piers) are cylindrical shafts having diameters larger than 24 in. (60 cm) which are drilled into the underlying soils, usually by large augers, and filled with concrete. These foundation units are capable of supporting loads which are many times greater than the load-carrying capacity of a single pile. Depending on the geographical location of the project, these installations may be termed *drilled shafts* or *caissons*. Support for superstructure loads is provided by extending the shaft through less competent soils down to a suitable soil bearing layer, or to bedrock, where the base of the shaft acts as a spread footing on the bearing layer. Additional load-carrying capacity can be derived from skin friction between the completed concrete shaft and the soils above the bearing stratum if these soils are not subject to future settlement with respect to the shaft.

In instances where the subsoils include sands below the groundwater table, a soil slurry is introduced into the shaft to hold the hole open during augering. In this case, concrete fill is placed by tremie from the bottom of the completed shaft excavation, displacing the slurry upward as the concrete placement progresses. Where the subsurface stratigraphy includes loose fill, soft clays, or organic soils such as peat, a casing is driven or twisted into the ground ahead of the auger to prevent squeezing of these materials in the shaft excavation, and the soil inside the casing is excavated by the auger. The casing is withdrawn as concrete placement progresses, always maintaining a positive head of fresh concrete up inside the casing.

Upon occasion, it may be feasible to gain additional frictional support by drilling the shaft several feet into bedrock, if the bedrock is within an economical distance from the ground surface. This type of installation is called a *rock-socketed pier* or *rock-socketed caisson*.

In cases where the soils overlying the bearing stratum are sufficiently stiff or cohesive to preclude caving, the base of the shaft may be enlarged by an underreaming tool to form a bell with a diameter approximately three times the diameter of the shaft. This type of foundation unit is often referred to as a *belled pier* or *belled caisson*. These belled piers have the advantage of supporting larger loads because of the increased bearing area at the base of the bell, while effecting economy of materials by using smaller-diameter shafts.

15.5. DESIGN CONSIDERATIONS

The selection of a technically suitable and economical foundation system for support of a building depends on a variety of factors, including the building configuration and structural loads to be supported, sensitivity of the structure to total and differential settlements, presence and depth of unsuitable soils, types of subsurface soils encountered, depth to the groundwater table, proximity to existing adjacent structures, and the potential influence of proposed future construction, among others. A detailed discussion of all of these and other factors is beyond the scope of this section; however, the most common factors encountered in the selection and design of building foundations are summarized below. Where typical dimensions or values are indicated, they are presented only to provide the reader with a sense of perspective and should not be used for actual design purposes. Since soil conditions are different at each site, and the configuration and requirements of planned structures vary widely, it is imperative that an experienced geotechnical engineer be engaged to undertake a thorough analysis of the project site and to provide specific design and construction recommendations for the proposed project.

Building Loads (see Chapter 9)

The building loads to be supported by the foundation system include the dead loads of the roof, floors, walls, and columns, the loads attributed to stationary mechanical equipment, and the live loads anticipated due to the intended use of the facility. While the dead loads are not difficult to determine, it should be noted that the live loads to be included in the analysis for selection and design of the foundations may vary, as discussed below.

While it is necessary to design the floors of the building for the maximum anticipated live load which may occur on any portion of the floor, economy in the foundation system may be realized if the live loads are reduced when they are calculated as contributing to the column loads. This can be evaluated by determining the percentage of the contributory floor area which will experience the design live loads at any one time. For example, the maximum live loads anticipated to be carried to columns in a typical office building may be on the order of 50 to 60 percent of the live loads used for design of the floor slab itself, since these floors are never totally loaded by furniture, equipment, files, and people.

In addition, since settlements of foundations supported on coarse-grained soils occur almost as quickly as the loads from the structure are applied, it is necessary to design the foundations for the maximum realistic live loads to be transmitted to the underlying bearing soils at any one time. On the other hand, settlements of foundations on fine-grained soils, such as clays, are a function of the time-dependent consolidation characteristics of the soil, which is defined primarily by its permeability. As a result, the appropriate live loads to be used in the design of foundations on these compressible fine-grained soils should be based on the average long-term live loads anticipated in the structure.

Frost Protection

Building foundations should be established below the anticipated depth of frost penetration, as measured from the lowest adjacent finished grade exposed to freezing temperatures, to prevent heaving of foundation elements. This frost penetration depth varies widely, depending on geographic location and climatic conditions. For example, the normal frost penetration depth in coastal areas of the Pacific Northwest area of the United States is approximately 15 to 18 in. (38 to 46 cm), while the frost depth in northern portions of New England can exceed 5 ft (1.5 m). An official in the Building Department of the municipality closest to the project site should be contacted if there is any question regarding the normal frost depth in the area of the proposed project.

Presence of Unsuitable Soils

As increased growth occurs in many areas, prime building sites become more scarce. It is therefore not unusual to encounter sites which may have a layer of loose natural soil, miscellaneous fill, or highly compressible soils, such as peat, extending to some depth below the ground surface. In such cases it may be possible to excavate the loose natural soils and replace and thoroughly recompact the same material in place if it is inorganic and generally coarse grained.

If the surficial layer consists of miscellaneous fill, peat, or other unsuitable soils, these materials cannot be used for support of structural loads and should be excavated and disposed of away from the building site. In such situations, the resultant excavation is normally backfilled with compacted granular material. The decision whether to employ this excavation and replacement technique is mainly a matter of economics, and depends on the cost of removal and disposal of the unsuitable material, as well as the cost of purchasing, placing, and compacting acceptable imported backfill. Experience has indicated that for structures such as office buildings, if the depth of material to be removed and replaced is greater than 6 to 8 ft (1.8 to 2.4 m), it is generally more economical to consider using deeper foundations and constructing the lowest floor as a structural slab supported by normally spaced columns.

It should be noted that if the unsuitable layer left in place consists of peat or organic material, such as household garbage, special precautions must be taken to protect against the migration of gases generated by the organic matter, such as methane, into the building.

Shallow Foundations

As indicated in Section 15.2, the ability of a soil stratum to support building loads depends primarily on the shear strength and compressibility of the soil. The bearing capacity of the soil is a function of the soil strength and the depth of embedment of the foundation in the soil stratum. The depth to which stresses are distributed to the bearing soils below the foundations is a linear function of the least plan dimension of the foundation element, therefore the bearing capacity of the soil is also directly related to the width of the footing.

Very narrow footings on both coarse-grained and fine-grained soils have a tendency to punch into the bearing stratum as a result of a bearing capacity failure in the soil. Therefore, most strip footings are recommended to be at least 18 in. (460 mm) in width and most isolated column footings are recommended to be at least 24 in. (600 mm) wide. A factor of safety of 3.0 against a bearing capacity failure is normally used when recommending maximum allowable soil bearing pressures for foundation design.

The estimated settlements to be experienced under the maximum allowable soil bearing pressure selected on the basis of bearing capacity considerations must be evaluated and this design bearing pressure reduced accordingly if the anticipated settlements cannot be tolerated by the structure. Typically buildings are capable of withstanding total settlements of up to 1 in. (25 mm) and differential settlements of 0.75 in. (19 mm) between normally spaced adjacent columns.

The depth of stress influence is also an important consideration in estimating the amount of settlement, particularly where the bearing stratum consists of compressible soils, such as clays. The configuration of the induced stresses in the soil beneath a footing is often called the *bulb of influence*. Generally the intensity of the transmitted stresses drops to about 8 percent of the soil bearing pressure applied by the footing at a depth below the footing equal to about twice the width of the footing. Consequently, if two footings are designed for the same soil bearing pressure, but the width of one footing is twice that of the other footing, the larger footing can be expected to settle twice as much as the smaller one, assuming similar soil conditions. In structures supported by spread footings on clays and having column loads which differ considerably, it is possible to minimize the differential settlements between the columns by adjusting the design soil bearing pressures for various footings, thereby equilibrating the anticipated total settlements at the column locations.

Stepped Footings

If below-grade spaces, such as electrical vaults or partial basements, are to be incorporated into the building design, it is important that wall and column footings be stepped down in the area of the below-grade space. The elevations of the bottoms of these footings should be designed to prevent stresses from an adjacent, higher footing overlapping and adding to the soil stresses induced by the lower footing. This typically can be accomplished if the bottom edge of each successively lower footing is designed to be above an imaginary plane sloped downward at 1.5:1 (horizontal:vertical) from the bottom edge of the adjacent higher footing. In some soil conditions use of a slope as steep as 1:1 (H:V) may be warranted, depending on the specific recommendations of the geotechnical engineer for the project.

Preloading and Surcharging

For some types of structures, such as large warehousing facilities, it is usually not economical to support the lowest floor slab structurally. If compressible materials underlie the floor area, it often is possible to support the building superstructure on deeper foundations and isolate the floor slab from the columns, allowing it to settle independently. Quite often floor slab settlements up to 2 to 3 in. (50 to 75 mm) can be tolerated without disrupting the efficient use of the facility.

At sites underlain by compressible soils, the anticipated lowest floor slab settlement may be excessive if it is supported on grade, particularly where the floor loads are high, as occurs in warehousing and some manufacturing facilities. In such cases, it is often possible to place a temporary fill over the building area to cause consolidation and settlements in the underlying soils prior to actual building construction. If the weight of the fill is about equal to the dead and live loads on the floor slab, the temporary fill is called a *preload*. If additional fill is placed so that the total fill weight is greater than the dead and live floor loads, the additional fill is called a *surcharge*.

The preload/surcharge fill is left in place while field observations are made of settlement platforms installed at the base of the fill, with risers extending up through the fill. By analyzing the results of the field settlement observations, it is possible to predict when all of the settlement induced by the fill will occur. Depending on the thickness and consolidation characteristics of the underlying compressible soils, this process may take as little as two to three weeks from completion of the preload/surcharge, but in some cases may require several months or more to occur. Once the preload/surcharge is removed, there usually is very little rebound in the underlying soils. Therefore, the lowest floor slab may be designed as a slab supported on grade and will usually experience only a minor amount of settlement, if any.

It may be expensive to purchase and place a preload/surcharge fill, and then remove and dispose of the material once the induced settlements are completed. However, in many circumstances granular base-course material is required for driveways and parking areas adjacent to the building. As a result, large savings can be realized by using the granular base-course material as the preload/surcharge fill in the building area, then moving and spreading the same material in the areas to be paved once the preload/surcharge period has been completed. Experience has shown that very often the amount of material required for the pavement base course is approximately equal to the volume of material required for the preload fill.

If the proposed building is adjacent to an existing structure, it is important to assess the effects of the preload/surcharge fill on the soils beneath the existing building so that settlements and potential distress to the existing structure can be avoided. In a similar vein, if an expansion of the proposed building is planned for construction in the future, it is expedient to extend the preload/surcharge fill a sufficient distance into the future expansion area so that preloading in the expansion area at a later date will not cause settlements or distress to the presently proposed structure.

Pile Foundations

The selection of the most economical pile foundation system for support of superstructure loads is dependent on the depth to suitable bearing materials, the types of piles available locally, the magnitude of the loads to be supported, and the cost per supported ton (kN) for each pile type. In general, the greatest economy is realized when the capacity of the piles is matched against the column loads so that each pile is loaded as close to the maximum allowable design load as possible, thereby effecting the greatest efficiency from the pile cluster. Except in special cases, it is advisable to analyze all of the column loads in the structure to select one specific pile type and diameter. Mixing pile types and sizes on a project may result in installing the wrong pile in some locations due to potential confusion in the field during construction. In addition, mixing pile types is not necessarily economical, since it may be necessary to mobilize different pile-driving hammers and other equipment.

Preaugering or Spudding

Advancing a pilot hole by augering prior to the installation of a pile may be required in instances where the pile must penetrate a denser layer overlying weak or compressible soils in order to achieve end-bearing resistance on or in a deeper bearing stratum. *Preaugering* is also used when a large number of piles are to be installed in a relatively small area and upward displacement of the building subgrade may result from the volume of soil displaced by the piles. In addition, preaugering is used where the vibrations resulting from driving piles from the ground surface may cause distress to adjacent structures.

Spudding is the process of advancing a pilot hole by driving a heavy steel section in order to penetrate buried obstructions which may be present beyond the normal reach of a backhoe.

Downdrag or Negative Skin Friction

If piles are to be installed through soil layers which are anticipated to settle under their own weight (such as recent fills) or due to the influence of future surface loads (such as built-up landscaping or materials stored adjacent to the structure), additional downward friction loads will be transmitted to the piles as the soil settles relative to the installed piles. This phenomenon is called *downdrag* or *negative skin friction*, and must be accounted for when determining the allowable capacity of the piles to support building loads.

Pile Hammer Selection

Depending on the type of pile material and the cross-sectional area of the pile, it is possible to split, broom, crack, or rupture a pile if the dynamic stresses induced during driving are excessive. As a rough rule of thumb only, the rated energy of the pile hammer in ft-lb should be approximately equal to 14 percent of the allowable pile design load expressed in pounds, or slightly greater. Notwithstanding this empirical criterion, a minimum rated energy of 15,000 ft-lb per hammer blow (20 kN-m per blow) is commonly used.

Prior to actual or production pile installation, the final penetration resistance in hammer blows per inch (hammer blows per cm) required to achieve the design pile load capacity should be determined based on the characteristics of the pile-driving hammer and cushion block configuration to be used by the contractor. This is commonly done using a compact computer program which simulates the hammer configuration and the subsurface soil properties. The program yields the ultimate pile capacity versus final penetration hammer blows per inch (blows per cm), as well as the maximum compressive and tensile stresses induced in the pile during driving.

Test Piles

For projects requiring a large number of high-capacity piles, it is common to perform from one to several pile load tests, in which single piles are driven at selected locations in the building area and subsequently loaded in increments to approximately twice the design load. The results of these tests are plotted as load versus vertical deflection curves, and analyzed to either verify the original pile design or modify it, as appropriate.

In some geographic areas the term *test pile* is erroneously used instead of *indicator pile*. Indicator piles are driven at the contractor's option at several locations on the site to determine the length(s) of piles to be ordered for the project. These indicator piles are not load tested.

Pile Spacing

Typically, piles in clusters are spaced a minimum of 2.5 to 3.0 diameters apart, center-to-center. This is done to promote *individual action* where support is derived by end-bearing and skin friction on the circumference of each pile. More closely spaced piles tend to act as a group, where skin friction occurs on the periphery of the total group configuration. The exception to this general practice occurs when pressure-injected footings are installed. Because of the size of the extruded concrete bulb bases for these units, the recommended minimum pile spacing is 54 in. [137 cm].

Pile Length Prediction

Other than calculating the length of piles deriving support solely from skin friction, it is difficult to accurately predict the depth of embedment necessary for end-bearing support in some soil strata, especially where the density or strength of the bearing soils tends to increase gradually with depth. As a result, it is recommended that the length of piles to be ordered for a project should be the responsibility of the pile contractor, who should have extensive local experience in installing piles in similar subsurface conditions. To aid the contractor in his evaluation, the logs of all of the subsurface explorations should also be made available, and the contract plans and specifications should designate the bearing stratum into which the piles are to be installed. In addition, the specifications should allow the contractor the opportunity to drive a reasonable number of indicator piles, if he so chooses.

15.6. RETAINING WALLS

Analysis of horizontal earth pressures is required for the structural design of basement walls and for walls to be constructed on the site for finished grade separations. In addition to horizontal earth pressures, large hydrostatic water pressures may act on the backs of these retaining walls if the soil backfill behind the walls is not fully drained. As a result, it is good practice to provide perforated drains surrounded by free-draining, coarse-grained soils at the base of all retaining walls. In general, soils containing more than 5 percent by weight passing the No. 200 sieve do not drain readily, and to be truly free-draining the amount of fines passing the No. 200 sieve should be limited to less than three percent. If the backfill material cannot be drained for some reason, the wall must be designed for the full hydrostatic water pressure calculated on the basis of the highest anticipated water level in the backfill.

Cantilevered Retaining Walls (Fig. 15.6.1.a)

For walls which are free to rotate outward slightly about the base (that is, walls which are not restrained at the top),

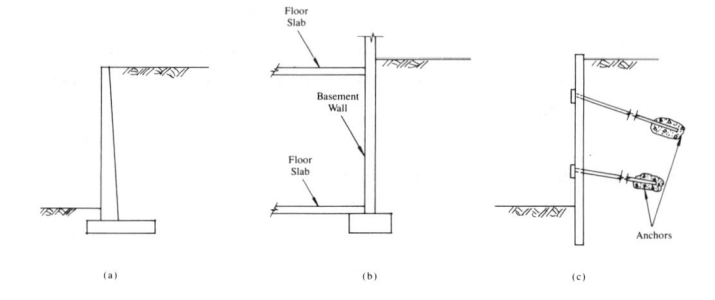

Fig. 15.6.1. Retaining walls. (a) Cantilevered retaining wall; (b) braced retaining wall; (c) tied-back retaining wall.

the Rankine active horizontal earth pressure condition is usually applicable for design. This "active" condition occurs in coarse-grained soils when the outward movement of the top of the wall is approximately equal to 0.5 percent of the wall height. For this condition, the horizontal earth pressure on the wall can be taken as a triangular distribution resulting from a fluid having an equivalent density of approximately one-third of the unit weight of the backfill soil. Since the active horizontal earth pressure is a function of the angle of internal friction of the backfill, it is necessary to complete the appropriate geotechnical analyses to determine the recommended design horizontal earth pressure for a specific project.

Braced Retaining Walls (Fig. 15.6.1.b and c)

The horizontal earth pressure imposed on the back of braced walls depends on the method of bracing and the sequence of backfilling. Some relatively shallow basement walls are constructed and braced by interior floor slabs prior to backfilling, while other deeper excavations may be supported by temporary or permanent wall systems which derive horizontal support by tied-back anchors drilled well back into the soils behind the wall. The tied-back wall technique is advantageous because it eliminates the need for interior horizontal or inclined structural braces and allows total access to the excavation for foundation and building construction. Because of varying soil conditions and local experience with tied-back retaining wall systems, it is important that the anticipated horizontal earth pressures be determined by a geotechnical engineer having extensive experience in the vicinity of the project site.

15.7. CONSTRUCTION CONSIDERATIONS

For even a thorough and detailed soil exploration program, borings are often located 100 feet (30 meters) or more apart, perhaps one at each corner of a proposed building. Natural soil deposits do not necessarily occur in well-defined horizontal layers, as illustrated in many textbooks. In nature, soil deposits can vary significantly in both the horizontal and vertical directions. Consequently, the soil explorations represent subsurface conditions only at the specific location they were made and typically may represent only about one ten-thousandth of the total soil affecting a project on the site. For economic reasons, practical foundation design must usually be based on this limited sampling of a nonhomogeneous natural soil material. As a result it should be expected that some variations and differences in subsurface conditions are likely to exist between exploration locations that could alter the validity of the original foundation design. Some of these variations are frequently exposed during construction excavations. If detected at this time it is often not too late to modify the design in a relatively economical manner that can make the difference between a successful foundation and one that is fraught with future problems.

It is very important, therefore, to continue the subsurface exploration program during the construction phase with observations by a qualified geotechnical engineer. In many circumstances it is advantageous to supplement visual observations during construction with additional exploration, testing, or other measurements pertinent to performance of the foundation design. The additional expense of such construction monitoring is typically a small fraction of the total construction cost and yet can often result in much larger cost savings through a more economical design and/or avoidance of expensive remedial repairs if post-construction problems arise.

To illustrate the reality of this situation, the Association of Soil and Foundation Engineers (ASFE) suggests, "expect the unexpected" during excavation and construction for foundations. Because such unexpected subsurface conditions often require additional expenditures for a properly constructed project, some contingency fund is advisable to accommodate such potential extra costs.

The remainder of this section will discuss briefly the various aspects of construction that can influence the performance and cost of the foundation design.

Site Preparation

Prior to placement of foundations for structures, good construction practice requires some preparation for essentially all project sites. Such preparation typically can include demolition of existing construction, clearing and grubbing of vegetation, removal of unsuitable materials, and earthwork grading such as excavation and/or fill placement.

Demolition of existing facilities such as buildings and pavements produces debris and rubble that requires disposal. Under most circumstances it is usually preferable to dispose of these materials off site. In some situations it may be reasonable to dispose of some types of rubble at select locations on site, provided only appropriate locations and placement techniques are utilized. Materials disposed on site should always be limited to durable mineral fragments (such as concrete or brick rubble) with negligible content of organic, wood, metallic, or plastic fragments. The mineral fragments should be placed so they are completely surrounded by soil fines to avoid nesting and large voids between larger fragments. Placement locations should be limited to areas outside of settlement-sensitive facilities such as buildings. Placement methods should conform to those described below for compacted fill.

The term *clearing and grubbing* is normally used to describe the site preparation construction operation of removing existing vegetation and related stumps and roots. Because organic materials decompose with time, these materials should not be left in place or buried by fills. They may be disposed by burying on site (if permitted) in nonstructural areas or hauling to an off-site disposal area.

Even after clearing and grubbing, the ground surface at most sites generally consists of a relatively thin zone of topsoil. This consists of a mixture of mineral matter weathered from the underlying parent soil or rock and partially decomposed organic material. The high organic content of these materials also renders them unsuitable as fill soils to underlie project facilities. The topsoil should be stripped (down to all-mineral soil or rock materials) and disposed off site. Alternatively, the stripped topsoil may be stockpiled for later use in landscaped areas.

On many sites there may exist surficial layers or pockets of materials (natural or man-placed) that for various reasons are unsuitable for use in engineered fills. Such material often includes (but is not limited to) problem soils discussed in Section 15.8, such as existing fill (including rubble and trash), highly organic or peat soils, and swelling soils. All such unsuitable soils should be excavated and disposed either off site or in specially designated areas on site where they are not likely to adversely affect the proposed project facilities. In rare instances it might be possible to process such materials on site to render them suitable for use in engineered fills, but such treatment is frequently cost prohibitive.

As a step in site preparation, earthwork operations generally consist of excavation (cut) of earth materials from one location and placement as fill at another location. For an economical design, it is desirable that cut and fill volumes at a site are close to equal (i.e., balance). This avoids the added expense of hauling borrow or import materials to the site or excess excavation away from the site.

Excavations

On-site excavations are generally required for most projects as part of earthwork operations and site grading and/or for placement of foundations below the ground surface. Excavation of earth materials is generally classified as soil on rock. Most definitions of *soil* versus *rock* relate to the degree of cementation between individual particles, which also affects the difficulty of excavating the material. From a construction consideration, *soil* is generally accepted to refer to earth materials that can readily be excavated by typical earthmoving equipment such as bulldozers, rubber-tired scrapers, backhoes, clamshell, or other power shovels.

Rock is generally defined as material which requires drilling and placement of explosives to break the rock into fragments that can then be handled by earthmoving equipment.

Using this distinction, the cost per unit volume for excavating rock can typically be 5 to 50 times that of soil. Therefore, it is usually economically advantageous to minimize or avoid altogether the need for rock excavation whenever possible. In reality, there is a continuous spectrum in degree of cementation and excavation difficulty between soil and rock. Some earth materials intermediate in character can often be broken into fragment sizes suitable for excavation using a process called *ripping*. This consists of tearing the material apart by one or more large metal ripper teeth mounted on large crawler-type tractors with hydraulic rams to exert downward pressure. Many rocklike materials have natural planes of weakness, sufficient weathering, and/or low degree of cementation such that they are rippable using appropriate equipment. Although unit volume costs for ripping are generally greater than for soil excavation, they can be significantly less than rock excavation requiring blasting.

The steepness at which excavation side slopes can stand without instability depends primarily on the strength of the earth materials, as well as secondary factors such as climate, height of slope, length of time, and others. Required slope inclinations for stable conditions can range from vertical for strong materials such as massive bedrock to 3H:1V (horizontal to vertical), or flatter, for relatively weak soils.

Adverse consequences of slope failure can range from a minor nuisance and expense of cleaning a few small slides to the major disaster of injury or death to personnel within the excavation. The factor of safety and degree of conservatism used in establishing slope inclinations should make appropriate consideration of the consequences of failure. Responsibility for safety of temporary slopes should belong to the contractor who is in the best position to constantly monitor them and take appropriate action to promote safety when required.

Particularly in urban areas, the presence of nearby facilities (e.g., buildings, streets, utilities, etc.) precludes sloping of excavation sides. Under these circumstances it may be necessary to use vertical slopes and provide temporary support of the excavation sides. Such temporary support systems must be designed to support anticipated lateral soil pressures. If the system permits lateral movement of the soil toward the excavation, the adjacent ground surface will settle, which could result in adverse effects on adjacent facilities. Consequently, design and installation of the bracing should be performed by professionals experienced in such matters.

Temporary *bracing* commonly consists of wood, metal, or concrete sheets placed to support the sides of the excavation. Additional structural members are often used to resist the lateral soil pressures. If these load-carrying members consist of struts or rakers placed within the excavation, they present the inconvenience of being in the way of construction of the permanent structure. To permit an open work area inside the excavation, load-carrying tensile struts called *tiebacks* can be drilled or driven into the soil outside the excavation.

If an excavation extends below the foundation level of an adjacent structure, it may be necessary to provide temporary support for that structure (*shoring*) during construction. In some situations it may be necessary to strengthen, replace or extend in depth the foundation of an existing structure using an operation referred to as *underpinning*. More detailed descriptions of methods used for temporary bracing of excavations, shoring, and underpinning is available in Ref. 15.4.

If a proposed building excavation will extend below the level of the groundwater, seepage into the excavation can adversely affect construction operations and possibly the long-term performance of the building foundations. In low-permeability soils such as clay, the volume of water seepage may be insignificant, but seepage pressures may create stability problems with the sides or base of the excavation. Disturbance to the foundation soils from the seepage pressures can also result in excessive postconstruction building settlement.

In soils of moderate to high permeability (such as silts and sands) the seepage volume can partially or completely fill the excavation, making construction of foundations virtually impossible. In addition the seepage pressures may not only disturb the soils, thereby increasing settlement, but can also erode the soils if they lack sufficient cohesion. This erosion can extend back into the soils away from the excavation in a process called *internal erosion* or *piping* that can threaten areas beyond the excavation itself.

To avoid most of these groundwater-related problems, it is generally desirable to lower the groundwater level within the proposed excavation. The results are most effective when the water level is lowered before the excavation is made. This can typically be accomplished by pumping from a system of wells or similar installations (see Ref. 15.5 for details). The water level can also be lowered as the excavation advances by pumping from shallow pits (*sumps*) extending slightly below the current temporary level of the general excavation. Although pumping from sumps may remove all free water from the excavation, in some soil conditions (e.g., stratified soils, lower permeabilities, etc.) this method may not be totally effective in eliminating excavation instability and soil disturbance from seepage pressures.

In some soil conditions, temporary or permanent lowering of the water table can result in excessive ground settlements that can extend some distance horizontally and adversely affect nearby structures. Planning, design, installation, and monitoring of dewatering operations should be performed by personnel experienced in these methods.

Fill Placement and Compaction

In numerous instances, excavated earth materials placed as fill have been responsible for major building damage as a result of excessive differential settlement, lateral pressures and deformation, and downslope movements or landslides. However, with proper placement and compaction of suitable materials, earthwork fill is capable of providing successful foundation support for multistory buildings, in many instances exceeding the quality of the natural site soils.

In general, the greater the density (dry unit weight) of a soil mass the more favorable its foundation support characteristics of high strength and low compressibility. Consequently, the engineered placement of fill utilizes mechanical compaction methods to achieve as high a density as practical for fill soils. This is best achieved by placement of the soil in relatively thin layers or *lifts*, typically not exceeding 4 to 12 inches (10 to 30 cm), with each lift thoroughly compacted prior to placing the next lift.

Compaction is accomplished by mechanical equipment suited to the specific soil type. For large volumes of fill in embankments, equipment usually consists of a heavy steel drum roller that is either self-propelled or mounted behind a towing vehicle such as a crawler tractor. Compaction of cohesive soils (silts and clays) is generally best accomplished by a sheepsfoot roller having radial protrusions (feet) extending from the face of the drum. Cohesionless soils (sands and gravels) are generally best compacted by a smooth steel drum roller with a vibratory action provided by a power source. Three to eight passes of an appropriate roller are generally required to achieve good compaction densities.

Where fill (or backfill) must be placed in locations with limited space (such as behind retaining walls and in utility trenches), large roller compactors cannot be used. In such limited areas cohesive soils can be compacted by smaller pneumatic or mechanical tampers and cohesionless soils by small vibratory rollers or plates. To achieve adequate compaction with these lower-energy compactors, it may be necessary to place fill in relatively thin lifts of 6 in. (150 mm) or less.

Standardized *compaction* or *moisture-density relation tests* (ASTM D-698 or D-1557) are typically used to evaluate the maximum dry density (MDD) that can be reasonably attained in the field for a specific soil. For all but highly permeable soils, these tests indicate that for a given compactive effort, the maximum dry density that can be achieved changes with the moisture content. If the soil is too dry, there is insufficient water to reduce bonding of soil solid particles and permit the mobility necessary for densification. However, if the soil is too wet, the void space between solid particles will be nearly filled with water, precluding further densification. The *optimum moisture content* (OMC) is that at which the maximum dry density (MDD) is achieved for a given compactive effort.

To assure that adequate compaction is accomplished in the field, a minimum percentage (typically 90 to 98 percent) of the maximum dry density (MDD) is specified. Field density tests are then taken during fill placement to verify the desired density. If the field moisture content of the fill material is too far above or below the optimum moisture content (OMC), the required density may be very difficult, or even impossible, to achieve. Consequently, quality control during fill placement is affected not only by the equipment and method used but also by close attention to the moisture content of the fill soil as it is placed. In many instances it is necessary to implement field wetting or drying operations to adjust the natural moisture content of excavated soils to near the OMC for compaction. It is generally easier and less expensive in the field to raise the moisture content by wetting than to lower it through drying. It may be uneconomical or even impossible to adequately compact moisture-sensitive soils that have a high natural moisture content or during periods of precipitation.

Prior to placing and compacting soil as fill, the natural ground to receive the fill should be adequately prepared. This includes removal of all organic and other unsuitable material as discussed previously under Site Preparation. The exposed surface to receive the fill should then be scarified, the soil moisture content should be adjusted to near OMC, and the fill should be compacted to the required dry density. This operation provides a good bond between the fill to be placed and the underlying natural soil materials. Where fill is to be placed on ground slopes steeper than 5H:1V (horizontal to vertical), the original natural ground should be excavated into natural soil materials to form steps or keys. Each step or key should have a maximum slope not exceeding 10H:1V and a minimum width at least two feet wider than the compaction equipment being used. Proper keying of soils is utilized to minimize the risk of downslope movement of fill at the contact with the natural ground surface.

A unit volume of soil excavated from a cut area may not produce exactly one unit volume of compacted fill because of differences in the density of the natural versus compacted materials. The resultant volume differences can range from zero to about 25 percent of shrinkage or swell, respectively referring to whether the excavated volume is greater or less than the compacted fill volume. These differences should be taken into consideration when estimating earthwork volumes, especially when attempting to balance cut and fill volumes. Because it is difficult to accurately predict in advance the actual compacted and natural densities, it is highly desirable to designate one or more areas of a site for a variable finished grade. These areas should be completed last to permit raising or lowering the grade, as necessary, to balance cut/fill volumes and absorb any inaccuracies in the estimated shrinkage factor.

Foundation Installations

The potential risk of soil variations between exploration locations and other unexpected subsurface conditions mandates a foundation verification program during construction. The most important step in the verification is that all natural soil surfaces to provide support for structural elements be observed by the geotechnical engineer who provided the foundation design recommendations. The purpose of this inspection is to verify that the soils exposed by excavation and designated to provide foundation support are of the type and quality assumed in the design. If zones or pockets of sub-standard soils exist between exploration locations, they are likely to be detected by this inspection. Appropriate action can then be taken to modify the design in a manner that will provide adequate foundation support.

Cast-in-place concrete for footing and slabs should be placed in direct contact with the undisturbed natural soils designated as suitable by the geotechnical engineer. Any soil disturbed or loosened by construction activities should be removed from excavations, by hand shoveling if necessary, prior to placing reinforcing steel or concrete. Free water or excessively wet soils should also be removed, if present. Compaction of loosened soils in lieu of removal should not be utilized unless approved by the geotechnical engineer.

15.8. PROBLEM SOILS

Some types of soil deposits are characterized by certain behavior that makes them notorious for their frequent damage to buildings as a result of excessive differential deformation. Because such soils are encountered in many parts of the world, the nature of these materials that tend to create structural damage will be discussed in the following section for some of the more common problem soils.

Fill

Many of man's building projects involve the movement of earth materials from one location to another to raise or lower the original natural ground surface. For example, it may be desirable to place fill materials to produce a level building area from terrain that is hilly or contains depressions or gullies. In many cases fill is placed to raise a low area above potential flood levels or for purposes of improved drainage.

In some respect man-placed fill materials have obtained an undeserved reputation for building damage. Numerous successful projects have been completed involving placement of extensive building complexes including multi-story buildings on significant volumes of fill with no resultant building damage. Conversely, many buildings have experienced extensive damage as a result of placement on even relatively small volumes of man-placed fill. The primary differences between such success and failure are the characteristics of the fill materials and the technique used for their placement.

All too often the sign placed on a vacant lot, "fill dirt wanted" is generally interpreted to read "dump your trash here." Such indiscriminately obtained fill material is likely to consist of those materials that were not desirable nor wanted elsewhere. Organic debris in such fill, such as topsoil, vegetation, roots, and garbage, is likely to decay with time. Such decay results in degradation and volume changes that often lead to differential settlements. Organic decay is also likely to produce foul odors and more dangerous and undesirable flammable gases such as methane. There have been numerous instances of such gases accumulating undetected in buildings until a spark ignited them, resulting in explosions causing damage, injuries, and even death.

Even fill consisting entirely of durable inorganic particles can experience damaging differential settlements. Particularly troublesome are larger-particle materials such as rubble debris consisting of concrete or brick, cobble- and boulder-size natural materials, and angular rock fragments resulting from excavations of bedrock using explosives (*shot rock*). When placed as fill these materials generally have relatively large voids between particles. With time, finer particles of adjacent natural or man-placed materials may migrate into these voids, resulting in an overall volume decrease causing settlement. Such migration can be especially troublesome if it is caused by flow of subsurface water. Such flow can carry fines completely away through the process of internal erosion or piping. This condition has been responsible for the failure of several earth-filled dams, resulting in extensive damage and loss of life. Even without the migration of fines, these predominantly large-particle fills often experience notable differential settlements with time as a result of gradual rearrangement of particles and crushing of point contacts where high stress concentrations occur.

Fill consisting of finer-grained, all-mineral soil particles is also prone to excessive differential settlement with time if it is not placed using appropriate engineering methods. These methods include: (1) proper preparation of the natural ground surface to receive the fill; (2) wetting or drying of the fill material to develop a moisture content conducive to proper compaction; and (3) placement of the fill material in relatively thin lifts (4 to 12 inches; 100 to 300 mm), with each lift thoroughly compacted prior to placing the next lift. A more detailed description of good fill placement technique and methods is discussed under Compaction in Section 15.7. Uncompacted or poorly compacted fill soils can also exhibit characteristics of collapsing soils, as discussed below.

The weight of soil fill relative to the weight of buildings is often misunderstood. Compacted soil fill weighs nearly as much as an equal volume of concrete, and a 3-foot (1-meter) thickness of fill places about as much weight on the foundation soils as a typical three-story residential or office building. Consequently, the weight of fill material placed at many sites often greatly exceeds the weight of buildings.

Compression of soft soils under the weight of placed fill usually results in relatively large settlements. Such soft soil deposits often exist in lowland areas where placement of fill is often desired to raise the site elevation. Major settlements may occur over a period of several months to several years after fill placement. Excessive differential settlements capable of causing severe building distress can result where fill berms are placed near exterior walls of buildings overlying soft, compressible soils.

Organic Soils and Peat

Relatively soft and plastic fine-grained natural soils with high organic content are prone to a significant amount of continuing settlement throughout the typical design life of structures. This phenomenon is referred to as *secondary settlement* and is a time-dependent behavior similar to creep deformations of other viscous materials.

The propensity of a soil for secondary settlement is approximately proportional to its organic content and water content. Peat soils, consisting almost entirely of organic materials and having water contents up to 1,000 percent, represent the extreme example of secondary settlement. Peat and other highly organic soils are generally considered unsuitable for support of buildings, necessitating the additional expense of removal of these soils by excavation or use of deep foundations. Even with buildings supported on deeper foundations, damaging differential settlements can result if fill materials are placed beneath, adjacent to, or near the buildings.

Collapsing Soils

Some natural soil deposits that exhibit only nominal settlements under typical foundation loads can suddenly experience much larger settlements if given access to water. This collapsing behavior is generally related to soils comprised mostly of bulky shaped grains (sand and nonplastic silt) but which are slightly cemented together by soluble compounds of more plastic, flake-shaped, clay particles. These soils usually have atypically high void ratios (low dry unit weight) and low moisture content (i.e., voids only partially saturated). Addition of more water eventually weakens the cementing agent, resulting in the collapsing behavior.

The extensive wind-blown silt soils (*loess*) that blanket much of Asia, North America and Eastern Europe, commonly exhibit a collapsing tendency. In arid or semi-arid regions wind-blown sands and silts, as well as cohesive alluvial fan and colluvial deposits, often exhibit similar behavior. Some residual soils, especially in tropical climates, can exhibit this condition.

Buildings placed on these soils may begin to settle significantly and differentially as a result of irrigation of lawns or plants adjacent to the structure. Poor surface drainage, downspouts, drains, leaking pipes, swimming pools, etc. can also provide water to trigger the collapse settlements.

Where collapsing soils are suspected, special soil testing should be performed by the geotechnical engineer to determine the relative potential for such problems. It may be necessary to utilize special foundation designs and other precautions to reduce risks of unacceptable settlements.

Swelling Soils

Fine-grained, plastic soils have a tendency to absorb water (when it is available) with a resultant increase in volume, or *swelling*. The potential for soil to swell generally increases with plasticity (i.e., plasticity index). The degree to which a soil will exhibit swelling in the field depends not only on its swell potential, but also on its initial water content and dry density, the stress (weight) on the soil, and the availability of water. Pressures of several tons per square foot can be exerted by a swelling soil, resulting in upward heaving of the soil and structures placed on it. Swelling is generally not uniform across a structure; consequently, differential heaving and structural damage typically occur.

The more severe problems with swelling soils generally occur in arid and semi-arid climates where evaporation normally keeps the water content of near-surface soils relatively low. Occasional rains provide water, resulting in seasonal swelling followed by later shrinkage as the soil volume decreases with water removal by evaporation during the dry season. If near-surface soils are protected from evaporation by shading from buildings and impervious surfaces such as pavements and slabs, moisture can accumulate to cause soil swelling. Because this process takes time to develop, detrimental effects on structures may not become apparent for several years. Deformation from swelling can also affect utilities, and if water-carrying conduits become broken and leak the situation is worsened.

Where swelling soils are suspected or known to occur, special testing and evaluation should be performed by the geotechnical engineer to develop a foundation design approach which reduces the risk of detrimental effects on the building.

Liquefaction

Ground shaking by moderate to strong earthquakes can cause a temporary loss in strength of loose sand soils below the groundwater level. With no shear strength these saturated soils behave as a liquid and become unable to support building loads, with resultant large settlements and occasional complete collapse of structures in bearing capacity failure. The strength loss can also result in lateral movement of the soil mass even on a nearly flat ground surface, with the potential for very extensive building damage.

Soil conditions with a potential for liquefaction are generally limited to geologically young deposits such as wind-blown, alluvial, or deltaic sands. Earthquakes having Richter magnitude of 5 or greater have generally been capable of inducing liquefaction in susceptible soils. At sites where soil and seismic conditions combine to produce a high risk of liquefaction, special evaluation should be made by the geotechnical engineer to estimate the risk and suggest mitigating measures. Although measures such as densification and drainage can be helpful in reducing the risk of liquefaction, they are frequently expensive to implement and may prove economically unfeasible except for more critical structures.

Permafrost

In colder climates much of the land area consists of a near-surface zone of permanently frozen ground (permafrost). Climatic conditions must maintain a mean soil temperature below freezing for permafrost to exist. The thickness of the permafrost layer varies from a few feet (meters) to hundreds of feet (meters) and is dependent on the thermal regime. Placement of structures on the frozen ground might alter the thermal regime and, especially with heated buildings, thaw the surface of the permafrost. Most permafrost contains a high water content and often ice lenses. When it thaws at the surface a quagmire of mud usually results and subsurface drainage is prevented by the underlying frozen ground. Structures supported on permafrost that has thawed often settle excessively and differentially. If the ground refreezes, damage can be increased through resultant heave. Placement of buildings in areas of permafrost must be carefully evaluated to either avoid a thaw of the ground or predict the effects of thawing in order that structures may be designed accordingly to obtain suitable foundation support.

REFERENCES

15.1. "Standard Test Method for Classification of Soils for Engineering Purposes," ASTM-D2487-85. *Annual Book of ASTM Standards*. American Society for Testing and Materials, Philadelphia, 1987, Vol. 04.08, pp. 395–408.

15.2 R. B. Peck, W. E. Hanson, and T. H. Thornburn. *Foundation Engineering*, 2nd Ed. John Wiley, New York, 1974, p. 43.

15.3 R. B. Peck, W. E. Hanson, and T. H. Thornburn. *Foundation Engineering*, 2nd Ed. John Wiley, New York, 1974, p. 188.

15.4. R. B. Peck, W. E. Hanson, and T. H. Thornburn. *Foundation Engineering*, 2nd Ed. John Wiley, New York, 1974, pp. 251–252, 447–471.

15.5. R. B. Peck, W. E. Hanson, and T. H. Thornburn. *Foundation Engineering*, 2nd Ed. John Wiley, New York, 1974, pp. 177–182.

SUGGESTIONS FOR FURTHER READING

Practical Guidelines for the Selection, Design and Installation of Piles. Committee on Deep Foundations American Society of Civil Engineering, New York, 1984.

J. E. Bowles. *Foundation Analysis and Design*, 4th Ed. McGraw-Hill, New York, 1988.

Department of the Navy. *Foundations and Earth Structures*. NAVFAC DM-7.2. US Government Printing Office, Washington, DC, 1982.

Department of the Navy. *Soil Mechanics*. NAVFAC DM-7.1. US Government Printing Office, Washington, DC, 1982.

R. B. Peck, W. E. Hanson, and T. H. Thornburn. *Foundation Engineering*, 2nd Ed. John Wiley, New York, 1974.

H. G. Poulos and E. H. Davis. *Pile Foundations Analysis and Design*. John Wiley, Brisbane, 1980.

M. J. Tomlinson. *Pile Design and Construction Practice*. Viewpoint Publications, London, 1977.

M. J. Tomlinson. *Foundation Design and Construction*, 5th Ed. Pitman, London, 1987.

L. Zeevaert. *Foundation Engineering for Difficult Subsoil Conditions*. Van Nostrand Reinhold, New York, 1983.

NOTE

A list of abbreviations of the units of measurement, definitions of these units, and conversion factors between British/American and metric units are given in the Appendix.

16
Noise Control

Anita Lawrence

Noise control is a very important aspect of building design, but it is often neglected, or thought to be amenable to adjustment if the completed building proves unsatisfactory. Unfortunately, such adjustments are unlikely to be successful and they are certain to be costly. Thus it is essential that building designers and supervisors thoroughly understand the principles involved.

16.1. SOUND AND SOUND PROPAGATION

Sound arises when the particles of a medium are caused to vibrate by a source. The simplest type of sound source is a small point in a large, unbounded medium. It may be thought of as a pulsating balloon; as the balloon increases in size it will produce a small increase in pressure in the surrounding air, and conversely, as it becomes smaller it causes a slight lowering of pressure, or rarefaction. These slight compressions and rarefactions, above and below atmospheric pressure, will be propagated as spherical waves away from the source, until such time as an obstruction is reached. The number of times per second that a complete cycle of oscillations occurs is called the *frequency f* of the sound, measured in Hertz (Hz). (Ref. 16.1) Sound that is audible to humans covers a frequency range of approximately 20 to 20,000 Hz.

Sound is not part of the electromagnetic spectrum and the energy travels relatively slowly—so slowly in fact that it is sometimes possible to perceive individual sound signals that have been reflected many times around a large room as distinct *echoes*. The speed of sound in any medium depends on its elasticity and density. In air, at normal room temperatures, the rate of propagation of sound energy, or the *speed of sound c*, is approximately 1130 ft/s (344 m/s). When a sound source oscillates rapidly, i.e., the higher its frequency, the shorter will be the distance between two particles undergoing the same *phase* of the

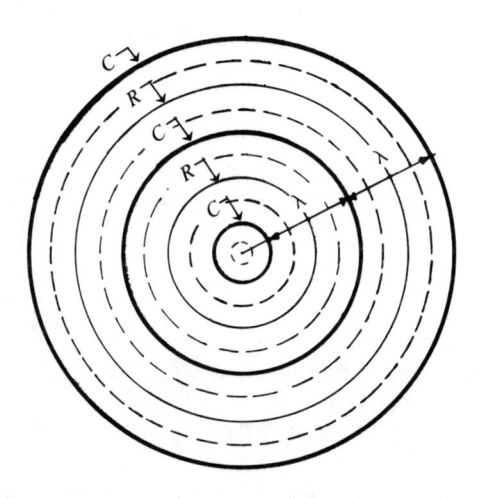

Fig. 16.1.1. Propagation of sound from a point source. C = compression, R = rarefaction, λ = wavelength (distance between two particles undergoing same phase of oscillation cycle).

oscillation cycle. This distance is called the *wavelength of the sound* λ (Fig. 16.1.1). The relationship between sound speed, frequency and wavelength is:

$$c = f\lambda \qquad (16.1)$$

Thus the range of wavelengths corresponding to audible frequencies, in air, is approximately 56 ft to 0.7 in. (17 m to 17 mm). This causes some difficulties in practice, since the low frequency sounds are of the same magnitude, or larger, than the dimensions of typical rooms or of typical barriers used out-of-doors, and thus they will tend to be diffracted in a complex manner, rather than undergo specular reflection as is the general case for light waves.

The quantity of sound produced by a source, its *sound power W*, is measured in *watts*, although the acoustic power of most audible sources is very small compared to their mechanical power. The rate at which sound energy flows through the medium, is called the *sound intensity I*, measured in watts/m^2; for a unidirectional flow from a point source of sound, the sound power flowing through a unit area normal to the direction of propagation is given by:

$$I = W/(4\pi r^2) \qquad (16.2)$$

where r is the distance from the source, in meters. This is the "inverse square law" relationship, which predicts a reduction in intensity proportional to the square of the distance between source and receiver. Until recently it has not been possible to measure sound intensity directly, and the quantity more commonly used to describe the quantity of sound is the *sound pressure*. As mentioned above, the passage of a sound wave causes rapid increases and decreases in pressure above and below atmospheric pressure; the root mean square of these pressure changes is called the sound pressure p, measured in Pascals. The relationship between sound pressure and sound intensity, for a freely progressing wave is

$$I = p^2/Z \qquad (16.3)$$

where Z is the *characteristic impedance* of the medium, and

$$Z = \rho c \qquad (16.4)$$

where ρ is the density of the medium, in kg/m^3, and c is the sound speed within it, in m/s.

16.2. SOUND PERCEPTION

The perception of sound by people involves a complex blend of physical, physiological, sensori-neural, and psycho-acoustic factors. Sound waves enter the ear canal and cause the *eardrum* (tympanic membrane) to vibrate. This causes vibration of three small bones in the middle ear, the *ossicles*, which in turn transmit the vibration to the *oval window* of the *cochlea*. The cochlea consists of a fluid-filled flat spiral of two and a half turns. It is subdivided into an upper and lower gallery partly by a bony structure and partly by a flexible *basilar membrane*. Another two membranes, *Reissner's* and the *tectorial membrane*, form a third cochlea cavity above the basilar membrane; this latter cavity contains a fluid which has a slightly different electric potential than the others. Some 20,000 sensory cells, called *hair cells* because of hairlike projections protruding from their upper ends, are supported by the basilar membrane. At least some of these hairs span to the underside of the tectorial membrane. A simplified diagram of the cochlea is shown in Fig. 16.2.1. As the basilar membrane is set into motion by the sound stimuli, the electrical conductivity of the hair cells is changed and neural pulses are transmitted along the audio nerve for processing by the brain. It is thought that sound of different frequencies causes different stimulation patterns in the basilar membrane, which is reflected in the pattern of neural impulses transmitted (Refs. 16.2, 16.3). At various stages of neural processing, the stimuli from both ears are combined, allowing for three-dimensional, *binaural perception*.

The more energy present in the sound waves, the greater will be the displacement of the basilar membrane. If the ear is subjected to excessively loud noise, particularly over a long period of time, some of the hair cells are damaged and eventually die, causing *sensori-neural deafness*, or *noise-induced hearing loss*. This is irreversible, and is usually most severe around 4,000 to 6,000 Hz, gradually extending to lower frequencies as excessive exposure to noise continues. The frequencies from about 1000 to 4000 Hz are particularly necessary for understanding speech, which means that people affected by noise-induced hearing loss are severely handicapped in normal social environments. Many people (except perhaps for some living in primitive societies), also suffer from decreased high-frequency sensitivity as they become older; this is called *presbycusis* (Ref. 16.4). The combined effects of excessive noise exposure and aging, plus the percentage of people with inherent otological defects, mean that in most populations there are likely to be several individuals with some type of impaired hearing.

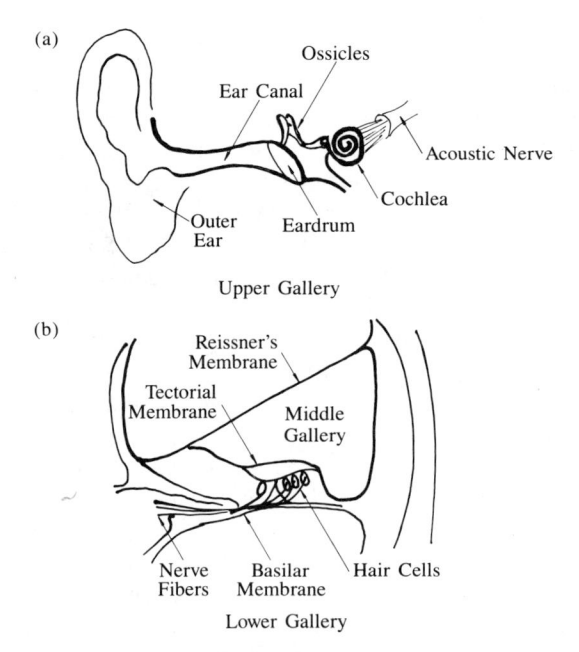

Fig. 16.2.1. Diagrams of the human ear. (a) Outer, middle, and inner ear; (b) detail of part of cochlea.

Decibels

Increments in sound intensity are perceived as equal when the ratio between successive intensity changes is kept constant; this suggests that a logarithmic scale is more suitable than a linear one. The unit used is the *decibel, dB*, and the reference levels for the ratios have been standardized internationally. The logarithmic expressions for sound power, intensity and pressure are as follows:

$$L_W = 10 \log (W/W_0) \quad (16.5)$$

where L_W is the sound power level, dB re 10^{-12} W
    W is the sound power, W
    W_0 is the reference sound power, 10^{-12} W

$$L_I = 10 \log (I/I_0) \quad (16.6)$$

where L_I is the sound intensity level, dB re 10^{-12} W/m^2
    I is the sound intensity, W/m^2
    I_0 is the reference sound intensity, 10^{-12} W/m^2

$$L_p = 10 \log (p^2/p_0^2) \quad (16.7)$$

where L_p is the sound pressure level, dB re 20 μPa
    p is the sound pressure, Pa
    p_0 is the reference sound pressure, 20 μPa

It will be realized from the above that decibels should always be accompanied by a specific reference; if none is specified, sound pressure level is assumed, since this is the quantity measured directly by a sound level meter. The audio range of sound pressure levels is approximately 0 to 120 dB, although at the most sensitive frequencies lower levels may be perceived and some of the most powerful sources, such as rocket motors, emit much higher levels.

The use of logarithmic scales requires the use of caution in calculations. For example, if there are two identical sound sources, each emitting 70 decibels sound pressure level, their combined level (assuming incoherent addition) will be 73 dB, not 140 dB. Conversely if one of the sources is switched off, the reduction will only be 3 decibels.

Loudness

People have varying sensitivity to sounds of different frequencies. They are most sensitive to sounds with frequencies around 3,000 Hz and much less sensitive to sound at the extremes of the audio range. So-called *equal loudness contours* were determined experimentally by asking large numbers of people to judge when pure tones (sinusoids) sounded as loud as a pure tone at 1,000 Hz. Sounds judged equally loud have the same *loudness level* in *phons* (Ref. 16.5). The shape of the contours of equal loudness varies considerably according to the level of the 1,000 Hz reference tone, becoming increasingly flat as the level increases. This led to the standardization of three *weighting networks*, A, B, and C, for sound level meters. Later loudness judgment experiments using bands of noise as stimuli found that the shape of the contours did not vary so much with the level of the reference sound (Ref. 16.6), and the A-weighting is now generally used to rank sound of any level with respect to average human perceptions of loudness. Fig. 16.2.2 shows the A-weighting curve.

16.3. SOUND ANALYSIS

Although the overall A-weighted sound pressure level of a sound, in dB(A), gives a reasonably satisfactory indication of its relative loudness; when designing for an appropriate acoustical environment, or attempting to carry out remedial measures, it is necessary to determine which frequency components of the sound are most important. In these cases sound spectrum analysis is necessary. It has been found, in a similar manner to loudness judgments, that people judge changes of sound frequency (or pitch) as equal when the ratios of the changes are kept constant. Thus a change in frequency from 500 to 1000 Hz is perceived as the same as a change from 1000 to 2000 Hz; such frequency changes from f to $2f$ are called *octave intervals*. Since the Hertz is a linear unit, frequency is usually plotted on a logarithmic scale.

Octaves, in acoustics, are described by their geometrical center frequencies; thus the octave centered on 1000 Hz extends from 707 to 1414 Hz. For more detailed analyses in architectural acoustics, one-third octaves are used. If a sound has equal energy at each frequency, it is called *white noise*, and the sound pressure level increases at 3 dB per octave. This is analogous to white light, see Fig. 16.2.2.

Most sound sources do not emit constant sound levels. (Some exceptions are machines, such as fans.) It becomes necessary to have some method of describing a sound with a time-varying level. One system is to determine the sound level exceeded for a certain percentage of a given time period; for example, the sound level exceeded for 10

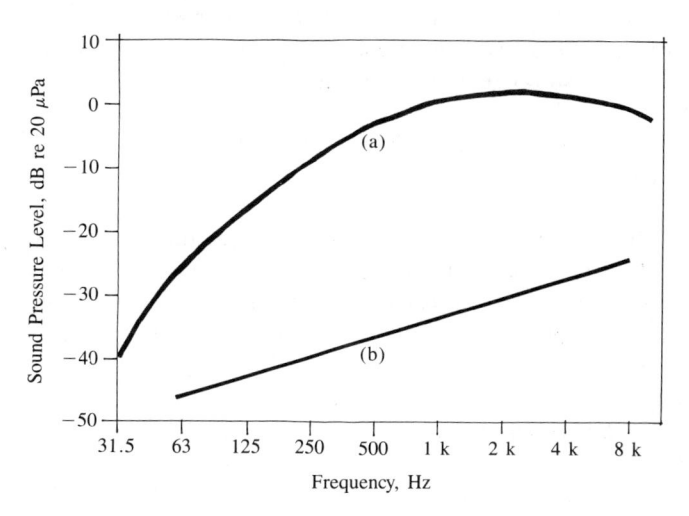

Fig. 16.2.2. Sound analysis. (a) A-weighting curve; (b) white noise (+3 dB per octave slope).

percent of the time represents the higher noise levels and is called $L_{10,T}$ dB (or, more usually, the A-weighted level is measured, which is described as $L_{A10,T}$ dB(A)). The sound level exceeded for 90 percent of the time is $L_{A90,T}$ dB(A) and represents the quietest levels; this is often termed the *background noise level*. An alternative descriptor is to find the level of a nonvarying sound that has the same total energy over the given time period. This is called the equivalent continuous A-weighted sound pressure level, $L_{Aeq,T}$.

$$L_{Aeq,T} = 10 \log_{10} \left[\frac{1}{t_2 - t_1} \int_{t_1}^{t_2} \frac{p_A^2(t)}{p_0^2} \, dt \right] dB(A)$$

(16.8)

This quantity may be measured directly with an integrating averaging sound level meter.

16.4. VIBRATION PERCEPTION

The main frequency range for vibration perception by people is from about 0.5 to 100 Hz. Below about 15 Hz, the main receptor is the nonauditory labyrinth, situated adjacent to the cochlea in the ear. Above this frequency the main response is through the skin. In addition to perception varying with frequency, the attitude of the body towards the motion is important (vertical, horizontal, sideways). The magnitude of the motion is usually quantified as the acceleration, m/s^2. Most research into human response to vibration has been related to the quality of ride in transportation vehicles or to pilot effectiveness under severe conditions. Three ranges of maximum exposure levels are recommended, the first relates to the preservation of health and safety, the second to the preservation of working efficiency, and the third to the preservation of comfort, which relates to the prevention of difficulties in writing, drinking, etc. (Refs. 16.7, 16.8, 16.9). However, for buildings it is recommended that the allowable vibration levels be set close to the threshold of perception. In some cases it is necessary to set building vibration limits to protect sensitive equipment; these may be as much as 5 times lower than human perception limits.

16.5. CRITERIA FOR ACCEPTABLE SOUND LEVELS IN BUILDINGS

There are two basic considerations in determining acceptable sound level criteria. The first is the provision of speech intelligibility, either in face-to-face situations or when using telecommunication systems; the second relates to annoyance.

Speech Intelligibility

The basic components of speech in any language are called *phonemes*, which are distinctive units of sound (Ref. 16.10). The words *sound* and *found* each have three phonemes, of which only the first is different. Vowel sounds contain the major part of the energy available in speech, although they do not contribute as much to comprehension as do the consonant sounds, which tend to have less energy and shorter durations as well as higher frequency spectra than the vowels. The overall speech frequency range is in the one-third octave bands centered from about 200 Hz to 6,300 Hz, the most important components for intelligibility lying between about 1,000 and 4,000 Hz. The power available in unaided human speech is limited, the long-term rms level of conversational speech being about 60 dB(A) at 3 feet (1 meter) from a typical male speaker.

For good speech intelligibility (see also Section 17.7), ideally each phoneme should be heard clearly; however, there are many redundancies in connected speech, and provided that the listener has normal hearing and is reasonably familiar with the language and the topic, the meaning may be understood in less than perfect conditions. Conversely, if the listener has a hearing loss or is not a native speaker of the language, or if the subject matter is unfamiliar, there is much less tolerance of background noise or other distorting influences, such as excessive *reverberation* (see Section 17.6). Excessive background noise will tend to mask the wanted speech signals; excessive reverberation (sounds being reflected many times around a room) has a similar effect.

Acceptable background sound levels for speech may be estimated using speech intelligibility calculations (Refs. 16.11, 16.12). Generally levels of 30 to 35 dB(A) are desirable, with levels up to 40 dB(A) usually being acceptable; see Table 16.1.

Annoyance Criteria

Annoyance caused by noise is difficult to quantify objectively. It is related to the disturbance caused to a wanted activity (or to a desired relaxation or sleep); it is related to the loudness of the intruding noise, but two noises may have the same loudness and yet not be equally annoying. Obviously, if a sound is inaudible it will not be annoying—this means that if background noises are moderate to high, individual noises will be masked. However, at night the general background noise level usually is lower, and the same individual noises may then become perceptible and thus annoying. It is important, therefore, in multifamily dwellings, hotels, and offices, that the background noise levels from air-conditioning, for example, are not too low, otherwise it becomes very expensive to provide sufficient sound attenuation between different occupancies. Table 16.1 gives some recommended sound levels for different types of activity in buildings (Ref. 16.13).

16.6. AIRBORNE SOUND TRANSMISSION

When a sound wave travelling through air encounters a boundary, such as the wall of a room, some of the energy

Table 16.1. Recommended Sound Levels in Buildings.

Building Type	$L_{A\,eq}$, dB(A)
Residential	
Living areas	30–40
Kitchens, bathrooms, etc.	35–40
Bedrooms	25–30
Hotels, Motels	
Foyers, bars, etc.	45–55
Dining rooms	40–45
Conference rooms	30–35
Bedrooms	30–35
Educational Buildings	
Classrooms, teaching laboratories	35–40
Lecture rooms (250 seat max.)	30–35
Laboratories, research	40–50
Assembly halls (over 250 seats)	25–30
Music rooms, drama studios	30–35
Libraries, reading areas	40–45
Public Buildings	
Hospital wards	30–40
Consulting rooms	40–45
Kitchens, service areas	45–50
Airport, railway and bus terminals	45–60
Court rooms	25–30
Museums	40–45
Restaurants	40–50
Indoor sports rooms	45–50
Department stores, supermarkets	45–55
Undercover car parks	55–65
Offices	
Private offices	35–40
General office areas	40–45
Drawing offices	40–50
Computer rooms	45–55
Public spaces	40–50

will be reflected back into the air, some will be transmitted into the wall, and some will then be transmitted from the wall into the space on the other side (an adjoining room, for example). The relative amounts of energy reflected and transmitted are determined by several factors, most of which are frequency dependent (Refs. 16.14, 16.15). In the mid-frequency range, the controlling factor is the relative impedance of air and of the boundary material; as shown in Eq. (16.4), the impedance Z is equal to the product of the medium's density and speed of sound in it. Since the speed of sound in a medium is itself related to its density and stiffness, impedance is strongly dependent on the density of a material. If the impedances are similar, most of the sound energy will be transferred from one medium to the other; conversely, if the impedances are dissimilar, most of the energy will be reflected back. Thus if sound travelling in air encounters a boundary that is dense and relatively stiff (concrete or brick, for example) most of the energy will be reflected back into the room and little will be transmitted (or absorbed) by the wall. The same impedance mismatch will occur on the boundary between the wall and the air on the other side; thus the *sound transmission loss* (STL) will be high. However, if the airborne sound encounters a medium such as a curtain, glass wool, etc., the impedances will be similar and most of the energy will be transmitted into the second medium (and again, transmitted to the air on the far side). In this case the sound transmission loss is low, and the *sound absorption*, as far as the source room is concerned, is high. It is important to realize that very little of the energy is really absorbed, that is, converted into another form of energy—it is simply transmitted from the source room. This type of energy transfer is called *Mass Law transmission*, and the STL increases by approximately 6 dB per doubling of surface density, and also by about 6 dB for each doubling of frequency (per octave). An approximate indication of the STL, R', in decibels, of a given homogeneous partition is found from:

$$R' = 20 \log (fM) + K \qquad (16.9)$$

where f is the frequency of the sound, Hz
           M is the surface density of the partition, lb/ft^2 (kg/m^2)
           K is a constant $= -34$ dB, M in lb/ft^2 (-47 dB, M in kg/m^2)

The Mass Law only applies in the frequency region where each part of the solid medium can be assumed to react independently. Sound energy in solid materials may set up flexural and shear waves, as well as the longitudinal waves which occur in gases. Finite-sized partitions are able to support many *resonances*—that is, if they are struck they will vibrate at preferred frequencies. These resonant frequencies depend on the dimensions of the partition and on the sound speed in the material. If an incident sound is of the same frequency as a panel resonance, the panel will vibrate in phase with the incident energy and most of the energy will be transmitted to the other side. At resonant frequencies the energy losses occur mainly through damping at the edges of the partition, and may be quite small. In practical cases, resonance transmission occurs in the lower frequency range, and at a frequency about twice that of the lowest resonant frequency the Mass Law effect becomes dominant.

Mass Law transmission continues until the *critical frequency* f_c is reached, and the *coincidence effect* occurs. As mentioned above, solids can support bending waves; the velocity of these waves varies with the frequency of the sound (unlike longitudinal waves, where velocity is independent of frequency). There will thus be some frequencies at which the bending wave in the solid will have the same wavelength as the projected wavelength of the airborne sound at a particular angle of incidence. When this occurs, the panel vibration will be in phase with the airborne sound, and little attenuation will occur. The critical frequency may be estimated from the following:

$$f_c = (c^2/1.8h) \times (\rho_p/E)^{1/2} \text{ Hz} \qquad (16.10)$$

where c is the velocity of sound in air, ft/s (m/s)
       h is the thickness of the panel, ft (m)
       ρ_p is the density of the material, lb/ft^3 (kg/m^3)
       E is Young's modulus, lb$_f$/ft^2 (N/m^2)

In practice, the coincidence effect is important only for relatively thin, lightweight materials such as plasterboard, plywood, glass, etc. It occurs at very low frequencies in thicker, masonry materials, and it is not discernable among the other resonant transmission effects. However, for lightweight panels it occurs typically around 1000 to 4000 Hz, important audio frequencies where the ear is very sensitive, and where considerable speech information is present. Fig. 16.6.1 illustrates the typical airborne sound transmission performance of a homogeneous, lightweight partition compared with that of a masonry wall.

Frequently constructions are used which incorporate double panels, e.g., double-glazed windows, cavity brick walls, etc. In this case the overall STL is less than the sum of the two panels, since they are partly coupled by the air in the cavity between them and by common surrounding materials (Ref. 16.16). In the Mass Law region, where the individual elements react independently, it is true that there will be four impedance boundaries, rather than the two of a single panel; theoretically, in this region, the STL will increase at 12 dB per octave. However, at low frequencies a mass-air-mass resonance occurs with elastic coupling between the panels and the air in the cavity. The approximate resonant frequency f_0 may be estimated from the following:

$$f_0 = F[(M_1 + M_2)/(M_1 M_2 d)]^{1/2} \quad (16.11)$$

where $F = 50$ in ft-lb units (60 in m-kg units)
          M_1, M_2 are the surface densities of the two skins, lb/ft^2 (kg/m^2)
          d is the thickness of the air cavity, ft (m)

For typical double-glazed windows, f_0 occurs in the low-frequency region and is seen as a pronounced dip in the STL curve. In addition, resonances can be set up over the length and height of the cavity and, in the high-frequency region, across its width. These resonances also contribute to lower STL values at the relevant frequencies. In the case of windows and other lightweight systems, it is advantageous to vary the surface density of the two panels, in order to avoid the coincidence dip occurring at the same frequency in both. Fig. 16.6.1 also shows a typical STL curve for a double-glazed window.

It can be seen that there are many factors which affect the sound transmission through building materials—some related to the material itself, but others to dimensions, fixing, etc. In practice, the sound transmission loss tends to be less than would be predicted from theoretical considerations, and it is always preferable to obtain data from laboratory measurements of STL for the type of construction proposed. However, even these tend to give optimistic results, since workmanship in practice may not be as good as in the sample tested. In addition, the samples tested are usually only 100 ft^2 (10 m^2) in area, which may vary considerably from the size of the construction as used in practice. The laboratory measurements are also designed to ensure uniform angles of incidence of the sound wave onto the panel (diffuse sound fields), since most materials have lower STL values for grazing angles of incidence. Diffuse sound fields do not usually occur in ordinary rooms, and this may also contribute to lower values of STL than expected. It is always prudent to require in situ measurement of the completed construction, and even more prudent to specify values of STL somewhat higher than the bare minimum required.

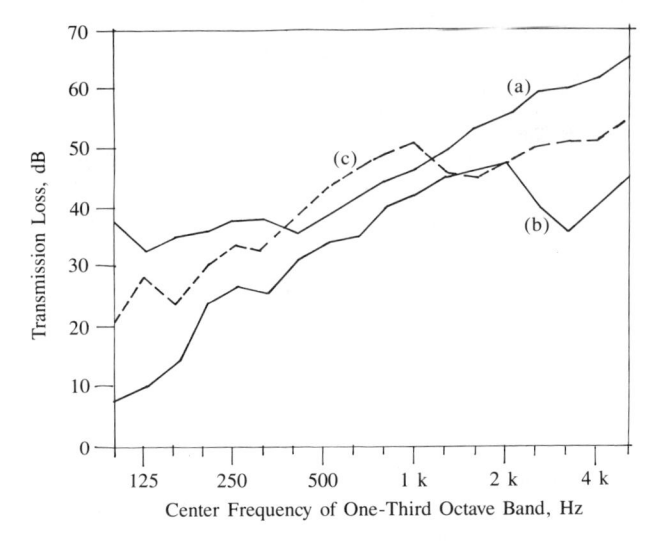

Fig. 16.6.1. Sound transmission loss variation with frequency. (a) Masonry wall (4 in. or 110 mm brickwork); (b) gypsum board on studwork; (c) double-glazed window with unequal thickness glazing ($\frac{1}{4}$ in. or 6 mm glass, 2 in. or 50 mm airspace, $\frac{3}{8}$ in. or 10 mm glass).

Another very important aspect of airborne sound transmission is the presence of any air paths, e.g., ventilation openings, cracks, etc., through which the airborne sound energy will travel with little or no attenuation. The average sound transmission loss of two or more elements, e.g. a brick wall with a door, will be dominated by the transmission through the weaker element. The average sound transmission loss, in decibels, is found from:

$$STL_{av} = -10 \log t_{av} \quad (16.12)$$

$$t_{av} = (S_1 t_1 + S_2 t_2 + \cdots + S_n t_n)/\sum S \quad (16.13)$$

where t_{av} is the average transmission coefficient
      $S_1, S_2, \cdots$ are the average surface areas of the different elements, ft^2 (m^2)
      $t_1, t_2, \cdots$ are the transmission coefficients of the different elements

$$t_i = 10^{-STL_i/10} \quad (16.14)$$

This calculation needs to be carried out for each frequency band of interest. It is important to remember that if an unglazed opening occupies 10 percent of the total surface area, the average STL cannot exceed 10 dB, no matter how high the STL of the remaining materials may be.

Rating Systems for Airborne Sound Transmission Loss

Although for critical situations, e.g., studio design, etc., it is desirable to consider the required STL value for each one-third octave band, comparing expected noise levels in adjacent areas and acceptable noise levels inside, for many rooms it is sufficient to specify some type of averaged value over certain frequency ranges. Standardized methods of averaging are available, using grading curves. In the United States (Ref. 16.17) and Australia (Ref. 16.18), the Sound Transmission Class curve is used (125 to 4000 Hz); a similarly shaped curve, but covering the frequency range from 100 to 3200 Hz, has been published by the International Standards Organisation, ISO (Ref. 16.19), and is used in parts of Europe. Basically, the measured STL values are compared with the standard curve, which has a slope of 9 dB per octave in the low frequencies, 3 dB per octave in the medium frequencies and is flat in the high frequencies. The grading curve is moved as high as possible, limited by specified maximum deficiencies of the measured curve below it, and the STL value at 500 Hz is the STC value (or R_w, ISO rating) of the construction. These curves are suitable for use for general commercial and domestic sound sources, although the lack of emphasis on low-frequency performance may mean that high-powered home audio systems may be transmitted at unacceptably high levels.

It has been suggested that the overall attenuation of a given construction could usefully be rated in dB(A). However, the dB(A) reduction depends on the spectrum of the source sound, and the latter would also have to be standardized for useful comparisons to be made.

16.7. STRUCTURE-BORNE AND IMPACT SOUND TRANSMISSION

Although the principle of energy transmission is the same for airborne and impact sound, the practical consequences are different. Structure-borne and impact sounds originate in the structure itself, from footsteps, banging doors, vibrating machines, ground vibration, etc. Since the impedances of most structural materials are similar, the energy will be transmitted for great distances with little attenuation, unless special construction techniques are used. As is the case for sound originating in air, attenuation occurs through reflections at impedance boundaries, and also through losses at joints, e.g., where a wall joins another wall at right angles, or at a wall-floor junction. The vibrating walls, floors, etc. act as airborne sound radiators in adjacent rooms.

Because of the redundancies and indeterminate boundary conditions in many buildings, the actual attenuations that will occur between the impact source and a receiver are difficult to predict, between 2 to 4 dB per joint can be expected (Ref. 16.20).

In order to reduce structure-borne vibration it is preferable to avoid its occurrence, for example, by placing machinery on properly designed vibration isolating mountings, by using resilient floor surfaces and by providing soft seals for doors, etc. Where structurally possible, elements should not be rigidly connected, but should be provided with resilient materials at joints to ensure impedance mismatching. The design of vibration isolators should be left to experts, since it is possible to enhance transmission from a machine to its supports (Ref. 16.21). The effectiveness of an isolator with low internal damping is given by:

$$T_v = 1/(f/f_0)^2 \qquad (16.15)$$

where T_v is the transmissibility
f is the frequency of vibration of the machine, Hz
f_0 is the resonant frequency of the isolator, Hz

Where $T > 1$, amplification of the vibration occurs, which not only means that the isolator is useless, but that the machine itself may be damaged. For T to be less than 1, it is clear that the resonant frequency of the isolator must be lower than the vibration frequency of the machine. This resonant frequency f_0 is dependent on the static deflection of the isolator:

$$f_0 = A(1/\delta_{st})^{1/2} \qquad (16.16)$$

where A = constant = 3.13, δ_{st} in in. (= 15.8, δ_{st} in mm)
δ_{st} = static deflection in. (mm)

To the building designer, the practical importance of these relationships is that the isolators must be correctly loaded and also that they must be able to deflect the required amount. In the case of machines with variable frequencies of vibration, for example, a compressor cycling on and off, it is necessary to provide sufficient damping to prevent undue transmission when $f = f_0$. Damping does, however, reduce the effectiveness of an isolator at higher frequencies. Another practical difficulty with machine isolation is that the above simplified relationships assume that the isolator supports are massive and do not vibrate; in modern multistory, lightweight construction this assumption is frequently not justified, and the resonant frequencies will be modified due to coupling. The actual attenuation will be less.

Rating Systems for Impact Sound Transmission

Measurement and rating of impact sound transmission is less well established than is the case for airborne sound.

There are as yet no standardized methods for measuring impact sound transmission in elements other than floors, and even this method is not universally accepted. The ISO (Ref. 16.22) requires the use of a standard tapping machine, the construction of which is carefully specified to insure standard impacting forces on the floor to be measured. Five brass or steel hammers of specified mass and drop sequentially hit the floor at intervals of approximately 100 ms. The average airborne sound pressure levels, caused by the floor radiation, are measured in the room below. The measurement is repeated with the machine located in different positions, taking into account the direction of beams, ribs, etc. The measurements may be made in a laboratory, in which case the floor test area should be between 100 and 200 ft^2 (10 and 20 m^2), or in situ in the building. The measured levels are corrected for absorption in the receiving room.

Floors measured according to the ISO standard may be rated using a reference curve (Ref. 16.23) which is approximately the inverse of the STC or R_w curves: it is flat in low frequencies, drops at 3 dB per octave in the mid-frequencies, and at 9 dB per octave in the high frequencies. The reference curve is shifted down as far as possible, while complying with deficiency limits; the value of the reference curve at 500 Hz is the single value rating number for the floor.

This method of measurement is criticized because the impacts produced by the machine do not represent the impacts of footsteps, etc. well. However, as yet no generally accepted replacement has been found. Although impact sound originating in walls and other building elements is also important, there are as yet no standard methods of measuring and assessing the attenuating performance of building elements against these sources.

Whole Building Vibration

Buildings may be excited into vibration by external forces, e.g., through their foundations if the ground is vibrating due to transportation such as underground trains and heavy vehicles, or blasting and piling operations, etc. In addition, tall, slender buildings are exposed to high wind forces and may sway laterally, alarming their occupants.

Buildings can be considered to be mass-spring systems, and have resonant frequencies dependent chiefly on their overall height, varying from about 10 Hz for low-rise buildings to less than 0.1 Hz for buildings over 60 stories in height. Building elements, such as typical floors, walls, etc. also have resonant frequencies, usually ranging from about 5 to 50 Hz.

Building occupants will be aware of vibration at levels much lower than those which are likely to cause any structural damage, and they may be disturbed by light fittings swaying and bath water moving in tall buildings affected by wind. They may also react adversely when lightweight building elements, and objects supported by them are caused to vibrate by high levels of airborne sound from nearby aircraft, heavy road vehicles, and trains.

16.8. BUILDING SERVICES NOISE CONTROL

There are many noise sources in building services, chiefly related to air handling and plumbing systems. The desirable method of overcoming these noise problems, by using low velocity air and liquid transport systems, is in conflict with the economic desire to reduce the space occupied by unprofitable ductwork and pipework as much as possible. Noise emitted by aerodynamic sources is proportional to the eighth power of the air velocity; thus if high velocity systems are used it is necessary to ensure that sufficient attenuators are provided (Ref. 16.24).

The major potential noise source in an air-handling system is the fan. Axial fans have most acoustic energy in their mid-frequencies, while centrifugal fans have most energy in the low frequencies, which are usually more difficult to attenuate. Rotation noise is caused each time a fan blade passes a certain point; this is a tonal sound, the frequency of which is the product of the fan speed in rpm and the number of blades. Another noise source is associated with turbulent flow caused by poor fan design. Fans produce the least overall noise levels when they are operating at their maximum efficiency; thus correct fan selection is very important.

Fan noise is transmitted throughout a building through the ductwork, with the noise travelling equally well with and against the air flow. Thus it is equally important to consider attenuation in the return and supply air systems. Quiet duct design implies avoiding turbulence, which means that abrupt changes of direction or restriction of flow, from control devices, dampers, etc., should be avoided, and the air terminal devices should be carefully selected. Duct pulsation may occur in high-velocity systems. This causes a low-frequency rumble which may be transmitted to lightweight ceilings, partitions, etc.

Attenuation may take the form of porous absorbent duct linings, plenum chambers and packaged silencers. The dimensions of such devices must be taken into account in the design of the building. Another common fault is insufficient space allowance for the mechanical services plant rooms; this may allow noise to bypass duct attenuators. Similarly, noise may be transmitted from one room to another through common ductwork; since the attenuation through duct walls is usually low it is important to avoid short lengths of common ductwork between noisy and quiet rooms.

Turbulent flow in fluids is another common noise source in buildings (Ref. 16.25). Although the pipes themselves may not be large, and thus not efficient sound radiators, if they are rigidly attached to large radiating surfaces, such as walls, ceilings, etc., the sound energy will be readily transmitted. Again, low velocities and the design of the pipework to ensure smooth flow are required. Cavitation is another common source of fluid noise. This arises when a local restriction in the flow path, caused by a valve, for example, results in a sudden velocity increase with a subsequent lowering of fluid pressure; when the restriction is passed, the velocity reduces and the vapor bubbles formed under the lowered pressure collapse. This results in a hissing sound. Water hammer occurs when a steady flow is suddenly interrupted, by a solenoid on an automatic washing machine, for example. Shock waves are reflected around the system.

Elevators and their plant rooms, including the switching devices are also potential noise sources. Plant rooms in particular should be carefully located away from noise-sensitive areas, and surrounded by sealed, highly attenuating construction.

16.9. NOISE AND THE BUILDING ENVELOPE

The noise levels in a building must be considered in relation to its surrounding environment. In many cases the occupants must be protected from excessive external noise levels originating from road traffic, aircraft, or nearby industry. (In some cases the building's neighbors must be protected from noise emanating from the building's plant and machinery.) In all cases, the attenuation afforded by the building envelope is critically dependent on whether or not natural ventilation is required, since, as stated earlier, the attenuation will be limited to 10 dB if more than 10 percent of the area consists of unglazed openings. Closed, openable windows will usually provide an average of about 20 dB attenuation, but if more than this is required, fixed and sealed windows will be necessary, and alternative means of ventilation will be needed.

The amount of attenuation required is determined by measuring, or predicting, the external noise levels at the relevant time periods and at relevant locations. If the building is only to be used during daytime, for example, evening and night-time noise levels, which are generally lower, are not relevant. The usual location for the noise-level measurement or prediction is near the building's facade.

Road traffic noise is the most common source of noise in urban situations, and there are several well-known methods of predicting its levels (Refs. 16.26, 16.27, 16.28) provided that data are available concerning vehicle flow rate, composition (percentage of heavy commercial vehicles), speed, etc. The time-varying levels are usually expressed in terms of $L_{A\,eq,\,T}$ or $L_{A10,\,T}$. The value of T may be 18 hours (from 0600 to 2400) or 24 hours, or, in some cases, related specifically to the times of use of the building. On busy roads, $L_{A\,eq,\,T}$ or $L_{A10,\,T}$ levels may range from 60 to 80 dB(A). A stream of vehicles travelling along a road propagates sound energy as from a line source, and the attenuation is only about 3 dB per doubling of distance from the source (not 6 dB as is the case with a point source). This means in practice that if it is feasible to locate a building 40 m rather than 20 m from a road, a reduction of 3 dB can be expected; however, a change from 200 m to 400 m separation will also only give a 3 dB attenuation due to distance, and would not usually be a sensible choice.

Topographical features such as hills can provide useful shielding from road traffic noise, as can buildings themselves. On a large site, planning may be used to shield noise-sensitive buildings from external noise sources; if only one building is involved, planning may be used to locate noise-sensitive rooms away from the noise source. For example, in dwellings, it is preferable to locate service rooms, such as bathrooms, laundries, and kitchens facing the roadway and the bedrooms, living rooms, and studies toward the rear, where the traffic noise levels may be 20 dB lower than at the front. Guidance for the selection of suitable types of construction to attenuate road traffic noise for different types of building is given in an Australian Standard (Ref. 16.29).

Purpose-built barriers are frequently built alongside busy highways. As well as assisting in reducing the required building attenuation they will also reduce noise levels in external areas nearby. However, in most cases the maximum attenuations achieved are of the order of 10 dB(A). The attenuation provided by a barrier may be estimated from geometrical considerations. Fig. 16.9.1 illustrates the principle involved, the greater the effective height of the barrier, the greater will be the sound reduction. This effective height is measured above the line of sight without the barrier in position, and it is obvious that barriers can usually only be effective for single-story buildings. The attenuation may be estimated from (Ref. 16.30)

$$N = 10(\log 20)X \qquad (16.17)$$

where N is the attenuation, dB re 20 μPa
$X = H^2/\lambda R$, (when $D \gg R \geq H$)
H = effective height of the barrier, ft (m)
λ = wavelength of sound considered, ft (m)
R = distance between source and barrier, ft (m)
D = distance between receiver and barrier, ft (m)

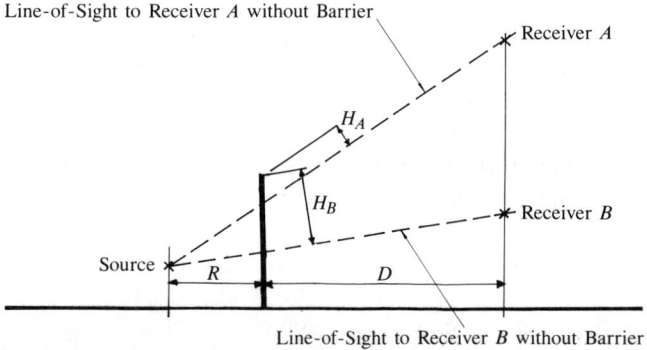

Fig. 16.9.1. Barrier geometry. H_A = effective height of barrier for Receiver A; H_B = effective height of barrier for Receiver B.

Alternatively, the attenuation may be assessed graphically, using the method of Maekawa (Ref. 16.31). (There are also more sophisticated methods of calculating barrier attenuation available; see Ref. 16.32.) It is essential that the barrier also be long, that is, the path-length of the sound transmitted around the ends must be much longer than that over the top; if this is not the case, the values for X must be calculated in the horizontal plane as well, and the total contributions added logarithmically.

Landscaping, such as tree and shrub planting, is erroneously thought to attenuate road traffic noise; this must be a psychological reaction, since measurements fail to show more than 1 or 2 dB reduction.

Aircraft are a common source of high noise levels near airports. Since aircraft are perceived as individual noise events, some sort of averaging is necessary to determine overall impact on people. There are several methods of determining aircraft noise impact; however, in general it is a combination of individual aircraft flyover noise level, the number of such occurrences in a given period, and the time of day at which they occur (frequently there is a penalty of 10 or more decibels for night-time flights). Although there is now strict noise emission legislation for new aircraft, and modern wide-bodied jets are less noisy than the older ones they are replacing, they still cause extremely high levels on the ground when they are landing and taking off. Many airport authorities prepare noise impact maps for the areas surrounding airports. One system, originally developed in the United States, is the Noise Exposure Forecast, NEF (Ref. 16.33) (adapted in Australia and called the Australian Noise Exposure Forecast, ANEF (Ref. 16.34)). These are produced by combining the "noise-prints" of all the aircraft types undertaking expected maneuvers around the airport at some future date; they are accompanied by recommended land-uses. Guidance for the type of construction required to achieve acceptable indoor sound levels for different types of building is given in an Australian Standard (Ref. 16.35).

The impact of railway noise on communities has not been studied as extensively worldwide as has that of road traffic and aircraft noise. In addition to airborne sound, ground vibration caused by the passage of trains, particularly freight trains, may cause annoyance. Track maintenance is also inherently noisy. The advent of very high speed trains has encouraged more attention to noise sources and acceptance criteria. Such trains were first introduced commercially in Japan, and environmental quality standards have been set at 70 dB(A) for residential areas (Ref. 16.36). Although the main sources of noise from conventional trains are the locomotive and the wheel-rail interaction, when trains travel at speeds over about 150 mph (250 km/h) aerodynamic noise is the chief problem.

The acceptable noise emission from industrial premises, entertainment centers, sporting complexes, and the like is frequently the subject of noise control legislation. This may take two forms; in one case, specific noise criteria are set, usually expressed as maximum dB(A) levels for different times of the day; in the other case, the preexisting background noise levels, expressed as the minimum L_{Aeq} or the L_{A90} level, at different times of the day, plus a margin of 5 dB(A), form the criteria. In both systems it is usual to penalize noises that are impulsive or that contain tonal components. The reason for the first penalty is that sound level meters set to read on fast response do not respond as quickly as the human ear to impulsive sounds with very fast rise times; the reason for the second penalty is that a tonal component in a sound makes it more noticeable and thereby more annoying (Refs. 16.37, 16.38).

Industrial noise usually originates from the operation of machinery and plant. Much of it is impulsive, resulting from the impact of metal parts on each other; some of it is tonal (from fans, etc.), and it may operate over 24-hour periods. It is best controlled at the source, by choosing quiet machinery and techniques. This has the added advantage of reducing the risk of employees suffering industrial hearing loss.

It is necessary to determine the noise emission of each item of plant and machinery, including materials handling equipment, and to estimate the overall noise level inside different parts of the building. It is preferable to use one-third octave band sound power levels for these calculations, and similar data should form part of the plant specifications. There are some difficulties inherent in estimating overall sound levels inside factory buildings, because of their unequal dimensions.

The emission of noise from industrial buildings may be predicted by taking into account the size of the radiating facades. No attenuation can be expected within a distance of a/π from a rectangular facade, where a is the smaller dimension; within b/π from the facade attenuation at the rate of 3 dB per doubling of distance should occur and after this distance the source can be assumed to be small or pointlike and an attenuation rate of 6 dB per doubling of distance may be expected. In the case of large industrial complexes, such as refineries, etc. it is necessary to calculate the total expected sound power level from all sources and to assign an acoustic center from which propagation may be determined. As is the case with surface transportation sources, topographical features and purpose-built barriers may be used to provide additional attenuation where required.

16.10. DETAILING, SUPERVISION, AND ACCEPTANCE TESTING

It must be emphasized that sound transmission in and around buildings is critically dependent on detailing and supervision. Frequently, much money is wasted and disappointing results are obtained because of the failure to understand the principles of sound transmission. Wherever there is an air path, there is an unobstructed path for airborne sound transmission; wherever structural elements are fixed rigidly together there is an unobstructed path for structure borne sound transmission.

As an example, the overall attenuation provided by installing a double-glazed, sealed window in a brick-veneer or cavity-brick wall is no better than with a single-glazed window if there is a path through the eaves and ceiling of a tiled-roof dwelling. A typical weakness in otherwise sound-attenuating construction is where pipes and cables for services pass through walls and floors. It is essential that the holes made for such services be as small as possible and that they be carefully sealed around the pipes and cables with nonhardening mastics. Doors are also potentially weak elements; where good sound attenuation between spaces is required it is essential that solid-core doors be used and provided with seals around all the perimeter. Return-air grilles in doors must be avoided. The acoustical consultant should form part of the design team and should be provided with detailed drawings for comment as they are developed.

It is desirable to include acceptance testing as part of the contract. There are now many acoustical standards available (Refs. 16.39, 16.40) (and, in some instances, regulations to be complied with). These set out methods of measurement, assessment, and reporting on results. The measurements are best carried out after completion of the building work, and it is desirable to allow sufficient time for this to be done. As mentioned earlier, although the sound transmission loss performance of building elements may be measured under laboratory conditions, it must be anticipated that lower performance will be obtained in practice, and this should be allowed for in design and specification.

Traditional methods of measuring sound transmission loss in situ rely on measurements of sound pressure level in adjacent spaces. However, although this gives the overall result, which is of most relevance, it does not usually enable discrimination between good and unsatisfactory elements to be made. For example, between two offices excessive sound may be transmitted through the partition, or through the suspended ceilings, or through a suspended floor, or through elements adjoining a common corridor. Recently another method of measuring sound transmission has been developed, using sound intensity rather than sound pressure (Ref. 16.41). Since sound intensity is a vector quantity, it is possible to tell from where the excessive sound is being transmitted. It is hoped that this method will be commonly available in the near future.

If structure-borne sound is the problem it is extremely difficult to correct; first, the source of the excessive transmission is not easily determined, and second, it may not be possible to insert flexible joints or isolating elements once the building is completed. Correct design, detailing, and supervision are particularly important in this area.

Much has been learned regarding the effects of sound within and around buildings over the last few decades. There are now many acoustical specialists available to assist building designers to achieve buildings that are quiet and free from excessive reverberation and vibration. However, they are frequently not able to assist in correcting faults in a completed building thus it is essential that they be consulted at the same time as structural and services engineers in order that such faults do not occur.

REFERENCES

16.1. A. Lawrence. *Acoustics and the Built Environment*, Ch. 1.1, 1.2. Elsevier, London, 1989.

16.2. G. Von Bekesy. *Experiments in Hearing*. McGraw Hill, New York, 1960.

16.3. Special issue on Hearing Research, *J. Acoust. Soc. Amer.*, **78**(1, Pt. 2), 295-388 (1985).

16.4. K. D. Kryter. *The Effects of Noise on Man*. Academic Press, New York, 1985.

16.5. H. Fletcher and W. A. Munson. "Loudness, Its Definition, Measurement and Calculation." *J. Acoust. Soc. Amer.*, **5**, 82-108 (1933).

16.6. D. W. Robinson and L. S. Little. "The Loudness of Octave Bands of Noise."*Acustica*, **14**, 24-35 (1964).

16.7. *Guide for the Evaluation of Human Exposure to Whole-Body Vibration*, ISO 2631-1978. International Standards Organisation, Geneva, 1978.

16.8. *American National Standard Guide for the Evaluation of Human Exposure to Whole-Body Vibration*. ANSI S3.18-1979. American National Standards Institute, New York, 1979.

16.9. *Vibration and Shock—Guide to the Evaluation of Human Exposure to Whole Body Vibration*. AS 2670-1983. Standards Australia, Sydney, 1983.

16.10. A. Lawrence. *Acoustics and the Built Environment*. Elsevier, London, 1989, Ch. 4.2.

16.11. *American National Standard for Rating Noise with Respect to Speech Interference*. ANSI S3.14-1977(R 1986). American National Standards Institute, New York, 1977.

16.12. *Acoustics—Methods of Assessing and Predicting Speech Privacy and Speech Intelligibility*. AS 2811-1985. Standards Australia, Sydney, 1985.

16.13. *Acoustics—Recommended Design Sound Levels and Reverberation Times for Building Interiors*. AS 2107-1987. Standards Australia, Sydney, 1987.

16.14. L. L. Beranek. "The Transmission and Radiation of Acoustic Waves by Solid Structures." *Noise Reduction*. McGraw Hill, New York, 1960, Ch. 13.

16.15. A. Lawrence. *Acoustics and the Built Environment*. Elsevier, London, 1985, Ch. 5.1.

16.16. J. D. Quirt. "Sound Transmission through Windows. I: Single and Double Glazing. II: Double and Triple Glazing." *J. Acoust. Soc. Amer.* **72**, 834-844 (1982); **74**, 534-542 (1983).

16.17. *Standard Classification for Determination of Sound Transmission Class*. ASTM E413. American Society for Testing and Materials, Philadelphia, 1977.

16.18. *Methods for Determination of Sound Transmission Class and Noise Isolation Class of Building Partitions*. AS 1276-1979. Standards Australia, Sydney, 1979.

16.19. *Acoustics—Rating of Sound Insulation in Buildings and of Building Elements—Part 1: Airborne Sound Insulation in Buildings and of Interior Building Elements*. ISO 717 Pt. 1. 1982. International Standards Organisation, Geneva, 1982.

16.20. R. J. M. Craik. "Damping of Building Structures." *App. Acoust.*, **14**, 347-359 (1981).

16.21. D. Muster and R. Plunkett. "Isolation of Vibrations." *Noise and Vibration Control*, L. L. Beranek, Ed. McGraw Hill, New York, 1971, Ch. 13.

16.22. *Acoustics—Measurement of Sound Insulation of Buildings and of Building Elements—Part VI: Laboratory Measurements of Impact Sound Insulation of Floors*. ISO 140-6, 1978. International Standards Organisation, Geneva, 1978.

16.23. *Acoustics—Rating of Sound Insulation in Buildings and of Build-*

ing Elements—Part 2: Impact Sound Insulation. ISO 717/2. International Standards Organisation, Geneva, 1982.
16.24. "Sound and Vibration Control." *ASHRAE Handbook*, Systems Volume. Amer. Soc. Heating, Refrig. and Air Cond. Engineers, Atlanta, 1980, Ch. 35.
16.25. D. B. Callaway. "Noise in Water and Steam Systems." *Handbook of Noise Control*, C. W. Harris, Ed. McGraw Hill, New York, 1957, Ch. 26.
16.26. *Calculation of Road Traffic Noise.* Dept. of the Environment, Welsh Office, Her. Maj. Stat. Off., London, 1988.
16.27. M. A. Burgess. "Noise Prediction for Urban Traffic Conditions—Related to Measurements in the Sydney Metropolitan Area." *App. Acoust.* **10**, 1–7 (1977).
16.28. *Highway Noise—A Design Guide for Prediction and Control.* Report 174. US Transport Research Board, Washington, 1976.
16.29. *Acoustics—Building Siting and Construction against Road Traffic Noise Intrusion.* AS 3671 Standards Australia, Sydney, 1989.
16.30. A. B. Lawrence. *Architectural Acoustics.* Elsevier, London, 1970, pp. 63–65.
16.31. Z. Maekawa. "Noise Reduction by Screens." *App. Acoust.*, **1**, 157–173 (1968).
16.32. U. J. Kurze. "Noise Reduction by Barriers." *J. Acoust. Soc. Amer.* **55**, 504–518 (1974).
16.33. W. J. Galloway and D. E. Bishop. *Noise Exposure Forecasts: Evolution, Evaluation, Extensions and Land use Interpretations. Final Report.* FAA-NO-70-9 United States Dept. of Transportation, Federal Aviation Administration, Office of Noise Abatement, Washington, DC, 1970.
16.34. A. H. Hede and R. B. Bullen. *Aircraft Noise in Australia: A Survey of Community Reaction.* Nat. Acoust. Lab. Report No. 88. Sydney, 1982.
16.35. *Acoustics—Aircraft Noise Intrusion—Building Siting and Construction.* AS 2021-1985. Standards Australia, Sydney, 1985.
16.36. T. Nimura, T. Sone, M. Ebata, and H. Matsumoto. "Noise Problems with High Speed Railways in Japan." *Noise Con. Eng.* **5**, 5–11 (1975).
16.37. *Acoustics—Description and Measurement of Community Noise Environments, Parts 1, 2, and 3.* ISO 1996/1, 2, and 3. International Standards Organisation, Geneva, 1987.
16.38. *Acoustics—Description and Measurement of Environmental Noise Parts 1, 2 and 3.* AS 1055/1, 2 and 3. Standards Australia, Sydney, 1984.
16.39. *Acoustics—Measurement of Sound Insulation in Buildings and of Building Elements: Parts I to VIII.* ISO 140. International Standards Organisation, Geneva, 1978.
16.40. *Methods for Field Measurement of the Reduction of Airborne Sound Transmission in Buildings.* AS 2253-1979. Standards Australia, Sydney, 1979.
16.41. A. Cops and M. Minten. "Comparative Study between the Sound Intensity Method and the Conventional Two-Room Method to Calculate the Sound Transmission Loss of Wall Constructions." *Noise Control Eng.*, **22**, 104–111 (1984).

SUGGESTIONS FOR FURTHER READING

A. Lawrence. *Acoustics and the Built Environment.* Elsevier, New York, 1989.

C. W. Harris (Ed.). *Handbook of Noise Control.* McGraw-Hill, New York, 1957.

L. E. Kinseler et al. *Fundamentals of Acoustics*, 3rd Ed. John Wiley, New York, 1982.

P. H. Parkin, H. R. Humphreys, and J. R. Cowell. *Acoustics, Noise, and Buildings*, 4th Ed. Faber, London, 1979.

NOTATION

c	speed of sound in air, ft/s (m/s)
dB(A)	A-weighted sound pressure level, dB re 20 μPa
f	frequency
f_c	critical frequency, Hz
f_0	resonant frequency, Hz
Hz	Hertz
I	sound intensity, watts/m^2
$L_{Aeq,T}$	equivalent continuous sound pressure level in time T, dB re 20 μPa
$L_{A10,T}$	sound pressure level exceeded 10 percent of the time T, dB re 20 μPa
$L_{A90,T}$	sound pressure level exceeded 90 percent of the time T, dB re 20 μPa
L_I	sound intensity level, dB re 10^{-12} W/m^2
L_p	sound pressure level, dB re 20 μPa
L_W	sound power level, dB re 10^{-12} W
p	sound pressure, Pa
STL	sound transmission loss, dB
T	measurement time period, hours
T_v	transmissibility
W	sound power, watts
Z	characteristic acoustic impedance
λ	wavelength of sound in air, ft (m)

A list of abbreviations of the units of measurement, and definitions of these units are given in the Appendix.

17

Room Acoustics

Louis A. Challis

The achievement of good listening conditions for an audience in an auditorium, church, court, or classroom necessitates low noise levels, appropriate sound distribution, and good sound definition at all listening positions. To achieve these basic requirements, one must start with an appropriate plan and understand how sound behaves in an enclosed space.

The reflection and absorption of sound in a space determines its characteristics and quality, and these characteristics are ultimately determined by the architectural design.

As both the volume or size of a hall and its potential occupancy increases, so too does the need for sound amplification. The provision of electronic amplification does not necessarily improve speech intelligibility, or the quality of the sound, unless the design of the amplification system is properly integrated with the architectural acoustical design.

17.1. PLANNING FOR ACOUSTICAL REQUIREMENTS

The achievement of good architectural acoustics is congruent with good planning. The process should start with the selection of the building site and continue through each subsequent stage of the design. An architect, engineer, or planner may well avoid potential design errors by adopting checklists in which the appropriate acoustical precautions are identified. A typical process will involve:

1. The selection of a site in the quietest possible surroundings consistent with the other planning requirements and financial constraints
2. The evaluation of the diurnal statistical variability of extraneous noise sources, through which the potential building façade design criteria may be appropriately assessed
3. The development of an appropriate design configuration which places those rooms requiring the quietest environment well away from the potential sources of intrusive noise
4. The selection of appropriate construction systems for the building envelope, with due consideration for the glazing, doors, entrances, air intake, and discharge penetrations for ventilation and exhaust systems
5. A comprehensive assessment of the potential noise and vibration sources within the building to ensure that the most appropriate barrier to airborne sound and structure-borne vibrations may be integrated into the design
6. An assessment of the design configuration for each type of room or space for which specific acoustical requirements are identified; this assessment should take into account background noise levels, the need for enhanced sound propagation requirements in terms of speech and/or music, or conversely, the attenuation requirements if sound intrusion needs to be minimized
7. The selection and distribution of absorptive and reflective surfaces and selection of materials to optimize the buildup, maintenance, or decay of sound within that room
8. The acoustical requirements for the air conditioning system and for the other mechanical services, in order to preclude an adverse impact on specific areas within the building (or even on adjacent buildings)
9. The design of electronic and electroacoustic systems associated with communications, computing

networks, speech amplification systems, emergency evacuation systems, electronic masking systems, or paging systems, in order to insure compliance with the fundamental acoustical requirements of each room or space within the building
10. The performance requirements, field or laboratory test requirements, and associated quality assurance programs for critical acoustical materials, products, services, or systems in the building to ensure that the basic design criteria will be achieved by each of the systems on the completion of the building
11. The development of an acoustical supervision program for the production of the elements during the various phases of construction, to ensure that contractors fulfill the specific acoustical requirements identified in the drawings and/or specifications; this program must incorporate intermediate as well as final acoustical performance test evaluations, through which the standards of nominated construction and assembly may be ensured.
12. Preparation of appropriate maintenance instructions and specifications for special construction, periodic inspection, special testing, and sources of replacement material relating to:
    (a) How the acoustical materials or special facings can be cleaned and redecorated, or alternatively with what materials they may be replaced
    (b) The acoustical characteristics and extent of specific surfaces, furnishings, carpets and underlay, absorptive screens or wall linings, acoustical murals or tapestries to maintain a specified level of sound absorption or variable absorption, where required
    (c) environmental requirements in terms of temperature and humidity, supply air, return air velocities and duct velocities, which have been adopted as specific design criteria for low noise areas, such as recording and television studios, auditoriums, or spaces with special electro-acoustic requirements
    (d) the range of electroacoustic design requirements for rooms in which assisted resonance, digital sound processors, or ambiophany has been provided, in order to achieve "variable acoustics"

The adoption and implementation of an appropriate acoustical checklist, which leads to the identification of potential problems at the earliest possible stages of the design, generally assists the designer to avoid the majority of the major acoustical pitfalls, which plague so many important architectural and industrial projects.

The use of such procedures usually proves to be just as important in the planning for industrial and transportation facilities, scholastic institutions and commercial buildings, as it is in the design of concert halls, radio and television studios and major governmental buildings.

17.2. BEHAVIOR OF SOUND IN AN ENCLOSED SPACE

When sound is generated in a room, its energy is radiated, reflected, and absorbed in a complex manner which depends on many factors. These include the shape, dimensions, and nature of construction of the room. Fig. 17.2.1 illustrates typical phenomena which may occur in any type of room or enclosed space and which are identified by the arrows. These phenomena are

1. Direct sound propagation, which is attenuated as a result of increasing distance between the source and the receiver
2. Primary reflection from adjacent walls or ceiling
3. Audience absorption of the direct sound
4. Absorption of the direct and reflected sound by absorptive or dissipative wall or ceiling surfaces
5. Multiple reflections from a reentrant reflection at the

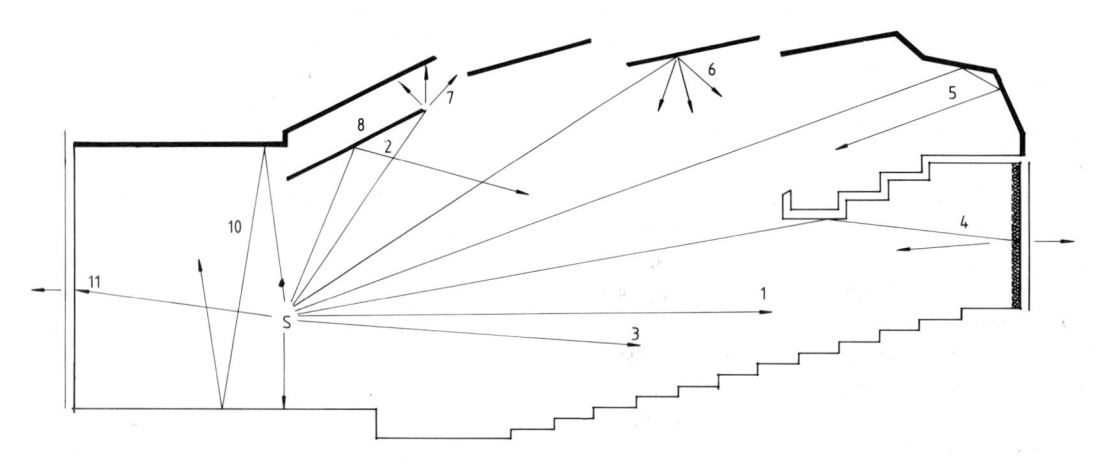

Fig. 17.2.1. The most important phenomena relevant to the design of auditoria, cinemas, courtrooms, atrium spaces, classrooms, and open planned offices. All require varying degrees of acoustical design and assessment. The key to these phenomena is listed in the text.

upper edge of the ceilings and walls (as well as between walls)
6. Sound dispersion by changes in the depth of sculpturing or angling of wall or ceiling surfaces
7. Edge diffraction from a primary sound reflector
8. Shadow zones behind large, free-standing or suspended sound reflectors
9. Panel resonance from timber flooring, thin glazing, or lightweight and thin wall or ceiling panels
10. Interreflection, standing waves, and local reverberation effects between parallel or closely spaced surfaces
11. Transmission of sound through the envelope to the external environment

When planning the acoustical criteria for auditoria, studios and lecture theaters there are a series of acoustical design objectives which require appropriate evaluation during the architectural and acoustical design (Table 17.1).

17.3. REFLECTION AND DIFFRACTION OF SOUND IN ROOMS

When a sound wave impinges on a stiff or heavy wall, most of the incident sound energy is reflected by the wall; a small portion of that energy is transmitted into and subsequently through the wall, where some of it is dissipated as heat, while a small proportion is radiated from its outer surface.

When a sound wave impinges on a lightweight wall or ceiling barrier constructed from porous materials such as fiberglass or mineral wool, the relationship between reflection, dissipation and propagation is significantly modified. The portion of incident energy reflected into the room is much lower, the portion transmitted is much higher, and most is dissipated by viscous losses within the capillary pores of the porous materials. The proportion of sound energy radiated through a lightweight or porous structure to the other side is therefore significantly higher.

Few commercial, residential, and industrial wall structures are very stiff. Even when they are relatively heavy, they still vibrate as a whole, or differentially, under the action of the acoustical pressure applied by the incident sound waves. Masonry, timber, or lightweight framed dry walls may be induced to vibrate like diaphragms that reflect and reradiate the incident sound energy back into the space from which it originated.

If we ignore the flanking components of sound energy through doors, windows, vents or apertures, most of the sound that is transmitted from one room to another is propagated in this way. Rigid, heavy, and thick walls are invariably better insulators, because they inhibit the propagation of sound energy more effectively than flexible, lightweight walls. On the other hand, a combination of rigid partitions on both sides of an absorptive, dissipative internal lining (such as fiberglass or mineral wool) generally achieves a higher level of sound attenuation in the speech frequency range than a typical solid masonry or concrete wall.

The Reflection of Sound

When a progressive or "free" sound wave (which is free from the influence of reflective surfaces) impinges on a uniform surface whose dimensions are large compared to the wavelength of the sound, its reflection conforms to the same physical principles as the reflection of light waves: the angle of reflection equals the angle of incidence, and the reflected sound ray lies in the plane of incidence.

The reflected sound rays follow the same paths that would result if a light ray was the source of energy. Large concave surfaces concentrate sound waves. They may be used to advantage as sound reflectors, but if used indiscriminately for aesthetic reasons, acoustical sound deficiencies result due to sound focusing within that space.

Conversely, a convex reflector spreads the reflected sound waves, and convex surfaces at the boundaries of a room diffuse the sound throughout the space (Fig. 17.3.1). For this reason, many large auditoriums and radio or broadcasting studios have been constructed with cylindrical or convex panels in the walls and ceilings as sound diffusing elements to disperse the sound waves smoothly (Ref. 17.1).

Acousticians often use the law of reflection to investigate the effects of various shapes on the sound distribution in a proposed room. These studies were previously conducted using graphical or optical procedures; but there are now a number of computer programs available (Ref. 17.2) which integrate the relevant laws of optical and geometrical acoustical theory to assess different aspects of the acoustics of the room. Some also incorporate procedures for assessing the electroacoustic requirements of the room.

Table 17.1. Acoustical Design Objectives for Auditoriums.

Clarity/intelligibility	Strong, uniform direct plus coplanar reflected sound
Balanced sound projection	Selective control of reflection from the lectern or stage to the audience
Cohesion for performers on the stage or podium	Control of stage reflections
Freedom from unwanted echoes and reflections strong envelopmental sound	Control of front to rear wall and unwanted side wall flutter echoes; optimization of side wall and proscenium reflections to ensure the proper space and time distribution of sound arriving from multiple locations within the hall
Early decay times and optimum reverberation times	Appropriate distribution of interior sound absorption and specifically the extent of audience sound absorption

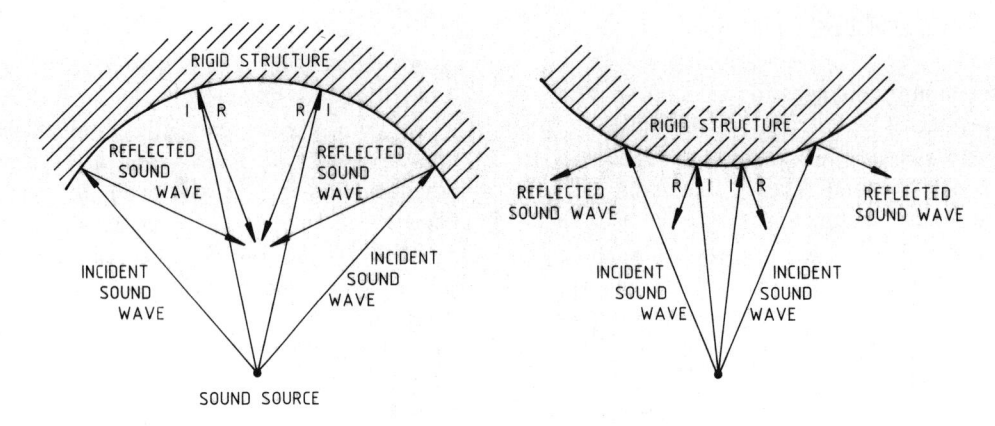

Fig. 17.3.1. Reflections of sound rays by convex and concave surfaces.

The Diffraction of Sound

While there are obvious analogies between the propagation of light and sound, there are also significant differences due to the frequency-related propagation of sound around obstacles and through apertures.

The laws of optics and acoustics are both based upon wave properties. However, because the wavelength of light is so small, optics can be handled by geometrical procedures based on rays. The longer sound waves produce diffraction, and this is a significant factor in physical acoustics.

Thus sound waves do not create sharp shadows or images like light waves. Unlike an optical wave, sound passing through a small aperture diffracts and reradiates as a hemispherical source after passing through that aperture.

Geometrical acoustics is similar to geometrical optics if the wavelengths of the sound are short compared to the dimensions of a room, or of an opening through which they pass, or of the reflecting surfaces on which they impinge. However, few room surfaces are large by comparison with the wavelength of low-pitched sounds. Therefore windows, doors, columns, beams, coffers, niches, or any form of ornamental relief, as well as areas of absorptive material, all introduce sound diffraction, which modifies both the direction and the magnitude of the reflected sound waves.

Diffraction of Sound from Reflective and Absorptive Surfaces

The science and art of room acoustics depends to a large extent on the diffraction effects that accompany the reflection of sound from various architectural features selected or integrated into the design of walls and ceilings.

The architectural, decorative, and functional sculpturing of wall and ceiling surfaces, which involve the use of beams, columns, and ornamental plaster elements, result in the creation of regular or irregular discontinuities in the boundary surfaces of the room. When sound impinges on these surfaces, complicated diffraction phenomena result (Ref. 17.3).

Discontinuities in the sound-absorptive treatment of a wall (such as the introduction of areas of absorptive material), as well as irregularities in the shape of a wall, diffract the incident sound waves. These acoustical discontinuities, or associated absorptive areas on the walls of a room, diffract or scatter incident sound waves and aid in diffusing the sound energy throughout the room. Most rooms which are regarded as acoustically well designed for speech, or for singing, or for other music that is intended to be clearly heard, normally achieve this through optimizing the level of sound diffusion (Ref. 17.4).

17.4. SOUND ABSORPTIVE MATERIALS

The rate at which sound is absorbed in a room is one of the principal factors in reducing noise, as well as in the control of reflection and reverberation. All materials used in the construction of buildings absorb some sound, but the most effective acoustical control invariably requires the use of materials that have been specially designed as sound absorbers.

Sound is absorbed by a mechanism which converts the sound into other forms of energy, and ultimately into heat. Most commercial sound-absorptive materials depend primarily on the porosity of their structure for their absorptive characteristics. Many man-made materials, such as fiberglass, mineral wools, and cellulose fibers formed into flexible blankets or semi-rigid or rigid boards have a multitude of small, deeply penetrating, interconnecting pores. The sound waves can readily propagate and penetrate between the interstices of their structure, where a portion of the sound energy is converted into heat by frictional and viscous resistance during the wave propagation.

The efficacy of sound absorption in such materials is dependent on the porosity and the thickness of the material, the frequency of the incident sound wave, and the extent to which the supporting or protecting facings modify or affect the incident sound energy. It is possible to achieve up to 100 percent sound absorption, but generally only over a portion of the range of frequencies under consideration.

Another mechanism by which sound energy may be absorbed is through the flexural vibration and dissipation of energy in panels, windows, floors, and walls (Refs. 17.5–17.7). The dissipative characteristics of even the heaviest wall or floor result in some sound absorption, even though it may be low.

Sound is also attenuated by the molecular absorption of air, which increases with increasing frequency of sound and also depends on the humidity in the air. With a large volume of air (in a large auditorium) this phenomenon may become significant, particularly if there are few other forms of sound absorption (Ref. 17.8).

In any auditorium the audience generally constitutes one of the most significant absorptive surfaces. Absorption depends on the rake angle of the floor and seating, the spacing of the seats (both longitudinally and laterally with respect to the source of sound energy), and most particularly on the mode of dress of the audience. Audiences in temperate climates wear more absorptive clothing than those in tropical climates, and this factor must be considered when assessing or nominating sound absorption coefficients for an audience in any architectural acoustical study (Ref. 17.9).

There are many acoustical materials which have been primarily developed to meet the requirements of commercial and industrial buildings. Most incorporate special facings, which may be resistant to dust, moisture, chemicals, or physical abuse. Sound absorptive materials have been designed for special applications in auditoriums, schools, swimming pools, gymnasiums, kitchens, factories, and plant rooms. The optimum use of these material makes it possible for speech to be heard clearly, and for music to be enjoyed to the fullest extent.

A wide range of commercial modular acoustical sound-absorptive products is now available for use in buildings. Most can be used in a variety of ways, only limited by the imagination of the user. There is no universal material that is best suited for all installations, and each project or design requires individual assessment in which all related physical, decorative, and functional properties of the materials must be given due consideration. Such evaluation should assess the following parameters:

1. The frequency distribution of the incident sound, and similarly the sound-absorption characteristics of the material to be used
2. The physical strength of the absorptive material and the mechanism through which it will be supported or fixed to the structure
3. The aesthetic characteristics of the material, particularly its light reflectance or conversely its light absorption
4. The flammability of the material, the extent to which it supports combustion, as well as its smoke development indices
5. The durability, weather and moisture resistance, resistance to rodents and other vermin, and the stability of its sound-absorption characteristics during its life (particularly if it is likely to require subsequent painting)
6. Its cost, and the adequacy and complexity of its installation

Determination of Sound Absorption Coefficients

There are two methods for evaluating the frequency-related sound absorption characteristics of sound absorptive materials.

One technique involves the use of an impedance tube, where the normal-incidence sound reflection coefficient may be determined through an evaluation of the standing wave phenomenon. The data provided by this procedure may be used to calculate the statistical absorption coefficients using the technique developed by Dubout and Davern (Ref. 17.11). This technique, although simple and generally inexpensive, may only provide limited data for some products and materials, and generally provides comparative data, rather than absolute data.

A second and more common technique is based on the use of reverberation chambers in which the material or sound absorptive system is placed or suspended to determine the extent to which it reduces the reverberation times when measured over a series of frequency band widths, which are normally one-third of an octave wide.

One major advantage of this measurement technique is that the reverberation chamber sound absorption coefficients are derived from a diffuse field assessment, which provides an average coefficient at each frequency and which is applicable for incident sound from all possible directions.

These coefficients are normally determined for absorption at one-third octave band center frequencies lying between 100 Hz and 5 kHz, and less frequently for frequencies as low as 63 Hz or as high as 8 kHz. The coefficients may be directly utilized for the computations of room reverberation times (Ref. 17.12).

Frequency Selective and Additive Systems

Many special or unusual materials and many absorptive systems, such as Helmholtz absorbers (Refs. 17.10, 17.13, and 17.14), perforated panel absorbers with small holes in thick panels and wide-spaced batten facings with narrow slots overlying cavities (Ref. 17.15), exhibit frequency-selective characteristics. These frequency-selective systems may prove advantageous when used as part of an overall system; however, they generally prove to be a liability when used as the dominant or single sound-absorptive system.

The narrow-frequency-selective sound-absorptive characteristics of most slotted or perforated acoustical facing systems may be broadened and substantially modified by the application of a sound absorptive fibrous mineral wool or fibreglass blanket in the cavity behind the facing (Ref. 17.16).

There are many situations where the nonuniformity or lack of appropriate sound absorption requires some form of corrective action. Historically those problems were solved in the old European castles and churches by hanging tapestries, suspending pennants, and by placing bottles or jugs in the walls with their open ends pointing into the rooms (Ref. 17.17). There are modern variants to these systems which utilize tapestries that have cavities behind or are backed by absorptive panels or quilts.

Another approach employs acoustical pennants and flags, and modular suspended absorbers; this is commonly used in swimming pools, gymnasiums, factories, and large atrium spaces. These devices are often adopted as a means of achieving reduced reverberation times, where other options or treatments have been rejected because of costs or complexity (Ref. 17.18).

17.5. RATING THE ACOUSTICAL ABSORPTIVITY OF MATERIALS

The efficiency of a material in absorbing acoustical energy at a specified frequency is defined as its sound absorption coefficient at that frequency. This quantity is the fractional part of the energy of an incident sound wave that is absorbed (not reflected) by the material. Thus if sound waves strike a material, and if 55 percent of the incident acoustical energy is absorbed and 45 percent of the energy is reflected, the absorption coefficient of the material is 0.55. Each square foot (or square meter) of this material is equivalent to 0.55 square feet (square meters) of a perfectly absorptive surface. The sabin is a measure of the sound absorption of a surface; it is the equivalent of 1 square foot of perfectly absorptive surface in imperial units (or 1 square meter in metric units). A surface of area S having an absorption coefficient alpha (α) has a total absorption of $S\alpha$ sabins.

The sabin is often referred to as a square-foot (or one square-meter) unit of sound absorption. The coefficient of sound absorption varies with the angle at which the sound wave strikes the material, particularly where the face and structure of the absorptive system is non-homogeneous.

Coefficients measured in a reverberation chamber, which are relevant in most other room environments, are the result of incident sound energy coming from all possible directions. The sound absorption coefficient determined for sound incident from all possible directions is called the *statistical sound absorption coefficient*, which is denoted by α_{st}. Measurements conducted in an impedance tube provide only normal-incidence sound absorption coefficients, but the statistical absorption coefficient can be derived from such data.

Since α_{st} varies with frequency, it has been common practice to list values at specific frequencies in tables of absorption coefficients, which are usually listed at frequencies of 125, 250, 500, 1000, 2000, and 4000 Hz. Most laboratories determine the sound absorption coefficients for materials, panels, ceilings and structures at the one-third octave band center frequencies lying between 100 Hz and 5 kHz (Ref. 17.19).

These absorption coefficients depend not only on the nature of the material, but also on other factors such as its thickness, as well as on the way in which the materials are used, suspended, protected or mounted, and most particularly on the depth of the air space behind the rear face of such systems (Ref. 17.20).

Noise Reduction Coefficient of Sound Absorptive Systems and Typical Sound Absorption Coefficients

The noise reduction coefficient, which is commonly abbreviated to NRC, is the average (to the nearest multiple of 0.05) of the measured absorption coefficients at the four octave-band center frequencies of 250, 500, 1000, and 2000 Hz. This number is often used to compare the efficacy of different materials for commercial noise-reduction applications in offices, schools, and auditoriums.

Although the NRC is convenient as a simple descriptor, its applicability is limited. It is preferable to select materials on the basis of the absorptive characteristics appropriate for the suppression of the type of noise which requires reduction. Typical sound absorption parameters at octave-band center frequencies are presented in Table 17.2.

17.6. GROWTH AND DECAY OF SOUND IN ROOMS

The reverberant sound level in a room is inversely proportional to the total amount of absorption produced by the air within that room and the amount of sound absorption at the room boundaries on the walls, floor, and ceiling. If the room incorporates a large amount of sound absorption, then the final equilibrium level is very quickly attained. Conversely, if there is only a small amount of absorption, the buildup of sound energy to the final state of equilibrium is relatively slow.

In precisely the same way, the decay of the sound level and sound energy in such a room is relatively slow, where there is little absorption. Such rooms are described as *live*, and in such rooms the application of simple acoustic ray theory is easily applied and generally provides acceptable results.

If a sound source is suddenly switched on in a live room (i.e, one in which there is relatively little sound-absorptive material), sound waves radiating from that source travel outward until they strike one or more of the boundaries of the room. Some of the energy is then absorbed, and the residual energy is reflected back into the room. This process of partial absorption and partial reflection continues until a state of equilibrium is established.

Table 17.2. Sound Absorption Coefficients for Typical Materials.

Octave-Band Center Frequency, Hz:	125	250	500	1000	2000	4000	8000
Audience in thick upholstered seats (per unit floor area)	.3	.4	.5	.4	.35	.3	.3
Acoustical mineral spray wool placed 1 in. (25 mm) thick on concrete	.1	.3	.65	.85	.9	.95	.9
Haircord carpet on felt underlay	.05	.05	.1	.2	.45	.65	.7
Heavyweight carpet without underlay on concrete floor	.02	.07	.16	.35	.55	.60	.65
Heavyweight wool carpet on very thick animal felt underlay	.11	.37	.77	.85	.83	.78	.8
$\frac{5}{8}$ in. (15 mm) thick fissured mineral wool based ceiling tile in No. 7 AMA mounting*	.4	.35	.4	.55	.65	.77	.8
2 in. (50 mm) thick semi-rigid fiber-glass panels with wool cloth facing cover fixed to solid backing	.25	0.6	1.0	1.0	1.0	1.0	0.9
$\frac{3}{16}$ in. (5 mm) thick glass windows in conventional aluminium frames	.35	.25	.15	.10	.07	.04	.03
Painted rendered brick wall $5\frac{1}{2}$ in. (130 mm) thick	.1	.05	.05	.06	.07	.08	.08
Perforated particleboard $\frac{5}{8}$ in. (16 mm) thick with $\frac{3}{8}$ in. (9 mm) holes at $1\frac{3}{8}$ in. (34 mm) centers spaced 3 in. (75 mm) from wall or floor	.15	.6	.45	.4	.38	.35	.3
Heavy woven woolen tapestry hanging 1 in. (25 mm) from wall, no backing	.03	.14	.32	.58	.7	.6	.55
Polished $\frac{3}{4}$ in. (19 mm) timber floor	.15	.11	.10	.07	.06	.06	.05
Steel-troweled concrete floor unpainted	.01	.01	.01	.01	.02	.02	.025

*AMA is the Acoustical Manufacturers Association of the United States of America.

Under these conditions, the rate at which acoustic energy is fed into the room equals the rate at which it is dissipated through the effects of sound absorption at the boundaries of the room, as well as through the sound-absorptive effects of the air in the room. After multiple successive reflections, the average energy density becomes constant throughout the room and the resulting sound field produced by these successive reflections is said to be *reverberant* and *diffuse*. Under such conditions, there should be equal probability at any instant of sound rays arriving from all directions at each point in the room. If there were no sound absorption in the room, the sound field would increase to an infinite intensity.

When dealing with relatively small enclosures with simple shapes, one can usually obtain an exact solution through wave analysis by solving the appropriate wave equation and using the known boundary conditions. A precise and exact analysis is not normally possible when one attempts to apply such theory to large, irregular enclosures. In such situations, useful information can however be obtained from the application of statistical techniques. Although such methods do not provide exact solutions, they do provide reasonably accurate values of sound level and generally such information suffices.

According to Sabine's definition of reverberation time (Ref. 17.21), which is the time, T_R (in seconds), taken for the sound pressure level to drop by 60 decibels* for a room of Volume V (in ft^3) and for a total absorption a (expressed in ft^2):

$$T_R = \frac{0.049V}{a} \quad (17.1)$$

Expressed in metric units, where V is in m^3 and a is in m^2:

$$T_R = \frac{0.161V}{a} \quad (17.2)$$

These equations define the average Sabine or statistical absorption coefficient $\overline{\alpha}$ in terms of the total surface area S:

$$a = S\overline{\alpha} \quad (17.3)$$

If all the surfaces of a room were perfect sound absorbers ($\overline{\alpha} = 1$), Eqs. (17.1) and (17.2) would still yield a finite value for the reverberation time. Obviously, with no reflected sound the reverberation time should be zero. In order to overcome this problem, a new approach must be sought for the analysis of sound in rooms in which the av-

*See Section 16.2 and Appendix A2 for a definition of *decibel*.

erage absorptive coefficient is no longer small. This usually occurs when $\bar{\alpha}$ exceeds a value of approximately 0.2.

For discrete components of energy impinging on a wall, floor, or ceiling surface, where some sound absorption takes place, and again during a subsequent reflection on another surface where similar absorption takes place, Sabine's equation may be redefined in terms of a *mean free path*, as well as in terms of the energy absorbed per second. From this it can be shown that the reverberation time may be redefined as

$$T_R = \frac{0.049V}{-S \log_e(1 - \bar{\alpha})} \quad (17.4)$$

in Imperial units. This equation was independently obtained by Eyring and by Norris and is generally known as the Norris-Eyring Reverberation Time Equation. It should be noted that if $\bar{\alpha} = 1$, then $T_R = 0$, as it should be. This differs from the Sabine Equations (17.1) and (17.2), where for small values of $\bar{\alpha}$, the term $[-S \log_e (1 - \bar{\alpha})]$ tends to $S\bar{\alpha}$.

The Eyring Reverberation Time Formula

As the volume of a room increases, and the extent of the absorption decreases, the effects of air absorption and of molecular absorption of the moisture (or water vapor) in that air result in a further significant change in the propagation and attenuation of the sound energy in that space.

Harris (Ref. 17.22) presented relevant data on the effects of that energy attenuation, which are reproduced in Tables 17.3a and 17.3b. Equations (17.1) and (17.2) can then be rewritten as:

$$T_R = 0.049 \frac{V}{a + 4mV} \quad (17.5)$$

in imperial units, or

$$T_R = 0.161 \frac{V}{a + 4mV} \quad (17.6)$$

in metric units, where

V = volume (ft³ or m³)

a = total absorption (ft² or m²)

m = attenuation constant for air (ft⁻¹ or m⁻¹).

When the reverberation time of a room is being evaluated and the extent of absorption is not small (i.e., $\bar{\alpha} > 0.2$), the Knudson and Harris version of Eyring's equation should be used to provide enhanced accuracy of calculation:

$$T_R = \frac{0.049V}{S[-2.30 \log_{10}(1 - \bar{\alpha})] + 4mV} \quad [17.7]$$

Table 17.3a. Values of Energy Attenuation Constant Multiplied by 4 for Air, 4 mV,* in British Units (1/foot).

Relative Humidity, %	Temperature, °F	2,000 Hz	4,000 Hz	6,300 Hz	8,000 Hz
30	59	0.0044	0.0148	0.0322	
	68	0.0036	0.0116	0.0256	
	77	0.0035	0.0095	0.0209	0.0410
	86	0.0034	0.0086	0.0172	
50	59	0.0030	0.0087	0.0191	
	68	0.0020	0.0074	0.0153	
	77	0.0029	0.0072	0.0135	0.0260
	86	0.0028	0.0071	0.0130	
70	50	0.0027	0.0068	0.0138	
	68	0.0026	0.0065	0.0122	
	77	0.0026	0.0064	0.0118	0.0184
	86	0.0025	0.0063	0.0117	

*m = energy attenuation constant for air (ft⁻¹)
V = volume of air
$4mV$ = energy attenuation of air, multiplied by 4.

Table 17.3b. Values of Energy Attenuation Constant Multiplied by 4 for Air, $4mV$,* in Metric Units (1/meter).

Relative Humidity, %	Temperature, °C	2,000 Hz	4,000 Hz	6,300 Hz	8,000 Hz
30	15	0.0143	0.0486	0.1056	
	20	0.0119	0.0379	0.0840	
	25	0.0114	0.0313	0.0685	0.1360
	30	0.0111	0.0281	0.0564	
50	15	0.0099	0.0286	0.0626	
	20	0.0096	0.0244	0.0503	
	25	0.0095	0.0235	0.0444	0.0860
	30	0.0092	0.0233	0.0426	
70	15	0.0088	0.0223	0.0454	
	20	0.0085	0.0213	0.0399	
	25	0.0084	0.0211	0.0388	0.0600
	30	0.0082	0.0207	0.0383	

*m = energy attenuation constant for air (m⁻¹)
V = volume of air
$4mV$ = energy attenuation of air, multiplied by 4

where S = total surface area of room, ft²

$\bar{\alpha}$ = average absorption coefficient of all the room surfaces

$4mV$ = energy attenuation constant for air multiplied by 4 × Volume

This equation is particularly significant when the room volume, the air absorption, and the extent of the sound absorption are all greater than normal. An examination of Tables 17.3a and 17.3b shows that this will make a major difference to the results computed by the Eyring equation if room volumes are large.

The Eyring equation does not provide accurate results where the sound-absorptive materials are distributed non-uniformly on only one or two surfaces within such a room.

The Fitzroy Reverberation Time Formula

The Eyring reverberation time formula presented above is based on the assumptions that the sound in the enclosure is uniformly distributed, and that the sound absorbing material is evenly distributed on all surfaces throughout the room; this results in a diffuse sound field.

The Eyring equation does not, however, take into account the effects of nonuniformly placed sound-absorbing materials, nor the results of echoes or room resonances. In point of fact, there are few situations in which the sound-absorbing materials are uniformly located around a room; more typical are offices where most or all of the sound-absorbing material is placed on the ceiling and floor. For such rooms the Eyring equation is not accurate, because the distribution of sound absorption is grossly nonuniform.

Fitzroy (Ref. 17.23) developed a more accurate empirical reverberation-time formula for rooms where the distribution of sound absorption is nonuniform. He developed it through ray acoustics, visualizing the sound field as simultaneous waves oscillating between the room's three perpendicular surfaces.

He postulated that a relationship exists between the three separate decay rates associated with each of these three sets of parallel surfaces, i.e., between the floor and the ceiling, between the side walls, and between the end walls, respectively, each being exposed to a specific proportion of the total sound energy distributed within the room. Assuming that the influence of each set of boundaries on the reverberation time was proportional to the ratio of the areas of the respective parallel surfaces to the total surface area of the room. Fitzroy modified the Eyring formula as follows:

$$T_R = \frac{S_x}{S}\left[\frac{0.049V}{S\log_e(1-\overline{\alpha}_x)^{-1}}\right] + \frac{S_y}{S}\left[\frac{0.049V}{S\log_e(1-\overline{\alpha}_y)^{-1}}\right] + \frac{S_z}{S}\left[\frac{0.049V}{S\log_e(1-\overline{\alpha}_z)^{-1}}\right]$$

[17.8]

where S_x is the side wall area, ft^2
S_y is the end wall area, ft^2
S_z is the floor and ceiling area, ft^2
S is the total wall area, ft^2
V is the room volume, ft^3
$\overline{\alpha}_x$, $\overline{\alpha}_y$ and $\overline{\alpha}_z$ are the average sound absorption coefficients of the x, y, and z area, respectively.

17.7. CLASSIFICATION OF AUDITORIUMS

The three main classes of auditoriums are those designed for:

1. Speech
2. Music
3. Multipurpose usage

The acoustical requirements for the optimum reception of speech differ significantly from those required for music, as do the environmental requirements for listening to speech and music. Typical auditoriums for speech are courtrooms, council chambers, classrooms, parliamentary chambers, conference halls, and lecture theaters. Auditoriums for music are typified by concert halls, opera houses, lyric theaters, and chamber music venues.

Churches constitute a special classification where the reception of speech is important, although acoustical designers of churches generally place a greater emphasis on the music-related characteristics than they should and consequently the ability to hear sermons is generally impaired. Town halls and school assembly halls are typical auditoriums in which speech and theatrical presentations are more common than musical concerts, and consequently the architect, the acoustician, and the client need to assess the relative importance of speech and music when nominating the design parameters in order to determine the most suitable acoustic environment.

Acoustics for Speech (see also Section 16.5)

When designing any auditorium, the nature and location of the source of sound are the primary design considerations. The level of unamplified speech normally ranges from a low whisper (30–35 dB(A)) to an assertive voice (70–75 dB(A)), when measured at a typical distance of 3 feet (1 m) in front of the orator. Actors occasionally raise their voices to 80–85 dB(A) at 3 ft (1 m), but the average voice levels are relatively low when compared with the levels produced by instruments, bands, or orchestras. As a consequence, many of the sounds important for speech intelligibility are relatively low in level.

The other important characteristic of speech is that its audibility (and intelligibility) by an audience requires clear reception of a rapid sequence of discrete sounds, most of relatively short duration. Intelligibility is thus determined both by the source power level and by the clarity with which the sound is propagated and heard. In designing a room for speech, both the loudness and the clarity of the sound must be optimized at all listening positions.

The primary factors which affect the speech intelligibility of an orator in a hall are described here.

1. The control of background noise within the audience listening area is the preeminent factor to ensure that the orator may be heard; if the background sound level is too high, each of the following attributes is nullified. The background sound level should preferably be less than 30dB(A) and ideally less than 25dB(A) (see Table 16.1).

2. The distance between the most remote member of the audience and the speaker (if his voice is unamplified) should ideally be less than 80 ft (24 m). This distance may be marginally increased in a lecture theater by side wall and ceiling reflective surfaces, and by raking of the seating upward from the orator.

3. A speaker's head and mouth, and thus his voice, are directional. This affects the potential shape of the audience area, both for the direct sound and the potential reflections, which may be gained from side walls and reflective ceiling surfaces. The directionality becomes more significant for high-frequency sounds, and particularly for sibilants and fricative consonants in human speech. Good intelligibility is possible with audience distances of up to 65 ft (20 m). A distance of 100 ft (30 m) is the extreme limit; beyond it sound amplification becomes an essential requirement.

4. The sound absorption of an audience is appreciable. It should therefore be seated on an appropriately raked or stepped floor to ensure appropriate visual and acoustical sight lines in order to reduce absorption of the orator's voice.

5. The provision of side wall and (more significantly) ceiling reflectors, provides a small but useful enhancement of speech intelligibility within an audience area, particularly when a fan-shaped or rectangular audience distribution has been selected. Such reflection can only be beneficial when the differential path length between the direct sound and the reflected sound is less than 20 ft (6 m). When the differential path length exceeds 20 ft (6 m) the direct and reflected components are no longer perceived as one, but as two distinct components. The primary reflective energy should be directed toward the most distant members of the audience to encompass the full width of the rearmost area. The width or minimum dimensions of the reflective ceiling panels should ideally be greater than 10 ft (3 m) in order to minimize edge diffraction effects, which become significant with panels of lesser dimensions. These panels may be of convex form in order to provide appropriate dispersion, or they may be segmented panels with intersecting surfaces to achieve the required level of dispersion. The absorption coefficients of the panels should be as small as possible in order to maximize the reflected energy.

6. When sound amplification becomes desirable (because of soft-spoken orators), or essential (because of the dimensions of the room or hall), the loudspeakers must be correctly positioned. The optimum position of a column loudspeaker system is directly over the head of the speaker. In this position there is minimum potential for acoustical feedback, minimum time delay between the direct sound and the amplified sound, maximum intelligibility and realism of the amplified sound.

An overhead loudspeaker position normally ensures minimum amplification at the closest seating positions, which would otherwise be subjected to excessive sound (with a podium-mounted speaker system), or to interference (when loudspeakers are placed on both sides of the stage). The position of the orator's microphone is extremely important. Lavalier microphones worn around the neck, hand-held or body-worn wireless microphones, and appropriately placed directional microphones on stands all offer specific advantages in terms of improved signal-to-noise ratio and reduced acoustical feedback from the main amplification system. They also offer a potential enhancement of the amplified voice signal, when correctly selected and utilized, to maintain appropriate uniformity of the orator's voice signal.

If loudspeakers are placed behind the orator's head (or sufficiently close to one or both sides), the likelihood of acoustical feedback or amplifier squeal is increased; this normally results in a significant degradation in voice quality. When such conditions occur, the microphone must be extremely directional, or it should be placed as close as possible to the orator's mouth.

7. There are many situations in council chambers, cinemas, concert halls, and auditoriums where elevation of the seats and/or step-downs in the ceiling (below galleries, projection boxes, passageways, and plant rooms) result in partial obstruction of the acoustical paths for sound enhancement. In these situations, and especially where sound shadows become significant, the architectural design should be reassessed. Alternatively, appropriate supplementary electronic amplification with special loudspeakers should be provided for the listeners affected (preferably with appropriate time delays to maintain the natural quality of the original sound).

8. The last, but not least, requirement for adequate speech intelligibility is the control of delayed reflections from distant surfaces and especially at the rear of a hall. Strong reflections with delay times greater than 20 milliseconds, or multiple reflections between opposing parallel surfaces, which create flutter echoes, should be avoided. The delayed reflections, sometimes described as near echoes, which have path differences of between 35 ft (11 m) and 70 ft (22 m) have the potential to degrade significantly the quality of audible speech and inhibit speech intelligibility at the rear of a hall.

These problems are generally minimized by the adoption of appropriately shaped ceilings (and/or side walls) which direct the sound energy toward a section of the audience, so that the resulting time delays are minimal. Problems from flutter echoes are normally minimized by adopting an absorptive surface for one of the pair of opposed walls, or by appropriately sculpturing their surfaces so that pronounced and well defined reflections and echoes are minimized.

Each of these phenomena has a significant effect on speech intelligibility. The shape and volume of an auditorium should be carefully considered in order to optimize its acoustical characteristics (Ref. 17.3).

Amplification of Music

The amplification of music in a large auditorium is generally a more difficult and far more complex task than the amplification of speech. While an orator may utilize a conventional microphone on a stand located directly in front of his or her head, or alternatively wear a lavalier microphone (one which is suspended around his or her neck), a multi-piece band or a large orchestra generally experience significant problems in terms of their ability to amplify each and every musician with the appropriate balance required for an effective primary amplification system. This problem can be overcome by using a series of overhead microphones supplemented by pressure-zone microphones (PZMs) appropriately placed on the floor adjacent to the quieter instruments (Ref. 17.24).

This approach generally proves to be successful, especially where a large, central, wide-range directional loudspeaker system is suspended over the stage on which the musicians are performing. This type of loudspeaker system is well suited for large circular, semi-circular, or similarly shaped auditoriums, in which musical presentations fulfill a secondary function to the more common uses, which include sporting events and/or oratory, or nonmusical primary functions.

Auditoriums may have reverberation times which are significantly shorter than the optimum values for musical, choral, or even operatic presentations. The acoustical characteristics of such a venue may be readily modified by electronic means to achieve an effective reverberation time significantly greater than its normal value. Current technology utilizing digital sound processors (Ref. 17.25), multiple amplifiers, and multiple speakers provides a practical and acoustically acceptable means of modifying the acoustical environment, as well as the quality of the amplified sound, to accord to a wide range of desirable and selected reverberant characteristics.

Concert Halls and Music Auditoriums

The acoustical design of a successful performing space for music or opera requires a complex synthesis of many of the basic requirements and techniques described above, together with more complex measurement and analysis techniques, particularly those based on the use of acoustical scale models (Refs. 17.26 and 17.27).

While the Sabine, Eyring, and Fitzroy equations provide reliable and accurate assessments of reverberation time, they give no information on the potential blend and distribution of primary and reflected sound in an auditorium. Experience is of assistance (Ref. 17.28); but as the complexity of the architectural design increases, or when the architect chooses an unusual configuration, the most effective analytical procedure available to the acoustician is to evaluate the necessary parameters with a scale model. The extent of the scale reduction is limited.

When the scaled frequencies exceed 50 kHz, the linearity of frequency scaling is affected by moisture in the air and by molecular absorption. In order to obviate these problems, specific precautions and appropriate facilities must be used (Ref. 17.26).

Models can be used to assess the efficacy of supplementary reflectors and the uniformity of early reflections, which are of special importance for musicians in an orchestra, particularly where the architectural shape of the auditorium makes it difficult to provide the normal reflecting surfaces over the orchestra.

Shapes of Auditoriums

One of the most significant factors affecting the performance of an auditorium is its shape, and the resulting relationship between the audience and the musicians, actors, singers, or orators on the stage.

Regular or rectangular shaped halls have specific benefits as auditoriums for music, but are generally ill suited for speech or presentation of drama. As the size of the auditorium and the distance between the source and the listener increases, the effects of air absorption and diminution of acoustical energy become increasingly important. Once the distance between acoustical source and listener exceeds 75 ft (25 m), it becomes necessary to choose a configuration of the audience and a shape for a hall which reduces the air volume within the space.

In order to achieve adequate sound levels, appropriate audibility, and good intelligibility at the rear of the hall, strict precautions must be taken to distribute the audience so as to reduce the effect of their sound absorption on the incident sound energy. This generally requires that:

1. Adequate lateral and/or overhead reflections of sound be provided to boost the sound energy at the rear of the hall
2. Sight lines be optimized by the adoption of raking seats
3. Unwanted reflections from the rear walls of the hall and from galleries and ceilings, where these generate unwanted reflections, be minimized

The provision of appropriate levels of supplementary diffusion on side walls and ceiling structures requires careful analysis. In critical designs, computer analysis or scale modeling should be adopted to assess the relationship between the primary sound wave and the multiple reflections produced from the walls, the floor, and the ceiling.

REFERENCES

17.1. J. E. Volkman. "Polycylindrical Diffusers in Room Acoustic Design." *J. Acoust. Soc. Am.*, **13**, 234 (1942).

17.2. *Modeler Design Program*. Bose Corporation, Framingham, MA, 1989.

17.3. J. P. Lochner and J. F. Burger. "The influence of Reflections on Auditorium Acoustics." *J. Sound and Vibration*, **1**(4), 426 (1964).

17.4. L. L. Beranek. *Music, Acoustics and Architecture*. John Wiley, New York, 1962, p. 454.

17.5. P. E. Sabine and L. G. Ramer. "Absorption—frequency Characteristics of Plywood Panels." *J. Acoust. Soc. Am.*, **20**, 267 (1948).

17.6. G. G. Sacerdote and A. Gigli. "Absorption of Sound by Resonant Panels." *J. Acoust. Soc. Am.*, **23**, 349 (1951).

17.7. E. C. Becker. "The Multiple Panel Sound Absorber." *J. Acoust. Soc. Am.*, **26**, 798 (1954).

17.8. V. Kurze and L. L. Beranek. *Sound Propagation Out Doors, Noise and Vibration Control*. McGraw-Hill, New York, 1971, p. 170.

17.9. L. L. Beranek. "Audience and Seat Absorption in Large Halls." *J. Acoust. Soc. Am.*, **32**, 661 (1960).

17.10. V. L. Jordan. "The Application of Helmholtz Resonators to Sound Absorbing Structures." *J. Acoust. Soc. Am.*, **19**, 92 (1947).

17.11. R. Dubout and W. Davern. "Calculation of Statistical Absorption Coefficient from Acoustic Impedance Tube Measurements." *Acustica*, **9**, 53 (1959).

17.12. *Measurement of Absorption Coefficients in Reverberation Room.* ISO-R354. International Standards Organisation, Geneva, 1963.

17.13. K. U. Ingard. "Perforated Facing and Sound Absorption." *J. Acoust. Soc. Am.*, **26**, 151 (1954).

17.14. E. E. Mikeska and R. N. Lane. "Measured Absorption Characteristics of Resonant Absorbers Employing Perforated Panel Facings." *J. Acoust. Soc. Am.*, **58**, 987 (1958).

17.15. J. M. Smith and C. W. Kosten. "Sound Absorption by Slit Resonators." *Acustica*, **1**, Ab 83 (1951).

17.16. D. B. Callaway and L. G. Ramer. "The Use of Perforated Facings in Designing Low Frequency Resonant Absorbers." *J. Acoust. Soc. Am.*, **24**, 319 (1952).

17.17. V. O. Knudsen and C. M. Harris. *Acoustical Designing in Architecture.* John Wiley, New York, 1968, p. 124.

17.18. T. J. Schultz and R. L. Kirkegaard. "Multipurpose Auditoria: An American Phenomenon." *Auditorium Acoustics*, R. Mackenzie (Ed.), Applied Science Publishers, London, 1975, Chapter 5.

17.19. *Standard Method of Test for Sound Absorption of Acoustical Materials in Reverberation Rooms.* ASTM C423. American Society for Testing and Materials, Philadelphia, 1977.

17.20. K. B. Ginn. *Architectural Acoustics.* Brüel & Kjaer, Naerum, Denmark, 1978, p. 53-60.

17.21. W. C. Sabine. *Collected Papers on Acoustics.* Harvard University Press, Cambridge, MA, 1922; reprinted by Dover, New York, 1964; Chapter 1.

17.22. C. M. Harris. "Absorption of Sound in Air Versus Humidity and Temperature." *J. Acoust. Soc. Am.*, **40**, 148-153 (1966).

17.23. D. Fitzroy. "Reverberation Formula Which Seems to Be Accurate with Non-Uniform Distribution of Absorption." *J. Acoust. Soc. Am.*, **31**, 893 (1959).

17.24. D. Andrews. "Pressure Zone Microphones, A Practical Application of the Pressure Zone Recording Process." Audio Eng. Soc. 66th Convention, Los Angeles, 1980.

17.25. L. A. Challis. "Award Winning Sound Processor." *Electronics Today International*, Sydney, p. 36-40 (April 1987).

17.26. R. H. Lyon and R. G. Cann. *Acoustical Scale Modelling—A Practical Course for Engineers and Architects.* Grozier Technical Systems, Boston, 1981.

17.27. L. A. Challis. "New Parliament House, Canberra—Acoustical Modelling of the House Chamber." *Bulletin of Aust. Acoust. Soc.*, **10**(3), 108-110 (1982).

17.28. P. S. Veneklasen. "Design Considerations from the Viewpoint of the Professional Consultant." *Auditorium Acoustics*, R. Mackenzie (Ed.), Applied Science Publishers, London, 1975, Chapter 4.

SUGGESTIONS FOR FURTHER READING

L. L. Beranek. *Music, Acoustics and Architecture.* John Wiley, New York, 1962.

D. Egan. *Architectural Acoustics.* McGraw-Hill, New York, 1988.

L. E. Kinseler et al. *Fundamentals of Acoustics*, 3rd Ed. John Wiley, New York, 1982.

A. B. Lawrence. *Architectural Acoustics.* Elsevier Applied Science, London, 1970.

P. Lord and D. Templeton. *The Architecture of Sound.* Architectural Press, London, 1986.

R. Mackenzie (Ed.). *Auditorium Acoustics*, Proceedings of an International Symposium on Architectural Acoustics held at Heriot-Watt University, Edinburgh. Applied Science, London, 1975.

NOTATION

a	total absorption, ft^2, m^2
$\log_e$	natural logarithm, to the base e
m	attenuation constant for air
s	total surface area ft^2, m^2
S_x	side-wall area, ft^2
S_y	end-wall area, ft^2
S_z	floor and ceiling area, ft^2
T_R	reverberation time, seconds
V	volume, ft^3, m^3
α	normal incidence sound absorption coefficient
α_{st}	statistical or random incidence sound absorption coefficient
$\bar{\alpha}$	average or statistical absorption coefficient
$\bar{\alpha}_x$	average sound absorption coefficient of side wall
$\bar{\alpha}_y$	average sound absorption coefficient of end wall
$\bar{\alpha}_z$	average sound absorption coefficient of floor and ceiling

A list of abbreviations of the units of measurement, and definitions of these units, are given in the Appendix.

18
Windows in Buildings

Baruch Givoni

The spectral qualities of different types of glass are first considered, and their potential use in the control of radiation. The thermal properties (U-values) of glazing are then discussed, and the efficiency of various shading devices. These aspects are important to ensure that windows do not cause overheating in summer.

The positive aspects of windows are considered in the rest of the chapter: windows as daylighting elements, windows as natural ventilation elements, and windows as solar heating elements in winter.

18.1. FUNCTIONS OF WINDOWS IN BUILDINGS

Windows fulfill many functions in buildings, such as providing contact with the outdoors (visual and auditory), views to attractive scenery (when available), natural ventilation, and daylighting. In addition they can serve as elements in passive solar heating and cooling systems.

Contact with the Outdoors. There is a common psychological need to be aware of what is going on outdoors: changes in weather, sunlight and passing clouds, variability and changes in surrounding vegetation (foliage and flowers), "information" on activities of people outside the building, and so on.

When the location of the building provides views to attractive scenery, either natural such as mountains, valleys, and waterfronts, or urban scenery, such as parks, attractive buildings, and streets, etc., the windows provide the ability to view these scenes. Sometimes, of course, there is also the need to shut out the outdoor environment: for privacy, to avoid noise, exclude daylight, etc. Thus windows, especially when openable, are the "natural" building elements which provide the contact with the outdoors and its control.

Natural Ventilation. Windows and doors leading to private outdoor areas such as porches are the building element by which natural ventilation is possible. Such ventilation is needed first of all for health reasons, to maintain a given indoor air quality in terms of odors, gases exhaled by people and emitted from materials, and in some cases also radioactive radon.

Ventilation is also essential during warm and hot seasons for thermal comfort, especially in humid regions where it may be desired during the whole day. Also in hot, dry regions natural ventilation is very desirable for direct physiological comfort during the evening and night hours. In addition to the direct sensory effect on human comfort, ventilation during the evening and night hours is needed in hot dry regions to hasten the cooling of the building's interior. The location, size, and design details of the windows have decisive effects on their effectiveness in securing good ventilation conditions for comfort and for the cooling of the building's structure.

Daylighting. Windows, clerestories, and often skylight in upper stories, are the source for daylighting of the interior. Such daylight is desired not only for energy conservation, but is usually considered superior psychologically to electrical lighting. Also in this case the location, size, and shading details of the windows determine the quality and quantity of the interior daylighting (see Section 19.6).

Passive Solar Heating. In winter, windows in the sunny walls (the south in the Northern Hemisphere) can play an important role in providing solar heating to the interior of buildings. Technically such passive solar heating is termed a *direct gain* system.

For an effective heating *system* it is not enough to have windows on the sunny side of the building. While any window in this orientation admits solar energy into the building, some additional elements are needed for satisfactory performance. Specifically, part of the solar energy penetrating into the building during the daytime has to be absorbed in some internal mass, in order to stabilize the indoor environment and to prevent too fast an elevation of the indoor temperature, which may lead to overheating and heat discomfort.

In residential buildings, which are occupied also during the evening and night hours, the stored energy should be released back to the interior to prevent too fast a drop of the indoor temperature. The performance characteristics of direct gain and the effects of various design details of the system on this performance are discussed in Sections 18.8 and 21.6.

Architectural Role of Glazed Areas and Shading Devices

Glazed openings in walls have traditionally been among the main means for articulating and defining the architectural character of a building. The overall fraction of the wall given up to windows, as well as the shape and distribution of the windows throughout the wall, are among the main elements of the architectural articulation of the facades of the building. More recently, mainly under the influence of Le Corbusier and Niemeyer, fixed shading devices in the forms of overhangs, fins, and "eggcrates", shading glazed areas and covering whole facades, became among the strongest architectural elements defining and characterizing a building.

18.2. SPECTRAL-OPTICAL PROPERTIES OF WINDOWS

Spectral Properties of Different Glasses (see also Section 3.2.)

A unique property of glass is its selective transparency to shortwave (solar) and longwave (thermal) radiation. Different types of glass transmit different fractions of the solar radiation spectrum, in the range of 0.4 to 2.5 μm (micrometer). At the same time all glasses are completely opaque to, and do absorb, the longwave radiation emitted from indoor surfaces. Part of the absorbed longwave radiation is transmitted back to the interior. Thus a greenhouse effect is created by the windows, namely transmission of solar radiation into the building while blocking and trapping indoors part of the longwave radiation.

By special treatments of the glazing it is possible to reflect back the longwave radiation emitted by the interior surfaces (low-emissivity glass) and thus to reduce the heat loss through the glazing. Such treatment is applied when the objective is to increase the greenhouse effect and to reduce the heat loss of the building in winter.

The result of the greenhouse effect is an elevation of the indoor temperature above the outdoor temperature beyond the level which results from penetration of solar radiation through open windows. This effect is, of course, in addition to the blocking of the convective heat loss (cooling through ventilation) by the glazing.

The solar spectrum can be divided into three main ranges: the ultraviolet (UV, wavelength below 0.4 μm), the visible spectrum (0.4–0.7 μm), and the infrared (IR, above 0.7 μm up to about 2.5 μm). Different glasses transmit different fractions of each one of these ranges.

The UV has a strong biological effect and also is responsible for fading of fabrics, colors, etc. but has negligible effect on thermal energy. The visible part of the solar spectrum provides the daylight, and the IR radiation produces only heat. When solar radiation impinges on a window glass, it is divided into three fractions. One part is reflected outward without any effect on the building's temperature. The second part is absorbed within the glass, raising its temperature, and the rest is transmitted, at the original wavelength, through the glazing into the building. While the function of all windows is to admit daylight into the building, any light inherently heats up the interior because all the transmitted solar energy is ultimately transformed inside the building into heat.

The different fractions of reflection, absorption, and transmission of the solar radiation spectrum are determined by the composition and/or treatment of the glass, and can be chosen to fulfill a wide range of ratios of light to heat transmission. The different ratios of light to heat transmission characterizing different types of glazing are achieved by modifying the amounts of different ranges of the solar spectrum which are either reflected, absorbed, or transmitted by the glass.

Types and Treatments of Glass

Window glasses can be broadly classified into several types, according to the selective transmission, reflection and absorption of different wavelength of radiation:

- Clear glass
- Heat-reflecting glass
- Low-emissivity (Low-*E*) glass
- Heat-absorbing glass
- Gray and colored glasses

Clear Glass. Clear glasses transmit the highest amounts of all the wavelengths of the solar spectrum. Consequently they transmit the highest amount of daylight, but they also cause the highest solar heat gain into the building, a property which in summer increases the cooling load on the building. In winter, however, such glasses may be the best for passive heating of the buildings by direct solar gain, especially if the heat loss through the windows at night is minimized by operable night insulation.

Control of the Reflected Radiation

The relative fraction of the reflected solar radiation depends not only on the type of the glass but also on the angle of incidence of the radiation. Between zero incidence angle (radiation normal to the glass) and about 40 degrees, the reflection from the two surfaces of a single clear glass is about 8 percent.

When the incidence angle is over 40 degrees the fraction of the reflected radiation increases gradually, till at 55 degrees it reaches about 15 percent, with a corresponding drop in the transmitted radiation. Over 55 degrees there is a larger progressive increase in the reflection and a sharper drop in the fraction of the transmitted radiation. At incidence angle of 80 degrees about 60 percent and at 85 degrees about 80 percent is reflected away. Specified values of reflection from different glasses are usually given for zero incidence angle. By different treatments of the glass it is possible to increase greatly the reflected radiation.

In different situations there might be opposite objectives with respect to the reflection (and transmission) of the infrared solar radiation. In solar-heated buildings the objective is to maximize the heat gain and therefore to minimize the reflection. On the other hand, in daylighted air-conditioned buildings the objective is to minimize the heat gain, while getting as much daylight as possible, an objective which can be achieved by enhanced reflection of the solar infrared radiation.

Heat-Reflecting Glass. Reflecting the infrared solar spectrum outward can reduce the solar heat gain more than the associated reduction of the transmitted light and thus improve the light-to-heat ratio. This can be achieved by heat-reflecting glass, which is produced by depositing a very fine semi-transparent metallic coating on the surface of the glass. The metallic coating reflects selectively a greater proportion of the solar infrared than of the visible portions of the solar radiation. By selective reflection of different ranges of the solar spectrum this glass minimizes the solar heat gain, although at some reduction of the transmitted daylight.

Low-Emissivity (Low-E) Glazing. Low-emissivity (low-E) glass has relatively high transmission of solar radiation but low emissivity, and correspondingly high reflectivity, for longwave (thermal) radiation. It is produced by deposition of a low-emissivity coating either on the glass itself or over a transparent plastic film stretched across an air space inside a sealed air space in a double glazed window, to protect it from damage and dirt.

Low-E glazing *reflects back to the indoor space* most (about 80 percent) of the longwave radiation (with wavelengths of 5 to 30 μm) while *transmitting* about 60 percent of the solar radiation. With the two sealed air spaces formed by the plastic film the U value of the glazing (1.3 W/m^2 °C, 0.23 Btu/h ft^2 °F) is much lower than that of a conventional double- or even triple-glazed window. The thermal effect of the low-E glazing is the opposite of that of the heat-reflecting glass, because it maximizes the solar heat gain.

Low-emissivity glass is presently manufactured on a relatively large scale in the USA and in Europe and is available from several major glass and window companies. The retail cost of the glass in the USA, with the coating over the glass, is about $22 per square meter more than that of conventional double glazed window.

Control of the Absorbed Radiation

The fraction of the absorbed radiation depends on the total thickness of the glass layers of the window and the type of the glass. Clear glass $\frac{1}{8}$ in. (3 mm) thick absorbs about 6 percent, and for each additional millimeter of thickness the absorption increases by about 2 percent of the impinging radiation. Specialized glasses can absorb a much greater fraction of the solar radiation.

Heat-Absorbing Glass. Heat-absorbing glass absorbs a greater fraction of the solar infrared than of the visible part of the spectrum. It is produced by increasing the iron content of the glass. Part of the absorbed radiation flows outward. As a result, the relative proportion of the visible spectrum (light) compared with the heat radiation which is transmitted through the glass increases. Heat-absorbing glass is used when it is desired to have daylight with as little heat gain as possible, which is usually the case in air-conditioned office buildings.

The absorbed radiation raises the temperature of the glass and part of the absorbed energy may be transferred to the interior by convection and longwave radiation. The actual fraction of the energy absorbed in heat-absorbing glass, which is transmitted ultimately to the interior, depends on the design details of the window. As heat-absorbing glass is used when it is desired to minimize the solar heat gain it is usually applied as the external layer of a double-glazed window, with the internal layer usually a clear glass. In this case most of the radiation absorbed at the external layer flows outward by convection and longwave radiation. The inward longwave radiation from the heat absorbing glass is intercepted by the inner layer of the window and only a small part of it is transferred to the interior.

Gray and Colored Glasses. Gray and colored glasses absorb more visible than infrared radiation. They are used mainly to reduce glare and excessive sunlight from large windows and glazed walls. The absorbed light elevates the glass temperature and consequently the heat flow inward due to convection and longwave radiation. Table 18.1 gives average values, derived from various sources, of the components and the total of the solar heat gain through a single-pane window made of some glasses (Ref. 18.1).

Table 18.1. Solar Gain through Some Single Glass Panes, Percent.

Glass Type	Direct Transmission	Absorbed Radiation	Total Heat Gain
Regular window glass	85	3	88
Clear glass	74	9	83
Light heat-absorbing glass	20	25	45
Gray glass	30	30	60
Heat-reflecting glass	38	17	55

Electrochromic Glazing

Recent developments in new glazing with new and changeable optical properties may lead to much better thermal performance, indoor comfort, and daylight conditions in buildings than was achievable with conventional glazing. In some cases patent-application procedures prevented discussion of the products. One such development is discussed here.

At the Electrooptics Technology Center of Tufts University, Professor Goldner is developing electrochromic glazing, termed the "smart window." The smart window can change its properties between two reversible states, a clear (transparent) and a colored (reflective) one, each having a different spectral reflectivity for solar radiation. The change from one state to the other is caused by the passage of a relatively small electrical current of alternating polarities (+3 or −3 volts). The optical state remains steady after the current has been stopped, till the reversed current is applied (Refs. 18.2 and 18.3).

In the clear state the transmissivities of the smart window are about 50 and 75 percent in the visible and in the IR portions of the solar spectrum, respectively. In the colored state the respective transmissivities are 20 and 5 percent.

18.3. THERMAL PROPERTIES (U VALUES) AND EFFECT OF WINDOWS (see also Chapter 20.)

The term *thermal properties* refers to the amount of heat flow by conduction through the windows due to the temperature difference between indoors and outdoors. This amount depends on three independent factors of the window system:

1. The existence and number of air spaces between glazing layers
2. The properties and/or treatments of the glazing material and surfaces
3. The materials and detailing of the window frames (not discussed in this chapter).

Effect of Air Spaces between Window Panes

Windows are available with a single pane of glass or with multiple panes, usually two or in cold countries three panes, with an air space (or spaces) between them. The air spaces add to the thermal resistance of the window, thus reducing its overall heat transfer coefficient (U value). The heat flow across the air space is by convection and radiation. The convection component depends to some extent on the width of the space. The radiation component can be reduced by special treatment (for heat reflection) of the glass. Consequently, the overall U value of windows can vary substantially between single-glazed windows and those with two and three panes. The typical U value of a single-pane window is about 1 Btu/h ft^2 °F (5–5.5 W/m^2 °C); for a double-glazed window with clear glass it is about 0.55 Btu/h ft^2 °F (3 W/m^2 °C); and for a triple-glazed window it is about 0.36 Btu/h ft^2 °F (2 W/m^2 °C).

Effect of Unshaded Windows on Cooling Loads of Air-Conditioned Buildings (Heat Gain through Unshaded Windows)

In air conditioned buildings, where air temperature is kept at the comfort level by the mechanical system, the windows determine to a very large extent the solar, as well as the conductive, heat gains and the resulting load on the cooling system and its energy consumption. The conductive heat gain through windows (Q_{cond}) is proportional to the glazing area (A_{glaz}) and the U value of the glazing, according to the known formula:

$$Q_{cond} = A_{glaz} U_{glaz}(T_i - T_o) \quad (18.1)$$

where T_i and T_o are the indoor and outdoor temperatures, respectively. The conductive heat gain through the glazing is independent of the orientation and the shading conditions of the windows.

On the other hand, the solar heat gain through windows depends to a very large extent on the shading conditions and, in the case of unshaded windows, also on the orientation of the windows. The effect of the orientation varies during the year and the relative solar gain at different orientations is quite different in summer and in winter.

Detailed information on the hourly and monthly design values of the solar heat gain through windows of different types at different orientations can be found in several books, such as the *ASHRAE Handbook of Fundamentals* (Ref. 18.4), the text by Stein, Reynolds, and McGuinness (Ref. 18.5), etc. Generally, however, the solar gain annual patterns in the different orientations can be summarized by the following statement:

> In summer the main solar gain is from Eastern (before noon) and Western (in the afternoon) windows. Solar gain through southern and northern windows in summer is much smaller. In winter the main solar gain is from the windows facing the Equator (southern windows in the Northern Hemisphere). Solar gain from eastern and western windows is much smaller. There is no direct solar gain from windows facing the poles (northern windows in the Northern Hemisphere), although some diffused and reflected solar radiation should be taken into account.

The Shading Coefficient of Unshaded Windows with Different Glazing

Although the solar gain through windows in air-conditioned buildings does not affect the indoor air temperature, which is maintained at the specified range by the mechanical system, it nevertheless has a significant impact on the overall comfort of the occupants of the building, and on the cooling load and energy consumption by the conditioning system.

Direct solar radiation on the occupants has an immediate effect on their comfort. In some situations, such as in winter in residential buildings, some direct radiation may be welcomed. In other situations, especially in nonresidential buildings such as offices and schools, direct solar penetration interferes adversely with the activities taking place in the building and therefore should be minimized or prevented.

Irrespective of the effect of the solar penetration on comfort it always increases the heat gain of the building. With different types and treatments of the glazing it is possible to modify the solar heat gain.

The solar heat gain through an unshaded window depends on the type (treatment) and thickness of the glazing. The highest solar gain, about 86 percent of the impinging (normal) radiation, would be through a thin ($\frac{1}{8}$ in., 3 mm) single layer of clear glass. A thicker glass absorbs more radiation, so less heat is transferred to the interior. Double glazing increases the fraction of the reflected radiation and consequently reduces, by about 10 percent, the transmitted solar energy.

Special treatments of the glazing, such as increasing the reflection or the absorption, can reduce appreciably the actual solar heat gain, even when the windows are not shaded. All these effects are expressed by the *shading coefficient* of the glazing, which is defined as the ratio between the solar gain through a given window glazing and the gain through a clear glass $\frac{1}{8}$ in. (3 mm) thick.

Values of the shading coefficient of various unshaded glazing types can be found in various books, such as the *ASHRAE Handbook of Fundamentals* (Ref. 18.4) etc. Typical values for some glazing types, are shown in Table 18.2 (averages from various sources).

Table 18.2. **Shading Coefficients of Some Glazing Types.**

Glazing	Shading Coefficient
Single Glasses	
Clear glass, $\frac{1}{8}$ in. (3 mm)	1.00
Clear glass, $\frac{3}{8}$ in. (10 mm)	0.90
Heat-absorbing glass, 3 mm	0.83
Heat-reflecting glass, 3 mm	0.50
Double Glazing, all $\frac{1}{8}$ in. (3 mm) thick	
Clear outside, clear inside	0.88
Heat-absorbing outside, clear inside	0.55
Heat-reflecting outside, clear inside	0.40

18.4. CHARACTERISTICS AND EFFICIENCY OF VARIOUS SHADING DEVICES

Shading devices can be divided broadly into two types: fixed and operable. Fixed shading is usually an integral part of the building's structure. Once built, its diurnal and annual shading pattern depends only on the incident angle of the sun's rays. Fixed shading devices cannot ensure complete adjustment of the shade to changing shading needs, although with proper design the overall performance can be reasonably good, especially with respect to windows facing the Equator (southern windows in the Northern Hemisphere). An obvious advantage of fixed shading is that it needs no handling by the occupants, and is also maintenance free.

The configuration of adjustable shading devices can be changed according to changing needs and therefore their performance can be much better than that of fixed devices. On the other hand their position has to be adjusted, daily or seasonally, to the changing patterns of the sun's motion and the shading needs. They usually also need maintenance to keep them in good condition.

Operable shading can be either external or internal to the glazing. From the thermal viewpoint there is a very significant difference in the performance of these two types and therefore they will be discussed separately.

Fixed Shading

There are two basic types of fixed shading devices: horizontal (overhangs) and vertical (fins). They can also be combined in different combinations, e.g., eggcrates (Ref. 18.6). Each one of the basic types casts a distinctive shade pattern, which can be plotted easily as a *shading mask*.

A shading mask shows the angles between the lower edges of the glass area (the reference points) and the edges of the shading device and the horizontal projection of the sky segment which is not blocked, from the viewpoint of the reference point, by a shading device. Thus the shading mask of an infinite horizontal overhang marks the vertical shadow angle and the solar altitude above which the sun rays will not reach any part of the glazing. The shading masks of vertical fins (extending far above the windows) mark the horizontal angles between the sun and the edges of the fins. When the sun is outside this section of the sky its rays will not reach the glazing.

Examples of shading masks of a horizontal overhang and vertical fins are shown in Figure 18.4.1 (Ref.18.1).

Efficiency of Fixed Shading in Different Orientations. Horizontal overhangs are most effective for southern windows (in the Northern Hemisphere). In summer they can block the sun, which is at a high position in the sky in summer, and admit radiation from the lower sun position in winter. There are, however, some problems during the spring and fall seasons. While the sun path has the same pattern on February 21 and October 21, February is cold

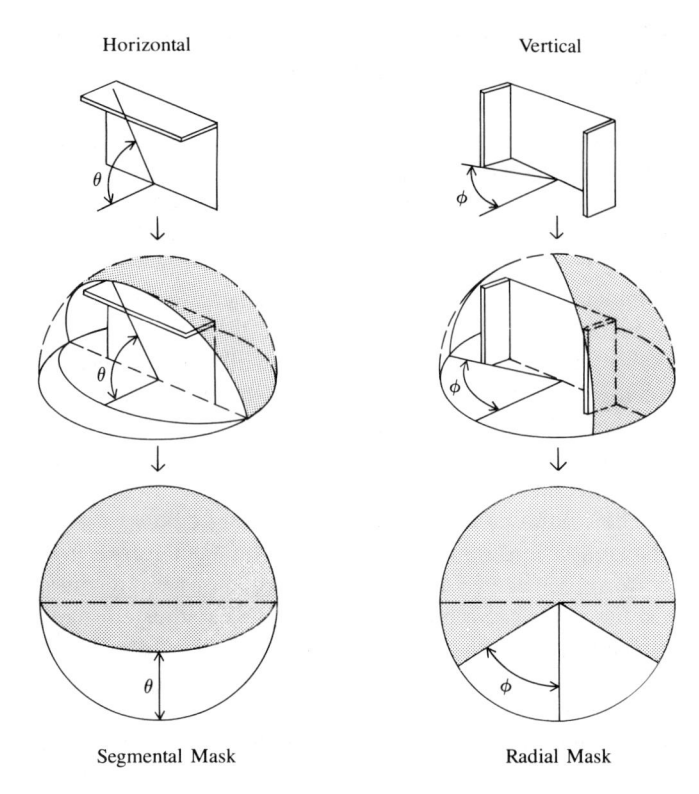

Fig. 18.4.1. Shading masks of horizontal overhang and of vertical fins.

in the Northern Hemisphere and solar heating is usually welcomed, while October may be a warm month and sun penetration may cause overheating.

Contrary to common belief, horizontal overhangs are more effective in summer than fixed vertical fins, even for eastern and western windows. In a study for Israeli conditions (latitude about 32 degrees) the shading efficiency of various shading devices under different orientations was computed (Ref. 18.1). The following shading devices were examined:

a. Horizontal shading extending only above the window (H)
b. Horizontal shading extending over the whole facade (Hoo)
c. Vertical shading perpendicular to the wall on both side of the window extending only up to its top (V)
d. Vertical shading as above but extending throughout the whole height of the building (Voo)
e. An eggcrate of perpendicular vertical and horizontal members (H + V)
f. A frame whose vertical members are oblique at 45 degrees toward the South (H + V_{45}).

Some results from this study are shown graphically in Figs. 18.4.2 and 18.4.3. The first shows diurnal patterns of impinging solar radiation on a square eastern window (3 × 3 ft or 1 × 1 m) with different fixed shading devices projecting over the window one-third of its dimension, in June, September, October, and December. Fig. 18.4.3 shows the effect of the projection depth of the various shading devices on the total impinging radiation in East and West orientations.

As can be seen from these figures the vertical fins normal to the wall exhibited the worst performance in summer as well as in winter. In summer, when the sun is nearly normal to the east wall most of the forenoon hours and to the west wall in the afternoon, fixed fins normal to the wall provide very little protection even at great depth. The horizontal overheads provided better, although insufficient, protection. In winter, on the other hand, the fins cast more shade on eastern and western windows than the horizontal overhangs.

The best annual performance of shading devices on eastern and western windows was exhibited by the frame with vertical fins oblique toward the south. On southern windows (in the Northern Hemisphere) the best shading is provided by a horizontal overhead extending well beyond the sides of the window.

At lower latitudes the relative disadvantage of vertical fins normal to the wall on eastern and western windows will even be greater. It should be noted, however, that long vertical fins turned toward the Equator (to the south in the Northern Hemisphere) would provide more effective shade in summer while permitting more sun penetration in winter. In fact, such oblique fins perform in a similar way to the frame with the oblique fin (H + V_{45}). Vertical fins are useful when applied to northern windows (in the Northern Hemisphere) especially at latitudes of 30–50 degrees, mainly because they can block the low sun from the northwest in the afternoon. As the morning sun is often desired even in summer, a single fin on the west side of the window may be better than symmetrical two fins.

Operable External Shading

External operable shading devices can be made of many materials and they have many forms. They include, inter alia, shutters, awnings, a variety of operable horizontal or vertical louvers, and also some types of venetian blinds rigid enough for use as external shades.

The geometrical configuration of operable shadings does not affect their performance. Whether horizontal or vertical they always can be so positioned as to cut off or to admit the sun's rays as desired at any particular time.

The color of *external* shading, when the glazing is *closed*, has very little effect on thermal performance but affects greatly the indoor lighting conditions. White and light-colored shades transmit more visible light to the interior than darker shades. Dark shades are heated while absorbing the radiation and emit more infrared radiation inward. However, this radiation is intercepted and absorbed by the glazing of the (closed) window.

When the windows are open, the infrared radiation from dark shades is transmitted directly to the interior. Consequently, when the windows are either open or closed, the

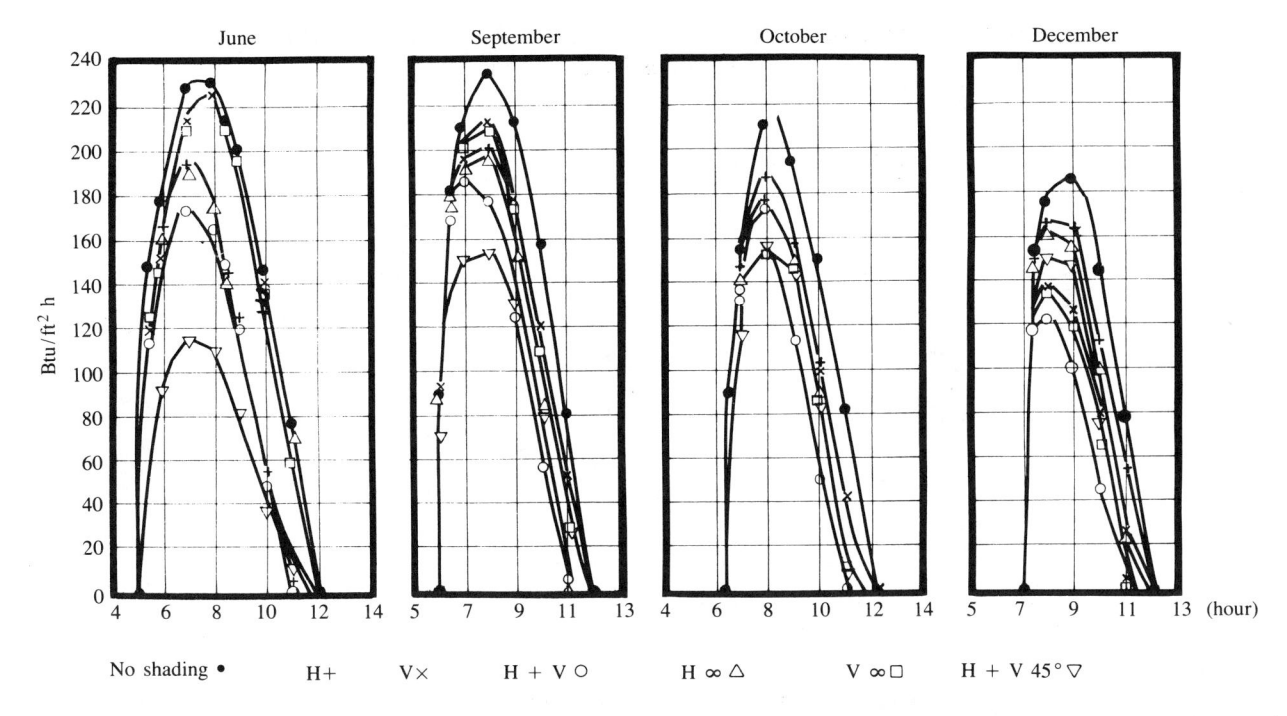

Fig. 18.4.2. Diurnal patterns of impinging solar radiation on a square eastern window with various fixed shading devices. (1 Btu/ft² h = 3.1546 W/m².)

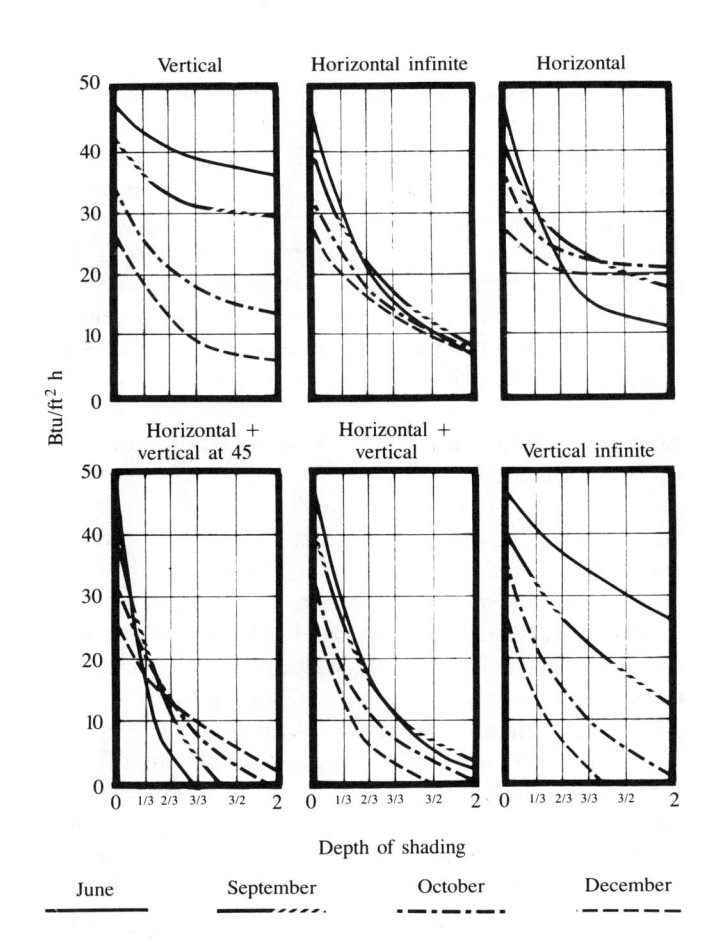

Fig. 18.4.3. Effect of projection depth of various fixed shading devices on the total impinging direct solar radiation. (1 Btu/ft² h = 3.1546 W/m².)

thermal performance of white and light-colored shading is better than those of dark shading devices. Therefore, in regions where ventilation is desirable together with prevention of solar radiation, as is often the case in hot regions with respect to western and eastern windows, white external shading is more advisable.

Operable Internal Shading

Internal shading devices, by definition, are inside the glazing and intercept the sun's rays *after* they pass through the glass. Consequently almost all the heat which is absorbed in the shade material is added to the solar heat gain. As a result, color has a significant effect on the performance of internal shading devices. Their overall thermal performance is much poorer than that of external shading. Still, they are very important and effective for indoor *sunlight* control.

In a study of Givoni and Hoffman (Ref. 18.7) a theoretical analysis was made of the components and the total solar heat transmitted through closed windows with external and internal venetian blinds, for two tilt angles of the slots, 30 and 45 degrees. When available, results of experimental studies elsewhere were compared to the calculated values. The solar gain through the glass-shade combinations was divided into two components:

1. The part transmitted after reflection between the slots
2. The total transmitted solar energy

In the case of internal shading the absorbed radiation is added to the solar gain. In case of external shading only 5

Table 18.3. Partitioned Heat Gain through Different Types of Shading and the Corresponding Shade Factors.

	Angle and Absorptivity of Blind		q_{tsg}		q_{in}		q_{in}, %	q_{in}, %, experimental
			W/m^2	$Btu/h\,ft^2$	W/m^2	$Btu/h\,ft^2$		
Internal	30°	0.2	76	24	197	62	43%	—
		0.4	58	18	261	83	57%	54%
		0.6	24	8	302	96	66%	—
	45°	0.2	52	17	183	58	39%	40%
		0.4	36	11	236	75	51%	51%
		0.6	12	4	245	90	62%	61%
External	30°	0.2	75	24	81	26	18%	—
		0.4	58	18	70	22	15%	—
		0.6	24	8	41	13	10%	—
	45°	0.2	52	17	59	19	13%	—
		0.4	36	11	47	15	10%	11%
		0.6	12	4	37	12	—	—

Impinging radiation = 460 W/m² = 146 Btu/h ft²
q_{tsg} = transmitted radiation through glass/shading combination
q_{in} = total solar heat gain (W/m² and Btu/h ft²)

percent of it is transferred inward. The results of this comparison are presented in Table 18.3 (Ref. 18.1).

18.5. EFFECT OF WINDOWS ON INDOOR TEMPERATURES

Effect of Unshaded Windows in Different Orientations

When a window is unshaded its quantitative effect on the indoor temperature depends on its orientation, according to the diurnal and annual patterns of solar radiation intensity on vertical surfaces. The differential radiation pattern on different orientations depends on the geographic latitude of the location of the building. In particular, a distinction should be made between near-equatorial latitudes (e.g., within about 15 degrees of the Equator) and higher latitudes. Within the Equatorial zone solar radiation on Northern and Southern walls is much smaller year-round than on eastern and western walls. In this zone the year-round air temperature is rather high, so that summer overheating is much more important than winter heating needs (except for locations at high elevation above sea level). Therefore, unshaded windows should be avoided as much as possible in easterly and westerly walls because they are sources of significant overheating of the interior.

It should be pointed out, however, that the Equatorial zone is within the Trade Winds belt, where wind direction is mainly from the East. Eastern windows are therefore very desirable in this zone for natural ventilation, which is essential for comfort in this high-humidity zone. The solution, of course, is in providing eastern windows with effective shading.

At higher latitudes the annual pattern of solar radiation of windows with different orientation is very different, especially where a southern window (in the Northern Hemisphere) is concerned. Here the window facing the Equator receives more radiation in winter, when heating is needed, than in summer. A window facing the Pole does not receive any radiation in winter, while getting a not insignificant amount in summer. The eastern and western windows receive much more radiation in summer than in winter.

These differential solar radiation patterns cause very different patterns of indoor temperature in rooms having windows in different orientations. This is illustrated in Fig. 18.5.1 (Ref. 18.8), which shows measured temperature patterns in models of unventilated rooms having a single unshaded window, facing different orientations. These measurements were taken at the Technion University in Haifa, Israel (Latitude about 32° N). The figure demonstrates clearly the dangers of overheating of unconditioned buildings from unshaded easterly windows.

Effect of Windows Shaded by Various Devices in Different Orientations

Shading devices can very significantly reduce the solar heat gain through windows, thus reducing the differential effect of the window's orientation. When well shaded, not only from direct solar radiation but also from radiation reflected from the surrounding area, the windows in any orientation transmit heat mainly by conduction, depending on the outdoor air temperature, which is the same in all orientations.

The combination of effective shading and natural ventilation, even at a low rate, can reduce the differences in the rate of indoor heating caused by windows of different orientations to an insignificant level, as is illustrated in Fig. 18.5.2 (Ref. 18.8). This figure shows indoor temperature patterns in the same models shown in Fig. 18.5.1, but when the windows were shaded by external dark venetian blinds.

The interaction between the effects of window orientations, shading, and ventilation conditions is illustrated in

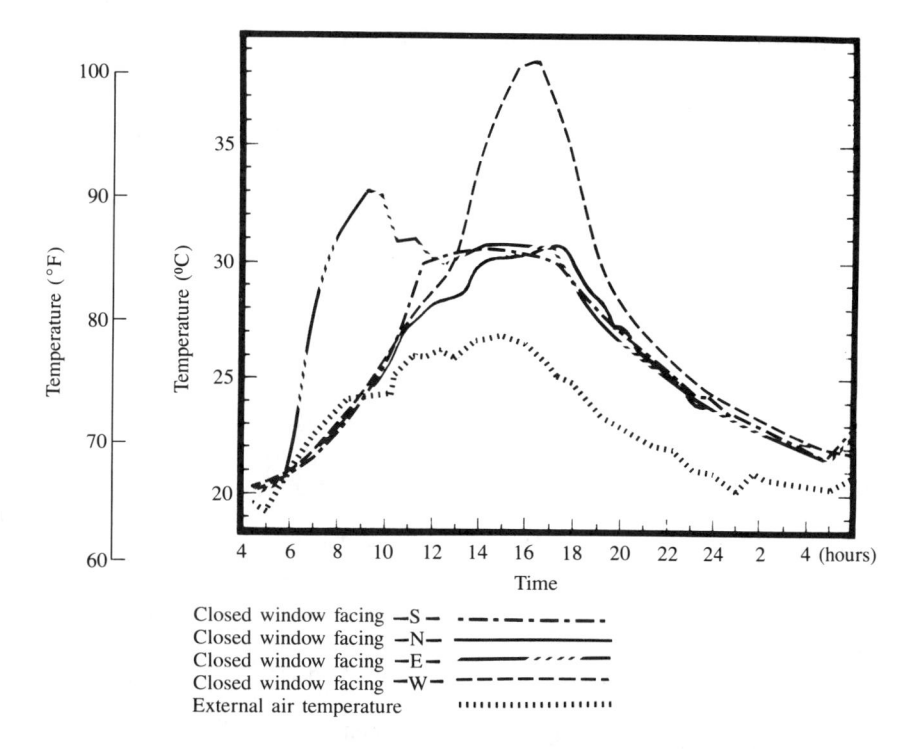

Fig. 18.5.1. Measured temperature patterns in models with unshaded windows in different orientations.

Table 18.4 (after Ref. 18.1). The table shows the differences between the indoor and outdoor maximum temperatures which were measured in the study at the Technion with the same models mentioned above, with different treatment of the windows.

Three natural ventilation conditions were applied: none, very low (through small slots), and high (windows open). The shading conditions were: none, external dark venetian blinds, external light-color (beige) blinds, internal dark and internal light-colored blinds. It can be seen from Table 18.4 that external effective shading, whether dark or light colored, can practically eliminate the effect of orientation on solar gain, as manifested by the heating effect of the windows.

With high ventilation rates through open windows solar energy enters the rooms but its effect on the indoor air temperature is minimal, because the excess heat is flushed away by the ventilation air. However, the penetrating radiation is absorbed in the indoor surfaces and materials, raising the indoor *radiant* temperature. During the night, when the wind often subsides, the absorbed radiation is released back to the indoor space and raises its temperature.

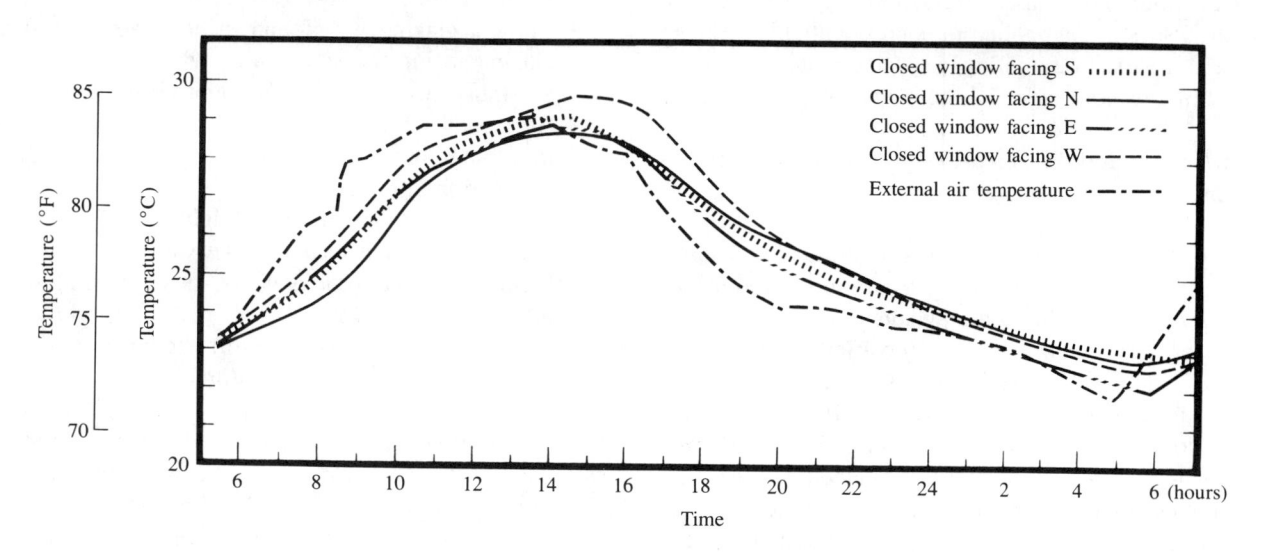

Fig. 18.5.2. Measured temperature patterns in models with windows in different orientations, with external venetian blinds.

Table 18.4. Differences between Indoor and Outdoor Maxima.

Shading	Ventilation	Temperature Difference, °C			
		East	West	North	South
None	Closed	5.9	11.3	3.5	3.5
	High	0.0	0.9	−0.4	0.4
	Low	4.0	7.7	2.2	5.7
External dark	Closed	0.0	0.5	−0.3	0.25
	High	0.3	0.45	0.25	0.65
External light	Closed	−0.3	0.3	−0.3	−0.1
	High	0.1	0.3	−0.2	0.0
Internal Dark	Closed	2.6	8.0	1.6	3.0
Internal light	Closed	1.7	6.5	0.6	1.5

1°C = 1.8°F

18.6. WINDOWS AS DAYLIGHTING ELEMENTS (see also Section 19.6)

Windows and other glazed areas in the building's envelope are the means by which the indoor space is lighted by solar radiation. Different types of openings have different lighting characteristics and are referred to by different terms (Refs. 18.9 and 18.10):

- Conventional *windows* are glazed openings in the walls with sill height of up to about 3 feet (1 meter).
- *Clerestories* are openings in the walls just below the ceiling, with sill height usually above eye level.
- *Skylights* are openings in the roof with horizontal glazed cover.
- *Roof monitors* are openings in the roof with vertical glazing and an opaque horizontal cover, elevated above the roof level.

The various types of glazed openings provide daylighting to all the different building types, residential as well as nonresidential. However, the functional problems of daylighting are different in these two classes of buildings. Generally, the issues of daylighting in nonresidential buildings are more complex. In the following, some issues involved in daylighting of nonresidential buildings are discussed.

Windows as Daylighting Elements in Nonresidential Buildings

One of the main differences between residential and nonresidential (commercial) buildings, from the viewpoint of building design and application of windows, is that the need for lighting for the performance of the various tasks which take place in most nonresidential buildings is much higher than in residential buildings. Natural daylighting can reduce the consumption of electricity for lighting and, as daylight is more efficient thermally than electrical lighting (more lumens per watt), the load imposed on the cooling system, whether mechanical or natural, can be smaller, depending on the control of the electrical lighting.

The Experimental Nonresidential Buildings Program in the USA. In 1979 the US Department of Energy (DOE) sponsored the Passive Solar Commercial Demonstration Program to determine the potential of passive solar technologies: daylighting as well as heating and cooling of buildings. Within the framework of this DOE Program 15, single-story new buildings were constructed and four existing buildings were retrofitted. The performance of all buildings was evaluated by several investigators. The results of this evaluation were summarized in two publications (Refs. 18.11 and 18.12).

Main Lessons from the DOE Study. The DOE Program has demonstrated that solar energy in the form of daylighting can be applied to *single-story* buildings of any size. Daylighting of the perimeter zone of the building can be provided by ordinary windows and/or clerestories. Roof monitors with south glazing and diffusing grids provided the best light for core areas of single-story buildings. Lighting of core areas of deep spaces also improves the quality of perimeter lighting by reducing excessive brightness contrast.

Under these conditions daylighting is cost effective and improves the quality of the indoor environment. With appropriate controls of the electrical lighting it can save lighting energy and reduce the cooling load. Daylighting is very cost-effective because of the high cost of electricity and the fact that lighting in nonresidential buildings is a major end-use energy component.

For effective daylighting the following design details were recommended:

- Windows should be equipped with shading devices which prevent direct sunbeam penetration and reflect it upward, toward the ceiling.
- Clerestories should either be shaded or have light shelves with sufficient depth to prevent direct sunbeam penetration and with their upper surface treated to reflect the beam upward.
- Vertical glazing was found to be superior to sloped glazing facing the sun, which was difficult to shade and thus caused direct-beam light penetration.
- Horizontal glazing (skylights) admitted excessive heat in summer and created complications for ceiling plenums and their content.
- Diffused light was the best. Light diffusion was provided by different means in the various experimental buildings: light-colored walls, ceilings, and special diffusing grids.
- Distributed small roof monitors provided better lighting than one large roof monitor.

Comments on Daylighting by Roof Monitors. In single-story nonresidential buildings (and/or the upper story of multistory buildings) roof monitors facing south (in the Northern Hemisphere) can provide high-quality daylight in very significant proportion to the total lighting needs, provided that the solar beam is reflected by suitable diffusers so that direct sunlight is prevented.

Daylighting by roof monitors can be applied regardless of the floor area size of the building. Therefore in single-story buildings the core area, where full electrical lighting has to be provided during the daytime, can be effectively eliminated. Occupants' satisfaction with the lighting conditions produced by south-facing monitors was very high in all of the buildings which have used such monitors.

18.7. WINDOWS AS NATURAL VENTILATION ELEMENTS (see also Section 10.6)

Ventilation Functions and Requirements

One of the primary purposes of windows is to provide natural ventilation, which is the flow of outdoor ("fresh") air through the building. Ventilation, however, serves three different functions which may call for different ventilation rates and patterns. The first is *health ventilation*, namely, maintaining the indoor air quality above a certain minimum level. The second is *comfort ventilation*, namely, providing human comfort in hot seasons by increasing the heat loss from the body, as well as preventing discomfort from excessive wetness of the skin. The third function is *structural cooling*, namely, cooling the building during the evening and night hours.

Health ventilation is needed at all times and its rate is the lowest. Usually about 0.5–1.0 air changes per hour in residential buildings would prevent unpleasant disagreeable odors. However, in some cases such as houses with heavy smoking or, in some places, a high concentration of radon gas emitted from the ground (or even from some building materials), the required ventilation rates would be much higher.

The airflow needed for thermal comfort is not directly related to the air change rates but to the air speed over the human body. As the flow is not homogeneous throughout the building but is usually concentrated in some indoor areas, it is possible by architectural design to obtain maximum air flow at the places in each room where people are located, for example, over the beds in a bedroom or over couches in living rooms, etc. Comfort ventilation is usually needed mostly during the daytime hours, especially in the afternoon when indoor temperature reaches its maximum, although in many warm and especially hot humid regions, it is desired also during the evening and night hours.

With continuous comfort cross-ventilation the indoor air temperature is very close to the outdoors, and no significant daytime temperature reduction is possible, e.g., by the use of high-mass construction. The function of structural cooling ventilation, on the other hand, is to lower the indoor *daytime temperature* well below the outdoor level. It should be provided only in the evening and night hours, while during the daytime hours the windows should be closed, to prevent entry of the outdoor hotter air. From the window design aspect structural cooling calls for directing the air flow near the surfaces of the mass, where the night coolness is stored.

Physical Mechanisms of Natural Ventilation

Natural ventilation of buildings can be generated by two different and independent forces:

1. By temperature difference between the indoor and the outdoor (thermosyphonic ventilation)
2. By the wind

Thermosyphonic Ventilation. When a vertical opening exists in a building, the air pressure on either side of its center is equal, and no air flow occurs at this level of the aperture, in spite of the temperature difference.

The pressure above and below the center, inside and outside, varies with height, but at different rates. The rate of pressure change is proportional to the density of the air and hence to its temperature. If the indoor air is warmer and therefore less dense, the indoor vertical pressure gradient is less than that outdoors. This means that inside the building there is an excess pressure at any level above the center and depression below it, compared with the vertical distribution of the air pressure outdoors. These pressure differences increase with vertical distance from the center of the aperture. At the upper section of the opening an excess pressure exists indoors and air is flowing outwards. At the lower section the excess pressure is outdoors and air is flowing inward.

When two openings are provided at different heights and the indoor temperature is again higher than outside, a similar pressure difference is formed. Excess indoor pressure builds up at the upper opening, where air flows outward, while a depression is created at the lower level, inducing an inward flow. When the indoor temperature is lower than outdoors, the positions are interchanged and the flow direction reversed.

The air flow F induced by the thermal force is proportional to the free area of the openings, A_w (m^2 or ft^2) and to the square root of the temperature difference dT (°C or °F) times the vertical distance between the centers of the upper and lower windows, h (m or ft) (Ref. 18.1).
In metric units:

$$F(\text{m}^3/\text{min. m}^2) = 7 A_w (h\, dT)^{0.5} \quad (18.2a)$$

and in British units:

$$F(\text{ft}^3/\text{min. ft}^2) = 9.4 A_w (h\, dT)^{0.5} \quad (18.2b)$$

The pressure difference dP (mm or in. water head) is given by the following formulas.
In metric units:

$$dP\,(\text{mm}) = h\, dT/0.85\,(T + 273) \quad (18.3a)$$

and in British units:

$$dP \text{ (in.)} = h \, dT/66(T + 460) \qquad (18.3b)$$

where T is the average temperature of the air column (°C or °F) and h is height (m or ft.).

Airflow Due to Wind Pressure. When wind is blowing against a building, the straight motion of the air is disturbed and the air is deflected around and above the building. The air pressure on the sides facing the wind is elevated above atmospheric pressure (pressure zone) and is reduced on the leeward side (suction zone). In this way pressure differences are created across the building.

When the wind is perpendicular to a rectangular building, the front wall is subject to pressure while the sides and rear are under suction. If the wind direction is oblique, the two upwind sides are under pressure and the two others are under suction. A flat roof is under suction in all cases.

The pressure difference between any two points on the building envelope determines the potential driving force for ventilation when openings are provided at these points. It may be expressed as a dimensionless pressure ratio, when related to the dynamic pressure exerted by the wind. This dynamic pressure, for ordinary temperature conditions, is given by (Ref. 18.1), in metric units:

$$dP = V^2/16 \qquad (18.4a)$$

and in British units:

$$dP = V^2/2000 \qquad (18.4b)$$

The pressure dP is in mm or in. of water and the wind velocity V is given in meters per second (metric) or in miles per hour (British).

The Combined Effect and Relative Importance of Wind and Thermal Force. The actual airflow in buildings results from the combined effect of thermal and wind pressure forces. The pressure gradient obtained across a given opening is the algebraic sum of the pressure differences generated by each force separately. The two forces may operate in the same or in opposite directions, depending on the direction of the wind and on whether the internal or external temperature is higher. The resulting airflow through the opening is proportional to the square root of the combined pressure difference. Therefore, even when the two forces are operating in the same direction, the resulting airflow can only be slightly higher (at most by 40 percent) than it would be with the greater force alone.

As the thermal force of ventilation depends on the product of the indoor-outdoor temperature difference and the height of the ventilation path (i.e., vertical distance between apertures), it is of practical importance only when one of these factors is of sufficient magnitude. In residential buildings the effective height of the ventilation path is very small, less than 6 ft 6 in. (2 m) in the average single-story apartment, so for an air flow of any practical use to be induced by thermal force there must be an appreciable difference between the indoor and outdoor temperatures. Such differences exist only in winter, and mostly in cold regions. Thus in summer the thermal force is usually too small to have any practical effect.

Window Design for Effective Natural Ventilation

Window Orientation with Respect to the Wind. It is generally believed that to have optimum ventilation conditions the inlet windows should face the wind directly, and that any deviation from this direction reduces the indoor air speed. However, a study by Givoni (Ref. 18.1) has shown that this is not always so. In some cases better conditions can be achieved when the wind is oblique to the inlet windows, particularly when good ventilation conditions are required in the whole area of a room.

In a room with two windows in opposite walls, where the inlet faces the wind directly, the main air stream flows straight from inlet to outlet and, apart from local turbulence at the corners of the outlet wall, the rest of the room is only slightly affected. Air speed is low along the side walls, particularly so at the corners of the inlet window wall. When the wind is oblique (e.g., at 45°) to the inlet opening of the same room, most of the air volume takes up a turbulent flow, circling motion around the room, increasing the air speed along the side walls and in the corners.

In contrast, if the two windows are located in adjacent walls, better ventilation is obtained with the wind perpendicular to the inlet window than when it is oblique and parallel to the inlet-outlet axis.

It can be concluded that better ventilation conditions are obtained when the air stream has to change direction within the room, than when the flow is direct from inlet to outlet. This conclusion is of great practical importance in regions where the prevailing wind direction is westerly or easterly.

These orientations are the most difficult from the point of view of shading. Having a building with a window with western orientation (facing the wind) may cause overheating by the sun. However, very good ventilation conditions are possible in regions with westerly winds, even when the long facade with the inlet windows is turned by 45° to the northwest or southwest, where the shading is much easier. When the wind direction is northwest or southwest, optimum ventilation conditions are achieved when the long facades are orientated toward the north or south, a direction which may also be preferable from the solar radiation viewpoint.

Window Size. The effect of the size of windows on ventilation depends to a great extent on whether the room is *cross-ventilated*. In rooms where windows are only in one wall, the size of the window will have little effect on the internal air velocity.

If the room is cross-ventilated, an increase in the size of

the windows increases the internal air speed, but only when both the inlet and outlet openings are increased. Increasing the inlet or outlet alone will only slightly affect the internal air motion. Even when the inlet and outlet are both increased, the increase in air speed is not proportional to the window size and the *rate* of velocity increase falls off.

Induced Cross-Ventilation in Rooms with One External Wall. When the wind is oblique to the window there is a gradient in the air pressure along the length of the wall, and thus the air can enter through one part of the window and leave through another. But when the wind is either perpendicular to or blowing from behind the window, pressure differences along the wall are too small for an increase in window size to have more than a slight effect.

Therefore, with common design of windows, a room with windows on one side only is poorly ventilated. However, when the wind direction is oblique to the external wall, there is a flow of air along and parallel to the length of the wall. It is possible to utilize the pressure gradient along the wall, by having in a given room two lateral windows, at the upwind and downwind sides of the room, and thus to improve on the ventilation conditions produced by a single window of the same area. But as the pressure gradients along a given wall of a room are relatively small, the resulting air flow is only moderate.

However, great improvement can be made in the ventilation conditions of such rooms by providing each one of the two windows with a *single* vertical projection (a fin), in a symmetrical pattern, preferably on the downwind side to the first (upwind) window and the upwind side of the second window (Refs. 18.1 and 18.13). In this way a positive pressure region is formed in front of the foremost window (with respect to the wind) and a suction in front of the rear window. Air then enters the room through the first window and leaves through the second, in effect creating cross-ventilation.

A similar effect is achieved by incorporating the projections necessary to create the pressure gradient as an integral part of the architectural and functional design. For example, balconies can be designed in conjunction with the openings (windows and doors) to utilize the side walls of the balconies as airflow control devices. The main difference between this arrangement and the previous one is that the positions of the pressure and suction areas are reversed and thus the internal air flow is from the downwind to the upwind window. It should be emphasized that, should the windows be provided with two projections on both sides, the whole effect is lost as the symmetry equalizes the pressure in front of the two windows, and so the driving force for ventilation is greatly reduced.

Effect of Fly-Screens. Fly-screens are essential in many parts of the world, particularly in the tropics. They may cause considerable reduction in air flow through windows, especially if the wind speed is low. Application of screens to a whole balcony in front of the openings improves the ventilation conditions compared with screens directly applied to the windows. The wind is able to penetrate the fly-screen through a larger area and then to contract toward the smaller doors or windows, free from obstruction. Application of screens to the outlet window or a rear balcony produces a smaller effect than the front screens.

18.8. WINDOWS AS SOLAR HEATING ELEMENTS (see also Section 21.6)

In winter, direct sun penetration through windows is a very effective method for heating buildings. However, effective utilization of the solar radiation calls for additional details (Refs. 18.14–18.18).

Direct Gain through Solar Windows

Buildings which are heated to a significant extent in winter by solar radiation penetrating through glazed openings are referred to as *direct gain* solar buildings. In direct gain buildings the inhabited spaces are heated by the sun, admitted through conventional windows, clerestories, roof monitors, skylights, etc. The mass of the building fabric itself acts as the necessary thermal storage material, to absorb and store excess solar energy during the sunny hours and release it back during the night.

Direct gain is the most efficient method to *collect* solar energy because the energy is collected at the lowest usable temperature, besides the benefits of daylight and view offered by sun facing glazing. Therefore it can be recommended that in all buildings ''solar'' windows will be included, with glazing area up to a certain limit, e.g., about 10–15 percent of the floor area of the heated space. Within this size limit it is also not too difficult to provide control means, such as movable shutters and/or insulation panels, to minimize heat loss in winter nights and overheating in summer.

The main factors limiting the size of solar glazing area are:

1. Diminishing utilization of the collected energy, beyond a given size of the solar windows
2. The increasing likelihood of overheating *during sunny days in winter* as the collectors' size increases; overheating can be minimized by venting out excess heat or by shading the solar glazing, but both ''solutions'' reduce the useable solar energy
3. Increased likelihood of overheating in summer from unwanted heat gain from the solar windows, as the window area increases; this problem can be solved by shading and/or insulating the solar glazing during the summer

The main factors related to the solar windows which affect the performance of ''Direct Gain'' buildings are:

- Location of solar windows
- Size of solar windows

- Choice of glazing type
- The amount and design details of the mass available for thermal storage
- Heat gain controls

Location of Solar Windows

The major advantage of direct gain systems is that significant amounts of solar energy may be collected through the elements which would be found in the building in any case, namely windows or roof monitors facing the sun (south in the Northern Hemisphere). A direct gain building is in effect a building where the largest fraction of all windows are in the wall facing the sun in winter.

Size of the Solar Windows

It is often tempting to make the area of solar windows as large as the building design allows, in order to maximize the penetrating solar energy during the heating season. However, such incoming solar radiation may raise the indoor temperature too much, and may then exceed comfort conditions, even in winter on sunny days. The problem can be more serious during the spring, summer, and fall seasons.

There are two other negative effects of too large glazing areas. First, the windows are usually the weakest point in the thermal quality of the building envelope, causing excessive heat loss in winter, mainly at night. From the solar energy utilization viewpoint the benefits from increasing size of glazing show diminishing returns, while the heat loss at night through the glazing is proportional to the glazing size, unless the area of the solar glazing is equipped with operable night insulation, or the glazing itself is of high intrinsic thermal resistance (transparent insulation, e.g., silicone foam).

Second, the penalty of summer overheating in regions with hot summers, from too large areas of solar glazing, may well be greater than the winter benefits. This penalty can also be eliminated by insulated operable shades which protect the building from daytime overheating while enabling fast cooling in the evenings by large, openable windows.

There is no single, simple computation method for arriving at the desired glazing size, taking into account all the various factors involved, but from experience with occupied residential buildings employing direct gain, the following rule of thumb gives guidance for the initial design.

In a region of hot summers, solar glazing should be about 10–15 percent of the total heated floor area. It may reach 35 percent in the solar rooms where it is located, as long as problems of glare, overheating, fading of fabrics, etc., are solved. Effective convective heat transfer should be secured between the solar and the nonsolar rooms, during the sunny hours, through large internal openings.

In cold regions larger solar glazing area (e.g., 20–25 percent of the heated area) may be appropriate, provided that high-thermal-resistance glazing is used (e.g., double glazing), together with the provision of effective night insulation.

Choice of the Glazing Type

Many different kinds of glazing are available. The properties of the glazing, which determine its performance as a solar collector, are:

- Average solar transmittance
- The effective U-value for conductive heat loss

As the main objective in solar buildings is to maximize the energy gain in winter, clear glass is the most effective. Single glass windows transmit more solar radiation than double glazing, but their heat conductance is much greater. Therefore in solar buildings double clear glass glazing would be the common low-cost choice. Use of heat-reflecting glazing, which reflects back the longwave thermal radiation emitted by the internal surfaces, would substantially increase the net heat gain, with a cost increase of about US $22 per square meter of the glazing.

Thermal Mass in Direct Gain Solar Buildings

Thermal mass "stores" energy from sunlit hours, to be given off back during the night. From the point of view of the daily cycle, only limited thicknesses of storage elements are useful, and this may determine the manner in which thermal mass is incorporated in the building's structural elements.

The heat capacity of masonry materials is a function of their specific heat, and of their mass. Since the specific heat of almost all masonry materials: concrete, brick, stone, adobe, etc., is similar, about 0.22 Btu/lb °F or 0.24 Wh/kg °C (see Table 20.1), the nominal heat capacity is essentially proportional to the total volume and the density of the material. Generally, the amount of heat capacity should be related to the amount of the penetrating solar radiation on clear days. In a given location this means that the minimum amount of heat storage should be related to the size of the solar glazing. For a given size of the solar glazing the performance of the building will improve with the increase in the amount of heat capacity, up to a given limit.

In a 24-hour cycle, a thickness of up to about 100 mm (4 in.) of concrete will be fully effective (Ref. 18.16). The minimum area of a storage element made of concrete should be at least 5 times the area of the glazing. If the thickness of the storage elements is greater, the area of concrete which will be required for effective storage will not decrease proportionately, due to the lower storage potential of the deeper layers. Other masonry materials, with lower thermal conductivity, will require even larger minimum area (and thinner layers) for effective thermal storage.

REFERENCES

18.1. B. Givoni. *Man, Climate and Architecture*. Van Nostrand Reinhold, New York, 1981.

18.2. R. B. Goldner and R. D. Rauh. "Electrochromic Materials for Controlled Radiant Energy Transfer in Buildings." *Soc. Photo-Optical Instrum. Eng.*, **428**, 38–44 (1983).
18.3. R. B. Goldner et al. "Thin Film Solid State Ionic Material for Electromic Smart Window™ Glass." *6th Int. Conf. on Solid State Ionics*, Garmisch-Parternkirchen, (FRG), Sept. 1987.
18.4 *ASHRAE Handbook—1985, Fundamentals*. American Society of Heating, Refrigerating and Air Conditioning Engineers, Atlanta, 1985.
18.5 B. Stein, J. S. Reynolds, and W. J. McGuinnes. *Mechanical and Electrical Equipment for Buildings*, 7th Ed. Wiley, New York, 1986.
18.6. V. Olglay and A. Olgyay. *Solar Control and Shading Devices*. Princeton University Press, Princeton, 1975.
18.7. B. Givoni and E. Hoffman. "Effect of Window Orientation on Indoor Air Temperature." *Architectural Science Review*, **9**, 80–83 (1966).
18.8. B. Givoni. "Laboratory Study of the Effect of Window Size and Location on Indoor Air Motion." *Architectural Science Review*, **8**, 42–46 (1965).
18.9. H. H. Bryan, W. M. Kroner, and R. P. Leslie. *Daylighting—A Resource Book*. Center for Architectural Research, Rensselaer Polytechnic Institute, Troy, New York, 1981.
18.10. B. H. Evans. *Daylight in Architecture*. McGraw-Hill, New York, 1981.
18.11. S. Ternoey, L. Bickle, C. Robbins, R. Busch, and K. McCord. *The Design of Energy Responsive Commercial Buildings*. Wiley, New York, 1985.
18.12. Burt Hill Kosar Rittlemann Assoc. and Min Kantvowitz Assoc. *Commercial Buildings Design: Integrating Climate, Comfort and Cost*. Van Nostrand Reinhold, New York, 1987.
18.13. S. Chandra, P. Fairey, and M. Houston. *A Handbook for Designing Ventilated Buildings*. Florida Solar Energy Center, Cape Caneveral, FL, 1983.
18.14. B. Givoni. "Integrated Passive Systems for Heating of Buildings by Solar Energy." *Architectural Science Review*, **24**, 24–41 (1981).
18.15. B. Givoni. "A Generalized Predictive Model for Direct Gain." *Passive Solar Journal*, **2**, 107–115 (1983).
18.16. B. Givoni. "The Effect of Heat Capacity in Direct Gain Buildings." *Passive Solar Journal*, **4**(1), 25–40 (1987).
18.17. R. W. Jones (Ed.). *Passive Solar Design Handbook*. Vol. 3. DOE/CS-0127/3. US Department of Energy, Washington, DC, 1982.
18.18. E. Mazria, *The Passive Solar Energy Book*. Rodale Press, Emmaus, PA, 1979.

SUGGESTIONS FOR FURTHER READING

D. Ander and M. Navvab. "Daylighting Impacts of Fenestration Controls." *Proceedings of the Eighth National Passive Solar Conference*. J. Hayes and D. A. Andrejko (Eds.), University of Delaware, Newark: American Section, International Solar Energy Society, 1983, pp. 175–180.

C. M. Ashley, D. C. Ashley, and L. F. Kinney. "Innovative, Efficient Daylighting Designs." *Proceedings of the Fifth National Passive Solar Conference*, J. Hayes and R. Snyder (Eds.), University of Delaware, Newark: American Section, International Solar Energy Society, 1980, pp. 1179–1182.

S. Daryanani. "Design Consideration for the Daylighting of New Commercial Buildings." *Energy and Buildings* **6**, 109–118 (1981).

R. Glover, "Daylighting Effects of Window Proportion, Location, and Ceiling Heights Predicted by Physical and Computer Models." *Proceedings of the Seventh National Passive Solar Conference*, J. Hayes and C. B. Winn (Eds.), University of Delaware, Newark: American Section, International Solar Energy Society, 1982, pp. 441–446.

S. R. Hastings and R. W. Crenshaw. *Window Design Strategies to Conserve Energy*. NBS Building Science Series 104. Superintendent of Documents, U.S. Government Printing Office, Washington, DC, 1977.

J. K. Holton. *Daylighting of Buildings*. National Bureau of Standards Report No. NBSIR 76-1098. Superintendent of Documents, U.S. Government Printing Office, Washington, DC, 1976.

R. G. Hopkinson (Ed.) "Sunlight in buildings." *Proceedings C.I.E. Intersessional Conference*, Newcastle-upon-Tyne, 1965.

R. Johnson, et al. "Glazing Energy Performance and Design Optimization with Daylighting." *Energy and Buildings*, **6**, 305–318 (1984).

J. Kendrick. "Daylight Variability in Rooms with Different Orientations." *General Proceedings of the 1983 International Daylighting Conference*, T. Vonier, (Ed.), Phoenix, AZ, 1983, pp. 21–28.

M. Magnusson. "Window Configuration: Designing for Daylighting and Productivity." *General Proceedings of the 1983 International Daylighting Conference*, T. Vonier (Ed.), Phoenix, AZ, 1983, pp. 155–160.

S. Matthews and P. Calthorpe. "Daylight as a Central Determinant of Design: How It Helped Shape a New TVA Office Building." *AIA Journal*, 86–92 (Sept. 1979).

D. Mirkovich. "'Light plenum' concept in office building design." *Proceedings of the Eighth National Passive Solar Conference*, J. Hayes and D. A. Andrejko (Eds.), University of Delaware, Newark: American Section, International Solar Energy Society, 1983, pp. 169–174.

F. Moore. "Sunlighting: Toward an Integration of Daylighting and Direct Gain Heating." *Proceedings of the Seventh National Passive Solar Conference*, J. Hayes and C. B. Winn (Eds.), University of Delaware, Newark: American Section, International Solar Energy Society, 1982, pp. 387–392.

E. Ne'eman. "A Comprehensive Approach to the Integration of Daylight and Electric Light in Buildings." *Energy and Buildings*, **6**, 97–108 (1984); at Conference, Feb. 16–18, 1983, Phoenix, AZ.

E. Ne'eman and D. Shrifteilig. "The Design of Openings for Given Daylight Requirements as a Function of a Topological Structure and Geometry of Light Admission." *Proceedings of the 19th CIE Session*, Kyoto, Bureau Central de la CIE, Paris, 1979, pp. 327–331.

W. Place, M. Fontoynont, and T. Howard. "Commercial Building Daylighting." *Proceedings of the Seventh National Passive Solar Conference*, J. Hayes and C. B. Winn (Eds.), University of Delaware, Newark: American Section, International Solar Energy Society, 1982, pp. 453–458.

C. L. Robbins. "Criteria and Goals in Planning for Sunlight and Daylight." *Proceedings of the 1979 National Conference on Technology for Energy Conference*. Information Transfer, Inc., Silver Spring, MD, 1979, pp. 330–334.

S. Selkowitz. "Daylighting and Passive Solar Buildings." *Proceedings of the Third National Passive Solar Conference*, H. Miller, M. Riordan, and D. Richards (Eds.), University of Delaware, Newark: American Section, International Solar Energy Society, 1979, pp. 271–281.

S. Selkowitz. "The Impact of Fenestration on Energy Use and Peak Loads in Daylighted Commercial Buildings." *Proceedings of the Eighth National Passive Solar Conference*, J. Hayes and D. A. Andrejko (Eds.), University of Delaware, Newark: American Section, International Solar Energy Society, 1983, pp. 187–192.

NOTATION

A	area
F	airflow
h	height
q, Q	quantity of heat
T	temperature
U-value	overall heat transfer coefficient

A list of abbreviations of the units of measurement, definitions of these units, and conversion factors between British/American and metric units are given in the Appendix.

19
Lighting

W. G. Julian

This chapter deals with lighting and the emphasis is placed on the use of light in workplaces, although mention is made of lighting for effect and atmosphere. The approach taken is to establish the criteria for good seeing conditions, to mention the technology which is available for those purposes, and to discuss some applications. This chapter draws heavily upon the recommendations of various national and international standards and, where possible, is independent of particular parochial practices.

19.1. THE OBJECTIVES OF LIGHTING DESIGN

The lighting of an interior or exterior space should ensure the safety of people in the space, facilitate the performance of visual tasks, and aid in the creation of an appropriate visual environment.

Safety is always important but the emphasis given to task performance and the appearance of the space will depend on the nature of the space. For example, the lighting considered suitable for an operating-theater table will place much more emphasis on lighting the task than on the appearance of the room, but in a theater foyer the priorities will be reversed. However, in almost all situations the designer should give consideration to both task performance and visual appearance, although there can be a variation in emphasis.

Lighting affects safety, task performance and the visual environment by changing the extent to which and the manner in which different elements of the space are revealed. Safety is ensured by making any hazards visible. Task performance is facilitated by making the relevant details of the task easy to see. Different visual environments can be created by changing the relative emphasis given to the various objects and surfaces in an interior. Different aspects of lighting influence the appearance of the elements in an interior in different ways and this section discusses the influence of each important aspect of lighting separately. However, lighting design involves integrating the various aspects of lighting into a unity appropriate to the design objectives.

The lighting system should therefore be so designed and installed as to effectively reveal the task and provide a safe and comfortable visual environment. The fulfillment of these objectives will often depend on the quality rather than the quantity of the lighting installed.

Efficient seeing of the task mainly depends on the adequate illumination of the task; freedom from unwanted reflections; the use of special techniques where appropriate; and that the luminances of the surroundings are correctly related to that of the task.

A safe and comfortable visual environment mainly depends on the avoidance of excessive illuminance variations; the absence of direct glare from lamps and luminaires; the correct luminance distribution on all surfaces; the use of suitable colors on the main surfaces; and the use of light sources with suitable color characteristics.

Careful attention to all of the above is of particular importance when visual tasks are critical and prolonged or are carried out under conditions of stress. Their fulfillment is also particularly important in the case of workers over the age of about fifty-five, since they are more readily affected by poor visual conditions than are younger people. However, the main visual defects of the older worker call for the use of correctly prescribed and fitted glasses rather than just the provision of more light (see also Section 19.5).

One of the fundamental decisions to be made when designing interior lighting is the relationship between daylight and electric light. It may be possible to rely on daylight during daytime and to design the electric lighting only for nighttime conditions; to use daylight as available but supplement it as required by electric lighting; or to ignore daylight and operate the building on electric lighting only. The decision as to which of these approaches should be adopted will be influenced by many considerations in addition to the lighting effects. For example, the energy consumption and costs involved, the possible building forms, and the need for a controlled environment are all relevant factors in determining the tradeoffs between daylight and electric light.

Decisions made on the use of daylight and electric light affect the lighting conditions produced and there is little doubt that given a choice people prefer to work by daylight and to enjoy a view. Windowless interiors are generally disliked, particularly if they are small, but may be accepted if there are good reasons for the interior to be windowless. People do not like the uncomfortable thermal conditions which extensive daylighting (or sunlighting) can produce, so it is usual to combine daylight and electric light to produce sufficient and suitable lighting on the task and in the room, by day and night. The electric lighting serves to supplement daylight when and where it is insufficient and the daylight contributes an element of variation and directional flow to the appearance of the interior. It is important to note that windows can be a source of direct disability glare and can sometimes cause a gloomy interior unless due regard is taken of the recommendations of the various standards which exist on lighting design.

19.2. THE VISUAL BASIS OF LIGHTING DESIGN

For working interiors the influence of the lighting upon work performance is very important. The performance of a given person for a given task is essentially a function both of the ability of that person to perform that task (task performance potential) and of the person's attitude toward performance of that task (task performance attitude).

Performance attitude determines to what extent the performance potential is effectively utilized and what the actual performance will be for a given performance potential. Attitude includes factors such as motivation, dedication, and concentration, all which are of a psychological or social nature and are beyond the scope of this book. Lighting, with all the other factors of the physical environment, may influence performance potential, but the influence upon actual performance is also dependent on the performance attitude.

Visual performance is the rate of information processed by the visual system as measured, for instance, by the speed and the accuracy with which the visual task (usually a part of another task) is performed. *Task visibility*, the measure of the ease, speed, and accuracy with which the task may be seen, may be considered as *visual performance potential*. It can be determined from measurements of visual performance at maximum level of task performance attitude.

The visibility of a visual task is generally determined by the visibility of the most difficult element that must be detected or recognized in order that the task may be performed. This detail is referred to as the *critical detail*. The visibility of the critical detail is a function of the difficulty experienced in discriminating it visually from the background against which it is seen and from other details in its immediate surroundings.

The visibility of a detail depends on many factors such as:

- Apparent size of the detail (the quotient of its size and the viewing distance)
- Luminance and color of the detail
- Adaptation luminance
- Contrast in luminance and color between the detail and its background
- Available observation time
- Form of the detail
- Similarity in form and texture between the detail in other details and the immediate surroundings
- Advance knowledge about the moment when the detail will appear in the visual field
- Position of the detail in the visual field
- Advance knowledge about the position of the detail in the visual field
- Experience with the visual task

In the achievement of good task visibility the most important lighting factor concerns the luminance of the task and the surroundings.

The luminance pattern of the visual field sets the level of adaptation of the visual system. This is the process by which the properties of the visual system are modified according to the luminances in the visual field: the final state is the *adaptation level*, expressed as a luminance— the *adaptation luminance*. In properly designed interiors the adaptation luminance can be taken as the average luminance in the central part of the visual field.

The properties of the visual system which are affected by the adaptation luminance are:

- Visual acuity or sharpness of vision, which is the capability of the system for discrimination between details or objects which are very close together, usually expressed by the apparent size of the smallest detail that can be discriminated

- Contrast sensitivity, which is the capability of the system for discrimination of small relative luminance differences, usually expressed by the reciprocal value of the minimum perceptible relative luminance difference
- The efficiency of the oculomotor functions for accommodation, convergence, pupilary contraction, eye movements, etc.

Visual acuity, contrast sensitivity, and oculomotor efficiency increase with increasing adaptation luminance up to a certain maximum level.

For tasks where the apparent size of the detail is critical with respect to task visibility, increased visual acuity due to increased luminances is of dominant importance for improving task visibility. When, however, the apparent size of the critical detail is far above the visual acuity threshold the contribution of increased visual acuity is negligible.

The two other factors mentioned above are also positively affected by an increase of the luminance, and they will result in improved task visibility only if these factors are critical with respect to the visibility of the task considered.

Since seeing depends upon being able to detect contrasts, it is important that contrast-diluting effects be avoided. *Disability glare* is the result of luminaires in the field, which reduce the contrasts available within the scene, for example, the effect produced by car headlights at night. Contrasts can also be diluted by reflection of light sources on gloss surfaces, as are experienced with gloss paper. These reflections are termed *unwanted reflections* or, sometimes, reflected glare.

An unsatisfactory luminance distribution in the scene may not cause physical disability, as mentioned above, but it may cause psychophysical effects, such as sensations of gloom or of inadequate light, distraction or discomfort. The discomfort effect caused by bright luminaires or windows is termed *discomfort glare*.

Note that while the objective is to produce appropriate luminances (hence, contrasts) for task visibility it is usual to express the requirements for lighting in terms of illuminances. These, in turn, should give rise to luminances and the desired task visibility. Thus, the majority of the recommendations made in lighting standards are in terms of illuminances (see, also, Section 19.4).

19.3. UNITS AND CONCEPTS

The mensuration system used in lighting is *photometry* and is a specialized subset of the more general system for the measurement of electromagnetic radiation—radiometry.

Photometry uses the same concepts as radiometry but has a peculiar system of units due, mainly, to historical reasons but also recognizing that the units are based on a human psychophysical response. The photometric units are radiometric ones weighted by the spectral response of the human visual system and a constant (the maximum luminous efficiency) which relates lumens to watts.

The fundamental unit is the *lumen*, which is the measure of *luminous flux*, Φ. Luminous flux is simply the visually useful power dissipated by a light source, but measured in lumens rather than watts. A monochromatic source at 555 nm wavelength producing 1 watt will also be producing 683 lm. At all other wavelengths the watts, multiplied by 683 are weighted by a number less than 1 because the visual system's response peaks at 555 nm and has the action spectrum $V(\lambda)$ shown in Fig. 19.3.1.

Flux is a scalar quantity and, in order to know how the flux is distributed in space, the *intensity I*, of the source is needed, together with a suitable coordinate system to define directions. Intensity is flux per unit solid angle (in a particular direction) and has the unit *candela* (lumen per steradian). Two common coordinate systems are in use—the C-γ system is usually used for indoor luminaires and roadlighting lanterns, and the B-β system for floodlights. Both systems specify measurement planes (designated C or B) and the angles of measurement within those planes (designated γ or β).

Luminance L is photometric brightness and is the area density of intensity, being the quotient of the intensity I of the source in a given direction and the projected area A of the source in the same direction. Luminance has the units candelas per square meter. Luminances are used to determine the *contrast* present in a scene and if relative luminance contrasts are used these correlate well with the perceived contrasts in the scene—that is, the contrast is the quotient of the difference in luminance and, say, the background luminance.

The luminances of surfaces are the result of the illuminance on the surface and the reflectance of that surface. *Illuminance E* is the area flux density on the surface, that is, it is the quotient of the flux Φ arriving and the area A upon which it falls. Illuminance has the unit of lumen per square meter or lux. *Reflectance* is the quotient of reflected to arriving flux and is, therefore, dimensionless.

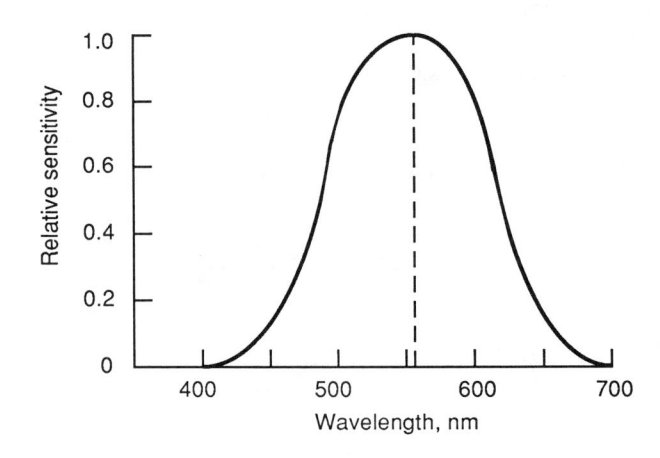

Fig. 19.3.1. The luminous efficiency function $V(\lambda)$ of the human visual system.

It is possible to show that for a surface normal to a source of intensity I but distant d meters, the illuminance E is I/d^2. If the normal to the surface is displaced from the direction of the source by an angle θ then the illuminance on the plane will be $I\cos\theta/d^2$.

The measurement of color is a more complex matter, especially if a system is needed which also indicates the perceived attributes of color. The CIE chromaticity system is used to measure color and it exists in a number of variants for different applications. In general, it has three values—a luminance value and two ratiometric cartesian coordinates which locate the color in a two-dimensional color space which represents all colors from white to the spectral locus. The representation, in the basic system is Yxy, where Y is the luminance value and x and y are the chromaticity coordinates. The system is based on a tristimulus interpretation of the visual system.

There also exist visual colorimetric systems based on the visual matching of standard color chips and the unknown color under a standard illuminant. The most common of these systems is the *Munsell* system, which is an atlas of colors using a nomenclature of hue (color), value (lightness), and chroma (saturation) as the three color coordinates.

19.4. LIGHTING STANDARDS AND THEIR BASES

The lighting level produced by a lighting system is usually quantified by the illuminance produced on a specified plane. In most cases this plane is the major plane of the tasks in the interior, and is commonly called the *working plane*. The illuminance provided affects both performance of the tasks and the appearance of the space.

The effect of lighting on work depends on the size of the critical details of the task and on their contrast with their background (Fig. 19.4.1). One particular task much used for laboratory investigations of visual performance consists of scanning an array of Landolt rings (Fig. 19.4.2a) and identifying those rings with gaps in a specified direction. By changing the size of the gap and the contrast of the ring with the background it is possible to vary the difficulty of the task over a wide range.

Three important points should be noted from Fig. 19.4.2b. The first is that increasing the illuminance on the task produces an increase in performance following a law of diminishing returns. The second is that the illuminance at which performance levels off is dependent on the visual difficulty of the task, that is, the smaller the size and the less the contrast of the task the higher the illuminance at which performance saturates. The third is that although increasing illuminance can increase task performance, it is not possible to bring a difficult visual task to the same level of performance as an easy visual task simply by increasing the illuminance.

In principle these effects occur for all tasks, although the exact relationship between the illuminance on the task and the performance achieved will vary with the nature of the task. There are two aspects of a task which are important in determining the effect of illuminance. One has already been mentioned—the task difficulty; the greater the visual difficulty the greater the importance of illuminance. The other is the extent to which the visual part of the task determines the overall performance. Where there is only a small visual component, as in audio typing, the influence of illuminance on overall task performance is likely to be small but where the visual component is a major element of the complete task, as in copy typing, then the illuminance provided will be important.

The specified illuminance for the task should be provided on an appropriate plane (horizontal, vertical, or inclined), with the worker standing or sitting in the normal working position.

Some tasks require illumination on more than one plane, although usually one predominates in importance. Allowance for the possibility of light being obstructed by the worker's body is particularly important when the task is on a vertical or an inclined plane.

Some standards specify single values for task illuminances, others single values with guidance on the use of higher or lower values depending upon the task, the operatives, and the need for speed or accuracy, and others give ranges with a method, based on the criteria mentioned above, for selecting which value should be used in the range. The latter method is used in the *IES Lighting Handbook* (Ref. 19.1). Table 19.1 indicates the illuminance ranges recommended by the CIE* for various task.

19.5. LIGHTING DESIGN METHODS

From the foregoing it is apparent that most lighting design, in terms of calculations, is undertaken as illuminance design and limited to the plane on which the task is carried out. Some of the quality aspects of the design may be checked after choices have been made on how task illuminances are to be achieved. In interior lighting a check may be made of the likelihood of discomfort glare and, possibly, of unwanted reflections in tasks. In exterior lighting, particularly roadlighting, checks may also be made of disability glare effects.

On the other hand some designers make decisions purely on the basis of the appearance of lighting equipment and the assumed appearance that the lighting will create without serious consideration of any task components. This is evident in many "prestige" areas, such as hotel foyers and rooms, where it may be impossible to read with comfort or speed. This approach to design usually involves no calculations and is sometimes slavish to ephemeral fads.

---

*CIE = *Commission Internationale de l'Éclairage* (International Commission on Illumination).

Lighting, size an

Lighting, size and contra

Lighting, size and contrast all affe

Lighting, size and contrast all affect the legibility to

Lighting, size and contrast all affect the legibility of text.

Lighting, size and contrast all affect the legibility of text. Lighting, size and contrast all

Lighting, size and contrast all affect the legibility of text. Lighting, size and contrast all affect the

Lighting, size and contrast all affect the legibility of text. Lighting, size and contrast all affect the legibility of text.

Lighting, size and contrast all affect the ability to read text. Lighting, size and contrast all affect the ability to read

Lighting, size and contrast all affect the legibility of text. Lighting, size and contrast all affect the legibility of text.

Lighting, size and contrast all affect the legibility of text. Lighting, size and contrast all affect the legibility of text.

Fig. 19.4.1. The effect of varying size and contrast of task details on ease of reading. Reading this under different lighting levels will demonstrate the dependence of seeing task detail on the illuminance provided on the task.

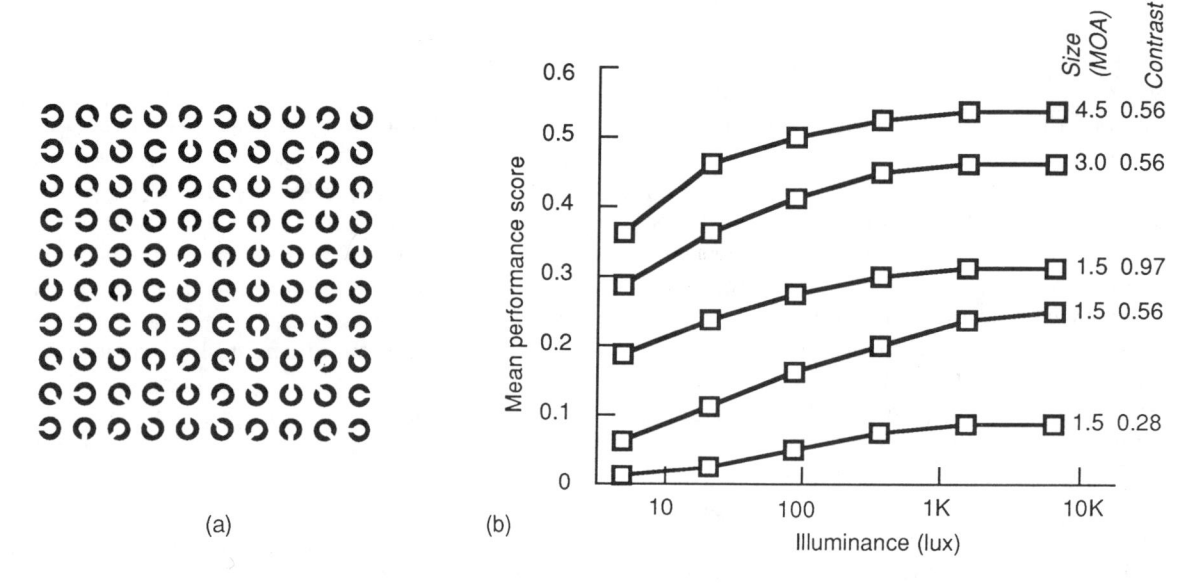

Fig. 19.4.2. (a) Landolt rings and (b) the mean performance scores for Landolt ring charts

Table 19.1. CIE Recommended Illuminance Ranges.

Illuminance Range, lux	Type of Task or Activity
20–30–50	Outdoor entrance areas
50–75–100	Circulation areas, simple orientation, short temporary visits
100–150–200	Rooms not continuously used, e.g., stores, cloak rooms, entrances
200–300–500	Tasks with simple visual requirements, e.g., rough machining, classrooms
300–500–750	Tasks with medium visual requirements, e.g., medium machining, offices
500–750–1000	Tasks with demanding visual requirements, e.g., testing, drawing offices
750–1000–1500	Tasks with difficult visual requirements, e.g., fine machining and assembly
1000–1500–2000	Tasks with special visual requirements, e.g., very fine inspection
>2000	Performance of very exacting visual tasks, e.g., surgery, microelectronics

Source: Guide on Interior Lighting (Ref. 19.2).

Obviously, good design must use the predictive design tools that have been developed, together with that special ability that makes a good designer. Unfortunately, there are few predictive tools to assist the designer with decisions about the quality and aesthetic aspects of design and the designer has to rely upon empirical advice in standards and upon experience.

Direct Illuminance

In terms of illuminance design (or calculation) the most common methods are the *point-by-point* and the *lumen method*. The former is used where the interreflected component of light is small, as in outdoor lighting, or in interiors with dark surfaces and direct-type luminaires. The method uses the inverse square law of illuminance and the cosine law to calculate direct illuminances at a point or on a grid of points.

The Lumen Method

When the illuminance at a point contains a significant contribution from light interreflected within a space, the point-by-point method would underestimate the illuminance. However, the calculation of the interreflected contribution is a tedious and time-consuming process and has not been practical or economical until the introduction of cheap computers and, since then, most applications still do not warrant such a procedure for routine calculations. It has been found that if a room is to be illuminated using a uniform array of luminaires, then the interreflected component of the light reaching the working plane in that room will be the same as for all other rooms with the same ratio of horizontal to vertical surface areas, for a given luminaire and mounting height. That ratio is called the *room index*. (Some countries use a *room cavity ratio* which is based on the reciprocal of the room index.)

That all rooms with the same room index behave in the same way means that the determination of planar illuminances in rooms can be simplified to providing a measure of the utilance of the installed lamp flux for a range of room indices. That measure is called variously the *utilization factor*, UF, or the *coefficient of utilization*. Account needs to be taken of light loss over the maintenance cycle of the lighting system by means of a depreciation term, such as, a *maintenance factor*, MF.

Since illuminance is defined as flux per unit area it follows that the illuminance predicted using this lumen method can be expressed as the utilized depreciated lamp flux per unit area of the plane being illuminated—the working plane. Mathematically, this is expressed as

$$E = \frac{\Phi \; UF \; MF}{A} \; \text{lux} \qquad (19.1)$$

The utilization factor is provided by manufacturers as tables for various combinations of room indices and, wall and ceiling and floor cavity reflectances. The maintenance factor can be found in various standards and guidance is provided for light loss from lamp lumen depreciation and dirt on luminaires and room surfaces.

It is usual to rearrange Eq. (19.1) to determine the required installed flux needed to achieve a specified illuminance. This then yields the number of required luminaires by dividing that flux by the product of the number of lamps per luminaire and the flux produced by one lamp. The luminaires are then spaced evenly throughout the ceiling and a check is made to insure that the spacing does not exceed a maximum that would invalidate the assumptions of the lumen method.

The lumen method is the most used calculation method in lighting design and requires only reliable data from manufacturers and a simple calculator. Variations on the method are also available by computer software suppliers. Some versions of the lumen method will also give average wall and ceiling luminances but without the assumed uniformity that is the case with the working plane.

It is not uncommon that interior design is achieved using only the lumen method. The surface luminances that result are achieved by chance, as part of the process of lighting the working plane. One of the advantages of using relatively high task illuminances is that the bounding surfaces of the room will receive more light and that the quality aspects of the space will be improved.

As has been suggested in the previous section, design should really be based on luminances and the contrasts or *apparent brightnesses* that result. Techniques have been developed to allow the rational design of the appearance of spaces by specifying the apparent brightness of elements and determining the flux that needs to be placed on the various surfaces to achieve the desired effect. These techniques are not without some difficulties, particularly in predicting the effects of interreflected flux and working with the very strong effect of lightness constancy. Nevertheless, such methods much more closely follow the objectives of the real design process than does simply the application of the lumen method.

In addition to achieving the desired illuminances or luminances for task visibility, the design process also calls for a check that the task areas are free from unwanted reflections, that the lighting system does not produce excessive distraction or discomfort, and that the luminance distribution does not result in a gloomy appearance. Standards and codes give guidance on how to achieve these objectives.

Daylight Illuminances

Daylighting design is usually illuminance-based and uses methods developed to calculate illuminances from standardized models of the sky luminance distribution. Some methods are equivalent to point-by-point calculations, while others are similar to the lumen method.

Computers have meant that the point-by-point approach can be used more easily than in the past. There are almost no design aids on assessing the quality aspects of daylit interiors and the designer is left to judgments based mainly on experience.

It has been mentioned that the point-by-point method can be used when the interreflected component of light is small. Outdoor floodlighting for display, sports, etc., is designed in this way. The design criteria are usually given in terms of illuminances on particular planes and with certain uniformities within these planes.

Sports Lighting

Sports lighting needs special consideration for both players and spectators. The task is rarely only a horizontal plane and vertical illuminances are very important. It is necessary to ensure that light comes from sufficiently many directions to adequately illuminate vertical surfaces and to eliminate strong shadows. Some sports involve fast-moving, small balls and high illuminances are needed, especially for competition matches, to allow the accurate tracking of fast-moving objects. Television broadcasting adds other special requirements, since the color and contrast tolerances of television cameras are much less than those of the human visual system. If long-focal-length lenses are used high illuminances toward camera positions are needed to maintain picture quality.

Roadlighting

Roadlighting is luminance-based because the driver's view of the road is at near-glancing angles to the road surface and a characteristic of matte surfaces that makes them appear almost glossy at those angles can be exploited to make the road surface appear bright. Therefore, objects can be made visible by their being seen silhouetted against the bright road surface. This technique works only for long, straight sections, since the viewing angle with respect to the normal to the road surface must be over 80°. Curves, intersections, pedestrian crossings, etc. are lit using an illuminance approach, where the aim is to light the objects so that they are seen in positive contrast against the road or other background surfaces.

Glare effects can be calculated for both road and other outdoor lighting. Because backgrounds tend to be very dark, excessive stray light into players' and drivers' eyes will cause disability by reducing the contrasts available in the scene and could lead to critical detail not being detected. Disability glare criteria exist for roadlighting calculations and for some sports lighting.

Obtrusive Light

Outdoor lighting can also impact other users because it is difficult to contain light to the area of interest and because, to achieve the lighting objectives, it is often necessary to mount the luminaires on high masts. By day these have an esthetic visual impact and by night the high luminances may cause distraction and/or disability to people in nearby properties. Spill light may also enter adjacent properties and, in particular, living and bedrooms. These effects can lead to considerable controversy when large outdoor lighting systems are proposed. It is difficult to develop criteria for these cases of amenity and social impact.

Spill light is also of concern around airports, since confusing light patterns can be produced, and astronomers are concerned about the disability effects produced by scattered light within the atmosphere from outdoor lighting, in particular, roadlighting.

Emergency Lighting

The safe evacuation of buildings and sports arenas requires that sufficient light be provided for the safe evacuation of occupants in the event of the failure of the main power supply. Most countries require *emergency evacuation lighting* in most classes of buildings, apart from individual dwellings. This lighting provides low-level light, usually by means of a battery supply, for, say, one or two hours to allow the safe evacuation of people. Statutory requirements usually indicate the required illuminances, those areas needed to be lit, and any associated illuminated exit signs.

Sports areas lit using discharge lamps also need provision to avoid panic in the event of a momentary interruption to supply. Either hot restrike techniques need to be applied or an anti-panic system based on filament lamps must be installed to provide instant, low-level lighting. This and other emergency lighting, for example in hospital operating theaters, is *not* the same as emergency evacuation lighting and is subject to separate design decisions, although the emergency supply for the various emergency lighting systems may be common.

Computer-Aided Design

Only the easy or the tedious problems have been attempted while the major issues in lighting remain untouched by computers. Many problems are unsolved because behavioral models do not exist.

Luminaire optical design is computer aided and the photometric testing of luminaires and the production of photometric data are automated and computer controlled. Trivial lighting design by the lumen method can be automated with little to be gained apart from the integration of lighting, electrical, and heat loads into electrical and energy design packages. Computers have allowed the extension of the lumen method into the calculation of direct surface illuminances from nonrectangular arrays of luminaires in nonrectangular rooms and the calculation of interreflected flux to varying degrees of accuracy, depending upon the subdivision of surfaces into smaller elements. However, the degree of accuracy may not depend upon the sophistication of the method of calculating the interreflection of flux but, rather, on the (in)adequacy of information on surface finishes, furnishing, etc. These extended lumen method systems allow the determination of surface luminances, and some packages include shaded, colored perspectives of the (possible) appearance of the lit space.

Outdoor lighting was an early beneficiary of computer-aided design, since it requires only point-by-point calculations due to the insignificance of interreflected flux. Color television demands good uniformity on all camera planes. While the calculations themselves are simple, the number of calculations for a large floodlighting system is beyond the capacity of accurate, economic manual methods. Instead, millions of trigonometric calculations are performed accurately and tirelessly by computer. However, this is not lighting design. The author has yet to hear of a design system which, given an arena and a catalogue of floodlights, will design the lighting. The design is done by an experienced person with the computational assistance of a computer. Floodlighting design is an enormous optimization problem.

Roadlighting physical parameters also benefit from computer-aided calculation, due mainly to the complex luminance factor of road surfaces, the intensity distribution of the luminaires, the three-dimensional spatial distribution of luminaires, road surface and observer, and the need to calculate road surface luminances. Again, the author is unaware of roadlighting optimization software, although fewer variables are involved than in a large floodlighting system. The disability glare effect of roadlighting can also be calculated, and it is an indicator of likely discomfort effects.

Other lighting quantities, such as cylindrical and semicylindrical illuminances and contrast rendering factors can be calculated: the latter only if task locations and characteristics and the detailed finishing of the environment are known, in addition to the choice of lighting system.

Computers also allow the detailed determination of indoor illuminances/luminances due to daylight (skylight and/or sunlight) from standard sky and sun models. The question, how well these models relate to reality is often avoided. In the future it is likely that daylighting design will be based on probabilities, rather than certainties. The dynamic nature of the sky makes other than probabilistic daylighting software is of dubious value, except in terms of very rough estimates of quantities.

Mention has been made of the determination of a discomfort glare indicator for roadlighting. Models exist for the discomfort effect in interior lighting from electric lighting, and these have been computerized, for example, the British Glare Index and the American Visual Comfort Probability. However, at present these have application in design only as go/no go indicators, since they are unrelated to any performance model of lighting. In fact, in some cases, too little "glare" may lead to a soporific lighting effect.

A number of large computer-aided design systems exist which aid in the design of energy efficient buildings. Provided that the objective is to produce energy efficient (empty-of-people) buildings these packages are fine. None has the sophistication to include the important quality aspects of lighting. That may be because some quality factors cannot be modeled, but if those that can be are included then the tradeoffs would no longer be simple ones, such as, more windows mean less electric lighting. In some cases, more windows mean more electric lighting (but no windows mean unhappy people). Until people are included, these systems should be treated with suspicion as design tools—they are suitable as methods of auditing likely energy use once the design has been determined.

Architects and lighting designers are excited about the fruits of new lamp technology: compact, low-wattage, high-lumen, good-color-rendering packages of light. However, most of these new sources are much less tolerant of environmental conditions than the older sources; for example, a relatively small change in environmental temperature can greatly affect the performance of these lamps.

What are needed, if designers are able to assert that they have met certain standards, are computer models to explore the impact of, say, the thermal design of a ceiling space on the performance of lamps. What are the tradeoffs, say, with the air-conditioning design? These issues will become more important as building owners demand performance from their environmental systems (and designers).

This brief overview of computer-aided lighting design has indicated that some areas of lighting design are adequately supplied with design aids while others are severely lacking. In particular, the physical aspects of both indoor and outdoor illuminance/luminance design are well understood. Some quality parameters in some applications, e.g., in roadlighting, are also well understood. Otherwise, it must be concluded that real computer-aided lighting design must await the development of robust models of psychophysical responses and also their relationships to visual performance. Without this knowledge the computer aid is really just a very fast, automated calculator. Claims to the contrary about lighting design software should be treated with skepticism.

Finally, before any software purchase is considered it is essential to know what models have been used in the software; what limitations it has (sensitivity to particular parameters, etc.); what assumptions are made if parameters are not specified; what correlation, if any, exists between predicted and prototype performance; what approximations have been employed in calculation processes (for example, methods of integration or interpolation); and what simplifications have been made to the (standard) model. These matters are sometimes not made clear. If they are not, then it would be wise to not consider the purchase.

19.6. LIGHT SOURCES

The aim of this section is to provide basic information on windows and luminaires. Maintenance of lighting equipment will be discussed in Section 19.9 as one of the considerations of lighting systems. The intention here, in the case of electric lighting, is to give sufficient information to demonstrate the differences between broad classes of equipment. It is not sufficiently precise for design purposes: manufacturers' data should always be consulted.

Daylight

Daylight is that light which is produced by the sun either directly (sunlight) or indirectly by the scattering effect of the atmosphere (skylight). Both sources can illuminate interiors directly through openings (windows, rooflights, etc.) or indirectly through the same openings but by light which has been reflected from external surfaces (the ground, building façades, parts of the window or rooflight, etc).

The sky is dynamic in its composition of water vapor and suspended particles, especially in areas near the ocean. The position of the sun varies throughout the day and year, influencing both the direction of daylight and its quantity (say, horizontal illuminance). The position of the sun can be accurately predicted for any location. The illuminance produced by the sun can be calculated provided that its position and the condition of the atmosphere are known, together with the geometry of the receiving surface relative to the sun.

The illuminance produced by standard sky conditions can be precisely calculated, but the difficulty is that the standard skies rarely if ever occur. Some models have been developed for intermediate sky conditions which allow the calculation of illuminances based on the probabilities of certain local atmospheric conditions.

Since the sky is dynamic it is impossible to use the concepts used in electric lighting of constant illuminances. Instantaneous illuminances are of little interest in the lighting of interiors over a day or a year. Instead, statistically likely quantities are used in order that assessments can be made of the adequacy of, say, the illuminances provided by daylight alone or on the tradeoffs involved in the various approaches that can be used for the integration of daylight and electric light. In the latter case it must be noted that simplistic illuminance (energy) studies are rarely satisfactory—it is essential that the quality of the luminous environment (the luminance distribution) be carefully assessed.

Electric Lamps

There are three basic types of electric lamp—incandescent, high pressure gas discharge, and low pressure gas discharge. Within each type there are a range of lamps available which differ in construction, wattage, luminous efficacy, color properties, cost, etc.

Incandescent lamps produce their light by means of thermal radiation, usually by the electrical heating of a tungsten filament to near its melting point. That is necessary because the efficacy (the quotient of lumens out to electrical watts in) is a function of filament temperature. So, too, is the life, and the incandescent lamp is a compromise between efficacy and life. The main advantages of incandescent lamps are their wide range of sizes and wattages, their dimability, and their simple control. Their main disadvantages are very low efficacies and short lives. A modification of the normal tungsten lamp is the introduction of a halogen into the lamp to produce the *tungsten halogen* lamp. This, due to the halogen regenerative cycle, results in lamps with higher efficacies, longer lives, and higher color temperatures (whiter) than normal incandescent lamps. They are also more compact and, in the low voltage versions, have small, compact filaments which facilitate the design of reflector systems with very good beam control.

The vapors of two metals, mercury and sodium, provide the bases for the high-pressure gas-discharge lamps. Mercury when operated at high pressures will produce a high output of visible radiation which, however, is unfortunately mainly in the blue-green region of the spectrum and is therefore unsuitable for applications where color is important. The lamp also produces ultraviolet radiation, which can be exploited by the use of a fluorescent coating on the outer envelope of the lamp to provide red radiation. This lamp is called the *mercury fluorescent lamp*. Another method for improving the color properties of the mercury lamp is to introduce other metals, as halides, into the arc tube. The so-called *metal halide lamp* can have excellent color properties depending upon the brew of metals used to fill the gaps in the mercury spectrum. The *high-pressure sodium lamp* produces a warm, golden white light and achieves high efficacies. It produces its whitish light by operating sodium vapor at very high pressures, resulting in spectral broadening of the otherwise monochromatic sodium spectral lines. In this lamp the tradeoff is between efficacy and the whiteness of the light produced. It is now replacing the mercury fluorescent lamp in most applications.

The low-pressure lamps are also based on the metals mercury and sodium, but there also exist, for display purposes, lamps based on discharges in inert gases, such as, neon and argon. The *low-pressure sodium lamp* has the highest efficacy of all lamps due to its monochromatic yellow radiation, but its application is limited to those cases where color discrimination is not considered important and where the cost of providing light is to be minimized.

The low-pressure mercury lamp is rarely used without a fluorescent coating because most of the radiation produced is ultraviolet. However, if *phosphors* are used on the inside of the lamp then the result is the familiar *tubular fluorescent lamp*. A wide range of colors is possible by the selection of appropriate halophosphates or the suitable mixing of narrow-band phosphors of the type used in color television picture tubes. The tubular fluorescent lamp, due to its high efficacy, low cost, etc. is the most used lamp in nondomestic applications. Recent developments in phosphors, filling gases, and control gear have led to compact fluorescent lamps.

The construction, operation, range of luminous efficacies, life and color properties of each lamp type are summarized in publications such as the *IES Lighting Handbook* (Ref. 19.1); an indication is given in Table 19.2. For information on a specific lamp the manufacturer's data should always be consulted.

Each basic lamp type can have a number of variations in construction. These variations can involve its shape, the number and type of caps it has, the presence of a fluorescent or diffusing coating on an outer envelope, the chemical composition of any fluorescent coating, and the provision of a reflector inside the lamp.

The operating details are concerned with such matters as runup time, reignition time, operating positions, and susceptibility to environmental conditions. Runup times and reignition times are important because most of the discharge lamps do not produce their maximum light output immediately after switch on. Usually several minutes are required before the maximum light output is achieved. Further, unless special circuits are used, high-pressure discharge lamps will not immediately reignite after an interruption of supply. Usually a period of several minutes is necessary for the lamp to cool before it will reignite. These factors limit the suitability of some lamp types for rapid switching and dimming. It is also worth noting that not all lamp types can operate in all positions and that some lamp types are sensitive to such external environmental factors as air temperature and vibrations.

The life of an electric lamp can have two distinct meanings, either the time after which the lamp ceases to operate, or the time after which the light output is so reduced that it is more economic to replace the lamp even though it is still functioning electrically. Typically, lamps with filaments fall into the first category but discharge lamps fall into the second. While defining the average life of lamps with filaments presents little problem, defining the life of a discharge lamp does, because it depends so strongly on the economic factors involved. Table 19.2 gives ranges of lamp life for each lamp type. A range of times is given for each lamp type because the time will vary with the construction and rating of the lamp used, even for lamps of the same type, and with such operating conditions as the voltage applied and the switching cycle.

Light sources that have their color point on or near the blackbody locus have a clear relationship between the (correlated) color temperature and the color appearance of the light source. Thus, lamps used for general lighting service and fluorescent lamps in particular, are classified according to their color temperature. The following three groups can be distinguished:

Color temperature	Color appearance	CIE color appearance group
< 3300 K	warm (yellowish) white	1
3300–5000 K	intermediate white	2
> 5000 K	cool (bluish) white	3

Although light sources having the same (correlated) color temperature will also have the same color appearance, this does not necessarily mean that colored surfaces will look the same under them, since surface color is due to selective

Table 19.2. Some Selected Lamp Characteristics.

Lamp	Luminous Efficacy,* lm/W	Lamp Life,** h	Color Appearance	CIE Color Rendering Group
Incandescent	8–18	1000–2000 (a)	warm	1A
Tungsten halogen	18–24	2000–4000 (a)	warm	1A
Mercury fluorescent	36–54	5000–10000 (b)	intermediate	3
Metal halide	66–84	5000–10000 (b)	depends upon choice	depends upon choice
High-pressure sodium	67–121	6000–12000 (b)	warm	2 or 4
Low-pressure sodium	101–175	6000–12000 (c)	monochromatic yellow	—

*These are lamp efficacies. Control gear losses must be considered for discharge lamps when calculating installed efficacy.
**Lamp life is subject to switching cycles, voltage, etc., as well as to various definitions. See the following notes:
(a) For lamps with filaments the life is expressed as the time after which 50 percent of a large sample of lamps will have failed.
(b) For these discharge lamps life is expressed as the time after which the light output of the lamp will have fallen 30 percent below the initial light output.
(c) For the low-pressure sodium discharge lamp, the life is related to a 30 percent reduction in luminous efficacy, rather than a 30 percent reduction in light output because for this lamp type the luminous efficacy tends to change with time rather than the light output.
Source: Code for Interior Lighting (Ref. 19.3).

reflection. In other words, those spectral wavelengths contained in the incident light that are reflected determine the color impression obtained from the surface.

This is satisfactory while the source is a thermal radiator and has a continuous spectrum (all wavelengths present). However, a selective radiator, such as a discharge lamp, emits light only in a selected number of spectral lines or bands, with the other wavelengths being absent.

That the color appearance obtained from such a light source can be "white" is explained by the theory of additive color mixing. Any spectral color together with its complementary color will produce white light and, as the complementary color itself is generally also present in the spectrum or can be obtained by mixing of two other spectral colors, it is possible to obtain white light by the combination of only two or three single wavelengths. Although the white light obtained may have a color appearance comparable with that of a thermal radiator and therefore can be assigned a correlated color temperature, surface colors illuminated by it may be difficult to distinguish, as most of the hues contained are absent in the light falling upon them.

The number, arrangement and relative power of the spectral lines or bands present in the visible part of the spectrum of a selective radiator determine how far a random selection of surface colors can be faithfully reproduced under this light. This is called the *color rendering capability* of the light source.

In 1965 the CIE developed a method for the quantitative assessment of the color rendering capability on the basis of eight test colors. (For some purposes the number of test colors is extended to fourteen.) First the correlated color temperature of the light source under test is assessed. Then, for each test color, the color appearance under the source is calculated as a percentage of that of a blackbody radiator of the same color temperature. The average result for the eight samples is the *general color rendering index* (R_a). It is a measure of the quality of "white" light sources. Table 19.3 shows the CIE color rendering groups and recommended applications.

The *control gear* which is associated with a discharge lamp should start the lamp, control the lamp current after ignition, and correct the power factor. Control gear consumes energy and for a given type, some circuits consume more than others. The efficacy of a lamp circuit as a whole depends on the total power taken by the lamp and the control gear. It is also necessary to consider the *power factor* of the circuit in order to minimize electricity charges and to ensure correct cable ratings.

The current and wattage ratings of cables, fuses and switchgear used in the lighting circuits must be related to the total current in the circuit. Allowance may be necessary for any increased currents and voltages during switching. Harmonic currents may be present and may increase the neutral current in a three-phase system.

All electric lamps operating from an alternating current supply have a time-varying (oscillating) light output. The source of the oscillation depends on the physical mechanisms by which the light is produced. For incandescent lamps, the oscillation is usually small because of the thermal inertia of the filament. For discharge lamps the oscillation can be more marked and depends on asymmetry and instability in the arc. For most light sources in most situations, the oscillation is not visible but when it does become visible the effect is called *flicker*. Flicker is a source of distraction and discomfort to people, particularly as it is easily detected by peripheral vision and thus cannot readily be avoided. Although sensitivity to flicker varies widely between individuals, the main factors which influence its perception are the frequency and the amplitude of the modulation and the area over which it occurs. Large amplitude modulations occurring over large areas at low frequencies are the most uncomfortable conditions. Small amplitude

Table 19.3. CIE Lamp Color Rendering Groups.

Color Rendering Group	Color Rendering Index Range	Color Appearance	Examples for Use — Preferred	Examples for Use — Acceptable
1A	$R_a \geq 90$	Warm, intermediate, and cool	Color matching, clinical examinations, picture galleries.	
1B	$80 \leq R_a < 90$	Warm to intermediate	Homes, hotels, restaurants, shops, offices, schools, hospitals.	
		Intermediate to cool	Printing, paint and textile industries, demanding industrial work	
2	$60 \leq R_a < 80$	Warm, intermediate and cool	Industrial buildings	Offices, schools
3	$40 \leq R_a < 60$		Rough industries	Industrial buildings
4	$20 \leq R_a < 40$			Rough industries

Source: Guide on Interior Lighting (Ref. 19.2).

oscillations over small areas may pass unnoticed. Modern electronic control gear operates at high frequencies, and this eliminates flicker effects.

The oscillation in light output from a lamp can produce a stroboscopic effect even when the oscillation is not visible. The stroboscopic effect is an illusion which makes a moving object appear to be stationary or moving in a different manner from that in which it is really moving. The strength of any stroboscopic effect depends on the frequency, regularity, and amplitude of luminous flux relative to the frequency and regularity of the movement of the object. The most dramatic effects will occur when the frequencies are matched or are multiples or submultiples of each other and the amplitude of modulation is large. Wherever a significant stroboscopic effect is possible the lighting should always be designed to minimize such effects for reasons of safety.

19.7. WINDOWS AND LUMINAIRES

Windows and Rooflights (see also Sections 3.18 to 3.20 and Chapter 18)

The majority of windows and rooflights employ transparent media (typically glass) which admit light. In most cases they are designed to admit direct skylight and reflected skylight and sunlight with some effort to eliminate the entry of direct sunlight, not only for thermal reasons, but to eliminate the areas of light luminance contrast which can result from patches of sunlight in working interiors.

The transparent window or rooflight allows surfaces in a room to "see" large area sources of light (the sky, ground etc.). These area sources illuminate the interior surfaces which in some cases may be the task areas and in others the bounding surfaces. Interreflection aids in the redistribution of light. There exist geometric relationships between the interior illuminances produced by the luminances of the sources (sky, ground etc.) visible from the point indoors. The luminance of a patch of sky seen by a point indoors can vary considerably (especially if white clouds are present). It can be seen that the calculation of illuminances is complicated by the dynamic nature of the sky, the constantly changing sun position, and the geometry of the point with respect to the window.

Diffusing windows and skylights can be treated in the same way as diffusing luminaires. Some people approximate clear glazed openings to various intensity distributions in order to use interior lighting calculation models for the prediction of daylight illuminances.

If intermediate statistical skies are to be used for design purposes, sophisticated software is necessary for the modeling of the sky luminance distribution and for the calculation of interior illuminances/luminances (using numerical integration).

It is wrong to think of the window (or rooflight) simply as a wall (or ceiling mounted) luminaire, since the part of the external, extended source which is visible (hence the characteristics of the "luminaire") will vary with the viewing position.

Luminaires

Luminaires can take many different forms, but all have to provide support, protection, and electrical connection to the lamp. The lighting function of luminaires is to redirect the lamp flux to where it is needed as efficiently as possible and to control unwanted effects, such as distraction, discomfort, and disability that views of bright parts of the luminaire or the lamp may cause. In addition, luminaires have to be safe during installation and operation and be able to withstand the surrounding ambient conditions. There are a number of international and national standards relating to the safety aspects of various luminaires, items used in the construction of luminaires, and the photometric testing of luminaires.

Light can be controlled by obstruction, diffusion, reflection, and refraction. Fig. 19.7.1 illustrates these methods. *Obstruction* (Fig. 19.7.1a) is used mainly for glare control, and the efficiency of the luminaire depends upon what is done on the interior. Obstruction provides protection from high luminances by the creation of *shielding* or *cutoff angles*. *Diffusion* (Fig. 19.7.1b) employs translucent materials to control glare by making the source area larger—a diffusing sphere around an incandescent lamp enormously increases its apparent area, so reducing the luminance of the source. Unfortunately, diffusion is very inefficient and is now usually limited to applications in domestic and decorative lighting.

Refraction exploits the light-bending abilities of transparent media with nonparallel surfaces. Ultraviolet-stable plastics have seen refractors replace almost all applications for diffusers. As can be seen in Fig. 19.7.1c, the prisms on this refractor provide upward light onto the ceiling, downward light toward the working plane, while limiting flux in those directions likely to cause distraction and discomfort. The bottom of the refractor is usually designed to make any image of the lamps appear much larger and, therefore, less bright. Because refractors are transparent they are more efficient than diffusers. Another advantage is that, because they effectively reduce the source luminance, they can be less of a problem than reflector systems when gloss horizontal tasks are involved.

Specular reflection (Fig. 19.7.1d) is also an efficient method for the redirection of lamp flux, especially if the area of the reflector is large compared with the source size—not always easily achieved with the size constraints placed on luminaires.

Specular reflection exploits the laws of reflection to allow the design of reflectors which both redirect flux in desired directions and which will not appear flashed when viewed from those directions which would result in distraction or glare. This beam control has made reflector systems popular in those applications where screen-based equipment is used. However, excessive downward light

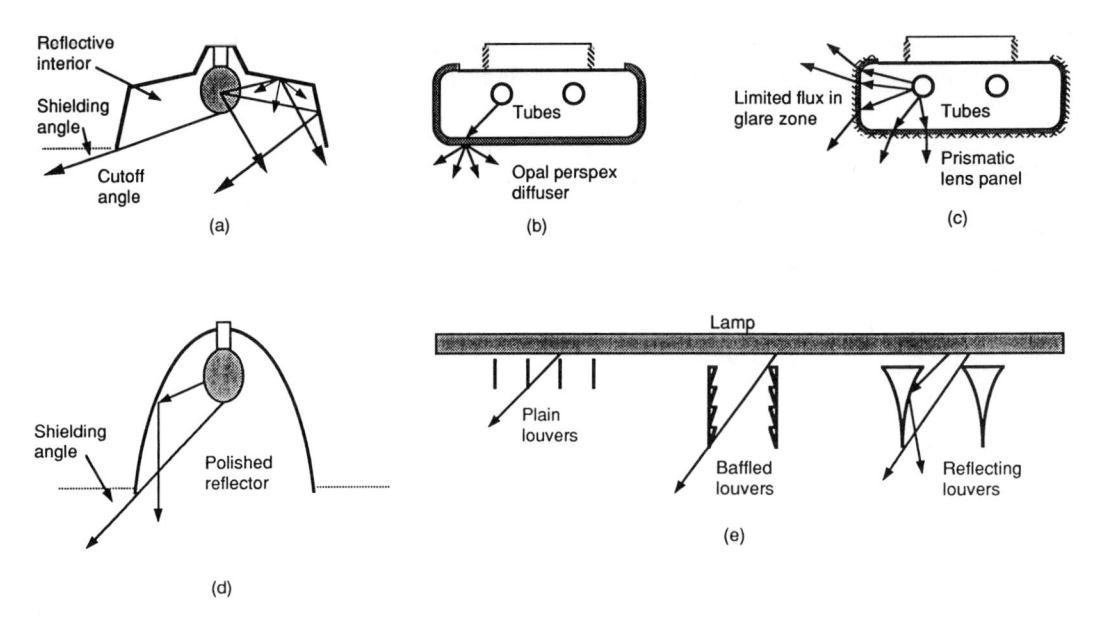

Fig. 19.7.1. Methods of light control used in luminaires. See the text for details. Some of the louver/reflector methods of control for use with tubular fluorescent lamps are shown in (e). Note that in all cases the objectives are to redirect lamp flux to where it is required and to minimize the flux in those directions which would result in glare to observers.

can, unless the room surfaces are separately lit, result in an underlit appearance to the space. As was noted in the previous paragraph, the open bottom of the reflector systems means that (near) horizontal tasks will, if glossy, image the bare lamp, with the result of contrast dilution of the task.

In general, reflectors and refractors are designed to place as much flux as possible, within the limits of glare control, to the side to maximize luminaire spacing while achieving good uniformity of horizontal illuminance. More flux is needed to the sides than directly below the luminaire due to both inverse and cosine law effects.

Lighting Control Systems

Control is an important part of any lighting system and can vary from a simple wall switch to being a part of a sophisticated computer-controlled, building management system. Whatever the method used, the aim of a control system is always to ensure that the lighting system is operating only when it is required, and that when it is, it is operating in the required state.

In principle, all light sources can be switched, but not all discharge lamps lend themselves to frequent switching due to restrike times. Switching can be achieved in a number of ways; the simplest is the manual switch. Remote switches using infrared transmitters with receivers on luminaires are also available. Lamps can also be switched by time switches or in response to the availability of daylight or the occupation of the interior. Photocells are used to sense the level of daylight available in an interior, while sensors of noise level, movement reflected radiation, and heat have all been used to detect people's presence in an interior. It is possible to send switching signals by low-voltage wiring or by high-frequency transmission pulses over the electrical supply wiring to control lighting. Individual luminaires can now be controlled, using inbuilt electronics, to respond in one of several different ways to the signals they receive. Such systems provide great flexibility in the way the lighting system can be used.

Dimming is required whenever the ability to steadily vary the illuminance in a room is desired. Tungsten filament lamps can be readily dimmed. Not all discharge lamps can be dimmed, and those that can, such as tubular fluorescent lamps, need special control gear. Dimming reduces the energy consumed by the lamp, but not necessarily in proportion to the light output, and usually changes its color properties. Many of the electronic developments mentioned in relation to switching can also be associated with dimming, including automatic response to daylight availability.

19.8. ENERGY CONSIDERATIONS

Significant savings in energy consumption and therefore in cost can be achieved by applying an energy-efficient design and operating approach to lighting systems. This is possible without reducing performance and visual satisfaction.

The use of daylight to supplement or replace electric light during the day in the window zones of interiors with side windows or over the entire area of spaces with rooflights can save energy for lighting. These savings should be balanced against the energy required to compensate the heat gains and losses through the daylight openings. Because of the extra heat exchange between the interior and the exterior through daylight openings, requirements on the air-conditioning will increase when the use of daylight is increased. The use of daylight therefore will be energy and cost-effective only if the savings on lighting are greater than the extra expenditure for air-conditioning (See also Sections 20.15 and 20.16). Further, it may be necessary to instal additional wall lighting to compensate for high window luminances, resulting in a reduced cost-benefit of some daylight/electric light integration.

Lamps and control gear of highest efficiency will minimize energy demands. In this respect attention must be given to the following lamp properties: color appearance; color rendering; luminance; luminous flux; lamp lumen depreciation; life; size; available luminaire types; starting and running up characteristics; dimming possibilities; etc. If the economic analysis justifies the investment it may be found that the recently developed electronic control gear for discharge lamps will yield energy savings, particularly when they are used with advanced control systems. In general, electronic gear yields higher circuit efficiencies due to high-frequency operation.

Luminaires should be selected which give the highest flux utilance, subject to achieving the required quality criteria for the lighting system. In this respect attention must be given to the following luminaire properties: suitability of the light distribution for that application; glare limitation; luminaire lumen depreciation due to dust and dirt collection or to discoloration of its materials; ease of cleaning and lamp exchange; mounting possibilities; appearance; etc.

Luminaire arrangement should preferably be such that the areas where the recommended illuminances are required are predominantly illuminated. In interiors where the work stations are known, fixed localized general lighting may be energy-efficient. If the location of the work stations is not known beforehand or is likely to change occasionally, a flexible mounting system may be provided that enables adaptation of the arrangement of the luminaires to the layout of the work stations.

Control of the electric lighting according to the required level at a given time and at a given place can be effective in energy saving. The level required depends on the available daylight, on the occupancy of the work station, on the tasks to be performed (requirements for work may be different from those for cleaning or the requirements at a given work station may vary in time depending on the tasks to be performed at that moment), and on the individual worker.

Proper maintenance procedures, including cleaning and group relamping at the most economic lamp life, can save costs and energy and can prolong the life of the system. Room surfaces should also be cleaned in order that their reflectances may be maintained. Glazing and any reflectors in daylighting systems must also be cleaned regularly.

Energy management in buildings involves control of internal and external heat gains and losses plus transportation of heat for use and disposal. Since the heat produced by the lighting forms part of the total heat load of the building it should be accounted for in the design of the air-conditioning system. It may prove effective to use return air luminaires which in general will make it easier to meet the comfort criteria for the indoor climate and which for most types of tubular fluorescent lamps may improve their luminous efficacy due to the controlled ambient temperature for the lamps.

There exist various methods for calculating the energy-efficiency of lighting systems, but the details of these are beyond the scope of this chapter. It should be noted that some methods take a simplistic view by considering only the lighting needed for task performance; however, it is essential that the whole environment be suitably lit for comfort and safety. Simplistic methods which ignore the quality aspects may lead to energy savings but at a cost in terms of productivity and/or safety. In most buildings the cost of lighting energy is a small fraction of the cost of the human resources.

19.9. LIGHTING MAINTENANCE

Maintenance of lighting systems keeps the performance of the system within the design limits, promotes safety, and, if considered at the design stage, can help to minimize the electrical load and capital costs. Maintenance includes replacement of failed or deteriorated lamps and control gear, and the cleaning of luminaires and room surfaces at suitable intervals.

Lighting systems need maintaining because without it they deteriorate. The light output from lamps decreases with time of operating until the lamp fails. Different lamp types deteriorate at different rates. Further, dirt deposition will occur on lamps, luminaires, and room surfaces.

There are two factors which need to be considered when determining the timing of lamp replacement, the change in light output, and the probability of lamp failure (see Section 19.6). Frequently it is desirable to replace discharge lamps even though they are still operating electrically, simply because the light output has fallen to an uneconomic level.

For the majority of systems the most sensible procedure is to replace all the lamps at planned intervals. This procedure, which is known as *group* or *bulk replacement*, has visual, electrical, and financial advantages over the alternative or replacing individual lamps as they fail. Visually, group replacement insures that the system maintains a uniform appearance. Electrically, group replacement reduces the risk of damage to the control gear caused by lamps nearing the end of their electrical life. Financially, by arranging that the lamp replacement will be associated with luminaire cleaning and doing it at a time when it will cause the minimum of disturbance to the activities in the interior, the cost of lamp replacement can be minimized. Group replacement is an appropriate procedure for routine maintenance. However, in any large system, a few lamps can be expected to fail prematurely and should be replaced promptly on an individual basis.

No matter whether lamps are replaced individually or in a group a decision has to be made about the replacement light source. As light source development proceeds there is a temptation to replace one light source with another which is superficially similar but of higher luminous efficacy. If this course of action is attempted, great care should be taken to establish that the replacement light source and the existing control gear are compatible, both physically and electrically. Before replacing any discharge light source with another of a different type, or the same type but from a different manufacturer, advice on compatibility should be sought from the manufacturers.

The timing and nature of lamp replacement is usually a matter of economic and managerial judgement and may well be determined by factors other than those directly related to the lighting. The proposed lamp replacement procedure should be considered during the design of the system.

The glazing in windows and rooflights also becomes dirty with time, reducing the transmittance of the system and the light admitted. The glazing can be soiled on the inside from the nature of the activity undertaken in the room and on the outside from the condition of the atmosphere and the degree to which the glazing is self-cleaning when it rains.

The light output of luminaires decreases progressively with time because of the accumulation of dust or other deposits on the transmitting and reflecting surfaces; and permanent discoloration of the transmitting and reflecting surfaces caused by age, by radiation from the lamps, or by corrosion in some atmospheres. The appropriate cleaning interval for luminaires and the lamps they contain is again an economic and managerial question. The factors that need to be considered are the cost and convenience of cleaning at a particular time and the prevailing efficiency of the system. As a general guide, luminaires should be cleaned at least once a year, but for some locations this will not be sufficient. It is usually advantageous to coordinate luminaire cleaning with lamp replacement if the latter is required. In planning a lighting system, it is important that provision be made for access to luminaires for lamp replacement and maintenance. Enclosed luminaires should be easy to open for cleaning, lamp replacement, etc., and movable parts should preferably be hinged or otherwise made captive.

The films of dust and dirt that deposit on all room surfaces and glazing will reduce transmittances and reflectances and affect the illuminance within a room. The rate and extent of the reduction depends upon many factors, including the texture of the surfaces, the inclinations of the surfaces, the location of the building in relation to industrial areas, the activities within the premises, atmospheric effects, and cleaning and renovation schedules.

It is important to remember that the illuminance on the working plane is a combination of direct light from the luminaires and diffusely reflected light from the ceiling and walls.

All lighting systems should be provided with a maintenance manual based on the "works as executed." This should include details of the luminaires installed, the lamps used in each luminaire (including type, wattage, color, etc.), any control devices used (e.g., dimmers), recommended cleaning and relamping cycles for various luminaires and lamps, and recommended cleaning cycles for windows, rooflights, and room surfaces. The owner should update the manual as a result of any subsequent additions and alterations to the lighting system. It is important that maintenance personnel use the manual to obviate problems due to the use of incorrect lamp types, wattages, colors, etc. The information contained in the maintenance manual can be used in computer-based planned maintenance and inventory control systems.

REFERENCES

19.1. J. Kaufman (Ed.). *IES Lighting Handbook*. Illuminating Engineering Society of North America, New York: *Reference Volume*, 1984; *Application Volume*, 1987.
19.2. *Guide on Interior Lighting*. Publication 29/2, Commission Internationale de l'Éclairage (CIE), Vienna, 1986.
19.3. *Code for Interior Lighting*. Chartered Institution of Building Services Engineers, London, 1984.

SUGGESTIONS FOR FURTHER READING

Code of Practice for Interior Lighting and the Visual Environment. AS 1680.1-1990. Standards Association of Australia, Sydney.
P. R. Boyce. *Human Factors in Lighting*. Applied Science, London, 1981.
W. G. Julian (Ed.). *Lighting Basic Concepts*, 4th Ed. Department of Architectural Science, University of Sydney, Sydney, 1984.
Various other publications of the Commission Internationale de l'Éclairage, the Illuminating Engineering Society of North America, the Lighting Division of the Chartered Institution of Building Services Engineers (of the United Kingdom), and the Standards Association of Australia.

NOTATION AND ABBREVIATIONS

A	area
CIE	Commission Internationale de l'Éclairage (International Commission on Illumination)
d	distance
E	illuminance
I	intensity
K	degree Kelvin
L	luminance
MF	maintenance factor
UF	utilization factor
θ	angle
λ	wavelength
Φ	luminous flux

A list of abbreviations of the units of measurement, and definitions of these units are given in the Appendix.

20
Heating and Cooling of Buildings

S. V. Szokolay

The various quantities used in the thermal design of buildings are defined. The various methods of heat transfer, the principles of psychrometry, and the use of the psychrometric chart are explained. This is then used to define the zone of thermal comfort for various climates.

Various aspects of the thermal behavior of buildings are examined, such as thermal insulation, condensation, and the calculation of heat losses and heat gains. The following sections are devoted to a discussion of the thermal design of buildings without the expenditure of thermal energy; and the use of mechanical ventilation, of heating and of air conditioning. The final section deals with energy conservation.

20.1. THERMAL QUANTITIES

Heat is a form of energy, appearing as molecular motion in substances or as electromagnetic radiation in space. It is measured in British thermal units (Btu). One Btu is the amount of heat required to elevate the temperature of 1 lb of water by 1°F. The SI metric unit of heat is the same as the unit of any form of energy or work: the joule (J). It is the work performed (or the capacity for such work, i.e., energy) when a unit force (newton, N) is acting over unit length (m); thus dimensionally it is N m. Its multiple, the kilojoule (1 kJ = 1000 J) is almost the same as a Btu: 1 kJ = 0.9478 Btu.

Temperature (T) can be considered as a symptom of the presence of heat in a substance; it is the measure of the thermal state of that substance. The Fahrenheit scale arbitrarily sets the melting point of ice at 32°F (some suggest that its zero point was set at what was then thought to be the lowest possible temperature), and 100°F is what was then thought to be the temperature of the human body. The Celsius scale (often referred to as "centigrade") has its zero at the freezing point and 100° at the boiling point of water (under normal atmospheric conditions):

$$°C = (5/9) \times (°F - 32)$$

The total absence of heat is the starting point of the Kelvin scale, the absolute zero. 0°C = 273.15°K. The temperature intervals of the Celsius and Kelvin scales are identical and in composite units of measurement K is often used as the temperature interval symbol, denoting a length of the scale, without specifying its position on the scale, to distinguish it from the °C, which denotes a point on the scale (Fig. 20.1.1). The absolute temperature scale which has the same intervals as the Fahrenheit degree is the Rankine scale. On this the freezing point of water is 459.67°R.

Specific heat capacity (c_p) gives the relationship between heat and temperature: it is the amount of heat energy required to cause a unit temperature increase of a unit mass of the substance. It is measured in units of Btu/lb °F, or in the SI unit of J/kg K (see Table 20.1).

Volumetric specific heat is a similar quantity, but it is based on unit volume and measured in Btu/ft^3 °F (J/m^3 K).

Density gives the relationship of mass and volume; it is the mass of a substance per unit volume, in lb/ft^3 or in kg/m^3 (see Table 20.1). In some cases the reciprocal of density may be convenient to use; this is referred to as the *specific volume*.

Thermal capacity is a property of a given body; it is the amount of heat required to cause unit temperature increase

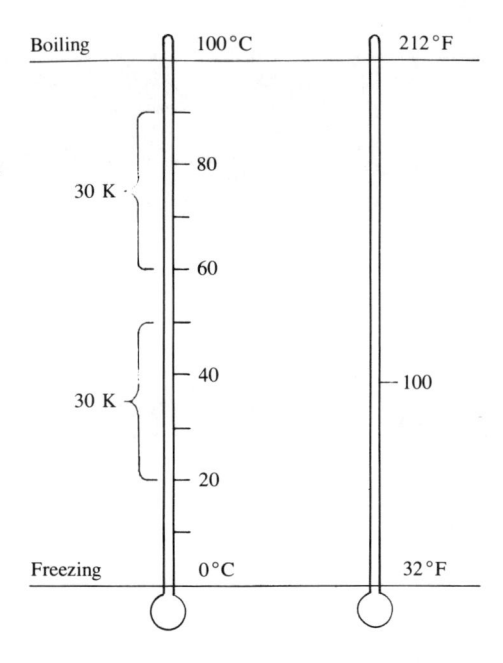

Fig. 20.1.1. Temperature scales. Note that °C gives a point on the scale, while K is used for a length of the scale, without specifying its position.

of that body. It is a product of its mass and the specific heat capacity of its material:

$$lb \times Btu/lb\ °F = Btu/°F \quad (kg \times J/kg\ K = J/K)$$

The *latent heat* of a substance is the amount of heat absorbed (or released) at a change of state (liquid to gaseous or solid to liquid) by a unit mass of that substance, without change in temperature, measured in Btu/lb (J/kg); e.g., for water:

latent heat of fusion (ice to water) at 32°F (0°C)	= 144 Btu/lb (335 kJ/kg)
latent heat of evaporation at 212°F (100°C)	= 972 Btu/lb (2261 kJ/kg)
same, at about 65°F (18°C)	= 1032 Btu/lb (2400 kJ/kg)

At a change in the reverse direction the same amount of heat is released.

Calorific value is the amount of heat released by a fuel (or food) material by its full combustion, which can be given on a unit mass or unit volume basis: Btu/lb or Btu/ft^3 (J/kg or J/m^3).

Heat flow rate or heat flux (Q) is usually measured in Btu/h. In SI units it is measured in the general unit of power, the watt (W), which is J/s. A special case is the *ton of refrigeration*, which is the cooling power (i.e., heat flux) provided by one short ton (2000 lb) of ice melting over 24 hours: 144 Btu/lb × 2,000 lb/24 h = 12,000 Btu/h = 200 Btu/min. This heat flux corresponds to 3517 W or about 3.5 kW (kilowatt).

The *density of heat flux*, or intensity, is measured in Btu/ft^2 h, or in W/m^2 in the SI, where it is used for all forms of energy flux, e.g., sound intensity as well as solar irradiance (1 W/m^2 = 0.317 Btu/ft^2 h).

20.2. HEAT TRANSFER

The *first law of thermodynamics* embodies the principle of conservation of energy. Heat and work are interconvertible; energy cannot be created or destroyed, only converted from one form into another; in any system the energy output must equal the energy input, unless there is a + or − storage component.

The *second law of thermodynamics* states that heat (energy) transfer can take place spontaneously in one direction only: from a hotter to a cooler body, or generally from a higher to a lower grade state. Only by an external energy input can a machine transfer heat against a gradient (e.g., in a refrigerator). The spontaneous heat transfer can take the form of conduction, convection, or radiation.

Conduction can take place within a body or between bodies in contact. It can be thought of as the spreading of molecular movement. The magnitude of such a flux will depend on:

1. The cross-sectional area A through which the heat can flow, taken as perpendicular to the direction of flow
2. The thickness or breadth b of the body, i.e., the length of the flow path
3. The temperature difference ΔT between the two points considered
4. A property of the material known as *conductivity*, or k-value (λ-value in the European literature)

Conductivity is given as the rate of heat flow through a unit area of a body of unit thickness, with unit temperature difference between the two sides, its unit is therefore Btu in./ft^2 h °F. In the American literature sometimes the thickness is also measured in ft, rather than in., thus the unit Btu ft/ft^2 h °F will, by cancellation, become Btu/ft h °F. The SI equivalent is W/m K. 1 W/m K = 6.93 Btu in./ft^2 h °F = 0.5778 Btu/ft h °F (see Table 20.1).

Resistivity (r) is the reciprocal of conductivity. Note that the *-ity* ending implies the property of a material, while the *-ance* ending refers to some property of a defined body.

Resistance (R) of a body is the product of its thickness (path-length of heat flow) and the resistivity of its material:

$$R = b \times r = b/k \quad (\text{ft}^2\ °F/Btu\ \text{or}\ m^2\ K/W)$$

This property is used to measure the performance of insulating materials and is often referred to as the *R-value*. For a multilayer building element the resistances of the layers are additive, e.g., for 3 layers: $R_{body} = R_1 + R_2 + R_3$. The reciprocal of the resistance is referred to as *conductance*: $C = 1/R_{body}$.

HEATING AND COOLING OF BUILDINGS

Table 20.1. Thermal Properties of Some Materials.

	Conductivity, Btu in./ft² h °F	Density, lb/ft³	Specific Heat, Btu/lb °F	Conductivity, W/m K	Density, kg/m³	Specific Heat, J/kg K
Wall Materials						
brickwork, outer leaf	5.83	106	0.19	0.840	1700	800
brickwork, inner leaf	4.30	106	0.19	0.620	1700	800
concrete, cast, dense	9.72	131	0.20	1.400	2100	840
concrete, cast, lightweight	2.64	75	0.24	0.380	1200	1000
concrete block, heavy	11.32	144	0.24	1.630	2300	1000
medium	3.54	87	0.24	0.510	1400	1000
light	1.32	37	0.24	0.190	600	1000
fiberboard (softboard)	0.42	19	0.24	0.060	300	1000
fibrous cement sheet	2.50	44	0.25	0.360	700	1050
fibrous cement decking	4.03	94	0.25	0.580	1500	1050
glass	7.64	156	0.20	1.100	2500	840
plasterboard	1.10	59	0.20	0.160	950	840
plywood	0.96	39	0.31	0.138	620	1300
stone: marble	13.90	156	0.21	2.000	2500	900
sandstone	9.00	125	0.19	1.300	2000	800
granite	16.00	162	0.19	2.300	2600	820
tile hanging	5.83	118	0.19	0.840	1900	800
timber: softwood	0.90	38	0.34	0.130	610	1420
hardwood	1.04	42	0.29	0.150	680	1200
wood chipboard	0.75	41	0.31	0.108	660	1300
Surfacing						
external rendering	3.47	81	0.24	0.500	1300	1000
plastering, dense	3.47	81	0.24	0.500	1300	1000
lightweight	1.10	37	0.24	0.160	600	1000
Roof and Floor Materials						
asphalt or bituminous felt	3.47	106	0.24	0.500	1700	1000
concrete slab, dense	7.85	125	0.24	1.130	2000	1000
concrete slab, aerated	1.10	31	0.20	0.160	500	840
metal deck	347	487	0.11	50	7800	480
screed	2.85	75	0.20	0.410	1200	840
stone chippings	6.67	112	0.24	0.960	1800	1000
tiles	5.83	119	0.19	0.840	1900	800
thatch (straw)	0.48	15	0.34	0.070	240	1420
timber boarding, wood blocks	0.97	40	0.29	0.140	640	1200
Insulating Materials						
cork	0.26	9	0.43	0.038	144	1800
EPS (expanded polystyrene slab)	0.24	1.56	0.33	0.035	25	1400
glass fiber: quilt	0.28	0.75	0.20	0.040	12	840
slab	0.24	1.56	0.24	0.035	25	1000
mineral fiber slab	0.24	2.18	0.24	0.035	35	1000
phenolic foam	0.28	1.87	0.33	0.040	30	1400
polyurethane board	0.17	1.87	0.33	0.025	30	1400
strawboard	0.64	22	0.35	0.093	350	1450
UF (urea-formaldehyde) foam	0.28	0.62	0.33	0.040	10	1400
wood wool slab	0.69	31	0.24	0.100	500	1000
Metals						
aluminum	1638	168	0.21	236	2700	877
brass	680	530	0.09	98	8500	380
copper	2666	556	0.09	384	8900	380
iron	542	493	0.10	78	7900	437
lead	257	705	0.03	37	11300	126
steel (mild)	326	487	0.11	47	7800	480
stainless steel	167	493	0.12	24	7900	510

For heat transfer from air to air the resistance of the two surfaces must also be taken into account:

$$R_{a-a} = R_{so} + R_{body} + R_{si}$$

where R_{so} and R_{si} are the outside and inside surface resistances, respectively (Fig. 20.2.1).

The reciprocal of this resistance is the *U-value*: $U = 1/R_{a-a}$ (Btu/ft² h °F or W/m²K). Tables often give the

326 HANDBOOK OF ARCHITECTURAL TECHNOLOGY

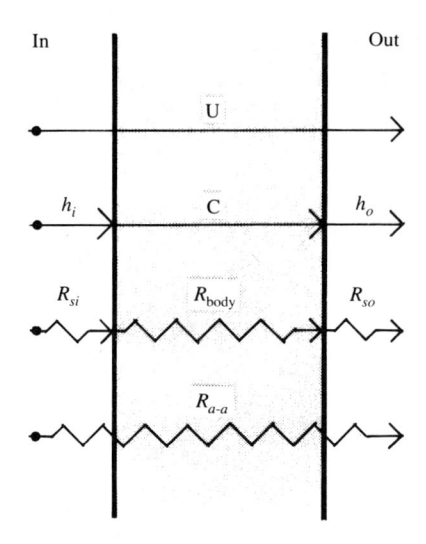

Fig. 20.2.1. Conductances and resistances. Resistances (the reciprocals of conductances) are additive.

surface conductance values, rather than surface resistances, denoted either h_o and h_i or f_o and f_i (where the f stands for film conductance):

$$R_{so} = 1/h_o = 1/f_o$$
$$R_{si} = 1/h_i = 1/f_i$$

The heat flux by conduction through an element will be given by

$$Q_c = A \times U \times \Delta T$$

where $\Delta T = T_o - T_i$. Note the suggested (but by no means generally used) sign convention: T_i is always negative; thus a negative Q_c will mean a heat loss.

Convection is the transfer of heat in a fluid (liquid or gas) by movement of fluid particles, but includes heat transfer from a solid surface into the fluid or vice versa. The heat flux in this case will be given by

$$Q_{cv} = A \times h_c \times \Delta T$$

where h_c is the convection coefficient in Btu/ft² h °F or W/m² K. Values of h_c for different conditions of either forced or free (natural) convection can be found in sources such as the *ASHRAE Handbook of Fundamentals* (Ref. 20.1).

The most often used values for average building surfaces are:

vertical surfaces: $h_c = 0.53$ Btu/ft² h °F
                                     (3.0 W/m²K)

horizontal, heat flow up: $h_c = 0.76$ (4.3)

horizontal, heat flow down: $h_c = 0.26$ (1.5)

Radiation can transfer heat from one body to another without any intervening medium, e.g., through space, in the form of electromagnetic waves. The relevant wavelength bands are:

light	380–700 nm
short infrared	700–2300 nm
long infrared	2300–10000 nm

(nm = nanometer, i.e., 10^{-9} m). The wavelength depends on the temperature of the emitting body. This radiation travels at the speed of light, 186,000 miles/s (3×10^8 m/s). On striking a surface some of the radiation may be reflected, some may be transmitted (if the body is transparent or translucent) and the remainder is absorbed, causing a heating effect.

The sum of the three coefficients, *reflectance, transmittance,* and *absorptance,* is always 1 (Fig. 20.2.2):

$$\rho + \tau + \alpha = 1 \qquad (20.1)$$

or for opaque materials:

$$\rho + \alpha = 1 \qquad (20.2)$$

The radiant emissive power of a perfect radiator (blackbody) is

$$E_b = \sigma \times T^4 \qquad (20.3)$$

where σ is the Stefan-Boltzmann constant, 0.1713×10^{-8} Btu/ft² h R^4 (5.67×10^{-8} W/m² K⁴). For ordinary bodies this will be modified by an *emittance* term. Emittance = absorptance ($\epsilon = \alpha$) for a given surface, for the same wavelength of radiation. However, in building problems *selective surfaces* are important, e.g., white paint at ordi-

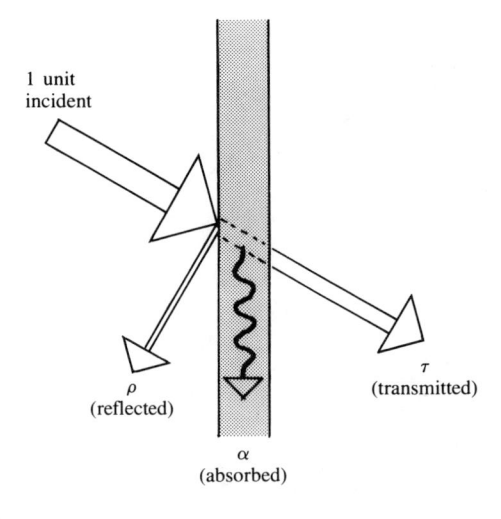

Fig. 20.2.2. The behavior of glass exposed to radiation:

$$\rho + \alpha + \tau = 1$$

nary temperatures (i.e., for long-wave infrared) would have an absorptance and emittance of about 0.9, but for the shorter solar wavelengths the absorptance is only some 0.3. Conversely, a copper oxide surface used on a solar collector may have a solar absorptance of 0.85, but an emittance of less than 0.1 at normal operating temperatures.

Radiant heat transfer between two equal and parallel surfaces will be proportionate to the difference in the fourth power of their absolute temperatures:

$$Q_r = \sigma \times A \times \epsilon_{eff} \times (T_1^4 - T_2^4) \quad (20.4)$$

where ϵ_{eff} is the *effective emittance*, the mean of the two surfaces and T_1 and T_2 are the absolute temperatures of the two surfaces.

In practical work a radiation coefficient h_r is often used, given in Btu/ft² h °F (W/m² K), with ordinary temperatures:

$$Q_r = A \times h_r \times (T_1 - T_2)$$

The value of this coefficient is

$$h_r = 1 \text{ Btu/ft}^2 \text{ h }°F \ (5.7 \text{ W/m}^2 \text{ K}) \times \epsilon_{eff}$$

around 68°F (20°C) and about

$$h_r = 0.8 \text{ Btu/ft}^2 \text{ h }°F \ (4.6 \text{ W/m}^2 \text{ K}) \times \epsilon_{eff}$$

around the freezing point.

20.3. PSYCHROMETRY

The atmosphere is a mixture of air and water vapor. The word *psychrometry* (from the Greek *psychros* = cold) originally meant the measurement of temperature, but today it refers to the study of air and water vapor mixtures and their changes. (Note the *r* in this word, which distinguishes it from *psychometry*, i.e., psychological measurement.)

Absolute humidity (AH, or moisture content) is a measure of the amount of water present in the air, per unit mass, expressed in gr/lb, i.e., grains of moisture per pound of dry air (g/kg, or grams per kilogram). Conversion: 1 g/kg = 7 gr/lb. In some cases the *humidity ratio* (HR is used instead of AH, measuring the same quantity, but using the same unit of mass in the numerator as in the denominator, i.e., lb/lb or kg/kg. This needs no conversion, as it is a dimensionless number, the same in both systems.

At any given temperature the air can only support a certain amount of moisture and no more. This is referred to as the *saturation humidity* (SH) and is measured in the same units as the absolute humidity. This can be plotted against the dry bulb (air) temperature (DBT), and this plot will form the basis of the psychrometric chart. The two main axes are: horizontal = DBT, vertical = HR (Fig. 20.3.1a).

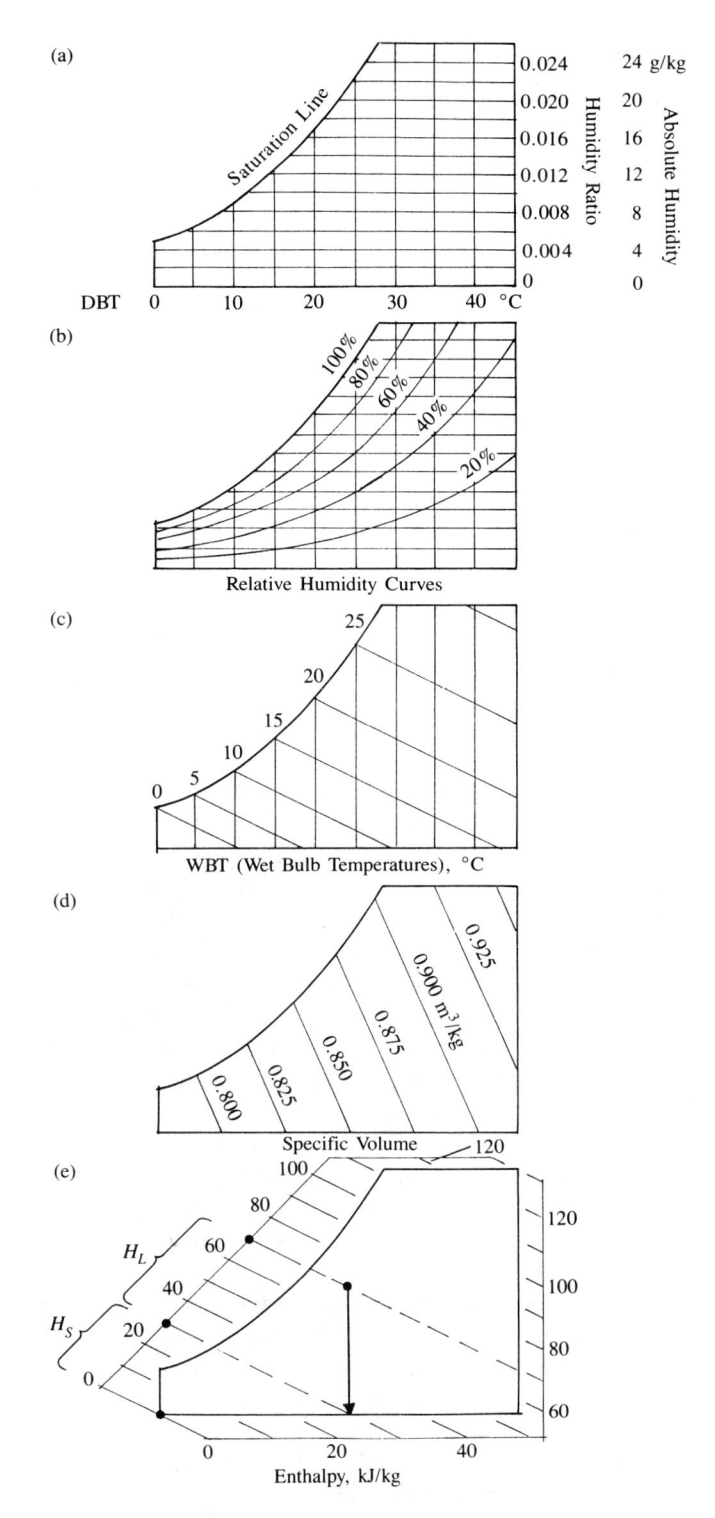

Fig. 20.3.1. Elements of the psychrometric chart. (a) Dry bulb temperature (DBT) and humidity ratio (HR), or absolute humidity (AH); (b) relative humidity (RH) curves; (c) wet bulb temperature (WBT) lines; (d) specific volume lines; (e) enthalpy or heat content, relative to dry air at 0 degree (in both °F and °C scales).

The term *vapor pressure* (p_v) refers to the partial pressure of water vapor present in the air volume considered, and it is linearly related to absolute humidity. It can be measured in any pressure unit, most often in psi (pounds per square inch) or kPa (kilopascals); 1 kPa = 0.145 psi. Saturation humidity can be expressed in terms of saturation vapor pressure (p_{vs}).

Relative humidity (RH) is an expression of the moisture content of a given atmosphere as a percentage of the saturation humidity at the same temperature:

$$RH = \frac{AH}{SH} \times 100 \text{ percent}$$

Some texts refer to this quantity as *percentage saturation* and define relative humidity in vapor-pressure terms:

$$RH = \frac{p_v}{p_{vs}} \times 100 \text{ percent}$$

Relative humidities are shown on the psychrometric chart by a series of curves plotted by the proportionate division of ordinates at any DBT point (Fig. 20.3.1b).

Wet bulb temperature (WBT) is measured by a *hygrometer* (from the Greek *ygros* = wet, moist), also referred to as a *psychrometer*. This consists of two thermometers mounted side by side. One measures the air (dry bulb) temperature (DBT). The other has its bulb wrapped in a wick, which is kept moist from a small reservoir. Maximum contact with air is ensured, in order to achieve the maximum possible evaporation rate. The *whirling hygrometer* is rotated around. The *Assman* or *aspirated hygrometer* is stationary and a small clockwork-driven propeller drives the air across the wet bulb. Evaporation from the wick will have a cooling effect and will cause a "wet bulb depression," i.e., a lower reading of temperature than the dry bulb. This cooling effect is proportional to the evaporation rate, which in turn depends on the vapor pressure of the atmosphere. When the atmosphere is saturated (RH = 100 percent) there can be no evaporation, thus no cooling effect, therefore the WBT reading will be the same as the DBT.

On the psychrometric chart the WBT is represented by sloping lines (Fig. 20.3.1c) which intersect with the same DBT line at the saturation curve. If the DBT and WBT values are measured by a hygrometer, the status point of the atmosphere can be located on the chart at the intersection of the DBT and WBT lines. Once this status point is located, a number of other characteristics can be read from the chart (Fig. 20.3.2). For example, if DBT = 90°F and WBT = 80°F, the status point is P, which indicates that the relative humidity (RH) is 66 percent and the humidity ratio (HR) is 0.020.

Specific volume is the reciprocal of density, given in ft^3/lb (m^3/kg) and on the chart (Fig. 20.3.1d) it is shown by another set of sloping lines (nearer to the vertical). This is useful in converting volumetric airflow quantities into mass-flow rates, e.g., in air-conditioning calculations.

Enthalpy (H) is the heat content of unit mass of the atmosphere, given in Btu/lb (kJ/kg), relative to the heat content of 0°F (0°C) dry air. Because of the different reference base the two values are not directly convertible. Enthalpy has two components, sensible heat and latent heat.

Sensible heat (H_s) is the heat content causing an increase in temperature. At any temperature (at normal atmospheric pressure) the sensible heat content of dry air is

$$H_s = 0.24 \times T(°F) \quad \text{or} \quad 1.005 \times T(°C)$$

where 0.24 Btu/lb °F (1.005 kJ/kg K) is the specific heat capacity of dry air.

Latent heat (H_L) is the heat content due to the presence of water vapor in the atmosphere. It is the heat that was required to evaporate the given amount of moisture (the latent heat of evaporation). Enthalpy is also indicated on the psychrometric chart. This would require a third set of sloping lines, near to, but not quite the same as the WBT lines. In order to avoid confusion, there are no enthalpy lines shown, but external scales are given on two sides. The enthalpy for any status point can be read by using a straightedge laid across the point and obtaining identical readings on both sides of the perimeter scale. For example, for the air condition represented by status point P,

the total enthalpy is: $H = 28$ Btu/lb (65 kJ/kg)
of which the sensible heat content is: $H_s = 17$ Btu/lb (39.5 kJ/kg)
latent heat content is the difference: $H_L = 11$ Btu/lb (25.5 kJ/kg)

(Fig. 20.3.1e). Figs. 20.3.2 and 20.3.3 present the complete psychrometric chart.

Psychrometric processes, i.e., changes in the conditions can be represented by the movement of the status point. Heating or cooling means the addition or removal of heat, without any addition or removal of moisture. The AH is not changing, only the DBT. The status point moves horizontally to the left (cooling) or to the right (heating) (Fig. 20.3.4a). Dehumidification can be achieved by cooling below the dewpoint. As the air is cooled and the status point reaches the saturation line, condensation would start (Fig. 20.3.4b). The DBT corresponding to this point is referred to as the *dewpoint temperature*.

In continued cooling the status point would move along the saturation curve. The reduction in the ordinate (the vertical HR scale) will represent the amount of moisture that would have condensed out. This process will reduce the moisture content (humidity ratio, HR) but will always end with 100 percent RH, a lower temperature but saturated air.

Adiabatic humidification takes place if water is evaporated into an air volume without any heat input or removal (i.e., adiabatically). This is the process in evaporative cooling. The latent heat of evaporation is taken from the air. The sensible heat content (H_s) is reduced and it is con-

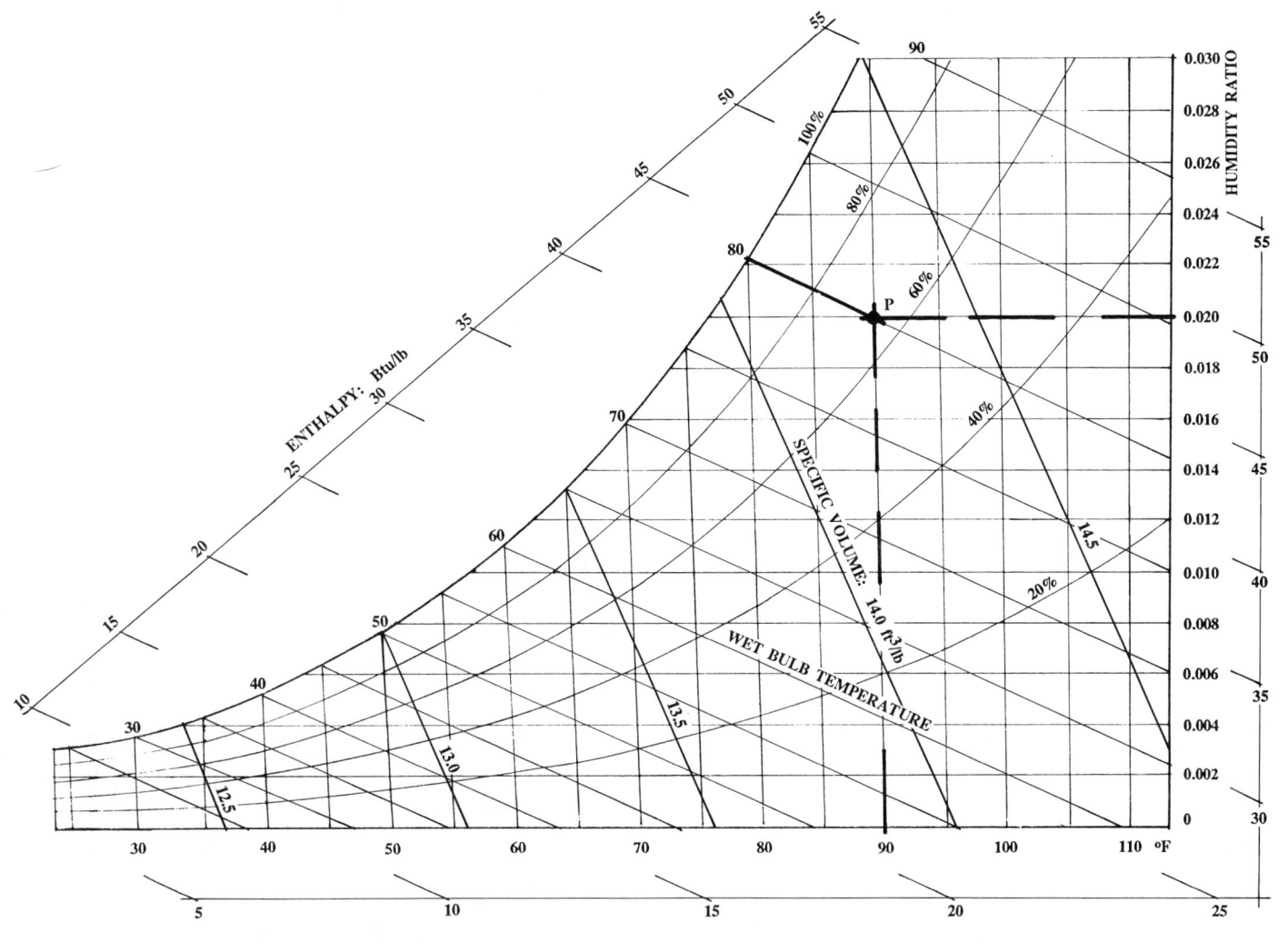

Fig. 20.3.2. Psychrometric chart in conventional American units.

verted to a latent heat content (H_L). The DBT is reduced, but the WBT remains constant: the status point will move up toward the left, along a WBT line (Fig. 20.3.4c).

Adiabatic dehumidification occurs when air is passed through some chemical sorbent (e.g., silica gel), which removes some of the moisture content by absorption or adsorption. The latent heat of evaporation is released in the process, the H_s is increased, while the total enthalpy H remains constant, with consequent increase in DBT. The status point moves down to the right along an enthalpy line (Fig. 20.3.4d).

Airflow can be characterized by the following quantities:

velocity, v in ft/min (m/s)
mass flow rate, $\dot{m}$ in lb/min (kg/s)
volume flow rate, vr in ft^3/min (m^3/s)

These quantities have the following relationships:

$$\dot{m} = vr \times \rho \quad (\text{lb/min} = \text{ft}^3/\text{min} \times \text{lb/ft}^3)$$
$$(\text{kg/s} = \text{m}^3/\text{s} \times \text{kg/m}^3)$$

where ρ is the density of air

$$\dot{m} = \frac{vr}{sv} \quad \left(\text{lb/min} = \frac{\text{ft}^3/\text{min}}{\text{ft}^3/\text{lb}}\right) \left(\text{kg/s} = \frac{\text{m}^3/\text{s}}{\text{m}^3/\text{kg}}\right)$$

where sv is the specific volume of air

$$vr = A \times v \quad (\text{ft}^3/\text{min} = \text{ft}^2 \times \text{ft/min})$$
$$(\text{m}^3/\text{s} = \text{m}^2 \times \text{m/s})$$

where A is the cross-sectional area available for the flow.

Mixing of two air streams of known temperature or enthalpy will result in a condition which can be determined by weighted averaging, according to the mass flow rate $\dot{m}$ (in lb/min or kg/s). For example, if the two air streams have (Fig. 20.3.4e)

mass flow rates $\dot{m}_1$ and $\dot{m}_2$ (indicated by points P_1 and P_2)
temperatures T_1 and T_2
enthalpies H_1 and H_2

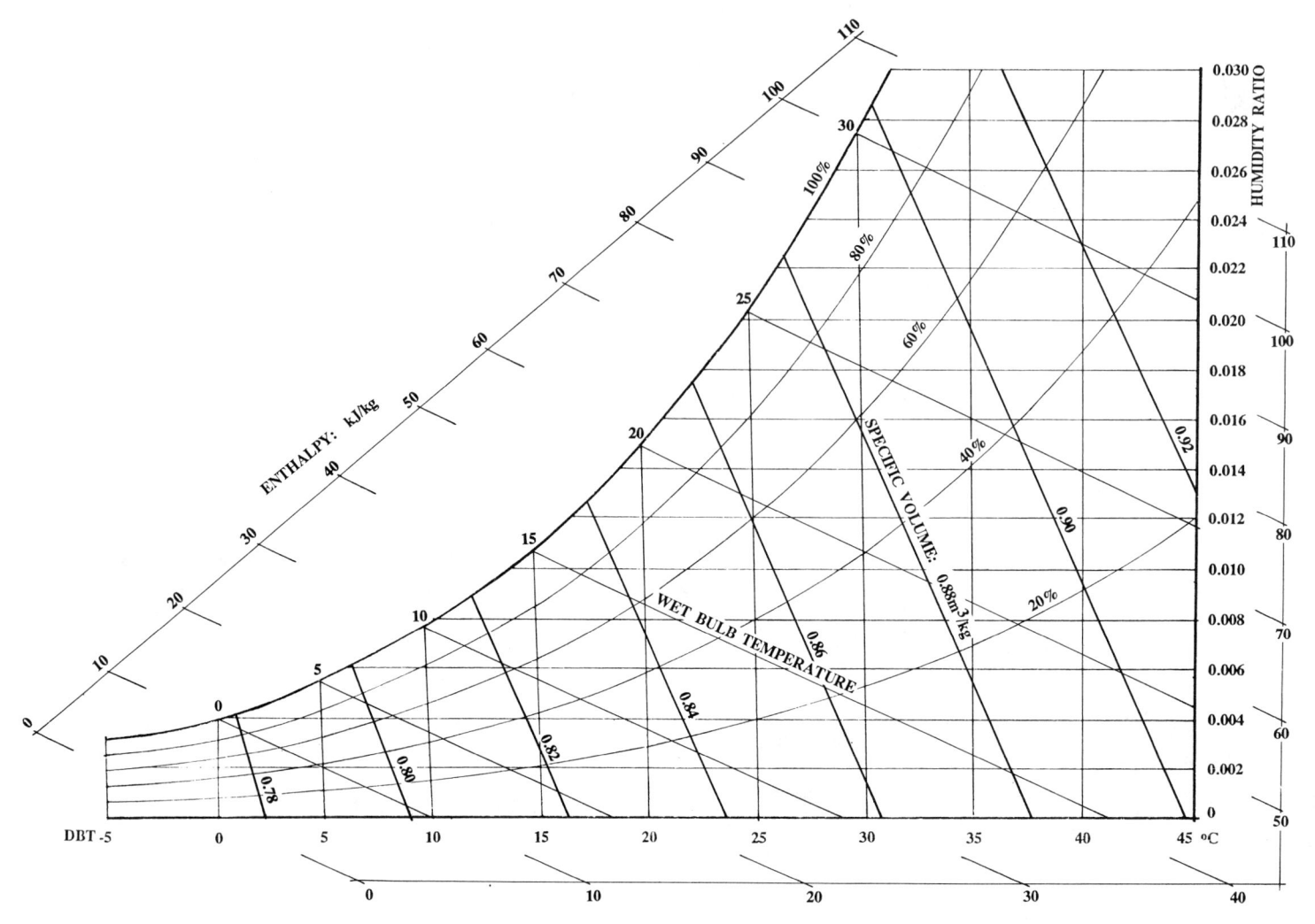

Fig. 20.3.3. Psychrometric chart in SI units.

the resultant mixture will have

$$\dot{m}_3 = \dot{m}_1 + \dot{m}_2 \text{ (at } P_3\text{)}$$

$$T_3 = \frac{\dot{m}_1 T_1 + \dot{m}_2 T_2}{\dot{m}_3}$$

$$H_3 = \frac{\dot{m}_1 H_1 + \dot{m}_2 H_2}{\dot{m}_3}$$

The status point of the mixture can also be determined on the psychrometric chart. If the status points of the two original air streams are connected by a straight line (Fig. 20.3.4e), the resultant status point will be on this line, nearer to the point of the larger $\dot{m}$. The length of this connecting line is to be divided in the proportions of $\dot{m}_1 : \dot{m}_2$.

20.4. THERMAL COMFORT

The human body is continuously producing heat by its metabolic processes, at a rate varying between 240 Btu/h (70 W) at sleep and 5100 Btu/h (1500 W) at very heavy work, depending on body size and activity level. It is often expressed in a relative unit, the met. This gives the heat production rate per unit body surface area: 1 met = 18 Btu/h ft^2 (= 58.2 W/m^2). The average person has a body surface of some 18.5 ft^2 (1.7 m^2), thus the heat output rate corresponding to 1 met would be about 360 Btu/h (100 W). Table 20.2 gives typical metabolic rates at various activities.

In order to maintain its normal temperature, the body must be able to dissipate the heat it produces, i.e., a thermal equilibrium must exist between the body and its environment:

$$M - E + R + Cd + Cv = 0 \qquad (20.5)$$

where M = metabolic rate
  E = evaporative cooling rate
  R = radiant heat input or loss
  Cd = conduction heat gain or loss
  Cv = convective heat gain or loss

HEATING AND COOLING OF BUILDINGS

Table 20.2. Metabolic Rates at Various Activities (Average Values).

Activity	met	Btu/h ft²	W/m²
sleeping	0.7	12.6	40.7
seated, at rest	1.0	18.0	58.2
walking: slowly (2 mph, 3.2 km/h)	2.0	36.0	116.4
fast (4 mph, 6.4 km/h)	3.8	68.4	221.2
work: house cleaning	2.7	48.6	157.1
cooking	1.8	32.4	104.8
typing	1.3	23.4	75.7
drafting	1.2	21.6	69.8
laboratory work	1.6	28.8	93.1
machine work: light	2.2	39.6	128.0
heavy	4.0	72.0	232.8
carpentry: hand sawing	4.4	79.2	256.0
planing	6.0	108.0	349.2
sports: golf	2.0	36.0	116.4
tennis	4.1	73.8	238.6
squash	6.1	109.8	355.0

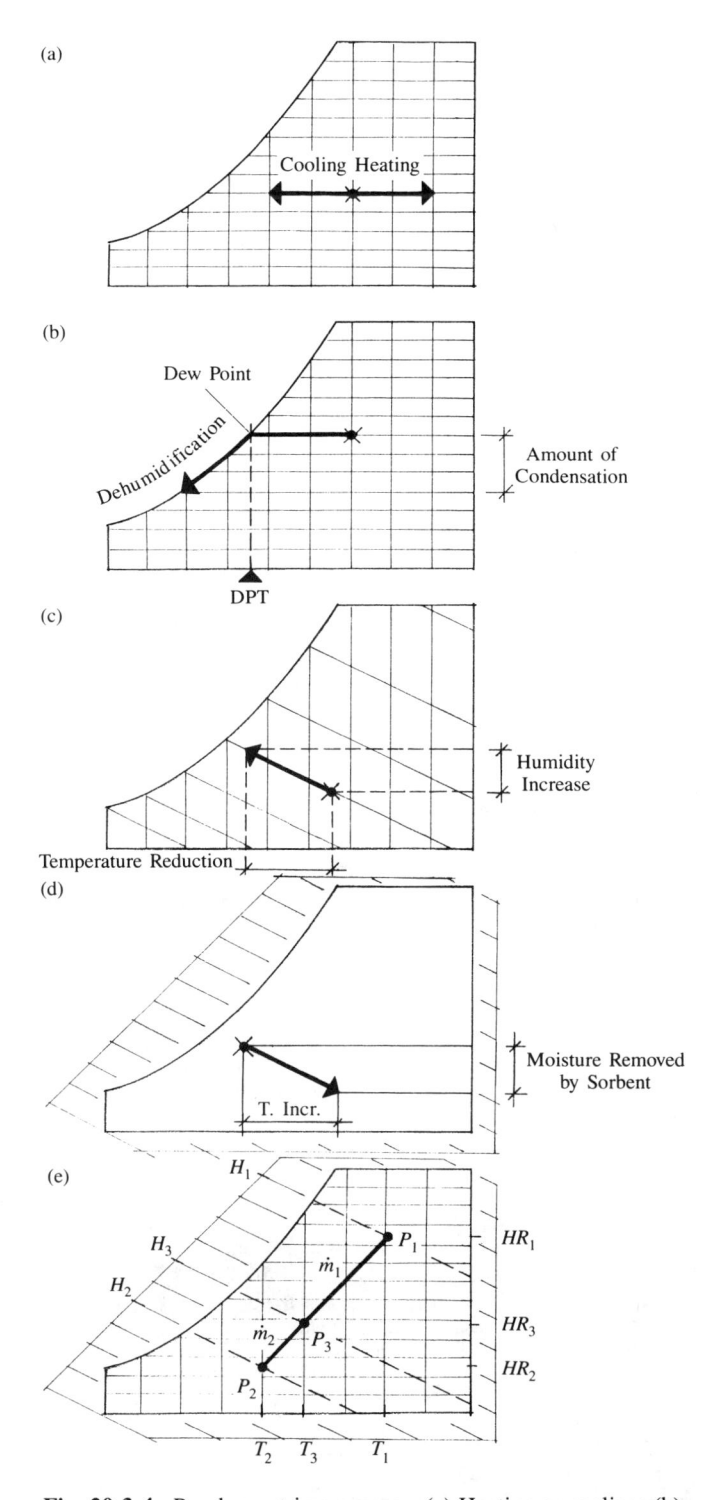

Fig. 20.3.4. Psychrometric processes. (a) Heating or cooling; (b) dehumidification by overcooling; (c) evaporative cooling; (d) dehumidification by sorbent; (e) mixing of two air streams.

A balance other than zero would produce a storage component: if positive, an increase, if negative, a decrease in body temperature. The body has very little tolerance for such temperature changes.

The deep body temperature is normally between 97 and 99°F (36 and 37°C), and the skin temperature is between 88 and 93°F (31 and 34°C). When the equilibrium is disturbed and the balance tends to be positive, *vasodilation* occurs, blood flow to the skin is increased, the skin temperature is elevated, thus heat dissipation is increased. When the balance tends to be negative, *vasoconstriction* reduces the blood flow to the skin, resulting in a lowered skin temperature, and thus heat dissipation is reduced. These *vasomotor* adjustments attempt to maintain the deep tissue temperature at its normal level.

Under overheated conditions, if vasodilation is insufficient, *evaporative regulation* (cooling) will be provided by sweat secretion. If this is unable to restore the balance, *hyperthermia* will occur: inevitable body heating, which may lead to heat stroke.

In cold (underheated) conditions, beyond vasoconstriction is the metabolic regulation zone, where the heat production of the body is increased either by involuntary shivering or by behavioral regulation: vigorous activity, or perhaps putting on more clothing. If these are also inadequate to restore the balance, *hypothermia*, inevitable body cooling, may be the result.

The heat dissipation rate, as well as our thermal sensation depends on four environmental variables: temperature, humidity, radiation, and air movement. In order to express the joint effect of some or all the four of these variables, a whole range of thermal comfort indices have been produced, starting with the *effective temperature* (ET) proposed by C. P. Yaglou in 1927 and adopted by the American Society of Heating, Refrigerating and Air Conditioning Engineers (ASHRAE). Over a dozen similar indices have been proposed by others (Ref. 20.2, Chapter 6).

The most recent and important index is the new *standard effective temperature* (SET, sometimes denoted ET*). It is defined on the psychrometric chart by a set of "equal comfort lines," which are practically vertical up to about 57°F (14°C), but become more and more sloping with increased

332 HANDBOOK OF ARCHITECTURAL TECHNOLOGY

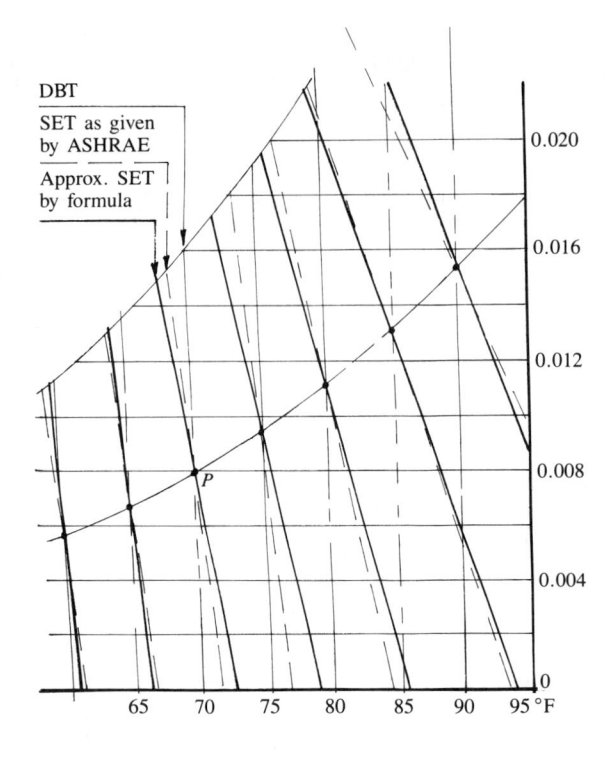

Fig. 20.4.1. Standard Effective Temperature, as given by ASHRAE, compared with the approximation by Eq. (20.6). For example, for point P, base line intercept $T = 70 + 23 \times (70 - 57) \times 0.008 = 72.4°F$.

temperatures (Fig. 20.4.1). This indicates that the influence of humidity is increasing at elevated temperatures, where evaporative cooling would be relied on, but is impaired by a high humidity.

The SET equal comfort lines are designated by (and coincide with) the DBT at the 50 percent RH curve. An approximation of the SET lines can be found by calculating the baseline intercept for any temperature T as:

$$T_{\text{intercept}} = T + 23 \times (T - 57) \times HR_T \quad (°F)$$
$$= T + 23 \times (T - 14) \times HR_T \quad (°C) \quad (20.6)$$

where HR_T is the humidity ratio at temperature T and 50 percent RH.

It has been suggested that for architectural purposes there is no point in amalgamating several of these environmental variables into one index, as each variable can be controlled by different means in building. Olgyay (Ref. 20.3) constructed his famous *bioclimatic chart* (Fig. 20.4.2) in order to show the interaction of the four environmental variables, while leaving each individually identifiable. He plotted a *comfort zone* on a chart with temperatures (DBT) on the vertical and relative humidities on the horizontal axes. For conditions above this zone air movement can provide a relief (elevate the top of the comfort zone), and for conditions below the zone solar radiation would be a remedy.

The parallel boundaries of the comfort zone (between

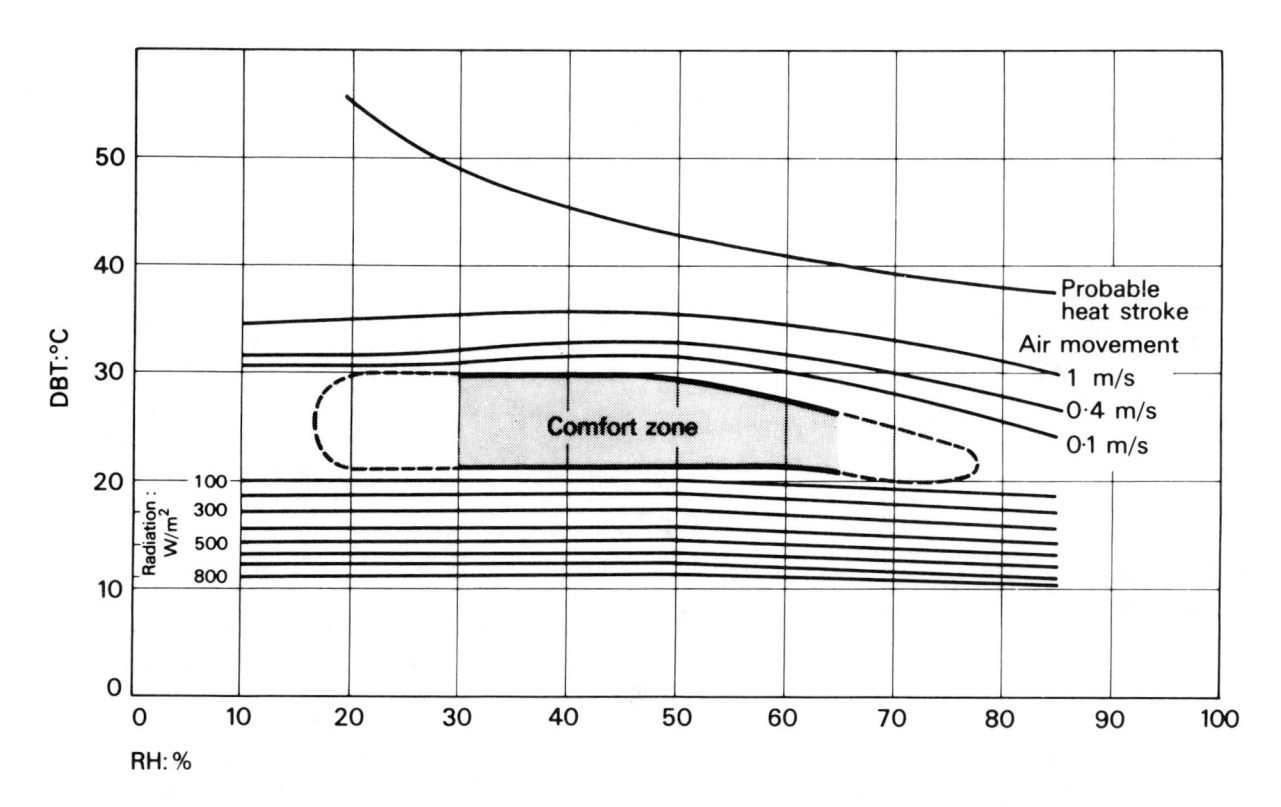

Fig. 20.4.2. The bioclimatic chart. Olgyay's original chart (Ref. 20.3) modified for warm climates.

about 25 and 50 percent RH) are at 70–82°F (20–27°C), and have been established for the USA, being valid for latitudes around 40°. It has been suggested that the zone should be moved up by 1°F for every 7° reduction in latitude (or by 1°C for every 12°). In the UK the limits are usually taken as 60–72°F (16–22°C). These limits are valid for sedentary workers (1 met) and should be reduced for people at heavy work or vigorous activity, such as sports, in accordance with the metabolic rates shown in Table 20.2.

A similar comfort zone can also be plotted on the psychrometric chart. Fig. 20.4.3 shows two such zones, one for summer and one for winter conditions, as defined by ASHRAE Comfort Standard 55R-74 (Ref. 20.4).

The work of Humphreys (Ref. 20.5) in England and Auliciems (Ref. 20.6) in Australia shows that the *thermal neutrality* of people (i.e., the theoretical centerpoint of the comfort zone) varies with the prevailing climate, as well as with the seasons. For people in nonconditioned (free-running) buildings the very simple linear function

$$T_n = 63.7 + 0.31 \times (T_0 - 32) \quad (°F)$$
$$= 17.6 + 0.31 \times T_0 \quad (°C) \quad (20.7)$$

gave a correlation coefficient of 0.88.

It has been suggested that the width of the zone can be taken as ±3.5°F (±2 K) about the neutrality temperature found from the above equation. This applies to people allowed to wear the clothes they find comfortable. The ASHRAE standard (Ref. 20.4), is applicable to lightly clothed individuals. Already in the 1930s research workers found it necessary to find a scale for the measurement of clothing insulation value. The clo unit has been devised, which corresponds to the insulation value of a 3-piece business suit with cotton underwear. 1 clo is equal to a cover over the whole body with a U-value of 1.13 Btu/ft^2 h °F (6.45 W/m^2 K). Table 20.3 gives the clo values of typical apparel.

The comfort zone, as defined above, gives the limits of comfort in terms of temperature and humidity, and is valid in the absence of radiation and with an air movement of less than 50 ft/min (0.25 m/s).

Some air movement is required under any circumstances. Even in winter, in a heated room, if the air velocity is less than about 20 ft/min (0.1 m/s), the occupants will judge the conditions to be stuffy. In such a heated room, however, the air movement should not exceed 50 ft/min (0.25 m/s), as that would be experienced as a draught, producing an unwanted cooling effect.

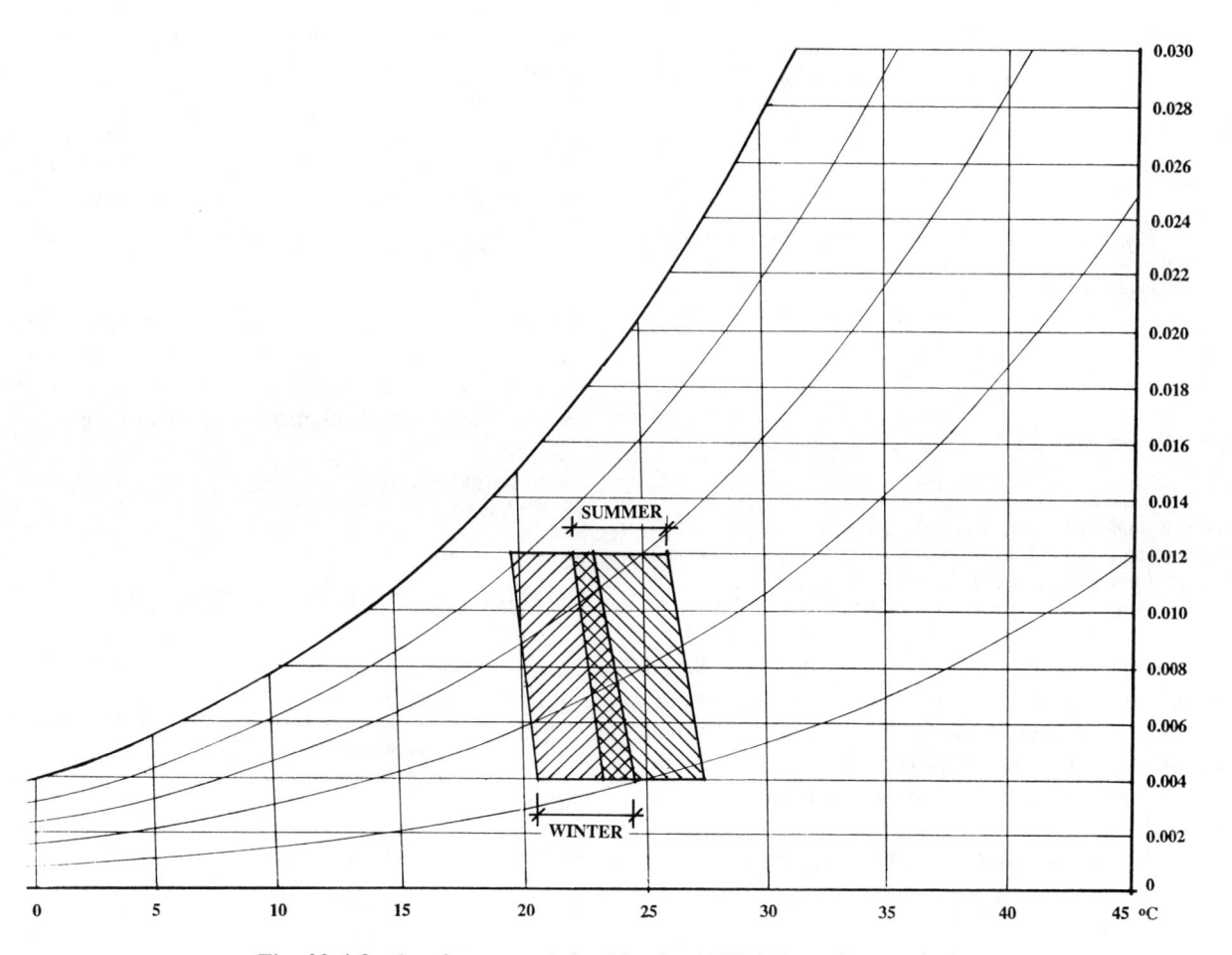

Fig. 20.4.3. Comfort zones defined by the ASHRAE comfort standard.

Table 20.3. Clo Units.

Ensembles

Men: socks, briefs, shoes,	
short sleeved shirt, light trousers	0.57
undershirt, shirt, pullover, light trousers	1.00
undershirt, shirt, warm trousers & jacket	1.18
Women: bra, panties, pantyhose, shoes,	
light dress	0.27
warm dress	0.73
warm blouse, slacks & sweater	1.20

Individual Items

shoes: sandals	0.02
normal	0.04
boots	0.08
underwear: long, upper	0.10
long, lower	0.10
sweater: light, short sleeves	0.16
long sleeves	0.19
heavy, short sleeves	0.33
long sleeves	0.37

Men		Women	
singlets	0.06	bra and panties	0.05
T-shirts	0.09	half slip	0.13
briefs	0.05	full slip	0.19
shirt,		blouse,	
light, short sleeves	0.14	light, short sleeves	0.18
long sleeves	0.22	long sleeves	0.22
heavy, short sleeves	0.25	heavy, short sleeves	0.26
long sleeves	0.29	long sleeves	0.29
(+5% for tie or turtleneck)		dress,	
vest, light	0.15	light, short sleeves	0.20
heavy	0.29	long sleeves	0.22
trousers, light	0.26	heavy, short sleeves	0.63
heavy	0.32	long sleeves	0.70
jacket, light	0.22	skirt, light	0.10
heavy	0.49	heavy	0.22
		(+5% if below, −5% if above knee)	
socks, short	0.04	jacket, light	0.17
knee-length, heavy	0.10	heavy	0.37
		stockings or pantyhose	0.01

Total clo = 0.82 × the sum of individual items.

Generally people's judgment of air velocities are:

up to 50 ft/min	(0.25 m/s)	unnoticed
50–100 ft/min	(0.25–0.5 m/s)	pleasant
100–200 ft/min	(0.5–1 m/s)	awareness of air movement
200–300 ft/min	(1–1.5 m/s)	unpleasant, draughty
above 300 ft/min	(above 1.5 m/s)	annoyingly draughty

This judgment, however, depends on temperature. When overheated conditions are experienced, air movement provides a relief; velocities up to 300 ft/min (1.5 m/s) may be welcome. Under cold conditions, air movement would produce a wind chill effect, which worsens the sensation of underheating.

The *wind chill index* (WCI) can be calculated as

$$\text{WCI} = (12.15 + 11.6\sqrt{v} - v) \times (33 - T) \quad (\text{W/m}^2) \quad (20.8)$$

where v = wind velocity in m/s
T = air temperature in °C

from which the equivalent *wind chill temperature* (WCT) can be found as

$$\text{WCT} = 33 - 0.03738 \times \text{WCI} \quad (°C) \quad (20.9)$$

The radiation field outdoors is usually dominated by the solar input, which is most often specified in terms of irradiance of a horizontal surface, in Btu/ft² h (W/m²). On average, every 13 Btu/ft² h irradiance would compensate for a temperature deficit of 1°F (=74 W/m² per °C).

In building interiors there is likely to be a complex radiation exchange pattern between surfaces of different temperatures, including the body surface of occupants. It would be difficult to identify vectorial radiation quantities, hence the concept of *mean radiant temperature* (MRT) is introduced. This is the average temperature of all surrounding surfaces, weighted by the solid angle subtended by each at the point of measurement. If this is less than the body surface temperature, then it allows heat dissipation. When MRT = DBT at comfortable temperatures, a modest amount of radiant heat dissipation occurs. When confronted by a cold surface, e.g., a windowpane in winter, the radiant heat loss becomes excessive and will be perceived as a draught, even if there is no measurable air movement.

The interrelationships among factors affecting thermal sensation are summarized in Table 20.4. These values can be used as a basis for compensatory measures.

20.5. CLIMATE

Weather is the term referring to the momentary state of the atmosphere. *Climate* is the integration in time (or the overall pattern) of weather conditions prevailing in a given location. The principal elements of climates are:

- Temperature
- Humidity

Table 20.4. Interrelationship of Thermal Factors.

Variable		Temp. compensation	Note
Air movement	each ft/min		
	above 30 ft/min	+1.0°F	max. 82°F
	each 0.005 m/s		
	above 0.15 m/s	+0.6°C	max. 28°C
Activity	each met increase	−4.5°F	min. 59°F
	(max. 3 met)	−2.5°C	min. 15°C
Clothing	each 0.1 clo added	−1.0°F	
		−0.6°C	
Radiation	each +1°F (+1°C)	−1.0°F	9.0°F
	in MRT	−1.0°C	5.0°F
			max. diff.

- Precipitation
- Sky conditions
- Solar radiation
- Winds

The earth receives most of its energy from the sun and it emits a similar amount of energy toward space, in the form of longwave infrared radiation. The heat emission potential is approximately uniform over the whole surface of the globe, but the solar radiation input is much greater in the equatorial regions than around the poles. The maximum shifts with the seasons between the Tropics of Cancer and Capricorn. It is this differential heating effect which is the main cause of all of our climatic phenomena. It causes atmospheric pressure differences (warmer air is lighter), with consequent movement of air masses, i.e., winds. Both these winds and ocean currents are mechanisms tending to even out differences in energy levels. Winds have been discussed in Chapter 10. Solar radiation is considered in Chapters 18, 21, and 22, while sky conditions were mentioned in Chapter 19. Here a classification of climates will be presented.

Numerous systems of climate classification are in use. Besides temperature, precipitation and its annual distribution are the main criteria for classification, which is often based on the local flora or agricultural potential. From the point of view of building design a classification based on thermal effects of the climate on humans is the most useful.

As indicated by the thermal balance equation given in the previous section, heat must be continuously dissipated from the human body. Climates can be classified according to the way they influence this heat dissipation.

If the heat dissipation is (or tends to be) excessive for all (or most) of the year, we refer to it as a *cold climate*. If the seasonal variation extends from underheating to overheating (i.e., from too much to insufficient heat dissipation) we speak about *temperate (moderate) climates*. Adjectives may indicate subtypes, eg: cool-temperate or warm-temperate.

In climates where the dominant human problem is overheating, two radically different climate types must be distinguished: hot-dry (or hot-arid) and warm humid.

Hot-dry climates occur primarily in the desert or semi-desert belts, between latitudes 15 and 30°, where the subtropic high-pressure zones (descending air masses) produce very little rain. Vegetation is sparse. Skies are clear, solar radiation is strong. Temperatures are high, but show very broad diurnal variations: 36–45°F (20–25 K) variation between day and night is not uncommon. Humidities are low; they may vary between 10 and 60 percent.

Warm-humid climates are usually found within 15° of the equator. These are characterized by frequent and heavy rainfall. Vegetation is luxuriant, but so is insect life. Skies are cloudy or hazy. In temperatures both the seasonal and the diurnal variations are very small. Temperatures are not as high as in the hot dry climates, but the high humidities (75–85 percent during the day) restrict the evaporative cooling mechanism of the skin and make conditions less tolerable.

It may be useful to distinguish some subcategories, as well as some special climate types, as shown in the following summary of climate types:

1. Cold
2. Temperate:
    (a) cool-temperate
    (b) warm-humid temperate
    (c) warm-dry temperate
3. Hot-dry:
    (a) maritime desert
4. Warm-humid:
    (a) warm-humid island climate
5. Composite or monsoon climate (seasonal variation between 3 and 4 above)
6. Tropical upland climate (cooler because of the altitude—around 3300 ft (1000 m) above sea level—but very strong solar radiation, because of the thin atmosphere).

Climatic zones cannot be defined by precise boundaries, a gradual transition is usually shown from one zone to the next.

20.6. CLIMATIC DATA

The problem in describing a climate is to find the balance between too little and too much data. Stating a single number, say 68°F (20°C), as the annual mean temperature of a location, provides very little information: it may be an average between 59 and 77°F (15 and 25°C) or between 32 and 104°F (0 and 40°C). At the other extreme, a presentation of 8760 temperature values (i.e., hourly values for the year), perhaps even for many years, would give an incomprehensible mass of data, with very little information content. A reasonable compromise is a presentation which gives monthly values of:

- Mean daily sunshine hours
- Cloud cover (tenths)
- Solar irradiation
- AM and PM values of relative humidity
- Mean wind speed and maximum gust
- Temperature: monthly mean, mean minimum, and mean maximum, supplemented by the 86th and 14th percentile values (those exceeded 1 day or 6 days per week)
- The standard deviation of daily means is given in brackets
- The number of frost days and heating and cooling degree-days

336 HANDBOOK OF ARCHITECTURAL TECHNOLOGY

The climate of a location may be represented by 12 monthly lines plotted on the psychrometric chart. Each line is defined by two points:

1. Mean minimum temperature with the AM relative humidity
2. Mean maximum temperature with the PM relative humidity

The 12 lines indicate the core of the area the climatic conditions would occupy. This can then be compared with the comfort zone determined by the following steps:

- Find the neutrality temperature by the expression

$$T_n = 63.7 + 0.31 \times (T_0 - 32) \quad (°F)$$

$$T_n = 17.6 + 0.31 \times T_0 \quad (°C) \qquad (20.10)$$

where T_0 is the annual mean temperature
- Mark this on the 50% RH curve of the chart
Mark the $T_n - 3.5$ and $T_n + 3.5°F$ ($T_n - 2$ and $T_n + 2°C$) points on the 50 percent curve

- Read the humidity ratio values for both and find the baseline intercept for the two side boundaries
- The top and bottom boundaries will be at the 0.012 and 0.004 HR levels, respectively

Fig. 20.6.1 shows four such climate plots: (a). A cold climate: Stockholm (Sweden). Temperatures are well below the comfort zone, rarely reach this zone, and never go above it. Generally, the climate fits this category if the mean temperature of the coldest month is below zero and the mean temperature of the warmest month remains below the comfort level.

(b). A temperate climate: Los Angeles (California). Afternoon temperatures exceed the upper comfort limit in three months, but the monthly means are within or below the comfort zone. A climate will be classified as temperate if winter monthly mean temperatures remain above the freezing point (although hourly temperatures may drop below this) and if summer monthly means remain below the upper comfort limit (although hourly values may exceed this).

(c). A hot-dry climate: Phoenix (Arizona). The lines ex-

STOCKHOLM

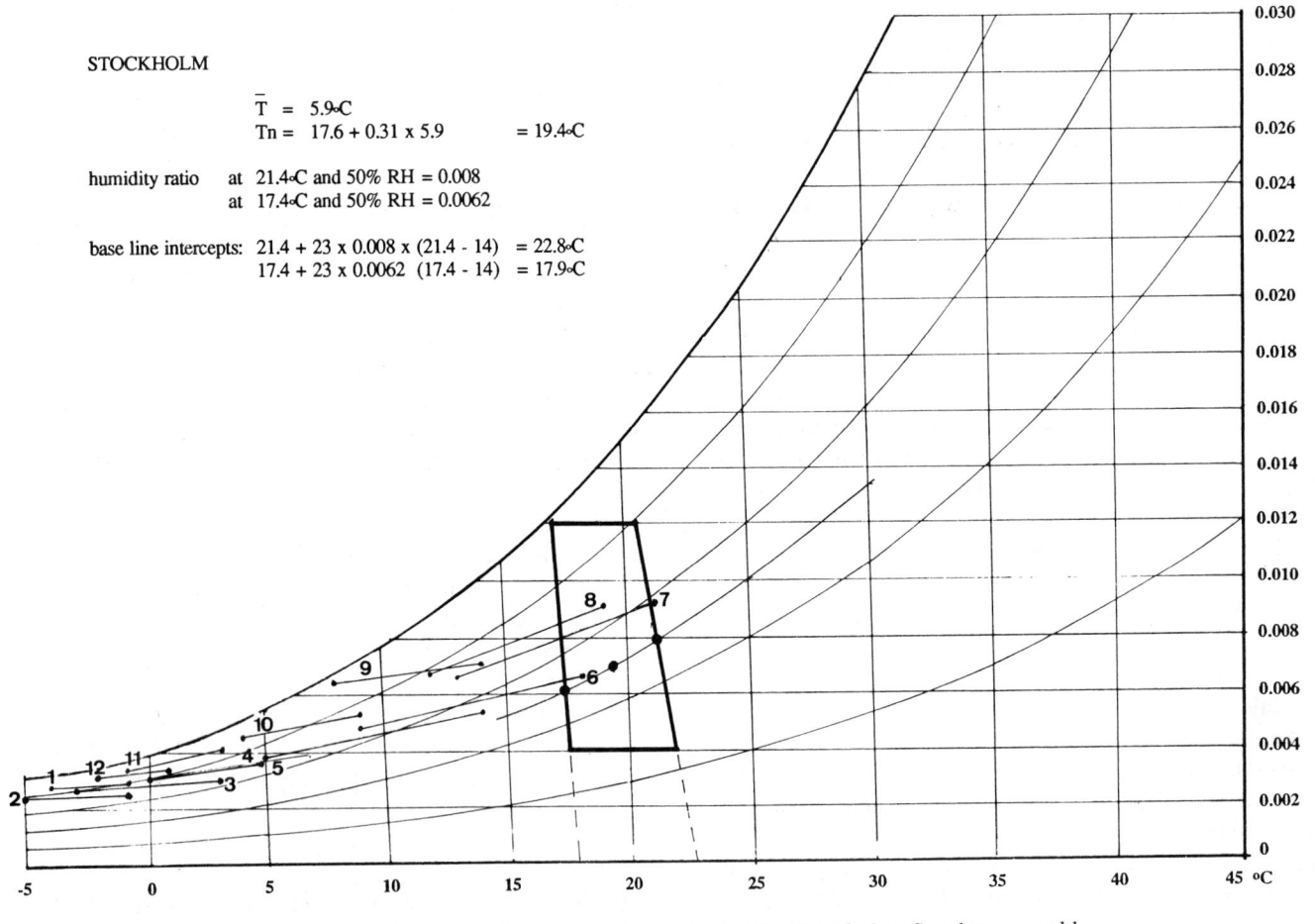

$\overline{T} = 5.9°C$
$T_n = 17.6 + 0.31 \times 5.9 = 19.4°C$

humidity ratio at 21.4°C and 50% RH = 0.008
 at 17.4°C and 50% RH = 0.0062

base line intercepts: 21.4 + 23 × 0.008 × (21.4 − 14) = 22.8°C
 17.4 + 23 × 0.0062 (17.4 − 14) = 17.9°C

Fig. 20.6.1. (a) Comfort zone and climate plot for Stockholm, Sweden: cold.

LOS ANGELES

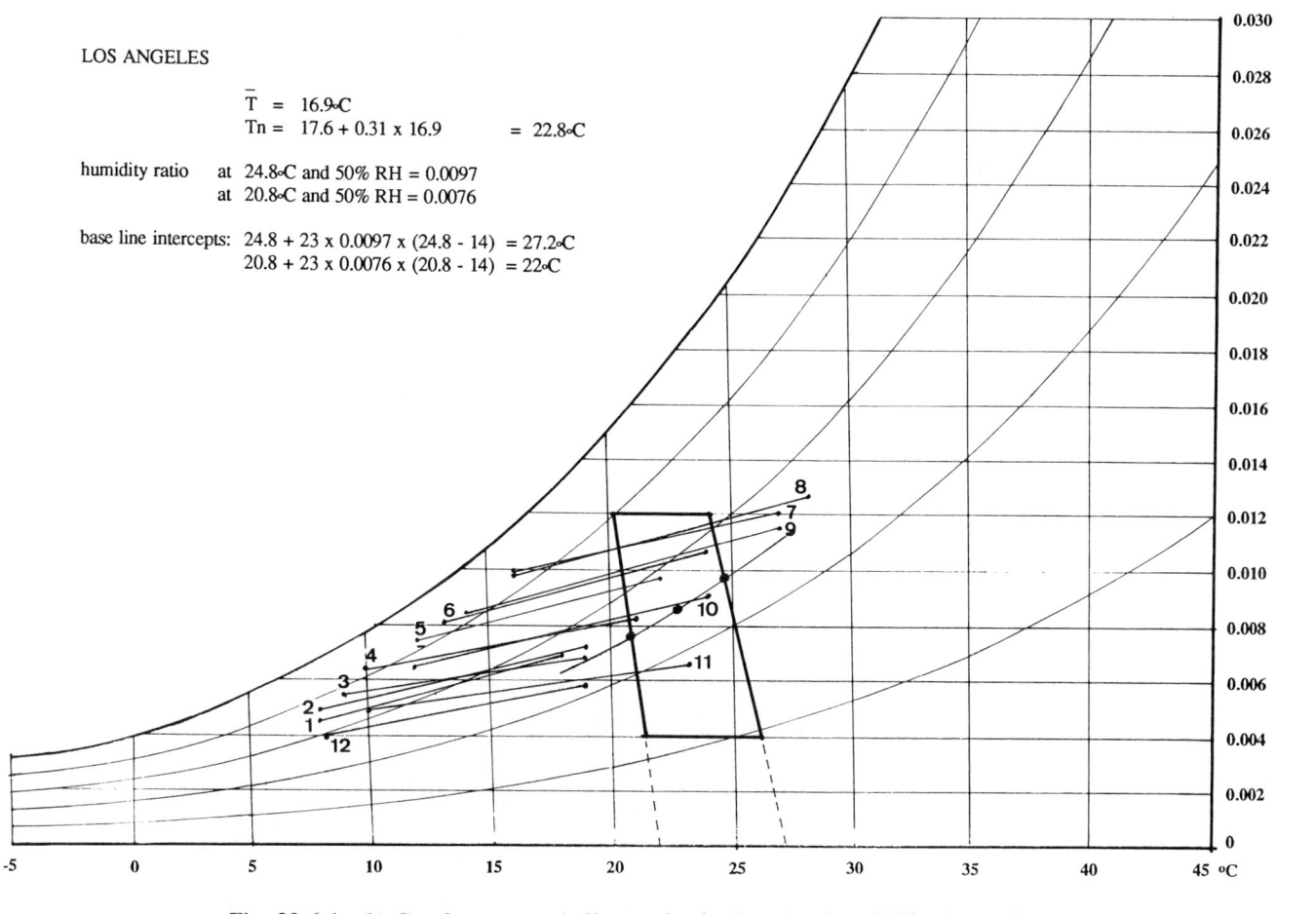

$\bar{T}$ = 16.9°C
T_n = 17.6 + 0.31 × 16.9 = 22.8°C

humidity ratio at 24.8°C and 50% RH = 0.0097
at 20.8°C and 50% RH = 0.0076

base line intercepts: 24.8 + 23 × 0.0097 × (24.8 − 14) = 27.2°C
20.8 + 23 × 0.0076 × (20.8 − 14) = 22°C

Fig. 20.6.1. (b) Comfort zone and climate plot for Los Angeles, California: Temperate.

tend well beyond the comfort zone, indicating overheating. The lines are long, indicating large diurnal variations. No line goes above the upper humidity limit. These climates are characterized by monthly means above the comfort level for at least four months, by the monthly mean range of temperatures generally greater than 20°F (12 K) and humidity ratios not exceeding 0.012.

(d). A warm-humid climate: Darwin (Australia). The lines are not only dominantly above comfort temperatures, but also well above the humidity limit, indicated by the top of the comfort zone. The lines are short: there is little diurnal variation. A climate fits this category if the monthly mean temperatures are above the comfort limit for at least six months, the mean range of temperatures is generally less than 18°F (10 K), and the humidity ratio is dominantly in excess of 0.012.

The term *microclimate* is used here on the scale of the individual building site. Local microclimatic effects can render the site climate quite different from the regional *macroclimate* usually depicted by published data. Factors affecting the microclimate are:

- Topography
- Ground surface
- Vegetation
- 3D objects

Only some examples of possible effects can be suggested: A low-lying site may be flood-prone, but may also suffer from fogs. Rainfall on the windward side of hills is increased, but it is decreased on the leeward side. A slope facing the equator will receive more radiation than the horizontal, but one with a polar orientation will receive less. A valley in the side of a mountain can be a channel for *katabatic winds*: cold air masses behaving in a way similar to water, i.e., flowing downhill. A bare ground usually means greater diurnal variation of temperature. Vegetation may provide shade and evaporative cooling. Large trees or adjacent buildings may overshadow the site. The designer must start with the macroclimatic data available from the nearest station and has to make an informed assessment of how the climate of the particular site may differ.

20.7. THERMAL INSULATION

The building envelope forms a barrier between the outdoor, often unfavorable conditions and the indoor controlled environment. It is a selective filter, which is in-

338 HANDBOOK OF ARCHITECTURAL TECHNOLOGY

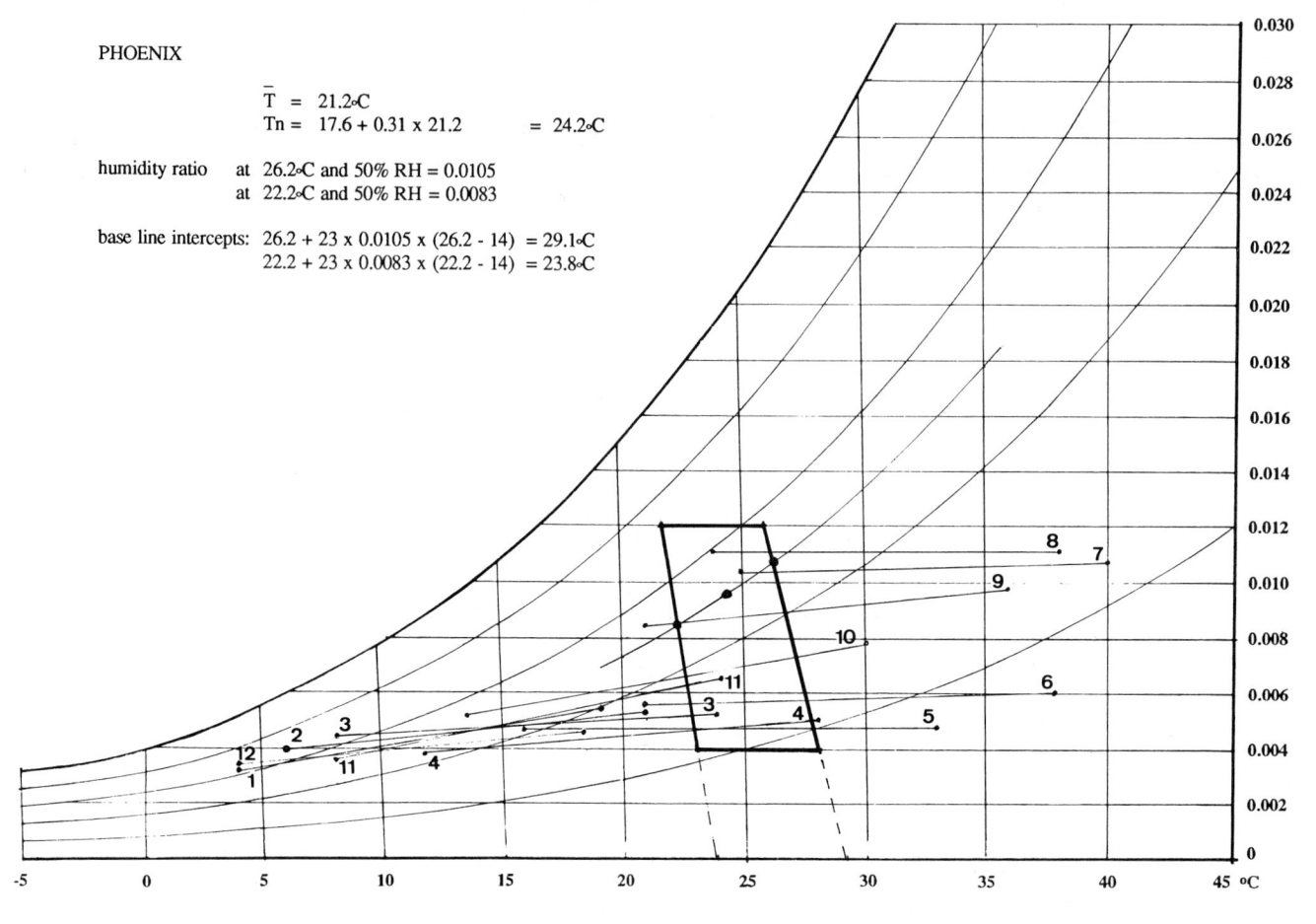

PHOENIX

$\overline{T} = 21.2°C$
$T_n = 17.6 + 0.31 \times 21.2 = 24.2°C$

humidity ratio at 26.2°C and 50% RH = 0.0105
at 22.2°C and 50% RH = 0.0083

base line intercepts: $26.2 + 23 \times 0.0105 \times (26.2 - 14) = 29.1°C$
$22.2 + 23 \times 0.0083 \times (22.2 - 14) = 23.8°C$

Fig. 20.6.1. (c) Comfort zone and climate plot for Phoenix, Arizona: hot-dry.

tended to admit the favorable influences (e.g., solar radiation or daylight), but exclude the unfavorable ones (e.g., cold winter winds), or at least control the flow of energy in the undesirable direction. Such an undesirable energy flow would be the heat loss from a heated building in winter or the heat gain of a cooled building in summer.

Thermal insulation can control this heat flow through elements of the building envelope. This can be of three kinds:

1. Reflective
2. Resistive
3. Capacitive

Reflective insulation, e.g., a bright aluminum foil, is useful where the mechanism of heat transfer is primarily radiation. This may be the case in the cavity of a wall or in an attic space between the top of the ceiling and the underside of the roof. Such a surface has both a low emittance and a low absorptance. It is equally effective whether it is used to line the emitting surface or the receiving surface. For the best effect both should be lined. One reflective surface facing an air space is equivalent to about 0.6 in. (15 mm) thickness of polystyrene and both faces lined with reflective surface would have the effect of an about 0.7 inch (18 mm) thick sheet of polystyrene. Reflective insulation has no effect if it is in contact with the surface from which or to which the radiation is to be controlled.

Resistive insulation. Of all common materials air has the lowest thermal conductivity. In an air-filled cavity conductive heat transfer is negligible: heat will be transferred by radiation and convection. The function of any material used for thermal insulation is to prevent convection. Fibrous or porous materials are used for this purpose, and the best ones are those that use the least amount of material per unit volume to encapsulate air in closed bubbles, i.e., a rigid foam structure, such as polystyrene or polyurethane (see Section 5.3).

The insulating property of a material is expressed by its conductivity (see Section 20.2), which may vary between the following limits:

Best rigid foam	0.17 Btu in./ft² h °F	(0.025 W/m K)
Timber (hardwood)	1.04	(0.15)
Dense concrete	11.30	(1.63)

DARWIN

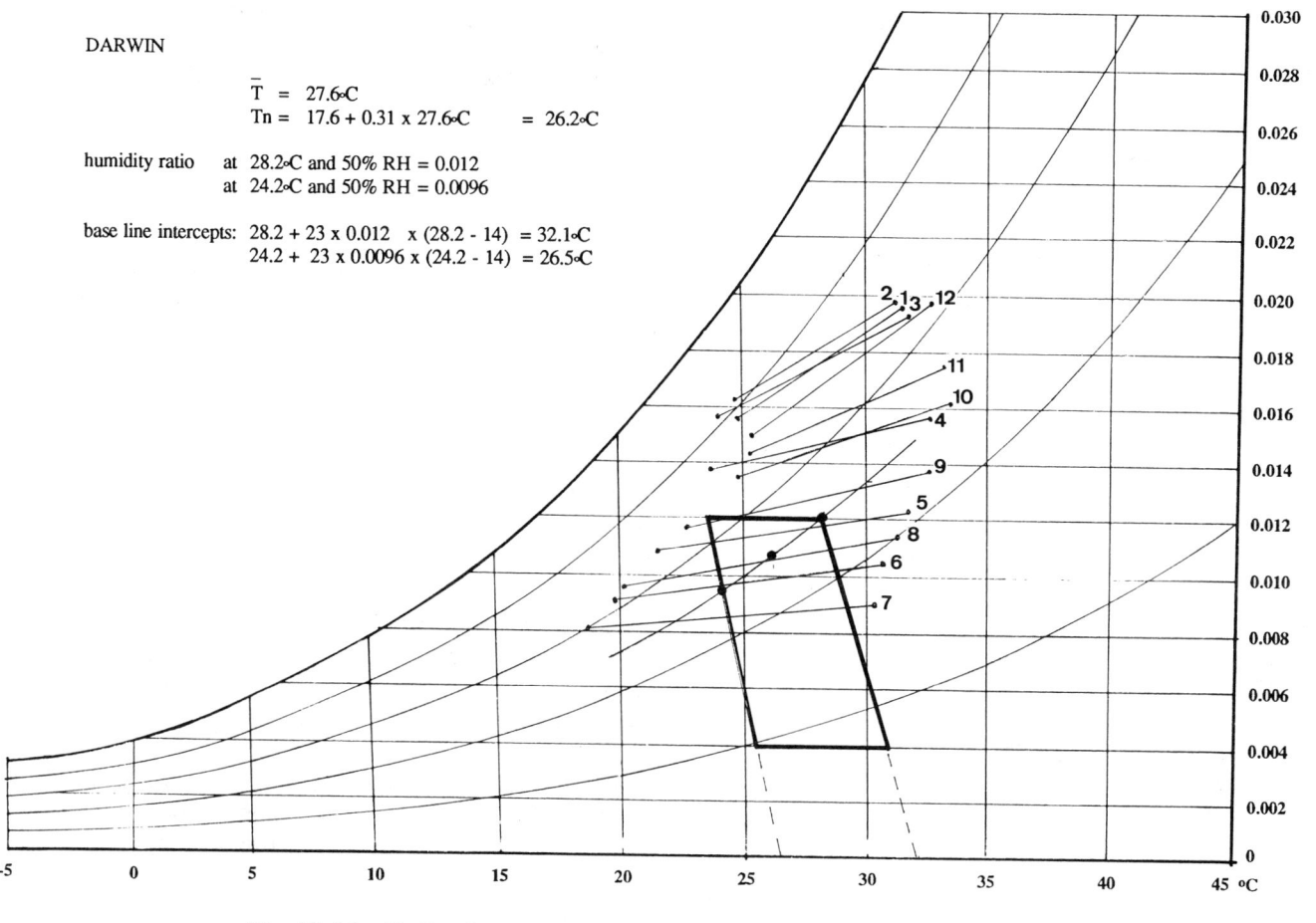

$\bar{T}$ = 27.6 °C
Tn = 17.6 + 0.31 x 27.6 °C = 26.2 °C

humidity ratio at 28.2 °C and 50% RH = 0.012
at 24.2 °C and 50% RH = 0.0096

base line intercepts: 28.2 + 23 x 0.012 x (28.2 - 14) = 32.1 °C
24.2 + 23 x 0.0096 x (24.2 - 14) = 26.5 °C

Fig. 20.6.1. (d) Comfort zone and climate plot for Darwin, Australia: warm-humid

---

The insulating effect of a particular sheet, or board, or layer of specified thickness is often stated in terms of its R-value ($R = b/k$); e.g., 2 in. (50 mm) glass wool:

$$k = 0.24 \text{ Btu in./ft}^2 \text{ h °F } (0.035 \text{ W/m K})$$

$$R = 2/0.24 = 8.33 \text{ ft}^2 \text{ h °F/Btu}$$

$$[R = 0.050/0.035 = 1.47 \text{ m}^2 \text{ K/W}]$$

If, for example, an R20 insulation is specified, this could mean

20 × 0.17 = 3.4 in. of polyurethane
20 × 0.24 = 4.8 in. of glass wool batt
20 × 0.64 = 12.8 in. of wood wool slab

In metric units the meaning is the same, but R-values are rarely used; performance is usually specified by the reciprocal, that is, the U-value.

The use of these materials reduces the heat flow rate and this effect is instantaneous, i.e., there is no delaying effect.

Capacitive insulation is influenced by the conductivity of the material, but the main factor is the thermal capacity of the element. This is the product of its surface density (lb/ft² or kg/m²) and the specific heat capacity of its material (Btu/lb °F or J/kg K). Compare the behavior of a 9 in. (220 mm) solid brick wall with that of a 0.4-in. (10-mm) thick slab of polystyrene. The U-values (or R-values) of the two elements are the same. If the temperatures were constant on both sides of these elements, the rate of heat flow would be exactly the same, i.e., the *steady state* behavior of the two elements is identical.

Significant differences occur under conditions of *periodic heat flow*. Fig. 20.7.1 shows the variation of heat flow rates through the two elements over a 24-hour period. The polystyrene is taken as of zero capacity. The peak of the heat flow through the brick wall is delayed by some 7 hours behind the peak of the zero-capacity wall. This delay is referred to as the *time lag* (ϕ). The other difference is the reduced amplitude of heat flow variation in the brick wall. The ratio of this amplitude (swing about the daily mean flow, sQ) to that of the zero-capacity wall (sQ_0) is known as the *decrement factor* (f) or amplitude decrement: $f = sQ/sQ_0$, a decimal fraction always less than 1 (except for very lightweight elements, for which it may be 1). If these two properties of an element are known, then the heat flow rate at any time through that element can be calculated. Fig. 20.7.2 shows the time lag and decrement factor values for solid homogeneous elements. For multilayer construction the data available are few and far between. Table 20.5 gives the U-values, time lag, and decrement factor values for numerous multilayer constructions, calculated using the program developed by the author. The table also shows for each element the values of *admittance* (Y), which is a measure of the ability of each element to absorb heat from or release heat into the interior. Dimensionally it is the same as the U-value: $Btu/ft^2\,h\,°F$ or $W/m^2\,K$. The total admittance of a room or a building is $qa = \Sigma\,(A \times Y)$

Reflective insulation is, in most cases, provided by a bright aluminum foil. As this is very vulnerable on its own, it is usually bonded either to a rigid sheet, such as a plasterboard (this would be fixed so that the foil-lined side faces the cavity), or to building paper.

Capacitive insulation is best provided by building elements also serving other purposes, such as a load-bearing brick or adobe wall or a reinforced concrete roof slab. The most important characteristic of these elements is their mass.

Resistive insulation comes in many shapes and sizes. Most building materials used for other purposes also have thermal insulating properties, even if not very good ones. Some materials are particularly designed for thermal insulation, but also serve other purposes (cellular terracotta blocks, lightweight aggregate or aerated concrete blocks, etc.).

Some organic-material rigid boards may also be consid-

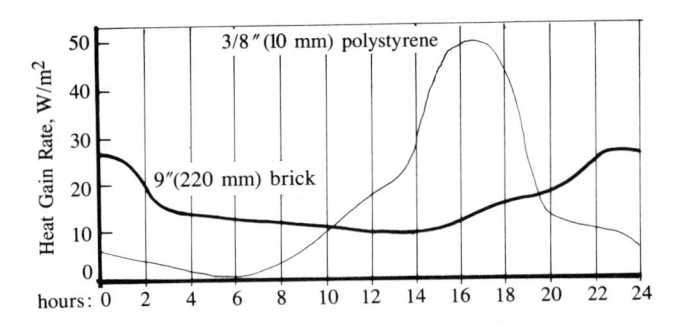

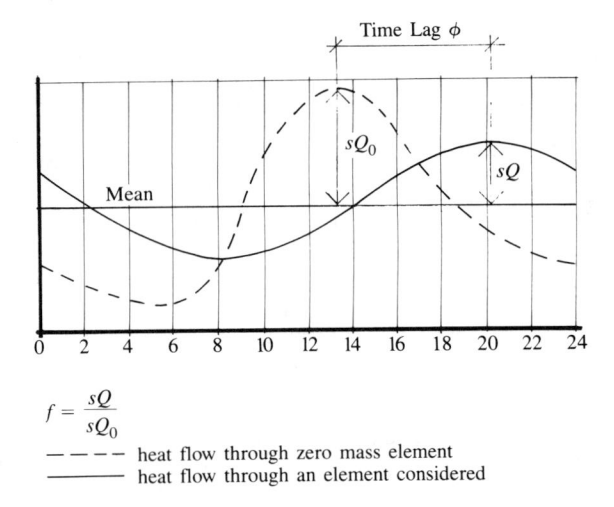

Fig. 20.7.1. Periodic heat flow. (a) Heat flow through two west-facing walls, one lightweight, one massive. (b) Definition of time-lag (ϕ) and decrement factor ($f = sQ/sQ_o$).

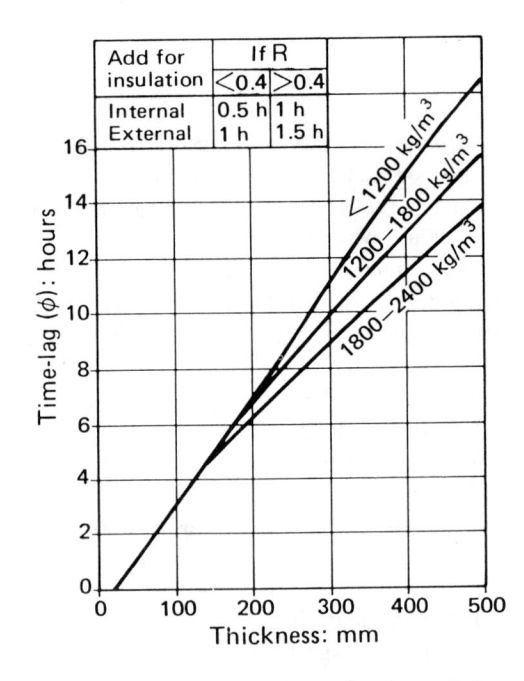

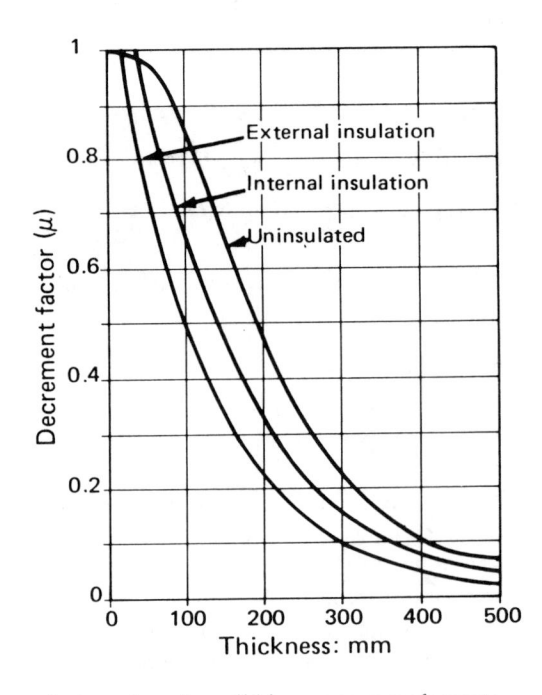

Fig. 20.7.2. Approximate time-lag and decrement factor values for solid homogeneous elements.

Table 20.5. Thermal Properties of Some Building Elements.

	U-value, Btu/ft² h °F	Admittance, Btu/ft² h °F	U-value W/m² K	Admittance, W/m² K	Time Lag, hours	Decrement Factor
Walls						
brick, single skin, 4.5 in. (110 mm)	0.58	0.74	3.28	4.2	2.6	0.87
9 in. (230 mm)	0.40	0.83	2.26	4.7	6.1	0.54
13 in. (335 mm)	0.30	0.83	1.73	4.7	9.4	0.29
brick, single skin, 4.5 in. (110 mm) plastered	0.53	0.72	3.02	4.1	3.0	0.83
9 in. (230 mm) plastered	0.38	0.79	2.14	4.5	6.5	0.49
13 in. (335 mm) plastered	0.32	0.79	1.79	4.5	9.9	0.26
brick, cavity, 11 in. (270 mm) plastered	0.26	0.77	1.47	4.4	7.7	0.44
same with 1 in. (25 mm) EPS in cavity	0.13	0.81	0.72	4.6	8.9	0.34
same with 1.5 in. (40 mm) EPS in cavity	0.10	0.83	0.55	4.7	9.1	0.32
same with 2 in. (50 mm) EPS in cavity	0.08	0.83	0.47	4.7	9.2	0.31
concrete block, solid, 8 in. (200 mm) + plasterboard	0.32	0.44	1.83	2.5	6.8	0.35
same but foil-backed plasterboard	0.25	0.32	1.40	1.82	7.0	0.32
same + 1 in. (25 mm) EPS (no cavity)	0.16	0.21	0.93	1.2	7.2	0.30
same but 1 in. (25 mm) cavity + 1 in. (25 mm) EPS + plasterboard	0.12	0.18	0.70	1.0	7.3	0.29
same but lightweight concrete	0.12	0.32	0.68	1.8	7.4	0.46
same but foil-backed plasterboard	0.11	0.26	0.61	1.5	7.7	0.42
same + 1 in. (25 mm) EPS (no cavity)	0.09	0.19	0.50	1.1	8.2	0.36
same but 1 in. (25 mm) cavity + 1 in. (25 mm) EPS + plasterboard	0.08	0.18	0.46	1.0	8.3	0.34
concrete block, hollow, 4 in. (100 mm) inside plastered	0.44	0.67	2.50	3.8	2.4	0.89
same, 8 in. (200 mm) inside plastered	0.43	0.72	2.42	4.1	3.0	0.83
concrete, dense, cast, 6 in. (150 mm)	0.61	0.93	3.48	5.3	4.0	0.70
same + 2 in. (50 mm) woodwool slab plastered	0.22	0.30	1.23	1.7	6.0	0.50
same but lightweight plaster	0.20	0.30	1.15	1.7	6.3	0.49
concrete, dense, cast, 8 in. (200 mm)	0.54	0.97	3.10	5.5	5.4	0.56
same + 2 in. (50 mm) woodwool slab plastered	0.21	0.39	1.18	2.2	7.7	0.36
same but lightweight plaster	0.19	0.30	1.11	1.7	7.6	0.35
concrete precast panel, 3 in. (75 mm)	0.75	0.86	4.28	4.9	1.9	0.91
same + 1 in. (25) cavity + 1 in. (25) EPS + plasterboard	0.15	0.18	0.84	1.0	3.0	0.82
concrete precast, 3 in. (75) + 1 in. (25) EPS + 6 in. (150 mm) lightweight concrete	0.10	0.40	0.58	2.3	8.7	0.41
same but 2 in. (50 mm) EPS	0.07	0.42	0.41	2.4	9.2	0.35
brick veneer, 4.5 in. (110 mm) + cavity + plasterboard	0.31	0.39	1.77	2.2	3.5	0.77
same but foil-backed plasterboard	0.24	0.30	1.36	1.7	3.7	0.75
same with 1 in. (25 mm) EPS or glass fiber	0.14	0.19	0.78	1.1	4.1	0.71
same with 2 in. (50 mm) EPS or glass fiber	0.09	0.16	0.50	0.9	4.3	0.69
same, 1 in. (25 mm) EPS + foil-backed plasterboard	0.12	0.18	0.69	1.0	4.1	0.71
block veneer, 4 in. (100 mm) + cavity + plasterboard	0.28	0.37	1.57	2.1	4.1	0.72
same but foil-backed plasterboard	0.22	0.30	1.24	1.7	4.3	0.69
same with 1 in. (25 mm) EPS or glass fiber	0.13	0.19	0.74	1.1	4.7	0.65
same with 2 in. (50 mm) EPS or glass fiber	0.08	0.16	0.48	0.9	4.9	0.62
same, 1 in. (25 mm) EPS + foil-backed plasterboard	0.12	0.18	0.66	1.0	4.7	0.64
framed, single fibrous cement or galvanized steel sheeting	0.91	0.92	5.16	5.2	0	1
same + cavity + plasterboard	0.39	0.39	2.20	2.2	0.3	1
same + 1 in. (25 mm) EPS or glass fiber	0.15	0.19	0.86	1.1	0.5	0.99
same + 2 in. (50 mm) EPS or glass fiber	0.09	0.16	0.53	0.9	0.7	0.99

(Continued on page 342)

Table 20.5. (Continued)

	U-value, Btu/ft² h °F	Admittance, Btu/ft² h °F	U-value W/m² K	Admittance, W/m² K	Time Lag, hours	Decrement Factor
Walls						
framed, 0.75 in. (20 mm) timber boarding	0.53	0.53	3.00	3.0	0.4	1
same + cavity + plasterboard	0.29	0.32	1.68	1.8	0.8	0.99
same + 1 in. (25 mm) EPS or glass fiber	0.13	0.18	0.76	1.0	1.0	0.99
same + 2 in. (50 mm) EPS or glass fiber	0.09	0.16	0.49	0.9	1.2	0.98
framed, tile-hanging + paper + cavity + 2 in. (50 mm) EPS + plasterboard	0.10	0.14	0.54	0.78	1.0	0.99
same but 4 in. (100 mm) EPS or glass fiber	0.06	0.12	0.32	0.71	1.0	0.99
wood frame, single 0.25 in. (6 mm) glass	0.88	0.88	5.0	5.0	0	1
double glazing	0.51	0.51	2.9	2.9	0	1
metal frame, single 0.25 in. (6 mm) glass	1.06	1.06	6.0	6.0	0	1
same but discontinuous frame	1.00	1.00	5.7	5.7	0	1
metal frame, double glazing	0.63	0.63	3.6	3.6	0	1
same but discontinuous frame	0.58	0.58	3.3	3.3	0	0
roof glazing, single 0.25 in. (6 mm) glass	1.16	1.16	6.6	6.6	0	1
double glazing	0.81	0.81	4.6	4.6	0	1
horizontal laylight + skylight,						
ventilated	0.67	0.67	3.8	3.8	0	1
unventilated	0.53	0.53	3.0	3.0	0	1
Roofs						
6 in. (150 mm) concrete slab, plastered, 75 screed + asphalt	0.32	0.79	1.8	4.5	8	0.33
same but lightweight concrete	0.18	0.41	0.84	2.3	5	0.77
1 in. (25 mm) timber deck, bituminous felt, plasterboard ceiling	0.32	0.33	1.81	1.9	0.9	0.99
same + 2 in. (50 mm) EPS	0.09	0.14	0.51	0.8	1.3	0.98
$\frac{3}{8}$ in. (10 mm) fibrous cement deck, asphalt, 0.5 in. (13 mm) fiberboard, cavity, fibrous cement ceiling	0.26	0.33	1.5	1.9	2.0	0.96
2 in. (50 mm) wood wool slab, 0.5 in. (13 mm) screed, 0.75 in. (20 mm) asphalt, cavity, plasterboard ceiling	0.18	0.25	1.0	1.4	3.0	0.93
0.5 in. (13 mm) fiberboard, 0.75 in. (20 mm) asphalt, cavity, $\frac{3}{8}$ in. (10 mm) foil-backed plasterboard	0.21	0.23	1.2	1.3	1	0.99
metal deck, bituminous felt, 1 in. (25 mm) EPS	0.19	0.21	1.1	1.2	1	0.99
same + 0.5 in. (13 mm) fiberboard + plasterboard ceiling	0.13	0.16	0.73	0.91	1	0.99
same but 2 in. (50 mm) EPS	0.08	0.13	0.48	0.75	1	0.98
corrugated fibrous cement sheet	0.86	0.86	4.9	4.9	0	1
same + attic + plasterboard ceiling	0.45	0.46	2.58	2.6	0.3	1
same + 2 in. (50 mm) EPS or glass fiber	0.10	0.18	0.55	1.0	0.7	0.99
tiles, underlayment + attic + plasterboard ceiling	0.46	0.46	2.59	2.6	0.5	1
same + 2 in. (50 mm) EPS or glass fiber	0.10	0.18	0.54	1.0	1.5	0.97
tiles, underlayment, 1 in. (25 mm) timber ceiling	0.34	0.37	1.91	2.1	1	0.99
same + 2 in. (50 mm) EPS or glass fiber	0.09	0.26	0.51	1.5	1.4	0.97
metal sheet (corrugated or profiled)	1.26	1.25	7.14	7.1	0	1
metal sheet + attic + plasterboard ceiling	0.45	0.46	2.54	2.6	0.3	1
same + 2 in. (50 mm) EPS or glass fiber	0.10	0.18	0.55	1.0	0.7	0.99
Floors						
suspended timber, bare or linoleum,						
10 × 10 ft (3 × 3 m)	0.18	0.35	1.05	2.0	0.7	0.99
25 × 25 ft (7.5 × 7.5 m)	0.12	0.35	0.68	2.0	0.8	0.98
50 × 25 ft (15 × 7.5 m)	0.11	0.35	0.61	2.0	0.8	0.98
50 × 50 ft (15 × 15 m)	0.08	0.35	0.45	2.0	0.9	0.97
100 × 50 ft (30 × 15 m)	0.07	0.35	0.39	2.0	0.9	0.97
200 × 50 ft (60 × 15 m)	0.06	0.35	0.37	2.0	1.0	0.97

Table 20.5. (*Continued*)

		U-value, Btu/ft² h °F	Admittance, Btu/ft² h °F	U-value W/m² K	Admittance, W/m² K	Time Lag, hours	Decrement Factor
Floors							
concrete slab on ground, 2 edges exposed							
10 × 10 ft	(3 × 3 m)	0.19	1.06	1.07	6.0	—	0.01
25 × 25 ft	(7.5 × 7.5 m)	0.08	1.06	0.45	6.0	—	0
50 × 25 ft	(15 × 7.5 m)	0.06	1.06	0.36	6.0	—	0
50 × 50 ft	(15 × 15 m)	0.04	1.06	0.26	6.0	—	0
100 × 50 ft	(30 × 15 m)	0.04	1.06	0.21	6.0	—	0
200 × 50 ft	(60 × 15 m)	0.03	1.06	0.18	6.0	—	0
concrete slab on ground, 4 edges exposed							
10 × 10 ft	(3 × 3 m)	0.26	1.06	1.47	6.0	—	0.02
25 × 25 ft	(7.5 × 7.5 m)	0.13	1.06	0.76	6.0	—	0.01
50 × 25 ft	(15 × 7.5 m)	0.11	1.06	0.62	6.0	—	0
50 × 50 ft	(15 × 15 m)	0.08	1.06	0.45	6.0	—	0
100 × 50 ft	(30 × 15 m)	0.06	1.06	0.36	6.0	—	0
200 × 50 ft	(60 × 15 m)	0.05	1.06	0.32	6.0	—	0

Note: EPS = expanded polystyrene.

ered in this category; e.g., a wood wool slab may be used exposed, for acoustic absorption, or may be cement rendered; strawboard may be rendered, but with a paper or vinyl facing it is often used for ceilings; a cork sheet or a wood (or cane) fiber softboard may provide a pin-up surface, as well as thermal insulation.

There is also a whole range of materials and products used specifically for insulation. Five categories can be distinguished:

1. Loose fills, e.g., cellulose fiber, exfoliated vermiculite
2. Quilts or blankets, e.g., fiberglass, mineral wool
3. Semi-rigid batts, e.g., fiberglass, mineral wool
4. Rigid boards, e.g., polystyrene, polyurethane, or the organic boards mentioned above
5. In situ foams (usually injected into cavities), e.g., polyurethane, urea-formaldehyde.

With the advent (and increase in popularity) of passive solar buildings (see Chapter 21), it has been realized that the best combination for the stability of the indoor climate is a heavy mass (capacitance) inside a layer of resistive insulation. During the last decade a number of techniques have been developed for the fixing and protective finishing of such external insulation.

Under steady-state conditions the sequence of layers in a constructional element does not affect the heat flow, but under variable conditions the dynamic response of an element strongly depends on this sequence. The important characteristic is the relative position of resistive and capacitive layers. For heat flow into a building a much larger time lag and reduced decrement factor is achieved by having the main storage mass (capacitive insulation) inside the resistive insulation layer. This would also drastically increase the admittance of the element, leading to a much more stable internal environment. For example:

	ϕ, hrs	f	admittance
4 in. (100 mm) reinforced concrete slab, with a membrane on top and 2 in. (50 mm) glass wool insulation under the slab	3.9	0.72	1.1
same, but insulation on top of the slab	4.9	0.49	6.2
brick-veneer wall: 4.5 in. (110 mm) brick cavity, 2 in. (50 mm) polystyrene, plasterboard	4.3	0.67	0.8
same, but inside out	5.1	0.52	5.2

In any reasonably constructed building envelope the weakest element, from the thermal point of view, is the window. The U-value of the best double glazed window, with a discontinuous frame (to prevent thermal bridging) would be 0.58 Btu/ft² h °F (3.3 W/m² K), which would be matched by a single-skin, 4.5 in. (110 mm) brick wall. The most ordinary single glazed, aluminum framed window would have a U-value as high as 1.06 Btu/ft² h °F (6 W/m² K). Thus, from the point of view of heat loss reduction, the smallest window would be the best. However, an equator-facing window would be an asset from the point of view of solar heat input, especially in winter. The problem is that the solar input may last 4 to 6 hours, while the inside-to-outside air-to-air heat loss continues over 24 hours. Indeed, the cumulative heat loss may exceed the total solar heat input. There are two possible solutions to this problem:

1. The use of optically transparent, but thermally highly insulative (high resistance) windows. Several types are under development; the most promising one

seems to be a clear silicone foam between two sheets of glass.
2. The use of night insulation, to reduce the U-value during all no-gain periods. This may take many forms, from heavy insulating curtains hung from a closed pelmet to some type of insulating shutter: sliding, hinged, or roller-type.

Cavity insulation, particularly filling the wall cavities with in situ foams, has been a controversial issue for some years. The purpose of the cavity is to prevent moisture penetration and it has been suggested that the cavity fill would break the discontinuity and allow moisture to get to the inner skin. It has now been shown that a good, continuous foam does not allow moisture penetration, but if gaps occur in the foam, e.g., around the cavity ties in a double brick wall, water could find its way through. Less fault-prone is the use of rigid foam boards (e.g., styrofoam) placed in the cavity as the wall is being built, attached to the outside face of the inner skin and still preserving a continuous cavity between it and the outer skin of brickwork.

20.8. CONDENSATION (see also Sections 7.3 and 7.5)

A problem which must be considered together with insulation is condensation. The problem can be best illustrated by an example: We have 73°F (23°C) and 50% RH air in a room. The dewpoint temperature of this air is about 54°F (12°C). If the air comes into contact with a surface at or below this temperature, condensation will occur. The most obvious example of this is the inside surface of a windowpane in winter. Many window frames include a condensation trough to catch the water running down the glass surface and discharge it to the outside through weepholes.

Such surface condensation is not too troublesome: it is visible, it can be dealt with. A more insidious problem is the *interstitial condensation* which occurs inside an element, perhaps inside a body of (porous) material. To continue the above example: if the outdoor temperature is 32°F (0°C), there will be a temperature gradient across the wall from 73 down to 32°F (from 23 down to 0°C). Somewhere within the wall there is a point at which the temperature drops to 54°F (12°C), where condensation would occur.

Water vapor in the room atmosphere has a much higher vapor pressure than the outdoor air; consequently it will migrate through the wall material toward the outside. Normal building materials have a very porous structure and offer little resistance to such vapor migration. If condensation occurs within a porous material, the pores may become filled with liquid water, the thermal insulation qualities of the material are reduced, the wall becomes colder, and therefore the condensation increases.

If this occurs in a roof, the occupants may believe that the roof is leaking. The wall (or other element) may become soaking wet, and may suffer structural damage. Wet rendering may support the growth of mildew and fungi. Wet plastering may separate from the base structure. A wet plasterboard ceiling may sag and ultimately fail by pulling through the nails used for fixing it. The problem is worst in low-income housing, where the building may be poorly insulated, so that the fabric is cold and the occupants close all vents to preserve the heat. Here also, portable kerosene heaters produce large quantities of vapor as a combustion product.

The remedy is to install a *vapor barrier* near the inside of the element. This may be polyethylene sheet, a foil-faced building paper or some impervious surface finish. The integrity and continuity of such a vapor barrier must be insured, as a crack or a puncture may defeat the purpose of the whole exercise. In rooms housing moisture-producing processes (e.g., kitchens or rooms of assembly, where people's moisture output may be very large), adequate ventilation must be provided to keep down the vapor pressure to manageable levels.

Condensation may also cause problems in a warm-humid climate in air-conditioned buildings. Here the problem is the penetration of vapor from the outside and its migration toward the inside. The vapor barrier here must be near the outside of the element. This rule can be generalized, to say that the vapor barrier should always be at or near the warm face of an element.

20.9. HEAT LOSS CALCULATION

The heat loss rate Q, e.g., in a winter situation, consists of two components, measured in Btu/h (W):

Q_c = conduction loss rate

Q_v = ventilation and infiltration loss rate

$$Q = Q_c + Q_v$$

Both depend on the temperature difference between outside and inside:

$$\Delta T = T_o - T_i$$

It may be useful to calculate first the *specific heat loss rate* q of the building, in Btu/h °F (W/K), which also has two components, conduction and ventilation:

$$q_c = \Sigma (A \times U)$$

i.e., the sum of area and U-value products for all elements of the envelope, and

$$q_v = 0.018 \times vr \ (\text{Btu/ft}^3 \ °F \times \text{ft}^3/h)$$
$$= 1200 \times vr \ (\text{J/m}^3 K \times \text{m}^3/s = W/K)$$
$$= 0.33 \times V \times N \ (\text{Wh/m}^3 K \times \text{m}^3/h = W/K)$$

where vr = ventilation rate
V = volume of space
N = number of air changes per hour

Then the specific heat loss rate is

$$q = q_c + q_v$$

and the total heat loss rate will be

$$Q = q \times \Delta T \quad \text{Btu/h °F} \times \text{°F} = \text{Btu/h}$$
$$(\text{W/K} \times \text{K} = \text{W})$$

For *calculating the heat loss from a building* it is advisable to use a tabulation, which can be referred to later, such as the following example for a simple house shown in Fig. 20.9.1:

Element	Construction	Area, ft^2	U-Value, Btu/ft^2 h °F	$A \times U$, Btu/h °F
Floor	slab on ground	1200	0.11	132
E wall	cavity brick, 1" EPS	240	0.13	31.2
S wall	cavity brick, 1" EPS	219	0.13	28.5
S window	double glazed, wood	80	0.51	40.8
S door	insulated, veneered	21	0.14	2.9
W wall	cavity brick, 1" EPS	240	0.13	31.2
N wall	cavity brick, 1" EPS	219	0.13	28.5
N window	double glazed, wood	80	0.51	40.8
N door	insulated, veneered	21	0.14	2.9
Roof	tiled, 2" EPS, plasterboard	1200	0.10	120

$q_c = 459$ Btu/h °F

or the same in SI units:

Element	Construction	Area, m^2	U-Value, W/m^2 K	$A \times U$, W/K
Floor	slab on ground	108	0.62	67
E wall	cavity brick, 25 mm EPS	21.6	0.72	15.6
S wall	cavity brick, 25 mm EPS	19.7	0.72	14.2
S window	double glazed, wood	7.2	2.9	20.9
S door	insulated, veneered	1.9	0.8	1.5
W wall	cavity brick, 25 mm EPS	21.6	0.72	15.6
N wall	cavity brick, 25 mm EPS	19.7	0.72	14.2
N window	double glazed, wood	7.2	2.9	20.9
N door	insulated, veneered	1.9	0.8	1.5
Roof	tiled, 50 mm EPS, plasterboard	108	0.54	58.3

$q_c = 230$ W/K

where EPS = expanded polystyrene. The two sets of figures slightly differ for reasons of rounding. The *U*-value of slab-on-ground floors depends on their perimeter length, thus it varies with size. *U*-values of pitched roofs are given for their horizontal projected area.

If the whole house is heated, internal walls can be ignored. The volume of this house is 9600 ft³ (260 m³). If

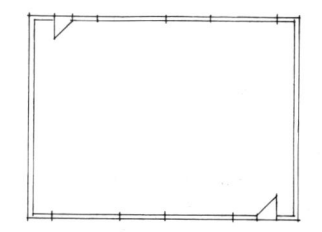

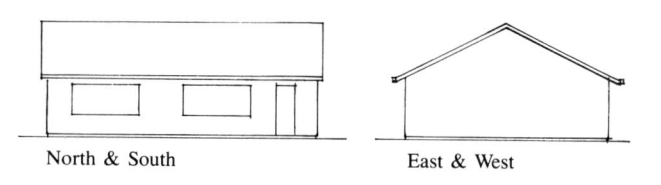

Fig. 20.9.1. A hypothetical small house used for a calculation example.

the infiltration and ventilation rate equals 2 air changes per hour then the ventilation heat loss rate will be:

$$q_v = 0.018 \times 2 \times 9600 \text{ ft}^3 = 346 \text{ Btu/h °F}$$
$$(= 0.33 \times 2 \times 260 \text{ m}^3 = 172 \text{ W/K})$$

thus the specific heat loss rate of the house will be

$$q = 459 + 346 = 805 \text{ Btu/h °F}$$
$$(= 230 + 172 = 402 \text{ W/K})$$

If we assume temperatures $T_i = 72°F$ (22°C) and $T_o = 32°F$ (0°C), then the rate of heat loss will be

$$Q = 805 \times (32 - 72) = -32{,}200 \text{ Btu/h}$$
$$(= 402 \times (0 - 22) = -8844 \text{ W})$$

(The outdoor design temperature is based on climatic data and it will be around the tenth or fifteenth percentile value of the T_o.) If the indoor temperature is to be maintained, heat must be supplied to the building at a similar rate, i.e., the above Q can be taken as the required rate of heating.

If there are any internal heat gains which are likely to be present whenever the internal temperature should be at its design value, then these can be subtracted from the Q value and the remainder will be the required heating rate. Such internal heat gain may be provided by lighting: the total wattage of the lighting installation (including the ballast load for gas discharge lamps, which is usually about 25 percent of the lamp wattage) becomes part of the Q_i.

For calculation in conventional units convert the watts as 1 W = 3.41 Btu/h. The heat output of people (see Table 20.2), machinery, and equipment will become part of the Q_i. The required mechanical heat input rate will be

$$Q_m = Q - Q_i$$

In domestic-scale buildings the value of Q is likely to be substantially greater than the Q_i, so the heat balance of the building will be dominated by the *envelope load*. In many other building types, such as places of assembly, dance halls, restaurants, and often also office buildings, the internal heat gain may dwarf the envelope losses. In this case we will speak of *internal load dominated buildings*.

If the building has significant-size windows of equatorial orientation, then the solar heat gain (Q_s) may also be taken into account to reduce the required heating rate, provided that the building has sufficient mass to absorb the solar radiation input, thus avoiding daytime overheating and excessive cooling down at night.

The 24-hour average solar irradiance G may be used for

Table 20.6. Solar Gain Factors

	Instantaneous (sgf)[c]	Alternating (asg)[d] Lightweight Building	Alternating (asg)[d] Heavyweight Building
Single Glazing			
clear $\frac{1}{4}''$ (6 mm) glass	0.76	0.64	0.47
surface tinted $\frac{1}{4}''$ (6 mm) glass	0.60	0.53	0.41
body tinted $\frac{1}{4}''$ (6 mm) glass	0.52	0.47	0.38
body tinted $\frac{3}{8}''$ (10 mm) glass	0.42	0.39	0.34
clear, with reflecting film	0.32	0.29	0.23
clear, with strongly reflecting film	0.21	0.19	0.16
clear, with tinted reflecting film	0.28	0.26	0.23
reflecting glass	0.36	0.33	0.27
strongly reflecting glass	0.18	0.17	0.15
Double Glazing (outer pane first)			
clear $\frac{1}{4}''$ (6 mm) + clear $\frac{1}{4}''$ (6 mm)	0.64	0.56	0.42
surface tinted + clear $\frac{1}{4}''$ (6 mm)	0.48	0.43	0.34
body tinted + clear $\frac{1}{4}''$ (6 mm)	0.40	0.37	0.30
body tinted $\frac{3}{8}''$ + clear $\frac{1}{4}''$ (10 + 6 mm)	0.30	0.28	0.24
reflecting + clear $\frac{1}{4}''$ (6 mm)	0.28	0.25	0.21
strongly reflecting + clear $\frac{1}{4}''$ (6 mm)	0.13	0.12	0.10
lightly reflecting sealed double unit	0.32	0.29	0.21
strongly reflecting sealed double unit	0.15	0.14	0.11
Single Glazing + External Shade			
clear $\frac{1}{4}''$ (6 mm) + light horizontal slats	0.16	0.11	0.09
+ light vertical slats	0.18	0.13	0.10
+ dark horizontal slats	0.13	0.09	0.08
+ holland blind	0.13	0.10	0.08
+ miniature louvers[a]	0.16	0.10	0.09
+ miniature louvers[b]	0.12	0.09	0.09
body tinted + light horizontal slats	0.13	0.09	0.08
+ light vertical slats	0.14	0.12	0.09
Double Glazing + External Shade			
clear + clear $\frac{1}{4}''$ + light horizontal slats	0.13	0.09	0.07
+ light vertical slats	0.15	0.10	0.08
+ light roller blind	0.10	0.09	0.07
+ miniature louvers[a]	0.12	0.07	0.06
+ miniature louvers[b]	0.09	0.06	0.06
+ dark horizontal slats	0.10	0.06	0.06
Single Glazing + Internal Shade			
clear $\frac{1}{4}''$ (6 mm) + light horizontal slats	0.31	0.28	0.24
+ light vertical slats	0.32	0.30	0.24
+ dark horizontal slats	0.35	0.36	0.34
+ linen blinds	0.20	0.18	0.14
body tinted + light slatted blinds	0.19	0.18	0.17
reflecting + light slatted blinds	0.14	0.14	0.12

[a] 1.5 mm spacing; width/spacing ratio: 0.85; blade tilt 20°; absorpt: 0.96.
[b] 1.1 mm spacing; width/spacing ratio: 1.15; blade tilt 20°; absorpt: 0.98.
[c] sgf = solar gain factor.
[d] asg = alternating solar gain.

each surface, from which the average solar gain can be calculated quite simply. For windows:

$$Q_s = A \times \overline{G} \times sgf$$

where sgf = solar gain factor (see Table 20.6); for opaque elements:

$$Q_s = A \times U \times \overline{G} \times \alpha \times R_{so}$$

where α = absorptance of each surface.

The product $G \times \alpha \times R_{so}$ is the temperature equivalent of the solar radiation, often referred to as the *sol-air excess temperature*, dT_e. (This is not a T but a ΔT quantity, in metric terms distinguished as K and not °C). If added to the outdoor temperature, it will give the *sol-air temperature*, $T_s = T_o + dT_e$, defined as the equivalent air temperature which would produce the same heat flow as the actual air temperature and the solar radiation combined.

The sol-air temperature concept can be explained another way, with reference to Fig. 20.9.2. A solid surface is exposed to solar radiation. The heat input is $G \times \alpha$. The surface is heated and its temperature (T_s) becomes higher than that of the adjacent air; thus there will be a heat loss.

This heat loss depends partly on the surface conductance (the reciprocal of surface resistance) and partly on the temperature difference: $1/R_{so} \times (T_s - T_o)$. The T_s will increase until an equilibrium is reached, i.e., until

$$\text{input} = \text{loss}$$
$$G \times \alpha = (T_s - T_o)/R_{so}$$

from which the T_s can be expressed:

$$T_s = T_o + G \times \alpha \times R_{so}$$

or, as $dT_e = T_s - T_o$ (by definition)

$$dT_e = G \times \alpha \times R_{so}$$

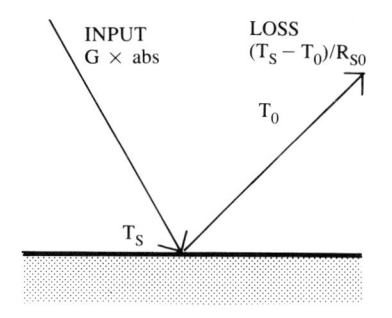

Fig. 20.9.2. Derivation of sol-air temperature.
T_s stabilizes when input $(G \times \alpha) = $ loss $[(T_s - T_o)/R_{so}]$
from which
$T_s = T_o + G \times \alpha \times R_{so}$
$dT_e = T_s - T_o = G \times \alpha \times R_{so}$
where T_s = sol-air (notional surface) temperature
T_o = outdoor air temperature
dT_e = sol-air excess temperature

This derivation ignores any conduction into the body (considers the surface only), so the actual surface temperature may be less than this T_s value, but the T_s value is valid as the notional temperature causing a heat flow into or through the body.

A building surface may also emit heat by radiation. Walls are usually facing other walls, other buildings, and other terrestrial surfaces, which are at comparable temperatures, thus the radiant heat emission would be negligible. A roof, however, faces the sky, which (when clear) is near the absolute zero temperature of outer space. For this reason an emission term is included in the above expression for a roof surface:

$$dT_e = (G \times \alpha - E) \times R_{so} \qquad (20.11)$$

The value of E is taken as between 28 Btu/ft² h (90 W/m²) for a clear sky and 6 Btu/ft² h (20 W/m²) for an overcast sky. The earlier tabulation can be extended to include the solar gain calculation for each element (G is calculated for latitude 42°):

Element	Area, ft²	U-Value	A × U, Btu/h °F	G, Btu/h ft²	α	sgf	R_{so}	Q_s, Btu/h
Floor	1200	0.11	132	—	—	—	—	—
E wall	240	0.13	31.2	15	0.4	—	0.34	63.6
S wall	219	0.13	28.5	38	0.4	—	0.34	147.3
S window	80	0.51	40.8	38	—	0.64	—	1945
S door	21	0.14	2.9	38	0.6	—	0.34	22.5
W wall	240	0.13	31.2	15	0.4	—	0.34	63.6
N wall	219	0.13	28.5	6	0.4	—	0.34	23.3
N window	80	0.51	40.8	6	—	0.64	—	307.2
N door	21	0.14	2.9	6	0.6	—	0.34	3.5
Roof	1200	0.10	120	21	0.3	—	0.23	173.9

$q_c = 459$ Btu/h °F

2750 Btu/h

or the same in SI units:

Element	Area, m²	U-Value	A × U, W/K	G, W/m²	α	sgf	R_{so}	Q_s W
Floor	108	0.62	67	—	—	—	—	—
E wall	21.6	0.72	15.6	47	0.4	—	0.06	17.6
S wall	19.7	0.72	14.2	119	0.4	—	0.06	40.6
S window	7.2	2.9	20.9	119	—	0.64	—	548.5
S door	1.9	0.8	1.5	119	0.6	—	0.06	6.4
W wall	21.6	0.72	15.6	47	0.4	—	0.06	17.6
N wall	19.7	0.72	14.2	20	0.4	—	0.06	6.8
N window	7.2	2.9	20.9	20	—	0.64	—	92.2
N door	1.9	0.8	1.5	20	0.6	—	0.06	1.1
Roof	108	0.54	58.3	66	0.3	—	0.04	46.2

q_c = 230 W/K   777 W

A graph of *heat flow rate versus temperature* can now be plotted (Fig. 20.9.3). Assume that the internal heat gain rate is 2730 Btu/h (800 W). The solar and internal gain is independent of temperature, thus it will be a horizontal line. The heat loss is represented by a sloping line, which intersects the horizontal axis at the design temperature. When $T_o = T_i$, then the heat loss is $Q = 0$. The slope of the line is given by q (Btu/h °F or W/K). It is sufficient to calculate its value for one point, as it is a linear function. This sloping line will intersect the heat gain line at a point, and the temperature corresponding to this point is referred to as the *balance-point temperature* T_b, at which the heat loss equals the gain, therefore no heating is required:

$$Q_s + Q_i + q(T_o - T_i) = 0 \quad (20.12)$$

From this expression the T_b can also be determined algebraically as the value of T_o at which the above expression is valid:

$$T_b = T_i - (Q_s + Q_i)/q \quad (20.13)$$

The concept of *degree-hours* is used to characterize the climate. If we have a recording of hourly temperatures and we set an arbitrary reference level (a base temperature), the area of the histogram below this level is the *cumulative temperature deficit* (Fig. 20.9.4), vertically: °F (K), horizontally: hours, thus the area is °F h (K h), i.e., degree-hours. If this reference level is taken as the above calculated T_b (balance-point temperature), then the number of degree-hours will be indicative of the heating requirement for the given period (degree-hours may be given for any time base, e.g., month or year). The degree-hour number is the climatic determinant and the specific heat loss rate is the building determinant:

Heating requirement = q × deg h

Btu/h °F × °F h = Btu

W/K × K h = Wh   (20.14)

Degree-day values are often published for base temperatures between 60 and 70°F (16 and 20°C) and, in the absence of more precise data, these numbers can be multiplied by 24, to get degree-hours. Degree-hours to any base temperature can be calculated if the standard deviation of the temperature distribution is known.

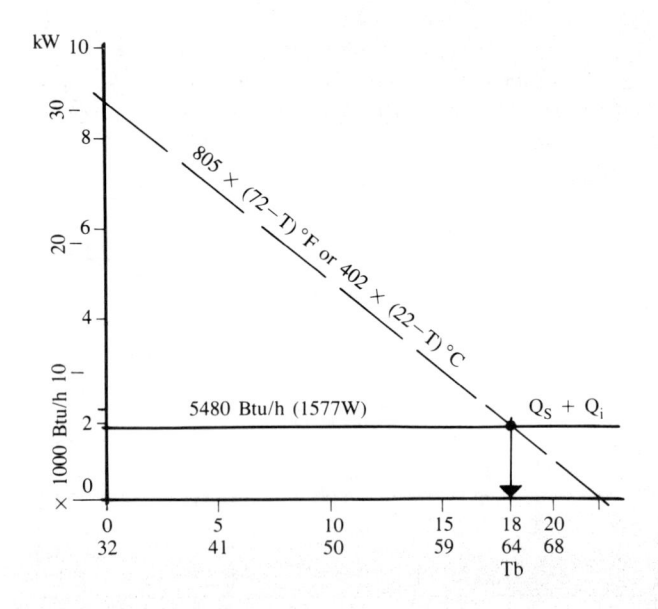

Fig. 20.9.3. A thermal balance graph, showing variation of heat flow (loss and gain) with outdoor temperature.

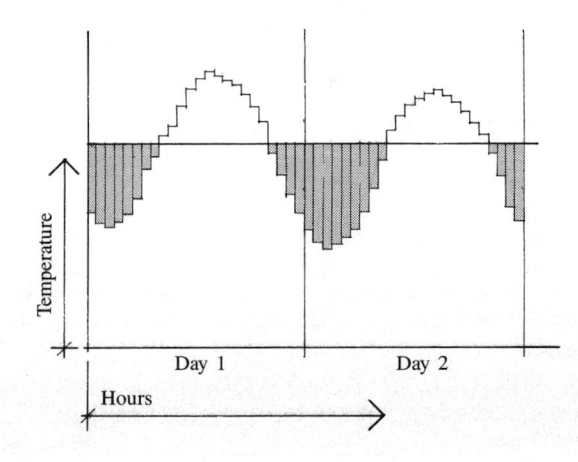

Fig. 20.9.4. Definition of (heating) degree-hours.

20.10. THERMAL BEHAVIOR OF BUILDINGS

The above calculation is based on *steady state* assumptions and is valid if both inside the outside temperatures are relatively constant and the heating system operates continuously. The expressions for such steady state heat flow are summarized in Table 20.7, where the component heat flows are shown as affected by the two climatic determinants, air temperature and solar radiation.

If the annual (seasonal) heating requirement is calculated by the above degree-hour method, it can be adjusted for intermittent heating by using the following three correction factors:

1. For length of working week:		c_1
7 days		1
5 days (weekend shutdown), massive buildings		0.85
lightweight buildings		0.75
2. For night shutdown:		c_2
continuous 24-hour heating		1
with night shutdown, if plant response:	quick	slow
building mass: light	0.55	0.70
medium	0.70	0.85
heavy	0.85	0.95
3. For length of working day:		c_3
if building mass:	light	heavy
occupied period:* 4 hours	0.68	0.96
8 hours	1	1
12 hours	1.25	1.02
16 hours	1.40	1.03

*As an allowance for heating up is included, use actual occupation period only

The building mass categories can be defined in terms of the *response factor*:

$$FR = (q_a + q_v)/(q_c + q_v)$$

For three divisions:

$$FR < 3 = \text{light}$$
$$3 < FR < 5 = \text{medium}$$
$$FR > 5 = \text{heavy}$$

For two divisions:

$$FR < 4 = \text{light}$$
$$FR > 4 = \text{heavy}$$

These adjustments give a rough approximation. For a more precise calculation capacitance effects must be calculated.

In the simplest case this can be done by using the *time lag* ϕ and *decrement factor f*, introduced in Section 20.7. The heat flow rate through a solid element at any time t will be the sum of the 24-hour mean heat flow $\overline{Q}$ and the deviation from (or swing about) this mean at that time (sQ_t). The two components are:

$$\overline{Q} = A \times U \times (\overline{T}_o - T_i) \quad (20.15)$$

$$sQ_t = A \times U \times f \times (T_{o(t-\phi)} - \overline{T}_o) \quad (20.16)$$

and the sum of the two is

$$Q_t = \overline{Q} + sQ_t$$
$$= A \times U \times [(\overline{T}_o - T_i) + f \times (T_{o(t-\phi)} - \overline{T}_o)]$$

$$(20.17)$$

In these expressions $T_{o(t-\phi)}$ is the outdoor temperature ϕ hours before time t; e.g., if $\phi = 5$ h and the calculation is done for 2 PM (14.00 h) then $T_{o(14-5)} = T_{o(9)}$, i.e., the 9 AM temperature value is to be used. In other words, due to the delaying effect of the wall, the 2 PM heat flow rate depends on the conditions at 9 AM. If solar radiation is to be taken into account, then the T_s values should be used in lieu of T_o.

The thermal behavior of a building depends on the heat flows through all elements of the envelope, as well as the ventilation heat flow and any internal gains. It is the configuration and the pattern of these heat flows that will determine the building's thermal response.

If for example, in a cold climate, there is a large solar gain through the windows and the total admittance of the building is small, the indoor temperature will rise (perhaps above the comfort limits), increasing the heat loss rate, until an equilibrium is achieved, i.e., the loss equals the gain.

Table 20.7. Steady State Heat Flow Expressions.

Air Temperature		Solar Radiation	
Ventilation	Conduction, All Elements	Opaque Elements	Windows
$Q_v = q_v \times \Delta T$	$Q_c = q_c \times \Delta T$	$Q_{so} = q_c \times dT_e$	$Q_{sw} = A \times G \times \text{sgf}$
$q_v = 1200 \times vr$	$q_c = \Sigma (A \times U)$	$dT_e = G \times \alpha \times R_{so}$	
$= 0.33 \times V \times N$	$\Delta T = T_o - T_i$	roofs:	
		$dT_e = (G \times \alpha - E) \times R_{so}$	

$$Q = (q_c + q_v) + \Delta T + Q_{so} + Q_{sw}$$

Or, in a hot climate, an increased roof insulation will reduce the conduction gain, thus insuring a lower indoor temperature. However, if for some reason (e.g., solar gain through windows or internal gain) the indoor temperature becomes higher than the outdoor, the same insulation would serve to prevent the heat dissipation, thus causing a further increase in indoor temperature.

20.11. THERMAL RESPONSE SIMULATION

The simplest method for finding the indoor temperatures in a building is the *admittance procedure*, which is based on the work of Mackey and Wright (Ref. 20.7) in the USA, in the 1940s, but developed by the British BRE (Building Research Establishment) (Ref. 20.8). The complex mathematics is relegated to the calculation of time lag ϕ, decrement factor f, and admittance Y for each element. Once these are known, the calculation is simple.

The underlying assumption is that in the absence of any solar and internal gain the indoor 24-hour mean temperature of a building will be the same as the outdoor mean. Any solar or internal gain must be dissipated by conduction and ventilation, both of which depend on the indoor–outdoor temperature difference. The indoor mean temperature will therefore be higher than the outdoor by a difference sufficient to create the required heat dissipation rate, to satisfy the equilibrium condition:

$$Q_s + Q_i + [q \times (\overline{T}_o - \overline{T}_i)] = 0 \quad (20.18)$$

from which the unknown $\overline{T}_i$ can be expressed:

$$\overline{T}_i = \overline{T}_o + (Q_s + Q_i)/q \quad (20.19)$$

The deviation from (or the swing about) this mean T_i at any time t can be found by calculating first the deviation of heat flow at that time from the day's mean. This will consist of six components:

	Building Parameter	Environmental Parameter
1. Ventilation	$sQ_v = 0.33 \times N \times V$	$\times (T_{0(t)} - T_0)$
2. Conduction, glass	$sQ_{cg} = A \times U$	$\times (T_{0(t)} - T_0)$
3. Conduction, solid	$sQ_{cs} = A \times U \times f$	$\times (T_{0(t-\phi)}) - T_0)$
4. Solar, glass	$sQ_{sg} = A \times asg$	$\times (G_{(t)} - G)$
5. Solar, solid	$sQ_{ss} = A \times U \times f \times R_{so} \times \alpha$	$\times (G_{(t-\phi)} - G)$
6. Internal	$sQ_i = Q_{i(t)} - Q_i$	

Items 4 and 5 must be considered separately for each surface, as the solar irradiance is different on each. The sum of these components gives the total swing in heat flow about the mean, at time t: $sQ_{(t)}$.

This swing in heat flow is either dissipated by ventilation or is stored in (or released from) the building fabric. These processes required a temperature difference and from the equilibrium expression the indoor temperature swing can be found. The ability of the fabric to absorb (or release) heat for unit temperature swing is measured by the total admittance:

$$q_a = \Sigma (A \times Y) \quad (20.20)$$

The equilibrium requirement is that at any time t the sum of any swings in heat gain, $sQ_{(t)}$, and the ventilation and heat storage swings must be zero:

$$sQ_{(t)} - [(q_a + q_v) \times (T_{i(t)} - \overline{T}_i)] = 0 \quad (20.21)$$

from which the indoor temperature can be expressed:

$$T_{i(t)} = \overline{T}_i + sQ_{(t)}/(q_a + q_v) \quad (20.22)$$

This method of calculation assumes that the ventilation rate is constant over the 24-hour period. A somewhat more involved calculation can take into account variable ventilation rates.

A number of other methods exist for the simulation of a building's thermal response. Most of these are based on some solution of an electrical resistance/capacitance network. Thermal insulation is represented by resistances and thermal storage capacity by capacitances. Voltage is analogous with temperatures. The mathematical solutions fall into two broad categories:

1. *Finite difference methods*, where the heat flows induced by environmental or occupancy changes are traced from point to point, with energy balances calculated for each point at frequent intervals; at its extreme the method may involve the solution of 10,000 simultaneous differential equations
2. *Response factor methods*, where the thermal response of a building element to a unit pulse is first calculated (the response factor of the element) and then the actual environmental and occupancy changes are applied to these response factors; a later development of this method produces a *building response factor*

All these methods, when numerous building elements are taken into account, become so cumbersome that their use becomes practicable only by computer programs. Many such programs are now available, ranging from quite simple ones running on a 64K PC, to very complicated large packages running on mainframe machines only. All such programs involve the use of some simplifying assumptions, especially when it comes to the simple description of a complex building. The user should be aware of the program's structure and algorithms, in order to make the right assumptions.

The qualities of such programs can be assessed in two ways:

1. *Validation*: comparison of the program's predictions with real life performance measurements, or with the

results of other recognized, previously validated programs, to see how accurate and how reliable these predictions are
2. *Evaluation*: to establish the usefulness and "user-friendliness" of the program, the ease of data input, the legibility of the output (how well this output conveys a meaning), and the relationship of the program to the normal working method of the architect

The latest developments attempt to link such predictive (simulation) packages to some architectural drafting (CAD) system, which would be used by architects for other reasons, e.g., as productivity tools. The program would then obtain the building geometry and dimensions from the graphics database, thus a considerable amount of user's time would be saved.

20.12. CLIMATIC DESIGN

As in Section 20.4, we establish the indoor thermal comfort requirements, and then (as in Sections 20.5 and 6) we survey the climatic conditions; the task is to design a building which ensures a set of indoor conditions as near as possible to those required. The tools to be used depend on the nature of the thermal problem, which determines the immediate objectives:

1. When cold discomfort (underheated) conditions prevail:
    (a) Minimize heat loss (insulation, air-tight construction to reduce infiltration, etc.)
    (b) Utilize heat gains from the sun and incidental internal sources
2. When hot discomfort (overheated) conditions prevail:
    (a) Prevent or reduce heat gains (e.g., shading, insulation)
    (b) Maximize heat dissipation
3. When conditions vary diurnally between hot and cold discomfort:
    (a) Even out variations (thermal capacity, i.e., mass effect)
    (b) Introduce flexibility or adjustment facility, (i) for cold and (ii) for hot periods

In the first instance six basic passive, or climatic design strategies can be considered:

1. Passive solar heating (see also Section 21.6)
2. Mass effect (thermal inertia or capacitive insulation) (see also Section 21.5)
3. Mass effect with night ventilation
4. Air movement effect (physiological cooling) (see also Section 10.6)
5. Evaporative cooling
6. Indirect evaporative cooling

Before any design work is started, i.e., at the predesign analysis stage, the potential of these strategies can be evaluated by using the psychometric chart. The comfort zone can be drawn (as in Section 20.4) and the climate can be represented (as in Section 20.6). Then the *control potential zones* for the above six strategies can be tested and the one which would cover most of the climate lines would be selected.

1. *Passive solar heating* will make thermally acceptable a range of outdoor conditions below the comfort zone, represented by an area to the left of this zone (Fig. 20.12.1a). The temperature limit can be established as a function of the mid-winter daily total irradiation (Btu/ft^2, W h/m^2) of the solar window (Dv):

$$T_0(\text{limit}) = T_n - 0.02 \times Dv \ (°F)$$
$$[= T_n - 0.0036 \times Dv \ (°C)]$$

e.g., if

neutrality temperature $T_n = 65.3°F \ (18.5°C)$
irradiation $Dv = 634 \ \text{Btu/ft}^2$
$(2000 \ \text{W h/m}^2)$

$$\begin{aligned} T_{0(\text{limit})} &= 65.3 - 0.02 \times 634 \\ &= 52.6°F \\ [&= 18.5 - 0.0036 \times 2000 \\ &= 11.3°C] \end{aligned}$$

$(52.6°F \simeq 11.3°C)$

2. *Mass effect* keeps the indoor temperature relatively constant when the outdoor varies. If the outdoor mean temperature, $(T_{\max} + T_{\min})/2$, is within the comfort zone then indoor comfort can be insured. Therefore the upper limit of the comfort potential zone for outdoor conditions will be half the diurnal range added to the upper comfort limit and marked on the 50 percent RH curve. In Fig. 20.12.1b:

$$T_3 = T_2 + 0.5 \times (T_{\max} - T_{\min}) \qquad (20.23)$$

The boundary of the control potential zone will be the set line corresponding to T_3. This can be approximated by the slope expression to give the baseline intercept:

$$\begin{aligned} T_{\text{intercept}} &= T_3 + 23 \times (T_3 - 57) \times HR_{T3} \ (°F) \\ &= T_3 + 23 \times (T_3 - 14) \times HR_{T3} \ (°C) \end{aligned}$$
$$(20.24)$$

where 23 is the slope constant.

The same logic can be applied to the underheated part of the day. The lower temperature limit will be

$$T_4 = T_1 - 0.5 \times (T_{\max} - T_{\min}) \qquad (20.25)$$

T_n = 65.3°F
limits: 62.3 - 68.3°F
intercepts: 62.3 + 23 × (62.3 - 57) × 0.0057 = 63°F
68.3 + 23 × (68.3 - 57) × 0.0078 = 70.3°F
$T_{o(limit)}$ = 65.3 - 0.02 × 634 = 52.6°F

with 634 Btu/ft².day

HUMIDITY RATIO

Fig. 20.12.1. Control potential zones: the potential of various thermal control strategies. (a) Passive solar heating.

The lower boundary is determined by the same slope expression as above.

Note that for overheated conditions a humidity ratio up to 0.014 will be acceptable, but not beyond the RH curve corresponding to the top left corner of the comfort zone.

3. *Mass effect with night ventilation* is a technique useful in overheated conditions only. If the building is adequately ventilated overnight, the stored heat will be dissipated and the indoor temperature will approach the minimum of the outdoor temperature. During the day the building would be closed to reduce the heat gain, thus the indoor mean would remain near the outdoor minimum. An effectiveness of 0.8 is assumed for this mechanism, hence the upper limit (Fig. 20.12.1b) will be set as

$$T_5 = T_2 + 0.8 \times (T_{max} - T_{min}) \quad (20.26)$$

The boundary can be constructed by the above slope expression.

4. *Air movement* produces a physiological cooling effect, which can be approximated as a function of the air velocity v:

$$dT = 0.054 \times v - 0.000045 \times v^2$$
$$(°F) \text{ (up to 600 ft/min)} \quad (20.27)$$
$$= 6 \times v - v^2 \quad (°C) \text{ (up to 3 m/s)}$$

As shown in Fig. 20.12.1c, this calculated dT value is added to T_2 and the result is T_3, the upper temperature limit at the 50 percent RH level. The boundary is determined by the same slope expression and is valid upward from the 0.012 HR level, up to the 90 percent RH curve. In very dry air evaporation from the skin is not restricted even with still air, so the improvement due to air movement is less. Consequently the baseline intercept will be halved for the boundary below 0.012 HR, e.g., if

$$T_2 = 78°F \quad (25.5°C) \quad \text{and} \quad v = 200 \text{ ft/min}$$
$$(= 1 \text{ m/s})$$

HEATING AND COOLING OF BUILDINGS 353

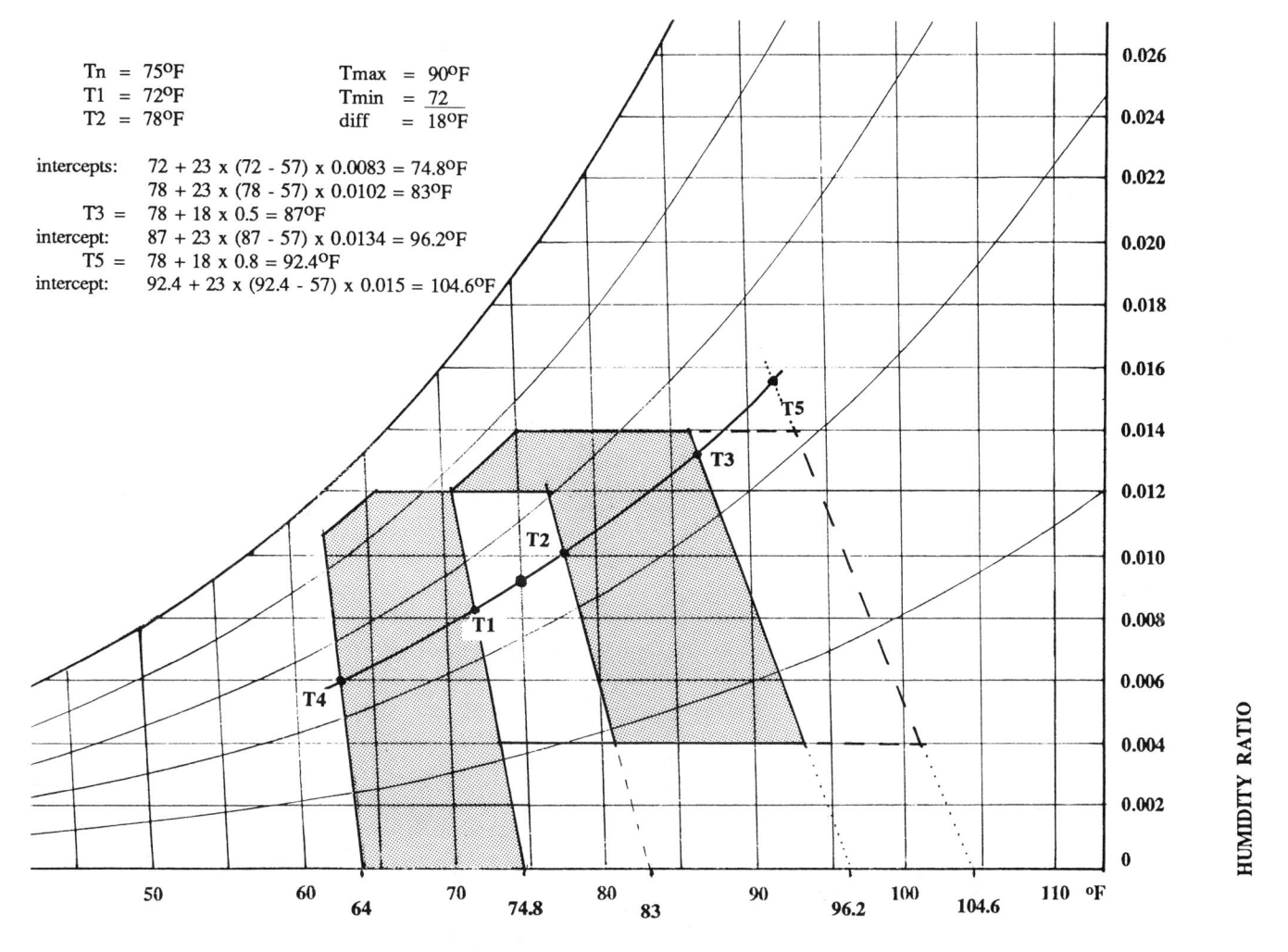

Tn = 75°F   Tmax = 90°F
T1 = 72°F   Tmin = 72
T2 = 78°F   diff = 18°F

intercepts: 72 + 23 × (72 − 57) × 0.0083 = 74.8°F
78 + 23 × (78 − 57) × 0.0102 = 83°F
T3 = 78 + 18 × 0.5 = 87°F
intercept: 87 + 23 × (87 − 57) × 0.0134 = 96.2°F
T5 = 78 + 18 × 0.8 = 92.4°F
intercept: 92.4 + 23 × (92.4 − 57) × 0.015 = 104.6°F

Fig. 20.12.1. Control potential zones: the potential of various thermal control strategies. (b) Mass effect (also with night ventilation).

then

$$T_3 = 78 + 9 = 87°F \quad (= 25.5 + 5 = 30.5°C)$$

and

$$T_{\text{intercept}} = 87 + 23 \times (87 - 57) \times 0.0136 = 96.4°F$$
$$= 30.5 + 23 \times (30.5 - 14) \times 0.0136$$
$$= 35.6°C$$

This will be used for projecting the boundary upward from T_3, but for the lower half the intercept will be at

$$87 + 9.4/2 = 91.7°F \quad (30.5 + 5.2/2 = 33.1°C)$$

Under warm conditions 200 ft/min (1 m/s) air velocity is perceived as pleasant and the limit for normal building occupancy is about 300 ft/min (1.5 m/s), hence these two control potential zones are shown in Fig. 20.12.1c.

5. *Evaporative cooling* is a particularly useful control strategy under hot-dry conditions. If a given volume of air is evaporatively cooled, its status point on the psychometric chart will move upward to the left, along a WBT line. Consequently the range of conditions, which can be brought to comfort level by evaporative cooling will be within an area downward to the right of the comfort zone, bounded by the WBT lines tangential to the two corners of the zone. Practical limitations restrict this cooling effect to about 22°F (12 K), thus the high-temperature boundary of the evaporative control potential zone will be $T_n + 22°F$ ($T_n + 12°C$) (Fig. 20.12.1d).

6. *Indirect evaporative cooling*, although not strictly a passive system, can be very useful when the humidities are higher. With high humidities the evaporative cooling potential is restricted and the addition of moisture would worsen the conditions. With this indirect system one air stream (usually the exhaust) is evaporatively cooled, and this will in turn cool the supply air stream through a plate (or rotary) heat exchanger, before it is discharged (Fig. 20.12.2). No moisture is added to the supply air stream,

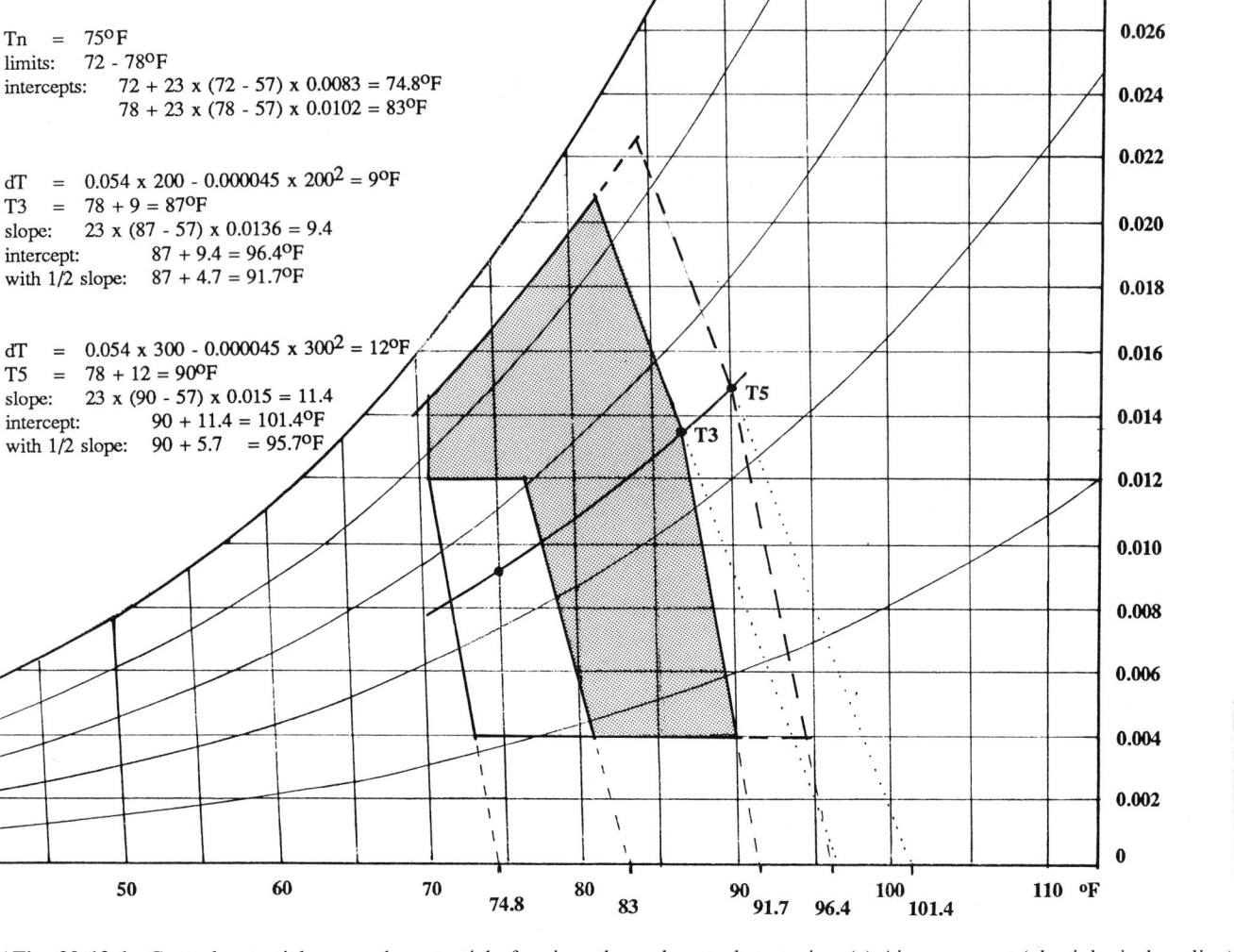

```
Tn       = 75°F
limits:  72 - 78°F
intercepts:  72 + 23 x (72 - 57) x 0.0083 = 74.8°F
             78 + 23 x (78 - 57) x 0.0102 = 83°F

dT       = 0.054 x 200 - 0.000045 x 200² = 9°F
T3       = 78 + 9 = 87°F
slope:    23 x (87 - 57) x 0.0136 = 9.4
intercept:          87 + 9.4 = 96.4°F
with 1/2 slope:     87 + 4.7 = 91.7°F

dT       = 0.054 x 300 - 0.000045 x 300² = 12°F
T5       = 78 + 12 = 90°F
slope:    23 x (90 - 57) x 0.015 = 11.4
intercept:          90 + 11.4 = 101.4°F
with 1/2 slope:     90 + 5.7  = 95.7°F
```

Fig. 20.12.1. Control potential zones: the potential of various thermal control strategies. (c) Air movement (physiological cooling).

so the top boundary of the control potential zone will be the 0.014 HR level. The upper temperature limit is also somewhat higher than for the direct system:

$$T_n + 27°F \quad (T_n + 15°C)$$

Once the appropriate control strategy is selected, the design can proceed and the task of the designer is to realize the potential of the selected method.

20.13. MECHANICAL VENTILATION

Where the passive controls are unable to ensure thermal comfort, some form of mechanical system will have to be relied on. The simplest of these are the mechanical ventilation systems.

Ventilation serves three distinctly different purposes:

1. Supply of fresh air/removal of used air
2. Removal of heat by air exchange
3. Physiological cooling.

These purposes may be combined, but may also be served by separate systems. A table-top fan or a ceiling fan may serve the last purpose, without supplying any fresh air. For this purpose the sensible air velocity is critical, whereas for the first two the volume flow rate (vr) is the important factor.

Ventilation (i.e., fresh air) requirements are established on an empirical basis. If the number of occupants is known, the required per capita air supply may vary between 8.5 and 46 CFM (ft³/min) (4 and 22 L/s), depending on occupancy density and processes to be accommodated. Some building regulations prescribe, e.g., for offices, a fresh air supply of 11 CFM (5 L/s) per person and then stipulate the number of persons to be counted per floor area (e.g., 1 person per 100 ft² or 10 m²). If the number of occupants is not known, the ventilation requirement may be specified in terms of the number of air changes per hour (N).

This can be converted into a volume flow (ventilation) rate (vr), if the volume of the room (ft³ or m³) is known:

$$vr = \frac{N \times V}{60} \text{ CFM}, \quad \text{if } V \text{ is in ft}^3$$

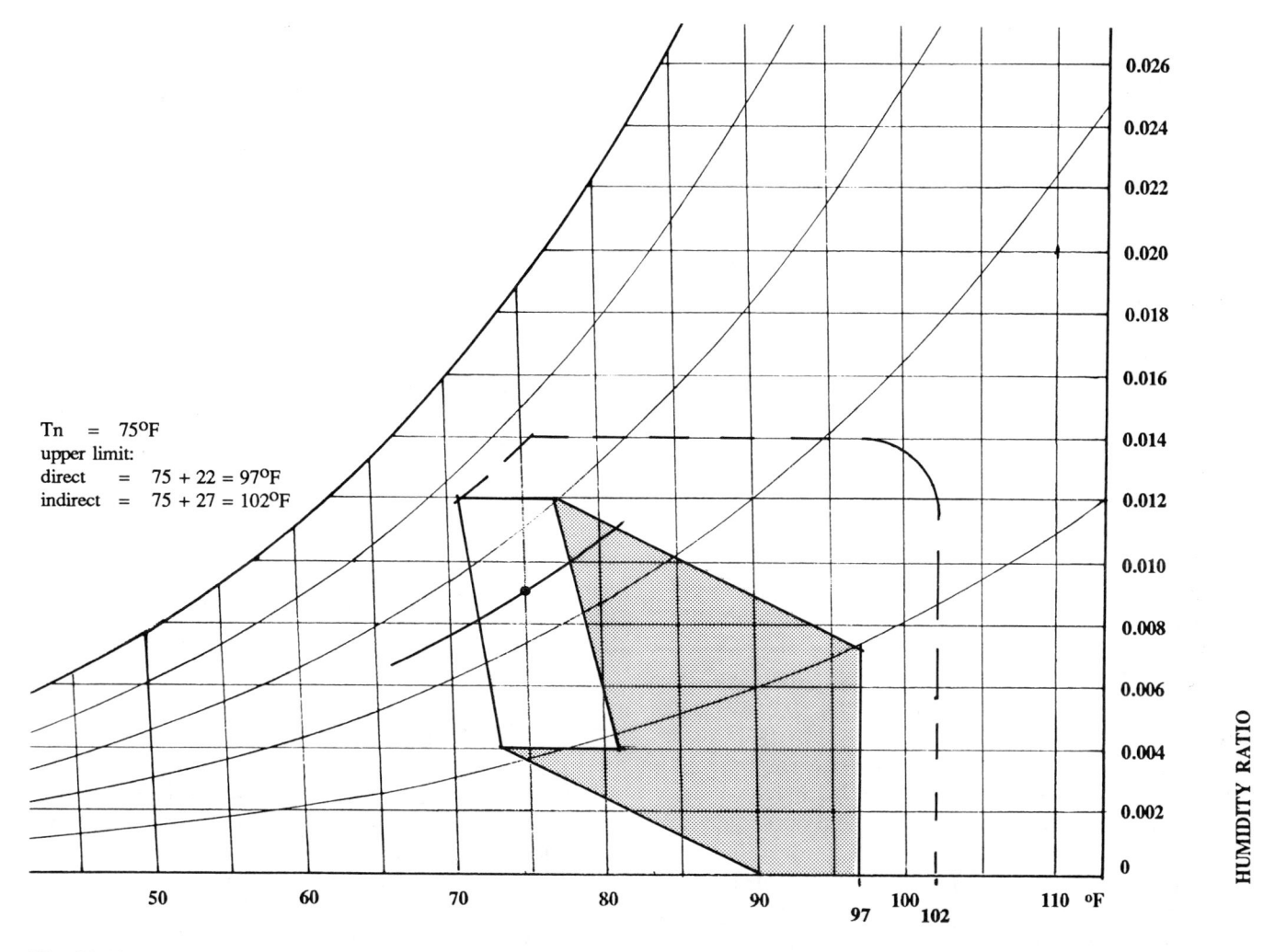

Fig. 20.12.1. Control potential zones: the potential of various thermal control strategies. (d) Evaporative cooling, direct and indirect.

$$vr = \frac{N \times V}{3600} \text{ m}^3/\text{s}, \text{ if } V \text{ is in m}^3 \quad (20.28)$$

Ventilation can be used to remove heat when the indoor temperature is higher than that outdoors. The heat removal capacity can be found by multiplying the vr with the specific heat of air and the temperature difference:

$$Q_v = vr \times 1.08 \times \Delta T \quad \text{(from CFM to Btu/h)}$$
$$= vr \times 1200 \times \Delta T \quad \text{(from m}^3\text{/s to W)}$$

$$(20.29)$$

where $\Delta T = T_0 - T_i$.

Three main types of mechanical ventilation systems can be distinguished.

1. *Extract* or *exhaust systems* are used at or near the source of some contamination, to remove it before it spreads through the building. Some everyday examples are the exhaust hood over a kitchen stove, or the exhaust system serving a toilet block. This system will create a negative pressure in the space served. When this equals the fan (blower) suction, no more air will be removed. It is therefore necessary to provide a relief vent or air intake grilles, possibly incorporated in doors or windows.

2. *Supply systems* bring in filtered outside air, and as this is pushed into the space, a positive pressure will be created. Relief vents must be provided to allow the exfil-

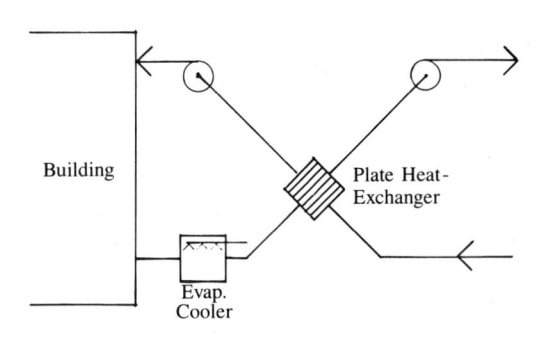

Fig. 20.12.2. Indirect evaporative cooler.

tration of surplus air. The system is useful where dust-free conditions must be ensured in a dusty environment. A special form of this is the fire ventilation, which forces air at high pressure: 2 in. or 50 mm wg (water gauge) or 500 Pa, into staircases or corridors, to keep these escape routes free of smoke.

3. *Balanced systems* have both supply and extract provided by mechanical means. The supply air vr is usually slightly higher than the extract rate, to prevent unwanted infiltration. These are the most expensive systems, but provide the greatest degree of flexibility; are rarely used on their own, but can form the basis of a warm air heating or of an air conditioning system.

The main components of any mechanical ventilation system are: fans (blowers), filters, ducts, and outlets.

Fans are used to move air around the building. They are almost always electrically driven. Two main types are most often used:

(a) Propeller or axial flow fans (the latter term is used when the fan operates within a cylindrical casing) are normally used for large air flow rates against a small pressure resistance.

(b) Centrifugal fans are used where the filters and an extensive ductwork create a large pressure resistance (or back-pressure). These are usually larger but quieter than the equivalent axial flow fan. Delivery capacities range from 600 to 160,000 CFM (0.3 to 75 m^3/s) and these fans can work against a backpressure of 0.1 to 6 in. wg (25 to 1500 Pa).

Filters in general use belong to one of three categories.

(a) Dry filters are usually of some porous or fibrous material, e.g., a fibrous pad which can be cleaned and reused or filter paper automatically wound from one roll to another across the duct whenever the operating length gets clogged up. A recent development is the multiple bag-type filter: several textile bags (similar to those used in vacuum cleaners) in parallel, providing a very large filter surface, thus low flow velocity and low resistance to air flow.

(b) Viscous impingement filters usually consist of a pad $\frac{3}{8}$ to 4 in. (10 to 100 mm) thick, e.g., metal turnings (or coiled plastic strips) between two wire meshes, dipped in oil: dust particles will adhere to the oily surface. The filter pads can be cleaned and reused, but there are also continuous operation endless loops, which go through a cleaning bath. These filters are effective down to about 10 μm particle size.

(c) Electrostatic filters rely on electrostatic attraction of ionized bodies: the air passes between ionizing rods, which have a static electrical charge of up to 12 kV. Any particles carried by the air stream become ionized and will adhere to the following plates of the opposite charge. These filters are effective down to about 0.01 μm particle size. To avoid rapid clogging up, it is useful to install a coarser dry prefilter.

Ducts are most often made of sheet metal (e.g., galvanized steel) and are of a rectangular cross-section. In recent years circular and oval flexible ducts, usually of plastic materials, became popular, mainly for the smaller sizes. Very large ducts, especially vertical risers, are often "builder's work," i.e., built in concrete or rendered brickwork.

Ducts carrying air substantially different in temperature from their environment should have a good thermal insulation.

Outlets can be louvered diffusers, with parallel straight blades, possibly quite long and narrow, or circular or square with concentric rings (or squares) of conical blades. In each case the blades may be fixed or adjustable. There may be a set of dampers behind the louvers, which are set once and for all during the commissioning of the system. A suspended ceiling may be perforated and serve as a diffuser from a pressurized ceiling plenum. Possibly the outlet, but often the return air grilles, may be combined with the luminaires, so that the heat output of the lamps can be removed before it enters the room. This would insure that the lamps operate at a reduced temperature, thus higher luminous efficacy and the lamp life is extended. Finally, there are several types of high-velocity outlets, with a longer throw, such as the personal air outlets used on aeroplanes.

20.14. HEATING

Heating of building spaces can be provided by local heating appliances, where fuel or some other form of energy is converted to heat in the space where it is needed. The energy source and the method of delivery may be:

- Electricity, by cables
- Gas, piped from public grid or externally stored bottle
- Oil, piped from external storage tank or in batch form, i.e., cans or bottles
- Solid fuel, (coal, coke, or wood) in batch form, i.e., cans, bins, baskets

Solid fuel appliances require a flue. Oil heaters may be portable, but larger, fixed units, as well as any gas-fired appliances, would require either a conventional vertical flue or a through-the-wall balanced flue, which has an air intake as well as a discharge opening.

Any central heating system consists of three main components:

1. The heat production plant, where the energy of some fuel is converted into heat
2. The distribution network
3. Heat emitters in the spaces served

Both the heat production and heat emission can be (and should be) controlled.

The choice of heat production plant depends on the heat transport fluid chosen. This may be air, water, or steam. Warm air is distributed by ductwork, water and steam by pipework. Air is heated by a central furnace (fired by a solid, liquid, or gaseous fuel), while hot water and steam are produced in boilers. Steam heating was popular early this century, but today it is only used as a heat transport fluid over longer distances, e.g., in district heating schemes. In such systems, each building served has a heat exchanger (calorifier), where water is heated; the local distribution within the building is performed by a water (hydronic) system.

The central heating boiler or furnace of a house is often located in the basement, but oil- or gas-fired boilers are also available in sizes which fit into a kitchen bench. At the domestic scale almost exclusively LTHW (low temperature hot water) systems are used, which are not pressurized and are open to the atmosphere through an expansion pipe and a feeder tank. The boiler output temperature is set between 150 and 190°F (66 and 90°C). The distribution pipework is usually $\frac{1}{2}$ in. (13 mm) copper and the circulation is driven by a small (40–60 W) pump. Fig. 20.14.1 shows a number of different piping arrangements. The emitters shown are of the pressed steel *panel radiator* type (a misnomer, as they emit heat primarily by convection), but a number of alternative emitters are also possible:

Convectors. Tubes carrying the hot water have fins or are attached to metal panels, which are within a casing with low- and high-level openings, through which a natural convection current (a thermosiphon circulation) will develop.

Fan-convectors. These are usually finned tubes through which the room air is circulated by a small electric fan.

Ceiling radiators. A pipe coil is bonded to the back of a metal ceiling panel, which is fixed flush with the rest of the ceiling. Ceiling radiators are usually operated with about 140°F (60°C) hot water.

Floor warming. A coil of $\frac{3}{8}$ or $\frac{1}{2}$ in. (10 or 13 mm) copper, polybutyl or high density polyethylene pipe is laid on the concrete floor slab and covered with an approx. 2 in. (50 mm) sand/cement screed. This system is operated with low-temperature hot water, not more than 100°F (38°C). This is perhaps the most comfortable form of heating. It is the only system which can produce an inverted temperature stratification, preferred by most people: slightly warmer at the foot than at the head level. It is an inherently slow response system, used mainly for spaces continuously oc-

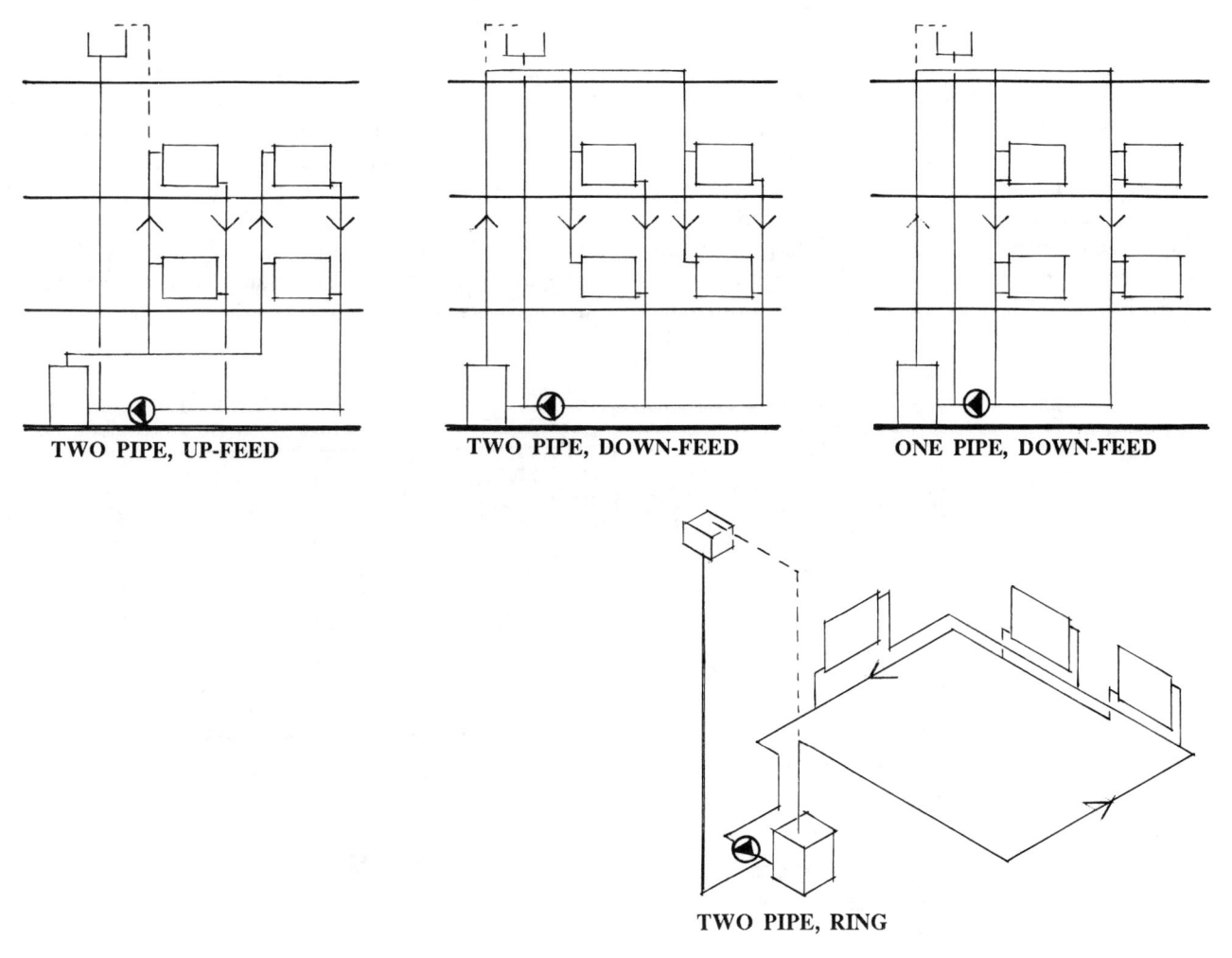

TWO PIPE, UP-FEED   **TWO PIPE, DOWN-FEED**   **ONE PIPE, DOWN-FEED**

TWO PIPE, RING

Fig. 20.14.1. Central-heating pipework systems.

cupied or heated. It may also be used to give a background heating, e.g., to produce a room temperature of about 60°F (15°C), which will then be topped up by some quick-response heat emitter, such as a fan-convector.

Warm air heating systems can readily be combined with mechanical ventilation systems and most air conditioning systems would also include a heating function. In such combined systems the air flow requirement for heat transport purposes is usually much larger than the fresh air requirement. The difference between the two quantities may be recirculated (Fig. 20.14.2).

20.15. AIR CONDITIONING

An air conditioning system supplies to the conditioned spaces an adequate quantity of air, which has been filtered, heated or cooled and its humidity controlled. The heart of an air conditioner is a refrigeration machine. In most cases this would be a compressor-type unit, but *absorption type refrigeration* machines are also used, especially in two situations:

1. Where low-grade waste heat is available
2. Where silent operation is required, e.g., for a refrigerator in a hotel bedroom

This is a binary system, where a refrigerant (e.g., ammonia, NH_3) is expelled from solution (in water, H_2O) by the application of heat. The heat source may be a small kerosene or gas flame, an electric heating element, or a heat exchanger supplied by hot water. Fig. 20.15.1 gives a diagrammatic representation of such a unit. The hot ammonia vapor dissipates its heat to the environment as it condenses. From a refrigerant reservoir the liquid ammonia

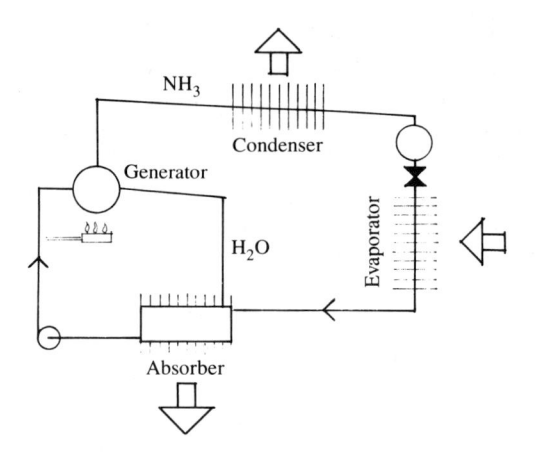

Fig. 20.15.1. An absorption refrigerator.

drips into the evaporator, where a reduced pressure exists. While evaporating, it will cool down and pick up heat from its environment. The ammonia vapor is then sucked back into solution in the absorber, where heat is released and dissipated.

The *compressor-type unit* (Fig. 20.15.2) uses a single fluid as a refrigerant, in the past usually a halocarbon (halogenated hydrocarbon), such as freon or R12. The closed loop is divided by the compressor and the pressure release (choke) valve into a high-pressure and a low-pressure part. As the refrigerant is compressed, its temperature is increased; thus it can dissipate some of its heat content to the environment, to a "sink." In the process it condenses. The resulting liquid slowly enters the evaporator (restricted by the choke valve) where a partial vacuum exists, due to the compressor's suction; it evaporates, cools and will pick up heat from its environment (from the "source").

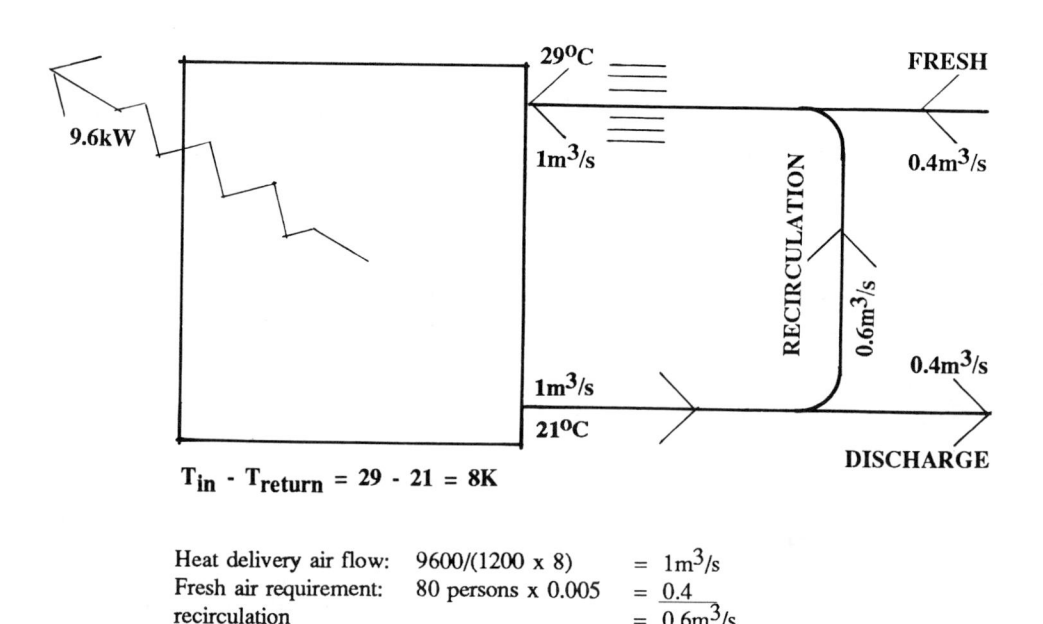

$T_{in} - T_{return} = 29 - 21 = 8K$

Heat delivery air flow: 9600/(1200 × 8) = 1 m³/s
Fresh air requirement: 80 persons × 0.005 = 0.4
recirculation = 0.6 m³/s

Fig. 20.14.2. A warm-air heating system, using both recirculated and fresh air.

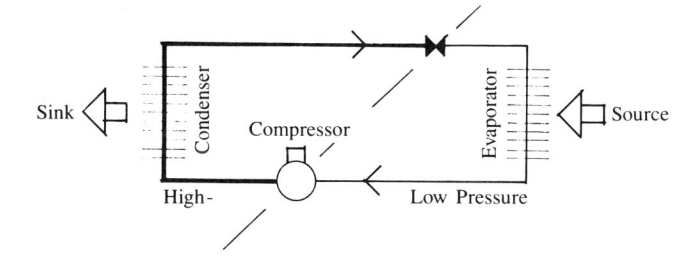

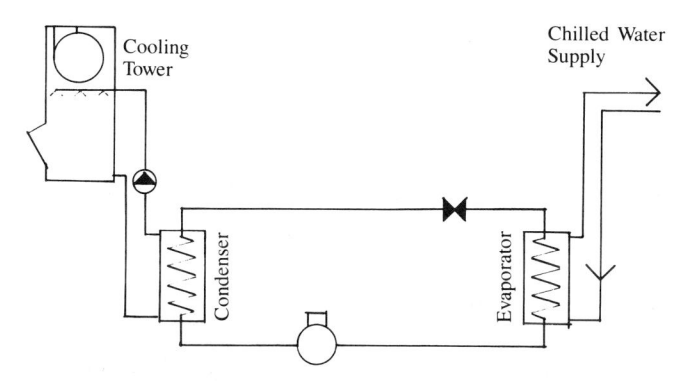

Fig. 20.15.2. A compression refrigerator and its adaptation as a water chiller.

The coefficient of performance is defined as

$$CoP = \frac{Q}{W} = \frac{\text{heat removed from source}}{\text{compressor work input}} \quad (20.30)$$

E.g., if a unit with a 1 kW compressor motor removes heat at a rate of 3.5 kW (= 1 ton of refrigeration) then $CoP = 3.5/1 = 3.5$.

Note: If the unit is used as a heat pump, i.e., for the purposes of gaining heat from a low-grade source, e.g., sea, river, wastewater, or even the atmosphere, then the CoP is defined differently:

$$CoP = \frac{Q'}{W} = \frac{\text{heat delivered to sink}}{\text{compressor work input}} \quad (20.31)$$

as in this case the compressor work input, converted to heat, is also part of the useful product, i.e., $Q' = Q + W$. Continuing the above example:

$$Q' = 3.5 + 1 = 4.5 \text{ kW}, \quad \text{thus} \quad CoP = 4.5/1 = 4.5$$

The evaporator and condenser coils are the heat intake and heat output heat exchangers and can be shaped to suit the particular application. In a domestic refrigerator the evaporator is usually a roll-bonded aluminum panel, with integral fluid channels, folded to form a freezer compartment, while the condenser is a set of finned tubes at the back of the refrigerator; these tubes are warm to the touch, and so they dissipate some heat to the room air.

HEATING AND COOLING OF BUILDINGS 359

In a *window-type packaged air conditioner* both heat exchangers are similar to an automobile radiator: fluid ways and a large fin surface in contact with air and air is forced through both by small fans (Fig. 20.15.3). The room air is forced through the evaporator coil, which is an air-to-fluid heat exchanger, while the outdoor air is driven through the condenser coil, which acts as a fluid-to-air heat exchanger.

In a *refrigerator serving a cold storage room*, the evaporator is a fan-coil unit, circulating the cold room air through the coil. The condenser coil may be air cooled, but for improved efficiency it is often water cooled. In this case we have a fluid-to-fluid heat exchanger. The cooling water is then circulated to a cooling tower, where it is sprayed through air, thus it is evaporatively cooled.

In a *large air-conditioning installation* the refrigeration machine may become a chilled water unit, where both heat exchangers are fluid-to-fluid. The evaporator end produces chilled water and the condenser end is cooled by a water circuit connected to a cooling tower. The chilled water is then distributed through insulated pipes to numerous fan-coil units or air-handling units serving various parts of the building. The air-cooling coil in such units is said to be *indirect*, i.e., a chilled-water circuit is inserted between the evaporator and the air, as opposed to the *direct evaporation coil*, where the air-cooling coil is the evaporator itself, where the refrigerant evaporates (e.g., in the packaged units mentioned above).

The terminology related to air-conditioning systems and components can be rather confusing, as various functional parts of a system are grouped together in a commercial product. In a domestic-scale packaged system, both in the window and the console type, all components are in one unit (Fig. 20.15.3). In a *split system* the compressor and condenser are outside, while the evaporator and its fan are only inside in a console unit (Fig. 20.15.4). The condenser in this case is an air-cooled, forced-draft, vertical-axis unit. The alternative would be a horizontal-axis or crossflow-type air-cooled condenser. The connecting pipework circulates the refrigerant itself (hence the distance restriction of about 30 ft or 10 m); thus the console is actually a direct expansion fan-coil unit.

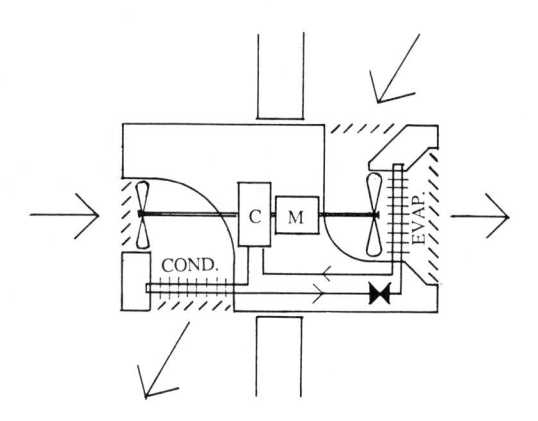

Fig. 20.15.3. A domestic-scale packaged air conditioner.

360 HANDBOOK OF ARCHITECTURAL TECHNOLOGY

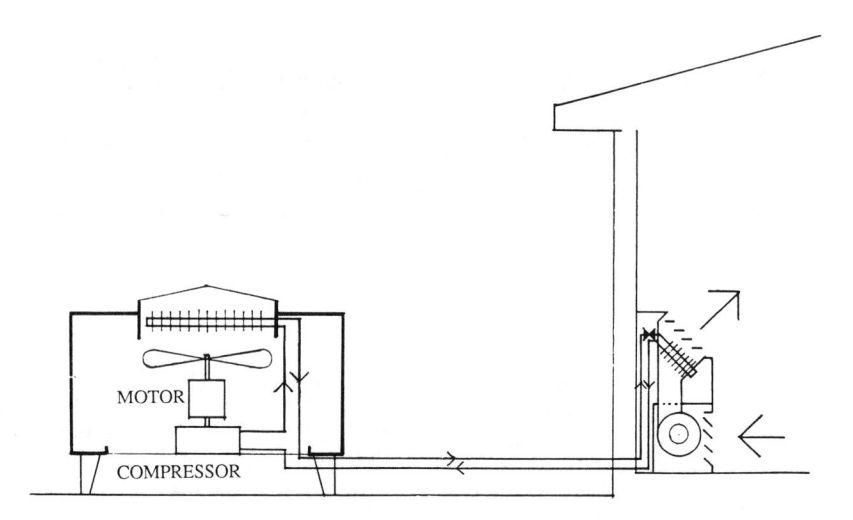

Fig. 20.15.4. A split-air conditioning system: the compressor and condenser are outside, while the evaporator and the fan are inside the building.

The difference between a fan-coil unit and an air-handling unit is only that the former term is used normally when it serves one room, without any ducts, and the latter is used when the output is distributed through ducts. An air-handling unit may include a filter, which the fan-coil unit would not. (This is almost like trying to define the difference between *tube* and *pipe*: there is no rule, and each individual instance must be learnt separately.)

The *central plant of an all-air system* is diagrammatically represented in Fig. 20.15.5, which has all possible components:

- Mixer (return air/fresh air)
- Filter
- Preheater coil
- Washer (humidifier)
- Cooling coil
- Eliminator plates (to remove droplets carried by the air stream)
- Heating (or reheating) coil
- Fan
- Silencer

Air-conditioning systems can be classified according to the following facets:

(a) Heat delivery system:
- All air
- Part air
- Air/water
- All water systems

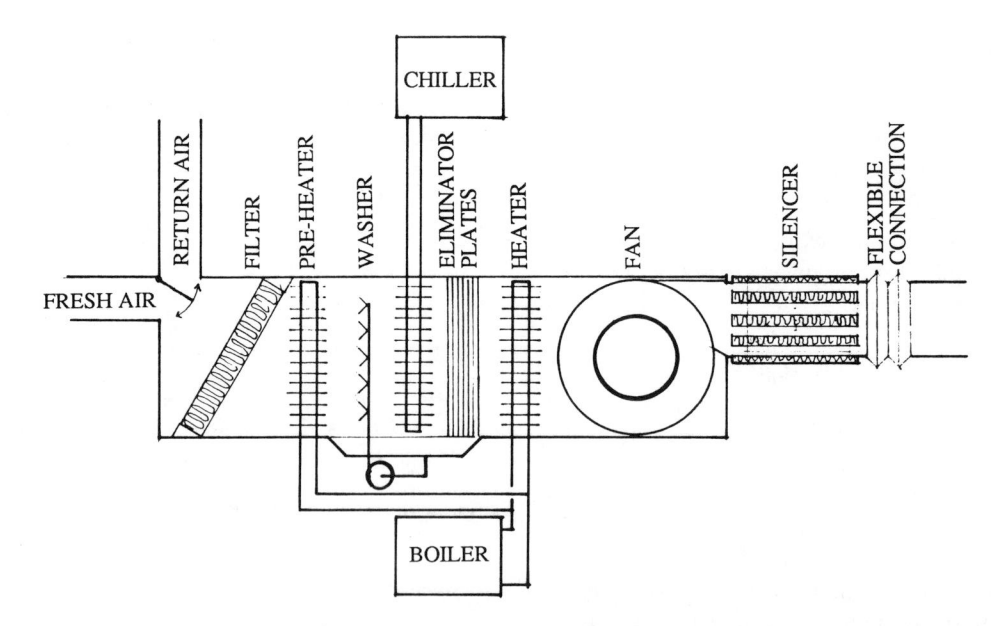

Fig. 20.15.5. A complete central air-handling system.

(b) Zoning:
- Single zone
- Multizone
- Local air handling

(c) Temperature control:
- Central
- Dual duct
- Variable volume
- Induction systems

(d) Air Velocity:
- Low: 600–1200 ft/min (3–6 m/s)
- High: 2300–4000 ft/min (12–20 m/s).

The number of permutations is very large, and new arrangements are continually being developed. Here only the most frequently used systems can be described.

1. *Packaged units system.* A central boiler provides hot water, a cooling tower provides cooling water and a central air intake supplies fresh air to numerous packaged units. Each of these has its own compressor, a water-cooled condenser, and a direct-expansion fan-coil unit.

2. *Local air-handling system.* This is similar to the packaged units system, but there is also a central chiller, i.e., a refrigeration unit producing chilled water. Its condenser end may have air-cooled condensing units or may be water cooled, served by a cooling tower. The local air-handling (fan-coil) units consist of a fan, a heating/cooling coil, filter, and return air intake. Fresh air may be supplied centrally, but each unit may have its own fresh-air intake through a perimeter wall.

The system just described is an all-water system, as all the heat is transported by water circulation. There is also a variant, which would be considered an air/water system. This has a larger air-handling unit for each floor (or each section) of the building, each of which may have several zones.

3. *Central, all-air, low-velocity system.* The entire plant is central, all the air is supplied to the building centrally through ductwork, and there is a duct system for return air, some of which is discharged, but much of it recirculated. Air is used as the primary heat transport fluid. The condition of all supply air is set at the central plant, but this plant may include a multizone unit, which would allow for different air conditions for each zone. The same fan and same coils would serve all zones, but the mixing proportions of cooled and heated air (or nonconditioned air, bypassing the coils) would be set separately for each zone by motorized dampers.

4. *Terminal reheat system.* All air is supplied centrally, but the plant has no heating coil. The air is usually overcooled and can be adjusted to the required condition by a heating element at the outlet or at a point serving several outlets in one zone. The heating element may be electric or may be a heater coil supplied by centrally produced hot water.

5. *Induction system.* This is a part-air system, where normally only the fresh air requirement is supplied centrally. The primary heating or cooling of this air also takes place centrally. Distribution is often through a high-velocity duct system, in an overconditioned state (i.e., overcooled in summer, overheated in winter). The outlet unit is arranged in such a way that a jet of the conditioned air induces an air intake from the room (a localized return air intake) and this return air is mixed with the conditioned air before being discharged into the room. This *induction unit* may or may not be fitted with a secondary heating or cooling coil, served with centrally heated or chilled water.

6. *Dual-duct system.* This is usually an all-air system and employs high-velocity ductwork. As the name suggests, there are two sets of ducts, taking centrally produced hot air and chilled air to the *mixing box* of each outlet. The mixing proportions are controlled by a room thermostat. This is the most luxurious system, giving an almost instant response to the flick of a switch, but also the most expensive, because of its dual ductwork and increased fan power, and also the most wasteful in energy terms. It was popular in the 1950s, but is rarely used today.

7. *Variable-volume system.* This is an all-air system where the air condition is set centrally. Each outlet is a *variable volume box*, controlled by a room thermostat. With increased load the air-supply volume is increased. Under no-load conditions the volume is reduced to its minimum, which is set as the fresh-air supply quantity. In energy terms this is the most economical system.

In any one building two or more of the above systems may be combined. For example, there may be a central all-air system serving the core of a building, while the perimeter zones are served by induction units or local air-handling units. Or, in a building which has both large general offices and small private offices, the former may be served by a central all-air system, while the latter are served by a variable volume system.

20.16. ENERGY CONSERVATION

The energy used in buildings is between 23 and 45 percent of the national total energy consumption in the various industrialized countries. The largest part of building energy use (50–75 percent) serves the purposes of thermal controls or HVAC, i.e., heating, ventilation, and air conditioning. The results of any energy conservation measure in building thermal controls can therefore be quite significant at the national level.

The individual building owner or manager may be more interested in the reduction of operating costs (i.e., the conservation of money) than in the conservation of energy. However, the two usually coincide: energy conservation means cost reduction, although cost reductions can be achieved by energy management without actual reduction of energy consumption.

The purpose of energy conservation can be served by many measures, depending on the nature of the building.

In *internal-load-dominated buildings* it often happens that even in winter, when the perimeter zone needs heating, the central zone would need cooling. Or, indeed, an equator-facing perimeter zone may also be overheated by solar gain, thus needing cooling, when the pole-facing side of the building needs heating. It does happen that the heating boilers and the air-conditioning chillers are working at the same time.

Substantial energy savings can be achieved by transferring the surplus heat from the central (or equator-facing) zone to the zone which requires heating. This can be done locally or at the central plant. The local solution would involve a large number of small heat transfer systems, e.g., exhausting air through a group of ten or twelve luminaires in the central zone by a small fan and ducting it to the perimeter zone, where it would be blown down at the inside face of the window. At the central plant level a heat exchanger would be introduced, using the exhaust air from the central zone to preheat the fresh-air intake. There is a multitude of similar possibilities; a little thought and modest expense can achieve quite large energy economies. This is good for the building owner, but also good for the earth as a whole.

In such buildings the envelope would have little influence on energy use, as long as it is reasonably well designed. For winter it is relatively easy to design a building envelope which (together with the fresh-air load) would produce a heat-loss rate of the same magnitude as the internal heat gains from lighting (see also Section 19.8), occupants, etc. The critical time for design of internal-load-dominated buildings is the summer. These usually have functions such that natural ventilation is not practicable (e.g., places of assembly, multistory offices), so that air conditioning must be relied on. Energy conservation can be achieved by reducing the air-conditioning load.

Insulation of the fabric is quite important, as the indoors will be kept at comfort temperatures when the outdoors is hot, causing a significant temperature gradient across the envelope. The phenomenon experienced in passively controlled buildings, where the insulation may prevent heat dissipation, would not occur here. It is an advisable practice to attempt to remove any sizable internal heat gain before it can contribute to the internal load, by using a local exhaust over heat sources. Beyond reducing internal gains (e.g., by using electric lamps of a much higher luminous efficacy) the most important measure is solar control.

In a badly designed building the *solar load* can be greater than all other loads together. This could be almost totally eliminated by the use of external shading devices (see Table 20.6 and Section 18.4). In recent years the use of solar control glasses became very popular (see also Sections 3.20 and 18.2). *Heat-absorbing glasses* would be almost useless: the glass itself becomes hot, thus a source of heat input into the building. *Reflective glasses* have a selective reflectance, which is a surface property. The best of these is gold-coated glass, which may have a transmittance of 0.4 for light but only about 0.1 for infrared (heat) radiation. It is vigorously marketed and it is quite fashionable. It does, however, have two problems. (1) It reduces daylighting of the interiors to about one-half of what it would be with ordinary glass, so that there will be a need for more electric lighting. Electric lighting is a double load: every watt used in the lamps must be matched by another watt in air conditioning to remove that heat input. (2) It is very antisocial. It can increase the radiant heat input of nearby buildings, it can substantially increase the sensible temperatures in adjacent outdoor spaces, and the visible light reflections can be the source of quite severe glare.

Internal-load-dominated buildings are often occupied only for short periods (e.g., auditoriums) and in most cases only for the normal working hours (offices). In winter the heating system would work intermittently, for 10 or 12 hours a day, or at least there would be a thermostat night-setback. When the building is unoccupied, there is no need for fresh-air supply, thus the fresh-air heating load is also eliminated. In this case a lightweight, insulated building would allow a shorter heating-up period, thus achieving a greater energy saving than a heavy, masonry-type building. For the latter, the heating-up period can be shortened by lightweight internal insulating linings. The surface temperature of these would closely follow the indoor air temperature. With a continuously occupied building intermittent heating is possible, if the building is of a heavy mass: this would bridge over the nonheating periods. If the building is continuously heated, the building mass is inconsequential.

In summer, intermittent occupancy would allow energy savings in a different way. The refrigeration plant could be switched off at night, but the fans should be left running whenever the temperature is lower outdoors than indoors. The building would thus be flushed with the cool night air, and the heat stored in the fabric would be removed. This is often referred to in air-conditioning jargon as an *economy cycle* operation. Where this is employed, a heavier building mass would be an advantage, as it would allow greater energy savings.

A heavier fabric offers an advantage for any air-conditioned building even if it does not lead to energy saving. The peak load would be significantly reduced (spread over a longer period), so that a smaller plant can be installed. As this would work longer hours, there may not be an energy saving, but the capital cost would be reduced. In many instances, where the electric utility company has a two-part tariff, namely, the user has to pay a fixed charge according to peak load, such reduction of the air-conditioning peak could also reduce the electricity bills. Money saving without actual energy conservation can be achieved by other means also.

Night storage systems are quite common for domestic hot water supply. Electricity is much cheaper at night: the off-peak tariff is usually only about one-half of the normal and often less. The generating capacity is there, the whole distribution infrastructure is there, but it is hardly used at night. Electric utilities have two major expense categories: (1) servicing the capital investment and (2) actual operating, generating costs. Most have a pricing policy whereby normal, day-time sales of power would pay for all capital-related costs, as well as its generating cost, but the off-peak tariff would only pay for generating costs.

This tariff can be made use of on a much larger scale. Several large office blocks have now a large water tank, in the order of 10,000 ft^3 (300 m^3). In winter this may be heated up to (say) 200°F (95°C) overnight and it will be used for space heating the next day, when its temperature may be depleted to (say) 110°F (45°C), thus the storage temperature range is 200 − 110°F = 90°F (95 − 45°C = 50 K). The amount of heat that can be stored in this system would be

10,000 ft^3 × 62.5 lb/ft^3 × 1 Btu/lb°F × 90°F × 0.000293 kWh/Btu = 16,481 kWh

or, in SI units,

300 m^3 × 1.16 kWh/m^{3}K × 50 K = 17,400 kWh

where 1.16 kWh/m^3 K is the specific heat capacity of water. (The two results are slightly different, as the two volumes are not exactly the same.) For a 10-hour heating period this could cope with a continuous load of some 1700 kW. If the electricity is 10¢/kWh during the day and 5¢/kWh at the off-peak rate, the saving could be 17,000 × 0.05 = $850 a single day!

In the summer a refrigeration machine operated overnight could freeze the whole volume of water, which would then be used for cooling the building the next day. The latent heat of fusion of water is 93 Wh/L, and the water can be used for cooling up to about 10°C, so there is an additional sensible heat storage capacity of 11.6 Wh/L, i.e., a total of (say) 104 Wh/L, which is 104 kWh/m^3. Thus the 300 m^3 ice/water system could provide 104 × 300 = 31,200 kWh cooling. In a 10-hour operation this could cope with a continuous cooling load of 3120 kW (approx. 890 tons of refrigeration). With the same electricity prices as above, the daily saving could be 31,200 × 0.05 = $1560! Even if we allow for system inefficiencies, the money saving could be quite substantial, although no energy has actually been saved.

Envelope-load-dominated buildings (i.e., buildings with little or no internal gain, e.g., houses and other small-scale buildings) offer a much greater scope to the architect or building designer. In many climates it is possible to design buildings which are completely passively controlled. In a cold climate the given temperatures cause a heat loss, but this can be counterbalanced by solar heat gains plus any internal gain that may exist. The designer's skill lies in achieving such a balance.

In moderate climates the task is similar for the winter, but the summer performance must also be kept in mind. It often happens that a house designed for (and successful in) the winter, will be badly overheated in the summer. The most obvious problem is solar gain through the windows, which should and could easily be eliminated. On equinox day the zenith angle of the sun at noon is the same as the geographical latitude (thus the altitude angle of the sun is 90° − latitude). By midsummer the sun moves 23.5° up from this position and by midwinter 23.5° down.

Consequently a fixed shading device (a canopy, a hood, or horizontal blades) over an equator-facing window will give an automatic seasonal adjustment. If, for example, the device is set to give complete shading at the equinox dates, it will fully exclude the sun for the summer half-year, but admit an amount increasing up to mid-winter and then decreasing to the spring equinox. No other orientation would allow such an automatic control, hence the recommendation that all major windows should face the equator. Seasonally variable control on any other orientation can only be achieved by adjustable shading devices, either manually operated or motorized, perhaps even computer-controlled.

The consequences of bad design may be excessive energy use, or thermal discomfort of the occupants, or both. If a design decision is made to have a passively controlled building, which has no active heating or cooling system, it will be difficult to talk about energy conservation. The building uses no energy. If it fails, the result may be discomfort, but still no energy use.

Some authors suggest the use of a notional energy consumption value for passively controlled buildings, i.e., what the energy consumption for heating and cooling of that building would be, to keep the indoor conditions within comfort limits, if it had a heating or cooling installation.

In several states of the USA, as well as in Australia, various methods are in use to calculate and set an annual energy consumption target for different building types and locations. If the designer succeeds in keeping the energy use of the building below this target value (or indeed, produces a building which works without energy use), the difference between the target and the actual use can be taken as energy conserved.

At least in relation to such envelope-load-dominated buildings the terms *climatic design*, *passive design*, or *energy conservation* have the same meaning. The following is a summary of variables at the designer's disposal, that would have an effect on the thermal performance, hence on the energy use of the building:

(a) Shape:
  • Surface-to-volume ratio
  • Aspect ratio and orientation
(b) Fabric:
  • Shading of surfaces (e.g., parasol roof)
  • Surface qualities (absorptance, emittance)
  • Thermal insulation (reflective, resistive)
  • Thermal inertia (capacitive insulation)
  • Relative position of resistive/capacitive layers

(c) Fenestration:
- Size, disposition, orientation of windows
- Special glasses, double (triple?) glazing
- Blinds, curtains (internal or between panes)
- Shading devices (external)
- Thermal shutters

(d) Ventilation:
- Air-exchange cooling: ventilation rate
- Physiological cooling: air velocity

Both affected by orientation, fenestration, closing mechanisms, insect screens, etc.

The dynamic pattern of heat flows can to some extent be determined by the designer, through the choice of elements with the appropriate time-lag, but where adjustment facilities are provided, (opening/closing of windows and vents, adjustment of shading devices, etc.) the user's behavior may radically influence the building's thermal performance and thus its energy consumption.

Ultimately, quite unexpected social, economic, and even psychological factors may influence energy consumption. A few typical examples are given below:

- Is the user responsible for paying the energy bills, or is someone else?
- Is the user in sympathy with the building, its passive controls and adjustments, or was it forced on him/her?
- If the users are employees, are the labor relations good or are the workers and management mutually suspicious or at loggerheads?

The architect may not have much influence over such factors, but it is good to be aware of them. If for example, it is known in advance that the users cannot be relied on to make the appropriate adjustments, then the architect should avoid making the success of the building dependent on such adjustments.

REFERENCES

20.1. *ASHRAE Handbook—Fundamentals.* American Society of Heating, Refrigerating and Air-Conditioning Engineers, Atlanta, 1985.
20.2. D. A. McIntyre. *Indoor Climate.* Applied Science, London, 1980.
20.3. V. Olgyay. *Design with Climate.* Princeton University Press, Princeton, NJ, 1963.
20.4. *ASHRAE Comfort Standard 55R-74.* American Society of Heating, Refrigerating and Air-Conditioning Engineers, New York, 1974.
20.5. M. A. Humphreys. "Outdoor Temperatures and Comfort Indoors." *Building Research and Practice.* **6**(2), 92–105 (1978); also Building Research Establishment, Current Paper 53/78.
20.6. A. Auliciems. "Psycho-Physiological Criteria for Global Thermal Zones of Building Design." *International Journal of Biometeorology,* **26**(Suppl. 2) 60–86 (1983).
20.7. C. O. Mackey and L. T. Wright. "Periodic Heat Flow—Homogeneous Walls or Roofs." *Heating, Piping and Air Conditioning,* **16**, 546–554 (1944).
20.8. E. Danter. "Periodic Heat Flow Characteristics of Simple Walls and Roofs." *Journal of the Institution of Heating and Ventilating Engineers,* **28**, 136–147 (1960).

DESIGN HANDBOOKS

ASHRAE HANDBOOK, published by the American Society of Heating, Refrigerating and Air-Conditioning Engineers, Atlanta in several parts, usually at four-year intervals:
Fundamentals
Systems and Applications
Equipment

CIBSE Guide, published by the Chartered Institution of Building Services Engineers, London, in several booklets, which are revised from time to time. Those most relevant to the thermal design of buildings are:
A1 *Environmental Criteria for Design*
A3 *Thermal Properties of Building Structures*
A5 *Thermal Response of Buildings*
A9 *Estimation of Plant Capacity*
B1 *Heating*
B2 *Air Conditioning Requirements*
B3 *Air Conditioning Systems and Equipment*
The CIBSE Guide was formerly known as the *IHVE Guide*.

SUGGESTIONS FOR FURTHER READING

H. J. Cowan and P. R. Smith. *Environmental Systems.* Van Nostrand Reinhold, New York, 1983.
B. Givoni. *Man, Climate and Architecture*, 2nd Ed. Van Nostrand Reinhold, New York, 1981.
J. R. Kell and P. L. Martin. *Faber and Kell's Heating and Air Conditioning of Buildings*, 6th Ed. Architectural Press, London, 1984.
K.-I. Kimura. *The Scientific Basis of Air Conditioning.* Applied Science, London, 1977.
T. A. Markus and E. N. Morris. *Buildings, Climate, and Energy.* Pitman, London, 1980.
S. V. Szokolay. *Environmental Science Handbook*, Construction Press, London, 1980.
J. Threlkeld. *Thermal Environmental Engineering.* Prentice Hall, Englewood Cliffs, NJ, 1970.

NOTATION

A	area	ft²	m²
AH	absolute humidity	gr/lb	g/kg
DBT	dry-bulb temperature	°F	°C
FR	response factor	—	—
G	global irradiance	Btu/ft² h	W/m²
H	heat content, enthalpy	Btu/lb	kJ/kg
H_L	latent heat content		
H_S	sensible heat content		
HR	humidity ratio		
MRT	mean radiant temperature	°F	°C
N	number of air changes per hour	—	—
Q	heat flow rate, heat flux	Btu/h	W
Q_c	conduction heat flow rate		
Q_{cv}	convection heat flow rate		
Q_i	internal (incidental) heat gain rate		
Q_m	mechanical heat input/removal rate		
Q_s	solar heat gain rate		
Q_v	ventilation heat flow rate		
R	thermal resistance	ft² h °F/Btu	m² K/W
R_{si}	inside surface resistance		
R_{so}	outside surface resistance		
RH	relative humidity	percent	percent
SH	saturation point, absolute humidity	gr/lb	g/kg

SET	standard effective temperature	°F	°C
T	temperature	°F	°C
T_i	indoor temperature		
T_n	neutrality temperature		
T_o	outdoor temperature		
T_s	sol-air temperature		
ΔT	temperature interval or difference	°F	K
dT_e	sol-air excess temperature	°F	K
U	air to air thermal transmittance	Btu/ft² h °F	W/m² K
V	volume (eg. of a room)	ft³	m³
WBT	wet-bulb temperature	°F	°C
Y	admittance	Btu/ft² h °F	W/m² K
b	breadth, thickness	in. (ft)	m
c_p	specific heat capacity	Btu/lb °F	J/kg K
f	decrement factor	—	—
h	heat transfer coefficient	Btu/ft² h °F	W/m² K
h_c	convection coefficient		
h_i	($=f_i$) inside surface (film) coeff.		
h_o	($=f_o$) outside surface (film) coeff.		
h_r	radiation coefficient		
k	conductivity ($=\lambda$)	Btu in./ft² h °F	W/m K
$\dot{m}$	mass flow rate	lb/min	kg/s
p_v	vapor pressure	lb/in.² (psi)	Pa (kPa)
p_{vs}	saturation vapor pressure		
q	specific heat loss (flow) rate	Btu/h °F	W/K
q_a	total admittance		
q_c	specific conduction heat flow rate		
q_v	specific ventilation heat flow rate		
r	resistivity	ft² h °F/Btu in.	m K/W
t	time	hour	hour
v	velocity	ft/min (fpm)	m/s
vr	volume flow (ventilation) rate	ft³/min (CFM)	m³/s (L/s)
α (alpha)	absorptance	—	—
ϵ (epsilon)	emittance	—	—
λ (lambda)	conductivity ($=k$)	Btu in./ft² h °F	W/m K
ρ (rho)	reflectance	—	—
τ (tau)	transmittance	—	—
ϕ (phi)	time lag	hour	hour

A list of abbreviations of the units of measurement, definitions of these units, and conversion factors between British/American and metric units are given in the Appendix.

21

Passive Solar Energy-Efficient Building Design

John A. Ballinger

The basic principles of the passive solar design of buildings has been known since the earliest times. The linking of this knowledge to scientific fact was not fully realized until the research work that followed the Second World War.

This chapter reviews the basic principles in the light of modern experience and provides guidelines to assist the designer and give direction to other more detailed text. Design techniques based on simple trouble free approach are the basis of this chapter, rather than the unusual and less well proven techniques. The three most commonly used passive solar heating techniques (direct gain, thermal storage walls, and sunspaces) are described with guidelines for their application.

21.1. INTRODUCTION

Passive solar architecture can be described as the utilization of the sun's energy together with the characteristics of a local climate to directly maintain thermally comfortable conditions in our buildings while minimizing energy consumption. Unlike many of the building technologies, good passive solar architecture is as much a matter of the art of design as it is of a knowledge of the technology. As with most architectural design matters, one cannot work without the other.

Today there is a considerable wealth of knowledge about the design of such buildings and many thousands of built examples, both modern and ancient; the writings of Watson (Ref. 21.1) and Shurcliff (Ref. 21.2) are typical of those written in the mid-seventies. Such publications give the reader a general overview of the variety of solutions that are possible. Some of these were designed that way intentionally, while others were purely accidental. The latter are rarely identified in the literature. On the whole unfortunately, the modern designer or builder has lost touch with the local environment and so designs in spite of the climate, and in spite of the sun in particular!

Even today, in spite of the great wealth of knowledge about solar design, much of the detailed thermal performance and interactions of our buildings are still not clearly understood. The research work being undertaken in many countries today involves continuing investigation, analysis and definition of the many complex thermal processes that take place in a building structure. There is still much to be done and many myths to be debunked. Thermal comfort standards accepted in the past for conditioned buildings have been found to be inappropriate for passive solar buildings. Research being undertaken today by scientists such as Winett et al. (Ref. 21.3) and Williamson and Coldicutt (Ref. 21.4) is reevaluating these measures and attempting to better match both the physical and psychological needs of the occupant to the design of the building. In spite of all this however there is sufficient knowledge to enable the designer to produce buildings far better thermally than the majority of those being built today.

There are two basic approaches to the utilization of solar energy in buildings—*active systems* and *passive systems*. Active systems, described in Chapter 22, are generally those that are very visible with collectors on roofs, pumps, plumbing, control systems, and storage tanks. Passive systems on the other hand are defined as those where the heat moves by natural means. A passive solar energy system is one which uses the materials of the building fabric as the collector, storage and energy transfer system with a minimum amount of mechanical equipment (low-powered fans for air movement are considered acceptable in a full passive system). This definition fits most of the simpler systems where heat is stored in the basic structure (walls, ceiling, or floor). There are also systems that have the heat storage as a permanent element within the building structure, such as nonstructural masonry, or water-filled drums or bottles. These are also classified as passive solar energy systems.

By way of analogy, let us consider a passive solar building as being a large combined solar collector/storage unit. The important parts of that unit are as follows:

(a) Glazed apertures exposed to the sun's path in winter but not in summer. The windows, if facing in the general direction of the equator, will do this job admirably.

(b) A means of collecting and storing the sun's energy which enters in winter—concrete or masonry floors with a heat conductive finish, masonry walls, water containers, or the like located in the sun's path. All of these work well to soak up the sun's heat and release it again when it gets cold.

(c) An insulated outer skin (outside walls, roof and floors as appropriate) to restrict the flow of that energy back to the cold exterior in winter and in from the outside in summer when it is so hot.

To plan a building using passive solar energy design principles one must first consider the aspects discussed in this chapter. The ideas that follow can be used in many building types besides residential. They can be applied to small workshops or factories, low-rise office buildings of only a few stories, schools, and community buildings—in fact, to any low-rise building situation. Some ideas will apply to very large buildings too. Not all the ideas included here are cost effective in the short term; however, often they are worthwhile because they make the building more comfortable for relatively little money. You will need to investigate each and then perhaps check them over with a quantity surveyor or building estimator.

21.2 HISTORICAL PERSPECTIVE

The basic principles of passive solar architecture have been well known throughout history; however, from time to time there have been a number of "dark ages" in the field of architecture and building when it seems that the knowledge is either lost or discarded. In terms of passive solar design, the last ten years have comprised an age of reenlightenment.

In looking back through history we find that the ancient Greeks venerated the sun and so the development of solar architecture encountered few cultural impediments. It was their commonly held belief that exposure to the sun nurtured good health. This knowledge and design understanding was lost in later periods of history, only to be rediscovered in the late 19th Century following the ills of the Industrial Revolution slums. According to Socrates, the ideal house could be designed to be cool in summer and warm in winter. That was 2500 years ago! Oribasius, an ancient medical authority, wrote that south-facing (facing toward the equator) areas were healthy places because of their exposure to the sun. He noted that north-facing areas were the least healthy, because they "do not receive much sun and when they do, the light falls obliquely without much vitality." Their solar architecture was based on a knowledge of the movement of the sun throughout the day and throughout the year. Butti and Perlin (Ref. 21.5) have researched and presented this aspect of our history from ancient times until the post–World War II period in a most interesting manner.

The activity in the promotion of solar housing prior to the Second World War was based on mainly local experience, with little formal scientific research. Designs were simple and tended to encourage extensive south-facing glass, double glazed in the colder climates. In the period following the Second World War there was a worldwide industrial expansion which resulted in abundant supplies of cheap energy. Also during that time experimental building stations were formed in many countries and scientists such as Van Straaten (Ref. 21.6) in South Africa, Givoni (Ref. 21.7) (the author of Chapter 18) in Israel and the USA, and J. W. Drysdale (Ref. 21.8) and R. O. Phillips (Ref. 21.9) in Australia began work on the long task of quantifying many of these ideas. There were of course many others in research establishments throughout the world undertaking similar work.

Most of this early work occurred at a time when energy was cheap and building materials expensive and scarce. It was so cheap then, that it became the norm to build a flimsy uninsulated enclosure and install a suitably sized (or oversized) machine to modify the indoor climate. Very few buildings were built appropriately for the climate. Hence the glass-box office building which we still build, and the unfortunately large picture window of the "American Dream Home." During that period from the late forties to the early seventies, energy costs were either considered to be insignificant or simply taken for granted.

Although the cost of energy in the developed countries is increasing, it is still relatively cheap. The oil supply scare of the 1970s has turned temporarily into an oil supply glut, resulting in relatively low world prices (Ref. 21.10). Even though the cost of energy has risen little in the developed countries relative to wages and cost of living, we are beginning to realize slowly that saving energy can mean significant monetary savings without sacrificing comfort levels, if the problem is tackled in a sensible manner. In most applications the passive use of solar energy in buildings is both cost efficient and energy conserving. There are much more appropriate uses for our high-grade energy sources of oil, gas, and electricity than low-grade heat situations such as hot water and space heating. Such energy sources should be reserved for those more appropriate uses such as transport, lighting, or chemical production, especially when solar energy can do the job or at least a substantial part of it.

21.3. SITE PLANNING AND ORIENTATION

If we are to make use of the sun's heat, then we must make sure it reaches our buildings when useful. Generally, the sun should be able to reach the collection area between 9 am and 3 pm in winter with as little obstruction and interference as possible. Trees on the site or the neighbor's site, or perhaps those you plan to put in, might shade the vital areas of the building. This needs to be checked and the building located to minimize any such interference. The shading effect of trees can be evaluated using techniques such as those by Sattler et al. (Ref. 21.11) which have been developed for use on personal computers.

In summer, there are often cool breezes which if directed through your building will help cool it. Likewise in winter, the cold winds should be deflected away from your building. With simple local information about your site, you can plan to optimize winter sun and summer breezes and block winter wind by careful placement of obstructions such as trees, fences, hedges, or garage. If your client has not yet bought a site, then look for one with the right aspect. Most important: remember to let the sun in from the south (the side facing the equator). Local weather bureau information will provide information for your area; however, check the site-specific wind patterns because other buildings, hills, or trees might deflect those breezes to another direction. Climate data are discussed in detail in Chapter 20, and their use is explained in this context.

Primitive man lived with his environment, without disruption or major change. He chose his shelter carefully and with knowledge of the climate. Today we have the power to move mountains; however, before we rush in and change everything, first we should select our site with care and with consideration for the intended use. Existing topography and obstructions will have a bearing on the siting of buildings for solar access, and so if considered early the designers task is much easier.

To obtain best use of the sun's energy, the designer must be aware of the pattern of the sun's movement as well as the specific considerations for building and site design. Detailed information on the position of the sun in any location is available in a wide range of literature; see, e.g., Refs. 21.9, 21.12, and 21.13. In reading the data, be aware that the altitude of the sun is the angle the sun makes with the horizon, while the azimuth of the sun is the angle in plan between true south/north and the direction of the sun.

Passive Solar Design

In the mid- to high latitudes the sun's path across the southern sky (in the northern hemisphere) is low in winter and high in summer, and so it is not difficult in most cases to design your building to:

- In winter, allow the sun to enter and warm the building and warm outdoor living areas
- In summer, prevent the sun from striking walls and roof or from penetrating to the inside

Windows facing toward the equator receive sunshine for most of the day in winter, and the desired period for access to the sun's rays in 9 AM to 3 PM because usually the heating value of the winter sun outside these hours is too low to consider worthwhile, although the psychological benefits may still make it attractive. The sun's energy reaching the earth's surface in summer is capable of providing overheating discomfort for a much longer period each day. Unwanted summer sunshine can be easily blocked on this side by an overhang, pergola, or other horizontal shading device, as discussed in Chapter 18.

Windows facing toward the east or west receive very little useful sun in the mornings and evenings during winter. However, in summer they receive a lot of the sun's energy, and because the sun is low in the sky it is difficult to screen it out with conventional shading devices. North-facing windows (facing away from the equator) receive no radiation in winter and very little in summer. The low evening sun in summer may cause problems, however, in the lower latitudes. From a design point of view, the most trouble-free orientation for windows is therefore in a southerly direction, with some northern windows for cross ventilation. All windows not facing toward the equator should be designed to minimize heat loss in cold climates as discussed in Chapter 20 and designed to minimize sun penetration in the summer months as described in Chapter 18.

Shading must be designed to achieve its purpose with a minimum of manual adjustment. The introduction of motorized devices should be considered carefully, weighing effectiveness against the additional cost and the problems of reliability. Experience has shown that design solutions that involve complex detail and externally mounted moving components are prone to excessive maintenance and periodic failure; the best solution is fixed shading devices, designed to suit the sun's movement. Harkness and Mehta (Ref. 21.14) have developed techniques for the design of such shading.

For efficient passive solar design, the main windows to rooms requiring heat should face in the general direction of the equator. Some flexibility of orientation is acceptable; however, it has been found that the optimum orientation is within 20 degrees either side of south (in the northern hemisphere). A building oriented outside this range loses the benefits of winter sun and gains the disadvantages of the summer sun. This is clearly demonstrated in Table 21.1, showing mean daily solar radiation incident on vertical surfaces in various directions for Latitude 34° south (Sydney, Australia). Similar patterns will be found in data for other

Table 21.1. Mean Daily Solar Radiation on Vertical Surfaces of Various Orientations.

Vertical Surface Oriented	Azimuth, Degrees	Jan	Feb	Mar	Apr	May	Jun	Jul	Aug	Sep	Oct	Nov	Dec	Avg.
S	180.0	8.1	6.4	5.2	4.0	3.0	2.5	2.8	3.8	5.2	6.5	8.3	9.2	5.4
SSE	157.5	8.7	7.2	5.5	4.1	3.0	2.5	2.8	3.8	5.4	7.2	9.1	10.0	5.8
SE	135.0	10.2	8.6	6.4	4.8	3.2	2.7	3.1	4.5	6.6	8.7	10.6	11.5	6.7
ESE	112.5	11.3	9.8	7.6	6.1	4.3	3.6	4.5	6.2	8.2	10.1	11.8	12.5	8.0
E	90.0	11.8	10.6	8.8	7.8	6.0	5.3	6.7	8.1	9.8	11.2	12.4	12.9	9.3
ENE	67.5	11.5	10.8	9.6	9.3	8.0	7.1	9.1	9.8	11.1	11.6	12.4	12.5	10.2
NE	45.0	10.7	10.4	10.0	10.6	10.0	9.0	11.4	11.2	11.9	11.4	11.6	11.4	10.8
NNE	22.5	9.3	9.6	10.2	11.7	12.0	10.7	13.5	12.2	12.3	10.8	10.4	9.9	11.1
N	0.0	8.5	9.0	10.5	12.6	13.3	11.4	14.3	12.6	12.6	10.1	9.5	9.2	11.2
NNW	−22.5	9.7	9.9	11.0	12.3	13.1	10.8	13.4	11.7	12.4	10.4	10.5	10.2	11.3
NW	−45.0	11.6	10.9	11.2	11.4	11.5	9.0	11.3	10.3	12.1	12.0	11.0	12.0	11.2
WNW	−67.5	12.8	11.4	10.9	10.2	9.5	7.1	8.9	8.9	11.4	11.1	13.0	13.3	10.7
W	−90.0	13.2	11.3	10.1	8.6	7.3	5.3	6.6	7.4	10.2	10.7	13.1	13.8	9.8
WSW	−112.5	12.7	10.5	8.7	6.8	5.2	3.8	4.6	5.8	8.6	9.7	12.5	13.4	8.5
SW	−135.0	11.4	9.0	7.1	5.1	3.6	2.7	3.2	4.5	6.9	8.5	11.1	12.1	7.1
SSW	−157.5	9.4	7.4	5.7	4.1	3.0	2.5	2.8	3.8	5.6	7.2	9.4	10.3	5.9
S	−180.0	8.1	6.4	5.2	4.0	3.0	2.5	2.8	3.8	5.2	6.5	8.3	9.2	5.4

Climate data for Sydney region, −34° Latitude. Average for years 1972–1976 computed from measured hourly global insolation on a horizontal surface, using a method by Bugler (Vitek, A.—University of New South Wales).
Source: Bugler, *Solar Energy*, **19**, 477, (1977).
[a] 1 MJ/m^2 day = 88 Btu/ft^2 day

locations (Ref. 21.12). Notice how the solar radiation received on a vertical surface facing NE or NW is almost the same year round (SE and SW in the northern hemisphere). The importance of orientation is self-evident!

If there is a preference, then common folklore in Australia suggests about 10 degrees east of north (in the northern hemisphere it should be east of south) is best to let some sun in for an early warmup in winter. This is also supported by authors such as Robinette and others (Ref. 21.16, pp. 192). Because orientation toward the equator is essential to passive solar design, it is important to choose a house block that allows such orientation of the windows to living areas within the house. Trees or buildings could block access to sunlight, and this needs to be checked when siting dwellings. The work of Sattler et al. (Ref. 21.11) and also Knowles (Ref. 21.15) will be helpful.

The orientation of a building is determined usually by the position of the windows and the proportion of the plan. Excluding the internal spaces at this point we aim to locate most glass on the equator-facing facade and design so that the north-south facades are larger than the east-west facades. In cold climates this proportion is important in terms of minimizing the exposed surface area and thus minimizing heat loss (this is discussed in greater detail in Section 21.14, Thermal Insulation). In the temperate and the hot-humid climates, however, it may be more important to consider shape in terms of design for the needs of natural ventilation. See also Chapter 18.

The relationship between a typical heating load profile and solar radiation incident on surfaces of different orientation is illustrated in Fig. 21.3.1 using data recorded in Sydney, Australia (Latitude 34° south). A diagram such as this is admittedly simplistic but it shows the effect of building shape and orientation very clearly. The elevation facing the equator (facing North in the Southern Hemisphere) is the only one that is able to combat the heating load without creating enormous penalties in the summer. In temperate climates, where winters are mild and summers hot, the orientation of some windows to the east and the west can be quite satisfactory provided there is adequate shading against the sun early or late in the day. In the more severe winter climates these windows tend to present a significant source of heat loss without any significant solar heat gain (unless the glazing system is multi-paned with sophisticated low-emittance glasses).

The way in which we plan our buildings affects the overall thermal efficiency. The greater the exposed external surface the greater the potential heat loss. A medium-density housing unit, for example, with other dwellings attached on each side, is subject to smaller heat losses per living unit than a single detached cottage, and likewise high-density multistory housing is subject to even smaller heat losses. In residential buildings this can be advantageous, provided the individual units have a reasonable access to sun during the day.

In high-density commercial buildings this compactness

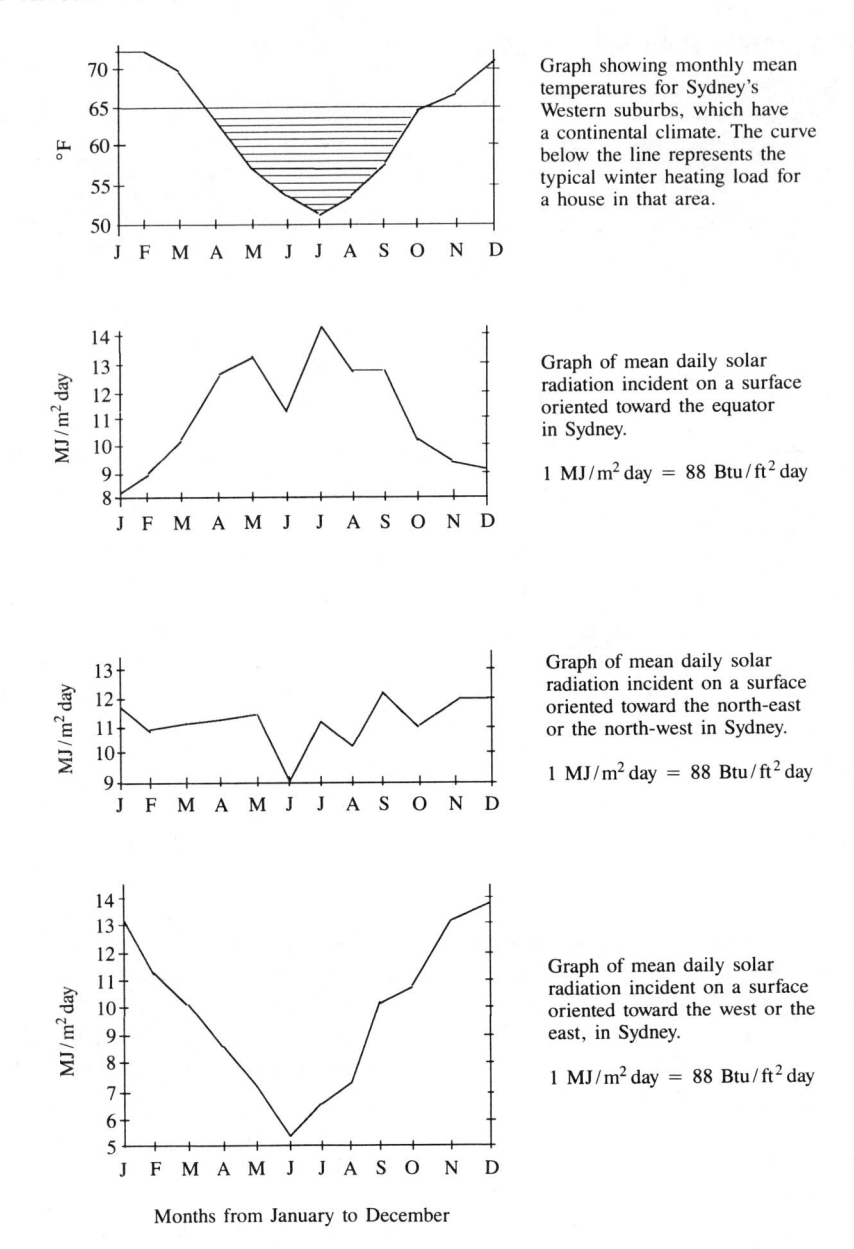

Fig. 21.3.1. Graph showing variation of solar radiation on vertical surfaces of different orientation.

Graph showing monthly mean temperatures for Sydney's Western suburbs, which have a continental climate. The curve below the line represents the typical winter heating load for a house in that area.

Graph of mean daily solar radiation incident on a surface oriented toward the equator in Sydney.

1 MJ/m² day = 88 Btu/ft² day

Graph of mean daily solar radiation incident on a surface oriented toward the north-east or the north-west in Sydney.

1 MJ/m² day = 88 Btu/ft² day

Graph of mean daily solar radiation incident on a surface oriented toward the west or the east, in Sydney.

1 MJ/m² day = 88 Btu/ft² day

Months from January to December

is usually a disadvantage, because it results in a year-round cooling load due to internally generated heat. The design of such buildings usually makes air conditioning mandatory if only to dissipate the trapped heat.

The solar gains in winter can be enhanced by the orientation and grouping of the various units. In developing these arrangements, it should be remembered that the sun is low in winter and high in summer. The exposure of a roof to solar radiation is therefore high in summer and light-colored surfaces will reflect much of that radiation (refer also to Chapter 18). All roofs should be well insulated, of course, to minimize heat losses, as discussed later.

Solar Access

What is Solar Access? Solar access has been described by Knowles (Ref. 21.15) as "allowing the sun to penetrate a building or be utilized by a solar collector on the surface of that building between 9 AM and 3 PM in mid-winter." There are varying degrees of solar access. There is *whole-site access*, where the area of yard to the south of the building, as well as the south wall and rooftop, are protected from shading by other buildings and vegetation in midwinter. *South-wall access* refers to the protection from shadows in midwinter of only the south facade, which includes the south roof and south wall.

Although whole-site access is desirable for outdoor garden use, it can be very costly in terms of the use of land and may not affect household energy use. Energy efficiency encompasses more than just energy savings in houses, and so the decreased density that results from whole-site access may not be justified. There is a third level of solar access, *rooftop access*, which aims to protect just the rooftop solar collector systems from shading at certain times. Although this level of solar access allows maximum density to be achieved, it forecloses too many options for future development. The definition of solar access depends on the definition of the solar collector (whether passive or active).

Protecting Solar Access. Two documented ways of protecting solar access are *solar envelopes* and *shadow masks*; the latter can be used in conjunction with a solar access butterfly (described later).

Solar Envelopes. The solar envelope concept has been studied extensively by Knowles at the University of Southern California and is defined as "the largest volumetric container over a land parcel that allows solar access to all adjacent neighbors within useful time constraints" (Ref. 21.15). A solar envelope defines the limiting volume for development of a site to provide nominated levels of solar access to adjacent sites, as shown below. The aim of the envelope is to protect solar access for the future.

Knowles's envelope is designed for whole-site solar access, which involves increased allotment size and therefore decreased density, which has development cost implications. All solar access protection techniques require some tradeoff between density and solar access. The Knowles envelope is generated using the altitude angles of the sun, at nominated times, to establish imaginary planes sloping inwards from their base on the boundaries of the site, as illustrated below. Differing levels of solar access can be achieved by raising or lowering the height from which sloping planes are generated (the *base plan height*).

Shadow Masks and the Solar Access Butterfly. The solar envelope is a form established in space and as such is difficult to visualize and to use in large-scale planning. The solar envelope is appropriate in existing built-up situations.

In order to consider topography and house orientation simultaneously, shadow masks and the access butterfly can be used.

The *shadow mask* principle takes into account factors such as gradient and orientation of slope and building orientation more easily than the solar envelope principle, while the *solar access butterfly* is a method which enables vegetation to be located to the south of a house without shading the equator-facing wall in winter.

Using the shadow mask and butterfly principles, large housing estates can be designed in plan to ensure solar access to each dwelling. The shadow mask is established for each dwelling for the position in which it is to be located. The composite mask that is formed is that of the shadow cast by a given building with a given orientation on a known slope and slope orientation. The shadow is a composite of the shadows cast at 9 AM, 12 noon, and 3 PM at the winter solstice (22nd December). It is during this time period that overshadowing of the north wall is unfavorable. If no overshadowing occurs at this time of the year, then active systems, such as rooftop hot water heaters, would not be shaded at any time of the year.

The composite shadow mask can be established by presenting the building, tree, or other object as a series of poles, finding the shadow length and direction cast by those poles, and connecting the pole shadows into a composite shadow mask.

Computer-based shadow-casting programs have been prepared by a number of different researchers, such as the computer module SOLPRO from the University of Sheffield (Ref. 21.17). Another program for the plotting of shadows cast by trees has been published by Sattler et al. in the journal *Solar Energy* (Ref. 21.11). Manual techniques to develop shadow masks for buildings of given dimensions are discussed by Robinette and others (Ref. 21.16) and Knowles (Ref. 21.15). The shadow masks show the maximum shadow that a building will cast and the limits of this shadow determine how close buildings may be placed together on any given slope.

The solar access butterfly shown in Fig. 21.3.2 can be used once the buildings have been located to determine where vegetation or other structures may be placed north of the house where shading may or may not be desirable. For example, shading of the north wall (but not the rooftop hot-water collector) may be desirable in summer. Therefore deciduous trees may be placed at appropriate distances from the north wall according to their height. Similarly, evergreen trees must be placed to prevent shading in winter. This is the reverse of the shadow mask principle, as it specifies zones where obstructions may not be higher than a nominated height for that distance from the south wall. The shadow mask and butterfly may overlap.

The solar access butterfly saves having to draw a shadow mask for each tree or other object located to the south of the building. The butterfly is made up of a series of height restriction lines at specified distances from the south wall of the building, depending on topography. For example, no object 10 feet (3 m) high can be placed closer to the south wall than the 10-foot (3 m) height line (unless it is a deciduous tree). The east and west extremities of the butterfly fall along the 9 AM and 3 PM winter solar azimuth angles drawn from the south facade of the building.

Site Planning for Solar Access. Protecting the solar access of houses has some important implications for overall site design. In order to achieve appropriate orientation of an energy-efficient house design, the design needs to relate to the block on which it is to be sited. Broadly speaking, there are four types of house lots which require different house design types.

A dwelling with its entry on the southern side and the living areas and major bedrooms facing the street is shown in Fig. 21.3.3. The south-facing outdoor space in such a dwelling will need to be screened from the street for privacy. In the case of a dwelling with the street on the northern side, where living areas and major bedrooms of an energy-efficient house could face the rear private yard, as in Fig. 21.3.4, then the southerly-facing yard is screened from street by house. In such a case the service areas (kitchen,

372 HANDBOOK OF ARCHITECTURAL TECHNOLOGY

Trees and buildings outside the butterfly can be as tall as desired, provided they do not shade the north facade of neighboring houses.

When a house is tilted off north (up to 20°), the butterfly is still drawn by using the 45° angles from north.

Plan of Solar Access Butterfly

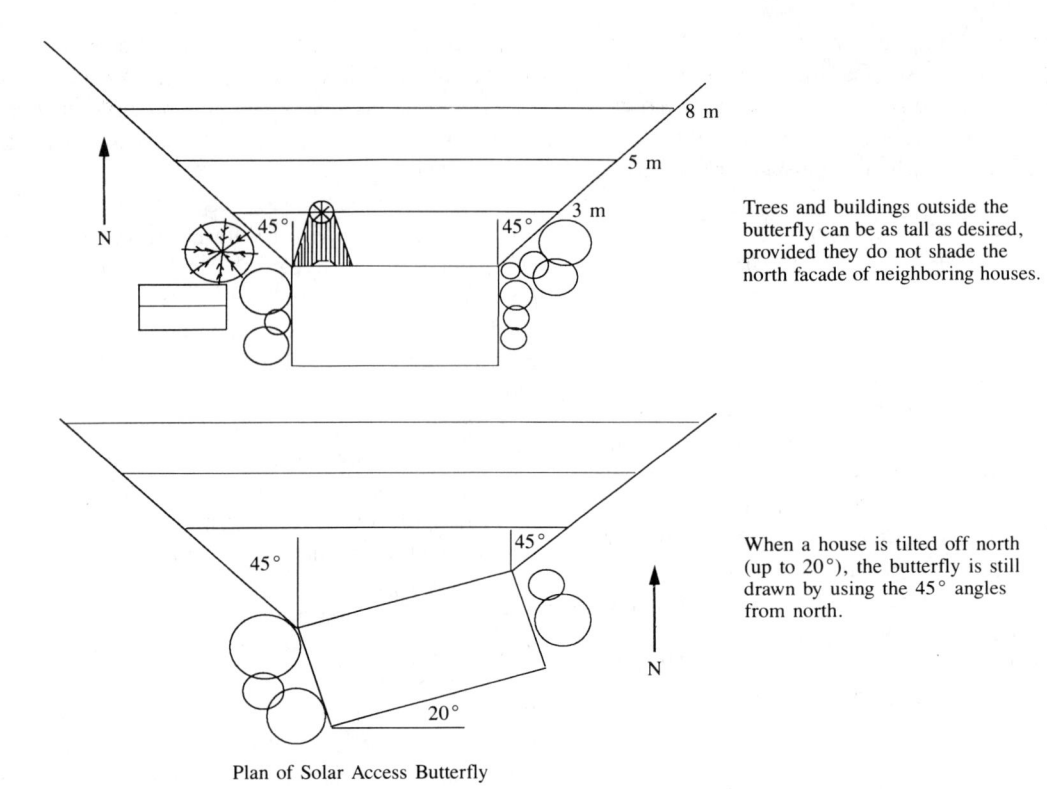

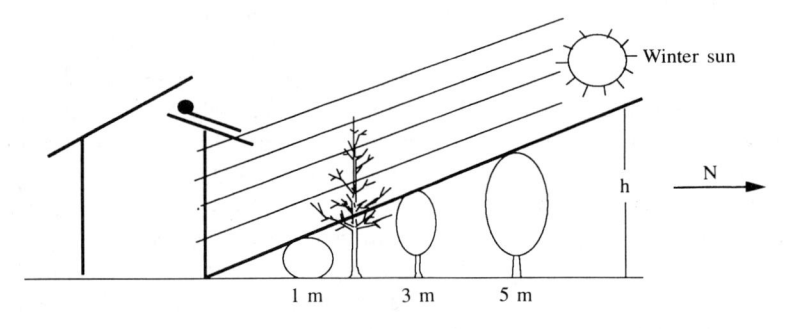

Solar Access Butterfly—Section

Fig. 21.3.2. Solar access butterfly.

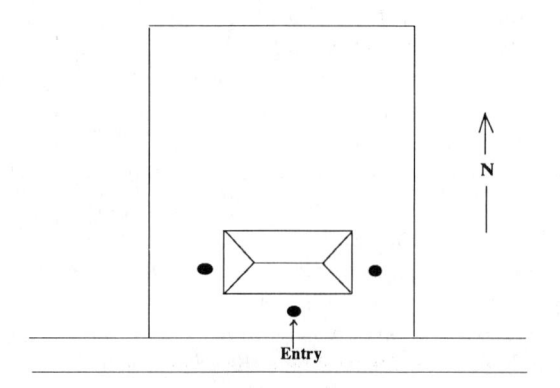

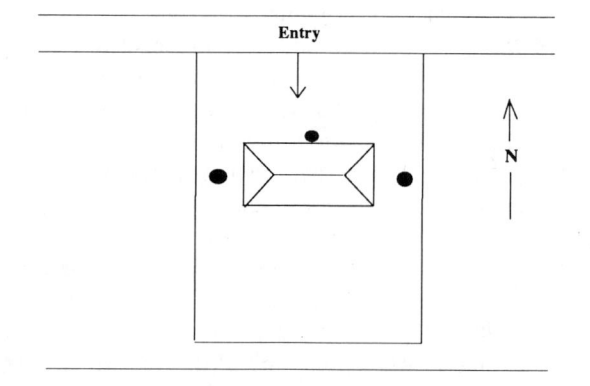

Fig. 21.3.3. South side entry.

Fig. 21.3.4. North side entry.

bathrooms) may have to face the street. The living area can be extended to street for public entry and presentation. This site is perhaps the easiest to work with in today's Western-style housing trends. In Fig. 21.3.5 the entry side of the dwelling faces in an easterly or westerly direction and the side of house faces the street, the south-facing outdoor space will need to be screened from the side facing the street. This arrangement also allows the designer to create a sense of entry private from the family areas of the house. Such lots may need to be wider to prevent shading from neighboring buildings to the south (this will depend on ground slope). In the case of lots where the road runs northeast or northwest a satisfactory design will be more difficult and so solutions will need to be considered individually.

Building Height and Setbacks. In most situations, existing setback regulations can be adapted to meet the solar access criteria. A standard setback from the street (building line) is the easiest means of protecting solar access, provided slope is constant. This, however, creates a monotonous streetscape and does not allow houses to be sited on the lot according to how outdoor spaces are to be used.

Landscaping

Trees, shrubs and other plants can have a beneficial effect on the microclimate as well as on the energy requirements of a house. Trees can block unfavorable winter winds and hence reduce heat loss, or they can funnel cooling summer breezes and hence reduce the cooling energy load. They can also provide shade to block unwanted summer solar radiation and improve the microclimate surrounding the building.

Deciduous trees and vines can be used to allow winter sun penetration and block summer sun. Methods of landscaping for energy efficiency are detailed by Robinette (Ref. 21.16), Olgyay (Ref. 21.18), and Moffat and Schiller (Ref. 21.19).

21.4. THERMAL INSULATION MATERIALS AND THEIR APPLICATION

Thermal insulation materials generally available for building purposes can be classified into two generic groups: bulk materials and reflective foil laminates (RFL). The first of these rely on the resistance of air trapped in pockets between the fibers of the blanket-type materials (mineral fiber materials) or the cells formed in the foamed structure of board or slab-type materials (usually made from plastics such as polystyrene and polyurethane foams). The second reflects radiant energy away from the object or surface being protected. The basic principles of heat transfer by radiation and conduction have been covered in Chapter 20 along with the principles of operation of such materials.

Thermal insulation in the outer fabric of a building is a vital component of an energy-efficient design strategy. The key to successful energy-efficient design is the control of heat flow through the external fabric. All the solar energy gained could be easily lost from an inadequately insulated building before it is able to be of benefit.

Roof Insulation. The major heat path in both cold and hot weather is through the roof. Generally the roof is the largest single exposed surface and is usually built of relatively lightweight materials. The basic insulation of roofs should be resistive material to minimize heat loss in the cold weather with the addition of a layer of reflective insulation under the roof cladding where summers are warm enough to cause overheating inside the building (most localities except those with cool summers). In predominantly warm-hot climates where no winter heating is required, the use of reflective insulation only may be appropriate. Reflective insulation has a greater resistance to heat flow down (summer) than to heat flow up (winter) because it resists radiant energy flow better than conductive flow (refer to Chapter 20). The use of resistive insulation will reduce the conductive losses available from any night-sky cooling effect or air cooling of the roof surface, which is undesirable in the warmer climates.

The air space below the reflective insulation in the attic space of a pitched roof need not be ventilated for summer where resistive insulation is included on top of the ceiling. The temperature of a ventilated roof space may be maintained at close to the outside air temperature and although this may be beneficial in summer to reduce heat buildup in the roof space, in cold weather it tends to negate any insulating contribution provided by the roof cladding and the associated reflective insulation. The difference in heat flow through a well insulated vented roof and a well insulated nonvented roof into the occupied space below is very small. The U-value of a pitched roof with only reflective insulation under the roof cladding is in the order of 6 Btu/ft^2 h °F (1.06 W/m^2 °C) for heat flow in an upward direction and 3.6 Btu/ft^2 h °F (0.64 W/m^2 °C) for heat flow in a downward direction (refer also to Chapter 20).

Wall Insulation. The insulating of framed external walls is generally not difficult because the outer cladding material is usually designed to be a barrier to moisture. In such construction it is important, however, to insure that a vapor barrier is installed on the warm side of the insulation layer,

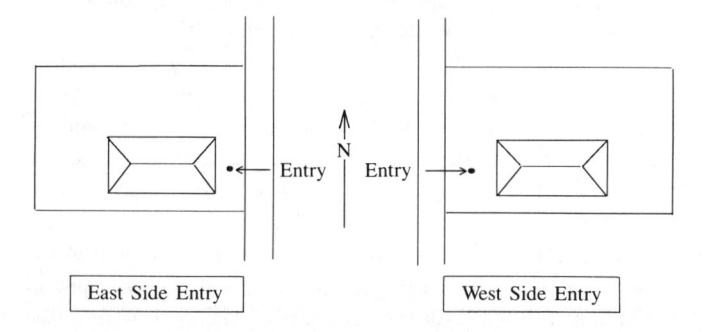

Fig. 21.3.5. East or west side entry.

as discussed in Chapter 20 (in cold climates this will be near the inside lining).

Heat bridges in frame construction can be a problem in cold climates and also extreme hot climates, especially where the framework is of metal. In such circumstances it is advisable to use an outer layer insulation that covers and thermally isolates the framework from the external cladding material. The issues concerning the insulation of double-skin cavity masonry walls and the transfer of moisture from one leaf to the other are discussed fully in Chapter 20.

Insulation of Framed Floors over Ventilated Crawl Spaces. In cold climates it is advisable to insulate the underside of framed lightweight floors. Generally the air space under such floors is ventilated to minimize problems caused by dampness. In winter months this results in such spaces being at temperatures close to ambient, thence the need to insulate to reduce heat losses down through the floor.

Insulation of Floor Slabs on Ground. In passive solar building design it should not be necessary to fully insulate between a concrete slab and the ground, except in extremely cold climates where in-floor central heating is being installed. The disadvantage of insulating the whole area under the floor slab is that the house is isolated from the ground, which in winter is warmer and in summer is cooler than the external air conditions. The free heat storage benefits of the ground under the building is lost if full insulation is used. Heat flow through floors is covered extensively in the BRE Digest No. 145 (Ref. 21.20).

A considerable amount of the heat lost through a concrete slab floor flows out through the edges of the slab because it is in much closer contact with the cold outside air, and so an alternative is to insulate the edge and the perimeter strip of the floor approximately 2 feet wide (600 mm). Such measures are not necessary in warmer climates such as the southeastern states of the USA, the temperate areas of southern Europe and much of the coastal part of Australia.

Perimeter floor slab insulation is recommended in areas of 3600 heating degree days to base 65°F (2000 degree days to base 18.3°C, SI units) or greater (refer Chapter 20 for a description of heating degree days), such insulation will help to reduce the loss of heat stored in the floor slab. Detailed information on the thickness and extent of underfloor insulation is given in ASHRAE Standard 90-75. When choosing to insulate floor slabs, consideration must be given to ground water heat losses and the problems of frost heave. Insulation can be used to minimize these effects.

The minimum insulation levels desirable in roofs, walls and floors will be determined by building codes and regulations in most countries (except Australia). Optimum levels on the other hand will be higher and will depend on the installed cost of the products being considered, the local cost of energy for space heating or cooling and the accepted discount rate for finance in the particular state or country.

Thermal insulation to restrict heat flow into and out of buildings has been well demonstrated to be economically worthwhile. In most situations the optimum levels of insulation will repay their capital outlay in energy savings over a short time. The improvement in thermal comfort compared to an uninsulated dwelling is quite significant, although it can be difficult to evaluate in economic terms when the users are accustomed to lower than average comfort standards. This is often the case in the most temperate climates where it is possible to manage with lower comfort levels. The value of energy savings over time can be determined using conventional discounting techniques as adequately described by Markus and Morris (Ref. 21.21).

21.5. THERMAL MASS AND ITS EFFECTS

Thermal mass incorporated in the construction of a building interior can improve thermal comfort and reduce energy consumption. Thermal comfort is improved by a reduction in the daily temperature swings and the maintenance of temperatures closer to the comfort zone, while energy consumption for heating and cooling can be reduced or even eliminated if the building is correctly designed. In spaces that are intermittently heated, as if often the case in temperate climates, thermal storage materials may have no significant effect on energy consumption. Thermal mass is especially important in hot-arid climates with high diurnal temperature swings, where the heat of the day can be stored for release at night to cool breezes on summer nights that will drain it away or to the interior space in winter to maintain comfort.

Let us review some important characteristics of materials that can store energy. First when energy is absorbed into a material it will rise in temperature. The effect of letting sun into a room that has no significant storage capacity will be to cause the room temperature to rise. If the room is well insulated then the rise will be quicker because little heat is lost.

If, on the other hand, the room surfaces comprise a significant area of high-storage-capacity material in the path of the sun, then some of the sun's energy entering the room will be absorbed without having any immediate effect on the temperature of the room. The temperature of the thermal mass will of course, rise and the heat energy is held until the temperature of the room begins to fall later after the sun is no longer entering the room.

The mean radiant temperature (MRT) of a room can be defined as the weighted average radiant temperature of all the surfaces in the room. If some surfaces are warmed by the sun's energy then the MRT will be higher and so we will sense that the room is warmer even though the air temperature may not have changed. The measure of this combined effect of both the air and the surface temperature is known as the *environmental temperature*. It is a useful measure of what we sense as thermal comfort and can be defined as $\frac{1}{3}$ air temperature + $\frac{2}{3}$ mean radiant temperature. Since the surface temperatures of a room have a significant bearing on our thermal comfort, we can utilize this by careful placement of heat storage materials.

If the thermal mass in the room has been cooled during the night, then during the day it will act as a sink and soak up the excess heat that flows into the room. In summer this can be very beneficial as a means of keeping the room cool (i.e., the environmental temperature is kept lower).

Where it is desirable to level out large swings in temperature from day to night, this can be achieved by the storage of heat from, say, the warmer part of the day until a later time when it can offset the colder temperature of the evening. The admittance values (Y-values) give an indication of the performance of elements in this respect. They can also be used in calculations to predict internal temperatures, using a technique known as the *admittance method*, described in Chapter 20.

From all this we can now make some recommendations about the desirability of thermal mass and its preferred qualities according to the climate of the location. In temperate climates and desert climates, which are usually arid, the desirable wall surfaces will have a low U-value, a low T-value, and a high Y-value. In areas where it is necessary to heat with auxiliary energy, it may be desirable to minimize all three values to maximize the heating effect when its needed.

Thermal Storage Capacity

When developing a thermal storage system or simply comparing materials it is useful to look at the storage capacity, which is sometimes referred to as the *volumetric heat capacity*, and the rate at which the material can take up and store heat (the Y-value). Some examples of common storage materials is given in Table 21.2.

From these values one can determine the heat storage capacity for a given temperature rise or, if the heat gain is known, how much will the material rise in temperature. In an ideal situation, for any room into which sunlight enters, the surface area of the thermal mass should be as large as possible, even where not directly exposed to solar radiation. It must, however, be well insulated from the outside so that it is mainly interacting with the interior.

In the case of a room that does not receive sunlight directly and is used and heated intermittently, then it is advisable to insulate any heavy material surfaces from the room. In such places large amounts of heat would just be soaked up by the thermal mass each time the heating is turned on and so the room might feel rather cool.

In the case of a building with a concrete slab floor on the ground, the ground underneath is being heated by the energy entering the slab from the room, either from solar energy or other energy sources such as space heaters. The ground adds to the thermal store of the floor slab where it is in contact with that slab. This is very useful in winter when there is plenty of solar radiation entering the house during the day. The heat is stored and then some is given back as the night time temperatures drop and the building begins to cool down. In summer the floor acts in the same way by soaking up the heat energy that gets into the house and so helping to keep the inside of temperatures down. The need for insulation under the slab and around the perimeter has been discussed in Section 21.4 earlier in this chapter.

The thermal behavior and energy consumption of 15 cottages was studied in a major research and demonstration project undertaken by this author and his research unit (Ref. 21.22). Each of the houses was typical of a particular construction type in Australia, and the plan layouts of some were also similar to permit cross comparisons of the results. Hourly data were collected from each dwelling over a three year period with the houses unoccupied for the first eight months. Graphs of the daily minimum and maximum temperatures recorded in four of the houses are illustrated in Figs. 21.5.1 to 21.5.4. Daily minimum and maximum temperatures in the living areas are plotted against similar outdoor temperature data over approximately 18 months during the occupied period. The impact of the various quantities of thermal mass in each house is shown by the marked reduction in the temperature swing and the general suppression of the temperature extremes. In each of the figures the data above the $X = Y$ line illustrates heat being returned to the interior of the space from the thermal mass at a time when the outdoor temperatures are low. The graphs show how each dwelling behaves under the same climatic influences. They are plots of the internal temperature against the outside temperature for each day using both the maximum and the minimum values. The data used include both summer and winter time measurements.

The cottage (#359) from which the data illustrated in Fig. 21.5.1 were derived is of standard timber frame construction with timber floor over a crawl space. The only insulation is 4-inch-thick glass fiber on the ceiling. The external cladding of this house is fibro-cement sheet, commonly used on many houses built in Eastern Australia in the 1940s and 50s, while the interior linings are $\frac{3}{8}$-inch (10-mm) plasterboard sheet. The living room windows are oriented to the west, south, and north (north windows have large fixed overhang). The results show that this house is unable to modify the external climate to any extent and in summer it is often hotter inside than outside!

Table 21.2. Thermal Properties of Some Common Building Materials.

Material	Density lb/ft³ (kg/m³)	Volumetric Heat Capacity; Btu/ft³ °F (J/m³ °C)
Materials Commonly Used for Thermal Storage:		
Water	62 (1000)	62 (4186)
Concrete	131 (2100)	26.2 (1764)
Brick	106 (1700)	20.1 (1360)
Stone: marble	156 (2500)	32.8 (2250)
Materials Not Suitable for Thermal Storage:		
Plasterboard	59 (950)	11.8 (798)
Timber	38 (610)	12.9 (866)
Glass fiber mat	1.5 (25)	0.37 (25)

Daily Extreme Temperature Points—Cottage #359

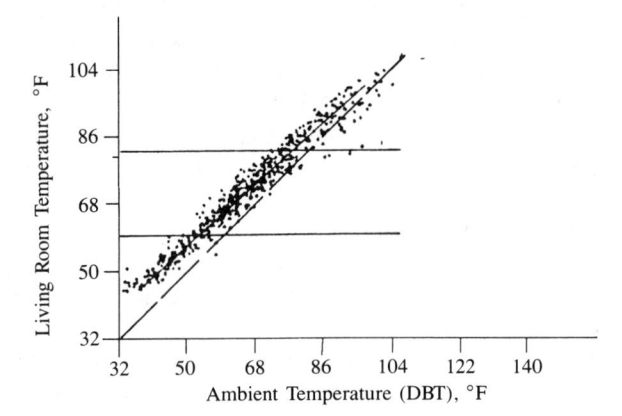

Fig. 21.5.1. Cottage #359, standard timber frame construction.

Daily Extreme Temperature Points—Cottage #351

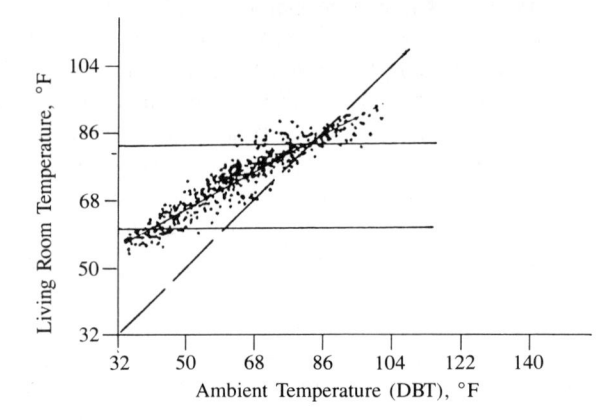

Fig. 21.5.3. Cottage #351, insulated timber frame with concrete slab floor.

The data illustrated in Fig. 21.5.2 is from a cottage (#357) of standard brick veneer construction also with a timber floor and ceiling insulation. This construction system is essentially a timber frame construction lined internally with plasterboard and with a single layer of brick built around the outside of the timber frame. The living room in this cottage has only equator-facing windows (north in Australia). The performance of this house is not significantly better because it still lacks an adequate amount of thermal storage material associated with the interior.

Figure 21.5.3 illustrates the results of data collected from a timber framed cottage (#351) with a concrete floor slab in direct contact with the ground. As with the others the internal linings are plasterboard and the ceiling is insulated with 4-inch (100-mm) thick glass fiber blanket. The exterior wall lining is $\frac{3}{8}$-inch (10-mm) thick compressed wood fiber planking laid over double-sided reflective foil insulation. All living area windows face toward the equator and the floor finish in hard vinyl tile with scatter rugs. The impact of the concrete floor slab is clear. The temperature swing is reduced and the interior conditions are buffered against the extremes of the outside. The ''narrowness'' of the cluster of dots shows that the concrete floor slab is acting in conjunction with the ground as a substantial heat sink.

The behavior of a traditional passive solar house is illustrated in Fig. 21.5.4. This cottage (#341) is constructed of double brick walls with the cavity filled with urea-formaldehyde foam. The floor is a concrete slab on ground similar to cottage #351 in Fig. 21.5.3. The roof is insulated similarly to the other houses and all living area windows face toward the equator (north). This house is the best in terms of overall thermal performance, as can be seen from the small number of dots above and below the accepted comfort lines. The dots in this example are clustered in a ''fatter'' pattern than those in Fig. 21.5.3, which displays the impact of the internal walls which are not ground connected. The energy stored in them must come from and go back into the interior space, thus causing the interior temperature to rise more slowly as the day warms up and to fall more slowly as the night comes on. It should be noted that some of the energy that enters the floor slab in both

Daily Extreme Temperature Points—Cottage #357

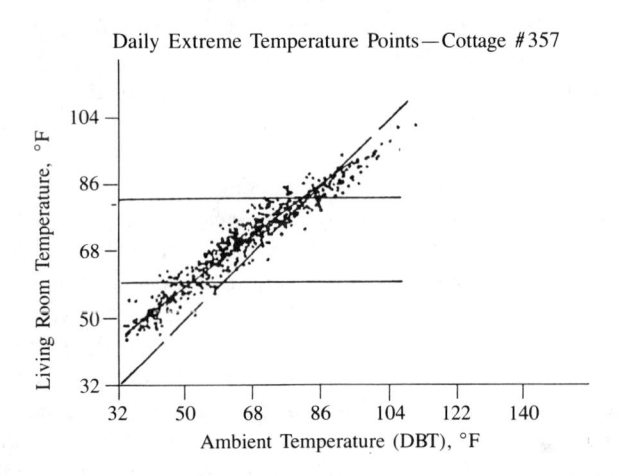

Fig. 21.5.2. Cottage #357, standard brick veneer construction.

Daily Extreme Temperature Points—Cottage #341

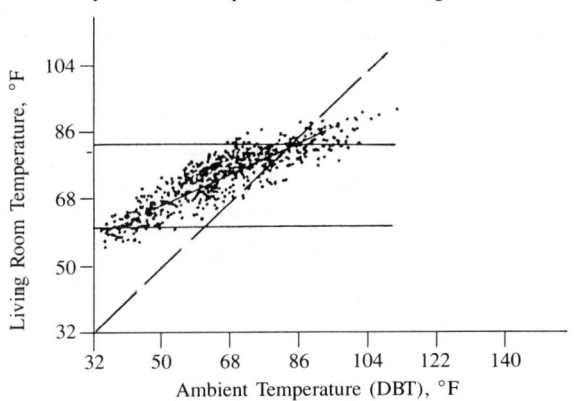

Fig. 21.5.4. Cottage #341, fully insulated double brick and concrete floor construction.

this example and that in Fig. 21.5.4 will flow away to the ground and be lost.

Interior Finishes and Furniture

The type of floor covering or finish used on a ground-connected floor (i.e., concrete slab, masonry, or stone paving) will have an important bearing on the way such a floor interacts thermally with the room. Materials such as carpet, cork, or foam-backed vinyl materials act as insulators (refer to chapter 5) and effectively reduce the internal admittance of the floor surface. During winter an undesirable temperature rise can occur in spaces without alternative thermal mass that are heated by the sun entering directly into the interior (this is known as a *direct gain* system and is discussed below) because such coverings reduce the admittance of heat into the floor slab. Likewise in summer a floor with an insulated covering is also less effective in acting as a heat sink to soak up the daily heat gains for disposal at night.

21.6. PASSIVE SOLAR HEATING SYSTEMS

A passive solar system can provide a substantial percentage of the heating needs of a building in most of the world climates. Its effectiveness will of course depend to some extent on the levels and duration of sunlight during the heating months. It has been demonstrated in the sunny-winter states of the USA (Ref. 21.2), in Mediterranean Europe, and in Australia (Ref. 21.24) that conventional heating loads can be reduced by as much as 90 percent in passive solar designed dwellings. Such systems are not additional to the building fabric but rather they comprise an integral part of the building. In this way the cost of a passive solar system is partly taken up in the cost of the building fabric. For this reason passive solar systems have a lower initial capital cost than active systems, either solar or fossil-fuel powered. Generally the maintenance is lower also, as there are usually fewer moving parts and the exposed materials are the building fabric.

The occupants of a passive solar building are generally more involved with the operation of the building and so have better control over the way in which they would like it to operate. Such control is usually quite simple; by way of operative blinds, shutters or curtains, adjustable shading perhaps for summer.

The diagrams in Fig. 21.6.1 illustrate the three systems for passive solar heating generally accepted today: direct gain, thermal storage walls (masonry or water), and attached sunspaces. They are described in what follows. Further information and design details can be found in all the literature on passive solar design listed in the bibliography. The reader will also find that opinions about precise details will vary from author to author in much the same way as opinion varies about construction details. Passive solar design does not have just one correct solution. Correct solutions are as varied as the designer's imagination.

Direct Gain

Direct gain systems are those where the solar radiation enters the habitable spaces via equator-facing windows and is absorbed by the materials inside the space for later dissipation when the ambient temperature falls. This is by far the most commonly used system and in spatial design terms the most flexible, because it can accommodate daylighting and views to the exterior as well as providing a source of heat. While it is the easiest for the designer to work with, it does have far more limitations than some of the other systems.

Direct Gain

Thermal Storage Wall

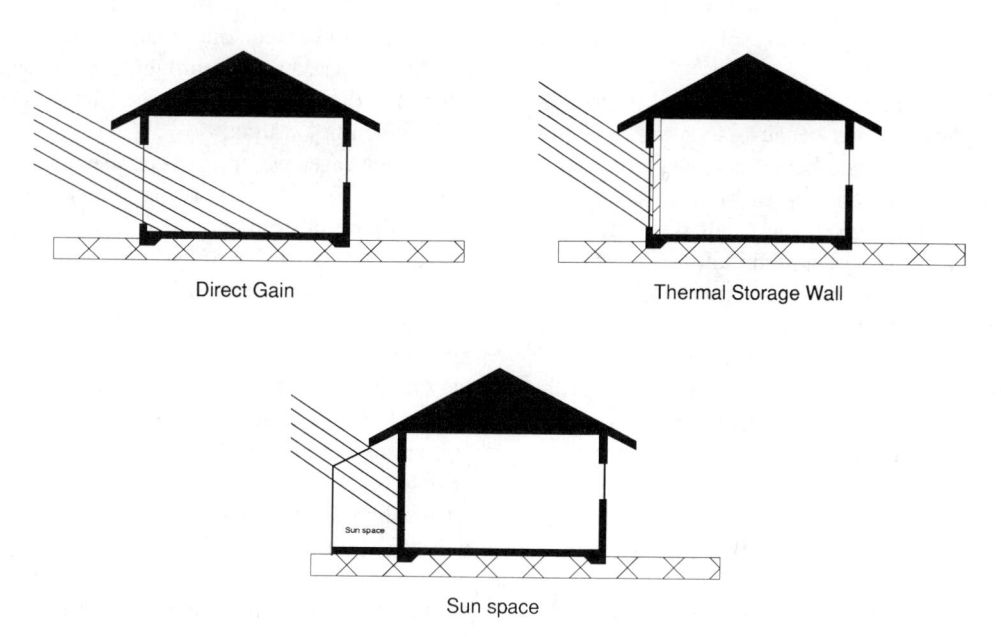

Sun space

Fig. 21.6.1. Three popular systems for passive solar heating

To operate effectively, the area of equator-facing direct gain window is closely related to the area of thermal storage materials within the space and the climate characteristics of the particular location. The thermal storage area must be matched to the incoming solar radiation to maintain a maximum diurnal temperature swing in the range of 8–10°F (5–6°C) for acceptable thermal comfort. Insufficient thermal storage could result in daytime overheating even in quite cold climates. In temperate climates, where heating loads are modest, this system should provide high levels of thermal comfort without significant auxiliary heating. But in very cold climates there is likely to be insufficient solar contribution due to the limitations of glass area, and it may be more appropriate to use a combination of systems (thermal storage wall or attached sunspace). Manual techniques for the design of appropriate window size and area of thermal storage material are given in many publications such the SLR-method by Balcomb (Ref. 21.24). Computer based calculation methods are also available such as SERI-RES (Ref. 21.25), CHEETAH (Ref. 21.26) and CALPAS (Ref. 21.27), to list only a few.

The equator-facing windows must be designed with appropriate shading and means of minimizing conductive heat loss as described in Chapters 18 and 20. Direct sunlight entering the space can be a problem in terms of fading of interior finishes and also glare for the occupants. The latter can be countered in most domestic situations by appropriate selection of surface finishes. Direct sunlight inside a room has many psychologically beneficial qualities which have been recognized down through the ages and so this should not be overlooked.

Roof-level glazing can provide a useful contribution to the equator-facing glass area, provided its thermal resistance is adequate to minimize heat losses. In temperate climates and those locations where the summers are quite hot it is important to avoid sloping glass. In any event all glass must be well shaded to stop the entry of summer sun as discussed in more detail later.

The floor is most commonly the main thermal storage medium in direct gain systems because so often it is the most economical place to locate heavy masonry materials. Unless there is an adequate amount of thermal storage in the walls of the space (perhaps at least half the walls) the floor should be of a material with a high thermal admittance (refer to Chapter 20) and have the least amount of thermally resistive covering (that is, carpets or cork tile). The surface should have a low reflectance to absorb as much of the incoming energy as possible. Where there is a significant thermal storage component in the walls, the floor may be more reflective to better distribute the sun's energy to the other heat storage surfaces.

Thermal Storage Wall (Trombe Wall)

Thermal Storage Wall systems usually comprise a dark-colored heavy wall (masonry, concrete, mud brick etc.) erected in the solar aperture with a double glass system mounted approximately 1 in. (20–30 mm) in front of the wall surface. The sun's radiation passes through the glass and is mostly absorbed by the dark surface of the wall (preferably with a high absorptance and a low emissivity). The amount of energy that is lost back through the glazing depends on the insulating properties of the glazing and the surface properties of the wall. Special surface coatings for thermal storage walls with low emissivity and high absorptivity are manufactured in North America specifically for this application.

The solar energy absorbed into the wall raises its temperature slowly throughout the day. By nighttime the heat has penetrated to the inside surface where it can radiate into the room raising the environmental temperature and so providing warmth to the occupants. The time taken for the heat to reach the inner surface depends on the thermal properties and thickness of the wall material, typically about 10 hours per foot thickness for masonry. The same design guidelines and computer-based design tools developed by various authors for correct sizing of direct gain systems usually also provide for thermal storage walls (Ref. 21.25 and 21.27).

In early examples a range of movable night insulation systems were employed, but Balcomb (Ref. 21.28) reports that experience has shown double glazing and selective surface coatings on the outer face of the thermal storage wall to be more reliable and cost effective. Current recommendations are that the air space between the glass and the wall surface should be well sealed. The earlier examples had various systems of venting either to the room being heated for winter or the outside to reject heat in summer.

Protection from solar radiation in the summer is best provided by some form of cover over the glazing. The protection that is appropriate for direct gain windows may not be sufficient to keep out the diffuse and the ground reflected radiation. Unwanted solar heat in direct gain heated spaces can be dissipated by natural ventilation, whereas in thermal storage walls it will be absorbed into the wall to heat the room when not wanted.

In some cases water has been used as the thermal storage material. This technique of passive solar heating is similar to the thermal storage wall except for a number of key points. The thermal storage capacity of water is approximately three times that of brickwork by volume (Refer to Table 20.1). While it is inexpensive as a material it is both difficult and relatively expensive to store securely. The time lag effect of water in containers is shorter than in masonry because it is a fluid; the transfer of energy is in part by conduction and in part by convection. Many examples built to date use water in vertical cylinders painted a dark color or finished with a selective coating as described for the thermal storage walls (Ref. 21.2). The cylinders can be placed with spaces between them to allow some solar radiation and daylight to penetrate directly into the space. The water storage walls generally perform better than thermal storage walls because the convection mixing of the water results in lower surface temperatures and a more even distribution of energy. Most of design tools that have been developed for use with thermal storage walls are also suitable for the design of water-based heat storage systems.

Current experience with this system indicates that it is not widely accepted in the residential building field, as the darkened wall covered with glass is considered rather ugly. Its use in the light commercial and industrial area such as warehouses and small scale industrial buildings is much more widely accepted.

Attached Sunspace

An attached sunspace system comprises an additional enclosure, usually with all surfaces glazed, attached to the equator-facing side of the building to be solar heated. The additional space so created can be used for various purposes that are suited to exposure to high levels of sunlight and a wider temperature range than aimed for inside the rest of the building. The built form of the sunspace may range from simple attachment to the face of the building to full integration into the building envelope. A number of sunspace configurations have been defined in the literature (Ref. 21.29) for use in design tool analysis. They are essentially variations on a theme that have been defined for computer modeling purposes. In reality, an attached sunspace is a room on the equator-facing side of a building with a significantly high glass area compared to the floor area (glass/floor ratio > 1).

The critical components of a sunspace solar heating system are the floor (usually ground connected), the wall separating the sunspace from the remainder of the building to be heated, and the area and nature of the glazing. The wall dividing the sunspace from the rest of the building is similar to the thermal storage wall described before. In this case the glass has been moved out to form an accessible space for other purposes, thus making the overall system more economically viable. The dividing wall can be either a solid mass, uninsulated, insulated on the inside, insulated on the outside, or simply lightweight heavily insulated. If the wall is of uninsulated heavy materials then the same rules apply as with the thermal storage wall. If on the other hand it is insulated, then a venting system is required to transport the collected heat to the interior of the building. The use of thermal mass materials inside the sunspace will help to modify the diurnal temperature swing.

In all locations except where summers are very cool, it is important to provide adequate through-ventilation to remove summer heat buildup (minimum vent area should be 10 percent of the total glass area for mild summer climates and more for warm to hot summer climates). In most areas where summers are warm (mean temperatures lie within the comfort range) it will be necessary to fully shade the glass area to avoid overheating and degradation of the interior surfaces and fitments. The preferred design for such areas is with a fixed opaque roof and only the vertical surfaces glazed. Even in colder climates there is likely to be problems with overheating in autumn as the sun is passing low in the sky and yet the temperatures are not commensurately lower. This can be overcome to some extent with suitable shading of the roof glass and the east and west glass, if present. Today the trend is to build such enclosures as a visual element in otherwise conventional building. Unfortunately, too often little thought is given to the protection of the glass areas from solar gain in summer; as a result there are many unsatisfactory buildings being built today.

In many applications an attached sunspace is used as a multilevel connecting space (lower floor with mezzanines above to the upper floors). In such cases the designer must be aware of the chimney effect of the tall space as the air in the sunspace will be much warmer than the remainder of the house. The design should allow for the cooler air inside to flow down to the lower area and out to the sunspace. With large glass areas overheating can be quite a serious problem without correct shading.

References

21.1. D. Watson. *Designing and Building a Solar House*. Garden Way Publishing, Charlotte, VT, 1977.

21.2. W. A. Shurcliff. *Solar Heated Buildings of North America: 120 Outstanding Examples*. Brick House Publishing Co., Harrisville, NH, 1978.

21.3. R. A. Winett, S. Q. Love, B. Stahl, D. E. Chinn, and I. N. Lickliter. "A Field-Based Approach to the Development of Comfort Standards, Energy Conservation Strategies and Media-Based Motivational Strategies: A Replication and Extension of Winter Findings." *ASHRAE Transactions*, 89(2B), 667–679 (1983).

21.4. T. Williamson and S. Coldicutt. "Environmental Response Logger." *Proc. CIB Conference, Healthy Buildings '88, Stockholm*, 3, 527–536 (1988).

21.5. K. Butti and J. Perlin. *A Golden Thread: 2500 years of Solar Architecture and Technology*. Marion Boyars, London, 1981.

21.6. J. F. Van Straaten. *Thermal Performance of Buildings*. Elsevier, London, 1967.

21.7. B. Givoni. *Man, Climate and Architecture*, 2nd Ed. Van Nostrand Reinhold, New York, 1976.

21.8. J. W. Drysdale. *Designing Houses for Australian Climates*. Experimental Building Station Bulletin No. 3, Sydney, 1947.

21.9. R. O. Phillips. *Sunshine and Shade in Australasia*. Experimental Building Station Bulletin No. 8, Sydney, 1948.

21.10. *Energy Policies and Programmes of the IEA Countries—1987 Review*. International Energy Agency, Paris, 1987.

21.11. M. A. Sattler, S. Sharples, and J. K. Page. "The Geometry of the Shading of Buildings by Various Tree Shapes." *Solar Energy*, 38(3), 187–201 (1987).

21.12. E. Mazria. *The Passive Solar Energy Book*. Rodale, Emmaus, PA 1979.

21.13. O. H. Koenigsburger, T. G. Ingersoll, A. Mayhew, and S. V. Szokolay. *Manual of Tropical Housing and Building*. Part 1: Climatic Design. Longman, London, 1973.

21.14. E. L. Harkness and M. L. Mehta. *Solar Radiation Control in Buildings*. Applied Science Publishers, London, 1978.

21.15. R. Knowles. *Energy and Form: An Ecological Approach to Urban Growth*. MIT Press, Cambridge, MA, 1974.

21.16. G. O. Robinette, (Ed.). *Landscape Planning for Energy Conservation*. Environmental Design Press, Reston, VA, 1977.

21.17. SOLPRO, computer module in the SCRIBE package by Ecotech, Sheffield (England).
21.18. V. Olgyay. *Design with Climate*. Princeton University Press, Princeton, NJ, 1963.
21.19. A. S. Moffat and M. Schiller. *Landscape Design That Saves Energy*, Wm. Morrow, New York, 1981.
21.20. *Heat Losses through Floors*. Building Research Establishment Digest No. 145. H. M. Stationery Office, London, 1972.
21.21. T. A. Markus and E. N. Morris. *Buildings, Climate and Energy*. Pitman, London, 1980.
21.22. J. A. Ballinger and M. G. Smart. "Bonnyrigg Solar Village." *Solar World Congress*, S. V. Szokolay (Ed.), Pergamon, Sydney, 1983.
21.23. J. A. Ballinger. *A Final Report of Passive Solar Housing for Sydney Growth Areas*. National Energy Research Development and Demonstration Council, Canberra, 1986.
21.24. J. D. Balcomb, R. J. Jones, C. E. Kosiewicz, G. S. Lazarus, R. D. McFarland, and W. O. Wray. *Passive Solar Design Handbook*, Vol. 3. American Solar Energy Society, New York, 1983.
21.25. SERI-RES (Solar Energy Research Institute Residential Energy Simulator), Thermal Analysis for Residential Buildings User's Manual. Solar Energy Research Institute, Golden, CO, 1981.
21.26. CHEETAH. A thermal response and energy load simulation program based on Thermal Response Factors, available for use on a microcomputer from Unisearch Limited, Kensington NSW 2033, Australia, 1988.
21.27. CALPAS. Energy evaluation tool. Californian Energy Commission, Sacramento, CA.
21.28. J. D. Balcomb, R. J. Jones, C. E. Kosiewicz, G. S. Lazarus, R. D. McFarland, and W. O. Wray. *Passive Solar Design Handbook*, Vol. 3. American Solar Energy Society, New York, 1983, pp. 98–100.
21.29. J. D. Balcomb, R. W. Jones, R. D. McFarland, and W. O. Wray. *Passive Solar Heating Analysis: A Design Manual*. American Society of Heating, Refrigerating and Air-Conditioning Engineers, Atlanta, GA, 1984.

SUGGESTIONS FOR FURTHER READING

D. Watson. *Designing and Building a Solar House*. Garden Way Publishing, Charlotte, VT, 1977.

K. Butti and J. Perlin. *A Golden Thread: 2500 years of Solar Architecture and Technology*. Marion Boyars, London, 1981.

J. F. Van Straaten. *Thermal Performance of Buildings*. Elsevier, London, 1967.

B. Givoni. *Man, Climate and Architecture*, 2nd Ed. Van Nostrand Reinhold, New York, 1976.

E. Mazria. *The Passive Solar Energy Book*. Rodale, Emmaus, PA, 1979.

O. H. Koenigsburger, T. G. Ingersoll, A. Mayhew, and S. V. Szokolay. *Manual of Tropical Housing and Building*. Part 1: Climatic Design. Longman, London, 1973.

R. Knowles. *Energy and Form: An Ecological Approach to Urban Growth*. MIT Press, Cambridge, MA, 1974.

V. Olgyay. *Design with Climate*. Princeton University Press, Princeton, NJ, 1963.

A. S. Moffat, M. Schiller. *Landscape Design That Saves Energy*. Wm. Morrow, New York, 1981.

T. A. Markus and E. N. Morris. *Buildings, Climate and Energy*. Pitman, London, 1980.

J. D. Balcomb, R. J. Jones, C. E. Kosiewicz, G. S. Lazarus, R. D. McFarland, and W. O. Wray. *Passive Solar Design Handbook*, Vol. 3. American Solar Energy Society, New York, 1983.

J. D. Balcomb, R. W. Jones, R. D. McFarland, and W. O. Wray. *Passive Solar Heating Analysis: A Design Manual*. American Society of Heating, Refrigerating and Air-Conditioning Engineers, Atlanta, GA 1984.

NOTE

A list of abbreviations of the units of measurement, definitions of these units, and conversion factors between British/American and metric units are given in the Appendix.

22

Active Solar Energy Systems

W. W. S. Charters and K. I. Guthrie

In this chapter attention is given to various aspects of components and systems falling under the generic category of active solar systems. Such systems require the provision of mechanical or electrical power in order to function. Typical application areas include swimming pool heating; hot water services; space heating and cooling; provision of stand-alone power supplies.

22.1. SOLAR THERMAL AND POWER SYSTEMS

Solar Thermal Systems

Incoming solar radiation can be transformed to thermal energy to perform a variety of heating tasks at various temperature levels. These include passive and active forms of solar space-heating systems for animal shelters and for human habitation, the provision of hot water for domestic, commercial, and industrial uses, the heating of indoor and outdoor swimming pools, and the provision of low-temperature process heat for industry (Ref. 22.1).

Generally, solar thermal collection devices can be divided into two main categories, of *nonconcentrating* and *concentrating*, the degree of concentration being dependent on the required temperature. As the concentration is increased for the higher temperature applications the requirement for tracking of the sun becomes increasingly important and the system costs escalate correspondingly (Ref. 22.2).

Solar thermal systems incorporate the solar collection elements, some form of thermal storage, and the associated pipework, pumps/fans, and controllers to complete the thermal circuits.

In this chapter a review will be made of the various solar thermal systems which have been developed for different domestic, commercial and industrial applications with emphasis being laid on those systems and system components which have been developed to the stage of commercial availability.

Solar Power Systems

In recent years (post-1980) there has been considerable interest in the provision of electrical power for houses in remote locations. Solar energy can be harnessed for this application either by tapping it indirectly through wind or solar thermal power systems, or directly through the use of photovoltaic panels. The latter option only will be considered here because of the emphasis in this text on domestic scale systems where photovoltaic generators provide the best option for small-scale standalone power supplies. These systems are always provided with battery storage and often backed by small diesel or petrol engine generating sets to ensure continuous reliable supply of power. Such

22.2. HOT WATER SERVICES AND SWIMMING POOL HEATING

On a worldwide basis it is likely that the provision of solar heated water is the single largest use of solar energy in the home and has the potential to save large quantities of conventional fuels in developed and developing nations alike.

Swimming Pool Heating

It is often not realized that in a temperate zone climate the energy requirement for heating an outdoor swimming pool may be well in excess of that required for house space heating. Because of this and with the advent of low-cost synthetic rubber (EPDM) strip collectors and clear polyethylene/ethylene vinyl acetate (PE/EVA) covers there has been a substantial increase in the market demand for solar swimming pool heating over the last few years.

The use of solar energy to heat water for hot water or pool heating is a most suitable means of utilizing solar energy to save fossil fuels. The energy savings possible vary according to local climatic conditions and the requirements for hot water.

A solar pool heating system can operate as a stand-alone, system which is suitable for most outdoor pools, or as a fuel saver for indoor pool heating. The supply of energy at the low temperatures required for swimming is an application which is undoubtedly economically viable in all climate zones where pool heating is required.

Energy and Temperature

The concepts of energy and temperature often cause confusion, and it is often thought that the "best" solar heater is the one that supplies the hottest water. This is not so. The most desirable system is the one that supplies the most energy at a usable temperature for the least cost.

In order to illustrate this point, Table 22.1 shows the energy and the temperature level required to be supplied to carry out some everyday tasks. Clearly, to heat a swimming pool will require a larger collector system than to boil a cup of water, but the type of collector can be much simpler and less expensive per unit area as it operates at a lower temperature.

22.3. SOLAR WATER HEATERS (see also Section 24.4)

Systems

System Components. A solar water heater is made up of a number of components fitted together to form a system. Most systems have some or all of the following components: collector(s), tank (storage), controller, pump, pipework (or other heat transfer mechanism) and a method of protection against freezing if the climate requires.

A well designed solar water heating system should be able to save more than half the water heating energy of a conventionally fueled system in colder temperate areas or supply almost all of the hot water in warmer tropical climates. In both locations a good system will deliver all the hot water required over most of summer; however, in temperate areas the variation in solar energy available from summer to winter causes a lower winter solar fraction (the fraction of the heat energy supplied by solar as compared to total heat energy).

System Types. The two main components are the collector(s) and tank and the type of system is described by their arrangement.

If the tank is situated above the collector(s) the water heated in the collector will *thermosyphon* from the collector to the tank. The colder water situated in the bottom of the tank will be drawn down into the collector(s) to replace the heated water; thus a circulation is set up while the sun is able to heat the water.

A thermosyphon system can have a tank mounted remote from the collector, generally inside the roof structure, or a tank mounted directly above the collectors external to the roof material (see Fig. 22.3.1).

A close-coupled thermosyphon system will have a greater heat loss from the tank in cold weather conditions than a remote thermosyphon system where the tank is mounted inside. However it is sometimes difficult to find sufficient space inside the roof for a remotely mounted tank. The thermosyphon is simple to operate; as long as it is installed correctly with the pipework maintaining its upward or downward slope it requires no pump or controller to operate it.

If, however, it is impossible to mount the tank above the collector, then a *pump* becomes necessary to maintain a flow through the collectors when the sun is shining. The storage tank is then mounted at a more convenient level and the pipework running to and from the collectors can be smaller, as it does not need to carry the full flow of water required at each household hot water use. In addition to the

Table 22.1. Heat and Temperature.

End Use	Thermal Energy Required	Usage Temperature
Boil 1 US quart (1 liter) of water	360 Btu (~360 kJ or 0.1 kWh)	212°F (100°C)
Heat 250 liters of water in a domestic hot water service	48,000 Btu (48,000 kJ or 13.3 kWh)	140°F (60°C)
Heat a domestic swimming pool from 68 to 77°F (from 20 to 25°C), if covered by a pool cover	1×10^6 Btu (~1×10^6 kJ or 275 kWh)	77°F (25°C)

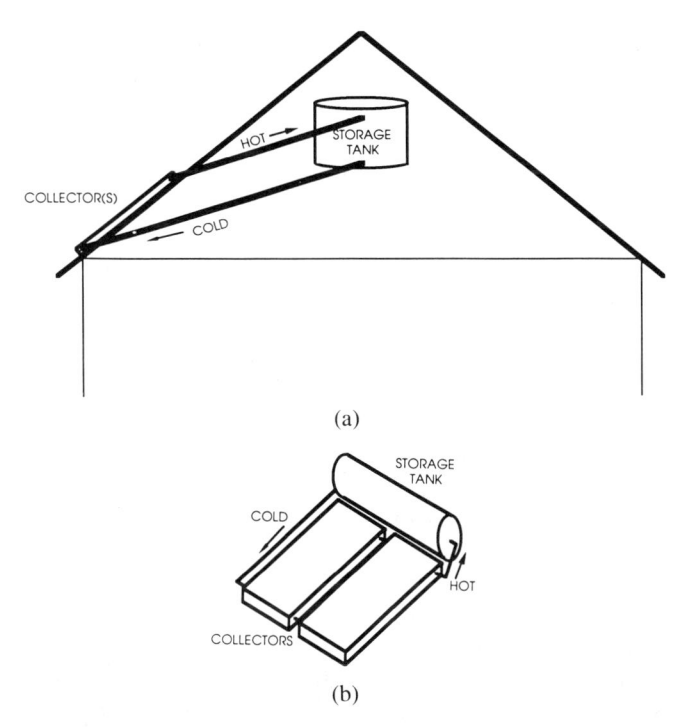

Fig. 22.3.1. Thermosyphon solar domestic water heaters. (a) Remote thermosyphon; (b) close-coupled thermosyphon.

extra cost of a pump, this type of system generally requires a *controller* to turn the pump on when the solar energy is sufficient to heat the water and off when it is insufficient (see Fig. 22.3.2).

The third type of system is the *integrated collector and storage system* (ICS). In this type of system the hot water is stored with the collector. The ICS system is also roof mounted but generally has greater overnight heat losses from the storage. As the top must remain transparent to solar radiation during the day it is difficult to insulate that surface (see Fig. 22.3.3).

Collector Types

A number of different types of collectors are available for water heaters. They are generally categorized as *flat plate*, *evacuated tube*, or *concentrating collectors*.

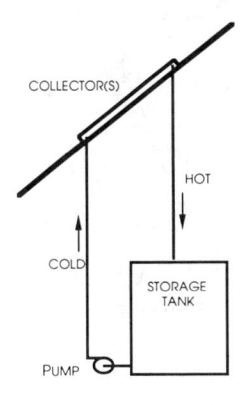

Fig. 22.3.2. Pumped solar domestic water heater.

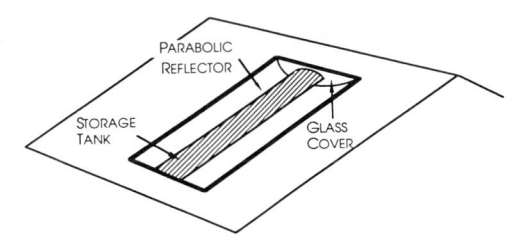

Fig. 22.3.3. Integrated collector and storage system (ICS).

Flat Plate Collectors. A flat plate collector is made up of an absorber with insulation behind and beside it, placed in a box with one or more transparent covers (see Fig. 22.3.4).

The absorber plate is generally made up of a grid of pipes with a metal plate fitted over the grid (fin-and-tube absorber, see Fig. 22.3.4a), or by two metal sheets fitted together with fluid passages pressed into the metal (flooded-plate absorber, see Fig. 22.3.4b). The plate is generally coated in a selective surface that will absorb a high percentage of incident solar radiation (typically over 90 percent) but re-emit only a small percentage (typically less than 10 percent) of the long-wave radiation from the hot surface. Black paint can be used and in some warmer locations may be more cost effective.

Solar radiation is absorbed by the plate and the energy is conducted along the fin to the water-carrying passages, where it heats the water. Insulation is placed at the back and sides of the collectors in order to minimize conduction heat losses.

The transparent cover system must transmit as much solar radiation as possible. However it must not degrade in sunlight (UV) and it must also seal the box effectively to prevent the ingress of rain water, which could wet the in-

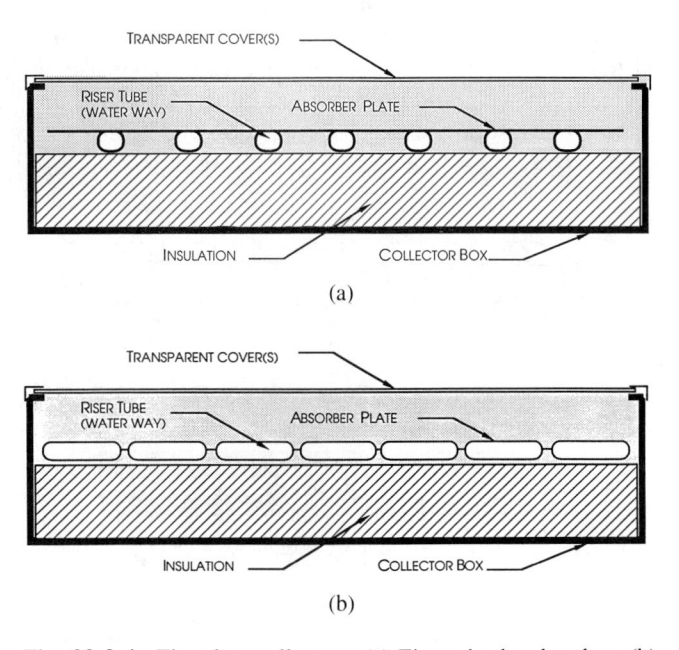

Fig. 22.3.4. Flat plate collectors. (a) Fin-and-tube absorber; (b) flooded-plate absorber.

sulation, rendering it useless. Covers can be made of glass or a variety of plastics.

Heat is lost from the absorber plate by conduction through the back and sides and by convection and radiation to the top. In a well designed collector using a selective surface, convection is the largest of the loss mechanisms (Ref. 22.4). In an endeavor to decrease the convection loss, more than one transparent cover is used by some manufacturers; others use convection suppression devices to limit the air movement in the air gap, thus decreasing the heat loss.

Evacuated Tube Collectors. Another method to prevent convection and conduction heat losses is to surround the absorber plate with a vacuum, so that radiation is the only mechanism which can cause heat loss from the absorber. As it is very difficult to maintain a vacuum surrounding a flat plate, because of the stresses in the transparent cover, the practical use of a vacuum is limited to tubular collectors.

Evacuated tube collectors consist of an absorber and a glass tube. The absorber may be made of glass with a selective surface sputtered on the outer layer (this is similar to an elongated vacuum flask, see Fig. 22.3.5a), or the absorber may be a metal fin-and-tube construction (see Fig. 22.3.5b). The use of a metal-to-glass seal is a potential weak spot, as the two materials expand at different rates upon heating, leading to stresses in the area of the seal. However, many manufacturers have overcome this problem.

At higher temperatures, evacuated tube collectors generally operate at a higher collection efficiency than flat plates; however, this is at the penalty of a higher cost due to a more complex manufacturing process.

Evacuated tubes are best mounted on a reflecting roof with a gap between the tubes so that the radiation incident on the roof is reflected back onto the tubes giving some degree of concentration of the solar energy available and making best use of the expensive tube (Ref. 22.5).

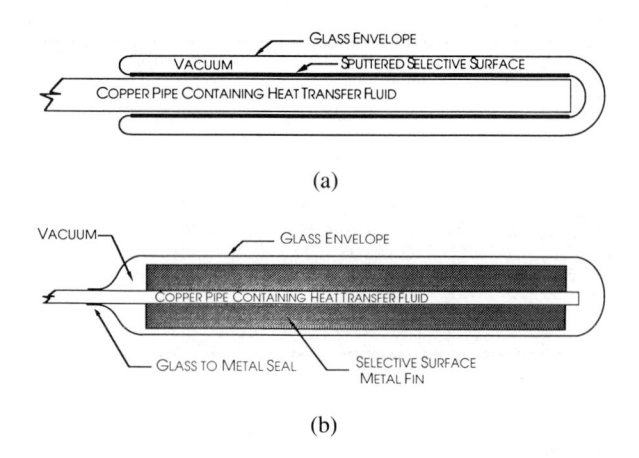

Fig. 22.3.5. Evacuated tube collectors. (a) "Vacuum flask" type; (b) metal fin-and-tube type.

Concentrating Collectors. A concentrating collector is made up of a reflector or lens which focuses the solar irradiation onto an absorber area smaller than that of the reflector or lens, thus concentrating the energy. The absorber can be a spot with a paraboloid reflector or a band with a parabolic trough reflector (see Fig. 22.3.6).

Concentrating collectors will collect radiation only from a small area of the sky. Typically they will absorb only the irradiation coming directly from the sun (called *direct* or *beam irradiation*) and will collect little, if any, of the diffuse irradiation reaching the collector after being scattered by clouds, fog, or smog or reflected by surrounding buildings or ground cover.

In clear conditions a concentrating collector will be able to gather energy at a higher temperature. This is useful if the energy can be stored at this high temperature. However, on overcast days little, if any, energy will be collected.

A concentrating collector must track the sun. A point focus collector must track on two axes, a line focus collector on only one. This produces extra levels of complexity in the design of the system and is the reason that point focus systems are not used at all for domestic hot water and only a few manufacturers use line focus collectors for home and commercial applications.

As the collectors will not work effectively on overcast days they are best suited to dry inland areas rather than wet coastal or tropical regions.

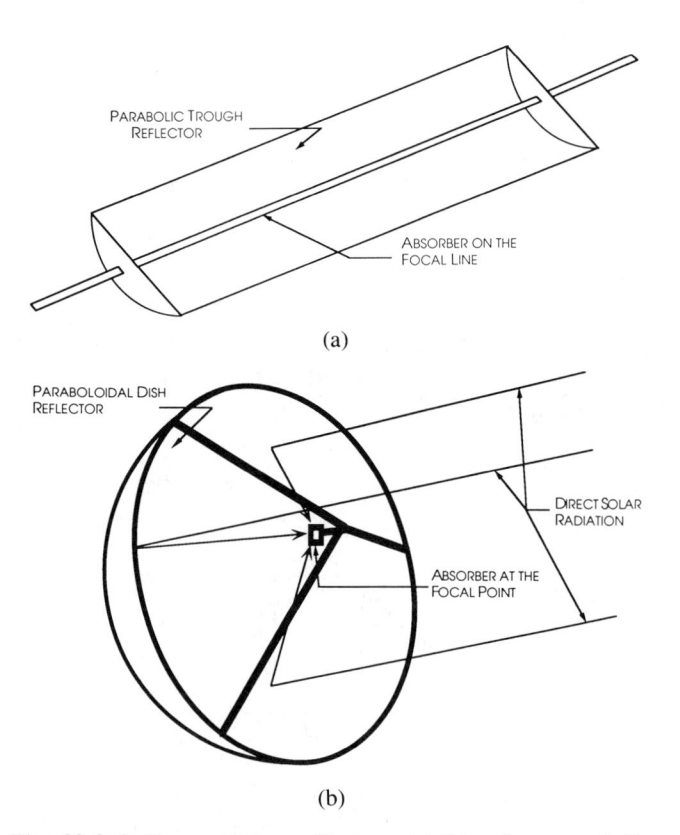

Fig. 22.3.6. Concentrating collectors. (a) Line focus parabolic trough; (b) point focus dish.

Solar Heat Pumps

Heat pumps driven by an electric motor can be used to upgrade ambient or waste energy available in large quantities but at low temperature to usable temperatures suitable for swimming pool heating or domestic hot water supply. A typical schematic of such a machine is shown in Fig. 22.3.7, where the main components are detailed.

Because the level of performance is heavily affected by the temperature lift required, i.e., the difference between the evaporator source and the condenser load, it is possible to substantially increase the performance by incorporating solar heating in the evaporator process. If this is done indirectly through heat exchange the device is called a *solar-assisted heat pump*. If it is done directly by combining the solar collector element and the evaporator into one unit the device is called a *solar-boosted heat pump* (Ref. 22.6).

Such solar-boosted units have been commercially produced in Australia for hot water systems and proved to be four times more effective than conventional electric immersion heaters. The same principle has been applied to gas-engine-driven solar-boosted heat pumps for heating an outdoor municipal swimming pool, with consequential reductions in gas consumption of 75 percent when compared with a conventional gas fired boiler of 75 percent thermal efficiency.

Hot Water Storage Cylinders

Once the energy is collected it must be stored in such a manner that it remains usable for a length of time depending upon the likely solar input on successive days. The hot water is therefore best stored in a well insulated cylinder.

The cylinder must contain the water pressure, resist corrosion, and maintain the temperature of the water stored within it. Thus the material of the cylinder must be chosen for strength and corrosion resistance and it must be packaged in an insulating layer and external jacket. Materials used for the inner container are generally copper, glass-lined mild steel, or stainless steel.

Copper is a very good material for corrosion resistance, as any potable water supply will have very little reaction with copper. However, it will only contain low-pressure water supplies and is generally only used in gravity feed storage tanks.

Glass- (vitreous-enamel-) lined mild steel containers offer good pressure resistance and reasonable corrosion resistance in good quality water supplies. Tanks of this type require an anode in order to reduce the risk of corrosion.

Stainless steel can be used, as it has good corrosion resistance and high strength. However, difficulty in fabrication means that it is currently only produced by a few manufacturers.

System Design Aspects

The water heater can be a direct system, where potable water is circulated through the collector and stored in the tank, or an indirect system, where there is a heat exchanger between the tank and collector or between the tank and the potable water. The use of a heat exchanger makes it easier to protect the collectors from freezing, as anti-freeze may be added to the heat transfer fluid. However, heat exchangers may add complexity and extra expense to the systems and can decrease stratification.

Stratification is the phenomenon that occurs when hotter water floats on colder water in the storage tank. Stratification is desirable, in that it allows more usable hot water for a given energy storage in the tank. For example, if a tank were stratified with the top half of the contents at 150°F (60°C) and the bottom half at 50°F (10°C) with a sharp thermocline at the boundary, then there is half a tank of water which is hot enough to use. If however, the tank is destratified all the contents would be at approximately 95°F (35°C), none of it usable for any household requirement.

Stratification can be enhanced by the use of diffusers on the cold water inlet and the flow and return line to the collectors. The diffusers are designed to decrease the entrance velocity of the water and thus reduce the mixing due to water flow into and out of the tank. The stratified tank would also return colder water to the collector than the mixed tank. This allows the collector to operate more efficiently, as heat losses are lower.

If the solar tank also contains an integral heater in it, the heating element must be located carefully to avoid unnecessary mixing of the water. There should be sufficient water above the element to allow enough hot water for days of poor solar radiation and sufficient below it so that cold water can be fed to the collectors to allow effective solar operation. The hot water from the collectors in a thermosyphon system should return at or below the element level as a general rule.

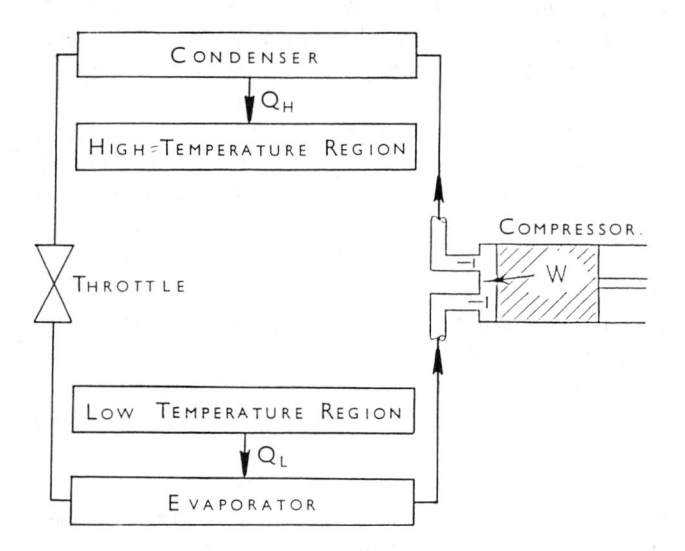

Fig. 22.3.7. Schematic sketch of vapor-compression heat pump.

Flow and Temperature Controllers. Various types of controller are used to ensure that the water heater operates as efficiently as possible and avoids problems due to freezing and overheating. A pump can be controlled at various levels of complexity from a simple time switch to a differential temperature controller.

A time clock is not generally suitable unless solar irradiation levels do not vary significantly from one day to the next. Another simple controller measures solar irradiation and energizes the pump circuit when the radiation is above a preset level. This takes no account of the tank temperature and may in fact circulate already hot water to the collectors, leading to wasted pumping power.

A differential temperature controller measures and compares the temperature in the tank and that of the collector. If the collector is hotter than the tank it will energize the pump to circulate the water. The temperature-sensing transducers and circuits must be suitably matched, and accurate, to ensure the pump runs only when it should. There must be sufficient hysteresis to ensure that the pump does not "short cycle," i.e., turn on and off too often. The hot sensor will generally be in a pocket in a pipe near the collector outlet, or it may be in a representative collector which has no water flowing through it. This second method measures the *stagnation temperature* of the collector and is used quite often in swimming pool heating solar systems.

Freeze Protection. A collector may be protected against freezing by a number of simple techniques:

1. Use of anti-freeze fluid in the collector circuit. This ensures that the collector cannot freeze, but requires the use of a heat exchanger to transfer the heat into the potable water.
2. Operation of the pump for a short time to replace the water in the collector with warmer water from the tank. This leads to a small loss of heat and requires power to the pump to be maintained and accuracy of the controller, to work effectively. However, it is used successfully in many installations.
3. Drainage of the collectors when the pump is not running. This ensures that the collectors are empty when a freezing condition occurs but all pipework must be installed to ensure that no part of the collector array is left with water in it.
4. Use of a valve which will drip water slowly at a low temperature. This will ensure a circulation of water in the collector and so prevent freezing.
5. Provision of low power electric elements in the collectors which are energized automatically if the collector temperatures falls to near freezing. This method requires electricity to be available and thermostat accuracy to ensure correct operation.

Over-Temperature Protection. Excessively hot water can cause a scalding hazard or possible damage to the tank material. A pumped system can be set so that the controller will not energize the pump if the tank is already at the maximum desired temperature. However, for a thermosyphon it is possible to increase the water temperature up to the boiling point if little water is withdrawn, e.g., while the household is away for vacation or if the system is being used at a substantially reduced load.

A thermosyphon can be protected from high temperatures by a thermostatic valve which will cut off the flow of water in the inlet pipe to the collector or by a thermostatic valve which will allow water to circulate through an uninsulated heat dump pipe if the water temperature is too high. Anti-scald mixing valves are also available to mix in cold water so as to give a constant maximum hot water temperature at the outlet.

Pumps. Pumps for solar systems should be chosen for the duty cycle requirement. Generally they operate in the domestic situation under a low-flow, low-head regime. However, the prime requirement is reliability when operating for long periods at high temperatures.

The pump should be sized to pump through the collectors a volume approximately equal to the daily average volume used in the household on an average solar day. This will enhance the required stratification in the tank.

Pipework. The materials used in pipework between the collector and the tank should be capable of withstanding the pressure and temperatures possibly developed under the worst operating conditions. They must also be passed by the local water supply authority as suitable to handle potable water, if a heat exchanger is not used.

A recent development has been the use of two small bore tubes bundled with control lines and insulated as a means of improving the installation time. This system is also ideal for low flow systems which enhance stratification and use very little pumping power (Ref. 22.7).

Sizing of Solar Systems. Systems can be sized by a number of methods, the most widespread of which is probably the *F*-Chart (Duffie and Beckmann) procedure and a number of modifications based on that method. These are available to run on microcomputers and can give fairly accurate forecasts of the likely performance of a system on a monthly basis. The optimum size will depend on a number of cost parameters, and most computer programs will optimize the system for the particular local conditions. However, for a standard domestic installation it is often best to buy a prepackaged system from a local supplier which is sized to suit the average household in the locality.

For larger households or households with more hot water required for household devices than is normal for that region, a system with both larger collector and storage should be specified. In general a person will use 40–50 US quarts, (40–50 liters) per day and each major appliance, e.g., dishwasher or clothes washer (if not self heating), will use as much as an extra person. The *preheat tank volume* should be sufficient for at least one full day's use.

System Tests. A number of tests have been developed throughout the world to assess the performance of a solar water heater under a given set of conditions (Refs. 22.8 and 22.9). Some of these test results can be extrapolated to other locations and loads (Refs. 22.10 and 22.11). However, most will only give a rating of one system against another at a given set of conditions. The Australian Standard tests (Refs. 22.9 and 22.13) are carried out over a range of conditions either outdoors or indoors under a solar simulator. From these test results it is possible to extrapolate to a range of locations and loads. Similar work is being carried out in Europe in an attempt to develop a shorter test procedure (Ref. 22.14).

Structural Considerations. A standard collector is generally of the order of 20 ft^2 (2 m^2) in area and will weigh approximately 77 lb (35 kg) when empty. When full it will hold only 2–3 US quarts of water weighing 4.5–6.5 lb (2–3 kg), giving a total of approximately 80 lb (40 kg). A solar collector array for domestic water heating would generally consist of two or three of these collectors. It is recommended that manufacturers' literature should be checked for exact weights.

The overall weight of the tank will of course depend on the volume of water is contains. One US quart (1 liter) of water weighs over 2 lb (1 kilogram), so a 300 US quart tank (300 liters) will weigh approximately 200 lb (80 kg) when empty and 880 lb (400 kg) when filled.

For a close-coupled thermosyphon and for an ICS this weight will need to be borne on the roof. For a remote thermosyphon the load will be carried within the ceiling.

Installation

Poor installation provides the main cause of complaints regarding inadequate performance of solar water heaters.

It is important that the installation be carried out by a competent tradesperson who has undergone a manufacturer's training program to correctly install the brand of equipment being used.

Siting. For best performance the collectors should be sited facing the equator (South in the Northern hemisphere, North in the Southern hemisphere) at a slope of approximately latitude angle. Deviation of up to 30° from the optimum direction will not significantly decrease the system performance. Deviation of 30–60° can be accommodated by installing additional collector area. The collectors should not be shaded for any substantial time of the day especially for three hours either side of solar noon.

The collector is quite often best integrated with the existing slope of the roof rather than incurring the extra cost of a frame to change the slope to latitude angle.

Thermosyphon systems require a minimum slope of 10° to operate properly, and the piping of a remote thermosyphon must have a constant slope of 1 in 10 minimum. It must not have any bends that could trap air, leading to a cessation of flow.

The water heater should of course be mounted in close proximity to the area of main hot water use (bathroom and kitchen) in order to minimize the pipe heat losses.

22.4. SWIMMING POOL HEATING

For many people the cost of heating a pool through conventional means such as gas, oil, or electricity is far too expensive to be considered. Besides conserving our natural energy sources, a solar pool heating system can provide a cost-effective and reliable answer for pool owners (domestic, public, or commercial) wishing to heat their swimming pools.

A solar system can reduce heating costs by as much as 70 percent for pools currently heated by oil, gas, or electricity. Local weather conditions usually dictate how much energy solar systems save. In temperate climates up to 5 to 6 months of swimming can be expected, an increase of 2–3 months, when using a properly designed and installed solar system without any boosting. In other areas the increase in swimming season and comfort will also be considerable.

Unlike a solar domestic water heating system where a collector and a storage vessel need to be purchased, the swimming pool is the heat store for a solar pool heating system so the additional requirements are only the collector, controller, pump, and associated plumbing fixtures. Another difference between pool and domestic water heating is that the pool heating load is only that required to maintain the temperature of the water, not to heat up replacement water.

As most of the heat loss occurs from the surface of the pool, the load to be supplied by a solar system is approximately proportional to the surface area. Heat is lost by convection, conduction, and radiation but mainly by evaporation; thus the use of a pool cover (a floating plastic blanket) will reduce heat losses considerably by reducing evaporation.

For example, a pool maintained at 80°F (27°C) will have a heat loss of 490 Btu/ft^2 day (4.9 MJ/m^2 day or 0.14 kWh/ft^2 day) if the air temperature is 68°F (20°C) and relative humidity 60 percent, or 850 Btu/ft^2 day (8.5 MJ/m^2 day or 0.24 kWh/ft^2 day) if the air temperature is 79°F (26°C) and relative humidity is 60 percent. However, by using a pool cover for 12 hours per day these figures are reduced to 260 Btu/ft^2 day (2.6 MJ/m^2 day) and 450 Btu/ft^2 day (4.5 MJ/m^2 day), or 0.07 and 0.13 kWh/ft^2 day.

This example illustrates the benefits of using a pool cover when the pool is not in use.

The use of a pool cover is also beneficial indoors, as it

reduces the amount of water vapor in the air and thus decreases condensation on windows and the building materials. The pool cover, however, adds an extra complication to the aspect of safety, and no-one should swim in the pool without the pool cover being totally removed. It is impossible to "surface" under a pool cover, as there is no access to air.

As the temperature at which heat is required in a swimming pool is quite low, it is generally most cost effective to use unglazed absorbers, as the glazing will approximately double the cost of most pool heating systems. Most unglazed systems on the market will produce similar output per square meter of absorber, so the collectors are quite often specified on the basis of area. Also as the pool heat load is approximately proportional to the pool surface area, the ratio of collector surface area to pool surface area is generally specified as being appropriate for particular pool types in particular locations.

Outdoor and Indoor Pools. It is generally found that for outdoor pools it is necessary to install a collector area of more than 50 percent of the pool surface area to give a suitable increase to the pool temperature. It is generally not cost effective to exceed 120 percent of the pool surface area, as the pool temperature will be limited by the lower performance of the collector at higher temperatures, due to larger heat losses. The use of larger pool heaters will, of course, allow faster heating of the water to comfortable temperatures after a bout of inclement weather may have cooled the pool to an unacceptable temperature.

Indoor pools generally require slightly higher temperatures and generally do not have the benefit of solar irradiation directly heating the water surface, so a larger solar heating array is generally required.

An indoor pool may also require the use of semi-glazed collectors if it is operated at higher temperatures, especially for therapeutic uses. A semi-glazed collector is one which has a transparent cover to reduce convection losses but does not have additional insulation and may well be vented to atmosphere.

A wide variety of commercially available solar systems now exist for swimming pool applications. Copper systems have been virtually superseded by unglazed plastic or rubber systems, which are not affected by the wide range of chemicals used to treat swimming pool water.

A variety of different rubbers and plastics are now widely used. Among them are ethylene-propylene-diene monomer (EPDM, synthetic rubber), Polyvinyl chloride (PVC) compounds, polyethylene, and polypropylene. It is important that the material be formulated for use as a pool heater, especially in order to avoid degradation due to ultraviolet light. The absorber is generally fabricated as a rigid panel or a flexible strip. A panel has the advantage of some degree of self-support, especially useful if mounted at a different angle to the roof. A strip, on the other hand, requires more support but has the advantage of flexibility in sizing.

It can be cut to fit the roof exactly and also fitted around chimney skylights, etc.

Plumbing Considerations. The solar heater can be plumbed into the filtration circuit or into a separate solar circuit. A completely separate circuit (see Fig. 22.4.1) is the most desirable option, but this can only be exercised if an outlet and return inlet is available.

If the system is to be plumbed into the existing filtration circuit, care must be taken to avoid problems caused by interaction with other devices on that circuit. In particular, the filter operating pressure should not be increased significantly by the addition of a solar heating system. A separate solar pump may be required if this is a problem or if the filter pump will not bear the extra load.

Figure 22.4.2, based on the Australian Standard (Ref. 22.12), shows three possible plumbing configurations which can be used to avoid most problems. Note that the pipe returning heated water to the filtration circuit must return before an auxiliary heater and also that a salt chlorinator (if fitted) must be immediately before the return to the pool inlet to avoid the build up of explosive chlorine gas, in any part of the circuit. Nonreturn valves should be placed in such a way so as to ensure that the collector does not backflush the filter into the pool when it drains. In areas prone to freezing, provision must be made to allow the system to drain down when not in operation.

Siting Features

The solar heater is best sited facing the equator. However, significant deviations to the west will not cause a significant loss of performance, and even the placement of the collector on a flat surface will still give good performance (Ref. 22.15). It is generally most cost effective to mount the collector flush with a suitably facing roof as near to the pool as possible. The site should remain unshaded for the greater part of the day, especially within three hours of solar noon.

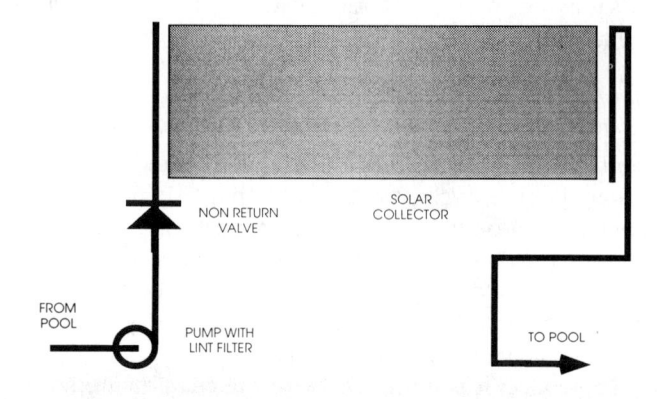

Fig. 22.4.1. Solar pool heating circuit separate from filtration circuit (from AS 3634-1989).

ACTIVE SOLAR ENERGY SYSTEMS 389

The collector should be mounted in such a way as to avoid trapping debris or moisture under the absorber, as this can lead to corrosion of metal roofing materials.

Regular visual inspection should be carried out to check for leakage, as chemicals used in pool water can cause corrosion or other damage to some roofing materials if left in contact for extended periods.

22.5. SOLAR SPACE HEATING AND COOLING

Solar Space Heating

The methods of providing solar-efficient design structures has been adequately covered in Chapter 21. Attention will be given here only to active solar heating and cooling systems for space conditioning in the house or office.

The basic components of an active system are:

1. An array of collectors
2. A heat storage system
3. Pumps and controls
4. An auxiliary heating system
5. A load

The arrangement of these components is shown schematically in Fig. 22.5.1. The lines joining the various components represent the pipes, or ducts, that carry the fluid from one section of the system to another. The most common fluids used for this task are water and air (Ref. 22.2).

Water-Based Heating Systems. Consider a system in which water is the heat transfer fluid and the storage system is a large tank of water. If the sun is shining the collector absorbs solar radiation, converts it to heat, and heats the water within the collector. An electronic controller senses the temperature in the collector and when this temperature is high enough that water flowing through the collector will be heated to a temperature higher than that of the storage tank water, the collector pump is turned on.

Water is then pumped from the storage tank through the collector, where it is heated, and then back to the storage tank. When insufficient solar radiation is available to heat the water passing through the collectors, the controller switches the pump off. In this manner energy is absorbed

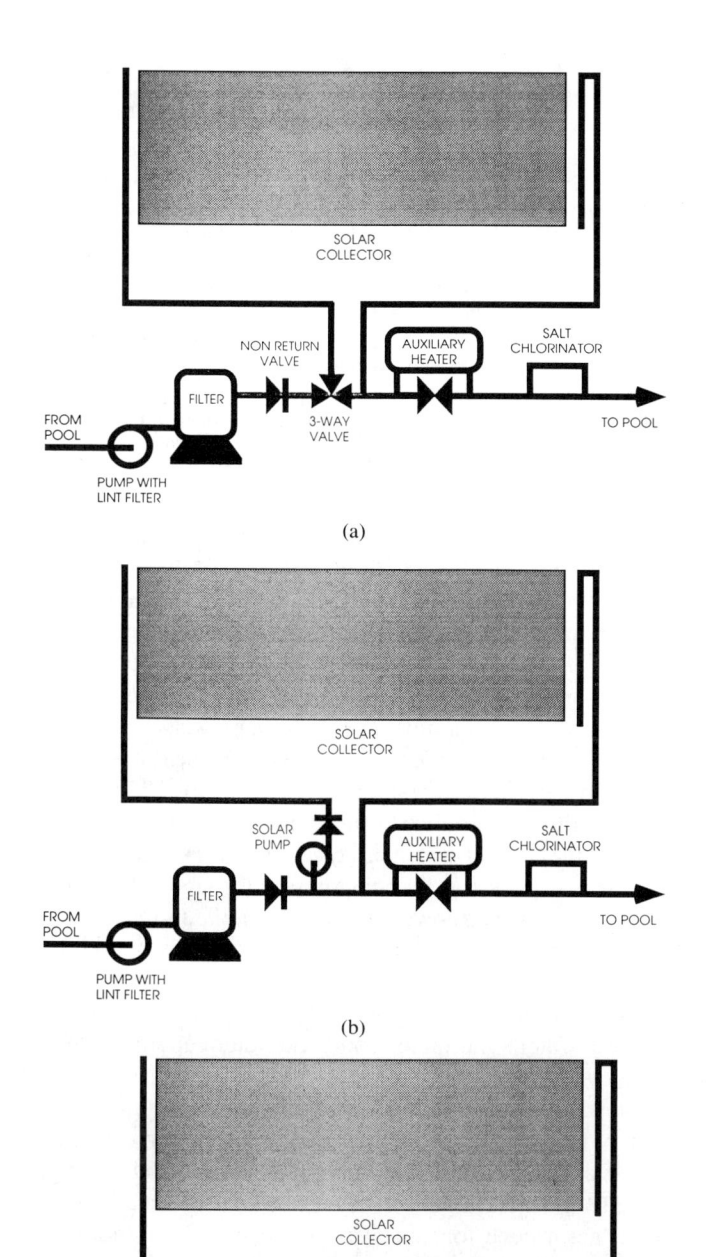

Fig. 22.4.2. Solar pool heating circuit integrated with filtration circuit. (a) Utilizing filtration pump; (b) utilizing a solar pump interlocked to run only when the filter pump is running; (c) utilizing an independent solar pump (from AS 3634-1989).

Structural Considerations. A solar pool heating collector will generally add little to the total weight of the roof, weighing between 1 and 2 lb/ft^2 (4 and 8 kg/m^2) when filled.

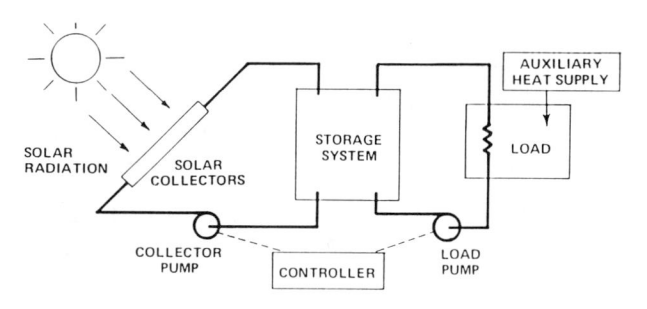

Fig. 22.5.1. Active solar energy collector system.

390 HANDBOOK OF ARCHITECTURAL TECHNOLOGY

when available, transformed to heat, and stored in the storage tank. When heat is required by the load a controller measures the water temperature available from the storage tank and compares this to the water temperature required by the load. If the storage tank temperature is higher, then energy is available from the storage tank. The load pump is turned on and hot fluid is passed from the storage tank. If there is no energy available from the storage tank, the controller turns on the auxiliary energy supply and so heat is provided to the load.

Air-Based Heating Systems. The basic arrangement of an air-based system is shown schematically in Fig. 22.5.2. Air, having been heated as it passes through the collectors, can be directed either to the rock bed storage unit or the load, depending on the load requirements. The flow paths are determined by a system of dampers. When the collectors are not operating and there is useful energy stored in the rock pile, the dampers may be arranged so that air is passed through the store and then to the load. If the storage is exhausted, an auxiliary heating unit must be used to meet the load requirements. The auxiliary heating system may be in series or parallel with the solar system.

Comparison of Air and Water Systems. The choice between an air-based or liquid-based system is a difficult design decision. For situations where heated air is the desired output (e.g., a space-heating application) air-based systems appear quite attractive because no heat exchangers are needed. However, water has much better thermal and heat transfer properties than air and so it is difficult to make a definite statement that one system is better than the other. Further comparisons between air and water systems are given in Table 22.2.

Solar Space Cooling

All conventional air conditioning systems (see Section 20.15) use an electric motor to drive a vapor compression refrigeration device using one of a range of chlorinated fluorocarbons as a working fluid. Although it is technically feasible to provide this electrical power by solar means using photovoltaic solar cells, the costs would generally be prohibitive. For this reason attention has been focussed on solar absorption cycle systems using lithium bromide and water, or water and ammonia as working fluids.

The solar energy collected in the form of heat is used to activate the cycle of operation, as shown in Fig. 22.5.3 for a typical lithium bromide/water chiller unit, so-called because of the chilled water produced which is used to provide the cooling effect by being passed through a water-to-air heat exchanger known as a *fan-coil unit*. In these units heat is added in the generator and the evaporator, and rejected in the condenser and the absorber. The operation of the unit depends on the capacity of the concentrated lithium bromide–water solution to absorb the water vapor produced in the evaporator.

For such units to work effectively the solar collectors must be capable of providing heat at generator temperatures in excess of 185°F (85°C) and preferably in the range 185–212°F (85–100°C). This means that high-quality collectors are needed for this task. For periods when the solar input is insufficient to provide the necessary heat input an

Table 22.2. Comparison of Air and Water Systems.

	Air System	Water System
Corrosion	Potentially low risk	Potentially high risk
Leakages	Unimportant if small	Any leak serious
Freezing damage	Very low risk	Potentially high risk
Boiling, pressure problems	None	Protection needed
Ducting, piping	Large space required for ducts; potentially high cost	Small fluid pipes Potentially low cost
Pump or blower requirements	Relatively high power	Low power
Storage volume	Larger than water systems	Smaller than air systems

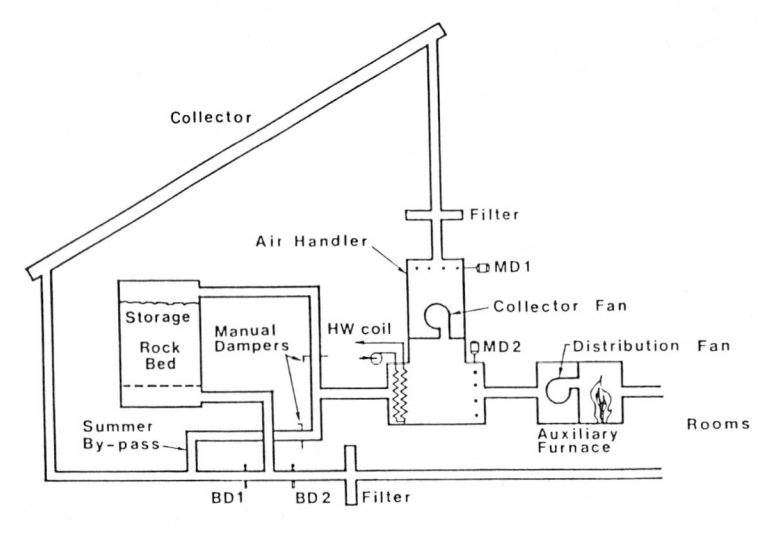

Fig. 22.5.2. Typical layout of solar air system.

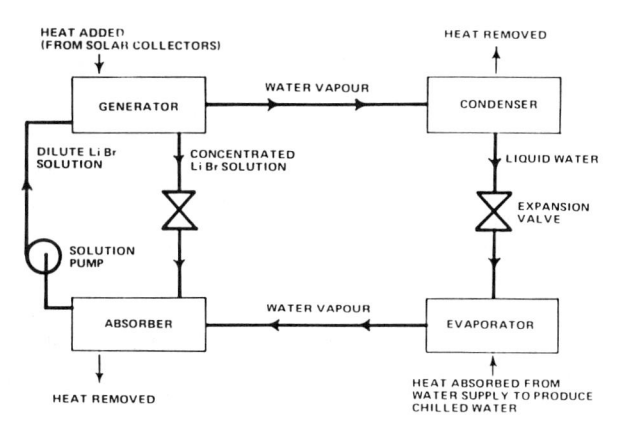

Fig. 22.5.3. Schematic diagram of LiBr/water chiller.

auxiliary heater can be provided, or the chilled water can be stored and recycled as required.

For most units a cooling tower is required to ensure adequate and effective heat rejection for the absorber and the condenser. Some modern commercial units have been designed with air-cooled absorbers and condensers, but such units require the minimum generator temperature to be raised from about 185°F (85°C) to temperatures approaching 211°F (92°C), and higher flow rates (kg solution per kg refrigerant) are used to guard against the possibility of crystallization.

To size and cost the solar arrays used for solar absorption chiller units a practical rule of thumb is to use 150 to 200 ft^2 (15 to 20 m^2) of collector for each ton of refrigeration capacity (i.e., per ~3.5 kW of cooling capacity).

22.6. STAND-ALONE POWER SUPPLIES

The costs associated with solar power systems are such that in many countries it is difficult for them to compete against grid electricity generated from conventional sources (see Chapter 23). On the other hand, if grid extension costs have to be provided by the potential customer, it is often more economic these days to install a stand-alone hybrid power system, an effective load management control device, and to use energy efficient appliances (Ref. 22.16).

Silicon solar cell arrays, both single crystal and polycrystalline, are becoming increasingly common for remote-area power supplies where it is vital to provide reliable, maintenance-free power. The basic solar photovoltaic power system consists of four main component parts (see Fig. 22.6.1).

1. The solar cell array of individual panels
2. A storage battery bank
3. Charge regulation
4. A blocking diode

The charge regulation is used to limit the battery voltage during periods of intense radiation, while the blocking diode is used to prevent the battery from discharging back into the solar array during the night when the electrical load is being met from the battery store (Ref. 22.17).

Sizing of Solar Systems

Because solar cell arrays are still relatively expensive at about US$6/peak watt, it is necessary to size the array as accurately as possible. For this exercise it is necessary to know the load characteristic, the battery storage capacity and the temporal pattern of solar radiation at the selected site. Virtually all solar power arrays are of fixed orientation and inclination angle, so they are subjected to considerable variations in input radiation on a daily and on a seasonal basis.

Experience accrued in Australia, on using remote-area solar power supplies, has shown that it is reasonable to expect the ratio of peak array output to 24-hour average load to vary from 6/1 to 9/1, provided the battery storage is sized to give 12 to 20 days' reserve capacity. On sites with a daily average solar radiation of the order of 2000 Btu/ft^2 (20 MJ/m^2) solar cells can compete with small diesel engines of up to 1 to 2 kW output (Ref. 22.18).

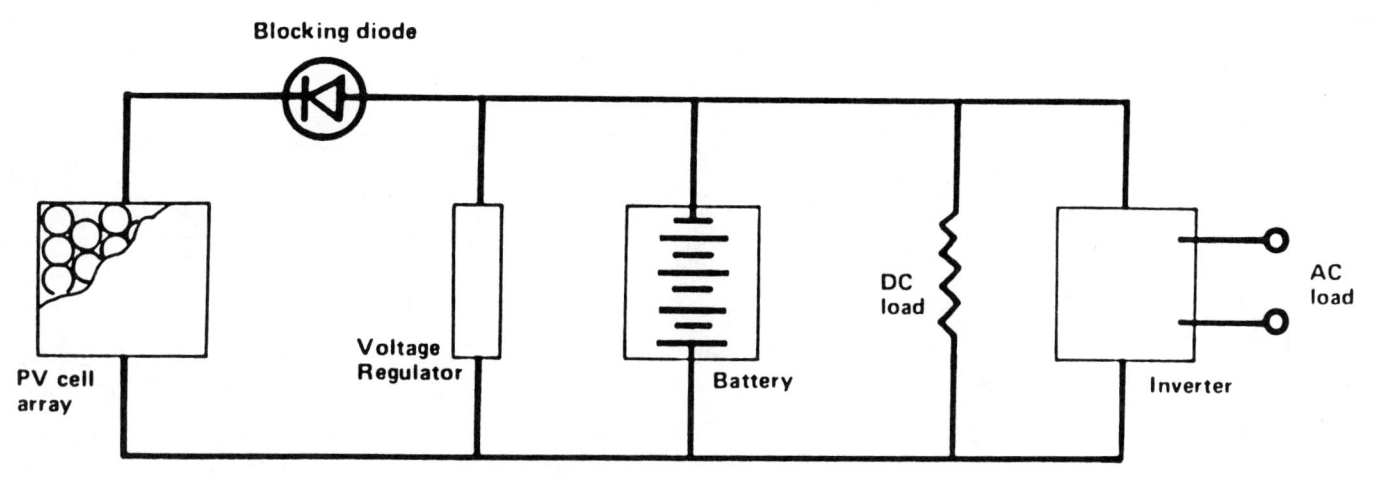

Fig. 22.6.1. Diagram of solar photovoltaic circuit.

REFERENCES

22.1. K. Butti and J. Perlin. *A Golden Thread*. Van Nostrand Reinhold, New York, 1979.

22.2. W. W. S. Charters and T. L. Pryor. *An Introduction to the Installation of Solar Energy Systems*. Victorian Solar Energy Council, Melbourne, Australia, 1982.

22.3. W. W. S. Charters and T. L. Pryor. *Theory and Design of Solar Thermal Systems*. Victorian Solar Energy Council, Melbourne, Australia, 1982.

22.4. J. A. Duffie and W. A. Beckman. *Solar Engineering of Thermal Processes*. John Wiley, New York, 1980.

22.5. W. B. Stine and R. W. Harrigan. *Solar Energy Fundamentals and Design with Computer Applications*. John Wiley, New York, 1985.

22.6. W. W. S. Charters and C. W. S. Dixon. "The Heat Pump Option—Use of Ambient Energy" *Solar '88 ANZSES Conference*, Melbourne, Australia, 1988.

22.7. K. G. T. Hollands, D. R. Richmond, and D. R. Mandelstam. "Re-engineering Domestic Hot Water Systems for Low Flow. *Proceedings Intersol '85*, Montreal, Canada, 1985, pp. 544–548.

22.8. ASHRAE. *Methods of Testing to Determine the Thermal Performance of Solar Domestic Water Heating Systems*. Standard 95-1981. American Society of Heating, Refrigerating and Ventilating Engineers, New York, 1981.

22.9. Standards Association of Australia. *Solar Water Heaters—Method of Test for Thermal Performance—Outdoor Test Method*. AS2984-1987. Sydney, 1987.

22.10. G. L. Morrison and H. N. Tran. "Correlation of Solar Water Heater Test Data." *Solar Energy*, **39**, 135–142 (1987).

22.11. S. A. Klein and A. H. Fanney. "A Rating Procedure for Solar Domestic Water Heating Systems." *ASME, J. Solar Energy Engineering*, **105** (Nov. 1983).

22.12. Standards Association of Australia. *Solar Heating Systems for Swimming Pools*. AS3634-1989. Sydney, 1989.

22.13. Standards Association of Australia. *Solar Water Heaters—Determination of Thermal Performance—Simulator Test Method*. AS2813-1985. Sydney, 1985.

22.14. W. B. Gillet and J. E. Bates. "DHW System Testing Procedures Discussion Document." Report on DHW, System Testing meeting, ISPRA February 1986. *Proceedings of Fourth G. S. T. G. Meeting*. Lisbon, 1986.

22.15. K. I. Guthrie. "The Optimum Direction and Slope of Unglazed Solar Pool Heating Collectors." *Solar '87, ANZSES Conference*. Canberra, Australia, 1987.

22.16. W. W. S. Charters. *Solar and Wind Power for Remote Areas and Rural Communities*. CSC (85) ENP-8. Commonwealth Science Council, London, 1985.

22.17. W. W. S. Charters. "Small Scale Stand Alone Power Supplies." *ISLANDS 88—Energy for Rural and Island Communities*. Hobart, Australia, 1988.

22.18. M. Mack. "Solar Power for Telecommunications." The Telecommunications Journal of Australia, **29**, 1 (1979).

SUGGESTIONS FOR FURTHER READING

E. Baker et al. *Solar Heating and Cooling Systems*. Pergamon Press, New York, 1984.

British Standards Institution. *Solar Heating Systems for Swimming Pools*. BS 6785. 1986. London, 1986.

J. C. V. Chinnappa, S. S. Murthy, M. V. K. Murthy, K. P. Stark. *Active Solar Cooling Systems*. James Cook University, Townsville, Australia, 1984.

D. M. Considine (Ed.). *Energy Technology Handbook*, Chapter 6, "Solar Energy Technology." McGraw-Hill, New York, 1977.

J. T. Czarnecki. *Swimming Pool Heating by Solar Energy*. Technical Report 19. CSIRO Division of Mechanical Engineering, Highett, Australia, 1978.

W. C. Dickinson and P. N. Cheremisinoff (Eds.). *Solar Energy Technology Handbook*. Marcel Dekker, New York and Basel, 1980.

R. C. Jordan and B. Y. H. Liu (Eds.). *Applications of Solar Energy for Heating and Cooling of Buildings*. GRP170. American Society of Heating, Refrigerating and Air Conditioning Engineers, New York, 1977.

J. F. Kreider and F. Kreith (Eds.). *Solar Energy Handbook*. McGraw-Hill, New York, 1981.

SRCC. *Test Methods and Minimum Standards for Certifying Solar Water Heating Systems*. Standard 200-82. Solar Rating and Certifying Corporation, Washington, DC (Revised February 1985).

NOTE

A list of abbreviations of the units of measurement, definitions of these units, and conversion factors between British/American and metric units are given in the Appendix.

23

Electricity in Buildings

Anthony D. Stokes

This chapter deals with electrical aspects of buildings. It includes a brief introduction to the methods of making simple electrical calculations. It deals with electrical power supply, including the possible need for in-house substations, the quality of supply availability for different purposes, the importance of standard installation codes to insure safety and the need for adequate lightning protection. Communications and other users of electrical space are also covered, together with some of the demands likely to be made in the near future, such as optical-fiber signalling, computer requirements for reduced electrical noise and "uninterruptible supply."

23.1. INTRODUCTION

Electricity has enormous power for both good and bad. The brilliant arc of the early lighthouse was a powerful lifesaver. The same kind of arc, burning uncontrolled within a building, is something to avoid at all costs. Starting in the late 1800s, electricity usage increased rapidly, first for lighting purposes and, a little later, as a driver of machinery. Accompanying this growth was a clear recognition of the need to ensure the safety of installations. To this end, all countries have a detailed installation code. In the USA, this is the NEC, National Electricity Code, which, with variations among the states, is the "bible" of the electrician. These codes are very detailed and the extremely low incidence of both fires caused electrically, and of electrocutions, is a tribute to their effectiveness.

In this chapter, the broad principles concerning electricity usage will be given. The aim is not to permit the architect so much to design the detail of an electrical installation, but rather to plan the spaces required and to discuss the possibilities during early negotiations with clients. Texts such as Porges (Ref. 23.1) and McGuinness et al. (Ref. 23.2) give information at the level required for more detailed electrical planning, while installation overviews can be found in Traister (Ref. 23.3) for 110-V systems and Petherbridge and Williams (Ref. 23.4) for 230-V installations.

Electricity has now so invaded our society that the capital cost of power distribution and communications networks is often as much as 10 percent of the cost of a large building. For electricity-intensive buildings, such as an electricity substation, computer center, telecommunications exchange, police, fire, medical, or other security business, the cost can be much higher.

In highly developed countries, the growth of electric power usage has tended to level out at between 2 and 4 kW per person. In Canada, where hydroelectric power is cheap, or Australia, where coal is cheap, electricity may frequently be used for heating as well as other purposes. In Europe, the tendency is to use fuels such as natural gas for heating and cooking, reserving to electricity those things for which it has an absolute supremacy, such as lighting and rotating machinery, including refrigerators, air conditioning, and elevators (lifts), leading to a lower electricity consumption. Communications networks continue to expand at a much faster rate than power usage, and now place major demands on the pathways into and within a large building. Communications, including radio and television, although small users of electric power and energy, are large users of electric space and materials.

23.2. FUNDAMENTALS

Three quantities are fundamental to any calculation of electric circuits: the *current I*, measured in amperes, the *voltage V*, measured in volts, and the *resistance* $R = V/I$, measured in ohms. An often used analogy is with fluid flow, where voltage is seen as the equivalent of pressure, current the equivalent of flow, and resistance akin to friction. The calculation of simple circuits, involving only direct currents and linear circuits, relies on three basic notions:

1. The sum of currents I_j entering from any one of j different directions into a node, or single point, is

$$\sum_{j=0}^{N} I_j = 0 \qquad (23.1)$$

2. The sum of voltages developed around a closed loop, consisting of N different elements, is

$$\sum_{j=0}^{N} V_j = 0 \qquad (23.2)$$

3. A complex circuit consisting of many interconnected loops and nodes can always be replaced by a simple equivalent consisting of a single voltage source and a single resistance; this is known as Thevenin's theorem

Almost all electric circuits that will be of interest to the architect are linear. It is anticipated here that the nonelectrical architect will only need to analyze circuits of relative simplicity so that the benefits of Thevenin's theorem will be available. This benefit will be complicated by the fact that normal electricity power supply is by alternating current, abbreviated as AC, at frequencies of 50 or 60 Hz. The use of AC allows transformers to step the voltage up and down. The power transmitted is determined by the product of the current flowing in the line and voltage difference between lines, and hence high voltages, up to 760 kV, are used for bulk power (e.g., Canada to New York). Depending on the circumstances, high voltages from 220 kV to 1,100 kV can be used for bulk power transmission. These high-voltage lines are the major pipelines that feed key substations. Substations vary enormously in size from a major focus that could occupy a land area of 1000 × 1000 ft (300 × 300 m) and supply a small city, to, at the other extreme, a pole-top or pad-mounted substation with a rating of 300 to 700 kVA, supplying perhaps 50 to 100 domestic consumers.

The analysis of AC circuits involves two extra linear elements, the *inductor* and the *capacitor*. These are devices that, unlike the resistor, can store electrical energy in the fields that they create. If we draw a mechanical analogy where velocity is the equivalent of current, then a car driving along a road at a velocity u has a kinetic energy $\frac{1}{2}mu^2$. To stop the car, this energy must be either converted into potential energy (coasting up a hill to a stop) or into heat (brake friction).

An inductor is an electrical device that stores magnetic energy in the flux which it creates in the surrounding air. In its simplest form, an inductance is simply a coil of wire. The inductance can be increased by coiling the wire onto a steel core, which focuses the flux and allows it to circulate with less magnetic resistance. The energy W stored in an inductance L is $W = \frac{1}{2}Li^2$, where L is the electrical equivalent of the mechanical mass m, and i is the instantaneous value of the current, which is constantly varying in AC circuits.

Perhaps the most common inductor of everyday life is the car ignition coil. The coil is charged with current by mechanically closing a switch (the distributor) to the battery. A short time later, the distributor rotates to a new position and the switch opens. Electrically, this is like an attempt to rapidly stop the moving car. A rapid increase in reverse acceleration is needed, which electrically is a large rise in voltage, $V_L = L(di/dt)$, where (di/dt) is the electrical "acceleration" and V_L is the electrical "force." The large rise in voltage, which can reach values of 30,000 V, is sufficient to flash the gap of the spark plug, so limiting any further increase in voltage and, instead, allowing an electrical current to continue to flow within the electrical coil. From the electrical point of view, the fact that this process ignites the fuel contained within the cylinder is entirely incidental.

The above electromechanical analogy emphasizes that the voltage across an inductance does not vary with the magnitude of the current, but with the rate of change of current in time, di/dt. It is exactly as in the mechanical analogy, where no force is needed to allow a moving mass m to continue traveling at a fixed velocity u. Forces are needed only when there is a rate of change of velocity du/dt to accelerate or decelerate the moving mass.

Similarly, for a capacitance C, the energy stored is $\frac{1}{2}CV^2$, where C is the electrical analogue of a mechanical spring. The current that flows in a capacitor is $i_C = C(dv/dt)$. Again, it is the time change of the electrical quantity, this time dv/dt, that is important. For this reason, we make a distinction between the instantaneous value of the current i and voltage, v, compared with their effective values I and V.

In a DC system, i_L and v_C do not change and hence i_C and v_L are always equal to I_C and V_L.

In an AC system, the current in an inductor alternates sinusoidally at a frequency f, so that $i_L = I_L \sin \omega t$, where $\omega = 2\pi f$ is called the *radian frequency*. The voltage across the inductor is $v_L = L(di_L/dt) = I_L \omega L \cos \omega t$. The same thing is true for a capacitor, with a voltage $v_C = V_C \sin \omega t$. The current through such a capacitor flows entirely in the air, or insulation space between the metal parts of the capacitor, and is $i_C = Cdv_C/dt = CV_C\omega \cos \omega t$.

The angle ωt is simply an angle that increases with time.

In a pictorial sense, it can be thought of as rotating at a constant speed in an anticlockwise direction. This idea has been used to considerably simplify the analysis of AC circuits, and is especially useful for circuits of the kind used for electricity supply. These circuits commonly include both resistance and inductance. For a current $i = I \cos \omega t$, the voltage drop across a resistor is $v_R = RI \cos \omega t$. Similarly, the voltage across an inductor is $v_L = LI\omega \sin \omega t$. The voltages v_R and v_L can be added directly because they are instantaneous values occurring at the same time. To do so would require the keeping of a continuous account of the voltage changes as they develop at different times. Instead, we make use of the fact that the two voltages vary in synchronism with each other, although they reach their maxima and minima at different times. For example, when $t = 0$, $\sin \omega t = 0$ and $v_L = 0$, but $\cos \omega t = 1$ and $v_R = RI$ is a maximum. In general, the sum of two such voltages can be represented as shown in Fig. 23.2.1, where $X_L = L\omega$ is the *reactance* of inductor L; similarly $X_C = 1/(\omega C)$ is the *reactance* of capacitor C. If for any reason one wished to know the instantaneous voltage across two or more such components, that voltage can be pictured as the horizontal projection of IZ, in Fig. 23.2.1, rotating around the circle at a speed ω. At time $t = 0$, the voltage would be IR. At time $t = 1/(4f)$, corresponding to $\omega t = \pi/2$ or $\sin \omega t = 1$, the voltage would be IX.

The magnitude of impedance Z is the ratio of the instantaneous maximum of power-frequency voltage to the instantaneous maximum of power-frequency current, that is, $Z = \sqrt{R^2 + X^2}$. The impedance of a combination of electrical elements takes a different value depending on frequency. However, unless one is dealing with the complication of harmonics, the impedance of a given network will be determined by the frequency of supply, which normally will be held to an accuracy equivalent to a loss, or gain, of a few seconds in a day. Electric clocks depend on such a high accuracy for the correct display of time over extended periods.

Associated with the impedance is the *power factor*, which is the cosine of the angle θ in Fig. 23.2.2. The power factor is used to determine how much average power will be consumed by the load, $P = I^2 Z \cos \theta = I^2 R$, compared with the power that simply oscillates between the power supply and the fields created by inductors and capacitors, $Q = I^2 2 \sin \theta \sin 2\omega t$. This ''oscillating'' power is a major

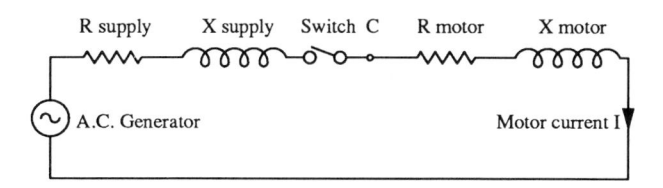

Fig. 23.2.2. Series electrical circuit. R denotes a resistance, X denotes a reactance, and I refers to the current flowing in the circuit. In this figure, A, B are the points of connection of the motor to the supply.

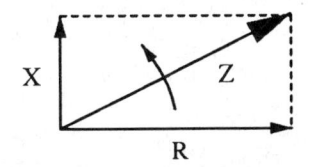

Fig. 23.2.1. Vector sum of resistive and reactive impedances. R = resistive voltage drop; X = total reactive voltage drop, which may include inductive and/or capacitive components; Z = combined impedance.

problem for a utility, since ordinary metering registers only the actual (real) power P of the load and records the oscillating part Q of the load as zero because it has, indeed, a zero average value. To supply the increased currents associated with this additional *reactive power* requires heavier transmission lines, and greater costs, than would be needed for a zero reactive power. In addition to the real and reactive powers P and Q, it is common to refer to equipment ratings in terms of the product of the rated current that can be passed through the device and the rated voltage. The VI product is called VA, kVA, or MVA, as appropriate. Transformers and switching equipment are examples of devices that have MVA ratings much larger than the actual power which they dissipate.

How might this problem of reactive power be of importance to the architect? Without complicating matters too much, the reactive power requirements of inductors and capacitors are equal and opposite. So, for an installation with a substantial motor load, presenting inductive reactive power demands, a bank of capacitors can be used in the main switchroom to confine the demands on wiring, for the supply of reactive power, to the building itself. Alternatively, the architect may insist that each motor, elevator, air-conditioning system, etc., of any size, be fitted with power-factor-correction capacitors to create a local balance. This is a better solution, since the reactive power of the capacitor is connected only when needed to balance that of the inductive (motor/other) load. Fluorescent lighting is also a significant user of reactive power and a significant generator of electrical harmonics. By the judicious use of capacitors, both the problems of supplying reactive power and the major effect of harmonics can be avoided.

Electrical circuits can be connected in series, as in Fig. 23.2.2, or in parallel, Fig. 23.2.3. Let us assume that the load represented by R_{motor} and X_{motor} of Fig. 23.2.2 is one phase of a three-phase induction-motor-driven air conditioner. The corresponding source impedance has the elements R_{source} and X_{source}, representing the connecting circuits to the utility's source of supply. The question to be answered in this example is, ''by how much will the voltage at the customers premises, point A, fall when the motor is switched on?'' If this voltage drop is too large then a flicker effect will be observed that may fall into one of three categories (Table 23.1). It may simply be observable, it may be irritating, or it may be so large as to be objection-

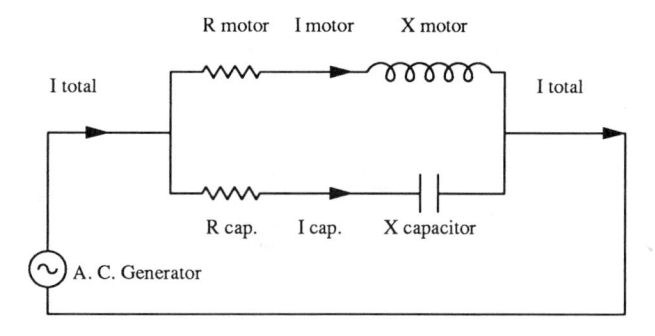

Fig. 23.2.3. Parallel electrical circuit. R denotes resistances, X denotes reactances, and I refers to current flowing in the appropriate circuit.

able. The values given in Table 23.1 are based on observer tests using a 60-W tungsten filament lamp. It is evident that the human response to flicker depends very much on the frequency of repetition. One will put up with much more when the flicker rate is say 1 per hour than 10 per second.

Section 23.10 gives a worked example, in tutorial style, of an actual calculation using the above problem as an example of a series AC circuit. Section 23.11 gives a similar treatment for the problem of power-factor correction as an example of an AC parallel circuit.

23.3. ELECTRIC POWER DISTRIBUTION

Electric power is nearly always generated at central stations and transmitted at high voltage to load centers where it is broken down with transformers to lower voltages for local distribution and to domestic voltage values for final supply. At each point of transformation, there will be switching and protection equipment grouped together as a substation.

The aim of such an approach is to reduce the currents transmitted to values usually less than about 4000 A. The effect is to minimize heat losses caused by transmission resistance to some 10 percent of the energy being transmitted. Another important aim is to limit the size of the currents that can flow in the event of a fault. Faults can range from a few hundred amperes to many tens of thousands. The momentary touching of conductors caused by the careless drilling of a wall space is an example of the

Table 23.1. Observer Responses to 60-W Tungsten Lamp Flicker Caused by Voltage Changes.

Repetition Frequency	Voltage Change, Percent, for the Onset of:		
	Observation	Irritation	Objection
30 per second	not seen	not seen	not seen
10 per second	0.4	0.7	1.0
5 per second	0.3	0.5	1.0
1 per second	0.4	0.7	1.6
1 per minute	0.6	1.7	5.2
1 per hour	3.0	6.0	8.0

first, and could produce momentary currents up to several thousand amperes if the site is close to a distribution focus (a substation). An excavator ripping into a high-voltage cable is an example of the second; this can result in momentary currents of over 100,000 A. Such currents may have a truly explosive effect, mechanically, thermally, and in their effect on the restoration of normal electricity supply. The electricity authority must cater for both extremes and all in between. The architect must recognize the possibilities in terms of the protection provided at points of electrical power focus.

Depending on the size of a building, the supply may be taken at high voltage to one or more substations within the building. As a rule of thumb, a building requiring more than 1000 kVA of electricity demand is likely to have such a substation, often within a basement or at ground level. It will be located in a separate room of approximately 12 ft (4 m) square.

If a new building is located in an area where electricity usage fully loads the existing utility equipment, the utility may require the installation of a substation in the building to serve the requirements of occupants and those of future customers in the area. Details of ownership and responsibility for the construction of the substation should be clarified at an early stage in overall planning.

The upper limit for a single substation is determined by the outgoing load currents. A large substation of 3 MVA will require an area of some 28 × 10 ft (8.5 × 3 m) and include many more outgoing circuits with their individual protective devices. Where several large substations are needed, these will be divided, more or less evenly, among

Fig. 23.3.1. Grosvenor Place, Sydney. (a) External view (Architect: Harry Seidler).

ELECTRICITY IN BUILDINGS 397

the floors of the building. Grosvenor Place, a 45-story tower in the center of Sydney, gives a modern example of such arrangements. Fig. 23.3.1a is an external view, while Fig. 23.3.1b gives an overview of the electrical supply network within the building. Individual transformers of 1.5 MVA are connected as parallel banks. Each weighs some 12,000 lb (5,500 kg) and is placed in position during construction of the steel framework. Such transformers are extremely reliable. Nevertheless, provision should be made for replacement access in the event of a failure.

Almost as important as making provision for replacement in the event of damage is the growing need to provide ample capacity in new buildings and to supplement services in existing buildings. In the mid-1980s the typical office used an electrical typewriter and a telephone. An average electricity demand was around 200 W/ft^2 (20 W/m^2). Today, so much more electrical equipment is being placed within the office, including computer-based word-processors, fax machines, desktop photocopiers, and the like that a very average figure for the 1990s will be at least 600 W/ft^2 (60 W/m^2). In Grosvenor Place, which is an up-market building with a variety of tenants, but in no sense an electrically intensive building, the measured demand during 1989 was 116 W/m^2. Figures of up to 200 W/m^2 are now being seriously planned for in electrically intensive applications.

Whereas the "cancer" of reinforced concrete has been a significant problem of large buildings during the decade past, the next decade is likely to see electrical strangulation as a major issue. Buildings will be in increasing difficulty if they do not have adequate space set aside to allow for additional services to be run through the building and the

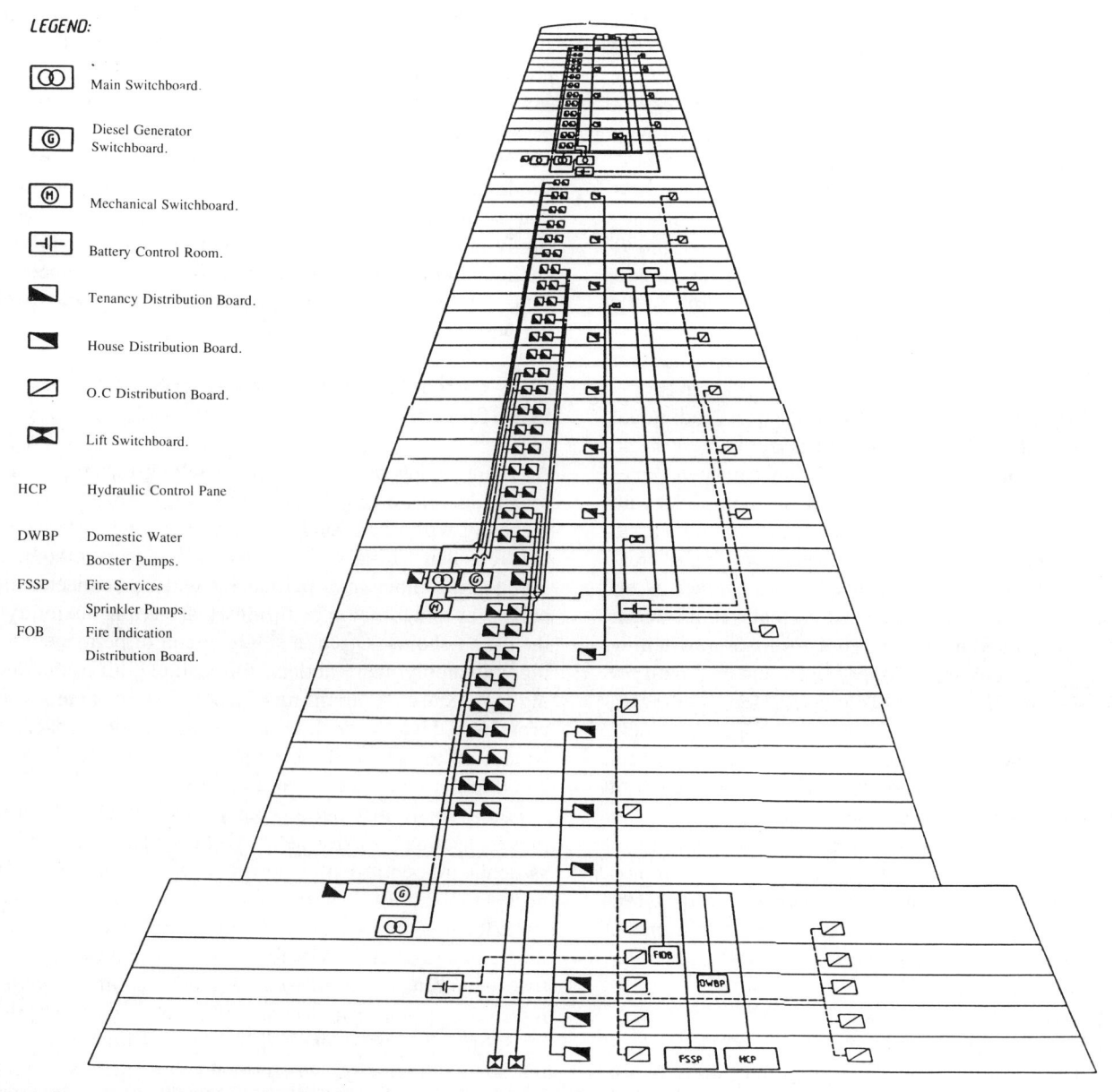

LEGEND:

- Main Switchboard.
- Diesel Generator Switchboard.
- Mechanical Switchboard.
- Battery Control Room.
- Tenancy Distribution Board.
- House Distribution Board.
- O.C Distribution Board.
- Lift Switchboard.

HCP Hydraulic Control Pane
DWBP Domestic Water Booster Pumps.
FSSP Fire Services Sprinkler Pumps.
FOB Fire Indication Distribution Board.

Fig. 23.3.1. Grosvenor Place, Sydney. (b) Electricity supply arrangement. (Reproduced by courtesy of the Electrical Consultants, Barry Webb and Associates, Pymble, Sydney.)

necessary space within their service areas for supplementary substation, switchboard, and control equipment. Tenants will increasingly desert buildings that have lost their electrical "wind".

23.4. THREE-PHASE, SINGLE-PHASE, AND LOAD BALANCING

High-voltage city supply is invariably arranged as a three-phase system in which there are effectively three generators mechanically coupled so that they run together at the same speed, but with their alternating output voltages shifted in time by an amount equal to one-third of the time of one cycle. When such a generating group feeds a set of three equal loads, for example, a three-phase water heater, the currents drawn in each phase are similarly shifted in time. Without going into the details, the three currents that supply the load are so arranged in time sequence that, when added together as instantaneous values of current, they sum to zero. By shifting the exact times at which the real power is supplied to the individual circuits, the three-phase system delivers power along each of the lines in such a way that the return current returns along the other two lines, each of which will, at a slightly different time, deliver their part of the total power. The situation is truly one where, electrically $I_1 + I_2 + I_3 = 0$, even though I_1, I_2, and I_3 may be, and, indeed are expected to be, equal in magnitude. For a balanced three-phase system the vectors I_1, I_2, and I_3 are spread equally around a circle.

The key advantage of the *balanced* three-phase system is that, at any instant, the sum of the outgoing currents is zero even though each does useful work in its individual load. Because the three currents add to zero, there is no need to provide individual return paths. A balanced three-phase load requires only three supply wires, compared with six of the same size for three separate loads. In both cases, a ground (earth) wire may also be needed for safety reasons. In addition, a single return wire, the *neutral*, is always run to take up any unbalanced currents, to allow for harmonics generated in some types of loads (switching power supplies, fluorescent lamps, etc.), and as a path for fault currents that flow when wiring has become damaged. Although the three-phase system is by far the most widely used, the same points hold true for any polyphase system with balanced loads. *Balanced* simply means that each of the polyphase elements of a grouped load is equal, or at least very nearly equal, to the others in the polyphase load.

Three-phase connections are by far the most common and are used when the load to be supplied exceeds a few kilowatts, for example, water heaters, air conditioners, large motors. In these cases, the load will also be a balanced three-phase load.

For smaller rated loads, only single-phase supply is used, in effect by connecting to only one of the equivalent generators referred to above. Each of the three limbs of the transformer terminates in a *neutral* point. The other points are called *actives*.

When single-phase loads are connected to a three-phase transformer, it is important to distribute the loads as evenly as possible among the three phases and to be sure that the neutral return conductor can safely carry the unbalanced currents. Although complete load balancing is unlikely in a given space, the combination of spaces and multiple loads does even out satisfactorily in practice.

When a system is being used with all three phases, it is common practice to nominate the voltage difference between phases as the basic value. For single-phase supply the voltage referred to is the active to neutral value. Thus, the one system can be described as 110/190 (North America), or 220/380 (Europe and Australia), where the first number is used for single-phase and the second for three-phase. To further confuse the picture, in some countries, especially where the lower voltage (110/190) supply is used, there are difficulties in supplying loads such as fluorescent lamps, and a two-wire system for single-phase supply is used, where one wire can be thought of as supplying +110 V while the second −110 V. In this case, the supply is quoted as 220 V, being the difference voltage between the two wires.

For most single houses and apartments, supply will be single-phase, the load being balanced by connecting other houses in the area to other phases. For a supply significantly in excess of 10 kVA, most utilities will require balancing within the installation and a three-phase connection. Thus any building significantly larger than a single dwelling will have three-phase supply.

23.5. CIRCUITS, SWITCHBOARDS AND SUBSTATIONS

A circuit is any run of permanent wiring that supplies an *outlet*, such as a plug socket or a lamp socket, or a permanently wired item such as a cooking range. *Permanent wiring* is that wiring which is installed as part of the building. Wiring other than permanent will be connected into outlets by plugs or other fittings that permit flexibility at the user's choice. Often, a single circuit of permanent wiring will supply many outlets, for example, all of the lighting for a house. A circuit runs back to a switchboard where protective devices, such as a fuse or circuit breaker, are connected to isolate the circuit in the event of short circuits, or the need to carry out repairs.

For a small installation, all of the circuits, lighting, power, heating, cooking, etc., will be supplied by a single switchboard controlled by a master switch and in turn connected to the utility's wiring. For larger installations, these switchboards will form only part of the network. It is common to have such a switchboard on every floor of a multistory building of substantial size, and the circuits are then referred to as *final subcircuits*. Final subcircuits are joined by *subcircuits*, or *submains*, to the next higher levels of the supply hierarchy, where again there will be switchboards in a treed structure (Fig. 23.5.1), leading finally to the main switchboard. In a substantial building, occupied

ELECTRICITY IN BUILDINGS 399

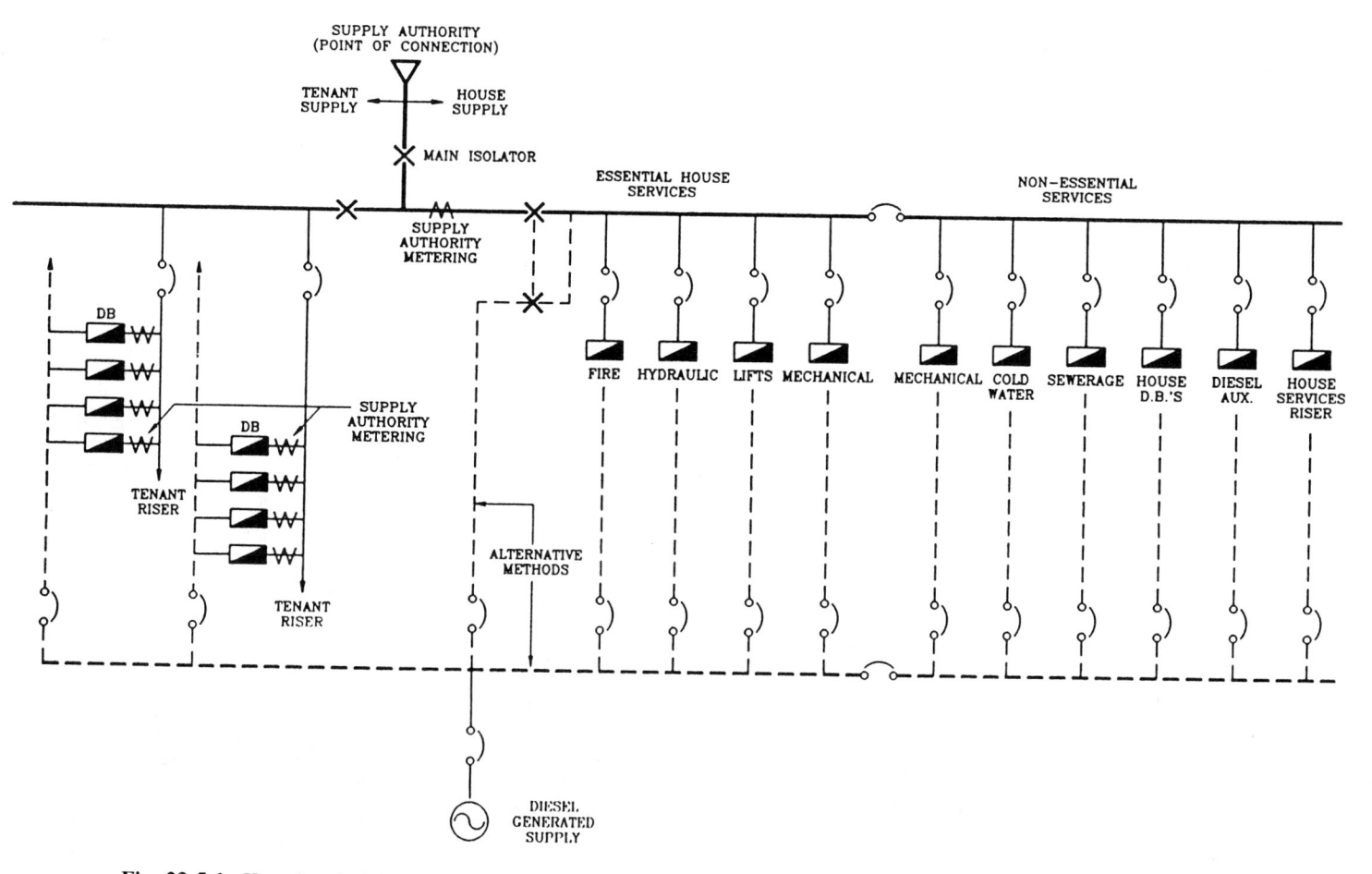

Fig. 23.5.1. Key electrical facilities within a major building. (Reproduced by courtesy of Barry Webb and Associates.)

by, say, 100 people, the main switchboard may be large enough to occupy its own service room and may include sophisticated control apparatus aimed at minimizing energy or peak load consumption to take advantage of local electricity tariffs.

When the load is high enough to warrant a transformation from a higher voltage for the incoming supply, the installation will also include a transformer and the switchboard/transformer combination becomes a substation.

Switchboards, and especially transformers, develop small but significant amounts of heat when drawing their rated currents. They cannot operate satisfactorily in a fully enclosed environment, but require good ventilation to limit temperature rises. They do not emit noxious fumes during normal operation, but can generate copious smoke and other unpleasant byproducts in the event of the rare arcing fault. For this reason, ventilation should be directed away from points where such byproducts could cause difficulties.

23.6. POWER DISTRIBUTION PATHS

The pathways for electric power distribution within a building are nowadays either completely hidden in offices, or managed in external ducts or trays for industrial buildings. For offices, the paths are often contained in decorative channels that hide the joints between structural parts. Although some building regulations do permit the embedding of suitably insulated wiring within the structure of walls, ceilings, and floors, this arrangement virtually excludes the possibility of easy change to meet future needs. Such measures should be used only for the last leap from a close-by duct to the final wall or ceiling outlet.

The details of building construction will ultimately be negotiated with electrical contractors. However, it is a good practice to ensure that the contractors lay draw wires within the electrical pathways. Draw wires do nothing but lie in wait. When needed, they are used to pull through additional wiring *and* a new draw wire, which lies in wait for the next occasion. With this in mind, it is also good practice to provide ample space at key turning points so that future drawing can be accomplished in stages, without binding at such turning points.

An example of an electric power pathway is given in Fig. 23.6.1. Here there are many circuits emanating from a substantial switchboard that controls the delivery of power to some 15 floors of a large building. Fig. 23.6.2 shows another aspect of the power pathways that are usually hidden within a false ceiling space, but in this instance pass from an unenclosed service area into the more fully finished parts of the building. While electric power circuits

Fig. 23.6.1. Electrical path ways leading from one of the main switchboards at the 13th level of Grosvenor Place. (Reproduced by courtesy of Barry Webb and Associates.)

Fig. 23.6.2. Electrical and other services within a false ceiling space. (Reproduced by courtesy of Barry Webb and Associates.)

cannot usually be combined with other circuits, such as telephone, fire protection, and signal (bells, etc.) wiring, these restrictions are often relaxed when double or multiple insulation covers are provided for the power wiring cables. In the application shown, all wiring has the necessary double cover of insulation and can be seen weaving its way among a variety of other services including air-conditioning and water. By providing a generous space within this false ceiling the architect has set the scene for further development of the building during its useful life.

23.7. LIGHTNING PROTECTION

For tall or exposed buildings, protection from attack by lightning is most important. Schonland's book *The Flight of Thunderbolts* (Ref. 23.5) is a fascinating and extremely readable account of the history of superstition, devastation, and eventual realization of the means for protection from lightning strikes.

The first line of protection is the *lightning conductor*, which projects above the building, receives the stroke, and transmits it to ground. The conductor does not need to have a large cross section; approximately $\frac{3}{8}$ inch (10 mm) diameter is quite sufficient. However, it must be firmly bonded to the building to resist electrodynamic forces. These are focused at points of change of direction. Such changes should be gradual and strongly locked in place.

It must not be thought that the lightning conductor will eliminate the presence of high voltages during the stroke. The cloud voltage may be 200,000,000 volts or more. The voltage at the tip of the lightning conductor can exceed 1,000,000 volts, albeit for the briefest of times (about 0.05 millisecond). Persons within the building can experience difficulty if the various service circuits (electricity, phone, signaling, etc.) are not correctly electrically bonded to the protection. Very large voltage differences can occur within the building and can be a source of danger to persons, and to equipment which is either in close proximity to, or in contact with, two or more services. Facsimile machines, or more particularly the state of health of connected facsimile machines, are sensitive indicators of installation quality after a lightning strike to a building. The whole matter of safe interconnection of lightning protection is a matter for experts and we do not attempt here to describe the details. Golde (Ref. 23.6) gives an excellent review of this complex subject.

23.8. COMMUNICATIONS

Within recent memory, communications were limited to the post, the telephone, the telegram, and the telex. Those days are gone. There is now a continuous spectrum including voice, data, facsimile, text, image, video and mobile communications. The telephone has assumed a key role linking this equipment; it is being joined by in-house systems of increasing complexity, often used to link computer facilities, and the local area network (LAN). For communications and computing systems, the copper conductor is being replaced by the optical fiber. On the horizon are superconductors, yet to emerge as useful products, but offering a new challenge both to power distribution and computer systems.

For many buildings, the implementation of a modern communications system can be integrated with the hidden highways used for other services. The electrical complexity of these systems is not accompanied by bulk; in fact, quite the opposite is true. Perhaps the most important factor to include in a building design is ease of access to the hidden highways so that updating can be achieved with a minimum use of the hammer drill and preferably simply by removing panels. Where such access is needed frequently, such as a computing center, the entire floor can be constructed as a raised platform with removable panels giving access to the space below. It is most important to allow spare space at the focal points of the communications system, whether that be a cubicle or a service room. The electrical strangulation referred to earlier in connection with electrical power services applies with even greater force to communications facilities, and, indeed, to surveillance and security. There is also the question of providing isolation for the services of different tenants. Tenants will be happy to share the same electrical power, but usually require separation for other electrical services. Sometimes, for example, in a building providing financial services, it may be necessary to offer a very high level of assurance that communications services are completely isolated and that the isolation is well protected.

During operation, the most important requirement of these systems is freedom from interference. Interference can take several forms. In the case of security signalling, entrance and exit monitoring of doors, and the like, the interference may take the form of physical attack, requiring armoring or other protection of both the terminal equipment and its interconnection to monitoring points. Interference may also take the form of theft of information. More insidious is the interference that occurs when electric signals from one circuit couple in an unwanted manner into the circuit of another. For example, the electrical noise of a powerful welder may cause very significant interference to broadcast signals, be they for entertainment or communication. Switching impulses on a power circuit may couple directly into a computer network and be counted there as an item of digital information or, in fact, misinformation.

The advent of the optical fiber as a communication connector for telecommunications, computer, and other information exchange purposes, will greatly ease the problem of interference, since electric signals do not couple directly into an optical fiber. Optical fibers also offer added security against theft, since they are much more difficult to tap into without damage and will also protect against the entry of lightning problems since the fiber is an excellent insulator. The optical fiber is also capable of huge bandwidth, which, roughly translated, means that very many circuits, including those of different kinds, can be sent along a single fiber. Optical fibers are an excellent means for point-to-point communication. They do not, at present, lend themselves to the multiple connections that copper allows. For example, in a heavily loaded telephone network a new service can be easily offered by means of a party line, that is, two phones connected directly in parallel and answering to the same number. With an optical fiber network, such a parallel connection has been commonly made by a piggyback method involving the conversion of optical signal to electric, making the parallel connection electrically and then constructing a new optical signal for the second path. Optical couplers for single to double paths are now available for research purposes, as are optical switching devices. Although they require skilled optical splicing techniques for successful couplings, one imagines that it will only be a matter of time before these techniques transform the optical communications highway into the profusion of interconnections that is now common in copper-based systems. Halley (Ref. 23.7) gives an overview of the uses of optical fibers in buildings.

23.9. QUALITY OF SUPPLY

Some questions relating to both quality of electrical supply and to quality of electrical loads within a building were discussed earlier. The architect usually cannot influence the quality of electricity supply that arrives at the building. However, it has become increasingly necessary to influence, and sometimes to control, the quality of electricity supply as it reaches sensitive loads.

Ordinary Supply Quality

The quality of the ordinary electricity supply will depend on many factors, but particularly on the state of development of the country. Sophisticated users expect an electrical supply at the flick of a switch, and will complain bitterly if a perfect supply is not available. In a less developed society, it is expected that supply will be available most, but not all of the time. In such a society, it is far more important to avoid the consequences of a complete splitup of the system into small, isolated fragments than to assure absolute availability.

Fragmentation, such as occurred in the famous New York blackout, leaves the network completely disconnected and unable to supply power even for the network's own essential purposes let alone for continued normal operation. To run up a complex system from a *black* start can take more than a day of intense activity. During such prolonged blackouts, the loss of an essential service is not only inconvenient in the extreme, but dangerous for security reasons and for the delivery of health care. Looting and other crimes are major problems during an extended power failure.

The ordinary supply in a sophisticated society will be available, for ordinary purposes, for years at a time with no hurtful absence. During thunderstorms, it is very likely that some areas of a large city will experience a few seconds absence of power while the network takes the necessary protective actions to guard against unavoidable overvoltages. These switching operations, together with other normal switching operations of a utility to facilitate, for example, maintenance, create a variety of supply variations. These can include:

1. Sags: drops in voltage sustained over at least one cycle (more than 8 to 10 milliseconds) and, in some cases lasting for more than a second. An IBM survey (Ref. 23.8) during 1980 to 1983 found that some kind of undervoltage occurred, on average, once every 2.1 days.
2. Surges: the same as sags, but with an increase in voltage. These are much less common than sags. The IBM survey (Ref. 23.8) showed an overvoltage once every 32.2 days, on average.
3. Failures: complete loss of power. Failures occur at nearly the same rate as surges but are also, commonly, of short duration. The IBM survey (Ref. 23.8) showed that some kind of outage occurred, on average, once every 50 days.
4. Other switching disturbances and spikes: a spike is a very short, but relatively high overvoltage that can sometimes reach 10 times or more the normal supply voltage during its short life. These were the most frequent disturbance found in the IBM survey (Ref. 23.8). Spikes were found once every two days, and other switching disturbances at a near-daily rate.

These excursions from the norm are almost always fleeting events that cause no difficulty to the ordinary user. The normal, longer-term, variations of voltage that are frequently considered acceptable are ±10 percent. Many countries nominate more than one tolerance; one as a target to achieve most of the time (often ±5 percent) and another for which corrective action is expected in the fullness of a "short" time. Supply outside these limits requires urgent action and may require disconnection for safety reasons. For example, induction motors can stall if supplied at significantly reduced voltage. Paradoxically, a stalled induction motor draws more than the usual current and can therefore burn out. However, for most users, the abnormalities of supply noted above are of no significance and go largely unnoticed.

Uninterruptible Supplies

Some users are very sensitive to loss of supply for even a second. Foremost among these are the users of computers. Computers hold information in the form of electric signals, or the state of an electric circuit. They can pass their information to the more permanent form of magnetic storage, but this is a time-consuming process, on the time scale on which computers work, and is usually done only when a job has been finished. A power failure that occurs before the making of a permanent record will lead to the loss of all electronically stored data. Computer companies and the large users of computing equipment have therefore a very keen interest in preventing even momentary losses of electricity supply.

Data handling rates can easily exceed a million items a second. If a spike, lasting only about a microsecond, enters a computer, it may corrupt the data or instruction stream and produce a stream of computer garbage. Fortunately it is easy to protect a computer against the entry of fast incoming disturbances that run directly in from the power network. It is much more difficult to guard against airborne signals that arrive in the same way as do radio and TV broadcasts. If expected, they may require special architectural treatment by way of electrical shielding. Similar treatment is needed for electronically sensitive defense and other users; this may require the construction of a complete metal envelope around the sensitive area. Such an envelope does not need to be load bearing; however, it must be capable of preventing the unwanted entry or escape of airborne electric signals.

The users of large rotating machinery also have a problem when an outage of more than a second occurs, due to the dropping out of hold-in relays. These relays keep the electricity supply connected to the large motors, while supply continues to be active. If supply is lost for more than a preset time, the relays open and disconnect the motor from the circuit. Such motors require special starting arrangements and cannot be simply left on line after a power failure.

Other groups concerned with an ultrareliable supply include those delivering health care, police, fire, security, and other services. Except where they involve a computer element, these services can usually tolerate an interruption of a few seconds. They require backup supply, but not of the same uninterruptible quality, and particularly not of the same narrow tolerances essential to the large computer user.

Fig. 23.9.1. A diesel-driven uninterruptible supply used to provide security of electricity supply for a large computing center. (Reproduced by courtesy of Holec Australia, Sydney.)

Modern methods for the protection of electricity supply in demanding conditions range from providing a backup sufficient to warn of an impending complete shutdown and to expect that permanent storage action be taken as a matter of urgency, to a full backup supply that will continue to generate electricity as long as the normal supply is absent. The short-life systems again tend to be focused on computer applications, while the fully independent arrangements can also be used by large computer operators and by most of the other target users requiring an effective 100-percent-available electricity supply. To be fully effective, these systems will be driven by a renewable fuel, usually diesel, and will be a full substitute for the normal supply. The most demanding are the computer systems that permit no interruption. These require rotating machinery that is on line at all times with spinning flywheel mechanisms that will immediately respond to a loss of supply quality. As the loss develops, within 1 to 2 seconds a diesel motor will be fired into action to recharge the flywheel. Power will continue to be delivered, as a replacement for the deficient normal supply, until that supply recovers. Automatic switching equipment will then revert to taking normal supply. Fig. 23.9.1 gives an example of a 1.5 MVA plant in the computing center of a large insurance company.

Such a system relies on two factors for its exceptional performance. Normal supply is generally very reliable. During the rare moments of unreliability there is an excellent expectation that the reserve supply will be in good order and can be used as a substitute. The expectation that both will be unserviceable at the same time has been estimated at once in 220 years for a particular system. Expectations of this kind are comforting, but are open to question.

Smaller systems, typically less than 200 kVA, are more frequently supplied by a large battery set. Modern batteries, if well maintained, have a life of perhaps 10 years, and such a system will adequately cope with the shutdown needs where the more demanding requirement of complete freedom from supply difficulties is not needed.

APPENDICES

23.10. FLICKER AS AN EXAMPLE OF A CALCULATION IN AN AC SERIES CIRCUIT

Virtually all three-phase loads are balanced, which means that they can be considered as three separate single-phase loads. We take the example of a 6-kW motor and use typical values for the starting and running conditions. The per-phase load of this motor is $6000/3 = 2000$ watts. A typical running power factor is $\cos\theta = 0.9$ so that $VI \cos\theta = 2000$. For a phase voltage of 240 V actually applied to the motor, this gives a "rated" motor running current of $I_{MR} = 2000/(240 \times 0.9) = 9.25$ A. During startup, the induction motor draws a much larger current than the running value, and it is this larger current that must be used in the flicker calculation. Again, typical values for the motor starting current are $I_{MS} = 6I_{MR} = 55.6$ A. The starting power factor is much smaller, with typical values of $\cos\theta = 0.29$. The motor impedance at start is $Z_{MS} = V/I_{MS}$ and with $V = 240$ volts this gives $Z_{MS} = 240/55.6$, or $Z_{MS} = 4.32$ ohms.

The values of R_M and X_M for this example, corresponding to R_{motor} and X_{motor} in Fig. 23.2.2, are, $R_M = Z_{MS}\cos\theta = 4.32 \times 0.29 = 1.25$ ohms, together with $X_M = \sqrt{Z_{MS}^2 - R_M^2} = 4.14$ ohms.

The source impedance will depend on how close the point of connection is to the local substation. For the purpose of the example we take $Z_S = 0.3 + j0.8$ ohms. With the switch closed we find the total circuit impedance is

$$Z_T = Z_S + Z_{MS} \tag{23.3}$$

$$= R_S + jX_S + R_M + jX_M \tag{23.4}$$

$$= 0.3 + 1.25 + j(0.8 + 4.14) \tag{23.5}$$

$$= 1.55 + j4.94 \text{ ohms} \tag{23.6}$$

giving a current of $I_T = I_M = 240/Z = 240/\sqrt{1.55^2 + 4.94^2} = 46.3$ A. In Eq. (23.4), the shorthand notation with a prefix j has been used to indicate that, while the reactive impedances X can be added together and, separately, the resistive parts R can be added together, the X's and R's cannot be mixed. The j indicates that the impedance is reactive. It is positive for an inductive reactance and negative for a capacitive one. The quantity j can be thought of as an operator that rotates an x-axis number in the x-y space to point in the y direction, that is, it rotates the x direction by 90 degrees into the y. Similarly, two such rotations, corresponding with j^2, rotate by 180 degrees. Since a positive x number, when rotated by 180 degrees, becomes a negative one, the idea has developed, and can be supported mathematically, that $j = \sqrt{-1}$.

To continue with the practical aspect of the example, the current I_M flowing in the motor develops a voltage of $I_M Z_M = 46.3 \times 4.32 = 200$ V. When the motor is switched on the voltage will drop from the previous value of 240 V to a new value of 200 V, for a 17 percent change. Clearly such a drop would cause objection even if repeated only at an hourly interval. The only solutions are to use a smaller air-conditioning plant, or to increase the size of the source conductors by approximately a factor of 2.

23.11. POWER-FACTOR CORRECTION IN AN AC PARALLEL CIRCUIT

For a series circuit, the voltages are summed to equal the source voltage. In a parallel circuit, each of the currents is summed to give the total (Fig. 23.2.3), that is, $I_T = I_{MR} + I_C$, where I_T has been used for I_{total}, I_{MR} for the running current of the motor, and I_C for the current flowing in the capacitive branch. The same voltage appears across each of the branches, so that $V_{MR} = V_C$, giving $I_{MR} = V_{MR}/Z_{MR}$ and $I_C = V_C/Z_C$.

Consider the motor of the previous example, but now running under steady conditions. Repeating the above calculations but for the running condition will show that the running impedance is $Z_{MR} = 23.3 + j4.94$ ohms, the running current is $I_{MR} = 9.02$ A, and the motor voltage, $V_{MR} = 234.4$ V, each per phase. Notice that the actual motor current $I_{MR} = 9.02$ A is slightly less than the rated value calculated in the previous section, because the actual motor voltage $V_{MR} = 234.4$ V is less than the assumed rated voltage of 240 V. We now include the effect of the parallel capacitive branch, recognizing that the resistance of most capacitors is so low that we usually take $R_C = 0$, leaving $Z_C = 0 + jX_C = -j/(\omega C)$. The total current I_T for this parallel circuit is,

$$I_T = V_T/Z_{MR} + V_T/Z_C \tag{23.7}$$

$$= V_T \frac{R_{MR} - jX_{MR}}{R_{MR}^2 + X_{MR}^2} + jV_T\omega C \tag{23.8}$$

$$= V_T \frac{R_{MR}}{R_{MR}^2 + X_{MR}^2} - V_T \frac{jX_{MR}}{R_{MR}^2 + X_{MR}^2} + jV_T\omega C \tag{23.9}$$

where the identities $j^2 = -1$ and $1/j = -j$ have been used. Although these equations have a bulky look to them, it will invariably be found simpler to deal with parallel circuits using the reciprocal of the impedances as in this example, even if it is necessary to expand them as in the second line of these last equations.

The practical point of the example can be seen in the last line, where by placing a capacitance with a value of

$$C = \frac{jX_{MR}}{(R_{MR}^2 + X_{MR}^2)\omega} \tag{23.10}$$

the total current drawn by the parallel pair of circuits is actually reduced below that drawn by the motor alone, to

$$I_T = V_T \frac{R_{MR}}{R_{MR}^2 + X_{MR}^2} \tag{23.11}$$

or $I_T = 8.3$ A, compared with the previous value of 9.02 A. Moreover, the utility will be spared the need to supply a total of some $Q = 2900$ VA of reactive power that simply oscillates back and forth between the main supply system and the magnetic field of the motor. This power still oscillates, but now between the capacitor and the motor.

While electricity distribution networks are often much more complex than has been shown by these two examples, they can often be approximated by simple circuits and treated as above.

REFERENCES

23.1. F. Porges (Ed.). *The Design of Electrical Services for Buildings*. John Wiley, New York, 1975.

23.2. W. J. McGuinness, B. Stein, and J. S. Reynolds. *Mechanical and Electrical Equipment for Buildings*, 6th Ed. John Wiley, New York, 1980.

23.3. J. E. Traister. *Electrical Design for Building Construction*. McGraw-Hill, New York, 1976.

23.4. K. Petherbridge and W. Williams. *Australian Electrical Wiring*, 2nd Ed., Vols. 1 and 2. McGraw-Hill, Sydney, 1981.

23.5. B. Schonland. *The Flight of Thunderbolts*. Clarendon Press, Oxford, 1964.

23.6. R. H. Golde. *Lightning Protection*. Edward Arnold, London, 1973.

23.7. P. Halley. *Optical Fibre Systems*. John Wiley, Chichester, England, 1987.

23.8. Salzer Technology Enterprises (Ed.). "Standards and Power Quality," in *UPS and Other Power Protection Equipment, An International, Indepth Study Report on the Technology, Products, Markets and Companies*, Chapter 11. Salzer Technology Enterprises Inc, Santa Monica, USA, February 1986.

SUGGESTIONS FOR FURTHER READING

F. Porges (Ed.). *The Design of Electrical Services for Buildings.* John Wiley, New York, 1975.

W. J. McGuinness, B. Stein, and J. S. Reynolds. *Mechanical and Electrical Equipment for Buildings*, 6th Ed. John Wiley, New York, 1980.

B. Y. Kinzey, Jr. and H. M. Sharp. *Environmental Technologies in Architecture.* Prentice-Hall, Englewood Cliffs, NJ, 1963.

G. J. Hughes (Ed.). *Electricity and Buildings.* Peter Peregrinus, Hitchin, England, 1984.

NOTATION

Symbol	Meaning of Symbol, and Name of Units in which it is Measured	Unit Abbreviation
C	Capacitance, microfarads	μF
f	Frequency, cycles per second, measured in hertz	Hz
I	Magnitude of the current waveform, amperes	A
i	*Instantaneous value in time of the current, amperes*	*A*
j	Electrical operator signifying a reactance value	
kVA	See VA; 1 kVA = 1,000 VA; kilo-volt-amperes	kVA
MVA	See VA; 1 MVA = 1,000,000 VA; mega-volt-amperes	MVA
L	Inductance, henries	H
P	Electrical power (real), watts	W
Q	Electrical reactive "power," volt-ampere-reactive	VAR
R	Resistance, ohms	Ω
V	Magnitude of the voltage waveform, volts	V
v	Instantaneous value in time of the voltage, volts	V
VA	Product of current through a device, volts × voltage across the device, amperes	VA
W	Average value of the electrical power, watts	W
X	Reactance, ohms	Ω
Z	Impedance, ohms	Ω
ω	Radian frequency, $\omega = 2\pi f$	sec^{-1}

24

Water Supply, Drainage, and Refuse Disposal

Max Sherrard and Kevin Bach

This chapter deals with the distribution of water and the removal of unwanted waters and refuse.
The quality of water required for water supply is discussed, followed by methods for heating water, and the layout and sizing of pipes required for the distribution of hot and cold water, including the water required for fire services. Roof, surface, and subsoil drainage is then considered, as well as sewerage, waste disposal, and refuse disposal.

24.1. WATER SUPPLY

Fitness for human consumption is obviously the most important prerequisite of any supply. Guarantees must be provided on freedom from harmful bacteria and, to a lesser extent, suspended matter. Deficiencies are remedied by the addition of chlorine and by filtration. Chlorine in excessive quantities can itself be quite unpleasant and harmful, and accordingly it is dosed under controlled conditions. In extreme cases, chlorine dosing may need to be incorporated into the reticulation (distribution) system of a project.

The degree of hardness ("ability to obtain a lather with soap") and/or the taste will vary, depending on the source of the water supply. Treatment for hardness will vary from ignoring it, to the installation of softening or treatment equipment within the building. This equipment is normally sized to suit only the water used for washing or drinking, as the case may be; thus the internal plumbing must be divided into separate systems, serving either the treated or nontreated outlets within the project.

Although the availability of pure water from the water supply authority's* mains in the street is assumed, potable water is available from other, somewhat limited sources.

*The authority may be city, county, or state, or specially constituted authority, such as a water board.

Rainwater, water pumped from the ground or rivers, must always be treated with suspicion, unless long established local custom and usage indicates otherwise.

24.2. WATER RETICULATION (DISTRIBUTION)

Pressure available at the time of maximum demand in the authority's mains decides how the reticulation (distribution) system within the building will be designed. Pressure is necessary to drive water through the reticulation system; there should be a residual pressure of 9 psi, corresponding to a head of 20 feet (6 m) at the most disadvantaged fitting. Depending on how high up a building the most disadvantaged fitting is situated, the available pressure is reduced by gravity and by the flow through pipes, bends, and valves. Smaller-bore pipes, due to their larger wetted perimeter compared to their cross-sectional area, use available pressure at a greater rate than larger-diameter pipes with the same flow.

Lack of adequate pressure may be overcome by introducing either a booster pump, a head tank, or both (Fig. 24.2.1).

A small project can be provided with adequate pressure by a boosting pump supplementing the existing pressure from the mains; however, the size of the authority's mains needs to be considered. If a significant pumped demand

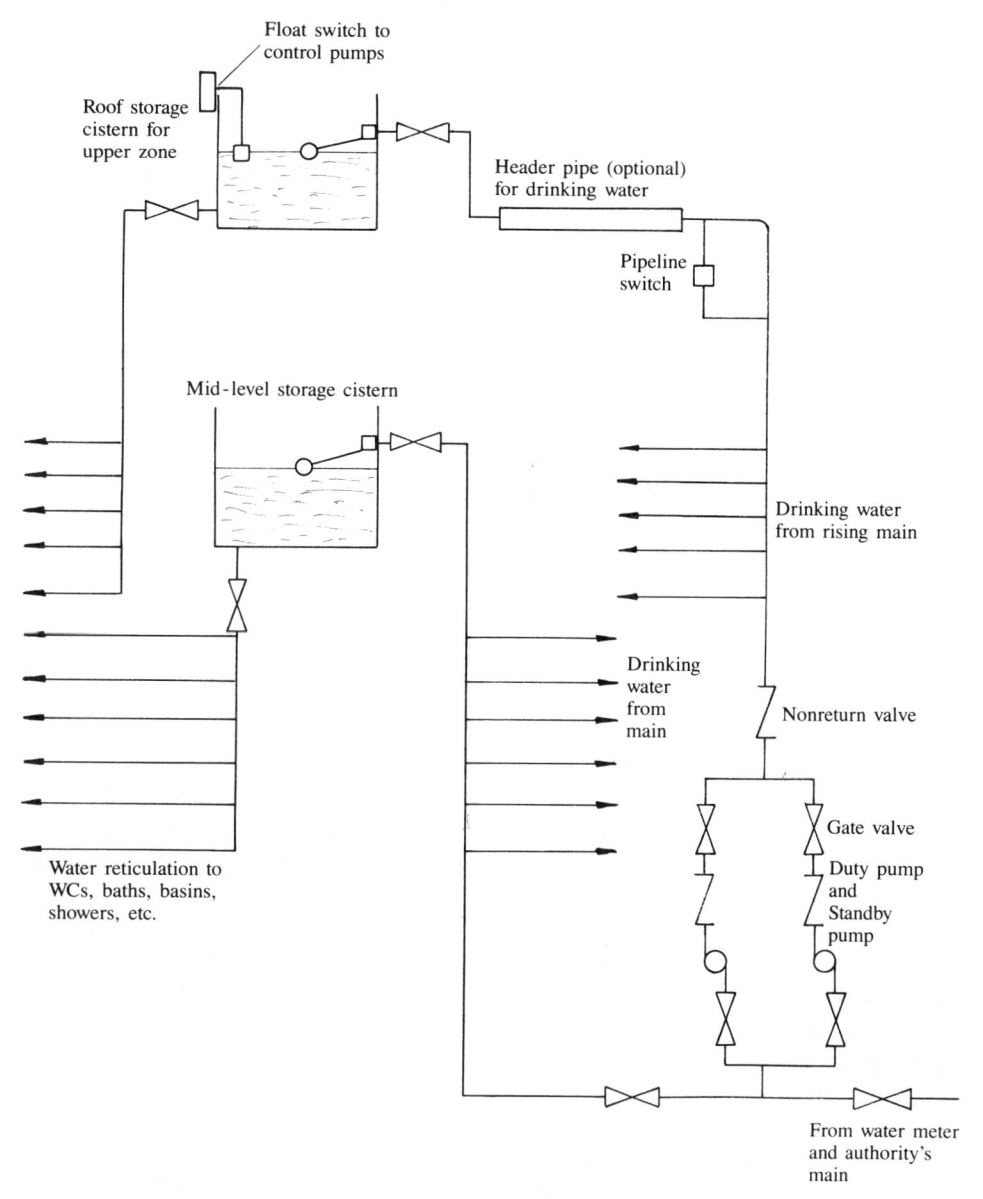

Fig. 24.2.1. Typical example of direct pumping from a main.

from the mains cannot be met, or nearby consumers may be inconvenienced, on-site storage should be introduced.

Some authorities require distribution from a head tank, even in areas of adequate pressure. This ensures a low uniform pressure to all fittings. Properly installed it prevents backsiphonage of potentially soiled water into the authority's mains; bidets, because of their design, are particularly susceptible to backsiphonage, and a break tank is frequently required.

For larger projects the installation of a head tank overcomes inadequate pressure in the supply mains. The size of the tank depends on the type of building and on its expected population.

Table 24.1, based on 24-hour usage, is satisfactory for a constantly maintained water supply. However, it should be adjusted if the water supply is subject to frequent interruption. For mixed classes of building the results should be added; for example, for an office with a canteen we need 10 + 2 = 12 US gals per worker per day.

Table 24.1. Water Storage Requirements for Buildings.

Class of Building	Water Storage Requirements	
	US Gals	Liters
Residential, per resident	24	90
Hotels, per guest	37	140
Office, per person	10	37
Restaurants, per meal	2	7
Schools, per pupil	7	27
Hospitals, per patient	37	140
Convalescent, per patient	30	115

Table 24.2. Water Usage by Fixture.

Fixture	Usage US Gallons	Liters
WC	2½	10
Shower	10	40
Bath	30	110
Hand basin	1	4
Kitchen sink	4	15

Alternatively, water usage can be determined from the average volume of water used by all the fixtures (Table 24.2).

Water tanks within buildings are generally sized to contain 1 to 2 days' usage. Excessive storage should be avoided, as the stored water may become stagnant. This problem can be overcome by distributing the drinking water directly from the supply pipe to the points, or feeding them from a smaller auxiliary tank. High buildings may need to be zoned to prevent the maximum pressure to any point exceeding 45 psi (a head of 100 ft or 30 m); this often coincides with the intermediate level of the mechanical plantrooms.

Water tanks may be fabricated from cast-steel panels (bolted together), lighter-gauge galvanized steel, or fiberglass. A tank that can be readily repaired is preferable. The tank should be covered to keep out dust and vermin.

24.3. COLD WATER

Pipes can be made from copper, plastic, steel, and lead (see Chapters 2 and 5). These materials are ranked in Table 24.3 for the attributes listed.

Copper piping is suited to the widest range of uses: hot and cold water, heating, gas, and drainage systems. The pipes may be joined with compression joints, soldered capillary joints, or directly by bronze welding or silver soldering. However, the last two are not suitable where vibration may occur, or the pipes are buried in the ground. Copper tubing is normally sized by its outside diameter; a choice of wall thicknesses is available. Chromium-plated copper tubing is acceptable for exposed pipework.

Table 24.3. Ranking of Materials for Cold-Water Pipes.

Property of Material	Copper	Plastic	Steel	Lead
Resistance to physical damage	2	0	3	1
Resistance to corrosion	1	3	1	0
Availability of sizes	3	2	2	1
Safety to consumers	2	3	2	0
Convenience of use	2	3	1	2

Ranking 3—best in group, 2—good, 1—moderate, 0—negligible, poor possession of property.

Plastic, like copper, has a smooth internal surface, offering low resistance to fluid flow. Unplasticized polyvinyl chloride (UPVC) pipes are suitable for both cold water and drainage systems, but should not be used for drainage taking a lot of hot water, because the pipes may soften. The pipes are jointed with a solvent cement applied to a socket-and-spigot joint. Plastic piping can be painted to improve its appearance when exposed.

Polyethylene piping is used for cold water services, frequently in underground applications where it can be conveniently placed in a ploughed trench. The use of this type of piping is almost universal in landscaping. Jointing is by means of compression fittings. Polyethylene piping is similarly unsuited to hot water, and as it is pervious to gas should not be used for this service.

Steel piping has a low initial cost, but because of its greater internal roughness it is hydraulically less efficient than copper or plastic. Jointing is by screwed or flanged joints, and these are less convenient than the methods used for plastic and copper pipes. Steel piping is available with a galvanized surface. This is normally used in water supply installations, although for heating or gas plain steel is frequently accepted.

Lead piping is susceptible to attack from soft water; small particles are picked up and carried in the water flow, and this makes it an unsuitable material for water supply pipes. The lime in lime or cement mortar corrodes lead pipe, but it can be protected by a dense tape wrapping. Although jointed easily with wiped soldered joints, its use as a piping material is very limited.

Pipes are fixed to walls, ceilings, and joists by clips or brackets, spaced to keep them in position. In services under pressure minor sagging is not important, but fixings should be located to avoid straining of the pipe. They should also be placed on each side of valves and intersections. For drain lines, however, sagging is not permissible, since continuous falls must be provided. Closely spaced adjustable suspenders must be provided for drains to insure that the correct gradient is maintained in the pipework.

Insulation of pipework is provided in areas subject to frost, to ensure continuity of supply and to guard against the damage caused by the internal freezing forces. Normally the areas requiring protection are the external services above ground, pipework in an uninsulated roof, and external faucets (taps) and meters. Local availability of materials determines the preferred methods of obtaining this necessary insulation.

The pipe sizes should meet the instantaneous demand or flow rate required at any particular fitting. Typical flow rates for a range of fittings are shown in Table 24.4. Pipes near to these fittings would then be sized for the sum of the instantaneous flow rates. Normally the diversity of demand will ensure that beyond the immediate vicinity of a particular complex, say, washroom, the pipework can be sized to suit the average flow conditions. The calculation of pipe sizes is discussed later in this section.

Table 24.4. Flow Rate from Sanitary and Kitchen Fittings.

	Instantaneous Flow Rate	
Fitting	US Gals/Min	Liters/Sec
WC flushing cistern	1.9	0.12
Wash basin	2.4	0.15
Wash basin with spray taps	0.6	0.04
Bath	4.8	0.30
Shower	1.9	0.12
Sink—$\frac{1}{2}$ in. (12 mm) faucets (taps)	3.2	0.20
Sink—$\frac{3}{4}$ in. (20 mm) faucets (taps)	4.8	0.30
Sink—1 in. (25 mm) faucets (taps)	9.5	0.60

Valves and Faucets (Taps)

Valves are used to control the use of a cold water system. They are installed systematically to isolate portions of a network so that it can be closed down for maintenance or other reasons. Normally, valves are similarly constructed to domestic faucets; however, the globe type should be used for very high-pressure applications, while gate valves can be used in low-pressure situations. When used in water supply, the valve stem is loose, so that it may act as a check valve at times of reverse flow in the pipeline, thus preventing possible backcontamination of the water supply. These valves are all of the screwdown type. Because of their relatively slow movement, they do not produce water hammer in the adjoining reticulation (distribution) system.

Faucets (taps) represent the user's contact point with the plumbing system, and they should be selected by the designer to suit the particular application. A bibcock is the conventional style, with a screwdown valve; however, a quick-action, lever-operated type can also be used. The pillar cock is similar; the pipe enters through the base and it can be mounted on the basin, either with its own outlet or combined with a hot-water pillar cock through a column spout. Spouts are available in many designs; those with an aerator or spray outlet result in the saving of a significant quantity of water (and also of fuel for heating the hot water). Piping and exposed taps are usually chrome plated.

Metering

Water supply is normally metered at the entry point into a building. Meters supplied and read by the water authority provide the basis for billing. Proprietors may also wish to monitor water usage, and further meters can be installed to particular portions of a building as required. A meter assembly normally would comprise a stop valve and meter; a check valve is included for larger installations, or if it is required by the authority. Meters are normally selected to be a size smaller than the entry pipe, to insure more accurate measurement of low flows. Because of the small length of the assembly, the head loss is insignificant. Suitable access to the water meter is required for the meter reading staff.

Maintenance

Maintenance to water supply systems is usually provided when it breaks down, rather than on a programmed regular scheme. The washers and/or glands of faucets need to be replaced to overcome leaks. Broken threads within a faucet can only be remedied by replacement of the part affected, or the whole of the fitting. If leaks within plumbing pipework are due to poor workmanship, they are normally discovered early in the life of the installation. However, leaks due to physical damage from an adjacent operation may occur later. Internal corrosion or deposition of carbonate salts reduces the efficiency of the system, eventually demanding replacement with a more resistant piping material, or installation of a water-softening device to remove the offending salt prior to its entering the private plumbing system.

Sizing

In calculating pipe sizes for either cold or hot water distribution, refer first to the minimum instantaneous demand flow rates as shown in Table 24.4. These should be totalled for the portion of the reticulation considered. This principle may be used throughout a system in calculating demand, but allowance for appropriate diversity leads to significant economies. For instance, as the network gets larger due to additional floors, pipes can be sized assuming successively 75 percent, 50 percent, and 25 percent of instantaneous demand. However, pipe sizes must increase in size as the system serves more points.

The diameter of the pipe required to give the calculated flow rate depends on the head available, the characteristics of the pipe's inner surfaces, the number of bends and valves, and the length of the pipe. The effect of bends, elbows, and tees can be incorporated by adding it to the equivalent pipe length (Table 24.5).

The available head is either provided by a booster pump or a head tank in the building, or it is obtained from the water authority's existing main in the street. This head is reduced by each stop valve in the line. The loss of head through a stop valve is dependent on its size and the flow

Table 24.5. Equivalent Resistance of Fittings.

Pipe Size		Equivalent Length of Pipe					
		Elbow		Tee		Faucet (Tap)	
in.	mm	ft	m	ft	m	ft	m
0.5	15	1.6	0.5	2.0	0.6	0.7	0.2
0.75	22	2.6	0.8	3.3	1.0	1.0	0.3
1	28	3.3	1.0	4.9	1.5	2.0	0.6
1.25	35	4.6	1.4	6.6	2.0	—	—
1.5	42	5.6	1.7	8.2	2.5	—	—
2.0	54	7.5	2.3	11.5	3.5	—	—

Note: The above table is based on the use of copper pipes. Galvanized steel is generally similar in equivalent resistance, although it has a lesser head loss in larger valves and faucets.

rate ($\frac{1}{2}$ in. SV loses 3 ft head at 3.1 US gal/min; 1 in. SV loses 6 ft at 11.4 US gal/min; 1$\frac{1}{2}$ in. SV loses 10 ft head at 36 US gal/min). The available head must therefore be considered for the most disadvantaged fitting (usually on the building's top floor).

Having determined the available head and the effective length of pipe, the head loss per foot can be calculated and the pipe size obtained from Fig. 24.3.1 or from the Thomas Box formula (Ref. 24.1):

$$q = \sqrt{\frac{9.65 \times d^5 \times H}{10^{12} \times L}} \quad \left[q = \sqrt{\frac{d^5 \times H}{25 \times L \times 10^5}} \right] \quad (24.1)$$

where q = discharge through pipe (US gal/min) [liters/sec]

d = diameter of pipe (in.) [mm]
H = head of water (ft) [m]
L = equivalent length of pipe (ft) [m]

The relative discharge capacity of pipes of various diameters is proportional to the square root of the fifth power of their diameters. Thus pipes can be sized without recourse to eq. (24.1) at each stage of a project. Table 24.6 sets out these data in usable form.

24.4. HOT WATER (SEE ALSO SECTIONS 22.2 AND 22.3)

Hot water is now considered an essential service. The energy source selected for heating depends partly on local factors, such as availability and cost, and partly on the suitability of the installation chosen for the particular project.

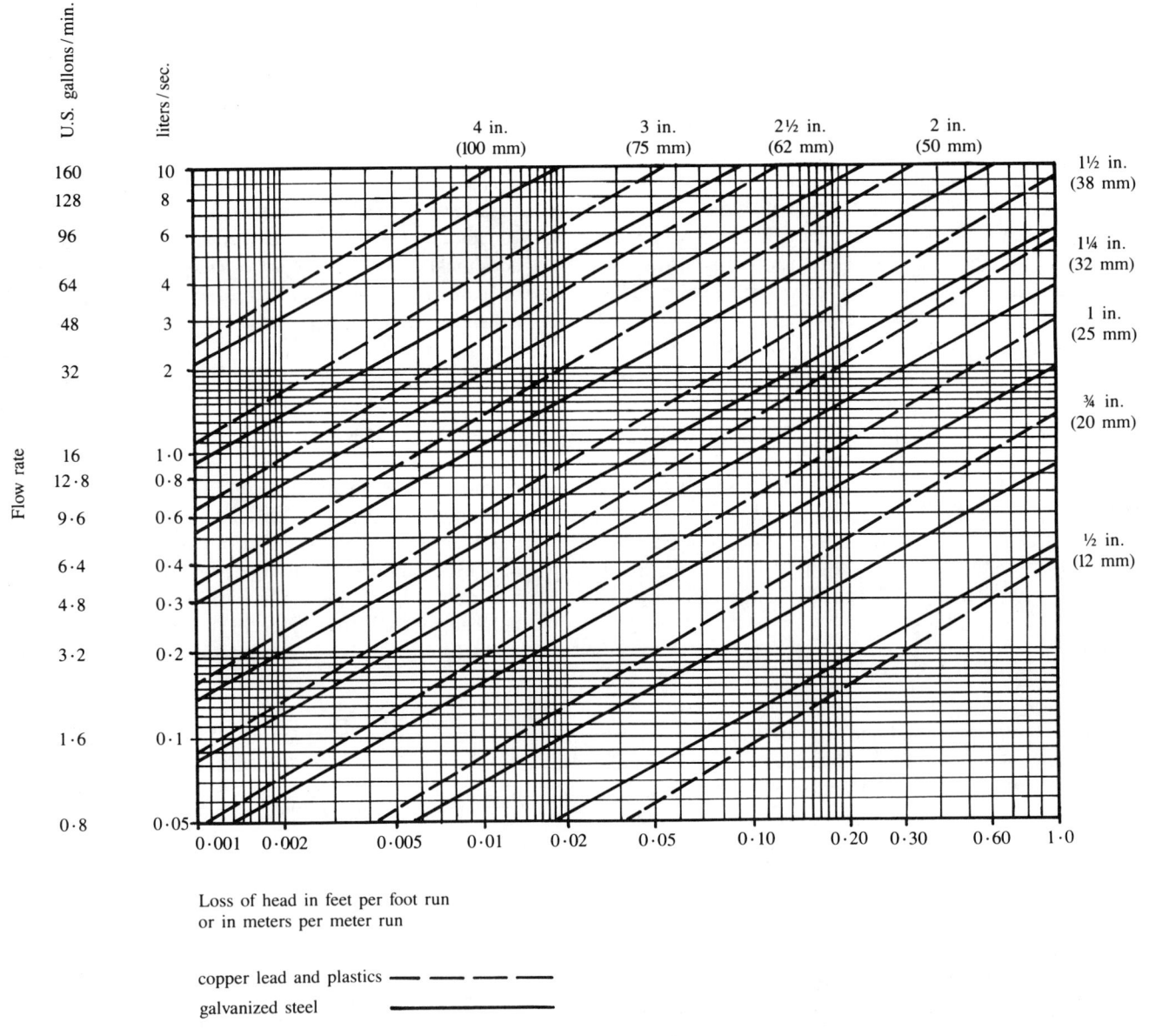

Fig. 24.3.1. Pipe sizing chart.

Table 24.6. Relative Capacity of Pipes.

Main Pipe Diameter		Number of Branch Pipes for Same Floor, with a Branch Pipe Diameter of:								
in.	mm	4 in. 100 mm	3 in. 75 mm	2.5 in. 65 mm	2 in. 50 mm	1.5 in. 40 mm	1.25 in. 32 mm	1 in. 25 mm	0.75 in. 20 mm	0.5 in. 15 mm
4	100	1	2	3	6	10	17	32	56	115
3	75		1	2	3	5	9	16	28	56
2.5	65			1	2	4	6	11	19	39
2	50				1	2	3	6	10	21
1.5	40					1	2	4	6	12
1.25	32						1	2	4	7
1	25							1	2	4
0.75	20								1	2
0.5	15									1

There are four basic types of water heater:

1. Instantaneous heaters
2. Storage heaters
3. Heat exchange units
4. Circulators or boilers

The *instantaneous heater* raises the water temperature as the water is used. *Storage units* contain hot water in a thermally insulated container ready for immediate use; replacement cold water is heated as the hot water is used. *Heat exchange units* consist of a thermally insulated container of static heated water in which is immersed a heat exchanger, generally in the form of a coil of copper tubing. As cold water passes through the heat exchanger it picks up heat from the stored water. The stored water reheats to its original temperature. *Circulators* or *boilers* heat water as it passes through the unit and the hot water is circulated by natural convection or circulating pump through the system. Each type has advantages and disadvantages (Table 24.7).

Planning of hot water systems should ensure that the distance between the hot water system or circulating pipe and the drawoff point is minimized. Local authorities frequently restrict this distance to about 30 ft (9 m) in order to save fuel and water. This restriction is also in the interest of the user's convenience.

Hot Water Storage

For centralized hot water systems, storage requirements are given in Table 24.8. Alternatively the quantity of hot water storage may be calculated from Table 24.9, which indicates usage at particular fittings.

The capacity and performance of a hot water heater is also dependent upon the heat input available. For electric immersion heaters, although their thermal efficiency is quite high, the efficiency is reduced when too small an element is fitted in a large storage heater. The heater selection should also be made considering that a longer life will be attained if the unit is not normally operating at peak load. Table 24.10 shows the recovery rate for water availability with various temperature rises.

Gas Heaters

Table 24.11 indicates hot water availability, based on town gas or natural gas as the fuel source.

With larger installations multiple hot water heaters are normally installed, which allow maintenance without the loss of the complete hot water service, and easier replacement.

Planning

Reticulation within large buildings is zoned, as for cold water, so that no outlets have a head greater than 100 feet (30 m). Larger installations may also be served by a centralized system. Some of the factors comparing these alternative systems are listed in Table 24.12.

Hot-water heaters may be supplemented by solar collectors (see Chapter 22). In warmer climates these roof-mounted units can make significant savings to overall fuel costs. However, prior to installation a calculation should be made of the full cost involved, including the additional investment in the solar collection system and its installation.

Some authorities provide electricity at reduced rates, based on the supply being provided in only off-peak periods. Such provisions need to be allowed for in considering the cost of alternative fuel sources.

For the installation of hot water heaters, allowance has to be made for the following associated features, as appropriate:

- Fresh air for oil or gas heaters
- A flue for spent gases
- A drain for heater overflow, with pressure relief (some authorities require there to be a visible discharge of dripping water into a tundish)

24.5. FIRE SERVICES (SEE ALSO CHAPTER 26)

This section offers an understanding of the services and associated equipment to be provided and incorporated in the construction of buildings for the purpose of extinguish-

Table 24.7. Hot Water System Comparison.

Property	Instantaneous	Storage	Heat Exchange	Boiler
Size	Small size can allow unobtrusive installation	Physically larger than instantaneous systems, requires more space	For comparable performance approximately twice the size of a storage unit is needed	Smaller than storage unit of comparable input, but requires a separate storage tank
Fuel supply	Needs much larger pipes or cables and creates heavy demand	Normal supply adequate and demand much lighter than for instantaneous system	Normal supply adequate and demand much lighter than for instantaneous system	Normal supply adequate and demand much lighter than instantaneous
Flow of hot water	Satisfactory use of only one tap at a time	Mains pressure units allow use of more than one faucet (tap) at a time. Reduced pressure units do not give true multipoint operation	Satisfactory use of only one faucet (tap) at a time	Depends on means used to provide circulation, pipe sizing, and pressure in installation
Quantity of hot water	Theoretically unlimited	Restricted to initial storage capacity, followed by delay, which may or may not be significant until reheated	Due to temperature differences between stored water at outlet of heat exchanger, only half of thermal content can be drawn at a useful temperature	Restricted to initial storage capacity of storage tank, which is supplied additional to the circulator, then a delay which may or may not be significant until reheated
Temperature of hot water	Entirely depends on: (1) Cold water temperature; (2) flow rate; (3) Adequacy of fuel supply	Constant for approx. 90% of capacity	Temperature drops dramatically after initial draw then progressively as draw continues. Unit suitable for warmer climates only	Depends on design and size of storage tank in relation to size of heater
Operation efficiency	Low standby losses. Gives higher operating efficiency, but generally no special hot water tariff applicable	Standby losses higher than for instantaneous system, but special hot water tariffs are available for most storage units	Standby losses slightly higher than storage as unit normally operates at higher temp. than storage	High heat losses from circulating hot water circuit and more extensive plumbing. High heat loss also if storage tank badly designed.

Modifications to these basic designs are necessary to suit their installation in hard-water districts.

Table 24.8. Hot Water Storage Requirement.

Type of Building	Storage per Person US Galls.	Liters
College (day)	1	4.5
Factories	6	23
Flats	1	4.5
Hotels (average)	10	36
Houses	12	45
Hospital		
General	6	27
Infectious	12	45
Nursing home	12	45
Hostels	9	32
Offices	1	4.5
Sports pavilions	10	36

ing or containing fires in their primary stages, and later as supplementary equipment to that of the Fire Authorities' equipment for completely extinguishing the fire.

The following services are listed in order of general importance, as considered at the planning stage of a building.

Table 24.9. Hot Water Usage by Fittings.

Fitting	Hot Water, US Gal	Liters
Hand basin	0.4	1.5
Hair wash basin	1.6	6
Shower	3.5	13
Bath	20	70
Washing machine	20	70
Washup sink	4	15
Cleaners sink	1.2	5

Table 24.10. Electric Heater Recovery Rate.

Heating Element, Watts (Continuous Rating)	Hot Water Availability					
	72°F Rise, US Gal	40°C Rise, Liters	90°F Rise, US Gal	50°C Rise, Liters	108°F Rise, US Gal	60°C Rise, Liters
1200	6.0	23	4.8	18	4.0	15
1500	7.7	29	6.0	23	5.0	19
1800	9.2	35	7.4	28	6.0	23
2000	10.3	39	8.2	31	6.9	26
2400	12.4	47	10.0	38	8.2	31
3000	15.9	60	12.7	48	10.6	40
3600	19.3	73	15.6	59	13.0	49
4800	25.9	98	20.6	78	17.2	65

Table 24.11. Hot Water Availability—Gas Heaters.

Nominal Size		Hourly Thermal Input			Hot Water at 90°F (50°C) Rise Over Peak Period at							
					1 Hr		2 Hr		4 Hr		6 Hr	
US Gal	Liters	kWh	Btu	MJ	US Gal	Liters	US Gal	Liters	US Gal	Liters	US Gal	Liters
25	90	6.94	23700	25	40	150	62	235	107	405	152	575
35	135	8.33	28440	30	53	199	79	301	133	505	187	709
50	170	8.33	28440	30	59	224	86	326	140	530	194	734
75	270	13.07	44560	47	95	361	139	527	227	859	314	1191

Briefly, these relate to the type of construction (flammability index of the building), the development's effect on the neighboring buildings and the occupation of the building. The fire services installed are provided principally to aid and assist the evacuation of the building by persons working in buildings and who have been trained, by the local Fire Department, in the technique of operating the fire equipment at their disposal. These people are called Fire Wardens and their job is to familiarize the occupants of the building of the evacuation procedures in the event of a fire.

In isolated areas, where developments are proposed and no support from public utilities is available, the type of firefighting facilities is of supreme importance, together with staff fully competent in this field.

Table 24.12. Large Hot Water System Comparison.

Centralized System	Local Unit Heaters
1. Provides large bulk storage for hospitals, hotels, etc.	1. May be installed close to the fittings to be installed, thus saving a lot of pipework.
2. One central boiler would require less maintenance than multiple heaters.	2. Saving of boiler house and fuel store space.
3. Cheaper fuel may be used.	3. Separate fuel connections to each heater.
4. Requires long lengths of secondary pipework (higher heat losses).	4. Greater risk of fire in building due to more gas or electric connections.
5. Less flue construction cost and no secondary heater.	5. Pumped circulation system may be avoided.

The services are categorized into two types: one where the equipment is manually applied, and the other where it is automatically activated by heat and smoke sensing devices.

Table 24.13 is a guide to the services needed for different types of buildings, their occupation and location.

Fire Hose Reels

Fire hose reels are designed and installed for use by the general public as a first aid measure in fighting any fire. Pressure flows are designed accordingly with a flow of 7 US gal/min (0.63 liters/second) at 40 psi (275 kPa). It is generally recognized that two hoses operating simultaneously are adequate for any system, providing a total fire hose reel flow of 14 US gal/min (1.26 liters/second). This must be added to the domestic demand to provide a total combined domestic/fire hose reel flow for the development.

Hose reels installed generally accommodate 120 ft (36 meters) of $\frac{3}{4}$ in. (20 mm) diameter hose. They should cover in a direct line all points on the floor at a radius of 80 ft (24 meters); this allows 40 ft (12 meters) to compensate for tenancy partitioning. Hose reels are recommended to be installed within 10 ft (3 meters) of the most familiar egress point or points from the building.

There are three options for piping installations of hose reels. Firstly, if an authority's water main is adjacent to the development and can be connected with a flow capable of the combined domestic and hose reel flow, then a single-pipe system is the most economic installation, since a common meter registers all water used which can be charged

Table 24.13. Fire Services Required.

Fire Hose Reels

Should be installed in all buildings which have a total floor area in excess of 5000 ft² (500 m²).

Fire Hydrants

Should be installed in all buildings which have a total floor area in excess of 20,000 ft² (2000 m²) or in each story of a building which has a rise in stories of more than 4, including basement carparking and roof areas which can be used by the public.

Fire Sprinkler Systems

Sprinkler systems should be installed in all buildings over 140 ft (42 meters) in height measured from the roof top plantrooms to the lowest floor providing egress to the street.

Buildings which exceed 380,000 ft² (38,000 m²), and are not compartmentalized into three-hour fire separated and isolated areas, should have a wet sprinkler system installed, and also any building which does not have fire separation between floors; for example, where escalators are installed, the two or more floors connected by escalators should have sprinklers installed.

Buildings which by nature of their occupation or their storage capacity are classified as a fire potential or hazard should be appraised independently.

In all these instances a fire study should be conducted by a person qualified or experienced in this work to appraise the proposed development.

Thermal and Smoke Detector Systems

These systems are normally installed in buildings of intermediate size, say between 80 ft (25 meters) and 140 ft (42 meters) in height; also in institutional buildings, such as hospitals, nursing homes, or homes for disabled persons.

---

accordingly. The only stipulation to this system, subject to proving the fire flows, is that no fire hose reels in the reticulated system are restricted by isolating valves, except at the water meter assembly master control valve.

The second method is only required in the special circumstances applicable to buildings in groups, where a domestic service is not required to all buildings, but hose reels are. In this instance a separate distribution system dedicated as a fire hose reel service is recommended, with a master control valve adjacent to the water meter, which can be padlocked in the ON position.

The third method is appropriate where a storage tank is required because of limited available flow or where no authority's supply is available. A storage tank of sufficient size with upper-level domestic drawoff and a dedicated lower-level drawoff for hose reels for a period of not less than 90 minutes is then generally an acceptable standard. An effective capacity of 1800 US gallons (6800 liters) would be required to serve solely the hose reels. A pump would also be required capable of the head differential between the most disadvantaged hose reel and the tank outlet, including friction loss of the pipework plus the 40 psi (270 kPa) pressure at the nozzle of the hose reel.

Fire Hydrants

In large building complexes, where fire hydrants are required to be installed and an authority's main is available, a separate distribution system is required; pipe sizing to all hydrant points is a minimum of 4 in. (100 mm). Hydrants are located adjacent to the hose reel positions, and should have a 120 ft (36 m) radius to all points of the floor.

The pipe flows to a hydrant and hydrant system vary considerably from one authority to another, but a basis for the design is 50 US gal/min (4.5 liters/second) at 40 psi (275 kPa) at the most hydraulically disadvantaged hydrant in the system.

If an authority's main is available it is recommended that the main be capable of delivering by pump or gravity a minimum flow of 250 US gal/min (22 liters/second). A pump may be necessary to increase the system to a maximum of 100 psi (650 kPa) to provide the required pressure of 40 psi (275 kPa) minimum at the most disadvantaged hydrant in the system.

If the authority's main is not able to provide a satisfactory flow, then a supply from a dam, river, sea, or subterranean water may be used, providing the known source is in excess of 250,000 US gallons (1 megaliter). If the source has an unknown capacity, a tank should be used to store an effective capacity of at least 250 US gallons/minute (22 liters/second) or 30,000 US gallons (118,000 liters) of 90 minutes usage. This capacity is adequate for a combined hydrant and hose reel system and in this instance it should be piped throughout the development in 4 in. (100 mm) pipe.

Where a fire authority has jurisdiction to combat fire, a booster valve is required, so that it has the capacity to increase pressure and flow to suit the hazard. This booster fitting should be compatible with that of the relevant Department (Brigade) and located within 50 ft (15 meters) of the boundary. If the fitting cannot be sited in this way, a series of suction fittings should be installed on the mains side of the booster valve. The normal requirement is 2 suction fittings for a 4 in. (100 mm) fire main and 4 fittings for larger mains.

If a hydrant system is required by legislation, or is desired, the hose connections are $2\frac{1}{2}$ in. (65 mm), which may be reduced to $1\frac{1}{2}$ in. (38 mm) for ease of unskilled use.

Detector Systems

Smoke and heat sensing devices are installed in buildings to raise an alarm if a fire breaks out which can be attended by a fire authority. This type of system does not extinguish the fire, but it can be integrated with wet or dry sprinkler systems activating water, gas, or foam for extinguishing the fire. These specialized systems may be required by the relevant authorities, or because of sensitive areas of occupation within building complexes. Whenever systems of this type are used, they should be installed by persons experienced in this field.

Sprinkler Systems

This method of automatic fire extinguishing is, if properly installed and maintained, a guaranteed method of putting out fires even in unoccupied buildings. The initial purpose of this system, mainly installed in large buildings or high rise buildings, is to contain the outbreak of fire until the building can be evacuated by all the occupants.

Sprinkler systems must be connected to a large water supply, either the authority's mains, storage tanks, dams, or rivers. The latter of these water supplies should have a minimum capacity of 250,000 US gallons (1 million liters). The minimum ordinary hazard fire sprinkler system drawing water from a static tank supply should have an effective capacity, for a duration of 90 minutes of operation, of 25,000 US gallons (90,000 liters).

Like the detector system, this type of system is connected to the local fire authority telephone alarm; it should have a booster connection similar to the hydrant system, so that the fire authority can add foam solutions to quickly extinguish the fire.

Fire Extinguishers

In all buildings, fire extinguishers are to be installed and maintained in accordance with the manufacturers' specifications.

The types used are dry powder, gas (CO_2), foam, and water-acid. These are portable, and installed on walls in common areas, in hose reel cupboards in or adjacent to electrical main boards and distribution boards, in main plantrooms for mechanical plant and elevator (lift) motor rooms and adjacent to escalator motor stations, in kitchens where commercial cooking is undertaken, and in carparking stations or areas.

For electrical fires dry powder or gas is to be used, and for most other applications pressurized foam is the most suitable for the variety of fire situations encountered. It is recommended that in commercial buildings 20 lb (9 kg) canisters should be used for all types of extinguishers.

In summarizing the fire protection systems installed in buildings, they should be installed by specialists in this field, all equipment should be positioned within the building for ease of operation and accessibility and accommodated within the architectural finishes. Hydrants and hose reels, including all associated equipment pumps, should be serviced every month. Detectors and sprinkler systems should be tested for operation every week, and extinguishers tested yearly and checked that they are fully charged.

24.6. ROOF, SURFACE, AND SUBSOIL DRAINAGE

Adequate provision for the collection and disposal of rainfall on the roofs of buildings is vital to ensure their continuing functional operation. To a lesser extent the management of rainfall on the surrounding areas will avoid nuisance flooding. Generally water below the ground will be present in small quantities only; it can nonetheless create great distress.

Roof Drainage (see also Section 7.2)

The roof drainage system must be able to cope with the peak rainfall intensity that may occur over quite a short period. Such peak intensities are predictable and are frequently quoted for a 5 min period, for a probability of occurring once in 5 or 100 years. The appropriate value is selected, depending on the importance of the building. Runoff from hail and snow will be less than from heavy rainstorms. However, if hail is frequent, further precautions may need to be taken against the potential buildup of hail impeding any water flow.

Roofs are drained by either eaves gutters, box gutters, or internal outlets.

In determining the catchment area which will flow to any outlet, allowance should be made for any adjacent wall areas which overshadow the roof, as windblown rain hitting this wall will also affect the roof. Normally an allowance of half the area of the wall should be added to the roof area.

Gutters exposed to direct sunlight are subject to significant thermal movement. Consequently, sufficient expansion joints should be provided to avoid thermal distortion affecting the gutters' performance. Expansion joints should be located at the maximum spacings as in Table 24.14, depending on the material used in the gutter fabrication.

Eaves gutters for small buildings are normally chosen from stock sizes; it is obviously preferable to adjust the design to the use of stock sizes wherever possible. Gutter size is dependent upon the slope of the gutter, distance of the outlet from the nearest downspout (downpipe) bend, and the location of the outlet in relation to the end of the gutter. Eaves gutters should never slope at less than 1 in

Table 24.14. Maximum Spacing of Expansion Joints.

Material	Maximum Spacing	
Aluminum	40 ft	12 m
Copper	25 ft	7 m
Fiber cement	60 ft	18 m
Galvanized steel	60 ft	18 m
Stainless steel	40 ft	12 m
Zinc	25 ft	7 m

480; however, if dust fallout or debris buildup is probable, the slope should be increased to 1 in 50. Outlets should be provided not more than 40 ft (12 m) apart. Leaf guards are essential to prevent outlets from becoming blocked. When the selected gutter has a higher fascia than the rear edge, overflow slots should be provided to reduce the potential damage. The proportions of either an eaves or a box gutter are hydraulically ideal when its width is twice the maximum expected depth of flow.

Box gutters should be at least 12 in. (300 mm) wide and constructed such that maintenance staff can safely walk along them. The minimum slope should be 1 in 180, and outlets should not be spaced further than 60 ft (18 m) apart. Increases to either of these aspects will improve the gutters performance.

The depth of a box gutter should be increased by 2 in. (50 mm) to provide freeboard, which will allow for ripples and turbulence in the water flow. Overflows are imperative with box gutters. They can be sized to cope with peaks in the rainfall or with the effect of a blockage of the outlet. In the former case an area of approximately 15 percent of the gutter discharge is adequate. The threshold to the overflow is located slightly above water level, and consequently the gutter depth needs to be increased to cope with the water backup in the time of a crisis.

As the discharge capacity of an outlet is increased by the depth of water above it, a box receiver, or sump constructed to the width of the gutter, is a convenient means of obtaining this increased depth; 12 in. (300 mm) is normally a satisfactory depth. However, if the gutter has a depth in excess of hydraulic requirements, this depth can be used to offset part of the box receivers' depth requirement. When conveniently located, say on the outside of the building, the box receiver can also incorporate the box gutter overflow.

Downspouts (downpipes) are preferably located externally. Provision should be made for clearing any chokage by means of a cleaning access near the base of the downpipe. For eaves gutters, round downspouts are selected to be half the gutter cross-sectional area. For box gutters the downspout size is determined by the size of the gutter or box-receiver discharging into it. Rectangular downspouts should have a 10 percent greater area than round pipes for serving the same catchment. The efficiency of the downspout is improved if a funnelled lead-in is incorporated, allowing a reduction of 10 percent of the downspout diameter to be made. To reduce swirl of the water entering the downpipe it should be placed no further than its diameter from a vertical face, that is, either the end of the gutter or to the side of the box receiver. When a downspout discharges onto a lower roof, a spreader should be placed at the foot of the downspout, to avoid surcharging of the lower roof.

If a grating or strainer is fitted to a rainwater outlet, then the total area of the perforations should be at least 150 percent of the calculated cross-sectional area of the outlet. The preferred design of such strainers is to project above the roof surface to help overcome the effect of accumulated debris. Drainage from flat areas without gutters requires separate consideration. The outlet diameter can be calculated from:

$$D = 0.69(Ap)^{0.5} \quad [D = 0.45(Ap)^{0.5}] \quad (24.2)$$

where D = diameter of outlet (in.) [mm]
       A = catchment area (ft^2) [m^2]
       p = rainfall intensity (in./hr) [mm/hr]

Stormwater Drainage

Underground stormwater pipes draining downspouts should have a larger diameter than that of the downspout. Such pipes should be laid at uniform grades in straight lines between inspection pits or drainage gulleys. If the downspout discharges directly into a gully, the pipe should terminate below the gully grating.

The sizing of underground drainage is dependent upon the selected rainfall intensity; however, as a guide, Table 24.15 provides an indication of pipeline capacity. The appropriate rainfall intensity should be obtained from local meteorological data. This table is based on the catchment areas being paved or roofed. If landscaped surfaces are

Table 24.15a. Underground Pipes—Nominal Stormwater Capacity (British/American Units).

Diameter, in.	Maximum Area (ft^2) That Can Be Drained by Pipes Laid at Indicated Gradients (Rainfall Intensity 4 in./hour)			
	1 in 50	1 in 100	1 in 50	1 in 200
4	2,700	1,850	1,600	1,400
6	7,500	5,400	4,300	3,200
8	16,100	11,800	9,700	8,050
10	29,000	20,500	16,100	14,000
12	46,200	32,250	26,900	23,650
15	82,800	58,000	47,300	38,700
18	109,000	86,000	70,000	57,000

Table 24.15b. Underground Pipes—Nominal Stormwater Capacity (Metric Units).

Diameter, mm	Maximum Area (m^2) That Can be Drained by Pipes Laid at Indicated Gradients (Rainfall Intensity 100 mm/hour)			
	1 in 50	1 in 100	1 in 150	1 in 200
100	250	175	150	130
150	700	500	400	300
200	1500	1100	900	750
250	2700	1900	1500	1300
300	4300	3000	2500	2200
375	7700	5400	4400	3600
450	10000	8000	6500	5300

contributing to the catchment also, then these may be included in the catchment area as approximately equivalent to 50 percent of their actual area.

Surface Drainage

Paved areas require to be sloped to adequately drain their surface. The selection of this rate of fall is awkward, as normally many constraints hinder a free choice of gradient. However the following Table 24.16 indicates minimum falls for various surfaces, to achieve reasonable drainage.

In some instances these crossfalls are of necessity exceeded; however, for important surfaces such as roads, they should be steepened by at least 20 percent.

Subsoil Drainage

Subsoil drainage in areas with a high water table or dampness is a vital part of any drainage installation. Excessive ground dampness can render a building unsuitable for habitation and/or cause damage to the building fabric and/or foundations, and to the surrounding paving.

In locations where excessive underground water occurs, tanking of the basement walls and floors is undertaken.

At the investigation stage of any project an assessment of the likelihood of underground water needs to be made and the means of collecting and disposing of it. In the absence of a geotechnical survey confirming the water table depth, various other techniques can be used to establish the probability of underground water, for example,

- Observing signs of dampness on the ground
- Observing stagnant water lying about
- Observing proximity of springs
- Experience of neighboring properties
- Observing water flowing in drains or streams even though no recent rain has fallen

Subsoil drainage is achieved by open-jointed pipework, frequently of unglazed clay, or perforated plastic, concrete, or clay piping. The plastic piping can have a "sock" of filter material surrounding it to prevent the ingress of fine material. Similarly, open joints can be protected by filter material. Normally, however, the transport of suspended material through subsoil drains ceases after a period from the initial installation.

If springs or other sources of water are discovered during excavation the system should be adjusted to take these into account. Normally subsoil drainage is laid under the basement floor to a regular pattern with branches feeding a main line ("herringbone" style), or to any other convenient pattern. The piping is normally of $2\frac{1}{2}$ in. (65 mm) diameter for branches, and 3–4 in. (75–100 mm) for principal runs. The spacing of the branch lines needs to take into account the other building construction details and the soil type. The following spacings are suggested, based on average conditions for different soil types:

Sand, sandy loam	not normally required
Loam	75 ft (25 m)
Loamy clay	45 ft (15 m)
Sandy clay	35 ft (12 m)
Clay	25 ft (8 m)

Subsoil drains are laid to low gradients without concern for self-cleansing velocities, frequently at 1 in 200 or flatter grades. The system normally discharges to a stormwater pit, fitted with a flap to prevent backflow from the stormwater system. In other instances the system can be carried to a natural point of discharge, or to its own sump for removal by a float-controlled pump. The design of the sump should include provision for some silt to be brought through the system.

As underground stormwater drainage lines excavated in, say, clay around a building intercept the movement of underground water, a subsoil drain can be placed in the common trench, or drainage can be achieved through a loose aggregate backfill to a short length, say, 10 ft (3 m) of subsoil drain projecting from a stormwater gully pit.

It is good practice, and often required to suit assumptions made in the structural design, for subsoil drainage to be placed in the backfill behind basement or retaining walls. These drains are laid similarly to those described above. To maximize the impact of subsoil drains on their underground environment, they are generally surrounded with a bed, 6 in. (150 mm) wide, of broken stone. Above this open-jointed material, a filter membrane is placed to insure that soil material from above does not choke the voids in the subsoil drain bedding. The filter membrane can comprise a geofabric, straw, or similar material. Behind basement and retaining walls the aggregate surround may be continued up to near surface level. Alternatively, a plastic egg-crated sheet material with filter fabric bonded to one side can be used as a cheaper alternative.

24.7. SEWERAGE AND WASTE DISPOSAL

In evaluating the requirements for this service it is important to be aware of the characteristics of the fixtures, both type and quantity, that will be connected to a specific type of piping and drainage system and the subsequent disposal of the effluent (Fig. 24.7.1). The following is a brief de-

Table 24.16. Minimum Crossfalls.

Earth surface	1 in 24
Gravel surface	1 in 36
Bituminous macadam surface	1 in 48
Asphaltic concrete paving	1 in 60
Concrete paving	1 in 60

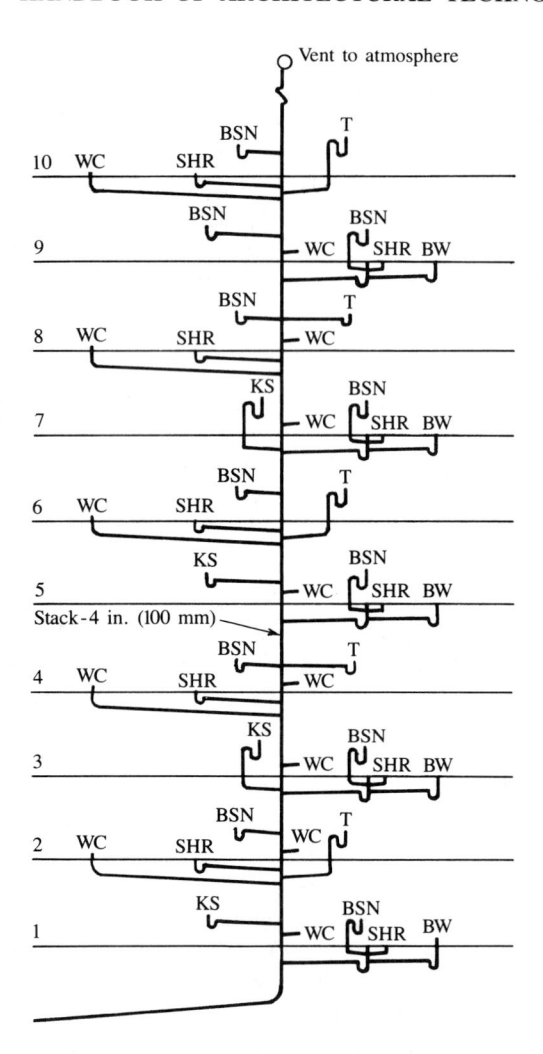

Fig. 24.7.1. Typical single-stack plumbing for residential building, using 4 in. (100 mm) stack. BSN = basin; BW = bath waste; KS = kitchen sink; SHR = shower; WC = water closet (toilet); T = tundish.

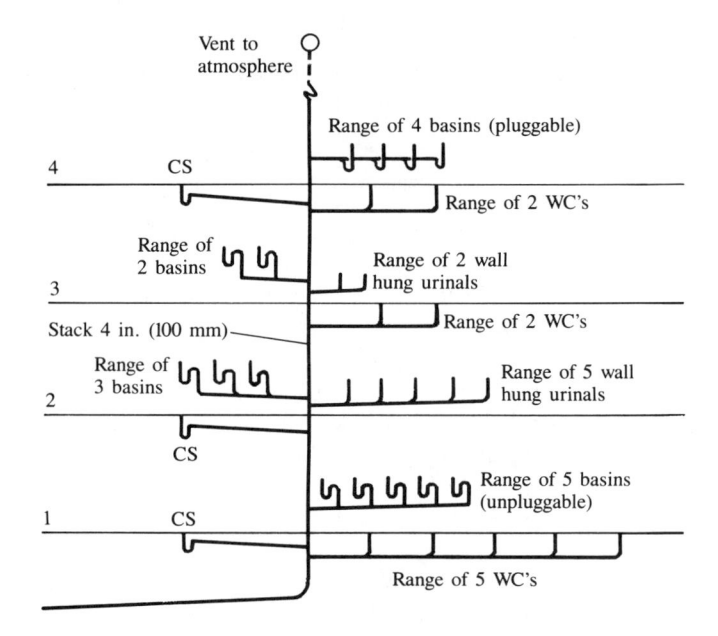

Fig. 24.7.2. Typical single-stack plumbing for commercial building, using 4 in. (100 mm) stack. CS = cleaner's sink; WC = water-closet (toilet).

scription of the requirements and methods of discharge to the authority's disposal treatment systems, the pretreatment that may be required for acceptance to the sewers, and, similarly, the requirements and acceptable standard of disposal for private sewage installations.

The average commercial development has four types of effluent which require evaluation (Fig. 24.7.2).

1. The connection to an authority's sewerage system will convey all sanitaryware, ablutions, washing facilities, and air conditioning wastes direct to the sewer via a sanitary plumbing soil and waste pipe system without pretreatment.

2. Where commercial kitchens or retail outlets require cooking of fats, this waste is to be piped separately to a collection pit or arrestor, which will retain the fats and grease for separate disposal by a sullage contractor. The outlet of this arrestor is then piped to the sewerage system.

3. In buildings where undercover carparking and car washing is required, these floor areas are to have a sep-arately piped drainage system, connected to an appropriately sized oil separator arrestor, which may incorporate a waste oil dump tank filled by a skimmer from the arrestor. A suction line is installed and terminated at a point where a waste disposal contractor can evacuate the dump tank as required.

4. Another effluent that may be encountered is subterranean water which may be classified as foul water. Because the development has below-ground floor levels, this must be collected by a system of subsoil piping graded to a collection well and pumpout pit, with a rising main discharging over a drainage outlet, connected to the sewer system (or, if permitted, connected to a stormwater system).

Miscellaneous equipment and fixtures normally installed in tenancy areas, such as photographic darkrooms, require a retention tank under the photographic sink of 25 US gal (100 liter) capacity to enable dilution of the chemicals to an acceptable level before discharge to the sewer system. In commercial kitchens, potato peelers discharge direct to a basket arrestor, and then to the sewer. Similarly, waste disposal units or macerators for vegetable disposal are connected direct to the sewer, but approval is normally required for commercially sized units, since they may affect the pH level of the sewer systems of some authorities.

Commercial photographic installations may require a silver recovery plant prior to discharge to the sewer system. All specialized equipment required to be installed and connected to the authority's sewer requires a chemical analysis, so that an appropriate pretreatment can be evaluated.

In private installations, such as remote resorts where no sewer system is available, a self-contained treatment or disposal plant should be installed. The first system to be considered, subject to the terrain and the absorbtion rate of the ground, which can be evaluated from geotechnic report, is a septic tank with an effluent holding tank or a system of transpiration trenches suitably sized to accommodate the demand. If an absorbtion trench is not available the effluent may be pumped to a pond or dam constructed an average of 3 ft (900 mm) deep, but with a large surface area for sun absorption and evaporation. In arid areas, where water is a critical issue, this evaporation dam may be recycled to a lawn-watering system at discrete hours.

Alternatively, a package sewage treatment plant can be sized to suit the maximum laminar flows of the system, or contained in a holding tank and pumped to the treatment plant at a constant rate. This method allows for the plant to be installed in a suitably remote location. A pond can also be used for storage of the treated effluent for recycling as previously discussed. The treatment plant basically is a steel tank divided into compartments where screens separate the solids for flocculation, and where air is injected into this chamber to lower the pH value and break down the solids. The effluent is then injected with chlorine to reduce the bacteria for discharge to the pond.

Soil and Waste Pipes

The design of the pipework collecting from all fixtures is based on graded pipework, whether in-ground or fixed to the building structure, to a point of discharge. The grades are generally 1:60 for soil and waste fixtures in ground, and reduce in grade with greater loads to 1:100 for larger mains. The average size main is 4 in. (100 mm) in diameter and increases to 6 in. (150 mm) diameter, when 10 or more water closets are being serviced. All fixtures and termination points such as floor wastes, need to have 3-in. (80-mm) deep water seals separating sewer odors from occupied areas. The sewers and sanitary plumbing stack systems are naturally aspirating (open ended), requiring venting to relieve the downdraught of discharge waste effluent.

To size the main soil stack and waste pipes, each fixture is assigned a value, in fixture unit points, which relate to the volume of water used at each fixture, and allow for the fact that not all fixtures will be in use at any one time. These loadings are given in Table 24.17. Soil stack sizes are given in Table 24.18, and sizes of waste pipes and stacks in Table 24.19.

The size of the sewer drain, apart from the fixture unit loading, is also governed by the hydraulic gradient of the pipes. Table 24.20 enables the design to be varied due to these grades.

The arrangement of fixtures is dependent on layout requirements and authority plumbing regulations. Typical arrangements for basic residential and commercial multi-story installations are shown in Figs. 24.7.1 and 24.7.2.

Table 24.17. Loadings for Soil Stacks and Waste Pipes.

Fixture	Fixture Units
Water closet	4
Slop hopper	4
Urinal	2 per 2 ft (600 mm) of trough or stall
Cleaner's sink	3
Sink	3
Commercial kitchen sink	4
Showers	2
Wash tub	3
Basin	1
Floor waste	1
Bathroom group	6

Table 24.18. Soil Stack Sizes.

Stack Size	Fixture Units
4 in. (100 mm)	350
5 in. (125 mm)	750
6 in. (150 mm)	1250
9 in. (225 mm)	3100

Table 24.19. Sizes of Waste Pipes or Waste Stacks.

Fixture	Size Outlet
Water closet	4 in. (100 mm) or 3 in. (80 mm) in domestic usage
Slop hopper	4 in. (100 mm)
Urinal	2 in. (50 mm) per 2 ft (600 mm) of trough, increasing to 4 in. (100 mm) for 8 ft (2.4 m) of trough
Cleaner's sink	2 in. (50 mm)
Sink	2 in. (50 mm) single and double bowl
Shower	2 in. (50 mm)
Basin	$1\frac{1}{2}$ in. (40 mm) or $1\frac{1}{4}$ in. (32 mm)
Wash tub	2 in. (50 mm)

Table 24.20. Sewer Pipes.

Pipe Diameter		Loading (Fixture Units) at the Indicated Grade			
in.	mm	1:20 or Steeper (to 45°)	1:40	1:60	1:80	1:100 or More
2	50	30	22			
$2\frac{1}{2}$	65	35	25			
3	80	40	30			
4	100	250	220	170	170	170
5	125	600	500	450	400	400
6	150	1050	900	800	700	700
8	200	2350	2000	1800	1600	1450
9	225	3300	2800	2450	2200	2000
12	300	6900	5900	5200	4600	4000

Offsets in stacks occur in most developments where drainage terminates at lower levels and stacks start at typical floors. The transition floors between these two zones normally require an offset in the stack in the horizontal plane (Fig. 24.7.3). Connection of fixtures in this area of pipework is restricted to a minimum of 8 ft (2.5 m) downstream of the main stack and 2 ft (600 mm) below the offset vertical bend. The lowest point of connection to the vertical stack is again 2 ft (600 mm). A relief vent sized to suit is also required after these offsets.

Vent Pipes

Vent pipes are fitted to stacks of the same size as the stack itself, and to waste pipes as equal in size to the waste outlet. If group vent pipes are proposed, the main vent is 2 in. (50 mm) and the branch vents may be $1\frac{1}{2}$ in. (40 mm). Vent pipes from water closets are 2 in. (50 mm). Main relief vent pipes are required in high rise buildings (Fig. 24.7.4). These relieve the stack at the base and join the stack below the roof, with also a branch relief being required every 9 floors as a cross-relief vent. These vents are sized both on fixture loading and height or length of the vent to the termination point (Table 24.21).

The maximum length of branches from the main drainage line is 20 ft (6 meters) without a vent, and this branch may connect a number of fixtures. However, for sanitary plumbing branches only one fixture can be connected, and branches are limited to a maximum length of 8 ft (2.5 meters) measured from the branch junction to the outlet of the fixture trap (Table 24.22).

24.8. REFUSE DISPOSAL

Storage and disposal of refuse (Table 24.23) by hygienic methods is vital for the health and amenity of a building's occupants. Refuse disposal may be either by individual garbage bins, or by a refuse chute to a communal container, to an incinerator, or to a holding container for automatic removal to a remote location for incineration.

With concern for the Earth's limited resources, much refuse is recycled. At the domestic level this normally requires separate storage of recycled wastes until collection. In industry, most wastes are retained, segregated, and taken (sometimes bought) by specialist recyclers. It is necessary to make allowance during the planning phase for any particular additional requirements that this may impose on the building.

An individual residence garbage tin is usually 1 ft 8 in. diameter by 2 ft 6 in. high (500 mm × 750 mm), holding 3.5 cu ft (0.93 m^3) of refuse after compaction. Garbage tins are normally used with plastic bag liners which can be readily removed and taken away by the authority's Cleansing Department. Planning provision requires access and ventilation, with provision for washing down.

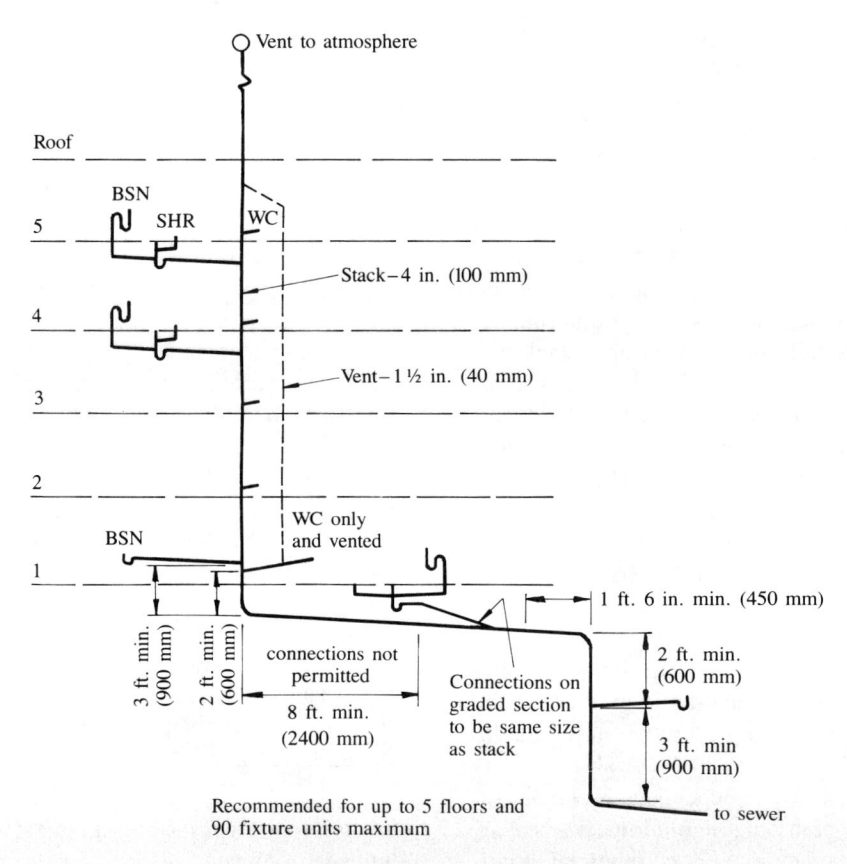

Fig. 24.7.3. Flat offsets required below the lowest connection, using 4 in. (100 mm) stack. BSN = basin; SHR = shower; WC = water closet (toilet).

WATER SUPPLY, DRAINAGE, AND REFUSE DISPOSAL 421

Table 24.22. Number of Fixture Traps Connected to a Vertical Stack at One Point Requiring a Horizontal Branch Vent.

Number	Diameter of Horizontal Branch Vent
2–20	2 in. (50 mm)
21–35	2½ in. (65 mm)
36–50	3 in. (80 mm)
More than 50	4 in. (100 mm)

Note: Fixture traps, *not* fixture units.

Table 24.23. Refuse from Residential, Commercial, or Industrial Buildings.

Residential	Commercial	Industrial
Food	Waste paper	As for other categories, plus:
Paper	Food	Toxic waste
Bottles	Cardboard	Offensive waste
Ashes		Dangerous waste
Tins		
Rags		
Cardboard		

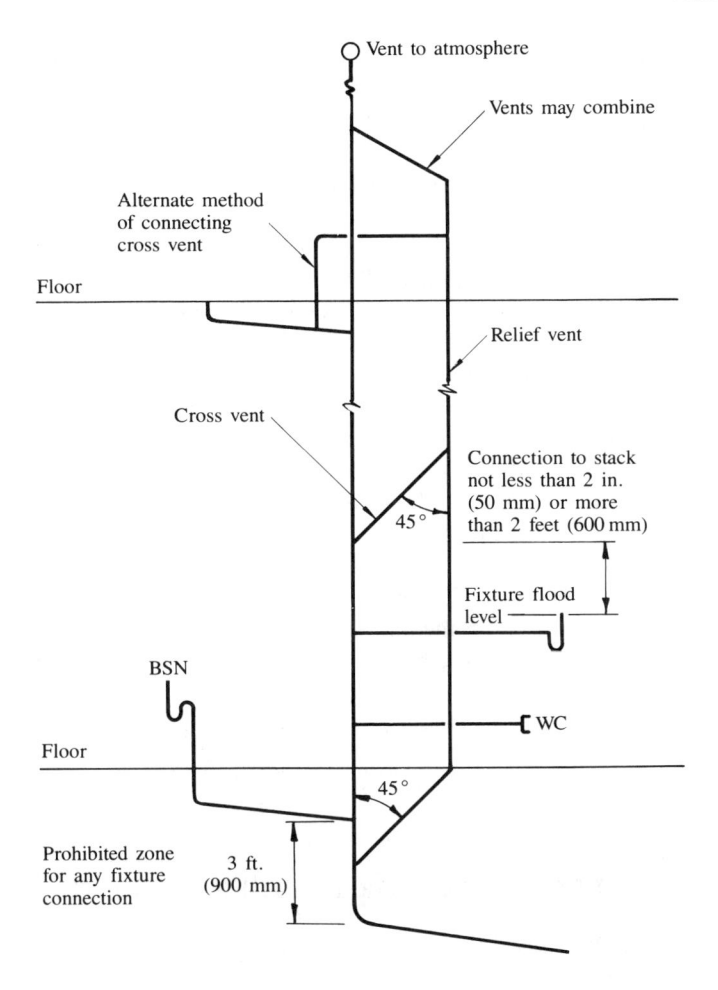

Fig. 24.7.4. Interconnection of stack and relief vent by cross vents.

In high-rise residential buildings some form of communal refuse disposal system is adopted. The design of the access hopper needs to take account of noise, dust, smoke, smells, hygiene, and rubbish falling from above. Hoppers should be situated in spaces which are well ventilated, may be cleaned, and will prevent any noise from disturbing adjacent tenants (Fig. 24.8.1). Chutes must be capable of internal cleaning. Dry methods using only stiff brushes are

Table 24.21a. Relief Pipe Sizes (British/American Units)

Soil Waste Stack Size, in.	Fixture Units Connected	\multicolumn{9}{c}{Maximum Length of Vent (ft) for Indicated Vent Diameter (in.)}
		1¼	1½	2	2½	3	4	5	6	8
2	12	30	70	200						
2½	28		30	100	300					
3	40			180	160	460				
4	350			20	80	210	820			
5	750				25	60	250	820		
6	1240					20	92	920		
8	2400						26	72	330	
9	3100							50	200	460

Table 24.21b. Relief Pipe Sizes (Metric Units)

Soil or Waste Stack Size, mm	Fixture Units Connected	\multicolumn{9}{c}{Maximum Length of Vent (m) for Indicated Vent Diameter (mm)}
		32	40	50	65	80	100	125	150	200
50	12	9	21	60						
65	28		9	30	90					
80	40			55	50	140				
100	350			6	25	65	250			
125	750				7	18	76	250		
150	1240					6	28	280		
200	2400						8	22	100	
225	3100							15	60	140

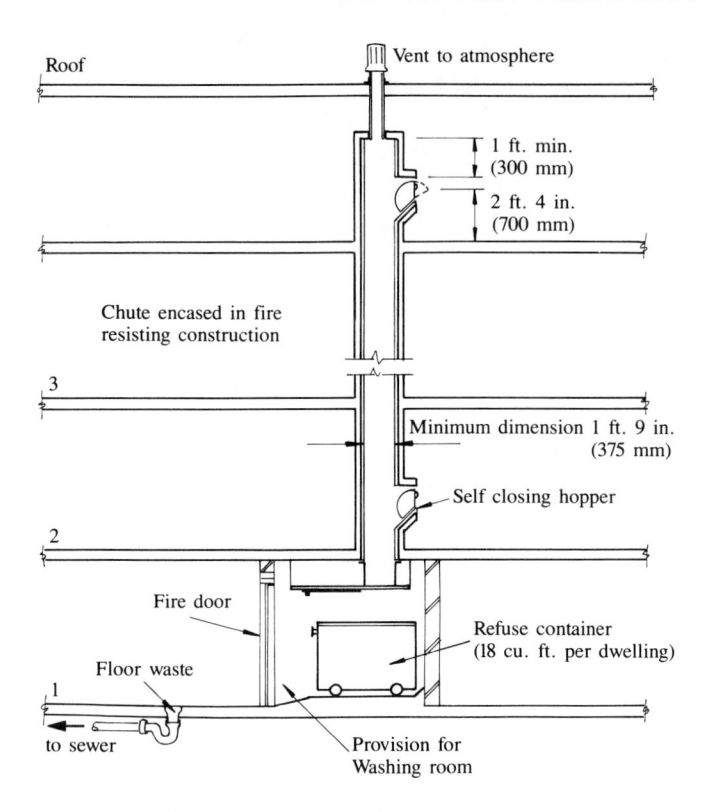

Fig. 24.8.1. Refuse chute arrangement.

preferred, as the risk of spreading disease is reduced in the absence of any residual water from the alternative wet-washing operations. Chutes should have internal dimensions of 1 ft 3 in. diameter or 1 ft 6 in. square (375 mm or 450 mm), to avoid refuse being hung up.

The chute ideally falls vertically through the building, although offsets of up to 20° may be tolerated to bring the chute to the container area. The chute must be capable of being closed at the base when the container is changed. Containers may be designed to incorporate compactors to provide more complete filling.

Areas where refuse is stored should be fireproofed, with provision to control any fire, and to enable easy and frequent cleaning. Ventilation is necessary to such areas, and to the chute, to ensure that smells do not accumulate. Accordingly, these areas should be constructed of robust, fire-rated, and easily cleaned materials and finishes, selected to be acid proof and not subject to corrosion.

Food-type refuse may be disposed through an electric sink grinder which, subject to the local authority's approval, discharges directly to the sewer. Larger models of sink grinders are available for catering and industrial applications. The disposal of metal, plastic, or glass containers is by the conventional garbage bin, or by a chute as described above.

A variation of the grinder system has been developed in Britain and France, involving a special sink with a grid and large-diameter waste pipe, which falls directly to a chamber at ground level. This system is able to handle bottles and tins. The refuse is then taken from the chamber either by a suction pipe to a central incinerator, or by a compactor truck.

In a further alternative to this scheme, which has been used in Sweden and Britain, the refuse falls in a common chute and is sucked to a central incinerator through a large-diameter pipe at regular intervals throughout the day. A modification to this scheme involves pulverizing the refuse before evacuating it to the central disposal location. Such central locations may be situated more than half a mile away from their collection point, thus allowing the construction of an incineration method with almost continuous operation and maximum efficiency.

REFERENCE

24.1. F. Hall. *Building Services and Equipment*, 3 Vol. Longman, London, 1977.

SUGGESTIONS FOR FURTHER READING

E. F. Brater. *Handbook of Hydraulics*. 6th Ed. McGraw-Hill, New York, 1976.

Tables for the Hydraulic Design of Pipes and Sewers, 4th Ed. Hydraulics Research Laboratory, Wallingford, England, 1983.

J. Lehr, S. Hurburt, B. Gallagher, and J. Voytek. *Design and Construction of Water Wells*. National Water Well Association and Van Nostrand Reinhold, New York, 1987.

G. Smethurst. *Basic Water Treatment*. Thomas Telford, London, 1988.

F. N. Kemmer (Ed.). *The Nalco Water Handbook*. McGraw-Hill, New York, 1979.

L. B. Escritt and W. D. Hawroth. *Sewerage and Sewage Treatment: International Practice*. Wiley, New York, 1984.

R. J. Puffett and L. J. Hossack. *Plumbing Services*. Vol. 1. *Basic Skills, Water Supply*. Vol. 2. *Waste Disposal, Roof Plumbing*. Vol. 3. *Gas Fitting*. McGraw-Hill, Sydney, 1989.

R. E. Bartlett and W. Madill. *Hydraulics for Public Health Engineers*. Elsevier, London, 1982.

NOTE

A list of abbreviations of the units of measurement, definitions of these units, and conversion factors between British/American and metric units are given in the Appendix.

25

The Movement of People and Goods

Peter R. Smith

The requirements for access and egress to and from buildings by both able-bodied and handicapped people are considered, both under normal conditions and in an emergency. These are based on the rates of arrival and departure, and the queues that are regarded as permissible.

All buildings must have corridors and stairways sufficiently wide to cope with the pedestrian traffic. Multistory buildings have in addition elevators, and sometimes also escalators and moving walkways.

The design of elevators (lifts) is discussed in some detail. The size and speed of the elevators depends on the size of the building and the expected traffic, as do the mechanical details of the installation. For tall buildings, zoning and skylobbies should be considered.

25.1 THE NEED FOR ACCESS AND EGRESS

Buildings are designed to contain and protect people and goods. Therefore it is essential that the people and goods have convenient access for normal use; that this access be controlled to prevent unauthorized entry of people or removal of goods; and that there be safe and rapid means of escape in the case of fire or emergency.

These requirements are often in conflict. Security (see Section 26.6) requires that the number of access points be restricted, and that the exit of goods be subject to inspection and surveillance. Convenience, and emergency egress, are better served by multiple and unrestricted points of access.

Size and Shape of Building

The significance of access as a criterion for planning, depends on the size and form of the building, as well as on its use.

People are capable of walking considerable distances on the same level, and most visitors will have walked at least several blocks to get to the building. Therefore it is unusual to provide any aids for horizontal movement except in very large buildings, such as airline or railroad terminals, in which the distances are large and the people may be carrying baggage.

Long, straight corridors can appear uninviting, both because of the long walking distance that they suggest, and also because they provide little visual stimulation along the way. It is necessary to provide some recognizable objective at the end of a long corridor, and preferably some variation in appearance along its length, to provide a sense of direction and also a sense of progress as one approaches the end. On the other hand, while a corridor with several bends, so that one end is not visible from the other, will provide more interest for browsing, there is the danger of losing one's sense of direction.

Since people are unwilling to walk up more than one or two stories, and the mobility-disabled are unable to change levels at all without very long ramps, elevators* are required for vertical transport in most public buildings. An elevator also allows easy transport of goods on trolleys, injured persons on stretchers, furniture and office equip-

---

*Elevator is the name commonly used in North America, while in Britain and other English-speaking regions, lift is preferred. Elevators (lifts) are devices legally capable of carrying passengers, even though some of them are designed mainly for freight. Dumbwaiters are small freight-only devices, which require less elaborate safety devices, and therefore are cheaper than elevators.

ment, cleaning equipment, and garbage cans. Therefore, although elevators are usually sized and located to serve the everyday needs of people entering and leaving a building, their design must also take account of these less frequent uses.

If there is heavy pedestrian traffic over a rise of only a few stories, escalators are likely to be the best solution for handling the bulk of the traffic. Passengers enter and leave an escalator with little interruption to their progress. The placing of the escalators establishes a travel path, and careful planning of a set of escalators can be used to determine the route its passengers follow.

In a tall building, vertical transporation is a major consideration in the design. In the design of the tallest buildings, the structural problems of vertical and wind loads, and the planning problems of fitting in enough elevators to serve the upper floors, are resolved together because the elevator shafts form a major and continuous vertical structural element.

Normal Access—Able-Bodied People

The majority of users are able to use stairs and read direction signs. Many of them will be familiar with the building. This explains why many poorly designed buildings still function fairly efficiently. Some buildings attract a high proportion of unfamiliar visitors, and in these cases easy direction-finding is particularly important.

Design of the normal access requires some knowledge of the origin and destination of the users. How will they approach the building? The entrance (or one of the entrances) should be obvious from each of the likely approach directions.

The security requirements of the building may dictate that each entrance (if there is more than one) directs the people through a main foyer. If entrances are on different levels, an escalator can be used to achieve this.

Although the security desk can be used to provide directions, and policy may require all visitors to go to that desk, nevertheless the direction of the elevators and the public areas of the building should be immediately apparent to the visitor. This saves the security staff time in giving directions, as well as making the visitor feel at ease in the building. It is also an advantage in security, to avoid having "lost" people wandering about the building.

Normal Access—Handicapped People

Visitors and regular users may have disabilities that make it more difficult for them to move about the building. The most obvious are mobility disabilities, requiring the use of a wheelchair or other walking aids. These are solved by the provision of ramps and elevators for change of level, adequate clearances at doorways and corners, suitable handrails, and suitable floor surfaces. People with small children in baby-carriages are, for these purposes, in the same category as those in wheelchairs. Details of requirements for access by the disabled are given in the appropriate specifications (Refs. 25.5 to 25.7).

Visual impairment is a greater disadvantage for a first-time visitor. In most cases the totally blind will require assistance until they are familiar with the building, although the provision of tactile maps and textured floor surfaces can provide some self-direction. Many visually impaired people are not totally blind, and can find their way provided it is not necessary to read directions, glare is avoided, and dangerous situations (such as the top of a stairway) are not encountered in unexpected locations.

The same provisions that make it easy for the partially sighted will also help those unable to read directions because of illiteracy, or because they do not understand the language. Signs consisting of well illuminated large arrows, numerals, and some of the simpler "international" symbols may be of assistance to both these groups.

Crowding is a serious disadvantage to all the groups described above. All of them require time to decide how to proceed, and space to move without hindering the able-bodied who wish to move faster. Space out of the main traffic route, or a ramp that does not attract traffic because it is more circuitous than a flight of steps, can be an aid to all the disabled and those who wish to move slowly.

Emergency Access and Egress

For normal access, the criteria are a convenient and pleasant path, with some provision of controlled entry. In an emergency, the criteria are a safe and easily found path, capable of accommodating the necessary numbers of people without causing panic. The emergency exits are generally unfamiliar, and people in an emergency situation cannot be relied upon to read signs apart from a simple "EXIT."

For these reasons, the emergency exit routes should lead unambiguously toward the street, or a safe refuge within the building. Requirements for emergency exit are laid down in the building codes, and they usually include provisions similar to the following:

- All exit doors should open in the direction of travel, without the need of a key
- The passage should be wide enough to accommodate the expected number of people without excessive crowding (see Section 25.3), and should not become narrower in the direction of travel
- Stairs coming down from upper floors and stairs coming up from a basement should not meet, but both discharge outside at ground level (so that two streams of people do not collide on the stairs)
- Stairs should remain smoke-free in a fire, by the use of self-closing doors, together with natural or forced ventilation; many codes require the stairs to be pressurized with fresh air to prevent smoke entry

Access for Goods and Equipment

There are three principal kinds of goods traffic in most nonwarehouse buildings—the supply of materials for the initial fitout, which usually overlaps with partial occupancy; the removal and supply of materials for subsequent tenancy changes or equipment replacement; and the day-to-day delivery of supplies and removal of rubbish. All three types must be catered for by the access system. The more occasional traffic can be allowed to cause some interruption to normal operations of the building, for example by taking some of the elevators out of normal service and using them as temporary freight elevators, out of peak hours. More routine operations such as delivery of supplies must be catered for with truck docks, temporary storage for unloaded material, and in most cases freight elevators away from the public areas.

Rubbish removal is often carried out at night, so that the normal passenger corridors and elevators can be used for this purpose. However, any canteens or restaurants in the building will produce food scraps, and special hygiene conditions will apply both to the food storage and preparation areas, and also to the temporary storage and removal of the rubbish.

25.2 RATES OF ARRIVAL AND DEPARTURE, AND QUEUEING

In the absence of any other influences, people should arrive at a building in a random manner. That does not imply a *uniform* rate of arrival; it implies that there will be variations from moment to moment. The mathematical representation of an arrival pattern is complicated because people are discrete units rather than a continuous variable, and it is not helpful to model a completely random pattern, because there are always external influences that make the real pattern nonrandom.

The arrival of *workers* at the building is concentrated in the period just before starting time, and if most of them come by bus or subway, there will be clusters as each bus or train arrives. The arrival pattern of *customers* follows a pattern depending on the nature of the business. The arrival pattern of workers in the elevator lobbies wanting to catch an elevator to leave the building depends on the quitting-time policy of the company.

Doorways, corridors, stairs, and escalators all handle people as a continuous stream. So long as the arrival rate does not exceed the rate at which they can pass through the doors, corridors, etc., there is virtually no queueing. If a bunch of people arrive at once, they must form a queue (either a well-organized line or a jumble of people, but technically it is a queue) to pass through. When people are crowded and cannot maintain their normal walking pace, the capacity of a doorway is reduced. If this bunch is the result of a bus arriving, the queue will probably disappear before the next bus arrives. If the doorway is just too small, the queue may persist for some time, and this is an obvious design fault.

Even with adequate doorways, occasional crowding is almost certain to occur, particularly if revolving doors or security checks limit the rate of progress. There must be somewhere for the waiting people to gather, off the main sidewalk (so as not to impede other pedestrians, and certainly so as not to spill onto the roadway), and preferably under cover in bad weather.

Elevators handle people in batches. Some passengers will always have to wait until an elevator car arrives. The size of the lobby must be adequate for those waiting at the worst time, as well as allowing space for the exiting passengers to leave the car before the new passengers board it. The size of elevator lobbies is discussed in Section 25.6 and Fig. 25.6.1.

25.3. SIZE AND CAPACITY OF CORRIDORS

The capacity of passageways to carry pedestrian traffic can only be determined by observation over large numbers of examples. Much of this research has been collected and presented by Tregenza in Ref. 25.1, which also contains an extensive bibliography on the subject.

Minimum Widths

A pedestrian requires a lane width of 21 to 24 in. (530 to 600 mm), which represents the width of the shoulders or elbows of a reasonably large person, plus a little clearance. A standard doorway is 2 ft. 8 in. (0.8 m) wide, so that any items designed to pass through a normal doorway do not exceed that width.

People using corridors or stairs can walk side by side, overtake, or pass people coming from the other direction on the basis of these imaginary lanes. Where the traffic flow is not the major consideration, a corridor should be at least wide enough to allow two people to pass in opposite directions without difficulty, and this requires about 4 ft (1200 mm). Although a straight corridor of this width also allows easy passage of a single wheelchair, it causes difficulties when a pedestrian has to pass a wheelchair, or another person carrying luggage, in the opposite direction. Two people walking abreast have to revert to single file when meeting someone coming the other way. Two wheelchairs or trolleys are not able to pass. Wheelchairs, trolleys, and long furniture items require additional width, or a splayed corner, to negotiate a right-angled bend.

The corridor width just described should not be used for more than a short distance. A width of 5 ft 6 in. to 6 ft (1.6 to 1.8 m) is a better minimum for more important traffic routes, and the estimated maximum traffic flow may require a greater width than this.

Obstructions reduce the effective width considerably. The most common obstructions are stationary people (in a queue or looking at shop windows), furniture and display

426 HANDBOOK OF ARCHITECTURAL TECHNOLOGY

Table 25.1. Pedestrian Traffic.

Item	Width, ft	Width, m
Pedestrian	2	0.6
Pedestrian with bags or trolley	3.3	1.0
Wheelchair, baby carriage	2.6	0.8

stands, and doorways. Most heavily trafficked pedestrian routes have a newsstand, potted plants, litter bins, and display windows. People often plan to meet after work by waiting in a passageway. When it is possible to predict the locations of these obstructions, additional space should be provided.

Table 25.1 shows the approximate widths of various items related to pedestrian traffic.

Widths Based on Traffic Flow

The minimum widths referred to above can be used if the traffic flow is not excessive. Most pedestrians walk at a speed of 3 to 6 ft/s (0.9 to 1.8 m/s) when unimpeded and alone. People walking in groups are slower, because they talk together and adopt the speed of the slowest in the group. There are also differences according to age and sex (related to size and fitness), and to the purpose of the journey (browsing, going somewhere pleasant or unpleasant).

When there is light traffic, people determine their own speed and their average speed and density determines the capacity of the route. When traffic is heavier, overtaking is difficult and the slower people determine the average speed. When traffic is very heavy, nobody can take normal steps, and the whole mass shuffles slowly or comes to a standstill. Two-way or cross traffic is less efficient than one-way traffic. This latter fact is important for the design of emergency exits, where there should be one-way traffic and usually no obstructions.

Figure 25.3.1 indicates the range of capacities of corridors, in persons per minute per lane width in the direction of travel, for various degrees of crowding. Fig. 25.3.2 gives a pictorial indication of various densities of pedestrian traffic. From the diagrams, it is obvious how greater crowding impedes the progress of all the users.

25.4. STAIRWAYS

People travel more slowly on stairs than on flat passageways, partly because of the additional energy needed to climb stairs, but mainly because of the restricted length of stride and the need to place the foot carefully on each step. Stairs are potentially dangerous, particularly for the infirm, and handrails are necessary. When the width of a flight is

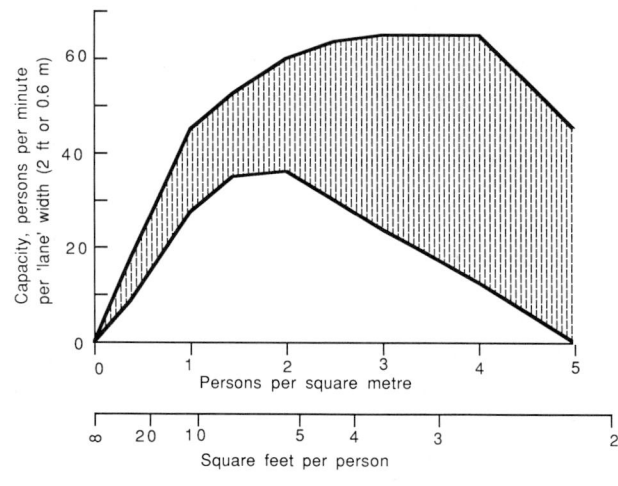

Fig. 25.3.1. The carrying capacity of passageways, expressed as persons per minute per "lane width," for various densities of crowding. In the left half of the diagram, the crowding is not enough to cause a significant loss of speed, and the capacity increases with the number of people using the passageway. Toward the right half, increased crowding causes the traffic to slow, and eventually the capacity is reduced.

The upper and lower lines represent approximately the range of values found by various experimenters (reported in Ref. 25.1). The upper values would be expected with unidirectional flow, with people who are physically fit and motivated to move without delay. The lower values would correspond to two-way traffic, with people of diverse ages including groups who wish to stay together and a mixture of "travelers" and "browsers."

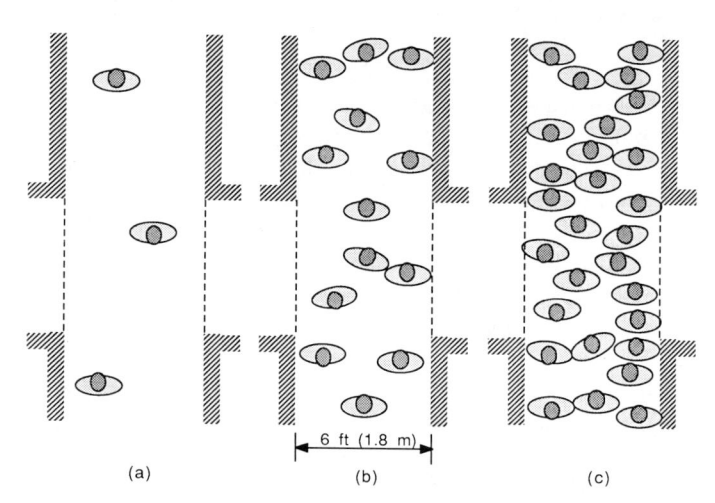

Fig. 25.3.2. (a) Pedestrians using a corridor at a density of 36 ft^2 per person (0.3 person per m^2) can walk freely, and easily avoid others walking in the same or the opposite direction without slowing. Cross-traffic of the same density would cause very little interference.

(b) A density of about 8 ft^2 per person (1.4 person per m^2) is the maximum for comfortable walking. It allows fairly free movement, although most walkers will reduce their speed and sometimes will have to balk to avoid another person. Two-way traffic causes more obstruction, particularly if there is no rule about keeping to one side. Cross-traffic would cause considerable disruption.

(c) A density of 3.6 ft^2 per person (3 persons per m^2) represents about the maximum capacity of a crowded passageway. All walkers are reduced to shuffling along, and are quite uncomfortable. Any cross-traffic, or an obstruction such as one person standing still, or a litter bin in the passageway, would cause chaos.

greater than about 6 ft. (1.8 m), a central handrail is also advisable, so that no person is more than arm's length from a handrail in the event of stumbling.

Building codes contain much detail about stairs, particularly stairs required for escape. They specify a range of acceptable values for treads and risers, usually based on an arbitrary rule. One such rule (illustrated in Fig. 25.4.1a) assumes that the length of a pace is 25 in. (620 mm), and since vertical movement is more difficult than horizontal movement, the sum of the tread and twice the rise should come to this value. Another rule states that the product of tread and rise should be 66 in.^{2} (42000 mm^2). Any such rule is obviously suspect on geometrical grounds, although there is also experimental evidence for some of the more commonly accepted proportions (Ref. 25.2, p. 88).

Any casual observation of people using stairs will reveal that some people take the stairs two at a time, indicating that the common values are much too conservative for at least part of the community. It is also widely accepted that people's bodies, and their feet, are larger now than they were a century or so ago, and therefore historically based rules should be treated with caution. Several principles, however, can be applied to all stair designs:

- The beginning and end of the stairs must be easily seen. Good lighting, handrails, change in floor finish,

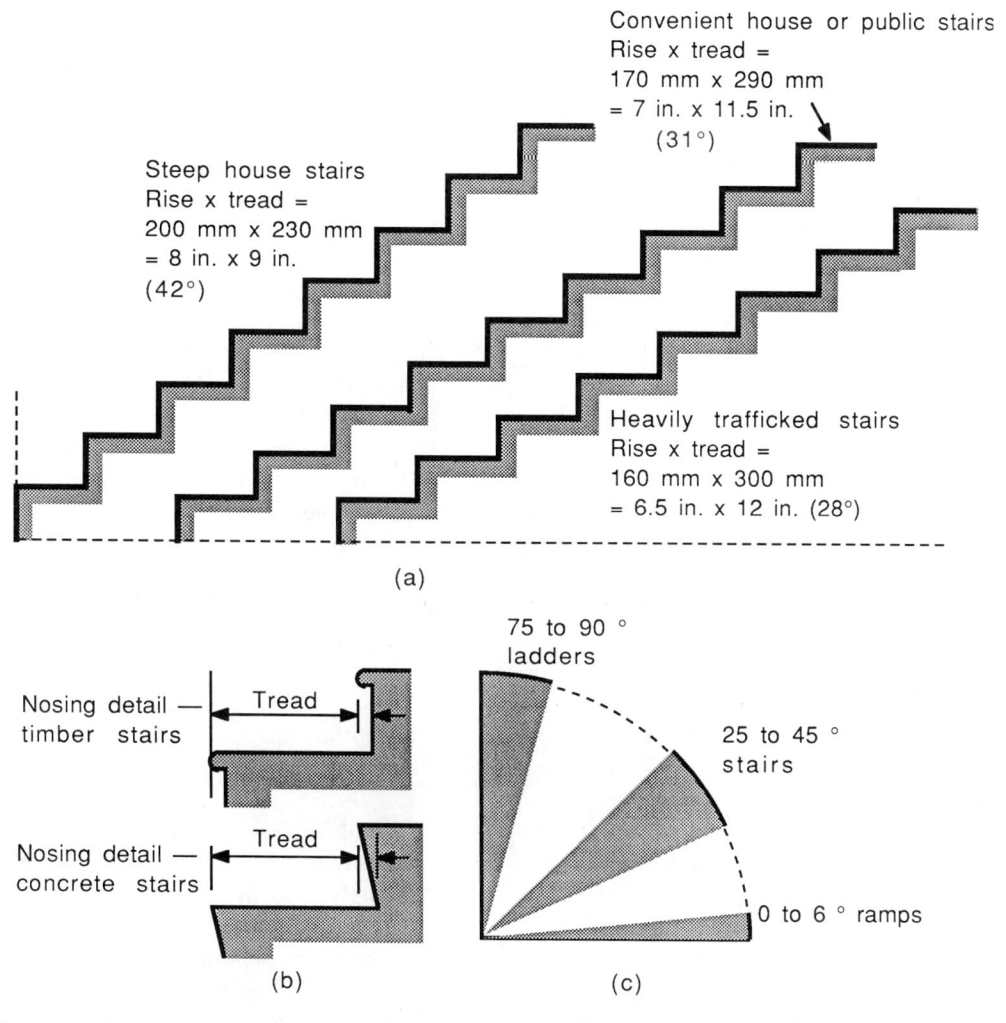

Fig. 25.4.1. (a) The proportion of tread to riser usually accepted as comfortable for stairs. If the tread is T and the rise is R, then $T + 2R$ should be about 25 in. (630 mm). For public buildings and heavy pedestrian traffic, stairs should be less steep. In houses, where the space taken by the stair is a significant consideration, and traffic is light, steeper proportions are commonly accepted.

(b) The effective tread length (called the *going* in Britain) is measured between equivalent points on two adjacent steps. The edge of each tread should form a *nosing* of about 1 to 2 in. (25 to 50 mm), to allow additional room for the toe or heel of the shoe. This adds to comfort when climbing upwards, but is of less advantage when descending.

(c) There is a practical range of angles in which ramps, stairs or ladders are usually built. Very flat stairs or steep ramps (in the range 6 to 25°) are less convenient and more dangerous than the preferred angles. Stairs above 45° are difficult to descend frontwards. Industrial stairs and ships' companionways are often in the steeper range, and are most safely descended backwards; but this requires the use of the handrails, so that nothing can be carried in the hands. Although *fixed* ladders are often constructed vertically, most users find them unpleasant to use. *Portable* ladders must have a slope, usually around 75°.

and no flight of less than three risers are some of the means of achieving this.

- Each step must be the same size as all the others in the flight. When a person begins to climb or descend stairs, the first few steps are most reliably located visually; but by placing the ball of the foot near the nosing (when descending), or the instep on the nosing (when climbing), it is easy to "feel" each step, using a combination of rhythm and peripheral vision to find each succeeding step, while using central vision to avoid other people and to locate the next landing. Uneven step dimensions reduce the effectiveness of the feeling process.
- The treads, particularly the nosings, must be nonslip under all conditions. This is hardest to achieve outdoors, in wet or freezing weather. Strips of carborundum or other hard, high-friction material can be inserted near the nosing to assist with friction. Watching a person descending a stair indicates that friction is required to slow the descent, and a loss of friction may cause a major accident. There is a similar requirement when ascending, but the consequences are usually less severe.

25.5. ESCALATORS AND MOVING WALKWAYS

An escalator or moving walk is a conveyor-belt for people. If the rate of arrival is not excessive, each passenger can step on immediately without waiting, be transported to the other end, and step off immediately. Only when the rate of arrival exceeds the transporting capacity is there any need to queue.

This advantage of instant service is achieved at a considerable cost in other capabilities. In the usual types of escalators and walkways, these limitations are as follows:

- Since the equipment does not stop, the passenger must be accelerated to full speed in the action of stepping on, that is in the length of one step. This effectively limits the speed of the machine to walking pace.
- Movement is linear, with passengers exiting in the order they entered. This means that each machine can only operate between two fixed points, unlike an elevator, which can have many intermediate stops.
- The angle of incline is limited. Therefore any significant vertical rise is accompanied by a far greater horizontal movement, whether this is desired or not. A moving walk (i.e., with a surface that does not form steps during its travel), can be built at any angle from horizontal to 15°. For escalators (which do form steps) the angle is normally 30°, and deviations from this are rare.
- Riding on an escalator requires a certain degree of agility and locomotor skill. It is not suitable for a wheelchair. A baby carriage or a small baggage trolley can be carried, with some inconvenience. It presents difficulty for the visually impaired, since it is necessary to observe the arrival of the treads. These disadvantages occur to a lesser degree with a moving walkway.
- Each machine operates in only one direction at a time, so that two-way traffic requires two separate escalators or walkways. However, in peak times one can be reversed, so that both operate in the major direction of travel.

Escalators are widely used to transport large numbers of people over a relatively short vertical distance. A single escalator has the same capacity as a large bank of elevators. There is little need for direction signs, since it is obvious where the escalator is going, and the passengers have the benefit of an uninterrupted view during their travel. By contrast, an elevator disappears behind closed doors and the passengers do not see the arrival floor until the doors open.

Escalators are also useful in the planning of a building with a large pedestrian traffic flow, in directing that flow in the desired direction. This principle is used to advantage in the airport terminal building at Charles de Gaulle Airport in Paris. Incoming and outgoing passengers are transported from one side to the other of the donut-shaped building, and also from one floor to another, by a number of escalators that criss-cross the hole in the donut. This is not only quicker but also more foolproof than directing people to go "halfway around and two floors down."

Horizontal moving walks are less common, mainly because people are more willing to walk horizontally than they are to walk up or down stairs. If the speed of the moving walk is the same as walking pace, there is no great time advantage in using it. There is the disadvantage that, once on the walk, one is not able to stop and browse until the next exit is reached.

The use of moving walks in buildings is limited to very large horizontal buildings, such as transportation terminals, where the advantages include the following:

- Long travel distances, so that walking is tiring for many people
- Many passengers are carrying baggage and may be fatigued from a long journey
- There are definite entry and exit points (such as the terminal lounges at an airport), and little need to stop between them
- Passengers in a hurry can walk on the moving walkway, thereby doubling their speed.

Urban People-Moving

The horizontal movement of people is receiving more interest in the field of urban design than in buildings. Railways, subways and bus lines carry most of the commuter traffic in large cities, while automobiles provide a more personalized service at the expense of large areas of land devoted to freeways and parking lots, and a higher fuel consumption than mass-transit systems.

Most short-distance transportation downtown is done on foot, which limits the practical distance between stops in the transit systems, or the distance between carparks and the destination of the user. The transit systems could operate faster, and perhaps with fewer lines, if there was another scale of transport between them and the pedestrian, and the carparks could be further from the center of downtown.

The conventional moving walkway, operating at pedestrian speed, does not offer enough advantage over walking. Experimental designs have been developed for accelerating moving walks, where the passenger enters at walking pace and is accelerated to four to five times that speed for most of the journey, and gently decelerated again before leaving. Other people-mover designs involve the use of vehicles, so that passengers have the opportunity to sit. Options include stopping to allow entry and exit; or slowing to allow stepping on or off; or a combination of slowing and a short moving walk that matches the speed of the slowed vehicle.

The treads of a moving walkway travel as an endless belt, returning to the original point by a path immediately under the walkway. Thus they can be installed in sidewalks or other public places with relatively little disruption to other traffic. Each one can be the length of a city block, so that the passengers can cross the road on foot, and the installation has minimal conflict with other traffic. In any system involving the use of vehicles, the vehicles must complete a round trip, thus interfering with roads and other pedestrian routes. These systems therefore usually have to operate either above or below grade. Escalators are used to take the passengers from ground level to the transport system level.

Mechanical Details

A moving walkway requires a firm, flat surface to stand on; close mechanical tolerances at the edges and exit point to prevent injury; and moving handrails to provide a means of maintaining balance. It is acceptable to stand on a flat surface that slopes up or down as much as 15° from the horizontal (1 in 3.7), since it is not necessary to walk, and there is a handrail to hold. By way of comparison, ramps within buildings are limited by building codes to a much flatter slope, usually 1 in 10 or 1 in 12.

The surface is formed from individual panels, usually of cast aluminum, hinged together as an endless chain. Outside the USA, some moving walks are built using reinforced-rubber conveyor belting running on closely spaced rollers. The ride is slightly uncomfortable, since the rollers can be felt as one's feet pass over them. There is also some danger of the passengers' feet or clothing being caught against the edges, or at the point of exit.

Escalators can be built steeper than moving walks because they form themselves into discrete horizontal steps. The industry standard is 30° (1 in 1.7), although in Europe some escalators are built at 35° inclination. The steps are about 14 in. (340 mm) deep (front to back) and 8 in. (200 mm) high. This is convenient for standing on, but much larger than a normal stairway. When an escalator is stopped, it forms a rather inconvenient stairway.

An escalator has the same requirements as a moving walk, and in addition the risers between the treads must be able to appear and disappear during the travel without trapping clothing or feet. The key to safety at the risers and the exits is the comb system. Both treads and risers have a grooved surface. A comb on the back of the tread engages the grooves in the riser, and a comb on the edge of the floor opening engages the grooves in the tread, so that any loose clothing or footwear is prevented from becoming caught.

In early escalators, the grooves and combs were about $\frac{1}{2}$ in. (12 mm) wide, which along with a considerable mechanical clearance caused some difficulty with small heels, umbrella tips, and children's toes. Modern treads are made of cast aluminum, with small and accurate grooves $\frac{1}{4}$ in. (6 mm) wide and minimum clearances.

Escalator treads run on wheels fore and aft, each pair of wheels following a different track. The geometry of the two tracks enables the treads to move either horizontally or along the slope, while maintaining a horizontal surface. They return underneath, thus requiring a considerable depth through the escalator enclosure. Moving walk treads are similar except they simply follow the slope of the walk, without forming risers.

Physical Sizes

Since the speed of escalators is fairly standard, their carrying capacity depends on the width. In the USA and Canada the width is given between the balustrades, while in Europe the tread width is used. The balustrade width is 8 in. (200 mm) greater than the tread width, since people are widest at the hips, and there is no point in making the expensive treads and mechanical components wider than necessary.

The common widths are 48 in. between balustrades (1000 mm treads), which fits two people per tread, and 32 in. between balustrades (600 mm treads), which takes one person comfortably per tread, and occasionally two.

Speeds and Capacities

The "standard" speed for escalators is 90 feet per minute (fpm) (0.45 m/s), measured in the direction of travel. Few people have difficulty in getting on at this speed. In public transport applications, the speed may be increased to 120 fpm (0.6 m/s) in peak hours. Experienced commuters who are in a hurry find this satisfactory. After peak hours the speed is reduced, because irregular users and the infirm may otherwise hesitate too long before getting on, thus negating any benefit of the higher speed. Moving walkways can run faster than escalators, mainly because it is easier to step onto a continuous flat surface than to have to identify a tread. Walkway speeds are commonly 180 fpm (0.9 m/s) if horizontal, reducing to 140 fpm (0.7 m/s) or less for a slope of 15°.

The capacity of an escalator or walkway depends on its speed and the degree of filling of the treads. It has been observed that passengers commonly fill escalators to about half their theoretical maximum capacity, although in some public transport applications the degree of filling is greater. Sometimes (as for example in the London underground) passengers are disciplined to stand on one side of the 48 in. escalators so that those in a greater hurry can walk past them on the other side. In this case it is possible to achieve a carrying capacity greater than 100% of the theoretical maximum.

Unlike elevators, where the length of travel reduces the peformance, the capacity of an escalator (Table 25.2) is independent of its length. (The longer escalator, of course, has more treads and is therefore a "bigger" escalator.)

25.6. ELEVATORS (LIFTS)

Although the escalator is the logical result of mechanizing a stairway, the elevator was actually invented earlier, because it evolved from earlier machines for elevating merchandise by mechanical or animal power. The elevator is the "batch process" of transporting people in buildings. In this respect its traffic pattern has much in common with a bus, which has a fixed route but only stops when there are passengers to get on or off.

One advantage that a modern elevator installation has over most other transport systems is that all the landing and car calls are processed by a central computer, which can assess the demands and dispatch the most appropriate car to answer each call. This results in a few calls not being answered in turn, with priority being given to handling the bulk of the traffic more expeditiously.

We noted earlier that a single escalator does not provide a full service, because it only operates in one direction. A single elevator can provide two-way service to a number of floors, but there are reasons why it is unlikely to provide a *satisfactory* service in most cases. The principal objections to a single elevator are the need for routine servicing, and the possibility of breakdown, either of which leave the building with no service at all. Of course it is possible for two elevators to be out of service simultaneously, but the probability of this happening is much lower than for one.

Criteria for Design of an Elevator Installation

Elevators are called on to serve different functions according to the size and nature of the building and their location in it. The most familiar are the passenger elevators which provide the principal passenger transport between levels in a multistory building, but may have a secondary role for carrying furniture or emergency personnel from time to time. Some elevators are used only occasionally to carry incapacitated people or goods in a low-rise building, or goods or vehicles or hospital patients or hotel guests with baggage. The criteria will therefore depend on the purpose.

An important requirement in providing an elevator service for a building is the location of the elevators (in one or more groups, depending on the size of the building) in relation to access from the entrances and also in relation to the layout of the upper floors. Since elevator shafts are normally vertical, their location on plan imposes a major constraint on every floor of the building. If the building is not of uniform height, at least one elevator group must be located in the tallest portion.

The main criteria for the design of an elevator group can be summarized under a few headings:

- *Capacity* to handle the passengers as they arrive, with minimum queueing, expressed as a percentage of the total building population that can be handled in the peak 5-minute period
- *Frequency* to provide an available car for arriving passengers without excessive waiting, expressed as the average time interval between cars
- *Car size* to handle the largest items required to be car-

Table 25.2. Typical Carrying Capacities of Escalators and Walkways.

	Width between Balustrades, in.	Tread Width, mm	Speed, fpm	Speed, m/s	Max. Capacity, Persons/ 5 min.	Nominal Capacity, Persons/ 5 min.
Escalator	32	600	90	0.45	425	170
			120	0.6	560	225
Escalator	48	1000	90	0.45	680	340
			120	0.6	900	450
Walkway	48	1000	180	0.9	1200	600
			140	0.7	900	450

fpm = feet per minute.

ried, for example, an occasional item of furniture, or a hospital bed with attendant, or a group of hotel guests with their baggage
- *Speed of total trip*, so that passengers do not preceive the total service as excessively slow

In addition there are many details that should be considered for the comfort and convenience of the users:

- A means of finding the elevator lobby that serves the user's destination floor. If there is only one zone of elevators, then a simple direction sign will suffice, but it is even better if at least one elevator door is visible from the entrance of the building. If there are multiple zones, then some signing is necessary in addition.
- Call buttons that are easy to find, and unambiguous for "up" and "down" calls. The location of the call buttons should encourage passengers to stand in a favorable position to watch all the cars in the group, and to move quickly to whichever comes first. The buttons should indicate that a call has been registered. People will become impatient more quickly if there is no indication that they are being served. If there are several buttons that all serve the same purpose, they must *all* light up to register a call, otherwise users will be uncertain whether they should press one or all the buttons.
- Lanterns, and an audible indication as well, to indicate which car is arriving and in which direction it will travel. The lanterns should be above head level to be visible above a crowd. When there is a computerized control system, the lantern can be illuminated as soon as the system has decided which car will arrive next. Early indication allows waiting passengers to move in the right direction, and can save a few seconds of loading time each time a car is loaded.
- Enough first-floor lobby space for the crowding that is expected at the up peak. Fig. 25.6.1 shows the usual recommendations.
- One set of buttons on the landing, and floor buttons in the car, should be at a level that can be reached by a person in a wheelchair, or a small child.

Layout of Elevator Groups

As mentioned previously, one elevator seldom provides a reliable service. In most cases, a group of three or more is needed to ensure that the waiting interval between them is not too great. To function as a group, the cars must all be close enough that an intending user can take whichever one arrives first. A moderately fast walking speed is 3 ft per second (0.9 m/s). If the landing doors are to remain open for 4 s, then an unobstructed person can walk briskly 12 ft (3.6 m) before they begin to close again. Obviously all the landing doors should be closer than this to all the waiting passengers, so that none feels anxious that the doors will close prematurely.

Two or three cars can conveniently be located side by side. There is no need to look over one's shoulder, and they are all close by. Four in a row or two opposite two are both acceptable for a group of four. Five in a row is beginning to be too long a distance to walk. There are some installations of six in a row where the door-open time has had to be increased because of the walking distances men-

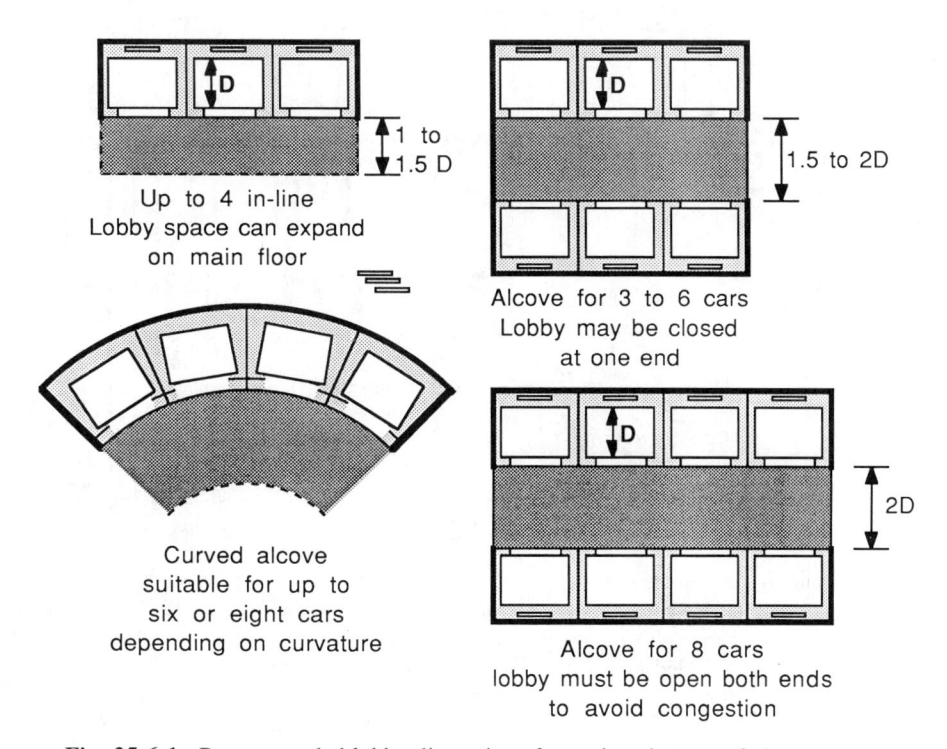

Up to 4 in-line
Lobby space can expand
on main floor
(1 to 1.5 D)

Curved alcove
suitable for up to
six or eight cars
depending on curvature

Alcove for 3 to 6 cars
Lobby may be closed
at one end
(1.5 to 2D)

Alcove for 8 cars
lobby must be open both ends
to avoid congestion
(2D)

Fig. 25.6.1. Recommended lobby dimensions for various layouts of elevator groups.

tioned above. Increasing the time spent at each landing reduces the performance of the group. Five, six, seven, or eight cars are best located opposite each other.

There are very few installations with more than eight cars in a group. With larger numbers of cars, one is not filled before the next arrives, and this causes confusion. The number of people waiting in the lobby becomes excessive. Zoning is likely to provide a better service.

Mechanical Details that Affect Performance

All elevator cars are guided by steel rails, and have a means of controlled raising and lowering of the car in response to calls. Virtually all modern machines are electrically powered. In most of them, an electric motor drives steel ropes that raise and lower the car.

Electric *traction machines* are suitable for most applications including high-speed and high-rise buildings. In a traction machine, the ropes are driven by friction over a sheave, with the car suspended on one end and a counterweight on the other. This reduces the total energy requirement for raising and lowering the car, although the energy required for accelerating and decelerating the combined mass of the car and counterweight is greater than if there were only the car. Fig. 25.6.2 shows various ways of arranging the roping. Different types of electric motors and drives are needed according to the speed required.

Most electric motors are designed to run on common alternating current (AC) run at one rated speed. Special starting equipment is needed to limit the current when starting large motors, and they are much more suited to constant operation than to stop-start conditions. Motors of this type are not ideally suited for operating elevators. Two-speed AC motors with automatic rheostatic control are used for elevator speeds up to 100 fpm (0.5 m/s), and give a comfort of ride and accuracy of leveling that is acceptable, but not great. Solid-state equipment now enables variable-frequency AC to be produced, which gives better speed control and allows AC motors to be used on medium-speed applications.

Much greater control over speed, acceleration, and retardation is available from a direct current (DC) motor, although the motor itself is much more expensive to manufacture. By varying the voltage, the speed can be infinitely varied. Until recently, the variable voltage was obtained from a motor-generator set (an AC motor driving a DC generator), the output voltage being controlled automatically by the controller of each elevator. One motor-generator set is needed for each elevator. The same controlled DC voltage can now be obtained using solid-state equipment which is quieter, uses less energy, and produces less waste heat.

The rotation speed of the traction sheave is relatively low. A 30-in. (750 mm) sheave driving an elevator at 400 fpm (2 m/s) turns at 50 rpm, whereas electric motors commonly operate at thousands of rpm. *Geared machines* use a worm-drive gearbox to match the characteristics of the motor and the load. However, it is possible to build a large-diameter DC motor that runs slow enough, and has enough torque, not to need a gearbox. By using 2:1 roping

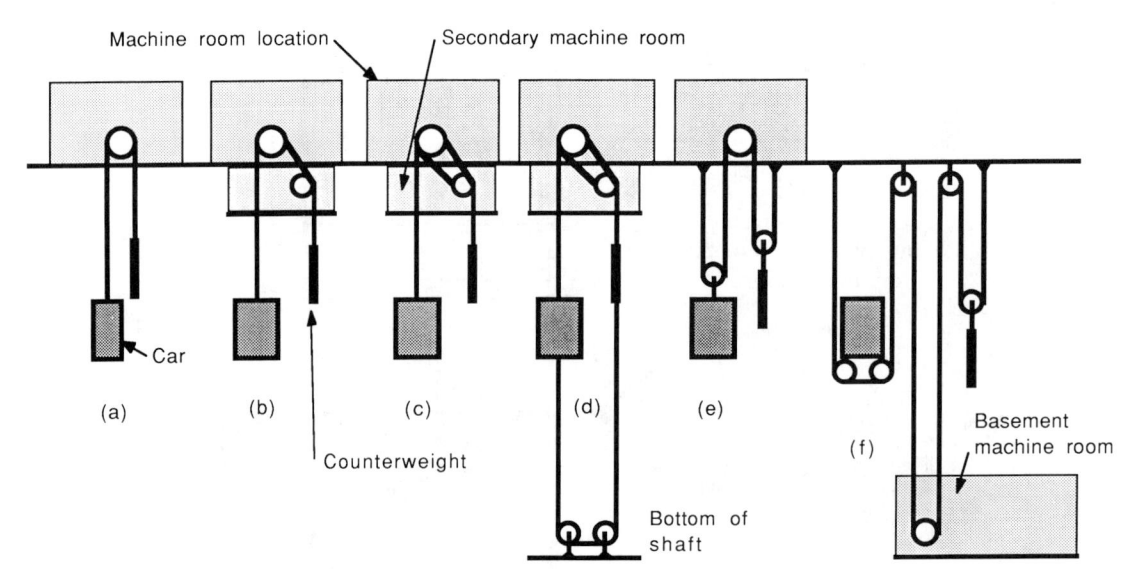

Fig. 25.6.2. Various ways of arranging the roping for traction-type elevators. (a) Single wrap using only the traction sheave. This is only possible for small cars because the distance between car and counterweight centers is limited. (b) Single wrap with divertor sheave. Allows more freedom in locating the counterweight. (c) Double wrap. The same as (b), except an extra wrap of the ropes gives more reliable traction. (d) Compensator ropes are added in tall buildings. The lower ropes are merely moving ballast to compensate for the weight of the moving hoist ropes. (e) 2:1 roping. The ropes move twice as fast as the car. This allows a gearless machine to be used on a slower car than would otherwise be feasible. (f) Underslung car. The machine room can be located in the basement, to reduce the height needed at the top of the building.

(see Fig. 25.6.2), the motor could operate at 100 rpm. *Gearless machines* are used for all high-rise, high-speed applications, giving smooth performance and lower maintenance costs than geared machines, although the initial cost is much higher.

Drum machines are useful for some low-speed, low-rise applications where there is no room for a counterweight. The machine is effectively a winch that lifts and lowers the car by winding the ropes onto a drum.

Hydraulic elevators are useful for low-speed, low-rise applications, particularly when there is no room for overhead machinery. The simplest form of hydraulic elevators utilize a straight hydraulic ram set into a hole below the shaft, which acts like a large hydraulic jack to raise and lower the car. A variation uses a hydraulic ram located in part of the shaft, which operates ropes to control the car. This does not require a deep hole. Fig. 25.6.3 illustrates both types. The hydraulic fluid is provided by a reservoir and electric pump located alongside the shaft. Hydraulic elevators were once powered by reticulated hydraulic power that was available from a utility company the same way as steam, water, gas and electricity are supplied, and some of these installations still exist.

The *doors* have a significant influence on the efficiency of an elevator installation. A significant amount of time is taken both in opening and closing the doors at each stop, and in loading and unloading the passengers.

Passengers load and unload fastest through wide doors. 48 in. (1200 mm) door widths are used for medium to large commercial elevators to allow two people to use the door side-by-side. Widths of 60 in. (1500 mm) can be used on larger cars for even easier access, while 36 in. (900 mm) doors are used on smaller cars, partly for economy and partly to save space in the elevator shaft. The relationship between the door type and the shaft width is shown in Fig. 25.6.4.

Wide doors, however, take a little longer to open and close. Elevator codes limit the kinetic energy of a closing door as a safety measure in case it collides with a late passenger, and therefore the doors are not permitted to close at excessive speeds. The slowest type of door, and also the one that takes up most width, is a single leaf sliding to one side (*single-slide*). Performance is improved slightly if two leaves both slide to the one side, one traveling twice as fast as the other, so that they both get to be open at the same time (*two-speed*). This arrangement takes up less width in the shaft (since the open doors only take up half the width of the opening), but because there are two car doors on parallel tracks, they take up more *depth* in the car. *Center-opening* doors are considerably faster, since each leaf only has to travel half the width of the opening. For very wide doors, a *two-speed center opening arrangement* is used. Fig. 25.6.4 illustrates the different arrangements.

The shape of the car also influences the efficiency with which it fills and empties. A wide shallow car is best for easy access, and causes least delay for passengers standing at the back who need to exit at the first stop. If taken to extremes, excessive width increases the length of the lobby, and it requires very wide doors to take advantage of the car width. Therefore most practical cars are just a little wider than deep. Special cars, such as those in a hospital, are more likely deeper, to accommodate a patient trolley.

Layout of Elevator Equipment

The usual arrangement for a traction machine is to have the machine room at the top of the shaft. A secondary machine room is needed to accommodate the divertor sheave at speeds greater than 700 fpm (3.5 m/s) (see Fig. 25.6.2). The top of the machine room is usually the highest part of the building, and determines the profile of any other mechanical rooms located on the roof. The safety provisions of elevator codes require an *overrun* at the top and bottom of the shaft, in which a car or counterweight can be decelerated by buffers if it travels past the bottom landing *at normal speed*. (If it exceeds normal operating speed by more than a nominated margin, usually 25 percent, the car safety device should stop the car by applying a braking force to the guide rails.) For high car speeds, the buffers are long hydraulic struts like those that cushion an airplane on landing.

For a constant rate of deceleration, the stroke of the buffer must increase with the square of the car speed. A similar clearance must be provided over the top of the car, in case the counterweight overruns and strikes its buffers. Buffers are not provided at the top of the shaft, since gravity will decelerate the car once the counterweight is brought to rest and takes the tension out of the ropes. Therefore,

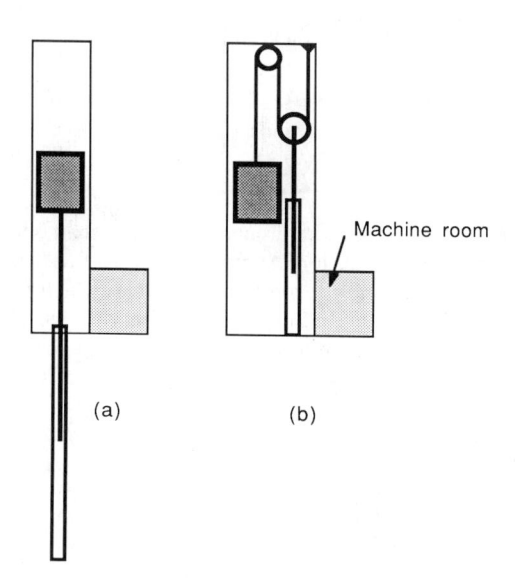

Fig. 25.6.3. Hydraulic elevators. (a) With a one-piece or telescopic ram beneath the car. The ram itself provides the overspeed and overtravel protection. (b) With the ram in the shaft, using a machine-chain or rope to operate the car itself. Normal safety devices are needed as with any rope-operated elevator.

(a) Single speed, single slide

(b) Two speed, single slide

(c) Two speed, center opening

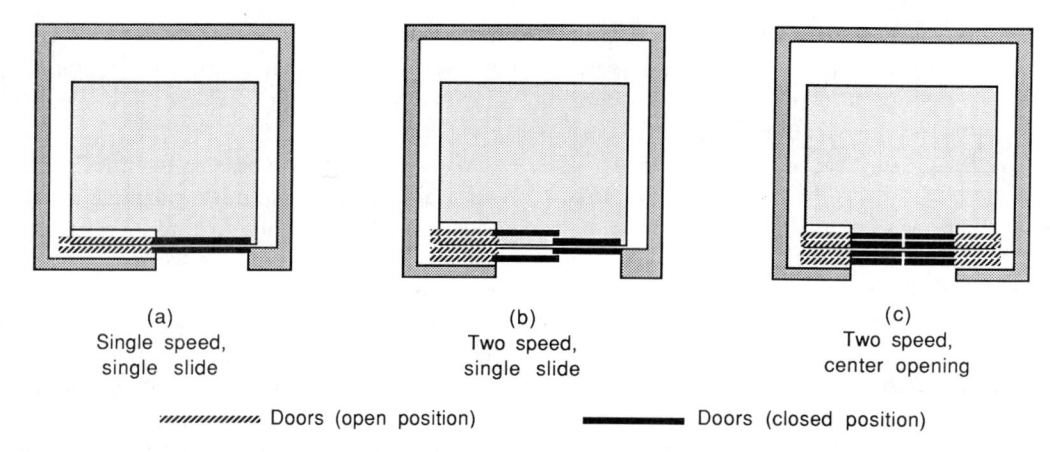

▓▓▓▓▓ Doors (open position)   ▬▬▬ Doors (closed position)

Fig. 25.6.4. Different arrangements of door openings for passenger cars. The landing and platform doors are always of the same type. Two-speed doors require less width, but more depth. Freight cars usually have vertical bi-parting doors (not shown), which allow full width access.

one of the consequences of high car speed is a large overrun requirement top and bottom of the shaft.

In addition to the mechanical clearances required, an allowance must be made for stretching of the ropes, and for a "refuge space" where a mechanic who might be working on top of the car can crouch down without striking any of the overhead structure. Elevator codes usually set the refuge space at 3 ft 6 in (1050 mm). Fig. 25.6.5 indicates the clearances needed.

The hoistway shaft has to accommodate the *outside* dimensions of the car, the counterweight, the guides for both car and counterweight, and an allowance for out-of-plumb in the construction. The latter depends on the accuracy expected from the builder. At least 2 in. (50 mm) should be allowed in a steel-framed or accurately built reinforced concrete building. Slip-formed concrete is a little more difficult to control for verticality, and an additional allowance may be necessary. Table 25.3 indicates the relationship between the inside car dimensions and the shaft dimensions.

The plan area needed for the machine room is about twice the area of the hoistway shaft. The machine room contains the traction machines themselves (motor and sheave, and gearbox if any, built into a single unit) sitting on beams directly above the shaft, the control equipment for each elevator, and the group control equipment. In modern installations the processing of calls and car-location information is carried out by solid-state computer equipment, which is compact but requires a clean and controlled environment. Current to the drive motors is also provided by solid-state electronic equipment, although in many existing installations this job is done by motor-generator sets which convert the normal three-phase alternating current to variable voltage direct current. All this equipment must be capable of being repaired or replaced. Hoist beams in the machine room ceiling permit the heavy items to be lifted and moved to a location above the lobby space. Hatchways through the machine room floor and the ceiling of the highest occupied floor permit items to be lowered to that floor, and then placed in one of the other elevators in the group to be taken to street level.

The secondary machine room floor occupies only the area of the shaft. It contains the divertor sheaves, and usually the governors. If there is no secondary floor, space must be found for the governors on the main machine room floor.

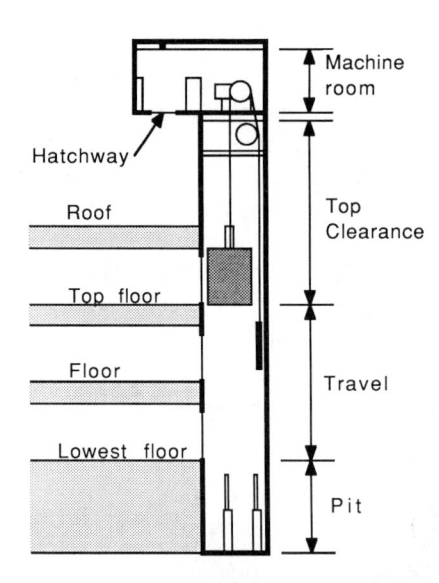

Fig. 25.6.5. Vertical section through an elevator shaft with electric traction machine at the top. Approximate dimensions are given below. They are assembled from several sources which give differing values, and should always be checked with the elevator manufacturers. The requirements also vary with car size.

Speed	Machine Room	Top clearance 1[a]	Top clearance 2[b]	Pit
100 fpm	8 ft	16 ft		4 ft.
(0.5 m/s)	(2.4 m)	(4.8 m)		(1.2 m)
200 fpm	9 ft	16 ft	21 ft	6 ft
(1 m/s)	(2.7 m)	(4.8 m)	(6.3 m)	(1.8 m)
400 fpm	9 ft	18 ft	23 ft	7 ft
(2 m/s)	(2.7 m)	(5.4 m)	(7.0 m)	(2.1 m)
800 fpm	10 ft		28 ft	14 ft
(4 m/s)	(3 m)		(8.4 m)	(4.2 m)
1200 fpm	10 ft		32 ft	20 ft
(6 m/s)	(3 m)		(9.6 m)	(6 m)

[a]Without secondary machine room
[b]With secondary machine room, usually only above 700 fpm (3.5 m/s)

THE MOVEMENT OF PEOPLE AND GOODS 435

Table 25.3. Approximate Sizes and Ratings of Elevator Cars.

| Capacity || Passengers || Inside, W × D || Shaft, W × D ||
lb	kg	Max.	Average	in.	mm	in.	mm
2000	900	12	10	68 × 51	1700 × 1300	89 × 83	2200 × 2100
2500	1150	16	13	82 × 51	2100 × 1300	102 × 83	2550 × 2100
3000	1350	20	16	82 × 55	2100 × 1400	102 × 88	2550 × 2200
3500	1600	24	19	82 × 66	2100 × 1650	102 × 96	2550 × 2400
4000	1800	28	22	92 × 66	2300 × 1650	114 × 96	2850 × 2400

25.7. ESTIMATING ELEVATOR PERFORMANCE

Speeds and Capacities

Elevators that run at speeds of 25 to 100 fpm (0.1 to 0.5 m/s) would be considered very slow, while high-speed cars in a tall building operate at 800 to 1800 fpm (4 to 9 m/s). A fast car has obvious advantages for a long travel distance, provided it can reach and maintain that speed for a significant part of the trip. For interfloor travel with short jumps, the maximum speed may not be achieved for most of the trip.

Elevator cars and machinery are rated by the manufacturers and the regulating authorities according to the weight they can carry, and this is converted to number of passengers on the nameplate. Approximate sizes and passenger ratings are given in Table 25.3. Actual dimensions can be varied to suit manufacturers' standards or special job requirements, although the maximum car area and passenger rating for any given load capacity is laid down in national or regional building codes. The car dimensions given in Table 25.3 are wide and shallow, to allow easy passenger access and maximum door width (the 82 in. car width allows 48 in. doors, the minimum size to allow comfortable two-lane passenger entry). Cars can be built narrower and deeper if stretcher accommodation is needed.

Performance and Performance Criteria

Each elevator car makes a series of round trips, terminating at the lobby. Trips do not necessarily extend to the highest floor each time. In the up-peak situation, the number of stops depends on the number of calls from passengers in the car or on the upper floors. Statistically, if there is an equal likelihood of any passenger wanting to go to any of the upper floors, the number of stops a car is likely to make on one trip is given by

$$P = F - F\left(1 - \frac{1}{F}\right)^C$$

where P = probable number of stops
 F = number of floors served above ground
 C = capacity of car on average trip (taken as no more than 80 percent of the maximum number of passengers)

At each stop, the car must decelerate, open the doors, allow passengers to exit, close the doors, and accelerate to speed. Then it travels at full speed to the next stop. A low-speed elevator will always reach full speed between floors, while a high-speed one may not do so when the distance between adjacent stops is less than several floors. Factors which influence the time taken for a round trip are therefore those described below.

- *Car size.* A larger car carries more people, who take more time to enter and leave the car, and also is likely to require more stops.
- *Car speed.* A faster car takes less time for the return trip, and for express sections of the journey. However, the improvement in round trip time is sometimes only marginal, since all other items in the trip time are unchanged.
- *Door opening and closing.* As described above, center-opening doors are the fastest, taking about 5.3 seconds for a 48-in. pair of doors. Two-speed doors opening to one side would take about 7.7 seconds

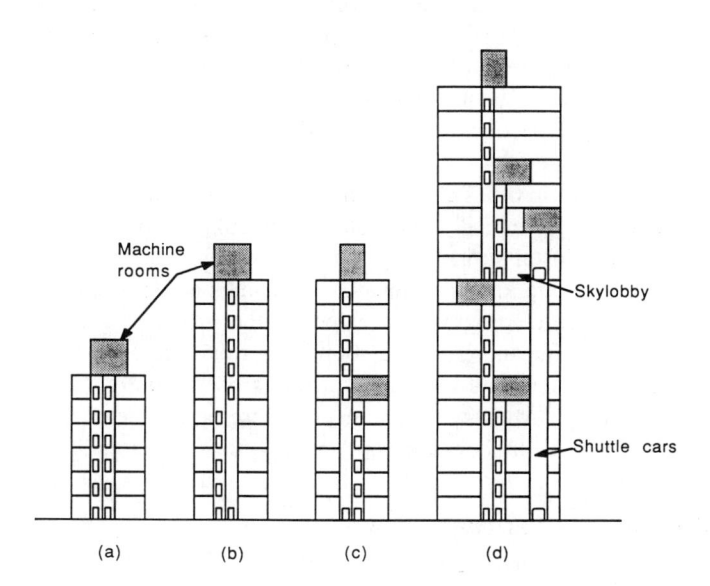

25.6.6. Possible zoning arrangements. (*Note:* the number of floors has been reduced for clarity.) (a) All cars serve all floors. (b) "Soft" zoning. All cars go past all floors, but the operating system divides them into zones. (c) "Hard" zoning. Low zone cars terminate with a separate machine room partway up the building. Space is made available on higher floors. (d) Skylobby system. Shuttle cars serve an upper lobby. Local elevators are repeated in the same plan position in each section of the building.

(Ref. 25.3, p. 64). With certain safeguards, it is permissible to begin opening the doors just before the car finally levels at the floor, thereby saving 1 second on each stop.

- *Floor standing and passenger transfer times.* Minimum standing times are suggested in Ref 25.3, p. 63, as 8 s at the lobby, 4 s at a floor for a landing call, and 2 s at a floor for a car call. The reason for the latter is that the passenger in the car is close to the door and ready to exit, while the passenger on the landing may have to walk a short distance after the car arrives. These times only allow a small number of passengers to transfer. The total time spent at each stop will be extended by about 1 s for each additional passenger transferring—a little more for narrow doors, a little less for wide doors. In special installations where the system is expected to handle trolleys, incapacitated persons, or any items that are slow to load, the landing times should be increased to avoid intimidating the users. The performance will be downgraded accordingly.

The design of an elevator system for a building involves choosing the number, size, speed and zoning of the elevator cars to satisfy the performance criteria, the most important of which are the handling capacity and the waiting interval. Table 24.4 indicates the range of speeds and car sizes likely to be used in various conditions.

Larger car sizes are appropriate for buildings with large areas per floor. Faster cars are appropriate for upper zones, where a significant part of the journey is spent traveling at full speed.

The design parameters for any particular installation should be determined knowing as much as possible about the expected use of the building (both initially and in the future), and the expectations of the users, both tenants and visitors. Table 25.5 lists some commonly used values, which can be no more than a guide.

To calculate the performance of a particular installation, it is necessary to estimate the round-trip time for one car. The average interval between cars is then

$$RTT/N$$

where *RTT* is the round trip time, in seconds, and *N* is the number of cars in the group

Table 25.5. Design Parameters for Elevators.

Building Type	Population Density ft²/Person	Population Density m²/Person	% Population Handled in 5 Minutes	Average Interval, Seconds
Offices:				
Prestige, single tenant	130	12	15–17	25–30
Investment, downtown	100–110	9–10	12–14	30–35
Investment, suburban	90–100	8–9	12–14	30–45
Apartments:				
Prestige	1.5 per bedroom		5–7	50–70
Midrange	2 per bedroom		6–8	60–80
Low rental	2–3 per bedroom		6–8	80–120
Hotels:				
4–5 star	1.5–2 per room		12–15	40–60
3 star and less	1.5–2 per room		10–12	50–70

As mentioned earlier, all the cars in a group must be located together so that an intending passenger has the chance of taking whichever one arrives first. The critical operating mode may be the morning up-peak traffic, the evening down-peak, or a combination of two-way and interfloor traffic during working hours. The capacity of the group to move passengers in the peak five-minute period is

$$N \times AVLOAD \times 300/RTT$$

where *AVLOAD* is the *average* load carried in each car under peak conditions (reckoned as not more than 80 percent of the nameplate load, since people will seldom pack a car to full capacity), and
300 seconds is five minutes

Round trip times can be determined from tables or charts prepared for typical conditions, or calculated for each individual installation taking into account as many relevant factors as are known. Elevator companies and consultants use computer programs to calculate the probable number of stops, and therefore the round trip times, and the handling capacity and interval of a series of alternative solutions to a particular requirement. There is no one correct solution. A number of acceptable solutions are considered

Table 25.4. Elevator Speeds and Car Sizes for Various Occupancies.

Travel Distance		Offices and Hotels, 16–20 Passenger Cars		Retail Stores 20–28 Passenger Cars		Apartments, 8–16 Passenger Cars	
ft	m	fpm	m/s	fpm	m/s	fpm	m/s
0–60	0–20	200–400	1–2	200	1	100	0.5
60–120	20–36	300–400	1.5–2	200–300	1–1.5	200	1
120–240	36–72	500–600	2.5–3	200–400	1–2	200–400	1–2
240–500	72–150	800–1000	4–5				

fpm = feet per minute.

in terms of cost, plan area, possible arrangements in groups, and in terms of the value that a particular level of service will add to the building.

For preliminary calculations, Fig. 25.7.1 provides a useful starting point. Taking the building as one zone, estimate the population, and the percentage of it to be handled in five minutes (expressed as a number of people). That number of people can be handled by a group of cars of a certain size that keep coming around at a certain interval. If the number is above the top of the chart, it would require very large cars at too-short intervals, and a zoned solution is indicated. Divide the building into a number of zones and try again for each zone.

Figure 25.7.2 gives an estimate of the round trip time for cars of different sizes and speeds, over different numbers of floors. It also indicates the 5-minute capacity of a single car operating as a local service. The capacity of a group is obtained by multiplying the capacity by the number of cars. If the car size and required interval is known, the required number of cars can be calculated from the round trip time graph.

Zoning

In most installations, the minimum number of elevators in a group is determined by the waiting interval between them (usually 3 or 4), while the maximum number is limited by the effective layout of a group around a lobby (usually 6 to 8). A building with a relatively small area per floor is likely to use smaller cars, and operate as a single zone up to about 20 stories. It is undesirable to have more than 20 stories in a single zone, as a passenger traveling to the upper floors spends too long in the elevator. If zones are used, they are likely to be of 10 or 12 stories. A building with a large area per floor is likely to use larger cars and have only 5 or 6 stories to a zone. If a building needs more than 8 cars, a zoned system will provide a better service for all users, except for interfloor traffic between zones, where it introduces the need to change cars.

Zoning reduces the round trip time dramatically for the lower zone, because those cars have less floors to serve. It also reduces the round trip time for the cars in the upper zones, because the number of stops is reduced. The express distance is travelled at full speed, and for a high-speed car it adds relatively little to the total time. Therefore passengers to upper floors have a shorter total trip (waiting time plus travel time). The round trip time is calculated for the number of stories where stops are possible, plus an addition for the nonstop travel distance of the express zone. Fig. 25.7.3 shows the *additional* time to be added. It can also be used to allow for the effect of a tall first floor.

Zoning may be achieved in one of two ways. With *soft zoning*, each elevator shaft extends the full height of the building, and landing doors are provided at all stories. However, the cars are programmed to operate in two groups. This arrangement has the advantage that the division between the zones can be changed at will. When one tenant expands and occupies stories in two separate zones, or when the density of traffic to some of the floors changes (usually as a result of change of tenancy), then the ability to rearrange the zoning is of considerable value. On the other hand, there is no advantage of reduced shaft area on higher floors.

With *hard zoning*, the shafts are constructed only as far as necessary to serve those floors that are part of each zone. If the motor rooms are at the top, then they are built at the top of each zone, usually coinciding with an intermediate mechanical plant room containing other services as well. The advantage is then that the space above each set of shafts is available for rental. It is not good office space (being in the middle of the building), but is usually capable of carrying heavier loads than the general floor area, and is therefore valuable for storage and strongrooms. The toilets and vertical ducts can be relocated to this area to free up more desirable space.

Skylobbies

In a very tall building (say 50 stories and up), the arrangement of the elevators and lobbies on the first few stories poses a considerable problem, and little space is left for the real use of the building. Buildings such as the Empire State Building in New York overcame this difficulty by having

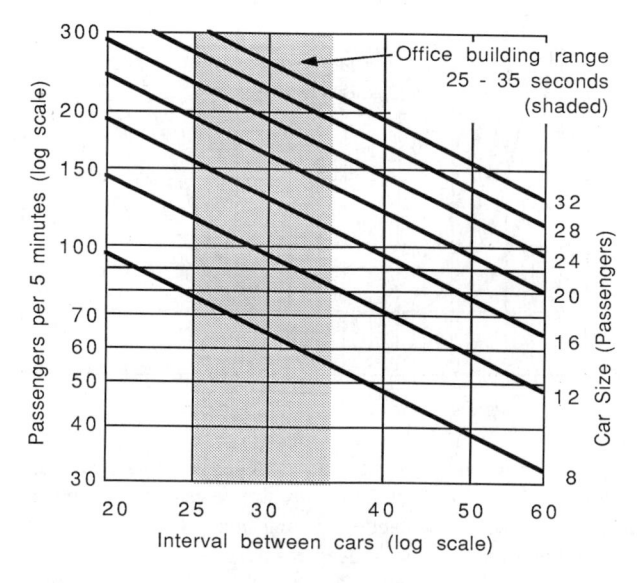

25.7.1. The five-minute handling capacity of sets of various sized elevator cars, plotted against the interval between them. First determine the required handling capacity of the group. Enter the graph from the left, and continue across to find the intersection of an acceptable car size and interval. If the required capacity is too high for an acceptable solution, try zoning. If it is too low, then the building is less than optimum size for elevatoring. Once a size and interval is determined, refer to Fig. 25.7.2 to determine the round-trip time of cars of various speeds. The number of cars required in the group is the round-trip time divided by the required interval.

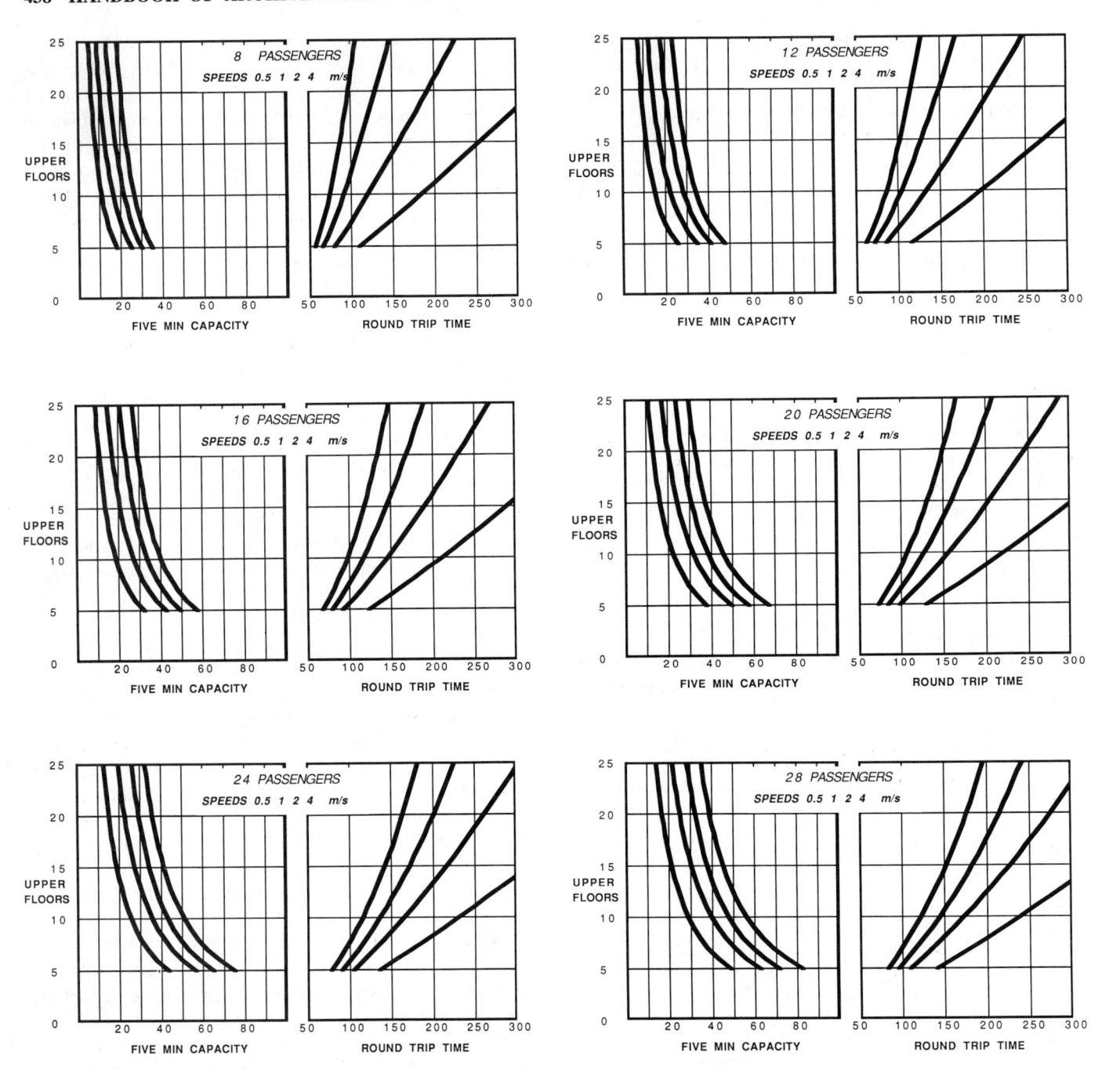

Fig. 25.7.2. The round trip time, and five-minute carrying capacity, for single elevator cars from 8 to 28 passenger nameplate capacity, and speeds from 100 to 800 fpm (0.5 to 4 m/s). All upper floors are assumed to have equal attraction. Figures are based on up peak conditions. Assumptions made about door operations and landing dwell times are intended to reflect good conditions. Slight to moderate downgrading is likely with nonstandard conditions such as extended door-open times and narrow or deep car shape.

larger floor areas at the lower levels, and setbacks as the building increases in height (Ref. 25.4). Setbacks were also part of the requirements of planning codes, to allow sunlight penetration into the streets. However, many modern buildings are designed as towers of uniform plan, set back on a large site or on a large podium, and the planning problem on the lower floors of a prismatic building of 50 stories or more becomes quite difficult. One way of relieving the problem is by the use of skylobbies.

In this system, a story about mid-height of the building, or two at third-points of the height, are designated as additional lobby floors. Passengers are carried to the upper lobbies in a group of shuttle cars. A separate set of zoned elevators travels up from each lobby, using the same plan

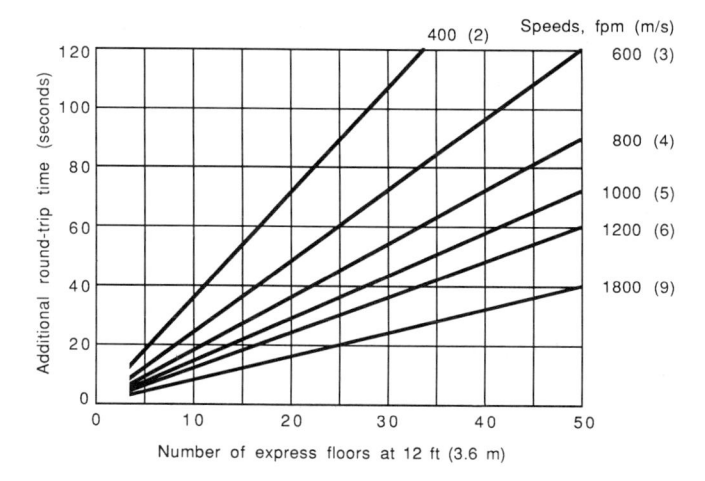

Fig. 25.7.3. Additional time to be added to the round-trip time when a car operates express through the lower floors of a building. The additional time is calculated as twice the distance divided by the speed, and therefore allows for both the up and down travel through the express zone at rated car speed.

positions as the group below it. (Appropriate structural provisions are needed to prevent an overrunning car in the upper group from colliding with the motor room serving cars in the lower part of the same shaft. Safety gear is also provided on the counterweight as well as the car.)

The same number of passengers have to be lifted from the ground-level lobby as if there were a conventional zoned system. However, the shuttle cars are much more efficient than normal cars because:

- They operate only between two floors, without intermediate stops
- They can be large (around 50 passengers), because there is no need for passengers in the rear of the car to exit first; while the area inside the car is proportional to the number of passengers, the structural and mechanical clearances around the perimeter do not vary greatly with size, so the *total* plan area taken by one car of 50 passengers is less than for two of 25 or three of 17 passengers
- They usually operate with doors on both ends of the car, so that passengers enter at one side, and exit at the other without turning around; returning passengers can enter from one side while the first passengers are leaving from the other side, without causing congestion. This saves time in loading and unloading.

Multilevel Elevator Cars

If the elevators take up too much floor space in a building, another solution is to use double-deck elevator cars, or even triple-deck cars. Although the maximum capacity of a double-deck car is twice that of a single-deck one, in practice one deck fills more quickly than the other, and the car departs with a slightly lower percentage of its total load than a conventional car would. The additional passengers mean that there is a probability of more stops per trip than a conventional car. These factors combine to give most double-deck cars a handling capacity closer to 150 percent of single-deck ones, rather than the 200 percent theoretically possible.

Multilevel cars are only appropriate for a large building, where the car size indicated by Fig. 25.7.1 would otherwise be at or above the largest size suitable for passenger service. The operating system is more complicated than usual, and it should be capable of operating in several modes to suit the needs of different times of the working day, or possibly of different occupants during the life of the building.

Up traffic is usually served by having two lobby levels, one each for the even-numbered and odd-numbered floors. This gives the most efficient use of the car, avoiding the need for both decks to stop at the same floor. A similar system can operate for the down-peak traffic, but for inter-floor traffic it must be possible for either deck to stop at any floor. For special purposes, the two decks of one elevator can be made to perform specific tasks. One deck can be fitted out as a goods elevator, for example, and programmed out of the passenger service. If there is an observation deck and a restaurant on the top two stories of the building, then an express elevator can be designed so that its two decks are entered from different foyers, one for each of the specialty floors. The patrons of each are unaware that they are sharing the elevator with the others. Each deck can be decorated differently, in keeping with the destination.

A limitation on the building design is that each story must be exactly the same height, at least in that part served by the multiple-deck cars. The overrun will be increased by one story if the lower deck must be able to serve the topmost floor, or vice versa. The machinery will be large, in keeping with the combined size of all the decks of each car (a double-deck 24 passenger car is in effect at 48-passenger car). The control equipment, as mentioned above, will of necessity be more complicated than for conventional cars; but as all new elevator systems are controlled by computer, this only requires more elaborate software and some mechanical interlocking between the decks.

REFERENCES

25.1. P. Tregenza. *The Design of Interior Circulation*. Crosby Lockwood Staples, London, 1976, 159 pp.
25.2. E. Neufert. *Architects' Data*. Crosby Lockwood Staples, London, 1970, pp. 88–90.
25.3. G. R. Strakosch. *Vertical Transportation: Elevators and Escalators.*, 2nd Ed. John Wiley, New York, 1982, 495 pp.
25.4. H. J. Cowan and P. R. Smith. *Environmental Systems*. Van Nostrand Reinhold, New York, 1983, 240 pp.

25.5. *American National Standard for Buildings and Facilities—Providing Accessibility and Usability for Physically Handicapped People.* ANSI A 117.1. American National Standards Institute, New York, 1986.

25.6. *Wheelchairs—Determination of Overall Dimensions, Mass, and Turning Space.* CSA Z323.4.2. Canadian Standards Association, Ottawa, 1986.

25.7. *Design for Access and Mobility, Part 1: General Requirements for Access—Buildings.* AS 1428.1. Standards Association of Australia, Sydney, 1988.

SUGGESTIONS FOR FURTHER READING

R. R. Adler. *Vertical Transportation for Buildings.* Elsevier, New York, 1970, 228 pp.

B. Stein, J. S. Reynolds, and W. J. McGuinness. *Mechanical and Electrical Equipment for Buildings*, 7th Ed. John Wiley, New York, 1986. Part VIII, "Transportation," pp. 1141–1227.

S. V. Szokolay. *Environmental Science Handbook.* Construction Press, Lancaster, UK, 1980, Sections 1.2, "Space Organisation," and 1.3, "Communications."

P. Tutt, and D. Adler. *New Metric Handbook* (replaces the *AJ Metric Handbook*). Architectural Press, London, 1979.

NOTE

A list of abbreviations of the units of measurement, definitions of these units, and conversion factors between British/American and metric units are given in the Appendix.

26
Safety in Buildings

T. Z. Harmathy

The minimum requirements for safety in buildings are laid down in building codes, and adequate fire protection is one of their main objectives. The insurer and the building designer look at the problem from different points of view, but both have to consider the acceptable level of financial risk.

The spread of a fire is described, from ignition to flashover and subsequent spreading. The various methods of defense against fire are then examined, and the smoke problem is considered. Finally the sociological and psychological factors that contribute to the incidence of fires are discussed.

The later part of the chapter deals with protection from crime. Security systems for small and for large buildings are considered separately, and the potential of electronic devices in "smart" buildings is examined. The final section deals with protection from floods and lightning.

26.1. Building Codes

The provision of safety is rooted in a perception of risk. According to Kaplan and Garrick (Ref. 26.1), a risk analysis consists of answering the following three questions:

1. What can happen?
2. How likely is it that that will happen?
3. If it does happen, how serious are the consequences?

The first question is concerned with the perilous scenario, the second with the probability of that scenario, and the third with the peril associated with it. Naturally, there can be several or many perilous scenarios. The risk is a statement of all answers to these three questions.

The minimum requirements for safety in buildings are usually dealt with in law by building codes and supplementary regulations (Ref. 26.2). They are intended to insure that the occupants of a building and of the neighboring buildings are not exposed to undue perils. Protection from structural collapse and fire, and sanitation (with respect to water supply, sewage, waste disposal, and air quality) are the principal subjects addressed in the building codes.

The building codes are model documents. They become legally binding only after their adoption by state, provincial, or municipal governments. The major North American building codes, such as the Uniform Building Code, the Standard Building Code, the Basic Building Code, and the National Building Code of Canada, are all similar as to their basic philosophies, yet they may contain widely different provisions.

The application of building code provisions may create some problems even with buildings that are more or less conventional. Most problems arise, however, with innovative designs or architectural styles. Many, though not all, of these innovative changes are advances in a true sense, intended to improve the quality of life, and disallowing them would amount to denying progress. The codes indeed allow the use of "equivalent" solutions. For example, the National Building Code of Canada says: "Materials, systems, equipment, and procedures not specifically described herein, or which vary from the specific requirements in this code, or for which no recognized test procedure has been established, may be used if it can be shown that the material, system, or equipment is suitable on the basis of past performance, or on the basis of acceptable tests or evaluation."

The problem with such equivalents is twofold. First,

there are many code requirements that have been adopted on historical grounds, and whose soundness has never been examined, let alone proved. Thus, demanding equivalence may mean perpetuating prejudiced preferences. Second, the prediction of performance from past experience has serious limitations. Many years may be required to produce a statistically significant record of events for analysis. Factors that gave rise to past events may no longer be present, and therefore the accumulated experience may not be suitable to establish probabilities of failures of current buildings, not to mention buildings now designed for future use. Clearly, those who decide on the acceptability of equivalents must to a great extent rely on the reputation of the designer.

In spite of the practical difficulties associated with deviating from code-sponsored solutions, it is generally agreed that, as science keeps expanding the frontiers of knowledge, more and more architects and engineers will opt for innovative designs. For this reason, and because the code-sponsored solutions are available from other sources, this chapter will handle the subject of safety mainly with a view to technical and financial optimization, without respect to the existence of applicable code regulations.

The structural safety of buildings is discussed in Chapters 11 to 15. Protection from crime, lightning, and floods will be considered briefly in Sections 26.6 and 26.7. The greater part of this chapter is devoted to the problem of protection from fire. Fire detectors and fire-fighting services installed in a building are discussed in Section 24.5.

26.2 PROTECTION FROM FIRE—SAFETY ASPECTS

Safety: As the Insurer sees it

For the insurer, fire safety has the connotation of acceptable level of financial risk. The main difficulty with the assessment of fire risk is the paucity of sufficiently detailed statistical data. To overcome this deficiency, insurance companies often resort to the so-called point scheme. In its original form, it was proposed by Gretener (Ref. 26.3) of the Swiss Fire Protection Association. It was later adopted in Austria, Italy, France, Belgium, and the Netherlands, and by the European Insurance Committee.

Gretener's point scheme consists of the assessment of a measure of risk, R, expressed as follows:

$$R = \frac{ap}{nsr} \quad (26.1)$$

where a = factor quantifying the tendency for a fire to start
p = factor quantifying inherent perils, such as those associated with building area and height, the nature and amount of combustible materials, their smoke-producing propensities, etc.
n = factor characterizing normal precautions, such as availability of water and the services of a fire brigade
s = factor concerned with special precautionary measures, such as use of detectors and sprinklers
r = fire resistance, as determined from standard fire tests

Values of a, p, n, and s are assigned by a group of experts, and the insurance premium is determined on the basis of the value of R.

Ramachandran (Ref. 26.4) and Watts (Ref. 26.5) mention a few more point schemes. Harvey (Ref. 26.6) describes a scheme prepared for computer execution. In North America, the best known point scheme is the National Bureau of Standards scheme for health care facilities (Ref. 26.7).

Safety: As the Building Designer Sees It

For the building designer, fire safety means a soundly engineered building, based on the understanding of the prevailing risks. The design decisions must address the risks associated with all phases of a fire: ignition, preflashover fire growth, fully developed fire, and intercompartmental fire spread. They must also address the smoke problem which may prevail in any phase of the fire.

The measures aimed at preventing the outbreak of fires or mitigating their consequences are related to (a) the layout and dimensioning of the building and its constituent parts, (b) the provision of safety devices and facilities, and (c) the selection of construction materials and products.

The Building before the Outbreak of Fire

Not too long ago, it was usual among researchers to study various fire-related phenomena as though the fire occurred in a space neatly isolated from the rest of the building. (Note: Fire researchers usually refer to building spaces as *compartments*. A compartment is defined as a building space, enclosed by walls, floor, and ceiling, which is most of the time separated from other spaces by a closed door or doors.) Because the temperature and draft conditions in the building at the outset of fire are of vital importance in the course the fire will take, it is not surprising that the results of earlier studies have not been fully borne out by observations of real-world fires.

The distribution of drafts prior to ignition is profoundly important. Drafts are brought about by two factors: temperature difference between the building interior and the outside atmosphere, and air leakage through the various compartment boundaries. Owing to the former, drafts are especially strong during the winter heating season.

The intensity and direction of air currents are illustrated in Fig. 26.2.1a. It shows the situation in a nine-story build-

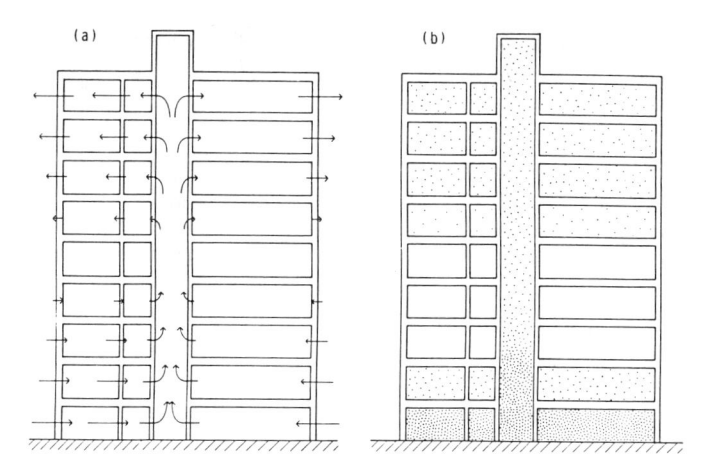

Figure 26.2.1. Air currents and smoke movement in a nine-story building. (a) Air currents. (b) Smoke distribution (fire on first floor).

ing on a calm winter day after the shutdown of the air handling system. If the leakage characteristics of the building envelope are uniform with height, air will infiltrate the building below its mid-height. After passing through one or more partitions, it will enter the vertical shafts (such as stairwells and elevator shafts), rise to the upper stories (the stack effect), and exfiltrate to the outside atmosphere. Strong winds, however, may substantially change the intensity and distribution of air currents.

The total rate of air infiltration (or exfiltration), V_a (lb h^{-1}, kg s^{-1}), can be expressed approximately as follows (Ref. 26.8):

$$V_a = \frac{\alpha \beta PC}{3T_a} \sqrt{g\left(1 - \frac{T_a}{T_i}\right) h_B^3} \qquad (26.2)$$

where α = equivalent orifice area for the outside walls (usually of the order of 0.0005), dimensionless
 β = orifice factor (about 0.6), dimensionless
 P = perimeter of the building, ft (m)
 C = constant (related to the gas constant), ~39.73 lb R ft^{-3} (353.5 kg K m^{-3})
 g = gravitational acceleration, 4.17 × 10^8 ft h^{-2} (9.9 m s^{-2})
 T_a = temperature of the outside atmosphere, R (K)
 T_i = temperature of building interior, R (K)
 R = degree of temperature on the Rankine scale (see Appendix)
 K = degree of temperature on the Kelvin scale (see Appendix)
 h_B = height of the building, ft (m)

As will be pointed out later, the rate of air infiltration is an important piece of information in designing measures to counter the dispersion of smoke in fire-stricken buildings.

26.3 SPREAD OF FIRE

Ignition

As at least four out of five fires start from small ignition sources (Ref. 26.9), the probability of fire outbreak in a building is directly related to the use of easily ignitable materials. The factors that control the ignition of an object are partly intrinsic to the material and its geometry, and partly extraneous. Their roles depend on whether the ignition is piloted or nonpiloted, i.e., whether the ignition occurs with or without the aid of flame, spark, or glowing wire.

Researchers have tried to shed light on the process of ignition by studying the conditions immediately preceding ignition, in terms of such material-intrinsic factors as the shape of the object, and the thermophysical and thermochemical properties of the material and its pyrolysis (thermal decomposition) products; and such extraneous factors as the ambient conditions and the nature and total energy of the ignition source.

Piloted ignition occurs when the flame remains attached to the surface of the material after the removal of the ignition source. For this to happen, the burning process must be capable of evolving energy at a rate sufficient (1) to maintain the temperature of the surface at the level of pyrolysis, (2) to provide heat for the pyrolysis* to proceed (the process that feeds the flame with gaseous fuel), and in addition (3) to compensate for the energy dispersion from the flame to the surroundings. Studies have indicated that the material's propensity for ignition is usually related to its thermal absorptivity (or thermal inertia), i.e., $\sqrt{k\rho c}$ (Btu ft^{-2} h$^{-1/2}$ R^{-1}; J m^{-2} s$^{-1/2}$ K^{-1}), where k is thermal conductivity, ρ is density, and c is specific heat.

This simple visualization of the post-ignition energy balance suggests that the most important factors abetting ignition are: (1) high radiant heat output by the flame, which in turn is determined by the flame's size and luminosity and by the heat of combustion of the gaseous pyrolysis products, (2) low pyrolysis temperature, (3) low heat of pyrolysis, and (4) low thermal absorptivity.

Studies conducted by deRis (Ref. 26.10), Lastrina et al. (Ref. 26.11), and Fernandez-Pello (Ref. 26.12) indicate that these are also the principal factors controlling the velocity of flame spread across the surface of an ignited object in the earliest stage of fire, when the spread is yet unaided by the burning of neighboring objects. One is led to believe, therefore, that products that tend to ignite easily also tend to burn rapidly at the onset of fire.

This rule becomes somewhat clouded, however, when applied to lightweight foam plastics of very low thermal absorptivity, to materials that melt on heating before reaching the temperature of pyrolysis, and to char-forming materials.

---
*Pyrolysis is chemical decomposition by heat.

With foam plastics, the energy of the ignition source and the surface area exposed to the source determine whether or not ignition will occur. Although the surface temperature of such materials will rise quickly to the level of pyrolysis if exposed to even a small energy source, the heat penetration will remain shallow and the rate of production of pyrolysis gases may not be sufficient to release, in combustion, energy at a rate necessary to keep the process going, following the removal of the pilot energy source. If, however, the energy of the ignition source is large enough to produce a sizeable initial flame, or the energy supply to the surface is augmented by radiative feedback from nearby burning objects, the flame will quickly spread over the entire surface of the material.

With melting materials (polyethylene, polypropylene, and polystyrene are prime examples), keeping the surface temperature at the level of pyrolysis may be difficult if their orientation is such that the melt flows away from the site of the flame.

With char-forming materials (of which cellulosics, such as wood and paper products, are of principal importance), pyrolysis produces a porous carbonaceous coating on the surface. If not removed continuously by oxidation, the char layer will gradually build up and, by blocking thermal feedback from the flame, will eventually quell the pyrolysis and thus cut off the fuel supply to the flame.

Even if the flaming combustion stops, char-forming materials may continue to undergo combustion of a different kind—smoldering. Whereas flaming combustion with these materials consists of three kinds of simultaneous reactions (gas phase combustion, pyrolysis, and char oxidation) smoldering consists of two kinds only: the consumption of the surface char by oxidation and the ongoing renewal of the char zone by pyrolysis, driven by the heat produced by the oxidation (Ref. 26.13). Cellulosic materials of complex surface structure and low thermal absorptivity, such as loose-fill cellulosic insulation, are especially prone to smoldering.

The so-called oxygen index test (Ref. 26.14) provides a convenient way of arranging materials according to their propensities for sustaining flaming combustion following ignition by a small-energy pilot flame. Table 26.1 gives the oxygen indices for the most common materials used in furnishings and in building construction. Unfortunately, the oxygen index does not reflect the increased or decreased propensity associated with the nature and energy of the ignition source, and the shape, mass, and surface texture of the material.

Another experimental procedure capable of yielding data relevant to the prediction of ignition and flame spread on materials was described more recently (Ref. 26.17).

Combustible materials are used in buildings either as furnishing items or as building components. When they serve in the latter role, they are usually protected by a noncombustible layer. Some may be used, however, as lining materials, or electric and plumbing fixtures. Thorough

Table 26.1. Oxygen Indices for a Few Common Materials (Refs. 26.15, 26.16).

Material	Oxygen Index*
Carbon, porous	55.9
Epoxy, conventional	19.8
Foam rubber	16.0
Neoprene	31.0
Polyamide (nylon)	29.0
Polycarbonate	26.0
Polyester (FRP)	18.2
Polyethylene	17.4
Polyisocyanurate foam, rigid	23.9
Polymethyl methacrylate	15.9
Polypropylene	17.4
Polystyrene	18.1
Polystyrene foam	18.8
Polystyrene foam, flame retardant	24.1
Polytetrafluoroethylene (teflon)	95.0
Polyvinyl chloride	46.6
Polyurethane foam, flexible	16.1
Polyurethane foam, rigid	15.3
Urea-formaldehyde	23.8
Wood, white pine	20.9
Wood, sugar maple	21.2
Wood, plywood	19.7

*Oxygen index = minimum oxygen concentration, expressed as volume percent, required to support flaming combustion.

knowledge of their ignitabilities will enable the building designer to select materials and products with a view to minimizing the probability of outbreak of fire.

Preflashover Fire Growth

Whether a small fire dies out or grows into a large fire depends on four factors: (1) the rate of heat release by the object first ignited, (2) the total fire load (i.e., the total mass of combustible materials) and the distribution of the fire load in the compartment, (3) the nature of compartment lining materials from the point of view of supporting combustion, and (4) the thermal absorptivity of the compartment boundaries (Table 26.2). If these factors are such as to create conditions favorable to unlimited fire growth, flashover will ensue (usually within 5 to 25 min) and the entire compartment will become involved in fire.

Table 26.2. Thermal Absorptivity of a Number of Common Building Materials (Ref. 26.56).

	Thermal Absorptivity $\sqrt{k\rho c}$	
Material	$Btu\, ft^{-2}\, h^{-1/2}\, R^{-1}$	$J\, m^{-2}\, s^{-1/2}\, K^{-1}$
Marble	6.67	2,270
Normal-weight concrete	6.44	2,190
Brick	4.46	1,520
Lightweight concrete, density 90.5 lb ft^{-3} (1450 kg m^{-3})	2.73	930
Plasterboard	2.18	740
Vermiculite plaster	1.96	670
Wood	1.28	440
Mineral wool	0.25	90

The time to flashover is a very important piece of information, because it indicates the maximum length of time that the occupants of the fire compartment have to escape or be rescued. For this reason, a thorough understanding of the chain of events connecting the ignition of the first object with flashover has been one of the major goals of theoretical and experimental fire research. The literature of the mathematical modeling of preflashover fires is quite voluminous by now; the principles of modeling have been outlined in many review articles (e.g., in Refs. 26.18 to 26.23).

In brief, there are three kinds of preflashover fire models: probabilistic models, modular (or zone) models, and field equation models. Among the three, the modular models are the most promising. They view the fire compartment as consisting of discrete control volumes (zones) of uniform process variables, and follow up the preflashover process by following up the fluxes of mass, momentum, and energy across the zone boundaries. These preflashover models have proved useful in the theoretical reconstruction of fire events. Their predictive capabilities, because of the inadequate knowledge of two important control volumes (burning object and fire plume) and the random nature of many input variables, are low as yet. Insight and common-sense reasoning still seem to have an edge over theory in predicting the progress of preflashover fires.

The first two of the mentioned factors affecting fire growth (the rate of heat release by the object first ignited, and the fire load and its distribution) relate largely to the compartment furnishings. They are subject to statistical probabilities and are beyond the control of the building designer. The designer does, on the other hand, have at least partial control over the other two factors: the burning characteristics of the lining materials and the thermal absorptivity of the compartment boundaries.

There is unfortunately no reliable performance test that can be used to predict the propensity of the lining materials to spread flames. For the sake of arranging the test results on a unique scale of merit, the standard tests are conducted under a specified set of conditions which rarely, if ever, coincide with those arising in advanced stages of preflashover fires.

Benjamin (Ref. 26.24) affirmed (with data borrowed from Castino et al., Ref. 26.25) that for lining materials the sequence of merit with respect to flame spread, as derived from the most widely used standard test (the ASTM E 84 tunnel test), is not necessarily valid under advanced preflashover conditions. This finding is not surprising if one considers that the rate of flame spread depends rather strongly on external radiation to the burning object, and that different materials respond differently to external radiation (Ref. 26.26).

The problems encountered with testing the flammability and flame spreading propensity of materials were reviewed by deRis (Ref. 26.27), who also offered novel solutions.

For some time following ignition, the first item ignited will burn in approximately the same way as it would in the open. Then, as the flames grow tall and perhaps other items ignite, the process of burning becomes more and more influenced by factors characteristic of the compartment as a whole. With increasing rapidity, a smoky layer of hot combustion and pyrolysis gases builds up below the ceiling. Intense radiant energy fluxes, originating mainly from the hot ceiling and the adjoining gas layer (Fig. 26.3.1), gradually heat up all objects in the compartment. As these energy fluxes reach a level of 17 to 27 kW m^{-2} (Ref. 26.28), all combustible objects ignite in a quick succession; flashover occurs.

A few fire scenarios of practical interest were surveyed by Benjamin (Ref. 26.24). He pointed out that combustible wall and ceiling linings might or might not play a significant part in the chain of events leading to flashover, depending on the total fire load, the nature and distribution of the combustible objects in the compartment, and location and size of the object first ignited. Bruce's experiments (Ref. 26.29) showed that the combustibility of the wall lining has little effect on the time to flashover if no piece of furniture is placed closer than 1.5 ft. (.45 m) to the walls. Further experimental studies (Refs. 26.30, 26.31) indicated that a temperature level of 930 to 1110 °F (500 to 600 °C) reached by the hot gas layer under the ceiling (Fig. 26.3.1) can be regarded as flashover criterion. Such a criterion is, however, of little practical utility unless the conditions for attaining the critical temperature level can be expressed in terms of the fire load and the geometric and thermal characteristics of the compartment boundaries.

Using the temperature of the hot gas layer as flashover criterion, Babrauskas (Ref. 26.32) and McCaffrey et al. (Ref. 26.33) developed criteria for assessing the likelihood of flashover. The latter workers suggested the following formula:

$$Q/(\sqrt{k\rho c}\, A_t \Phi)^{1/2} \geq C \qquad (26.3)$$

where Q = rate of heat release by the fire, Btu h^{-1} (W)

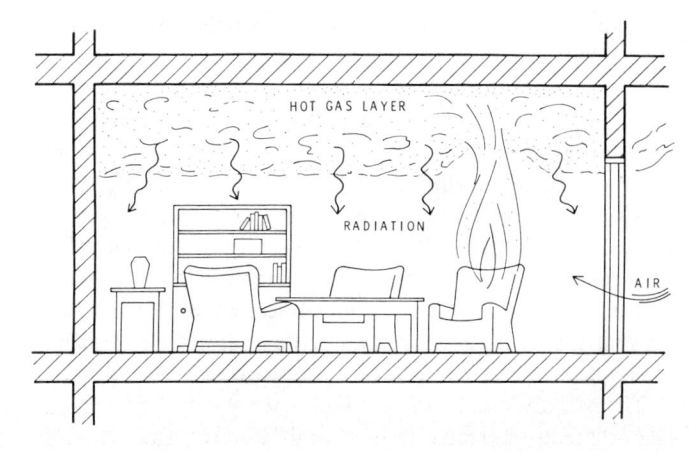

Figure 26.3.1. Preflashover fire.

A_t = total surface area of the fire compartment, ft² (m²)

$\sqrt{k\rho c}$ = thermal absorptivity of the compartment boundaries, Btu ft⁻² h⁻¹/² R⁻¹ (J m⁻² s⁻¹/² K⁻¹)

The value of the constant C is

$$C = \begin{cases} 1740 \text{ Btu}^{1/2} \text{ R}^{1/2} \text{ lb}^{-1/2} \text{ h}^{-1/4} \\ 8100 \text{ J}^{1/2} \text{ K}^{1/2} \text{ kg}^{-1/2} \text{ s}^{-1/4} \end{cases}$$

Φ (lb h⁻¹; kg s⁻¹) is the ventilation factor, which quantifies the rate of inflow of air into the fire compartment. This parameter assumes a minimum value when the air flow rate is not augmented by drafts. In this case

$$\Phi_{min} = \rho_a A_v \sqrt{g h_v} \qquad (26.4)$$

where ρ_a = density of atmospheric air (~ 0.0755 lb ft⁻³ at 68°F; 1.21 kg m⁻³ at 20°C)

A_v = area of ventilation opening (window or door), ft² (m²)

h_v = height of the ventilation opening, ft (m)

Equation (26.3) makes it possible to estimate whether the burning of a large piece of furniture (e.g., an armchair, a bed) can lead to flashover. The rate of heat evolution from the burning of such an object can be assessed from available data (Ref. 26.34) or from an experimental burn test (Ref. 26.32). Of particular interest is the contribution of the thermal absorptivity of the compartment boundaries, $\sqrt{k\rho c}$, to the likelihood of flashover. (Typical values of the thermal absorptivities of common construction materials are listed in Table 26.2.) Eq. (26.3) indicates an increased likelihood of flashover for compartments lined with good insulation, i.e., with materials of low thermal absorptivity.

It is clear from the preceding discussions that fire safety in a building can be greatly increased by circumspect design. The designer knows the intended use of the buildings and therefore has at least a rough idea of the types of articles that are to be placed in the various compartments. He can add valuable minutes to the time of flashover by not specifying combustible linings in those rooms that are most likely to be furnished with fabric-covered (upholstered) items, or in which clothing articles are kept or stored. He can further improve the level of fire safety by providing closets or built-in cabinets for the storage of clothing articles or paper products. In the design of theaters, lecture rooms, atria, lounges, etc., he can specify slightly elevated or recessed walkways or built-in planters along the walls that are to be lined with combustible materials, and thus prevent the occupants or interior decorator from placing upholstered furniture close to those walls.

The probability that the fire will reach the flashover stage can be greatly reduced by the installation of detecting and suppressing devices. Photoelectric and ionization smoke detectors are more suitable for use in residential buildings than thermal or flame detectors. With the use of smoke detectors, the human losses in residential buildings can be reduced by as much as 40 to 50 percent (Refs. 26.35, 26.36).

Except for high-rise buildings and buildings with large open floor arrangements, the use of a sprinkler system (see Section 24.5) is, as a rule, an optional measure. Yet its use is often rewarded by the reduction of certain building code requirements and by lower insurance premiums. Recent studies have indicated (Refs. 26.36, 26.37) that mandating the use of sprinklers for single-family dwellings is not justifiable on economic grounds.

Fully Developed Fires

Even though fires may occasionally spread from one compartment to another during the preflashover stage, the flashover is usually regarded as marking the beginning of the fire's propensity for spread. Consequently, the potential of a fire for intercompartmental spread depends primarily on its characteristics during the phase of fully developed burning.

Once the fire has grown beyond flashover, human survival in the fire compartment is no longer possible. The design strategy is to prevent intercompartmental fire spread.

It has been traditional to visualize the spread of a fire as resulting from a successive destruction of (or by heat transmission through) the compartment boundaries. Statistical data do not fully support this concept. It appears (Ref. 26.38) that only one out of five fires will reach the stage of flashover. Of those fires that develop beyond flashover, 35 percent will not spread, and about 55 percent will spread by convection: by the advance of flames and hot gases.

Clearly, the defense against the spread of fully developed fires must have two components: (1) countering the potential of fire for spread by destruction, and (2) countering its potential for spread by convection.

26.4 DEFENSE AGAINST THE SPREAD OF FIRE (see also Section 24.5)

Defense Against Fire Spread by Destruction

The defense against the spread of fire by the destruction of (or heat transmission through) compartment boundaries consists of using building elements (such as walls, floors, beams, and columns) of sufficient fire resistance. Since the fire resistance requirement must be commensurate with the fire's destructive potential, the design to counter spread by destruction should, in principle, be a two-step procedure: (1) assessment of the destructive potential of the fully developed fire, and (2) selection of building elements that have proved to possess fire resistant qualities adequate under the circumstances.

The fire resistant quality of a building element is usually determined by subjecting a representative specimen of the element to a standard fire test, ASTM E 119 in North America. In this test, the specimen is exposed (on one side or the other, dependent on its use in the building) to the hot gases of a large furnace whose temperature is controlled to follow a unique course. The test is carried on until the specimen "fails" (in a way specified in the standard) either structurally or thermally (i.e., by heat transmission). The time of failure quantifies the fire resistance of the building element.

Nowadays performing such tests is not necessary for a large number of building elements. Their fire resistances can be assessed by calculations (see, e.g., Refs. 26.39 to 26.43) based on heat transmission and structural analyses, and on the knowledge of material behavior at elevated temperatures (see, e.g., Refs. 26.44 to 26.47).

Unfortunately, in present practice fire resistance requirements are usually allotted on the basis of building code provisions rather than engineering considerations. The fire resistance requirements specified in the building codes have developed mainly from tradition or from rough estimates of the expected fire severities, assumed to be proportional to the fire load (mass of combustible materials). It has been known since the mid-1950s, however, that the fire load is only one of several parameters on which the severity (destructive potential) of real-world fires depends.

Clearly, specifying fire resistance requirements in terms of performance in test fires is justifiable only if (1) the destructive potential of real-world fires can be defined as a function of all significant parameters, and (2) the relationship between the performance of building elements in real-world fires and standard test fires is understood.

Several ways of replacing the building code provisions by more reasonable fire resistance requirements have been suggested during the years. The best known among them are Ingberg's method (Ref. 26.48), Law's method (Ref. 26.49), Pettersson's method (Ref. 26.50), and the DIN method (Ref. 26.51, 26.52). Based on experimental findings, simple formulas or procedures are presented in these methods for the calculation of fire resistance requirements. These formulas or procedures do not take account of all parameters that are known to have a significant effect on the severity of fires.

A recent method, based on the normalized heat load concept (Ref. 26.53), offers the advantage of providing an insight into the performance of building elements in both real-world fires and test fires. The accuracy of this concept was proved out in a multitude of compartment burnout experiments (Ref. 26.54). It comes as no surprise, therefore, that the assessment of fire resistance requirements based on this concept is more reliable than assessments based on previous methods (Ref. 26.55).

The normalized heat load is defined as the total heat absorbed by a unit area of an enclosure during an exposure to fire (real-world fire or test fire), divided by the thermal absorptivity of the enclosure boundaries. It has been shown that, for a given building element, equal values of the normalized heat load represent equal harms done by any two fires, however dissimilar they may be as to their temperature histories. The normalized heat load can, therefore, be regarded as a quantifier of the destructive potential of fire.

For real-world compartment fires, the normalized heat load depends largely on the following variables (Ref. 26.56):

A_F = floor area of the compartment on fire, ft² (m²)

A_t = total surface area of the compartment, ft² (m²)

h_c = height of the compartment, ft (m)

$\sqrt{k\rho c}$ = thermal absorptivity of the compartment boundaries, Btu ft⁻² h⁻¹ᐟ² R⁻¹ (J m⁻² s⁻¹ᐟ² K⁻¹)

Φ = ventilation factor, lb h⁻¹ (kg s⁻¹)

L = specific fire load (mass of combustibles per unit floor area), lb ft⁻² (kg m⁻²)

Since cellulosic materials (particularly wood) still form the bulk of the combustibles in buildings, the specific fire load is looked upon as expressing the mass of wood per unit floor area. (Note: If there are substantial quantities of noncellulosic materials present, multiply their mass by their heat of combustion, and divide it by the heat of combustion of wood.)

The ventilation factor and the specific fire load are random variables. In the calculation scheme to be shown, the ventilation factor will be taken into account with its most adverse value, its minimum, Eq. (26.4).

Information on the specific fire load, developed from Swedish data (Ref. 26.57), is presented for a few building occupancies in Table 26.3. The arithmetic means L_m and the standard deviations, σ_L are listed.

Table 26.3. Information on Specific Fire Load, Estimated from Swedish Data (Ref. 26.57).*

	Specific Fire Load			
	Mean, L_m		Standard Deviation, σ_L	
Occupancy	lb ft⁻²	kg m⁻²	lb ft⁻²	kg m⁻²
Dwelling	6.17	30.1	0.90	4.4
Office	5.08	24.8	1.76	8.6
School	3.59	17.5	1.05	5.1
Hospital	5.15	25.1	1.60	7.8
Hotel	2.99	14.6	0.86	4.2

*The tabulated values are, on the whole, representative of the occupancies shown. Discrepancies in specific fire load values reported in various publications are attributable to differences in sampling and evaluation techniques, and the estimation of that part of the fire load which is not accessible to combustion.

In a preliminary assessment of the fire resistance requirements, all compartments in the building can be regarded as essentially square in shape. Thus the average surface area of the compartments can be calculated as

$$A_t = 2A_F + 4h_C\sqrt{A_F} \qquad (26.5)$$

If the compartment boundaries are formed by different materials, the thermal absorptivity should be interpreted as a surface-averaged value and calculated as

$$\sqrt{k\rho c} = \frac{1}{A_t}(A_1\sqrt{k_1\rho_1 c_1} + A_2\sqrt{k_2\rho_2 c_2} + \cdots) \qquad (26.6)$$

in which the numerical subscripts refer to the various materials and to the surfaces formed by them. (The thermal absorptivities of common construction materials have been listed in Table 26.2.)

The normalized heat load on the compartment boundaries, for the most adverse (minimum) value of the ventilation factor and the arithmetic mean of the specific fire load, can be expressed by the following semi-empirical equation (Ref. 26.58):

$$H' = C_1 \frac{(11.0\delta + 1.6)A_F L_m}{A_t\sqrt{k\rho c} + C_2\sqrt{\Phi_{min} A_F L_m}} \qquad (26.7)$$

in which

$$C_1 = \begin{cases} 456 \text{ Btu lb}^{-1} \\ 1.06 \times 10^6 \text{ J kg}^{-1} \end{cases}$$

$$C_2 = \begin{cases} 0.223 \text{ Btu lb}^{-1} \text{ R}^{-1} \\ 935 \text{ J kg}^{-1} \text{ K}^{-1} \end{cases}$$

H' = normalized heat load for the compartment (or any of the compartment boundaries) in a real-world fire (for $L = L_m$ and $\Phi = \Phi_{min}$), $h^{1/2}$ R $(s^{1/2}$K$)$

and

$$\delta = \begin{cases} C_3\sqrt{(h_C^3/\Phi_{min})} \\ 1 \end{cases} \text{ whichever is less} \qquad (26.8)$$

where

$$C_3 = \begin{cases} 11.8 \text{ lb}^{1/2} \text{ ft}^{-3/2} \text{ h}^{-1/2} \\ 0.79 \text{ kg}^{1/2} \text{ m}^{-3/2} \text{ s}^{-1/2} \end{cases}$$

δ is a dimensionless, semi-empirical factor.

The coefficient of variation for the uncertainty associated with the use of Eqs. (26.7) and (26.8) is 0.101 (Ref. 26.54).

Since in a standard fire test the furnace temperature follows a prescribed course, the normalized heat load imposed on a building element (compartment boundary) in a test fire is a unique function of the duration of the test which, if the test is carried on up to the point of failure, is equal to the fire resistance of the building element. The relationship between the fire resistance and the normalized heat load in a test fire is

$$\tau = 0.11 + C_4 H'' + C_5(H'')^2 \qquad (26.9)$$

in which

$$C_4 = \begin{cases} 5.33 \times 10^{-4} \text{ h}^{1/2} \text{ R}^{-1} \\ 0.16 \times 10^4 \text{ h s}^{-1/2} \text{ K}^{-1} \end{cases}$$

$$C_5 = \begin{cases} 14.44 \times 10^{-8} \text{ R}^{-2} \\ 0.13 \times 10^{-9} \text{ h s}^{-1} \text{ K}^{-2} \end{cases}$$

τ = fire resistance (or duration of test fire), h

H'' = normalized heat load on the building element in a standard fire test, $h^{1/2}$ R $(s^{1/2}$ K$)$

In Eq. (26.9) the fire resistance is expressed in terms of the normalized heat load (rather than the normalized heat load in terms of the fire resistance) for convenience in determining the fire resistance requirements.

The fire resistance (i.e., the result of the fire test) is also a random quantity. The coefficient of variation for τ is about 0.1 (Ref. 26.59).

The fire resistance requirement is clearly the value of τ at which $H'' \geq H'$.

Employing well-known reliability-based design procedures (Refs. 26.60, 26.61), the following formulas have been developed for the calculation of fire resistance requirements (Ref. 26.62):

$$\tau_d = 0.11 + C_4 H_d'' + C_5(H_d'')^2 \qquad (26.10)$$

in which

$$H_d'' = H' \exp\left[\beta\sqrt{\Omega_1^2 + 0.09^2 + 0.101^2}\right] \qquad (26.11)$$

and, in Eq. (26.11),

$$\Omega_1 = \frac{\sigma_L}{L_m} \frac{A_t\sqrt{k\rho c} + \frac{C_2}{2}\sqrt{\Phi_{min} A_F L_m}}{A_t\sqrt{k\rho c} + C_2\sqrt{\Phi_{min} A_F L_m}} \qquad (26.12)$$

Under the square root sign in Eq. (26.11), the first and second terms express the uncertainties due to the random nature of the specific fire load and the result of the standard fire test, respectively. The third term expresses the uncertainty associated with the use of Eqs. (26.7) and (26.8).

In Eqs. (26.10) and (26.11), the d subscripts indicate design values, and β is a dimensionless factor, a function of the allowed failure probability, P_f (dimensionless). This function is shown in Fig. 26.4.1.

When deciding on the allowable failure probability, the expected magnitude of human and property losses resulting from a failure is the most important consideration. Prescribing values of P_f applicable to various situations would normally be considered as a task for the writers of building regulations.

After selecting a value for P_f, the fire resistance requirement is calculated from Eqs. (26.7), (26.8), and (26.10) to (26.12). A numerical example of the calculations has been presented in Ref. 26.63.

Statistical data indicate that, with the present construction practices, less than 10 percent of fully developed fires are likely to spread by the destruction of compartment boundaries. This being so, very little additional safety is gained by increasing the fire resistance requirements (Ref. 26.38).

Defense against Fire Spread by Convection

The fully developed period of a compartment fire lasts usually no longer than 30 min. In fact, a vigorously burning fire that lasts longer than 30 min is almost certain indication of spread beyond the compartment of fire origin. As pointed out earlier, the most common mode of spread is convection.

Four factors have a major influence on the extent and direction of fire spread: (1) the potential of fire for convective spread, as quantified by the μ-factor (to be discussed), (2) the presence of a means of passage for the flames and hot gases, (3) the intensity and direction of drafts in the building, and (4) the nature of the lining materials along the path of spread.

The presence of easily pyrolyzing materials in the fire compartment, and ventilation conditions that are conducive to a massive combustion of the pyrolysis products outside the compartment boundaries (e.g., outside the doors or windows) present a very grave danger of fire spread, irrespective of the support the outside combustion can get from drafts and combustible materials along the path of spread.

A dimensionless factor has been introduced to characterize the potential of a compartment fire to spread by convection (Ref. 26.56). It is denoted by μ and defined as

$$\mu = \frac{\text{rate of heat evolution outside the fire compartment}}{\text{total rate of heat evolution from the fire load}}$$

(26.13)

For cellulosics (mainly wood and paper products), which are still the most abundant combustibles in buildings, the approximate expression for μ is

$$\mu = 0.879(1 - \delta) \quad (26.14)$$

For other fuels see Ref. 26.56.

Char-forming plastics behave very similarly to cellulosics in fires. On the other hand, the behavior of non-charring

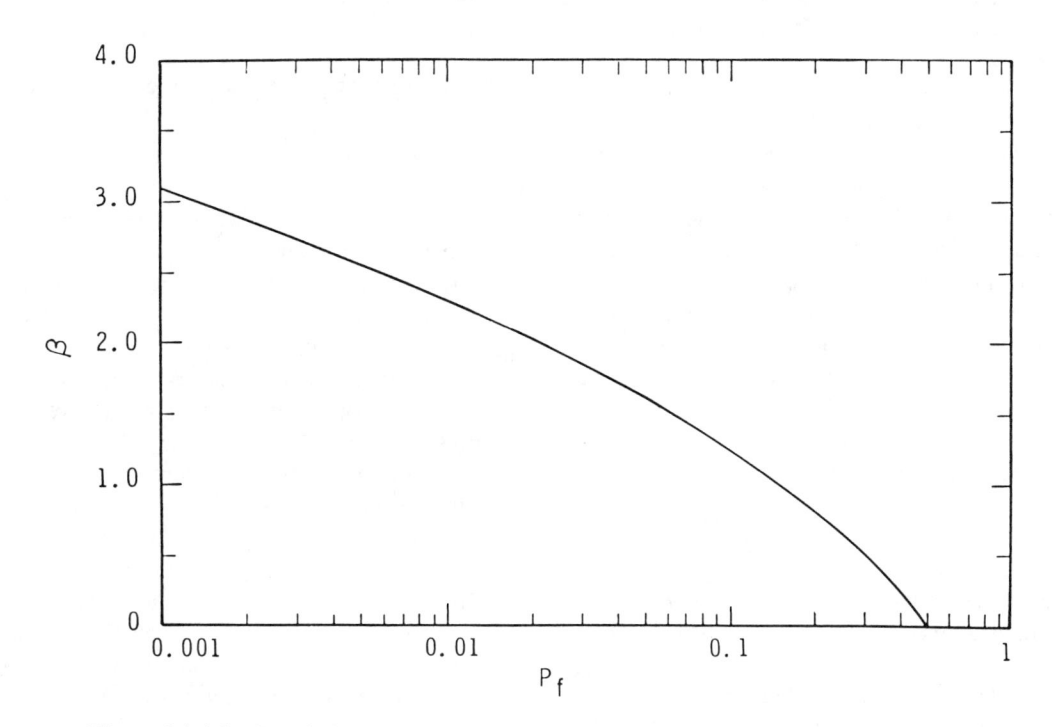

Figure 26.4.1. Correlation between the factor β and the probability of failure in fire, P_f.

plastics is quite different. To gain a thorough understanding of the dangers associated with fires of these two groups of fuels, two series of theoretical studies were conducted (Ref. 26.56). The spread potentials by both destruction (as quantified by the normalized heat load) and convection (quantified by the μ-factor) were studied. The following conclusions were drawn:

1. From the point of view of potential for spread by convection, fires of cellulosics are usually less dangerous than fires of noncharring plastics. From the point of view of potential for spread by destruction, the opposite is true.

2. The potential of fires to spread by convection decreases with increasing ventilation if the fire load consists of noncharring plastics, and increases with ventilation if the fire load consists of cellulosics.

3. For any kind of fire load, the potential for spread by destruction decreases with increasing ventilation, be it natural ventilation (through broken windows, or open or burned-out doors) or forced ventilation (e.g., by drafts).

The most common path for a fire to spread by convection is a door left open by the fleeing tenants. Fire experts agree that in large buildings the simplest and most effective way of countering fire spread is to separate the various occupancy units by self-closing doors. Some building codes have already made the use of self-closing doors mandatory in high-rise buildings.

The spread of fire can at times be traced back to the penetration of floors and walls by plastic drain, waste and vent pipes, and by electric cables. Techniques of impeding fire spread through penetrations have been studied and various solutions offered (Refs. 26.64 to 26.66).

Cavities within some structural elements and roof spaces can also abet the spread of fire. A variety of methods of fabricating and erecting cavity barriers and fire stops have been suggested (Refs. 26.67, 26.68).

Drafts play a very important part in the spread of fire. As discussed in the section "The Building before the Outbreak of Fire" (Section 26.2), it is usually during the winter heating season that the strongest drafts arise. It comes as no surprise, therefore, that winter is the season of the worst fire incidents. The path of fire spread usually coincides with the path of air currents (see Fig. 26.2a). Thus, if fire breaks out in a compartment below the mid-height of a tall building, it will (if a door is open) enter the corridor, and later it may rise through the vertical shafts to the floor above. This is why self-closing doors are especially effective below the mid-height of high-rise buildings.

In the upper stories, on the other hand, the fire tends to spread toward the building envelope, so that the use of self-closing doors is less beneficial. On reaching the building envelope, the flames issuing from the broken windows may ignite the exterior cladding, if it is combustible, or may break the windows above and set the compartment on the next floor aflame.

A systematic investigation conducted in Australia (Ref. 26.69) confirmed an earlier British finding that less than 2-ft (0.6-m) wide projections over the windows of a multistory building do not prevent the vertical advance of flames from window to window. It was found, however, that projections wider than 4 ft (1.2 m) are effective in keeping the flames away from the facade and in reducing thermal radiation to the windows above to an acceptable level.

Clearly, continuous balconies and open corridors can play an important part in preventing the spread of fire along the building facade. Unfortunately, continuous balconies and open corridors are rarely employed nowadays even for residential buildings, because they cut down the light reaching the interior, increase the building costs, and may be considered to be undesirable from the point of view of aesthetics and security.

Simple flame deflectors (Ref. 26.70) could provide the same degree of protection as continuous balconies or open corridors, without the mentioned drawbacks. They have been visualized as light metal panels mounted vertically above each window and held in vertical position by a fusible part, possibly a nut. These panels turn down to a horizontal position when activated by the flames issuing from the windows below.

The nature of the lining materials in the corridors may also be an important factor in intercompartmental fire spread. Experimental studies (Refs. 26.71 to 26.74) showed only a limited success in correlating the rate of fire spread in corridors with the results of standard flame spread tests (ASTM E 84) conducted on combustible linings. The presence of combustible linings is, however, not an absolute prerequisite for spread. The propensity for spread is determined primarily by the conditions in the fire compartment which feeds the flames and hot gases into the corridor.

26.5 SMOKE, AND FIRE SAFETY DECISIONS

The Smoke Problem

Fire statistics reveal that more people die in burning buildings from inhalation of toxic gases than from heat-inflicted injuries. Even in deaths that are caused by burns, smoke is often a contributing factor. Dense smoke obscures the vision of the occupants and prevents them from reaching safety. There are good reasons to believe (Ref. 26.75) that obscuration of vision is the principal threat to life safety in building fires.

The gravity of the smoke problem depends on three factors. These are, in order of importance: (1) the extent to which materials of high smoke-producing propensity are used, (2) the intensity of drafts in the building at the time of fire, and (3) the toxicity of the pyrolysis and combustion products of the building's combustible contents.

A number of experimental techniques for measuring the smoke-producing propensity of materials have been reviewed by Hilado and Murphy (Ref. 26.76). It appears that the experimental results depend not only on the chemical composition of the material but also on such factors as the nature and amount of additives, the density and thickness of the sample material, and ventilation. Representative values developed by a gravimetric technique (Refs. 26.76, 26.77) are listed in Table 26.4.

The effect of the intensity and direction of drafts on smoke spread is, in a way, similar to their effect on fire spread. Yet, smoke is not a combustion-carrying medium but merely an aggregate of fire gases and airborne particles. It is therefore much more mobile than the fire that breeds it, and may disperse throughout the building in a matter of minutes, even if the ventilation or air-conditioning system is shut off.

It is, of course, essential to have smoke or thermal detectors installed on the exhaust side of the ventilation or air-conditioning system. Surveillance of this kind will enable specific actions to be taken: shutting off the system and closing the dampers (Ref. 26.78).

The distribution of air currents that arise in a nine-story building during the winter heating season (after the shutdown of the air-handling system) was described earlier and illustrated in Fig. 26.2.1a. Fig. 26.2.1b shows how the same air currents would distribute smoke on the various levels of the building within a mere 10 to 15 min from the start of a fire on the first floor.

A door that remains closed during a fire is an effective barrier not only against the spread of fire but also against the spread of smoke. A numerical example worked out for a 20-story building, with fire occurring in the winter on the first floor, indicated that the rate of smoke spread could be reduced by a factor of at least 30 by closing the door of the fire compartment. Further reduction could be achieved by applying a strip of intumescent material, (a material that swells in a fire, e.g., one described in Ref. 26.79), to the edges of the door.

Table 26.4. Representative Values of the Smoke-Producing Characteristics of Selected Materials (Refs. 26.76, 26.77).

Material	Percent Smoke, Based on Original Weight
Acrylic, unidentified	0.33
Linoleum	0.52
Polycarbonate	0.89–1.34
Polychloroprene rubber, filled, fire retardant	0.80
Polyester, brominated, reinforced	1.70
Polymethyl methacrylate	0.08
Polypropylene, fire retardant	1.64
Polystyrene	4.86
Polyvinyl chloride, flooring	0.21
Polyvinyl chloride, flexible, fire retardant	2.36
Polyvinyl chloride, rigid	1.33
Wood, hard	0.05–0.13
Wood, soft	0.08–0.23
Wood, board	0.06–0.57

There is no unified approach as yet to the problem of how to restrict the use of materials on the basis of their propensities to generate toxic gases. The most likely reason is that carbon monoxide, which may be produced by the incomplete combustion of any organic material, is still the number one killer. Accumulated data indicate (Ref. 26.80), however, that other toxic gases, such as hydrogen cyanide, hydrogen chloride, nitrogen dioxide, and sulfur dioxide, may be the cause of fire deaths and injuries more often than is commonly believed.

The most obvious step the building designer can take to alleviate the smoke problem is to avoid specifying materials that are known to be heavy smoke producers or generate highly toxic combustion or pyrolysis products. Yet, this passive method of defense is rarely sufficient. From among the active methods, three will be discussed here briefly: smoke dilution, provision of refuge areas, and pressurization.

In milder climates, where the stack effect in smoke dispersion may not be significant, the technique of diluting the smoke is often used in keeping certain vital areas of the building, such as lobbies and stairwells, free of heavy smoke. It has been suggested (Ref. 26.81) that dilution with fresh air in a 100 to 1 proportion will insure relatively safe conditions with respect to both visibility and toxicity. The information needed to design a smoke dilution system includes the equivalent orifice area (mentioned in connection with Eq. 26.2) for the boundaries of the space to be kept free of smoke, and the rate of smoke generation by the fire. (The latter can be estimated as described in Ref. 26.82.)

The time for evacuating a building is approximately proportional to the building height (Refs. 26.83, 26.84) and, depending on the occupant concentration, may take longer than the average duration of a compartment fire. Complete evacuation of a building taller than about 10 to 15 stories is, therefore, not practicable. The danger of exposing the occupants to smoke can be greatly reduced by providing pressurized refuge areas (preferably in the vicinity of stairwells), where the occupants can stay in relative safety for the duration of the fire. The required rate of air supply to these areas is not likely to be determined by the leakage characteristics of their boundaries, but rather by the need for maintaining tolerable conditions for the assembled occupants. The required minimum flow rate of fresh air is about 15 ft^3 min^{-1} (.45 m^3 min^{-1}) per person.

The most effective way of preventing the spread of smoke is to pressurize the building or some major parts of it. Smoke travel through the vertical shafts (stairwells, elevator shafts, etc.) to the upper floors can be countered by raising the pressure in the vertical shafts above the level of the outside atmosphere. The required minimum rate of air flow to pressurize the building is approximately three times the total rate of air infiltration into the building (see Eq. (26.2)). The pressure difference against which the fans have to work is equal to the difference between the pressure of the outside atmosphere and the shaft pressure on the ground floor level (Ref. 26.82). In not-too-tall buildings, pressurization can be most conveniently achieved by injecting outside air into all vertical shafts at the top of the building.

A supplement to the National Building Code of Canada (Ref. 26.85) contains an exhaustive survey of measures for safety from smoke in high buildings. Some of them are just common-sense solutions and impose very little restriction on the building design.

Logic Trees and Tradeoffs

The National Fire Protection Association (NFPA) developed a decision tree (Ref. 26.19) to aid the designer in making fire safety decisions. Fig. 26.5.1 shows the top two or three levels of the decision tree. Each level represents means of achieving the goal at the next higher level.

The purpose of the decision tree is to visualize various ways of working toward some well defined fire safety objectives, e.g., protecting the building's occupants, its contents, and the neighbors. These objectives are met if ignition is prevented OR if, given ignition, the fire is managed. An OR gate is represented by the symbol ⊕. When, to achieve a certain objective, all elements below a gate are needed, an AND gate is used, which is represented by the symbol ⊙.

The Prevent Fire Ignition branch of the tree is essentially a kind of fire prevention code. Since, for success, most of the events shown in this branch require continuous monitoring, fire prevention is for the most part a responsibility of the owners or occupants. However, by incorporating certain features into the building, the designer can assist the owners or occupants.

Since the occurrence of ignition is not fully preventable, the Manage Fire Impact branch also plays a significant part in reaching the overall objective. This branch may be looked upon as a building design code. The impact of the fire can be handled through either the Manage Fire branch OR the Manage Exposed branch. Naturally, by following both of these routes the probability of success is higher.

Managing the fire can be accomplished by (1) controlling the burning process, (2) suppressing the fire, or (3) controlling the fire by passive (built-in) safety measures. Here, again, the OR gate is used, indicating that the designer may have a choice as to which route to follow.

The NFPA decision tree was conceived as a guide for choosing between various alternatives toward achieving the overall goal. However, it could also be used in a quantitative sense, if information on the probabilities of success with all the alternatives were available. Similar decision trees may serve as logic diagrams in making cost-benefit decisions. Thor and Sedin (Ref. 26.86) used this technique to study methods of minimizing fire and smoke damage in one-story industrial buildings.

A decision logic of considerable practical utility has been developed recently (Ref. 26.38). It is based on the premise that as long as the expected annual fire losses (the sum of human losses—deaths and injuries—and property losses, both expressed in monetary terms) are the same, any set of fire safety measures is equivalent to any other set. The report provides a collection of input data applicable to dwellings, apartments, hotels, motels, health care buildings, office buildings, and educational buildings. The input information is composed partly of data taken from US census and fire statistics, and partly of Delphi assessments.

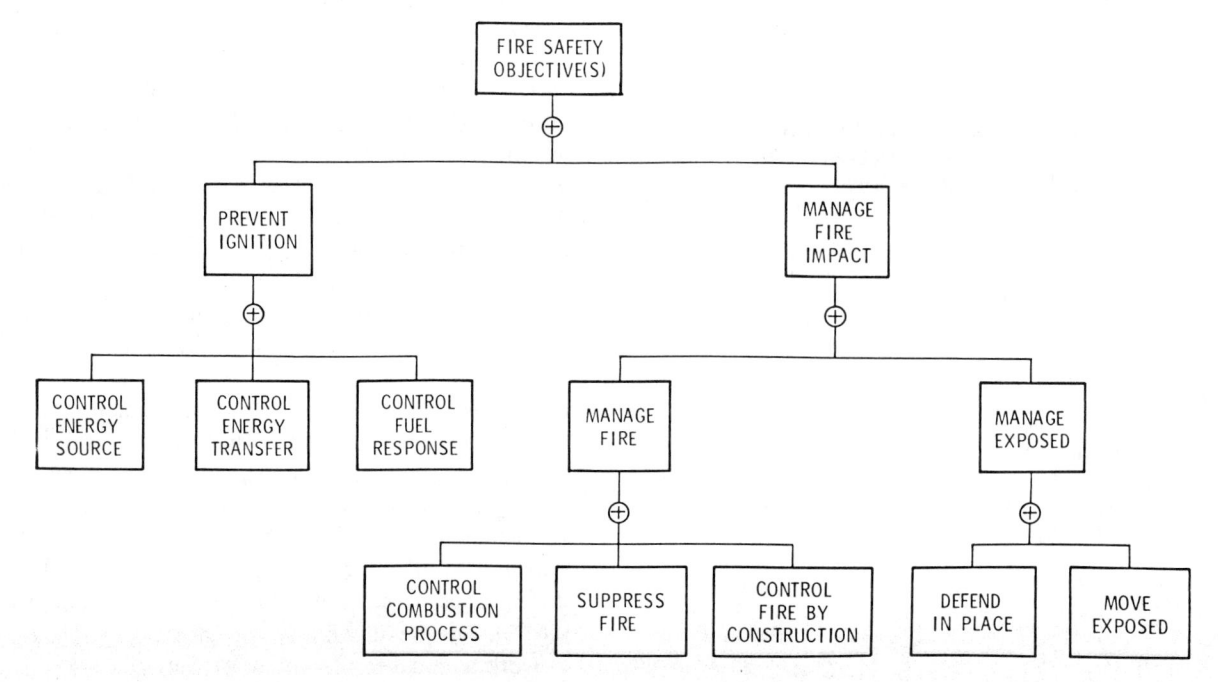

Figure 26.5.1. The top two or three levels of the NFPA decision tree.

(The Delphi technique is a systematic development of quantitative answers to complex problems by a group of experts; see Refs. 26.87, 26.88.)

The report presents the results of a large number of sample calculations. Some of the more interesting conclusions are as follows:

1. The practical fire safety goal (which precludes the possibility of intercompartmental fire spread) can be approximated in some cases by the use of smoke detectors alone, in others by the combined use of smoke detectors and self-closing doors.

2. Trying to improve fire safety by increasing the fire resistance requirements would be a futile effort.

3. If the equality of fire loss expectations is regarded as the criterion of equivalence of fire safety measures, then the building code requirements may be relaxed for office and educational buildings, but they should be strengthened for hotels and motels.

In large buildings a high degree of fire safety can be achieved by incorporating the fire safety system into the overall building automation system. This subject will be further discussed under the heading Protection from Crime, Section 26.6.

Psychological and Sociological Factors

Statistics show that human frailties and undesirable behavioral patterns are responsible for the majority of building fires. Thus the question, how much fire safety is really necessary, cannot be answered without considering some psychological and sociological factors. Countless examples show that some people can live safely in extremely flammable shacks, while others fall victim to fire in modern buildings equipped with all amenities and fire safety facilities.

Clearly, there would be no need for most fire safety measures if society consisted only of people with a high sense of social responsibility. A striking example that there is a profound human factor behind the statistical data was given in a British report (Ref. 26.89). It revealed that the high fire losses in an area with a low level of household amenities did not decrease after a massive redevelopment, including provision of amenities.

The high incidence of fires in modern times is due largely to malice and negligence, which are symptoms of a deficient sense of responsibility. It manifests itself in various ways, and is the source of the troubles that plague today's society. Education is the cure. Problems that have a strong social component cannot be solved by technology alone.

26.6. PROTECTION FROM CRIME

Paucity of Regulatory Measures

While protection against fire has always been a central issue in building regulations, protection against crime has so far received little attention. There are no code regulations outlining minimum security standards. It is a relatively new requirement in some model building codes that entrance doors and windows not too high above the ground be manufactured to resist forced entry.

Apparently, protection from crime is on the whole regarded as the responsibility of the owner, whether he uses the building as residence or runs it for income.

The paucity of regulatory measures aimed at crime prevention does not reflect public apathy. The alarming incidence of crime is very much on the public mind. Crime statistics reveal (Ref. 26.90) that in the United States:

- An average of 19,000 persons are murdered every year, while the fire deaths average only about 6,000
- About 1.3 million violent crimes (excluding murder) are committed annually, while the fire-related injuries amount only to 100,000
- Just under 5 million burglaries, robberies, instances of shoplifting, and other larceny thefts from buildings are reported every year, while building fires known to fire departments average fewer than 1 million

The problems of protecting people and property from criminal acts are not necessarily parallel for small buildings (detached one- and two-family dwellings) and large, multi-occupant buildings (such as apartment buildings, health care facilities, or educational and office buildings). Consequently, the practical approaches to crime prevention may be quite different for small and large buildings.

Security Systems for Small Buildings

In order to remain competitive in the housing market, developers rarely offer for sale one- and two-family houses equipped for crime prevention. In some crime-stricken areas, however, they may find it profitable to install iron grilles over the windows, or to surround a new development with security fences or high walls, so that the future occupants can opt for protecting the points of access to the community by hired guards. For lack of prearranged or built-in safeguards, the community may organize a mutual protection scheme, a so-called neighborhood watch. Most families living in suburban areas believe, however, that they would be better off fending for themselves. Overlooking the protection that a four-legged guard may offer, many will decide to equip their homes with a burglar alarm system (Refs. 26.91 to 26.93).

All security systems consist essentially of three major components: (1) *sensors*, the eyes or ears of the system; (2) the *central processing unit*, the "brain" of the system and an interface between the operator and the system; and (3) the *response device*, the device that executes the protective measure (e.g., the alarm itself). With simpler security devices that serve one particular purpose (e.g., a battery-powered door alarm), no central processing unit is necessary; the sensor and the response device (alarm) are combined into a single unit.

There are two types of security systems: (1) *perimeter surveillance systems*, designed to detect intrusion through the building envelope, and (2) *area surveillance systems*, designed to reveal an intruder already inside the building.

Magnetic contacts or switches are the most frequently used sensors for perimeter surveillance. Window foils, glass breakage sensors, glass breakage sound detectors, or wired window screens may also be used to detect intrusion through windows.

Sensors for area surveillance are designed to spot an intruder moving inside the house. With ultrasonic or microwave motion detectors, a signal will be sent to the central processing unit when the wave pattern generated by the detector is disturbed by a person entering the field. Infrared photocell detectors signal when an invisible light beam issued by the detector is disrupted. Passive infrared detectors react to the body heat of an intruder. The likelihood of false alarm is greatly reduced by the use of dual technology detectors which combine a microwave or ultrasonic detector with a passive infrared device.

The best place for mounting a sensor for area surveillance is some busy space in the building, such as the hallway.

The central processing unit handles the sensor signals and, when called for, activates the response device. Some sophisticated units will also alert others (relatives, friends, or a monitoring agency) through an automatic telephone dialer.

With lights or a digital readout, the processing unit informs the occupants of the status of the alarm system and (possibly) of past events. This is the place where the system can be "armed" and "disarmed" (i.e., turned on and off). Arming or disarming is usually done with a key or a code. The processing unit delays the activation of the response device to allow the occupants enough time to leave the house after switching the system on, or to disarm it after returning home.

The sensors are, as a rule, hooked up to the processing unit by concealed wiring. With wireless systems, radio transmitters provide the link.

The response device consists of a bell or siren, mounted usually in the attic. The processing unit may be programmed to shut off a wailing siren within 15 minutes.

Equipping the alarm system with backup batteries is essential for reliable operation.

Security Systems for Large Buildings

The occupants of small buildings are usually related, or at least know and trust one another. They all have a key, or know the code, to arm and disarm the security system, so that unauthorized entry amounts to forcible intrusion.

In large buildings, the occupants know little about one another, even less about one another's sphere of personal or business acquaintances. Unless guards keep the entrances under surveillance, the occupants must share the responsibility for protecting the building against intruders.

In many apartment and office buildings, the entrance doors are permanently locked, and the occupants enter the building using their keys. These doors are equipped with an electric latch bolt release that can be activated from any of the occupancy units. A visitor, to gain admittance, is required to identify himself to one of the occupants through a two-way communication system between the entrance hall and the occupancy units.

In many office buildings, visitors may only enter a reception area, and only those working in the building are granted access to the rest of the building. As with small buildings, there are two ways of providing security in the restricted areas: (1) by a perimeter surveillance system, and (2) by an area surveillance system.

In large buildings, perimeter surveillance is usually provided by access control systems (Refs. 26.91, 26.92, 26.94 to 26.96). The traditional methods of access control (guard service, lock and key, common code pushbutton lock, common code key pad entry system, etc.) are replaced in modern buildings by microprocessor-controlled, individual-code card access systems.

The most widely used systems employ magnetic stripe or magnetic dot cards, Weigand cards, or proximity cards (Ref. 26.94 to 26.96). The systems employing the last mentioned cards are the most advanced, but also the most expensive.

Like the security systems in small buildings, the card access system consists of three major components: (1) sensors, namely, the card readers; (2) the central processing unit, which interfaces with the sensors and response devices as well as with the operator, "decides" on granting or denying access, and, dependent on the sophistication of the system, may perform some other functions; and (3) the response devices, namely, latch bolt releases and an alarm which sounds warning in case of intrusion.

A stand-alone access control unit consists of one to eight readers and a microprocessor of limited programmability. A large-capacity and sophisticated on-line unit can handle a minimum of 32 readers. The readers are linked to a central computer which, in addition to performing the basic functions of a central processing unit, can also perform a host of other functions. For example, it can check if a door is left open too long or detect if forced entry has occurred, it can lock or unlock doors at specified times, and it can collect, store, and periodically output data for record or bookkeeping purposes (Ref. 26.96). It can be programmed to grant access to certain areas for certain persons only, and only within predetermined periods of time. And it can be reprogrammed any time to reflect changed circumstances.

The state-of-the-art tool for area surveillance is the closed-circuit television (CCTV) system (Refs. 26.92, 26.97). The television cameras serve as the eyes of the system. Typically, they are placed in parking areas, entryways, elevator lobbies, and stairways. The more expensive systems employ silicon intensifier target (SIT) cameras (suitable for low-light environments), which may also be equipped with zoom lenses and pan/tilt mechanisms. The video monitors (black-and-white or color) are usually located in a dimly lit control room. It may be of some advantage to have the screens remain blank until something happens. The lighting up of the screen will alert the guard.

It is vitally important to provide all kinds of security system with back-up power source.

"Smart" Buildings

A powerful central processing unit may do a lot more than just coordinate the security of a building. It can also be used for a host of additional functions (Refs. 26.91, 26.98, 26.99), such as:

- With respect to fire safety: to monitor the status of all heat and smoke detectors, manual pull stations, and sprinkler release relays; in case of fire, to cause the elevators to home to a predetermined floor and shut down; to close all fire doors and open some others necessary for evacuation; to initiate smoke control measures (such as shutting down the air handling system and pressurizing the stairwells); and to alert the security guards or the fire department.
- With respect to elevators, escalators, moving walkways, and automatic doors: to schedule the operation in such a way as to prevent crowding and save energy; to detect and record faults in the people mover system.
- With respect to the heating, ventilating, and air conditioning system: to provide thermal comfort, humidity control, and adequate ventilation; to execute scheduled setbacks during off-hours, possibly with local overrides; to arrange for optimum starts and stops for large equipment; to detect and record faults in the system.
- With respect to lighting: to provide optimum lighting, scheduled on-off switching or dimming, possibly with local overrides in response to sensor signals

The list could go on and on.

The adjective *smart* started to appear in 1984 with reference to buildings in which microprocessor technology is utilized for surveilling and controlling the normal functioning of the building and for taking care of emergency situations. However, the adjective *automated* might be more appropriate. With the steady increase of the price of hired help, there is hardly any doubt that building automation looks ahead to a bright future.

26.7. PROTECTION FROM FLOODS AND LIGHTNING

Being local problems, protection against floods and lightning do not readily fit into such all-purpose documents as building codes.

In the United States, county ordinances enforce the National Flood Insurance Act. Maps prepared by the Department of Housing and Urban Development Flood Insurance Administration designate the flood hazard areas, divide them (depending on the gravity of hazard) into various zones, and prescribe the minimum elevation of habitable floors (i.e., floors used for living purposes) above a mean water level. Fill may be used in some areas, but in the coastal high hazard zones the house must be constructed on piling or columns. The space under the house may be used for utility room, garage, screened porch, etc., and may be enclosed by walls, provided that they are of a flimsy kind that collapses under a load presented by high tide or wave action, or by winds stronger than 100 mph (160 km/h). The ordinances also cover the electrical and gas installations, as well the water supply, sanitary sewers, and septic tanks.

Protection from lightning is generally regarded as the responsibility of the building owner. Whether or not lightning protection is advisable depends on the value of the so-called risk index (Ref. 26.100), to be calculated from a point scheme. The following factors are rated:

- Type of structure
- Type of construction
- Location of building in relation to other buildings
- Topography
- Building occupancy and contents
- Lightning frequency

The point values to be assigned to these factors are tabulated (Ref. 26.100), and range from 1 to 5 or from 1 to 10. The values for the last mentioned factor have been based on maps showing the average annual thunderstorm days in the area of concern (see, e.g., Ref. 26.101 for the U.S., Ref. 26.100 for Canada).

In general, there is no need for protection against lightning if the risk index indicates light to moderate risk (i.e., it is less than 3). Acceptable techniques of providing protection to buildings rated as moderate to severe risks are detailed in Refs. 26.100 and 26.101. The protection system consist of air terminals or intercepting conductors, down conductors, and ground electrodes. All components of the system are usually made from copper, aluminum, or stainless steel.

REFERENCES

26.1. S. Kaplan and B. J. Garrick. "On the Quantitative Definition of Risk." *Risk Analysis*, **1**(1), 11-27 (1981).

26.2. A. G. Wilson. "Design of Buildings for Safety and Health." *Engineering Journal*, **56**(4), 33-37 (1973).

26.3. M. Gretener. "Attempt to Calculate the Fire Risk of Industrial and Other Objects." *3rd Intl. Fire Protection Symp.*, Eindhoven, 1968.

26.4. G. Ramachandran. "A Review of Mathematical Models for Assessing Fire Risk." *Fire Prevention*, **149**, 28-32 (May 1982).

26.5. J. M. Watts, Jr. "Fire Risk Assessment Schedules." *The SFPE Handbook of Fire Protection Engineering*, Chapter 4-11. Soci-

ety of Fire Protection Engineers/National Fire Protection Association, Boston/Quincy, MA, 1988, pp. 4-89 to 4-102.
26.6. C. S. Harvey. "Using the Computer as an Interface between the Authority and the Jurisdiction." *Fire Journal*, **79**(1), 27-69 (1985).
26.7. H. E. Nelson and A. J. Shibe. "A System for Fire Safety Evaluation of Health Care Facilities." NBSIR 78-1555. National Bureau of Standards, Washington, DC, 1980.
26.8. J. H. McGuire and G. T. Tamura. "Simple Analysis of Smoke-Flow Problems in High Buildings." *Fire Technology*, **11**(1), 15-22 (1975).
26.9. W. G. Berl and B. M. Halpin. "Fire-Related Fatalities: An Analysis of Their Demography, Physical Origins, and Medical Causes." *Fire Standards and Safety*, A. F. Robertson (Ed.), ASTM STP 614, American Society for Testing and Materials, Philadelphia, PA, 1976, pp. 26-54.
26.10. J. N. deRis. "Spread of Laminar Diffusion Flame." *12th Symp. (Intl.) on Combustion*. The Combustion Institute, Pittsburgh, PA, 1969, pp. 241-252.
26.11. F. A. Lastrina, R. S. Magee, and R. F. McAlevy, III. Flame spread over fuel beds: Solid-phase energy considerations. *13th Symp. (Intl.) on Combustion*, The Combustion Institute, Pittsburgh, PA, 1971, pp. 935-948.
26.12. A. C. Fernandez-Pello. "A Theoretical Model for the Upward Laminar Spread of Flames over Vertical Fuel Surfaces." *Combustion and Flame*, **31**(2), 135-148 (1978).
26.13. T. Z. Harmathy. "Burning, Pyrolysis, Combustion and Char-Oxidation: Need for Clarifying Terminology." *Fire and Materials*, **8**(4), 224-226 (1984).
26.14. C. P. Fenimore and F. J. Martin. "Candle-Type Test for Flammability of Polymers." *Modern Plastics*, **44**(3), 141-192 (1966).
26.15. C. J. Hilado. *Flammability Handbook for Plastics*. Technomic Publ., Stamford, CT, 1969, p. 40.
26.16. Y. Tsuchiya and K. Sumi. "Smoke Producing Characteristics of Materials." *J. Fire and Flammability*, **5**(1), 64-75 (1974).
26.17. J. G. Quintiere and M. T. Harkleroad. "New Concept for Measuring Flame Spread Properties." *Fire Safety: Science and Engineering*, ASTM STP 882, T. Z. Harmathy (Ed.), American Society for Testing and Materials, Philadelphia, PA, 1985, pp. 239-267.
26.18. R. Pape and T. E. Waterman. "Understanding and Modeling Preflashover Compartment Fires." *Design of Buildings for Fire Safety*, ASTM STP 685, E. E. Smith and T. Z. Harmathy (Eds.), American Society for Testing and Materials, Philadelphia, PA, 1979, pp. 106-138.
26.19. H. J. Roux and G. N. Berlin. "Toward Knowledge-Based Fire Safety System." *Design of Buildings for Fire Safety*, ASTM STP 685, E. E. Smith and T. Z. Harmathy (Eds.), American Society for Testing and Materials, Philadelphia, PA, 1979, pp. 3-13.
26.20. W. W. Jones. "A Review of Compartment Fire Models." IR 83-2684. National Bureau of Standards, Washington, DC, 1983.
26.21. J. S. Parikh and J. R. Beyreis. "Survey of the State of the Art of Mathematical Fire Modeling." *SFPE Bulletin*, 5-8 (March 1985).
26.22. D. Drysdale. *Fire Dynamics*. John Wiley, New York, 1985.
26.23. J. Quintiere. "Analytical Methods for Firesafety Design." *Fire Technology*, **24**(4), 333-352 (1988).
26.24. I. A. Benjamin. "Development of a Room Fire Test." *Fire Standards and Safety*, ASTM STP 614, A. F. Robertson (Ed.), American Society for Testing and Materials, Philadelphia, PA, 1976, p. 300-311.
26.25. G. T. Castino, J. R. Beyreis, and W. S. Metes. "Flammability Studies of Cellular Plastics and Other Building materials Used for Interior Finish." File Subject 723, Underwriters Laboratories Inc., Northbrook, IL, 1975.
26.26. A. Tewarson and F. Tamanini. "Research and Development for a Laboratory-Scale Flammability Test Method for Cellular Plastics." FMRC Serial No. 22524, Factory Mutual Engineering, Boston, MA, August 1976.
26.27. J. deRis. "Flammability Testing State-of-the-Art." *Fire and Materials*, **9**(2), 75-80 (1985).
26.28. J. B. Fang. "Fire Buildup in a Room and the Role of Interior Finish Materials." NBS Technical Note 879, National Bureau of Standards, Washington, DC, 1975.
26.29. H. D. Bruce. "Experimental Dwelling-Room Fires." Report No. 1941, Forest Products Laboratory, Madison, WI, 1959.
26.30. D. Gross. "The Measurement and Correlation of Fire Growth in a Room." *Proceedings of Symp. on Full-Scale Tests*, Research and Development Center, Lancaster, PA, 1974.
26.31. G. Hagglund, R. Jansson, and B. Onnermark. "Fire Development in Residential Rooms after Ignition from Nuclear Explosions." F.O.A. Rapport C 20016-D6 (A3), Forsvarets Forskningsanstalt, Stockholm, Sweden, 1974.
26.32. V. Babrauskas. "Estimating Room Flashover." *Fire Technology*, **16**(2), 94-103 (1980).
26.33. B. J. McCaffrey, J. G. Quintiere, and M. F. Harkleroad. "Estimating Room Temperatures and the Likelihood of Flashover Using Fire Test Data Correlations." Center for Fire Research, National Bureau of Standards, Washington, DC, 1980.
26.34. J. Quintiere. "Growth of Fire in Building Compartments." *Fire Standards and Safety*, ASTM STP 614, A. F. Robertson (Ed.), American Society for Testing and Materials, Philadelphia, PA, 1977, pp. 131-167.
26.35. A. Gomberg, B. Buchbinder, and F. L. Offensend. "Evaluating Alternative Strategies for Reducing Residential Fire Loss—The Fire Loss Model." NBSIR 82-2551, National Bureau of Standards, Washington, DC, 1982, 61 pp.
26.36. R. T. Ruegg and S. K. Fuller. "A Benefit-Cost Model of Residential Fire Sprinkler Systems." Technical Note 1203, National Bureau of Standards, Washington, DC, 1984, 122 pp.
26.37. T. Z. Harmathy. "On the Economics of Mandatory Sprinklering of Dwellings." *Fire Technology*, **24**(3), 245-261 (1988).
26.38. T. Z. Harmathy et al. "A Decision Logic for Trading between Fire Safety Measures." *Fire and Materials*, **14**(1), 1-10 (1989).
26.39. A. H. Gustaferro. "Design of Prestressed Concrete for Fire Resistance." *J. Prestressed Concrete Inst.*, **18**(6), 102-116 (1973).
26.40. T. T. Lie. "Temperature Distributions in Fire-Exposed Building Columns." *J. Heat Transfer*, **99**(1), 113-119 (1977).
26.41. B. Bresler. "Analytical Prediction of Structural Response to Fire." *Fire Safety J.*, **9**(1), 103-117 (1985).
26.42. "Structural fire safety. CIB W14 Workshop Report." *Fire Safety J.*, **10**(2), 77-137 (1986).
26.43. "Guide for Determining the Fire Endurance of Concrete Elements." ACI 216R-81, American Concrete Institute, Detroit, MI, 1987, 44 pp.
26.44. Y. Anderberg et al. "Properties of Materials at High Temperatures—Steel." Report LUTVDG/(TVBB-3088), ISSN 0282-3756, Lund Institute of Technology, Lund, Sweden, 1983, 135 pp.
26.45. U. Schneider. "Modeling of Concrete Behaviour at High Temperatures." *Design of Structures against Fire*, R. D. Anchor, H. L. Malhotra, and J. A. Purkiss (Eds.), Elsevier Applied Science, London, 1986, pp. 53-69.
26.46. E. L. Schaffer, F. E. Woeste, D. A. Bender, and C. M. Marx. "Strength and Fire Endurance of Glued-Laminated Timber Beams." *Design of Structures against Fire*, R. D. Anchor, H. L. Malhotra, and J. A. Purkiss (Eds.), Elsevier Applied Science, London, 1986, pp. 71-85.
26.47. T. Z. Harmathy. "Properties of Building Materials." *The SFPE Handbook of Fire Protection Engineering*, Chapter 1-26. Society of Fire Protection Engineers/National Fire Protection Association, Boston/Quincy, MA, 1988, pp. 1-378 to 1-391.
26.48. S. H. Ingberg. "Tests of Severity of Building Fires." *NFPA Quarterly*, **22**(1), 43-61 (1928).
26.49. M. Law. "A Relationship between Fire Grading and Building

Design and Contents." Fire Research Note No. 877, Joint Fire Research Organisation, Borehamwood, England, 1971, 43 pp.
26.50. O. Pettersson. "The Connection between a Real Fire Exposure and the Heating Conditions According to Standard Fire Resistance Tests—with Special Application to Steel Structures." Bulletin No. 39, Division of Structural Mechanics and Concrete Construction, Lund Institute of Technology, Lund, Sweden, 1975, 86 pp.
26.51. "Structural Fire Protection in Industrial Building Construction. Part 1: Required Fire Resistance Period; Part 2: Determination of the Burning Factor m; Appendix 1 to Part 1: Calorific Value and m-Factors." Draft in manuscript form, DIN 19230, Deutsches Institut für Normung, Berlin, 1978.
26.52. M. Kersken-Bradley. "Probabilistic Concepts in Fire Engineering." *Design of Structures against Fire*, R. D. Anchor, H. L. Malhotra, and J. A. Purkiss (Eds.), Elsevier Applied Science, London, 1986, pp. 21–39.
26.53. T. Z. Harmathy. "The Fire Resistance Test and Its Relation to Real-World Fires." *Fire and Materials*, **5**(3), 112–122 (1981).
26.54. J. R. Mehaffey and T. Z. Harmathy. "Thermal Response of Compartment Boundaries to Fire." *Proceedings of First Intntl. Symp. on Fire Safety Science*, Gaithersburg, MD, 1985, pp. 111–118.
26.55. T. Z. Harmathy. "On the Equivalent Fire Exposure." *Fire and Materials*, **11**(2), 95–104 (1987).
26.56. T. Z. Harmathy. "Fire Severity: Basis of Fire Safety Design." *Fire Safety of Concrete Structures*, ACI SP-80, American Concrete Institute, Detroit, MI, 1983, pp. 115–149.
26.57. O. Pettersson, S. E. Magnusson, and J. Thor. "Fire Engineering Design of Steel Structures." Publication No. 50, Swedish Institute of Steel Construction, Stockholm, Sweden, 1976.
26.58. J. R. Mehaffey and T. Z. Harmathy. "Assessment of Fire Resistance Requirements." *Fire Technology*, **17**(4), 221–237 (1981).
26.59. ASTM E05.11 Task Group. "Repeatability and Reproducibility of Results of ASTM E 119 Fire Tests." Research Report No. E5-1003, American Society for Testing and Materials, Philadelphia, PA, 1982.
26.60. C. A. Cornell. "A Probability-Based Structural Code." *ACI Journal, Proceedings*, **66**(12), 974–985 (1969).
26.61. J. J. Zahn. "Reliability-Based Design Procedures for Wood Structures." *Forest Products J.*, **27**(3), 21–28 (1977).
26.62. T. Z. Harmathy and J. R. Mehaffey. "Design of Buildings for Prescribed Levels of Structural Fire Safety." ASTM STP 882, *Fire Safety: Science and Engineering*, T. Z. Harmathy (Ed.), American Society for Testing and Materials, Philadelphia, PA, 1985, pp. 160–175.
26.63. T. Z. Harmathy. "How Much Fire Resistance Is Really Needed?" *Concrete International*, **10**(12) 40–44, (1988).
26.64. J. H. McGuire. "Penetration of Fire Partitions by Plastic DWV Pipe." *Fire Technology*, **9**(1), 5–14 (1973).
26.65. J. H. McGuire. "Small-Scale Fire Tests of Walls Penetrated by Telephone Cables." *Fire Technology*, **11**(2), 73–79 (1975).
26.66. K. K. Choi. "Fire Stops for Plastic Pipe." *Fire Technology*, **23**(4), 267–279 (1987).
26.67. F. Spiegelhalter. "Guide to Design of Cavity Barriers and Fire Stops." BRE Current Paper No. CP 7/77, Building Research Establishment, Fire Research Station, Borehamwood, England, 1977.
26.68. K. K. Choi and W. Taylor. "Combustibility of Insulation in Cavity Walls." *J. Fire Sciences*, **2**(3), 179–188 (1984).
26.69. "Horizontal Projections in the Prevention of Spread of Fire from Storey to Storey." Report No. TR52/75/397, Commonwealth Experimental Building Station, Sydney, Australia, 1971.
26.70. T. Z. Harmathy. "Design of Buildings for Fire Safety—Part II." *Fire Technology*, **12**(3), pp. 219–236 (1976).
26.71. E. L. Schaffer and H. W. Eickner. "Corridor Wall Linings—Effect on Fire Performance." *Fire Technology*, **1**(4), 243–255 (1965).
26.72. J. H. McGuire. "The Spread of Fire in Corridors." *Fire Technology*, **4**(2), 103–108 (1968).
26.73. W. J. Christian and T. E. Waterman. "Fire Behavior of Interior Finish Materials." *Fire Technology*, **6**(3), 165–178 (1970).
26.74. T. E. Waterman. "Corridor Flame Spread." *Fire Journal*, **67**(6), 66–72 (1973).
26.75. R. Friedman. "Quantification of Threat from a Rapidly Growing Fire in Terms of Relative Material Properties." *Fire and Materials*, **2**(1), 27–33 (1978).
26.76. C. J. Hilado and R. M. Murphy. "Fire Response of Organic Polymeric Materials (Organic Materials in Fire: Combustibility)." *Design of Buildings for Fire Safety*, ASTM STP 685, E. E. Smith and T. Z. Harmathy (Eds.), American Society for Testing and Materials, Philadelphia, PA, 1979, pp. 76–105.
26.77. C. J. Hilado and H. J. Cumming. "Studies with Arapahoe Smoke Chamber." *J. Fire and Flammability*, **8**(3), 300–308 (1977).
26.78. "Early Detection of Fires in Ventilation and Air Conditioning Systems." *Cerberus Alarm*, No. 102 (December 1987), pp. 1–3.
26.79. "Palusol Fire-Board." B557e-2.74. Badische Anilin- und Soda-Fabrik, Mannheim, Germany, 1974.
26.80. K. Sumi and Y. Tsuchiya. "Toxicity of Decomposition Products." *J. Combustion Toxicology*, **2**(3), 213–225 (1975).
26.81. J. H. McGuire, G. T. Tamura, and A. G. Wilson. "Factors in Controlling Smoke in High Buildings." *Fire Hazards in Buildings*, ASHRAE Symposium Bulletin, San Francisco, CA, January 1970, pp. 8–13.
26.82. T. Z. Harmathy. "Building Design and the Fire Hazard." *Wood and Fiber*, **9**(2), 127–144 (1977).
26.83. M. Galbreath. "Time of Evacuation by Stairs in High Buildings." *Fire Fighting in Canada*, **13**(1), 6–10 (1969).
26.84. J. L. Pauls. "Movement of People." *The SFPE Handbook of Fire Protection Engineering*, Chapter 1-15. Society of Fire Protection Engineers/National Fire Protection Association, Boston/Quincy, MA, 1988, pp. 1–246 to 1–268.
26.85. Associate Committee on the National Building Code. "Measures for Fire Safety in High Buildings." NRCC 13366, National Research Council of Canada, Ottawa, 1973.
26.86. J. Thor and G. Sedin. "Fire Risk Evaluation and Cost Benefit of Fire Protective Measures in Industrial Buildings." *Fire Safety J.*, **2**(3), 153–166 (1979/80).
26.87. N. C. Dalkey. "The Delphi Method: An Experimental Study of Group Opinion." Report RM-5888-PR, Rand Corporation, Santa Monica, CA, 1969, 79 pp.
26.88. T. Z. Harmathy. "The Delphi Method—A Complement to Research." *Fire and Materials*, **6**(2), 76–79 (1982).
26.89. "House Fires and Social Conditions." Building Research Establishment, UK, *BRE News*, Autumn 1979, p. 49.
26.90. A. Norton. "When Security Provisions Threaten Firesafety." *Fire Journal*, **82**(6), 40–77 (1988).
26.91. G. Underwood. *The Security of Buildings*. The Architectural Press, London, 1984.
26.92. L. Monroe. "How Secure Is Your Building." *Buildings*, 100–103 (April 1985).
26.93. D. Stevenson. "Home Secure Home." *Canadian Consumer*, **18**(7), 31–37 (1988).
26.94. W. C. Miller. "Entry, Exit, and More . . . Total Building Access Control." *Building Operating Management*, 46–50 (August 1984).
26.95. T. Callen. "The Microprocessor Effect on Access Control Systems." *Building Operating Management*, 78–80 (June 1985).
26.96. P. S. Hamblin. "Card Access Systems—No Longer Limited to Larger Buildings." *Building Operating Management*, 68–74 (February 1986).

26.97. V. Houk. "Closed-Circuit Television Systems." *Building Operating Management*, 32–34 (August 1984).

26.98. M. Lynn. "Retrofitting Security Systems into Existing Buildings." *Building Operating Management*, 22–25 (June 1985).

26.99. A. D. McKinley. "Modern Building Services—More than Computerized HVAC." *ASHRAE Transactions*, **94**(Part 1), 934–947 (1988).

26.100. *Installation Code for Lightning Protection Systems*, CAN/CSA-B72-M87, Canadian Standards Association, Rexdale, ON (Canada), March 1987.

26.101. W. C. Hart and E. W. Malone. *Lightning and Lightning Protection*. Multivolume EMC Encyclopedia Series, Vol. IV, Don White Consultants, Inc., Gainsville, VA, 1979.

SUGGESTIONS FOR FURTHER READING

The SFPE Handbook of Fire Protection Engineering. Society of Fire Protection Engineers/National Fire Protection Association, Boston, MA, 1988.

D. Drysdale. *Fire Dynamics*. Wiley, New York, 1985.

R. D. Anchor, H. L. Malhotra, and J. R. Purkiss (Eds.). *Design of Structures against Fire*. Elsevier, London, 1986.

Guide for Determining the Fire Endurance of Buildings. ACI 216R-81. American Concrete Institute, Detroit, 1987.

G. Underwood. *The Security of Buildings*. Architectural Press, London, 1984.

NOTATION

All symbols are defined before or after the equation in which they first appear. Only the more important symbols are included in this list, and those that appear in more than one section in this chapter.

A_F	floor area of the fire compartment, ft^2 (m^2)
A_t	total surface area of the fire compartment, ft^2 (m^2)
A_v	area of ventilation opening (window, door), ft^2 (m^2)
g	gravitational acceleration, 4.17×10^8 ft h^{-2} (9.8 m s^{-2})
h_c	height of fire compartment, ft (m)
h_v	height of ventilation opening, ft (m)
H'	normalized heat load on the compartment (or any of the compartment boundaries) in a real-world fire (for $L = L_m$ and $\Phi = \Phi_{min}$), h$^{1/2}$ R (s$^{1/2}$ K)
H''	normalized heat load on the building element in a standard fire test, h$^{1/2}$ R (s$^{1/2}$ K)
$\sqrt{k\rho c}$	thermal absorptivity of the compartment boundaries, Btu ft^{-2} h$^{-1/2}$ R^{-1} (J m^{-2} s$^{-1/2}$ K^{-1})
L	Specific fire load (mass of combustibles per unit floor area) lb ft^{-2} (kg m^{-2})
P_f	failure probability, dimensionless
β	factor in Eq. (26.11), dimensionless
δ	factor defined by Eq. (26.8), dimensionless
μ	factor quantifying the potential of fully developed fire for spread by convection, dimensionless
ρ_a	density of atmospheric air, ~ 0.0755 lb ft^{-3} at 68°F (1.21 kg m^{-3} at 20°C)
σ_L	standard deviation for the specific fire load, same dimension as specified fire load, L
τ	fire resistance (or duration of standard test fire), h
Φ	ventilation factor, lb h^{-1}, kg s^{-1}

Subscripts

d	design value
m	arithmetic mean
min	minimum

A list of abbreviations of the units of measurement, definitions of these units, and conversion factors between British/American and metric units are given in the Appendix.

Appendix
Units of Measurement

A.1 ABBREVIATIONS USED FOR UNITS OF MEASUREMENT

A	ampere
Btu	British thermal unit
C	Celsius (Centigrade)
CFM	cubic feet per minute
cd	candela
db	decibel
F	Fahrenheit
fpm	feet per minute
ft	foot
ft^2	square foot
ft^3	cubic foot
G	giga (= 1,000,000,000)
g	gram
gr	grain
h	hour
in.	inch
in.^{2}	square inch
in.^{3}	cubic inch
J	joule
K	Kelvin; degree Kelvin; kilopound (=1,000 pound)
k	kilo (= 1,000); kilopound
kg	kilogram
kip	kilopound
kJ	kilojoule
km	kilometer
kN	kilonewton
kPa	kilopascal
ksi	kilopounds per square inch (= 1,000 psi)
kW	kilowatt
kWh	kilowatt-hour (= 3.6 MJ)
L, l	liter
lb	pound
lm	lumen
M	mega (= 1,000,000)
MJ	megajoule
MN	meganewton
MPa	megapascal
MW	megawatt
m	meter
m^2	square meter
m^3	cubic meter
m (prefix)	milli (= 0.001)
mm	millimeter
min	minute
mph	miles per hour
N	newton
n	nano (= 0.000 000 001)
nm	nanometer
Pa	pascal
pcf	pound per cubic foot
plf	pound per linear foot
psf	pound per square foot
psi	pound per square inch
R	Rankine; degree Rankine
s	second
sec	second
V	volt
wg	water gauge (measured in in. or mm)
W	watt
μ	micro (= 0.000 001)
μm	micrometer (formerly called micron)
Ω	ohm
°	degree
′	minute (particularly for circular measure)
″	second (particularly for circular measure); inch
#	number (designation of size in a standard gauge); pound

A.2 DEFINITIONS OF UNITS, AND CONVERSION FACTORS BETWEEN BRITISH/AMERICAN AND METRIC UNITS

Length and Thickness

In British/American units the standard is 1 foot (ft) = 12 inches (in.). For long distances, 1 mile = 5280 ft.

In metric units the standard is 1 meter (m).

1 km = 1,000 m; 1 m = 1,000 mm; 1 mm = 1,000 μm; 1 μm = 1,000 nm.

1 mile = 1.609 km
1 km = 0.62137 miles
1 m = 3.281 ft = 39.37 in.
1 ft = 0.3048 m
1 in. = 25.4 mm

The diameter of thin wires and of thin sheets of metal or plastic is often designated by a gauge number, which is an arbitrary scale. There are many gauge number systems, devised for particular industries, or for particular countries or cities. A widely used system is the US Standard Gauge.

Inch and Metric Equivalents of the US Standard Gauge.

Gauge Number	inches	millimeters
10	0.1345	3.42
12	0.1046	2.66
14	0.0747	1.90
16	0.0598	1.52
18	0.0478	1.21
20	0.0359	0.912
22	0.0299	0.759
24	0.0239	0.607
26	0.0179	0.455
28	0.0149	0.378

Area

1 m^2 = 10.764 ft^2
1 ft^2 = 0.0929 m^2

One square meter = 10 square feet is a common approximation.

Volume and Capacity

There is no difference in principle between the measures of volume (cubic foot, cubic meter), and the measures of capacity (gallon, quart, liter [L or l]).

1 ft^3 = 0.02832 m^3
1 m^3 = 35.315 ft^3

1 US gallon = 4 quarts = 3.7854 liters
1 liter = 0.001 m^3
 = 0.264 US gallons = 1.057 US quarts
 = 0.220 (British) Imperial gallons

One liter = 1 US quart is a common approximation.

Section Modulus

The section modulus of a structural member has the dimension (length)^3, and its dimensions are therefore the same as for volume (ft^3, in.^{3}, m^3, or mm^3).

Second Moment of Area (Moment of Inertia)

The second moment of area of a structural member has the dimension (length)^4. It is generally (although incorrectly) called the moment of inertia.

1 ft^4 = 0.008 631 m^4
1 in.^{4} = 416,231 mm^4
1 m^4 = 115.862 ft^4 = 2,402,510 in.^{4}
1 mm^4 = 2.402 × 10^{-6} in.^{4}

Mass

In British/American units the standard is
1 pound (lb) = 16 ounces (oz) = 7000 grains (gr).

In metric units the standard is
1 kilogram (kg) = 1000 grams (g).

1 lb = 0.4536 kg   1 kg = 2.205 lb
1 gr = 64.8 mg   1 g = 15.4 gr

Density (Unit Weight of Materials) and Specific Gravity

Density is mass per unit volume. It is also called the unit weight of materials, although it is strictly the unit mass (see entry for "Weight" below).

1 lb/ft^3 = 16.018 kg/m^3 1 kg/m^3 = 0.064 243 lb/ft^3

The abbreviation pcf is sometimes used for lb/ft^3.

Specific gravity is the ratio of the mass or weight of a substance to the mass or weight of an equal volume of water. Since a kilogram is defined as the mass of 1 liter (= 0.001 m^3) of water, the density of materials in kg/L is numerically equal to their specific gravity.

Density in kg/m^3 = 1000 × specific gravity
Density in lb/ft^3 = 62.425 × specific gravity

Weight and Force

In British/American units the standard is the pound-force (lbf), usually just called the pound (lb). It is the force of a mass of one pound under the action of the earth's gravity at sea-level, and thus also its weight. For larger forces, 1 kilopound (kip or K or k) = 1000 lb, or 1 (short) ton = 2000 lb.

In the old metric units, similarly, the standard was the kilogram-force (kgf, or simply kg).

The SI System (*Système International d'Unités*), which has now been introduced as the standard for measurements in most countries, and is also the recognized metric system in the USA, uses a different concept. A newton (N) is the force exerted by 1 kilogram (*not* 1 gram) under the action of an acceleration of 1 m/sec^2 (*not* the acceleration due to gravity). This makes the system universal. It can be used on the top of a mountain, or in a spaceship; however, it is less convenient for architects and engineers working on the earth's surface.

For larger forces,

$$1 \text{ MN} = 1000 \text{ kN} \quad 1 \text{ kN} = 1000 \text{ N}.$$

$$1 \text{ lb} = 4.448 \text{ N} \quad 1 \text{ N} = 0.2248 \text{ lb}$$
$$1 \text{ kip} = 4.448 \text{ kN} \quad 1 \text{ kN} = 0.2248 \text{ kip}$$

Pressure and Stress

Pressure and stress are both force per unit area. The British/American units most frequently used in the design of buildings are

1 kilopound per square inch (ksi) = 1000 pound per square inch (psi)

and 1 psi = 144 pound per square foot (psf).

The corresponding SI unit is the pascal (Pa), where

$$1 \text{ Pa} = 1 \text{ N/m}^2.$$

For larger pressures and stresses,

1MPa = 1000 kPa = 1 MN/mm^2 1 kPa = 1000 Pa.

In most European countries, the pascal is used only for fluid pressure, and the customary units for stress are the kN/m^2 (= 1 kPa) and the N/mm^2 (= 1 MPa).

$$1 \text{ psf} = 47.880 \text{ Pa} \quad 1 \text{ kPa} = 20.885 \text{ psf}$$
$$1 \text{ psi} = 6.895 \text{ kPa} \quad 1 \text{ kPa} = 0.1450 \text{ psi}$$
$$1 \text{ ksi} = 6.895 \text{ MPa} \quad 1 \text{ MPa} = 0.1450 \text{ ksi}$$

In meteorological work, the millibar (mb); the atmosphere (atm), i.e., standard atmospheric pressure at sea level; and the height of the mercury column in a barometer at 1 atm are still used:

$$1 \text{ mb} = 0.1 \text{ kPa} = 0.0145 \text{ psi}$$
$$1 \text{ atm} = 101.3 \text{ kPa} = 14.69 \text{ psi}$$
$$1 \text{ atm} = 760 \text{ mm of mercury} = 30 \text{ in. of mercury}$$

The "head" of water is used for calculations on water supply and disposal:

$$1 \text{ ft head of water} = 0.4327 \text{ psi} = 2.984 \text{ kPa}$$
$$1 \text{ m head of water} = 1.419 \text{ psi} = 9.789 \text{ kPa}$$

Angular Measure

Angles are commonly measured in degrees (°), minutes ('), and seconds (").

$$60'' = 1' \text{ and } 60' = 1°$$
$$360° = \text{the circumference of a complete circle}$$
$$90° = 1 \text{ right angle}.$$

This is an arbitrary measure, and for certain mathematical calculations (see Chapter 1) an absolute measure is required. One radian is defined as the angle subtended at the center of a circle by an arc equal in length to its radius. The circumference of a circle is 2π times its radius. Therefore,

$$1 \text{ radian} = 360/2\pi = 57.2958 \text{ degrees} = 57°17'45''.$$

The steradian is the corresponding three-dimensional measure. It is defined as the solid angle subtended at the center of a sphere by an area of its surface numerically equal to the square of its radius. It is used, for example, in illumination design (see Chapter 19).

Time and Frequency

Time is measured in days, hours (h), minutes (min), and seconds (s or sec). The year varies in length.

$$1 \text{ min} = 60 \text{ sec} \quad 1 \text{ h} = 60 \text{ min} = 3600 \text{ sec}$$
$$1 \text{ day} = 24 \text{ h} = 1{,}440 \text{ min} = 86{,}400 \text{ sec}$$

Frequency is the inverse of time. It is measured in cycles per second. This unit is called a hertz.

1 hertz (Hz) = 1 cycle per second = 60 cycles per minute.

Temperature

In British/American units temperature is measured by the Fahrenheit (F) scale. Its zero point was fixed by the temperature at which a then widely used freezing mixture solidified, and its hundred-degree point by the human body temperature, as it was thought to be at the time (1714).

The Celsius (C) scale, also called the centigrade scale, is used with the metric system. Its zero point is the freezing point of water, and its hundred-degree point the boiling point of water.

$$0°C = 32°F \qquad 100°C = 212°F$$
$$°F = \frac{9}{5}°C + 32 \qquad °C = \frac{5}{9}(°F - 32)$$

Absolute zero is the lowest temperature (theoretically) attainable. It occurs at $-459.6°F$ and $-273.15°C$. The Rankine (R) and the Kelvin (K) scales are the same as the Fahrenheit and the Celsius scales, but their zero point is absolute zero. The degree sign is omitted for degrees Rankine and degrees Kelvin:

$$R = °F + 459.6$$
$$K = °C + 273.15$$

For temperature differences, only the relative size of the degree is important:

$$1 K = 1°C = 1.8°F = 1.8 R$$

Speed and Velocity

In British/American units, this is measured in feet per minute (ft/min) or in miles per hour (mph). In metric units it is measured in meters per second (m/s) or in kilometers per hour (km/h).

$$1 \text{ ft/min} = 0.00508 \text{ m/s} = 0.018\,288 \text{ km/h}$$
$$1 \text{ mph} = 1.609 \text{ km/h} = 0.447 \text{ m/s}$$
$$1 \text{ m/s} = 3.6 \text{ km/h} = 196.85 \text{ ft/min} = 2.237 \text{ mph}$$

Energy

All systems of measurement use the joule (J) for electrical energy. The SI system uses the joule for all forms of energy, including heat energy, but the British thermal unit (Btu) is used in conjunction with the British/American units. The calorie (cal), which was the unit of heat energy in the old metric system, is also still used.

The joule is a small unit, and kilojoules and megajoules are frequently used.

$$1 \text{ MJ} = 1000 \text{ kJ} \qquad 1 \text{ kJ} = 1000 \text{ J}$$
$$1 \text{ Btu} = 1.055 \text{ kJ} \qquad 1 \text{ kJ} = 0.984 \text{ Btu} = 239 \text{ cal}$$

1 Btu = 1 kJ is a common approximation.

Another frequently employed unit is the kilowatt-hour:

$$1 \text{ kWh} = 3.6 \text{ MJ}$$

Power and Heat Flow

All systems of measurement use

$$\text{watts (W)} = \text{joules per second (J/s)}$$

as units of electrical power. The SI system uses watts for all forms of power, including heat flow. In conjunction with British/American units, Btu/h are used for general thermal calculations, and tons of refrigeration for air conditioning. Horsepower are used for mechanical power.

$$1 \text{ MW} = 1000 \text{ kW} \qquad 1 \text{ kW} = 1000 \text{ W}$$
$$1 \text{ W} = 3.412 \text{ Btu/h} \qquad 1 \text{ Btu/h} = 0.293 \text{ W}$$

Some other conversions are:

$$1 \text{ kW} = 3412 \text{ Btu/h} = 860 \text{ kcal/h} = 239 \text{ cal/s}$$
$$= 0.284 \text{ tons of refrigeration}$$
$$= 1.341 \text{ British/American horsepower}$$
$$= 1.360 \text{ metric horsepower}$$

Power and Heat Flow per Unit Area

This is measured in Btu/h ft^2 in British/American units, and in W/m^2 in SI metric units.

$$1 \text{ Btu/h ft}^2 = 3.155 \text{ W/m}^2$$
$$1 \text{ W/m}^2 = 0.3170 \text{ Btu/h ft}^2$$

The met is a unit used in the literature on thermal comfort. It gives the average heat production rate per unit human body surface area, and it is taken as

$$1 \text{ met} = 18 \text{ Btu/h ft}^2 = 58.2 \text{ W/m}^2$$

Specific Heat (Heat Capacity per Unit Mass)

This is measured in British thermal units per pound per degree Fahrenheit (or Rankine), or in kilojoules per kilogram per degree Kelvin (or Celsius):

$$1 \text{ Btu/lb °F} = 4.1868 \text{ kJ/kg K}$$
$$1 \text{ kJ/kg K} = 0.2388 \text{ Btu/lb °F}$$

Thermal Conductivity (k-Value)

This is the property of a material to conduct heat through a unit area and unit thickness. In metric SI units it is measured in W/m K. In British/American units it can similarly be measured in Btu/h ft °F, but Btu in./h ft^2 °F is often more convenient, because heat flow is measured per square foot, and thickness in inches:

$$1 \text{ Btu in./h ft}^2 \text{ °F} = 0.1442 \text{ W/m K}$$
$$1 \text{ Btu/h ft °F} = 1.731 \text{ W/m K}$$

$$1 \text{ W/m K} = 6.933 \text{ Btu in./h ft}^2 \text{ °F}$$
$$= 0.5778 \text{ Btu/h ft °F}$$

Thermal Conductance, Transmittance, or Admittance (Heat Transfer Coefficient or *U*-Value)

This is the property of a given thickness of material, or an assembly of materials, forming a wall, floor or roof, to transmit heat through a unit surface. It is measured in Btu/h ft² °F or in W/m² K.

$$1 \text{ Btu/h ft}^2 \text{ °F} = 5.678 \text{ W/m}^2 \text{ K}$$
$$1 \text{ W/m}^2 \text{ K} = 0.1761 \text{ Btu/h ft}^2 \text{ °F}$$

Thermal Resistance (*R*-Value)

This is the reciprocal of the thermal conductance.

$$1 \text{ ft}^2 \text{ °F h/Btu} = 0.1761 \text{ m}^2 \text{ K/W}$$
$$1 \text{ m}^2 \text{ K/W} = 5.678 \text{ ft}^2 \text{ °F h/Btu}$$

Electrical Units

These are the same in all systems of measurement. The ampere (A), which measures electrical current, is the basic unit, from which the others are derived.

The volt (V) measures potential difference (or "voltage").

The ohm (Ω) measures electrical resistance.

$$\Omega = \text{V/A}.$$

The watt (W), which measures power, was also originally an electrical unit. W = V A for direct current (DC).

Units for Illumination Design

The fundamental unit is the lumen (lm), which is the measure of luminous flux from a light source, the illumination equivalent of power flow; it thus corresponds to the watt (W).

The intensity of a light source is measured in candela:

$$1 \text{ candela} = 1 \text{ lumen per steradian}$$

(see "Angular Measure," above)

The illuminance of a surface is measured in lux (lx):

$$1 \text{ lux} = 1 \text{ lumen/m}^2$$

These units have been accepted by the principal national bodies, including the Illuminating Engineering Society of North America. However, an older system based on the British/American units is still in use:

1 footcandle = 10.76 lux   1 lux = 0.093 footcandles

Acoustic Units

Sound pressure and sound power are measured in decibel. This a logarithmic ratio (Section 16.2), not an absolute unit. However, it can be made an absolute unit by referring it to a base measured in pascal (Pa) for sound pressure, or in watt (W) for sound power (Section 16.2).

Sound absorption is measured in sabin. The dimensions of the original sabin were square feet. A metric sabin is used for metric calculations; the two are related like ft² and m²:

$$1 \text{ foot sabin} = 0.0929 \text{ metric sabin}$$
$$1 \text{ metric sabin} = 10.764 \text{ foot sabin}$$

Index to Contributors

R. M. Aynsley, **133**
K. Bach, **406**
J. Ballinger, **366**
A. D. Bendtsen, **53**
R. E. Bucknam, **252**
L. Challis, **281**
W. W. S. Charters, **381**
H. J. Cowan, **1, 10, 26, 79, 148, 459, 464**
D. Freas, **53, 228**
T. M. Gavin, **252**
B. Givoni, **293**
K. I. Guthrie, **381**
T. Z. Harmathy, **441**

W. Julian, **308**
A. Lawrence, **269**
B. Martin, **92, 100**
M. Mehta, **193**
R. C. Moody, **228**
S. N. Pollalis, **115**
D. L. Schodek, **115**
J. M. Sherrard, **406**
P. R. Smith, **1, 10, 26, 79, 148, 423**
A. D. Stokes, **393**
S. V. Szokolay, **323**
L. Tall, **178**
F. Wilson, **108**

Index to Authors Cited

The numbers refer to the page where authors or, in the case of anonymous publications, the sponsoring organizations are cited. If there are several citations on the same page, the number is given in square brackets behind the page number.

M. Abramowitz, 9
D. A. Abrams, 51
Acoustical Society of America, 279
D. Adler, 440
R. R. Adler, 440
Agriculture, U. S. Department of, 78
Air Conditioning Engineers, American Society of Heating, Refrigerating and (ASHRAE), 147, 280, 307, 364[3], 392
W. Alexander, 25
C. B. Allendorfer, 9
Aluminum Association, Washington DC, 25
Aluminum Manufacturer's Association, Architectural, 107
America, Brick Institute of 99[3], 107[7]
American Architectural Manufacturers' Association, Des Plaines, IL, 90
American Concrete Institute, Detroit (ACI), 51[2], 226[4], 456, 458
American Hardboard Association, Palatine IL, 78[2]
American Institute of Steel Construction, Chicago (AISC), 191[2], 192[2], 226
American Institute of Timber Construction, Englewood CO (AITC), 78, 146, 251[5], 251[2]
American National Standards Institute, New York (ANSI), 78[2], 132, 251, 279, 440
American Plywood Association, Tacoma WA, 78, 250[2], 251
American Society for Testing and Materials, Philadelphia (ASTM), 24[31], 25[6], 51[46], 52[25], 78, 90[3], 250, 268, 279, 292, 457
American Society of Civil Engineers, New York (ASCE), 147[2], 191, 250[2], 268
American Society of Heating, Refrigerating, and Air Conditioning Engineers (ASHRAE), Atlanta GA, 147, 280, 307, 364[3], 392
American Welding Society, Miami, 192
R. Amon, 227
G. G. Amoroso, 51
J. Amrhein, 226
D. Ander, 307
Y. Anderberg, 456
R. D. Anchor, 458
D. Andrews, 292
Architectural Aluminum Manufacturers' Association, Chicago, 107
Architectural Manufacturers' Association, American, 90
Ove Arup and Partners, 177
ASCE, 147[2], 191, 250[1], 268
M. F. Ashby, 25
C. M. Ashley, 307
D. C. Ashley, 307
ASHRAE, 107, 147, 280, 307, 364[3], 392
A. J. Ashurst, 51

ASTM, 24[31], 25[6], 51[46], 52[25], 78, 90[3], 250, 268, 279, 292, 457
S. M. Atlas, 90
A. Auliciems, 364
(Australian) Experimental Building Station, 99[2], 457
Australian Timber Research Institute, 250, 251
Australian Uniform Building Regulations Coordinating Committee, 107
Australia, Standards Association of, 132[2], 147, 192, 226, 250[2], 279[4], 280[4], 392[3], 440
R. Aynsley, 147[2]

V. Babrauskar, 456
J. A. Baird, 250
E. Baker, 392
J. D. Balcomb, 380[3]
J. A. Ballinger, 380[2]
K. E. Bates, 392
C. Beall, 52, 226
J. J. Beaudoin, 91
A. Beck, 9
J. K. Beck, 227
V. Beck, 147
E. C. Becker, 291
W. A. Beckman, 392
L. S. Beedle, 192
D. A. Bender, 456
I. A. Benjamin, 456
L. L. Beranek, 279, 291[3], 292
W. G. Berl, 456
G. N. Berlin, 456
J. R. Beyers, 456[2]
L. Bickle, 307
R. E. Billow, 117
A. Blaga, 91
F. G. H. Blyth, 51
M. Boas, 9
R. H. Bogue, 52
BOCA National Building Code, 132
Bose Corporation, Framingham MA, 291
K. R. Bootle, 78
J. E. Bowles, 268
P. R. Boyce, 322
A. W. Brace, 24
E. F. Brater, 422
B. Bresler, 456
D. E. Breyer, 250, 251
Brick Institute of America, Reston, VA, 99[3], 107[7]

467

INDEX TO AUTHORS CITED

(British) Building Research Establishment, 51, 99[10], 107[8], 457
(British) Department of the Environment, 280
(British) Hydraulics Research Laboratory, 422
British Standards Institution 51[2], 99[2], 107, 132[2], 147, 192, 226, 227, 392
(British) Timber Research and Development Association, 250, 251
R. Brown, 114
H. D. Bruce, 456
H. H. Bryan, 301
J. A. Brydson, 90
B. Buchbinder, 456
Building Code, California State, 132
Building Code, Commonwealth of Massachusetts State, 132
Building Code of Chicago, 132
Building Code of the City of New York, 132
Building Codes and Regulations, Directory of State, 132
Building Materials Advisory Board, New York, 114
Building Officials and Code Administrators International, BOCA National Building Code, Country Club Hills IL, 132
Building Regulations Coordinating Council, Australian Uniform, 107
Building Research Establishment, Garston, England, 51, 99[10], 107[8], 457
Building Research Studies and Documentation, International Council for (CIB), 250, 456
Building Services Engineers, Chartered Institution of, 322, 364
Building Station, Experimental, Sydney, 99[2], 457
R. B. Bullen, 280
J. F. Burger, 291
H. Burgess, 78
M. A. Burgess, 280
Burt Hill Kosar Rittlemann, 307
R. Busch, 307
K. Butti, 379, 380, 392

California Energy Commission, Sacramento, 380
California State Building Code, 132
D. B. Callawey, 280, 292
T. Callen, 457
J. H. Callendar, 132
R. Calthorpe, 307
(Canadian) Institute for Research in Construction, 99[8], 107[16]
(Canadian) Laminated Timber Institute, 250, 251
(Canadian) National Building Code, 132, 147, 250, 457
Canadian Standards Association, 191, 226, 250[2], 440, 458
Canadian Wood Council, Ottawa, 250
R. G. Cann, 292
N. B. Carruthers, 137
G. T. Castino, 456
J. Cermak, 147
M. Chadnoff, 78
L. A. Challis, 292[2]
R. E. Chambers, 91
S. Chandra, 147, 307
Chartered Institution of Building Services Engineers, London, 322, 364
W. W. S. Charters, 392[5]
P. N. Cheremisinoff, 392
Chicago, Building Code of, 132
J. C. V. Chinappa, 392
D. E. Chinn, 379
K. K. Choi, 457[2]
W. J. Christian, 457
CIB, 250, 456
CIE, 322
Civil Engineers, American Society of, 147[2], 191, 250[2], 268
A. Clark, 147
B. L. Clarke, 51
Coastal Construction Manual, Federal Emergency Management Agency, Washington, 146
N. Cobb, 147
S. Coldicutt, 379
R. Coleman, 177
M. P. Collins, 237
Commerce, U. S. Department of, 78
Commission Internationale de l'Éclairage (CIE), 322
Commonwealth of Massachusetts State Building Code, 132

Concrete Institute, American, 51[2], 226[4], 456, 458
Concrete Masonry Association, National, Herndon VA, 227
H. S. Conover, 117
D. M. Considine, 392
CONSTRADO, London, 192
Constructional Steelwork Research and Development Organization, London (CONSTRADO), 192
J. P. Cook, 91
A. Cops, 280
C. A. Cornell, 457
Council on Tall Buildings and Urban Habitat, Bethlehem PA, 157[2]
H. J. Cowan, 9[2], 177[5], 226, 364, 439
J. R. Cowell, 280
R. J. M. Craik, 279
R. W. Crenshaw, 307
H. J. Critchfield, 147
H. J. Cumming, 447
W. G. Curtin, 227
J. T. Czarnecki, 392

N. C. Dalkley, 457
E. Danter, 364
S. Daryanani, 307
A. Davenport, 147
W. Davern, 392
E. H. Davis, 268
J. E. Deedham, 227
L. O. Degelman, 147
Department of the Environment, London, 280
H. E. Desch, 78
J. N. de Ris, 456[2]
Deutsches Institut für Normung (DIN), 457
W. Dickey, 227
W. C. Dickinson, 392
A. G. H. Dietz, 91, 250
R. Dillingham, 147
DIN (German Standards Institute), 457
Division of Building Research, National Research Council of Canada, see Institute for Research in Construction
C. W. S. Dixon, 392
Directory of State Building Codes and Regulations, Herndon VA, 132
P. Drew, 177[2]
D. Drysdale, 456, 458
J. W. Drysdale, 379
R. Dubout, 292
J. Duffie, 392

M. Ebata, 280
H. D. Eberhart,
Ecotech, Sheffield, England, 380
R. Edwards, 147
D. Egan, 292
H. W. Eickner, 457
B. Ellingwood, 132[2]
Emergency Management Agency, Federal, 146
Energy Agency, International, Paris, 379
Energy Commission, California, 380
Environment, Department of, London, 280
L. B. Escritt, 422
R. W. Eshelby, 251
B. H. Evans, 307
R. J. Evans, 251
Experimental Building Station, Sydney, 99[2], 457

C. Faber, 177
K. F. Faherty, 250
P. Fairey, 307
J. B. Fang, 456
A. H. Fanney, 392
V. Fassina, 51
Federal Aviation Administration, Washington, 280
Federal Emergency Management Agency, Washington, 146
E. B. Feldman, 117
C. P. Fenimore, 456
A. C. Fernandez-Pello, 456

R. L. Finney, 9
Fire Protection Association, National, Boston, 458
Fire Protection Engineers, Society of, 458
First International Conference on Lightweight Structures, Sydney, 177
D. Fitzroy, 292
H. Fletcher, 279
R. S. Fling, 226
M. G. Fontana, 25
M. Fontoyrant, 307
Forest Products Association, National, Washington, 28, 250[2]
Forest Products Laboratory, Madison WI, 107[2], 250
Forest Products Research Laboratory, England, 78[2]
J. Frados, 91
J. Francis, 147
A. D. Freas, 250
M. H. Freitag, 51
R. Friedman, 457
A. Frisch, 146
A. C. Frost, 52
T. Fujita, 146
S. K. Fuller, 456

T. V. Galambos, 192
M. Glbreath, 457
B. Gallagher, 422
L. Garding, 9
B. J. Garrida, 455
R. Geiger, 146
A. Gigli, 291
W. B. Gillett, 392
K. B. Ginn,
B. Givoni, 306, 307[5], 364, 379, 380
R. Glover, 307
K. A. Godfrey, 226
R. B. Goldner, 307[2]
A. Gomberg, 456
B. Gorenc, 192
E. Gossard, 146
M. Grayson, 52
D. W. Green, 78
N. D. Greene, 25
M. Gretener, 455
D. S. Gromola, 250
D. Gross, 456
D. Guise, 177
G. Gurfinkel, 250
A. H. Gustaferro, 456
K. I. Guthrie, 392

G. Hagglund, 456
A. S. Hall, 327
F. Hall, 422
P. Halley, 404
B. M. Halpin, 456
P. S. Hamblin, 457
G. Hans, 250
W. E. Hanson, 268
Hardboard Association, American, 78[2]
F. Harkleroad, 456
M. T. Harkleroad, 456
E. L. Harkness, 379
T. Z. Harmathy, 456[4], 457[10]
R. W. Harrigan, 392
C. M. Harris, 280, 292[2]
W. C. Hart, 458[2]
C. S. Harvey, 456
N. Hassoun, 226
S. R. Hastings, 307
W. D. Haworth, 422
J. Heading, 9
A. H. Hede, 280
J. Heger, 91
J. L. Heiman, 107
A. Hendry, 226
T. Herzog, 177

L. R. Higgins, 117
C. J. Hilado, 456, 457[2]
L. Hogben, 9
K. G. T. Hollands, 392
J. K. Holton, 307
R. G. Hopkinson, 307
L. J. Hossack, 422
E. L. Houghton, 147
V. Houk, 458
M. Houston, 307
T. Howard, 307
R. Hoyle, 250
G. J. Hughes, 405
M. A. Humphreys, 364
R. H. Humphreys, 280
S. Hurburt, 422
Hydraulics Research Laboratory, Wallingford, England, 422

IABSE, 132
K. U. Ingard, 292
S. H. Ingberg, 456
T. G. Ingersoll, 379, 380
Institute for Research in Construction, National Research Council, Canada, 99[8], 107[16]
International Conference of Building Officials, Uniform Building Code, Whittier CA, 90, 132, 226[2]
International Conference on Lightweight Structures, Sydney, 177
International Council for Building Research Studies and Documentation (CIB), Rotterdam, 250, 456
International Energy Agency, Paris, 379
International Standards Organization, Geneva, 99, 279[4], 280[2], 292
International Symposium on Pneumatic Structures, 177
International Association for Bridge and Structural Engineering (IABSE), Zurich, 132
C. Irwin, 147
N. Isyumov, 147

R. Jansson, 456
D. R. H. Jones, 25
R. J. Jones, 380
R. W. Jones, 307, 380
W. W. Jones, 456
J. Johnson, 226
R. Johnson, 307
S. M. Johnson, 191
W. G. Johnson, 9
R. C. Jordan, 392
V. L. Jordan, 292
W. G. Julian, 322

P. Kaplan, 455
A. Kareen, 147
J. Kaufman, 322
T. C. Kavanagh, 191
F. J. Keenan, 250
R. R. Kell, 364
F. N. Kemmer, 422
J. Kendrick, 307
M. Kersken-Bradley, 457
K.-I. Kimura, 364
L. F. Kinney, 407
L. E. Kinseler, 280, 292
B. Y. Kinzey, 405
D. W. Kirk, 227
R. L. Kirkegaard, 292
S. A. Klein, 392
M. Kline, 9
R. Knowles 379, 380
V. O. Knudsen, 292
O. H. Koenigsberger, 379, 380
C. E. Kosiewicz, 380
C. W. Kosten, 292
J. F. Kreider, 392
F. Kreith, 392
W. M. Kroner, 307

470 INDEX TO AUTHORS CITED

R. Kropfli, 146
K. D. Kryster, 279
U. J. Kurze, 280
V. Kurze, 291

R. Lambourne, 91
Laminated Timber Institute of Canada, 250, 251
R. N. Lane, 292
F. A. Lastrina, 456
G. M. Lavers, 78
M. Law, 456
A. Lawrence, 279[3], 280[2], 292
F. M. Lea, 51
K. Leet, 226
J. Lehr, 422
R. P. Leslie, 307
M. Levy, 177
H. S. Lew, 132
M. Lewin, 90
T. J. Lewis, 24
W. H. Lewis, 91, 117
I. N. Lickliter, 379
M. Liddament, 147
Lighting, International Commission on (CIE), 322
Lightweight Structures, First International Conference on, 177
T. T. Lie, 456
T. Y. Lin, 132, 177, 226
B. Y. H. Liu, 392
J. P. Locher, 291
P. Lord, 292
S. Q. Love, 379
P. M. Lurie, 192
M. Lynn, 458
R. H. Lyon, 292

R. F. McAlevy, 456
B. J. McCaffrey, 456
K. McCord, 307
J. McDonald, 146
R. McGrath, 52
W. J. McGuiness, 307, 404, 405, 440
J. H. McGuire, 456, 457[4]
D. A. McIntyre, 364
R. D. MacFarland, 380[2]
M. Mack, 392
R. Mackenzie, 292
C. O. Mackey, 364
A. D. McKinley, 458
R. McTaggart, 107
Q. Madill, 422
Z. Maekawa, 280
R. S. Magee, 456
M. Magnusson, 307
S. E. Magnusson, 457
Z. Makowski, 177
H. L. Malhotra, 458
E. W. Malone, 458
R. Mancher, 9
D. R. Madelstam, 392
T. A. Markus, 364, 380
B. Martin, 107
F. J. Martin, 456
P. L. Martin, 364
C. M. Marx, 456
Massachusetts State Building Code, Commonwealth of, 132
Materials, American Society for Testing and (ASTM), 24[31], 25[6], 51[46], 52[25], 78, 90[3], 268, 279, 292, 457
S. Mathews, 307
H. Matsumoto, 280
A. Mayhew, 379, 380
E. Mazria, 307, 379, 380
J. R. Mehaffey, 457[2]
K. Mehta, 147[2]
M. L. Mehta, 379
W. Melbourne, 147

W. S. Metes, 456
C. J. Mettem, 251
Midwest Plan Service, Iowa State University, Ames, 250
E. E. Mikeska, 292
V. V. Mikhailov, 51
L. Miller, 146
W. C. Miller, 457
Min Kantvowitz and Associates, 307
J. Minor, 146
M. Minten, 280
D. Mirkovich, 307
D. Mitchell, 227
J. Mock, 226
A. S. Moffat, 380
L. Moilett, 91
L. Monroe, 457
P. Montella, 91
R. C. Moody, 250
F. Moore, 307
W. Moore, 177
J. Morgan, 147
E. N. Morris, 364, 380
G. L. Morrison, 392
L. C. Morrow, 117
W. A. Munson, 279
R. M. Murphy, 457
M. V. K. Murthy, 392
S. S. Murthy, 392
S. Muster, 279

National Building Code, BOCA, 132
National Building Code of Canada, 132, 147, 250, 457
National Building Technology Centre, Sydney, see Experimental Building Station
National Bureau of Standards, Washington, 78 107[5], 251
National Concrete Masonry Association, Herndon VA, 227
National Fire Protection Association, Boston, 458
National Forest Products Association, Washington, 78, 250[2]
National Particle Board Association, Gaithersburg MD, 78[2]
M. Navvab, 307
Navy, U. S. Department of the, 268[2]
E. Ne'eman, 307[2]
H. E. Nelson, 456
P. L. Nervi, 177
E. Neufert, 439
A. M. Neville, 52
B. G. Neville, 226[2]
J. R. Newman, 9
New York, Building Code of, 132
New Zealand, Standards Association of, 132
T. Nimura, 280
A. Norton, 457

C. O. Oakley, 9
F. L. Offensend, 456
A. Olgyay, 307
V. Olgyay, 307, 364, 380
H. Olin, 91, 117
B. Onnermark, 456
A. K. Osborne, 25
Ove Arup and Partners, 177
E. C. Ozelton, 250

J. K. Page, 379
R. Panek, 91
R. Pape, 456
J. S. Parikh, 456
P. H. Parkin, 280
Particleboard Association, National, Gaithersburg VA, 78[2]
J. L. Pauls, 457
E. Pearce, 90
R. B. Peck, 268
A. Penwarden, 147
J. Perlin, 379, 380, 392
R. Persson, 52

J. Peter, 52
J. Peterka, 147
K. Petherbridge, 404
O. Petterson, 457[2]
R. Peyret, 147
A. Pflüger, 177
R. O. Phillips, 379
S. U. Pillai, 227
J. Pitts, 52
W. Place, 307
R. Plunkett, 279
Plywood Association, American, 78, 250[2], 251
Pneumatic Structures, International Symposium on, 177
H. W. Pollack, 25
D. Popovicz, 52
F. Porges, 404, 405
H. G. Poulos, 268
T. L. Pryor, 392[2]
R. J. Puffett, 422
J. R. Purkiss, 458

J. G. Quintiere, 456[4]
J. D. Quirt, 279

G. Ramachandran, 455
G. S. Ramaswamy, 177
L. G. Ramer, 291, 292
B. V. Rangan, 227
R. D. Rank, 307
J. Rearson, 147
J. M. Redheffer, 9
T. Reinhold, 147
C. E. Reynolds, 227
J. S. Reynolds, 307, 404, 405, 440
D. R. Richmond, 392
C. L. Robbins, 307[2]
J. J. Roberts, 227
G. O. Robinette, 379
I. H. Rose, 9
H. J. Roux, 456
R. T. Ruegg, 456

P. E. Sabine, 291
W. C. Sabine, 292
G. G. Sacerdoti, 291
S. Sahlin, 52
C. G. Salmon, 177, 226
M. Salvadori, 177
Salzer Technology Enterprises, Santa Monica CA, 404
M. A. Sattler, 379
R. Scanlan, 147
E. L. Schaffer, 250, 456, 457
M. Schiller, 380
Schmidt, 91, 117
R. Schneider, 227
U. Schneider, 456
D. L. Schodek, 177
B. Schonland, 404
T. J. Schultz, 292
Scientific American, 9
Sealants and Waterproofers Institute, Chicago, 91
A. B. Searle, 52
P. E. Secker, 24
G. Sedin, 457
S. Selkowitz, 307[2]
R. J. Shaffer, 52
H. M. Sharp, 405
S. Sharples, 379
C. Shaw, 147
G. Shaw, 227
P. G. Sheasby, 24
G. E. Sherwood, 250
A. J. Shibe, 456
L. L. Shreir, 25
D. Shrifteilig, 307

W. A. Shurcliff, 379
E. Simin, 146
M. G. Smart, 380
G. Smethurst, 422
B. A. Smith, 114
J. M. Smith, 292
P. R. Smith, 9, 364, 439
Society of Fire Protection Engineers, 458
I. S. Sokolnikoff, 9
Solar Energy Research Institute, Golden CO, 380
Solar Rating and Certifying Corporation, Washington DC, 392
L. A. Soltis, 250
T. Sone, 280
Southern Pine Marketing Council, New Orleans LA, 250
F. Spiegelhalter, 457
B. Stahl, 379
Standards Association of Australia, 132[2], 147, 192, 226, 250[2], 279[4], 280[4], 392[3], 440
Standards Association, Canadian, 191, 226, 250[2], 440, 458
Standards Association of New Zealand, 132
Standards Institute, American National, 78[2], 132, 251, 279, 440
Standards Institute, German (DIN), 457
Standards Institution, British, 99[2], 107, 132[2], 147, 192, 227, 392
Standards, National Bureau of, Washington DC, 78, 107[5], 251
Standards Organization, International, Geneva, 99, 279[4], 280[2], 292
K. P. Stark, 392
Steel Construction, American Institute of (AISC), 191[2], 192[2], 226
Steel Research and Development Organization, Constructional, London (CONSTRADO), 192
I. A. Stegun, 9
B. Stein, 307, 404, 405, 440
E. Stein, 132
D. Stevenson, 457
W. B. Stine, 392
S. D. Stotesbury, 132, 177, 226
G. R. Strakosch, 439
R. Strauch, 146
A. Street, 25
V. L. Streeter, 147
R. Stroh, 250
K. Sumi, 456, 457
M. Swami, 147
S. V. Szokolay, 364, 379, 380, 440

L. Tall, 191, 192
Tall Buildings, Council on, 147[2]
F. Tamamini, 456
G. T. Tamura, 456
T. Taylor, 147
W. Taylor, 457
W. H. Taylor, 52
D. Templeton, 292
S. Ternoey, 307
Testing and Materials, American Society for (ASTM), 24[31], 25[6], 51[46], 52[25], 78, 90[3], 250, 268, 279, 292, 457
A. Tewarson, 456
P. Thiery, 90
G. N. Thomas, 9
J. Thor, 457[2]
T. H. Thornburn, 268
J. Threlkeld, 264
Timber Construction, American Institute of, 78, 146, 250[5], 251[2]
Timber Engineering Company, New York, 250
Timber Research and Development Association, London, 250, 251
Timber Research Institute, Australian, 250, 251
R. Tinyou, 192
M. J. Tomlinson, 268.2?
E. Torroja, 177
J. E. Traister, 404
N. H. Tran, 392
Transport Research Board, U. S., 280
J. P. Trembley, 9
P. Trengenza, 439
Truss Plate Institute, Madison WI, 250[3], 251[2]
T. Tschanz, 147

INDEX TO AUTHORS CITED

Y. Tsuchiya, 456
P. Tutt, 440

G. Underwood, 457, 458
Uniform Building Code, International Conference of Building Officials, Whittier CA, 90, 132, 226[3]
Unisearch, Sydney, 380
U. S. Department of Agriculture, 78
U. S. Department of Commerce, 78
U. S. Department of the Navy, 268[2]
U. S. Transport Research Board, Washington DC, 280

J. F. van Straaten, 379, 380
L. H. Van Vlack, 25
P. C. Varley, 25
P. S. Veneklassen, 292
B. Vickery, 147
J. E. Volkman, 291
G. Von Bekesy, 279
J. Voytek, 422

F. F. Waangard, 250
R. F. Warner, 227

T. E. Waterman, 456, 457[2]
E. H. Waters, 107
D. Watson, 379, 380
J. M. Watts, 455
B. D. Weiss, 192
Welding Society, American, 192
Western Wood Products Association, Portland OR, 250
R. N. White, 177
R. L. Wiegel, 132
W. Williams, 404
T. Williamson, 250, 379
A. G. Wilson, 455
F. Wilson, 114[2]
E. M. Winkler, 52
R. A. Winnett, 379
F. Woeste, 250, 456
Wood Council, Canadian, 250
W. O. Wray, 380[2]
L. T. Wright, 364

L. N. Zaccaro, 9
J. J. Zahn, 457
L. Zeewart, 268

Subject Index

The numbers in normal type refer to the page where reference is made to the subject; in a few instances this continues on the subsequent page.
Numbers in bold type denote major references which may continue for several pages, for the entire section, or the entire chapter.

abrasion resistance of concrete aggregate, 36
abrasion resistance of plastics, 84
abrasion testing, 112
ABS, 82
absolute humidity, 327
absorbed sound, 273
absorber plate, 383
absorptance, thermal, 326
absorption refrigerator, 358
absorptive materials, 284, 287
absorptive surfaces, 281
absorptivity, thermal, 438–448
AC 394, 432
accelerators for concrete, 41
acceptable frequency of elevator service, 430, 436
acceptance testing for sound attenuation, 279
access control for security, 454
access to buildings, 424, 425
ACI Code, 193
acid refractories, 14
acoustic insulation, 23, 273, 275
acoustic models, 291
acoustic plaster, 32
acoustics, **269, 281**
acrylics, 82, 85, 86, 87, 90, 170
acrylonitrile butadiene styrene, 82
active solar energy systems, **373**
activity, physical, of persons in a room, **331,** 334
adaptation luminance, 309
adhesives, 24, 31, **87,** 248
adiabatic dehumidification, 328
admittance, thermal, 340, **341,** 375
admittance method of passive solar design, 375
adobe, 48, 340
aerated concrete, 43, 340
aerodynamic damping, 141
aerodynamics, 138–140
A-frames (roof structures), 234
afwillite, 33
age-hardening, 16
aging, 16, 21, 33
aggregate for concrete,
   coarse, 35
   fine, 35
   lightweight, 35, 340, 345
aggregate reaction (with cement), 35

airborne sound transmission, 272, 281
air changes, number of, 345
air conditioners, 358-361
air conditioning, 144, 344, 356, **358,** 418, 455
   location of exhaust stacks, 146
   noise from, 272, 276, 281
air conditioning ducts, 87, 276, 451
aircraft noise, 278
air currents due to a fire, 443
air entraining agents, 34, **40,** 41
air exhaust systems, 355
air extract systems, 355
air filters, 356
air filtration, 355
air flow, 144, 329, **334**
air infiltration, 144, 443
air intakes and exhausts, location of, 146
air movement for thermal comfort, 144, 329, **344,** 353
air, velocity of
   in air conditioning ducts, 361
   in room, 334
AISC Manual, 179, 218
alabaster, 32
alarm systems, 453
alclad, 21
alkali-aggregate reaction, 35
alkali-paint reaction, 90
alkyd resins, 83, 90
allowable stress, 178–186
allowable stress design, 178
alloys, 12, 17, 18, 22
alloys of aluminum, **20**
alloy steels, **17**
alpha iron, 12, 15
alternating current, 394
alternating solar gain, 346
alumina, 18
aluminium, *see* aluminum
aluminous cement, 34
aluminum, 11, 16, 17, **18,** 19, **20,** 24, 150
   thermal movement of, 95
aluminum alloys, **20**
aluminum foil, 20, 87, 340, 341, 342
aluminum powder, 33
American Concrete Institute, 193
American Institute of Steel Construction, 179, 218

SUBJECT INDEX

American National Standards, 116, 134, 248
American Society for Testing and Materials, 24, 33, 35, 37, 38, 40, 51, 70, 90, 111, 252, 256, 265, 268, 292, 445, 450
American Society of Heating, Refrigerating, and Air Conditioning Engineers, 296, 307, 326, 332, 333, 374
American standard lumber sizes, 71
American standard steel sections, 14
ammonia, 358, 390
amplification of music, 290
anchorage of reinforcement, 204
anchorage of retaining walls, 262
anemometers, 137
angle of incline
   for escalators, 428
   for ladders, 427
   for ramps, 427
   for stairs, 427
anhydrite, 32
anhydrous gypsum plaster, 32
anisotropy of timber, 55
annealing, 16, 21
annoyance criteria (for noise), 272
annual rings in timber, 55
annual value (of past, present, and future expenditure on a building), 111
annulus, 5
anodizing, 17, **21**, 24
ANSI, 116, 134, 146, 248
anticyclones, 133
antimony oxide, 90
apartments, 432, 452, 454; *see also* dwellings
APP, 102
apparent brightness, 313
arch action in masonry walls, 159
arched roofs, 169, 171, 173, 174, 176, 234, 244, 245
arches, 164, 165, 169, 234, 244
area surveillance system, 454
areas of geometric figures and solids, 5–8
argillaceous limestone, 27
argillaceous sandstone, 27
argon, 11, 23
artificial light, *see* electric light
ASHRAE, 296, 307, 326, 332, 333, 374
asphalt, 86, 96, 101, 102, 342
asphalt shingles, 86, 101
Assman hygrometer, 328
assumptions made in reinforced concrete design, 196
ASTM standards, 24, 33, 35, 37, 38, 40, 51, 70, 90, 111, 252, 256, 265, 268, 292, 445, 456
atactic polypropylene, 102
atomic number, 10
atomic weight, 10
atoms, 11
atriums, 446
attached sun spaces for passive solar heating, 379
attenuation of noise, 273–278
attics, 342
audience absorption of sound, 281, 285
auditorium shape, 291
auditoriums, 289, 291, 362
   design of, **281**
   for music, 290, 291,
   for speech, 289
augered piles, 214, 258
augers, 255, 261
austenite, 15, 18
automatic doors, 424, 455
average, 4, 39
A-weighted sound pressure level, 271
axial flow fans, 356

baby carriages, 424
backfill, 265
background noise, 272
backup diesel-driven plant for uninterruptible power supply, 403
bag of cement, 36
baggage, 428
bakelite, 82
balanced reinforced concrete sections, 196
balconies in a fire, 450
barriers for noise attenuation, 278
bar sizes for metric bars, 194
bar sizes for standard (inch-sized) bars, 194
basement walls, 213
basic refractories, 14
baths, 409, 418
batts of insulation, 343
bauxite, 18, 34
beam-and-stringer grade lumber, 70
beam-columns, **185**, 212
beam theory for trusses, 160
beams, 14, 44, 45, 70, 149, **151**, 167, 168, **181, 195**, 230, 239
bearing joint, 186
bearing stress, 187
bedding of tiles, 96
bending moment coefficients for beams and one-way slabs, theoretical, 156–159
bending moment coefficients, empirical (for reinforced concrete design), 205–206
bending moment coefficient tables
   for cantilevers, 156
   for continuous beams, 158
   for fixed-ended beams, 157
   for simply supported beams, 156
bending moments, 151, 181–186, 198–199, 209, 217, 225
bending strength of timber, 60, 61, 65
bending stress in materials, 151, 182, 196
bending, theory of, 151
bentonite, 89
benzene, 79, 80, 89
Bernoulli's equation, 140
Bessemer process, 14
béton brut, 41
billets of steel, 14
binaural perception, 270
binomial series, 2
bioclimatic chart, 332
bitumen, 86, 96, 99, 101, 102
bituminous felt, 86, 103, 342
black-body radiator, 326
bleeding of concrete, 40
blinds, 346
blocks, concrete, 43, 44, 94, 95, 206, 341
blooms of steel, 14
blow molding of plastics, 84
bluff body aerodynamics, **138**
boards of lumber (timber), 70
body-worn microphones, 290
BOCA National Building Code, 116
body-tinted glass, 50, 295, 296, 346
boilers, 411, 412
bolted connections, 187, 246
bolts, 23, 186, 233
bond between steel and concrete, 14, 44
bond breaker (in movement joints), 97
bonding of bricks and blocks, 44
bond stress in reinforced concrete, 204
booster pump, 406, 407
bore holes, 255
boundary layer (of air), 134, 136
box gutters, 415
bracing (during erection), 249, 264
brass, 22
brazing, 23, 24
breeze, 144
brick veneer, 45, 341
bricks
   clay, **44**, 95, 325, 340, 375, 444
   concrete, 43, 47
   sand-lime, 47, 95

SUBJECT INDEX

brickwork growth, 45
brightness, 313
British thermal unit, 462
brittleness, 13, 26, 49
broken windows in a fire, 450
bronze, 22, 31
Btu, 459, 462
buckling, 150, 175, 179, 181, 183, 212
buffers for elevators, 433
buffeting by wind, 141
Building Code Requirements for Reinforced Concrete (ACI 318-83), 193
building codes, 116, 441
building materials, **10, 26, 61, 79**
    weight of, 117
building services, 109, 168, **354, 381, 393, 406, 423**
    noise control, 276
built-in beams, 153, 154, 157
built-up felt roofing, 102
bulk density, 36
burglar alarms, 453
burglaries, 453
bush hammering, 42
butadiene, 82, 87, 90
butterfly, solar access, 371, 372
butt joint, 96, 187
buttresses, 172

cables, 167, 170, 172, 173, 176, 216, 217
cable-stayed beams, 167, 170
cable-stayed cantilevers, 170
CADD, 191, 315
cadmium plating, 23
caissons, 214, 258
calcareous limestone, 27
calcareous sandstone, 27
calcium carbonate, 27, 29, 32, 33
calcium chloride 40, 41
calcium silicate, 33
calcium-silicate bricks, 47
calcium sulfoaluminate, 33
calculation of fire resistance, 447–449
call buttons for elevators, 431
calorific value, 324
cambium, 54
candela, 310, 463
cantilevers, 152, 156, 170
capacitative thermal insulation, 338–340
capacitor, electric, 394
capacity of elevators, 436, 438
capacity of escalators, 430
capacity of moving walkways, 430
carbon, 11, 13, 15, 18
carbonation, 93
carbon chains, 80
carbon monoxide, 451
carbon rings, 80
carpets, 85
carrying capacity of elevators, 436, 438
carrying capacity of escalators, 430
carrying capacity of moving walkways, 430
car size of elevators, 430, 431, 435
case hardening, 16
cast-in-place piles, 214, 257
cast iron, 14
cathedral glass, 49
caulking, 86, 87
cavitation, 276
cavity ratio, room (for lighting design), 313
cavity walls, 45, 104, 341, 342, 375, 450
CCTV, 454
cedar, 60, 74, 81, 89
ceiling distribution of services, 109, 399
ceiling load, 125
ceiling plenum, 356

ceiling radiators, 357
ceiling reflectors, 290
ceilings for timber buildings, 240
ceilings, sound transmission through, 276, 279
ceiling tiles, 76
cellular concrete, 43
celluloid, 82
cellulose, 55
cellulose acetate, 82, 87
cellulose plastics, 82, 87
cellulosic materials, 55, 444
Celsius, 323, 462
cement, 33
cement chemistry, 33
cementite, 15
cement-lime mortar, 32, 34, 47, 94, 95
cement mortar, 34, 47
cement paint, 34, 90
cement plaster, 34
centigrade, 323, 462
central heating, 357
central processing unit for fire protection and security, 453
central refuse incinerator, 422
centrifugal fans, 356
ceramic-coated opaque glass, 49
ceramics, 10, **36**
char-forming materials, 443, 444, 449
char-forming plastics, 449
chimney plumes, 146
chlorinated rubber, 90
chlorine, 11, 406
chloroprene, 98
chromium, 10, 17, 18
churches, 244, 289
chutes for garbage, 421, 422
CIE, 311, 313, 318, 322
cladding, 104, 142
clay, 33, 44, 89, 253, 417
cleaning colored cement, 34
clearance for elevators, 434
clear coatings, 90
clear glass, 49, 295, 306
clear sky, 347
clearstory windows, 302
clear timber, 64, 74, 78
clerestories, 302
climate, 133, 334–339
climatic data, 335
climatic design, **351**
clinker bricks, 45
clo, 333, **334**
closed-circuit television, 454
clothing, 334
cloud cover, 335
coal heating, 356
coarse aggregate, 35
coarse-grained soil, 232
coatings, clear, 90
coefficient(s)
    of thermal expansion of metals, 19
    of utilization, 313
    of variation, 4
cohesion in soils, 254, 256
cohesive concrete mix, 38
cohesive soils, 254, 256
cold climate, 335, 336
cold rolling, 14, 15, 19
cold water, *see* water
cold water pipes, 408
cold working, 16, 21
collapsing soils, 267
color, 308
    of venetian blinds that is thermally desirable, 301–302
colored cement, 34, 43
colored glass, 49

476 SUBJECT INDEX

colorimetric systems, 311
color matching, 311
color mixing, 318
color rendering, 318
color temperature, 317
colour, see color
columbium, 11, 18
columns, 149, 167, 168, **183, 211,** 231, 232
    elimination of, at ground floor level, 169
    subject to axial load and bending moment, 185, 212
combustible materials, 444
comfort in climbing stairs, 427
comfort, thermal, 144, **330,** 332, 333, 455
comfort zone, thermal, 332, 333, 336–339
communications (telephones, facsimile machine, computers), **401**
compaction, 253, 264, 266
compartments, fire, 442, 444, 446, 447
COM-PLY, 76
composite beams and slabs, 218
composite columns, 221
composite construction of steel and reinforced concrete, **218**
composite decks, 220
compressibility of soils, 254, 259
compressible fillers for joints, 93
compression flanges of steel beams, 180–183
compression members, 167, 168, **183, 211,** 231, 232
compression molding, 84
compressive strength
    of concrete, 38, 39, 193
    of timber, 60, 61, 64
compressor-type refrigeration unit, 358
computer-aided design
    for direct solar gain, 378
    for lighting design, 315
    for shadow-casting programs, 371
    for structural design and drawing, 191
    for thermal design, 350
computers, 109, 191, 315, 350, 397, 402, 403, 453
    data handling rates, 402
    ease of relocation, 109
    uninterruptible power supply, 402, 403
computing networks, 401
concave sound reflectors, 283
concentrated loads, 118, 119, 152, 156–158
concert halls, 291
concrete, **23,** 193
    maximum strain in, 196
    no fines, 35
    reinforced, weight of, 117
    thermal properties, 325, 338, 340–343, 444
concrete additives, 33, 40
concrete aggregates, **34**
    classification, 35
    coarse, 35
    fine, 35
    particle size, 35
concrete blocks and bricks, 43, 44, 47, 94, 95, 206, 341
concrete cover, 203
concrete decks, weight of, 117
concrete domes, 169, 172
concrete paint, 34, 89, 90
concrete piles, 214, 257
concrete slabs on grade (on ground), 106, 343, 374–376
concrete slabs, suspended, **205**
concrete strength, 38, 39, 193
concrete structures, **193**
concrete surface finish, **41**
condensate, exclusion of, 102, 344
condensation, 100, 344
conductance, thermal, 324
conduction, thermal, 330, 387
conductivity, thermal, 324
cone, 7
conference halls, 289
connections for timber, 246, 247

connectors for timber, 232
conservatory for passive solar heating, 379
consolidation, 254
continuous beams, 153, 255, 158, 159, 166
contraction joints, 93
contrast, visual, 10, 312
control gear (for lamps), 318, 320, 321
control joints, 45
convection, 326, 330, 387, 446, 449
convectors, 357
conversion of aluminous cement, 34
convex sound reflectors, 284
cooling of buildings, **358**
copper, 11, 17, 19, **22,** 86, 385, 401, 408
cork, 85, 98, 325
corridors, 423, **425**
corrosion protection, **16,** 89
corrugated fibrous cement sheet, 342
corrugated metal, 17, 20, 101, 342
COR-TEN, 18
cosine law, 322, 320
cost, relative contribution to the, by vertical loads and by horizontal loads, 168
cost, first, 111
cost, life-cycle, 111
cotton, 85, 176
counterweights for elevators, 432
cover of concrete over reinforcement, 203
crack control in reinforced concrete, 203
cracking, 29, 33
crawl spaces under timber floors, 106, 237, 373
creep
    of concrete, 202
    of plastics, 84
    of timber, 67
creosote, 69
crime protection, **453**
critical points in a phase diagram, 15
cross falls in surface drainage, 417
cross ventilation, 304
crown of arch or dome, 165, 171
crown glass, 49
crystal structure, 11–13
cumulative temperature deficit, 348
curing membrane, 40
curing of concrete, **36,** 40
curing of plastics, 87
current, electric, 394
curtains, 344
curtain walls, 18, 20, 22
curved glulam structures, 234
curved roofs, snow load on, 125, 126
cyclones, 133
cylindrical structures, 173, 174

damage from high winds, 133, 134
dampers
    in air conditioning ducts, 356, 451
    for vibration control, 276
damping of aerodynamic vibrations, 141
damping of structure-borne vibrations, 375
damp-proof courses, 20, 22, 46, 105, 106
daylight, 309, 314, 316, 320
daylight illuminance, 314
daylighting, 293, 302, 314, 316, 320
dB, 271
dB (A), 271
DC, 394, 432
dead loads, **116,** 195, 209
deafness, 270
decay of timber, 58, 69
decibel, 271, 463
deciduous trees for sun penetration, 373
decrement factor in heat flow calculations, 339, 340, **341,** 343, 349
deep foundations, 257

defense against the spread of fire, **446**
deflection
 of aluminum, 20
 of concrete, **202**
 of plastics, 84
 of steel, 183
 of timber, 59
deformation, 11-16, **92**
degree-days, 348
degree-hours, 348
dehumidification, 328, 331
Delphi assessments, 452, 453
density, 323, 460
 of concrete aggregate, 36
 of lightweight concrete, 43
 of metals, 19
 of plastics, 82, 84
 of timber and wood products, 57, 60-63, 76
density of pedestrian traffic, 426
desert climate, 325
design assumptions for reinforced concrete, 196
design
 of composite beams, **218**
 of columns, **221**
 of load-bearing masonry walls, **221**
 of prestressed concrete, **216**
 of reinforced concrete beams, **196**
 of reinforced concrete columns, **211**
 of reinforced concrete slabs, **196, 205**
 of steel beams, **181**
 of steel columns, **183**
 of steel ties, **180**
deterioration of concrete surfaces, 42
deterioration of natural stone, **28**
dew point, 100, 328, 344
diagonal compression, 200
diagonal tension, 200
differentiation table, 3
diffraction of sound, 283, 284
diffusing luminaires, 319
diffusing windows, 319
diffusion of light, 319
dimension lumber, 70, 71
dimmers, 322
dimming, 320
diorite, 27
direct current, 394
direct gain of solar heat, 294, 305
direct glare, 308
direct illuminance, 313
direct gain method of passive solar heating, 294, **305**, 368, **377**
dirt (on windows and/or lamps), 322
disability glare, 310
disabled people, 424
discomfort glare, 310, 315
disintegration of concrete in a fire, 35
dislocation (in a crystal), 12
dispersion of gaseous wastes, 146
dispersion of sound, 283
dissipative surfaces (in an auditorium), 282
distemper, 88
distributed loads, 118, 119
distribution of electric power, **396**
district heating, 357
diurnal variation of temperature, 335
dolerite, 27
dolomite, 27, 48
domes, 169, 171, 172, 244, 245
door left open in a fire, 450
doors, 20, 424, 450, 451, 455
 automatic, 424, 455
 as barriers against smoke, 451
 for elevator cars, 433, 434
double-deck elevators, 439
double glazing, 50, 295, 296, 306, 342, 346

double shear, 186
double tees (prestressed concrete), 216
doubly reinforced concrete beams, 198
Douglas fir, 55, 57, 60, 61, 64
downpipes, *see* downspouts
downspouts, 18, 22, 84, 416
downwash (of air), 142
draft conditions in a fire, 442, 450
drafty, 334
drainage, 104, 254, 262, **415**
drained joint, 104
draught, draughty, *see* draft, drafty
draw wires for electric conduits, 399
dressed lumber, 70
driving rain, 100, 103
dry bulb temperature, 327
drywall construction, 32, 86, 90
ductility, 13, 178
ducts for ventilation and air conditioning, 276, 356
dumbwaiters, 423
durability, 16, 26, 57, 83, 85, 90, **108**
Dutch cone penetrometer, 256
dwellings, 447, 452; *see also* apartments
dyes, 21, 90
dynamic loads, 122, 141

e, 1-3
ear, structure of, 270
earlywood, 55
earthenware, 47
earth pressure, 122
earthquake loads, 120-122, **129**
earthquakes, 120, 121, 267
eaves, 101, 105, 140
 projecting, 140
eaves gutters, 415
echoes, 283
"economy cycle" in air conditioning, 362
effective emittance, thermal, 327
effective length of steel columns, 184
effective temperature, 331
efflorescence, 29, 45, 113
eggcrate shading, 294, 298
egress from building, 424, 451
elasticity, 12, 19, 59, 62, 150, 178, 183, 194
elasticity, modulus of, 13, 150
 of aluminum, 19
 of concrete, 196
 of plastics, 84
 of steel, 19
 of wood, 59-62, 64, 66
elastomeric membranes, 85, 102
elastomers, 86, 87
electric circuits in parallel, 395, 396
electric circuits in series, 395
electric current, 394
electric heaters for hot water, 413
electric impedance, 395
electric lamps, **316**
electric light, 309, **316**
electric lighting, heat load due to, 362
electric outlet, 398
electric power distribution, **396**
electric power distribution paths, **399**
electric resistance, 394
electric sink grinder for refuse, 421
electric switchboard, 397-399
electric voltage, 394
electric wiring, 398
electricity in buildings, **393**
electricity tariffs, 362
electrochemical series of metals, 17
electrochromic glazing, 296
electrodes for welding, 23, 187
electrolyte, 17, 22

electromagnetic waves, 269, 326
electrons, 10, 11
electrostatic filters, 356
elements, 11
elevator lobbies, 431
elevators, 168, 277, 423, **430**
  doors for, 433, 434
  speeds, 435, 436, 438
  wind effects on, 146
elimination of interior columns, 167, 168, 169
  at ground level, 169
EMC, 56
emergency lighting, 314
emittance, thermal, 326
emulsion paints, 88
encastré beams, 153, 154, 157
end-bearing piles, 214, 257
end laps for roof sheets, 101
energy conservation, 320, **361, 366,** 455
energy required for hot water, 382
enthalpy, 328, 329
entrained air (in concrete), 40
entrapped air (in concrete), 40
environment, luminous, 316
environment, visual, 308
environmental impact, 142
environmental technology, **323, 366, 381, 393, 406, 423, 441**
environmental temperature, 374
environmental wind effects, 142
EPDM, 387
epoxy, 31, 83, 85, 87, 90
equilibrium, 148
equilibrium moisture content, 56
equivalent stress block for reinforced concrete beam, 197
erection of timber structures, 249
escalators, 423, **428**
escalators
  carrying capacities, 429, 430
  mechanical details, 429
  sizes, 429
  speeds, 429
escape in case of fire or emergency, 423, 424
estimate of slab self-weight, 117
ET, 331
ethane, 80
ethylene, 80, 82
ethylene-propyleme-diene monomer, 387
ettringite, 33, 41
Euler formula, 150
Euler load, 150, 183
eutectic, 15
eutectoid, 15
evacuated tube solar collectors, 383
evacuation lighting, 314
evacuation of building, 424, 451
evaporation, heat loss by, 387
evaporative cooling, 330, 331, 351, 353
excavation, 263
exclusion of condensate, 102, 106
exclusion of water and condensation, **100**
exfiltration of air, 443
exhaust fans, wind effects on, 146
exhaust of air, location of, 146
exhaust systems, 355
exit doors to open without key, 424
exits, 424
expanded polystyrene, 80, 341, 342
expanded polyurethane, 81
expansion joints, 93, 94, 95
expansion jonts for gutters, 415
expansion
  of brickwork, 45, 93, 94, 95
  of concrete, 33, 41, 93, 95
  of metals, 95
  of stone, 95
  of timber, 57, 93, 95

expansive cement, 41
explosive rivets, 23
exposed aggregate, 42, 43
exterior-type plywood, 248
external shading, 297–301, 346
external walls, 103
extract systems (for air), 355
extrusion, 19, 20, 22, 45, 83
Eyring reverberation time formula, 288

fabrication
  of aluminum alloys, 19, 23
  of concrete, 38, 43
  of plastics, 83
  of steel, 14, 23
  of steel structures, 189, 191
  of timber, **69,** 229
fabrics in fires, 441
fabric structures, 176
face brick, 45
factor of safety, 182, 195
Fahrenheit, 323, 461
failure modes of reinforced concrete, 195
failure of electric power, 401
failure path through bolt holes, 180
fan-convectors, 357
fan noise, 276
fans, 346, 451
fasteners for timber, 232
fatigue strength, 65
faucets, 409
F-chart for sizing solar water systems, 386
feldspar, 27, 48
fenestration, see windows
ferrite, 15
fiberboard, 76, 77, 235
fiberglass, 83
fiber saturation point of timber, 56
fibers, optical, 401
fibre, see fiber
fibrous cement sheets, 342
fibrous plaster, 32
fill (for foundations), 264, 266
fillers for movement joints, 98, 99
fillet weld, 187
filters for air, 356, 360
filtration of air, 355
fine aggregate, 35
fine-grained soils, 253, 254, 267
fineness of cement, 33
fire compartments, 442, 444, 446, 447
fire, design for protection from, **442**
fire detector systems, 414
fire extinguishers, 415
fire fighting, water supply for, **411**
fire hose reels, 413, 414
fire hydrants, 414
fire load, 447–449
fire protection, 32, 168, **441**
fire resistance, 19, 35, 45, 69, 84, 99, **446**
fire retardants
  for carpets, 85
  for plastics, 84
  for timber, 69, 90
fire safety, 442
fire sprinkler systems, 414, 415, 446
fire ventilation (at above-normal pressure), 356
first cost, 111
fixed-ended beams, 153, 154, 157
fixed shading, 297–300
fixture units, 419
flakeboard, 234, 235
flame detectors, 414, 446, 450, 455
flame retardants
  for carpets, 85

for plastics, 84
for timber, 69, 90
flaming combustion, 444
flammability of materials, 285, **444**
flange, limitation on width of,
for composite sections, 218
for reinforced concrete sections, 200
for steel sections, 179
flashings, 20, 22
flashover, 445
flat plate solar collectors, 383
flat plates (reinforced concrete), 207, 208
flat roofs, 101, 118
flat slabs (reinforced concrete), 207, 208
flexible joints, 153, 155, 160, 162, 166, 172
flicker, 318, 396, 403
flint, 27
float glass, 49
floating floors, 118; *see also* isolation of vibrations
floating swimming pool blanket, 387
floodlighting, 315
floods, protection from, 455
floor covering materials, 84, **85**
floor distribution of services, 109, 399, 401
floor loads, 124
flooring, 74, 113, 342, 343
floors for timber-framed buildings, 238, 239
flow rates from sanitary and kitchen fittings, 409
fluorescent lamps, 316, 317
flutter echoes, 290
flux
heat, 324
lamp, 320
luminous, 310, 313
flux for brick-making, 45
for steel-making, 14
for welding, brazing and soldering, 23, 24
fly screens, effect on natural ventilation, 305
flywheel in standby electric plant, 403
foam insulation, 81, 338, 341-344, 373
footcandle, 463
footings, **213, 256**
formaldehyde, 82
foundation loads, 127
foundations, **252**
for light-frame timber buildings, 237
fountains, 145
fractions, conversion to decimals, 8
fracture, 11-13
frames, multi-story, steel or concrete, 119, 121, 124, 128, 130, 141, **164,** 167, 168, 179, 204, 205
frames, timber, for houses, 45, 236, 242, 243, 342, 373-376
freestone, 28
freeze protection
for solar hot-water, 386
for water pipes, 408
freezing, 335
freon, 358
frequency, 269, 461
frequency of elevator service, acceptable, 430, 436
frequency-selective sound absorbers, 285
fresco technique, 88
friction, internal, in cohesionless soils, 254
friction joint, 186
friction piles, 214, 257
frog (on brick), 45
frost, 335
frosted glass, 49
frost heave, 93, 259
frost protection of foundations, 259
function of joints, 94
furniture, 109
in fires, 446

gage numbers, 460
gages, conversion to inches and millimeters, 460

gales, 144
gallons, 460
galvanized iron or steel, 16, 24, 89, 342, 356, 408
galvanizing, 16
gamma iron, 15
garbage tins, 420
gas heaters for hot water, 411, 413
gas heating, 356
gaskets, 87, **97,** 104
gauge numbers, 460
gauges, conversion to inches and millimeters, 460
Gaussian distribution, 4, 8
gearless elevators, 432, 433
geodesic domes, 172
geometrical acoustics, 284
geometry, 5-8
girders, 70, 159, 178, 181, 182, 218-220, 230; *see also* beams
glare control, 319
glare
direct, 308
disability, 310
discomfort, 310, 315
glass, **48, 294,** 319
thermal properties, 325
glass aggregate for concrete, 43
glass fibers, 83, 176, 325, 341, 342, 375
glass-reinforced plastics, 83, 235
glass wool, 339
glazing of clay tiles, 48
glazing of windows, 40, 296, 306, 322, 346
glue, 71, 84, 87
glued-laminated timber, 71
Glulam (timber), 71, 231, 244
gneiss, 28, 31
going (on stairs), 427
gold, 11, 17, 22
gold-coated glass, 362
gradation of soil, 23
grade, slabs on, 106
grading lumber (timber), 70
graffito, 33, 34
grain of timber, 68-70
grain (unit of mass or weight), 460
granite, 27, 28, 31
gravel, 232
gravity loads, 115
gray glass, 295, 296
Greek "passive solar" design, 367
greenhouse effect, 49
greenhouses for passive solar heating, 379
groove weld, 187
ground-supported floors, 106
groundwater, 106, 264
GRP, 83
guide rails for elevators, 433
gust of wind, 134, 335
gutters, 18, 22, 415
gypsum, 32
gypsum drywall construction, 32, 86, 90
gypsum plaster, 32
gyration, radius of, 150, 181

halide lamps, 316, 317
halocarbons, 358
handicapped people, 424
handrails, need for, 426, 429
hardboard, 76, 78
hard-drawn high-tensile steel wire, 16, 172, 216
hardening of cement, 33
hardness, 15, 60, 61
hardness of water, 406
hardwood, 53, 71, 78
hard zoning of elevators, 435
headers, 44
head of water, 406, 461
hearing loss, 270

SUBJECT INDEX

heartwood, 54
heat-absorbing glass, 50, 295, 346, 362
heat bridges in frame construction, 373
heat detectors, 414, 446, 450, 455
heat exchange units for hot water supply, 411, 412
heat flow rate, 324
heat flux, 324
heating and cooling of buildings, **323**, 366, 381
heating of buildings, **356**
heating-up period, 362
heat loss calculations, **344**
heat pumps, 359, 385
heat-reflecting glass, 50, 295, 296, 346
heat-sensing detectors, 414
heat stroke, 331, 332
heat transfer, **324**
heat-treatable and non-heat-treatable aluminum alloys, 21
heat treatment of aluminum alloys, 21
heat treatment of steel, 15, 16
heavy timber buildings, **242**
heliarc welding, 23
helium, 11, 23
Helmholtz absorbers, 285
hemihydrate gypsum plaster, 32
hemispherical arches, 165, 234
hemispherical domes, 171
hertz, 269, 461
hiding power of paint, 88
high-early-strength cement, 33, 40
high-pressure sodium lamps, 316
high-strength concrete, 41, 193, 216
high-strength low-alloy steels, 18
high-tensile steel wire, hard-drawn, 16, 172, 216
high-velocity ducts, 361
HIPS, 82
histogram, 4
hollow concrete or terracotta blocks, 48, 206
hollow-core slabs, 216
honeycomb of paper with plywood facings, 235
hoppers for garbage, 421
horizontal loads, 115, **128**
horizontal reactions, 148, 162–165, 172–175
horizontal shading, 298-301
hospitals, 119, 121, 447, 452
   uninterruptible power supply, 402
hot-arid climate, 335, 338, 378
hot-dry climate, 335, 338, 378
hotels, 436, 447, 452
hot rolling, 14, 19
hot-water storage cylinders for solar systems, 385
hot-water storage requirements, 412
hot-water storage tanks, 22, 383, 411
hot-water supply, solar, 22, 381, **382**, 411
hot-water systems, 381, **382, 410, 412, 413**
hot water usage, 412
human body temperature, 331
human ear, 270
humidifier for air conditioning plant, 360
humidity, 101, 144, 327, 328, 334, 335
humidity ratio, 327, 336–339
hurricanes, 133
hydrated lime, 32
hydration
   of cement, 33, 34, 41
   of lime, 32
   of gypsum, 32
hydraulic elevators, 433
hydraulic services, **406**
hydrochloric acid, 34
hydrogen cyanide, 451
hygrometer, 328
hyperbolic functions, 2–4
hyperbolic paraboloids, 175
hyperboloids, 175
hyperthermia, 331

hypothermia, 331
Hz, 269

I-beams and joists, 14, 181, 182, 218–220, 229
ice, 93, 100
ICS, 383
identification index for (timber) sheathing panels, 248
igneous rocks, 26–28
ignition of a fire, 443
illuminance, 308, 310, 312–314, 316
illumination, 311
illumination design, **308**
impact, environmental, 142
impact loads, 119
impact sound, 275
impact sound transmission, 275
impact strength of timber, 60, 61
impedance, electric, 395
impedance (of sound), 270, 273
incandescent lamps, 316
inclination of roofs for exclusion of rainwater, 101
incline, angle of,
   for escalators, 428
   for ladders, 427
   for ramps, 427
   for stairs, 427
index, room, 313
inertia, moment of, 101, 202, 360
inertia, thermal, 351, 443
incinerator for refuse, 422
inductor, electric, 394
industrial noise, 278
infiltration of air, 144, 443, 451
infinite series, 3
infrared radiation, 295, 326, 330, 335
ingot of steel, 14
injection molding, 84
instantaneous solar gain factor, 346
insulating materials, cement-based, 43
insulating materials, thermal properties of, 325
insulation, *see* insulation, sound, *and* insulation, thermal
insulation bats, 82, 83, 87
insulation board, 76
insulation for solar windows, for use during the night only, 306
insulation for water pipes, 408
insulation, sound, 23, 273, 275
insulation, thermal, 20, 43, 86, 102, 103, 106, 118, **337, 341**, 362, **373**, 408
insurance against fire, 442
intakes of air, location of, 146
integral waterproofers for concrete, 41
integration table, 3–4
integrated collector and storage systems for solar hot water, 383
intelligibility of sound, 272, 283, 290
intensity of heat, flux, 324
intensity of sound, 270, 271
interference in electrical and computer transmissions, 401
intermittent heating, 362
internal friction, 254
internal shading, 299, 300, 346
International Conference of Building Officials, 116
International Standards Organization, 99, 275, 276, 279, 280
inter-reflection of sound, 283
interstitial condensation, 344
interval between elevator cars, 436, 437
intumescence, 84, 90, 451
iron, 11, 12, **14**, 15
I-shapes (of steel), 179–191
ISO, 99, 275, 276, 279, 280
isolation of vibrations, 275

joint fillers, 98, 99
jointing, 23, 32, 34, 44, 86, **92**

joints, 23, 32, 34, 44, 86, **92**
   function of, 94
joist floors, reinforced concrete, 48, 206
joists, 48, 70, 206, 229; *see also* beams
joule, 462

k, K, 459, 461, 462
katabatic winds, 337
Keene's cement, 32
Kelly ball test, 38
Kelvin, 323, 462
keratin, 32
kevlar, 176
kiln, 32, 33, 45
kip, 461
kitchens, 417–422
kJ, 462
kN, 461
knots in timber, 68–70
kPa, 462
ksi, 461
k-value, 324
kWh, 462

lacquer, 89, 90
ladders, 427
laminated glass, 50
laminated paperboard, 77
laminated timber, 71, 72, 80
lamp flux, 320
lamp life, 317, 321
lamp replacement, 321, 322
lamps
   electric, 316, 317
     fluorescent, 316, 317
     incandescent, 316, 317
LAN, 401
Landolt rings, 311
landscaping (effect on noise), 278
landscaping for passive solar design, 373
landslide, 254
lanterns to indicate elevator arrival, 431
lap joints, 96, 187
laps for roof sheets, 101
latent heat, 324, 328
lateral loads, 115
lateral support of compression flange, 181, 183
latewood, 55
latex, 86
Lavalier microphones, 290
lay-in ceiling panels, 76
lay lights, 342
LCC, 111
lead, 11, 17, 19, **23**, 24, 408
lecture rooms, theaters, 289, 290, 448
life cycle costing, 111
life expectancy, 108
lifts, *see* elevators
light-frame timber buildings, 236
lighting, **308**
lighting design, 311, 455
lighting maintenance, 313, **321**
lighting standards, 311
lighting units, 310, 463
lightning protection, 400, 455
light sources, **316**
lightweight aggregate, 35, 340, 444
lightweight construction and energy conservation, 349, 362
lignin, 55
lime, 31
lime mortar, 31, 46, 47
lime putty, 32
limestone, 27–29, 31, 33, 35, 48
limewash, 32
limit states design, 178, 190

lining materials, propensity to spread flames, 445
linoleum, 85, 451
linseed oil, 85, 86, 88
lintels, 44, 45, 46
liter, litre, 461
lithium bromide, 390
live loads, 116, 119, 124, 195, 208
load and resistance factor design, 190
load balancing
   electric, 398
   prestressed concrete, 217
load-bearing masonry, 45, 149, **221**
load-bearing walls, 149
load factor, 190, 195
load, fire, 447–449
loads, **115**, 259
lobbies for elevators, 431, 454
local buckling, 179, 190
location of air intakes and exhausts, 146
loess, 267
logarithms, 2
log houses, 242
long columns, 150
longest-spanning structures, 172
loss of prestress, 216
loudness, 271
loudspeakers, 290, 291
loudspeakers with time delay, 290
louvered diffusers, 356
louver/reflectors for luminaires, 320, 356
louvers, 346, 356
low-alloy steel, 18
low-E glazing, 295
low-emissivity glazing, 295
low-heat portland cement, 33
low-pressure sodium lamps, 317
low-temperature hot-water systems, 357
LFRD, 190
LTHW, 357
lucite, 82
lumber, **69, 228**
lumber grade marks, 248
lumen, 310, 313, 463
lumen (in wood), 55
lumen method, 313
luminaire, 308, 313, 319
luminance, 308, 310, 314, 316, 319
luminance distribution, 316, 319
luminous environment, 316
luminous flux, 310, 313
lux, 310, 313, 463
λ-value, 324

machine room location for elevators, 432–435
machine stress rating of lumber (timber), 71
macroclimate, 337
magnesium, 11, 21
magnesium oxychloride, 34
magnesite flooring, 34
maintenance, 46, **108**
maintenance factor, 313, 321
maintenance of electric power supply, 402
maintenance of water supply system, 409
manganese, 11, 21
marble, 27, 28, 31, 444
martensite, 15
Martin-Héroult process, 18, 19
masks, shading, 298, 371
masonry cement, 32, 34, 47, 94, 95
masonry domes, 172
mass effect (thermal), 351-353, **374**
massive construction and energy conservation, 349, 362
mass law of sound transmission, 273
mass, thermal 351–353, **374**
mastics, 31, 86, 93

482 SUBJECT INDEX

materials, **10, 26, 61, 79**
mathematics, **1**
matte glass, 49
maximum permissible stress, 178–186
maximum steel ratio for concrete, 197
maximum strain of concrete, 196
maximum and minimum temperatures, 335, 336
MDF, 77
mean (of data), 4, 39
mean radiant temperature, 334, 374
measurements, units of, **459**
mechanical and electrical equipment of buildings, **323, 381, 393, 423**
mechanical details
    of elevators, 432
    of escalators, 429
mechanical properties of wood, 58, **60, 61**
mechanical ventilation, **354**
medium-density fiberboard, 77
melamine formaldehyde, 83, 84, 87
melting materials (in a fire), 444
melting point of metals, 19
membrane, tympanic (ear drum), 270
membranes, 175, 176
Mercalli scale, 121
mercury fluorescent lamps, 316
met, 330, **331**, 462
metabolic rate, 330, **331**
metal deck forms in composite construction, 220, 325
metal halide lamps, 316
metals, **10**
metamorphic rocks, 26–28
metering of water, 409
methane, 80
metric reinforcing bars (US and Canada), 194
mica, 27, 89
microclimate, 337
microphones, 290, 291
mill-type buildings, 179, 243
mineral fibers, 343, 373
mineral wool, 343, 373, 444
minimum and maximum temperature, 335, 336
minimum crossfalls for surface drainage, 417
minimum steel ratio for concrete, 197
minimum width of corridors, 425
mirrors, 49
mixing of concrete, **36**
MJ, 462
MMI, 121
mobile homes, 78
models for auditoriums, 291
modes of failure of reinforced concrete, 195
Modified Mercalli scale, 121
modulus of elasticity, 13, 150
    of aluminum, 19
    of concrete, 196
    of plastics, 84
    of steel, 19
    of wood, 59, 60, 61, 62, 64, 66
modulus of rupture of timber, 59, 65, 66
modulus, section, 151
moisture content
    of concrete aggregate, 35, 36
    of soil, 253
    of wood, **56**, 60, 61, 62
moisture damage, 16, 58, **100**, 113
moisture movement, 95, 249; *see also* shrinkage *and* creep
moment, 148
moment, bending, 151, 181–186, 198, 199, 209, 217, 225
moment of area, second, 151
moment of inertia, 151, 181, 202
monolithically poured concrete slab and beam assembly, 200
monomer, 79, 81
monsoon climate, 335
mortar, 33, 34, 46, 86, 93
movable night insulation, 378

movement joints, **92**
movement of air for thermal comfort, 144, 329, **344**, 353
movement of people and goods, **423**
movement of the sun, daily, 368
moving loads, 119
moving walkways, 428, 430
MPa, 461
MRT, 334, 374
MSR, 71
mud bricks, 48
multi-level elevator cars, 439
multistory frames, 119, 121, 124, 128, 130, 141, **164,** 167, 168, 179, 204, 205
Munsell color system, 311
Muntz metal, 22
music amplification, 290
music auditoriums, 291
muskeg, 253

nails, 231, 233, 246
nanometer, 326, 460
National Climatic Data Center, Greenville NC, 136
natural light, *see* daylight
natural logarithms, 2
natural stone, **26**, 32, 34, 35, 93, 325
natural ventilation, 144, 293, 303, 351, 368
    effect of fly screens on, 305
    effect on noise transmission, 277
negative bending moment, 151
neoprene, 98, 176
neutral axis, 151
neutrality temperature, 336
newton, 461
nickel, 17, 18
nickel silver, 22
night (additional thermal) insulation, movable, 374, 378
night shutdown (for energy economy), 349, 362
night-sky cooling, 373
night-storage system for hot water, 362
night ventilation, 351, 353
niobium, 11, 18
nitriding, 16
no-fines concrete, 35
noise, **269**
    from air conditioning, 272, 276
    from fans, 276
    from plumbing, 276
noise attenuation, 273, 275–278
noise attenuation barriers, 278
noise control, **269**
noise control legislation, 278
Noise Reduction Coefficient, 286
non-ferrous metals, **22**
non-slip treads on stairs, 428
normalized heat load, 447–449
normalizing, 16
nosing of stairs, 427
notation, 9, 25, 52, 78, 91, 147, 177, 192, 280, 292, 322, 364–365, 405, 458, 459
NRC, 286
number of air changes, 345
number of members in a statically determinate truss, 160, 169, 172
nylon, 82, 85, 176

obtrusive light, 314
occupancy loads, 116, 118, 119, 124
octave interval, 271
office buildings, 108, 109, 111, 119, 396, 397, 401, 436, 447, 452, 454
off-peak electricity tariff, 362
oleoresinous paint, 88
oil heating, 356
oil, linseed, 85, 86, 88
oil paint, 88

Olgyay's bioclimatic chart, 332
one-way mirror, 49
one-way slabs, 205
oolitic limestone, 27
opacity of paint, 88
opal glass, 89
open-web joists, 221
operable external shading, 298–301
operable internal shading, 299–301
operable night insulation for solar windows, 306
optical fibers, 401
organic soils, 253, 263, 267
orientation of buildings, 368–370
orientation of windows, 296, 297, 300, 304
oriented strand board, 75
ornamental plaster, effect on acoustics, 284
outlet, electric, 398
overcast sky, 347
over-reinforced sections, 195
over-temperature protection for hot-water systems, 386
oxidation, 10, 14, 16, 21, 23, 24
oxygen, 10, 11, 16
oxygen index, 444

paint, 17, **88**
panel radiator, 357
panel resonance, 283
pans, plastic, as concrete forms, 206
paperboard, 77
parabolic dish solar collectors, 384
parabolic trough solar collectors, 384
particle board (woodchip board), 77, 78, 84, 235
particulates, wind transport of, 146
partitions, 20, 273, 276
    weight of, 118
pascal, 461
passive solar design, **366**
passive solar heating, 293, 351, 352, 363, **366, 377**
patina, 17
pearlite, 15, 16
peat, 93, 253, 259, 267
pedestrians
    loads due to, 118, 119
    wind effects on, 142–144
pedestrian traffic, 424–430
penetration test, 256
penetrometer, 256
people-moving, 423, 428
perception of sound, 270
perimeter floor slab insulation, 374
perimeter surveillance system, 454
perimeter zone for air conditioning, 362
periodic heat flow, 339, 340
periodic table, 11
perlite, 32
permafrost, 268
permeability, 254
permissible stress, *see* allowable stress
perspex, 82
PF, 82
phenol, 83
phenol formaldehyde, 82, 87
pH level of waste water, 418
phosphors (used in lamps), 317
phosphorus, 11, 14, 18
phoneme, 272
photocells, 320, 381, 391
photovoltaic cells, 381, **391**
photographic installations, waste water from, 418
physiological cooling, 351, 354
piers, 214, 258
pigments, 21, 34, **88**
pile caps, 257
pile-driving hammers, 258, 261
piles, 214, 257, 261

pin joints, 155, 160, 162–166, 172
pipes, 22, 84, 87, 408
pisé, 48
pitched roofs, 101, 345
pitch of roofs for exclusion of rainwater, 101
pit for elevators, 434
placing of concrete, **36**, 38
plaster
    cement, 33, 41, 45
    gypsum, 37
    ornamental, effect on acoustics, 284
plasterboard, 32, 45, 341, 342, 375, 444
plastering, 32, 34, 45, 325
plaster of Paris, 32
plastic deformation, 11–13
plastic design of steel structures, 179, 190
plasticity
    of metals, 12, 190
    of plastics, 79
    of soil, 253, 267
plasticizers, 80, 83, 88
plastic pans as concrete forms, 206
plastics, 10, 17, 23, **79**
    in fires, 449, 450
plastic water pipes, 408
plate girders, 189
plenum, 109, 356
plexiglas, 82
plumbing, 112, 418–420, 444
    for solar swimming pool heaters, 387
    noise from, 276
plumes from chimneys, 146
plywood, 24, 75, 78, 87, 234, 235, 248
pneumatic structures, 176
Poisson's ratio for timber, 59, 62
pole and post frame buildings, 243
poles, 232
polyacetal, 82
polyamide, 82
polycarbonate, 82, 84, 451
polyester, 83, 85, 87, 176
polyethylene, 82, 86, 87, 93, 98, 388, 408, 444, 450
polymer, 79, 81
polymer-cement concrete, 85
polymer concrete, 84
polymer-impregnated concrete, 85
polymethyl methacrylate, 82
polypropylene, 82, 102, 386, 444, 450
polystyrene, 80–82, 325, 339, 341–343, 373, 444, 450
polysulfide, 87, 96
polyurethane, 83, 87, 90, 93, 96, 98, 325, 339, 343, 373
polyvinyl acetate, 82, 86, 88, 90
polyvinyl chloride, 79, 81, 84, 85, 176, 386, 408, 451
ponding, 115, 125
pool cover, 387
porcelain enamel, 17
porewater pressure, 254
porphyry, 27, 28
portal frames, 161–164, 179
portland cement, 33
positive bending moment, 151
post and timber grade, 70
posts, 70, 231
post-tensioning, 216
power distribution, 109, **396**
power distribution paths, **399**
power factor, electric, 318, 396, 404
power, sound, 270, 271
power supplies, stand-alone, 381, **391**
power systems, 109
pozzolan, 34
Pratt trusses, 161
precast concrete, 43, 216
precipitation, 33; *see also* rain *and* snow
prefabricated housing, 78

484 SUBJECT INDEX

preheater coil, 360
preliminary design, 149, 151, 179
pre-painted steel tubes, 17, 174
present value, 111
preservation of natural stone, **30**
preservation technology, 30, 112
pressure due to wind, 126, 127, 140
pressure-injected footings, 258
pressure, sound, 270, 271
pressure, soil, on retaining walls, 262
pressure-zone microphones, 291
pressurization of refuge areas and staircases to keep them free from smoke, 424, 451
prestressed cable networks, 175
prestressed concrete, **215**
prestressed membranes, 175
pretensioning, 216
primary beams, 159, 206
primer (paint), 89
progressive collapse, 226
propeller fans, 356
protected walls, 104
protection
    from crime, **453**
    from fire, **442**
    from floods, 455
    of wood, **68**
psi, 461
psychological factors in fire protection, 453
psychrometer, 328
psychrometric chart, 327, 329-331, 333, 336-339
psychrometry, **327**
puddling process, 14
pumps for water supply, 382, 386, 406, 407
pumping of concrete, 38
pumping of groundwater, 264
punching shear, 215
purlins, 70, 183
putty, window, 86
PVA, 82, 86, 88, 90
PVC, 79, 81, 84, 85, 176, 386, 408, 451
pyramid, area and volume of, 8
pyrolysis, 443-445, 450
PZMs 291

quadratic equations, 2
quality of electricity supply, **401**
quantities for thermal measurement, **323**, 461-463
quarry tiles, 48
quartersawn wood, 74
quartzite, 28, 31
quasistatic wind load, 142
quenching, 15, 16, 21
queues, 425
quicklime, 31
quilts of insulation, 343

radian measure, 1, 461
radiant heat, 330
radiant temperature, mean, 334
radiation
    infrared, 295, 326, 330, 335
    solar, 365, 369
    thermal, 326, 335, 387
    ultraviolet, 68, 86, 89, 112, 316, 317, 383
radiator, black body, 326
radiator (for heating), 357
radius of gyration, 150, 181
rafters, 209
raft footings, 214
railings, 128
rain, 100, 103, 337, 383
    washing of stone surfaces, 30
rain gauge, 100

rain penetration, 46
rainscreen, 104
rainwater, 406
ramps, 423, 427
Rankine (temperature scale), 323, 443, 462
rapid-hardening cement, 33
rating system
    for acoustical absorptivity of materials, 286
    for airborne sound transmission loss, 275
    for impact sound transmission loss, 275
rayon, 85
readability of exposed aggregate, 43
recommended sound levels, 273
reconstituted wood, 75
recycling of waste, 420
red cedar, 60, 61, 74, 89
reduction of live loads with height, 124, 132
redwood, 64, 74, 89
reentrant reflections of sound, 282
reflectance
    thermal, 326
    visual, 310
reflecting films (on glass), 346
reflecting glass, 50, 295, 296, 346, 362
reflection
    of light, 49, 319
    of solar radiation, 295
    of sound, 282, 283
reflective foil laminates, 20, 340, 373
reflective surfaces, 281
reflective thermal insulation, 20, 102, 103, 338, 340, 373
refraction, 319
refractory bricks, 14
refrigeration, 358
refuge areas in case of fire, 451
"refuge space" for elevator mechanics, 434
refuse, **420**
reinforced blockwork, brickwork, 44-47, 221, 225
reinforced concrete design, **193**
reinforced concrete joist floors, 48, 206
reinforced concrete slabs on grade (on ground), 106, 343, 374-376
reinforced concrete slabs, suspended, **205**
reinforced concrete, weight of, 117
reinforcement for concrete, 194
reinforcing bar sizes, 194
relative humidity, 101, 144, 328, 335
rendering, 32, 34, 45, 325
repair of natural stone, **30**
replacement of lamps, 321
representative soil samples, 255, 256
resin, 82, 88, 90
resistance
    electric, 394
    thermal, 324
resistance factor (structural steel design), 180
resistive thermal insulation, 338, 340, **341**
resistivity, thermal, 324
resonance, 273, 283
response factor, thermal, 349
restoration of buildings, 30-32, 112
retaining walls, 122, 127, 213, **262**
retarder, 32, 41, 42
reverberation, 272
reverberation chamber, 285
reverberation time, 283, **286**
Reynolds number, 138-140
RFL, 373
ribbed reinforced concrete slabs, 48, 206
rigid frames, 162, 179, 188, 189
rigid joints, 153, 154, 162, 166, 172
rivets, 23, 186
risers (on stairs), 427
road traffic noise, 297
robberies, prevention of, 453
robustness of construction, 226

roller shutters, 344
roll roofing, 101, 113
Roman concrete, 41
Roman numerals, equivalents in ordinary numbers, 8
Ronan Point Tower collapse, 226
roof drainage, 101, 415
roofing, 101–103, 113, 342, 373
    uplift on, 127, 133, 134
rooflights, 302, 319, 342, 378
roof monitors for daylighting, 302
roof pitch, 101
roof screed, 103
roofs, loads on, 124
roof slope, 101
roof structures for timber-framed buildings, 240, 241
roof trusses, 161, 179
room acoustics, **281**
room cavity ratio (for lighting design), 313
room index (dto), 313
round timber, 73
roundtrip time for elevators, 436, 438
rubber (including synthetic rubber), 23, 85–87, 98, 99, 102, 176, 387
ruled surfaces, 175
rust, 16
R scale (Rankine temperature scale), 323, 443, 462
R-value, 324, 339, 463

sabin, 286, 463
Sabine reverberation time formula, 287
saddle surfaces, 174–176
safety glass, 50
safety in buildings, **441**
sags in electric power, 402
saltation (wind transport of particles), 145
salt glaze, 48
SAN, 82
sand, 27, 35, 232
sand-lime bricks, 47
sandstone, 27, 28, 30, 35
sandwich cores, 235
sandwich panels, 234, 235
sanitary fittings and plumbing, 18, 84, 418–420
sarking, 102, 103
saturation, degree of
    of concrete aggregate, 36
    of soil, 253
saturation humidity, 327
SBS, 102
scenery (shorter-life interior fittings), 108
school assembly halls, 289
school rooms, 289
Schwedler domes, 172
screed on flat roofs, 103, 325
screws, 246
sealants, **86**, 93, **96**, 104
sealing strips, 86, 97
sealing tapes, 86, 97
seasoning of timber, 70
second law of thermodynamics, 324
second moment of area, 151
section modulus, 151, 181, 460
sector, 5, 6,
secondary beams, 159, 206
security, 423, 424, 453
sedimentary marble, 28
sedimentary rocks, 26, 27
seepage, 264
segment, 5, 6
segregation of concrete, 38
seismic zones, 122
selective surfaces, thermal, 326, 378, 383, 384
self-closing fire doors, 424
self-weight
    of concrete slabs, 117

    of steel decks, 117
    of timber decks, 117
sensors for security systems, 453
series, mathematical, 2, 3
serpentine, 28
service core, 168, 434
service ducts, 220, 276, 359
    metal deck forms used for, 220
service loads, 115, 149
services, building, 108, 168, **354, 381, 393, 406, 423**
setbacks in buildings for solar access, 373
setting of cement, 33
settlement of foundations, 93, 254, 260, 266
sewerage and waste disposal, **417**
sewer pipes, 419
sewer system, 418–422
sgraffito, 33, 34
shade trees, 368, 373
shading coefficients, 297
shading devices, 50, 294, 297–301, 346, 363
shading masks, 298, 371
shadow masks, 298, 371
shadows, 371; *see also* shading
shadow zones for sound, 290
shakes (defect in wood), 69, 70
shakes (roof covering), 74, 101
shale, 27, 33
shallow domes, 72
shallow foundations, 256, 260
shape of auditoriums, 291
shape of compressive stress distribution curve in concrete, 196
shear connectors for composite construction, 218, 219, 221
shear force, 151, 181, 200, 209, 210, 218, 219
shear in steel sections, checking for, 181, 182
shear plates for timber connections, 246
shear reinforcement for concrete, 201
shear strength
    of concrete, 200
    of soil, 254
    of steel, 182
    of timber, 60, 61
shear stress
    in concrete, 201
    in structural steel, 182
shear walls, 213, 224
sheathing with fiberboard, 76
shellac, 90
shell, building (the most durable part), 108
shell structures, 169, 171–174
sherardizing, 16
shielded metal arc welding, 187, 188
shingles
    asphalt, 86, 101
    wooden, 74, 89, 101
short columns, 149
showers, 409, 418
shrinkage, 32, 41, 44, 47, 57, 93, 95, 203, 208, 249
shrinkage-compensating cement, 41
shutdown of heating on weekend for energy economy, 349
shutters, 344
shutting down the air conditioning system in case of fire, 451
side-wall reflectors, 290
siding, 45, 74, 89
sight lines, 291
silencer (for air conditioning system), 360
silica, 27, 31, 33, 35, 48
siliceous limestone, 27
siliceous sandstone, 27
silicon, 11, 21
silicone, 31, 83, 86, 96, 98, 176, 306
silicon photovoltaic cells, 391
silk, 85
silt, 93, 253
silver, 11, 17, 22, 24
silver solder, 24

simply supported beams, 151, 152, 155–157, 166
    beams with cantilever overhangs, 152–154
single-phase electric supply, 398
single shear, 186
single-stack plumbing, 418
singly reinforced concrete beams, 196
sink grinders for food refuse, 421
site planning for solar access, 368, 371
size of elevator cars, 430, 431, 435
sizing
    of soil stacks, 419
    of solar water systems, 386
    of subsoil drains, 417
    of underground pipes for stormwater, 416
    of waste pipes, 419
    of water pipes, 409–411
sky, 347
sky conditions, 335
skylight (scattered sunlight), 316
skylights (windows), 302, 319, 342, 378
skylobbies, 437
slabs on grade, 106, 343, 374–376
slabs on ground, 106, 343, 374–376
slag, 14
slate, 28, 31, 101
slats of shading devices, 346
slender columns, 150, 183, 212
slenderness ratio for buckling, 150, 184
slope of roofs required for exclusion of rain, 101
sloping grain of timber, 69
slump test for concrete, 37
"smart" buildings, 455
smoke, **450**
smoke detectors, 414, 446, 455
smoke dilution, 451
smoke dispersion, 146, 451
smoke distribution in a building, 443
smoke-free stairs, 424, 451
smoke-producing characteristics of materials, 451
snow, 100, 125, 126
    drifts due to wind, 145
snow loads, 115, 118, 125, 126
sodium lamps, 316, 317
softwood, 53, 70, 71, 78, 89
soft zoning of elevators, 435
soil analysis, 252
soil exploration, **255**
soil movement, 93
soil stack sizes, 419
sol-air excess temperature, 345, 347
sol-air temperature, 345, 347
solar access, 370
solar access butterfly, 371, 372
solar-assisted heat pumps, 385
solar-boosted heat pumps, 385
solar cells, 391
solar collectors, concentrating, 381, **384**
solar collectors, non-concentrating, 22, 381, **383**
solar-control glass, 50, 294
solar envelopes, 371
solar gain factor, 346
solar gain through glass, 296, 300, 301, 346
solar heating, 293, **305**, 377, 389
solar heat pumps, 385
solar heat, storage of, 306
solar hot-water supply, 22, 381, **382**, 411
solar radiation, 335, 369
solar space cooling, 385, 389
solar space heating, 305, **377**, **389**
solar windows, 305, 306, 377
    operable night insulation for, 306
soldering, 23, 24
solid-fuel heating, 356
solid walls (without cavities), exclusion of rain, 103
solution heat treatment of aluminum alloys, 21

sorbent dehumidification, 331
sound, **269**, **281**
sound absorption, 272, 284
sound absorption coefficient, 285, 287
sound-absorptive materials, **284**
sound analysis, 271
sound attenuation, 273, 275–278
sound attenuation of windows, 51
sound diffusion, 284
sound diffraction, 283
sound dispersion, 283
sound insulation, 23, 273, 275
sound intensity, 270, 271
sound level meter, 271
sound levels, recommended, 273
sound power, 270, 271
sound pressure, 270, 271
sound reflection, 283
soundness of cement, 33
sound perception, 270
sound propagation, 269
sound shadows, 283
sound transmission 272, 274, 275
sound transmission loss, 273–275
sound transmitted by air-conditioning ducts, 276
space frames, 148, **169**, 171, 174
space heating and cooling, **356**, **358**, **377**, **381**, **389**
specific fire load, 447–449
specific gravity
    of concrete aggregates, 36
    of lightweight concretes, 43
    of metals, 19
    of plastics, 82, 84
    of timber and wood products, 57, 60–63, 76
specific heat capacity, 323, 339
specific heat loss rate, 344
specific volume, 32, 328
specified compressive strength of concrete, 38, 39, 193
specular reflection, 319
speech auditoriums, 289
speech intelligibility, 272, 283, 290
speed
    of sound, 269
    of elevators, 435, 436, 438
    of escalators, 429
    of moving walkways, 430
sphere, area and volume of, 6
spill light (from sporting events &c), 314
spirit varnish, 90
spirit, white, 88
split-ring connectors for timber, 232, 246
sports lighting, 314
spread of fire, **443**
springings of arches and domes, 165, 169, 171
springwood, 33
sprinkler systems, 414, 415, 456
stack effect, 451
stacks for air conditioning, 146
stagger of bolts, 80
stain (for wood), 90
stainless steel, 17, **18**, 19, 31, 176, 385
stairs, 423, **426**, 451, 454
stanchions, 14, 183
stand-alone power supplies, 381, **391**
standard deviation, 4, 39
standard effective temperature, 331, 332
standard gauge (gage), 460
standard lumber (timber), sizes, 7
standard penetration test, 256
standard steel sections, 14, 178
standard test fires, 447–449
standing waves, 283
statically determinate beams, 151
statically determinate structures, 148
statically indeterminate structures, 148

SUBJECT INDEX

static electricity in carpets, 85
static equilibrium, 148
static loads, 115
static wind loads, 120, 121, 125, 127, 128, 141, 142
statistical sound absorption coefficient, 386
statistical terms, definition of, 4
steady-state heat flow, 339, **349**
steam heating, 357
steel, 14, **15, 17,** 19, 150, **178**
    corrosion protection of, 16–18
steel bar sizes, 194
steel decks, weight of, 117
steel domes, 171, 172
steel, heat treatment of, 15, 16
steel, manufacture of, 14
steel piles, 257
steel pipes for water supply, 408
steel reinforcement for concrete, 194
steel structures, **178**
steel, thermal movement, 95
steel, thermal properties, 325
steel tubes, 14, 171, 174
steel wire drawing, 16, 172
steepness of stairs, 427
Stefan-Boltzman law, 326
stepped footings, 260
steradian, 310, 461
stiffeners for plate girders, 190
stirrups, 201
STL, 273
stone, classification of, **26**
stone, natural, **26,** 32, 34, 35, 93, 325
stone veneer, **31**
stoneware, 47
storage capacity, thermal, 374, **375**
storage mass (capacitative insulation), 340, 343
storage of solar heat, 306, 378
stormwater drainage, 416
strain
    definition of, 13
    maximum of concrete, 196
strain hardening, 16, 21
streamline flow, 138
strength
    definition, 13
    of concrete, 38, 39, 193
    of concrete aggregate, 36
    of timber, 59–66
strength reduction factor for reinforced concrete, 195
stress, definition of, 13
stress relieving, 16, 21
stressed-skin panels, 234, 235
stress-grading of lumber (timber), 70, 71, 230
stretchers, 44
stringers, 60, 234
strips, sealing, 97
stroboscopic effect, 319
Strouhal number, 140
structural analysis, 149
structural design (*versus* structural analysis), 149
structural members, 149, **155**
structural systems, **148**
structure-borne sound transmission, 275
structure of timber, 53
structures, **148, 178, 193, 228, 252**
struts, 167, 168, **183, 211,** 231, 232
studs, 206, 240
styrene, 80, 81
styrene-acrylonitrile copolymer, 82
styrene-butadiene, 87, 90, 98
styrene-butadiene-styrene, 102
subflorescence, 113
submerged-arc welding, 187
subsidence of foundations, 93
subsoil drainage, 417

substations, electric, 394, 396
substrate (to which paint adheres), 88
suction due to wind, 127, 140
sulfate attack, 93
sulfate resistant cement, see both under *portland cement*, 34, and under *aluminuous cement*, 34
sulfuric acid, 21, 29
sulphate, *see* sulfate
summation of series, 2–3
summerwood, 55
sunlight, 309, 316
sunshine hours, data on, 335
sun's movement (in relation to passive solar design), 368
sunspace, attached, for passive solar heating, 379
superplasticizers (for producing high-strength concrete), 40
supply systems for air, 355
surface drainage, 417
surface drainage, minimum crossfalls, 417
surface-tinted glass, 346
surges in electric power, 402
surveillance (for crime protection), 454
suspended acoustical absorbers, 286
suspended floors
    concrete, 106, 107, 205–210, 218–221
    timber, 106, 229–231, 238
suspension structures, 171–173
sweating (as evaporative cooling), 331
swelling of bricks, 45, 93–95
swelling of soils, 267
swimming pools
    blankets, 387
    heating, 381, 382, **387**
    paint, 90
switchboard, electric, 397–399
synthetic rubber, *see* rubber

tanks for hot-water storage, 22, 383, 411
tapes, sealing, 86
taps (for water), *see* faucets
task, illuminance for, 313
task performance, visual, 308
T-beams
    composite construction, 218
    reinforced concrete, 199
tearing resistance of plastics, 84
teflon, 176
telephones, 397, 401
television
    closed-circuit, 454
    lighting for, 314, 315
tempera painting, 88
temperate climate, 335, 337
temperature, 323, 327, 328, 331, 334, 461
temperature, color, 317
temperature conditions at the outset of a fire, 442
temperature movement, 93, 203, 208
temperature of the human body, 331
tempered glass, 50
tempering (of metals), 16
tendons (in prestressed concrete), 215, 216
tensile strength of timber, 60, 61
tension members, 149, 150, 180
tents, 176
terracotta, 48, 206, 340
terrazzo, 43
testing of building materials, 111
thatch, 101, 325
theft, prevention of, 453
theaters (theatres), 289–291, 446
theory of bending, 151
thermal absorptance, 326
thermal absorptivity, 438–448
thermal admittance, 340, **341,** 375
thermal capacity, 323

SUBJECT INDEX

thermal comfort, 144, **330,** 332, 333, 455
thermal conductance, 324
thermal conduction, 324
thermal conductivity, 324
thermal emittance, 326
thermal expansion, 95
thermal expansion coefficients of aluminum, copper, lead and steel, 19
thermal fire detectors, 414, 446
thermal inertia, 351, 443
thermal insulation, 20, 43, 86, 102, 103, 106, 118, **337, 341,** 362, **373**
   movable, 344, 378
thermal mass, 351–3, **374**
thermal movement, 95, 101, 104
thermal properties of materials, 50, 58, **325,** 375
thermal quantities, definition of, **323,** 461–463
thermal radiation, 295, 326, 335, 387
thermal reflectance, 326
thermal resistance, 324
thermal resistivity, 324
thermal response of building to variable heat flow, 350
thermal selective surfaces, 326, 378, 383, 384
thermal storage 375
thermal storage capacity, 374, 375
thermal storage in cylinders containing water, 378
thermal storage walls, **378**
thermal transmittance, 326
thermodynamics, laws of, 324
thermoplastic materials, **79,** 102
thermosetting materials, 79, **82**
thermosyphon, 382, 387
thermosyphonic ventilation, 303
Thevenin's theorem, 394
thinner for paint, 88
third-point loading, 159
three-phase electric supply, 398
throat (cut under window sills), 30
throat (of weld), 24, 188
thunderstorms, effect on electricity supply, 402
tiebacks, 264
ties, 149, 150, 180
tiles, 48, 101, 342
   bedding of, 96
   joints between, 96
timber, **53, 228**
   for specific references to timber see also lumber and wood
timber decks, weight of, 117
timber fasteners, 232
timber flooring, 74, 238, 239, 342, 373
timber-framed houses, 45, 236, 242, 243, 342, 373–6
timber, thermal properties of, 58, 325, 338, 341, 342, 375
timber piles, 257
timber structures, **228**
time-delayed loudspeakers, 290
time lag of insulation, 340, **341,** 343, 349
tin, 11, 22, 24
titanium dioxide white, 88, 89
ton of refrigeration, 363, 462
toothed metal plate connectors for timber, 233, 246
toothed steel reinforcing strips for timber, 232
top clearance for elevators, 434
topcoat of paint, 89
tornadoes, 134
torsion, 181, 202
torus, 7
toughened glass, 50
toughness, definition of, 13
toxicity of smoke, 450
tracheids, 53
traction-type elevators, 432
traffic flow, 426
trains, very fast, noise from, 278
transformer, electric, 394, 397, 399
transmission of solar radiation, 295
transmission of structure-borne sound, 275
transmittance, thermal, 326

transmitted sound, 273
transparency of glass, reason for, 49
transportation of concrete, 38, 44
trapezoid, 6
travertine, 27, 28, 31
treads of stairs, 427
trees for shading, 368, 373
triangular load distribution, 159
triangulated domes, 172
triangulated trusses, 160, 161
triaxial test, 254
trigonometry, 1–4
triple-deck elevators, 439
triple glazing, 50, 296
Trombe walls, 378
tropical climate, 335
tropical cyclones, 133
trusses, **155,** 172, 174, 230, 233
tube concept for tall buildings, 168
tubes, steel, 14, 171, 174
tubular fluorescent lamps, 317
tufa (rock), 27
tungsten halogen lamps, 316
turbulence, 140, 141, 276
turbulent wake flow, 140, 141
turpentine, 88
two-way slabs, 207, 208
typhoons, 133

UF, 82, 325
ultimate strength, 179, 194
   method for reinforced concrete design, 194
ultramarine, 88
   synthetic, 88
ultraviolet radiation, 68, 86, 89, 112, 316, 317, 383
undercoat of paint, 89
underfloor distribution of services, 109
underground pipes for stormwater, 416
underlayment, 102, 103, 118, 342
under-reinforced concrete sections, 195
underslung elevator cars, 432
undisturbed soil samples, 256
Uniform Building Code, 116
uniformly distributed loads, 118, 119, 153–159
uninterruptible electric power supply, 402
units of measurement, **459**
unit weights
   of building materials, 117
   of concrete aggregate, 36
   of partitions, 118
   of soil, 253
unplasticized polyvinyl chloride, 408
unshaded windows, 296, 300
unsound aggregate particles, 35
upholstered furniture in a fire, 446
uplift on roofs, 127, 133, 134
UPVC, 408
urban people-moving, 428
urea, 83
urea formaldehyde, 82, 85, 87, 325, 343, 376
urinals, 18, 19, 419
USA Building Codes, 115, **116**
US National Weather Service, 134, 136
US Standard Gauge (Gage), 460
utilization factor (for electric lamps), 313
UV, 68, 86, 89, 112, 316, 317, 383
U-value, 325, 339, **341,** 344, 463
U-values of windows, 296, 306, 341, 342, 373, 375

vacuum flask solar collector, 384
value, annual, 111
value, present, 111
valves for control of water supply, 409
vanadium, 11, 18

vapor barriers, 20, 84, 102, 103, 105, 344, 373
vapor-compression heat pump, 385
vapor pressure, 327
vapor, water, 100, 327
varnish, 90
Vebe test, 37
vehicle for paint, 88
velocities of elevators, 435, 436, 438
velocity of air, 334, 361
velocity of sound, 269
veneer, brick or stone, 31, 45
veneer lumber (timber), 72
veneer/particle composite panels, 76
venetian blinds, 300-302
    best color for, 301, 302
vented roof space, 102, 103, 373
vented wall space, 105
ventilated crawl spaces under timber floors, 373
ventilation, 144, 293, 303, 329, 344, 351, 356, 358, 364, 368
ventilation conditions conducive to combustion, 449
ventilation factor for fire spread, 446
ventilation mechanical, 354
ventilation of roof space, 102, 103, 373
ventilation rate, 345
ventilation thermosyphonic, 303
vent pipes, 420, 421
vermiculite, 32, 343, 444
vertical loads, 115
vertical shading, 298, 299
vibration absorption, 23
vibration perception, 272
vibrations, structure-borne, 275, 281
Vicat test, 33
Vierendeel girder, 166, 169
vinyl butyral, 50
vinyl chloride, 79, 81
viscous impingement filters, 356
visual performance, 309
visual task, 308
vitrification, 45
void ratio of concrete aggregate, 36
    of soil, 253
voltage, 394
volumes of geometric solids, 6–8
volumetric specific heat, 323
vortex shedding, 140, 141

waferboard, 75
waffle slabs, 208
wall coverings, 112
walls
    exclusion of water, 103
    masonry, 28, 44, 46, **221**
    reinforced concrete, **212**
    thermal insulation, 341, 342, 373
    timber, 238
warm-air heating, 356, 358
warm-humid climate, 335, 339
Warren trusses, 161
washer (for air), 360
waste pipe sizes, 419
wastes, gaseous, wind dispersion of, 146
water
    distribution, **406**
    exclusion of, **100**
    usage, 408
water accumulation, 115, 125
water-based paints, 32, 88
water-cement ratio of concrete, 36, 40
water closets, 409, 418
waterglass, 30
water hammer, 277
water pipes, 408
waterproofers for concrete, 41
waterproofing materials, 86
waterproofing membranes, 86
water-reducing admixtures for concrete, 40
water reticulation, **406**
water spray, wind-driven, 145
water storage requirement in buildings, 407
water supply, **406**
    for fire fighting, **411**
    pumps, 382, 386, 406, 407
water vapor, 100, 344
watt, 310, 393, 397, 462, 463
wavelength, 269, 326
wax, 90
WCI, 143
WCs, 409, 418
wear (abrasion), 112
weather, 334
weathering, 17, 18, 29, 42, 57, 68
weatherboard, *see* siding
weathering steel, 18
weatherometer, 84, 111
web of steel section, 180
weekend shutdown for energy economy, 349
weepholes, 46
Weibull distribution, 137, 138
weights
    of building materials, 117
    of concrete aggregate, 36
    of concrete slabs, 117
    of partitions, 118
    of soil, 253
    of steel decks, 117
    of timber decks, 117
welded connections, 187, 188
welded wire fabric, 194
welding, 23, 84, 187
well-graded soil, 252
wet-bulb temperature, 327, 328
wetting agent, 43, 88
wheelchairs, 424–426, 431
whirling hygrometer, 328
white cement, 34, 42
white noise, 271
white paint, 32, 88, 89
white spirit, 88
whitewash, 32
whiting, 89
width of corridors, 425, 426
width of escalators, 429, 430
willy-willys, 134
wind-borne debris, 133, 134
wind-chill index, 143, 334
wind climate, 133, 335
wind dispersion of gaseous wastes, 146
wind effects, **133**, 337
wind frequency data, 136–138
wind loads, **120**, 121, 125, 127, 128, **141**, 167, 195
windowless interiors, 309
window putty, 86
windows, **293**, 319, 320, 343, 453
    broken, in a fire, 450
    heat and sound insulation of, 50, 296, 306, 343, 364
    metal, 20
windows as solar heating elements, 305, 306, 377
window-type packaged air conditioners, 359
wind pressure, 126, 127, 140
wind speed, 135, 136
wind transport of particulates, 145
wind tunnel studies, 142, 143
wired glass, 49
wiring, electric, 398
wood, 53, **228**, 444, 450
    thermal properties, 58, 325, 338, 341, 342, 375
woodchip board, 77, 78, 84, 235
wood wool, 339, 341, 343

wool, 85
workability of concrete, 37
work hardening, 16
working loads, 115, 149
working stress method for reinforced concrete design, 194
work station, 109
wrought aluminum alloys, 20
wrought iron, 14

X rays, 23
yield strength of steel, 181, 183, 196
zinc, 11, 16, 17, 21, 23, 24, 89
zincalume sheet, 16
zinc chromate, 89
zinc tetroxychromate, 89
zoning of elevators, 432, **437**